VOLUME 1

SOURCES OF THE AMERICAN REPUBLIC

A DOCUMENTARY HISTORY OF POLITICS, SOCIETY AND THOUGHT

SOURCES OF THE AMERICAN REPUBLIC

A Documentary History of Politics, Society, and Thought

Volume 1

MARVIN MEYERS, The University of Chicago

ALEXANDER KERN, The State University of Iowa

JOHN G. CAWELTI, The University of Chicago

Critical Readers:

Thomas C. Cochran, University of Pennsylvania
Carl N. Degler, Vassar College
Weymouth T. Jordan, The Florida State University
Chase C. Mooney, Indiana University
Russel B. Nye, Michigan State University
Kramer J. Rohfleisch, San Diego State College

SCOTT, FORESMAN AND COMPANY

CHICAGO, ATLANTA, DALLAS, PALO ALTO, FAIR LAWN, N.J.

Cover photo: Wood eagle, attributed to Schimmel.
National Gallery of Art, Index of American Design.

PREFACE

Why do historians, professional and amateur, find the study of history fascinating and instructive, while beginning students often find it routine and dull? For many reasons, of course. Obviously, the initiate knows where he stands, has the broad outline in his head, and so can go on to interesting questions ranging from detective puzzles to philosophic riddles. The novice is struggling to acquire the rudiments of his subject. In this struggle no miracles of progress are possible.

Yet first inquiries in history *can* be exciting. The sympathy and intellectual curiosity of the student can be engaged at an early stage. Good teachers have always done this, whatever their educational materials. Good textbooks help. Why not add the very materials that stimulate the interest and pleasure of the teachers themselves: the original sources and the analyses of scholarly interpreters? From these materials the student gains an immediate sense of the mind and character, custom and practice, of past generations. Of equal or greater importance, he confronts the issues of the past in a fresh way. The arguments of the participants—sometimes great arguments—give a reality to historical decisions that no summary alone can quite recapture. The student himself becomes a kind of participant observer in the history of his nation. Not incidentally, he gains a liberal education in the social sciences from the excellent examples of political, social, economic, and cultural inquiry offered by the originals and by the commentaries of expert historical judges. Finally, by relating sources to text and comparing professional judgments, the student acquires some critical awareness of the "making" of history by historians.

All these good things can come only in modest measure. This is still only a beginning. But it is a good beginning: one that stirs interest, promotes learning, and whets the appetite for further historical study.

In common with a growing number of our professional colleagues, we have drawn from classroom experience a profound conviction that the original sources of the American Republic are indispensable materials for teaching the history of politics, society, and thought in the United States. We have found other volumes of selected readings useful in various ways, yet never wholly adequate to our purposes. We have learned from our predecessors, from our experience, and from each other. The results are offered here in the hope that they represent not merely a change but an improvement in the selection, organization, and presentation of source materials for United States history.

The general character of the volumes will be apparent from an inspection of the Table of Contents. Sources are conceived in their widest sense, as a record of the elements and forces that shaped a special kind of order in America. The American Republic is understood as a commonwealth of citizens doing political business, but also as a social and cultural entity. In the two volumes, we have ordered the sources in six large parts or units, each representing a significant stage of American historical development from the first colonial settlements to the present. Within each part we have organized first a sequence of chapters corresponding to the commonly recognized periods of political and social history, and then two comprehensive chapters, one recording main currents of thought and culture, the other sampling major historical interpretations of an era. Thus each part progresses from the record of particular social conditions and public affairs to the general ideas and values underlying a wide span of history, concluding with the alternative judgments of leading scholars. We have tried to preserve both the continuity and the range of American history in a flexible form that will permit different teachers to make their own varying uses of the materials. Our arrangement moves from the concrete and practical to the general and reflective; but others may with perfect ease reverse the order or adopt any combination that suits their teaching purposes. The part and chapter organization and the detailed descriptive Table of Contents will show the possibilities at a glance. Thus some may wish to begin with the relevant interpretations; some may wish to combine appropriate intellectual and cultural documents with the more concrete political and social history—e.g., Puritan theology with New England settlement; most, we expect, will prefer to take things in the order given.

We have given the volumes the subtitle "a documentary history" in the belief that the editorial matter—part introductions, chapter introductions, and headnotes—does considerably more than identify the specific items. Our effort has been to relate the sources to the broad flow of history, to point up the distinctive contribution of each document, and to suggest persistent themes and significant disjunctions among the documents. Whether or not the volumes are used in association with a textbook, they have a considerable measure of self-sufficiency. Sources are placed in historical context for those mainly interested in the narrative development; and arguments are juxtaposed to counterarguments with editorial indications of relevant issues for those primarily concerned with the problems of American democracy.

Of the selection and editing of particular sources one need say little in advance. The proof is in the reading. Aware of the varieties of taste and judgment among teachers and the varieties of capacity among students, we have tried to preserve a balance without attempting the self-defeating task of pleasing everyone. Each reading was chosen for its historical significance, for its intrinsic interest, and for its value as a teaching instrument. The classics are well represented, in as full a form as space permitted; but we have regularly introduced fresh materials that seemed appropriate and useful from our own research and teaching experience. We do not pretend to have mastered the insoluble problem of "coverage" versus "intensity." Our minimum requirements were that the most important subjects and points of view be sampled and that each selection be of sufficient length to show the *development* of an argument, observation, or idea. The editors share a strong conviction that a collection of bits and pieces, of mere illustrative footnotes to history, makes weak stuff for an historical education at the college level.

The close and continuing collaboration of the editors gives the volumes the character of a joint product. We have sought expert advice and gained substantially from it; but finally we have consulted among ourselves and made our own decisions in the hope of preserving a coherence of organization and approach that is sometimes lacking in collective ventures. Alexander Kern supplied the original idea for the book. Kern and Marvin Meyers laid out the general design, with the assistance of John Cawelti. Meyers assumed primary responsibility for selections and editorial matter in the chapters dealing with political and social history; and with the assistance of Kern he handled the historical interpretations and drafted the part introductions. Kern and Cawelti proposed the selections and editorial matter for the chapters in intellectual and cultural history. But finally all important decisions followed the discussion and agreement of the three editors.

We wish to express our gratitude for the criticisms and suggestions, both general and detailed, of Dr. Thomas C. Cochran of the University of Pennsylvania, Dr. I. Bernard Cohen of Harvard University, Dr. Carl Degler of Vassar College, Dr. Weymouth T. Jordan of the Florida State University, Dr. Chase C. Mooney of Indiana University, Dr. Russel B. Nye of Michigan State University, and Dr. Kramer J. Rohfleisch of San Diego State College. These critical readers not only gave us valuable suggestions based on their expert knowledge but also helped to supplement our own limited experience of teaching needs and possibilities. The enterprising staff of the College Department of Scott, Foresman and Company skillfully relieved us of many burdens and offered vigorous guidance at every stage of the work.

We gratefully acknowledge the contribution of our colleagues and students in the College of the University of Chicago and at the State University of Iowa, who have helped to shape our views of history and pedagogy as partially reflected in the present volumes. Edith Cooper Meyers, Jean Borduer Kern, and Elizabeth Cawelti gave a measure of assistance for which there is (and was) no price.

Marvin Meyers
Alexander Kern
John G. Cawelti

Part One

The Colonial Background: 1607 to 1763

CHAPTER 2   THE AMERICAN MIND IN THE MAKING

Part Three

Democratic Growth and the Sectional Conflict: 1825 to 1865

PART ONE

The Colonial Background

1607-1763

Colonial America was the offspring of Europe, particularly of England. Working within the framework of the British Empire, the colonists adapted English ideas, institutions, and customs to the American environment. Although other peoples from the British Isles and Northern Europe came and left their lasting mark, nevertheless the original and dominant heritage was English. The tradition of liberty under law, expressed in the English constitution and common law, had given direction to colonial politics and government. Valued elements of the English heritage included limited executive power, representative institutions, individual rights, trial by jury and impartial justice, and local administration and a decentralized militia as opposed to a large bureaucracy and a standing army.

The colonists came to a vast, wild, isolated country where men had to rely substantially upon their own wits and energies to survive. They could find opportunities to improve their fortunes by opening new lands, new enterprises, whole new communities. Especially on the frontiers, men of varied nationalities and social origins came together and learned to manage for themselves. The tendency of colonial history was to give fuller expression to liberty and equality in politics and society. By 1763 the American provinces provided—so far as they were their own masters—an unprecedented measure of popular rule, religious toleration, civil liberty, and social-economic opportunity.

The passage of European beliefs to America further influenced colonial life. The dissenting Calvinist faith carried to New England by the Puritans inspired the effort to create "Godly Commonwealths" where strict Biblical standards of morality would be enforced by the joint authority of magistrates and clergy. As Puritans prospered in the New World, however, and spread out onto new lands, their religious faith lost much of its vigor and frequently became translated into a secular faith in frugality, industry, and perseverance. The European intellectual influence on America came also from philosophers like John Locke, who defended novel doctrines that were to guide American revolutionists—doctrines like the idea of equal natural rights to life, liberty, and property and of limited government based on the consent of the governed. Still, while English and Continental ideas provided the intellectual sources of the new movement, American experiences in mastering nature and creating new societies certainly strengthened the trend toward actually establishing new freedoms and individual rights.

Viewing the colonial past as the background of an independent nation, we emphasize the internal life of the colonies. That the Americans could develop their own distinctive life already suggests something about the character of the British Empire. Edmund Burke's eloquence states—and overstates—an important truth about the Empire: "through a wise and salutary neglect, a generous nature has been suffered to take her own way to perfection." In effect, a federal empire had evolved between 1607 and 1763, with King and Parliament and their agents regulating general concerns—trade, war, diplomacy, Indian relations—and provincial authorities largely controlling the mass of local affairs. It was not a perfect system. But in the stormy years of conflict after 1763 Americans looked back on the "old empire" as a golden age, and they drew heavily on imperial experience when they founded their own federal union.

Chronological Chart: 1607 to 1763

THE AMERICAN SCENE . . . .

POLITICAL

1607 Jamestown settled by London Company.

1619 1st legislature in New World met in Jamestown.
1620 Pilgrims landed at Plymouth.
1624 New Netherland (New York) settled by Dutch.
1630 Settlement of Massachusetts Bay began.
1634 Maryland settled by proprietor Lord Baltimore.
1635 Connecticut valley settled.
1636 Roger Williams founded Providence.
1637 New Haven founded.
1639 "Fundamental Orders of Connecticut," 1st colonial constitution, adopted.
1643 New England Confederation formed for common defense.
1651 Navigation Act passed by Cromwell's Parliament.
1653 North Carolina settled by Virginian migrants.
1660 1st of four Navigation Acts (1660, 1663, 1673, 1696) passed by Parliament.
1663 Carolina granted by charter to eight proprietors.
1664 New Netherland seized by English.
The Jerseys granted to Berkeley and Carteret.
1670 Charleston, S.C., founded.
1676 Bacon's Rebellion in Virginia.
1679 New Hampshire made a royal colony.
1682 Pennsylvania founded by Quaker William Penn.
1686 Dominion of New England formed by Andros.
1689 Andros deposed; Dominion of New England ended.
1689–1697 King William's War.
1696 Board of Trade for the Plantations named by William III.
1699 Woolens Act passed by Parliament.
1702 East and West Jersey united.
1702–1713 Queen Anne's War.

1713 North and South Carolina formally separated.
1718 New Orleans founded by the French.
c1720 French began fortification of Mississippi valley.

1729 North and South Carolina became royal colonies.
1732 Georgia charter granted to 21 "trustees."
Hat Act passed by Parliament.
1733 Molasses Act passed by Parliament.

1744–1748 King George's War.
1750 Iron Act passed by Parliament.

1754 Albany Congress convened.
1755 General Braddock defeated by French and Indians.
1756–1763 French and Indian War.
1763 Treaty of Paris ceded to England the French territories of Canada, the trans-Appalachian West (to the Mississippi), and the Spanish Floridas.

ECONOMIC AND SOCIAL

1612 1st successful tobacco crop planted in Virgina.
1619 1st export of Virginia tobacco sent to England.
1st Negro slaves (20) imported into Virginia.
1623 Plymouth colonists began cultivation of corn.
1626 Wheat successfully cultivated in New Netherland.

c1635 Famous "triangular trade" between New England (fish and lumber), the West Indies (sugar, molasses, rum), and England (finished goods) began.

1643 1st colonial woolen mill founded at Rowley, Mass.
1644 1st Boston ship built.
Lynn (Mass.) iron works founded.
1654 1st Jews arrive in New Amsterdam (New York).
1660 Estimated colonial population: 84,800.

1664 Colonial horse racing began at Newmarket Course, L.I.
1670–1690 Sharp growth of Virginia aristocracy.

1683 1st German settlers founded Germantown, Pa.
1685 French Huguenots settled throughout colonies following revocation of the Edict of Nantes.
1692 Salem witch trials.
1696 Royal African Company's monopoly of slave trade ended; "triangular trade" began between colonies (fish), the West Indies (rum), and West Africa (slaves).
1st successful rice crop produced in South Carolina.

1705 Virginia Black Code restricted Negroes' privileges.
1710 Great German migration to middle colonies began.
1714 Scotch-Irish migration to Pennsylvania began.
1716 1st colonial theater built in Williamsburg, Va.
1721 1st smallpox inoculations given in Boston.
1725 Estimated slave population: 75,000.

1730 Estimated colonial population: 654,950.
1732 Scotch-Irish began migration down the Shenandoah valley into Virginia, the Carolinas, and Georgia.

1735 Peter Zenger's libel trial promoted freedom of the press.
1750–1751 Christopher Gist explored the Ohio country.
1752 Hallam's American Company set up repertory theater to tour colonies.

1760 French and Indian War business boom reached peak.
1763 Estimated colonial population: 1,650,000 (Philadelphia 24,000; Boston 16,000; New York 14,000; Charleston 10,000; Newport 8,000).

INTELLECTUAL

1609 Church of England established by law in Virginia.
1611 1st Presbyterians arrived in Virginia.

1620 Separatist Congregational church founded at Plymouth.
1630 Puritan Congregational church founded at Salem.
1633 Boston Latin School, 1st secondary school in America, founded.
1636 Harvard College founded.
1638 1st colonial printing press set up at Cambridge.
1642–1647 Compulsory school laws enacted by Massachusetts.
1644 Roger Williams' *The Bloudy Tenent* published.

1656–1657 1st Quakers arrived in New England.
1659 Quakers hanged on Boston Common.
1662 Massachusetts' Halfway Covenant liberalized church membership, blurring distinction between elect and others.
1668 1st Baptists exiled from Massachusetts.

1682 Pennsylvania established freedom of religion.
1687 1st Anglican service in Boston conducted.
1688 Quakers made 1st formal protest against slavery.
1693 William and Mary College founded.

1701 Yale College founded.

1706 1st Anglican parish in Connecticut formed at Stratford.
1714 Cotton Mather publicly espoused Copernican system.

1726 Revivalist Log College founded at Neshaminy, Pa.
1727 Jonathan Edwards minister at Northampton.
1731 1st colonial circulating library founded by Benjamin Franklin in Philadelphia.
1732 *Poor Richard's Almanac* began publication.
1734-1750 The "Great Awakening."

1743 American Philosophical Society founded.
1751–1789 Georgian architecture became fashionable.
1752 Franklin's kite experiment performed.
1754 Columbia University founded as "King's College."
1755 University of Pennsylvania chartered as 1st non-sectarian college in America.

1608 French founded Quebec.
1609 Twelve Years' Truce gave Dutch independence.
1618–1648 Thirty Years' War.
1620 Francis Bacon published *Novum Organum*.
1625 Grotius published *On the Law of War and Peace*.
1630 Galileo popularized the Copernican theory.

1635 French Academy founded by Cardinal Richelieu.

1637 Descartes published *Discourse on Method*, accepting "reason" as the sole authority.
1642–1649 English civil wars; Charles I beheaded.
1643–1715 Reign of Louis XIV of France.
1649–1659 English Commonwealth and Protectorate.
1652 Capetown founded by Dutch.
1660 "Restoration" of Stuart King Charles II.
1661 Bombay seized by the English.
1662 Royal Society (for science) founded.
1664 French East India and West India Companies founded.

1682 La Salle claims Louisiana territory for France.
1687 Newton published gravitational theory.
1688–1689 Glorious Revolution deposed James II in favor of William and Mary, ending absolutism in England.
1690 John Locke's social contract theory published.
1694 Bank of England founded.

1701 Jethro Tull invented the seed-drill plow.

1705 Newcomen developed the steam pump.
1707 England and Scotland united as Great Britain.
1713 Treaty of Utrecht gave England Gibraltar, Hudson Bay, Newfoundland, and Acadia.
1721–1742 Robert Walpole, as 1st English prime minister, fostered colonial policy of "salutary neglect."

1733 John Kay invented the flying shuttle.
1736 John and Charles Wesley founded Methodism.
1740–1786 Frederick II, the Great, king of Prussia.

1752 Great Britain adopted Gregorian calendar.

1755 Samuel Johnson's English *Dictionary* published.
1756–1763 Seven Years' War.
1760–1820 George III, king of England.
1762 Rousseau published the *Social Contract*.

CHAPTER 1

From Wilderness to Commonwealth

Christopher Columbus was not the first European to reach America. Norse adventurers had made the trip some five hundred years before 1492. But the Columbian discoveries effectively opened communications between the Old World and the New. Spanish conquistadors of the sixteenth century—men like Cortés and Pizarro—carved out an American empire stretching from the Gulf of Mexico over the Caribbean area, Central America, and much of South America. In Mexico and Peru the Spaniards found the high civilizations of the Aztec and Inca with their fabulous supplies of gold and silver. American treasure enriched both the adventurers and the Spanish nation and stimulated the commercial and industrial growth of Europe.

The incredible success of the Spanish empire focused the attention of the Western European nations on the New World. By the end of the sixteenth century, Tudor England had consolidated its national power, mastered the Spanish Armada (1588), and accumulated enough private wealth to finance successful colonial enterprises in America. The spirit of adventure ran high in Elizabethan England, and there were strong political, economic, and religious motives to direct men's energies into empire building. Engaged in a sharp competition with Spain, France, and Holland for world commercial supremacy, the English originally saw in America a captive market for their manufactures, especially woolen cloth; a source of treasure and of strategically important imports such as tar and ship timber; a way to develop a great merchant marine; an outlet for "surplus" population; and a potential route to the Orient. Missionary zeal strengthened political and economic motives.

Similar purposes were shared by England's rivals, but England alone had large numbers of citizens ready to try their fortunes in the New World. Between 1607 and 1642—a time of political and religious troubles in England—some 65,000 adventurous spirits went out to the British West Indies and the mainland colonies. In Spanish America a small European elite dominated a large Indian population. New France (Canada) remained a sparsely settled outpost dedicated to conversion of the Indians and largely dependent on the fur trade. In British North America, however, Englishmen ruled over Englishmen according to English principles, and this fact helps to explain the unique political, social, and economic developments that shaped the future American republic.

The joint-stock trading company, which had proved an effective instrument for financing and managing English commercial ventures in Russia and the Near East, became the initial agency for planting colonies in Virginia and Massachusetts Bay. A later and more common English colonizing device was the proprietary charter employed in Maryland, Pennsylvania, Delaware, and for a time in New York, the Carolinas, the Jerseys, and Georgia. Under this arrangement a wealthy individual or group—a Calvert or a Penn, for example—undertook to plant an American colony, receiving from the crown a grant of territory and extensive political authority. By these several grants the crown conveyed a portion of its possessions and powers to particular private subjects in order to make the American domain serviceable to king and nation.

The wilderness of eastern North America concealed no wonders of Indian civilization such as the Spanish found to the south. Scattered tribes of the Algonquin family (a group identified by common linguistic traits) met the English everywhere along the Atlantic coast, with varying combinations of awe and friendliness, suspicion and hostility. The North American Indians had no stores or mines of precious metals to yield to conquerors, nor would they ever be effectively reduced to a servile labor force for the Europeans. The founders of the early seventeenth-century colonies in Virginia and Massachusetts thus faced a merciless struggle with nature for survival in the wilderness. In Virginia two thirds of the first party died within a few months; at Plymouth perhaps half of the original Pilgrim settlers survived their first New England winter. It was necessary to learn how to deal with a strange physical environment and a "savage" people. There was little margin for error. It was equally important to forget some common notions: in the case of Virginia, for example, to forget many of the original economic goals of the company promoters and to meet the new country on its own terms. This the Virginians did when they adopted Indian corn as a subsistence crop (a lesson all English colonists learned from the natives) and—the decisive choice—when they based their economy on the cultivation of tobacco, another Indian crop which had gained great favor in the English market.

COLONIAL EVOLUTION

The conventional grouping of the colonies by geographic areas—New England, the Middle Colonies, and the South—makes a good deal of sense, if we remember some obvious limitations. In important respects the several North American colonies followed a common pattern. Through the seventeenth century the great mass of settlers were Englishmen of roughly similar social origins: yeomen, craftsmen, shopkeepers, clerks, and laborers. Virginia did receive some English gentry (as did Massachusetts), but critical scholarship has adjudged the picture of early Virginia as the refuge of Cavalier aristocrats largely a myth. Settlers brought with them a common English heritage. They had to master a common wilderness environment and meet the same sort of Indian resistance, although the later settlements like Pennsylvania (1682) could draw upon the experience and supplies of established neighbors. In some measure all the colonies felt the threat of imperial rivals: the French to the north and west, the Spanish to the south. All lived within the same imperial framework, on terms that varied more by individual colonies than by geographical regions. Indeed, within each section the differences among colonies were sometimes as impressive as the resemblances. The contrast was dramatic, for example, between North Carolina with its rough society of small farmers and South Carolina with its growing mass of Negro slaves and its princely merchant-planter class. Rhode Island, for another case, seemed a queer, dark country to its seventeenth-century New England neighbors.

Nevertheless, there remains a set of significant traits characterizing each of the geographical sections. The Southern colonies can be identified by their almost exclusively rural and agrarian society. The landed aristocracy that evolved in the tidewater areas was marked off sharply not only from their servile laborers but from the independent farmers of the back country, including (after 1732) many German and Scotch-Irish immigrants. Charleston, South Carolina, was the only Southern commercial center of major consequence. The plantation slavery system certainly helps to explain this one-sided development, which has always proved costly to the South. A heavy fixed investment in land and slaves tied up capital, while the very presence of slavery discouraged the immigration of free workers into the coastal regions where cities, commerce, and industry might have flourished.

New England is most readily identified as Puritan country. Both the Pilgrim "Separatists" of Plymouth and the far more numerous and important Puritan founders of Massachusetts Bay and Connecticut were religious reformers who sought a new land where they and their church brethren might live and worship according to their special understanding of God's law for man. Economic motives were not unimportant, as we can learn even from the devout Pilgrim leader William Bradford, who explains that economic hardships suffered by the Pilgrim exiles in Holland threatened the existence of the congregation and—among other causes—made a fresh beginning in America necessary.

The Puritans were not unique among American colonists in allying church and state, nor were their legal regulations of private conduct essentially different from those, say, of early Virginia. What did distinguish the early New England settlers was their profound sense of being a chosen people with a mission to build a New Zion in the wilderness. If we emphasize religious aspects of Puritan New England, however, it is not to suggest that the colonists despised worldly interests. The early Puritans were highly practical men who made a success of community-building, fighting, farming, fishing, shipbuilding, and trading. Along the coast the fishing towns sent ships to the Newfoundland banks in pursuit of cod, a fish so highly valued that it earned a place on the Massachusetts coat of arms. Boston became the first important commercial town in the American colonies. Bostonians traded fish, timber, and provisions to the West Indies; built, sold, and sailed merchant ships; and later took a leading part in the "triangular trade," exchanging New England rum for African slaves for West Indian sugar and molasses.

Perhaps colonial Pennsylvania best represents the distinctive features of the Middle Colonies, although it must be recognized that neighboring New York, for example, with its strong element of Dutch culture and its Hudson valley manors running to the hundreds of thousands of acres, was substantially different. Religious purposes were of particular importance for the Quaker proprietors of Pennsylvania, as they had been earlier for the New England Puritans and for the Catholic Calverts of Maryland. William Penn envisioned a colony where the sorely persecuted Quakers might live and worship in the light of their "gentle persuasion." Penn's pacific Indian policy and his exceptional toleration of religious differences recalled the earlier approach of Roger Williams in Rhode Island. The "Frame of Government" approved by the proprietor in 1682 introduced a relatively democratic political system, and the early legal codes of Pennsylvania tempered with Quaker mercy the harsh justice then common in England and the other colonies. Of exceptional importance were Penn's liberal land policies— as compared with those of other proprietors—and his highly successful efforts to attract plain, hard-working folk from the British Isles and the European continent, many of them Rhineland Germans, some of them members of radical Protestant sects such as the Amish, Dunkards, Mennonites, and Moravians. The Quaker colony, with New York, came to represent the full ethnic range of Western Europe, while New England and the seaboard South remained essentially English in background.

THE IMPERIAL ORDER

Certainly we would have a distorted view of colonial experience if we were to judge the British Empire entirely by the impassioned arguments of the 1760's and 1770's, after imperial policy had taken a new direction. A century and a half of colonial life had developed a proud and self-willed people who valued *both* their own provincial communities *and* the empire which had made it possible for them to grow and prosper as free men. Note one revealing episode: more than six months after Lexington and Concord the officers of General Washington's mess still regularly drank to the health of George III.

During the first half century or so of colonial history there was little system in the British Empire. Private promoters, as we have seen, were chartered to finance, settle, manage, and defend new colonies in America. For most of the promoters, beginning with the Virginia Company, the venture proved a sorry bargain: the investment was heavy and the returns, if any, slow, uncertain, and slight. Charter terms normally called for some form of popular representation, and the promoters introduced legislative assemblies that steadily increased their powers over the span of colonial history. After the early attempts at corporate ownership and management of economic enterprises were abandoned, the settlers assumed major responsibility for clearing and cultivating lands, building and regulating settlements, initiating commerce, shipping, and manufactures. In short, they took responsibility for conducting the domestic, economic, and social affairs of America.

From the beginning, ultimate authority over the colonies rested with the crown. Colonial acts could be disallowed in England, colonial judgments could be reversed, and colonial charters could, by due process, be revoked. One important method for bringing the colonies under tighter control was to convert corporate and proprietary settlements into royal colonies, ruled by a crown-appointed governor. This step was taken first in Virginia as early as 1624 and was repeated later in New Hampshire (1680), New York (1685), Massachusetts (1691), North and South Carolina (1729), and Georgia (1752). The king and his advisers gave detailed instructions to the royal governors and could thus coordinate imperial policy more effectively. Colonial legislatures, however, exerted strong counterpressures on the governors by gradually taking hold of the purse strings.

The English prized their American colonies for many reasons, but above all for their economic value. From the middle years of the seventeenth century, acts of trade and navigation and the administrative machinery for enforcing them became the main business of imperial policy. Parliament, which was becoming master of the English government, framed these economic regulations largely under the influence of the rising commercial and industrial interests in England. The system was based upon the mercantilist theory that a nation gained wealth and strength by multiplying its exports, minimizing its imports from foreigners, controlling strategic raw materials, enlarging its merchant marine, and broadly by accumulating precious metals from a favorable balance of trade. The effects of the mercantilist system are difficult to measure. Colonial economic freedom was limited in a way that probably increased the cost of American imports and decreased the price of the colonies' most valuable exports. On the other hand, the colonists had privileged access to the imperial market, received the protection of English naval and military power, participated in the benefits of the shipping regulations, and received some outright contributions in the form of bounties. When the trade laws pinched too hard, as in the case of the Molasses Act of 1733, they found ways of evading the rules, sometimes with the connivance of imperial officials.

Whether because of or in spite of the British imperial system, the American colonies grew and prospered mightily. The striking fact is, most observers agree, that it was not the mercantilist system as such that provoked colonial rebellion but the novel attempt by Parliament to tax the colonies for revenue. The record of this new departure and its consequences we shall consider in Part II.

Planting the Wilderness

THE VIRGINIA EXPERIENCE

1

TOIL OR TREASURE: A SEARCH FOR A PROFITABLE LIVELIHOOD
from *Proceedings of the English Colony,* 1612

By the opening of the seventeenth century, England had become a first-rank maritime and commercial power with the means and the ambition to seek its own place in the Western World. Dreams of gold and of a Northwest Passage to the Orient inspired English colonizing schemes; so too did calculations of commercial profit, designs for the expansion of national power, and—quoting from the first Virginia charter—a zeal to bring "the infidels and savages" to "the true knowledge and worship of God" and to "human civility."

After several poorly planned colonial ventures had met disaster, King James I (1603-1625) granted a charter to a company of London merchants who organized and financed what became the first permanent English settlement in America: the Virginia colony, established at Jamestown in 1607. Under the Virginia charter of 1606 the king authorized "certain knights, gentlemen, merchants, and other adventurers [i.e., investors]" to take up and develop lands in "that part of America, commonly called Virginia, and other parts and territories in *America*, either appertaining unto us, or which are not now actually possessed by any *Christian* prince or people." The original grant to the London group of the Virginia Company covered ten thousand square miles of territory along the Atlantic coast, between the thirty-fourth and forty-first parallels. In 1609, the boundaries were redefined, giving Virginia a claim to a four-hundred-mile strip of land that reached "from sea to sea, west and northwest."

Thus the crown assigned to a private commercial company the task of founding a new empire in America. The investors and enterprisers of the company were promised their reward in the form of land, natural resources, and exclusive trading rights.

The colonial gentlemen and soldiers—friends of Captain John Smith—who recorded the *Proceedings of the English Colony* were keenly aware of the contrasts between the Spanish and English experience in founding an American empire. The Spaniards had found fabulous stores of treasure in Mexico and South America, and they found populous and highly developed Indian civilizations in their American domains. The Virginians found neither. The "gold" they shipped to England proved to be fool's gold. The Indians they encountered were scattered, poor, and relatively primitive tribes. Combining the devices of trade, diplomacy, and war, the English settlers sought to secure themselves against Indian attack and to obtain from the natives cleared land and essential food supplies. There were no quick fortunes to be made in Virginia.

The plain record of early Virginia which follows shows how the first generation tried to adapt ends and means to the conditions of the North American wilderness. If some leaders persisted in the quest for gold and a Northwest Passage, others recognized that Virginia must, by hard work, "bring to perfection the commodities of the country." Early efforts were made to produce such export commodities as tar, pitch, glass, soap ashes, and lumber, but it took a great deal of driving by John Smith and other leaders to keep the motley group of settlers at such laborious tasks. Since the Virginia Company, down to 1619, owned the lands and claimed all the surplus produce of the colony, there was little economic incentive for the settlers.

This project to establish a colony under the direction of the Virginia Company was modified by later charters of 1609 and 1612, which gave fuller political control to the company stockholders. In 1624, the company lost its charter, and Virginia came directly under royal authority.

The 10 of September 1608, by the election of the Council, and request of the company, Captain Smith received the letters patents, and took upon him the place of President, which till then by no means he would accept, though he were often importuned thereunto. . . .

. . . the church was repaired, the storehouse re-covered, building prepared for the supply we expected. . . . The whole company every Saturday exercised in a field prepared for that purpose; the boats trimmed for trade, which in their journey encountered the second supply [the company's ship from England], that brought them back to discover the country of Monacan.

How or why Captain Newport obtained such a private commission as not to return without a lump of gold, a certainty of the south sea, or one of the lost company of Sir Walter Raleigh, I know not. . . . As for the coronation of Powhatan, and his presents of basin, ewer, bed, clothes, and such costly novelties, they had been much better well spared than so ill spent, for we had his favor much better only for a poor piece of copper, till this stately kind of soliciting made him so much overvalue himself that he respected us as much as nothing at all.

As for the hiring of the Poles and Dutch, to make pitch and tar, glass, mills, and soap-ashes, was most necessary and well. But to send them and seventy more without victual to work was

Text: William Simmonds (ed.), "The Proceedings of the English Colonie in Virginia," in Captain John Smith, *Works,* ed. Edward Arber ("The English Scholar's Library No. 16" [Birmingham, 1884]), pp. 121-22, 124-27, 147-48. The spelling and punctuation have been modernized.

not so well considered; yet this could not have hurt us had they been 200, though then we were 130 that wanted for ourselves. For we had the savages in that decorum (their harvest being newly gathered) that we feared not to get victual sufficient had we been 500.

Now was there no way to make us miserable but to neglect that time to make our provision, whilst it was to be had, the which was done to perform this strange discovery but more strange coronation. To lose that time, spend that victual we had, tire and starve our men, having no means to carry victual, munition, the hurt or sick, but their own backs, how or by whom they were invented I know not. . . .

The next day came Powhatan. Smith delivered his message of the presents sent him, and redelivered him Namontack, desiring him come to his Father Newport to accept those presents and conclude their revenge against the Monacans. Whereunto the subtle savage thus replied:

If your king has sent me presents, I also am a king and this my land. 8 days I will stay to receive them. Your father is to come to me, not I to him, nor yet to your fort, neither will I bite at such a bait. As for the Monacans, I can revenge my own injuries, and as for Atquanuchuck, where you say your brother was slain, it is a contrary way from those parts you suppose it. But for any salt water beyond the mountains, the relations you have had from my people are false.

Whereupon he began to draw plots upon the ground, according to his discourse, of all those regions.

Many other discourses they had (yet both desirous to give each other content in complemental courtesies), and so Captain Smith returned with this answer.

Upon this, Captain Newport sent his presents by water, which is near 100 miles, with 50 of the best shot himself went by land, which is but 12 miles, where he met with our 3 barges to transport him over.

All things being fit for the day of his coronation, the presents were brought, his basin, ewer, bed, and furniture set up, his scarlet cloak and apparel (with much ado) put on him, (being persuaded by Namontack they would do him no hurt). But a foul trouble there was to make him kneel to receive his crown. He, neither knowing the majesty nor meaning of a crown, nor bending of the knee, endured so many persuasions, examples, and instructions as tired them all. At last, by leaning hard on his shoulders, he a little stooped, and Newport put the crown on his head, when, by the warning of a pistol, the boats were prepared with such a volley of shot that the king start up in a horrible fear till he saw all was well. Then, remembering himself to congratulate their kindness, he gave his old shoes and his mantle to Captain Newport.

But perceiving his purpose was to discover the Monacans, he labored to divert his resolution, refusing to lend him either men or guides more than Namontack. And so, after some complemental kindness on both sides, in requital of his presents, he presented Newport with a heap of wheat ears that might contain 7 or 8 bushels, and as much more we bought, ready dressed, in the town, wherewith we returned to the fort.

The ship having disburdened herself of 70 persons, with the first gentlewoman and woman servant that arrived in our colony, Captain Newport with all the Council, and 120 chosen men, set forward for the discovery of Monacan, leaving the President at the fort with 80 (such as they were) to reload the ship.

Arriving at the falls, we marched by land some forty miles in 2 days and a half, and so returned down to the same path we went. Two towns we discovered of the Monacans, the people neither using us well nor ill, yet for our security we took one of their petty Werowances [chiefs] and lead him bound, to conduct us the way.

And in our return searched many places we supposed mines, about which we spent some time in refining, having one William Callicut, a refiner, fitted for that purpose. From that crust of earth we digged, he persuaded us to believe he extracted some small quantity of silver (and not unlikely better stuff might be had for the digging). With this poor trial, we were contented to leave this fair, fertile, well-watered country.

Coming to the falls, the savages fained there were diverse ships come into the bay to kill them at Jamestown. Trade they would not, and find their corn we could not, for they had hid it in the woods; and being thus deluded, we arrived at Jamestown, half sick, all complaining and tired with toil, famine, and discontent to have only but discovered our gilded hopes and such fruitless certainties, as the President foretold us.

No sooner were we landed but the President dispersed many as were able, some for glass, others for pitch, tar, and soap ashes, leaving them with the fort, to the Council's oversight.

But 30 of us he conducted 5 miles from the fort to learn to make clapboard, cut down trees, and lay in woods. Amongst the rest, he had chosen Gabriell Beadell and John Russell, the only two gallants of this last supply and both proper gentlemen. Strange were these pleasures to their conditions; yet lodging, eating, drinking, working, or playing, they doing but as the President, all these things were carried so pleasantly, as within a week, they became masters, making it their delight to hear the trees thunder as they fell. But the axes so oft blistered their tender fingers that commonly every third blow had a loud oath to drown the echo, for remedy of which sin the President devised how to have every man's oaths numbered, and at night, for every oath to have a can of water poured down his sleeve. With which, every offender was so washed (himself and all) that a man should scarce hear an oath in a week.

By this, let no man think that the President or these gentlemen spent their times as common wood-hackers, at felling of trees or suchlike other labors, or that they were pressed to anything as hirelings or common slaves, for what they did (being but once a little inured), it seemed, and they conceited it, only as a pleasure and a recreation. Yet 30 or 40 of such voluntary gentlemen would do more in a day than 100 of the rest that must be pressed to it by compulsion. Master Scrivener, Captain Waldo, and Captain Winne at the fort, every one in like manner carefully regarded their charge.

The President, returning from among the woods, seeing the time consumed and no provision gotten, (and the ship lay idle and would do nothing) presently embarked himself in the discovery barge, giving order to the Council to send Mr. Percy after him with the next barge that arrived at the fort. 2 barges he had himself, and 20 men. But arriving at Chickahamina, that dogged nation was too well acquainted with our wants, refusing to trade, with as much scorn and insolence as they could express. The President, perceiving it was Powhatan's policy to starve us, told them he came not so much for their corn as to revenge his imprisonment and the death of his men murdered by them. And so landing his men, and ready to charge them, they immediately fled. But then they sent their ambassadors with corn, fish, fowl, or what they had, to make their peace; (their corn being that year bad) they complained extremely of their own wants, yet fraughted our boats with 100 bushels of corn and, in like manner Mr. Percy's, that not long after us arrived. They having done the best they could to content us, within 4 or 5 days we returned to Jamestown. . . .

Those temporal [temporizing] proceedings to some may seem too charitable to such a daily daring treacherous people [i.e., the Indians]; to others unpleasant that we washed not the ground with their bloods nor showed such strange inventions in mangling, murdering, ransacking, and destroying (as did the Spaniards) the simple bodies of those ignorant souls; nor delightful because not stuffed with relations of heaps and mines of gold and silver, nor such rare commodities as the Portugals and Spaniards found in the East and West Indies. The want whereof hath begot us, that were the first undertakers, no less scorn and contempt than their noble conquests and valiant adventures (beautified with it), praise and honor. Too much, I confess, the world cannot attribute to their ever memorable merit. And to clear us from the world's blind ignorant censure, these few words may suffice to any reasonable understanding.

It was the Spaniards good hap to happen in those parts where were infinite numbers of people who had manured the ground with that providence that it afforded victual at all times; and time had brought them to that perfection; they had the use of gold and silver, and the most of such commodities as their countries afforded: so that what the Spaniard got was only the spoil and pillage of those country people, and not the labors of their own hands.

But had those fruitful countries been as savage, as barbarous, as ill-peopled, as little planted, labored, and manured, as Virginia; their proper labors, it is likely, would have produced as small

profit as ours. But had Virginia been peopled, planted, manured, and adorned with such store of precious jewels and rich commodities as was the Indies, then, had we not gotten and done as much as by their examples might be expected from us, the world might then have traduced us and our merits, and have made shame and infamy our recompense and reward.

But we chanced in a land even as God made it. Where we found only an idle, improvident, scattered people, ignorant of the knowledge of gold, or silver, or any commodities; and careless of anything but from hand to mouth, but for baubles of no worth; nothing to encourage us but what accidentally we found nature afforded. Which ere we could bring to recompense our pains, defray our charges, and satisfy our adventurers [investors]; we were to discover the country, subdue the people, bring them to be tractable, civil and industrious, and teach them trades, that the fruits of their labors might make us recompense, or plant such colonies of our own that must first make provision how to live of themselves ere they can bring to perfection the commodities of the country: which doubtless will be as commodious for England as the West Indies for Spain if it be rightly managed; notwithstanding all our homebred opinions that will argue the contrary, as formerly suchlike have done against the Spaniards and Portugals.

But to conclude, against all rumor of opinion, I only say this for those that the three first years began this plantation: notwithstanding all their factions, mutinies, and miseries, so gently corrected and well prevented, peruse the Spanish *Decades*, the relations of M. Hacklut; and tell me how many ever, with such small means as a barge of 2 tons, sometimes with 7, 8, 9, or but at most 15 men, did ever discover so many fair and navigable rivers, subject so many several kings, people, and nations to obedience and contribution, with so little bloodshed.

And if in the search of those countries, we had happened where wealth had been, we had as surely had it, as obedience and contribution; but if we have overskipped it, we will not envy them that shall chance to find it. Yet can we not but lament it was our ill fortune to end when we had but only learned how to begin and found the right course how to proceed. . . .

2 **POWDERED WIFE: THE STARVING TIME IN VIRGINIA**

from John Smith, *General Historie of Virginia*, 1624

The "starving time" was a critical moment in the history of Virginia. When Lord Delaware's supply ships arrived from England in 1610, the scattered and desperate

Jamestown colony was at the point of abandoning America. Perhaps sixty survivors remained of the nine hundred settlers who had landed since 1607. No other episode reveals more clearly what a precarious venture it was for several hundred Englishmen to plant a colony in the wilderness.

Captain John Smith (1580-1631), most famous of the Jamestown founders, compiled this grim account of death and depravity from eyewitness reports, adding his grateful reflection on "God's infinite providence." Once a soldier of fortune, Smith joined the first Virginia expedition as a member of the colonial council and served as an imperious president of the colony from 1608 to 1609. He proved a bold, resourceful frontier fighter, trader, and taskmaster. Smith's continual quarrels with rival leaders were carried over into his writings on Virginia; thus he is a partisan but still a colorful and informative guide for students of early colonial life.

Captain Smith returned to England in 1609. After several years of exploring and charting the New England coast in the service of the Plymouth Company, he settled down to a life of authorship. Smith's publications on America include: *A True Relation* (1608), *A Description of New England* (1616), and *The General Historie of Virginia, New England and the Summer Isles* (1624).

[1609] Now we all found the loss of Captain Smith [i.e., the author], yea, his greatest maligners could now curse his loss: as for corn provision and contribution from the savages, we had nothing but mortal wounds with clubs and arrows; as for our hogs, hens, goats, sheep, horse, or what lived, our commanders, officers, and savages daily consumed them, some small proportions sometimes we tasted till all was devoured; then swords, arms, pieces, or anything, we traded with the savages, whose cruel fingers were so oft imbrewed in our bloods that what by their cruelty, our Governor's indiscretion, and the loss of our ships, of five hundred [people] within six months after Captain Smith's departure, there remained not past sixty men, women, and children, most miserable and poor creatures; and those were preserved, for the most part, by roots, herbs, acorns, walnuts, berries, now and then a little fish. They that had starch in these extremities made no small use of it; yea, even the very skins of our horses.

Nay, so great was our famine that a savage we slew and buried the poorer sort took him up again and eat him; and so did divers one another boiled and stewed with roots and herbs. And one amongst the rest did kill his wife, powdered [salted] her, and had eaten part of her before it was known, for which he was executed, as he well deserved. Now whether she was better roasted, boiled or carbonadoed, I know not, but of such a dish as powdered wife I never heard of.

This was that time, which still to this day we called the starving time; it were too vile to say and scarce to be believed, what we endured. But the occasion was our own for want of providence, industry and government, and not the barrenness and defect of the country, as is generally supposed. . . . This in ten days more, would have supplanted us all with death.

But God that would not this country should be unplanted, sent Sir Thomas Gates, and Sir George Sommers with one hundred and fifty people most happily preserved by the Bermudas to preserve us. . . .

When these two noble knights did see our miseries, being but strangers in that country, and could understand no more of the cause, but by conjecture of our clamors and complaints, of accusing and excusing one another, they embarked us with themselves, with the best means they could, and abandoning Jamestown, set sail for England, whereby you may see the event of the government of the former commanders left to themselves, although they had lived there many years, as formerly hath been spoken (who hindered now their proceedings, Captain Smith being gone).

At noon they fell to the Ile of Hogs, and the next morning to Mulberrypoint, at what time they descried the long-boat of the Lord la Ware, for God would not have it [Virginia] so abandoned. For this honorable Lord, then governor of the country, met them with three ships exceedingly well furnished with all necessaries fitting, who again returned them to the abandoned Jamestown. . . .

His Lordship arrived the ninth of June 1610, accompanied with Sir Ferdinando Waynman, Captain Houlcroft, Captain Lawson, and diverse other gentlemen of sort; the tenth he came up with his fleet, went on shore, heard a sermon, read his commission, and entered into consultation for the good of the colony, in which secret

Text: Captain John Smith, "The General Historie of Virginia &c.," *Works,* ed. Edward Arber ("The English Scholar's Library No. 16" [Birmingham, 1884]), pp. 498-501. The spelling and punctuation have been modernized.

counsel we will a little leave them, that we may duly observe the revealed counsel of God.

He that shall but turn up his eye, and behold the spangled canopy of heaven, or shall but cast down his eye, and consider the embroidered carpet of the earth, and withal shall mark how the heavens hear the earth, and the earth the corn and oil, and they relieve the necessities of man, that man will acknowledge God's infinite providence. But he that shall further observe how God incline all casual events to work the necessary help of his saints, must needs adore the Lord's infinite goodness.

Never had any people more just cause to cast themselves at the very footstool of God and to reverence his mercy, than this distressed colony, for if God had not sent Sir Thomas Gates from the Bermudas, within four days they had almost been famished; if God had not directed the heart of that noble knight to save the fort from firing at their shipping [i.e., from being set on fire at their embarkation] for many were very importunate to have burnt it, they had been destitute of a present harbour and succour. If they had abandoned the fort any longer time, and had not so soon returned, questionless the Indians would have destroyed the fort, which had been the means of our safeties amongst them and a terror. If they had set sail sooner, and had launched into the vast ocean, who would have promised they should have incountered the fleet of the Lord la Ware, especially when they made for Newfoundland, as they intended, a course contrary to our Navy approaching. If the Lord la Ware had not brought with him a years provision, what comfort would those poor souls have received, to have been relanded to a second distruction? This was the arm of the Lord of Hosts, who would have his people pass the Red Sea and Wilderness, and then to possess the land of Canaan. It was divinely spoken of heathen Socrates, If God for man be careful, why should man be over-distrustful? . . .

THE PLYMOUTH EXPERIENCE

3 PILGRIMS' PROGRESS

from William Bradford, *Plimouth Plantation*, 1609-1620

English rulers, beginning with King Henry VIII, (1509-1547) had aligned their country with the Protestant Reformation then sweeping over northern Europe. They rejected papal authority and established the National Church of England as a halfway house between traditional Catholicism and radical Protestantism. Neither Queen Elizabeth (1558-1603) nor her Stuart successor James I would tolerate further agitation of religious questions by zealous religious reformers. (See Chapter 2 for further information on Puritanism.)

Faced with severe persecution, the dissenting congregation of the English town of Scrooby—which shared much of Puritan doctrine but demanded separation from the Anglican Church—began (1607-1609) the long pilgrimage that led to Holland and finally to Plymouth in New England.

William Bradford (1590-1657), self-educated son of a yeoman farmer, joined Pastor John Robinson's Scrooby "Separatists" and became the master spirit of the Plymouth colony. For thirty years he served as governor. Bradford's manuscript history of migration and settlement (first published in 1856) is one of the enduring colonial documents, reflecting his own simplicity and sagacity, his piety and moral force. Above all, one sees in the Bradford history the religious purposes that led the Pilgrims and many other early colonists to seek the New Zion in "a hideous and desolate wilderness."

Financed by a group of London promotors, the Pilgrim exiles made their way from Holland back to England, boarded the *Mayflower*, and set a course for Virginia. (The Virginia Company had granted the Pilgrims permission to found an independent settlement within the limits of its colony.) Accident brought the Pilgrims to Cape Cod in New England. After exploring the nearby coast they moved into the permanent site at Plymouth on Christmas of 1620.

The suffering and quiet heroism of the first year in New England are movingly recounted by Bradford. Here, as in Virginia, a few men cut off from civilization were compelled to master a strange and harsh environment. The cost of failure would be extinction of the colony. Certainly the profound religious faith of the Pilgrims helped to sustain the settlement; but they could not have succeeded without excellent leaders like Bradford and Elder William Brewster or without the timely aid and instruction provided by friendly Indians.

Because they had no legal authority to settle at Plymouth—and for other reasons given by Bradford—the Pilgrim leaders drew up and signed a document stating their consent to form a civil society and to obey its laws. This *Mayflower Compact* of 1620 formed a precedent for the principle that government should be based on written agreements, the principle embodied a century and a half later in the new state and federal constitutions of independent America.

Holland: Decision for the New World

After they had lived in this city [Leyden] about some 11 or 12 years (which is the more observable, being the whole time of that famous truce between that state and the Spaniards) and sundry of them were taken away by death; and many others began to be well stricken in years (the grave mistress experience having taught them many things) those prudent governors, with sundry of the sagest members began both deeply to apprehend their present dangers, and wisely to foresee the future and think of timely remedy. In the agitation of their thoughts, and much discourse of things hereabout, at length they began to incline to this conclusion, of removal to some other place. Not out of any newfangledness, or other suchlike giddy humour by which men are oftentimes transported to their great hurt and danger, but for sundry weighty and solid reasons, some of the chief of which I will here briefly touch. And first, they saw and found by experience the hardness of the place and country to be such as few in comparison would come to them, and fewer that would bide it out and continue with them. For many that came to them, and many more that desired to be with them, could not endure that great labor and hard fare, with other inconveniences which they underwent and were contented with. But though they loved their persons, approved their cause, and honored their sufferings, yet they left them, as it were weeping as Orpah did her mother-in-law Naomi. . . .

. . . But that which was more lamentable, and of all sorrows most heavy to be borne, was that many of their children, by these occasions, and the great licentiousness of youth in that country, and the manifold temptations of the place, were drawn away by evil examples into extravagant and dangerous courses, getting the reins off their necks and departing from their parents. Some became soldiers, others took upon them far voyages by sea, and other some worse courses, tending to dissoluteness, and the danger of their souls, to the great grief of their parents and dishonor of God. So that they saw their posterity would be in danger to degenerate and be corrupted.

Lastly, (and which was not least) a great hope and inward zeal they had of laying some good foundation (or at least to make some way thereunto) for the propagating and advancing the gospel of the Kingdom of Christ in those remote parts of the world; yea, though they should be but even as stepping stones unto others for the performing of so great a work.

These and some other like reasons moved them to undertake this resolution of their removal, the which they afterward prosecuted with so great difficulties, as by the sequel will appear.

The place they had thoughts on was some of those vast and unpeopled countries of America, which are fruitful, and fit for habitation, being devoid of all civil inhabitants, where there are only savage and brutish men which range up and down little otherwise than the wild beasts of the same. This proposition being made public and coming to the scanning of all, it raised many variable opinions amongst men and caused many fears and doubts amongst themselves. Some from their reasons and hopes conceived, labored to stir up and encourage the rest to undertake and prosecute the same; others again, out of their fears, objected against it and sought to divert from it, alleging many things, and those neither unreasonable nor unprobable. . . .

It was answered that all great and honorable actions are accompanied with great difficulties, and must be both enterprised and overcome with answerable courages. It was granted the dangers were great but not desperate; the difficulties were many but not invincible. For though there were many of them likely, yet they were not certain; it might be sundry of the things feared might never befall; others, by provident care and the use of good means, might in a great measure be prevented; and all of them (through the help of God) by fortitude and patience might either be borne or overcome. True it was that such attempts were not to be made and undertaken without good ground and reason, not rashly or lightly as many have done for curiosity or hope of gain, etc. But their condition was not ordinary; their ends were good and honorable; their calling lawful and urgent, and therefore they might expect the

Text: William Bradford, *Bradford's History of Plimouth Plantation* (Boston: Wright & Potter Printing Co., State Printers, 1901), pp. 29-30, 32-35, 93-97, 109-12, 114-16. The spelling and punctuation have been modernized.

blessing of God in their proceeding. Yea, though they should lose their lives in this action, yet might they have comfort in the same, and their endeavors would be honorable. . . . After many other particular things answered and alleged on both sides, it was fully concluded by the major part to put this design in execution, and to prosecute it by the best means they could. . . .

Arrival

. . . [1620] But to omit other things, (that I may be brief), after long beating at sea, they fell with that land which is called Cape Cod, the which being made and certainly known to be it, they were not a little joyful. . . .

Being thus arrived in a good harbor and brought safe to land, they fell upon their knees and blessed the God of heaven, who had brought them over the vast and furious ocean and delivered them from all the perils and miseries thereof, again to set their feet on the firm and stable earth, their proper element. . . .

But here I cannot but stay and make a pause, and stand half amazed at this poor peoples' present condition; and so I think will the reader too, when he well considers the same. Being thus passed the vast ocean and a sea of troubles before in their preparation (as may be remembered by that which went before), they had now no friends to welcome them, nor inns to entertain or refresh their weatherbeaten bodies, no houses or much less towns to repair to, to seek for succor. It is recorded in Scripture, as a mercy to the apostle and his shipwrecked company, that the barbarians showed them no small kindness in refreshing them, but these savage barbarians, when they met with them (as after will appear) were readier to fill their sides full of arrows than otherwise. And for the season it was winter, and they that know the winters of that country know them to be sharp and violent and subject to cruel and fierce storms, dangerous to travel to known places, much more to search an unknown coast. Besides, what could they see but a hideous and desolate wilderness, full of wild beasts and wild men, and what multitudes there might be of them they knew not. Neither could they, as it were, go up to the top of Pisgah, to view from this wilderness a more goodly country to feed their hopes, for which way soever they turned their eyes (save upward to the heavens) they could have little solace or content in respect of any outward objects. For summer being done, all things stand upon them with a weatherbeaten face, and the whole country, full of woods and thickets, represented a wild and savage hue. If they looked

behind them, there was the mighty ocean which they had passed, and was now as a main bar and gulf to separate them from all the civil parts of the world. If it be said they had a ship to succor them, it is true. But what heard they daily from the master and company but that with speed they should look out a place with their shallop where they would be at some near distance, for the season was such as he would not stir from thence till a safe harbor was discovered by them where they would be and he might go without danger; and that victuals consumed apace, but he must and would keep sufficient for themselves and their return. Yea, it was muttered by some that if they got not a place in time they would turn them and their goods ashore and leave them. Let it also be considered what weak hopes of supply and succor they left behind them that might bear up their minds in this sad condition and trials they were under, and they could not but be very small. It is true, indeed, the affections and love of their brethren at Leyden was cordial and entire towards them, but they had little power to help them or themselves. . . . What could now sustain them but the spirit of God and his grace? May not and ought not the children of these fathers rightly say: *Our fathers were Englishmen which came over this great ocean and were ready to perish in this wilderness, but they cried unto the Lord, and he heard their voice, and looked on their adversity, etc. Let them therefore praise the Lord because he is good and his mercies endure forever. Yea, let them which have been redeemed of the Lord show how he hath delivered them from the hand of the oppressor. When they wandered in the desert [and] wilderness out of the way, and found no city to dwell in, both hungry, and thirsty, their soul was overwhelmed in them. Let them confess before the Lord his loving kindness and his wonderful works before the sons of men.* . . .

The Mayflower Compact

I shall, a little, return back and begin with a combination made by them before they came ashore, being the first foundation of their government in this place, occasioned partly by the discontented and mutinous speeches that some of the strangers amongst them had let fall from them in the ship: that when they came ashore they would use their own liberty, for none had power to command them, the patent they had being for Virginia, and not for New England, which belonged to another government, with which the Virginia Company had nothing to do. And partly that such an act by them done (this their condition considered) might be as firm as any patent, and in some respects more sure.

The form was as follows.

In the name of God, Amen. We whose names are underwritten, the loyal subjects of our dread sovereign Lord, King James, by the grace of God, of Great Britain, France, and Ireland, king, defender of the faith, etc., having undertaken, for the glory of God, and advancement of the Christian faith, and honor of our king and country, a voyage to plant the first colony in the northern parts of Virginia, do by these presents solemnly and mutually in the presence of God, and one of another, covenant and combine ourselves together into a civil body politic, for our better ordering and preservation and furtherance of the ends aforesaid; and by virtue hereof to enact, constitute, and frame such just and equal laws, ordinances, acts, constitutions, and offices, from time to time, as shall be thought most meet and convenient for the general good of the Colony, unto which we promise all due submission and obedience. In witness whereof we have hereunder subscribed our names at Cape Cod the 11 of November, in the year of the reign of our sovereign Lord, King James, of England, France, and Ireland, the eighteenth, and of Scotland the fifty-fourth. Anno Dom. 1620.

Year of Trial, 1620-1621

After this they chose, or rather confirmed, Mr. John Carver (a man godly and well approved amongst them) their Governor for that year. And after they had provided a place for their goods, or common store, (which were long in unloading for want of boats, foulness of the winter weather, and sickness of divers,) and begun some small cottages for their habitation as time would admit, they met and consulted of laws and orders, both for their civil and military government, as the necessity of their condition did require, still adding thereunto as urgent occasion in several times and as cases did require.

In these hard and difficult beginnings, they found some discontents and murmurings arise amongst some and mutinous speeches and carriages in other, but they were soon quelled and overcome by the wisdom, patience, and just and equal carriage of things by the Governor and better part, which clave faithfully together in the main. But that which was most sad and lamentable was that, in 2 or 3 months time, half of their company died, especially in January and February, being the depth of winter and wanting houses and other comforts, being infected with the scurvy and other diseases which this long voyage

and their inaccommodate condition had brought upon them. So, as there died sometimes 2 or 3 of a day in the aforesaid time that, of 100 and odd persons, scarce 50 remained. And of these, in the time of most distress, there was but 6 or 7 sound persons, who, to their great commendations be it spoken, spared no pains, night nor day, but with abundance of toil and hazard of their own health, fetched them wood, made them fires, dressed them meat, made their beds, washed their loathsome clothes, clothed and unclothed them; in a word, did all the homely and necessary offices for them which dainty and queasy stomachs cannot endure to hear named; and all this willingly and cheerfully without any grudging in the least, showing herein their true love unto their friends and brethren. A rare example and worthy to be remembered.

Two of these 7 were Mr. William Brewster, their reverend Elder, and Miles Standish, their captain and military commander, unto whom myself and many others were much beholden in our low and sick condition. And yet the Lord so upheld these persons, as in this general calamity they were not at all infected either with sickness, or lameness. And what I have said of these, I may say of many others who died in this general visitation; and others yet living, that while they had health, yea, or any strength continuing, they were not wanting to any that had need of them. And I doubt not but their recompense is with the Lord. . . .

All this while the Indians came skulking about them and would sometimes show themselves aloof of, but when any approached near them, they would run away. And once they stole away their tools where they had been at work and were gone to dinner. But about the *16 of March* a certain Indian came boldly amongst them and spoke to them in broken English, which they could well understand, but marveled at it. At length they understood, by discourse with him, that he was not of these parts, but belonged to the eastern parts, where some English ships came to fish, with whom he was acquainted, and could name sundry of them by their names, amongst whom he had got his language. He became profitable to them in acquainting them with many things concerning the state of the country in the east parts where he lived, which was afterwards profitable unto them; as also of the people here, of their names, number, and strength, of their situation and distance from this place, and who was chief amongst them. His name was *Samasett*. He told them also of another Indian whose name was *Squanto*, a native of this place who had been in England and could speak better English than himself. Being, after some time of entertainment and gifts, dismissed, a while after he came again, and 5 more with him, and they brought again all the tools that were stolen away before, and made way for the coming of their great sachem, called *Massasoit*, who, about 4 *or* 5 *days after*, came with the chief of his friends and other attendance, with the aforesaid *Squanto*. With whom, after friendly entertainment and some gifts given him, they made a peace with him (which hath now continued this 24 years). . . .

After these things he returned to his place called *Sowams*, some 40 *miles* from this place, but *Squanto* continued with them and was their interpreter and was a special instrument sent of God for their good beyond their expectation. He directed them how to set their corn, where to take fish, and to procure other commodities, and was also their pilot to bring them to unknown places for their profit, and never left them till he died. . . .

Evolution of Colonial Society

THE SOUTHERN COLONIES

4

THE FIRST AMERICAN LEGISLATURE

from *Proceedings of the Virginia Assembly*, 1619

The evolution of Virginia from a wilderness outpost to a stable agrarian community proceeded slowly and uncertainly for a generation. Decisive for the economic progress of the colony was the distribution of company lands among the settlers in fifty- and one hundred-acre tracts, carried out in 1619 by Sir George Yeardley, the new governor. This was one of a series of company measures that dissolved the original corporate system and established private ownership as the permanent basis of Virginia's farming economy.

An important step toward political maturity was taken at the same time when Governor Yeardley convened the first representative assembly in English America. This meeting of the elected House of Burgesses (as it came to be known) with the appointed governor and council in the summer of 1619 marked the end of quasi-military rule in Virginia. Although the new representative body had a voice in Virginia affairs, it was still far less than an independent legislature. Both the governor and the English company could reject its acts, and the company could impose policies without securing colonial consent. Yet an example of representative government had been introduced, however cautiously, and this procedure would be followed and developed in all the colonies.

The proceedings of the first American legislature offer a glimpse of prominent Virginia institutions, interests, and attitudes. Of particular interest are the laws that govern moral and religious conduct, showing the tight association between the Anglican Church and the civil government. Note too the assembly's "humble suit" for greater powers. This issue would become a central theme of colonial politics.

A Report of the manner of proceeding in the General Assembly convened at James city in Virginia, July 30, 1619, consisting of the Governor, the Counsel of Estate and two Burgesses elected out of each Incorporation and Plantation, and being dissolved the 4th of August next ensuing. . . .

The most convenient place we could find to sit in was the choir of the church where Sir George Yeardley, the Governor, being set down in his accustomed place, those of the Counsel of Estate

sat next him on both hands, except only the Secretary then appointed Speaker, who sat right before him, John Twine, clerk of the General Assembly, being placed next the Speaker; and Thomas Pierse, the Sergeant, standing at the bar to be ready for any service the Assembly should

Text: "Proceedings of the First Assembly of Virginia, Held July 20, 1619," *Colonial Records of Virginia,* Virginia Senate Document Extra (Richmond, 1874), pp. 9-11, 13-14, 19-23, 25-28, 31-32. The spelling and punctuation have been modernized.

command him. But for as much as men's affairs do little prosper where God's service is neglected, all the Burgesses took their places in the choir till a prayer was said by Mr. Bucke, the Minister, that it would please God to guide and sanctify all our proceedings to his own glory and the good of this plantation. Prayer being ended, to the intent that, as we had begun at God Almighty, so we might proceed with awful and due respect towards the Lieutenant, our most gracious and dread Sovereign, all the Burgesses were entreated to retire themselves into the body of the church, which being done, before they were fully admitted, they were called in order and by name, and so every man (none staggering at it) took the oath of supremacy and entered the Assembly. . . .

. . . The Speaker, who for a long time has been extreme sickly and therefore not able to pass through long harangues, delivered in brief to the whole assembly the occasions of their meeting. Which done he read unto them the commission for establishing the Counsel of Estate and the General Assembly, wherein their duties were described to the life.

Having thus prepared them he read over unto them the great Charter, or commission of privileges, orders and laws, sent by Sir George Yeardley out of England, which, for the more ease of the committees having divided into four books, he read the former two the same forenoon for expedition's sake a second time over, and so they were referred to the perusal of two committees, which did reciprocally consider of either and accordingly brought in their opinions. But some may here object to what end we should presume to refer that to the examination of committees, which the Counsel and Company in England had already resolved to be perfect, and did expect nothing but our assent thereunto. To this we answer that we did it not to the end to correct or control anything therein contained, but only in case we should find ought not perfectly squaring with the state of this Colony, or any law which did press or bind too hard, that we might, by way of humble petition, seek to have it redressed, especially because this great Charter is to bind us and our heirs forever. . . .

Here begin the laws drawn out of the Instructions given by his Majesty's Counsel of Virginia in England to my lord la Warre, Captain Argall and Sir George Yeardley, knight.

By this present General Assembly be it enacted that no injury or oppression be wrought by the English against the Indians whereby the present peace might be disturbed and ancient quarrels might be revived. . . .

First, in detestation of idleness, be it enacted that if any man be found to live as an idler or renegade, though a freedman, it shall be lawful for that Incorporation or Plantation to which he belongeth to appoint him a master to serve for wages, till he show apparent signs of amendment. . . .

As touching the instruction of drawing some of the better disposed of the Indians to converse with our people and to live and labor amongst them, the Assembly, who know well their dispositions, think it fit to enjoin, least to counsel those of the Colony, neither utterly to reject them nor yet to draw them to come in. But in case they will of themselves come voluntarily to places well peopled, there to do service in killing of deer, fishing, beating of corn and other works, that then five or six may be admitted into every such place, and no more, and that with the consent of the Governor. Provided that good guard in the night be kept upon them, for generally (though some amongst many may prove good) they are a most treacherous people, and quickly gone when they have done a villainy. And it were fit a house were built for them to lodge in apart by themselves, and lone inhabitants by no means to entertain them.

Be it enacted by this present assembly that for laying a surer foundation of the conversion of the Indians to Christian religion, each town, city, borough, and particular plantation do obtain unto themselves by just means a certain number of the natives' children to be educated by them in true religion and civil course of life—of which children the most towardly boys in wit and graces of nature to be brought up by them in the first elements of literature, so to be fitted for the college intended for them, that from thence they may be sent to that work of conversion. . . .

Be it further ordained by this General Assembly, and we do by these presents enact that all contracts made in England between the owners of the land and their tenants and servants which they shall send hither, may be caused to be duly performed, and that the offenders be punished as the Governor and Counsel of Estate shall think just and convenient.

Be it established also by this present Assembly that no crafty or advantageous means be suffered to be put in practice for the enticing away the tenants or servants of any particular plantation from the place where they are seated. And that it shall be the duty of the Governor and Counsel of Estate most severely to punish both the seducers and the seduced, and to return these latter into their former places. . . .

. . . And for encouragement of particular hundreds, as Smithe's hundred, Martin's hundred,

Lawnes' hundred, and the like, it is agreed that what commodities are reaped upon any of these several Colonies, it shall be lawful for them to return the same to their own adventurers [investors]. Provided that the same commodity be of their own growing without trading with any other, in one entire lump and not dispersed. . . .

A third sort of laws, such as may issue out of every man's private conceit.

It shall be free for every man to trade with the Indians, servants only excepted, upon pain of whipping. . . .

That no man do sell or give any Indians any piece, shot or powder, or any other arms, offensive or defensive upon pain of being held a traitor to the Colony, and of being hanged as soon as the fact is proved, without all redemption. . . .

All ministers shall duly read divine service, and exercise their ministerial function according to the ecclesiastical laws and orders of the Church of England, and every Sunday in the afternoon shall catechize such as are not yet ripe to come to the Communion. And whosoever of them shall be found negligent or faulty in this kind shall be subject to the censure of the Governor and Counsel of Estate.

The ministers and church wardens shall seek to present all ungodly disorders, the committers whereof. If, upon good admonitions and mild reproof, they will not forbear the said scandalous offenses [such] as suspicions of whoredoms, dishonest company keeping with women and suchlike, they are to be presented and punished accordingly.

If any person, after two warnings, do not amend his or her life in point of evident suspicion of incontinency or of the commission of any other enormous sins, that then he or she be presented by the church wardens and suspended for a time from the church by the minister. In which interim, if the same person do not amend and humbly submit him or herself to the church, he is then fully to be excommunicate, and soon after a writ or warrant to be sent from the Governor for the apprehending of his person and seizing on all his goods. Provided always that all the ministers do meet once a quarter, namely, at the feast of St. Michael the Archangel of the nativity of our Saviour, of the Annunciation of the blessed Virgin, and about midsummer at James city or any other place where the Governor shall reside, to determine whom it is fit to excommunicate, and that they first present their opinion to the Governor ere they proceed to the act of excommunication. . . .

All persons whatsoever upon the Sabbath day shall frequent divine service and sermons both forenoon and afternoon, and all such as bear arms shall bring their pieces, swords, powder, and shot. And everyone that shall transgress this law shall forfeit three shillings a time to the use of the church, all lawful and necessary impediments excepted. But if a servant, in this case, shall willfully neglect his master's command he shall suffer bodily punishment.

No maid or woman servant, either now resident in the Colony or hereafter to come, shall contract herself in marriage without either the consent of her parents, or of her master or mistress, or of the magistrate and minister of the place both together. And whatsoever minister shall marry or contract any such persons without some of the foresaid consents shall be subject to the severe censure of the Governor and Counsel of Estate. . . .

The General Assembly doth humbly beseech the said Treasurer, Counsel and Company, that albeit it belongeth to them only to allow or to abrogate any laws which we shall here make, and that it is their right so to do, yet that it would please them not to take it in ill part if these laws which we have now brought to light do pass current and be of force till such time as we may know their farther pleasure out of England. For otherwise, this people (who now at length have gotten the reins of former servitude into their own swinge [control]) would in short time grow so insolent, as they would shake off all government, and there would be no living among them.

Their last humble suit is that the said Counsel and company would be pleased, so soon as they shall find it convenient, to make good their promise set down at the conclusion of their commission for establishing the Counsel of Estate and the General Assembly, namely, that they will give us power to allow or disallow of their orders of court, as his Majesty hath given them power to allow or to reject our laws.

In sum, Sir George Yeardley, the governor, prorogued the said General Assembly till the first of March, which is to fall out this present year of 1619, and in the mean season dissolved the same.

5

TOBACCO AND TRADE IN MARYLAND

from George Alsop, *Maryland*, 1666

Maryland was the first of the proprietary colonies in America. In 1632 the crown made a grant of territory and far-reaching political powers to George Calvert, first Lord Baltimore. This Maryland charter was taken up by his son and heir, Cecilius. In the case of Virginia, the responsibilities and rewards of planting an American colony had been assigned to a commercial company. The Maryland enterprise was placed in the hands of one wealthy individual proprietor.

The Calverts were leading English Catholics in an age when the Roman Church suffered oppressive restraints. Thus the proprietors saw in Maryland a refuge and a missionary base for Catholics, as well as a source of economic gain. It soon became clear, however, that Protestant settlers would outnumber Catholics; and the early adoption of a policy of partial religious toleration was important in securing the rights of the Catholic minority.

George Alsop, an obscure Englishman, came to Maryland in 1658 as an indentured servant. He was bound to service for four years to repay his master the cost of passage and maintenance. This was the system under which most of the labor for Virginia and Maryland tobacco plantations was supplied during the seventeenth century.

Alsop's sketch of early Maryland agriculture and trade, published after his return to England, shows the primary importance of tobacco in the economy of the Chesapeake Bay region. So valuable was this staple that it served the colonists as a form of money. More significant than the petty New England traders tartly described by Alsop were the London merchants who shipped and marketed most of the Chesapeake tobacco crop and supplied the planters with imports on credit. In the absence of urban trading centers, as Alsop notes, much of the commerce with Maryland (and Virginia) was conducted by the costly method of sending trading vessels up the streams to collect tobacco from the several plantations.

The three main commodities this country [Maryland] affords for traffic are tobacco, furs, and flesh. Furs and skins, as beavers, otters, muskrats, raccoons, wildcats, and elk or buffalo, with diverse others, . . . were first made vendible by the Indians of the country and sold to the inhabitant and by them to the merchant, and so transported into England and other places where it becomes most commodious.

Tobacco is the only solid staple commodity of this province. The use of it was first found out by the Indians many ages ago and transferred into Christendom by that great discoverer of America, Columbus. It's generally made by all the inhabitants of this province, and between the months of March and April they sow the seed (which is much smaller than mustard-seed) in small beds and patches digged up and made so by art, and about May the plants commonly appear green in those beds. In June they are transplanted from their beds and set in little hillocks in distant rows, dug up for the same purpose; some twice or thrice they are weeded and succoured from their illegitimate leaves that would be peeping out from the body of the stalk. They top the several plants as they find occasion in their predominating rankness. About the middle of September they cut

the tobacco down and carry it into houses (made for that purpose) to bring it to its purity. And after it has attained, by a convenient attendance upon time, to its perfection, it is then tied up in bundles and packed into hogsheads and then laid by for the trade.

Between November and January there arrives in this province shipping to the number of twenty sail and upwards, all merchantmen loaded with commodities to traffic and dispose of, trucking with the planter for silks, Hollands, serges, and broadcloths, with other necessary goods, prized at such and such rates as shall be judged on is fair and legal, for tobacco at so much the pound, and advantage on both sides considered; the planter for his work, and the merchant for adventuring himself and his commodity into so far a country. Thus is the trade on both sides drove on with a fair and honest decorum.

The inhabitants of this province are seldom or never put to the affrightment of being robbed of their money, nor to dirty their fingers by telling of vast sums. They have more bags to carry corn

Text: George Alsop, *A Character of the Province of Maryland* ("Fund Publication No. 15, Maryland Historical Society," Baltimore, 1880), pp. 66-69. The spelling and punctuation have been modernized.

than coin; and though they want, but why should I call that a want which is only a necessary miss? the very effects of the dirt of this province affords as great a profit to the general inhabitant as the gold of Peru doth to the straight-breeched commonalty of the Spaniard.

Our shops and exchanges of Maryland are the merchants' storehouses, where with few words and protestations goods are bought and delivered, not like those shopkeepers' boys in London that continually cry, "What do ye lack Sir? What d'ye buy?" yelping with so wide a mouth as if some apothecary had hired their mouths to stand open to catch gnats and vagabond flys in.

Tobacco is the current coin of Maryland, and will sooner purchase commodities from the merchant than money. I must confess the New England men that trade into this province had rather have fat pork for their goods than tobacco or furs, which I conceive is because their bodies being fast bound up with the cords of restringent zeal, they are fain to make use of the lineaments of this non-Canaanite creature physically to loosen them . . .

Madeira wines, sugars, salt, wicker chairs, and tin candlesticks is the most of the commodities they bring in. They arrive in Maryland about September, being most of them ketches and barks, and such small vessels, and those dispersing themselves into several small creeks of this province to sell and dispose of their commodities where they know the market is most fit for their small adventures. . . .

6

PIEDMONT VS. TIDEWATER: BACON'S REBELLION

from *A True Narrative of the Late Rebellion*, 1677

Between the founding of Jamestown and the outbreak of Bacon's Rebellion in 1676, Virginia had developed a social order dominated by the large tobacco planters of the tidewater region. The royal governor and his planter allies effectively controlled the offices, the favors (such as land grants), and the policies of the colonial government. Many historians find the underlying causes of Bacon's Rebellion in the economic and political grievances which western farmers felt and which they attributed to the colonial aristocracy in general and to the arbitrary regime of Governor William Berkeley in particular.

As for the immediate cause, the rebellion arose out of urgent Indian troubles in the back country. The imperiled frontier settlers vainly demanded that Governor William Berkeley authorize a campaign against the Indians. Leading the angry western men was Nathaniel Bacon, an Englishman of distinguished family who had come to Virginia in 1673, received an appointment to the colonial council, and taken up land beyond the fall line. Bacon and his followers marched against the Indians without a commission from the governor, and Bacon was proclaimed a rebel. Widespread popular discontent forced Governor Berkeley to call for long-deferred elections to the House of Burgesses. When Bacon appeared to claim his seat, he was arrested but then released. Returning with a fighting force, Bacon compelled the governor to sign his military commission.

Again Bacon marched west against the Indians; again he was proclaimed a rebel by the governor; and again he occupied Jamestown, this time instituting a reform government. Governor Berkeley's army recaptured the seat of government only to lose it once more to the rebels, who burned Jamestown. In October of 1676, Nathaniel Bacon died, probably of malaria, and his movement soon disintegrated. Twenty-three rebel leaders were executed, and many others lost their estates. Bacon's Rebellion effected no basic changes in the government of Virginia, but two immediate improvements did follow. The high-handed Governor Berkeley was forced out of office by a royal commission sent from England, and a treaty with the Indians brought relief to the western settlements.

The first part of the following selection from the narrative of the commissioners describes the beginning of Bacon's Rebellion; the second part shows how the rebellion, after Bacon's arrest and subsequent release by Governor Berkeley, moved into an all-out offensive; and the third part depicts how, after the siege and burning of Jamestown by the rebels, the rebellion broadened into an attempt to overthrow the Berkeley government but collapsed upon the death of Bacon.

The Rise of the Rebellion

The unsatisfied people, finding themselves still liable to the Indian cruelties, and the cries of their wives and children growing grievous and intolerable to them, gave out in speeches that they were resolved to plant tobacco rather than pay the tax for maintaining of forts, and that the erecting of them was a great grievance, juggle and cheat, and of no more use or service to them than another plantation with men at it, and that it was merely a design of the grandees to engross all their tobacco into their own hands.

Thus the sense of this oppression and the dread of a common approaching calamity made the giddy-headed multitude mad and precipitated them upon that rash overture of running out upon the Indians themselves, at their own voluntary charge and hazard of their lives and fortunes. Only they first by petition humbly craved leave or commission to be led by any commander or commanders as the governor should please to appoint over them to be their chieftain or general. But instead of granting this petition, the governor by proclamation under great penalty, forbade the like petitioning for the future.

This made the people jealous that the governor for the lucre of the beaver and otter trade, etc., with the Indians, rather sought to protect the Indians than them, since after public proclamation prohibiting all trade with the Indians (they complain), he privately gave commission to some of his friends to truck with them, and that those persons furnished the Indians with powder, shot, etc., so that they were better provided than his Majesty's subjects.

The people of Charles City County (near Merchants Hope), being denied a commission by the governor although he was truly informed (as by a letter of his to his Majesty he confesseth) of several formidable bodies of Indians coming down on the heads of James River within 50 or 60 miles of the English plantations, and knew not where the storm would light, they begin to beat up drums for volunteers to go out against the Indians and so continued sundry days drawing into arms, the magistrates being either so remiss or of the same faction that they suffered this disaster without contradiction or endeavoring to prevent so dangerous a beginning and going on.

The rout being got together now wanted nor waited for nothing but one to head and lead them out on their design. It so happened that one Nathaniel Bacon Jr., a person whose lost and desperate fortunes had thrown him into that remote part of the world about 14 months before and framed him fit for such a purpose, as by the sequel will appear, which may make a short character of him no impertinent digression.

He was a person whose erratic fortune had carried and shewn him many foreign parts and of no obscure family. Upon his first coming into Virginia, he was made one of the Council, the reason of that advancement (all on a sudden) being best known to the governor, which honor made him the more considerable in the eye of the vulgar, and gave some advantage to his pernicious designs. He was said to be about four or five and thirty years of age, indifferent tall but slender, blackhaired and of an ominous, pensive, melancholy aspect, of a pestilent and prevalent logical discourse tending to atheism in most companies, not given to much talk or to make sudden replies, of a most imperious and dangerous hidden pride of heart, despising the wisest of his neighbors for their ignorance, and very ambitious and arrogant. But all these things lay hid in him till after he was a councillor, and until he became powerful and popular.

Now this man, being in company with one Crews, Isham, and Bird, who growing to a height of drinking and making the sadness of the times their discourse, and the fear they all lived in because of the Susquahanocks who had settled a little above the Falls of James River and committed many murders upon them, among whom Bacon's overseer happened to be one, Crews and the rest persuaded Mr. Bacon to go over and see the soldiers on the other side James River and to take a quantity of rum with them to give the men to drink, which they did, and (as Crews, etc., had before laid the plot with the soldiers) they all at once in field shouted and cried out, a Bacon! a Bacon! a Bacon! which taking fire with his ambition and spirit of faction and popularity, easily prevailed on him to resolve to head them, his friends endeavoring to fix him the faster to his resolves by telling him that they would also go along with him to take revenge upon the Indians, and drink damnation to their souls to be true to him, and if he could not obtain a commission they would assist him as well and as much as if he had one, to which Bacon agreed.

This forwardness of Bacon's greatly cheered and animated the people, who looked upon him as the only patron of the country and preserver of their lives and fortunes.

Text: "A True Narrative of the Rise, Progresse, and Cessation of the Late Rebellion in Virginia, Most Humbly and Impartially Reported by His Majestyes Commissioners Appointed to Enquire into the Affaires of the Said Colony," *The Virginia Magazine of History and Biography*, IV (1896), pp. 121-25, 129-30, 149-53. The spelling and punctuation have been modernized.

For he pretended and boasted what great service he would do for the country in destroying the common enemy, securing their lives and estates, liberties, and such like fair frauds, he subtly and secretly insinuated by his own instruments over all the country, which he seduced the vulgar and most ignorant people to believe (two-thirds of each county being of that sort) so that their whole hearts and hopes were set now upon Bacon. Next he charges the governor as negligent and wicked, treacherous and incapable, the laws and taxes as unjust and oppressive and cries up absolute necessity of redress.

Thus Bacon encouraged the tumult and as the unquiet crowd follow and adhere to him, he listeth them as they come in upon a large paper, writing their name circular wise, that their ring leaders might not be found out.

Having conjured them into this circle, given them brandy to wind up the charm, and enjoined them by an oath to stick fast together and to him, and the oath being administered, he went and infected New Kent County ripe for rebellion.

Bacon having got about 300 men together in arms prepared to go out against the Indians, the governor and his friends endeavor to divert his designs, but cannot.

He proclaims Bacon and his followers rebels and mutineers for going forth against the Indians without a commission, and (getting a company of gentlemen together) the governor marcheth up to the Falls of James River to pursue and take Bacon, or to seize him at his return, but all in vain, for Bacon had got over the river with his forces and, hastening away into the woods, went directly and fell upon the Indians and killed some of them who were our best friends of Indians and had fought against the Susquahanocks, enemies to the English. . . .

Extorting the Commission

Bacon attending at town for a commission (which the governor is said to have promised him) and being delayed or put off, was secretly whispered to by some of his friends that those delays would endanger his life, and that if speedily he endeavored not to prevent it, there was a conspiracy to murder him on such a night, upon which he privately leaves the town. Now whether this was only a raised rumor of Bacon's, or a real truth we cannot determine, but being raised after Bacon was gone, we suppose it false.

He no sooner was come to the upper parts of James River, but the impatient people run to him to ask how affairs stood, exclaiming still more and more against the Indians and desired to know

if he had yet a commission and, understanding he had or could not obtain any, they began to set up their throats in one common cry of oaths and curses and cried out aloud that they would either have a commission for Bacon that they might serve under his conduct or else they would pull down the town or do worse to some if they had it not, and if Bacon would go but with them they would get him a commission. Thus the raging tumult came down to town (sitting the assembly) and Bacon at the head of them, having entered the town, he seizes and secures the principal places and avenues, sets sentinels and sends forth scouts, so that no place could be more securely guarded.

Having so done, he draws up all his men in arms against the state house where the governor, Council, and Burgesses were then assembled and sitting, and sends in to the Assembly to know if now they would grant him a commission, which Sr. Wm. Berkeley utterly refused and, rising from his chair of judicature, came down to Bacon and told him to his face and before all his men that he was a rebel and a traitor, etc., and should have no commission and, uncovering his naked bosom before him, required that some of his men might shoot him before ever he would be drawn to sign or consent to a commission for such a rebel as Bacon. . . . Much hurrying, solicitation and importunity is used on all sides to the governor to grant Bacon a commission. At last the governor consents, a commission is drawn up and sent him, he dislikes it, they pray him to draw or direct one himself and the governor should sign it. Whereupon Bacon draws up the contents of a commission according to his own mind, and returns it to the clerk to prepare one by which is done, liked of and received.

After the governor had signed the principal commission to Bacon, he is also pleased to sign 30 commissions more [blank] for officers that were to serve under him. . . .

Triumph and Death

Bacon goes next to Green Spring and, during his stay thereabouts, draws a protest or oath against the governor and his party, which is said to be imposed on the people and taken by above 600 at once in Glouster County and also forced upon others in several parts of the country and is as follows:

Bacon's Oath of Fidelity

Whereas Sir William Berkeley, Knight, late Governor of Virginia, hath in a most barbarous and abominable manner exposed and betrayed our lives, and for greediness of sordid gain did defer our just defense and hinder all the loyal endeavors of his Majesty's faithful subjects; and further when the country did raise a sufficient force for the effectual proceeding against the Indian enemy, he did, contrary to all equity and justice and the tenors of his commission, endeavor to oppose the said forces by himself and the Assembly set forth: of which attempts being several times defeated by the people's abhorrence of so bloody a design, he left the country in a small vessel, it being unknown to all people to what parts of the world he did repair, and whereas, as our army upon his departure betaking themselves to the care of the frontiers, did march out against the Indians and obtain so great a victory as hath in a manner finished all the disaster and almost resettled the country in a happy peace, yet notwithstanding Sir Wm. Berkeley, with forces raised in Accomack, did invade the country with acts of hostility, with all intentions to persecute the said army with these aforesaid reasons, as also having betrayed his trust to the king by flying from his seat of judicature, and acting wholly contrary to his commission. We protest against him unanimously as a traitor and most pernicious enemy to the public, and further we swear that in all places of his Majesty's Colony of Virginia we will oppose and prosecute him with all our endeavors by all acts of hostility as occasion shall present, and further, whereas plotting and wishing in his heart a total ruin and destruction of this poor colony he hath endeavored to set the heart of our sovereign against us by false information and lies, requesting forces of his majesty wherewith to compel and subdue us, hindering, intercepting, and preventing all our remonstrances for peace, which might have gone home in our justification, as also hindering of our sending home of agents in the people's behalf which was the most humble and earnest request of the people at first, we do further declare and swear that we think it absolutely consisting with our allegiance and loyalty to treat with and discourse with the said forces and commissioners with all submission to his Majesty. But otherwise, if it shall so prove that notwithstanding all entreaties and offers we shall make, they shall offer to land by force, in our own defense to fly together as in a common calamity and jointly with the present army now under the command of General Bacon, to stand or fall in the defense of him and the country in so just a cause, and in all places to oppose their proceedings (only until such time as his Majesty by our agents shall fully understand the miser-able case of the country, and the justice of our proceedings) which most just request if they shall refuse and by force endeavor to enter the country, we are resolved to uphold the country as long as we can and never to absent and join with any such army whatever, and lastly in case of utmost extremity rather than submit to any so miserable a slavery (when none can longer defend ourselves, our lives and liberties) to acquit the colony rather than submit to so unheard of injustice, and this we all swear in the presence of Almighty God as unfeignedly and freely as ever we desire of him for happiness to come.

By the General.

The governor and his forces being gone, Bacon orders the shore to be guarded all along, to observe their motions, and as they moved to follow them and prevent them from landing or having any provisions sent on board them.

Bacon now begins to show a more merciless severity and absolute authority than formerly, plundering and imprisoning many and condemning some by power of martial law. . . .

Now Bacon finding that his soldiers' insolences growing so great and intolerable to the people (of whom they made no due distinction) and finding their actings to reflect on himself, he did not only betake himself to a strict discipline over his men but also to more moderate courses himself.

Releasing some prisoners, pardoning others that were condemned, and calling those to account against whom any complaints came for seizures or plundering their estates without his order or knowledge.

This prosperous rebel, concluding now the day his own, marcheth with his army into Glouster County, intending to visit all the northern part of Virginia to understand the state of them and to settle affairs after his own measures. . . .

But before he could arrive to the perfection of his designs (which none but the eye of omniscience could penetrate) providence did that which no other hand durst (or at least did) do and cut him off.

He lay sick at one Mr. Pates in Glouster County of the bloody flux, and (as Mr. Pate himself affirms) accompanied with a lousy disease, so that the swarms of vermin that bred in his body he could not destroy but by throwing his shirts into the fire as often as he shifted himself.

He died much dissatisfied in mind, inquiring ever and anon after the arrival of the frigates and forces from England, and asking if his guards were strong about the house.

7
LUBBERLAND: THE BACK COUNTRY OF NORTH CAROLINA

from William Byrd, *History of the Dividing Line*, 1728

None of the romantic images of the colonial South or the frontier fit the Carolina "Lubberland" sketched caustically by William Byrd II (1674-1744) of Westover Plantation, Virginia. Surveying the Virginia-North Carolina boundary, Byrd observed a land of indolence, ignorance, crudity, disorder—an unhealthy backwater of American life. Backwaters of this sort appeared in almost every phase of frontier settlement. Yet to balance the picture one must recall the many thousands of pioneers who brought courage and enterprise to the task of settling the southern back country during the nineteenth century.

The world of William Byrd was as remote as possible from "Lubberland." Heir to a substantial Virginia estate, he combined business initiative with political influence to amass some 179,440 acres in his lifetime. His Westover mansion, with its fine gardens and its broad lawn sloping to the river, was a Virginia showpiece; his manor house was furnished with the costliest furniture and paintings, cut glass, and silver imported from England. His 3600-volume library was one of the finest of colonial collections. Byrd studied law in England, residing there some fifteen years, and traveled on the Continent. In Virginia he not only directed his expansive estates but also, as one of the high aristocracy of the colony, served in the House of Burgesses, the Governor's Council, and several lucrative administrative offices.

Byrd's *History of the Dividing Line* and his *A Progress to the Mines* are vivid accounts of nature, travel, society, and economy in the early eighteenth-century South. First published in 1841, they have been reissued several times since. His candid diaries, now in print, record in detail the occupation and pleasures of a Virginia gentleman at home and abroad.

. . . The Sabbath happened very opportunely to give some ease to our jaded people, who rested religiously from every work but that of cooking the kettle. We observed very few cornfields in our walks, and those very small, which seemed the stranger to us, because we could see no other tokens of husbandry or improvement. But, upon further inquiry, we were given to understand people only made corn for themselves and not for their stocks, which know very well how to get their own living.

Both cattle and hogs ramble in the neighboring marshes and swamps, where they maintain themselves the whole winter long, and are not fetched home till the spring. Thus these indolent wretches, during one half of the year, lose the advantage of the milk of their cattle, as well as their dung, and many of the poor creatures perish in the mire, into the bargain, by this ill management.

Some, who pique themselves more upon industry than their neighbors, will, now and then, in compliment to their cattle, cut down a tree whose limbs are loaden with the moss afore-

mentioned. The trouble would be too great to climb the tree in order to gather this provender, but the shortest way (which in this country is always counted the best) is to fell it, just like the lazy Indians, who do the same by such trees as bear fruit, and so make one harvest for all. By this bad husbandry milk is so scarce in the winter season that, were a big-bellied woman to long for it, she would lose her longing. And, in truth, I believe this is often the case and, at the same time, a very good reason why so many people in this province are marked with a custard complexion.

The only business here is raising of hogs, which is managed with the least trouble, and affords the diet they are most fond of. The truth of it is, the inhabitants of N[orth] Carolina devour so much swine's flesh, that it fills them full of gross humors. For want too of a constant supply of salt, they are commonly obliged to eat it fresh, and that begets the highest taint of scurvy. Thus, whenever a severe cold happens to constitutions thus vitiated, 'tis apt to improve into the yaws, called there very justly the country-distemper. This has all the symptoms of the pox, with this aggravation, that no preparation of mercury will touch it. First it seizes the throat, next the palate, and lastly shows its spite to the

Text: William Byrd, "History of the Dividing Line," *The Writings of Colonel William Byrd*, ed. John Spencer Bassett (New York: Doubleday, Page & Co., 1901), pp. 44-47, 75-76, 79-81, 87. The spelling and punctuation have been modernized.

poor nose, of which 'tis apt, in a small time, treacherously to undermine the foundation.

This calamity is so common and familiar here, that it ceases to be a scandal, and in the disputes that happen about beauty, the noses have in some companies much ado to carry it. Nay, 'tis said that once, after three good pork years, a motion had like to have been made in the House of Burgesses, that a man with a nose should be incapable of holding any place of profit in the province, which extraordinary motion could never have been intended without some hopes of a majority.

Thus, considering the foul and pernicious effects of eating swine's flesh in a hot country, it was wisely forbidden and made an abomination to the Jews, who lived much in the same latitude with Carolina. . . .

We had encamped so early that we found time in the evening to walk near half a mile into the woods. There we came upon a family of mulattoes that called themselves free, though by the shyness of the master of the house, who took care to keep least in sight, their freedom seemed a little doubtful. It is certain many slaves shelter themselves in this obscure part of the world, nor will any of their righteous neighbors discover them. On the contrary, they find their account in settling such fugitives on some out-of-the-way corner of their land, to raise stocks for a mean and inconsiderable share, well knowing their condition makes it necessary for them to submit to any terms.

Nor were these worthy borderers content to shelter runaway slaves, but debtors and criminals have often met with the like indulgence. But if the government of North Carolina has encouraged this unneighborly policy in order to increase their people, it is no more than what ancient Rome did before them, which was made a city of refuge for all debtors and fugitives, and from that wretched beginning grew up in time to be mistress of a great part of the world. And, considering how fortune delights in bringing great things out of small, who knows but Carolina may, one time or other, come to be the seat of some other great empire? . . .

Surely there is no place in the world where the inhabitants live with less labor than in N[orth] Carolina. It approaches nearer to the description of lubberland than any other, by the great felicity of the climate, the easiness of raising provisions, and the slothfulness of the people.

Indian corn is of so great increase, that a little pains will subsist a very large family with bread, and then they may have meat without any pains at all by the help of the low grounds and the great variety of mast that grows on the highland. The men, for their parts, just like the Indians, impose all the work upon the poor women. They make their wives rise out of their beds early in the morning, at the same time that they lie and snore, till the sun has run one-third of his course, and dispersed all the unwholesome damps. Then, after stretching and yawning for half an hour, they light their pipes and, under the protection of a cloud of smoke, venture out into the open air; though, if it happens to be never so little cold, they quickly return shivering into the chimney corner. When the weather is mild, they stand leaning with both their arms upon the cornfield fence, and gravely consider whether they had best go and take a small heat at the hoe, but generally find reasons to put it off till another time.

Thus they loiter away their lives, like Solomon's sluggard, with their arms across and, at the winding up of the year, scarcely have bread to eat.

To speak the truth, 'tis a thorough aversion to labor that makes people file off to N. Carolina, where plenty and a warm sun confirm them in their disposition to laziness for their whole lives. . . .

This town [Edenton, N.C.] is situate on the north side of Albermarle Sound, which is there about 5 miles over. A dirty slash runs all along the back of it, which in the summer is a foul annoyance, and furnishes abundance of that Carolina plague, mosquitoes. There may be 40 or 50 houses, most of them small and built without expense. A citizen here is counted extravagant if he has ambition enough to aspire to a brick chimney. Justice herself is but indifferently lodged, the court house having much the air of a common tobacco house. I believe this is the only metropolis in the Christian or Mahometan world, where there is neither church, chapel, mosque, synagogue, or any other place of public worship of any sect or religion whatsoever.

What little devotion there may happen to be is much more private than their vices. The people seem easy without a minister, as long as they are exempted from paying him. Sometimes the society for propagating the gospel has had the charity to send over missionaries to this country, but unfortunately, the priest has been too lewd for the people or, which oftener happens, they too lewd for the priest. For these reasons these reverend gentlemen have always left their flocks as arrant heathen as they found them. Thus much, however, may be said for the inhabitants of Edenton, that not a soul has the least taint of hypocrisy, or superstition, acting very frankly and above board in all their excesses.

Provisions here are extremely cheap and extremely good, so that people may live plentifully at a trifling expense. Nothing is dear but law, physic, and strong drink, which are all bad in their kind, and the last they get with so much difficulty, that they are never guilty of the sin of suffering it to sour upon their hands. Their vanity generally lies not so much in having a handsome dining room, as a handsome house of office: in this kind of structure they are really extravagant.

They are rarely guilty of flattering or making any court to their governors, but treat them with all the excesses of freedom and familiarity. They are of opinion their rulers would be apt to grow insolent if they grew rich, and for that reason take care to keep them poorer, and more dependent, if possible, than the saints in New England used to do their governors. They have very little coin, so they are forced to carry on their home traffic with paper money. This is the only cash that will tarry in the country, and for that reason the discount goes on increasing between that and real money, and will do so to the end of the chapter. . . .

The line cut William Spight's plantation in two, leaving little more than his dwelling house and orchard in Virginia. Sundry other plantations were split in the same unlucky manner, which made the owners accountable to both governments. Wherever we passed, we constantly found the borderers laid it to heart if their land was taken into Virginia. They chose much rather to belong to Carolina, where they pay no tribute, either to God or to Caesar.

Another reason was, that the government there is so loose, and the laws so feebly executed, that, like those in the neighborhood of Sidon formerly, every one does just what seems good in his own eyes. If the governor's hands have been weak in that province, under the authority of the lord proprietors, much weaker then were the hands of the magistrate, who, though he might have had virtue enough to endeavor to punish offenders, which very rarely happened, yet that virtue had been quite impotent, for want of ability to put it in execution.

Besides, there might have been some danger, perhaps, in venturing to be so rigorous for fear of undergoing the fate of an honest justice in Corotuck precinct. This bold magistrate, it seems, taking upon him to order a fellow to the stocks for being disorderly in his drink was, for his intemperate zeal, carried thither himself, and narrowly escaped being whipped by the rabble into the bargain. . . .

8

GENTLE FOLK AND SIMPLE FOLK IN VIRGINIA: CROSSING THE LINE

from Devereux Jarratt, *Life*, 1806

The *Life* of the Reverend Devereux Jarratt (1733-1801) has been called by a leading scholar, Professor Douglass Adair, "the most interesting autobiography written in eighteenth-century Virginia." As Adair points out, "Jarratt's life was lived on both sides of the class line that divided the gentry from the common people in the Old Dominion and the most popular feat of his career was to cross that line." In this case history of social mobility it was the established church of Virginia that offered the son of a carpenter and small landowner his upward passage into the gentry.

Jarratt's tale tells much of the intellectual and moral as well as the social condition of mid-eighteenth-century Virginia. Thus a boy of nineteen brought up to the plough and ax and offering but a smattering of elementary learning could set up as a country schoolmaster and something of a local wonder. To make an impression of his first assignment, Jarratt obtained from a slave a third-hand periwig, the "distinguishing badge of *gentle folk*." As he moved from family to family, Jarratt acquired a "religious concern"—partly by reflecting on the irreligion of his hosts—and painfully educated himself in the rudiments of theology by reading the stray sermons and Biblical commentaries that came to hand. At twenty-five, with the patronage of the local gentry, the gifted and ambitious schoolmaster put himself to the task of gaining a liberal education and preparing for the ministry. In 1762 he sailed for England to take orders in the Anglican Church and returned to Virginia the following year to claim a parish. Thus began a career of vigorous service to the Episcopal Church in Virginia that seemed for a time to promise a great religious awakening. But the American Revolution and the disestablishment of the state church by Jefferson, Madison, and others made Jarratt's last decades a time of trial and seeming failure.

I was born in *New Kent,* a county in Virginia, about 25 miles below Richmond, on January 6th, 1732-3, O.S. I was the youngest child of *Robert Jarratt* and *Sarah* his wife. . . .

My father was brought up to the trade of a carpenter, at which he wrought till the very day before he died. He was a mild, inoffensive man, and much respected among his neighbors. My mother was the daughter of Joseph Bradley, of *Charles City,* a county bordering on *New Kent.* None of my ancestors, on either side, were either rich or great, but had the character of honesty and industry, by which they lived in credit among their neighbors, free from real want, and above the frowns of the world. This was also the habit, in which my parents were. They always had plenty of plain food and raiment, wholesome and good, suitable to their humble station, and the times in which they lived. Our food was altogether the produce of the farm, or plantation, except a little sugar, which was rarly used; and our raiment was altogether my mother's manufacture, except our hats and *shoes,* the *latter* of which we never put on, but in the winter season. We made no use of *tea* or *coffee* for breakfast, or at any other time; nor did I know a single family that made any use of them. Meat, bread and milk was the ordinary food of all my acquaintance. I suppose the *richer sort* might make use of *those* and other luxuries, but to such people I had no access. We were accustomed to look upon, what were called *gentle folks,* as beings of a superior order. For my part, I was quite shy of *them,* and kept off at a humble distance. A *periwig,* in those days, was a distinguishing badge of *gentle folk*—and when I saw a man riding the road, near our house, with a wig on, it would so alarm my fears, and give me such a disagreeable feeling, that, I dare say, I would run off, as for my life. Such ideas of the difference between *gentle* and *simple,* were, I believe, universal among all of my rank and age. . . .

My parents neither sought nor expected any titles, honors, or great things, either for themselves or children. Their highest ambition was to teach their children to read, write, and understand the fundamental rules of arithmetic. I remember also, they taught us short prayers, and made us very perfect in repeating the *Church Catechism.* They wished us all to be brought up in some honest calling, that we might earn our bread, by the sweat of our brow, as they did. Two of their children died in infancy, before I was born; and only four lived to years of maturity, three sons and a daughter. I was a great favorite, as being the youngest.

When I was between six and seven years of age, I had the misfortune to lose my father, by a very sudden stroke. I remember, on the morning, in which he died, I saw him go out of the house, about his business, as usual, and by nine o'clock I saw him expiring in his chamber. His sudden exit was attributed to his taking a dose of *tartar emetic,* as he complained of being something unwell. The remembrance of *this event,* has made me cautious of *tartar* all my days. I never knowingly took a grain of it; though I suspected that a physician once gave me some of it, in disguise, but it almost put an end to me. It brought on the same symptoms of the cramp and cold sweat, which came on my father, just before he expired—but I, being of a stronger constitution than he, survived the attack.

My father, dying so suddenly and unexpectedly, had made no will; the consequence was that my elder brother, *Robert,* heired all the landed estate. Of the perishable estate an equal division was made, and my part, as well as the rest, amounted to 25£. current money of Virginia, which I was to receive at the age of twenty-one. This sum would be thought very trifling, at this day, but then it was justly reckoned much more considerable, as all family necessaries were so much cheaper, than now. A horse, which would now sell for 20£. might be bought then for 5£.: a good cow and a calf for a pistole, and other things in proportion. I mention these things to shew the difference of the times, and the great fluctuation of human affairs. . . .

At a very early period, as I have been told, I discovered a pregnancy of genius, in some things, not very common, and was frequently called *parson;* and some of my friends would sometimes say they thought I would be a *parson.* I can myself remember *this;* and can now recollect that the retentiveness of my memory was very extraordinary. Before I knew the letters of the alphabet, I could repeat a whole chapter in the Bible, at a few times hearing it read, especially if the subject of it struck my fancy. . . .

At 8 or 9 years old, I was sent to an English school in the neighbourhood:—and I continued to go to one teacher and other, as opportunity served, (though not without great interruptions) till I was 12 or 13. In this time I learned to read in the Bible, (though but indifferently) and to write a sorry scrawl, and acquired some knowledge of Arithmetic. With this small fund, I left school; and my mother dying about this time, no farther care was bestowed on my education.

Text: Douglass Adair (ed.), "The Autobiography of the Reverend Devereux Jarratt, 1732-1763," *William and Mary Quarterly; A Magazine of Early American History,* IX (July 1952), 360-71, 373-75, 378-81, 388-89, 391-93 *passim.*

I now fell into the hands of my eldest brother. In his way, he was exceeding kind to me. He allowed me in all the indulgences a depraved nature, and an evil heart could desire. I mean, he was at no pains to correct my morals, or restrain me from any of the vices of the times. I followed the way of my own heart, and walked in the sight of mine own eyes, not considering, as every one ought, *that for all these things God would bring me into judgment*. While with my brother, I was employed in three kinds of business. 1. In keeping and exercising race-horses for the turf. 2. In taking care of, and preparing gamecocks for a match and main. 3. In ploughing, harrowing and other plantation work. The two first were then agreeable enough—but the last, in which I was the most constantly employed, was very irksome. Thus I continued, till about 17 years of age, when I was allowed to quit the plow, and to betake myself to the business of a carpenter, with my second brother *Joseph*. But he was fractious, and often had recourse to hard words and severe blows. These I did not at all relish: but I continued to labour with him till the latter end of the year 1750, or 1751.

Before I proceed, I must take a little time to reflect on the danger of my situation, at that period. During the 5 or 6 years, I continued with my brothers, I do not remember ever to have seen or heard any thing of a religious nature; or that tended to turn my attention to the great concerns of eternity. I know not, that I ever heard any serious conversation respecting God and Christ, Heaven and Hell. There was a church, in the parish, within three miles of me, and a great many people attended it every Sunday. But I went not once in a year. . . .

In circumstance so unpromising, it is not very wonderful, that I remained ignorant of God, and careless about religion. I only copied the example of my *elders* and *superiors;* and the example of such has great influence, especially a bad example. But so far were those, who ought to have set me a good example, and restrained me from the company, the *conversation* and the *practice* of the ungodly, from doing so, that, by precept and example, I was directly led into all *these,* and encouraged therein. *Cards, racing, dancing, &c.* which are still the favourite sport and diversion of the wicked and ungodly, were then much in vogue. In these I partook, as far as my time and circumstances would permit, as well on Sundays as any other day. In these I vainly sought my felicity, but never found. . . .

I was not contented with the small degree of learning I had acquired, and wished for more knowledge, especially in figures. My friends and acquaintance, I dare say, thought me a topping scholar—but I knew better. I had not gone far in Arithmetic, and was very superficial in the rules I had been hurried through. To understand figures well, we reckoned the height of learning. Philosophy, Rhetoric, Logic, &c. we never heard of. There were no books on such subjects among us. *Arithmetic* was all and all. To acquire this, I borrowed a plain book, in manuscript; and while the horse, with which I harrowed or ploughed, was grazing an hour or two at noon, I frequently spent the time in application to that book. And being now of an age for better discovering the nature of things, I made a greater progress in the real knowledge and use of figures, in one month, than I had done in years, while at school. But I had no thought, then, of commencing a teacher: yet, while at the *plough,* or *ax,* I seemed out of my element. Neither of *these,* as time evinced, was the *business,* for *which* I was designed, and to which providence gradually opened, and prepared the way.

One of the most remote means, as I consider it, which led me to the station, which I now fill, was my being called from the *ax* to the *quill.* This took place, in the 19th year of my age, when I was thinking of nothing less. I was so well skilled in the *Division of Crops,* the *Rule of Three,* and *Practice,* that, you may be sure, the fame of my learning sounded far. One *Jacob Moon,* living in Albermarle county, about one hundred miles from New Kent, had also heard how learned I was. He, being a native of New Kent, and perhaps, prejudiced in favour of his old county folk, sent me word, that he should be glad to employ me as a schoolmaster, and supposed I might get as many pupils, in his neighbourhood, as would make it worth my while to set up a school. I readily embraced the proposal, and soon packed up my *all,* which consisted in such things, as made no great baggage, for I think I carried the whole on my back, except one shirt. In this plight, I took my departure from the place of my nativity. My whole dress and apparel consisted in a pair of coarse breeches, one or two oznaburgs shirts, a pair of shoes and stockings, an old felt hat, a bear skin *coat,* which, by the by, was the first coat I ever had made for me, since my childhood. And that I might appear something more than common, in a strange place, and be counted somebody, I got me an old wig, which, perhaps being cast off by the master, had become the property of his slave, and from the slave it was conveyed to me. But people were not obliged, you know, to ask how I came by it, and, I suppose, I was wise enough not to tell them. I had not, however, a farthing of money, and I believe, I had never owned five shillings cash in all my life. I had neither *horse* nor *saddle;* but my brother lent me *both*, which I was to return in a month or two. On the second or third day, after I sat out, I arrived at *Moon's* place or residence. *Moon* was then an overseer for Col. Richard Cocke, of *Surrey* county. We soon entered on the business of raising a school. But I quickly discovered the number of pupils would be far short of what I had been made to expect. The prospect was gloomy and forbidding, at that time, nor did it brighten much for some years, yet I have reason to adore the providence of God, that brought me here.

I opened my little school, though the promised income, as might be foreseen, would scarce afford me clothing of the coarsest sort. However I was content with a little, which I could call my own. I behaved so well in my new station, that I gained the confidence of *Moon,* so far, that he trusted me with as much checks, as made me two new shirts. This was something better than I had been used to before. I considered myself well of, as I never looked for, or expected great matters. . . .

With respect to religious advantages, my situation was not at all mended, but rather worse. Moon's family, in which I lived, were just as ignorant of religion, as I was, and as careless about it. And as Albemarle was then nearly a frontier county, the manners of the people were generally more rough and uncivilized, than in the more interior parts of the country. In the interior counties, there were churches and ministers to perform divine service every Sunday. But in Albemarle, there was no minister of any persuasion, or any public worship, within many miles. The Sabbath day was usually spent in *sporting:* and whether *this* was right or wrong, I believe, no one questioned. . . .

When my year expired, at Moon's . . . I thought it advisable to move my quarters, and get a school at another place. I did so. Here again my expectation failed me, as my *second* school was less profitable than the *first*. . . .

I went now to board with a gentleman, whose name was *Cannon.* He was a man of great possessions, in lands, slaves, &c. &c. As I had been always very shy of *gentlefolk,* and had never been accustomed to the company and conversation of the rich, you may imagine, how awkwardly, and with what confusion, I entered his house. There was another very fearful circumstance, which added to my perplexity: for I had been told, that the lady of the house was a *New-light,* and of sentiments so rigid and severe, that all levities of every kind must be banished from her presence, and every species of ungodliness must

expect a sharp reproof from her. I was put upon some serious reflections, and considerations, how to demean myself, in her presence, so as to give no cause for reproof, and also induce the pious matron to think I was not destitute of religion. This put me upon a *project* entirely new to me, I mean, *to act the hypocrite.* I had no intention of being religious, but wished to appear so, in order to gain her good opinion. O how thoughtless—how inconsiderate—how foolish is man! While I restrained myself, that I might appear fair in the eyes of a worm, like myself—I considered not that I was, at all time, exposed to the view of that Holy Being, to whom I must render an account for all my words and actions. . . .

The custom of this lady was, as I soon discovered, to read a sermon, in *Flavel,* every night—to which she wished me to attend. I had, indeed, little relish for such entertainment, yet, agreeable to my purpose of playing the hypocrite, and gaining a favourable opinion, I affected a very close attention. And that I might excel in this art, and more effectually answer my purpose, I would sometimes, after a long discourse was finished (Flavel's sermon's being all lengthy) ask her to read another—though, probably, I understood not the tenth part of what was read. Flavel's sermons are too experimental and evangelical, for one, so ignorant of divine things, as I was, to comprehend. . . .

But it pleased God, on a certain night, while she was reading, as usual, to draw out my attention, and fix it on the subject, in a manner unknown to me before. The text of the sermon was, *"Then opened he their understanding:"* From which words were pointed out, what new discoveries would open to the eye of the mind, by means of spiritual illumination, &c. The subject was naturally as dark to me, as any of the former, and yet I felt myself imprest with it, and saw my personal interest in the solemn truths—and truths I believed them to be: But, at the same time, I was conscious, that I was a stranger to that spiritual illumination and its consequent discoveries, and, of course, was yet in a dark and dangerous state. I must have known before this, that I was a sinner, and all things were not right with me, but nothing ever came home to my heart, so as to make a lasting impression, till now. The impression followed me to bed—arose with me in the morning, and haunted me from place to place, till I resolved to forsake my sins, and try to save my soul.—But my resolution was made in my own strength, for I had not yet learned how weak and frail we are by nature, and that all our sufficiency is of God. . . .

This was the state, in which I was, at the conclusion of that year—when necessity obliged me to change my place of abode. I mentioned above, that my *school* here was small, and the *income* about 7£. and I found it would be still less, should I continue another year. So I looked out for a school some where else. *Moon* wished to employ me again, and I went there, with the prospect of having a greater number of pupils, than before. I now got a school of twelve or thirteen scholars, at twenty shillings per scholar, which was the usual price, in those days. I again boarded with *Moon* all that year. . . .

I was myself, at that time, but little acquainted with the principles of the church. Nor did I understand the meaning of many scriptures, which I read, but I understood enough to know that except we *repent*, we must perish—and except a man be *born again*, he cannot see the kingdom of God. These truths I insisted on, in the family, and especially the necessity of being *born again*. This they did not deny, "We must all be born again", said they, "but that is to be after we are dead".

I wished to be better acquainted with the meaning of the scriptures. I wanted some instructor. I had not a single book in the world, nor was I able to buy any books, had I known of any for sale. But, by some means, I got hold of a little old book, in a smoky condition, which I found to be *Russel's* seven sermons. I borrowed the book, and read the sermons again and again. This book was of much service to me; and I remember I was deeply imprest with the account of *Francis Spira*, which is given in one of the Sermons. But I still wanted help in understanding the scriptures. I had never heard of any expositor, nor did I know there was any such in the universe: yet I thought it necessary there should be a book of that sort. Mentioning, perhaps, my desire of an expositor to some person, I was told of a very large *book*, belonging to a gentleman, about five or six miles distant across the river, *which* explained all the New Testament. I resolved to get the reading of that book, if possible. By my living so long with Mr. Cannon, and the resort of gentlemen to his house, I had worn off some of my clownish rusticity, and had become less shy of persons in the upper ranks of life. I, therefore, determined on a visit to the gentleman, who owned the book, and in a short time went to his house. Here I found no less a treasure, than that most excellent *exposition*, called *Burkett* on the New Testament. I asked the loan of it, which was readily granted. And, taking up the *folio* in my arms, I brought home the prize. I was wonderfully pleased with the book, not only

for the light and instruction I gained by it, but also because I found the *writer* to have been a minister of the Church—hoping this circumstance would gain the attention of the family to such parts, as I should wish them to hear me read. But it was not so. As I had no candle, my custom was, in an evening, to sit down flat on the hearth, erect the volume on the end of a chest, which stood near, and, by the light of the fire, read till near midnight. It pleased God mightily to improve my understanding, by these means—and I soon became, what was called a good reader, and my relish for books and reading greatly increased. . . .

My annual income, as already said, had been very small, yet, by frugality, I had saved enough to procure me a small poney and a saddle. I began also to get some credit in a store, and having prospect of getting 13£. at the end of that year, ventured to go in debt for a tolerable suit of cloths—my linen, on Sundays, was finer than formerly, and I began, no doubt, to be a little too vain, and to think more highly of myself, than I ought. . . .

For some time before this period, I began to exercise my talents for the good of souls. I had acquired a considerable knowledge of Divinity and some gift in *extempore* prayer—and in reading with readiness and propriety, I had much improved. I was thought to read any book well, but especially books of sermons and treatises on religious subjects. I acquired the gift of extempore prayer, by officiating as chaplain in Mr. Cannon's family, from the first time family prayer was set up in it, which was shortly after my becoming a member of it the second time.

The way in which I exercised my talents was by appointing meetings, every sunday when the minister was not to preach in the neighbourhood. In these meetings, I used to make prayer, sing Watts' Hymns and Psalms, and read some lively and practical discourse. Considerable congregations used to attend those meetings: solemn attention was paid—impressions were frequently made on the hearers, and I hope some good was done. . . .

Having continued this exercise for some time, several of my friends wished me to turn my attention toward the ministry, suggesting I had talents suitable for such an office, and that I might be of more service by devoting myself entirely to the preaching of the gospel. But I looked upon the idea as fanciful, and paid little regard to suggestions of that sort. Not that I was averse to the office—but how it was possible I could be qualified, so as to be admitted to it, I had no conception—I was wholly among the *Presby-*

terians—had received all my knowledge of religion from them, was peculiarly attached to them and their Church and had no notion then of being a minister or member of any other. I had never examined the principles of the *Church of England,* and by what I knew of the lives and preaching of the Clergy, I had imbibed strong prejudices against that Church—I know also that the *Presbyterians* required the knowledge of the Latin, Greek, &c. in all, who took part with them in the Ministry. This obstacle appeared insuperable, as I was totally ignorant of *these* languages, and without the means of acquiring the knowledge of them.

I had, by this time taught school five or six years, and was under such a character as a teacher, that I suppose, I could have got business any where. Having stayed with Mr. Cannon as long as convenient, I went into Cumberland, and set up a school at Mr. Thomas Tabb's, a gentleman who had lately joined the Presbyterians. I boarded in his house, performed the office of chaplain in the family, morning and evening, and still kept up the custom of meeting on sundays, either at my school-house or other private houses. Here I was living when *N. Davies,* a gentleman of Cumberland, solicited, and obtained a young man from the college of *New Jersey,* to come to his house to instruct his son, in the *Latin* &c. This young man's name was *Alexander Martin,* who, after the Revolution was repeatedly elected governor in North Carolina, and is, at this time one of the members of Congress—I was now more than ever pressed on by my friends, to turn my attention to the ministry; and, for this purpose, they advised me to put myself under the tuition of *Mr. Martin.* I was still without money, perhaps I had not twenty shillings in cash—for, of late, I had laid out what money I could spare, in buying books —and a very good collection of Divinity, Poetry, &c. I had got, the want of money was the only obstacle in the way—but the hand of Providence interposed, and removed it. Mr. *John Cannon,* with whom I had lived, and Capt. *John Hunter,* uncle to Mr. *Martin,* kindly offered me such assistance, as should enable me to go through my studies. This they did unsolicited, and *gratis* —Such a generous proposal I could not reject, and, in a little while, entered Mr. *Martin's* school, as his pupil, being then twenty-five years and four months old—or thereabout.

I had never seen the rudiments of the Latin tongue, in all my life, nor had I learned a word in any grammar whatever. But such was the strength of my memory then, that in eight days, I could so perfectly repeat every part of the grammar, that I began to construe, give the parts

of speech, rules, &c. In seven months, I began to read *Suetonius,* one of the most difficult Latin authors in prose—in a word, I acquired such knowledge of the Latin and Greek, in that year, that my generous friends were released from their burden—as I was capable of improving myself, and teaching others also. . . .

It was in the spring, 1762, when I quit my school, and began to prepare for an immediate entrance into Holy Orders. Not in the *Presbyterian,* as first intended, but in the *Church* of England—I first obtained a title to a parish— next waited on the Governor of Virginia, and then on the Rev. Mr. *William Robinson,* the Bishop of London's Commissary. From both I obtained such papers as were necessary to carry to the Bishop—I had all things ready in May, and agreed for my passage with a William Ashburn, Captain of a Ship, called the *Everton*—but, by one hindrance and another, I did not sail for England till some time in the October following. . . .

[Upon arriving in England] I waited on the bishop of London, as soon as I could, and put all my papers in his hand. He read them, and told me my credentials were very authentic, and refered me to his chaplain, Dr. *Fortin,* for examination—but told me there would be no ordination till Christmas. I said, my wish was to be dispatched sooner, as I never had the small pox, I was in great danger every day I staid in the city. His reply was, he could not have ordinations every day.—I knew I must wait his leisure, and so took my leave of his lordship, for that time. I then waited on Dr. *Fortin,* and past my trials before him with approbation, and he promised to present me to the bishop. He did so, and I was ordained deacon, in the King's chapel, at Christmas, in the year 1762, after I had staid in London about four weeks. There were several others ordained at the same time, all Englishmen, except myself. Some of these had studied at *Oxford,* and some at Cambridge. We all, by appointment, waited on the bishop, in the afternoon of the same day, on which we had been ordained. We were received very politely, and, I remember, he addrest himself to us in words to this effect— that he had never been so well pleased with any ordination before, as he then was—"Your performances, at your examination, which I have now in hand, *said he,* are all well done;" and, fixing his eyes on me, added, "especially yours from Virginia." 'You may be sure it was very gratifying to me, to find myself, who had never seen the inside of a college, or any other public seminary, one hour in my life, thus distinguished, and placed before *Oxonians* and *Cantabrigians.*

The bishop of *Chester* was to hold an ordination, in the city, the Sunday following, and I requested and obtained from my lord of London, letters dismissory to him. And, having passed my trials before his chaplain, I was ordained priest, by the bishop of Chester, just one week after I had been ordained a deacon.

By the 10th of January, 1763, I had all my letters of ordination, &c. ready for returning back to Virginia. . . .

We had a long passage, and were at short allowance for water, almost the whole way. But, by the blessing of God, I had the pleasure of treading on my native soil the first sunday in July, 1763; and after an absence of about nine months. For all the favors I met with; during this period, and for all the dangers I escaped let the name of the Lord have all the thanks, praise and adoration, which are so justly due.

I landed in York-Town, early on the Sunday morning, and taking breakfast at an inn, I went up York river, in a boat, in order to wait on the commissary. I waited also on the governor of Virginia. Then, having seen my friends in New-Kent, I went in quest of a parish. . . .

I was now introduced into a new station in life, which called for new exertions, and I applied myself to the several duties of my office, according to the best of my judgment—But the manner, in which I conducted myself—the means I used for the salvation of souls, and the success of my labours, will be the subject of another letter—And indeed, it would appear impious, in me, if I did not stop, a while, in his place, to pour out my soul, in ardent gratitude and praise, to that indulgent *Being,* who endowed me with such faculties of body and mind, as I have possest, and still possess—who, at all times, hath given me food to eat and raiment to put on, suited to the various stations and conditions of my life—raised me from the depths of obscurity and the lowest walks of life, to some degree of eminence and usefulness among men—provided friends for me, both at home and abroad—by sea and land, and on both sides the *Atlantic.* But above all, am I bound to bless and magnify his goodness and mercy, in bringing me out of a state of darkness, guilt and bondage to sin and satan, to a state of light and knowledge, and set me at liberty from the worst of tyrants, through Jesus Christ—and giving me a good hope, through grace, that, when I have served him, in this generation, according to his will, I shall rest from my labors, in the peaceful regions of everlasting felicity, when time shall be no more.

THE NEW ENGLAND COLONIES

9

PLYMOUTH PLANTATION

from William Bradford, *Plimouth Plantation,* 1623-1644

The direct influence of the Pilgrims upon American history was relatively slight. Plymouth was soon overshadowed and, in 1691, was absorbed by the neighboring Massachusetts Bay Colony of the Puritans. Yet the Plymouth experience—as related by Governor Bradford—is instructive on many matters relevant to other New England settlements. Here was a typical experiment in creating a "Godly Commonwealth" in the American forest. (On Bradford, see Document 3. Chapter 2 presents the ideas underlying the "Godly Commonwealth" of the Puritans.)

Originally Plymouth, like early Jamestown, was to be a corporate enterprise. For seven years all ownership was to rest in the company that financed the venture; then assets were to be distributed among the shareholders. By 1623, however, the Plymouth colonists found the corporate system unworkable. They gained independence from their English backers after 1627 and permanently established private ownership of land. Governor Bradford shrewdly observes the contrasting effects of the two forms of economic organization.

The final passages on the dispersion of the Plymouth congregation suggest two persistent themes of early New England history: the steady displacement of religious by secular motives and controls, and the continuous process of forming new settlements by the detachment of organized groups from the older centers. Under this latter system, the town became the basic political unit throughout New England. (See Document 158 for a view of the New England town as it appeared some two centuries later.)

Of Collective Farming

. . . [1623] At length, after much debate of things, the Governor (with the advice of the chiefest amongst them) gave way that they should set corn, every man for his own particular, and in that regard trust to themselves; in all other things to go on in the general [collective] way as before. And so assigned to every family a parcel of land, according to the proportion of their number for that end, only for present use (but made no division for inheritance), and ranged all boys and youth under some family. This had very good success for it made all hands very industrious, so as much more corn was planted than otherwise would have been by any means the Governor or any other could use, and saved him a great deal of trouble, and gave far better content. The women now went willingly into the field and took their little ones with them to set corn, which before would allege weakness and inability, whom to have compelled would have been thought great tyranny and oppression.

The experience that was had in this common course and condition, tried sundry years and that amongst godly and sober men, may well evince they [the] vanity of that conceit of Plato's and other ancients, applauded by some of later times, that the taking away of property and bringing in community into a commonwealth, would make them happy and flourishing, as if they were wiser than God. For this community (so far as it was) was found to breed much confusion and discontent and retard much employment that would have been to their benefit and comfort. For the young men that were most able and fit for labor and service did repine that they should spend their time and strength to work for other men's wives and children, without any recompense. The strong, or man of parts, had no more in division of victuals and clothes than he that was weak and not able to do a quarter the other could; this was thought injustice. The aged and graver men to be ranked and equalized in labors and victuals, clothes, etc., with the meaner and younger sort, thought it some indignity and disrespect unto them. And for men's wives to be commanded to do service for other men, as dressing their meat, washing their clothes, etc., they deemed it a kind of slavery, neither could many husbands well brook it. Upon the point all being to have alike, and all to do alike, they thought themselves in the like condition and one as good as another; and so, if it did not cut off those relations that God hath set amongst men, yet it did at least much diminish and take of the mutual respects that should be preserved amongst them. And would have been worse if they had been men of

another condition. Let none object this is men's corruption and nothing to the course itself. I answer, seeing all men have this corruption in them, God in his wisdom saw another course fitter for them. . . .

Of Saints and Sinners

[1642] Marvelous it may be to see and consider how some kind of wickedness did grow and break forth here in a land where the same was so much witnessed against, and so narrowly looked unto, and severely punished when it was known; as in no place more, or so much that I have known or heard of; insomuch as they have been somewhat censured, even by moderate and good men, for their severity in punishments. And yet all this could not suppress the breaking out of sundry notorious sins (as this year, besides other, gives us too many sad precedents and instances), especially drunkenness and uncleanness; not only incontinency between persons unmarried, for which many, both men and women have been punished sharply enough, but some married persons also. But that which is worse, even sodomy and buggery (things fearful to name), have broke forth in this land oftener than once. I say it may justly be marveled at and cause us to fear and tremble at the consideration of our corrupt natures, which are so hardly bridled, subdued, and mortified; nay, cannot by any other means but the powerful work and grace of God's spirit. But (besides this) one reason may be that the Devil may carry a greater spite against the churches of Christ and the gospel here, by how much the more they indeavor to preserve holiness and purity amongst them, and strictly punisheth the contrary when it ariseth either in church or commonwealth, that he might cast a blemish and stain upon them in the eyes of [the] world, who use to be rash in judgment. I would rather think thus, than that Satan hath more power in these heathen lands, as some have thought, than in more Christian nations, especially over God's servants in them.

Another reason may be, that it may be in this case as it is with waters when their streams are stopped or dammed up, when they get passage they flow with more violence and make more noise and disturbance than when they are suffered to run quietly in their own channels. So wickedness being here more stopped by strict laws, and the same more nearly looked unto, so as it cannot run in a common road of liberty as it would

Text: William Bradford, *Bradford's History of Plimouth Plantation* (Boston: Wright & Potter Printing Co., State Printers, 1901), pp. 162-64, 459-61, 507-09. The spelling and punctuation have been modernized.

and is inclined; it searches everywhere, and at last breaks out where it gets vent.

A third reason may be, here (as I am verily persuaded) is not more evils in this kind, nor nothing near so many by proportion as in other places; but they are here more discovered and seen and made public by due search, inquisition, and due punishment; for the churches look narrowly to their members, and the magistrates over all, more strictly than in other places. Besides, here the people are but few in comparison of other places, which are full and populous and lie hid, as it were, in a wood or thicket, and many horrible evils by that means are never seen nor known; whereas here they are, as it were, brought into the light and set in the plain field, or rather on a hill, made conspicuous to the view of all. . . .

Of the Dispersion

[1644] Many having left this place (as is before noted) by reason of the straightness and barrenness of the same, and their finding of better accommodations elsewhere, more suitable to their ends and minds; and sundry others still upon every occasion desiring their dismissions, the church began seriously to think whether it were not better jointly to remove to some other place than to be thus weakened and as it were insensibly dissolved. Many meetings and much consultation was held hereabout, and diverse were men's minds and opinions. Some were still for staying together in this place, alleging men might here live, if they would be content with their condition; and that it was not for want or necessity so much that they removed as for the enriching of themselves. Others were resolute upon removal, and so signified that here they could not stay, but if the church did not remove, they must. Insomuch as many were swayed, rather than there

should be a dissolution, to condescend to a removal if a fit place could be found that might more conveniently and comfortably receive the whole, with such accession of others as might come to them for their better strength and subsistence, and some such like cautions and limitations. So as, with the aforesaid provisos, the greater part consented to a removal to a place called Nawsett, which had been superficially viewed and the good will of the purchasers (to whom it belonged) obtained, with some addition thereto from the court. But now they began to see their error, that they had given away already the best and most commodious places to others, and now wanted themselves, for this place was about fifty miles from hence, and at an outside of the country, remote from all society; also, that it would prove so strait, as it would not be competent to receive the whole body, much less be capable of any addition or increase; so as (at least in a short time) they should be worse there then they are now here. The which, with sundry other like considerations and inconveniences, made them change their resolutions. But such as were before resolved upon removal took advantage of this agreement and went on notwithstanding, neither could the rest hinder them, they having made some beginning.

And thus was this poor church left, like an ancient mother, grown old, and forsaken of her children (though not in their affections), yet in regard of their bodily presence and personal helpfulness. Her ancient members being most of them worn away by death, and these of later time being like children translated into other families, and she like a widow left only to trust in God. Thus she that had made many rich became herself poor. . . .

10   PURITAN ARISTOCRACY: THE LIMITS OF POPULAR LIBERTY

from John Winthrop, *History of New England*, 1645

The Massachusetts Bay colony was founded in 1630 by English Puritan dissenters. Acute religious and political persecution in England—the prelude to the bloody civil war of 1642-1644—drove some 25,000 settlers to New England in the "Great Migration" of 1630-1640. For many, especially among the leaders, Massachusetts represented a promised land where God's elect might create a "Bible Commonwealth," free from the persecutions and corruptions of old England. There was no promise of freedom for all but only for those who shared the Puritan faith and discipline.

The legal basis for the Massachusetts Bay colony was a royal charter issued (1629) to an English company of merchants and other investors with Puritan sympathies. A small group of company officers and freemen (stockholders)—all zealous Puritans—were authorized to carry the charter to New England and to rule the colony according to the charter terms. Thus, by converting a company charter into a frame of government,

Massachusetts Bay became in large measure a self-governing colony under the general authority of the crown.

The ruling officers and freemen of the company in America were only a handful among the thousands of original settlers. Slowly and reluctantly they acceded to demands for a wider distribution of political rights, although they continued to believe that the good Puritan society could be achieved only under the firm governance of the wise and godly few, the eminent leaders of church and state.

John Winthrop (1588-1649) represented the ruling Puritan aristocracy. Educated at Cambridge University and trained in the law, Winthrop was a substantial member of the English gentry with profound Puritan convictions and a high ambition to build a "Godly Commonwealth" in the American wilderness. He was the first governor of Massachusetts Bay and was recalled to the office repeatedly during his life in America.

In his "Little Speech on Liberty" reprinted below, Winthrop defended what finally proved to be a losing cause when he insisted that the freemen and their delegates in the General Court, or legislature, should quietly submit to the authority of the magistrates (the governor, deputy, and council of assistants). He contended that though they were called to office by the people, the magistrates nevertheless derived from God their authority to govern and judge men "by rules of God's laws and our own."

The immediate occasion for the speech was an angry quarrel between Deputy Governor Winthrop and some defiant men of the town of Hingham over the appointment of a militia captain. However, as Winthrop explains in his excellent journal, behind the quarrel lay the growing popular demand "that magistracy must be no other, in effect, than a ministerial [i.e., administrative] office, and all authority both legislative, consultative, and judicial, must be exercised by the people in their body representative."

I suppose something may be expected from me upon this charge [of exceeding the powers of deputy governor] that is befallen me, which moves me to speak now to you; yet I intend not to intermeddle in the proceedings of the court, or with any of the persons concerned therein. Only I bless God, that I see an issue of this troublesome business. I also acknowledge the justice of the court and, for mine own part, I am well satisfied. I was publicly charged and I am publicly and legally acquitted, which is all I did expect or desire. And though this be sufficient for my justification before men, yet not so before the God who hath seen so much amiss in my dispensations (and even in this affair) as calls me to be humble. For to be publicly and criminally charged in this court is matter of humiliation (and I desire to make a right use of it), notwithstanding I be thus acquitted. If her father had spit in her face, (saith the Lord concerning Miriam,) should she not have been ashamed seven days? Shame had lien upon her, whatever the occasion had been. I am unwilling to stay you from your urgent affairs, yet give me leave (upon this special occasion) to speak a little more to this assembly. It may be of some good use to inform and rectify the judgments of some of the people, and may prevent such distempers as have arisen amongst us. The great questions that have troubled the country are about the authority of the magistrates and the liberty of the people. It is yourselves who have called us to this office, and being called by

you, we have our authority from God in way of an ordinance such as hath the image of God eminently stamped upon it, the contempt and violation whereof hath been vindicated with examples of divine vengeance. I entreat you to consider that when you choose magistrates you take them from among yourselves, men subject to like passions as you are. Therefore, when you see infirmities in us you should reflect upon your own and that would make you bear the more with us and not be severe censurers of the failings of your magistrates, when you have continual experience of the like infirmities in yourselves and others. We account him a good servant who breaks not his covenant. The covenant between you and us is the oath you have taken of us which is to this purpose: that we shall govern you and judge your causes by the rules of God's laws and our own, according to our best skill. When you agree with a workman to build you a ship or house, etc., he undertakes as well for his skill as for his faithfulness, for it is his profession and you pay him for both. But when you call one to be a magistrate, he doth not profess nor undertake to have sufficient skill for that office nor can you furnish him with gifts, etc., therefore you must run the hazard of his skill and ability. But if he fail in faithfulness, which by his oath he is bound

Text: John Winthrop, *The History of New England from 1630 to 1649,* ed. James Savage (Boston: Little, Brown & Co., 1853), II, 279-82. The spelling and punctuation have been modernized.

unto, that he must answer for. If it fall out that the case be clear to common apprehension and the rule clear also, if he transgress here, the error is not in the skill but in the evil of the will: it must be required of him. But if the case be doubtful, or the rule doubtful to men of such understanding and parts as your magistrates are, if your magistrates should err here, yourselves must bear it.

For the other point concerning liberty, I observe a great mistake in the country about that. There is a twofold liberty, natural (I mean as our nature is now corrupt) and civil or federal. The first is common to man with beasts and other creatures. By this, man as he stands in relation to man simply hath liberty to do what he lists; it is a liberty to evil as well as to good. This liberty is incompatible and inconsistent with authority, and cannot endure the least restraint of the most just authority. The exercise and maintaining of this liberty makes men grow more evil and in time to be worse than brute beasts: *omnes sumus licentia deteriores.* This is that great enemy of truth and peace, that wild beast which all the ordinances of God are bent against, to restrain and subdue it. The other kind of liberty I call civil or federal; it may also be termed moral, in reference to the covenant between God and man in the moral law, and the politic covenants and constitutions amongst men themselves. This liberty is the proper end and object of authority, and cannot subsist without it; and it is a liberty to that only which is good, just, honest. This liberty you are to stand for, with the hazard (not only of your goods, but) of your lives, if need be. Whatsoever crosseth this, is not authority but a distemper thereof. This liberty is maintained and exercised in a way of subjection to authority; it is of the same kind of liberty wherewith Christ hath made us free. The woman's own choice makes such a man her husband; yet being so chosen, he is her lord and she is to be subject to him, yet in a way of liberty not of bondage; and a true wife accounts her subjection her honor and freedom and would not think her condition safe and free but in her subjection to her husband's authority. Such is the liberty of the church under the authority of Christ, her king and husband; his yoke is so easy and sweet to her as a bride's ornaments; and if through forwardness or wantonness, etc., she shake it off at any time, she is at no rest in her spirit until she take it up again; and whether her lord smiles upon her and embraceth her in his arms, or whether he frowns or rebukes or smites her, she apprehends the sweetness of his love in all and is refreshed, supported, and instructed by every such dispensation of his authority over her. On the other side, ye know who they are that complain of this yoke and say, let us break their bands, etc., we will not have this man to rule over us. Even so, brethren, it will be between you and your magistrates. If you stand for your natural corrupt liberties and will do what is good in your own eyes, you will not endure the least weight of authority, but will murmur and oppose and be always striving to shake off that yoke; but if you will be satisfied to enjoy such civil and lawful liberties, such as Christ allows you, then will you quietly and cheerfully submit unto that authority which is set over you, in all the administrations of it, for your good. Wherein, if we fail at any time, we hope we shall be willing (by God's assistance) to hearken to good advice from any of you, or in any other way of God; so shall your liberties be preserved in upholding the honor and power of authority amongst you.

11 | **WEDDINGS AND RED RIBBONS: LIFE IN CONNECTICUT**

from Sarah Kemble Knight, *Journal,* 1704

Mrs. Sarah Kemble Knight (1666-1727), daughter of a Boston merchant, was a vigorous and versatile woman of affairs whose journal of a trip on horseback from Boston to New York and back in 1704-1705 provides a richly detailed view of ordinary life in the early eighteenth century. Traveling with such company as she could find along the primitive roads of southern New England and New York—a strenuous and sometimes risky adventure in those days—this competent colonial lady was engaged along the way in the business of settling an estate, probably that of her late shipmaster husband. Later, Madam Knight conducted a school in her home and may well have taught the young Benjamin Franklin his letters. She settled finally in Connecticut, where she bought lands, maintained an inn, and accumulated an estate valued at £1800.

Her observations of New Haven, Connecticut, reprinted in the following selection, range from marriage customs to business practices. Note especially the system, then widespread in the colonies, of using local commodities and even Indian wampum as a form of currency.

Madam Knight's portrayal of a tobacco-spitting "bumpkin" buying bits of finery for his shy "Jone Tawdry" would not have pleased those rigid Puritans, John Davenport and Theophilus Eaton, who founded the New Haven colony in 1639. There, as in Massachusetts Bay, the founders planned a community that united church and state to enforce God's rules for men. The Connecticut colony, which absorbed New Haven in 1665, maintained a close church-state alliance through the eighteenth century even as popular ways became more secular and liberal.

Madam Knight's manuscript journal was first published in 1825 and has been reprinted in several later editions.

. . . They are governed by the same laws as we in Boston (or little differing), throughout this whole colony of Connecticut, and much the same way of church government, and many of them good, sociable people, and I hope religious too: but a little too much independent in their principles and, as I have been told, were formerly in their zeal very rigid in their administrations towards such as their laws made offenders, even to a harmless kiss or innocent merriment among young people. Whipping being a frequent and counted an easy punishment about which, as other crimes, the judges were absolute in their sentences. . . .

Their diversions in this part of the country are on lecture days and training days mostly: on the former there is riding from town to town.

And on training days the youth divert themselves by shooting at the target as they call it (but it very much resembles a pillory), where he that hits nearest the white has some yards of red ribbon presented him, which being tied to his hatband, the two ends streaming down his back, he is led away in triumph with great applause, as the winners of the Olympiac Games. They generally marry very young, the males oftener, as I am told, under twenty than above; they generally make public weddings and have a way something singular (as they say) in some of them, viz. Just before joining hands the bridegroom quits the place, who is soon followed by the bridesmen, and as it were, dragged back to duty—being the reverse to the former practice among us, to steal Miss Pride.

There are great plenty of oysters all along by the seaside, as far as I rode in the colony, and those very good. And they generally lived very well and comfortably in their families. But too indulgent (especially the farmers) to their slaves, suffering too great familiarity from them, permitting them to sit at table and eat with them (as they say to save time). . . .

There are everywhere in the towns as I passed, a number of Indians, the natives of the country, and are the most savage of all the savages of that kind that I had ever seen, little or no care taken (as I heard upon enquiry) to make them otherwise. They have in some places lands of their own and governed by laws of their own making; —they marry many wives and at pleasure put them away and on the least dislike or fickle humor on either side; saying *stand away* to one another is a sufficient divorce. And indeed those uncomely *Stand aways* are too much in vogue among the English in this (indulgent colony) as their records plentifully prove, and that on very trivial matters, of which some have been told me but are not proper to be related by a female pen, though some of that foolish sex have had too large a share in the story. . . .

They give the title of merchant to every trader, who rate their goods according to the time and specie they pay in: viz. pay, money, pay as money, and trusting. *Pay* is grain, pork, beef, etc., at the prices set by the General Court that year; *money* is Pieces of Eight, Ryals, or Boston or Bay shillings (as they call them), or good hard money, as sometimes silver coin is termed by them; also Wampum, viz. Indian beads which serves for change. *Pay as money* is provisions, as aforesaid one-third cheaper than as the Assembly or General Court sets it; and *trust* as they and the merchants agree for time.

Now, when the buyer comes to ask for a commodity, sometimes before the merchant answers that he has it, he says, "Is your pay ready?" Perhaps the chap replies "Yes"; "What do you pay in?" says the merchant. The buyer having answered, then the price is set; as suppose he wants a sixpenny knife, in pay it is 12d—in pay as money eight pence, and hard money its own price, viz. 6d. It seems a very intricate way of trade and what *Lex Mercatoria* had not thought of.

Text: Sarah Kemble Knight, *The Private Journal of a Journey from Boston to New York in the Year 1704,* ed. William Law Learned (Albany, N.Y.: Frank H. Little, 1865), pp. 49-50, 52-60. The spelling and punctuation have been modernized.

Being at a merchant's house, in comes a tall country fellow with his alfogeos [bag or pouch] full of tobacco, for they seldom lose their cud but keep chewing and spitting as long as their eyes are open—he advanced to the middle of the room, makes an awkward nod, and spitting a large deal of aromatic tincture, he gave a scrape with his shovel-like shoe, leaving a small shovel full of dirt on the floor, made a full stop, hugging his own pretty body with his hands under his arms, stood staring round him like a cat let out of a basket. At last, like the creature Balaam rode on, he opened his mouth and said: "Have you any ribbon for hatbands to sell I pray?" The questions and answers about the pay being past, the ribbon is brought and opened. Bumpkin simpers, cries, "It's confounded gay I vow"; and beckoning to the door, in comes Jone Tawdry, dropping about 50 curtsies and stands by him; he shows her the ribbon. "Law you," says she, "it's right gent, do you take it, 'tis dreadful pretty." Then she enquires, "Have you any hood silk I pray?" which being brought and bought, "Have you any thread silk to sew it with," says she, which being accommodated with, they de-

parted. They generally stand, after they come in, a great while speechless and sometimes don't say a word till they are asked what they want, which I impute to the awe they stand in of the merchants, who they are constantly almost indebted to, and must take what they bring without liberty to choose for themselves; but they serve them as well, making the merchants stay long enough for their pay. . . .

Their chief red-letter day is St. Election, which is annually observed according to charter to choose their governor, a blessing they can never be thankful enough for, as they will find if ever it be their hard fortune to lose it. The present governor in Connecticut is the Honorable John Winthrop, Esq., a gentleman of an ancient and honorable family whose father was governor here sometime before, and his grandfather had been governor of the Massachusetts. This gentleman is a very courteous and affable person, much given to hospitality and has by his good services gained the affections of the people as much as any who had been before him in that post. . . .

12   THE NEW BOSTON: DECLINE OF PURITAN AUSTERITY

from Andrew Burnaby, *Travels*, 1760

The tight Puritan world of Winthrop and John Cotton was already changing character when Madam Knight recorded her observations at the turn of the century. By 1760 the Reverend Andrew Burnaby, Vicar of Greenwich, England, saw in Boston a busy commercial port town of almost twenty thousand. A wealthy upper class of merchants and professionals had replaced the old elite of ministers and magistrates. They built and furnished elegant homes and cultivated the refinements and moderate pleasures of polite society. The church, originally the heart of the community, had lost its unity and much of its power. In short, Boston had grown prosperous and worldly.

The sea provided the way to wealth for Boston and the lesser New England ports. Enterprising merchants shipped lumber, fish, rum, whale oil, and other local products to the West Indies, England, the Mediterranean, and the African Gold Coast. They imported and distributed sugar, molasses, salt, wine, English manufactures, and slaves. Large profits were made from shipbuilding and from the carrying trade.

The Massachusetts countryside changed less rapidly and radically than did the metropolis. Yeoman farmers drew a comfortable subsistence from their one or two hundred acres and followed simple, largely self-sufficient ways. The country custom of "tarrying" struck the Reverend Mr. Burnaby as a pleasant, practical, and usually innocent diversion.

Boston, the metropolis of Massachusetts-Bay, in New England, is one of the largest and most

Text: Andrew Burnaby, *Burnaby's Travels Through North America* ("Source Books of American History," New York: A. Wessels Co., 1904), pp. 132-34, 138-42. The spelling and punctuation have been modernized.

flourishing towns in North America. It is situated upon a peninsula, or rather an island joined to the continent by an isthmus or narrow neck of land half a mile in length, at the bottom of a spacious and noble harbor, defended from the sea by a number of small islands. The length of it is nearly two miles, and the breadth of it half a one; and it is supposed to contain 3000 houses, and 18 or 20,000 inhabitants. . . .

. . . The buildings in Boston are in general good; the streets are open and spacious and well-paved; and the whole has much the air of some of our best county towns in England. The country round about it is exceedingly delightful; and from a hill, which stands close to the town, where there is a beacon erected to alarm the neighborhood in case of any surprise, is one of the finest prospects, the most beautifully variegated and richly grouped of any without exception that I have ever seen.

The chief public buildings are three churches; thirteen or fourteen meeting-houses; the governor's palace; the court-house, or exchange; Faneuils Hall; a linen-manufacturing-house; a work-house; a bridewell; a public granary; and a very fine wharf, at least half a mile long, undertaken at the expense of a number of private gentlemen for the advantage of unloading and loading vessels. Most of these buildings are handsome: the church, called King's Chapel, is exceedingly elegant, and fitted up in the Corinthian taste. There is also an elegant private concert room, highly finished in the Ionic manner. . . .

The established religion here, as in all the other provinces of New England, is that of the congregationalists; a religion different in some trifling articles, though none very material, from the presbyterian. There are besides these, however, great numbers of people of different persuasions, particularly of the religion of the Church of England, which seems to gain ground and to become more fashionable every day. A church has been lately erected at Cambridge within sight of the college, which has greatly alarmed the congregationalists, who consider it as the most fatal stroke that could possibly have been levelled at their religion. . . .

Arts and sciences seem to have made a greater progress here than in any other part of America. Harvard College has been founded above a hundred years; and although it is not upon a perfect plan, yet it has produced a very good effect. The arts are undeniably forwarder in Massachusetts Bay than either in Pennsylvania or New York. The public buildings are more elegant, and there is a more general turn for music, painting, and the *belles lettres.*

The character of the inhabitants of this province is much improved, in comparison of what it was, but Puritanism and a spirit of persecution is not yet totally extinguished. The gentry of both sexes are hospitable and good-natured; there is an air of civility in their behavior, but it is constrained by formality and preciseness. Even the women, though easiness of carriage is peculiarly characteristic of their nature, appear here with more stiffness and reserve than in the other colonies. They are formed with symmetry, are handsome, and have fair and delicate complexions but are said universally, and even proverbially, to have very indifferent teeth.

The lower class of the people are more in the extreme of this character and, which is constantly mentioned as singularly peculiar to them, are impertinently curious and inquisitive. . . .

Singular situations and manners will be productive of singular customs, but frequently such as, upon slight examination, may appear to be the effects of mere grossness of character will, upon deeper research, be found to proceed from simplicity and innocence. A very extraordinary method of courtship which is sometimes practiced amongst the lower people of this province, and is called "tarrying," has given occasion to this reflection. When a man is enamoured of a young woman and wishes to marry her, he proposes the affair to her parents (without whose consent no marriage in this colony can take place); if they have no objection, they allow him to tarry with her one night in order to make his court to her. At their usual time the old couple retire to bed, leaving the young ones to settle matters as they can, who, after having sat up as long as they think proper, get into bed together also, but without pulling off their under-garments, in order to prevent scandal. If the parties agree, it is all very well. The banns are published, and they are married without delay. If not, they part, and possibly never see each other again, unless, which is an accident that seldom happens, the forsaken fair-one prove pregnant, and then the man is obliged to marry her, under pain of excommunication. . . .

THE MIDDLE COLONIES

13

MODERATE EXPECTATIONS: TOWN AND COUNTRY IN PENNSYLVANIA

from William Penn, *A Further Account of Pennsylvania,* 1685

William Penn (1644-1718), proprietor of Pennsylvania, brought not only great wealth but also wisdom and humanity to the task of founding an American colony. Son of an

English admiral and court favorite, Penn defied his family and risked persecution when, as a young man, he joined the Society of Friends, or Quakers. This radical sect, created out of the religious ferment of the Cromwell era, preached the doctrine of the "inner light" by which God revealed Himself directly to every man. Quaker social teachings emphasized the values of simplicity, equality, charity, nonviolence, and toleration. To the authorities of Old and New England, Quakers represented a grave threat to religious orthodoxy and social order. (See Document 23 for an example of Quaker persecution.)

In 1681 King Charles II granted William Penn the land west of the Delaware River. Employing his own fortune and the invested funds of wealthy English Quakers, Penn established a colony where sorely oppressed Quakers could find refuge, where Quaker principles could be realized, and where the proprietor and the investors might reap handsome rewards. The Quaker colony under Penn's guidance was distinctive for its relatively democratic government, its large measure of religious toleration, and its fair and peaceful Indian policy.

Settlers were attracted from England and Wales and from the European continent, especially Germany. Several promotional tracts by Penn, like the one reprinted here, were published in Dutch and German as well as English. These generally accurate descriptions invited to Pennsylvania immigrants who desired a fair chance to prosper in the New World, if they would be "moderate in expectation" and "count on labor before a crop."

. . . The people are a collection of diverse nations in Europe as French, Dutch, Germans, Swedes, Danes, Finns, Scotch, Irish, and English, and of the last equal to all the rest; and, which is admirable, not a reflection on that account. But as they are of one kind and in one place and under one allegiance, so they live like people of one country, which civil union has had a considerable influence towards the prosperity of that place.

II. Philadelphia and our intended metropolis, as I formerly writ, is two miles long and a mile broad, and at each end it lies that mile upon a navigable river. The situation high and dry, yet replenished with running streams. Besides the High Street that runs in the middle from river to river and is an hundred foot broad, it has eight streets more that run the same course, the least of which is fifty foot in breadth. And besides Broad Street, which crosseth the town in the middle and is also an hundred foot wide, there are twenty streets more that run the same course, and are also fifty foot broad. . . .

III. I mentioned in my last account that from my arrival, in eighty-two, to the date thereof, being ten months, we had got up four-score houses at our town and that some villages were settled about it. From that time to my coming away, which was a year within a few weeks, the town advanced to three hundred and fifty-seven houses, diverse of them large, well built, with good cellars, three stories, and some with balconies.

Text: William Penn, *A Further Account of the Province of Pennsylvania* (London?, 1685), pp. 2-6, 17-18, 20. The spelling and punctuation have been modernized.

IV. There is also a fair key [wharf] of about three hundred foot square, built by Samuel Carpenter, to which a ship of five hundred tons may lay her broadside, and others intend to follow his example. We have also a ropewalk made by B. Wilcox, and cordage for shipping already spun at it.

V. There inhabits most sorts of useful tradesmen as carpenters, joiners, bricklayers, masons, plasterers, plumbers, smiths, glaziers, tailors, shoemakers, butchers, bakers, brewers, glovers, tanners, fellmongers, wheelwrights, millwrights, shipwrights, boatwrights, ropemakers, sailmakers, blockmakers, turners, etc.

VI. There are two markets every week and two fairs every year. In other places markets also, as at Chester and Newcastle.

VII. Seven ordinaries for the entertainment of strangers and workmen that are not housekeepers and a good meal to be had for sixpence, sterl.

VIII. The hours for work and meals to labourers are fixed and known by ring of bell.

IX. After nine at night the officers go the rounds and no person, without very good cause, suffered to be at any public house that is not a lodger. . . .

XI. Some vessels have been here built and many boats, and by that means a ready conveniency for passage of people and goods.

XII. Diverse brickerys going on, many cellars already stoned or bricked and some brick houses going up.

XIII. The town is well-furnished with convenient mills; and what with their garden plats (the least half an acre), the fish of the river, and their labour to the countryman who begins to pay with the provisions of his own growth, they live comfortably.

XIV. The improvement of the place is best measured by the advance of value upon every man's lot. I will venture to say that the worst lot in the town, without any improvement upon it, is worth four times more than it was when it was laid out, and the best forty. And though it seems unequal that the absent should be thus benefited by the improvements of those that are upon the place, especially when they have served no office, run no hazard, nor as yet defrayed any public charge, yet this advantage does certainly redound to them, and whoever they are they are great debtors to the country, of which I shall now speak more at large.

Of Country Settlements

1. We do settle in the way of townships or villages, each of which contains 5,000 acres, in square, and at least ten families, the regulation of the country being a family to each five hundred acres. Some townships have more, where the interests of the people is less than that quantity, which often falls out.

2. Many that had right to more land were at first covetous to have their whole quantity without regard to this way of settlement, though by such wilderness vacancies, they had ruined the country, and then our interest of course. I had in my view society, assistance, busy commerce, instruction of youth, government of peoples, manners, conveniency of religious assembling, encouragement of mechanics, distinct and beaten roads, and it has answered in all those respects, I think, to an universal content. . . .

4. I said nothing in my last of any number of townships but there are at least fifty settled before my leaving those parts, which was in the month called August, 1684.

5. I visited many of them and found them much advanced in their improvements. Houses over their heads and garden plots, coverts for their cattle, an increase of stock, and several enclosures in corn, especially the first commerce; and I may say of some poor men was the beginnings of an estate, the difference of laboring for themselves and for others, of an inheritance and a rack lease, being never better understood. . . .

Of the Natives

1. Because many stories have been prejudicially propagated as if we were upon ill terms with the natives and sometimes, like Job's kindred, all cut off but the messenger that bought the tidings, I think it requisite to say thus much, that as there never was any such messenger, so the dead people were alive at our last advices, so far are we from ill terms with the natives, that we have lived in great friendship. I have made seven purchases, and in pay and presents they have received at least twelve hundred pounds of me. Our humanity has obliged them so far that they generally leave their guns at home when they come to our settlements; they offer us no affront, not so much as to one of our dogs; and if any of them break our laws, they submit to be punished by them: and to this they have tied themselves by an obligation under their hands. We leave not the least indignity to them unrebuked, nor wrong unsatisfied. Justice gains and awes them. They have some great men amongst them, I mean for wisdom, truth and justice. I refer to my former account about their laws, manners, and religious rites.

Of the Government

The government is according to the words of the Grant as near to the English as conveniently may be: In the whole, we aim at duty to the King, the preservation of right to all, the suppression of vice, and encouragement of virtue and arts; with liberty to all people to worship Almighty God, according to their faith and persuasion. . . .

Now for you that think of going thither, I have this to say by way of caution: if an hair of our heads falls not to the ground without the providence of God, remember your removal is of greater moment. Wherefore have a due reverence and regard to his good Providence, as becomes a people that profess a belief in Providence. Go clear in yourselves and of all others. Be moderate in expectation, count on labour before a crop, and cost before gain, for such persons will best endure difficulties, if they come, and bear the success, as well as find the comfort that usually follow such considerate undertakings.

14   THE AMERICAN IMMIGRANT: THE LOT OF INDENTURED SERVANTS

from Gottlieb Mittelberger, *Journey to Pennsylvania*, 1750

The migration of Europeans to North America began in 1607 and has not yet ceased. During most of the seventeenth century the great body of immigrants were English, the Dutch of New Amsterdam being the major exception. But from the late years of that century, and especially after 1710, important new stock was added to the colonial population. Most numerous among the non-English arrivals were the African slaves, the Scotch-Irish, and the Germans, but sprinklings were also to be found of Swedes, Finns, Welsh, French Huguenots, and Jews. Although the American people at the time of the Revolution were still predominantly English in background, they had already become a nation of many nations. "Here," the French observer Crèvecoeur remarked, "all nations are melted into a new race of men."

Pennsylvania was from the beginning a heterogeneous society, as William Penn's account shows. (See Document 13.) Some Dutch and Swedish settlers were in the area when the colony was established, and early migrations brought men from many parts of Northern Europe and the British Isles. Germantown, settled in 1683, was the earliest center of Germans from the Rhineland region, which was to supply perhaps one third of Pennsylvania's population by the eve of the Revolution. Moreover, these thousands of Germans—and Scotch-Irish too—who entered the New World through Pennsylvania gradually made their way south (after 1732) through the Shenandoah Valley to settle the back country of Maryland, Virginia, the Carolinas, and Georgia.

Most of the eighteenth-century German immigrants to Pennsylvania came as "redemptioners," a type of indentured servant. Peasants and artisans, lacking funds to pay their passage, were sold by the ship captains to masters who required labor on farms or in homes and shops. Normally the redemptioner was bound to serve for three to five years. He was neither a slave nor a free worker but something in between. At the end of his term he would receive clothes, some equipment, and fifty acres of land.

Gottlieb Mittelberger, who came to Pennsylvania in 1750 as a schoolmaster and organist, describes bitterly the hardships of the redemptioners through the long, miserable voyage and the longer period of backbreaking service opening new lands. The thousands who ignored his warnings found plenty of hardships but also, finally, a decent life as independent farmers. An eye for good soils and a talent for farming made these ancestors of the "Pennsylvania Dutch" one of the most successful colonial immigrant groups. More than others, they tended to stick together, preserve their native language, customs, and beliefs, and stay out of politics. German craftsmen developed two of the most important devices for the winning of the west: the "long rifle" and the Conestoga covered wagon.

Both in Rotterdam and in Amsterdam the people are packed densely, like herrings so to say, in the large sea vessels. One person receives a place of scarcely 2 feet width and 6 feet length in the bedstead, while many a ship carries four to six hundred souls; not to mention the innumerable implements, tools, provisions, water-barrels and other things which likewise occupy much space.

On account of contrary winds it takes the ships sometimes 2, 3 and 4 weeks to make the trip from Holland to Kaupp [Cowes] in England. But when the wind is good, they get there in 8 days or even sooner. Everything is examined there and the custom-duties paid, whence it comes that the ships ride there 8, 10 to 14 days and even longer at anchor, till they have taken in their full cargoes. During that time every one is compelled to spend his last remaining money and to consume his little stock of provisions which had been reserved for the sea; so that most passengers, finding themselves on the ocean

where they would be in greater need of them, must greatly suffer from hunger and want. Many suffer want already on the water between Holland and Old England.

When the ships have for the last time weighed their anchors near the city of Kaupp [Cowes] in Old England, the real misery begins with the long voyage. For from there the ships, unless they have good wind, must often sail 8, 9, 10 to 12 weeks before they reach Philadelphia. But even with the best wind the voyage lasts 7 weeks.

But during the voyage there is on board these ships terrible misery, stench, fumes, horror, vomiting, many kinds of seasickness, fever, dysentery, headache, heat, constipation, boils, scurvy, cancer, mouth-rot, and the like, all of which come from old and sharply salted food and meat, also from very bad and foul water, so that many die miserably.

Add to this want of provisions, hunger, thirst, frost, heat, dampness, anxiety, want, afflictions and lamentations, together with other trouble, as c. v. the lice abound so frightfully, especially on sick people, that they can be scraped off the body. The misery reaches the climax when a gale rages for 2 or 3 nights and days, so that

Text: Gottlieb Mittelberger, *Journey to Pennsylvania in the Year 1750 and Return to Germany in the Year 1754,* trans. Carl Theo. Eben (Philadelphia: John Jos. McVey, 1898), pp. 19-20, 22, 24-31.

every one believes that the ship will go to the bottom with all human beings on board. In such a visitation the people cry and pray most piteously. . . .

Many sigh and cry: "Oh, that I were at home again, and if I had to lie in my pig-sty!" Or they say: "O God, if I only had a piece of good bread, or a good fresh drop of water." Many people whimper, sigh and cry piteously for their homes; most of them get home-sick. Many hundred people necessarily die and perish in such misery and must be cast into the sea, which drives their relatives or those who persuaded them to undertake the journey, to such despair that it is almost impossible to pacify and console them. In a word, the sighing and crying and lamenting on board the ship continues night and day so as to cause the hearts even of the most hardened to bleed when they hear it. . . .

At length, when, after a long and tedious voyage, the ships come in sight of land, so that the promontories can be seen, which the people were so eager and anxious to see, all creep from below on deck to see the land from afar, and they weep for joy, and pray and sing, thanking and praising God. The sight of the land makes the people on board the ship, especially the sick and the half-dead, alive again, so that their hearts leap within them; they shout and rejoice, and are content to bear their misery in patience, in the hope that they may soon reach the land in safety. But alas!

When the ships have landed at Philadelphia after their long voyage, no one is permitted to leave them except those who pay for their passage or can give good security; the others, who cannot pay, must remain on board the ships till they are purchased, and are released from the ships by their purchasers. The sick always fare the worst, for the healthy are naturally preferred and purchased first; and so the sick and wretched must often remain on board in front of the city for 2 or 3 weeks, and frequently die, whereas many a one, if he could pay his debt and were permitted to leave the ship immediately, might recover and remain alive. . . .

The sale of human beings in the market on board the ship is carried on thus: Every day Englishmen, Dutchmen and High-German people come from the city of Philadelphia and other places, in part from a great distance, say 20, 30, or 40 hours away, and go on board the newly arrived ship that has brought and offers for sale passengers from Europe, and select among the healthy persons such as they deem suitable for their business, and bargain with them how long they will serve for their passage money, which most of them are still in debt for. When they have come to an agreement, it happens that adult persons bind themselves in writing to serve 3, 4, 5 or 6 years for the amount due by them, according to their age and strength. But very young people, from 10 to 15 years, must serve till they are 21 years old.

Many parents must sell and trade away their children like so many head of cattle; for if their children take the debt upon themselves, the parents can leave the ship free and unrestrained; but as the parents often do not know where and to what people their children are going, it often happens that such parents and children, after leaving the ship, do not see each other again for many years, perhaps no more in all their lives. . . .

It often happens that whole families, husband, wife, and children, are separated by being sold to different purchasers, especially when they have not paid any part of their passage money.

When a husband or wife has died at sea, when the ship has made more than half of her trip, the survivor must pay or serve not only for himself or herself, but also for the deceased.

When both parents have died over half-way at sea, their children, especially when they are young and have nothing to pawn or to pay, must stand for their own and their parents' passage, and serve till they are 21 years old. When one has served his or her term, he or she is entitled to a new suit of clothes at parting; and if it has been so stipulated, a man gets in addition a horse, a woman, a cow.

When a serf has an opportunity to marry in this country, he or she must pay for each year which he or she would have yet to serve, 5 to 6 pounds. But many a one who has thus purchased and paid for his bride, has subsequently repented his bargain, so that he would gladly have returned his exorbitantly dear ware, and lost the money besides.

If some one in this country runs away from his master, who has treated him harshly, he cannot get far. Good provision has been made for such cases, so that a runaway is soon recovered. He who detains or returns a deserter receives a good reward.

If such a runaway has been away from his master one day, he must serve for it as a punishment a week, for a week a month, and for a month half a year. But if the master will not keep the runaway after he has got him back, he may sell him for so many years as he would have to serve him yet.

Work and labor in this new and wild land are very hard and manifold, and many a one who came there in his old age must work very hard to his end for his bread. I will not speak of young people. Work mostly consists in cutting wood, felling oak-trees, rooting out, or as they say there, clearing large tracts of forest. Such forests, being cleared, are then laid out for fields and meadows. From the best hewn wood, fences are made around the new fields; for there all meadows, orchards and fruit-fields are surrounded and fenced in with planks made of thickly-split wood, laid one above the other, as in zigzag lines, and within such enclosures, horses, cattle, and sheep are permitted to graze. Our Europeans, who are purchased, must always work hard, for new fields are constantly laid out; and so they learn that stumps of oak-trees are in America certainly as hard as in Germany. In this hot land they fully experience in their own persons what God has imposed on man for his sin and disobedience: for in Genesis we read the words: In the sweat of thy brow shalt thou eat bread. Who therefore wishes to earn his bread in a Christian and honest way, and cannot earn it in his fatherland otherwise than by the work of his hands, let him do so in his own country and not in America; for he will not fare better in America. However hard he may be compelled to work in his fatherland, he will surely find it quite as hard, if not harder, in the new country. Besides, there is not only the long and arduous journey lasting half a year, during which he has to suffer, more than with the hardest work; he has also spent about 200 florins which no one will refund to him. If he has so much money, it will slip out of his hands; if he has it not, he must work his debt off as a slave and poor serf. Therefore let every one stay in his own country and support himself and his family honestly. Besides I say that those who suffer themselves to be persuaded and enticed away by the man-thieves, are very foolish if they believe that roasted pigeons will fly into their mouths in America or Pennsylvania without their working for them.

15

NEW YORK POLITICS: GOVERNOR, COUNCIL, AND ASSEMBLY
from William Smith, *History of New York*, 1756

New Netherland was founded in 1624 by the Dutch West India Company and remained a Dutch colony until conquered in 1664 by the English forces of the Duke of York, the future King James II. Following the overthrow of James in England's Glorious Revolution of 1688, and the parallel Leisler Revolution in the colony (1689-1691), New York was ruled by an appointed royal governor and council and an assembly elected by the freemen of the colony. General supervisory power rested in the English imperial government, dominated after 1688 by Parliament.

William Smith (1728-1793) was a prominent participant in the colonial affairs described in his *History of New York*. A lawyer and jurist, he served for many years on the colonial council but worked actively on the Whig side in New York politics. (The Whigs supported the power of the legislature and opposed the legal establishment of the Anglican Church.) Faced with the difficult choice of loyalty or revolution in 1776, Smith tried to straddle the fence but finally in 1783 went into exile, ending his career as Chief Justice of England's Canadian colony.

The selections from Smith's *History* reprinted here sketch some distinguishing features of eighteenth-century New York politics. Dutch pioneers had been joined by French, Scotch-Irish, German, and English colonists (including migrants from New England). Together they had pushed up the Hudson Valley from New York to Albany (an important fur-trading center) and out onto Long Island. New York City itself contained over twenty different nationalities and sects. Thus New York, even more than Pennsylvania, represented a variety of peoples and ways.

Unlike Pennsylvania, however, New York had since Dutch times developed an imposing, close-knit, landed aristocracy, which dominated much of the Hudson Valley. Vast family estates—that of the Van Rensselaers occupied 700,000 acres—were organized as manors on the English model, employing long-term tenants to work the land. Political favoritism was the main source of these semi-feudal domains. The landed magnates, in close alliance with the wealthy merchants of the city of New York, controlled local government and provided leadership for the contending factions in colonial politics.

Throughout the eighteenth century the struggle of the elected assembly for greater authority formed the central theme of New York politics. Above all, as Smith's *History* shows, the legislature was bidding with some success for control of the purse. In this as in many matters of procedure and substance the members of the assembly adopted for themselves the example of the English Parliament, thereby moving in the direction of colonial self-government.

The Political State

This colony, as a part of the king's dominions, is subject to the controul of the British parliament; but its more immediate government is vested in a governour, council and general assembly.

The governours-in-chief, who are always appointed by the king's commission, under the great seal of Great Britain, enjoy a vast plenitude of power, as may be seen in their patents, which are nearly the same. . . .

The instructions received with the commission, are explanatory of the patent, and regulate the governour's conduct on almost every common contingency.

The salary, generally granted to the governour by the instructions, is 1,200*l*. sterling out of the revenue here; but that being an insufficient fund, the assembly, in lieu of it, give him annually 1,560*l*. currency. The perquisites perhaps amount to as much more.

This office was formerly very lucrative, but becomes daily less considerable, because almost all the valuable tracts of land are already taken up.

The council, when full, consists of twelve members, appointed by the king's mandamus and sign manual. All their privileges and powers are contained in the instructions. They are a privy council to the governour in acts of civil government; and take the same oath administered to the king's council in England. The tenure of their places is extremely precarious, and yet their influence upon the publick measures very considerable. In the grant of all patents the governour is bound to consult them, and regularly they cannot pass the seal without their advice.

They enjoy a legislative power, as the lords do in parliament; and exercise also judicial authority upon writs of error and appeals. They are convened by the governour; and he is always present when they sit as a court or privy council, which is ordinarily at the fort. In their legislative capacity, they meet without the governour, and always at the city hall. . . . Their proceedings are very formal, and in many respects they imitate the example of the lords. Their messages to the assembly are carried by one of their own members, and the house always rises at his entrance and receives them standing. The council never publish their legislative minutes; but the assembly always print their own votes; nor do either of these houses permit strangers to be present at their conventions. . . .

The general assembly consists of twenty-seven representatives, chosen by the people, in pursuance of a writ of summons issued by the governour. . . .

I need not enlarge upon the customs of the general assembly, for they take the practice of the British house of commons for their model, and vary from them in but very few instances. . . .

The continuance of our assemblies was unlimited till the political struggles, which took rise in Mr. Cosby's administration, forced Mr. Clarke, who succeeded him, to pass the act restricting them to three years; but this was repealed by the king, and a septennial law enacted soon after the arrival of governour Clinton, which is still in full force.

No colony, upon the continent, has formerly suffered more than ours, in the opinion of the king's ministers. This has been owing to the ill impressions made by our governours, who are scarce ever disengaged from disputes with the lower house. Our representatives, agreeable to the general sense of their constituents, are tenacious in their opinion that the inhabitants of this colony are entitled to all the privileges of Englishmen; that they have a right to participate in the legislative power, and that the session of assemblies here is wisely substituted instead of a representation in parliament, which, all things considered, would, at this remote distance, be extremely inconvenient and dangerous. The governours, on the other hand, in general, entertain political sentiments of a quite different nature. All the immunities we enjoy, according to them, not only flow from, but absolutely depend upon, the mere grace and will of the crown. It is easy to conceive that contentions must naturally attend such a contradiction of sentiments. Most of our disputes, however, relate to the support of government. Before lord Cornbury's embezzlements, the revenue was established for a long period, but afterwards reduced to a few years. The violent measures, in Mr. Cosby's time, led the assembly to the scheme of an annual provision. These are the words of that much famed address of

Text: William Smith, *History of New York* (Albany, N.Y.: Ryer Schermerhorn, 1815), pp. 350-51, 364-66, 368-71.

the house, to lieutenant governour Clarke, on the 8th of September, 1737, previous to the change.

"The true causes of the deficiency of the revenue, we believe, are too well known to your honour, to make it necessary for us to say much on that head. Had the conspicuous loyalty of the inhabitants of this province met with a suitable treatment in return: it is not unlikely, but we should now be weak enough to act like others before us, in being lavish beyond our abilities, and raising sums unnecessary to be given; and continued the donation, like them, for a longer time than what was convenient for the safety of the inhabitants: but experience has shown the imprudence of such a conduct, and the miserable condition to which the province is reduced renders the raising of large sums very difficult, if not impracticable. We therefore beg leave to be plain with your honour, and hope you will not take it amiss, when we tell you that you are not to expect that we either will raise sums unfit to be raised; or put what we shall raise into the power of a governour to misapply, if we can prevent it; nor shall we make up any other deficiencies, than what we conceive are fit and just to be paid; or continue what support or revenue we shall raise for any longer time than one year. Nor do we think it convenient to do even that, until such laws are passed, as we conceive necessary for the safety of the inhabitants of this colony, who have reposed a trust in us for that only purpose,

and which we are sure you will think it reasonable we should act agreeable to, and by the grace of God we will endeavour not to deceive them."

The sentiments of this address still prevail among the people, and therefore the success of the present solicitations, for a permanent, indefinite, support, will probably be in vain.

The matter has been often litigated with great fervency on both sides, and the example of the British parliament urged as a precedent for our imitation. To this it is answered, that the particular state of this province differs so widely from that of their mother country that we ought not in this respect to follow the custom of the commons. Our constitution, as some observe, is so imperfect in numberless instances, that the rights of the people lie, even now, at the mere mercy of their governours; and granting a perpetual support, it is thought, would be in reality little less than the loss of every thing dear to them. . . .

By gradual advances, at seasonable junctures, we might have introduced such amendments as would, at this day, have established a sound and well fortified political frame; but through our utter neglect of education, the ancient assemblies consisted of plain, illiterate husbandmen, whose views seldom extended farther than to the regulation of highways, the destruction of wolves, wild cats, and foxes, and the advancement of the other little interests of the particular counties which they were chosen to represent.

The Imperial System

THE AMERICAN VIEW OF EMPIRE

16

REASONS AND MOTIVES FOR THE ALBANY PLAN

from Benjamin Franklin, "Reasons and Motives on Which the Albany Plan Was Formed," 1754

The growth of the colonies from wilderness outposts to thriving provincial societies came about within the framework of the British Empire. By the mid-eighteenth century each of the thirteen colonies had developed a significant measure of local self-government, subject to the general superintendence of the English Parliament in matters that concerned the empire as a whole—especially trade, foreign policy, Indian relations, and territorial expansion. The missing link in this political structure was a centralized intercolonial institution—some organization which would represent the several colonies and act for them in matters too large for the separate colonial legislatures to handle independently or too difficult for Parliament to act upon wisely so far from the American scene. Effective defense against the French, for instance, called for a united front instead of the situation in which each colony supported military operations as much or as little as it chose.

The colonists of Massachusetts Bay, Plymouth, Connecticut, and New Haven had anticipated such an intercolonial agency when they formed the New England Confederation (1643-1684) to deal primarily with common problems of defense. In a very different fashion, James II had in 1686-1687 forcibly combined the New England colonies, New York, and the Jerseys into the Dominion of New England, under the autocratic rule of an appointed governor, Sir Edmund Andros; but this experiment in consolidation collapsed with the Glorious Revolution of 1688.

The most ambitious and promising scheme for uniting the colonies was the Albany Plan of Union, formulated by Benjamin Franklin. On the eve of the French and Indian War in 1754, seven colonies sent delegates to a congress at Albany, New York. For reasons outlined in the following document, they adopted Franklin's plan for a common government empowered to manage Indian relations, acquire lands, form and regulate new settlements, organize military defense, and to levy duties and taxes for these purposes. The government would be in the hands of a Grand Council chosen by the several colonial assemblies and a President-General appointed and supported by the crown. Although the scheme was rejected both by England and the colonial legislatures—each side feared that it would concede too much—the Albany Congress had contributed a useful precedent for the future American confederation.

The commissioners from a number of the northern colonies, being met at Albany, and considering the difficulties that have always attended the most necessary general measures for the common defence, or for the annoyance of the enemy, when they were to be carried through the several particular Assemblies of all the colonies; some Assemblies being before at variance with their governors or councils, and the several branches of the government not on terms of doing business with each other; others taking the opportunity, when their concurrence is wanted, to push for favourite laws, powers, or points, that they think could not at other times be obtained, and so creating disputes and quarrels; one Assembly waiting to see what another will do, being afraid of doing more than its share, or desirous of doing less, or refusing to do any thing because its country is not at present so much exposed as others, or because another will reap more immediate advantage; from one or other of which causes, the Assemblies of six out of seven colonies applied to, had granted no assistance to Virginia, when lately invaded by the French, though purposely convened, and the importance of the occasion earnestly urged upon them;—considering moreover, that one principal encouragement to the French, in invading and insulting the British American dominions, was their knowledge of our disunited state, and of our weakness arising from such want of union; and that from hence different colonies were, at different times, extremely harassed, and put to great expense both of blood and treasure, who would have remained in peace, if the enemy had had cause to fear the drawing on themselves the resentment and power of the whole;—the said commissioners, considering also the present encroachments of the French, and the mischievous consequences that may be expected from them, if not opposed with our

force, came to an unanimous resolution: *That a union of the colonies is absolutely necessary for their preservation.*

The manner of forming and establishing this union was the next point. When it was considered, that the colonies were seldom all in equal danger at the same time, or equally near the danger, or equally sensible of it; that some of them had particular interests to manage, with which a union might interfere; and that they were extremely jealous of each other; it was thought impracticable to obtain a joint agreement of all the colonies to a union, in which the expense and burthen of defending any of them should be divided among them all; and if ever acts of Assembly in all the colonies could be obtained for that purpose, yet as any colony, on the least dissatisfaction, might repeal its own act, and thereby withdraw itself from the union, it would not be a stable one, or such as could be depended on; for if only one colony should, on any disgust, withdraw itself, others might think it unjust and unequal, that they, by continuing in the union, should be at the expense of defending a colony, which refused to bear its proportionable part, and would therefore one after another withdraw, till the whole crumbled into its original parts. Therefore the commissioners came to another previous resolution, *That it was necessary the Union should be established by act of Parliament.*

They then proceeded to sketch out a *Plan of Union,* which they did in a plain and concise manner, just sufficient to show their sentiments of the kind of union, that would best suit the circumstances of the colonies, be most agreeable to the people, and most effectually promote his

Text: Benjamin Franklin, *Complete Works,* ed. John Bigelow (New York: G. P. Putnam's Sons, 1887), II, pp. 350-53.

Majesty's service, and the general interest of the British empire. This was respectfully sent to the Assemblies of the several colonies for their consideration, and to receive such alterations and improvements as they should think fit and necessary; after which it was proposed to be transmitted to England to be perfected, and the establishment of it there humbly solicited.

This was as much as the commissioners could do. . . .

17

IMPERIAL PARTNERSHIP: COLONIAL CONTROL OF TAXATION, COLONIAL REPRESENTATION IN PARLIAMENT

from Benjamin Franklin, Letters to Governor Shirley, December 18 and 22, 1754

A revision of the Albany Plan proposed by William Shirley, the royal governor of Massachusetts (1741-1757), moved Benjamin Franklin to examine the nature of the British Empire from the colonial point of view. In a series of penetrating letters to Governor Shirley, written a decade before the Stamp Act crisis, Franklin tried to explain how the colonists could be at once passionate defenders of self-government—especially where the taxing power was concerned—and loyal subjects of the crown.

His argument for colonial representation in Parliament, to be followed by a general alteration of the system of economic regulation, envisioned an imperial commonwealth beyond the grasp of his contemporaries. English leaders had no intention of admitting troublesome colonials into imperial councils or sacrificing the advantages of their trade laws. Americans concentrated their efforts on defending the rights of their several colonial legislatures until they finally created their own Continental Congress to conduct the common business first of resistance and then of revolution.

Franklin played a large role in colonial and imperial politics. He was clerk of the Pennsylvania Assembly from 1736 to 1751 and a delegate for Philadelphia from 1751 to 1764. He held high office in the imperial administration as Deputy Postmaster for the colonies and spent many years in England as colonial agent (in effect, a "lobbyist" in Parliament) for Pennsylvania, Georgia, New Jersey, and Massachusetts. After 1775 he served the Continental Congress in many important capacities. His diplomatic success in securing French aid during the Revolution was an incalculable contribution to American independence.

On the imposition of direct taxes upon the colonies without their consent.

Wednesday Morning [December 18, 1754.]

SIR,

I mentioned it yesterday to your Excellency as my opinion, that excluding the *people* of the colonies from all share in the choice of the grand council, would probably give extreme dissatisfaction, as well as the taxing them by act of Parliament, where they have no representative. In matters of general concern to the people, and especially where burthens are to be laid upon them, it is of use to consider, as well what they will be apt to think and say, as what they ought to think; I shall therefore, as your Excellency requires it of me, briefly mention what of either kind occurs to me on this occasion.

First they will say, and perhaps with justice, that the body of the people in the colonies are as loyal, and as firmly attached to the present

Text: Benjamin Franklin, *Complete Works,* ed. John Bigelow (New York: G. P. Putnam's Sons, 1887), II, 377-87.

constitution, and reigning family, as any subjects in the king's dominions.

That there is no reason to doubt the readiness and willingness of the representatives they may choose, to grant from time to time such supplies for the defence of the country, as shall be judged necessary, so far as their abilities will allow.

That the people in the colonies, who are to feel the immediate mischiefs of invasion and conquest by an enemy in the loss of their estates, lives and liberties, are likely to be better judges of the quantity of forces necessary to be raised and maintained, forts to be built and supported, and of their own abilities to bear the expence, than the parliament of England at so great a distance.

That governors often come to the colonies merely to make fortunes, with which they intend to return to Britain; are not always men of the best abilities or integrity; have many of them no estates here, nor any natural connexions with us, that should make them heartily concerned for our welfare; and might possibly be fond of raising and keeping up more forces than necessary, from the profits accruing to themselves, and to make provision for their friends and dependants.

That the counsellors in most of the colonies being appointed by the crown, on the recommendation of governors, are often of small estates, frequently dependant on the governors for offices, and therefore too much under influence.

That there is therefore great reason to be jealous of a power in such governors and councils, to raise such sums as they shall judge necessary, by draft on the lords of the treasury, to be afterwards laid on the colonies by act of parliament, and paid by the people here; since they might abuse it by projecting useless expeditions, harassing the people, and taking them from their labour to execute such projects, merely to create offices and employments, and gratify their dependants, and divide profits.

That the parliament of England is at a great distance, subject to be misinformed and misled by such Governors and Councils, whose united interests might probably secure them against the effect of any complaint from hence.

That it is supposed an undoubted right of Englishmen, not to be taxed but by their own consent given through their representatives.

That the colonies have no representatives in parliament.

That to propose taxing them by parliament, and refuse them the liberty of choosing a representative council, to meet in the colonies, and consider and judge of the necessity of any general tax, and the quantum, shews suspicion of their loyalty to the crown, or of their regard for their country, or of their common sense and understanding, which they have not deserved.

That compelling the colonies to pay money without their consent, would be rather like raising contributions in an enemy's country, than taxing of Englishmen for their own public benefit.

That it would be treating them as a conquered people, and not as true British subjects.

That a tax laid by the representatives of the colonies might easily be lessened as the occasions should lessen, but being once laid by parliament under the influence of the representations made by Governors, would probably be kept up and continued for the benefit of Governors, to the grievous burthen and discouragement of the colonies, and prevention of their growth and increase.

That a power in Governors to march the inhabitants from one end of the British and French colonies to the other, being a country of at least 1500 square miles, without the approbation or the consent of their representatives first obtained, such expeditions might be grievous and ruinous to the people, and would put them on footing with the subjects of France in Canada, that now groan under such oppression from their Governor, who for two years past has harassed them with long and destructive marches to Ohio.

That if the colonies in a body may be well governed by governors and councils appointed by the crown, without representatives, particular colonies may as well or better be so governed; a tax may be laid upon them all by act of parliament for support of government, and their assemblies may be dismissed as an useless part of the constitution. . . .

That the British colonies bordering on the French are properly frontiers of the British empire; and the frontiers of an empire are properly defended at the joint expence of the body of the people in such empire: It would now be thought hard by act of parliament to oblige the Cinque Ports or seacoasts of Britain to maintain the whole navy, because they are more immediately defended by it, not allowing them at the same time a vote in choosing members of the parliament; and if the frontiers in America bear the expence of their own defence, it seems hard to allow them no share in voting the money, judging of the necessity and sum, or advising the measures.

That besides the taxes necessary for the defence of the frontiers, the colonies pay yearly great sums to the mother-country unnoticed: For taxes paid in Britain by the land holder or artificer, must enter into and increase the price of the produce of land and of manufactures made of it; and great part of this is paid by consumers in the colonies, who thereby pay a considerable part of the British taxes. . . .

In short, as we are not suffered to regulate our trade, and restrain the importation and consumption of British superfluities (as Britain can the consumption of foreign superfluities) our whole wealth centers finally amongst the merchants and inhabitants of Britain, and if we make them richer, and enable them better to pay their taxes, it is nearly the same as being taxed ourselves, and equally beneficial to the crown.

These kind of secondary taxes, however, we do not complain of, though we have no share in the laying, or disposing of them; but to pay immediate heavy taxes, in the laying, appropriation, and disposition of which we have no part, and which perhaps we may know to be as unnecessary, as grievous, must seem hard measure to Englishmen, who cannot conceive, that by hazarding their lives and fortunes, in subduing and settling new countries, extending the dominion, and increasing the commerce of the mother nation, they have forfeited the native rights of Britons, which they think ought rather to be given to them, as due to such merit, if they had been before in a state of slavery. . . .

Your Excellency's most obedient,
and most humble servant,
B. Franklin.

On the subject of uniting the colonies more intimately with Great Britain by allowing them representatives in parliament.

Boston, Dec. 22, 1754.

SIR,

Since the conversation your Excellency was pleased to honour me with, on the subject of *uniting the colonies* more intimately with Great Britain, by allowing them *representatives in parliament*, I have something further considered that matter, and am of opinion, that such a union would be very acceptable to the colonies, provided they had a reasonable number of representatives allowed them; and that all the old acts of Parliament restraining the trade or cramping the manufactures of the colonies be at the same time repealed, and the British subjects *on this side the water* put, in those respects, on the same footing with those in Great Britain, till the new Parliament, representing the whole, shall think it for the interest of the whole to reënact some or all of them. It is not that I imagine so many representatives will be allowed the colonies, as to have any great weight by their numbers; but I think there might be sufficient to occasion those laws to be better and more impartially considered, and perhaps to overcome the interest of a petty corporation, or of any particular set of artificers or traders in England, who heretofore seem, in some instances, to have been more regarded than all the colonies, or than was consistent with the general interest, or best national good. I think too, that the government of the colonies by a parliament, in which they are fairly represented, would be vastly more agreeable to the people, than the method lately attempted to be introduced by royal instructions, as well as more agreeable to the nature of an English constitution, and to English liberty; and that such laws as now seem to bear hard on the colonies, would (when judged by such a Parliament for the best interest of the whole) be more cheerfully submitted to, and more easily executed.

I should hope too, that by such a union, the people of Great Britain, and the people of the colonies, would learn to consider themselves, as not belonging to a different community with different interests, but to one community with one interest; which I imagine would contribute to strengthen the whole, and greatly lessen the danger of future separations. . . .

Now I look on the colonies as so many counties gained to Great Britain, and more advantageous to it than if they had been gained out of the seas around its coasts, and joined to its land: For being in different climates, they afford greater variety of produce, and being separated by the ocean, they increase much more its shipping and seamen; and since they are all included in the British empire, which has only extended itself by their means; and the strength and wealth of the parts are the strength and wealth of the whole; what imports it to the general state, whether a merchant, a smith, or a hatter, grow rich in Old or New England? And if, through increase of people, two smiths are wanted for one employed before, why may not the *new* smith be allowed to live and thrive in the *new* country, as well as the *old* one in the *old*? In fine, why should the countenance of a state be *partially* afforded to its people, unless it be most in favour of those who have most merit? And if there be any difference, those who have most contributed to enlarge Britain's empire and commerce, increase her strength, her wealth, and the numbers of her people, at the risk of their own lives and private fortunes in new and strange countries, methinks ought rather to expect some preference. With the greatest respect and esteem, I have the honour to be

Your Excellency's most obedient
and most humble servant,
B. Franklin.

BRITISH COLONIALISM

18 THE MERCANTILIST SYSTEM

from Adam Smith, *The Wealth of Nations,* 1776

By the middle of the eighteenth century, England had worked out a thoroughgoing system of imperial economic regulation. The main objects of this mercantilist system were (1) to promote the military and maritime strength of England and the empire,

(2) to give English merchants and manufacturers a monopolistic position in colonial markets, (3) to draw to England colonial products wanted for use or resale and exclude commodities which English producers could supply, and (4) to prevent the development of certain colonial manufactures which would offer competition to English industry. A series of parliamentary measures effectively beginning with the Navigation Act of 1660 established the framework of the system. Enforcement was entrusted in part to English "admiralty courts" and after 1696 to "vice-admiralty courts" and governors in the colonies.

To what extent the Acts of Trade and Navigation were violated and to what extent they placed an economic burden on the colonists are both disputed questions. (Certainly the ill-advised Molasses Act of 1733, which attempted to cut off imports of sugar, molasses, and rum from the French and Dutch West Indies, was generally evaded by merchants of the North American colonies.) For a masterful contemporary analysis of the workings and consequences of the British mercantilist system, we turn to Adam Smith's economic classic *The Wealth of Nations*, first published in 1776. Smith (1723-1790), a Scottish professor of moral philosophy, severely criticizes British imperial economic policy on the basis of his *laissez-faire*, or free-trade, principles; yet he is careful to point out offsetting colonial benefits, especially by comparison with the more restrictive systems of other imperial powers. Few of Smith's countrymen agreed that the mercantilist policy sacrificed English as well as colonial welfare to the special interests of merchants and manufacturers in the colonial trade.

. . . In the disposal of their surplus produce, or of what is over and above their own consumption, the English colonies have been more favoured, and have been allowed a more extensive market, than those of any other European nation. Every European nation has endeavoured more or less to monopolize to itself the commerce of its colonies, and, upon that account, has prohibited the ships of foreign nations from trading to them, and has prohibited them from importing European goods from any foreign nation. But the manner in which this monopoly has been exercised in different nations has been very different.

Some nations have given up the whole commerce of their colonies to an exclusive company, of whom the colonies were obliged to buy all such European goods as they wanted, and to whom they were obliged to sell the whole of their own surplus produce. . . . Of all the expedients that can well be contrived to stunt the natural growth of a new colony, that of an exclusive company is undoubtedly the most effectual. This, however, has been the policy of Holland, though their company, in the course of the present century, has given up in many respects the exertion of their exclusive privilege. . . .

Other nations, without establishing an exclusive company, have confined the whole commerce of their colonies to a particular port of the mother country, from whence no ship was allowed to sail, but either in a fleet and at a particular season, or, if single, in consequence of a particular licence, which in most cases was very well paid for. . . . This, however, till within these few years, had always been the policy of Spain, and the price of all European goods, accordingly,

is said to have been enormous in the Spanish West Indies. . . .

Other nations leave the trade of their colonies free to all their subjects, who may carry it on from all the different ports of the mother country, and who have occasion for no other licence than the common dispatches of the customhouse. In this case the number and dispersed situation of the different traders renders it impossible for them to enter into any general combination, and their competition is sufficient to hinder them from making very exorbitant profits. Under so liberal a policy the colonies are enabled both to sell their own produce and to buy the goods of Europe at a reasonable price. But since the dissolution of the Plymouth company, when our colonies were but in their infancy, this has always been the policy of England. It has generally too been that of France, and has been uniformly so since the dissolution of what, in England, is commonly called their Mississippi company. The profits of the trade, therefore, which France and England carry on with their colonies, though no doubt somewhat higher than if the competition was free to all other nations, are, however, by no means exorbitant; and the price of European goods accordingly is not extravagantly high in the greater part of the colonies of either of those nations.

In the exportation of their own surplus produce too, it is only with regard to certain commodities that the colonies of Great Britain are confined to the market of the mother country. These com-

Text: Adam Smith, "Wealth of Nations," *Works,* ed. Dugald Stewart (London: Strahan and Preston, 1811), III, 375-91.

modities having been enumerated in the act of navigation and in some other subsequent acts, have upon that account been called *enumerated commodities*. The rest are called *non-enumerated;* and may be exported directly to other countries, provided it is in British or Plantation ships, of which the owners and three-fourths of the mariners are British subjects.

Among the non-enumerated commodities are some of the most important productions of America and the West Indies; grain of all sorts, lumber, salt provisions, fish, sugar, and rum.

Grain is naturally the first and principal object of the culture of all new colonies. By allowing them a very extensive market for it, the law encourages them to extend this culture much beyond the consumption of a thinly inhabited country, and thus to provide beforehand an ample subsistence for a continually increasing population.

In a country quite covered with wood, where timber consequently is of little or no value, the expence of clearing the ground is the principal obstacle to improvement. By allowing the colonies a very extensive market for their lumber, the law endeavours to facilitate improvement by raising the price of a commodity which would otherwise be of little value, and thereby enabling them to make some profit of what would otherwise be mere expence. . . .

To increase the shipping and naval power of Great Britain, by the extension of the fisheries of our colonies, is an object which the legislature seems to have had almost constantly in view. Those fisheries, upon this account, have had all the encouragement which freedom can give them, and they have flourished accordingly. The New England fishery in particular was, . . . one of the most important, perhaps, in the world. . . .

If the whole surplus produce of America in grain of all sorts, in salt provisions, and in fish, had been put into the enumeration, and thereby forced into the market of Great Britain, it would have interfered too much with the produce of the industry of our own people. It was probably not so much from any regard to the interest of America, as from a jealousy of this interference, that those important commodities have not only been kept out of the enumeration, but that the importation into Great Britain of all grain, except rice, and of salt provisions, has, in the ordinary state of the law, been prohibited. . . .

The enumerated commodities are of two sorts: first, such as are either the peculiar produce of America, or as cannot be produced, or at least are not produced, in the mother country. Of this kind are, molasses, coffee, cacao-nuts, tobacco, pimento, ginger, whalefins, raw silk, cotton-wool, beaver, and other peltry of America, indigo, fustic, and other dying woods: secondly, such as are not the peculiar produce of America, but which are and may be produced in the mother country, though not in such quantities as to supply the greater part of her demand, which is principally supplied from foreign countries. Of this kind are all naval stores, masts, yards, and bowsprits, tar, pitch, and turpentine, pig and bar iron, copper ore, hides and skins, pot and pearl ashes. The largest importation of commodities of the first kind could not discourage the growth or interfere with the sale of any part of the produce of the mother country. By confining them to the home market, our merchants, it was expected, would not only be enabled to buy them cheaper in the Plantations, and consequently to sell them with a better profit at home, but to establish between the Plantations and foreign countries an advantageous carrying trade, of which Great Britain was necessarily to be the center or emporium, as the European country into which those commodities were first to be imported. . . .

The most perfect freedom of trade is permitted between the British colonies of America and the West Indies, both in the enumerated and in the non-enumerated commodities. Those colonies are now become so populous and thriving, that each of them finds in some of the others a great and extensive market for every part of its produce. All of them taken together, they make a great internal market for the produce of one another.

The liberality of England, however, towards the trade of her colonies has been confined chiefly to what concerns the market for their produce, either in its rude state, or in what may be called the very first stage of manufacture. The more advanced or more refined manufactures even of the colony produce, the merchants and manufactures of Great Britain chuse to reserve to themselves, and have prevailed upon the legislature to prevent their establishment in the colonies, sometimes by high duties, and sometimes by absolute prohibitions. . . .

While Great Britain encourages in America the manufactures of pig and bar iron, by exempting them from duties to which the like commodities are subject when imported from any other country, she imposes an absolute prohibition upon the erection of steel furnaces and slitmills in any of her American plantations. She will not suffer her colonists to work in those more refined manufactures even for their own consumption; but insists upon their purchasing of her merchants and manufacturers all goods of this kind which they have occasion for.

She prohibits the exportation from one province to another by water, . . . by land upon horseback or in a cart, of hats, of wools and woolen goods, of the produce of America; a regulation which effectually prevents the establishment of any manufacture of such commodities for distant sale, and confines the industry of her colonists in this way to such coarse and household manufactures, as a private family commonly makes for its own use, or for that of some of its neighbours in the same province.

To prohibit a great people, however, from making all that they can of every part of their own produce, or from employing their stock and industry in the way that they judge most advantageous to themselves, is a manifest violation of the most sacred rights of mankind. Unjust, however, as such prohibitions may be, they have not hitherto been very hurtful to the colonies. Land is still so cheap, and, consequently, labour so dear among them, that they can import from the mother country, almost all the more refined or more advanced manufactures cheaper than they could make them for themselves. Though they had not, therefore, been prohibited from establishing such manufactures, yet in their present state of improvement, a regard to their own interest would, probably, have prevented them from doing so. In their present state of improvement, those prohibitions, perhaps, without cramping their industry, or restraining it from any employment to which it would have gone of its own accord, are only impertinent badges of slavery imposed upon them, without any sufficient reason, by the groundless jealousy of the merchants and manufacturers of the mother country. In a more advanced state they might be really oppressive and insupportable.

Great Britain too, as she confines to her own market some of the most important productions of the colonies, so in compensation she gives to some of them an advantage in that market; sometimes by imposing higher duties upon the like productions when imported from other countries, and sometimes by giving bounties upon their importation from the colonies. In the first way she gives an advantage in the home-market to the sugar, tobacco, and iron of her own colonies, and in the second to their raw silk, to their hemp and flax, to their indigo, to their naval-stores, and to their building-timber. . . .

With regard to the importation of goods from Europe, England has likewise dealt more liberally with her colonies than any other nation.

Great Britain allows a part, almost always the half, generally a larger portion, and sometimes the whole of the duty which is paid upon the importation of foreign goods, to be drawn back upon their exportation to any foreign country. . . .

Our colonies, however, are by no means independent foreign countries; and Great Britain having assumed to herself the exclusive right of supplying them with all goods from Europe, might have forced them (in the same manner as other countries have done their colonies) to receive such goods, loaded with all the same duties which they paid in the mother country. But, on the contrary, till 1763, the same drawbacks were paid upon the exportation of the greater part of foreign goods to our colonies as to any independent foreign country. In 1763, indeed, by the 4th of Geo. III. c. 15. this indulgence was a good deal abated, . . . Before this law, many different sorts of foreign goods might have been bought cheaper in the plantations than in the mother country; and some may still.

Of the greater part of the regulations concerning the colony trade, the merchants who carry it on, it must be observed, have been the principal advisers. We must not wonder, therefore, if, in the greater part of them, their interest has been more considered than either that of the colonies or that of the mother country. In their exclusive privilege of supplying the colonies with all the goods which they wanted from Europe, and of purchasing all such parts of their surplus produce as could not interfere with any of the trades which they themselves carried on at home, the interest of the colonies was sacrificed to the interest of those merchants. . . .

But though the policy of Great Britain with regard to the trade of her colonies has been dictated by the same mercantile spirit as that of other nations, it has, however, upon the whole, been less illiberal and oppressive than that of any of them. . . .

19 THE POLITICAL SYSTEM

from Thomas Pownall, *Administration of the British Colonies*, 1764

Just as British imperial policy was facing grave new problems, Thomas Pownall, in his *The Administration of the British Colonies* (1764), voiced the hope that statesmen "would be naturally led into the true system of government, by following *with the powers of the state*, where the actual and *real powers of the system of things* lead to." Pownall, in short, believed that there was a principle of imperial organization *implicit* in the existing relations of the American colonies to the mother country which should be made *explicit* in a reorganized empire. He wanted to unify and tighten imperial administration, to preserve the chartered rights and liberties of the colonial "corporations," and to draw colonial representatives into a grand imperial Parliament.

In the passages reprinted below, Pownall presents his view of the empire as it might be if his reforms were realized and adds his economic justification for holding colonies. We can find here the outlook of an experienced and enlightened imperial administrator who had first come to America in 1753, serving successively as secretary to the governor of New York, observer for the English Board of Trade, lieutenant governor of New Jersey, liberal and effective governor of Massachusetts during the war years, 1757-1760, and finally governor of South Carolina. After his return to England, Pownall held a seat in the House of Commons for over a decade. His book went through six editions.

The first step that [a reformed imperial] administration would take to fix the basis of an established, permanent and effective system of government for the mother country and the Colonies, must be made by some *leading measure*, which shall, on real fact, and by actual representation of the parties concerned, examine into the various interests which have arisen, the various claims which are derived from those interests, and the various rights that may, or may not, be admitted, as founded on these, and as consistent with the general government and interest of the whole. . . .

If this measure be adopted, *a general bill of rights*, and an act for the establishment of government and commerce on a great plan of union, will be brought forward; the colonies will be considered as so many corporations, not without, but united to, the realm; they will be left in all the free and full possession of their several rights and liberties, as by grant, charter, or commissions given; yet, for every power which they exercise or possess, they will depend upon the government of the whole, and upon Great Britain as the center. Great Britain, as the center of this system, of which the colonies by actual union shall become organized, not annexed parts, must be the center of attraction to which these colonies, in the administration of every power of their government, in the exercise of their judicial powers, in the execution of their laws, and in every operation of their trade must tend. They will remain under the constant influence of the attraction of this center; and cannot move, but that every direction of such movement will converge to

Text: Thomas Pownall, *The Administration of the British Colonies*, 5th ed. (London: J. Walter, 1774), I, 28-29, 39-42.

the same. And as it is not more necessary to preserve the several governments subordinate in their respective orbs, than it is essential to the preservation of the whole empire to keep them disconnected and independent of each other, *they must be guarded by this union against having or forming any principle of coherence with each other, above that whereby they cohere to this center, this first mover.* They should alway remain incapable of any coherence, or of so conspiring amongst themselves, as to create any other equal force which might recoil back on this first mover. Policy acting upon a system of civil union, may easily and constitutionally provide against all this. The colonies and provinces, as they stand at present, are under the best form as to this point, which they can be under. They are under the best frame and disposition for the government of the general and supreme power (duly applied) to take place, having at present no other principle of civil union between each other, than that by which they naturally are, and in policy should be, in communion with Great Britain, as the common center of all. The different manner in which they are settled; the different modes under which they live; the different forms of charters, grants, and frames of government they possess; the various principles of repulsion that these create; the different interests which they actuate; the different religious interests by which they are actuated; the rivalship and jealousies which arise from hence; and the impracticability of reconciling and accommodating these incompatible ideas and claims, will keep them for ever so, so long as the spirit of civil policy remains, and is exerted to the forming and maintaining of this system of union. . . .

CHAPTER 2

The American Mind in the Making

In the seventeenth century, the period in which most of the American colonies were founded, the dominant American intellectual movement was Puritanism, which was centered in the New England colonies. The other colonies—most of their efforts concentrated on the physical problems of taming a wilderness—had almost no intellectual life of their own until the eighteenth century. In the late seventeenth century the influence of Puritanism rapidly declined, even in New England, and the intellectual movement known as the Enlightenment became dominant in the American colonies and remained to influence the entire eighteenth century.

PURITANISM

Because both Puritanism and the Enlightenment originated in European religious and philosophical movements, we must briefly cross the water and go back one century in time to begin our story. The Protestant Reformation produced two great religious systems: that of the German Martin Luther (1483-1546) and that of the Swiss John Calvin (1509-1564). In the seventeenth century, Calvinism became the dominant dissenting faith in England and came into conflict with the legally established Anglican Church. Two religious groups derived from Calvinism were instrumental in the colonization of America: the Pilgrims who settled at Plymouth and the Puritans of the Massachusetts Bay Colony. Both Pilgrims and Puritans came to America during the 1630's and 1640's to get away from the Anglican Church. However, the Pilgrims were members of a small religious sect which had little influence, while the Puritans belonged to what was, after the court and established church, the most powerful social and intellectual force in England, so powerful that by the middle of the seventeenth century it had produced a revolution and brought about the execution of King Charles I.

Since Puritanism was an offshoot of Calvinism, an understanding of the Puritan colonists' intellectual life requires some comprehension of Calvin's doctrines. Both Calvin and the Puritans insisted on the supreme authority of the Bible and believed that it was a sufficient guide to the solution of man's problems and the understanding of his role in the universe. As they interpreted it, the Bible said that man had been created by God to enjoy eternal bliss. But the first man, Adam, committed the unforgivable crime of disobeying his Creator's single command, not to eat the fruit of the Tree of Knowledge. And "In Adam's fall, we sinned all": Adam's *original sin* made all his descendants sinful *by nature* and therefore unable to save themselves from eternal damnation.

Despite His just wrath at man's evil nature, however, God was also merciful, and He allowed His only son, Christ, to atone for man's sin by dying on the Cross. Unfortunately, even this sacrifice was not sufficient to wipe out the full immensity of man's evil, and thus, according to Calvin, only a few men could be saved from Hell. One might think that the selection of these few would depend on the performance of religious and moral duties in this life, but such was not the case for Calvin. Because God was absolutely sovereign (*i.e.*, his power was not limited by any other will) and man was innately unable to save himself, God arbitrarily selected certain individuals, giving them the supernatural assistance they needed to free themselves from sin. This supernatural assistance to the sinner was to come in the form of an actual experience of God's power.

Now let us attach the proper names to these ideas: God's choosing those to be saved was known as *Election,* and the chosen were the *Elect* or the *Saints;* since election supposedly took place before the beginning of time, it was an act of *Predestination;* the supernatural assistance God gave to the elect was called *Grace,* while the experience of grace was known as *Conversion.* Finally, the converted man was thought to be one of the *Regenerate.* With these ideas in mind we can turn to the development of Puritanism in America.

The Puritans came to America in order to establish a *Godly Commonwealth,* wherein they might live according to what they took to be God's will. The doctrine of salvation through grace did not absolve man from the performance of religious and moral duties, even though these would not save his soul. On the contrary, the only sign that a man had been elected by God was his ability to free himself from sin and live a holy and upright life. The Godly Commonwealth's ideas and institutions, therefore, sprang from the desire to live in accordance with God's will as communicated to man through the Bible. This was, to the Puritans, the only true Christian liberty. They believed that if men would not voluntarily follow God's commands, they should be forced to do so for the good of their own souls. Their intense commitment to this belief led them to religious intolerance and persecution. Although they came to America to find religious liberty for themselves, they would not tolerate dissent from their own religious beliefs; men like Roger Williams (c1603-1683) and the Quakers were forced to leave the Puritan colonies or face imprisonment and death.

The Puritans were convinced that the way to heaven was not easy and that sinful man obviously needed all the assistance he could get. Yet how could man-made laws and rules do any good if a soul could be saved only through God's grace? This was a paradox the Puritans never solved, and the attempt to deal with it ultimately led them away from Calvinism.

The doctrine of the *Covenant* was the Puritan's main attempt to solve the paradoxical relationship of God's grace and the laws of the Godly Commonwealth. Justifying their doctrine by reference to the Biblical covenants of God with Adam, Noah, and others, the New England theologians asserted, in effect, that God had made a special covenant with the Puritans, who, like the Biblical Israelites, were a chosen people. The implication was that every Puritan colonist was one of the elect and, with the proper effort, could win God's grace. Thus, they argued, the church should exercise a strict supervision of politics, society, and intellectual life in the Godly Commonwealth.

This doctrine led to a very close relationship between church and state, which was justified by the argument that the church had an obligation to ensure that the commonwealth's political leaders were properly chosen and trained. An unregenerate person could hardly rule in accordance with God's will, and therefore one of the colony's most important laws was that only a church member could vote and hold office.

The practical result of Puritan political ideas was an aristocratic society in which power was concentrated in the hands of a few individuals. But unlike the English aristocracy of birth, the Puritan aristocracy was based on religious excellence. In theory and to a considerable extent in practice, the most powerful men in New England were the clergy, a highly educated intellectual elite. And since a man did not have to be a member of an hereditary aristocracy to become a minister, the Puritan system made it possible for some men of lower-middle class origin to rise to positions of great authority. This American idea of a *moral and religious aristocracy* as opposed to an aristocracy of birth had very important consequences in the eighteenth century and helped New England become a center of revolutionary activity. Even in the seventeenth century, the Puritan's concept of aristocracy led to considerable misunderstanding between them and some of their co-religionists in England (see Document 22).

Although some intense religious movements have discouraged the development of learning and science, this was not the case with the Puritans. In fact, they had the only thriving intellectual life in the seventeenth-century colonies. Their leaders were among the most learned men of the time. And since they believed it to be man's duty to find out as much as possible about God's creation, education and science were strongly encouraged. However, their science was a very limited one, for they believed that God could and did intervene directly in nature. This belief made it impossible for them to accept the modern idea that nature obeys regular laws which can be discovered through experiment and the use of man's reason. According to Puritan theory, science would inevitably lead man to a greater sense of the wonders and mystery of nature and nature's God.

THE ENLIGHTENMENT

Unfortunately for the Puritans, science, as it developed in the late seventeenth and early eighteenth centuries, did not lead man to a greater sense of his helplessness before the wonders of God's creation. On the contrary, more and more men came to believe that they could understand and manipulate their environment in order to create a better earthly life. By the end of the seventeenth century, Puritanism was on the decline as an intellectual force in America, and the great English and Continental philosophers of the great intellectual movement known as the Enlightenment had taken the place of Puritan theologians as the source of American ideas.

The key ideas of the Enlightenment clustered around two terms: *reason* and *nature*. The Puritans had believed man's reason to be worth little, incapacitated as it was by his innate depravity, and they thought of nature as God's creation, controlled by His inscrutable Will. In the eighteenth century a dramatically new attitude gradually replaced this God-centered orientation. The men of the Enlightenment cast aside Revelation (*i.e.*, the Bible) and turned to nature and society with new interest, seeking for the principles and laws that controlled them.

The Enlightenment developed a belief called *deism*, which involved a new conception of God's role in the Universe. The Puritan God was a definite personality whose control over nature and history was *direct* and *continual*. The God of deism, on the other hand, was an impersonal master engineer who had given the creation certain laws. Once the processes of nature had been started, He no longer interfered but let these natural processes follow automatically the laws He had given them. These laws were the *natural laws* which the men of the Enlightenment dreamed of discovering through reason and experiment. Men hoped that an understanding of the natural laws which governed both nature and society would lead to a re-creation of man's environment and ultimately to happiness in this life, a goal that had been beyond man's wildest dreams for over sixteen centuries.

This new optimism about the possibilities of human life led to a great broadening of men's interests. Benjamin Franklin (1706-1790), who is in many ways a representative man of the Enlightenment, was a businessman, writer, scientist, inventor, politician, philosopher, educational thinker, diplomat, and founder of libraries, clubs, scientific associations, fire companies, police forces, and even governments. By contrast, even the broadest of the Puritans, Cotton Mather (1663-1728), seems narrow and otherworldly.

Since men's interests had turned from God to the study of nature and society, the Enlightenment's most significant and lasting contribution to American thought was in the realm of political and social ideas. In fact, the European ideas that hit eighteenth-century America with the greatest impact were those of the group of English and European political philosophers who came to be known as the *social contract philosophers*. The most important thinkers of this group were Thomas Hobbes (1588-1679), John Locke (1632-1704), and Jean Jacques Rousseau (1712-1778). In contrast to the medieval idea that rulers derived their authority from God, these philosophers asserted that the authority came from a *Social Contract*.

Society was considered by the men of the Enlightenment to be a man-made rather than a God-made thing. They had good reason for thinking so, for the establishing of the colonies in the American wilderness had involved a good many agreements like the "Mayflower Compact" to establish the colonial governments. Thus it was a logical step for the contract philosophers to imagine a pre-social state, when men lived without any social institutions of any kind. They called this the *State of Nature*.[1] In the state of nature, these philosophers argued, all men had the same rights to each others' lives and property. It is evident that in such a state, without any authority to preserve the peace, men would soon destroy one another. For this reason society had to be created, and this event must have involved some kind of agreement among the individuals coming together to form a society. This agreement was the social contract.

The important implications of this theory for American thought were two: first, if governments are created so that men may live a more peaceful and happy life

---

[1] The idea of the *state of nature* was also derived from a medieval concept of man's natural state: the state in which Adam lived before the fall. For some of the contract philosophers, the idea remained only a philosophical concept, but others believed the state of nature to have been an actual historical event.

than is possible in the state of nature, then there are obligations for the rulers as well as for the ruled. Government is a kind of trusteeship established for definite ends, rather than a divinely established authority with unlimited powers. Second, the idea of the contract implied that government is created and derives its authority from the *consent* or will of the governed.

Another idea growing out of the social contract theory became very important in the American Enlightenment. Some early formulations of the theory insisted that men gave up all their *Natural Rights* (*i.e.*, those rights all men possessed equally in the state of nature) when a social authority was created. At the end of the seventeenth century, however, John Locke, the English philosopher whose influence was most pervasive in eighteenth-century America, argued that certain natural rights were *inalienable* and could not be forsworn in the social contract. This implied that rulers had to protect certain rights, an argument that later found its way into the Declaration of Independence.

Interestingly enough, the social contract argument first appeared in America in the sermons of a New England minister (see Document 32), but as grievances with England increased, the ideas spread through the colonies to become the dominant theme in the agitation which led to the revolution.

The Enlightenment was the first nation-wide intellectual movement in America. While Puritanism had been strongest in New England, the ideas of the Enlightenment were held by men all over the country—from Washington and Jefferson in the South and Franklin in the middle colonies to the Adamses in New England. Even many pious individuals who were out of sympathy with the religious ideas of men like Franklin were strongly influenced by their orientation toward the problems of this world. Although English and European philosophers developed most of the significant ideas, it was Americans who translated the Enlightenment into practical politics and actually made one of the first recorded social contracts, the Constitution of the United States.

THE GREAT AWAKENING

Although the ideals of the Enlightenment rapidly undermined the Godly Commonwealth, especially among social and intellectual leaders, the intense religious consciousness of Puritanism was not yet dead. Throughout the early eighteenth century it smoldered fitfully in rural areas until, in 1734, it burst into flame in the first American religious revival, the *Great Awakening*. Led by a man who was not only the most brilliant American thinker of his age but also a true spiritual descendant of the Calvinists—Jonathan Edwards (1703-1758)—the Great Awakening was at first a kind of religious reaction against the worldly orientation of the Enlightenment. As it gathered steam, however, spreading across the United States with startling intensity, it developed into a complex popular movement. Revivalism flared up, died down, and then burst out again throughout most of the rest of the eighteenth century, strongly contrasting with the even tenor of the Enlightenment. The Great Awakening is thus one of the most fascinating intellectual events of pre-revolutionary America, bodying forth both the dying agonies of Puritanism and a fitful prophecy of things to come.

The Puritan Synthesis

THE GODLY COMMONWEALTH

20 THE WAY TO HEAVEN: PURITAN SELF-DISCIPLINE

from Thomas Shepard, "The Way to Heaven," 1655

The Puritan ideal of the Godly Commonwealth was a system of religious, philosophical, and political ideas organized around the quest for salvation. As this selection vividly illustrates, the way to heaven was no primrose path in the minds of the Puritans. In fact, the very essence of Puritanism was struggle—against the wilderness, against oneself, against the world and the Devil.

Thomas Shepard (1605-1699), the author of "The Way to Heaven," was, like most early Puritan ministers, born in England. To escape the persecutions of the high churchmen of the Church of England, he came to New England in 1635, when the Massachusetts Bay Colony was just getting under way. As minister at Cambridge, Mass., he became a founder of Harvard College and one of the important leaders of the Godly Commonwealth. He was a great preacher, and his book *The Sincere Convert*, from which the following selection is taken, was extremely popular, running through twenty editions between 1641 and 1812.

In "The Way to Heaven," Shepard outlines the things a man must become and the things he must avoid if he wishes to be saved. It should be observed that the religious virtues emphasized have a considerable application to the secular life. Humiliation, faith, and opposition can easily be translated into willingness to work, hope for success, and industry and perseverance. As the colonies became better established and the economic opportunities of the New World more apparent, the Puritans applied the same kind of moral energy to the pursuit of economic salvation in this world as to preparation for the next.

"The Way to Heaven" is also an excellent illustration of Puritan ideas about art and rhetoric. The style is essentially straightforward and plain, because the Puritans believed that when men wrote about true and holy things, their statements needed no refinement or fancy rhetorical tricks. There is abundant and vivid use of figures of speech in the selection, but these come either from plain everyday life or from the Bible. A good example is the striking metaphor "Jesus Christ is not got with a wet finger," which expresses Shepard's belief that salvation does not come from merely fingering the pages of the Bible.

The Gate is strait, and therefore a man must sweat and strive to enter; both the entrance is difficult and the progress of salvation too. Jesus Christ is not got with a wet finger. It is not wishing and desiring to be saved will bring men to Heaven; Hell's mouth is full of good wishes. It is not shedding a Tear at a Sermon, or blubbering now and then in a corner, and saying over thy prayers, and crying God's Mercy for thy sins will save thee. It is not a "Lord, have mercy upon us," will do thee good. It is not coming constantly to church; these are easy matters. But it is a tough Work, a wonderful hard Matter to be saved. Hence the Way to Heaven is compared to a race, where a man must put forth all his strength and stretch every limb and all to get forward. Hence

a Christian's Life is compared to wrestling, Eph. vi. 12. All the policy and power of Hell buckle together against a Christian, therefore he must look to himself, or else he falls. Hence it is compared to fighting, II. Tim. iv. 7, as Man must fight against the Devil, the World, himself, who shoot poisoned Bullets in the Soul, where a Man must kill or be killed. God hath not lined the Way to Heaven with Velvet, nor strewed it with Rushes. He will never feed a slothful humor in man, who will be saved if Christ and Heaven will drop into their mouths, and if any would bear their charges thither. If Christ might be bought for a few cold Wishes and lazy Desires, he would be of small reckoning among men, who would say: "Lightly come, lightly go." Indeed Christ's Yoke is easy in itself, and when a man is got into Christ, nothing is so sweet; but for a carnal dull heart, it is hard to draw in it: For,

Text: Thomas Shepard, *The Sincere Convert* (London: Thomas Mabb, 1664), pp. 99-106. The spelling has been modernized.

There are four strait Gates which every one must pass through before he can enter into Heaven.

1. There is the strait Gate of Humiliation. God saveth none but first he humbleth them. Now it is hard for a heart as stiff as a stake to bow, as hard as a stone to bleed for the least prick, not to mourn for one sin, but all sins; and not for a fit, but all man's life-time. Oh it is hard for a man to suffer himself to be loaden with sin, and prest to death for sin, so as never to love sin more, but to spit in the face of that which he once loved as dearly as his life. It is easy to drop a tear or two, and be Sermon-sick; but to have a heart rent for sin, and from sin, this is true Humiliation, and this is hard.

2. The strait Gate of Faith. It is an easy matter to presume but hard to believe in Christ. It is easy for a man that was never humbled to believe and say: " 'Tis but believing." But it is an hard matter for a man humbled when he sees all his sins in order before him, the Devil and Conscience roaring upon him, and crying out against him, and God frowning upon him; now to call God Father is an hard Work. Judas had rather be hanged than believe. It is hard to see a Christ as a Rock to stand upon, when we are overwhelmed with sorrow of heart for sin. It is hard to prize Christ above ten thousand worlds of pearl. 'Tis hard to desire Christ and nothing but Christ; hard to follow Christ all the day long, and never be quiet till he is got in thine arms, and then with Simeon to say: "Lord, now lettest thou thy servant depart in peace."

3. The strait Gate of Repentance. It is an easy Matter for a man to confess himself to be a sinner, and to cry to God for forgiveness until next time. But to have a bitter sorrow, and so to turn from all sin, and to return to God, and all the ways of God, which is true Repentance indeed; this is hard.

4. The strait Gate of Opposition of Devils, the World, and a Man's own self, who knocks a Man down when he begins to look towards Christ and Heaven.

Hence learn that every easy way to Heaven is a false way, although Ministers should preach it out of their pulpits, and Angels should publish it out of Heaven.

Now there are nine easy Ways to Heaven (as men think) all of which lead to Hell.

1. The common broad Way, wherein a whole parish may all go abreadth in it; tell these people they shall be damned; their answer is, "Then woe to many more besides me."

2. The Way of Civil Education; whereby many wild natures are by little and little tamed, and like wolves are chained up easily while they are young.

3. Balaam's Way of good Wishes; whereby many people will confess their ignorance, forgetfulness, and that they can not make such shows as others do, but they thank God their hearts are as good, and God for his part accepts (say they) the will for the deed. And, "My son, give me thine heart;" the heart is all in all, and so long they hope to do well enough. Poor deluded Creatures, thus to think to break through Armies of Sins, Devils, Temptations, and to break open the very Gates of Heaven with a few good Wishes! They think to come to their journey's end without legs, because their hearts are good to God.

4. The Way of Formality; whereby men rest in the performance of most or of all external duties without inward life. Every man must have some religion, some fig-leaves to hide their nakedness. Now this religion must be either true religion, or the false one; if the true he must either take up the power of it, but that he will not, because it is burdensome; or the form of it, and this being easy, men embrace it as their God, and will rather lose their lives than their religion thus taken up. This Form of Religion is the easiest religion in the world; partly because it easeth men of trouble of conscience, quieting that. Thou hast sinned, said Conscience, and God is offended; take a Book and pray, keep thy Conscience better, and bring thy Bible with thee. Now Conscience is silent, being charmed down with the Form of Religion, as the Devil is driven away (as they say) with Holy Water; partly also because the Form of Religion credits a man, partly because it is easy in itself; it's of a light carriage, being but the shadow and picture of the substance of religion; as now, what an easy matter is it to come to Church! They hear (at least outwardly) very attentively an hour or more, and then to turn to a proof, and to turn down a leaf, here's the Form. But now to spend Saturday-night and all the whole Sabbath Day-morning, in trimming the Lamp, and in getting Oil in the Heart to meet the Bridegroom the next Day, and so meet him in the Word, and there to tremble at the Voice of God, and suck the breast while it is open, and when the Word is done, to go aside privately and there to chew upon the Word, there to lament with tears all the vain thoughts in duties, deadness in hearing—this is hard, because this is the Power of Godliness, and this men will not take up. So for private praying what an easy matter is it for a man to say over a few prayers out of some devout Book, or to repeat some old prayer got by heart since a child, or to have two or three short-winded Wishes for God's Mercy in the morning and at

night! this Form is easy. But now to prepare the heart by serious meditation of God and man's self before he prays, then to come to God with a bleeding, hunger-starved heart, not only with a desire but with a warrant, "I must have such or such a Mercy," and there to wrestle with God, although it be an hour or two together for a Blessing—this is too hard. Men think none do thus and therefore they will not.

5. The Way of Presumption; whereby men having seen their sins, catch hold easily upon God's Mercy, and snatch comforts before they are reached out unto them. There is no word of comfort in the Book of God intended for such as regard Iniquity in their Hearts, though they do not act it in their lives. Their only comfort is that the Sentence of Damnation is not yet executed upon them.

6. The Way of Sloth; whereby men lie still and say "God must do all." If the Lord would set up a Pulpit at the ale-house door, it may be they would hear oftener. If God will always thunder, they will always pray; if he strike them now and then with sickness, God shall be paid with good words and promises enough, that they will be better if they live; but as long as Peace lasts they will run to Hell as fast as they can; and if God will not catch them they care not, they will not return.

7. The Way of Carelessness, when men feeling many difficulties pass through some of them, but not all, and what they can not get now, they feed themselves with a false hope they shall hereafter. They are content to be called Precisians and Fools, and crazy Brains, but they want Brokenness of Heart, and they will pray (it may be) for it, and pass by that difficulty; but to keep the wound always open, this they will not do, to be always sighing for help, and never to give themselves rest till their hearts are humbled; that they will not. These have a Name to live, yet are dead.

8. The Way of Moderation or honest Discretion, which indeed is nothing but Luke-warmness of the Soul, and that is when a man contrives and cuts out such a way to Heaven, as he may be hated of none, but please all, and so do any thing for a quiet life and so sleep in a whole skin. The Lord saith: "He that will live godly must suffer persecution." No, not so, Lord. Surely (think they) if men were discreet and wise, it would prevent a great deal of trouble and opposition in good Courses; this man will commend those that are most zealous, if they were wise; if he meet with a black-mouthed Swearer, he will not reprove him, lest he be displeased with him; if he meet with an honest Man, he'll yield to all he saith, that so he may commend him; and when he meets them both together, they shall be both alike welcome (whatever he thinks) to his house and table, because he would fain be at peace with all men.

9. And lastly, The Way of Self-Love; whereby a man fearing terribly he shall be damned, useth diligently all means whereby he shall be saved. Here is the strongest difficulty of all, to row against the Stream, and to hate a man's self, and then to follow Christ fully.

21

THE CHOSEN PEOPLE: THE PURITANS' COVENANT WITH GOD

from Peter Bulkeley, *The Gospel-Covenant*, 1651

By means of the doctrine of the Covenant, the Puritans attempted to reconcile the Calvinistic idea of salvation through grace with man's efforts to save himself through the Godly Commonwealth. This doctrine implied that the New England colonists had a special covenant with God; therefore a man could be assured of salvation if he became a full member of the Godly Commonwealth. In this selection Peter Bulkeley, a founder and minister of Concord, Mass., explains the importance of the covenant with God. He points out that men possess both benefits and special responsibilities when they are living under the covenant.

Although in Bulkeley's formulation the doctrine of the covenant was still in harmony with Calvin's idea of the *elect* (see pp. 59-60), there was an increasing tendency to insist that if a man performed religious and moral duties in this life, God was obligated to take his soul to Heaven. This idea directly contradicted the Calvinistic tenets of the *absolute sovereignty of God, predestination,* and *election* and paved the way for the less rigorous and otherworldly religious ideas of the American Enlightenment.

Peter Bulkeley (1583-1659) was educated at Cambridge, England, and for twenty-one years was rector of a Bedfordshire parish. Being removed from this post by Archbishop Laud for nonconformity to the Church of England, he left England (c1634). After a brief stay at Cambridge, Mass., "he carried a good number of planters with him up further into the woods" and founded the town of Concord, where he remained as its first minister until his death. He was noted for his benevolence as well as for his strict virtues and strong adherence to theocracy.

Seeing this is one of the blessings of the covenant of grace, to have God above us and over us, to guide and rule us, this must teach us when we enter into covenant with God, not to count our condition then a state of liberty, as if we might then walk after our own desires, and ways, as if there were none to command us and rule over us. Indeed, there is a spiritual liberty from our enemies, but there is subjection required to the Lord. We must not look only after gifts, mercies, kindnesses, pardon, and such tokens and pledges of grace, but look also for this, to be under God, and to set up Him on high to be a God and Lord over us; And let us not count this our misery, but our blessedness, that we are brought under His gracious government. Herein the Lord showeth His marvelous kindness, that He will take the care of us. Would we not wonder to see such a Prince as Solomon, to take his subjects' children to tutor them and train them up under him? Now we are but poor ants and worms upon earth, but the Lord of heaven offereth to take the government of us upon Himself; This is infinite mercy; whither would our unruly hearts carry us? if He should leave us to ourselves? Who is there that hath an experience of the sinful evils that are in his heart, but will acknowledge this to be a benefit, that the Lord should rule over him with an out-stretched arm? If God leave Hezekiah but a little, how is his heart lift up with pride, so that he must have a Prophet sent to him on purpose to humble him? If God leave David to himself, to what evils is he not ready to fall? And is there not the same spirit in us? The more contrariety and opposition that there is in us to the will of God, the greater mercy it is that He will be King over us. Learn therefore to count it no small blessing, and when God beginneth with us to overrule the rebelliousness of our hearts, and to bring them into order, take heed that we spurn not with the heel, nor lift up ourselves: But let us humble ourselves, and submit ourselves to Him, that He may take the guidance of us into His own hands. Hear the rod and kiss it, and take it as a mercy, that He is pleased to take the care of us, to correct our wanderings, and bring us back into the ways of our own peace. Take heed of walking contrary, lest He say to us, as to the *Israelites*, that *He will reign over us no more.*

For trial and examination, whether we be a people in Covenant with God, and have taken Him to be our God; For if God be our God, then He must be God over us, and above us, He must rule us, and we must be ruled and governed by Him.

How may we know that the Lord hath taken us into His government, and that we are ruled by Him alone?

By these four things we may know it.

First, Where the Lord sets Himself over a people, He frames them unto a willing and voluntary subjection unto Him, that they desire nothing more than to be under His government, they count this their felicity, that they have the Lord over them, to govern them. As the servants of Solomon were counted happy that they might stand before him, and minister unto him; so it is the happiness of God's people, that they are under Him, and in subjection unto Him: The Lord's government is not a Pharaoh-like tyranny, to rule them with rigour, and make them sigh and groan, but it is a government of peace; He rules them by love, as He first wins them by love. He conquers them indeed by a mighty strong hand, but withal He draws them by the cords of love. He overcometh our evil with the abundance of His goodness; therefore His spirit, though sometime it be called a *spirit of power*, yet it is also a *spirit of love, joy, and peace;* though the spirit put forth His power in vanquishing our *enemies* that held us in bondage, yet it overcometh *us* by love, making us to see what a blessed thing it is to have the Lord to be over us. Thus when the Lord is in Covenant with a people, they follow Him not forcedly, but as far as they are sanctified by grace, they submit willingly to His regiment. Therefore those that can be drawn to nothing that is good, but by compulsion and constraint, it is a sign that they are not under the gracious government of the Lord God.

Secondly, If God be God over us, governing us by the government of His grace, we must yield Him universal obedience in all things. He must not be over us in one thing, and under us in another, but He must be over us in every thing;

Text: Peter Bulkeley, *The Gospel-Covenant* (London: Matthew Simmons, 1651), pp. 218-23. The spelling has been modernized.

God's authority is cast away by refusing obedience to one Commandment, as well as by refusing obedience unto all. His authority is seen in one, as well as in another. And he that breaketh one, doth in effect break all, as James 2:11. When God cometh to rule, He cometh with power, to cast down *every stronghold,* and *every* high thought that is exalted against the power of Christ. He cometh to lay waste the whole kingdom of sin; all must down, not a stone left of that Babel. The Lord will reign in the whole soul, He will have no God, no King with Him. And therefore herein look unto it, if He be God over us, He alone must rule over us, and no other with Him. Consider whether God's dominion hath its full extent in us; whether there be not some corruption which thou desirest to be spared in: Canst thou give up thyself wholly to the power of grace, to be ruled by it? Canst thou part with thy Absalom, thy beloved lust, and be content that God should set up His kingdom in thy whole soul? Then is God over thee, and thou in covenant with Him. But if thou canst not submit that the life of some darling lust should go; if there be any sin that is dearer to thee, than to obey God; if thou hast thy exceptions, and reservations, and wilt not yield universal obedience, then art thou an alien from God and His Covenant; God is no God unto thee, nor art thou one of His people.

Thirdly, Where the Lord governeth and setteth up His kingdom over the soul, He carries and lifts up the heart to an higher pitch, and above that which flesh and blood could or would attain unto. And that both in the things themselves, and the ends which they aim at in them. He makes a man undertake such things as his own heart would refuse and turn from, as Ezek. 3:14, he was very backward to preach to the Jews, and yet when he saw it was the Lord's mind, he submitted. So Paul (Rom. 15:20.) *enforced himself* to preach the Gospel, yet it was not a constrained force, but the love of Christ constrained him, 2 Cor. 5. So Moses, though at the first very loath to go to Pharaoh, yet when the power of grace prevailed in him, he contends with Pharaoh as with his equal in the cause of God, and would not yield to the fierceness of the King, not for an hoof; so though he fled from the serpent at the first sight, yet at God's commandment he taketh it up in his hand. This also we see in Abraham when he was commanded to sacrifice his own son, though he loved him, yet he loved God more, and therefore obeyed, which nature alone could never have done. In all these they wrought against the stream, doing that which flesh and blood could never have done. Again,

the power of God's grace in His government lifts up the soul to higher ends and aims, than flesh and blood can attain unto. The kingdom of God's grace, is called the *kingdom of heaven,* His aims and ends are on high, not earthly but heavenly; His government is an heavenly regiment, the Lord governeth the hearts of His people to the same end which He hath propounded to Himself. God's ends and our ends meet in one, which is the glorifying of His Name. This putteth the difference between all formal hypocrites, and those that are ruled by the spirit of grace: hypocrites are ruled by their own spirit, and they never aim at higher than their own ends, their own honour, credit, profit, etc. Though their *actions* may be *spiritual,* yet their *ends* are *carnal;* but when God taketh the heart into His guidance, then He maketh us to set up Him as highest in the throne, and all is done for His honour. It makes a man to use and employ himself, wisdom, strength, riches, credit, and esteem in the Church, and all for God, not for himself; God is his last end in every thing, as most worthy to be glorified by all. Indeed a man in Covenant with God may do many things for himself, aiming at the furtherance of his own good both spiritual and temporal, and also aim at the good of other men, but this is not in opposition, but in subordination to God and His glory; that last and main end must sway all other ends. Nothing must be done to cross and hinder His glory; this is the government of God's Grace. Consider how God's Spirit guides thy heart to those things, and aims, that flesh and blood cannot at all reach unto; for if thou hast only thine own end and aim then thou art thine own, and not under the government of God.

Fourthly, The government of God's grace causeth the peace of God to lodge in that soul in which it ruleth. Rom. 14:17. *The kingdom of God is righteousness, peace, and joy in the Holy Ghost.* Grace and peace go hand in hand; There is a reign and rule of grace, Rom. 5:21. And so there is of peace, Col. 3:15. As under the reign of Solomon, there was abundance of peace, so there is under the government of Christ, He is the King of Salem. And the more the soul is subjected unto His government, the more peace it finds. And that may be seen in these two things.

First, In the dispensations and administrations of God's providence, though things go cross against us, we meet with many troubles, God's providences seem to cross His promises; yet there is peace to the soul in it; therefore saith Christ, Job. 16, last. *In the world you shall have trouble, but in Me you shall have peace.* Certain it is, that if ever our hearts be out of quiet, it is because there is some sedition and traitorous conspiracy, which hath been rising up against the kingdom of Christ, and this works trouble; but where the soul is subjected to the regiment of grace, it maketh it to rest in peace; In all wrongs, injuries, and crosses, it knows the Lord will right them; In all wants, it knows that He will provide; In all kind of trials, that He will with the temptation give an issue in due time. But the heart that is unsubdued to God's kingdom, is ready to fret against God, and sit down discontented when any thing crosseth him.

Secondly, As it resteth in peace under the dispensations of God's providences, so it rests in peace in regard of the spiritual enemies of our salvation, which fight against our souls. Whatsoever threatens our ruin, the soul shrouds itself under the wing of the Almighty and concludes with the Prophet, Isa. 33:22. *The Lord is my Judge, He is my King, and He will save me.* Let us examine ourselves by these things, and we may see whether we be under the government of God, and so whether we be in Covenant with Him.

This may serve for a rule of direction, and withal for a ground of consolation to the Lord's servants; when they feel the strength of their corruptions working in them, and their lust prevailing against them, that they make them groan, and cry with Paul. *O wretched man that I am,* etc., when they find themselves foiled again and again, and can get no help against those evils, let them fly to this promise of grace; let them lay this promise of the covenant before them, and remember what the Lord hath said, *I will rule over you with a mighty hand,* Ezek. 20:33. Remember the Lord of His promise, and claim it, that it may be made good unto thee. And say, Lord, thou hath promised, that Thou wilt rule over me; why is it then that these tyrants rule and reign in my soul? Why doth unbelief, pride, worldliness rule? Thus make we our refuge to the throne of Grace, and then as the Lord will fulfill the other promises of His covenant, so He will also fulfill this, and will rule us by His Grace; He will come and plead the cause of His people against all their enemies, and say as Isa. 52:5, *What have I to do here, that My people are taken away for nought? they that rule over them make them to howl,* etc. His meaning is as if He should say, What do you mean, Egypt and Asbur, to trouble My people, that you put Me also to trouble in rescuing them? Let them alone, or else I will make you feel My power, etc. So it is in the enemies of our souls, when we are forced to howl unto God, by reason of the bondage of our corruptions, He will set us free, He himself will be a God over us, to rule us by His Spirit.

This being one of the blessings of the covenant of Grace, to have God to be Lord over us, let us then all be admonished to give up ourselves to the regiment of His grace.

22

PURITAN ARISTOCRACY: CHURCH AND STATE IN THE GODLY COMMONWEALTH

from John Cotton, Letter to Lord Saye and Sele, 1636

The relationship between church and state was very close in the Godly Commonwealth and became a subject of considerable misunderstanding between the colonists and Puritan circles in England. The law that only church members might vote and hold office in the Massachusetts Bay Colony was a particular subject of dispute. Lord Saye and Sele, a noble English Puritan, had contemplated migrating to the Colony but, disturbed at what he had heard of its political and social system, wrote to John Cotton, one of the Godly Commonwealth's leading clergymen. In reply, Cotton gave a classic exposition of American Puritan political theory.

Lord Saye and Sele was concerned that the law granting full citizenship only to church members would allow anyone, regardless of hereditary social position, to become a political leader. This, he feared, would overthrow the traditional English aristocracy and lead the Godly Commonwealth into "distractions, and popular confusions" or to that worst of all political horrors, democracy. The church, he feared, would become dominant in all things and allow no authority to the secular aristocracy which was, in the worthy lord's mind, the chief bulwark against the excesses of democracy.

Cotton replies that though church and state are partially separate in function, the church has a basic responsibility to prepare "fit instruments both to rule, and to choose rulers." He agrees with Lord Saye and Sele that democracy is not a fit government for men but insists that the church is the best bulwark against popular usurpation of secular authority and has the further duty of helping the state to make rules in accordance with God's will. Therefore the church and state ought to maintain each other by aiming at "authority in magistrates, liberty in peoples, purity in the church." Though Cotton saw no conflict in these three principles, it was not long before the Puritan authority was challenged by a broader concept of "liberty in people" than the Puritan doctrine, which implied that the only true liberty is living according to God's will as interpreted by Puritan leaders.

John Cotton (1585-1652) was educated at Cambridge, England, and about 1612 became a vicar in Boston, Lincolnshire, where he remained twenty years, moving more and more in doctrine and practice toward Puritanism. He was finally informed against for not kneeling at the sacrament and was cited to appear in 1633 before Archbishop Laud in the Court of High Commission. He hid in London and then fled to the New England Boston (which had been named in compliment to him), where he became teacher of the First Church, a post he held until his death. Here he enjoyed a wide reputation for erudition and Puritan piety, wrote prolifically, and came to wield immense influence over New England affairs. He conducted an extended controversy with Roger Williams, whose banishment from Massachusetts Bay he approved. (See Document 24.)

Right honourable,

. . . It is very suitable to God's all-sufficient wisdom, and to the fullness and perfection of Holy Scriptures, not only to prescribe perfect rules for the right ordering of a private man's soul to everlasting blessedness with himself, but also for the right ordering of a man's family, yea, of the commonwealth too, so far as both of them are subordinate to spiritual ends, and yet avoid both the church's usurpation upon civil jurisdictions, *in ordine ad spiritualia,* and the commonwealth's invasion upon ecclesiastical administrations, *in ordine* to civil peace, and conformity to the civil state. God's institutions (such as the government of church and of commonwealth be) may be close and compact, and co-ordinate one to another, and yet not confounded. God hath so framed the state of church government and ordinances, that they may be compatible to any commonwealth, though never so much disordered in his frame. But yet when a commonwealth hath liberty to mould his own frame (*scripture plenitudinem adoro*) I conceive the scripture hath given full direction for the right ordering of the same, and that, in such sort as may best maintain the euexia of the church. . . . It is better that the commonwealth be fashioned to the setting forth of God's house, which is his church, than to accommodate the church frame to the civil state. Democracy, I do not conceive that ever God did ordain as a fit government either for church or commonwealth. If the people be governors, who shall be governed? As for mon-

archy, and aristocracy, they are both of them clearly approved, and directed in Scripture, yet so as referreth the sovereignty to himself, and setteth up Theocracy in both, as the best form of government in the commonwealth, as well as in the church.

The law, which your Lordship instanceth in (that none shall be chosen to magistracy among us but a church member) was made and enacted before I came into the country; but I have hitherto wanted sufficient light to plead against it. 1st. The rule that directeth the choice of supreme governors is of like equity and weight in all magistrates, that one of their brethren (not a stranger) should be set over them, Deut. 17:15; and Jethro's counsel to Moses was approved of God, that the judges, and officers to be set over the people, should be men fearing God, Exod. 18:21.; and Solomon maketh it the joy of a commonwealth, when the righteous are in authority, and their mourning when the wicked rule, Prov. 29:21, Job 34:30. . . .

When your Lordship doubteth [fears], that this course will draw all things under the determination of the church, *in ordine ad spiritualia* (seeing the church is to determine who shall be members, and none but a member may have to do in the government of a commonwealth) be pleased (I pray you) to conceive, that magistrates are neither chosen to office in the church, nor do govern by directions from the church, but by civil laws, and those enacted in general courts, and executed in courts of justice, by the governors and assistants. In all which, the church (as the church) hath nothing to do; only, it prepareth fit instruments both to rule, and to choose rulers, which is no ambition in the church, nor dishonor to the commonwealth; the apostle, on the con-

Text: John Cotton, "Letter to Lord Saye and Sele," in Thomas Hutchinson, *History of Massachusetts Bay* (Boston: Thomas & John Fleet, 1764), I (Appendix III), 496-501.

trary, thought it a great dishonor and reproach to the church of Christ, if it were not able to yield able judges to hear and determine all causes amongst their brethren, I Cor. 6:1-5, which place alone seemeth to me fully to decide this question; for it plainly holdeth forth this argument: It is a shame to the church to want able judges of civil matter (as v. 5.) and an audacious act in any church member voluntarily to go for judgment, otherwhere than before the saints (as v. 1.) then it will be no arrogance nor folly in church members, nor prejudice to the commonwealth, if voluntarily they never choose any civil judges, but from amongst the saints, such as church members are called to be. But the former is clear; and how then can the latter be avoided? If this therefore be (as your Lordship rightly conceiveth one of the main objections if not the only one) which hindereth this commonwealth from the entertainment of the propositions of those worthy gentlemen, we entreat them, in the name of the Lord Jesus, to consider, in meekness of wisdom, it is not any conceit or will of ours, but the holy counsel and will of the Lord Jesus (whom they seek to serve as well as we) that overruleth us in this case: and we trust will overrule them also, that the Lord only may be exalted amongst all his servants. What pity and grief were it, that the observance of the will of Christ should hinder good things from us!

But your Lordship doubteth, that if such a rule were necessary, then the church estate and the best ordered commonwealth in the world were not compatible. But let not your Lordship so conceive. For, the church submitteth itself to all the laws and ordinances of men, in what commonwealth soever they come to dwell. But it is one thing, to submit unto what they have no calling to reform; another thing, voluntarily to ordain a form of government, which to the best dis-

cerning of many of us (for I speak not of myself) is expressly contrary to rule. Nor need your Lordship fear (which yet I speak with submission to your Lordship's better judgment) that this course will lay such a foundation, as nothing but a mere democracy can be built upon it. Bodine confesseth, that though it be *status popularis,* where a people choose their own governors; yet the government is not a democracy, if it be administered, not by the people, but by the governors, whether one (for then it is a monarchy, though elective) or by many, for then (as you know) it is aristocracy. In which respect it is, that church government is justly denied . . . to be democratical, though the people choose their own officers and rulers.

Nor need we fear, that this course will, in time, cast the commonwealth into distractions, and popular confusions. For (under correction) these three things do not undermine, but do mutually and strongly maintain one another (even those three which we principally aim at) authority in magistrates, liberty in people, purity in the church. Purity, preserved in the church, will preserve well-ordered liberty in the people, and both of them establish well-balanced authority in the magistrates. God is the Author of all these three, and neither is Himself the God of confusion, nor are His ways the ways of confusion, but of peace. . . .

Now the Lord Jesus Christ (the prince of peace) keep and bless your Lordship, and dispose of all your times and talents to His best advantage: and let the covenant of His grace and peace rest upon your honourable family and posterity throughout all generations.

Thus, humbly craving pardon for my boldness and length, I take leave and rest,

Your Honours to serve in Christ Jesus.

23

A LIMITED LIBERTY: PERSECUTION OF THE QUAKERS

from The Quaker Petition to King Charles II, 1661

The Puritan idea of liberty did not include liberty of conscience or freedom of religion, and one of the most basic and continuous challenges to the Godly Commonwealth came from individuals and groups who did not accept the religious ideas of the Puritans. The Puritan leaders responded to these challenges with what could be called at best a tragically misplaced vigor. Religious dissenters were not tolerated within the boundaries of the Godly Commonwealth, and if they persisted in coming in, they were first subjected to great indignities, then imprisoned and tortured, and finally, in some cases, executed.

The following document, a petition of grievances to King Charles II by members of the anti-Puritan Quaker faith residing in New England, gives eloquent testimony to both the courage and the persistence of the dissenters.

A declaration of some part of the sufferings of the People of God in scorn called Quakers, from the Professors in New England, only for the exercise of their consciences to the Lord, and obeying and confessing to the truth, as in his light he had discovered it to them:

1. Two honest and innocent women stripped stark naked, and searched after an inhuman manner.

2. Twelve strangers in that country, but free-born of this nation, received twenty-three whippings, the most of them being with a whip of three cords with knots at the ends, and laid on with as much strength as could be by the arm of their executioner, the stripes amounting to three hundred and seventy.

3. Eighteen inhabitants of the country, being freeborn English, received twenty-three whippings, the stripes amounting to two hundred and fifty.

4. Sixty-four imprisonments of the Lord's People, for their obedience to his will, amounting to five hundred and nineteen weeks, much of it being very cold weather, and the inhabitants kept in prison in harvest time, which was very much to their loss; besides many more imprisoned, of which time we cannot give a just account.

5. Two beaten with pitched ropes, the blows amounting to an hundred and thirty-nine, by which one of them was brought near unto death, much of his body being beaten like unto a jelly, and one of their doctors, a member of their church, who saw him, said, it would be a miracle if ever he recovered, he expecting the flesh should rot off the bones, who afterwards was banished upon pain of death. There are many witnesses of this there.

6. Also an innocent man, an inhabitant of Boston, they banished from his wife and children, and put to seek an habitation in the winter, and in case he returned again, he was to be kept prisoner during his life, and for returning again he was put in prison, and hath been now a prisoner above a year.

7. Twenty-five banishments upon the penalties of being whipped, or having their ears cut, or branded in the hand, if they returned.

8. Fines laid upon the inhabitants for meeting together, and edifying one another, as the

Text: Joseph Besse, *A Collection of the Sufferings of the People Called Quakers* (London: Luke Hinde, 1753), **I,** xxx-xxxii.

Saints ever did; and for refusing to swear, it being contrary to Christ's Command, amounting to about a thousand pounds, beside what they have done since that we have not heard of. Many families, in which there are many children, are almost ruined by their unmerciful proceedings.

9. Five kept fifteen days in all, without food, and fifty-eight days shut up close by the gaoler, and had none that he knew of; and from some of them he stopt up the windows, hindering them from convenient air.

10. One laid neck and heels in irons for sixteen hours.

11. One very deeply burnt in the right hand with the letter (H) after he had been whipt with above thirty stripes.

12. One chained to a log of wood the most part of twenty days, in an open prison, in the winter time.

13. Five appeals to England denied at Boston.

14. Three had their right ears cut by the hangman in the prison, the door being barred, and not a friend suffered to be present while it was doing, though some much desired it.

15. One of the inhabitants of Salem, who since is banished upon pain of death, had one half of his house and land seized on while he was in prison, a month before he knew of it.

16. At a General Court in Boston they made an order, that those who had not wherewithal to answer the fines that were laid upon them for their consciences, should be sold for bondmen and bondwomen to Barbadoes, Virginia, or any of the English plantations.

17. Eighteen of the People of God were at several times banished upon pain of death; six of them were their own inhabitants, two of which being very aged people, and well known among their neighbors to be of honest conversation, being banished from their houses and families, and put upon travelling and other hardships, soon ended their days, whose death we can do no less than charge upon the rulers of Boston, they being the occasion of it.

18. Also three of the servants of the Lord they put to death, all of them for obedience to the truth, in the testimony of it, against the wicked rulers and laws at Boston.

19. And since they have banished four more upon pain of death, and twenty-four of the inhabitants of Salem were presented, and more fines called for, and their goods seized on to the value

of forty pounds for meeting together in the fear of God, and some for refusing to swear.

These things, O King! from time to time have we patiently suffered, and not for the transgression of any just or righteous law, either pertaining to the Worship of God, or the Civil Government of England, but simply and barely for our consciences to God, of which we can more at large give thee, or whom thou mayst order, a full account (if thou will let us have admission to thee, who are banished upon pain of death, and have had our ears cut, who are some of us in England attending upon thee) both of the causes of our sufferings, and the manner of their disorderly and illegal proceedings against us; they began with immodesty, went on in inhumanity and cruelty, and were not satisfied until they had the blood of three of the martyrs of Jesus: revenge for all which we do not seek, but lay them before thee, considering thou hast been well acquainted with sufferings, and so mayst the better consider them that suffer, and mayst for the future restrain the violence of these rulers of New England, having power in thy hands, they being but the children of the family of which thou art Chief Ruler, who have in divers their proceedings forfeited their Patent,

as upon strict inquiry in many particulars will appear.

And this, O King! we are assured of, that in time to come it will not repent thee, if by a close rebuke thou stoppest the bloody proceedings of these bloody persecutors, for in so doing thou wilt engage the hearts of many honest people unto thee both there and here, and for such works of mercy the blessing is obtained; and showing it is the way to prosper: We are witnesses of these things, who

Besides many long imprisonments, and many cruel whippings, had our ears cut,

JOHN ROUSE,
JOHN COPELAND.

Besides many long imprisonments, divers cruel whippings, with the seizing on our goods, are banished upon pain of death, and some of us do wait here in England, and desire that we may have an order to return in peace to our families,

SAMUEL SHATTOCK, JOSIAH SOUTHICK, NICHOLAS PHELPS, JOSEPH NICHOLSON, JANE NICHOLSON.

24 A DEBATE ON LIBERTY OF CONSCIENCE

from John Cotton, *The Answer,* 1644
from Roger Williams, *The Bloudy Tenent,* 1644

The Puritan spokesmen did their best to defend on the highest principles their persecution of religious dissenters, and, in fact, these persecutions were doubly intense because they were motivated by the deepest religious conviction. It is difficult to translate religious fanaticism into rational argument, however, and most of the Puritan apologies have a rather forced air. John Cotton, for example, argued that individuals who dissented from Puritan beliefs were really going against their own consciences, for the conscience, implanted by God, could not possibly lead a man to go against the truth, i.e., the Puritan dogmas. Therefore, according to Cotton, when the Puritans persecuted dissenters, they were not really interfering with liberty of conscience but punishing individuals for not following *their own* consciences.

Roger Williams was perhaps the ideal man to see through this rather frightening sophistry, for he was one of the few men in history who have consistently done what their consciences tell them to, regardless of the consequences. Born and educated in England, like most of the Puritan leaders, Williams first landed in New England in 1631. He was offered a post at the church of Salem, Mass., but objecting to what he called its lack of separation from the corrupt Church of England, he went to Plymouth, the Pilgrim colony, where he remained for a year or so. Returning to Salem in 1633, he accepted a ministerial post this time, beginning a fascinating career of agitation against the doctrines of the colony's leading ministers. His criticism of the church leaders not only went against their religious views but threatened their political position. Their resultant hostility made necessary Williams' famous flight to the Narragansett Indian country in the middle of winter. After this adventurous episode he founded the colony of Providence (Rhode Island) with some other dissenters. This colony became one of the first American communities with religious freedom.

In his later life (from 1643 to 1652) Williams engaged in an extended controversy about religious freedom with that same John Cotton who had been one of his leading opponents and one of the chief Puritan apologists of persecution. Williams himself was an extremely religious man; his faith was similar to that of the Puritans in all essentials but that of liberty of conscience. He believed not only that persecution was against the express words and example of Christ but also that for the church to assume the secular power necessary for enforcement of religious conformity would inevitably lead to its corruption. In the following selections, Williams and Cotton debate the question of persecution for religious beliefs. The first selection, although not from Cotton's books attacking Williams, is a concise statement of his defense of persecution. In the second selection, Williams argues specifically against Cotton's defense in the form of a dialog between Peace and Truth from *The Bloudy Tenent of Persecution for Cause of Conscience* (1644).

The Argument of John Cotton

The question . . . is, whether persecution for cause of conscience be not against the doctrine of Jesus Christ the King of Kings.

Now by persecution for cause of conscience, I conceive you mean, either for professing some point of doctrine which you believe in conscience to be the truth, or for practicing some work which in conscience you believe to be a religious duty.

Now in points of doctrine some are fundamental, without right belief whereof a man cannot be saved: Others are circumstantial or less principal, wherein men may differ in judgment, without prejudice of salvation on either part.

In like sort, in points of practice, some concern the weightier duties of the law, as, what God we worship, and with what kind of worship; whether such, as if it be right, fellowship with God is held; if corrupt, fellowship with Him is lost.

Again, in points of doctrine and worship less principal: either they are held forth in a meek and peaceable way, though the things be erroneous or unlawful; or they are held forth with such arrogance and impetuousness, as tendeth and reacheth (even of itself) to the disturbance of civil peace.

Finally, let me add this one distinction more: when we are persecuted for conscience sake, it is either for conscience rightly informed, or for erroneous and blind conscience.

These things premised, I would lay down mine answer to the question in certain conclusions.

First, it is not lawful to persecute any for conscience sake rightly informed; for in persecuting such, Christ himself is persecuted in them. Acts 9:4.

Secondly, for an erroneous and blind conscience, (even in fundamental and weighty points)

Text: John Cotton, "The Answer of Mr. John Cotton in New England, to the Aforesaid Arguments Against Persecution for Cause of Conscience Professedly Maintaining Persecution for Cause of Conscience," in *Publications of the Narragansett Club* (Providence, 1867), III, 41-42. Roger Williams, "The Bloudy Tenent of Persecution for Cause of Conscience," in *Publications of the Narragansett Club* (Providence, 1867), III, 81, 217-20.

it is not lawful to persecute any, till after admonition once or twice: and so the Apostle directeth, Titus 3:10. and giveth the reason, that in fundamental and principal points of doctrine or worship, the word of God in such things is so clear, that he cannot but be convinced in conscience of the dangerous errour of his way, after once or twice admonition, wisely and faithfully dispensed. And then if any one persist, it is not out of conscience, but against his conscience, as the Apostle saith, verse 11. He is subverted and sinneth, being condemned of himself, that is, of his own conscience. So that if such a man after such admonition shall still persist in the errour of his way, and be therefore punished, he is not persecuted for cause of conscience, but for sinning against his own conscience.

The Argument of Roger Williams

Peace. Now the last distinction is this: "Persecution for conscience is either for a rightly informed conscience, or a blind and erroneous conscience."

Truth. Indeed, both these consciences are persecuted; but lamentably blind and erroneous will those consciences shortly appear to be, which out of zeal for God, as is pretended, have persecuted either. . . .

. . . As God needeth not the help of a material sword of steel to assist the sword of the Spirit in the affairs of conscience, so those men, those magistrates, yea, that commonwealth which makes such magistrates, must needs have power and authority from Christ Jesus to sit as judge, and to determine in all the great controversies concerning doctrine, discipline, government, etc.

And then I ask, whether upon this ground it must not evidently follow, that—

Either there is no lawful commonwealth, nor civil state of men in the world, which is not qualified with this spiritual discerning: and then also, that the very commonweal [i.e., the People] hath more light concerning the church of Christ, than the church itself.

Or, that the commonweal and magistrates thereof, must judge and punish as they are persuaded in their own belief and conscience, be their conscience paganish, Turkish, or antichristian. What is this but to confound heaven and earth together, and not only to take away the being of Christianity out of the world, but to take away all civility, and the world out of the world, and to lay all upon heaps of confusion? . . .

Peace. Yea; but, say they, the godly will not persist in heresy, or turbulent schism, when they are convinced in conscience, etc.

Truth. Sweet Peace, if the civil court and magistracy must judge, as before I have written, and those civil courts are as lawful, consisting of natural men as of godly persons, then what consequences necessarily will follow I have before mentioned. And I add, according to this conclusion it must follow, that, if the most godly persons yield not to once or twice admonition, as is maintained by the answerer [John Cotton], they must necessarily be esteemed obstinate persons; for if they were godly, saith he, they would yield. Must it not then be said, as it was by one passing sentence of banishment upon some whose godliness was acknowledged, that he that commanded the judge not to respect the poor in the cause of judgment, commands him not to respect the holy or the godly person?

Hence I could name the place and time when a godly man, a most desirable person for his trade etc., yet something different in conscience, propounded his willingness and desire to come to dwell in a certain town in New England; it was answered by a chief of the place, "This man differs from us; and we desire not to be troubled." So that in conclusion, for no other reason in the world, the poor man, though godly, useful, and peaceable, could not be admitted to a civil being and habitation on the common earth, in that wilderness, amongst them. . . .

Peace. Mr. Cotton concludes with a confident persuasion of having removed the grounds of that great error, viz., that persons are not to be persecuted for cause of conscience.

Truth. And I believe, dear Peace, it shall appear to them that, with fear and trembling at the word of the Lord, examine these passages, that the charge of error reboundeth back, even such an error as may well be called, The Bloody Tenent—so directly contradicting the spirit, and mind, and practice of the Prince of peace; so deeply guilty of the blood of souls, compelled and forced to hypocrisy in a spiritual and soul-rape; so deeply guilty of the blood of the souls under the altar, persecuted in all ages for the cause of conscience, and so destructive to the civil peace and welfare of all kingdoms, countries, and commonwealths.

Peace. To this conclusion, dear Truth, I heartily subscribe, and know the God, the Spirit, the Prince, the angels, and all the true awaked sons of peace, will call thee blessed. . . .

Truth. . . . But hark, what noise is this?

Peace. These are the doleful drums, and shrill-sounding trumpets, the roaring, murdering cannons, the shouts of conquerors, the groans of wounded, dying, slaughtered righteous with the wicked. Dear Truth, how long? how long these dreadful sounds and direful sights? how long before my glad return and restitution?

Truth. Sweet Peace, who will believe my true report? yet true it is, if I were once believed, blessed Truth and Peace should not so soon be parted.

Peace. Dear Truth, what welcome hast thou found of late beyond thy former times, or present expectations?

Truth. Alas! my welcome changes as the times, and strongest swords and arms prevail: were I believed in this: that Christ is not delighted with the blood of men, but shed his own for his bloodiest enemies—that by the word of Christ no man for gainsaying Christ, or joining with the enemy anti-christ, should be molested with the civil sword. Were this foundation laid as the Magna Charta of highest liberties, and good security given on all hands for the preservation of it, how soon should every brow and house be stuck with olive branches?

Peace. This heavenly invitation makes me bold once more to crave thy patient ear and holy tongue. Error's impatient and soon tired, but thou art light, and like the Father of lights, unwearied in thy shinings. . . .

PURITAN SCIENCE

25

AMAZING MAGNETISM: THE WONDERS OF NATURE'S GOD

from Cotton Mather, *The Christian Philosopher*, 1721

Sir Isaac Newton (1642-1727) was both a devoutly religious man and the scientist who made the most important breakthrough of the seventeenth century with the formulation of the laws of motion. Likewise, the Puritans, despite their intense concentration on the way to heaven, were earnest scientists. However, one of their most important beliefs made it impossible for them to accept the modern idea of scientific research. This belief was the doctrine of *God's special providence,* or the direct intervention of God in natural processes. Science, which depends on the assumption that nature follows regular laws, is ultimately impossible if an inscrutable deity is constantly intervening in natural processes. This poses the problem of how scientific investigation was reconciled with the Puritan belief in God's special providence.

The following selection gives one answer. Cotton Mather, an important Puritan clergyman, was a firm believer in special providences. But he was also an exponent of science, a corresponding member of the Royal Society, and an advocate of inoculation against smallpox at a time when medicine was often considered a sinful interference with the will of God. Mather attempted to harmonize science and religion in *The Christian Philosopher.* In this work he claims that man can understand and make laws about *some* natural processes (such as magnetism) but can never hope to understand *all* the wonders of nature's God. This position is only too obviously a defensive one, however, for if *some* natural processes operate according to law, why not *all* such processes?

Science won a more thorough-going acceptance in America during the eighteenth century. For this development, see Benjamin Franklin, Document 30.

Cotton Mather (1663-1728) was born in Boston, the son of a Puritan minister, Increase Mather, and grandson of leading Puritan ministers, John Cotton and Richard Mather. A precocious lad, he was incredibly pious and industrious. At the age of seven or eight, he tells us, he was composing forms of prayer for his schoolmates and rebuking them for "their wicked *words* and *ways.*" At eleven he wrote and spoke Latin fluently, had read the New Testament in Greek, and had begun the study of Hebrew. From Harvard he received his B.A. degree in 1678 at the age of fourteen, the youngest graduate then on record. After taking his M.A. in 1681, he assisted his father at North Church in Boston and became associate minister in 1685. There he remained all his life, marrying three times, burying most of his fifteen children, and preaching thousands of sermons. He wrote and published 444 separate pieces. He was so prolific as a writer that he has come to represent to many people the whole story of American Puritanism.

Mather rose to become the most influential man in the city of Boston, always vigorously intent upon preserving the old New England theocratic institutions. He defended the decisions of the Salem witchcraft trials (1692), and the later revulsion among the people against the trials caused him to be cruelly denounced. In attempting a delaying action in the early eighteenth century against the new forces of the Enlightenment, he was fighting a losing battle.

Such an unaccountable thing there is as the magnetism of the earth. A principle very different from that of gravity.

The operations of this amazing principle, are principally discovered in the communion that iron has with the loadstone; a rough, coarse, unsightly stone, but of more value than all the diamonds and jewels in the universe. . . .

In every magnet there are two poles, the one pointing to the north, and the other to the south.

The poles, in divers parts of the globe, are diversely inclined towards the center of the earth.

These poles, tho contrary to one another, do mutually help towards the magnet's attraction, and suspension of iron.

If a stone be cut or broke into ever so many pieces, there are these two poles in each of the pieces.

Text: Cotton Mather, *The Christian Philosopher* (Charlestown, Mass.: Middlesex Bookstore, 1815), 112-26.

If two magnets are spherical, one will conform itself to the other, so as either of them would do to the earth; and after they have so turned themselves, they will endeavor to approach each other; but placed in a contrary position, they avoid each other.

If a magnet be cut through the axis, the segments of the stone, which before were joined, will now avoid and fly each other.

If the magnet be cut by a section perpendicular to its axis, the two points, which before were conjoined, will become contrary poles; one in one, t'other in t'other segment.

Iron receives vertue from the magnet, by application to it, or barely from an approach near it, though it do not touch it; and the iron receives this vertue variously, according to the parts of the stone it is made to approach to. . . .

Once for all, gentlemen philosophers, the magnet has quite puzzled you. It shall then be no indecent anticipation of what should have been observed at the conclusion of this collection, here to demand it of you, that you glorify the infinite creator of this, and of all things, as incomprehensible. You must acknowledge that human reason is too feeble, too narrow a thing to comprehend the infinite God. The words of our excellent Boyle deserve to be recited on this occasion: "Such is the natural imbecility of the human intellect, that the most piercing wits and excellent mathematicians are forced to confess, that not only their own reason, but that of mankind, may be puzzled and nonplused about quantity, which is an object of contemplation natural, nay, mathematical. Wherefore why should we think it unfit to be believed, and to be acknowledged, that in the attributes of God . . . there should be some things which our finite understandings cannot clearly comprehend? And we who cannot clearly comprehend how in ourselves two such distant natures, as that of a gross body and an immaterial spirit should be so united as to make up one man, why should we grudge to have our reason pupil to an Omniscient Instructor, Who can teach us such things, as neither our own mere reason, nor any others, could ever have discovered to us?" . . .

It is then evident, that all mankind is to this day in the dark as to the ultimate parts of quantity. . . .

. . . There is hardly any one thing in the world, the essence whereof we can perfectly comprehend. But then to the natural imbecility of reason, add the moral depravations of it, by our fall from God, and the ascendant which a corrupt and vicious will has obtained over it, how much ought this consideration to warn us against the conduct of an unhumbled understanding in things relating to the Kingdom of God? I am not out of my way, I have had a magnet all this while steering of this digression: I am now returning to that.

. . . To fall down before a stone, and say, *Thou art a God,* would be an idolatry, that none but a soul more senseless than a stone could be guilty of. But then it would be a very agreeable homage unto the Glorious God, for me to see much of Him in such a wonderful stone as the magnet. They have done well to call it the loadstone, that is to say, the lead-stone: *May it lead me unto Thee, O my God and my Saviour!* magnetism is in this like to gravity, that it leads us to God and brings us very near to Him. When we see magnetism in its operation, we must say, *This is the Work of God!* And of the stone, which has proved of such vast use in the affairs of the waters that cover the sea, and will ere long do its part in bringing it about that the glory of the Lord shall cover the earth, we must say, *Great God, this is a wonderful Gift of Thine unto the World!*

A New Age: The Enlightenment

POOR RICHARD'S PROGRESS: BENJAMIN FRANKLIN

That extraordinary American, Benjamin Franklin (1706-1790), was a major representative of the American Enlightenment. Franklin was born and spent his early life in Boston, the hub of the Godly Commonwealth. He was raised on Puritanism and throughout his life retained much of the moral earnestness and sense of duty that were second nature to the Puritans. As he tells us in his *Autobiography*, however, he was very sceptical of the Calvinistic tenets of predestination, election, eternal damnation, and salvation through grace. After a brief flirtation with deism, an eighteenth-century philosophical religion (see pp. 60-61), Franklin settled down with a creed that emphasized the social rather than the spiritual virtues.

Significantly, Franklin chose to be a printer, a vital occupation in an age when ideas and their communication were stimulating revolutionary changes in man's outlook. Also, he moved from older, more conservative Boston to the thriving new community of Philadelphia, a city which later became the first capital of the new American nation.

Franklin was one of the great men of the eighteenth century, renowned far beyond the boundaries of the colonies he helped to form into a nation. John Adams once noted that Franklin was more famous among his contemporaries than Sir Isaac Newton, Frederick the Great, or Voltaire. Franklin's publishing ventures in Philadelphia grew successful so rapidly that by the age of forty-two he had made enough money to retire from active business. After his rise from rags to riches, he became a leading colonial politician, then a revolutionary statesman, and finally a dean of international diplomacy. The infinite variety of his activities can be suggested by scenes in which he is flying a kite to determine the electrical nature of lightning, standing before the House of Commons to plead the American objections to taxation without representation, working in his office as postmaster general of the colonies to put the postal system on a profitable basis, reposing in the halls of Versailles and being revered by the ladies and noblemen of the court of Louis XVI, and invoking guidance from the Supreme Being in deliberation of the American Constitutional Convention.

The following selections illustrate both the breadth of Franklin's interests and the kind of ideas that were rapidly replacing Puritanism as the dominant intellectual influence in eighteenth-century America.

26

THE END OF PURITANISM: SOCIAL UTILITY AS THE STANDARD OF VALUE

from Benjamin Franklin, *Autobiography*, 1771

Franklin's *Autobiography* is particularly interesting not only because it offers the story of his life and a statement of his views on many matters but also because it was used throughout the nineteenth century by many American parents as a moral guide for children.

In this selection Franklin sums up briefly his religious experiences and ideas. Especially significant is the fact that he apparently chose his creed on the basis of its usefulness in the search for a good life. This utilitarian way of looking at religion is practically the opposite of the Puritan outlook, for it implies that a man can accept or reject revelation (i.e., the word of God as revealed through the Bible) by the criteria of reason.

Before I enter upon my public Appearance in Business it may be well to let you know the then State of my Mind, with regard to my Principles and Morals, that you may see how far those influenc'd the future Events of my Life. My Parent's [*sic*] had early given me religious Impressions, and brought me through my Childhood piously in the Dissenting Way. But I was scarce 15 when, after doubting by turns of several Points as I found them disputed in the different Books I read, I began to doubt of Revelation it self. Some Books against Deism fell into my Hands; they were said to be the Substance of Sermons preached at Boyle's Lectures. It happened that they wrought an Effect on me quite contrary to what was intended by them: For the Arguments of the Deists which were quoted to be refuted, appeared to me much Stronger than the Refutations. In short I soon became a thorough Deist. My Arguments perverted some others, particularly Collins and Ralph: but each of them having afterwards wrong'd me greatly without the least Compunction and recollecting Keith's Conduct towards me, (who was another Freethinker) and my own towards Vernon and Miss Read, which at Times gave me great Trouble, I began to suspect that this Doc-

Text: Benjamin Franklin, *Works*, ed. John Bigelow (New York: G. P. Putnam's Sons, 1887), I, 137-40.

trine tho' it might be true, was not very useful. —My London Pamphlet, which had for its Motto these Lines of Dryden

Whatever is, is right. Tho' purblind Man
Sees but a Part of the Chain, the nearest Link,
His Eyes not carrying to the equal Beam,
That poises all, above.

And from the Attributes of God, his infinite Wisdom, Goodness and Power concluded that nothing could possibly be wrong in the World, and that Vice and Virtue were empty Distinctions, no such Things existing: appear'd now not so clever a Performance as I once thought it; and I doubted whether some Error had not insinuated itself unperceiv'd, into my Argument, so as to infect all that follow'd, as is common in metaphysical Reasonings.—I grew convinc'd that *Truth*, *Sincerity* and *Integrity* in Dealings between Man and Man, were of the utmost Importance to the Felicity of Life, and I form'd written Resolutions, (which still remain in my Journal Book) to practice them everwhile I lived. Revelation had indeed no weight with me as such; but I entertain'd an Opinion, that tho' certain Actions might not be bad *because* they were forbidden by it, or good *because* it commanded them; yet probably those Actions might be forbidden *because* they were bad for us, or commanded *because* they were beneficial to us, in their own Natures, all the Circumstances of things considered. And this Persuasion, with the kind hand of Providence, or some guardian Angel, or accidental favourable Circumstances and Situations, or all together, preserved me (thro' this dangerous Time of Youth and the hazardous Situations I was sometimes in among Strangers, remote from the Eye and Advice of my Father) without any *wilful* gross Immorality or Injustice that might have been expected from my Want of Religion. I say *wilful,* because the Instances I have mentioned, had something of *Necessity* in them, from my Youth, Inexperience, and the Knavery of others. I had therefore a tolerable Character to begin the World with, I valued it properly, and determin'd to preserve it.

27

THE WAY TO WEALTH: INDUSTRY, PRUDENCE, AND FRUGALITY AS RULES FOR SUCCESS

from Benjamin Franklin, *The Way to Wealth,* 1757

Franklin's *The Way to Wealth* first appeared as a preface to one of his most famous printing ventures, *Poor Richard's Almanac,* and was later reprinted separately. This early success manual started an American tradition that can be traced down to such a recent publication as *Fortune* magazine's *The Art of Success* (1956). Franklin's guide was so successful that by 1889 it had been reprinted at least four hundred times in a great variety of languages, including Chinese.

By comparing *The Way to Wealth* with such a Puritan moral guide as "The Way to Heaven" (Document 20), one can see clearly how the Puritan rules for spiritual salvation have been transmuted into secular terms. And since the economic virtues stressed by Franklin came out of a religious tradition, there was a tendency for economic success to be equated with moral and spiritual uprightness. This close association of morality and money-making has been an important theme in American intellectual life.

In preaching "the way to wealth," Franklin himself, unlike many of his disciples, did not look upon financial success as man's ultimate goal. His own career with its many interests beyond the pursuit of wealth belies this. Probably he felt that presenting the hope of financial wealth was a good way to instill in his fellow countrymen the socially valuable virtues of industry, prudence, and temperance. No doubt he was also conscious of the popularity of these ideas with the hard-working farmers who bought his almanac.

. . . I stopt my Horse lately where a great Number of People were collected at a Vendue of Merchant Goods. The Hour of Sale not being come, they were conversing on the Badness of the Times, and one of the Company call'd to a plain clean old Man, with white Locks, *Pray, Father* Abraham, *what think you of the Times? Won't these heavy Taxes quite ruin the Country? How shall we ever be able to pay them? What would you advise us to?*——Father *Abraham* stood up, and reply'd, If you'd have my Advice, I'll give it you in short, for a *Word to the Wise is enough,* and *many Words won't fill a Bushel,* as *Poor Richard* says. They join'd in desiring him to speak his Mind, and gathering round him, he proceeded as follows;

"Friends, says he, and Neighbours, the Taxes are indeed very heavy, and if those laid on by the Government were the only Ones we had to pay, we might more easily discharge them; but we have many others, and much more grievous to some of us. We are taxed twice as much by our *Idleness,* three times as much by our *Pride,* and four times as much by our *Folly,* and from these Taxes the Commissioners cannot ease or deliver us by allowing an Abatement. However let us hearken to good Advice, and something may be done for us; *God helps them that help themselves,* as *Poor Richard* says, in his Almanack of 1733.

It would be thought a hard Government that should tax its People one tenth Part of their *Time,* to be employed in its Service. But *Idleness* taxes many of us much more, if we reckon all that is spent in absolute *Sloth,* or doing of nothing, with that which is spent in idle Employments or Amusements, that amount to nothing. *Sloth,* by bringing on Diseases, absolutely shortens Life. *Sloth, like Rust, consumes faster*

Text: Benjamin Franklin, *Works,* ed. John Bigelow (New York: G. P. Putnam's Sons, 1887), I, 441-52.

than Labour wears, while the used Key is always bright, as *Poor Richard* says. But *dost thou love Life, then do not squander Time, for that's the Stuff Life is made of,* as *Poor Richard* says.— How much more than is necessary do we spend in Sleep! forgetting that *The sleeping Fox catches no Poultry,* and that *there will be sleeping enough in the Grave,* as *Poor Richard* says. If Time be of all Things the most precious, *wasting Time* must be, as *Poor Richard* says, *the greatest Prodigality,* since, as he elsewhere tells us, *Lost Time is never found again;* and what we call *Time-enough, always proves little enough:* Let us then up and be doing, and doing to the Purpose; so by Diligence shall we do more with less Perplexity. *Sloth makes all Things difficult, but Industry all easy,* as *Poor Richard* says; and *He that riseth late, must trot all Day, and shall scarce overtake his Business at Night.* While *Laziness travels so slowly, that Poverty soon overtakes him,* as we read in *Poor Richard,* who adds, *Drive thy Business, let not that drive thee;* and *Early to Bed, and early to rise, makes a Man healthy, wealthy and wise....* So much for Industry, my Friends, and Attention to one's own Business; but to these we must add *Frugality,* if we would make our *Industry* more certainly successful. A Man may, if he knows not how to save as he gets, *keep his Nose all his Life to the Grindstone,* and die not worth a *Groat* at last. *A fat Kitchen makes a lean Will,* as *Poor Richard* says; and,

Many Estates are spent in the Getting,
Since Women for Tea forsook Spinning and
  Knitting,
And Men for Punch forsook Hewing and
  Splitting.

If you would be wealthy, says he, in another Almanack, *think of Saving as well as of Getting: The* Indies *have not made* Spain *rich, because her* Outgoes *are greater than her* Incomes. Away then with your expensive Follies, and you will

not have so much Cause to complain of hard Times, heavy Taxes, and chargeable Families; for, as *Poor Dick* says,

Women and Wine, Game and Deceit,
Make the Wealth small, and the Wants great.

And farther, *What maintains one Vice, would bring up two Children.* You may think perhaps, That a *little* Tea, or a *little* Punch now and then, Diet a *little* more costly, Clothes a *little* finer, and a *little* Entertainment now and then, can be no *great* Matter; but remember what *Poor Richard* says, *Many a* Little *makes a Mickle;* and farther, *Beware of* little *Expences; a small Leak will sink a great Ship;* and again, *Who Dainties love, shall Beggars prove;* and moreover, *Fools make Feasts, and wise Men eat them....* And now to conclude, *Experience keeps a dear School, but Fools will learn in no other, and scarce in that;* for it is true, *we may give Advice, but we cannot give Conduct,* as *Poor Richard* says: However, remember this, *They that won't be counselled, can't be helped,* as *Poor Richard* says: And farther, That *if you will not hear Reason, she'll surely rap your Knuckles.*

Thus the old Gentleman ended his Harangue. The People heard it, and approved the Doctrine and immediately practised the contrary, just as if it had been a common Sermon; for the Vendue opened, and they began to buy extravagantly, notwithstanding all his Cautions, and their own Fear of Taxes....

... However, I resolved to be the better for the Echo of it; and though I had at first determined to buy Stuff for a new Coat, I went away resolved to wear my old One a little longer. *Reader,* if thou wilt do the same, thy Profit will be as great as mine.

  I am, as ever,
    Thine to serve thee,
July 7, 1757.   RICHARD SAUNDERS.

28

A NEW EDUCATIONAL PHILOSOPHY: EDUCATION AS A PREPARATION FOR LIFE

from Benjamin Franklin, *Idea of the English School,* 1751

This selection presents Franklin's pioneer statement of what has come to be an extremely important American educational philosophy. Puritan education was based on the study of the Greek and Latin classics in the original languages, along with intensive reading of the Bible and study of theology. Here Franklin applies the same criterion of social utility to education that he did to religion. Feeling that the teaching of the dead languages was unnecessary, he developed a curriculum which he believed would provide the proper balance of useful and ornamental skills. Franklin's educational thinking foreshadows many later American educational developments such as vocational schooling and even, in some respects, "progressive" education.

Sketch'd out for the Consideration of the Trustees of the Philadelphia Academy [1751]

It is expected that every Scholar to be admitted into this School, be at least able to pronounce and divide the Syllables in Reading, and to write a legible Hand. None to be receiv'd that are under   Years of Age.

First or Lowest Class

Let the first Class learn the *English Grammar* Rules, and at the same time let particular Care be taken to improve them in *Orthography*. . . .

The Third Class

to be taught Speaking properly and gracefully, which is near of Kin to good Reading, and naturally follows it in the Studies of Youth. . . . For their farther Improvement, and a little to vary their Studies, let them now begin to read *History*, after having got by Heart a short Table of the principal Epochas in Chronology. They may begin with *Rollin's Antient and Roman Histories,* and proceed at proper Hours as they go thro' the subsequent Classes, with the best Histories of our own Nation and Colonies. Let Emulation be excited among the Boys by giving, Weekly, little Prizes, or other small Encouragements to those who are able to give the best Account of what they have read, as to Times, Places, Names of Persons, &c. This will make them read with Attention, and imprint the History well in their Memories. In remarking on the History, the Master will have fine Opportunities of instilling Instruction of various Kinds, and improving the Morals as well as the Understandings of Youth.

The Natural and Mechanic History contain'd in the *Spectacle de la Nature*, might also be begun in this Class, and continued thro' the subsequent Classes by other Books of the same Kind: For next to the Knowledge of *Duty*, this Kind of Knowledge is certainly the most useful, as well as the most entertaining. The Merchant may thereby be enabled better to understand many Commodities in Trade; the Handicraftsman to improve his Business by new Instruments, Mixtures and Materials; and frequently Hints are given of new Manufactures, or new Methods of improving Land, that may be set on foot greatly to the Advantage of a Country.

The Fourth Class

to be taught Composition. Writing one's own Language well, is the next necessary Accomplishment after good Speaking. . . .

Fifth Class

To improve the Youth in *Composition,* they may now, besides continuing to write Letters, begin to write little Essays in Prose, and sometimes in Verse, not to make them Poets, but for this Reason, that nothing acquaints a Lad so speedily with Variety of Expression, as the Necessity of finding such Words and Phrases as will suit with the Measure, Sound, and Rhime of Verse, and at the same time well express the Sentiment. . . .

Sixth Class

In this Class, besides continuing the Studies of the preceding, in History, Rhetoric, Logic, Moral and Natural Philosophy, the best *English* Authors may be read and explain'd. . . . The Hours of each Day are to be divided and dispos'd in such a Manner, as that some Classes may be with the Writing-Master, improving their Hands, others with the Mathematical Master, learning Arithmetick, Accompts, Geography, Use of the Globes, Drawing, Mechanicks, &c.; while the rest are in the *English* School, under the *English* Master's Care.

Thus instructed, Youth will come out of this School fitted for learning any Business, Calling or Profession, except such wherein Languages are required; and tho' unacquainted with any antient or foreign Tongue, they will be Masters of their own, which is of more immediate and general Use; and withal will have attain'd many other valuable Accomplishments; the Time usually spent in acquiring those Languages, often without Success, being here employ'd in laying such a Foundation of Knowledge and Ability, as, properly improv'd, may qualify them to pass thro' and execute the several Offices of civil Life, with Advantage and Reputation to themselves and Country.

B. F.

Text: Benjamin Franklin, *Writings,* ed. Albert H. Smyth (New York: Macmillan Co., 1907), III, 21-29.

29

NEW SOCIAL INSTITUTIONS: THE VOLUNTARY FIRE ASSOCIATION

from Benjamin Franklin, *Autobiography*, 1771

The following selection illustrates an important eighteenth-century contribution to American political ideas and institutions. Democratic ideas in America were stimulated by opposition to an all-powerful central authority such as the English king or the Puritan church. If the powers of government are limited, however, how are the social tasks which require the organization and cooperation of many individuals to be accomplished? The American answer to this problem was the voluntary association, in the creation of which Benjamin Franklin was a pioneer. In addition to the volunteer fire department described in this selection, Franklin also assisted in founding a subscription library, a more effective police force, a philosophical and scientific association, and a club, the Junto, for the promotion of such projects.

The importance of the voluntary associations for American life was great. One significant implication was the hope that human problems could gradually be solved by the cooperation of reasonable individuals. The voluntary associations of the eighteenth century also paved the way for that most important nineteenth- and twentieth-century American institution, the corporation.

. . . About this time I wrote a paper (first to be read in Junto, but it was afterward publish'd) on the different accidents and carelessnesses by which houses were set on fire, with cautions against them, and means proposed of avoiding them. This was much spoken of as a useful piece, and gave rise to a project, which soon followed it, of forming a company for the more ready extinguishing of fires, and mutual assistance in removing and securing of goods when in danger. Associates in this scheme were presently found, amounting to thirty. Our articles of agreement oblig'd every member to keep always in good order, and fit for use, a certain number of leather buckets, with strong bags and baskets (for packing and transporting of goods), which were to be brought to every fire; and we agreed to meet once a month and spend a social evening together, in discoursing and communicating such ideas as occurred to us upon the subject of fires as might be useful in our conduct on such occasions.

Text: Benjamin Franklin, *Works*, ed. John Bigelow (New York: G. P. Putnam's Sons, 1887), I, 204-05.

The utility of this institution soon appeared, and many more desiring to be admitted than we thought convenient for one company, they were advised to form another, which was accordingly done; and this went on, one new company being formed after another, till they became so numerous as to include most of the inhabitants who were men of property; and now, at the time of my writing this, tho' upward of fifty years since its establishment, that which I first formed, called the Union Fire Company, still subsists and flourishes, tho' the first members are all deceas'd but myself and one, who is older by a year than I am. The small fines that have been paid by members for absence at the monthly meetings have been apply'd to the purchase of fire-engines, ladders, fire-hooks, and other useful implements for each company, so that I question whether there is a city in the world better provided with the means of putting a stop to beginning conflagrations; and, in fact, since these institutions, the city has never lost by fire more than one or two houses at a time, and the flames have often been extinguished before the house in which they began has been half consumed.

30

THE RISE OF EXPERIMENTAL SCIENCE

from Benjamin Franklin, *Autobiography*, 1771

The following selection from Benjamin Franklin's *Autobiography* illustrates new developments in scientific ideas which can be compared with Puritan scientific beliefs, as exemplified in Cotton Mather's "Of Magnetism" (Document 25). Franklin's willingness to attempt new experiments and qualify existing ideas is an indication of the rise of experimentalism in science; his openness of mind contrasts with Mather's desire to fit natural phenomena into the preconceived system of Puritan theology. Franklin made his attitude quite clear in a letter to Peter Collinson, dated August 14, 1747:

> I have lately written two long Letters to you on the Subject of Electricity. . . . On some further Experiments since I have observ'd a Phenomenon or two, that I cannot at present account for on the Principle laid down in those Letters, and am therefore become a little diffident of my Hypothesis, and asham'd that I have express'd myself in so positive a manner. In going on with these Experiments how many pretty Systems do we build which we soon find ourselves oblig'd to destroy!

This new attitude of the Enlightenment, increasingly victorious in both Europe and America, was instrumental in bringing about the great scientific progress made in the eighteenth, nineteenth, and twentieth centuries.

In 1746, being at Boston, I met there with a Dr. Spence, who was lately arrived from Scotland, and show'd me some electric experiments. They were imperfectly perform'd, as he was not very expert; but, being on a subject quite new to me, they equally surpris'd and pleased me. Soon after my return to Philadelphia, our library company receiv'd from Mr. P. Collinson, Fellow of the Royal Society of London, a present of a glass tube, with some account of the use of it in making such experiments. I eagerly seized the opportunity of repeating what I had seen at Boston; and, by much practice, acquir'd great readiness in performing those, also, which we had an account of from England, adding a number of new ones. I say much practice, for my house was continually full, for some time, with people who came to see these new wonders.

To divide a little this incumbrance among my friends, I caused a number of similar tubes to be blown at our glass-house, with which they furnish'd themselves, so that we had at length several performers. Among these, the principal was Mr. Kinnersley, an ingenious neighbor, who, being out of business, I encouraged to undertake showing the experiments for money, and drew up for him two lectures, in which the experiments were rang'd in such order, and accompanied with such explanations in such method, as that the foregoing should assist in comprehending the following. He procur'd an elegant apparatus for the purpose, in which all the little machines that I had roughly made for myself were nicely form'd by instrument-makers. His lectures were well attended, and gave great satisfaction; and after some time he went thro' the colonies, exhibiting them in every capital town, and pick'd up some money. In the West India Islands, indeed, it was with difficulty the experiments could be made, from the general moisture of the air.

Oblig'd as we were to Mr. Collinson for his present of the tube, etc., I thought it right he should be inform'd of our success in using it, and wrote him several letters containing accounts of our experiments. He got them read in the Royal Society, where they were not at first thought worth so much notice as to be printed in their Transactions. One paper, which I wrote for Mr. Kinnersley, on the sameness of lightning with electricity, I sent to Dr. Mitchel, an acquaintance of mine, and one of the members also of that society, who wrote me word that it had been read, but was laughed at by the connoisseurs. The papers, however, being shown to Dr. Fothergill, he thought them of too much value to be stifled, and advis'd the printing of them. Mr. Collinson then gave them to *Cave* for publication in his Gentleman's Magazine; but he chose to print them separately in a pamphlet, and Dr. Fothergill wrote the preface. Cave, it seems, judged rightly for his profit, for by the additions that arrived afterward they swell'd, to a quarto volume, which has had five editions, and cost him nothing for copy-money.

It was, however, some time before those papers were much taken notice of in England. A copy of them happening to fall into the hands of the Count de Buffon, a philosopher deservedly of great reputation in France, and, indeed, all over Europe, he prevailed with M. Dalibard to translate them into French, and they were printed at Paris. The publication offended the Abbé Nollet, preceptor in Natural Philosophy to the royal family, and an able experimenter, who had form'd and publish'd a theory of electricity, which then had the general vogue. He could not at first believe that such a work came from America, and said it must have been fabricated by his enemies at Paris, to decry his system. Afterwards, having been assur'd that there really existed such a person as Franklin at Philadelphia, which he had doubted, he wrote and published a volume of Letters, chiefly address'd

Text: Benjamin Franklin, *Works*, ed. John Bigelow (New York: G. P. Putnam's Sons, 1887), I, 276-81.

to me, defending his theory, and denying the verity of my experiments, and of the positions deduc'd from them.

I once purpos'd answering the abbé, and actually began the answer; but, on consideration that my writings contain'd a description of experiments which any one might repeat and verify, and if not to be verifi'd, could not be defended; or of observations offer'd as conjectures, and not delivered dogmatically, therefore not laying me under any obligation to defend them; and reflecting that a dispute between two persons, writing in different languages, might be lengthened greatly by mistranslations, and thence misconceptions of one another's meaning, much of one of the abbé's letters being founded on an error in the translation, I concluded to let my papers shift for themselves, believing it was better to spend what time I could spare from public business in making new experiments, than in disputing about those already made. I therefore never answered M. Nollet, and the event gave me no cause to repent my silence; for my friend M. le Roy, of the Royal Academy of Sciences, took up my cause and refuted him; my book was translated into the Italian, German, and Latin languages; and the doctrine it contain'd was by degrees universally adopted by the philosophers of Europe, in preference to that of the abbé; so that he lived to see himself the last of his sect, except Monsieur B——, of Paris, his *élève* and immediate disciple.

What gave my book the more sudden and general celebrity, was the success of one of its proposed experiments, made by Messrs. Dalibard and De Lor at Marly, for drawing lightning from the clouds. This engag'd the public attention every where. M. de Lor, who had an apparatus for experimental philosophy, and lectur'd in that branch of science, undertook to repeat what he called the *Philadelphia Experiments;* and, after they were performed before the king and court, all the curious of Paris flocked to see them. I will not swell this narrative with an account of that capital experiment, nor of the infinite pleasure I receiv'd in the success of a similar one I made soon after with a kite at Philadelphia, as both are to be found in the histories of electricity.

Dr. Wright, an English physician, when at Paris, wrote to a friend, who was of the Royal Society, an account of the high esteem my experiments were in among the learned abroad, and of their wonder that my writings had been so little noticed in England. The Society, on this, resum'd the consideration of the letters that had been read to them; and the celebrated Dr. Watson drew up a summary account of them, and of all I had afterwards sent to England on the subject, which he accompanied with some praise of the writer. This summary was then printed in their Transactions; and some members of the Society in London, particularly the very ingenious Mr. Canton, having verified the experiment of procuring lightning from the clouds by a pointed rod, and acquainting them with the success, they soon made me more than amends for the slight with which they had before treated me. Without my having made any application for that honour, they chose me a member, and voted that I should be excus'd the customary payments, which would have amounted to twenty-five guineas; and ever since have given me their Transactions gratis. They also presented me with the gold medal of Sir Godfrey Copley for the year 1753, the delivery of which was accompanied by a very handsome speech of the president, Lord Macclesfield, wherein I was highly honoured.

HUMANITARIANISM

31   THE PROBLEM OF SLAVERY

from John Woolman, "On the Keeping of Negroes," 1772

Although slavery was a critical moral problem for Americans from the beginning, the issue was largely avoided until the mid-eighteenth century. The Quaker John Woolman (1720-1772) played an important role in the awakening of the American conscience to this problem. A devoutly religious man, Woolman, born in Northampton, New Jersey, became a speaker in 1741 at a Quaker meeting, one of those assemblages of Friends for divine communion where no clergy presides and any layman who feels the inspiration may pray or minister to his fellow men. In 1746 he set out with a companion to visit Quakers in the backwoods of Virginia; afterwards he spent most of his life in journeys throughout the colonies from New England to the Carolinas, testifying to the Friends what was in his mind and spirit.

In the course of his travels, Woolman grew greatly disturbed by the treatment of Negroes in the South and spoke and wrote of the moral wrong of slavery. One of his disciples, Benjamin Lundy, inspired the famed William Lloyd Garrison to devote his life to the abolition movement. However, this selection from Woolman's works shows Woolman not as a radical social reformer but as one who attempted to appeal to the consciences of other individuals to correct a wrong which God would certainly not ignore in the final reckoning.

Although Woolman was far more otherworldly in his religious beliefs than the men of the Enlightenment, his arguments show still another aspect of the more secular orientation of eighteenth-century religious thought, even in the case of an intensely pious man. It is also interesting that Woolman employs a version of the natural rights argument derived from the social contract theory (see pp. 61-62).

If we seriously consider that liberty is the right of innocent men; that the mighty God is a refuge for the oppressed; that in reality we are indebted to them; that they being set free are still liable to the penalties of our laws, and as likely to have punishment for their crimes as other people; this may answer all our objections. And to retain them in perpetual servitude, without just cause for it, will produce effects, in the event, more grievous than setting them free would do, when a real love to truth and equity was the motive to it.

Our authority over them stands originally in a purchase made from those who, as to the general, obtained theirs by unrighteousness. Whenever we have recourse to such authority it tends more or less to obstruct the channels through which the perfect plant in us receives nourishment.

There is a principle which is pure placed in the human mind, which in different places and ages hath had different names; it is, however, pure, and proceeds from God. It is deep and inward, confined to no forms of religion, nor excluded from any, where the heart stands in perfect sincerity. In whomsoever this takes root and grows, of what nation soever, they become brethren, in the best sense of the expression. Using ourselves to take ways which appear most easy to us, when inconsistent with that purity which is without beginning, we thereby set up a government of our own, and deny obedience to Him whose service is true liberty.

He that hath a servant, made so wrongfully, and knows it to be so, when he treats him otherwise than a free man, when he reaps the benefit of his labor without paying him such wages as are reasonably due to free men for the like service, clothes excepted, these things though done in calmness, without any show of disorder, do yet deprave the mind in like manner and with as great certainty as prevailing cold congeals water. These steps taken by masters, and their conduct striking the minds of their children whilst young, leave less room for that which is good to work upon them. The customs of their parents, their neighbors, and the people with whom they converse, working upon their minds, and they, from thence,

conceiving ideas of things and modes of conduct, the entrance into their hearts becomes, in a great measure, shut up against the gentle movings of uncreated purity.

From one age to another the gloom grows thicker and darker, till error gets established by general opinion, that whoever attends to perfect goodness and remains under the melting influence of it finds a path unknown to many, and sees the necessity to lean upon the arm of divine strength, and dwell alone, or with a few, in the right committing their cause to Him who is a refuge for his people in all their troubles.

Where, through the agreement of a multitude, some channels of justice are stopped, and men may support their characters as just men by being just to a party, there is great danger of contracting an alliance with that spirit which stands in opposition to the God of love, and spreads discord, trouble, and vexation among such who give up to the influence of it.

Negroes are our fellow-creatures, and their present condition amongst us requires our serious consideration. We know not the time when those scales in which mountains are weighed may turn. The Parent of mankind is gracious, his care is over his smallest creatures, and a multitude of men escape not his notice. And though many of them are trodden down and despised, yet he remembers them; he seeth their affliction, and looketh upon the spreading increasing exaltation of the oppressor. He turns the channels of power, humbles the most haughty people, and gives deliverance to the oppressed at such periods as are consistent with his infinite justice and goodness. And wherever gain is preferred to equity, and wrong things publicly encouraged to that degree that wickedness takes root and spreads wide amongst the inhabitants of a country, there is real cause for sorrow to all such whose love to mankind stands on a true principle and who wisely consider the end and event of things.

Text: John Woolman, "Considerations on the Keeping of Negroes," *The Journal and Essays,* ed. Amelia M. Gummere (New York: Macmillan Co., 1922), pp. 380-81. Printed by permission of The Macmillan Company.

32

THE SOCIAL CONTRACT: THE RIGHT OF REVOLUTION

from John Wise, A *Vindication*, 1717
from Jonathan Mayhew, *Unlimited Submission*, 1750

Although Puritan political and social theory was non-democratic, its concept of a religious and moral aristocracy had certain democratic tendencies in that it allowed men of lowly origins to rise to positions of aristocratic authority in the Godly Commonwealth. In addition, the physical problems of colonization not only developed independence and self-reliance in the colonists but also made it increasingly difficult for the Puritan aristocrats to set up a central political and religious authority. For this reason, even the churches of the Godly Commonwealth had been organized into separate congregations which strongly resisted any attempts to limit their independence.

With the decline of Puritanism in the late seventeenth century, various efforts were made by the Puritan leaders to set up a central religious body to enforce official dogma in the individual congregations. One such attempt aroused the animosity of John Wise, minister of Ipswich, Mass., who turned to the social contract philosophers of the Enlightenment (see pp. 61-62) for arguments to defend the independence of his congregation.

In this selection from his *A Vindication of the Government of New England Churches* (1717), Wise summarized the social contract ideas. In part of the selection, he considers man in a state of nature (see pp. 61-62) and describes the "immunities" or rights that have been given man by God: (1) that man is the subject of the inner law of nature in that he has been given "reason" whereby he can discover and follow the best rules for him to live by; (2) that he has the right to follow his reason, to live without authority, and to have equality with other men. These rights exist without qualification only in the pre-social state of nature, however, and, in part, Wise points out that men must give up certain of their natural rights to exist in a "civil" state (i.e., after the social contract has created a society). Wise argues, however, that though man must give up some of his rights, all government depends on the people's consent, and governors must therefore "engage to take care of the Common Peace, and Welfare."

Wise was, so far as we know, the first American to employ the social contract argument, but it was not long before others picked the argument up. As grievances with England increased, the social contract became a dominant theme of attacks upon the colonial policies of George III and his parliament. It was not long before these attacks were carried a step further—to the assertion that rulers who fail to protect the common welfare must be replaced, by revolution if necessary. On January 30, 1750, Jonathan Mayhew, like Wise a New England preacher, presented the argument for the right of revolution in a fiery discourse on "Unlimited Submission and Non-resistance to the Higher Powers," from which the second extract is taken.

John Wise

[A] I shall consider Man in a state of Natural Being, as a Free-Born Subject under the Crown of Heaven, and owing Homage to none but God himself. It is certain Civil Government . . . must needs be acknowledged to the Effect of Humane Free-Compacts and not of Divine Institution; it is the Produce of Mans Reason, of Humane and Rational Combinations, and not from any direct Orders of Infinite Wisdom. . . . Government is

Text: John Wise, "A Vindication of the Government of New England Churches," in *Old South Leaflets* (Boston: Directors of the Old South Work, n.d.), VII, 281-88. Jonathan Mayhew, *A Discourse Concerning Unlimited Submission and Non-Resistance to the Higher Powers* (Boston: Hall and Goss, 1818), p. 36.

not formed by Nature, as other Births or Productions; If it were, it would be the same in all Countries; because Nature keeps the same Method, in the same thing in all Climates. . . . But to proceed under the head of a State of Natural Being, I shall more distinctly Explain the State of Human Nature in its Original Capacity, as Man is placed on Earth by his Maker, and Cloathed with many Investitures, and Immunities which properly belong to Man separately considered.

1. The Prime Immunity of Mans State, is that he is most properly the Subject of the Law of Nature. He is the Favourite Animal on Earth; in that this Part of Gods Image, *viz.* Reason is Congenate with his Nature, wherein by a Law

Immutable, Instampt upon his Frame, God has provided a Rule for Men in all their Actions, obliging each one to the performance of that which is Right, not only as to Justice, but likewise as to all other Moral Vertues, the which is nothing but the Dictate of Right Reason founded in the Soul of Man. . . . That which is to be drawn from Mans Reason, flowing from the true Current of that Faculty, when unperverted, may be said to be the Law of Nature; . . . So that the meaning is, when we acknowledge the Law of Nature to be the dictate of Right Reason, we must mean that the Understanding of Man is Endowed with such a power, as to be able, from the Contemplation of humane Condition to discover a necessity of Living agreeably with this Law: And likewise to find out some Principle, by which the Precepts of it, may be clearly and solidly Demonstrated. The way to discover the Law of Nature in our own state, is by a narrow Watch, and accurate Contemplation of our Natural Condition, and propensions. . . . If a Man any ways doubts, whether what he is going to do to another Man be agreeable to the Law of Nature, then let him suppose himself to be in that other Mans Room; And by this Rule effectually Executed. A Man must be a very dull Scholar to Nature not to make Proficiency in the Knowledge of her Laws. . . .

2. The Second Great Immunity of Man is an Original Liberty Instampt upon his Rational Nature. He that intrudes upon this Liberty, Violates the Law of Nature. . . .

[a] The Internal Native Liberty of Mans Nature in general implies, a faculty of Doing or Omitting things according to the Direction of his Judgment. But in a more special meaning, this Liberty does not consist in a loose and ungovernable Freedom, or in an unbounded Licence of Acting. Such Licence is disagreeing with the condition and dignity of Man, and would make Man of a lower and meaner Constitution than Bruit Creatures; who in all their Liberties are kept under a better and more Rational Government, by their Instincts. Therefore as *Plutarch* says, *Those persons only who live in Obedience to Reason, are worthy to be accounted free: they alone live as they Will, who have learnt what they ought to Will.* So that the true Natural Liberty of Man, such as really and truely agrees to him, must be understood, as he is Guided and Restrained by the Tyes of Reason, and Laws of Nature; all the rest is Brutal, if not worse.

[b] Mans External Personal, Natural Liberty, Antecedent to all Humane parts, or Alliances must also be considered. And so every Man must be conceived to be perfectly in his own Power

and disposal, and not to be controuled by the Authority of any other. And thus every Man, must be acknowledged equal to every Man, since all Subjection and all Command are equally banished on both sides; and considering all Men thus at Liberty, every Man has a Prerogative to Judge for himself, *viz.* What shall be most for his Behoof, Happiness and Well-being.

[c] The Third Capital Immunity belonging to Mans Nature, is an equality amongst Men; Which is not to be denied by the Law of Nature, till Man has Resigned himself with all his Rights for the sake of a Civil State; and then his Personal Liberty and Equality is to be cherished, and perserved to the highest degree, as will consist with all just distinctions amongst Men of Honour, and shall be agreeable with the publick Good. . . .

And thus we come,

[B] To consider Man in a Civil State of Being; wherein we shall observe the great difference between a Natural, and Political State; for in the Latter State many Great disproportions appear, or at least many obvious distinctions are soon made amongst Men; which Doctrine is to be laid open under a few heads.

1. Every Man considered in a Natural State, must be allowed to be Free, and at his own dispose; yet to suit Mans Inclinations to Society; And in a peculiar manner to gratify the necessity he is in of publick Rule and Order, he is Impelled to enter into a Civil Community; and Divests himself of his Natural Freedom, and puts himself under Government; which amongst other things Comprehends the Power of Life and Death over Him; together with Authority to Injoyn him some things to which he has an utter Aversation, and to prohibit him other things, for which he may have as strong an Inclination; so that he may be often under this Authority, obliged to Sacrifice his Private, for the Publick Good. So that though Man is inclined to Society, yet he is driven to a Combination by great necessity. For that the true and leading Cause of forming Governments, and yielding up Natural Liberty, and throwing Mans Equality into a Common Pile to be new Cast by the Rules of fellowship; was really and truly to guard themselves against the Injuries Men were lyable to Interchangeably; for none so Good to Man as Man, and yet none a greater Enemy. So that,

2. The first Humane Subject and Original of Civil Power is the People. For as they have a Power every Man over himself in a Natural State, so upon a Combination they can and do bequeath this Power unto others; and settle it according

as their united discretion shall Determine. For that this is very plain, that when the Subject of Sovereign Power is quite Extinct, that Power returns to the People again. And when they are free, they may set up what species of Government they please; or if they rather incline to it, they may subside into a State of Natural Being, if it be plainly for the best. . . .

Let us conceive in our Mind a multitude of Men, all Naturally Free & Equal; going about voluntarily, to Erect themselves into a new Common-Wealth. Now their Condition being such, to bring themselves into a Politick Body, they must needs Enter into divers Covenants.

1. They must Interchangeably each Man Covenant to joyn in one lasting Society, that they may be capable to concert the measures of their safety, by a Publick Vote.

2. A Vote or Decree must then nextly pass to set up some Particular species of Government over them. And if they are joyned in their first Compact upon absolute Terms to stand to the Decision of the first Vote concerning the Species of Government: Then all are bound by the Majority to acquiesce in that particular Form thereby settled, though their own private Opinion, incline them to some other Model.

3. After a Decree has specified the Particular form of Government, then there will be need of a New Covenant, whereby those on whom Sovereignty is conferred, engage to take care of the Common Peace, and Welfare. And the Subjects on the other hand, to yield them faithful Obedience. . . .

Jonathan Mayhew

We may very safely assert these two things in general, without undermining government: One is, that no civil rulers are to be obeyed when they enjoin things that are inconsistent with the commands of God. All such disobedience is lawful and glorious; particularly if persons refuse to comply with any *legal establishment of religion,* because it is a gross perversion and corruption—as to doctrine, worship, and discipline—of a pure and divine religion, brought from heaven to earth by the Son of God,—the only King and Head of the Christian church,—and propagated through the world by his inspired apostles. All commands running counter to the declared will of the Supreme Legislator of heaven and earth are null and void, and therefore disobedience to them is a duty, not a crime. . . . Another thing that may be asserted with equal truth and safety is, that no government is to be submitted to at the expense of that which is the sole end of all government—the common good and safety of society. Because, to submit in this case, if it should ever happen, would evidently be to set up the means as more valuable and above the end, than which there cannot be a greater solecism and contradiction. The only reason of the institution of civil government, and the only rational ground of submission to it, is the common safety and utility. If, therefore, in any case, the common safety and utility would not be promoted by submission to government, but the contrary, there is no ground or motive for obedience and submission, but for the contrary.

The Great Awakening

THE UNFASHIONABLE PHILOSOPHER: JONATHAN EDWARDS

Though the name of Billy Graham is known to almost all adult Americans, the man who initiated the first American revival movement and who was probably the greatest philosopher we have produced, is almost forgotten by all but specialists in the study of American culture and philosophy. Jonathan Edwards was born in East Windsor, Conn., on October 5, 1703, and was educated at Yale. He was already a full-fledged philosopher by the age of sixteen, when he wrote down for his own personal edification an incredibly brilliant brief statement of the philosophical theory now known as Idealism. Becoming minister at Northampton, Mass., in 1726, he remained there until 1750 when his congregation dismissed him as a result of incidents growing out of the revival, called the *Great Awakening*, which he had started. From 1751 to 1757 his life was spent as a missionary to the Indians at the frontier post of Stockbridge, Mass. In this unlikely spot he composed several philosophical treatises defending Calvinistic doctrine. In 1757 he was chosen to be president of the College of New Jersey (now Princeton University), but he died of smallpox on March 22, 1758, within three months of assuming office.

In an age when *reason* and *nature* were words on every man's lips, Jonathan Edwards was deeply and unflinchingly committed to God. All of his brilliance was devoted to a hopeless cause: the reconciliation of predestination, original sin, salvation through grace, and all the Calvinistic tenets with eighteenth-century developments in science and philosophy. Philosophically speaking, he accomplished his task, but men like Franklin just did not want to believe in the absolute sovereignty of God, and even the most brilliant of philosophers could not bring such men back to the Puritan fold.

Though his work had little success among political and intellectual leaders, Edwards started a kind of popular movement that has had a continual impact on American culture: the revival (see p. 62 and Documents 37 and 107).

33

THE SOVEREIGNTY OF GOD: INTENSE RELIGIOUS CONSCIOUSNESS

from Jonathan Edwards, *Personal Narrative*, 1739

Jonathan Edwards was particularly suited to start "The Great Awakening," as the American religious revival of 1734-1750 has come to be called. His own religious convictions were passionately held, and he could find emotional satisfaction and peace in the harshest of the Calvinistic doctrines. This selection from his *Personal Narrative*, an autobiographical document, makes vividly clear that the intense religious consciousness of the Puritans had not entirely died out in the eighteenth century.

From my childhood up, my mind had been full of objections against the doctrine of God's sovereignty, in choosing whom he would to eternal life, and rejecting whom he pleased; leaving them eternally to perish, and be everlastingly tormented in hell. It used to appear like a horrible doctrine to me. But I remember the time very well, when I seemed to be convinced, and fully satisfied, as to this sovereignty of God, and his justice in thus eternally disposing of men, according to his sovereign pleasure. But never could give an account, how, or by what means, I was thus convinced, not in the least imagining at the time, nor a long time after, that there was any extraordinary influence of God's Spirit in it; but only that now I saw further, and my reason apprehended the justice and reasonableness of it. However, my mind rested in it; and it put an end to all those cavils and objections. And there has been a wonderful alteration in my mind, in respect to the doctrine of God's sovereignty, from that day to this; so that I scarce ever have found so much as the rising of an objection against it, in the most absolute sense, in God's shewing mercy to whom he will shew mercy, and hardening whom he will. God's absolute sovereignty and justice, with respect to salvation and damnation, is what my mind seems to rest assured of, as much as of any thing that I see with my eyes; at least it is so at times. But I have often, since that first conviction, had quite another kind of sense of God's sovereignty than I had then. I have often since had not only a conviction, but a delightful conviction. The doctrine has very often appeared exceeding pleasant, bright, and

sweet. Absolute sovereignty is what I love to ascribe to God. . . .

My wickedness, as I am in myself, has long appeared to me perfectly ineffable, and swallowing up all thought and imagination; like an infinite deluge, or mountain over my head. I know not how to express better what my sins appear to me to be, than by heaping infinite upon infinite, and multiplying infinite by infinite. Very often, for these many years, these expressions are in my mind, and in my mouth, "Infinite upon infinite . . . Infinite upon infinite!" When I look into my heart, and take a view of my wickedness, it looks like an abyss infinitely deeper than hell. And it appears to me, that were it not for free grace, exalted and raised up to the infinite height of all the fulness and glory of the great Jehovah, and the arm of his power and grace stretched forth in all the majesty of his power, and in all the glory of his sovereignty, I should appear sunk down in my sins below hell itself; far beyond the sight of every thing, but the eye of sovereign grace, that can pierce even down to such a depth. And yet it seems to me, that my conviction of sin is exceeding small, and faint; it is enough to amaze me, that I have no more sense of my sin. I know certainly, that I have very little sense of my sinfulness. When I have had turns of weeping and crying for my sins I thought I knew at the time, that my repentance was nothing to my sin.

Text: Jonathan Edwards, *The Works of President Edwards* (New York: Robt. Carter and Bros., 1881), I, 15.

34

THE HARD SELL AND THE SOFT SELL: TWO REVIVAL SERMONS

from Jonathan Edwards, Two Sermons, 1741

The Great Awakening (see p. 62) was spread both by terrifying sermons describing the wrath of God and the horrors of eternal damnation and by softer appeals stressing God's love and the advantages of becoming one of the regenerate—a person who has experienced intense religious conversion. These two selections are both from sermons by Jonathan Edwards, given in the full flush of the Great Awakening. "Sinners in the Hands of an Angry God" is a classic example of the hell-fire-and-brimstone school of preaching, yet has considerable literary merit. One witness to the actual preaching of this sermon has written of its effect: "There was such a breathing of distress, and weeping, that the preacher was obliged to speak to the people and desire silence, that he might be heard."

Sinners in the Hands of an Angry God

The bow of God's wrath is bent, and the arrow made ready on the string, and justice bends the arrow at your heart, and strains the bow, and it is nothing but the mere pleasure of God, and that of an angry God, without any promise or obligation at all, that keeps the arrow one moment from being made drunk with your blood. Thus all you that never passed under a great change of heart, by the mighty power of the Spirit of God upon your souls; all you that were never born again, and made new creatures, and raised from being dead in sin, to a state of new, and before altogether unexperienced light and life, are in the hands of an angry God. However you may have reformed your life in many things, and may have had religious affections, and may keep up a form of religion in your families and closets, and in the house of God, it is nothing but his mere pleasure that keeps you from being this moment swallowed up in everlasting destruction. However unconvinced you may now be of the truth of what you hear, by and by you will be fully convinced of it. Those that are gone from being in the like circumstances with you, see that it was so with them; for destruction came suddenly upon most of them; when they expected nothing of it, and while they were saying, Peace and safety: now they see, that those things on which they depended for peace and safety, were nothing but thin air and empty shadows.

The God that holds you over the pit of hell, much as one holds a spider, or some loathsome insect over the fire, abhors you, and is dreadfully provoked: his wrath towards you burns like fire; he looks upon you as worthy of nothing else, but to be cast into the fire; he is of purer eyes than to bear to have you in his sight; you are ten thousand times more abominable in his eyes, than the most hateful venomous serpent is in ours. You have offended him infinitely more than ever a stubborn rebel did his prince; and yet it is nothing but his hand that holds you from falling into the fire every moment. It is to be ascribed to nothing else, that you did not go to hell the last night; that you was suffered to awake again in this world, after you closed your eyes to sleep. And there is no other reason to be given, why you have not dropped into hell since you arose in the morning, but that God's hand has held you up. There is no other reason to be given why you have not gone to hell, since you have sat here in the house of God, provoking his pure eyes by your sinful wicked manner of attending his solemn worship. Yea, there is nothing else that is to be given as a reason why you do not this very moment drop down into hell.

O sinner! Consider the fearful danger you are in: it is a great furnace of wrath, a wide and bottomless pit, full of the fire of wrath, that you are held over in the hand of that God, whose wrath is provoked and incensed as much against you, as against many of the damned in hell. You hang by a slender thread, with the flames of divine wrath flashing about it, and ready every moment to singe it, and burn it asunder; and you have no interest in any Mediator, and nothing to lay hold of to save yourself, nothing to keep off the flames of wrath, nothing of your own, nothing that you ever have done, nothing that you can do, to induce God to spare you one moment.

The Peace Which Christ Gives

I invite you now to a better portion. There are better things provided for the sinful miserable children of men. There is a surer comfort and more durable peace: comfort that you may enjoy in a state of safety and on a sure foundation:

Text: Jonathan Edwards, *The Works of President Edwards* (New York: Robt. Carter and Bros., 1881), IV, 318, 437.

a peace and rest that you may enjoy with reason and with your eyes open; having all your sins forgiven, your greatest and most aggravated transgressions blotted out as a cloud, and buried as in the depths of the sea, that they may never be found more; and being not only forgiven, but accepted to favor; being the objects of God's complacence and delight; being taken into God's family and made his children; and having good evidence that your names were written on the heart of Christ before the world was made, and that you have an interest in that covenant of grace that is well ordered in all things and sure; wherein is promised no less than life and immortality, an inheritance incorruptible and undefiled, a crown of glory that fades not away; being in such circumstances, that nothing shall be able to prevent your being happy to all eternity; having for the foundation of your hope, that love of God which is from eternity unto eternity; and his promise and oath, and his omnipotent power, things infinitely firmer than mountains of brass. The mountains shall depart, and the hills be removed, yea, the heavens shall vanish away like smoke, and the earth shall wax old like a garment, yet these things will never be abolished.

In such a state as this you will have a foundation of peace and rest through all changes, and in times of the greatest uproar and outward calamity be defended from all storms, and dwell above the floods, Psalm xxxii. 6, 7; and you shall be at peace with every thing, and God will make all his creatures throughout all parts of his dominion, to befriend you, Job v. 19, 24. You need not be afraid of any thing that your enemies can do unto you, Psalm iii. 5, 6. Those things that now are most terrible to you, viz., death, judgment, and eternity, will then be most comfortable, the most sweet and pleasant objects of your contemplation, at least there will be reason that they should be so. Hearken therefore to the friendly counsel that is given you this day, turn your feet into the way of peace, forsake the foolish and live; forsake those things which are no other than the devil's baits, and seek after this excellent peace and rest of Jesus Christ, that peace of God which passes all understanding. Taste and see; never was any disappointed that made a trial, Prov. xxiv. 13, 14. You will not only find those spiritual comforts that Christ offers you to be of a surpassing sweetness for the present, but they will be to your soul as the dawning light that shines more and more to the perfect day; and the issue of all will be your arrival in heaven, that land of rest, those regions of everlasting joy, where your peace and happiness will be perfect, without the least mixture of trouble or affliction, and never be interrupted nor have an end.

35

THE EFFECT OF THE REVIVAL: CONVERSIONS IN NORTHAMPTON

from Jonathan Edwards, *Narrative of Surprising Conversions*, 1735

By 1735, under Jonathan Edwards' ministry, sudden conversions in Northampton, Mass., reached thirty-five a week. But the emotional hysteria generated by Edwards' preaching did not find favor with everyone. Revivalism was strenuously attacked by many important clergymen, and in 1750, after a tragic case of suicide that had some connection with the Northampton revival, Edwards was dismissed from his Northampton ministry. In the midst of the furor, Edwards prepared a letter to a fellow minister to explain and defend his methods. In this document Edwards described how emotional outbursts result when God gives the convert a new supernatural sense through which he can directly perceive God's truth, mercy, and love and, in contrast, his own vile wickedness. The sudden opening of this new sense throws the convert into a state of violent and mixed emotions. This attempt to find what could be called a psychological explanation of the process of religious conversion is one of the many reflections of eighteenth-century science and philosophy in Edwards' thought.

The revivalist techniques and beliefs of Edwards and his followers came to be known as the "New Light" as opposed to the "Old Light" of the more conservative clergy. The struggle between New Lights and Old Lights developed into a division in the church which is still reflected in the controversy in religious circles that invariably develops around a figure like Billy Graham. Perhaps the crowning irony of Edwards' tragic career was the turn that the New Light took in the hands of many of its later leaders, who unleashed a virulent attack on the intellect itself as the false religion of "Pharisee-teachers." (See Document 37.)

My Letter to a Brother
[the Reverend Benjamin Colman]

May 30. 35.

Dear Sir

In answer to your Desire, I here send you a Particular account of the Present Extraordinary circumstances of this Town, & the neighbouring Towns with Respect to Religion. . . .

A Concern about the Great things of Religion began, about the Latter End of December, & the beginning of January, to Prevail abundantly in the Town, till in a very Little Time it became universal throughout the Town, among old and young, & from the highest to the Lowest; all seemed to be siezed with a deep concern about their Eternal salvation; all the Talk in all companies, & upon occasions was upon the things of Religion, and no other talk was anywhere Relished; & scarcely a single Person in the whole Town was Left unconcerned about the Great things of the Eternal World: Those that were wont to be the vainest, & Loosest Persons in Town seemed in General to be siezed with strong convictions: Those that were most disposed to contemn vital & Experimental Religion, & those that had the Greatest Conceit of their own Reason: the highest Families in the Town, & the oldest Persons in the Town, and many Little Children were affected Remarkeably; no one Family that I know of, & scarcely a Person has been Exempt & the Spirit of God went on in his saving Influences, to the appearance of all Human Reason & Charity, in a truly wonderfull and astonishing manner. The news of it filled the neighbouring Towns with Talk, & there were many in them that scoffed and made a Ridicule of the Religion that appeared in Northampton; But it was observable that it was very frequent & Common that those of other Towns that came into this Town, & observed how it was here, were Greatly affected, and went home with wounded spirits, & were never more able to Shake off the Impression that it made upon them, till at Length there began to appear a General concern in several of the Towns in the County: in the month of march the People in new Hadley seemed to be siezed with a deep concern about their salvation, all as it were at once, which has Continued in a very Great degree Ever since: about the same time there began to appear the Like Concern in the west Part of Suffield, which has since spread

into all Parts of the Town. It next began to appear at Sunderland, & soon became universal, & to a very Great Degree. about the same Time it began to appear in Part of Deerfield, Called Green River, & since has filled the Town. It began to appear also at a part of Hatfield, and after that the whole Town in the second week in April seemed to be siezed at once, & there is a Great & General concern there. . . .

People are brought off from Inordinate Engagedness after the World, & have been Ready to Run into the other Extreme of too much neglecting their worldly Business & to mind nothing but Religion. Those that are under Convictions are Put upon it Earnestly to Enquire what they shall do to be saved, & diligently to use appointed means of Grace, and apply themselves to all known duty. & those that obtain Hope themselves, & the Charity of others Concerning their Good Estate, Generally seem to be brought to A Great Sense of their own Exceeding misery in a natural Condition, & their utter helplessness, & Insufficiency for themselves, & their Exceeding wickedness & Guiltiness in the sight of God; it seldom fails but that Each one seems to think himself worse than any body Else, & they are brought to see that they deserue no mercy of God, that all their Prayers & Pains are Exceeding worthless & Polluted, & that God, notwithstanding all that they have done, or can do, may Justly Execute his Eternal wrath upon them, & they seem to be brought to a Lively sense of the Excellency of Jesus Christ & his sufficiency & willingness to save sinners, & to be much weaned in their affections from the world, & to have their Hearts filled with Love to God and Christ, and a disposition to Lie in the dust before him. they seem to have Given them a Lively Conviction of the Truth of the Gospel, & the divine authority of the Holy Scriptures; tho they cant have the Excercise of this at all Times alike, nor Indeed of any other Grace. they seem to be brought to abhor themselves for the sins of their Past Life, & to Long to be holy, & to Live holily, & to Gods Glory; but at the same time complain that they can do nothing, they are poor Impotent Creatures, utterly Insufficient to Glorify their Creatour & Redeemer. They Commonly seem to be much more sensible of their own wickedness after their Conversion then before, so that they are often Humbled by it, it seems to them that they are Really become more wicked, when at the same time they are Evidently full of a Gracious Spirit: Their Remaining sin seems to be their very Great Burthen, & many of them seem to Long after Heaven, that there they may be Rid of sin. They Generally seem to be united in dear Love,

Text: Jonathan Edwards, *Representative Selections*, ed. Clarence H. Faust and Thomas H. Johnson (New York: American Book Co., 1935), pp. 73-80, 82-84.

and affection one to another, & to have a Love to all mankind: I never saw the Christian spirit in Love to Enemies so Exemplified, in all my Life as I have seen it within this Half year. . . .

The Experiences of some Persons Lately amongst [us] have been beyond almost all that Ever I heard or Read of. There is a Pious woman in this Town that is a very modest Bashfull Person, that was moved by what she heard of the Experiences of others Earnestly to seek to God to give her more clear manifestations of himself, and Evidences of her own Good Estate, & God answer'd her Request, and Gradually gave her more & more of a sense of his Glory & Love, which she had with Intermissions for several days, till one morning the week before Last she had it to a more than ordinary degree, and it Prevaild more & more till towards the middle of the day, till her nature began to sink vnder it, as she was alone in the House; but there came sombody into the House, & found her in an unusual, Extraordinary frame She Expressed what she saw & felt to him; it came to that at Last that they Raised the neighbours, they were afraid she would die; I went up to see her & found her Perfectly sober & in the Exer[c]ise of her Reason, but having her nature seemingly overborn & sinking, and when she could speak Expressing in a manner that cant be described the sense she had of the Glory of God, and Particularly of such & such Perfections, & her own vnworthiness, her Longing to Lie in the dust, sometimes her Longing to Go to be with Christ, & crying out of the Excellency of Christ, & the wonderfullness of his dying Love; & so she continued for Hours together tho not alwaies in the same degree. . . .

There Lately Came up hither a Couple of ministers from Connecticut viz. Mr Lord of Preston, & Mr Owen of Groton, who had heard of the Extraordinary circumstances of this & the neighbouring Towns, who had heard the affair well Represented by some, & also had heard many Reports Greatly to its disadvantage, who came on purpose to see & satisfy themselves; & that they might thoroughly Acquaint themselves, went about, & spent Good Part of a day, in hearing the accounts of many of our new Converts, & Examining of them; which was Greatly to their satisfaction & they took Particular notice, among other things of the modesty with which Persons Gave account of themselves, & said that the one half was not told them, & could not be told them; & that if they Renounced these Persons Experiences they must Renounce Christianity it self. and Mr Owen said Particularly as to their Impressions on their Imaginations, they were quite different from what had been Represented, &

that they were no more than might naturally be Expected in such cases.

Thus sir I have Given you a Particular account of this affair which satan has so much misrepresented in the Countrey. This is a true account of the matter as far as I have Opportunity to Know, & I suppose I am vnder Greater advantages to Know than any Person Living. Having been thus Long in the account, I forbear to make Reflections, or to Guess what God is about to do; I Leave this to you, and shall only say, as I desire alwaies to say from my Heart *To God be all the Glory whose work alone it is;* & Let him have an Interest in your Prayers, who so much needs divine help at that day, & is your affectionate Brother,

& Humble servant,
Jth Edwards.

Northampton May 30. 1735.

Since I wrote the foregoing Letter, there has Happen'd a thing of a very awfull nature in the Town; My Uncle Hawley, the Last Sabbath day morning, Laid violent Hands on himself, & Put an End to his Life, by Cutting his own throat. He had been for a Considerable Time Greatly Concern'd about the Condition of his soul; till, by the ordering of a sovereign Providence he was suffered to fall into deep melancholly, a distemper that the Family are very Prone to; he was much overpowered by it; the devil took the advantage & drove him into despairing thoughts: he was Kept very much awake a nights, so that he had but very Little sleep for two months. till he seemed not to have his Faculties in his own Power: he was in a Great measure Past a Capacity of Receiving advice, or being Reason'd with. the Coroners Inquest Judged him delirious. Satan seems to be in a Great Rage, at this Extraordinary breaking forth of the work of God. I hope it is because he knows that he has but a short time: doubtless he had a Great Reach, in this violent attack of his against the whole affair. We have appointed a day of Fasting in the Town this week, by Reason of this & other appearances of satans Rage amongst us against Poor souls. I yesterday saw a woman that belongs to Durham, who says there is a Considerable Revival of Religion there.

I am   yours   &c—
J.E.

Northampton June 3. 1735.

36 THE VOICE OF REASON: OPPOSITION TO THE GREAT AWAKENING

from Charles Chauncy, *Enthusiasm Describ'd and Caution'd Against*, 1742

The Old Light opposition to the New Light revival technique (see headnote, Document 35) centered in old, firmly rooted seaboard communities like Boston. The battle between the two "Lights" is typical of the complexity of popular movements in America. On the one hand, the revival movement was a reaction against more secular Enlightenment religious beliefs. On the other hand, revivalism was a social movement, pointing up the vague opposition that was growing between the aristocratic gentry of the towns and plantations and the lower-status groups of the frontier areas. For the Great Awakening led to a clash between the aristocratic and highly educated clergy, who opposed emotionalism in religion, and the revivalists, whose religious views made emotion more important than learning. At odds, then, were a group of religious reactionaries who tended to be socially and politically more democratic (the New Lights) and a group of religious liberals who were socially and politically aristocratic.

An example of the Old Light reaction to the revivalism of the Great Awakening can be seen in this selection from a sermon by Charles Chauncy, a leading clergyman of Boston. Chauncy's religious views were strongly influenced by the Enlightenment, resembling in many respects those of Benjamin Franklin, and he is often viewed by historians as a precursor of Unitarianism. Socially and intellectually, however, Chauncy was a conservative gentleman, and reading between the lines of his attack on religious enthusiasm, we can feel the educated aristocrat's disgust at, and suspicion of, the emotional hysteria of the lower-class mob.

. . . [The] Enthusiast is one who has a conceit of himself as a person favored with the extraordinary presence of the Deity. He mistakes the workings of his own passions for divine communications, and fancies himself immediately inspired by the Spirit of God, when all the while, he is under no other influence than that of an over-heated imagination.

The cause of this enthusiasm is a bad temperament of the blood and spirits; 'tis properly a disease, a sort of madness, and there are few, perhaps none at all, but are subject to it; though none are so much in danger of it as those in whom melancholy is the prevailing ingredient in their constitution. In these it often reigns, and sometimes to so great a degree that they are really beside themselves, acting as truly by the blind impetus of a wild fancy, as though they had neither reason nor understanding.

And various are the ways in which their enthusiasm discovers itself.

Sometimes, it may be seen in their countenance. A certain wildness is discernable in their general look and air, especially when their imaginations are moved and fired.

Sometimes, it strangely loosens their tongues and gives them such an energy, as well as flu-

ency and volubility in speaking, as they themselves, by their utmost efforts, can't so much as imitate, when they are not under the enthusiastic influence.

Sometimes, it affects their bodies, throws them into convulsions and distortions, into quakings and tremblings. This was formerly common among the people called Quakers. I was myself, when a lad, an eye-witness to such violent agitations and foamings in a boisterous female speaker as I could not behold but with surprise and wonder.

Sometimes, it will unaccountably mix itself with their conduct and give it such a tincture of that which is freakish or furious as none can have an idea of, but those who have seen the behavior of a person in a frenzy.

Sometimes, it appears in their imaginary peculiar intimacy with heaven. They are, in their own opinion, the special favorites of God, have more familiar converse with Him than other good men, and receive immediate, extraordinary communications from Him. The thoughts which suddenly rise up in their minds, they take for suggestions of the Spirit; their very fancies are divine illuminations; nor are they strongly inclined to anything, but 'tis an impulse from God, a plain revelation of His will.

And what extravagances, in this temper of mind, are they not capable of, and under the

Text: Charles Chauncy, Enthusiasm Describ'd and Caution'd Against (Boston: J. Draper, 1742), pp. 3-7.

specious pretext, too, of paying obedience to the authority of God? Many have fancied themselves acting by immediate warrant from heaven, while they have been committing the most undoubted wickedness. There is indeed scarce anything so wild, either in speculation or practice, but they have given in to it. They have, in many instances, been blasphemers of God and open disturbers of the peace of the world.

But in nothing does the enthusiasm of these persons discover itself more than in the disregard they express to the dictates of reason. They are above the force of argument, beyond conviction from a calm and sober address to their understandings. As for them, they are distinguished persons; God himself speaks inwardly and immediately to their souls. "They see the light infused into their understandings, and cannot be mistaken; 'tis clear and visible there, like the light of bright sunshine; shows itself and needs no other proof but its own evidence. They feel the hand of God moving them within and the impulses of His Spirit, and cannot be mistaken in what they feel. Thus they support themselves, and are sure reason hath nothing to do with what they see and feel. What they have a sensible experience of, admits no doubt, needs no probation." And in vain will you endeavor to convince such persons of any mistakes they are fallen into. They are certainly in the right, and know themselves to be so. They have the Spirit opening their understandings and revealing the truth to them. They believe only as he has taught them: and to suspect they are in the wrong is to do dishonor to the Spirit; 'tis to oppose his dictates, to set up their own wisdom in opposition to his, and shut their eyes against that light with which he has shined into their souls. They are not, therefore, capable of being argued with; you had as good reason with the wind.

And as the natural consequence of their being thus sure of everything, they are not only infinitely stiff and tenacious, but impatient of contradiction, censorious, and uncharitable; they encourage a good opinion of none but such as are in their way of thinking and speaking. Those, to be sure, who venture to debate with them about their errors and mistakes, their weaknesses and indiscretions, run the hazard of being stigmatized by them as poor unconverted wretches, without the Spirit, under the government of carnal reason, enemies to God and religion, and in the broad way to hell.

They are likewise positive and dogmatical, vainly fond of their own imaginations, and invincibly set upon propagating them; and in the doing of this, their powers being awakened and put as it were, upon the stretch, from the strong impressions they are under that they are authorized by the immediate command of God himself, they sometimes exert themselves with a sort of ecstatic violence; and 'tis this that gives them the advantage, among the less knowing and judicious of those who are modest, suspicious of themselves, and not too assuming in matters of conscience and salvation. The extraordinary fervor of their minds, accompanied with uncommon bodily motions and an excessive confidence and assurance, gains them great reputation among the populace, who speak of them as men of God in distinction from all others, and too commonly hearken to and revere their dictates, as though they really were, as they pretend, immediately communicated to them from the Divine Spirit.

This is the nature of Enthusiasm, and this its operation, in a less or greater degree, in all who are under the influence of. 'Tis a kind of religious frenzy, and evidently discovers itself to be so whenever it rises to any great height.

And much to be pitied are the persons who are seized with it. Our compassion commonly works towards those who, while under distraction, fondly imagine themselves to be kings and emperors; and the like pity is really due to those who, under the power of enthusiasm, fancy themselves to be prophets, inspired of God and immediately called and commissioned by him to deliver his messages to the world. And though they should run into disorders and act in a manner that cannot but be condemned, they should notwithstanding be treated with tenderness and lenity; and the rather, because they do not commonly act so much under the influence of a bad mind as a deluded imagination. And who more worthy of Christian pity than those who, under the notion of serving God and the interest of religion, are filled with zeal and exert themselves to the utmost while all the time they are hurting and wounding the very cause they take so much pains to advance. 'Tis really a pitiable case; and though the honesty of their intentions won't legitimate their bad actions, yet it very much alleviates their guilt. We should think as favorably of them as may be and be dispos'd to judge with mercy, as we would hope to obtain mercy.

37

THE GREAT AWAKENING STRIKES BACK: OPPOSITION TO RELIGIOUS RATIONALISM

from Gilbert Tennent, *The Danger of an Unconverted Ministry*, 1740

Because most of the conservative clergy (see Document 36) and the more important colleges opposed religious emotionalism, the revivalist New Lights were forced to found their own schools to recruit and train their brethren. The most important of these schools was the "Log College," founded in 1726 in a log cabin in Bucks County, Pennsylvania, by William Tennent (1673-1745). Tennent's son, Gilbert (1703-1764), was educated by his father at the school and went on to become one of the leading revivalists of the Great Awakening. Gilbert himself had undergone a violent religious conversion and was convinced that such a religious experience was essential for a preacher. Therefore, in sermons like this selection, he attacked the highly educated clergy who refused to have any part of the emotional hysteria connected with revivalism.

The struggle between the Old Lights and the New Lights was so violent that there was considerable raiding of congregations back and forth to find converts. Tennent justifies such religious banditry on the ground that an unconverted clergy, such as the educated but emotionally uncommitted "Pharisee-Teachers," could not possibly help their congregations to salvation.

Ironically, the "Log College" is of considerable importance in the history of American education; it was the grandfather of what is now known as Princeton University.

But possibly some may again object against Persons going to hear others, besides their own Ministers; . . . Again it may be objected, That the aforesaid Practice tends to grieve our Parish-Minister, and to break Congregations in Pieces.

I answer, If our Parish-Minister be grieved at our greater Good, or prefers his Credit before it; then he has good Cause to grieve over his own Rottenness and Hypocrisie. And as for Breaking of Congregations into Pieces, upon the Account of People's Going from Place to Place, to hear the Word, with a view to get greater Good; that spiritual Blindness and Death, that so generally prevails, will put this out of Danger. It is but a very few, that have got any spiritual Relish; the most will venture their Souls with any Formalist, and be well satisfied with the sapless Discourses of such dead Drones. . . .

I would conclude my present Meditations upon this Subject, by Exhorting

All those who enjoy a faithful Ministry, to a speedy and sincere Improvement of so rare and valuable a Privilege; lest by their foolish Ingratitude the Righteous GOD be provok'd, to remove the Means they enjoy, or his Blessing from them, and so at last to expose them in another State to Enduring and greater Miseries. For surely, these Sins which are committed against greater Light and Mercy, are more presumptuous, un-

grateful, and inexcusable; there is in them a greater Contempt of GOD's Authority, and Slight of his Mercy; those Evils do awfully violate the Conscience, and declare a Love to Sin as Sin; such Transgressors do rush upon the Bosses of GOD's Bucker, they court Destruction without a Covering, and embrace their own Ruin with open Arms. And therefore according to the Nature of Justice, which proportions Sinners Pains, according to the Number and Heinousness of their Crimes, and the Declaration of Divine truth, you must expect an enflamed Damnation: Surely, it shall be more tolerable for *Sodom* and *Gommorah*, in the Day of the LORD, than for you, except ye repent.

And let gracious Souls be exhorted, to express the most tender Pity over such as have none but Pharisee-Teachers; and that in the Manner before described: To which the Example of our LORD in the Text before us, be an inducing and effectual Incitement; as well as the gracious and immense Rewards, which follow upon so generous and noble a Charity, in this and the next State.

And let those who live under the Ministry of dead Men, whether they have got the Form of Religion or not, repair to the Living, where they may be edified. Let who will, oppose it. What famous Mr. *Jenner* observes upon this Head, is most just, 'That if there be any godly Souls, or any that desires the Salvation of his Soul, and lives under a blind Guide, he cannot go out (of his Parish) without giving very great Offence;

Text: Gilbert Tennent, *The Danger of an Unconverted Ministry Considered in a Sermon on Mark VI, 34* (Philadelphia: Benjamin Franklin, 1740).

it will be tho't a Giddiness, and a Slighting of his own Minister at home. When People came out of every Parish round about, to *John* [The Baptist], no Question but this bred Heart-burning against *John*, ay, and Ill-will against those People, that would not be satisfied with that Teaching they had in their own Synagogues.' Thus far he. But tho' your Neighbors growl against you, and reproach you for doing your Duty, in seeking your Souls Good; bear their unjust Censures with Christian Meekness, and persevere; as knowing that Suffering is the Lot of Christ's Followers, and that spiritual Benefits do infinitely overbalance all temporal Difficulties.

And O! that vacant Congregations would take due Care in the Choice of their Ministers! Here indeed they should hasten slowly. The Church of Ephesus [In Paul's Epistle] is commended, for Trying them which said they were Apostles, and were not; and for finding them Liars. Hypocrits are against all Knowing of others, and Judging, in order to hide their own Filthiness; like Thieves they flee a Search, because of their stolen Goods. But the more they endeavour to hide, the more they expose their Shame. Does not the spiritual Man judge all Things? Tho' he cannot know the States of subtil Hypocrits infallibly; yet may he not give a near Guess, who are the sons of *Sceva*, by their Manner of Praying, Preaching, and Living? Many Pharisee-Teachers have got a long fine string of Prayer by Heart, so that they are never at a Loss about it; their Prayers and Preachings are generally of a Length, and both as dead as a Stone, and without all Savour. I beseech you, my dear Brethren, to consider, That there is no Probability of your getting Good, by the Ministry of Pharisees. For they are no Shepherds (no faithful ones) in Christ's Account. They are as good as none, nay, worse than none, upon some Accounts. For take them first and last, and they generally do more Hurt than Good. They serve to keep better out of the Places where they live; nay, when the Life of Piety comes near their Quarters, they rise up in Arms against it, consult, contrive and combine in their Conclaves against it, as a common Enemy, that discovers and condemns their Craft and Hypocrisie. And with what Art, Rhetorick, and Appearances of Piety, will they varnish their Opposition of Christ's Kingdom? As the Magicians imitated the Works of *Moses,* so do false Apostles, and deceitful Workers, the Apostles of Christ.

I shall conclude this Discourse with the Words of the Apostle *Paul 2, Cor.* 11:14-15.

And no Marvel; for Satan himself is transformed into an Angel of Light: Therefore it is no great Thing if his Ministers also be transformed as the Ministers of Righteousness; whose End shall be according to their Works.

CHAPTER 3

Interpretations of the Colonial

Background

Perhaps the most distinguished of American historical works have been written about the period before the formation of the Union. Heroic deeds of explorers and conquerors, encounters with exotic peoples in the wilderness, the clash of mighty empires: these have been themes for narrative writing on the grand scale by such men as William H. Prescott (1796-1859), historian of the Spanish conquistadors, and Francis Parkman (1823-1893), whose stirring volumes on France and England in North America are classics of American prose. Their politically minded contemporary George Bancroft (1800-1891), educated in the spirit of German romantic thought and of Jacksonian Democracy, transformed the colonial past into an inspiring story of the fulfillment of ancestral ideals of liberty and democracy.

Colonial historiography in the grand manner has continued into the twentieth century, although the vision has grown tamer, the scholarship cooler and more critical, and the style plainer. Among the comprehensive modern works based on lifelong study of the sources, one might single out Charles McLean Andrews' multi-volume *The Colonial Period of American History* and Lawrence Henry Gipson's massive survey, *The British Empire before the American Revolution*.

Selections from shorter writings by both these authors indicate their perspectives on colonial America. Although Andrews as well as Gipson considers the whole range of colonial and imperial development, Andrews' approach is well represented by his attempt to show how the frontier environment differentiated Americans from Britons and prepared them for independence. Gipson's studies, on the other hand, have been marked by their emphasis on the whole of the

British imperial framework and by his admiration for "the grandeur of the Old British Empire."

Studies of the colonial period by American scholars influenced both by Frederick Jackson Turner's "frontier thesis" and by a concern for finding the beginnings of the future nation have focused more on American conditions, experiences, and ideas than on the British context. Some recent writers on economic history—notably Lawrence A. Harper (The English Navigation Laws) and Curtis P. Nettels (The Roots of American Civilization)—would challenge Gipson's view, insisting upon the adverse economic consequences of imperial policy.

Comparing these recent works of professional scholarship with Francis Parkman's brilliant but no less learned "literary" history, one can appreciate the striking change in American historical writing from the nineteenth century to the twentieth. In Parkman's dramatic image, the struggle between France and England for control of North America becomes an opposition between two sets of national principles and traditions, two types of national character. Parkman, so to speak, votes with the liberal, practical, Protestant English but feels with the romantic, feudal, Catholic French—saving some of his sympathy for the heroic virtues of the savage.

No unified interpretation of the whole of colonial thought begins to do justice to the complexities of the subject. The history of ideas too easily can become a dry genealogy of doctrines or a facile reduction of ideas to external circumstances, motives, or effects. Perry Miller has earned an eminent place among the modern students of colonial intellectual history for his masterful analyses of the changing content of Puritan thought. In his studies of the "covenant theology," represented by the selection printed below, Miller probes beneath the popular image of Puritanism as a moral attitude or feeling to discover a not quite successful effort of the seventeenth-century Puritan mind to reconcile Calvinist theology with the reason and science of the new European philosophies. Thus the splitting of eighteenth-century New England thought into the rationalism of a John Wise and the unconditional Calvinism of a Jonathan Edwards is seen by Miller as a consequence of this unresolved conflict in the "covenant theology." The work of Perry Miller has had an important influence in the turning of colonial intellectual history away from the old debate between "ancestor-worshipers"—writers largely concerned with doing honor to the New England Fathers—and "debunkers" who were equally concerned with exposing the undemocratic and illiberal dogmatism of the "blue-nose" Puritans.

38

FRANCE AND ENGLAND IN AMERICA

from Francis Parkman, Montcalm and Wolfe, 1885

The "flowering of New England" in the first half of the nineteenth century created an excitingly original American literature from the pens of Emerson, Thoreau, Hawthorne, and others. The literary generation that succeeded the Concord group had less creative verve, and some of its highest accomplishments came in the realm of narrative history.

In 1851 a Bostonian of the "Brahmin" order, still in his twenties, brought out the first volume of what was to become the epic of the American wilderness. Francis Parkman's History of the Conspiracy of Pontiac, the source of the following selection, foreshadowed his great history of France and England in North America, published in nine volumes between 1865 and 1892. In the preface to the earlier work Parkman argued that a history such as he projected could not be drawn from documents alone but demanded "familiar acquaintance with the men and scenery of the wilderness." Parkman's travels to the wild regions of the North and West gave authenticity to his writings. His vision seriously impaired, Parkman had to dictate the narrative to a secretary after the documents had been read to him.

Parkman's masterful portrait of the struggle for North America from the early French explorations to the English triumph of 1763 went through numerous editions, reaching the lettered public to an extent that would now be rare indeed for works of original historical scholarship.

The French claimed all America, from the Alleghanies to the Rocky Mountains, and from Mexico and Florida to the North Pole, except only the ill-defined possessions of the English on the borders of Hudson Bay; and to these vast regions, with adjacent islands, they gave the general name of New France. They controlled the highways of the continent, for they held its two great rivers. First, they had seized the St. Lawrence, and then planted themselves at the mouth of the Mississippi. Canada at the north, and Louisiana at the south, were the keys of a boundless interior, rich with incalculable possibilities. The English colonies, ranged along the Atlantic coast, had no royal road to the great inland, and were, in a manner, shut between the mountains and the sea. At the middle of the century they numbered in all, from Georgia to Maine, about eleven hundred and sixty thousand white inhabitants. By the census of 1754 Canada had but fifty-five thousand. Add those of Louisiana and Acadia, and the whole white population under the French flag might be something more than eighty thousand. Here is an enormous disparity; and hence it has been argued that the success of the English colonies and the failure of the French was not due to difference of religious and political systems, but simply to numerical preponderance. But this preponderance itself grew out of a difference of systems. We have said before, and it cannot be said too often, that in making Canada a citadel of the state religion,—a holy of holies of exclusive Roman Catholic orthodoxy,—the clerical monitors of the Crown robbed their country of a trans-Atlantic empire. New France could not grow with a priest on guard at the gate to let in none but such as pleased him. One of the ablest of Canadian governors, La Galissonière, seeing the feebleness of the colony compared with the vastness of its claims, advised the King to send ten thousand peasants to occupy the valley of the Ohio, and hold back the British swarm that was just then pushing its advance-guard over the Alleghanies. It needed no effort of the King to people his waste domain, not with ten thousand peasants, but with twenty times ten thousand Frenchmen of every station,—the most indus-

trious, most instructed, most disciplined by adversity and capable of self-rule, that the country could boast. While La Galissonière was asking for colonists, the agents of the Crown, set on by priestly fanaticism, or designing selfishness masked with fanaticism, were pouring volleys of musketry into Huguenot congregations, imprisoning for life those innocent of all but their faith,—the men in the galleys, the women in the pestiferous dungeons of Aigues Mortes,—hanging their ministers, kidnapping their children, and reviving, in short, the dragonnades. Now, as in the past century, many of the victims escaped to the British colonies, and became a part of them. The Huguenots would have hailed as a boon the permission to emigrate under the fleur-de-lis, and build up a Protestant France in the valleys of the West. It would have been a bane of absolutism, but a national glory; would have set bounds to English colonization, and changed the face of the continent. The opportunity was spurned. The dominant Church clung to its policy of rule and ruin. France built its best colony on a principle of exclusion, and failed; England reversed the system, and succeeded.

I have shown elsewhere the aspects of Canada, where a rigid scion of the old European tree was set to grow in the wilderness. The military Governor, holding his miniature Court on the rock of Quebec; the feudal proprietors, whose domains lined the shores of the St. Lawrence; the peasant; the roving bushranger; the half-tamed savage, with crucifix and scalping-knife; priests; friars; nuns; and soldiers,—mingled to form a society the most picturesque on the continent. What distinguished it from the France that produced it was a total absence of revolt against the laws of its being,—an absolute conservatism, an unquestioning acceptance of Church and King. The Canadian, ignorant of everything but what the priest saw fit to teach him, had never heard of Voltaire; and if he had known him, would have thought him a devil. He had, it is true, a spirit of insubordination born of the freedom of the

Text: Francis Parkman, *Montcalm and Wolfe* (Boston: Little, Brown & Co., 1885), I, 20-35 *passim.*

forest; but if his instincts rebelled, his mind and soul were passively submissive. The unchecked control of a hierarchy robbed him of the independence of intellect and character, without which, under the conditions of modern life, a people must resign itself to a position of inferiority. Yet Canada had a vigor of her own. It was not in spiritual deference only that she differed from the country of her birth. Whatever she had caught of its corruptions, she had caught nothing of its effeminacy. The mass of her people lived in a rude poverty,—not abject, like the peasant of old France, nor ground down by the tax-gatherer; while those of the higher ranks—all more or less engaged in pursuits of war or adventure, and inured to rough journeyings and forest exposures—were rugged as their climate. Even the French regular troops, sent out to defend the colony, caught its hardy spirit, and set an example of stubborn fighting which their comrades at home did not always emulate.

Canada lay ensconced behind rocks and forests. All along her southern boundaries, between her and her English foes, lay a broad tract of wilderness, shaggy with primeval woods. Innumerable streams gurgled beneath their shadows; innumerable lakes gleamed in the fiery sunsets; innumerable mountains bared their rocky foreheads to the wind. These wastes were ranged by her savage allies, Micmacs, Etechémins, Abenakis, Caughnawagas; and no enemy could steal upon her unawares. Through the midst of them stretched Lake Champlain, pointing straight to the heart of the British settlements,—a watery thoroughfare of mutual attack, and the only approach by which, without a long *détour* by wilderness or sea, a hostile army could come within striking distance of the colony. The French advance post of Fort Frederic, called Crown Point by the English, barred the narrows of the lake, which thence spread northward to the portals of Canada guarded by Fort St. Jean. Southwestward, some fourteen hundred miles as a bird flies, and twice as far by the practicable routes of travel, was Louisiana, the second of the two heads of New France; while between lay the realms of solitude where the Mississippi rolled its sullen tide, and the Ohio wound its belt of silver through the verdant woodlands. . . .

The thirteen British colonies were alike insomuch as they all had representative governments, and a basis of English law. But the differences among them were great. Some were purely English; others were made up of various races, though the Anglo-Saxon was always predominant. Some had one prevailing religious creed; others had many creeds. Some had charters, and some had

not. In most cases the governor was appointed by the Crown; in Pennsylvania and Maryland he was appointed by a feudal proprietor, and in Connecticut and Rhode Island he was chosen by the people. The differences of disposition and character were still greater than those of form.

The four northern colonies, known collectively as New England, were an exception to the general rule of diversity. The smallest, Rhode Island, had features all its own; but the rest were substantially one in nature and origin. The principal among them, Massachusetts, may serve as the type of all. It was a mosaic of little village republics, firmly cemented together, and formed into a single body politic through representatives sent to the "General Court" at Boston. Its government, originally theocratic, now tended to democracy, ballasted as yet by strong traditions of respect for established worth and ability, as well as by the influence of certain families prominent in affairs for generations. Yet there were no distinct class-lines, and popular power, like popular education, was widely diffused. Practically, Massachusetts was almost independent of the mother-country. Its people were purely English, of sound yeoman stock, with an abundant leaven drawn from the best of the Puritan gentry; but their original character had been somewhat modified by changed conditions of life. A harsh and exacting creed, with its stiff formalism and its prohibition of wholesome recreation, excess in the pursuit of gain,—the only resource left to energies robbed of their natural play; the struggle for existence on a hard and barren soil; and the isolation of a narrow village life—joined to produce, in the meaner sort, qualities which were unpleasant, and sometimes repulsive. . . . The staple of character was a sturdy conscientiousness, an undespairing courage, patriotism, public spirit, sagacity, and a strong good sense. . . . They were conspicuous, moreover, for intellectual activity, and were by no means without intellectual eminence. Massachusetts had produced at least two men whose fame had crossed the sea,—Edwards, who out of the grim theology of Calvin mounted to sublime heights of mystical speculation; and Franklin, famous already by his discoveries in electricity. On the other hand, there were few genuine New Englanders who, however personally modest, could divest themselves of the notion that they belonged to a people in an especial manner the object of divine approval; and this self-righteousness, along with certain other traits, failed to commend the Puritan colonies to the favor of their fellows. Then, as now, New England was best known to her neighbors by her worst side.

In one point, however, she found general applause. She was regarded as the most military among the British colonies. This reputation was well founded, and is easily explained. More than all the rest, she lay open to attack. The long waving line of the New England border, with its lonely hamlets and scattered farms, extended from the Kennebec to beyond the Connecticut, and was everywhere vulnerable to the guns and tomahawks of the neighboring French and their savage allies. . . . Fighting had been a necessity with her, and she had met the emergency after a method extremely defective, but the best that circumstances would permit. Having no trained officers and no disciplined soldiers, and being too poor to maintain either, she borrowed her warriors from the workshop and the plough, and officered them with lawyers, merchants, mechanics or farmers. To compare them with good regular troops would be folly; but they did, on the whole, better than could have been expected. . . .

The great colony of Virginia stood in strong contrast to New England. In both the population was English; but the one was Puritan with Roundhead traditions, and the other, so far as concerned its governing class, Anglican with Cavalier traditions. In the one, every man, woman, and child could read and write; in the other, Sir William Berkeley once thanked God that there were no free schools, and no prospects of any for a century. The hope had found fruition. The lower classes of Virginia were as untaught as the warmest friend of popular ignorance could wish. New England had a native literature more than respectable under the circumstances, while Virginia had none; numerous industries, while Virginia was all agriculture, with but a single crop; a homogeneous society and a democratic spirit, while her rival was an aristocracy. Virginian society was distinctly stratified. On the lowest level were the negro slaves, nearly as numerous as all the rest together; next, the indented servants and the poor whites, of low origin, good-humored, but boisterous, and sometimes vicious; next, the small and despised class of tradesmen and mechanics; next, the farmers and lesser planters, who were mainly of good English stock, and who merged insensibly into the ruling class of the great landowners. It was these last who represented the colony and made the laws. They may be described as English country squires transplanted to a warm climate and turned slave-masters. . . . What they wanted in schooling was supplied by an education which books alone would have been impotent to give, the education which came with the possession and exercise of political power, and the sense of a position to maintain, joined to a bold spirit of independence and a patriotic attachment to the Old Dominion. They were few in number; they raced, gambled, drank, and swore; they did everything that in Puritan eyes was most reprehensible; and in the day of need they gave the United Colonies a body of statesmen and orators which had no equal on the continent. A vigorous aristocracy favors the growth of personal eminence, even in those who are not of it, but only near it.

The essential antagonism of Virginia and New England was afterwards to become, and to remain for a century, an element of the first influence in American history. Each might have learned much from the other; but neither did so till, at last, the strife of their contending principles shook the continent. Pennsylvania differed widely from both. She was a conglomerate of creeds and races,—English, Irish, Germans, Dutch, and Swedes; Quakers, Lutherans, Presbyterians, Romanists, Moravians, and a variety of nondescript sects. The Quakers prevailed in the eastern districts; quiet, industrious, virtuous, and serenely obstinate. The Germans were strongest towards the centre of the colony, and were chiefly peasants; successful farmers, but dull, ignorant, and superstitious. Towards the west were the Irish, of whom some were Celts, always quarrelling with their German neighbors, who detested them; but the greater part were Protestants of Scotch descent, from Ulster; a vigorous border population. Virginia and New England had each a strong distinctive character. Pennsylvania, with her heterogeneous population, had none. but that which she owed to the sober neutral tints of Quaker existence. A more thriving colony there was not on the continent. Life, if monotonous, was smooth and contented. Trade and the arts grew. Philadelphia, next to Boston, was the largest town in British America; and was, moreover, the intellectual centre of the middle and southern colonies. Unfortunately, for her credit in the approaching war, the Quaker influence made Pennsylvania noncombatant. . . .

New York had not as yet reached the relative prominence which her geographical position and inherent strength afterwards gave her. The English, joined to the Dutch, the original settlers, were the dominant population; but a half-score of other languages were spoken in the province, the chief among them being that of the Huguenot French in the southern parts, and that of the Germans on the Mohawk. In religion, the province was divided between the Anglican Church, with government support and popular dislike, and numerous dissenting sects, chiefly Lutherans, Independents, Presbyterians, and members of the

Dutch Reformed Church. The little city of New York, like its great successor, was the most cosmopolitan place on the continent, and probably the gayest. It had, in abundance, balls, concerts, theatricals, and evening clubs, with plentiful dances and other amusements for the poorer classes. Thither in the winter months came the great hereditary proprietors on the Hudson; for the old Dutch feudality still held its own, and the manors of Van Rensselaer, Cortland, and Livingston, with their seigniorial privileges, and the great estates and numerous tenantry of the Schuylers and other leading families, formed the basis of an aristocracy, some of whose members had done good service to the province, and were destined to do more. Pennsylvania was feudal in form, and not in spirit; Virginia in spirit, and not in form; New England in neither; and New York largely in both. This social crystallization had, it is true, many opponents. In politics, as in religion, there were sharp antagonisms and frequent quarrels. They centred in the city; for in the well-stocked dwellings of the Dutch farmers along the Hudson there reigned a tranquil and prosperous routine; and the Dutch border town of Albany had not its like in America for unruffled conservatism and quaint picturesqueness.

Of the other colonies, the briefest mention will suffice: New Jersey, with its wholesome population of farmers; tobacco-growing Maryland, which, but for its proprietary government and numerous Roman Catholics, might pass for another Virginia, inferior in growth, and less decisive in features; Delaware, a modest appendage of Pennsylvania; wild and rude North Carolina; and, farther on, South Carolina and Georgia, too remote from the seat of war to take a noteworthy part in it. The attitude of these various colonies towards each other is hardly conceivable to an American of the present time. They had no political tie except a common allegiance to the British Crown. Communication between them was difficult and slow, by rough roads traced often through primeval forests. Between some of them there was less of sympathy than of jealousy kindled by conflicting interests or perpetual disputes concerning boundaries.

The patriotism of the colonist was bounded by the lines of his government, except in the compact and kindred colonies of New England, which were socially united, though politically distinct. The country of the New Yorker was New York, and the country of the Virginian was Virginia. The New England colonies had once confederated; but, kindred as they were, they had long ago dropped apart. William Penn proposed a plan of colonial union wholly fruitless. James II. tried to unite all the northern colonies under one government; but the attempt came to naught. Each stood aloof, jealously independent. At rare intervals, under the pressure of an emergency, some of them would try to act in concert; and, except in New England, the results had been most discouraging. Nor was it this segregation only that unfitted them for war. They were all subject to popular legislatures, through whom alone money and men could be raised; and these elective bodies were sometimes factious and selfish, and not always either far-sighted or reasonable. Moreover, they were in a state of ceaseless friction with their governors, who represented the king, or, what was worse, the feudal proprietary. These disputes, though varying in intensity, were found everywhere except in the two small colonies which chose their own governors; and they were premonitions of the movement towards independence which ended in the war of Revolution . . .

In Canada there was no popular legislature to embarrass the central power. The people, like an army, obeyed the word of command,—a military advantage beyond all price.

Divided in government; divided in origin, feelings, and principles; jealous of each other, jealous of the Crown; the people at war with the executive, and, by the fermentation of internal politics, blinded to an outward danger that seemed remote and vague,—such were the conditions under which the British colonies drifted into a war that was to decide the fate of the continent.

This war was the strife of a united and concentred few against a divided and discordant many. It was the strife, too, of the past against the future; of the old against the new; of moral and intellectual torpor against moral and intellectual life; of barren absolutism against a liberty, crude, incoherent, and chaotic, yet full of prolific vitality.

39

THE GRANDEUR OF THE OLD EMPIRE

from Lawrence Henry Gipson, *The British Empire in the Eighteenth Century*, 1952

Lawrence Henry Gipson, Professor Emeritus of History at Lehigh University, completed the nine volumes of his chief work, *The British Empire before the American*

Revolution, over a period of twenty years from 1936 to 1956. This exhaustive history views the mid-eighteenth century empire from the English center, looking out to the colonial parts. Other works of note are his biography, *Jared Ingersoll: A Study of American Loyalism* (1920) and a recent contribution to the New American Nation series, *The Coming of the Revolution, 1763-1775* (1954).

The following selection is taken from Gipson's Inaugural Lecture as Harmsworth Professor of American History at the University of Oxford, delivered in November 1951. Here one sees the Old Empire as it appears to a thoroughly sympathetic scholar, and one meets the interesting suggestion that the American Revolution can best be understood as the ironic consequence of Britain's imperial achievements: first in nurturing proud and prosperous colonies, then in defeating the French and so eliminating the external menace that had kept Americans loyal to the empire.

In view of the weighty indictment of Great Britain in 1775 by American colonials in charging that they not only had been misgoverned but governed despotically, it is important to examine briefly the sort of governments they possessed in the latter half of the eighteenth century. The chief executive in each colony, whether continental or island, was a so-called governor, or a deputy governor or lieutenant governor as the case might be. But the powers that he possessed might differ sharply between governor and governor. In all the colonies, with one exception, he or his deputy was expected to reside in the colony; but with respect to Newfoundland he was in 1750 a naval captain with his official residence on board a warship; thus his authority over the settlers on the island could be exerted only sporadically; for he came to the harbour of St. John's in the spring and returned home in the fall after convoying the sack ships loaded with cod to Spain or Portugal. In Nova Scotia he was an officer in the land forces, and in the other royal colonies he might or might not be a civilian. Commissioned and instructed by the King in Council, the royal governor's constitutional authority was therefore determined by the nature of his commission and the instructions that he received. Outside of Newfoundland all royal governors were provided with a council that shared with them certain powers and beyond that acted in an advisory capacity. As the representative of the King, the royal governor, as a rule, occupied a position of great dignity and influence within his province. In contrast, the governor of a corporate colony—elected annually to office by the freemen of the colony, as in the case of Connecticut, or by the General Assembly as was true in Rhode Island—possessed very little authority; since he was neither commissioned by the Crown nor instructed by it except under unusual circumstances, he felt obliged at all times to make sure, if he expected to retain office, that his official acts were in harmony not only with the laws of the colony but the temper of public opinion there. Occupying a position midway between the governor of a royal colony and that of a corporate colony was the governor of a proprietorial province, who was commissioned and instructed by the Proprietor or Proprietors living in England, after the person selected for this post had secured the royal approval.

As to the colonial legislatures, there was also much divergency exhibited. One thing they had in common, however, was their power and aggressiveness in matters of public interest and the degree to which they took Parliament as their model. In all the older colonies, with the exception of Pennsylvania and Delaware, the Assembly was bicameral; in all of them, where there were two chambers, taxation measures originated in the lower house, the members of which were chosen by the freemen. Since the chief source of public funds was the taxes, which were necessary to maintain the local government, the latter could be quickly paralysed if the legislature refused to vote them. Here was the chief weapon in the eighteenth century for making the governor, whether royal or proprietorial, submissive to the will of that body, despite the fact that in the case of Virginia this officer's salary was automatically paid out of the export duty on tobacco. Labouring under such limitations a governor might be disagreeable but hardly despotic. In other words, if the governor in obedience to his instructions or otherwise sought to carry out an unpopular policy he was almost sure to find himself deadlocked with at least the lower house of his assembly and at times even with the upper house, and, therefore, in a position of isolation and total weakness in the performance of his duties. He might therefore feel impelled, unless his instructions specifically forbade his doing so, to approve bills that, although demanded by the people of the province where he presided and passed by both chambers of the Assembly, were from his personal

Text: Lawrence Henry Gipson, *The British Empire in the Eighteenth Century* (Oxford: Clarendon Press, 1952), pp. 9-12, 14-18, 23-25.

view and that of the home Government against the interests of the mother country and even of the rest of the Empire. On the other hand, he might, but at his peril, refuse his assent to legislation.

Here one may point out the existence of a safeguard that was designed to give a certain unity to all legislation passed in the various assemblies within the Empire. The laws of every colony—with the exception of the statutes of the two corporate colonies of Connecticut and Rhode Island and of the proprietary of Maryland—had to be sent to England after receiving the signature of the governor, in order to be submitted for final acceptance or rejection to the King's Privy Council. No colonial law that in the judgement of this body was in serious opposition to the constitution, statutes, or policy of the mother country would be approved. To arrive at a valid conclusion regarding each measure the Lords Commissioners of Trade and Plantations, better known as the Board of Trade, was given the primary responsibility of making an examination of the great mass of colonial legislation. In this laborious task they were aided not only by the agents appointed by the colonies to represent their interests in London but also by both the Attorney-General and Solicitor-General or by their own legal counsel. Thereupon the Board would frame a so-called 'representation' that was forwarded to the Lords of the Committee of the Council; the latter in turn would recommend to the Privy Council itself the appropriate action to be taken. Cumbersome as was this procedure for approving or disapproving colonial legislation, it was certainly done in a spirit of judicial detachment and was doubtless the best method that could be devised under the circumstances for giving a certain coherence to the work of the large number of semi-autonomous law-making bodies within the Empire in 1750. . . .

The trade and navigation system calls for special comment at this point. In its essence it was, as we find it in the middle of the eighteenth century, a politico-economic system designed, among other purposes behind it, to make the mother country the centre of commercial activities within the Empire, to maintain the vitality and prosperity of certain of her home industries which were the source of much of her economic strength, to encourage, on the one hand, the growth of British sea-power, and to guard, on the other, against foreign competition in the Empire's carrying trade; further, it aimed to make the Empire economically self-contained with respect to essential things. This system has commonly been called mercantilism; but the word carries so many connotations that

for our purposes it would perhaps be better to call it—as Provost G. N. Clark in his *Wealth of England* has well denominated it—protectionism. This system was slowly evolved, so far as the Empire was concerned, with the gradual growth of the latter. With the expansion of the Empire, in other words, there took place a corresponding expansion in the restrictions and encouragements that taken together made up the system. By the year 1750 it had all but reached its maturity and rested upon an impressive body of parliamentary statutes. Whatever may have been the narrow insular purposes of those who in the seventeenth century first laid down the framework for it, it is clear that by the middle of the eighteenth century it was geared to the view of realizing the broad objectives of a prosperous and, in so far as was possible, as previously noted, a self-contained Empire. In forbidding foreign shipping to have access to colonial ports and markets and at the same time in encouraging the ship-building and carrying trades in the colonies, it had by the period under discussion made possible the creation of an imperial merchant marine that was doubtless equal to, if not greater than, the combined shipping of the French and Spanish Empires; it had also contributed to the building up of the Royal Navy to a point where it bore the same relation to the united navies of France and Spain that the merchant marine had attained with respect to the combined shipping of these countries.

In some ways protectionism, it is clear, worked a hardship on portions of the Empire in favour of certain key industries in Great Britain. . . . When the well-established British beaver-hat industry was later threatened with extinction by outside competition, the Hat Act of 1732 was passed which forbade the export of beaver-hats made in any British colony and limited the number of apprentices there that might learn this art. Likewise, in the year 1750, when the English iron industry was confronted with great unsold surpluses of iron and ironware and widespread unemployment and distress among the workers, the Iron Act was passed that sought vainly to check the expansion of the American steel and iron industry and to direct the efforts of American iron-masters chiefly to the production of pig- and bar-iron for export to England. Yet, in describing the working of the system with its restrictions, we must not fail to mention at the same time, the great encouragement through bonuses offered to colonials to produce certain articles, such as ship timber, naval stores, indigo, silk, and potash.

What Britain virtually said to her colonies and dependencies was, 'You must not destroy a useful industry in the mother country, which affords you protection, in order to profit by the suffering that this would entail. Rather turn your attention to supplying the Empire with those things that it needs but must otherwise bring in from outside. This useful function we will heartily promote among you.' Here we have an example of empire-planning, of the welfare empire, long before men began to write treatises for or against state-planning or the welfare-state.

The channelling of many colonial exports and most colonial imports was also characteristic of the protectionist system. It was designed to make Great Britain the entrepôt for the Empire. As a result, all ship timber, as well as potash, furs and skins, tobacco, rice with some concessions, sugar, cotton, raw wool, molasses, copper, and iron that left a colony could be exported directly only to the mother country or to another colony. Likewise, goods secured in Europe and intended for the American market, with minor exceptions, had to be carried first to Great Britain for the payment of duties and for certification. These trade regulations were held to be a proper colonial contribution for maritime protection and thus for the support of the Royal Navy.

The many restrictions, it is clear, were, while certainly considered a nuisance by colonials, not such as to prevent phenomenal economic development within almost all parts of the Empire, accompanied by widespread prosperity. Reference has been made to the vast expansion of the merchant marine, with the building and operation of hundreds of ships by colonials. By 1750 the output of ore from the mines of Great Britain and her colonies and of pig-iron, bar-iron, and steel from the furnaces and forges had also dwarfed that of any other nation or empire, as did the production for export of woollen goods from the looms of England, corn and meat products from the farms of the British Isles and the colonies, and tobacco and rice from the latter. Further, the Empire had a great surplus of furs, deer-skins, and fish, both herring and cod; it was self-sufficient not only in linen goods produced chiefly in Ireland and Great Britain but in building materials for ships—including any quantity of oak for the hulls, white pine for the great masts and yardarms, all from the forests of the northern colonies, and also tar, pitch, and turpentine from the yellow pine of the Carolinas—and it was more than self-sufficient in sugar drawn from the West Indies, but not in molasses, out of which rum was distilled. While the true age of coal was still to come, so far as industry was concerned, enormous deposits of this were being worked in England and Scotland and were only awaiting exploitation in western Pennsylvania. Moreover, in England and Lowland Scotland almost every town boasted the production of some speciality, be it cotton goods, then known as Manchester goods, copper-ware, pottery, porcelain, silk goods, and other articles that had acquired more than local renown. As a result, and despite the fact of the presence of the poor and distressed in every part of the Empire, most people within it were adequately clothed, nourished, and sheltered and the more enterprising or more fortunate were so in profusion. Thus flourishing in peace, the Empire, by reason of its immense resources, was powerful and dreaded in time of war. . . .

But the Empire of the middle of the eighteenth century had its Achilles' heel. Ironically enough, a certain weakness, a certain instability, was embedded in the very texture of its finest flowering —in the very freedom of its institutions and buoyancy of a great and inspiring tradition that had made possible this flowering. Growing by leaps and bounds, the old British continental colonies that had been weak and dependent in the seventeenth century were by the middle of the eighteenth—taken as a group—strong, wealthy, very self-conscious, and dynamic. They had needed the protection afforded by the mother country in the days of their infancy and likewise later during the period of what might be called their adolescence. With French Canada to the north of them and Spanish Florida to the south, and to the westward stretching from the Appalachian Mountains to the Mississippi River a vast sort of no-man's land where dwelt thousands of fierce aborigines subject to French influence, there were the best of reasons why centrifugal tendencies latent within the old Empire were little in evidence in 1750. But once these menaces were removed as the result of what in my writings I call the Great War for the Empire of 1754-63 and of the Treaty of Paris that terminated it, the whole psychological attitude of American colonials towards Great Britain underwent nothing less than a revolution.

Before 1750 no colonial assembly had been prepared or disposed to challenge seriously the principle that authority with respect to all questions affecting the constitution of the colony in question and that of the Empire in general was concentrated in the King's Privy Council or, after the Revolution of 1688, that its final source was the King's High Court of Parliament. As late as 1754, but in the midst of a general alarm, when commissioners from various colonies, with the encouragement of the Board of Trade, met at Albany, New York, and there attempted to work out some practicable plan that would permit the British inhabitants of North America to present a solid front in face of what they with good reason felt were the French aggressions on their borders, the delegates significantly agreed that the proper procedure was to appeal to the *Parliament* so to alter the constitutional bases of their colonial governments as to make possible a binding union for the purposes of defence. Foremost among the architects of this Albany Plan of Union was Benjamin Franklin. To him it was apparent at the time that it was Parliament *alone* which was sufficiently clothed with power to change existing constitutional arrangements within the Empire.

However, with the Anglo-French war in North America coming to a triumphant conclusion, a new note was struck there—a note that doubtless would never have been heard had France, instead, won the war and had achieved the purpose of confining the British colonials to a narrow strip of the north Atlantic seaboard. It may be stated with candour that this change in attitude among most British colonials did not come as the result of any conduct on the part of the government of the mother country that in all honesty could be called either despotic or tyrannical, freely as this was charged between the years 1761 and 1775, as well as long afterwards even up to our own days.

40

THE FRONTIER AND THE AMERICAN COLONIES

from Charles McLean Andrews, *The Colonial Background of the American Revolution,* 1931

Charles McLean Andrews' *The Colonial Period of American History* (4 volumes, 1934-1938) is less notable for striking new interpretations than for soundness and breadth of scholarship. An earlier historical essay from which the following passages are taken—*The Colonial Background of the American Revolution*—presents a bolder conception of the patterns of colonial development that prepared Americans to strike for independence. Note the difference between this view of the American frontier as the breeding ground of independence and Gipson's emphasis upon a shift of colonial interest with the British conquest of French Canada (Document 39).

Such was England at the time of her trouble with the colonies: a land of two nations, one privileged, wealthy, and honored, divinely invested, as it were, with the right to rule; the other unprivileged, poor, and ignored, and according to the views of the time predestined by the eternal law to be ruled. The colonists faced an old country, with a highly developed and complex social organization, which was growing each year more and more industrialized, and in which manufactures, trade, and commerce—marks of a social and industrial state—were considered more important than agriculture; a country where the real conditions of an agricultural land like America were very imperfectly understood, and where rights based on history, law, and the possession of property were cultivated to the almost complete atrophy of those that were merely human. They faced a dominant aristocracy, composed of less than one-fiftieth of the male population of the kingdom, sensitive, exclusive, and inclined to arrogance, deeply concerned for their land, business profits, and other vested interests, and caring but little for the finer spiritual aspects of

Text: Charles McLean Andrews, The Colonial Background of the American Revolution, rev. ed. (New Haven, Conn.: Yale University Press, 1931), pp. 194-99.

art, literature, and religion. They faced a stubborn ruling minority, which exercised political power, monopolized the offices of state, dominated parliament, and indirectly determined the policies of ministries and shaped legislation to the advantage of their class. They faced a parliament, whose supremacy was unchallenged, for the nation as a whole had little control over its deliberations and was not recognized as exercising any appreciable influence on the conduct of affairs.

In contrast to this highly conventionalized social class, with its stereotyped, unprogressive system of thought and government, stood the American colonies forming in large part an agricultural frontier, with an environment that was favorable to the development of man as an individual rather than as a member of society. Frontiersmen have always awakened slowly to the importance of the communal interest. Distrustful of outside law and authority, suspicious of centralized government, and determined to enjoy entire liberty of action in domestic concerns, they have been wont to employ emergency methods, whenever convinced that in no other way could they obtain justice or secure relief. From Bacon's rebellion to the Regulators' War and from the activities of the Green Mountain Boys of Vermont, in opposing the authority of New York, to the vigilance committees of San Francisco in the early days of the American occupation of California, has the frontier exhibited a fearless and aggressive individualism.

Frontier settlers and pioneer communities, located far from the seats of organized authority, have developed their own ideas of government and have been accustomed to act upon the theory that the state was created by voluntary compact between contracting parties possessed of various inherent rights. This theory of the social compact has played a very important part in the history of American institutions, because of the constant presence of the frontier as the population moved westward, and has found itself expressed in various forms from the Mayflower Compact and the plantation covenants of the New England towns, through the agreements of the transient frontier states during the Revolution, to the schemes adopted by the local committees of Texas in 1835 and the vigilance committees of California in 1851 and 1856. Though before 1776 each of the British colonies in America had a well-ordered and stable form of government of its own, that government (except in Connecticut and Rhode Island) was not of its own devising, and there was always existent an undercurrent of the frontier spirit—call it democratic if you will, though the word is not well chosen—which, though more or less dormant in the towns and the tidewater plantations, was insurgent in many parts of the back country and the mountain valleys, and omnipresent in New England, where (so all-pervading was the habit of expressing opinions) it unconsciously determined political thought and shaped political action.

But not the whole of the colonial area was frontier in life and character. The older section along the coast was made up of cities and towns in the North and of plantations in the South, where lived representatives of a wealthy and leisure class, commercially minded and conservatively inclined and given to oligarchic methods of government; while west of the "fall line" or head of navigation of the rivers flowing into the Atlantic a new frontier was in the making. Between the people of these two sections, as well as between the classes of the older region—the propertied and those without property, the conservatives and the radicals, the franchised and the unfranchised—there was beginning that time-honored and irrepressible conflict which was to play so prominent a part not only in the Revolution but also from that time to the present day in the history of the United States. However, during the colonial period, so predominantly was the whole area agricultural and so strong were the traditions of individualism already established that, in contrast with the temperament of the mother country, the prevailing spirit everywhere was that of the frontier. In all parts of this area, in varying degrees of intensity, the conviction existed that a people so far away from the ultimate source of authority had a right to control their own political institutions. Our colonists cared less for efficient government than they did for self-government, and they paid less attention to the defense of their own borders and the preservation of law and order at home than they did to the securing of the right to govern themselves. Probably few if any among them realized the significance of their own promptings, and certain is it that no one in official England grasped the fact that the only way to save the colonies to the mother country was to grant them some measure of responsible government. The logic of historical processes is generally hidden even from the far-seeing men of any given age.

The territory of the new West, from the Lake Champlain to South Carolina—notably along the Susquehanna, in western Maryland, and in the Shenandoah Valley of Virginia—formed the frontier, properly so called, of the colonial area, and its occupants were too far removed from political and social contact with Great Britain to be much concerned with her affairs. It was in New England that the first cry of protest was raised against the policy of the mother country. There the towns—in most instances agricultural communities, dominated by the Congregational system of church organization—were accustomed to manage their own affairs. Glorying in their town and freemen's meetings, their ecclesiastical societies, their proprietary gatherings for the distribution and management of their lands, and the fact that they gave to every voting inhabitant an opportunity to take some part in the management of affairs, they were overcharged, as it were, with the spirit of self-government. Even their trainbands elected their minor officers, and placed in command men who sympathized with the radical, and often irresponsible, views of the rank and file. Connecticut, in particular, having always been free from interference by the crown and resident crown officials and having had fewer points of contact with Great Britain than had any of the other colonies, was filled with the spirit and practice of independency and held that the opinion of the individual was a fundamental factor in the life of a people.

Thus the environment of the New Englander produced an atmosphere of individualism that was congenial to the growth of the doctrine of natural rights independent of law, convention, and tradition, and was hostile to all ideas based on history, precedent, and man-made statute. These colonists fought with every species of difficulty that nature could place in their path—climate, stubbornness of the soil, amazing forests, and a stone-strewn earth—and they conquered nature because they were freemen, not slaves. Such an experience had its certain effect. "God and nature brought us into the world free men," said the Wallingford fathers, "and by solemn charter, compact, and agreement we came into the English constitution." Such a statement as this could not have been understood by a member of the British ministry or of parliament or by a legal adviser of the crown, and all of them would have called it meaningless, as from a constitutional point of view it was. They would have found similar views, uttered here and there in formal resolutions and private correspondence, not only unintelligible but positively dangerous and have dismissed them as merely the mouthings of theorists and radicals. Their attitude is well summed up in the remark of a contemporary Englishman, who in commenting on the preamble to the Declaration of Independence said that the American gentry assumed to themselves the inalienable right of talking nonsense. . . .

41 THE PURITAN MIND

from Perry Miller, *Errand into the Wilderness*, 1956

Perry Miller's essay, "The Marrow of Puritan Divinity," presents an approach to New England intellectual history that was prefigured in the author's *Orthodoxy in Massachusetts* (1933) and developed in two searching volumes on *The New England Mind* (1939, 1953). Taking Puritan thought on its own terms, Miller finds the "covenant" doctrine (see pp. 59-60 and Document 21) to be of central importance as the link between the Calvinist theology of early New England thinkers and what he insists was their responsiveness to problems raised by the radically new teachings of Enlightenment philosophy and science, of innovators like Bacon, Descartes, and Hobbes.

The introduction to *The Puritans* (1938), a collection of sources edited by Perry Miller and Thomas H. Johnson, further emphasizes the intellectual breadth of the early Puritans as children of the late Elizabethan Age. In addition to the volume *Errand into the Wilderness* (1956), from which the following essay is drawn, Miller has written a stimulating intellectual biography, *Jonathan Edwards* (1949), that makes substantial claims for the "New Light" minister as an original philosopher. Mr. Miller is Professor of American Literature at Harvard University.

I have not attempted in this account of the covenant theology to give more than a rapid survey; the summary of each point could easily be amplified, and revealing quotations multiplied indefinitely. But in even as compressed a treatment as this, the bent of the thought becomes clear. In every position there is a remarkable consistency of tone, a resolute determination to solve the riddles of Calvinist theology, as far as may be possible by the ingenuity of man or the subterfuges of metaphysics, in a reasonable, comprehensible fashion, and yet at the same time to preserve, in form at least, the essential structure of Calvinism. To understand why these men should have been driven by this urgency, it is necessary to remember what was taking place in

Text: Perry Miller, *Errand into the Wilderness*, pp. 92-98. Reprinted by permission of the publishers from Perry Miller, *Errand into the Wilderness*. Cambridge, Mass.: Harvard University Press, Copyright 1956 by The President and Fellows of Harvard College.

the intellectual life of Europe at the time, in science, in politics, in the work of Bacon, of Descartes, and of Hobbes. Within the limits of their particular theology, within the framework of their creed, these Puritans were responding to the same impulses as their philosophical contemporaries. They were seeking to understand, to draw up explicable laws, to form clear and distinct ideas, to bring order and logic into the universe. They could not interpret it as extension and movement as did Descartes. They could not reduce it to atoms as did Hobbes. They could not deify its natural construction as did the Newtonians. But oddly enough they could take many steps in the same direction once they had seized upon their fundamental discovery that God has voluntarily engaged Himself to regular, ascertainable procedures. The rest followed surely and easily from this premise: the validity of reason in man, the regularity of secondary causes in nature, the harmony of knowledge and faith, the coincidence of the arbitrary with inherent goodness, the intimate connection between grace and the incitements that generate grace, the necessity for moral responsibility and activity. Everywhere along the line the method of the divine dispensation, while authorized only by God and remaining under His constant control, is actually synchronized with a completely scientific account. God works grace in the soul, not by compulsion, but by persuasion and reasonable inducements, by the sermon of the minister which penetrates the sinner's mind. Was the real cause God working through the sermon, or was it the sermon itself? The authors had no hesitancy in saying that the sermon was simply the efficient cause and that God was the final cause, but they were delighted to find that God's activity could take the form of a natural stimulus. This seemed to make religion doubly secure and to enhance it by the addition of comprehensibility. . . .

The achievement of this theology was that it did everything that could be done to confine the unconfinable God in human terms. It transformed the revealed Word from an exaction arbitrarily imposed by a conqueror into a treaty of mutual obligation. But it never forgot that at the long last God is not to be fathomed, understood, or described with absolute certainty. Such certainty as we do have is temporary, the result of an agreement, of God's having consented to be bound in the main by such and such conditions, of His condescending for the moment to speak the language of men. There is no absolute guarantee that *all* His manifestations will appear within the scope of the covenant. The essence of Calvinism and the essence of Puritanism is the hidden God, the unknowable, the unpredictable. In this sense the Puritans were indeed Calvinists. They hedged the undiscoverable Essence about with a much more elaborate frame than did Calvin. They muffled it and cloaked it (to borrow Cotton's phrase), they cabined it and circumscribed it up to a point; and though the point was far beyond anything Calvin would have allowed, there was still a limit beyond which even the federal theologians could not go. They could not say that natural law was immutable and eternal, though they might say it was generally reliable. They might say that God's justice was for all intents and purposes the same as human justice, but they could not say that it was invariably the same. Always they had to leave a loophole, they had to be wary and circumspect; for behind the panorama of the world, behind the covenant and behind the Scriptures there loomed an inconceivable being about whom no man could confidently predict anything, who might day in and

day out deal with man in stated forms and then suddenly strike without warning and scatter the world into bits. There was no telling with unqualified certitude what He might do; there was only the rule of thumb, the working agreement that by and large He would save and reject according to reason and justice as we understand the words. For ordinary purposes this was enough; we could feel fairly secure, we need not be too distraught. But the Puritan, as long as he remained a Puritan, could never banish entirely from his mind the sense of something mysterious and terrible, of something that leaped when least expected, something that upset all regularizations and defied all logic, something behind appearances that could not be tamed and brought to heel by men. The covenant thought kept this divine liberty at several removes, placed it on a theoretical plane, robbed it of much of its terror, but it could not do away with it entirely. . . .

For Preston and the Puritan theologians of the covenant it was enough that God had consented to reason and had made an effort to fit His will to the requirements of abstract justice. They would not dogmatize further about His essence, and they felt that no man had a right to. They would expound the laws of reason and the laws of nature step by step with Taylor, they would extol justice and virtue as much as he, but they would not affirm that these human constructions, these intellectual values, were necessarily part and parcel of the cosmos. God's will coincides roughly with such conceptions, but not always exactly. The universe is almost always regular and orderly, but there is the one chance in a million, the one inexplicable accident, the one fact that will not fit into any scheme. There is every so often the apparently good man who cannot be saved or the hopeless wretch who is lifted from the gutter to glory in spite of all that we think appropriate. "If he take pleasure to breathe in a man, there is nothing can hinder him, it will blow upon the most noysome dunghill in any place, and be never a whit the more defiled." In a Christian community the machinery of conversion is set up, the covenant proposed, the terms made explicit, the means set in order, and yet in spite of all the best intentions this or that individual may never be able to join the covenant. And there is no explaining why, except that it is God's pleasure to withhold the ability from that particular man. Even the godly, after they have become partakers of the covenant, will not dwell in happiness and comfort. . . .

The Puritan wished to bring his theology into harmony with science and reason wherever they might be made to coincide, but he could never lose his hunger for the inward exultation that came from a union with God which, though it might be brought about by natural causes, was yet something supernatural, something different from the causes, something which was bestowed only at the pleasure of God. Faith adds no new doctrine, teaches us no new facts, is not an addition to the contents of the mind. . . .

To be wise unto sobriety was the purpose of this theology, to elucidate the laws of God's universe, but to keep a wary eye upon the unpredictability, the mystery of God. The evidence of subsequent history, both in England and in New England, would seem to be that it failed. Eventually the ideas which it introduced into the creed, reinforced by the triumph of Newtonian physics, displaced the theology in the estimation of such men as Charles Chauncy. The moral of this episode in the story is, I think, that the Calvinism to which the Puritans were ostensibly dedicated was already in the process of far-reaching modification at the hands of English theologians before it was transported to Massachusetts. The men who directed the intellectual life of seventeenth-century New England left Cambridge and London when their tradition was in the first flush of transformation. They did not depart until into that tradition, under the guise of a doctrine of covenants made by God with man, there had been injected many ideas which derived, not from theology and revelation, but from law, from the study of nature, from the principles of a reason and common sense. As time went on, the incompatibility of these ideas with the official confession was bound to become more apparent. Seen in this light, the development of rationalism in eighteenth-century New England is not a phe-

nomenon produced entirely by the stimulation of imported ideas. The intellectual life of American Puritans in the seventeenth century was by no means so sparse and monotonous as it has sometimes been accused of being. The pristine doctrine was not rigorous, ironclad, and inflexible; it had in it the elements of complexity, the seeds of future growth, making for diversity and contradiction. That period which is sometimes spoken of as the "glacial age" was not an era of intellectual dearth and philosophical sterility, but one of slow progression toward the ultimate separation of the diverse attitudes which had somehow been awkwardly and unwittingly put together in the covenant theology of Ames, Preston, and Sibbes. It was, therefore, no accident, no violent break in the course of New England thought, that John Wise should shift the grounds for defending Congregationalism from the Bible to the laws of reason and nature and to the character of the social compact. It is also not surprising to find that when Jonathan Edwards came to feel that rationalism and ethics had stifled the doctrine of God's sovereignty and dethroned the doctrine of grace, he threw over the whole covenant scheme, repudiated the conception of transmission of sin by judicial imputation, declared God unfettered by any agreement or obligation, made grace irresistible, and annihilated the natural ability of man. It was Jonathan Edwards who went back to the doctrine from which the tradition had started: went back, not to what the first generation of New Englanders had held, but to Calvin, and who became, therefore, the first consistent and authentic Calvinist in New England.

PART
TWO

The Revolution and the New

Republic

1763-1825

On July 4, 1826, John Adams and Thomas Jefferson died, just half a century after the adoption of the Declaration of Independence. Some days before his death Jefferson reflected with profound satisfaction upon the achievement of the Revolutionary generation: "All eyes are opened, or opening, to the rights of man. The general spread of the light of science has already laid open to every view the palpable truth, that the mass of mankind has not been born with saddles on their backs, nor a favored few booted and spurred, ready to ride them legitimately, by the grace of God." These were not the vain musings of old age. In two generations America had traveled the long road from colonial dependence to stable nationhood. The bold experiment in republican self-government according to the principles of the Declaration of Independence—the experiment to which Jefferson and Adams devoted their lives—had created a flourishing new order in the New World.

This bold experiment of 1776 was undertaken most reluctantly. In 1763 the American colonists showed no serious signs of disloyalty to an empire that left them ample room for economic growth and local self-government. As grievances mounted under the new imperial program of taxation, regulation, and control, however, Americans faced a succession of fateful choices. To accept and obey the novel requirements of Crown and Parliament would, they felt, expose their liberties and property to arbitrary control. To assert their rights as colonists, as Englishmen, as men, would create dangerous conflicts with an established and respected authority. The leaders of colonial opinion chose to fight. Each crisis from the Stamp Act quarrel of 1765 to the skirmishing at Lexington and Concord a decade later seemed to open fresh ways and means toward independence. By July 4, 1776, the representatives of the colonies had decided to stake everything on a bid for nationhood.

The several colonies learned by painful experience that they could not each stand alone against the English. A more perfect union was required to make their protests effective, to conduct the struggle for independence, and to make independence stick. Again a most reluctant citizenry conquered its fears of centralized power to establish a firm Union with authority to meet the common problems of the independent states—problems once handled by the imperial regime. The Articles of Confederation, which left the general government under the final control of sovereign states, provided a transition to the Constitution of 1787.

After 1789 Americans fought out their differences within the framework of the Constitution. Parties arose over the issues of broad or narrow construction, of centralized or decentralized power, of agrarian or commercial-industrial predominance, of French or English sympathies. A decade of Hamiltonian nationalism was ended with the "Revolution of 1800" and the triumph of the Jeffersonian Republicans. Following the War of 1812, the tide of opinion turned again toward the broad use of national powers to stimulate and direct economic development. The old political alignment of Federalists and Republicans disappeared, and party lines remained blurred until Andrew Jackson emerged in 1828 as the leader of a powerful new Democratic coalition.

The half-century from the Revolution to 1825 was overwhelmingly a political age. The establishment of the independent republic was the great concern that enlisted the creative energies of the nation. Confronted with urgent and exciting political tasks, the best talents of America spent themselves in reasoning out solutions—and helping to give them effect. Jefferson, Madison, Hamilton, Adams, Marshall: these are at once the political and the intellectual greats of the early Republic. The boundary between significant thought and effective action is thinner here than in any other era of American history.

Chronological Chart: 1763 to 1825

THE AMERICAN SCENE . . . .

POLITICAL

1764 Parliament passed Sugar Act and tightened enforcement of the customs service.
1765 Stamp Act passed; Stamp Act Congress convened.
1767 Townshend Acts passed.
1768 British troops occupied Boston.
1770 "Boston Massacre," *March 5.*
1773 Tea Act passed; "Boston Tea Party," *Dec. 16.*
1774 "Intolerable Acts" passed.
1st Continental Congress met in Philadelphia, *Sept. 5.*
1775 Battles of Lexington and Concord, *April 19.*
2nd Continental Congress convened, *May 10.*
1776 Declaration of Independence, *July 4.*
1777 Vermont became an independent state.
1778 France and the U.S. signed treaty of alliance.
1781 Articles of Confederation ratified by 13 states.
Cornwallis surrendered to Washington at Yorktown.
1783 Treaty of Paris ended Revolutionary War.
1785 Ordinance of 1785 passed by Congress.
1786 Annapolis Convention convened.
1786-1787 Shays' Rebellion in western Massachusetts.
1787 Northwest Ordinance enacted by Congress.
Constitutional Convention met in Philadelphia, *May-Sept.*
1787-1788 Constitution ratified by 11 states.
1789-1797 George Washington, president.
1790 Hamilton's debt plan enacted by Congress.
1791 1st Bank of the United States established.
1792 Bill of Rights ratified.
1793 "Citizen Genet" affair.
1794 Jay's Treaty with Britain signed.
1795 Pinckney's Treaty with Spain signed.
1797-1801 John Adams, president.
1797 "XYZ" affair.
1798 Alien and Sedition Acts passed, *June-July.*
Kentucky and Virginia Resolutions, *Nov.-Dec.*
1801-1809 Thomas Jefferson, president.
1801-1804 Tripolitan War.
1803 *Marbury* vs. *Madison* decision.
1806 1st Non-Importation Act passed, *April 18.*
1807 Aaron Burr's conspiracy trial held.
Embargo Act passed, *Dec. 22.*
1808 African slave trade ended by law, *Jan. 1.*
1809 Non-Intercourse Act passed, *March 1.*
1809-1817 James Madison, president
1810 Macon's Bill No. 2 enacted.
1812-1814 War of 1812.
1814 Hartford Convention of New England states met.
1816 2nd Bank of the United States chartered.
1817-1825 James Monroe, president.
1817 Rush-Bagot Agreement signed.
1818 Convention of 1818 signed.
1819 *McCulloch* vs. *Maryland* decision.
1820 Missouri Compromise passed.
1823 Monroe Doctrine announced.
1825 John Quincy Adams elected president.

ECONOMIC AND SOCIAL

1763-1765 Business slump followed French and Indian War.

1767 Cotton successfully raised in South Carolina.
1769 Watauga settlement established in Tennessee.
Daniel Boone entered Kentucky.

1775 1st antislavery society formed by Franklin and Rush.
Daniel Boone founded Boonesborough, Ky.
U.S. began outproducing England and Wales in pig iron.
1776-1783 Wartime deficit financing caused business boom.

1781 Bank of North America chartered by Congress.

1784-1788 1st major American depression resulted from unstable commerce and the British banking crisis of 1784.
1785 1st American turnpike authorized by Virginia.
1786-1788 New Ohio Co., Scioto Co., and Symmes Co. formed for settlement of upper Ohio valley.
1787 1st American cotton mill founded at Beverly, Mass.

1789-1800 Prosperity resulted from European war demand for American produce and shipping.
1790 1st U.S. census: 3,929,627.
1792 New York Stock Exchange founded.
1793 Eli Whitney invented the cotton gin, causing spectacular rise in cotton production in the lower South.

1801-1811 Trade expanded until 1807, dropped during blockades and embargo of 1807-1808, then revived 1809-1811.
1803 Louisiana Purchase expanded U.S. by 140%.
1804-1806 Lewis and Clark explored the Far Northwest.
1806-1807 Pike explored Colorado and New Mexico.
1807 Fulton's steamboat made successful Hudson run.
1808-1814 Non-Intercourse policy and War of 1812 stimulated domestic manufacturing.

1811 Steamboats entered upon Ohio-Mississippi rivers.
1812-1814 Foreign trade shrank to all-time low.
1813 "Waltham system" of textile manufacturing begun, featuring power operation, large capital investment, and employment of unskilled labor.

1818 Cumberland Road completed to Wheeling.
1819-1822 1st major banking crisis caused collapse of land speculations and general depression of business.
1820 U.S. census: 9,638,453 (7.2% urban).
1825 Erie Canal officially opened.

INTELLECTUAL

1765 1st medical school in America founded at College of Philadelphia.
1766 1st Methodist society in America formed in New York.

1776 Thomas Paine's *Common Sense* published, *Jan.*
1779 Phi Beta Kappa founded at William and Mary College.
1st Universalist church formed at Gloucester, Mass.
1780 American Academy of Arts and Sciences chartered.
1783 Enrollment at Yale, highest in U.S., reached 270.
1785 1st state college, University of Georgia, founded.

c1789–1820 "Roman Revival" architecture became vogue.
1790 Duncan Phyfe opened furniture shop in New York.
1791 William Bartram's *Travels* published.
1792 H. H. Brackenridge's *Modern Chivalry* published.
1793 "Connecticut Wits," a group of nationalistic poets, published *American Poems*.
1794 Thomas Paine's *Age of Reason* published.

1797 Frontier camp-meeting revivals began great vogue.
1798–1801 Charles Brockden Brown published his series of Gothic romances.
1802 Ohio enabling act set principle of granting each Western state two townships for a university.
1803 Boston's 1st Roman Catholic Church dedicated.

1809 Washington Irving's *History of New York by Diedrich Knickerbocker* published; the name "Knickerbocker school" was given to New York writers like Irving, Bryant, Cooper.
1812 Benjamin Rush's *Medical Inquiries and Observations upon the Diseases of the Mind* published.

1818 *American Journal of Science and Arts* founded.
1819 Unitarian Church founded by W. E. Channing.
University of Virginia founded as 1st U.S. college not requiring chapel attendance or religious profession.
c1820–1860 "Greek Revival" architecture became vogue.
1823 James Fenimore Cooper's *The Pioneers* published.

1764 James Hargreaves invented the spinning jenny.
1765 Diderot's rationalistic *Encyclopedia* completed.
1768–1771 Captain Cook made 1st voyage to the Pacific.
1768–1774 Catherine II's Russia expanded in Turkish war.
1769 James Watt invented the modern steam engine.
1772, 1793, 1795 Poland partitioned by Prussia, Russia, and Austria.
1774–1792 Louis XVI, king of France.
1774–1785 Warren Hastings, Governor-General of British India, initiated social and economic reforms.
1776 Adam Smith's *Wealth of Nations* published.
1778 Voltaire and Rousseau died.
1778–1779 France, Holland, and Spain declared war on England, during American Revolution.
1781 Immanuel Kant's *Critique of Pure Reason* ushered in philosophical idealism of the Romantic Age.
1785 Edmund Cartwright invented the power loom.

1788 Australia settled by English convict colonists.
1789 The Bastille stormed, marking start of the French Revolution, *July 14.*

1792–1797 War of the First Coalition against France.
1793 Louis XVI and Marie Antoinette executed in Paris.
1793–1794 The Reign of Terror in France.

1796–1798 General Bonaparte campaigned in Italy and Egypt.
1798 Malthus' *Essay on Population* published.
1799–1804 Napoleon Bonaparte, First Consul of France.
1800 Alessandro Volta developed the electric battery.
1801 Great Britain and Ireland became United Kingdom.
1804 Napoleon crowned Emperor of the French.
1806 Napoleon issued the Berlin Decree, *Nov. 21.*
1807 Britain issued Orders in Council, *Jan. 7, Nov. 11.*
Napoleon issued the Milan Decree, *Dec. 17.*

1809–1825 South and Central American nations won independence from Spain and Portugal.
1814–1831 Scott's "Waverley novels" published.
1814 Napoleon exiled to Elba; Congress of Vienna met.
1815 Napoleon returned, met defeat at Waterloo, and was exiled to St. Helena, *Mar.-June.*
Quadruple Alliance and Holy Alliance signed.
1817 British Coercion Acts suspended *habeas corpus.*

1819 Singapore founded by Sir Stamford Raffles.
1820 Congress of Troppau quelled liberalism in Naples.
1821 Greece declared independence from Turkish rule.
1822 Congress of Verona crushed Spanish reformers.
1825 World's 1st railway line opened in England.

CHAPTER 4

The Struggle for Independence:

1763 to 1783

A NEW IMPERIAL COURSE

The year 1763 was a year of triumph for the British Empire. The arch-rival, France, had been defeated in India and driven from the North American continent in the Seven Years' War of 1756-1763. (The conflict in America was known as the French and Indian War.) Britain ruled the seas and held sway over the greatest empire in the history of the western world. For many Americans the war had been a grand common enterprise. As Benjamin Franklin wrote in 1760: "No one can more sincerely rejoice than I do, on the reduction of Canada, and this is not merely as I am a colonist, but as I am a Briton."

The rejoicing quickly ended when the English faced up to the costs and responsibilities of their American conquests—and when the colonists in turn faced a determined British effort to secure their new frontiers in Canada and the Mississippi Valley, to enforce the system of commercial controls, and to support the needed troops and officials in part by taxing the Americans. Ironically—as Professor Lawrence Gipson maintains in Document 39—the achievement of British supremacy in North America reduced the colonists' dependence on England for protection against hostile French and Spanish neighbors and thus freed the Americans to defy British demands even at the risk of open conflict. The glorious French and Indian War itself had left a residue of resentment. In many English eyes the Americans had fought too little and paid too little and had shown an unpatriotic tendency to seek profits by trading with the enemy, especially through West Indian ports. One effort to penalize that trade, the issuing of broad search warrants (called Writs of Assistance), provoked in Massachusetts the first great protest statement of the Revolutionary era: James Otis' plea in 1761 for the rights of Englishmen against the arbitrary exercise of Parliamentary power.

Thus in 1763 the British Empire was set on a fatal new course by King George III and his first minister, George Grenville. Parliament, which had previously exercised direct authority over the American colonies mainly in the field of external commerce, now asserted its power in a series of provocative acts touching vital internal affairs of the Americans. The Proclamation of 1763 was issued by the British government as part of a new policy to restrain westward migration in the interest of frontier defense but also in the interest of English land speculators and fur traders. The Currency Act of 1764 applied to all the colonies a prohibition on the issue of paper money which had previously been limited to New England. The Quartering Act of 1765 required the colonists to house British troops in public and private buildings when barracks were lacking and to furnish part of their provisions.

Most important were the acts designed to raise a revenue for the support of soldiers and royal officials, together with new measures expanding and strengthening the enforcement machinery. The Revenue (or Sugar) Act of 1764 was followed by the explosive Stamp Act of 1765 and the Townshend Acts of 1767. Under the new program, tax revenues did begin to flow into the hands of royal officials, and the whole system of commercial regulations was administered with unprecedented vigor and efficiency. There was one drastic consequence which had not been anticipated seriously by imperial policy-makers: they had stirred up a hornet's nest in America.

PROTEST TO REVOLUTION

The Old Empire before 1763 was not all peace and harmony. If Americans generally prospered under British rule, the mercantilist system still created serious conflicts of economic interest between colony and metropolis—as one may judge from Adam Smith's analysis (Document 18) or Benjamin Franklin's (Document 17). If loyalty to Crown and Empire generally persisted even through a decade of bitter quarreling after 1763, it was not an unconditional loyalty. Americans had won a large measure of freedom and self-government within the Empire. They claimed the "rights of Englishmen" under the British Constitution and the privileges provided in their colonial charters as essential terms of their membership in the Empire. To make them choose between their accustomed liberties and powers, on the one hand, and their imperial loyalty, on the other, would be a dangerous experiment, as some English critics of Parliamentary policy explained. The risk would be compounded if a set of colonies with important differences and misunderstandings within and among themselves should recognize a common external danger and form a common front.

The colonial protest movement was born with the arrival of Grenville's new imperial measures. Enforcement of the Revenue Act of 1764 began to pinch colonial merchants. The Quartering Act of 1765 was met with defiance by the New York Assembly, leading Parliament to order a blanket veto on all legislative acts until the assembly capitulated. The Stamp Act provoked a major crisis.

Urged on by Patrick Henry, the Virginia House of Burgesses sounded the alarm. Their "Virginia Resolves," attacking Parliamentary taxation of the colonies, were echoed throughout colonial America. Massachusetts, constant partner of Virginia in leading the discontented, responded with a call for an intercolonial congress. Delegates sent by nine colonial assemblies met in New York in October 1765 to declare their right as Englishmen to tax themselves through their own representatives. (See Document 44.) Of great consequence was the simple fact that the several colonies had convened *on their own initiative*—without benefit of imperial authority—to present a united protest.

Not only did the colonists devise a precedent for combining forces in extra-legal assemblies; they discovered the effectiveness of direct action. From Boston to Charleston, crowds of angry colonists intimidated the appointed stamp distributors. Men rioted in the streets, tore down houses, hanged and burned their enemies in effigy, forced resignations from the distributors of stamps, raised liberty poles, and toasted "Liberty, Property, and no Stamp Duty." (The "mobs," it should be noted, as well as the radical Sons of Liberty, were not a wild rabble: they were organized and more or less controlled by responsible members of provincial society—merchants, lawyers, and the like.) The net effects of the protest were to make the Stamp Act a dead letter, to provide the colonists with experience in organizing a resistant movement, and to give them a sense of their collective power.

Repeal of the Stamp Act (1766) brought a brief pause to the colonial protest movement; New York went so far as to vote statues to William Pitt and George III. But news of the Townshend Acts (1767), imposing new import duties and establishing an American Board of Customs Commissioners at Boston, again spurred Americans into action. Townsmen swore off tea and other imported luxuries; women gathered in each other's houses to spin and weave their "home-spun"; merchants of the leading ports adopted non-importation agreements, which cooperative citizens enforced by boycotts, threats, and occasional applications of tar and feathers. Ammunition for the protest against Parliamentary taxation was supplied by the Circular Letter from the Massachusetts Assembly to the other colonies (Document 46). Faced with dissolution of their assembly, the unrepentant Massachusetts leaders gathered an extra-legal convention from the towns to voice their opposition.

The arrival of British troops in Boston (October 1768) to support the anxious customs commissioners introduced a new and dangerous source of friction. The ensuing "Boston Massacre" of March 5, 1770, may be reduced in retrospect to a bloody snowball fight; but the news of such an encounter, spread assiduously through the colonies, aroused the fear that colonial protests would be silenced by a standing army of redcoats.

Removal of the troops and repeal of the Townshend duties (1770) quieted resistance for awhile. Leaders like Sam Adams and Joseph Warren in Massachusetts and Patrick Henry, Thomas Jefferson, and Richard Henry Lee in Virginia improved their time by initiating committees of correspondence to tighten the links among the towns and the colonies. Then the passage of the Tea Act (1773), granting the English East India Company the privilege of marketing tea directly in America, provoked a new crisis. When Governor Thomas Hutchinson of Massachusetts refused the popular demand that the tea ships be sent away without unloading, a band of "Indians" mixed a potent salt-water brew in Boston Harbor.

Parliament replied with the Coercive (or Intolerable) Acts of 1774, designed to punish and overawe the unruly Bostonians. Instead, the disciplinary measures served to unify the colonies in resistance and bring their delegates together at Philadelphia in the first Continental Congress (September 1774). From this point on, the movement toward revolution gained momentum rapidly. Rejecting Joseph Galloway's plea for loyalty and compromise, the Congress asserted in effect that the colonial legislatures were competent to manage their own internal affairs (including, of course, the laying of taxes) without Parliamentary intervention. A Continental Association was formed to cut off commercial relations with England.

And the several colonies, Massachusetts in the lead, began to look to their militias for defense.

The encounter between Minutemen and British troops at Lexington and Concord (April 19, 1775) broadened into the colonial siege of Boston and finally, in July of 1776, into an open war for independence directed by the second Continental Congress.

The way from protest to revolution had been marked by the successive measures of the new imperial policy. These were met by colonial resistance, which led in turn to British acts of coercion. In the course of opposition the colonists had made effective use of existing political machinery—their assemblies, town meetings, and militias, for example—and had devised new institutions outside the formal imperial system for their purposes: Sons of Liberty, associations to enforce economic boycotts, provincial Committees of Public Safety, Committees of Correspondence, and—most important—intercolonial congresses. When the moment came for declaring independence, the essential units of an American political system were at hand: provincial legislatures which had been managing their own affairs for months, a makeshift army fighting at Boston under General Washington; and a Continental Congress already exercising the powers of a common government.

As independent institutions evolved out of old colonial forms and recent protest organizations, so the principles of the Revolution developed from old ideas and traditions which had been given fresh meanings and applications in the debate of 1763-1776. A flood of speeches, pamphlets, and resolutions by such remarkable leaders of opinion as the Adamses, John Dickinson, Thomas Jefferson, and Patrick Henry instructed the colonists in their rights—at first in their traditional right to tax themselves, later in their right to manage all internal affairs through their elected representatives. In *Common Sense,* published in January 1776 (Document 49), Tom Paine moved the debate to a new level with his arguments on the evils of monarchy in general and the "sullen tempered Pharaoh of England" in particular; on the absurdity "in supposing a Continent to be perpetually governed by an island"; and on the urgent mission of America to give mankind a new example of free, republican government. Finally the great Declaration of Independence rested the American case for revolution on the universal grounds that governments are established by consent of the governed to secure the equal rights of man and may be overthrown when they betray their trust.

THE REVOLUTION

The last group of documents, 51-54, illustrates the terrible difficulties the new republic experienced in making good its claim to independence. With raw troops, weak finances, and scant supplies the loosely united Americans had to match forces with the leading power of the world. They found a priceless leader in Washington. In France they found an arsenal and later an indispensable ally, committed by its own national interests to the defeat of England. The Atlantic Ocean separating the English home base from the fighting front served Americans well; so did a spacious, decentralized country that gave them room to retreat and England an enormous bite to swallow. Although Tory enemies made trouble (especially in New York and the Carolinas) and Patriot friends sometimes placed local and private interests above the common cause, the American people nevertheless sustained the eight-year struggle and won recognition of their independence in the peace of 1783.

To complete their victory, as Washington warned (Document 54), Americans still faced the task of joining the states in a firm republican union.

Great Britain's New Imperial Course

<big>42</big> DEBT AND TAXES: THE BRITISH CASE

from Thomas Whately, *Considerations*, 1766

Great conquests come at great cost. The brilliant triumphs of the British in the Seven Years' War (1756-1763) brought vast territorial gains—in Canada, Cape Breton Island, the Mississippi and Ohio valleys, and Florida, in India and the West Indies, and on the African Senegal—but these triumphs also brought hard responsibilities and a swollen national debt of £130,000,000. By virtue of its costly victories, the British Empire of 1763 faced a new practical situation. Government leaders like George Grenville, Chancellor of the Exchequer (1763-1765), were ready to map a new imperial course adapted to that situation. Expert advisers like Thomas Whately, a permanent Treasury official, could be called upon to pen sharp pamphlets in defense of the program that would secure the expansive American frontiers, tighten the system of trade regulation, and especially shift more of the imperial tax burden to British Americans.

Thomas Whately's *Considerations on the Trade and Finances of This Kingdom* (1766) represents the reasoning of those who shaped, administered, and supported the new imperial policies. In their eyes a great war had been fought primarily in behalf of their North American colonies. The colonies, they believed, enjoyed the fruits of victory without sharing the costs. Such arguments would be convincing to Englishmen who observed that the American customs service failed to pay even its operating expenses; that the bill for defending the American frontier with ten thousand soldiers would exceed £300,000 a year; that English landowners were being taxed about a third of their incomes to meet the oppressive public debt. Practical arguments of the Americans concerning the "hidden taxes" exacted under the mercantilist system or their inability to pay new levies failed to sway official opinion. Colonial appeals to principle—"no taxation without representation"—seemed to them absurd. Were not Americans "virtually" represented by members of Parliament, who acted for the whole Empire, not for the relatively few constituents who elected them?

Edmund Burke (see Document 43) and other Parliamentary critics of the new course could not persuade the imperial authorities that they might seek a revenue in America only to lose an empire.

That the Wealth and the Power of *Great Britain* depend upon its Trade, is a Proposition, which it would be equally absurd in these times to dispute or to prove: It was not indeed apprehended that they were so great as they have been found to be, we did not ourselves know our own Strength, till the Vigour of the last War [the Seven Years' War] applied the Resources of that Wealth, and exerted the Efforts of that Power; in the progress of it many Acquisitions highly beneficial to Commerce were made; and the most important of them were secured by the Peace; but on the other hand, the Abilities of this Country were stretched to their utmost extent, and beyond their natural Tone: Trade must suffer in proportion; for the Price both of Labour and Materials was enhanced by the Number and the Weight of the new Taxes, and by the sudden and extraordinary demand which the Ruin of the *French* Navigation brought upon *Great Britain:* in consequence of which, rival Nations who were not before, may now be able in many articles to undersell us at Foreign Markets, and even become Competitors at our own. Both public and private Credit were at the same time oppressed by the vast and rapid encrease of the National Debt: the Value of the Stocks being sunk by the quantity of them, Scarcity of Money and high Rates of Interest ensued; and the large unfunded Debt which remained behind, aggravated the Evil, and affected every Money-

Text: Thomas Whately, *Considerations on the Trade and Finances of This Kingdom* (London: G. Wilkie, 1766), pp. 3-4, 68-82.

transaction. These are Circumstances of very serious concern, and important to the decision of any enquiry into our national Situation: . . .

But of all the Measures which were pursued for the Benefit of Trade, those were by far the most important which respected the Colonies, who have been of late the Darling Object of their Mother Country's Care: We are not yet recovered from a War undertaken solely for their Protection: Every Object for which it was begun, is accomplished; and still greater are obtained than at first were even thought of; but whatever may be the Value of the Acquisitions in *America*, the immediate Benefit of them is to the Colonies; and this Country feels it only in their Prosperity; for though the Accessions of Trade and of Territory which were obtained by the Peace, are so many Additions to the Empire and the Commerce of *Great Britain* at large, yet they principally affect that Part of her Dominions, and that Branch of her Trade, to which they immediately relate. To improve these Advantages, and to forward still further the peculiar Interests of the Colonies, was the chief Aim of the Administration in the Period now before me. . . .

Were there no other Ground to require a Revenue from the Colonies, then as a Return for these Obligations, it would alone be a sufficient Foundation: Add to these the Advantages obtained for them by the Peace; add the Debt incurred by a War undertaken for their Defense only; the Distress thereby brought upon the Finances, upon the Credit both publick and private, upon the Trade, and upon the People of this Country; and it must be acknowledged that no Time was ever so seasonable for claiming their Assistance. The Distribution is too unequal, of Benefits only to the Colonies, and of all the Burthens upon the Mother Country; and yet no more was desired, than that they should contribute to the Preservation of the Advantages they have received, and take upon themselves a small Share of the Establishment necessary for their own Protection: Upon these Principles several new Taxes were laid upon the Colonies: Many of them were indeed, as I have already shewn, rather Regulations of Trade than Funds of Revenue: But some were intended to answer both Purposes: In others the Produce was the principal Object; and yet even the most productive of all, were of that Kind which is perhaps more tender of Trade than any other: The same Sum could not have been raised with so little Oppression by Impost as by Stamp Duties, for they do not affect some Articles of Commerce more than others; they do not even fall upon

Men of any particular Denomination: They are heavy upon none, because they are paid only occasionally; and they are collected with more Ease to the Subject than any; . . .

But it was never intended to impose on them any Share of the National Debt: They were never called upon to defray any Part of our domestic civil Expences: The Legislature only required of them to contribute to the Support of those Establishments, which are equally interesting to all the Subjects of *Great Britain*. The Charge of the Navy, Army, and Ordinance, of *Africa*, and of *America*, is about 3,000,000*l. per ann.* These surely are general; they are as important to the Colonies as to the Mother Country; as necessary to their Protection, as conducive to their Welfare, as to our own: If all share the Benefit, they should also share the Burthen; the Whole ought not to be born by a Part: The *Americans* are in Number a Fifth of the *British* Subjects; yet the Aid required of them was in the Proportion only of about one in twenty; and to make it still more easy, the Expenditure was restrained to that Country. . . .

. . . We have their All, they say; all that they can gain, all that they can raise is sent hither, to purchase *British* Manufactures, and we must therefore be content to see their Demand diminished, by so much as any Revenue we require may amount to: But does their All really even center in *Great Britain?* Their illicit Trade was computed during the last Peace to be about a Third of their actual Imports; and the Money diverted from that to the Support of the Establishment, is certainly no national Loss: Of the Supply from hence, a Third is also supposed to be in foreign Commodities; so that upon these Calculations, the British Manufactures do not amount in Value to one-Half of the *American* Consumption; and the utmost Force therefore of the Argument is, that we lose a Vent for 80,000*l.* worth of Manufactures, by getting an Accession of 160,000*l.* to the Revenue. . . .

The Argument is nearly the same, it is only weaker, when instead of the Consumption of the Colonies, the Consequence of that Consumption, their Debt to this Country, is pleaded, and the new Duties are represented as depriving them of the Means of discharging it: This Complaint would be just, if a Revenue had been exacted from them, without furnishing them with Resources for raising it; but the Peace, and the Measures taken since for improving the Advantages of it, have done much more: For it would be rating the Cessions made by *France* very low indeed, if the Security which is the Consequence of them; if the vast Accession of Territory; if the Intercourse opened with the *Indians,* their greater Demand for Cloathing, Arms, Spirits, and other Commodities, and the Monopoly of their Return in Beaver, Furs, and all Sorts of Peltry; if the Improvements of the Cod, Seal, and Sea-Cow Fishery; the Establishment of the Right to cut Log-wood; the Facilities obtained in the *Spanish* Trade by the Approximation of our Settlements to theirs; and the other Acquisitions of the Peace; were not all together valued to the *Americans* alone, at a Sum much larger than the Revenue expected from them. In this Enumeration I have not included such Articles as have lately received particular Encouragement; the Whale Fishery, the Rice, the Hemp and Flax, and the Timber; nor the Preference shewn in so many Instances to the Produce of our Islands, over that of Foreign Plantations. By all these Means we have encreased the Abilities of the Colonies, to purchase our Manufactures, to make Returns for the Supply, and to discharge their Debts in *Great Britain:* All Objections therefore to the Taxing them, as affecting their Trade, are resolvable at last into a Complaint, that we have not done more for them. We have opened to them new Funds of Wealth; and if we apply'd a Part of it to the National Service, the Deduction was only from our Boon, not from their Property: That after all Taxes paid, if all had continued, would have been greater than ever; and the Commerce said to be oppressed, would, upon the Whole, have been far more flourishing than if no Duties had been laid, and at the same Time none of the above-mentioned Advantages given. . . .

Nor is this the only Fund lately provided for them: The Encrease of the Establishments there furnishes them with another, which alone would more than ballance the Account: For those Establishments during the late Peace did not amount to 100,000*l. per ann.* and at present they are about 350,000*l.* exclusive of the Naval Expence which also is greater than it was, and exclusive of Extraordinaries, which in every Part of that Service are augmented; including these, the Charge must be between four and five hundred thousand Pounds *per ann.* and though the Whole is not spent in that Country, the Cloathing, Arms and other Articles being provided here; yet no Deductions, however liberal, will reduce the actual Expenditure in *America* near so low as 160,000*l.* and whatever the Excess may be above that Sum, it must be remitted thither from *Great Britain;* whatever may be the Amount, it is at the least four Times as much as it used to be: So that on this Ground also the Colonies are enriched; and they are here again upon the Whole in much

better Circumstances, than if there had been no additional Taxes, and at the same Time no additional Establishments. . . .

The only remaining Argument worth Notice, is, that Restraints being laid upon the Trade of the Colonies, they ought therefore to be exempted from contributing to the Revenue: A very general Argument indeed, equally applicable to all Times, and to all Taxes; but which would not be a just Inference even from a Supposition that they had no other Trade than to their Mother Country; and is preposterous when applied to a People, whose Lands through all their various Soils and Climates are luxuriantly rich in almost all the Productions of the Earth, who besides their inexhaustible Fisheries, and besides their Intercourse with *Great Britain,* carry on a most extensive Traffick with the *West-Indies,* with *Africa,* and with all Parts of *Europe* to the Southward of Cape *Finesterre;* and whose Seas are from all these Causes throng'd with Ships, and their Rivers floating with Commerce. This flourishing State of their Commerce contradicts all the Complaints which have been made of the Restraints laid upon it: For such Restraints have subsisted from a very early Period, and under them that Trade has been established and enlarged, which it is now pretended they oppress: They must have been more oppressive upon Infant Colonies; yet they never prevented their Growth; on the contrary they have been found at all Times, and in all Circumstances, to be indispensably necessary; and in reality, the Acts of Trade do no more than express an implied Condition, which is the first Principle of Colonization; for no State would ever have allowed its Subjects to remove into a distant Part of its Dominions, if it were thereby to be deprived of their Services and Usefulness: At home their Consumption and their Labour were all for the Benefit of the Country they lived in; Commodities raised, Manufactures made, or foreign Merchandize imported there, were their only possible Supply: There only, or by Exportation from thence, could they find a Vent for so much of their own Produce as they wished to dispose of; and they were thus by their Situation alone the Means by which Industry, Navigation, and Revenue, were supported. Upon their Migration, this Necessity ceased: They might then supply themselves from other Places; and give to Foreigners the Carriage, the Use, and the Advantage of their Produce. To prevent such a Perversion, the Acts of Trade confine them in several Respects, and to a certain Degree, only to the same Circumstances in which their Fellow Subjects continue; and compel them by Law to be as serviceable to their

Country, as they were before obliged to be by Situation. And that exclusive Trade with their Colonies, which is claimed with more or less Rigour by all the *European* Powers, is not an injurious Monopoly established by Force; but is a due Exercise of that indisputable Right which every State, in Exclusion of all others, has to the Services of its own Subjects. Nor was the Exercise of it ever supposed to imply an Exemption from Taxes: . . .

If from what has been said it appears, that no Principle of Finance or of Commerce forbids the Taxing of the Colonies for the Purposes of Revenue only; it must on the other Hand be admitted that the Circumstances of this Country [England] call for every Aid which any of its Subjects can give: And there was a peculiar Propriety in requiring it from the *Americans,* who have contributed so little and for whom so much had been done: . . .

43

GREAT EMPIRES AND LITTLE MINDS: A BRITISH CONCILIATOR

from Edmund Burke, *Conciliation with the Colonies,* 1775

America had her Tories, England her Whigs: great Whigs.

The great Whig, Edmund Burke, would class Whately (Document 42) and his superiors among the "vulgar and mechanical politicians" who "think that nothing exists but what is gross and material." On the contrary, Burke insisted, that "mysterious whole," the British Empire, had been held together by the spirit of the English Constitution. Burke's image of an imperial commonwealth, united not by force or paper regulations but essentially by the traditional principles of free Englishmen, may suggest one reason for the painful hesitation of most Americans in taking the final step to independence. Burke's great "Conciliation" speech in the English House of Commons (March 22, 1775), from which the following selection is taken, reviewed the circumstances of colonial history which had shaped Americans into a special breed of Englishmen. He understood that Americans, though reluctant, were capable of striking for independence, and he pleaded with Parliament to restore imperial harmony by recognizing the right of the colonies to tax themselves.

No outsider was better equipped than Edmund Burke (1729-1797) to understand the Americans. His Whig party principles, and perhaps his Irish origins, made him a sympathetic judge, while his editorial duties for the *Annual Register,* his position as colonial agent for New York, and his role as a leading Whig spokesman in Parliament required close knowledge of American affairs. Distinguished for his eloquent criticisms of British actions in Ireland and India as well as in America, Burke later wrote and spoke with equal brilliance in attacking the French Revolution of 1789. Burke has been both praised and blamed as a father of the "conservative" outlook, with its emphasis on tradition and experience—not abstract theory—as the best guides to political action.

. . . My hold of the colonies is in the close affection which grows from common names, from kindred blood, from similar privileges, and equal protection. These are ties which, though light as air, are as strong as links of iron. Let the colonists always keep the idea of their civil rights associated with your government,—they will cling and grapple to you, and no force under heaven will be of power to tear them from their allegiance. But let it be once understood that your government may be one thing, and their

Text: Edmund Burke, "Speech on Moving His Resolutions for Conciliation with the Colonies," *Works* ("Bohn's Standard Library" [London: George Bell & Sons, 1889]), I, 508-09.

privileges another, that these two things may exist without any mutual relation, the cement is gone—the cohesion is loosened—and everything hastens to decay and dissolution. As long as you have the wisdom to keep the sovereign authority of this country as the sanctuary of liberty, the sacred temple consecrated to our common faith, wherever the chosen race and sons of England worship freedom, they will turn their faces towards you. The more they multiply, the more friends you will have; the more ardently they love liberty, the more perfect will be their obedience. Slavery they can have anywhere. It is a weed that grows in every soil. They may have it from Spain; they may have it from Prussia. But, until you become lost to all feeling of your true interest and your natural dignity, freedom they can have from none but you. This is the commodity of price of which you have the monopoly. This is the true Act of Navigation which binds to you the commerce of the colonies, and through them secures to you the wealth of the world. Deny them this participation of freedom, and you break that sole bond which originally made, and must still preserve, the unity of the empire. Do not entertain so weak an imagination as that your registers and your bonds, your affidavits and your sufferances, your cockets and your clearances, are what form the great securities of your commerce. Do not dream that your letters of office, and your instructions, and your suspending clauses, are the things that hold together the great contexture of the mysterious whole. These things do not make your government. Dead instruments, passive tools as they are, it is the spirit of the English communion that gives all their life and efficacy to them. It is the spirit of the English Constitution which, infused through the mighty mass, pervades, feeds, unites, invigorates, vivifies every part of the empire, even down to the minutest member. . . .

All this, I know well enough, will sound wild and chimerical to the profane herd of those vulgar and mechanical politicians who have no place among us; a sort of people who think that nothing exists but what is gross and material, and who, therefore, far from being qualified to be directors of the great movement of empire, are not fit to turn a wheel in the machine. But to men truly initiated and rightly taught, these ruling and master principles which, in the opinion of such men as I have mentioned, have no substantial existence, are in truth everything, and all in all. Magnanimity in politics is not seldom the truest wisdom; and a great empire and little minds go ill together. If we are conscious of our station, and glow with zeal to fill our places as becomes our station and ourselves, we ought to auspicate all our public proceedings on America with the old warning of the church, *Sursum corda!* We ought to elevate our minds to the greatness of that trust to which the order of providence has called us. By adverting to the dignity of this high calling our ancestors have turned a savage wilderness into a glorious empire, and have made the most extensive and the only honorable conquests —not by destroying, but by promoting the wealth, the number, the happiness of the human race. Let us get an American revenue as we have got an American empire. English privileges have made it all that it is; English privileges alone will make it all it can be. . . .

Reluctant Rebels: Degrees of Separation

44

A DECLARATION OF COLONIAL RIGHTS

from "Declaration of Rights of the Stamp Act Congress," October 19, 1765

The Stamp Act (1765) rounded out a series of Parliamentary measures lately designed by George Grenville and his political friends to draw revenue from America. Following the Sugar (or Revenue) Act of 1764, the Stamp Tax confronted the American colonists with a new and alarming prospect. Henceforth, it seemed, the Parliament in Westminster not only would enforce its trade laws rigorously but would lay a heavy hand upon affairs previously left, in fact if not in theory, largely under the control of colonial legislatures. Above all, the Stamp Act would undermine that hard-won and most prized privilege of the colonial governments: the power of the purse.

It mattered little to the colonists that Englishmen at home were used to paying a stamp tax on legal documents, newspapers, almanacs, playing cards, and other printed matter. Nor did it soothe colonial feelings when prominent native Americans were chosen to distribute the stamped paper. The Stamp Act appeared to many throughout the colonies as it did to a rising young Boston lawyer, John Adams, who wrote in his diary of "that enormous engine fabricated by the British Parliament, for battering down all the rights and liberties of America." "Our presses have groaned," Adams observed, "our pulpits have thundered, our legislatures have resolved, our towns have voted, the crown officers have everywhere trembled."

The American protest went beyond talk: merchants of the leading commercial cities agreed to boycott British goods; Sons of Liberty were organized in towns and villages; angry mobs intimidated the tax collectors and effectively nullified the Stamp Act. Parliament had touched a raw nerve, and Americans quickly found a common voice, a common will to organize and act.

In October 1765, nine colonies sent delegates to the Stamp Act Congress in New York. There, "upon mature deliberation," they declared their rights and grievances. No doubt their protestations of loyalty to the crown and of "all due subordination" to Parliament were genuine. Yet the ringing assertion of their right to tax themselves contained the prophecy of revolution.

Saturday, Oct. 19th, 1765, A. M.—The congress met according to adjournment, and resumed, &c. as yesterday; and upon mature deliberation, agreed to the following declarations of the rights and grievances of the colonists in America, which were ordered to be inserted:

The members of this congress, sincerely devoted, with the warmest sentiments of affection and duty to his majesty's person and government; inviolably attached to the present happy establishment of the protestant succession; and with minds deeply impressed by a sense of the present and impending misfortunes of the British colonies on this continent; having considered as maturely as time would permit, the circumstances of the said colonies, esteem it our indispensable duty to make the following declarations, of our humble opinion, respecting the most essential rights and liberties of the colonists, and of the grievances under which they labor, by reason of several late acts of parliament.

1st. That his majesty's subjects in these colonies, owe the same allegiance to the crown of Great Britain, that is owing from his subjects born within the realm, and all due subordination to that august body, the parliament of Great Britain.

2d. That his majesty's liege subjects in these colonies are entitled to all the inherent rights and privileges of his natural born subjects within the kingdom of Great Britain.

3d. That it is inseparably essential to the freedom of a people, and the undoubted rights of Englishmen, that no taxes should be imposed on them, but with their own consent, given personally, or by their representatives.

4th. That the people of these colonies are not, and from their local circumstances, cannot be, represented in the house of commons in Great Britain.

5th. That the only representatives of the people of these colonies, are persons chosen therein, by themselves; and that no taxes ever have been,

Text: Hezekiah Niles (ed.), *Principles and Acts of the Revolution in America* (Baltimore: H. Niles, 1822), pp. 456-57.

or can be constitutionally imposed on them, but by their respective legislatures.

6th. That all supplies to the crown, being free gifts of the people, it is unreasonable and inconsistent with the principles and spirit of the British constitution, for the people of Great Britain to grant to his majesty the property of the colonists.

7th. That trial by jury is the inherent and invaluable right of every British subject in these colonies.

8th. That the late act of parliament, entitled, An act for granting and applying certain stamp duties, and other duties in the British colonies and plantations in America, &c. by imposing taxes on the inhabitants of these, colonies, and the said act, and several other acts, by extending the jurisdiction of the courts of admiralty beyond its ancient limits, have a manifest tendency to subvert the rights and liberties of the colonists.

9th. That the duties imposed by several late acts of parliament, from the peculiar circumstances of these colonies, will be extremely burthensome and grevious, and from the scarcity of specie, the payment of them absolutely impracticable.

10th. That as the profits of the trade of these colonies ultimately centre in Great Britain, to pay for the manufactures which they are obliged to take from thence, they eventually contribute very largely to all supplies granted there to the crown.

11th. That the restrictions imposed by several late acts of parliament, on the trade of these colonies, will render them unable to purchase the manufactures of Great Britain.

12th. That the increase, prosperity and happiness of these colonies, depend on the full and free enjoyment of their rights and liberties, and an intercourse, with Great Britain, mutually affectionate and advantageous.

13th. That it is the right of the British subjects in these colonies, to petition the king or either house of parliament.

Lastly, That it is the indispensable duty of these colonies to the best of sovereigns, to the mother country, and to themselves, to endeavor, by a loyal and dutiful address to his majesty, and humble application to both houses of parliament, to procure the repeal of the act for granting and applying certain stamp duties, of all clauses

of any other acts of parliament, whereby the jurisdiction of the admiralty is extended as aforesaid, and of the other late acts for the restriction of the American commerce.

45

PARLIAMENT'S REPEAL AND DECLARATION

from "The Declaratory Act," March 18, 1766

"Magnanimity in politics," Burke argued in 1775, "is not seldom the truest wisdom." For a moment, in 1766, it must have seemed to American colonists that Parliament either had discovered this lofty principle of government or had bowed beneath the storm of colonial resistance to the Stamp Act. For in March of 1766 the supreme legislature of the mighty British Empire repealed the year-old tax measure.

A passing acquaintance with Parliamentary affairs would have taught the American observer that the repealers were not moved by terror. For reasons of internal English politics, King George III swung his support from George Grenville to the Marquis of Rockingham as Cabinet head. Rockingham led a political faction (the Old Whigs) opposed to the Stamp Act as a troublesome measure with unfavorable effects on English trade. A show of magnanimity in the act of repeal was soon obscured by the accompanying Declaratory Act, which summarily asserted the supremacy of Parliament and the dependency of the colonial legislatures "in all cases whatsoever." With the passage of the Townshend duties in 1767, it became clear that the comprehensive powers claimed by Parliament in the Declaratory Act included the power to lay new taxes without colonial consent.

An act for the better securing the dependency of his Majesty's dominions in America upon the crown and parliament of Great Britain.

WHEREAS *several of the houses of representatives in his Majesty's colonies and plantations in* America, *have of late, against law, claimed to themselves, or to the general assemblies of the same, the sole and exclusive right of imposing duties and taxes upon his Majesty's subjects in the said colonies and plantations; and have, in pursuance of such claim, passed certain votes, resolutions, and orders, derogatory to the legislative authority of parliament, and inconsistent with the dependency of the said colonies and plantations upon the crown of* Great Britain: . . . be it declared . . . , That the said colonies and plantations in *America* have been, are, and of right ought to be, subordinate unto, and dependent upon the imperial crown and parliament of *Great Britain;* and that the King's majesty, by

and with the advice and consent of the lords spiritual and temporal, and commons of *Great Britain,* in parliament assembled, had, hath, and of right ought to have, full power and authority to make laws and statutes of sufficient force and validity to bind the colonies and people of *America,* subjects of the crown of *Great Britain,* in all cases whatsoever.

II. And be it further declared . . . , That all resolutions, votes, orders, and proceedings, in any of the said colonies or plantations, whereby the power and authority of the parliament of *Great Britain,* to make laws and statutes as aforesaid, is denied, or drawn into question, are, and are hereby declared to be, utterly null and void to all intents and purposes whatsoever.

Text: John Raithby (ed.), *The Statutes at Large of England and of Great Britain* (London: George Eyre and Andrew Strahan, 1811), XII, 480.

46

COLONY TO COLONY: THE RIGHTS OF ENGLISHMEN

from "Circular Letter from the House of Representatives of Massachusetts-Bay," February 11, 1768

Each new measure of Parliament in pursuit of its post-1763 imperial aims moved the colonists to further acts of resistance, to broader and firmer forms of organization, to more insistent statements of their rights.

The repeal of the Stamp Act, so hopefully received in America, was followed in 1767 by the laying of colonial import duties on paper, paint, lead and glass, among English products, and on tea. Charles Townshend, the new Chancellor of the Exchequer, hoped in this way to raise an American revenue and yet avoid colonial objections to the imposition of "internal taxes" (such as the Stamp Tax). With the enlarged revenues, royal officials in America might be supported directly, free of financial dependence on self-willed colonial legislatures.

Equally significant was Townshend's determination to enforce stringently the new revenue act and indeed the whole system of mercantile regulations and taxes. An American Board of Customs Commissioners was established in Boston with ample powers to reorganize, expand, and direct the activities of the imperial customs service.

Undoubtedly the Board did its work well—perhaps too well. Collections multiplied, to the substantial benefit of a swarm of royal officials; but at the same time harassed colonial merchants and their sympathizers were put in an ugly mood. Direct acts of resistance and obstruction moved the fearful commissioners to demand military protection, with consequences that can be learned from Document 47.

Once again the merchants of the leading cities applied economic pressures through their non-importation agreements of 1768-1769. Once again political leaders presented a common front against taxation without representation. In February 1768, the Massachusetts Assembly approved a Circular Letter drafted by the fiery Sam Adams and addressed to all the colonial assemblies of North America. Familiar American arguments, with some new ones, were advanced with vigor: that the colonists remained loyal to the King, "our common head and father"; that they acknowledged the supremacy of Parliament; but that the Parliament itself was bound by the British Constitution to recognize man's "right in nature" to yield his property only by his own free consent.

By May, three other colonial assemblies had voted their endorsement, and a fourth, Virginia, had drafted its own letter of concurrence and support. The Massachusetts Assembly was dissolved by Governor Francis Bernard; and when its deputies refused to rescind the Circular Letter, a new Assembly was again dissolved on angry orders from England. Massachusetts gave no signs of submission but only shifted the location of the protest movement to the towns and to extra-legal associations.

Province of the Massachusetts-Bay,
Feb. 11, 1768.

SIR,

The House of Representatives of this province have taken into their serious consideration the great difficulties that must accrue to themselves and their constituents, by the operation of the several Acts of Parliament imposing duties and taxes on the American colonies.

As it is a subject in which every colony is deeply interested, they have no reason to doubt but your House is duly impressed with its importance; and that such constitutional measures will be come into as are proper. It seems to be necessary, that all possible care should be taken that the representations of the several assemblies, upon so delicate a point, should harmonize with each other: the House therefore hope that this letter will be candidly considered in no other light

Text: John Almon (ed.), *A Collection of Interesting, Authentic Papers, Relative to the Dispute Between Great Britain and America; Shewing the Causes and Progress of That Misunderstanding, from 1764 to 1775* (London: J. Almon, 1777), pp. 191-93.

than as expressing a disposition freely to communicate their mind to a sister colony, upon a common concern, in the same manner as they would be glad to receive the sentiments of your, or any other House of Assembly on the continent.

The House have humbly represented to the Ministry their own sentiments: that his Majesty's High Court of Parliament is the supreme legislative power over the whole empire: that in all free states the constitution is fixed: and as the supreme legislative derives its power and authority from the constitution, it cannot overleap the bounds of it, without destroying its foundation: that the constitution ascertains and limits both sovereignty and allegiance: and therefore his Majesty's American subjects who acknowledge themselves bound by the ties of allegiance, have an equitable claim to the full enjoyment of the fundamental rules of the British constitution: that it is an essential unalterable right in nature, ingrafted into the British constitution as a fundamental law, and ever held sacred and irrevocable by the subjects within the realm, that what a man hath honestly acquired is absolutely his own which he may freely give, but cannot be taken from him without his consent: that the American subjects may therefore, exclusive of any consideration of charter rights, with a decent firmness adapted to the character of freemen and subjects, assert this natural constitutional right.

It is moreover their humble opinion, which they express with the greatest deference to the wisdom of the parliament; that the acts made there, imposing duties on the people of . this province, with the sole and express purpose of raising a revenue, are infringements of their natural and constitutional rights; because, as they are not represented in the British parliament, his Majesty's commons in Britain by those acts grant their property without their consent.

This House further are of opinion, that their constituents, considering their local circumstances, cannot by any possibility be represented in the Parliament; and that it will for ever be impracticable that they should be equally represented there, and consequently not at all; being separated by an ocean of a thousand leagues: that his Majesty's royal predecessors, for this reason, were graciously pleased to form a subordinate legislative here, that their subjects might enjoy the unalienable right of a representation. Also that considering the utter impracticability of their ever being fully and equally represented in parliament, and the great expence that must unavoidably attend even a partial representation there, this House think, that a taxation of their constituents, even without their consent, grievous as it is, would be preferable to any representation that could be admitted for them there.

Upon these principles, and also considering that were the right in the parliament ever so clear, yet for obvious reasons it would be beyond the rule of equity, that their constituents should be taxed on the manufactures of Great Britain here, in addition to the duties they pay for them in England, and other advantages arising to Great Britain from the acts of trade; this House have preferred a humble, dutiful, and loyal petition to our most gracious sovereign, and made such representation to his Majesty's ministers, as they apprehend would tend to obtain redress.

They have also submitted to consideration, whether any people can be said to enjoy any degree of freedom, if the crown, in addition to its undoubted authority of constituting a governor, should appoint him such a stipend as it shall judge proper, without the consent of the people, and at their expence: and whether, while the judges of the land, and other civil officers, hold not their commissions during good behaviour, their having salaries appointed for them by the crown, independant of the people, hath not a tendency to subvert the principles of equity, and endanger the happiness and security of the subject.

In addition to these measures, the House have wrote a letter to their agent, Mr. De Berdt, the sentiments of which he is directed to lay before the ministry; wherein they take notice of the hardship of the act for preventing mutiny and desertion; which requires the governor and council to provide enumerated articles for the King's marching troops, and the people to pay the expence: and also the commission of the gentlemen appointed commissioners of the customs to reside in America, which authorizes them to make as many appointments as they think fit, and to pay the appointees what sums they please, for whose mal-conduct they are not accountable: from whence it may happen, that officers of the crown may be multiplied to such a degree, as to become dangerous to the liberty of the people, by virtue of a commission which doth not appear to this House to derive any such advantages to trade as many have been led to expect.

These are the sentiments and proceedings of this house: and as they have too much reason to believe, that the enemies of the colonies have represented them to his Majesty's ministers and the parliament as factious, disloyal, and having a disposition to make themselves independent of the mother country, they have taken occasion, in the most humble terms, to assure his Majesty and his ministers, that with regard to the people of this province, and, as they doubt not, of all the colonies, that the charge is unjust.

The House is fully satisfied, that your assembly is too generous and enlarged in sentiment to believe, that this letter proceeds from an ambition of taking the lead, or dictating to the other assemblies: they freely submit their opinion to the judgment of others; and shall take it kind in your House to point out to them any thing further that may be thought necessary.

This House cannot conclude without expressing their firm confidence in the King, our common head, and father, that the united and dutiful supplications of his distressed American subjects will meet with his royal and favourable acceptance.

47

LOBSTERBACKS AND CUSTOMS RACKETEERS

from Anon., "A Journal of the Times," 1768-1769

In 1768 the rumblings of popular discontent in Boston alarmed the Royal Governor, Francis Bernard, and the new customs commissioners. Following a riot provoked by official seizure of John Hancock's sloop *Liberty* (June 10, 1768), the commissioners retreated to Castle William in the harbor and sent out urgent calls for troops (June 15).

Months later, the home authorities agreed to this extraordinary peacetime measure. Beginning in October 1768, the citizens of Boston found growing numbers of red-coated soldiers (nicknamed "lobsterbacks") camped on their Common and lodged in Faneuil Hall. The "Boston Massacre" of March 5, 1770, was the dramatic climax to a long series of conflicts between townsmen and British soldiers. This street brawl that got out of control left a handful of casualties and a heritage of bitter memories.

Certain anonymous Yankees skilled in controversial writing spread the news of Boston under military rule throughout the Empire. A daily journal of events and comments was secretly prepared in Boston, sent to Holt's *New York Journal* for Thursday publication, reprinted Saturday by the *Pennsylvania Chronicle*, then copied by the *Boston Evening Post* and other colonial and English journals. Menacing lobsterbacks and grasping customs racketeers were made notorious throughout British North America.

October 29, 1768

The inhabitants of this town have been of late greatly insulted and abused by some of the officers and soldiers, several have been assaulted on frivolous pretences, and put under guard without any lawful warrant for so doing. A physician of the town walking the streets the other evening, was jostled by an officer, when a scuffle ensued; he was afterwards met by the same officer in company with another, both as yet unknown, who repeated his blows, and as is supposed gave him a stroke with a pistol, which so wounded him as to endanger his life. A tradesman of this town on going under the rails of the Common in his way home, had a thrust in the breast with a bayonet from a soldier; another person passing the street was struck with a musket; and the last evening a merchant of the town was struck down by an officer who went into the coffee-house, several gentlemen following him in, and expostulating with the officers, were treated in the most ungenteel manner; but the most atrocious offence and alarming behaviour was that of a captain, the last evening, who in company with two other officers, endeavoured to persuade some Negro servants to ill-treat and abuse their masters, assuring them that the soldiers were come to procure their freedoms, and that with their help and assistance they should be able to drive all the Liberty Boys to the devil; with discourse of the like import, tending to

excite an insurrection. Depositions are now taking before the magistrates, and prosecutions at common law are intended, the inhabitants being determined to oppose by the law such proceedings, apprehending it the most honourable as well as the most safe and effectual method of obtaining satisfaction and redress; at the same time they have a right to expect that General Gage will not remain an unconcerned spectator of such a conduct in any under his command.—*Here Americans you may behold some of the first fruits springing up from that root of bitterness a standing army. Troops are quartered upon us in a time of peace, on pretence of preserving order in a town that was as orderly before their arrival as any one large town in the whole extent of his Majesty's dominions; and a little time will discover whether we are to be governed by the martial or the common law of the land.* . . .

March 28, 1769

The charge and vexation of clearing out vessels coasting from one part of the province to another, is a growing evil.—The master of a vessel, owned at Duxbury, a town in the port of Boston, to which harbour the coasters go and return in about a fortnight, having taken some necessaries on board for the people dwelling there, was, as all others are, obliged to clear out, &c. The charge of which amounted to three dollars; a large tax upon the English merchandize transported from port to port, in the course of a year, and a great discouragement to our trade and navigation,—Sufferances must be obtained at the custom-house, before shot, powder, rum,

Text: Oliver Morton Dickerson (ed.), *Boston Under Military Rule, 1768-1769, as Revealed in "A Journal of the Times"* (Boston: Chapman & Grimes, 1936), pp. 15-16, 84, 102.

sugar, molasses and any triffling articles are taken into a coaster: A brazier of this town put a bar of steel on board one of these boats for a customer, and offered to swear it was English; this was not satisfactory, unless he would swear to the very vessel this bar was imported in; this could not be done by him, as the steel in his store had been mixt; the skipper was therefore prevented from receiving it on board, and obliged to return it back to the brazier: A merchant of this town, was put to the like difficulty, respecting a box of Bristol glass, and another relative to a chest of English tea: And we are told, that in consequence of orders from the C—m—rs [Commissioners], it is required at the custom house, when a barrel of sugar, rum, and a few pounds of coffee, &c. &c. &c. are reported for shipping to any place even in this harbour, that instead of the usual certificate from the merchant, that those goods were legally imported and had paid the imposed duties, the vender of such articles must make oath, as to the vessel it was imported in; and also the *purchaser*, that they are the same; and even the *truckman* is to give evidence that such goods have been put on board those coasters.—*The confusion which must be occasioned by such before unheard of requirements, in a new country, whose settlers are scattered along an extensive sea shore, and are constantly needing supplies, are as obvious, as the illegality and impolicy of those and such like proceedings of the American B—d of C—rs* [Board of Commissioners]. . . .

May 22, 1769

It has been justly observed. "That the colony trade is in a measure, a system of art and restriction; yet the very principle may be destroy'd by multiplying to excess, the means of securing it." The present trade of America has of late years, been embarrassed beyond description, with the multiplicity and intricacy of regulations and ordinances; our late M—n—rs [Ministers], from whom we must exclude the Rockingham Administration, seem to be possessed with something hardly short of a rage, for regulation and restriction; they have extended to us their several acts of Parliaments, calculated to prevent a contraband trade with their French neighbours,

multiplied bonds, certificates, affidavits, warrants, sufferances, cockets, &c. and every species of custom-house officers, both upon the land and water; have supported the new regulations with such severe penalties, and extended them without the least consideration of circumstances to so many objects, that American commerce is expiring under them. Upon the first appointment of an American Board of C—s—ms [Customs], it was trumpetted to the merchants, by the tools of power, that it was an institution calculated to *retrieve the trade* from many of its present embarrassments; and that some of the colonies agents in London, were so well satisfied, that the residence of the C—m—rs [Commissioners] in any trading province would be greatly advantageous to its commerce, as to offer in behalf of their constituents a large sum of money, to obtain the preferrence.—Our merchants however, were by no means disposed to hearken to such delusory insinuations; they considered the project of an American revenue, to be wholly founded upon anti-commercial principles; and that a set of men sent among us to support this project, and riot upon its produce, must become as obnoxious, as the exercise of their power would be distressing.—Their conjectures were soon realized; to say nothing of the haughty imperious, indelicate behaviour of the B—d [Board of Customs] as men, their whole official conduct has been such, as lead people to consider them as the greatest political curses that could have been sent among us.—This B—d soon gave being to such an innumerable train of under officers, &c. that the whole revenue raised by the late duties, has been scarcely sufficient to satiate their craving appetites; but the monies drained from our merchants, distressing as it has been, is the least part of our sufferings; they have, with the advice and assistance of G— B— [Governor Bernard] and the cabal, gone into every measure that has appeared to us most likely to cramp and lessen both a provincial and foreign trade, by which we have been so impoverished; that thro' necessity, as well as resentment, our farmers and mechanics, are lopping off many articles of superfluities, and going into such manufactures as may be carried on here to the greatest advantage. . . .

48

A CASE FOR LOYALTY

from Joseph Galloway, *The American Rebellion*, 1780, and *Journals of the Continental Congress*, 1774

With the repeal of the Townshend duties (excepting that on tea) in 1770, imperial relations entered a brief period of comparative calm. By 1772 storm winds were rising again, however; and the Tea Act of May 1773, followed by the Boston Tea Party in December, brought on a raging crisis—one that only revolution would resolve.

Parliament's reply to the rough Tea Party in Boston Harbor was a set of four "Coercive Acts" designed to punish Massachusetts and give a sobering example to all colonists. The port of Boston was closed, the Massachusetts charter was altered, town meetings were curtailed, and once more British troops were called in. Although it dealt with affairs outside the colonies, the "Quebec Act" (which gave Canada a highly centralized government under crown control and provided its French Catholic citizens with a privileged position) was construed by the aroused Americans as a threat to the Protestant religion and to representative government.

At the prompting of Virginia's popular leaders, who had initiated intercolonial committees of correspondence in 1773, a Continental Congress was summoned to Philadelphia in September 1774 to state again the rights and grievances of the colonists and to adopt a common course of action. Among the delegates were not a few moderates like Joseph Galloway. Speaker of the Pennsylvania Assembly since 1766, a wealthy and influential figure in provincial society, Galloway hoped for reconciliation and deeply feared the consequences of radical words and measures. For a time Galloway's compromise plan of union seemed to have a chance of adoption, but the bold counsels and shrewd maneuvers of the Adamses and their radical allies proved more convincing. To Galloway's dismay, the First Continental Congress approved the "Suffolk Resolves," a declaration by a Massachusetts convention denying the binding force of Parliament's Coercive Acts; and the Congress went on to adopt the "Association," an agreement among the colonies to put economic pressure upon England by enforcing a strict boycott of English goods and markets throughout the continent.

When the Second Continental Congress met in May of 1775 there was no longer a place for Galloway. Blood had been spilled at Lexington and Concord, and the leading questions before the house were as much military as political. Many moderates were drawn reluctantly into the Patriot cause, but Galloway was one of those who could not stomach rebellion and chose the Loyalist side. He saw his estates confiscated during the war and ended his days a British pensioner in exile.

Galloway's sketch of the machinations of the Radicals reveals, of course, his own choleric feelings; yet it would be difficult to overstate the importance of such leaders as Sam and John Adams and Patrick Henry in organizing the colonial protest movement and moving it forward to the point of no return. To them, acceptance of the Galloway plan—in substance not unlike Franklin's Albany Plan of 1756—would only have postponed the inevitable showdown until the Patriot movement lost its momentum.

On the Patriot Machine

Upon the meeting of Congress, two parties were immediately formed, with different views, and determined to act upon different principles. One intended candidly and clearly to define American rights, and explicitly and dutifully to petition for the remedy which would redress the grievances justly complained of—to form a more solid and constitutional union between the two countries, and to avoid every measure which tended to sedition, or acts of violent opposition. The other consisted of persons whose design, from the beginning of their opposition to the Stamp Act, was to throw off all subordination and connexion with Great-Britain; who meant by

Texts: Joseph Galloway, Historical and Political Reflections on the Rise and Progress of the American Rebellion (London: G. Wilkie, 1780), pp. 66-70. Worthington C. Ford (ed.), Journals of the Continental Congress, 1774-1789 (Washington, D.C.: Government Printing Office, 1904), I, 45-48, 49-51.

every fiction, falsehood and fraud, to delude the people from their due allegiance, to throw the subsisting Governments into anarchy, to incite the ignorant and vulgar to arms, and with those arms to establish American Independence. The one were men of loyal principles, and possessed the greatest fortunes in America; the other were congregational and presbyterian republicans, or men of bankrupt fortunes, overwhelmed in debt to the British merchants. The first suspected the designs of the last, and were therefore cautious; but as they meant to do nothing but what was reasonable and just, they were open and ingenuous. The second, fearing the opposition of the first, were secret and hypocritical, and left no art, no falsehood, no fraud unessayed to conceal their intentions. The loyalists rested, for the most part, on the defensive, and opposed, with success, every measure which tended to violent opposition. Motions were made, debated and rejected, and nothing was carried by either.

While the two parties in Congress remained thus during three weeks on an equal balance, the republicans were calling to their assistance the aid of their factions without. Continual expresses were employed between Philadelphia and Boston. These were under the management of Samuel Adams—a man, who though by no means remarkable for brilliant abilities, yet is equal to most men in popular intrigue, and the management of a faction. He eats little, drinks little, sleeps little, thinks much, and is most decisive and indefatigable in the pursuit of his objects. It was this man, who by his superior application managed at once the faction in Congress at Philadelphia, and the factions in New England. Whatever these patriots in Congress wished to have done by their colleagues without, to induce General Gage, then at the head of his Majesty's army at Boston, to give them a pretext for violent opposition, or to promote their measures in Congress, Mr. Adams advised and directed to be done; and when done, it was dispatched by express to Congress. By one of these expresses came the inflammatory resolves of the county of Suffolk, which contained a complete declaration of war against Great-Britain. . . .

Upon these resolves being read, a motion was made that the Congress should give them their sanction. Long and warm debates ensued between the parties. At this time the republican faction in Congress had provided a mob, ready to execute their secret orders. The cruel practice of tarring and feathering had been long since introduced. This lessened the firmness of some of the loyalists; the vote was put and carried. Two of the dissenting members presumed to offer their protest against it in writing, which was negatived. They next insisted that the tender of their protest and its negative should be entered on the minutes; this was also rejected.

By this treasonable vote the foundation of military resistance throughout America was effectually laid. The example was now set by the people of Suffolk, and the measure was approved of by those who called themselves the representatives of all America. The loyal party, although they knew a great majority of the colonists were averse to the measure, perceived the improbability of stemming the torrent. They had no authority, no means in their own power to resist it; they saw those who held the powers of Government inactive spectators, and either shrinking from their duty, or uniting in the measures of sedition; they saw the flame of rebellion spreading with more rapidity in a province under the eye of his Majesty's army than in any other; and that no effectual measures were taking by Govern-

ment in Britain to suppress it; and yet, as a petition to his Majesty had been ordered to be brought in, they resolved to continue their exertions. They hoped to prevail in stating the rights of America on just and constitutional principles; in proposing a plan for uniting the two countries on those principles, and in a clear, definitive and decent prayer, to ask for what a majority of the colonies wished to obtain; and as they had no reason to doubt the success of this measure in a British Parliament, they further hoped, that it would stop the effusion of blood and the ruin of their country.

With this view, as well as to probe the ultimate design of the republicans, and to know with certainty whether any proposal, short of the absolute independence of the Colonies, would satisfy them, a plan of union was drawn by a member of the loyal party [Galloway], and approved by the rest. It was so formed as to leave no room for any reasonable objection on the part of the republicans, if they meant to be united to Great Britain on any grounds whatever. It included a restoration of all their rights, and a redress of all their grievances, on constitutional principles; and it accorded with all the instructions given to them as members of Congress.

Speech Delivered by Joseph Galloway in the Continental Congress, September 28, 1774

. . . Desirous as I am to promote the freedom of the Colonies, and to prevent the mischiefs which will attend a military contest with Great-Britain, I must intreat you to desert the measures which have been so injudiciously and ineffectually pursued by antecedent Assemblies. Let us thoroughly investigate the subject matter in dispute, and endeavour to find from that investigation the means of perfect and permanent redress. In whatever we do, let us be particular and explicit, and not wander in general allegations. These will lead us to no point, nor can produce any relief; they are besides dishonourable and insidious. I would therefore acknowledge the necessity of the supreme authority of Parliament over the Colonies, because it is a proposition which we cannot deny without manifest contradiction, while we confess that we are subjects of the British Government; and if we do not approve of a representation in Parliament, let us ask for a participation in the freedom and power of the English constitution in some other mode of incorporation: for I am convinced, by long attention to the subject, that let us deliberate, and try what other expedients we may, we shall find none that can give to the Colonies substantial freedom, but some such incorporation. I therefore beseech you, by the respect you are bound to pay to the instructions of your constituents, by the regard you have for the honour and safety of your country, and as you wish to avoid a war with Great-Britain, which must terminate, at all events in the ruin of America, not to rely on a denial of the authority of Parliament, a refusal to be represented, and on a non-importation agreement; because whatever protestations, in that case, may be made to the contrary, it will prove to the world that we intend to throw off our allegiance to the State, and to involve the two countries in all the horrors of a civil war.

With a view to promote the measure I have so earnestly recommended, I have prepared the draught of a plan for uniting America more intimately, in constitutional policy, with Great Britain. . . .

A Plan of a Proposed Union between Great Britain and the Colonies, September 28, 1774.

That a British and American legislature, for regulating the administration of the general affairs of America, be proposed and established in America, including all the said colonies; within, and under which government, each colony shall retain its present constitution, and powers of regulating and governing its own internal police, in all cases what[so]ever.

That the said government be administered by a President General, to be appointed by the King, and a grand Council, to be chosen by the Representatives of the people of the several colonies, in their respective assemblies, once in every three years. . . .

That the Grand Council shall meet once in every year, if they shall think it necessary, and oftener, if occasions shall require, at such time

and place as they shall adjourn to, at the last preceding meeting, or as they shall be called to meet at, by the President-General, on any emergency.

That the grand Council shall have power to choose their Speaker, and shall hold and exercise all the like rights, liberties and privileges, as are held and exercised by and in the House of Commons of Great-Britain.

That the President-General shall hold his office during the pleasure of the King, and his assent shall be requisite to all acts of the Grand Council, and it shall be his office and duty to cause them to be carried into execution.

That the President-General, by and with the advice and consent of the Grand-Council, hold and exercise all the legislative rights, powers, and authorities, necessary for regulating and administering all the general police and affairs of the colonies, in which Great-Britain and the colonies, or any of them, the colonies in general, or more than one colony, are in any manner concerned, as well civil and criminal as commercial.

That the said President-General and the Grand Council, be an inferior and distinct branch of the British legislature, united and incorporated with it, for the aforesaid general purposes; and that any of the said general regulations may originate and be formed and digested, either in the Parliament of Great Britain, or in the said Grand Council, and being prepared, transmitted to the other for their approbation or dissent; and that the assent of both shall be requisite to the validity of all such general acts or statutes.

That in time of war, all bills for granting aid to the crown, prepared by the Grand Council, and approved by the President-General, shall be valid and passed into a law, without the assent of the British Parliament.

49   THE COMMON SENSE OF REVOLUTION

from Thomas Paine, *Common Sense*, January 10, 1776

Since the adoption of a new imperial policy in 1763, Americans had rioted, organized, resolved, boycotted, ostracized, and met in Continental Congress; and finally, on April 19, 1775, Yankee minutemen had skirmished with a force of British regulars on Lexington Green. Men like Franklin, Patrick Henry, and Sam Adams had set their sights on independence well before the fighting started. Yet for most influential Americans, revolution was a dreadful prospect that could be faced only by degrees. A year after Lexington, John Adams still wondered when his timid colleagues in the Continental Congress would risk a declaration of independence.

The appeal of the Stamp Act Congress (1765) had challenged the authority of Parliament to lay taxes for revenue, and Benjamin Franklin in his soothing testimony before the House of Commons made it seem that only "internal" taxation offended the colonists. The "external" taxes of the Townshend Act (1767) proved no more palatable. In steady progression the Americans enlarged their claims until, in 1774, the Continental Congress declared the right of the provincial assemblies to legislate "in all cases of taxation and internal polity," while giving their consent "cheerfully" to the continued operation of imperial trade regulations. The Second Continental Congress formed an army and conducted military operations and, at the same time, sent an olive branch petition to the King, asking him to right their wrongs and recognize their governments as coordinate branches of a British commonwealth.

In this setting a recently arrived Englishman, Thomas Paine (1737-1809), published his *Common Sense* on January 10, 1776. At last independence was openly demanded as the necessary and desirable end; Paine's words caught fire. It is estimated that more than 100,000 copies of his pamphlet circulated among the colonists within a few months of publication. One can never establish the precise effect of such appeals, yet clearly Paine did much to undermine colonial loyalty to the Crown and to create a popular demand for an independent republican government.

Paine's *American Crisis* papers of 1776-1783 helped to sustain confidence during "the times that try men's souls." He published *The Rights of Man* (1791-1792) in defense of the French Revolution and sat for a time in the French National Convention; he also sat for ten months in a French prison under the Reign of Terror. His unorthodox deist views, expressed in *The Age of Reason*, alienated his adopted countrymen after his return to America in 1802.

Thoughts on the Present State of American Affairs.

In the following pages I offer nothing more than simple facts, plain arguments, and common sense: and have no other preliminaries to settle with the reader, than that he will divest himself of prejudice and prepossession, and suffer his reason and his feelings to determine for themselves: that he will put on, or rather that he will not put off, the true character of a man, and generously enlarge his views beyond the present day.

Volumes have been written on the subject of the struggle between England and America. Men of all ranks have embarked in the controversy, from different motives, and with various designs; but all have been ineffectual, and the period of debate is closed. Arms as the last resource decide the contest; the appeal was the choice of the King, and the Continent has accepted the challenge. . . .

The Sun never shined on a cause of greater worth. 'Tis not the affair of a City, a County, a Province, or a Kingdom; but of a Continent— of at least one-eighth part of the habitable Globe. 'Tis not the concern of a day, a year, or an age; posterity are virtually involved in the contest, and will be more or less affected even to the end of time, by the proceedings now. Now is the seed-time of Continental union, faith and honour. The least fracture now will be like a name engraved with the point of a pin on the tender rind of a young oak; the wound would enlarge with the tree, and posterity read it in full-grown characters.

By referring the matter from argument to arms, a new era for politics is struck—a new method of thinking hath arisen. All plans, proposals, &c. prior to the nineteenth of April [1775], *i.e.*

to the commencement of hostilities, are like the almanacks of the last year; which tho' proper then, are superceded and useless now. Whatever was advanced by the advocates on either side of the question then, terminated in one and the same point, viz. a union with Great Britain; the only difference between the parties was the method of effecting it; the one proposing force, the other friendship; but it hath so far happened that the first hath failed, and the second hath withdrawn her influence.

As much hath been said of the advantages of reconciliation, which, like an agreeable dream, hath passed away and left us as we were, it is but right that we should examine the contrary side of the argument, and enquire into some of the many material injuries which these Colonies sustain, and always will sustain, by being connected with and dependant on Great-Britain. To examine that connection and dependance, on the principles of nature and common sense, to see what we have to trust to, if separated, and what we are to expect, if dependant.

I have heard it asserted by some, that as America has flourished under her former connection with Great-Britain, the same connection is necessary towards her future happiness, and will always have the same effect. Nothing can be more fallacious than this kind of argument. We may as well assert that because a child has thrived upon milk, that it is never to have meat, or that the first twenty years of our lives is to become a precedent for the next twenty. But even this is admitting more than is true; for I answer roundly,

Text: Thomas Paine, *Writings*, ed. Moncure D. Conway (New York: G. P. Putnam's Sons, 1894), I, 84-92, 99-101.

that America would have flourished as much, and probably much more, had no European power taken any notice of her. The commerce by which she hath enriched herself are the necessaries of life, and will always have a market while eating is the custom of Europe.

But she has protected us, say some. That she hath engrossed us is true, and defended the Continent at our expense as well as her own, is admitted; and she would have defended Turkey from the same motive, *viz.* for the sake of trade and dominion.

Alas! we have been long led away by ancient prejudices and made large sacrifices to superstition. We have boasted the protection of Great Britain, without considering, that her motive was *interest* not *attachment*; and that she did not protect us from *our enemies* on *our account*; but from *her enemies* on *her own account*, from those who had no quarrel with us on any *other account*, and who will always be our enemies on the *same account*. Let Britain waive her pretensions to the Continent, or the Continent throw off the dependance, and we should be at peace with France and Spain, were they at war with Britain. . . .

But Britain is the parent country, say some. Then the more shame upon her conduct. Even brutes do not devour their young, nor savages make war upon their families; Wherefore, the assertion, if true, turns to her reproach; but it happens not to be true, or only partly so, and the phrase *parent* or *mother country* hath been jesuitically adopted by the King and his parasites, with a low papistical design of gaining an unfair bias on the credulous weakness of our minds. Europe, and not England, is the parent country of America. This new World hath been the asylum for the persecuted lovers of civil and religious liberty from *every part* of Europe. Hither have they fled, not from the tender embraces of the mother, but from the cruelty of the monster; and it is so far true of England, that the same tyranny which drove the first emigrants from home, pursues their descendants still.

In this extensive quarter of the globe, we forget the narrow limits of three hundred and sixty miles (the extent of England) and carry our friendship on a larger scale; we claim brotherhood with every European Christian, and triumph in the generosity of the sentiment. . . .

Much hath been said of the united strength of Britain and the Colonies, that in conjunction they might bid defiance to the world: But this is mere presumption; the fate of war is uncertain, neither do the expressions mean any thing; for this continent would never suffer itself to be drained of inhabitants, to support the British arms in either Asia, Africa, or Europe.

Besides, what have we to do with setting the world at defiance? Our plan is commerce, and that, well attended to, will secure us the peace and friendship of all Europe; because it is the interest of all Europe to have America a free port. Her trade will always be a protection, and her barrenness of gold and silver secure her from invaders. . . .

. . . As Europe is our market for trade, we ought to form no partial connection with any part of it. It is the true interest of America to steer clear of European contentions, which she never can do, while, by her dependance on Britain, she is made the make-weight in the scale of British politics.

Europe is too thickly planted with Kingdoms to be long at peace, and whenever a war breaks out between England and any foreign power, the trade of America goes to ruin, *because of her connection with Britain*. The next war may not turn out like the last, and should it not, the advocates for reconciliation now will be wishing for separation then, because neutrality in that case would be a safer convoy than a man of war. Every thing that is right or reasonable pleads for separation. The blood of the slain, the weeping voice of nature cries, 'TIS TIME TO PART. Even the distance at which the Almighty hath placed England and America is a strong and natural proof that the authority of the one over the other, was never the design of Heaven. The time likewise at which the Continent was discovered, adds weight to the argument, and the manner in which it was peopled, encreases the force of it. The Reformation was preceded by the discovery of America: As if the Almighty graciously meant to open a sanctuary to the persecuted in future years, when home should afford neither friendship nor safety. . . .

Men of passive tempers look somewhat lightly over the offences of Great Britain, and, still hoping for the best, are apt to call out, *Come, come, we shall be friends again for all this.* But examine the passions and feelings of mankind: bring the doctrine of reconciliation to the touchstone of nature, and then tell me whether you can hereafter love, honour, and faithfully serve the power that hath carried fire and sword into your land? If you cannot do all these, then are you only deceiving yourselves, and by your delay bringing ruin upon posterity. Your future connection with Britain, whom you can neither love nor honour, will be forced and unnatural, and being formed only on the plan of present convenience, will in a little time fall into a relapse more wretched than the first. But if you say, you can still pass the violations over, then I ask, hath your house been burnt? Hath your property been destroyed before your face? Are your wife and children destitute of a bed to lie on, or bread to live on? Have you lost a parent or a child by their hands, and yourself the ruined and wretched survivor? If you have not, then are you not a judge of those who have. But if you have, and can still shake hands with the murderers, then are you unworthy the name of husband, father, friend, or lover, and whatever may be your rank or title in life, you have the heart of a coward, and the spirit of a sycophant. . . .

As to government matters, 'tis not in the power of Britain to do this continent justice: the business of it will soon be too weighty and intricate to be managed with any tolerable degree of convenience, by a power so distant from us, and so very ignorant of us; for if they cannot conquer us, they cannot govern us. To be always running three or four thousand miles with a tale or a petition, waiting four or five months for an answer, which, when obtained, requires five or six more to explain it in, will in a few years be looked upon as folly and childishness. There was a time when it was proper, and there is a proper time for it to cease.

Small islands not capable of protecting themselves are the proper objects for government to take under their care; but there is something absurd, in supposing a Continent to be perpetually governed by an island. In no instance hath nature made the satellite larger than its primary planet; and as England and America, with respect to each other, reverse the common order of nature, it is evident that they belong to different systems. England to Europe: America to itself.

I am not induced by motives of pride, party, or resentment to espouse the doctrine of separation and independence; I am clearly, positively, and conscientiously persuaded that it is the true interest of this Continent to be so; that every thing short of *that* is mere patchwork, that it can afford no lasting felicity,—that it is leaving the sword to our children, and shrinking back at a time when a little more, a little further, would have rendered this Continent the glory of the earth. . . .

The object contended for, ought always to bear some just proportion to the expense. The removal of North, or the whole detestable junto, is a matter unworthy the millions we have expended. A temporary stoppage of trade was an inconvenience, which would have sufficiently balanced the repeal of all the acts complained of, had such repeals been obtained; but if the whole

Continent must take up arms, if every man must be a soldier, 'tis scarcely worth our while to fight against a contemptible ministry only. Dearly, dearly do we pay for the repeal of the acts, if that is all we fight for; for, in a just estimation 'tis as great a folly to pay a Bunker-hill price for law as for land. . . . No man was a warmer wisher for a reconciliation than myself, before the fatal nineteenth of April, 1775, but the moment the event of that day was made known, I rejected the hardened, sullen-tempered Pharaoh of England for ever; and disdain the wretch, that with the pretended title of FATHER OF HIS PEOPLE can unfeelingly hear of their slaughter, and composedly sleep with their blood upon his soul. . . .

A government of our own is our natural right: and when a man seriously reflects on the precariousness of human affairs, he will become convinced, that it is infinitely wiser and safer, to form a constitution of our own in a cool deliberate manner, while we have it in our power, than to trust such an interesting event to time and chance. . . . Should the government of America return again into the hands of Britain, the tottering situation of things will be a temptation for some desperate adventurer to try his fortune; and in such a case, what relief can Britain give? Ere she could hear the news, the fatal business might be done; and ourselves suffering like the wretched Britons under the oppression of the Conqueror. Ye that oppose independance now, ye know not what ye do: ye are opening a door to eternal tyranny, by keeping vacant the seat of government. There are thousands and tens of thousands, who would think it glorious to expel from the Continent, that barbarous and hellish power, which hath stirred up the Indians and the Negroes to destroy us; the cruelty hath a double guilt; it is dealing brutally by us, and treacherously by them.

To talk of friendship with those in whom our reason forbids us to have faith, and our affections wounded thro' a thousand pores instruct us to detest, is madness and folly. Everyday wears out the little remains of kindred between us and them; and can there be any reason to hope, that as the relationship expires, the affection will increase, or that we shall agree better when we have ten times more and greater concerns to quarrel over than ever?

Ye that tell us of harmony and reconciliation, can ye restore to us the time that is past? Can ye give to prostitution its former innocence? neither can ye reconcile Britain and America. The last cord now is broken, the people of England are presenting addresses against us. There are injuries which nature cannot forgive; she would cease to be nature if she did. As well can the lover forgive the ravisher of his mistress, as the Continent forgive the murders of Britain. The Almighty hath implanted in us these unextinguishable feelings for good and wise purposes. They are the Guardians of his Image in our hearts. They distinguish us from the herd of common animals. The social compact would dissolve, and justice be extirpated from the earth, or have only a casual existence were we callous to the touches of affection. The robber and the murderer would often escape unpunished, did not the injuries which our tempers sustain, provoke us into justice.

O! ye that love mankind! Ye that dare oppose not only the tyranny but the tyrant, stand forth! Every spot of the old world is overrun with oppression. Freedom hath been hunted round the Globe. Asia and Africa have long expelled her. Europe regards her like a stranger, and England hath given her warning to depart. O! receive the fugitive, and prepare in time an asylum for mankind.

50

THE DECLARATION OF INDEPENDENCE IN CONGRESS, JULY 4, 1776

The halfway revolution begun in April 1775 could not long continue. Through the early months of 1776 Americans were drawn to Paine's incendiary logic: either they must capitulate—as a substantial minority of loyalists did—or they must drive on to independence.

In mid-May of 1776 the Virginia Burgesses instructed their delegates in Congress to move for independence; at the same time Congress advised the several colonies to establish their own governments. Finally on July 2, while the British General William Howe was landing troops on Staten Island (New York), Congress took the great leap: Richard Henry Lee's resolution for independence, before the house since June 7, was adopted. In the meantime Jefferson had drafted a declaration of independence with advice from John Adams, Benjamin Franklin, and others. On July 4 the formal Declaration, still essentially Jefferson's creation, was adopted.

The Declaration has been construed as everything from a bid for foreign aid to a précis of philosopher John Locke's *Essay Concerning the True Original, Extent and End of Civil Government.* Jefferson, in later years, gave perhaps the most convincing account of the background of the Declaration: it was meant simply "to place before mankind the common sense of the subject in terms so plain and firm as to command their assent"; it drew its authority from "the harmonizing sentiments of the day." In brief, the Declaration "was intended to be an expression of the American mind."

The principles of equal rights derived from the laws of nature, of popular sovereignty, and of limited government were laid down not only to justify revolution but also— Lincoln later argued—to provide "a standard maxim for free society which should be familiar to all and revered by all; constantly looked to, constantly labored for, and even though never perfectly attained, constantly approximated."

The unanimous Declaration of the thirteen united States of America,

When in the Course of human events, it becomes necessary for one people to dissolve the political bands which have connected them with another, and to assume among the Powers of the earth, the separate and equal station to which the Laws of Nature and of Nature's God entitle them, a decent respect to the opinions of mankind requires that they should declare the causes which impel them to the separation.

We hold these truths to be self-evident, that all men are created equal, that they are endowed by their Creator with certain unalienable Rights, that among these are Life, Liberty and the pursuit of Happiness. That to secure these rights, Governments are instituted among Men, deriving their just powers from the consent of the governed, That whenever any Form of Government becomes destructive of these ends, it is the Right of the People to alter or to abolish it, and to institute new Government, laying its foundation on such principles and organizing its powers in such form, as to them shall seem most likely to effect their Safety and Happiness. Prudence, indeed, will dictate that Governments long established should not be changed for light and transient causes; and accordingly all experience hath shown, that mankind are more disposed to suffer, while evils are sufferable, than to right themselves by abolishing the forms to which they are accustomed. But when a long train of abuses and usurpations, pursuing invariably the same Object evinces a design to reduce them under absolute Despotism, it is their right, it is their duty, to throw off such Government, and to provide new Guards for their future security.—Such has been the patient sufferance of these Colonies; and such is now the necessity which constrains them to alter their former Systems of Government. The history of the present King of Great Britain is a history of repeated injuries and usurpations, all having in direct object the establishment of an absolute Tyranny over these States. To prove this, let Facts be submitted to a candid world.

He has refused his Assent to Laws, the most wholesome and necessary for the public good.

He has forbidden his Governors to pass Laws of immediate and pressing importance, unless suspended in their operation till his Assent should be obtained; and when so suspended, he has utterly neglected to attend to them.

He has refused to pass other Laws for the accommodation of large districts of people, unless those people would relinquish the right of Representation in the Legislature, a right inestimable to them and formidable to tyrants only.

He has called together legislative bodies at places unusual, uncomfortable, and distant from the depository of their Public Records, for the sole purpose of fatiguing them into compliance with his measures.

He has dissolved Representative Houses repeatedly, for opposing with manly firmness his invasions on the rights of the people.

He has refused for a long time, after such dissolutions, to cause others to be elected; whereby the Legislative Powers, incapable of Annihilation, have returned to the People at large for their exercise; the State remaining in the mean time exposed to all the dangers of invasion from without, and convulsions within.

He has endeavoured to prevent the population of these States; for that purpose obstructing the Laws for Naturalization of Foreigners; refusing to pass others to encourage their migrations hither, and raising the conditions of new Appropriations of Lands.

He has obstructed the Administration of Justice, by refusing his Assent to Laws for establishing Judiciary Powers.

He has made Judges dependent on his Will alone, for the tenure of their offices, and the amount and payment of their salaries.

He has erected a multitude of New Offices, and sent hither swarms of Officers to harass our people, and eat out their substance.

He has kept among us, in times of peace, Standing Armies without the Consent of our legislatures.

He has affected to render the Military independent of and superior to the Civil Power.

He has combined with others to subject us to a jurisdiction foreign to our constitution, and unacknowledged by our laws; giving his Assent to their acts of pretended Legislation:

For quartering large bodies of armed troops among us:

For protecting them, by a mock Trial, from Punishment for any Murders which they should commit on the Inhabitants of these States:

For cutting off our Trade with all parts of the world:

For imposing taxes on us without our Consent:

For depriving us in many cases, of the benefits of Trial by Jury:

For transporting us beyond Seas to be tried for pretended offences:

For abolishing the free System of English Laws in a neighbouring Province, establishing therein an Arbitrary government, and enlarging its Boundaries so as to render it at once an example and fit instrument for introducing the same absolute rule into these Colonies:

For taking away our Charters, abolishing our most valuable Laws, and altering fundamentally the Forms of our Governments:

For suspending our own Legislatures, and declaring themselves invested with Power to legislate for us in all cases whatsoever.

He has abdicated Government here, by declaring us out of his Protection and waging War against us.

He has plundered our seas, ravaged our Coasts, burnt our towns, and destroyed the lives of our people.

He is at this time transporting large armies of foreign mercenaries to compleat the works of death, desolation and tyranny, already begun with circumstances of Cruelty & perfidy scarcely paralleled in the most barbarous ages, and totally unworthy the Head of a civilized nation.

He has constrained our fellow Citizens taken Captive on the high Seas to bear Arms against their Country, to become the executioners of their friends and Brethren, or to fall themselves by their Hands.

He has excited domestic insurrections amongst us, and has endeavoured to bring on the inhabitants of our frontiers, the merciless Indian Savages, whose known rule of warfare, is an undistinguished destruction of all ages, sexes, and conditions.

In every stage of these Oppressions We have Petitioned for Redress in the most humble terms: Our repeated Petitions have been answered only by repeated injury. A Prince, whose character is thus marked by every act which may define a Tyrant, is unfit to be the ruler of a free people.

Nor have We been wanting in attentions to our Brittish brethren. We have warned them from time to time of attempts by their legislature to extend an unwarrantable jurisdiction over us. We have reminded them of the circumstances of our emigration and settlement here. We have appealed to their native justice and magnanimity, and we have conjured them by the ties of our common kindred to disavow these usurpations which, would inevitably interrupt our connections and correspondence. They too have been deaf to the voice of justice and of consanguinity. We must, therefore, acquiesce in the necessity, which denounces our Separation, and hold them, as we hold the rest of mankind, Enemies in War, in Peace Friends.

We, therefore, the Representatives of the united States of America, in General Congress, Assembled, appealing to the Supreme Judge of the world for the rectitude of our intentions, do, in the Name, and by authority of the good People of these Colonies, solemnly publish and declare, That these United Colonies are, and of Right ought to be Free and Independent States; that they are Absolved from all Allegiance to the British Crown, and that all political connection between them and the State of Great Britain, is and ought to be totally dissolved; and that as Free and Independent States, they have full power to levy War, conclude Peace, contract Alliances, establish Commerce, and to do all other Acts and Things which Independent States may of right do. And for the support of this Declaration, with a firm reliance on the Protection of Divine Providence, we mutually pledge to each other our Lives, our Fortunes and our sacred Honor.

The American Revolution

51

WE CONQUER BY A DRAWN GAME: STRATEGY OF SPACE

from Thomas Paine, *The Crisis*, 1777

Tom Paine's second *Crisis* paper (January 13, 1777) was published when the American prospect in war seemed very bleak. Nominally addressed to the British General Howe, his appeal was certainly intended for those patriots whose souls had been tried by a succession of punishing defeats.

General Washington, with a motley army of "embattled farmers," had been driven from New York and chased across New Jersey into Pennsylvania. Apart from Washington's dramatic strike at Trenton on Christmas night of 1776, the principal military achievement of the Continentals in that year had been simply—but significantly—holding the army together. As Paine feared, General Howe was in a position to take almost anything he pleased, including the rebel capital of Philadelphia. (The occupation of Philadelphia came in September 1777.)

The turning of the tide came only by degrees, and many causes were at work: among others, the leadership of Washington, the indispensable aid of France (at first in money and supplies, and from 1778 in men and ships), and the mistakes of British generals. Tom Paine, no expert military strategist but a sharp political observer, emphasized two vital American advantages: a country too broad and decentralized to be secured by an expeditionary force, and a countryside full of irreconcilable rebels. His moral for discouraged patriots was that they might lose many battles and still—if they would retreat, endure, return—win the war: "We conquer by a drawn game."

. . . By what means, may I ask, do you [Lord Howe] expect to conquer America? If you could not effect it in the summer, when our army was less than yours, nor in the winter, when we had none, how are you to do it? In point of generalship you have been outwitted, and in point of fortitude outdone; your advantages turn out to your loss, and show us that it is in our power to ruin you by gifts: like a game of drafts, we can move out of *one* square to let you come in, in order that we may afterwards take two or three

Text: Thomas Paine, *Writings*, ed. Moncure D. Conway (New York: G. P. Putnam's Sons, 1894), 1, 179, 189-92.

for one; and as we can always keep a double corner for ourselves, we can always prevent a total defeat. You cannot be so insensible as not to see that we have two to one the advantage of you, because we conquer by a drawn game, and you lose by it. Burgoyne might have taught your lordship this knowledge; he has been long a student in the doctrine of chances.

I have no other idea of conquering countries than by subduing the armies which defend them: have you done this, or can you do it? If you have not, it would be civil in you to let your proclamations alone for the present; otherwise, you will ruin more tories by your grace and favor, than you will whigs by your arms.

Were you to obtain possession of this city [Philadelphia], you would not know what to do with it more than to plunder it. To hold it in the manner you hold New-York, would be an additional dead weight upon your hands: and if a general conquest is your object, you had better be without the city than with it. When you have defeated all our armies, the cities will fall into your hands of themselves; but to creep into them in the manner you got into Princeton, Trenton, &c. is like robbing an orchard in the night before the fruit be ripe, and running away in the morning. Your experiment in the Jerseys is sufficient to teach you that you have something more to do than barely to get into other people's houses; and your new converts, to whom you promised all manner of protection, and seduced into new guilt by pardoning them from their former virtues, must begin to have a very contemptible opinion both of your power and your policy. Your authority in the Jerseys is now reduced to the small circle which your army occupies, and your proclamation is no where else seen unless it be to be laughed at. The mighty subduers of the continent have retreated into a nutshell, and the proud forgivers of our sins are fled from those they came to pardon; and all this at a time when they were despatching vessel after vessel to England with the great news of every day. In short, you have managed your Jersey expedition so very dexterously, that the dead only are conquerors, because none will dispute the ground with them.

In all the wars which you have formerly been concerned in you had only armies to contend with; in this case you have both an army and a country to combat with. In former wars, the countries followed the fate of their capitals; Canada fell with Quebec, and Minorca with Port Mahon or St. Phillips; by subduing those, the conquerors opened a way into, and became masters of the country: here it is otherwise; if you get possession of a city here, you are obliged to shut yourselves up in it, and can make no other use of it, than to spend your country's money in. This is all the advantage you have drawn from New-York; and you would draw less from Philadelphia, because it requres more force to keep it, and is much further from the sea. A pretty figure you and the tories would cut in this city, with a river full of ice, and a town full of fire; for the immediate consequence of your getting here would be, that you would be cannonaded out again, and the tories be obliged to make good the damage; and this sooner or later will be the fate of New-York.

I wish to see the city saved, not so much from military as from natural motives. 'Tis the hiding place of women and children, and lord Howe's proper business is with our armies. When I put all the circumstances together which ought to be taken, I laugh at your notion of conquering America. Because you lived in a little country, where an army might run over the whole in a few days, and where a single company of soldiers might put a multitude to the rout, you expected to find it the same here. It is plain that you brought over with you all the narrow notions you were bred up with, and imagined that a proclamation in the king's name was to do great things; but Englishmen always travel for knowledge, and your lordship, I hope, will return, if you return at all, much wiser than you came. . . .

. . . Were you to garrison the places you might march over, in order to secure their subjection, (for remember you can do it by no other means,) your army would be like a stream of water running to nothing. By the time you extended from New-York to Virginia, you would be reduced to a string of drops not capable of hanging together; while we, by retreating from state to state, like a river turning back upon itself, would acquire strength in the same proportion as you lost it, and in the end be capable of overwhelming you. The country, in the meantime, would suffer, but it is a day of suffering, and we ought to expect it. What we contend for is worthy the affliction we may go through. If we get but bread to eat, and any kind of raiment to put on, we ought not only to be contented, but thankful. More than *that* we ought not to look for, and less than *that* heaven has not yet suffered us to want.

52

WINTER OF DESPAIR: VALLEY FORGE

from George Washington, Letter to Benj. Harrison, December 23, 1777

George Washington (1732-1799) assumed command of the colonial forces besieging British-occupied Boston in July of 1775 and completed his first mission some eight months later when General Gage abandoned the city. The next comparable American success would be a long time coming.

With only scant supplies and green troops at his command, Washington could not form and execute his own grand strategy. The initiative lay with the superior military power, and American commanders could only obstruct, retreat, harass, and wait for openings such as they found at Saratoga, New York (October 17, 1777), where General Burgoyne's isolated army was overwhelmed, and finally at Yorktown, Virginia (October 17, 1781), where the trapped Cornwallis met disaster.

Washington's responsibilities as Commander in Chief were political as well as military. He waged a ceaseless war with Congress and the states for supplies and men. He pleaded with Congress to abandon its faith in the militia ("To place any dependence upon militia is assuredly resting upon a broken staff") and give him regular soldiers whose terms of enlistment would not run out in the midst of battle. If Washington was not a brilliant general, he was a great leader who held the revolutionary forces together under seemingly impossible conditions. His report to Congress from winter quarters at Valley Forge (1777-1778) provides a moving record of the hungry, ragged, half-frozen army and the high-spirited general who would not let Congress forget the human and military costs of parsimony and neglect.

To the President of Congress, Valley Forge, December 23, 1777.

. . . Since the month of July we have had no assistance from the quartermaster-general, and to want of assistance from this department the commissary-general charges great part of his deficiency. To this I am to add, that, notwithstanding it is a standing order and often repeated, that the troops shall always have two days' provisions by them, that they might be ready at any sudden call; yet an opportunity has scarcely ever offered, of taking an advantage of the enemy, that has not been either totally obstructed, or greatly impeded, on this account. And this, the great and crying evil, is not all. The soap, vinegar, and other articles allowed by Congress, we see none of, nor have we seen them, I believe, since the battle of Brandywine. The first, indeed, we have no little occasion for; few men having more than one shirt, many only the moiety of one, and some none at all. In addition to which, as a proof of the little benefit received from a clothier-general, and as a further proof of the inability of an army, under the circumstances of this, to perform the common duties of soldiers (besides a number of men confined to hospitals for want of shoes, and others in farmers' houses on the

same account,) we have, by a field return this day made, no less than two thousand eight hundred and ninety-eight men now in camp unfit for duty, because they are barefoot and otherwise naked. By the same return it appears, that our whole strength in Continental troops, including the eastern brigades, which have joined us since the surrender of General Burgoyne, exclusive of the Maryland troops sent to Wilmington, amounts to no more than eight thousand two hundred in camp fit for duty; notwithstanding which, and that since the 4th instant, our numbers fit for duty, from the hardships and exposures they have undergone, particularly on account of blankets (numbers having been obliged, and still are, to sit up all night by fires, instead of taking comfortable rest in a natural and common way), have decreased near two thousand men.

We find gentlemen, without knowing whether the army was really going into winter-quarters or not (for I am sure no resolution of mine would warrant the Remonstrance) reprobating the measure as much as if they thought the soldiers were made of sticks or stones, and equally insensible of frost and snow; and moreover, as if they conceived it easily practicable for an inferior army, under the disadvantages I have described ours to be, which are by no means exaggerated to confine a superior one, in all respects well-appointed and provided for a winter's cam-

Text: George Washington, *Writings,* ed. John C. Fitzpatrick ("George Washington Bicentennial Edition" [Washington, D.C.: Government Printing Office, 1933]), X, 194-96.

paign, within the city of Philadelphia, and to cover from depredation and waste the States of Pennsylvania and Jersey. But what makes this matter still more extraordinary in my eye is, that these very gentlemen,—who were well apprized of the nakedness of the troops from ocular demonstration, who thought their own soldiers worse clad than others, and who advised me near a month ago to postpone the execution of a plan I was about to adopt, in consequence of a resolve of Congress for seizing clothes, under strong assurances that an ample supply would be collected in ten days agreeably to a decree of the State (not one article of which by the by, is yet come to hand),—should think a winter's campaign, and the covering of these States from the invasion of an enemy, so easy and practicable a business. I can assure those gentlemen, that it is a much easier and less distressing thing to draw remonstrances in a comfortable room by a good fireside, than to occupy a cold, bleak hill, and sleep under frost and snow, without clothes or blankets. However, although they seem to have little feeling for the naked and distressed soldiers, I feel superabundantly for them, and, from my soul, I pity those miseries, which it is neither in my power to relieve or prevent. . . .

53

SPECULATION, PECULATION, IDLENESS: THE GENERAL'S DESPAIR

from George Washington, Letter to Benj. Harrison, December 18, 1778

Washington served the Revolution without pay. A noble cause, he believed, demanded everything a man could give. He did not hesitate to judge others by his own extraordinary standard of devotion: the soldier who deserted or went home when his term ran out; the legislator, state or continental, who timidly avoided laying the heavy taxes needed to sustain the war; the merchant or farmer who sold to the enemy or profiteered at the expense of his countrymen; the politician who placed the interests of his own state or estate above the common cause. Reading Washington's wartime communications, one sometimes wonders how the war was won.

Great numbers of Americans did, of course, redeem the pledge of "our lives, our fortunes and our sacred honor" given in the Declaration. Moreover, the line between public interest and private gain was not always clear. The merchants, for example, who founded new fortunes by fitting out privateers to prey on British shipping, entered a desperately risky business which ruined more men than it profited; and when their financial gamble succeeded, enemy ships were knocked out, and the captured cargoes provided needed resources for the patriot cause. If farmers asked a heavy price for their scarce commodities, they did for a time accept the paper money and public certificates of an impoverished government which might not live to fulfill its promises. Indeed, the whole system of printing floods of paper money (some $240 million in "Continentals" and almost as much in state bills) served as a crude form of public taxation when other means failed. The money slipped in value as it changed hands until in 1780 Congress offered to redeem the paper bills at the rate of forty Continentals to one silver dollar. Literally, in some cases, the money was not worth the paper it was printed on.

Washington's censures could not erase selfishness and indifference; yet his words and still more his example helped to nourish public virtue and to keep before Americans the ideal of an independent union.

To Benjamin Harrison, Speaker of the House of Delegates of Virginia, Philadelphia, December 30, 1778.

. . . If I was to be called upon to draw a picture of the times and of Men, from what I have seen, and heard, and in part know, I should in one word say that idleness, dissipation & extravagance seems to have laid fast hold of most of them.— That speculation—peculation—and an insatiable thirst for riches seems to have got the better of every other consideration and almost of every order of Men.—That party disputes and personal quarrels are the great business of the day whilst the momentous concerns of an empire—a great and accumulated debt—ruined finances—depreciated money—and want of credit (which in their consequences is the want of everything) are but secondary considerations and postponed from day to day—from week to week as if our

Text: George Washington, *Writings*, ed. John C. Fitzpatrick ("George Washington Bicentennial Edition" [Washington, D.C.: Government Printing Office, 1936]), XIII, 466-468.

affairs wear the most promising aspect—after drawing this picture, which from my Soul I believe to be a true one, I need not repeat to you that I am alarmed and wish to see my Country men roused.—I have no resentments, nor do I mean to point at any particular characters,—this I can declare upon my honor for I have every attention paid me by Congress that I can possibly expect and have reason to think that I stand well in their estimation, but in the present situation of things I cannot help asking—Where is Mason—Wythe—Jefferson—Nicholas—Pendleton—Nelson—and another I could name—and why, if you are sufficiently impressed with your danger do you not (as New York has done in the case of Mr. Jay) send an extra member or two for at least a certain limited time till the great business of the Nation is put upon a more respectable and happy establishment.—Your Money is now sinking 5 pr. ct. a day in this city; and I shall not be surprised

if in the course of a few months a total stop is put to the currency of it.—And yet an Assembly—a concert—a Dinner—or supper (that will cost three or four hundred pounds) will not only take Men off from acting in but even from thinking of this business while a great part of the Officers of the Army from absolute necessity are quitting the service and the more virtuous few rather than do this are sinking by sure degrees into beggary and want.—I again repeat to you that this is not an exaggerated acct.; that it is an alarming one I do not deny, and confess to you that I feel more real distress on acct. of the prest. appearances of things than I have done at any one time since the commencement of the dispute—but it is time to bid you once more adieu. Providence has heretofore taken me up when all other means and hope seemed to be departing from me in this. I will confide.—

54

THE COMPLETION OF INDEPENDENCE

from George Washington, "Circular Letter to Governors," June 8, 1783

The British army band at Yorktown in 1781 played "The World Turned Upside Down" as the soldiers stacked their arms; this defeat was indeed the end of any serious military effort to restore the old regime in America. To make their independence stick, Americans now faced the difficult diplomatic task of negotiating a favorable peace and the still more trying political task of establishing a stable union of the states. Benjamin Franklin—a skilled and knowing bargainer—with his associates John Jay and John Adams achieved a substantial diplomatic triumph in the Treaty of Paris (September 3, 1783). American independence was formally recognized; and the new republic gained a spacious country from Canada to the Floridas, from the Atlantic to the Mississippi.

The political task of founding a nation was mastered only by degrees. Down to 1781 the Continental Congress was the common authority for joining, more or less, the efforts of the states. The weakness and timidity of Congress seemed most extreme to the Commander in Chief (as one may note in the sequence of Washington documents, 52-53) but not only to him. Congress itself proposed Articles of Confederation (1777) which assigned important powers over war, diplomacy, finance, interstate disputes, Indian relations, and the like to the central legislature, although they left the states "sovereign" and required the cooperation of state governments for the raising of men and money. Adoption of even this mild form of confederation was resisted until 1781, due partly to popular jealousy of a strong central power and partly to an angry conflict between states with large western land claims and those without.

In June of 1783, with hostilities ended and a treaty in the making, Washington looked forward to retirement after eight years of devoted service. His long command experience had impressed him deeply with the need for a continental union strong enough to maintain and defend itself. What he had seen in the last years of the war, after military victory was assured, had been alarming. Disgruntled soldiers, doubting that Congress would ever compensate them for their sacrifices, approached Washington with schemes for a military *coup d'état* that would establish the General as a limited monarch or simply force Congress to meet their demands. Washington scotched such designs; but he used his great prestige with Congress to obtain concessions for his soldiers, and as in the case of the following Circular Letter, he urged the states to secure their precarious national union before it was too late. Note the interesting resemblance between arguments offered in 1783 and the unity appeal of Washington's Farewell Address of 1796 (Document 69).

Circular Letter to the Governors of All the States on Disbanding the Army.

June 8, 1783

The great object, for which I had the honor to hold an appointment in the service of my country, being accomplished, I am now preparing to resign it into the hands of Congress, and to return to that domestic retirement, which, it is well known, I left with the greatest reluctance; a retirement for which I have never ceased to sigh, through a long and painful absence, and in which (remote from the noise and trouble of the world) I meditate to pass the remainder of my life, in a state of undisturbed repose. But before I carry this resolution into effect, I think it a duty incumbent on me to make this my last official communication; to congratulate you on the glorious events which Heaven has been pleased to produce in our favor; to offer my sentiments respecting some important subjects, which appear to me to be intimately connected with the tranquillity of the United States; to take my leave of your Excellency as a public character; and to give my final blessing to that country, in whose service I have spent the prime of my life, for whose sake I have consumed so many anxious days and watchful nights, and whose happiness, being extremely dear to me, will always constitute no inconsiderable part of my own.

Impressed with the liveliest sensibility on this pleasing occasion, I will claim the indulgence of dilating the more copiously on the subjects of our mutual felicitation. When we consider the magnitude of the prize we contended for, the doubtful nature of the contest, and the favorable manner in which it has terminated, we shall find the greatest possible reason for gratitude and rejoicing. This is a theme that will afford infinite delight to every benevolent and liberal mind, whether the event in contemplation be considered as the source of present enjoyment, or the parent of future happiness; and we shall have equal occasion to felicitate ourselves on the lot which Providence has assigned us, whether we view it in a natural, a political, or moral point of light.

The citizens of America, placed in the most enviable condition, as the sole lords and proprietors of a vast tract of continent, comprehending all the various soils and climates of the world, and abounding with all the necessaries and conveniences of life, are now, by the late satisfactory pacification, acknowledged to be possessed of absolute freedom and independency. They are, from this period, to be considered as the actors on a most conspicuous theatre, which seems to be peculiarly designated by Providence for the display of human greatness and felicity. Here they are not only surrounded with every thing, which can contribute to the completion of private and domestic enjoyment; but Heaven has crowned all its other blessings, by giving a fairer opportunity for political happiness, than any other nation has ever been favored with. Nothing can illustrate these observations more forcibly, than a recollection of the happy conjuncture of times and circumstances, under which our republic assumed its rank among the nations. The foundation of our empire was not laid in the gloomy age of ignorance and superstition; but at an epoch when the rights of mankind were better understood and more clearly defined, than at any former period. The researches of the human mind after social happiness have been carried to a great extent; the treasures of knowledge, acquired by the labors of philosophers, sages, and legislators, through a long succession of years, are laid open for our use, and their collected wisdom may be happily applied in the establishment of our forms of government. The free cultivation of letters, the unbounded extension of commerce, the progressive refinement of manners, the growing liberality of sentiment, and, above all, the pure and benign light of Revelation, have had a meliorating influence on mankind and increased the blessings of society. At this auspicious period, the United States came into existence as a nation; and, if their citizens should not be completely free and happy, the fault will be entirely their own.

Such is our situation, and such are our prospects; but notwithstanding the cup of blessing is thus reached out to us; notwithstanding happiness is ours, if we have a disposition to seize the occasion and make it our own; yet it appears to me there is an option still left to the United States of America, that it is in their choice, and depends upon their conduct, whether they will be respectable and prosperous, or contemptible and miserable, as a nation. This is the time of their political probation; this is the moment when the eyes of the whole world are turned upon them; this is the moment to establish or ruin their national character for ever; this is the favorable moment to give such a tone to our federal government, as will enable it to answer the ends of its institution, or this may be the ill-fated moment for relaxing the powers of the Union, annihilating the cement of the confederation, and exposing us to become the sport of European

Text: George Washington, *Writings,* ed. John C. Fitzpatrick ("George Washington Bicentennial Edition" [Washington, D.C.: Government Printing Office, 1938]), XXVI, 483-87, 494-96.

politics, which may play one State against another, to prevent their growing importance, and to serve their own interested purposes. For, according to the system of policy the States shall adopt at this moment, they will stand or fall; and by their confirmation or lapse it is yet to be decided, whether the revolution must ultimately be considered as a blessing or a curse; a blessing or a curse, not to the present age alone, for with our fate will the destiny of unborn millions be involved. . . .

There are four things, which, I humbly conceive, are essential to the well-being, I may even venture to say, to the existence of the United States, as an independent power.

First. An indissoluble union of the States under one federal head.

Secondly. A sacred regard to public justice.

Thirdly. The adoption of a proper peace establishment; and,

Fourthly. The prevalence of that pacific and friendly disposition among the people of the United States, which will induce them to forget their local prejudices and policies; to make those mutual concessions, which are requisite to the general prosperity; and, in some instances, to sacrifice their individual advantages to the interest of the community.

These are the pillars on which the glorious fabric of our independency and national character must be supported. Liberty is the basis; and whoever would dare to sap the foundation, or overturn the structure, under whatever spacious pretext he may attempt it, will merit the bitterest execration, and the severest punishment, which can be inflicted by his injured country. . . .

. . . . Here I might speak with the more confidence, from my actual observations; and, if it would not swell this letter (already too prolix) beyond the bounds I had prescribed to myself, I could demonstrate to every mind open to convic-

tion, that in less time, and with much less expense, than has been incurred, the war might have been brought to the same happy conclusion, if the resources of the continent could have been properly drawn forth; that the distresses and disappointments, which have very often occurred, have, in too many instances, resulted more from a want of energy in the Continental government, than a deficiency of means in the particular States; that the enefficacy of measures arising from the want of an adequate authority in the supreme power, from a partial compliance with the requisitions of Congress in some of the States, and from a failure of punctuality in others, while it tended to damp the zeal of those, which were more willing to exert themselves, served also to accumulate the expenses of the war, and to frustrate the best concerted plans; and that the discouragement occasioned by the complicated difficulties and embarrassments, in which our affairs were by this means involved, would have long ago produced the dissolution of any army, less patient, less virtuous, and less persevering, than that which I have had the honor to command. . . .

I now make it my earnest prayer, that God would have you and the State over which you preside, in his holy protection; that he would incline the hearts of the citizens to cultivate a spirit of subordination and obedience to government; to entertain a brotherly affection and love for one another, for their fellow citizens of the United States at large, and particularly for their brethren who have served in the field; and finally, that he would most graciously be pleased to dispose us all to do justice, to love mercy, and to demean ourselves with that charity, humility, and pacific temper of mind, which were the characteristics of the Divine Author of our blessed religion, and without an humble imitation of whose example in these things, we can never hope to be a happy nation.

CHAPTER 5

A More Perfect Union: 1783 to 1789

The French Revolution of 1789 led to Robespierre and then to Napoleon. The American Revolution of 1776 led to Washington, Adams, Jefferson, Madison—to succession of elected presidents administering a constitutional republic. The sharpness of the contrast has suggested to some scholars that the American Revolution was not properly a revolution at all but a colonial war for independence. Revolution or not, the American struggle from 1776 to 1783 did establish within a few years a new regime that would endure, despite the terrible Civil War of the 1860's, down to our time.

THE INDEPENDENT STATES

When revolution came, American society was not thrown into chaos. No void was left between the old regimes and the new. Within the states, well-organized movements led by responsible and politically experienced colonists assumed control and promptly founded constitutional governments. Disputes between "democratic" and "aristocratic" elements were serious, as Professor Jensen (Document 108) and other authorities maintain, yet rarely so grave as to drive men into resistance. The main enemy in 1776 was an external power represented in America by an invading army and its sympathizers.

The work of state constitution-making progressed rapidly in the midst of war. By July of 1777 all the states but three lived under written constitutions of their own devising. With extraordinary uniformity, Americans committed themselves to a republican system of government embodying the common principles of the Declaration of Independence. The source of political authority was the consent of the people. The end was the safety and happiness of the people, to be realized by securing their inherent rights to life, liberty, and property. The agents were the more or less direct representatives of the majority of society. Much of the political controversy of the time turned on this last point; but it was primarily an argument over "more or less," not over the principle of popular rule as such.

The new state governments were almost as similar in basic form as in purpose. The dominant concern apparent in the several constitutions was to control abuses of political power by a wide variety of institutional arrangements. Provision of a written constitution was in itself a primary source of restraint. Specific guarantees of civil liberties and due process of law, stated in a bill of rights, characterized the new constitutions. Regular and frequent elections (one-year terms of office were common) would keep government close to the constituency; and the branch of government closest to the people—the legislative—was given greatest power. On similar reasoning, the most feared branch—the executive—was left comparatively weak. Still, the constitution-makers hoped to achieve additional security against governmental tyranny from the separation of powers into three distinct branches which would check and balance each other and from the almost universal subdivision of the legislatures into two houses. The judicial branch in particular gained a measure of independence from its long term of office: seven states provided tenure during good behavior.

The new forms of government, bearing a strong resemblance to their colonial predecessors, were plainly of the democratic type. Some limitations on popular rule were provided by the varying property qualifications required of voters and of officeholders. Recent researches indicate that only a small proportion of citizens was excluded from voting by these restrictions. Disproportionate representation of the seaboard areas was, however, a legitimate grievance of the western counties in most Southern states. The most significant change in the direction of democracy was the immediate consequence of independence: home authorities, in some degree dependent on the people, displaced the whole apparatus of imperial authority in the states. (Some leading problems of the state governments are discussed by Jefferson in Document 55.)

Only with the greatest reluctance did the citizens of the several states concede to a new federal authority any of the powers they had assumed. This is perhaps the surest sign of the loyalty and confidence the new republics had won, or at least had carried over, from the old colonial governments.

CONFEDERATION AND CONSTITUTION

With the founding of new state commonwealths, Americans met the responsibilities of independence promptly and, on the whole, wisely. The hardly less compelling task of joining forces in a continental union proved a severe trial. Loyalty to the states came naturally for men who had long thought of themselves either as British citizens or as Virginians, Yorkers, Yankees, and the like. Attachment to the American union was an acquired sentiment. Not even the necessities of the Revolutionary War could persuade Americans to entrust adequate powers to their central authority, as Washington's eloquent pleas for support testify (Documents 52-54).

Yet the problem of union could not be evaded. Formerly the imperial authority had handled those concerns affecting the whole continent and demanding a common policy: defense, diplomacy, Indian relations, Western lands, external commerce, interstate conflicts, and more. Independence put responsibility in American hands. Most wanted the strength of union without the risk of raising a new oppressive central power.

In 1777 the Continental Congress approved the Articles of Confederation and submitted the instrument to the state legislatures for adoption. Interstate quarrels over Western land claims, especially the sharp dispute between Virginia and Maryland over the cession of Virginia's vast domain to the union, postponed ratification of the Articles until 1781. The Confederation provided a halfway house to federal union. The preamble defined the form of association as a "firm league of friendship" among the several states, and Article II explicitly pronounced that "Each state retains its sovereignty, freedom, and independence." In the Confederation Congress, the principal ruling body, each state held one vote. Amendments required the unanimous consent of the states. Although important central powers over such matters as war, diplomacy, and Indian affairs were assigned to Congress, these functions proved difficult to exercise. Positive action on all important matters required the assent of nine states. To raise men or money, the indispensables of government, Congress could only requisition the states and hope for compliance. There was no separate executive to provide strong leadership.

The record of the Confederation government from 1781 to 1788 was not a glorious one, although many writers have challenged the view that the union was *in extremis* when the new Constitution was formed. In foreign affairs the position of America was symbolized by the taunting suggestion of a British Foreign Secretary that the Confederation send out thirteen ambassadors since the general government seemed incapable of enforcing its agreements. The public finances were in sorry shape. Denied the power to lay import duties, Congress had to coax the states to meet tax requisitions (with limited success), seek more foreign loans, issue certificates of indebtedness, and in effect repudiate much of the domestic war debt by letting the Continental money sink to nothing. Power to regulate commerce had been withheld from Congress, and the states pursued their own varying designs, leading to such domestic trade wars as that between New York and New Jersey.

The most conspicuous achievement of the Confederation government was the adoption of a constructive policy for distributing Western lands among settlers (the Ordinance of 1785) and for initiating new states in the territories (the Northwest Ordinance of 1787). In practice, Congress responded to lobby pressures and to its own desperate financial needs by selling off millions of acres to speculating land companies at a few cents an acre. Congress gained some revenue, a few men reaped large profits, and thousands of settlers moved across the mountains to open a new West. Other accomplishments of the Confederation might be listed, yet the basic judgment seems to be that of its most sympathetic interpreter, historian Merrill Jensen: "The Congress of the United States had no power over either the states or their citizens. Hence, each state could govern itself as it pleased" (Document 108).

Few Americans were satisfied with the Articles of Confederation. Efforts to strengthen the government drew wide support, only to fail under an amendment procedure requiring unanimous consent. The grievances of specific economic interest groups—public creditors, for example, or merchants—supplied one of the motives for the movement toward a constitutional convention, as some writers have emphasized. Yet any American who wished his country strong, secure, and prosperous as the condition of his own "safety and happiness," if not for nobler reasons, could find an interest in reforming the central government. The question was how far to go toward nationalizing the political system.

Men like Washington and John Jay among the elder statesmen and Hamilton and Madison among the young reformers were convinced of the need for basic changes in the Confederation. The Annapolis Convention, in 1786, proposed a general convention to consider how the Confederation might be rendered "adequate to the exigencies of the Union." The "little Rebellion" of Daniel Shays in Massachusetts (1786-1787) raised visions of impending anarchy before the eyes of many solid citizens and so heightened their concern for constitutional reform. All the states but Rhode Island sent delegates to Philadelphia in the spring of 1787. Few of the sponsors expected what they got the following September: a new plan of union, ready for submission to state ratifying conventions.

Between December 1787 and July 1788 all the states but Rhode Island and North Carolina ratified the Constitution. The process was not smooth and easy. Important differences had emerged behind the closed doors of the Philadelphia meetings. Large states and small disputed over their relative importance in the new system, until the Connecticut (or Great) Compromise gave each group part of its demands: equal representation of states in the Senate, and proportional representation of numbers in the House. An elaborate compromise balanced the claims of Northern and Southern states. Finally, a large majority of the Convention supported Benjamin Franklin's view, that an actual imperfect constitution satisfying many of their pressing needs was far preferable to an endless quest for the ideal scheme (Document 59). In the state ratifying conventions the controversy grew more severe. Impassioned critics like Patrick Henry and Richard Henry Lee prophesied the death of liberty. The flaw most commonly attacked, however, was the absence of a bill of rights, and many conventions urged the adoption of amendments while voting for ratification. In the first Congress to meet under the Constitution, James Madison, a leading draughtsman and advocate of the original document, drew up the Bill of Rights. By the end of 1791, the first ten amendments had been ratified.

The Constitution has been called a bundle of compromises. Certainly no single interest or view was wholly satisfied, and many specific provisions did represent a middle term between opposing requirements. The most creative of the compromises was the formation of a federal union, combining state authority over local affairs—and these included vital concerns of life, liberty, and property—with a national government authorized in specific ways "to form a more perfect union, establish justice, insure domestic tranquility, provide for the common defense, promote the general welfare, and secure the blessings of liberty to ourselves and our posterity."

Underlying the compromises of the Constitution were certain fundamental agreements, as Professor Edmund Morgan argues (Document 110). The general government, no less than the state regimes, was to be republican in basis, end, and form. The founders had in view a government resting on the consent of the governed which would be strong enough to serve the needs of a growing nation and yet could not destroy the rights of men.

When the newly elected government began to assemble in New York on March 4, 1789, America was still far from the millennium. Of great significance was the willingness of dissenters to work within the system as a loyal opposition. No body of irreconcilables conspired to restore the old regime. Hard fights were still to be fought over the direction the new republic would take. But the Constitution proved a tough and flexible instrument which could be adapted to political changes in the face of changing times.

The First Republic: States in Confederation

TOWARD LIBERTY AND EQUALITY

55

GOVERNMENT AND LAW IN VIRGINIA

from Thomas Jefferson, *Notes on the State of Virginia*, 1782

Compared with other revolutions, the change of regimes in America was a remarkably regular and orderly affair. The course of events in Virginia fairly represents the general pattern. In May of 1776 the provincial Convention, already wielding the powers of government, appointed a committee to draft a constitution. Before the end of June a constitution was adopted by the representatives, opening with a memorable declaration of rights that summed up the principles of free, democratic government as understood by the Revolutionary generation. Thus, before the Declaration of Independence, Virginia had established a new political authority under its own fundamental laws. By the close of 1776 eight states had completed this process of establishing constitutional governments.

Thomas Jefferson (1743-1826) prepared his comprehensive *Notes on the State of Virginia* from 1781 to 1782 at the request of the Secretary of the French legation in Philadelphia. His informed discussion ranges from geography and natural history to manners and morals. Of particular interest here are the chapters delineating the new political order in Virginia. The commentary reflects both Jefferson's experience as a state legislator and governor and his reflections as a philosophic student of politics.

Jefferson's criticisms of limited voting rights and unequal sectional representation suggest that political democracy was indeed a source of controversy in the new states. Yet he finds other fundamental problems that would remain even if the voting scheme were perfectly democratic.

Virginia was typical of the independent states in leaving the task of making and ratifying the constitution to the regular legislature. Only Massachusetts (1780) and New Hampshire (1784) called distinct constitutional conventions and then submitted the result to popular referendums. Jefferson's objections to the Virginia procedure recall the principle of the Declaration: that government rests upon a social compact defining the ends and limits of political power. Thus a written constitution based directly upon popular consent is needed to keep government—even democratic government—within its proper bounds. Jefferson was especially concerned with the problem since Virginia, sharing the general preference of the states, had concentrated powers in the legislative branch.

QUERY XIII.

The constitution of the State and its several charters?

. . . In each state separately a new form of government was established. Of ours particularly the following are the outlines. The executive powers are lodged in the hands of a governor, chosen annually, and incapable of acting more than three years in seven. He is assisted by a council of eight members. The judiciary powers are divided among several courts, as will be hereafter explained. Legislation is exercised by two houses of assembly, the one called the house of Delegates, composed of two members from each county, chosen annually by the citizens, possessing an estate for life in 100 acres of uninhabited land, or 25 acres with a house on it, or in a house or lot in some town: the other called the Senate, consisting of 24 members, chosen quadrennially

by the same electors, who for this purpose are distributed into 24 districts. The concurrence of both houses is necessary to the passage of a law. They have the appointment of the governor and council, the judges of the superior courts, auditors, attorney general, treasurer, register of the land office, and delegates to congress. . . .

This constitution was formed when we were new and unexperienced in the science of government. It was the first, too, which was formed in the whole United States. No wonder then that time and trial have discovered very capital defects in it.

Text: Thomas Jefferson, "Notes on the State of Virginia," *Writings,* ed. Paul Leicester Ford (New York: G. P. Putnam's Sons, 1894), III, 214-226, 229, 235, 242-244, 251-255, 261-266.

1. The majority of the men in the state, who pay and fight for its support, are unrepresented in the legislature, the roll of freeholders entitled to vote, not including generally the half of those on the roll of the militia, or of the tax-gatherers.

2. Among those who share the representation, the shares are very unequal. Thus the county of Warwick, with only one hundred fighting men, has an equal representation with the county of Loudon, which has 1746. So that every man in Warwick has as much influence in the government as 17 men in Loudon. But lest it should be thought that an equal interspersion of small among large counties, through the whole state, may prevent any danger of injury to particular parts of it, we will divide it into districts, and shew the proportions of land, of fighting men, and of representation in each: [see below]

An inspection of this table will supply the place of commentaries on it. It will appear at once that nineteen thousand men, living below the falls of the rivers, possess half of the senate, and want four members only of possessing a majority of the house of delegates; a want more than supplied by the vicinity of their situation to the seat of government, and of course the greater degree of convenience and punctuality with which their members may and will attend in the legislature. These nineteen thousand, therefore, living in one part of the country, give law to upwards of thirty thousand living in another, and appoint all their chief officers executive and judiciary. From the difference of their situation and circumstances, their interests will often be very different.

3. The senate is, by its constitution, too homogenous with the house of delegates. Being chosen by the same electors, at the same time, and out of the same subjects, the choice falls of course on men of the same description. The purpose of establishing different houses of legislation is to introduce the influence of different interests or different principles. Thus in Great Britain it is said their constitution relies on the house of commons for honesty, and the lords for wisdom; which would be a rational reliance, if honesty were to be bought with money, and if wisdom were hereditary. In some of the American States, the delegates and senators are so chosen, as that the first represent the persons, and the second the property of the State. But with us, wealth and wisdom have equal chance for admission into both houses. We do not, therefore, derive from the separation of our legislature into two houses, those benefits which a proper complication of principles is capable of producing, and those which alone can compensate the evils which may be produced by their dissensions.

4. All the powers of government, legislative, executive, and judiciary, result to the legislative body. The concentrating these in the same hands is precisely the definition of despotic government. It will be no alleviation that these powers will be exercised by a plurality of hands, and not by a single one. 173 despots would surely be as oppressive as one. Let those who doubt it turn their eyes on the republic of Venice. As little will it avail us that they are chosen by ourselves. An *elective despotism* was not the government we fought for, but one which should not only be founded on free principles, but in which the powers of government should be so divided and balanced among several bodies of magistracy, as that no one could transcend their legal limits, without being effectually checked and restrained by the others. For this reason that convention, which passed the ordinance of government, laid its foundation on this basis, that the legislative, executive and judiciary departments should be separate and distinct, so that no person should exercise the powers of more than one of them at the same time. But no barrier was provided between these several powers. The judiciary and executive members were left dependent on the legislative, for their subsistence in office, and some of them for their continuance in it. If

	Square miles	Fighting men	Delegates	Senators
Between the sea-coast and falls of the rivers	11,205	19,012	71	12
Between the falls of the rivers and Blue Ridge of mountains	18,759	18,828	46	8
Between the Blue Ridge and the Alleghany	11,911	7,673	16	2
Between the Alleghany and Ohio..	79,650	4,458	16	2
Total	121,525	49,971	149	24

therefore the legislature assumes executive and judiciary powers, no opposition is likely to be made; nor, if made, can it be effectual; because in that case they may put their proceedings into the form of an act of assembly, which will render them obligatory on the other branches. They have accordingly in many instances, decided rights which should have been left to judiciary controversy: and the direction of the executive, during the whole time of their session, is becoming habitual and familiar. And this is done with no ill intention. The views of the present members are perfectly upright. When they are led out of their regular province, it is by art in others, and inadvertence in themselves. And this will probably be the case for some time to come. But it will not be a very long time. Mankind soon learn to make interested uses of every right and power which they possess, or may assume. The public money and public liberty, intended to have been deposited with three branches of magistracy, but found inadvertently to be in the hands of one only, will soon be discovered to be sources of wealth and dominion to those who hold them; distinguished, too, by this tempting circumstance, that they are the instrument, as well as the object, of acquisition. With money we will get men, said Caesar, and with men we will get money. Nor should our assembly be deluded by the integrity of their own purposes, and conclude that these unlimited powers will never be abused, because themselves are not disposed to abuse them. They should look forward to a time, and that not a distant one, when a corruption in this, as in the country from which we derive our origin, will have seized the heads of government, and be spread by them through the body of the people; when they will purchase the voices of the people, and make them pay the price. Human nature is the same on every side of the Atlantic, and will be alike influenced by the same causes. The time to guard against corruption and tyranny, is before they shall have gotten hold of us. It is better to keep the wolf out of the fold, than to trust to drawing his teeth and talons after he shall have entered. To render these considerations the more cogent, we must observe in addition:

5. That the ordinary legislature may alter the constitution itself. On the discontinuance of assemblies, it became necessary to substitute in their place some other body, competent to the ordinary business of government, and to the calling forth the powers of the State for the maintenance of our opposition to Great Britain. Conventions were therefore introduced, consisting of two delegates from each county, meeting together and forming one house, on the plan of the former house of Burgesses, to whose places they succeeded. These were at first chosen anew for every particular session. But in March 1775, they recommended to the people to choose a convention, which should continue in office a year. This was done, accordingly, in April 1775, and in the July following that convention passed an ordinance for the election of delegates in the month of April annually. It is well known, that in July 1775, a separation from Great Britain and establishment of republican government, had never yet entered into any person's mind. A convention, therefore, chosen under that ordinance, cannot be said to have been chosen for the purposes which certainly did not exist in the minds of those who passed it. Under this ordinance, at the annual election in April 1776, a convention for the year was chosen. Independance, and the establishment of a new form of government, were not even yet the objects of the people at large. . . . So that the electors of April 1776, no more than the legislators of July 1775, not thinking of independance and a permanent republic, could not mean to vest in these delegates powers of establishing them or any authorities other than those of the ordinary legislature. So far as a temporary organization of government was necessary to render our opposition energetic, so far their organization was valid. But they received in their creation no powers but what were given to every legislature before and since. They could not, therefore, pass an act transcendent to the powers of other legislatures. If the present assembly pass an act, and declare it shall be irrevocable by subsequent assemblies, the declaration is merely void, and the act repealable, as other acts are. So far, and no farther authorized, they organized the government by the ordinance entitled a Constitution or Form of government. It pretends to no higher authority than the other ordinance of the same session; it does not say that it shall be perpetual; that it shall be unalterable by other legislatures; that it shall be transcendent above the powers of those who they knew would have equal power with themselves. . . . The other states in the union have been of opinion that to render a form of government unalterable by ordinary acts of assembly, the people must delegate persons with special powers. They have accordingly chosen special conventions to form and fix their governments. The individuals then who maintain the contrary opinion in this country, should have the modesty to suppose it possible that they may be wrong, and the rest of America right. But if there be only a possibility of their

being wrong, if only a plausible doubt remains of the validity of the ordinance of government, is it not better to remove that doubt by placing it on a bottom which none will dispute? If they be right we shall only have the unnecessary trouble of meeting once in convention. If they be wrong, they expose us to the hazard of having no fundamental rights at all. True it is, this is no time for deliberating on forms of government. While an enemy is within our bowels, the first object is to expel him. But when this shall be done, when peace shall be established, and leisure given us for intrenching within good forms, the rights for which we have bled, let no man be found indolent enough to decline a little more trouble for placing them beyond the reach of question. . . .

QUERY XIV.

The administration of justice and the description of the laws?

. . . Many of the laws which were in force during the monarchy being relative merely to that form of government, or inculcating principles inconsistent with republicanism, the first assembly which met after the establishment of the commonwealth, appointed a committee to revise the whole code, to reduce it into proper form and volume, and report it to the assembly. This work has been executed by three gentlemen [Jefferson, Wythe and Pendleton], and reported; but probably will not be taken up till a restoration of peace shall leave to the legislature leisure to go through such a work.

The plan of the revisal was this. The common law of England, by which is meant that part of the English law which was anterior to the date of the oldest statutes extant, is made the basis of the work. It was thought dangerous to attempt to reduce it to a text; it was therefore left to be collected from the usual monuments of it. Necessary alterations in that, and so much of the whole body of the British statutes, and of acts of assembly, as were thought proper to be

retained, were digested into 126 new acts, in which simplicity of style was aimed at, as far as was safe. The following are the most remarkable alterations proposed:

To change the rules of descent, so as that the lands of any person dying intestate shall be divisible equally among all his children, or other representatives, in equal degree. . . .

To establish religious freedom on the broadest bottom.

To emancipate all slaves born after passing the act. The bill reported by the revisers does not itself contain this proposition; but an amendment containing it was prepared, to be offered to the legislature whenever the bill should be taken up, and further directing, that they should continue with their parents to a certain age, then be brought up, at the public expence, to tillage, arts, or sciences, according to their geniusses, till the females should be eighteen, and the males twenty-one years of age, when they should be colonized to such place as the circumstances of the time should render most proper, sending them out with arms, implements of houshold and of the handicraft arts, seeds, pairs of the useful domestic animals, &c. to declare them a free and independant people, and extend to them our alliance and protection, till they shall have acquired strength; and to send vessels at the same time to other parts of the world for an equal number of white inhabitants; to induce whom to migrate hither, proper encouragements were to be proposed. It will probably be asked, Why not retain and incorporate the blacks into the state, and thus save the expense of supplying by importation of white settlers, the vacancies they will leave? Deep-rooted prejudices entertained by the whites; ten thousand recollections, by the blacks, of the injuries they have sustained; new provocations; the real distinctions which nature has made; and many other circumstances will divide us into parties, and produce convulsions, which will probably never end but in the extermination of the one or the other race. . . .

PERILOUS FREEDOM: TWO VIEWS OF SHAYS' REBELLION

In the 1780's Massachusetts farmers in common with their neighbors of Rhode Island and other states were feeling the effects of a postwar depression. The old Continental paper money was worthless, hard cash was scarce, and the tax burden fell heavily on landed property. Many farmers faced the prospect of losing their holdings for failure to pay their debts and taxes.

Protest meetings throughout the state demanded relief in the form of paper money, tax reforms, and "stay" laws to postpone court actions against delinquent debtors. Similar campaigns had won substantial concessions in more than half of the states. When the Massachusetts legislature failed to meet these demands, a movement mainly concentrated in the interior counties and led by Daniel Shays, a Revolutionary veteran, turned to direct action. Mobs forcibly closed the courts at Northampton, Worcester,

Springfield, and elsewhere: this was one sure way to protect debtors from the penalties of the law. In December of 1786, Shays gathered some twelve hundred armed followers for an attack on the federal arsenal at Springfield. This time he was met and routed by the state militia. By the end of February the rebellion had been crushed. The legislature pardoned all but a few leaders and eventually granted even Shays a pardon. At the next election Governor James Bowdoin, who had put down the rebellion, was defeated by John Hancock. The new legislature made modest concessions to the discontented farmers.

56

THE MAD CRY OF THE MOB

from Abigail Adams, Letter to Thomas Jefferson, January 2, 1787

Abigail, wife of John Adams, reported the events of Shays' Rebellion to Thomas Jefferson, then the American minister in Paris. Her reactions were those of many leading citizens who took the disturbances as a warning that "the mad cry of the mob" might endanger property and order, although Mrs. Adams was far calmer and more understanding than those who dropped dark hints of monarchy and military coups as the necessary remedies. Shays' rebellion provided both an incentive and an argument for the movement leading to a strong national government as the sole alternative to anarchy.

. . . With regard to the Tumults in my Native state which you inquire about, I wish I could say that report had exagerated them. It is too true Sir that they have been carried to so allarming a Height as to stop the Courts of justice in several Counties. Ignorant, wrestless desperadoes, without conscience or principals, have led a deluded multitude to follow their standard, under pretence of grievances which have no existance but in their immaginations. Some of them were crying out for a paper currency, some for an equal distribution of property, some were for annihilating all debts, others complaning that the Senate was a useless Branch of Government, that the Court of common pleas was unnecessary, and that the sitting of the General Court in Boston was a grievence. By this list you will see the materials which compose this rebellion, and the necessity there is of the wisest and most vigorus measures to quell and suppress it. Instead of that laudible spirit which you approve, which makes a people watchfull over their Liberties and alert in the defence of them, these mobish insurgents are for sapping the foundation, and distroying the whole fabrick at once. —But as these people make only a small part of the state, when compared to the more sensible and judicious, and altho they create a just allarm and give much trouble and uneasiness, I cannot help flattering myself that they will prove sallutary to the state at large, by leading to an investigation of the causes which have pro-

duced these commotions. Luxery and extravagance both in furniture and dress had pervaded all orders of our Countrymen and women, and was hastning fast to sap their independance by involving every class of citizens in distress, and accumulating debts upon them which they were unable to discharge. Vanity was becoming a more powerfull principal than patriotism. The lower order of the community were prest for taxes, and tho possest of landed property they were unable to answer the demand, whilst those who possest money were fearfull of lending, least the mad cry of the mob should force the Legislature upon a measure very different from the touch of Midas.

By the papers I send you, you will see the beneficial effects already produced. An act of the Legislature laying duties of 15 per cent upon many articles of British manufacture and totally prohibiting others—a number of Vollunteers Lawyers physicians and Merchants from Boston made up a party of Light horse commanded by Col. Hitchbourn, Leit. Col. Jackson and Higgenson, and went out in persuit of the insurgents and were fortunate enough to take 3 of their principal Leaders, Shattucks Parker and Page. Shattucks defended himself and was wounded in his knee with a broadsword. He is in Jail in Boston and will no doubt be made an example of. . . .

Text: Thomas Jefferson, *Papers,* ed. Julian P. Boyd (Princeton, N.J.: Princeton University Press, 1955), XI, 86-87.

57

A LITTLE REBELLION NOW AND THEN

from Thomas Jefferson, Letter to James Madison, January 30, 1787

Jefferson, commenting on the news of Shays' Rebellion to his friend Madison, refused to take alarm. His philosophy left room for "a little rebellion now and then" as a way of arresting the tendency of governments to grow corrupt and of arousing general concern for public affairs. Far more serious to Jefferson were John Jay's pending negotiations with Spain, which would abandon American rights to navigate the Mississippi River in return for commercial privileges in Spanish ports. This, Jefferson insisted, would drive the trans-Appalachian settlers to secession and sacrifice a vast and valuable domain. Under a storm of protest Jay's negotiations were cut off.

. . . I am impatient to learn your sentiments on the late troubles in the Eastern states. So far as I have yet seen, they do not appear to threaten serious consequences. Those states have suffered by the stoppage of the channels of their commerce, which have not yet found other issues. This must render money scarce, and make the people uneasy. This uneasiness has produced acts absolutely unjustifiable: but I hope they will provoke no severities from their governments. A consciousness of those in power that their administration of the public affairs has been honest, may perhaps produce too great a degree of indignation: and those characters wherein fear predominates over hope may apprehend too much from these instances of irregularity. They may conclude too hastily that nature has formed man insusceptible of any other government but that of force, a conclusion not founded in truth, nor experience. Societies exist under three forms sufficiently distinguishable. 1. Without government, as among our Indians. 2. Under governments wherein the will of every one has a just influence, as in the case in England in a slight degree, and in our states in a great one. 3. Under governments of force: as in the case in all other monarchies and in most of the other republics. To have an idea of the curse of existence under these last, they must be seen. It is a government of wolves over sheep. It is a problem, not clear in my mind, that the 1st. condition is not the best. But I believe it to be inconsistent with any great degree of population. The second state has a great deal of good in it.

Text: Thomas Jefferson, Writings, ed. Paul Leicester Ford (New York: G. P. Putnam's Sons, 1894), IV, 361-63.

The mass of mankind under that enjoys a precious degree of liberty and happiness. It has it's evils too: the principal of which is the turbulence to which it is subject. But weigh this against the oppressions of monarchy, and it becomes nothing. *Malo periculosam libertatem quam quietam servitutem.* [I prefer perilous liberty to quiet servitude] Even this evil is productive of good. It prevents the degeneracy of government, and nourishes a general attention to the public affairs. I hold it that a little rebellion now and then is a good thing, and as necessary in the political world as storms in the physical. Unsuccessful rebellions indeed generally establish the incroachments on the rights of the people which have produced them. An observation of this truth should render honest republican governors so mild in their punishment of rebellions, as not to discourage them too much. It is a medicine necessary for the sound health of government. If these transactions give me no uneasiness, I feel very differently at another peice of intelligence, to wit, the possibility that the navigation of the Missisipi may be abandoned to Spain. I never had any interest Westward of the Alleghaney; and I never will have any. But I have had great opportunities of knowing the character of the people who inhabit that country. And I will venture to say that the act which abandons the navigation of the Missisipi is an act of separation between the Eastern and Western country. It is a relinquishment of five parts out of eight of the territory of the United States, an abandonment of the fairest subject for the paiment of our public debts, and the chaining those debts on our own necks *in perpetuum.* . . .

THE NEW TERRITORIES

58

NORTHWEST ORDINANCE OF 1787

from *Northwest Ordinance*, 1787

The reputation of the Confederation government (1781-1788) has improved markedly in the past generation, although very few present historians would care to undo the work of the Constitutional Convention of 1787, which overthrew the Confederation. The "Critical Period" under the Articles of Confederation was not, it seems, so chaotic and desperate a time as Federalist sources and earlier interpreters showed it to be. And many of the troubles of the "first republic"—problems of foreign commerce and public finance, of military and diplomatic weakness, of Indian disturbances and inter-state rivalries—were less a reflection on specific political arrangements than they were a reflection of the intrinsic difficulties of a struggling new nation confronting the task of establishing its independence.

With these conditions understood, one still must emphasize the failures of the Con-federation regime in meeting the great common problems of the states. Yet the most significant achievement of the general government in this period was the introduction of a system for the settlement, organization, and eventual absorption of the West. One can hardly overestimate the importance of the decision to treat the country beyond the Alleghenies not as the colonial domain of the original states but as the potential source of equal partners in statehood.

During and after the Revolution speculative land promoters directed a great migration of bold spirits across the mountains. By 1790 there were 120,000 Americans in the West, mainly concentrated in the future states of Kentucky and Tennessee. Virginia and the other states with Western land claims began to cede their holdings to the Confederation in 1781, although the process was not completed until Georgia made its final cession in 1802. Thus responsibility for planning and directing Western development fell to the Confederation Congress. Since most of the land south of the Ohio quickly passed into private or company hands, the exercise of Congressional authority was largely directed toward the Old Northwest, an area including what are now the states of Ohio, Indiana, Illinois, Michigan, and Wisconsin.

The first major public action was the passage of Jefferson's Ordinance of 1784, a democratic scheme providing for the rapid assumption of self-governing powers by numerous small territories. This was followed by the Ordinance of 1785, which applied the New England township scheme to the survey and sale of public lands. In advance of settlement, the government would lay out rectangular townships of thirty-six sections, each containing one square mile (or 640 acres). This became the basic plan for future public land divisions; however, the plan had only slight *immediate* effect, for millions of acres of the best land had already been disposed of at bargain prices to land speculators or had been reserved by the states as bounty for their Revolutionary veterans.

The urgent demands of Western settlers together with the skillful lobbying of the Ohio and Scioto Land Companies led Congress to pass the Northwest Ordinance of 1787. Superseding the earlier Jefferson plan for territorial government, the Northwest Ordinance provided for fewer and larger territories (three to five) and for a slower transition from Congressional to local control. It remained a fundamentally democratic plan for forming new states, however, and it included significant provisions for the maintenance of civil liberties, for the advancement of education, and for the exclusion of slavery. The first Congress under the new Constitution confirmed the action of the Confederation. The main terms of the Ordinance are printed in the selection below.

Section 1. *Be it ordained by the United States in Congress assembled,* That the said Territory for the purpose of temporary government, be one district, subject, however, to be divided into two districts, as future circumstances may, in the opinion of Congress, make it expedient. . . .

Sec. 3. *Be it ordained by the authority afore-said,* That there shall be appointed, from time to

Text: Salmon P. Chase (ed.), *The Statutes of Ohio and of the Northwestern Territory, Adopted or Enacted from 1788 to 1833 Inclusive; Together with the Ordinance of 1787* (Cincinnati: Corey & Fairbank, 1833), I, 66-69 *passim.*

time, by Congress, a governor, whose commission shall continue in force for the term of three years, unless sooner revoked by Congress; he shall reside in the district, and have a freehold estate therein, in one thousand acres of land, while in the exercise of his office.

Sec. 4. There shall be appointed from time to time, by Congress, a secretary, whose commission shall continue in force for four years, unless sooner revoked; he shall reside in the districts, and have a freehold estate therein, in five hundred acres of land, while in the exercise of his office. It shall be his duty to keep and preserve the acts and laws passed by the legislature, and the public records of the district, and the proceedings of the governor in his executive department, and transmit authentic copies of such acts and proceedings every six months to the Secretary of Congress. There shall also be appointed a court, to consist of three judges, any two of whom to form a court, who shall have a common-law jurisdiction and reside in the district, and have each therein a freehold estate, in five hundred acres of land, while in the exercise of their offices; and their commissions shall continue in force during good behavior.

Sec. 5. The governor and judges, or a majority of them, shall adopt and publish in the district such laws of the original states, criminal and civil, as may be necessary, and best suited to the circumstances of the district, and report them to Congress from time to time, which laws shall be in force in the district until the organization of the general assembly therein, unless disapproved of by Congress; but afterward the legislature shall have authority to alter them as they shall think fit. . . .

Sec. 9. So soon as there shall be five thousand free male inhabitants, of full age, in the district, upon giving proof thereof to the governor, they shall receive authority, with time and place, to elect representatives from their counties or townships, to represent them in the general assembly: *Provided,* That for every five hundred free male inhabitants there shall be one representative, and so on, progressively, with the number of free male inhabitants, shall the right of representation increase, until the number of representatives shall amount to twenty-five; after which the number and proportion of representatives shall be regulated by the legislature: *Provided,* That no person be eligible or qualified to act as a representative unless he shall have been a citizen of one of the United States three years, and be a resident in the district, or unless he shall have resided in the district three years; and, in either case, shall likewise hold in his own right, in fee-simple,

two hundred acres of land within the same: *Provided also,* That a freehold in fifty acres of land in the district, having been a citizen of one of the states, and being resident in the district, or the like freehold and two years' residence in the district, shall be necessary to qualify a man as an elector of a representative.

Sec. 10. The representatives thus elected shall serve for the term of two years; and in case of the death of a representative, or removal from office, the governor shall issue a writ to the county or township, for which he was a member, to elect another in his stead, to serve for the residue of the term.

Sec. 11. The general assembly, or legislature, shall consist of the governor, legislative council, and a house of representatives. The legislative council shall consist of five members, to continue in office five years, unless sooner removed by Congress; any three of them to be a quorum; and the members of the council shall be nominated and appointed in the following manner, to wit: As soon as representatives shall be elected the governor shall appoint a time and place for them to meet together, and when met they shall nominate ten persons, resident in the district, and each possessed of a freehold in five hundred acres of land, and return their names to Congress, five of whom Congress shall appoint and commission to serve as aforesaid; and whenever a vacancy shall happen in the Council, by death or removal from office, the house of representatives shall nominate two persons, qualified as aforesaid, for each vacancy, and return their names to Congress, one of whom Congress shall appoint and commission for the residue of the term; and every five years, four months at least before the expiration of the time of service of the members of the council, the said house shall nominate ten persons, qualified as aforesaid, and return their names to Congress, five of whom Congress shall appoint and commission to serve as members of the council five years, unless sooner removed. And the governor, legislative council, and house of representatives shall have authority to make laws in all cases for the good government of the district, not repugnant to the principles and articles in this ordinance established and declared. And all bills, having passed by a majority in the house, and by a majority in the council, shall be referred to the governor for his assent; but no bill, or legislative act whatever, shall be of any force ·without his assent. The governor shall have power to convene, prorogue, and dissolve the general assembly when, in his opinion, it shall be expedient. . . .

Sec. 14. It is hereby ordained and declared, by the authority aforesaid, that the following articles shall be considered as articles of compact between the original states and the people and states in the said territory, and forever remain unalterable, unless by common consent, to wit:

Article I

No person, demeaning himself in a peaceable and orderly manner, shall ever be molested on account of his mode of worship, or religious sentiments, in the said territory.

Article II

The inhabitants of the said territory shall always be entitled to the benefits of the writs of habeas corpus and of the trial by jury, of a proportionate representation of the people in the legislature, and of judicial proceedings according to the course of the common law. All persons shall be bailable, unless for capital offenses, where the proof shall be evident, or the presumption great. All fines shall be moderate; and no cruel or unusual punishment shall be inflicted. No man shall be deprived of his liberty or property, but by the judgment of his peers, or the law of the land, and, should the public exigencies make it necessary, for the common preservation, to take any person's property, or to demand his particular services, full compensation shall be made for the same. And, in the just preservation of rights and property, it is understood and declared that no law ought ever to be made or have force in the said territory that shall, in any manner whatever, interfere with or affect private contracts, or engagements, bona fide, and without fraud previously formed.

Article III

Religion, morality, and knowledge being necessary to good government and the happiness of mankind, schools and the means of education shall forever be encouraged. The utmost good faith shall always be observed toward the Indians; their lands and property shall never be taken from them without their consent; and in their property, rights, and liberty they never shall be invaded or disturbed unless in just and lawful wars authorized by Congress; but laws founded in justice and humanity shall, from time to time, be made, for preventing wrongs being done to them and for preserving peace and friendship with them.

Article IV

The said territory, and the states which may be formed therein, shall forever remain a part of this confederacy of the United States of America, subject to the Articles of Confederation, and to such alterations therein as shall be constitutionally made; and to all the acts and ordinances of the United States in Congress assembled, conformable thereto. The inhabitants and settlers in the said territory shall be subject to pay a part of the federal debts contracted, or to be contracted, and a proportional part of the expenses of government to be apportioned on them by Congress, according to the same common rule and measure by which apportionments thereof shall be made on the other states; and the taxes for paying their proportion shall be laid and levied by the authority and direction of the legislatures of the district, or districts, or new states, as in the original states, within the time agreed upon by the United States in Congress assembled. The legislatures of those districts, or new states, shall never interfere with the primary disposal of the soil by the United States in Congress assembled, nor with any regulations Congress may find necessary for securing the title in such soil to the bona fide purchasers. No tax shall be imposed on lands the property of the United States; and in no case shall nonresident proprietors be taxed higher than residents. The navigable waters leading into the Mississippi and Saint Lawrence, and the carrying places between the same, shall be common highways, and forever free, as well to the inhabitants of the said territory as to the citizens of the United States, and those of any other states that may be admitted into the confederacy, without any tax, impost, or duty therefor.

Article V

There shall be formed in the said territory not less than three nor more than five states. . . . And whenever any of the said states shall have sixty thousand free inhabitants therein, such state shall be admitted by its delegates into the Congress of the United States, on an equal footing with the original states, in all respects whatever; and shall be at liberty to form a permanent constitution and state government: *Provided,* The constitution and government, so to be formed, shall be republican, and in conformity to the principles contained in these articles, and, so far as it can be consistent with the general interest of the confederacy, such admission shall be allowed at an earlier period, and when there may be a less number of free inhabitants in the state than sixty thousand.

Article VI

There shall be neither slavery nor involuntary servitude in the said territory, otherwise than in the punishment of crimes, whereof the party shall have been duly convicted: *Provided always,* That any person escaping into the same, from whom labor or service is lawfully claimed in any one of the original states, such fugitive may be lawfully reclaimed, and conveyed to the person claiming his or her labor or service as aforesaid. . . .

Done by the United States, in Congress assembled, the 13th day of July, in the year of our Lord 1787, and of their sovereignty and independence the twelfth.

Birth of a Nation

59

BENJAMIN FRANKLIN ON THE GREAT COMPROMISE

from James Madison, *Debates of the Constitutional Convention,* 1787

The political system of the Articles of Confederation lasted from 1781 to 1788, an era viewed by some writers—contemporary and modern—as "The Critical Period" in the life of the new nation, by others as a time of social vigor and democratic progress. Certainly the Articles created a weak central government, reflecting the hostility of the Revolutionary generation toward concentration of power and their strong attachment to the several states. The weakness of the Confederation was painfully clear in matters of diplomacy, defense, commercial regulation, and public finance. Its virtues were primarily those of the constituent states, which held the major share of power under the system.

A determined movement to strengthen the union gathered support in the 1780's. At Annapolis in 1786 delegates from five states met long enough to call for a general convention at Philadelphia in May of next year. The Philadelphia convention, they proposed, should recommend ways "to render the constitution of the Federal Government adequate to the exigencies of the Union." Between May 25 and September 17, 1787, the Convention shaped a new Constitution of the United States. Only a newly framed government referred to the people for adoption could save the union from chaos, the Founders insisted.

On the course of constitution-making, see Edmund Morgan's discussion in Document 110. The closing remarks of the venerable Doctor Franklin capture some of the spirit of the Founding Fathers. They approached their task with brave hopes for the future of the republican experiment but also with a prudent regard for political realities. The delegates had compromised their differences to make a sound Constitution that would, if well administered, serve the urgent needs of the nation. Let them not risk everything, Franklin counseled, by demanding an unattainable perfection.

The speech is taken from James Madison's notes, first published posthumously in 1840. The meetings of the Constitutional Convention were held behind closed doors and no official record of debates was kept.

Monday, September 17, 1787: In Convention

The engrossed Constitution being read,

Doctor FRANKLIN rose with a speech in his hand, which he had reduced to writing for his own conveniency, and which Mr. Wilson read in the words following.

Mr. President

I confess that there are several parts of this constitution which I do not at present approve,

Text: James Madison, "Journal of the Constitutional Convention," *Writings,* ed. Gaillard Hunt (New York: G. P. Putnam's Sons, 1903), IV, 472-75, 482-83.

but I am not sure I shall never approve them: For having lived long, I have experienced many instances of being obliged by better information, or fuller consideration, to change opinions even on important subjects, which I once thought right, but found to be otherwise. It is therefore that the older I grow, the more apt I am to doubt my own judgment, and to pay more respect to the judgment of others. Most men indeed as well as most sects in Religion, think themselves in possession of all truth, and that wherever others differ from them it is so far error. Steele a Protestant in a Dedication tells the Pope, that the only difference between our Churches in their opinions of the certainty of their doctrines is, the Church of Rome is infallible and the Church of England is never in the wrong. But though many private persons think almost as highly of their own infallibility as of that of their sect, few express it so naturally as a certain french lady, who in a dispute with her sister, said "I don't know how it happens, Sister but I meet with no body but myself, that's always in the right—*Il n'y a que moi qui a toujours raison.*"

In these sentiments, Sir, I agree to this Constitution with all its faults, if they are such; because I think a general Government necessary for us, and there is no form of Government but what may be a blessing to the people if well administered, and believe farther that this is likely to be well administered for a course of years, and can only end in Despotism, as other forms have done before it, when the people shall became so corrupted as to need despotic Government, being incapable of any other. I doubt too whether any other Convention we can obtain, may be able to make a better Constitution. For when you assemble a number of men to have the advantage of their joint wisdom, you inevitably assemble with those men, all their prejudices, their passions, their errors of opinion, their local interests, and their selfish views. From such an assembly can a perfect production be expected? It therefore astonishes me, Sir, to find this system approaching so near to perfection as it does; and I think it will astonish our enemies, who are waiting with confidence to hear that our councils are confounded like those of the Builders of Babel; and that our States are on the point of separation, only to meet hereafter for the purpose of cutting one another's throats. Thus I consent, Sir, to this Constitution because I expect no better, and because I am not sure, that it is not the best. The opinions I have had of its errors, I sacrifice to the public good. I have never whispered a syllable of them abroad. Within these walls they were born, and here they shall die. If every one of us in returning to our Constituents were to report the objections he has had to it, and endeavor to gain partizans in support of them, we might prevent its being generally received, and thereby lose all the salutary effects & great advantages resulting naturally in our favor among foreign Nations as well as among ourselves, from our real or apparent unanimity. Much of the strength & efficiency of any Government in procuring and securing happiness to the people, depends, on opinion, on the general opinion of the goodness of the Government, as well as of the wisdom and integrity of its Governors. I hope therefore that for our own sakes as a part of the people, and for the sake of posterity, we shall act heartily and unanimously in recommending this Constitution (if approved by Congress & confirmed by the Conventions) wherever our influence may extend, and turn our future thoughts & endeavors to the means of having it well administered.

On the whole, Sir, I can not help expressing a wish that every member of the Convention who may still have objections to it, would with me, on this occasion doubt a little of his own infallibility, and to make manifest our unanimity, put his name to this instrument. . . .

Whilst the last members were signing it Doctor FRANKLIN looking towards the President's Chair, at the back of which a rising sun happened to be painted, observed to a few members near him, that Painters had found it difficult to distinguish in their art a rising from a setting sun. I have, said he, . . . often in the course of the Session, and the vicisitudes of my hopes and fears as to its issue, looked at that behind the President without being able to tell whether it was rising or setting: But now at length I have the happiness to know that it is a rising and not a setting Sun.

The Constitution being signed by all the members except Mr. [Edmund] Randolph [of Virginia], Mr. Mason, and Mr. Gerry who declined giving it the sanction of their names, the Convention dissolved itself by an Adjournment sine die—

60 THE CONSTITUTION OF THE UNITED STATES

The new Constitution was signed by thirty-nine of the delegates. Gerry of Massachusetts and Randolph and Mason of Virginia, dissented. Others, like Luther Martin of Maryland and Yates and Lansing of New York, expressed their disapproval by walking out on the Convention before the business was concluded. The completed instrument was the work of many hands, but James Madison has earned the title of "Father of the Constitution" for his distinguished work in the debates and proceedings of the Convention.

The Confederation Congress received the proposed Constitution with mixed reactions. To avoid a knockdown fight that would weaken chances of popular approval, the advocates of the new system persuaded Congress simply to advise the states to elect ratifying conventions where the issue could be resolved. Three states (Delaware, New Jersey, Georgia) approved quickly and unanimously. Elsewhere—notably in New Hampshire, Massachusetts, Virginia, and New York—the issue was closely contested. Indeed, North Carolina and Rhode Island postponed ratification until after the new government had been established. The ninth state, New Hampshire, ratified on June 21, 1788. This met the requirements for adoption set by the Convention. The Confederation Congress closed its career when it named New York as the provisional seat of government, called for elections, and fixed the date (March 4, 1789) for the meeting of the new Congress.

We the People of the United States, in Order to form a more perfect Union, establish Justice, insure domestic Tranquility, provide for the common defence, promote the general Welfare, and secure the Blessings of Liberty to ourselves and our Posterity, do ordain and establish this Constitution for the United States of America.

ARTICLE I.

Section 1.

All legislative Powers herein granted shall be vested in a Congress of the United States, which shall consist of a Senate and House of Representatives.

Section 2.

The House of Representatives shall be composed of Members chosen every second Year by the People of the several States, and the Electors in each State shall have the Qualifications requisite for Electors of the most numerous Branch of the State Legislature.

No Person shall be a Representative who shall not have attained to the Age of twenty five Years, and been seven Years a Citizen of the United States, and who shall not, when elected, be an Inhabitant of that State in which he shall be chosen.

Representatives and direct Taxes shall be apportioned among the several States which may be included within this Union, according to their respective Numbers, which shall be determined by adding to the whole Number of free Persons, including those bound to Service for a Term of Years, and excluding Indians not taxed, three fifths of all other Persons.[1] The actual Enumeration shall be made within three Years after the first Meeting of the Congress of the United States, and within every subsequent Term of ten Years, in such Manner as they shall by Law direct. The Number of Representatives shall not exceed one for every thirty Thousand, but each State shall have at Least one Representative; and until such enumeration shall be made, the State of New

Hampshire shall be entitled to chuse three, Massachusetts eight, Rhode-Island and Providence Plantations one, Connecticut five, New-York six, New Jersey four, Pennsylvania eight, Delaware one, Maryland six, Virginia ten, North Carolina five, South Carolina five, and Georgia three.

When vacancies happen in the Representation from any State, the Executive Authority thereof shall issue Writs of Election to fill such Vacancies.

The House of Representatives shall chuse their Speaker and other Officers; and shall have the sole Power of Impeachment.

Section 3.

The Senate of the United States shall be composed of two Senators from each State, chosen by the Legislature thereof, for six Years; and each Senator shall have one Vote.

Immediately after they shall be assembled in Consequence of the first Election, they shall be divided as equally as may be into three Classes. The Seats of the Senators of the first Class shall be vacated at the Expiration of the second Year, of the second Class at the Expiration of the fourth Year, and of the third Class at the Expiration of the sixth Year, so that one third may be chosen every second Year; and if Vacancies happen by Resignation, or otherwise, during the Recess of the Legislature of any State, the Executive thereof may make temporary Appointments until the next Meeting of the Legislature, which shall then fill such Vacancies.[2]

No Person shall be a Senator who shall not have attained to the Age of thirty Years, and been nine Years a Citizen of the United States, and who shall not, when elected, be an Inhabitant of that State for which he shall be chosen.

The Vice President of the United States shall be President of the Senate, but shall have no Vote, unless they be equally divided.

The Senate shall chuse their other Officers, and also a President pro tempore, in the Absence of the Vice President, or when he shall exercise the Office of President of the United States.

The Senate shall have the sole Power to try all Impeachments. When sitting for that Purpose,

[1] Modified by Amendment XIV, Section 2.
[2] Provisions changed by Amendment XVII.

they shall be on Oath or Affirmation. When the President of the United States is tried the Chief Justice shall preside: And no Person shall be convicted without the Concurrence of two thirds of the Members present.

Judgment in Cases of Impeachment shall not extend further than to removal from Office, and disqualification to hold and enjoy any Office of honor, Trust or Profit under the United States: but the Party convicted shall nevertheless be liable and subject to Indictment, Trial, Judgment and Punishment, according to Law.

Section 4.

The Times, Places and Manner of holding Elections for Senators and Representatives, shall be prescribed in each State by the Legislature thereof; but the Congress may at any time by Law make or alter such Regulations, except as to the Places of chusing Senators.

The Congress shall assemble at least once in every Year, and such Meeting shall be on the first Monday in December, unless they shall by Law appoint a different Day.[3]

Section 5.

Each House shall be the Judge of the Elections, Returns and Qualifications of its own Members, and a Majority of each shall constitute a Quorum to do Business; but a smaller Number may adjourn from day to day, and may be authorized to compel the Attendance of absent Members, in such Manner, and under such Penalties as each House may provide.

Each House may determine the Rules of its Proceedings, punish its Members for disorderly Behaviour, and, with the Concurrence of two thirds, expel a Member.

Each House shall keep a Journal of its Proceedings, and from time to time publish the same, excepting such Parts as may in their Judgment require Secrecy; and the Yeas and Nays of the Members of either House on any question shall, at the Desire of one fifth of those Present, be entered on the Journal.

Neither House, during the Session of Congress, shall, without the Consent of the other, adjourn for more than three days, nor to any other Place than that in which the two Houses shall be sitting.

Section 6.

The Senators and Representatives shall receive a Compensation for their Services, to be ascertained by Law, and paid out of the Treasury of the United States. They shall in all Cases, except Treason, Felony and Breach of the Peace, be privileged from Arrest during their Attendance at the Session of their respective Houses, and in going to and returning from the same; and for any Speech or Debate in either House, they shall not be questioned in any other Place.

No Senator or Representative shall, during the Time for which he was elected, be appointed to any civil Office under the Authority of the United States, which shall have been created, or the Emoluments whereof shall have been encreased during such time; and no Person holding any Office under the United States, shall be a Member of either House during his Continuance in Office.

Section 7.

All Bills for raising Revenue shall originate in the House of Representatives; but the Senate may propose or concur with Amendments as on other Bills.

Every Bill which shall have passed the House of Representatives and the Senate, shall, before it become a Law, be presented to the President of the United States; If he approve he shall sign it, but if not he shall return it, with his Objections to that House in which it shall have originated, who shall enter the Objections at large on their Journal, and proceed to reconsider it. If after such Reconsideration two thirds of that House shall agree to pass the Bill, it shall be sent, together with the Objections, to the other House, by which it shall likewise be reconsidered, and if approved by two thirds of that House, it shall become a Law. But in all such Cases the Votes of both Houses shall be determined by yeas and Nays, and the Names of the Persons voting for and against the Bill shall be entered on the Journal of each House respectively. If any Bill shall not be returned by the President within ten Days (Sundays excepted) after it shall have been presented to him, the Same shall be a Law, in like Manner as if he had signed it, unless the Congress by their Adjournment prevent its Return, in which Case it shall not be a Law.

Every Order, Resolution, or Vote to which the Concurrence of the Senate and House of Representatives may be necessary (except on a question of Adjournment) shall be presented to the President of the United States; and before the Same shall take Effect, shall be approved by him, or being disapproved by him, shall be repassed by two thirds of the Senate and House of Representatives, according to the Rules and Limitations prescribed in the Case of a Bill.

---

[3] Provision changed by Amendment XX, Section 2.

Section 8.

The Congress shall have Power To lay and collect Taxes, Duties, Imposts and Excises, to pay the Debts and provide for the common Defence and general Welfare of the United States; but all Duties, Imposts and Excises shall be uniform throughout the United States;

To borrow Money on the credit of the United States;

To regulate Commerce with foreign Nations, and among the several States, and with the Indian Tribes;

To establish an uniform Rule of Naturalization, and uniform Laws on the subject of Bankruptcies throughout the United States;

To coin Money, regulate the Value thereof, and of foreign Coin, and fix the Standard of Weights and Measures;

To provide for the Punishment of counterfeiting the Securities and current Coin of the United States;

To establish Post Offices and post Roads;

To promote the Progress of Science and useful Arts, by securing for limited Times to Authors and Inventors the exclusive Right to their respective Writings and Discoveries;

To constitute Tribunals inferior to the supreme Court;

To define and punish Piracies and Felonies committed on the high Seas, and Offences against the Law of Nations;

To declare War, grant Letters of Marque and Reprisal, and make Rules concerning Captures on Land and Water;

To raise and support Armies, but no Appropriation of Money to that Use shall be for a longer Term than two Years;

To provide and maintain a Navy;

To make Rules for the Government and Regulation of the land and naval Forces;

To provide for calling forth the Militia to execute the Laws of the Union, suppress Insurrections and repel Invasions;

To provide for organizing, arming, and disciplining, the Militia, and for governing such Part of them as may be employed in the Service of the United States, reserving to the States respectively, the Appointment of the Officers, and the Authority of training the Militia according to the discipline prescribed by Congress;

To exercise exclusive Legislation in all Cases whatsoever, over such District (not exceeding ten Miles square) as may, by Cession of particular States, and the Acceptance of Congress, become the Seat of the Government of the United States, and to exercise like Authority over all Places purchased by the Consent of the Legislature of the State in which the Same shall be, for the Erection of Forts, Magazines, Arsenals, dock-Yards, and other needful Buildings;—And

To make all Laws which shall be necessary and proper for carrying into Execution the foregoing Powers, and all other Powers vested by this Constitution in the Government of the United States. or in any Department or Officer thereof.

Section 9.

The Migration or Importation of such Persons as any of the States now existing shall think proper to admit, shall not be prohibited by the Congress prior to the Year one thousand eight hundred and eight, but a Tax or duty may be imposed on such Importation, not exceeding ten dollars for each Person.

The Privilege of the Writ of Habeas Corpus shall not be suspended, unless when in Cases of Rebellion or Invasion the public Safety may require it.

No Bill of Attainder or ex post facto Law shall be passed.

No Capitation, or other direct, Tax shall be laid, unless in Proportion to the Census or Enumeration herein before directed to be taken.

No Tax or Duty shall be laid on Articles exported from any State.

No Preference shall be given by any Regulation of Commerce or Revenue to the Ports of one State over those of another: nor shall Vessels bound to, or from, one State, be obliged to enter, clear, or pay Duties in another.

No Money shall be drawn from the Treasury, but in Consequence of Appropriations made by Law; and a regular Statement and Account of the Receipts and Expenditures of all public Money shall be published from time to time.

No Title of Nobility shall be granted by the United States: And no Person holding any Office of Profit or Trust under them, shall, without the Consent of the Congress, accept of any present, Emolument, Office, or Title, of any kind whatever, from any King, Prince, or foreign State.

Section 10.

No State shall enter into any Treaty, Alliance, or Confederation; grant Letters of Marque and Reprisal; coin Money; emit Bills of Credit; make any Thing but gold and silver Coin a Tender in Payment of Debts; pass any Bill of Attainder, ex post facto Law, or Law impairing the Obligation of Contracts, or grant any Title of Nobility.

No State shall, without the Consent of the Congress, lay any Imposts or Duties on Imports or Exports, except what may be absolutely necessary for executing it's inspection Laws: and the net Produce of all Duties and Imposts, laid by any State on Imports or Exports, shall be for the Use of the Treasury of the United States; and all such Laws shall be subject to the Revision and Controul of the Congress.

No State shall, without the Consent of Congress, lay any Duty of Tonnage, keep Troops, or Ships of War in time of Peace, enter into any Agreement or Compact with another State, or with a foreign Power, or engage in War, unless actually invaded, or in such imminent Danger as will not admit of delay.

ARTICLE II.

Section 1.

The executive Power shall be vested in a President of the United States of America. He shall hold his Office during the Term of four Years, and, together with the Vice President, chosen for the same Term, be elected, as follows:

Each State shall appoint, in such Manner as the Legislature thereof may direct, a Number of Electors, equal to the whole Number of Senators and Representatives to which the State may be entitled in the Congress: but no Senator or Representative, or Person holding an Office of Trust or Profit under the United States, shall be appointed an Elector.

The Electors shall meet in their respective States, and vote by Ballot for two Persons, of whom one at least shall not be an Inhabitant of the same State with themselves. And they shall make a List of all the Persons voted for, and of the Number of Votes for each; which List they shall sign and certify, and transmit sealed to the Seat of the Government of the United States, directed to the President of the Senate. The President of the Senate shall, in the Presence of the Senate and House of Representatives, open all the Certificates, and the Votes shall then be counted. The Person having the greatest Number of Votes shall be the President, if such Number be a Majority of the whole Number of Electors appointed; and if there be more than one who have such Majority, and have an equal Number of Votes, then the House of Representatives shall immediately chuse by Ballot one of them for President; and if no Person have a Majority, then from the five highest on the List the said House shall in like Manner chuse the President. But in chusing the President, the Votes shall be taken by States, the Representation from each State having one Vote; A quorum for this Purpose shall consist of a Member or Members from two thirds of the States, and a Majority of all the States shall be necessary to a Choice. In every Case, after the Choice of the President,

the Person having the greatest Number of Votes of the Electors shall be the Vice President. But if there should remain two or more who have equal Votes, the Senate shall chuse from them by Ballot the Vice President.[4]

The Congress may determine the Time of chusing the Electors, and the Day on which they shall give their Votes; which Day shall be the same throughout the United States.

No Person except a natural born Citizen, or a Citizen of the United States, at the time of the Adoption of this Constitution, shall be eligible to the Office of President; neither shall any Person be eligible to that Office who shall not have attained to the Age of thirty five Years, and been fourteen Years a Resident within the United States.

In Case of the Removal of the President from Office, or of his Death, Resignation, or Inability to discharge the Powers and Duties of the said Office, the Same shall devolve on the Vice President, and the Congress may by Law provide for the Case of Removal, Death, Resignation or Inability, both of the President and Vice President, declaring what Officer shall then act as President, and such Officer shall act accordingly, until the Disability be removed, or a President shall be elected.

The President shall, at stated Times, receive for his Services, a Compensation, which shall neither be encreased nor diminished during the Period for which he shall have been elected, and he shall not receive within that Period any other Emolument from the United States, or any of them.

Before he enter on the Execution of his Office, he shall take the following Oath or Affirmation: —"I do solemnly swear (or affirm) that I will faithfully execute the Office of President of the United States, and will to the best of my Ability, preserve, protect and defend the Constitution of the United States."

Section 2.

The President shall be Commander in Chief of the Army and Navy of the United States, and of the Militia of the several States, when called into the actual Service of the United States; he may require the Opinion, in writing, of the principal Officer in each of the executive Departments, upon any Subject relating to the Duties of their respective Offices, and he shall have Power to grant Reprieves and Pardons for Offences against the United States, except in Cases of Impeachment.

[4] Provisions superseded by Amendment XII.

He shall have Power, by and with the Advice and Consent of the Senate, to make Treaties, provided two thirds of the Senators present concur; and he shall nominate, and by and with the Advice and Consent of the Senate, shall appoint Ambassadors, other public Ministers and Consuls, Judges of the supreme Court, and all other Officers of the United States, whose Appointments are not herein otherwise provided for, and which shall be established by Law: but the Congress may by Law vest the Appointment of such inferior Officers, as they think proper in the President alone, in the Courts of Law, or in the Heads of Departments.

The President shall have Power to fill up all Vacancies that may happen during the Recess of the Senate, by granting Commissions which shall expire at the End of their next Session.

Section 3.

He shall from time to time give to the Congress Information of the State of the Union, and recommend to their Consideration such Measures as he shall judge necessary and expedient; he may, on extraordinary Occasions, convene both Houses, or either of them, and in Case of Disagreement between them, with Respect to the Time of Adjournment, he may adjourn them to such Time as he shall think proper; he shall receive Ambassadors and other public Ministers; he shall take Care that the Laws be faithfully executed, and shall Commission all the Officers of the United States.

Section 4.

The President, Vice President and all civil Officers of the United States, shall be removed from Office on Impeachment for, and Conviction of, Treason, Bribery, or other high Crimes and Misdemeanors.

ARTICLE III.

Section 1.

The judicial Power of the United States, shall be vested in one supreme Court, and in such inferior Courts as the Congress may from time to time ordain and establish. The Judges, both of the supreme and inferior Courts, shall hold their Offices during good Behaviour, and shall, at stated Times, receive for their Services, a Compensation, which shall not be diminished during their Continuance in Office.

Section 2.

The judicial Power shall extend to all Cases, in Law and Equity, arising under this Con-

5 Clause changed by Amendment XI.

stitution, the Laws of the United States, and Treaties made, or which shall be made, under their Authority;—to all Cases affecting Ambassadors, other public Ministers and Consuls;— to all Cases of admiralty and maritime Jurisdiction;—to Controversies to which the United States shall be a Party;—to Controversies between two or more States;—between a State and Citizens of another State;—between Citizens of different States,—between Citizens of the same State claiming Lands under Grants of different States, and between a State, or the Citizens thereof, and foreign States, Citizens or Subjects.[5]

In all Cases affecting Ambassadors, other public Ministers and Consuls, and those in which a State shall be Party, the supreme Court shall have original Jurisdiction. In all the other Cases before mentioned, the supreme Court shall have appellate Jurisdiction, both as to Law and Fact, with such Exceptions, and under such Regulations as the Congress shall make.

The Trial of all Crimes, except in Cases of Impeachment, shall be by Jury; and such Trial shall be held in the State where the said Crimes shall have been committed; but when not committed within any State, the Trial shall be at such Place or Places as the Congress may by Law have directed.

Section 3.

Treason against the United States, shall consist only in levying War against them, or in adhering to their Enemies, giving them Aid and Comfort. No person shall be convicted of Treason unless on the Testimony of two Witnesses to the same overt Act, or on Confession in open Court.

The Congress shall have Power to declare the Punishment of Treason, but no Attainder of Treason shall work Corruption of Blood, or Forfeiture except during the Life of the Person attainted.

ARTICLE IV.

Section 1.

Full Faith and Credit shall be given in each State to the public Acts, Records, and judicial Proceedings of every other State. And the Congress may by general Laws prescribe the Manner in which such Acts, Records and Proceedings shall be proved, and the Effect thereof.

Section 2.

The Citizens of each State shall be entitled to all Privileges and Immunities of Citizens in the several States.

A Person charged in any State with Treason, Felony, or other Crime, who shall flee from Justice; and be found in another State, shall on

Demand of the executive Authority of the State from which he fled, be delivered up, to be removed to the State having Jurisdiction of the Crime.

No Person held to Service or Labour in one State, under the Laws thereof, escaping into another, shall, in Consequence of any Law or Regulation therein, be discharged from such Service or Labour, but shall be delivered up on Claim of the Party to whom such Service or Labour may be due.

Section 3.

New States may be admitted by the Congress into this Union; but no new State shall be formed or erected within the Jurisdiction of any other State; nor any State be formed by the Junction of two or more States, or Parts of States, without the Consent of the Legislatures of the States concerned as well as of the Congress.

The Congress shall have Power to dispose of and make all needful Rules and Regulations respecting the Territory or other Property belonging to the United States; and nothing in this Constitution shall be so construed as to Prejudice any Claims of the United States, or of any particular State.

Section 4.

The United States shall guarantee to every State in this Union a Republican Form of Government, and shall protect each of them against Invasion; and on Application of the Legislature, or of the Executive (when the Legislature cannot be convened) against domestic Violence.

ARTICLE V.

The Congress, whenever two thirds of both Houses shall deem it necessary, shall propose Amendments to this Constitution, or, on the Application of the Legislatures of two thirds of the several States, shall call a Convention for proposing Amendments, which, in either Case, shall be valid to all Intents and Purposes, as Part of this Constitution, when ratified by the Legislatures of three fourths of the several States, or by Conventions in three fourths thereof, as the one or the other Mode of Ratification may be proposed by the Congress; Provided that no Amendment which may be made prior to the Year One thousand eight hundred and eight shall in any Manner affect the first and fourth Clauses in the Ninth Section of the first Article; and that no State, without its Consent, shall be deprived of its equal Suffrage in the Senate.

ARTICLE VI.

All Debts contracted and Engagements entered into, before the Adoption of this Constitution, shall be as valid against the United States under this Constitution, as under the Confederation.

This Constitution, and the Laws of the United States which shall be made in Pursuance thereof; and all Treaties made, or which shall be made, under the Authority of the United States, shall be the supreme Law of the Land; and the Judges in every State shall be bound thereby, any Thing in the Constitution or Laws of any State to the Contrary notwithstanding.

The Senators and Representatives before mentioned, and the Members of the several State Legislatures, and all executive and judicial Officers, both of the United States and of the several States, shall be bound by Oath or Affirmation, to support this Constitution; but no religious Test shall ever be required as a Qualification to any Office or public Trust under the United States.

ARTICLE VII.

The Ratification of the Conventions of nine States, shall be sufficient for the Establishment of this Constitution between the States so ratifying the Same.

done in Convention by the Unanimous Consent of the States present the Seventeenth Day of September in the Year of our Lord one thousand seven hundred and Eighty seven and of the Independance of the United States of America the Twelfth[6] IN WITNESS whereof We have hereunto subscribed our Names,

> Go: WASHINGTON—Presidt
> and deputy from Virginia

AMENDMENTS TO THE CONSTITUTION

[AMENDMENT I]

Congress shall make no law respecting an establishment of religion, or prohibiting the free exercise thereof; or abridging the freedom of speech, or of the press; or the right of the people peaceably to assemble, and to petition the Government for a redress of grievances.

[6] The Constitution was submitted on September 17, 1787, by the Constitutional Convention, was ratified by the conventions of several states at various dates up to May 29, 1790, and became effective on March 4, 1789.

[AMENDMENT II]

A well regulated Militia being necessary to the security of a free State, the right of the people to keep and bear Arms, shall not be infringed.

[AMENDMENT III]

No Soldier shall, in time of peace be quartered in any house, without the consent of the Owner, nor in time of war, but in a manner to be prescribed by law.

[AMENDMENT IV]

The right of the people to be secure in their persons, houses, papers, and effects, against unreasonable searches and seizures, shall not be violated, and no Warrants shall issue, but upon probable cause, supported by Oath or affirmation, and particularly describing the place to be searched, and the persons or things to be seized.

[AMENDMENT V]

No person shall be held to answer for a capital, or otherwise infamous crime, unless on a presentment or indictment of a Grand Jury, except in cases arising in the land or naval forces, or in the Militia, when in actual service in time of War or public danger; nor shall any person be subject for the same offense to be twice put in jeopardy of life or limb; nor shall be compelled in any criminal case to be a witness against himself, nor be deprived of life, liberty, or property, without due process of law; nor shall private property be taken for public use, without just compensation.

[AMENDMENT VI]

In all criminal prosecutions, the accused shall enjoy the right to a speedy and public trial, by an impartial jury of the State and district wherein the crime shall have been committed, which district shall have been previously ascertained by law, and to be informed of the nature and cause of the accusation; to be confronted with the witnesses against him; to have compulsory process for obtaining witnesses in his favor, and to have the Assistance of Counsel for his defence.

[AMENDMENT VII]

In Suits at common law, where the value in controversy shall exceed twenty dollars, the right of trial by jury shall be preserved, and no fact tried by a jury, shall be otherwise re-examined in any Court of the United States, than according to the rules of the common law.

[7] The first ten amendments were all proposed by Congress on September 25, 1789, and were ratified and adoption certified on December 15, 1791.

[8] Proposed by Congress on March 4, 1794, and declared ratified on January 8, 1798.

[AMENDMENT VIII]

Excessive bail shall not be required, nor excessive fines imposed, nor cruel and unusual punishments inflicted.

[AMENDMENT IX]

The enumeration in the Constitution, of certain rights, shall not be construed to deny or disparage others retained by the people.

[AMENDMENT X]

The powers not delegated to the United States by the Constitution, nor prohibited by it to the States, are reserved to the States respectively, or to the people.[7]

[AMENDMENT XI]

The Judicial power of the United States shall not be construed to extend to any suit in law or equity, commenced or prosecuted against one of the United States by Citizens of another State, or by Citizens or Subjects of any Foreign State.[8]

[AMENDMENT XII]

The Electors shall meet in their respective states, and vote by ballot for President and Vice-President, one of whom, at least, shall not be an inhabitant of the same state with themselves; they shall name in their ballots the person voted for as President, and in distinct ballots the person voted for as Vice-President, and they shall make distinct lists of all persons voted for as President, and of all persons voted for as Vice-President, and of the number of votes for each, which lists they shall sign and certify, and transmit sealed to the seat of the government of the United States, directed to the President of the Senate;—The President of the Senate shall, in the presence of the Senate and House of Representatives, open all the certificates and the votes shall then be counted;—The person having the greatest number of votes for President, shall be the President, if such number be a majority of the whole number of Electors appointed; and if no person have such majority, then from the persons having the highest numbers not exceeding three on the list of those voted for as President, the House of Representatives shall choose immediately, by ballot, the President. But in choosing the President, the votes shall be taken by states, the representation from each state having one vote; a quorum for this purpose shall consist of a member or members from two-thirds of the states, and a majority of all the states shall be necessary to a choice. And if the House of Representatives shall not choose a President whenever the right of choice shall devolve upon them, before the fourth day of March next following, then the Vice-President shall act as President, as in the case of the death or other constitutional disability of the President.—The person having the greatest number of votes as Vice-President, shall be the Vice-President, if such number be a majority of the whole number of Electors appointed, and if no person have a majority, then from the two highest numbers on the list, the Senate shall choose the Vice-President; a quorum for the purpose shall consist of two-thirds of the whole number of Senators, and a majority of the whole number shall be necessary to a choice. But no person constitutionally ineligible to the office of President shall be eligible to that of Vice-President of the United States.[9]

[AMENDMENT XIII]

Section 1.

Neither slavery nor involuntary servitude, except as a punishment for crime whereof the party shall have been duly convicted, shall exist within the United States, or any place subject to their jurisdiction.

Section 2.

Congress shall have power to enforce this article by appropriate legislation.[10]

[AMENDMENT XIV]

Section 1.

All persons born or naturalized in the United States, and subject to the jurisdiction thereof, are citizens of the United States and of the State wherein they reside. No State shall make or enforce any law which shall abridge the privileges or immunities of citizens of the United States; nor shall any State deprive any person of life, liberty, or property, without due process of law; nor deny to any person within its jurisdiction the equal protection of the laws.

Section 2.

Representatives shall be apportioned among the several States according to their respective numbers, counting the whole number of persons in each State, excluding Indians not taxed. But when the right to vote at any election for the choice of electors for President and Vice-President of the United States, Representatives in Congress, the Executive and Judicial officers of a State, or the members of the Legislature thereof, is denied to any of the male inhabitants of such State, being twenty-one years of age, and citizens of the United States, or in any way abridged, except for participation in rebellion, or

other crime, the basis of representation therein shall be reduced in the proportion which the number of such male citizens shall bear to the whole number of male citizens twenty-one years of age in such State.

Section 3.

No person shall be a Senator or Representative in Congress, or elector of President and Vice President, or hold any office, civil or military, under the United States, or under any State, who, having previously taken an oath, as a member of Congress, or as an officer of the United States, or as a member of any State legislature, or as an executive or judicial officer of any State, to support the Constitution of the United States, shall have engaged in insurrection or rebellion against the same, or given aid or comfort to the enemies thereof. But Congress may by a vote of two-thirds of each House, remove such disability.

Section 4.

The validity of the public debt of the United States, authorized by law, including debts incurred for payment of pensions and bounties for services in suppressing insurrection or rebellion, shall not be questioned. But neither the United States nor any State shall assume or pay any debt or obligation incurred in aid of insurrection or rebellion against the United States, or any claim for the loss or emancipation of any slave; but all such debts, obligations and claims shall be held illegal and void.

Section 5.

The Congress shall have power to enforce, by appropriate legislation, the provisions of this article.[11]

[AMENDMENT XV]

Section 1.

The right of citizens of the United States to vote shall not be denied or abridged by the United States or by any State on account of race, color, or previous condition of servitude.

Section 2.

The Congress shall have power to enforce this article by appropriate legislation.[12]

[9] Proposed by Congress on December 9, 1803; declared ratified on September 25, 1804; supplemented by Amendment XX.

[10] Proposed by Congress on January 31, 1865; declared ratified on December 18, 1865.

[11] Proposed by Congress on June 13, 1866; declared ratified on July 28, 1868.

[12] Proposed by Congress on February 26, 1869; declared ratified on March 30, 1870.

[AMENDMENT XVI]

The Congress shall have power to lay and collect taxes on incomes, from whatever source derived, without apportionment among the several States, and without regard to any census or enumeration.[13]

[AMENDMENT XVII]

The Senate of the United States shall be composed of two Senators from each State, elected by the people thereof, for six years; and each Senator shall have one vote. The electors in each State shall have the qualifications requisite for electors of the most numerous branch of the State legislatures.

When vacancies happen in the representation of any State in the Senate, the executive authority of such State shall issue writs of election to fill such vacancies: *Provided,* That the legislature of any State may empower the executive thereof to make temporary appointments until the people fill the vacancies by election as the legislature may direct.

This amendment shall not be so construed as to affect the election or term of any Senator chosen before it becomes valid as part of the Constitution.[14]

[AMENDMENT XVIII]

Section 1.

After one year from the ratification of this article the manufacture, sale, or transportation of intoxicating liquors within, the importation thereof into, or the exportation thereof from the United States and all territory subject to the jurisdiction thereof for beverage purposes is hereby prohibited.

Section 2.

The Congress and the several States shall have concurrent power to enforce this article by appropriate legislation.

Section 3.

This article shall be inoperative unless it shall have been ratified as an amendment to the Constitution by the legislatures of the several States, as provided in the Constitution, within seven

[13] Proposed by Congress on July 12, 1909; declared ratified on February 25, 1913.

[14] Proposed by Congress on May 13, 1912; declared ratified on May 31, 1913.

[15] Proposed by Congress on December 18, 1917; declared ratified on January 29, 1919. Repealed by Amendment XXI.

[16] Proposed by Congress on June 4, 1919; declared ratified on August 26, 1920.

years from the date of the submission hereof to the States by the Congress.[15]

[AMENDMENT XIX]

The right of citizens of the United States to vote shall not be denied or abridged by the United States or by any State on account of sex.

Congress shall have power to enforce this article by appropriate legislation.[16]

[AMENDMENT XX]

Section 1.

The terms of the President and Vice President shall end at noon on the 20th day of January, and the terms of Senators and Representatives at noon on the 3d day of January, of the years in which such terms would have ended if this article had not been ratified; and the terms of their successors shall then begin.

Section 2.

The Congress shall assemble at least once in every year, and such meeting shall begin at noon on the 3d day of January, unless they shall by law appoint a different day.

Section 3.

If, at the time fixed for the beginning of the term of the President, the President elect shall have died, the Vice President elect shall become President. If a President shall not have been chosen before the time fixed for the beginning of his term, or if the President elect shall have failed to qualify, then the Vice President elect shall act as President until a President shall have qualified; and the Congress may by law provide for the case wherein neither a President elect nor a Vice President elect shall have qualified, declaring who shall then act as President, or the manner in which one who is to act shall be selected, and such person shall act accordingly until a President or Vice President shall have qualified.

Section 4.

The Congress may by law provide for the case of the death of any of the persons from whom the House of Representatives may choose a President whenever the right of choice shall have devolved upon them, and for the case of the death of any of the persons from whom the Senate may choose a Vice President whenever the right of choice shall have devolved upon them.

Section 5.

Sections 1 and 2 shall take effect on the 15th day of October following the ratification of this article.

Section 6.

This article shall be inoperative unless it shall have been ratified as an amendment to the Constitution by the legislatures of three-fourths of the several States within seven years from the date of its submission.[17]

[AMENDMENT XXI]

Section 1.

The eighteenth article of amendment to the Constitution of the United States is hereby repealed.

Section 2.

The transportation or importation into any States, Territory, or possession of the United States for delivery or use therein of intoxicating liquors, in violation of the laws thereof, is hereby prohibited.

Section 3.

This article shall be inoperative unless it shall have been ratified as an amendment to the Constitution by conventions in the several States, as provided in the Constitution, within seven years from the date of the submission hereof to the States by the Congress.[18]

[AMENDMENT XXII]

Section 1.

No person shall be elected to the office of the President more than twice, and no person who has held the office of President, or acted as President, for more than two years of a term to which some other person was elected President shall be elected to the office of the President more than once. But this Article shall not apply to any person holding the office of President when this Article was proposed by the Congress, and shall not prevent any person who may be holding the office of President, or acting as President, during the term within which this Article becomes operative from holding the office of President or acting as President during the remainder of such term.

Section 2.

This article shall be inoperative unless it shall have been ratified as an amendment to the Constitution by the legislatures of three-fourths of the several States within seven years from the date of its submission to the States by Congress.[19]

[17] Proposed by Congress on March 2, 1932; declared ratified on February 6, 1933.
[18] Proposed by Congress on February 20, 1933; declared ratified on December 5, 1933.
[19] Proposed by Congress on March 24, 1947; declared ratified on March 1, 1951.

The Meaning of the Constitution

THE FEDERALIST PAPERS

Both sides gained important victories in the heated and often bitter controversy over ratification of the Constitution. The Federalists—as the defenders of the proposed government called themselves—won acceptance of the new regime. The Anti-Federalist opposition successfully united public opinion in support of a series of amendments that Madison later condensed into the Bill of Rights (Amendments I-X, ratified in 1791).

Many of the arguments made in the ratification debates still hold historical interest. One contribution, *The Federalist*, has permanent value as the fundamental commentary on the meaning of the Constitution and as a penetrating discussion of the problems of federalism and popular government in America.

Nowhere was the fight for the Constitution more doubtful than in the New York ratifying convention, which met through June and July of 1788. The skillful leadership of Hamilton and a few other prominent Federalist delegates helped to win over a hostile convention by a bare majority of three votes. Anticipating a severe struggle, Hamilton in the fall of 1787 proposed to Madison and John Jay the publication in the New York *Independent Journal* of a series of papers defending the Constitution. Under the pressure of newspaper deadlines the three men, but principally Hamilton and Madison, issued the masterly *Federalist* papers, seventy-seven in all, under the pseudonyms of first "A Citizen of New York," then "Publius." Eight more papers were added when they were collected in book form.

Their broad purpose was stated in the first paper. The very existence of the union was in mortal danger. Americans were charged with the responsibility "by their conduct and example, to decide the important question, whether societies of men are really capable or not of establishing good government from reflection and choice, or whether they are forever destined to depend for their political constitutions on accident and force." Publius would therefore offer arguments and evidence to promote "a judicious estimate of our true interests." The discussion would include: the utility of the union; the insufficiency of the Confederation to preserve that union; the necessity of an "energetic" government; the conformity of the proposed Constitution to true republican principles; and the security the Constitution would afford to the preservation of republican government, to liberty, and to property.

The eighty-five *Federalist* papers do not have the unity of a systematic discourse. They were newspaper essays turned out serially by three quite different men to explain and justify the specific provisions of the Constitution and to meet current objections. Hamilton, we know, preferred a "high-toned" centralized government closer to the English model; Madison was soon to join the Republican opposition to Hamilton's policies and constitutional interpretations. Yet with the constitutional experiment at stake they could present an impressively consistent analysis of the problems facing Americans under the Confederation and of the criteria for "a republican remedy."

61

FACTION: THE REPUBLICAN DISEASE

from James Madison, *The Federalist*, No. 10, 1787

The Federalist No. 10 has been singled out as a key to the thought of the Founding Fathers, at least since historian Charles Beard (1874-1948) claimed this paper as a basic source of his own economic interpretation of the Constitution (and of politics in general). Madison's brilliant analysis of faction as the natural disease of popular governments has provoked sharp disputes among students of the Constitution and of American political thought. Does the discussion of the economic basis of faction suggest that the Founding Fathers were themselves property-conscious conservatives who supported the Constitution as an instrument of class rule? Does Madison's defense of the representative principle and the large, diverse republic as remedies for faction constitute a rejection of democracy? Does Madison's analysis of the competition of factions eliminate the idea of the common good as an effective political guide, in favor of the view that politics consists solely in a process of bargaining among interest groups? However one answers these disputed questions, he will find in Madison's tight argument a priceless introduction to the thought of the Founders and to the nature of the American political order.

The Same Subject Continued.

Among the numerous advantages promised by a well constructed union, none deserves to be more accurately developed than its tendency to break and control the violence of faction. The friend of popular governments, never finds himself so much alarmed for their character and fate, as when he contemplates their propensity to this dangerous vice. He will not fail, therefore, to set a due value on any plan which, without violating the principles to which he is attached, provides a proper cure for it. The instability, injustice, and confusion, introduced into the public councils, have, in truth, been the mortal diseases under which popular governments have

Text: *The Federalist and Other Constitutional Papers*, ed. E. H. Scott (Chicago: Albert, Scott & Co., 1894), pp. 53-60.

everywhere perished; as they continue to be the favourite and fruitful topics from which the adversaries to liberty derive their most specious declamations. The valuable improvements made by the American constitutions on the popular models, both ancient and modern, cannot certainly be too much admired; but it would be an unwarrantable partiality, to contend that they have as effectually obviated the danger on this side, as was wished and expected. Complaints are everywhere heard from our most considerate and virtuous citizens, equally the friends of public and private faith, and of public and personal liberty, that our governments are too unstable; that the public good is disregarded in the conflicts of rival parties; and the measures are too often decided, not according to the rules of justice, and the rights of the minor party, but by the superiour force of an interested and overbearing majority. However anxiously we may wish that these complaints had no foundation, the evidence of known facts will not permit us to deny that they are in some degree true. It will be found, indeed, on a candid review of our situation, that some of the distresses under which we labour, have been erroneously charged on the operation of our governments; but it will be found, at the same time, that other causes will not alone account for many of our heaviest misfortunes; and, particularly, for that prevailing and increasing distrust of public engagements, and alarm for private rights, which are echoed from one end of the continent to the other. These must be chiefly, if not wholly, effects of the unsteadiness and injustice, with which a factious spirit has tainted our public administrations.

By a faction, I understand a number of citizens, whether amounting to a majority or minority of the whole, who are united and actuated by some common impulse of passion, or of interest, adverse to the rights of other citizens, or to the permanent and aggregate interests of the community.

There are two methods of curing the mischiefs of faction: The one, by removing its causes; the other, by controlling its effects.

There are again two methods of removing the causes of faction: The one, by destroying the liberty which is essential to its existence; the other, by giving to every citizen the same opinions, the same passions, and the same interests.

It could never be more truly said, than of the first remedy, that it was worse than the disease. Liberty is to faction what air is to fire, an aliment, without which it instantly expires. But it could not be a less folly to abolish liberty, which is essential to political life because it nourishes faction, than it would be to wish the annihilation of air, which is essential to animal life, because it imparts to fire its destructive agency.

The second expedient is as impracticable, as the first would be unwise. As long as the reason of man continues fallible, and he is at liberty to exercise it, different opinions will be formed. As long as the connection subsists between his reason and his self-love, his opinions and his passions will have a reciprocal influence on each other; and the former will be objects to which the latter will attach themselves. The diversity in the faculties of men, from which the rights of property originate, is not less an insuperable obstacle to an uniformity of interests. The protection of these faculties is the first object of government. From the protection of different and unequal faculties of acquiring property, the possession of different degrees and kinds of property immediately results; and from the influence of these on the sentiments and views of the respective proprietors, ensues a division of the society into different interests and parties.

The latent causes of faction are thus sown in the nature of man; and we see them every where brought into different degrees of activity, according to the different circumstances of civil society. A zeal for different opinions concerning religion, concerning government, and many other points, as well of speculation as of practice; an attachment to different leaders, ambitiously contending for pre-eminence and power; or to persons of other descriptions, whose fortunes have been interesting to the human passions, have, in turn, divided mankind into parties, inflamed them with mutual animosity, and rendered them much more disposed to vex and oppress each other, than to co-operate for their common good. So strong is this propensity of mankind, to fall into mutual animosities, that where no substantial occasion presents itself, the most frivolous and fanciful distinctions have been sufficient to kindle their unfriendly passions, and excite their most violent conflicts. But the most common and durable source of factions, has been the various and unequal distribution of property. Those who hold, and those who are without property, have ever formed distinct interests in society. Those who are creditors, and those who are debtors, fall under a like discrimination. A landed interest, a manufacturing interest, a mercantile interest, a moneyed interest, with many lesser interests, grow up of necessity in civilized nations, and divide them into different classes, actuated by different sentiments and views. The regulation of these various and interfering interests forms the principal task of modern legislation, and involves the spirit of party and faction in the necessary and ordinary operations of government.

No man is allowed to be a judge in his own cause; because his interest will certainly bias his judgment, and, not improbably, corrupt his integrity. With equal, nay, with greater reason, a body of men are unfit to be both judges and parties at the same time; yet what are many of the most important acts of legislation, but so many judicial determinations, not indeed concerning the rights of single persons, but concerning the rights of large bodies of citizens? and what are the different classes of legislators, but advocates and parties to the causes which they determine? Is a law proposed concerning private debts? It is a question to which the creditors are parties on one side, and the debtors on the other. Justice ought to hold the balance between them. Yet the parties are, and must be, themselves the judges: and the most numerous party, or, in other words, the most powerful faction, must be expected to prevail. Shall domestic manufactures be encouraged, and in what degree, by restrictions on foreign manufactures? are questions which would be differently decided by the landed and the manufacturing classes; and probably by neither with a sole regard to justice and the public good. The apportionment of taxes, on the various descriptions of property, is an act which seems to require the most exact impartiality; yet there is, perhaps, no legislative act, in which greater opportunity and temptation are given to a predominant party, to trample on the rules of justice. Every shilling, with which they overburden the inferiour number, is a shilling saved to their own pockets.

It is in vain to say, that enlightened statesmen will be able to adjust these clashing interests, and render them all subservient to the public good. Enlightened statesmen will not always be at the helm: nor, in many cases, can such an adjustment be made at all, without taking into view indirect and remote considerations, which will rarely prevail over the immediate interest which one party may find in disregarding the rights of another, or the good of the whole.

The inference to which we are brought is, that the *causes* of faction cannot be removed; and that relief is only to be sought in the means of controlling its *effects*.

If a faction consists of less than a majority, relief is supplied by the republican principle, which enables the majority to defeat its sinister views, by regular vote. It may clog the administration, it may convulse the society; but it will be unable to execute and mask its violence under the forms of the constitution. When a majority is included in a faction, the form of popular government, on the other hand, enables it to sacrifice to its ruling passion or interest, both the public good and the rights of other citizens. To secure the public good, and private rights, against the danger of such a faction, and at the same time to preserve the spirit and the form of popular government, is then the great object to which our inquiries are directed. Let me add, that it is the great desideratum, by which alone this form of government can be rescued from the opprobrium under which it has so long laboured, and be recommended to the esteem and adoption of mankind.

By what means is this object attainable? Evidently by one of two only. Either the existence of the same passion or interest in a majority, at the same time must be prevented; or the majority, having such coexistent passion or interest, must be rendered, by their number and local situation, unable to concert and carry into effect schemes of oppression. If the impulse and the opportunity be suffered to coincide, we well know, that neither moral nor religious motives can be relied on as an adequate control. They are not found to be such on the injustice and violence of individuals, and lose their efficacy in proportion to the number combined together; that is, in proportion as their efficacy becomes needful.

From this view of the subject, it may be concluded, that a pure democracy, by which I mean a society consisting of a small number of citizens, who assemble and administer the government in person, can admit of no cure from the mischiefs of faction. A common passion or interest will, in almost every case, be felt by a majority of the whole; a communication and concert, results from the form of government itself; and there is nothing to check the inducements to sacrifice the weaker party, or an obnoxious individual. Hence it is, that such democracies have ever been spectacles of turbulence and contention; have ever been found incompatible with personal security, or the rights of property; and have, in general, been as short in their lives, as they have been violent in their deaths. Theoretic politicians, who have patronized this species of government, have erroneously supposed, that by reducing mankind to a perfect equality in their political rights, they would, at the same time, be perfectly equalized and assimilated in their possessions, their opinions, and their passions.

A republic, by which I mean a government in which the scheme of representation takes place, opens a different prospect, and promises the cure for which we are seeking. Let us examine the points in which it varies from pure democracy, and we shall comprehend both the nature of the cure and the efficacy which it must derive from the union.

The two great points of difference, between a democracy and a republic, are, first, the delegation of the government, in the latter, to a small number of citizens elected by the rest; secondly, the greater number of citizens, and greater sphere of country, over which the latter may be extended.

The effect of the first difference is, on the one hand, to refine and enlarge the public views, by passing them through the medium of a chosen body of citizens, whose wisdom may best discern the true interest of their country, and whose patriotism and love of justice, will be least likely to sacrifice it to temporary or partial considerations. Under such a regulation, it may well happen, that the public voice, pronounced by the representatives of the people, will be more consonant to the public good, than if pronounced by the people themselves, convened for the purpose. On the other hand, the effect may be inverted. Men of factious tempers, of local prejudices, or of sinister designs, may by intrigue, by corruption, or by other means, first obtain the suffrages, and then betray the interests of the people. The question resulting is, whether small or extensive republics are most favourable to the election of proper guardians of the public weal; and it is clearly decided in favour of the latter by two obvious considerations.

In the first place, it is to be remarked, that however small the republic may be, the representatives must be raised to a certain number, in order to guard against the cabals of a few; and that however large it may be, they must be limited to a certain number, in order to guard against the confusion of a multitude. Hence, the number of representatives in the two cases not being in proportion to that of the constituents, and being proportionally greatest in the small republic, it follows, that if the proportion of fit characters be not less in the large than in the small republic, the former will present a greater option, and consequently a greater probability of a fit choice.

In the next place, as each representative will be chosen by a greater number of citizens in the large than in the small republic, it will be more difficult for unworthy candidates to practice with success the vicious arts, by which elections are too often carried; and the suffrages of the people being more free, will be more likely to centre in men who possess the most attractive merit, and the most diffusive and established characters.

It must be confessed, that in this, as in most other cases, there is a mean, on both sides of which inconveniences will be found to lie. By enlarging too much the number of electors, you render the representative too little acquainted with all their local circumstances and lesser interests; as by reducing it too much, you render him unduly attached to these, and too little fit to comprehend and pursue great and national objects. The federal constitution forms a happy combination in this respect; the great and aggregate interests being referred to the national; the local and particular to the state legislatures.

The other point of difference is, the greater number of citizens, and extent of territory, which may be brought within the compass of republican, than of democratic government; and it is this circumstance principally which renders factious

combinations less to be dreaded in the former, than in the latter. The smaller the society, the fewer probably will be the distinct parties and interests composing it; the fewer the distinct parties and interests, the more frequently will a majority be found of the same party; and the smaller the number of individuals composing a majority, and the smaller the compass within which they are placed, the more easily will they concert and execute their plans of oppression. Extend the sphere, and you take in a greater variety of parties and interests; you make it less probable that a majority of the whole will have a common motive to invade the rights of other citizens; or if such a common motive exists, it will be more difficult for all who feel it to discover their own strength, and to act in unison with each other. Besides other impediments, it may be remarked, that where there is a consciousness of unjust or dishonourable purposes, communication is always checked by distrust, in proportion to the number whose concurrence is necessary.

Hence, it clearly appears, that the same advantage, which a republic has over a democracy, in controlling the effects of faction, is enjoyed by a large over a small republic—is enjoyed by the union over the states composing it. Does this advantage consist in the substitution of representatives, whose enlightened views and virtuous sentiments render them superiour to local prejudices, and to schemes of injustice? It will not be denied, that the representation of the union will be most likely to possess these requisite endowments. Does it consist in the greater security afforded by a greater variety of parties, against the event of any one party being able to outnumber and oppress the rest? In an equal degree does the increased variety of parties, comprised within the union, increase this security. Does it, in fine, consist in the greater obstacles opposed to the concert and accomplishment of the secret wishes of an unjust and interested majority? Here, again, the extent of the union gives it the most palpable advantage.

The influence of factious leaders may kindle a flame within their particular states, but will be unable to spread a general conflagration through the other states; a religious sect may degenerate into a political faction in a part of the confederacy; but the variety of sects dispersed over the entire face of it, must secure the national councils against any danger from that source; a rage for paper money, for an abolition of debts, for an equal division of property, or for any other improper or wicked project, will be less apt to pervade the whole body of the union, than a particular member of it; in the same proportion as such a malady is more likely to taint a particular county or district, than an entire state.

In the extent and proper structure of the union, therefore, we behold a republican remedy for the diseases most incident to republican government. And according to the degree of pleasure and pride we feel in being republicans, ought to be our zeal in cherishing the spirit, and supporting the character of federalists.

PUBLIUS.

62

THE SUPREME LAW OF THE LAND

from Alexander Hamilton, *The Federalist*, No. 15, 1787

Hamilton's *Federalist* No. 15 goes to the root of the federal problem. Perhaps the youthful Hamilton, embroiled in the ratification fight, exaggerated the evils of the "Critical Period." His statement of the essential distinction between the Articles of Confederation and the new Constitution, as two ways of relating the center to the parts of a complex political community, is a model of accuracy. The Confederation, Hamilton maintained, was essentially an alliance of sovereign governments. The Constitution would create a national government with direct authority over individual citizens. *The Federalist* No. 15 considers the nature and consequences of this crucial difference, with the obvious purpose of establishing the superiority of the Constitutional system. Hamilton's discussion is directly related to the "keystone clause" (in Article VI), stating that the Constitution, the laws of the United States made "in pursuance thereof," and all treaties made under the national authority "shall be the supreme law of the land."

Other *Federalist* papers, especially Madison's No. 39, develop the principles of federation embodied in the Constitution. The central government gives law directly to the people *within* the sphere of powers assigned to it by the Constitution. Other powers not assigned remain with the states; and the states moreover figure as distinct units in the apportionment of Senate seats, in the ratification and amendment procedures, and in other significant ways. This problem of the proper relationship between central and local governments seems to be a permanent issue of American politics. Much of the Revolutionary debate turned on this question. It has been argued fiercely in the ratification fight, in the party battles of the early republic, in the great sectional struggle of the nineteenth century, and—with somewhat less intensity—in every serious dispute over domestic policy down to our time.

To the People of the State of New York:

In the course of the preceding papers, I have endeavored, my fellow-citizens, to place before you, in a clear and convincing light, the importance of Union to your political safety and happiness. I have unfolded to you a complication of dangers to which you would be exposed, should you permit that sacred knot which binds the people of America together to be severed or dissolved by ambition or by avarice, by jealousy or by misrepresentation. In the sequel of the inquiry through which I propose to accompany you, the truths intended to be inculcated will receive further confirmation from facts and arguments hitherto unnoticed. If the road over which you will still have to pass should in some places appear to you tedious or irksome, you will recollect that you are in quest of information on a subject the most momentous which can engage the attention of a free people, that the field through which you have to travel is in itself spacious, and that the difficulties of the journey have been unnecessarily increased by the mazes with which sophistry has beset the way. It will be my aim to remove the obstacles from your progress in as compendious a manner as it can be done, without sacrificing utility to despatch.

In pursuance of the plan which I have laid down for the discussion of the subject, the point next in order to be examined is the "insufficiency of the present Confederation to the preservation of the Union." It may perhaps be asked what need there is of reasoning or proof to illustrate a position which is not either controverted or doubted, to which the understandings and feelings of all classes of men assent, and which in substance is admitted by the opponents as well as by the friends of the new Constitution. It must in truth be acknowledged that, however these may differ in other respects, they in general appear to harmonize in this sentiment, at least,

Text: *The Federalist and Other Constitutional Papers*, ed. E. H. Scott (Chicago: Albert, Scott & Co., 1894), pp. 80-87.

that there are material imperfections in our national system, and that something is necessary to be done to rescue us from impending anarchy. The facts that support this opinion are no longer objects of speculation. They have forced themselves upon the sensibility of the people at large, and have at length extorted from those, whose mistaken policy has had the principal share in precipitating the extremity at which we are arrived, a reluctant confession of the reality of those defects in the scheme of our federal government, which have been long pointed out and regretted by the intelligent friends of the Union.

We may indeed with propriety be said to have reached almost the last stage of national humiliation. There is scarcely any thing that can wound the pride or degrade the character of an independent nation which we do not experience. Are there engagements to the performance of which we are held by every tie respectable among men? These are the subjects of constant and unblushing violation. Do we owe debts to foreigners and to our own citizens contracted in a time of imminent peril for the preservation of our political existence? These remain without any proper or satisfactory provision for their discharge. Have we valuable territories and important posts in the possession of a foreign power which, by express stipulations, ought long since to have been surrendered? These are still retained, to the prejudice of our interests, not less than of our rights. Are we in a condition to resent or to repel the aggression? We have neither troops, nor treasury, nor government [for the Union]. Are we even in a condition to remonstrate with dignity? The just imputations on our own faith, in respect to the same treaty, ought first to be removed. Are we entitled by nature and compact to a free participation in the navigation of the Mississippi? Spain excludes us from it. Is public credit an indispensable resource in time of public danger? We seem to have abandoned its cause as desperate and irretrievable. Is commerce of importance to national wealth? Ours is at the lowest point of declension. Is respectability in the eyes of foreign powers a safeguard against foreign encroachments? The imbecility of our government even forbids them to treat with us. Our ambassadors abroad are the mere pageants of mimic sovereignty. Is a violent and unnatural decrease in the value of land a symptom of national distress? The price of improved land in most parts of the country is much lower than can be accounted for by the quantity of waste land at market, and can only be fully explained by that want of private and public confidence, which are so alarmingly prevalent among all ranks, and which have a direct tendency to depreciate property of every kind. Is private credit the friend and patron of industry? That most useful kind which relates to borrowing and lending is reduced within the narrowest limits, and this still more from an opinion of insecurity than from the scarcity of money. To shorten an enumeration of particulars which can afford neither pleasure nor instruction, it may in general be demanded, what indication is there of national disorder, poverty, and insignificance that could befall a community so peculiarly blessed with natural advantages as we are, which does not form a part of the dark catalogue of our public misfortunes?

This is the melancholy situation to which we have been brought by those very maxims and councils which would now deter us from adopting the proposed Constitution; and which, not content with having conducted us to the brink of a precipice, seem resolved to plunge us into the abyss that awaits us below. Here, my countrymen, impelled by every motive that ought to influence an enlightened people, let us make a firm stand for our safety, our tranquillity, our dignity, our reputation. Let us at last break the fatal charm which has too long seduced us from the paths of felicity and prosperity.

It is true, as has been before observed, that facts, too stubborn to be resisted, have produced a species of general assent to the abstract proposition that there exist material defects in our national system; but the usefulness of the concession, on the part of the old adversaries of federal measures, is destroyed by a strenuous opposition to a remedy, upon the only principles that can give it a chance of success. While they admit that the government of the United States is destitute of energy, they contend against conferring upon it those powers which are requisite to supply that energy. They seem still to aim at things repugnant and irreconcilable; at an augmentation of federal authority, without a diminution of State authority; at sovereignty in the Union, and complete independence in the members. They still, in fine, seem to cherish with blind devotion the political monster of an *imperium in imperio*. This renders a full display of the principal defects of the Confederation necessary, in order to show that the evils we experience do not proceed from minute or partial imperfections, but from fundamental errors in the structure of the building, which cannot be amended otherwise than by an alteration in the first principles and main pillars of the fabric.

The great and radical vice in the construction of the existing Confederation is in the principle of LEGISLATION for STATES or GOVERNMENTS, in their CORPORATE or COLLECTIVE CAPACITIES, and as contradistinguished from the INDIVIDUALS of which they consist. Though this principle does not run through all the powers delegated to the Union, yet it pervades and governs those on which the efficacy of the rest depends. Except as to the rule of appointment, the United States has an indefinite discretion to make requisitions for men and money; but they have no authority to raise either, by regulations extending to the individual citizens of America. The consequence of this is, that though in theory their resolutions concerning those objects are laws, constitutionally binding on the members of the Union, yet in practice they are mere recommendations which the States observe or disregard at their option.

It is a singular instance of the capriciousness of the human mind, that after all the admonitions we have had from experience on this head, there should still be found men who object to the new Constitution, for deviating from a principle which has been found the bane of the old, and which is in itself evidently incompatible with the idea of GOVERNMENT; a principle, in short, which, if it is to be executed at all, must substitute the violent and sanguinary agency of the sword to the mild influence of the magistracy.

There is nothing absurd or impracticable in the idea of a league or alliance between independent nations for certain defined purposes precisely stated in a treaty regulating all the details of time, place, circumstance, and quantity; leaving nothing to future discretion; and depending for its execution on the good faith of the parties. Compacts of this kind exist among all civilized nations, subject to the usual vicissitudes of peace and war, of observance and nonobservance, as the interests or passions of the contracting powers dictate. In the early part of the present century there was an epidemical rage in Europe for this species of compacts, from which the politicians of the times fondly hoped for benefits which were never realized. With a view to establishing the equilibrium of power and the peace of that part of the world, all the resources of negotiation were exhausted, and triple and quadruple alliances were formed; but they were scarcely formed before they were broken, giving an instructive but afflicting lesson to mankind, how little dependence is to be placed on treaties which have no other sanction than the obligations of good faith, and which oppose general considerations of peace and justice to the impulse of any immediate interest or passion.

If the particular States in this country are disposed to stand in a similar relation to each other, and to drop the project of a general DISCRETIONARY SUPERINTENDENCE, the scheme would indeed be pernicious, and would entail upon us all the mischiefs which have been enumerated under the first head; but it would have the merit of being, at least, consistent and practicable. Abandoning all views towards a confederate government, this would bring us to a simple alliance offensive and defensive; and would place us in a situation to be alternate friends and enemies of each other, as our mutual jealousies and rivalships, nourished by the intrigues of foreign nations, should prescribe to us.

But if we are unwilling to be placed in this perilous situation; if we still will adhere to the design of a national government, or, which is the same thing, of a superintending power, under the direction of a common council, we must resolve to incorporate into our plan those ingredients which may be considered as forming the characteristic difference between a league and a government; we must extend the authority of the Union to the persons of the citizens,—the only proper objects of government.

Government implies the power of making laws. It is essential to the idea of a law, that it be attended with a sanction; or, in other words, a penalty or punishment for disobedience. If there be no penalty annexed to disobedience, the resolutions or commands which pretend to be laws will, in fact, amount to nothing more than advice or recommendation. This penalty, whatever it may be, can only be inflicted in two ways: by the agency of the courts and ministers of justice, or by military force; by the COERCION of the magistracy, or by the COERCION of arms. The first kind can evidently apply only to men; the last kind must of necessity, be employed against bodies politic, or communities, or States. It is evident that there is no process of a court by which the observance of the laws can, in the last resort, be enforced. Sentences may be denounced against them for violations of their duty; but these sentences can only be carried into execution by the sword. In an association where the general authority is confined to the collective bodies of the communities that compose it, every breach of the laws must involve a state of war; and military execution must become the only instrument of civil obedience. Such a state of things can certainly not deserve the name of government, nor would any prudent man choose to commit his happiness to it.

There was a time when we were told that breaches, by the States, of the regulations of the federal authority were not to be expected; that a sense of common interest would preside over the conduct of the respective members, and would beget a full compliance with all the constitutional requisitions of the Union. This language, at the present day, would appear as wild as a great part of what we now hear from the same quarter will be thought, when we shall have received further lessons from that best oracle of wisdom, experience. It at all times betrayed an ignorance of the true springs by which human conduct is actuated, and belied the original inducements to the establishment of civil power. Why has government been instituted at all? Because the passions of men will not conform to the dictates of reason and justice, without constraint. Has it been found that bodies of men act with more rectitude or greater disinterestedness than individuals? The contrary of this has been inferred by all accurate observers of the conduct of mankind; and the inference is founded upon obvious reasons. Regard to reputation has a less active influence, when the infamy of a bad action is to be divided among a number, than when it is to fall singly upon one. A spirit of faction, which is apt to mingle its poison in the deliberations of all bodies of men, will often hurry the persons of whom they are composed into improprieties and excesses, for which they would blush in a private capacity.

In addition to all this, there is, in the nature of sovereign power, an impatience of control, that disposes those who are invested with the exercise of it, to look with an evil eye upon all external attempts to restrain or direct its operations. From this spirit it happens, that in every political association which is formed upon the principle of uniting in a common interest a number of lesser sovereignties, there will be found a kind of eccentric tendency in the subordinate or inferior orbs, by the operation of which there will be a perpetual effort in each to fly off from the common centre. This tendency is not difficult to be accounted for. It has its origin in the love of power. Power controlled or abridged is almost always the rival and enemy of that power by which it is controlled or abridged. This simple proposition will teach us, how little reason there is to expect, that the persons intrusted with the administration of the affairs of the particular members of a confederacy will at all times be ready, with perfect good-humor, and an unbiased regard to the public weal, to execute the resolutions or decrees of the general authority. The reverse of this results from the constitution of human nature.

If, therefore, the measures of the Confederacy cannot be executed without the intervention of the particular administrations, there will be little prospect of their being executed at all. The rulers of the respective members, whether they have a constitutional right to do it or not, will undertake to judge of the propriety of the measures themselves. They will consider the conformity of the thing proposed or required to their immediate interests or aims; the momentary conveniences or inconveniences that would attend its adoption. All this will be done; and in a spirit of interested and suspicious scrutiny, without that knowledge of national circumstances and reasons of state, which is essential to a right judgment, and with that strong predilection in favor of local objects, which can hardly fail to mislead the decision. The same process must be repeated in every member of which the body is constituted; and the execution of the plans, framed by the councils of the whole, will always fluctuate on the discretion of the ill-informed and prejudiced opinion of every part. Those who have been conversant in the proceedings of popular assemblies; who have seen how difficult it often is, where there is no exterior pressure of circumstances, to bring them to harmonious resolutions on important points, will readily conceive how impossible it must be to induce a number of such assemblies, deliberating at a distance from each other, at different times, and under different impressions, long to coöperate in the same views and pursuits.

In our case, the concurrence of thirteen distinct sovereign wills is requisite, under the Confederation, to the complete execution of every important measure that proceeds from the Union. It has happened as was to have been foreseen. The measures of the Union have not been executed; the delinquencies of the States have, step by step, matured themselves to an extreme, which has, at length, arrested all the wheels of the national government, and brought them to an awful stand. Congress at this time scarcely possess the means of keeping up the forms of administration, till the States can have time to agree upon a more substantial substitute for the present shadow of a federal government. Things did not come to this desperate extremity at once. The causes which have been specified produced at first only unequal and disproportionate degrees of compliance with the requisitions of the Union. The greater deficiencies of some States furnished the pretext of example and the temptation of interest to the complying, or to the least delinquent States. Why should we do more in proportion than those who are embarked with us in the same political voyage? Why should we consent to bear more than our proper share of the common burden? These were suggestions which human selfishness could not withstand, and which even speculative men, who looked forward to remote consequences, could not, without hesitation, combat. Each State, yielding to the persuasive voice of immediate interest or convenience, has successively withdrawn its support, till the frail and tottering edifice seems ready to fall upon our heads, and to crush us beneath its ruins.

63

CHECKS AND BALANCES

from James Madison, *The Federalist*, No. 51, 1788

Jefferson's criticism of the imperfect separation of powers in Virginia (Document 55) reminds us that the principle of dividing government into distinct branches—executive, legislative, and judicial—as a means of holding political power in check was no invention of the Founding Fathers. In part the principle reflected institutions and practices that had evolved in the colonies. More important, the separation of powers and the system of checks and balances seemed to the *Federalist* authors "essential to the preservation of liberty" in a popular regime.

The Federalist No. 51, in common with other papers, proceeds from a tough appraisal of human nature to a policy of "supplying, by opposite and rival interests, the defect of better motives." As one recent commentator translated this, the Founding Fathers acted on the maxim "If you can't be good, be careful." Although they labored to expand the powers of the national government, they had not abandoned the traditional American view—so prominent in the Revolutionary era—that men with power in their hands can never be above suspicion. Popular elections, the Founders thought, were a necessary but not sufficient defense against tyranny. The representatives of the majority might themselves establish—in Jefferson's phrase—an "elective despotism."

To the People of the State of New York:

To what expedient, then, shall we finally resort, for maintaining in practice the necessary partition of power among the several departments [executive, legislative, and judicial], as laid down in the Constitution? The only answer that can be given is, that as all these exterior provisions are found to be inadequate, the defect must be supplied, by so contriving the interior structure of the government as that its several constituent parts may, by their mutual relations, be the means of keeping each other in their proper places. Without presuming to undertake a full development of this important idea, I will hazard a few general observations, which may perhaps place it in a clearer light, and enable us to form a more correct judgment of the principles and structure of the government planned by the convention.

In order to lay a due foundation for that separate and distinct exercise of the different powers of government, which to a certain extent is admitted on all hands to be essential to the preservation of liberty, it is evident that each department should have a will of its own; and consequently should be so constituted that the members of each should have as little agency as possible in the appointment of the members of the others. Were this principle rigorously adhered to, it would require that all the appointments for the supreme executive, legislative, and judiciary magistracies should be drawn from the same fountain of authority, the people, through channels having no communication whatever with one another. Perhaps such a plan of constructing the several departments would be less difficult in practice than it may in contemplation appear. Some difficulties, however, and some additional expense would attend the execution of it. Some deviations, therefore, from the principle must be admitted. In the constitution of the judiciary department in particular, it might be inexpedient to insist rigorously on the principle: first, because peculiar qualifications being essential in the members, the primary consideration ought to be to select that mode of choice which best secures these qualifications; secondly, because the permanent tenure by which the appointments are held in that department, must soon destroy all sense of dependence on the authority conferring them.

Text: *The Federalist and Other Constitutional Papers*, ed. E. H. Scott (Chicago: Albert, Scott & Co., 1894), pp. 285-90. Although *The Federalist* No. 51 has conventionally been assigned to Hamilton or Madison in twentieth-century editions of the papers, there is convincing evidence in favor of Madison's authorship. See Douglass Adair, "The Authorship of the Disputed Federalist Papers: Part II," *William and Mary Quarterly*, I (July 1944), 235-64.

It is equally evident, that the members of each department should be as little dependent as possible on those of the others, for the emoluments annexed to their offices. Were the executive magistrate, or the judges, not independent of the legislature in this particular, their independence in every other would be merely nominal.

But the great security against a gradual concentration of the several powers in the same department, consists in giving to those who administer each department the necessary constitutional means and personal motives to resist encroachments of the others. The provision for defence must in this, as in all other cases, be made commensurate to the danger of attack. Ambition must be made to counteract ambition. The interest of the man must be connected with the constitutional rights of the place. It may be a reflection on human nature, that such devices should be necessary to control the abuses of government. But what is government itself, but the greatest of all reflections on human nature? If men were angels, no government would be necessary. If angels were to govern men, neither external nor internal controls on government would be necessary. In framing a government which is to be administered by men over men, the great difficulty lies in this: you must first enable the government to control the governed; and in the next place oblige it to control itself. A dependence on the people is, no doubt, the primary control on the government; but experience has taught mankind the necessity of auxiliary precautions.

This policy of supplying, by opposite and rival interests, the defect of better motives, might be traced through the whole system of human affairs, private as well as public. We see it particularly displayed in all the subordinate distributions of power, where the constant aim is to divide and arrange the several offices in such a manner as that each may be a check on the other—that the private interest of every individual may be a sentinel over the public rights. These inventions of prudence cannot be less requisite in the distribution of the supreme powers of the State.

But it is not possible to give to each department an equal power of self-defence. In republican government, the legislative authority necessarily predominates. The remedy for this inconveniency is to divide the legislature into different branches; and to render them, by different modes of election and different principles of action, as little connected with each other as the nature of their common functions and their common dependence on the society will admit. It may even be necessary to guard against dangerous encroachments by still further precautions. As the weight of the legislative authority requires that it should be thus divided, the weakness of the executive may require, on the other hand, that it should be fortified. An absolute negative on the legislature appears, at first view, to be the natural defence with which the executive magistrate should be armed. But perhaps it would be neither altogether safe nor alone sufficient. On ordinary occasions it might not be exerted with the requisite firmness, and on extraordinary occasions it might be perfidiously abused. May not this defect of an absolute negative be supplied by some qualified connection between this weaker department and the weaker branch of the stronger department, by which the latter may be led to support the constitutional rights of the former, without being too much detached from the rights of its own department?

If the principles on which these observations are founded be just, as I persuade myself they are, and they be applied as a criterion to the several State constitutions, and to the federal Constitution, it will be found that if the latter does not perfectly correspond with them, the former are infinitely less able to bear such a test.

There are, moreover, two considerations particularly applicable to the federal system of America, which place that system in a very interesting point of view.

First. In a single republic, all the power surrendered by the people is submitted to the administration of a single government; and the usurpations are guarded against by a division of the government into distinct and separate departments. In the compound republic of America, the power surrendered by the people is first divided between two distinct governments, and then the portion allotted to each subdivided among distinct and separate departments. Hence a double security arises to the rights of the people. The different governments will control each other, at the same time that each will be controlled by itself.

Second. It is of great importance in a republic not only to guard the society against the oppression of its rulers, but to guard one part of the society against the injustice of the other part. Different interests necessarily exist in different classes of citizens. If a majority be united by a common interest, the rights of the minority will be insecure. There are but two methods of providing against this evil: the one by creating a will in the community independent of the majority— that is, of the society itself; the other, by comprehending in the society so many separate descriptions of citizens as will render an unjust combination of a majority of the whole very improbable, if not impracticable. The first method prevails in all governments possessing an hereditary or self-appointed authority. This, at best, is but a precarious security; because a power independent of the society may as well espouse the unjust views of the major, as the rightful interests of the minor party, and may possibly be turned against both parties. The second method will be exemplified in the federal republic of the United States. Whilst all authority in it will be derived from and dependent on the society, the society itself will be broken into so many parts, interests, and classes of citizens, that the rights of individuals, or of the minority, will be in little danger from interested combinations of the majority. In a free government the security for civil rights must be the same as that for religious rights. It consists in the one case in the multiplicity of interests, and in the other in the multiplicity of sects. The degree of security in both cases will depend on the number of interests and sects; and this may be presumed to depend on the extent of country and number of people comprehended under the same government. This view of the subject must particularly recommend a proper federal system to all the sincere and considerate friends of republican government, since it shows that in exact proportion as the territory of the Union may be formed into more circumscribed Confederacies, or States, oppressive combinations of a majority will be facilitated; the best security, under the republican forms, for the rights of every class of citizens, will be diminished; and consequently the stability and independence of some member of the government, the only other security, must be proportionally increased. Justice is the end of government. It is the end of civil society. It ever has been and ever will be pursued until it be obtained, or until liberty be lost in the pursuit. In a society under the forms of which the stronger faction can readily unite and oppress the weaker, anarchy may as truly be said to reign as in a state of nature, where the weaker individual is not secured against the violence of the stronger; and as, in the latter state, even the stronger individuals are prompted, by the uncertainty of their condition, to submit to a government which may protect the weak as well as themselves; so, in the former state, will the more powerful factions or parties be gradually induced, by a like motive, to wish for a government which will protect all parties, the weaker as well as the more powerful. It can be little doubted that if the State of Rhode Island was separated from the Confederacy and left to itself, the insecurity of rights under the popular form of government within such narrow limits would be displayed by such reiterated oppressions of factious majorities that some power altogether independent of the people would soon be called for by the voice of the very factions whose misrule had proved the necessity of it. In the extended republic of the United States, and among the great variety of interests, parties, and sects which it embraces, a coalition of a majority of the whole society could seldom take place on any other principles than those of justice and the general good; whilst there being thus less danger to a minor from the will of a major party, there must be less pretext, also, to provide for the security of the former, by introducing into the government a will not dependent on the latter, or, in other words, a will independent of the society itself. It is no less certain than it is important, notwithstanding the contrary opinions which have been entertained, that the larger the society, provided it lie within a practical sphere, the more duly capable it will be of self-government. And happily for the *republican cause*, the practicable sphere may be carried to a very great extent, by a judicious modification and mixture of the *federal principle*.

AN ANTI-FEDERALIST ARGUMENT

64

COUNTER-REVOLUTION: THE MENACE OF THE CONSTITUTION

from Patrick Henry, Speech in the Virginia Ratifying Convention, 1788

The movement favoring adoption of the Constitution could claim great American names, including those of Washington and Franklin, and brilliant talents such as Madison and Hamilton offered. If the Anti-Federalist notables in most states were rather less distinguished, the opposition leaders in Virginia were formidable indeed. They included Patrick Henry, the intoxicating orator and adroit politician of Revolutionary fame; Richard Henry Lee, a veteran leader in the councils of the union, whose *Letters from a Federal Farmer* gave the Anti-Federalists their most effective campaign document; and George Mason, eminent among the "Republican Gentlemen" who guided Virginia affairs and the principal author of the state's Declaration of Rights (1776).

When the opposing forces met at Richmond in June 1788 to determine the fate of the new Constitution (a successful union lacking the most populous state was scarcely thinkable), one crucial shift had occurred. The influential Governor Edmund Randolph, who had refused to sign the Constitution at Philadelphia, now joined forces with Madison, George Wythe, John Marshall, Edmund Pendleton, and other Federalist luminaries. Washington lent his endorsement but not his presence. Jefferson, still in France, was claimed by both sides. His letters show a gradual change of view in favor of ratifying the Constitution while recommending amendments, especially a bill of rights.

Patrick Henry thundered his denunciations of the Constitutional Convention in language that recalled his polemics of Revolutionary days. His rhetoric was more extravagant than that of sober Anti-Federalists like Mason; some of his charges were simply wild shots; but essentially he voiced the fears and resentments of all who opposed the Constitution as an instrument of national consolidation. The states would be destroyed. Liberty and property would be exposed to the will of a distant and unfriendly central power. The real choice, Henry argued with some justice and some exaggeration, lay between two ideals: a simple, decentralized country which left men and localities largely free to act for themselves; or "a great, mighty, and splendid nation."

On June 26, 1788, Virginia ratified the new Constitution, but only by a margin of ten votes. Following the example set by Massachusetts and observed by nearly all the subsequent conventions, the Virginia body recommended the adoption of a bill of rights and other amendments.

Mr. HENRY. Mr. Chairman, the public mind, as well as my own, is extremely uneasy at the proposed change of government. Give me leave to form one of the number of those who wish to be thoroughly acquainted with the reasons of this perilous and uneasy situation, and why we are brought hither to decide on this great national question. I consider myself as the servant of the people of this commonwealth, as a sentinel over their rights, liberty, and happiness. I represent their feelings when I say that they are exceedingly uneasy at being brought from that state of full security, which they enjoyed, to the present delusive appearance of things. A year ago, the minds of our citizens were at perfect repose. Before the meeting of the late federal Convention at Philadelphia, a general peace and a universal tranquillity prevailed in this country; but, since that period, they are exceedingly uneasy and disquieted. When I wished for an appointment to this Convention, my mind was extremely agitated for the situation of public affairs. I conceived the republic to be in extreme danger. If our situation be thus uneasy, whence has arisen this fearful jeopardy? It arises from this fatal system; it arises from a proposal to change our government—a proposal that goes to the utter annihilation of the most solemn engagements of the states. . . .

. . . Make the best of this new government— say it is composed by any thing but inspiration —you ought to be extremely cautious, watchful, jealous of your liberty; for, instead of securing your rights, you may lose them forever. If a wrong step be now made, the republic may be lost forever. If this new government will not come up to the expectation of the people, and they shall be disappointed, their liberty will be lost, and tyranny must and will arise. I repeat it again, and I beg gentlemen to consider, that a wrong step, made now, will plunge us into misery, and our republic will be lost. It will be necessary for this Convention to have a faithful historical detail of the facts that preceded the session of the federal Convention, and the reasons that actuated its members in proposing an entire alteration of government, and to demonstrate the dangers that awaited us. If they were of such awful magnitude as to warrant a proposal so extremely perilous as this, I must assert, that this Convention has an absolute right to a thorough discovery of every circumstance relative to this great event. And here I would make this inquiry of those worthy characters who composed a part of the late federal Convention. I am sure they were fully impressed with the necessity of forming a great consolidated government, instead of a confederation. That this is a consolidated government is demonstrably clear; and the danger of such a government is, to my mind, very strik-

Text: Jonathan Elliot (ed.), *The Debates in the Several State Conventions on the Adoption of the Federal Constitution* (Washington, D.C.: J. Elliot, 1840), III, 21-22, 44-46, 53-54, 58-60, 65-66.

ing. I have the highest veneration for those gentlemen; but, sir, give me leave to demand, What right had they to say, *We, the people?* My political curiosity, exclusive of my anxious solicitude for the public welfare, leads me to ask: Who authorized them to speak the language of, *We, the people,* instead of, *We, the states?* States are the characteristics and the soul of a confederation. If the states be not the agents of this compact, it must be one great, consolidated, national government, of the people of all the states. . . .

. . . Here is a resolution as radical as that which separated us from Great Britain. It is radical in this transition; our rights and privileges are endangered, and the sovereignty of the states will be relinquished: and cannot we plainly see that this is actually the case? The rights of conscience, trial by jury, liberty of the press, all your immunities and franchises, all pretensions to human rights and privileges, are rendered insecure, if not lost, by this change, so loudly talked of by some, and inconsiderately by others. Is this tame. relinquishment of rights worthy of freemen? Is it worthy of that manly fortitude that ought to characterize republicans? It is said eight states have adopted this plan. I declare that if twelve states and a half had adopted it, I would, with manly firmness, and in spite of an erring world, reject it. You are not to inquire how your trade may be increased, nor how you are to become a great and powerful people, but how your liberties can be secured; for liberty ought to be the direct end of your government. . . .

. . . We are come hither to preserve the poor commonwealth of Virginia, if it can be possibly done: something must be done to preserve your liberty and mine. The Confederation, this same despised government, merits, in my opinion, the highest encomium: it carried us through a long and dangerous war; it rendered us victorious in that bloody conflict with a powerful nation; it has secured us a territory greater than any European monarch possesses: and shall a government which has been thus strong and vigorous, be accused of imbecility, and abandoned for want of energy? Consider what you are about to do before you part with the government. Take longer time in reckoning things; revolutions like this have happened in almost every country in Europe; similar examples are to be found in ancient Greece and ancient Rome—instances of the people losing their liberty by their own carelessness and the ambition of a few. We are cautioned by the honorable gentleman, who presides, against faction and turbulence. I acknowledge that licentiousness is dangerous, and that it ought to be provided against: I acknowledge, also, the new

form of government may effectually prevent it: yet there is another thing it will as effectually do—it will oppress and ruin the people. . . .

. . . An opinion has gone forth, we find, that we are contemptible people: the time has been when we were thought otherwise. Under the same despised government, we commanded the respect of all Europe: wherefore are we now reckoned otherwise? The American spirit has fled from hence: it has gone to regions where it has never been expected; it has gone to the people of France, in search of a splendid government—a strong, energetic government. Shall we imitate the example of those nations who have gone from a simple to a splendid government? Are those nations more worthy of our imitation? What can make an adequate satisfaction to them for the loss they have suffered in attaining such a government—for the loss of their liberty? If we admit this consolidated government, it will be because we like a great, splendid one. Some way or other we must be a great and mighty empire; we must have an army, and a navy, and a number of things. When the American spirit was in its youth, the language of America was different: liberty, sir, was then the primary object. We are descended from a people whose government was founded on liberty: our glorious forefathers of Great Britain made liberty the foundation of every thing. That country is become a great, mighty, and splendid nation; not because their government is strong and energetic, but, sir, because liberty is its direct end and foundation. We drew the spirit of liberty from our British ancestors: by that spirit we have triumphed over every difficulty. But now, sir, the American spirit, assisted by the ropes and chains of consolidation, is about to convert this country into a powerful and mighty empire. If you make the citizens of this country agree to become the subjects of one great consolidated empire of America, your government will not have sufficient energy to keep them together. Such a government is incompatible with the genius of republicanism. There will be no checks, no real balances, in this government. What can avail your specious, imaginary balances, your rope-dancing, chain-rattling, ridiculous ideal checks and contrivances? But, sir, we are not feared by foreigners; we do not make nations tremble. Would this constitute happiness, or secure liberty? I trust, sir, our political hemisphere will ever direct their operations to the security of those objects.

Consider our situation, sir: go to the poor man, and ask him what he does. He will inform you that he enjoys the fruits of his labor, under his own fig-tree, with his wife and children around him, in peace and security. Go to every other member of society,—you will find the same tranquil ease and content; you will find no alarms or disturbances. Why, then, tell us of danger, to terrify us into an adoption of this new form of government? And yet who knows the dangers that this new system may produce? They are out of the sight of the common people: they cannot foresee latent consequences. I dread the operation of it on the middling and lower classes of people: it is for them I fear the adoption of this system. I fear I tire the patience of the committee; but I beg to be indulged with a few more observations. When I thus profess myself an advocate for the liberty of the people, I shall be told I am a designing man, that I am to be a great man, that I am to be a demagogue; and many similar illiberal insinuations will be thrown out: but, sir, conscious rectitude outweighs those things with me. I see great jeopardy in this new government. I see none from our present one. . . .

This Constitution is said to have beautiful features; but when I come to examine these features, sir, they appear to me horribly frightful. Among other deformities, it has an awful squinting; it squints towards monarchy; and does not this raise indignation in the breast of every true American?

Your President may easily become king. Your Senate is so imperfectly constructed that your dearest rights may be sacrificed by what may be a small minority; and a very small minority may continue forever unchangeably this government, although horridly defective. Where are your checks in this government? Your strongholds will be in the hands of your enemies. It is on a supposition that your American governors shall be honest, that all the good qualities of this government are founded, but its defective and imperfect construction puts it in their power to perpetrate the worst of mischiefs, should they be bad men; and, sir, would not all the world, from the eastern to the western hemisphere, blame our distracted folly in resting our rights upon the contingency of our rulers being good or bad? Show me that age and country where the rights and liberties of the people were placed on the sole chance of their rulers being good men, without a consequent loss of liberty! I say that the loss of that dearest privilege has ever followed, with absolute certainty, every such mad attempt.

If your American chief be a man of ambition and abilities, how easy is it for him to render himself absolute! The army is in his hands, and if he be a man of address, it will be attached to him, and it will be the subject of long meditation with him to seize the first auspicious moment to accomplish his design; and, sir, will the American spirit solely relieve you when this happens? I would rather infinitely—and I am sure most of this Convention are of the same opinion—have a king, lords, and commons, than a government so replete with such insupportable evils. If we make a king, we may prescribe the rules by which he shall rule his people, and interpose such checks as shall prevent him from infringing them; but the President, in the field, at the head of his army, can prescribe the terms on which he shall reign master, so far that it will puzzle any American ever to get his neck from under the galling yoke. I cannot with patience think of this idea. If ever he violates the laws, one of two things will happen: he will come at the head of his army, to carry every thing before him; or he will give bail, or do what Mr. Chief Justice will order him. If he be guilty, will not the recollection of his crimes teach him to make one bold push for the American throne? Will not the immense difference between being master of every thing, and being ignominiously tried and punished, powerfully excite him to make this bold push? But, sir, where is the existing force to punish him? Can he not, at the head of his army, beat down every opposition? Away with your President! we shall have a king: the army will salute him monarch: your militia will leave you, and assist in making him king, and fight against you: and what have you to oppose this force? What will then become of you and your rights? Will not absolute despotism ensue? . . .

I beg pardon of this house for having taken up more time than came to my share, and I thank them for the patience and polite attention with which I have been heard. If I shall be in the minority, I shall have those painful sensations which arise from a conviction of *being overpowered in a good cause.* Yet I will be a peaceable citizen. My head, my hand, and my heart, shall be at liberty to retrieve the loss of liberty, and remove the defects of that system in a constitutional way. I wish not to go to violence, but will wait with hopes that the spirit which predominated in the revolution is not yet gone, nor the cause of those who are attached to the revolution yet lost. I shall therefore patiently wait in expectation of seeing that government changed, so as to be compatible with the safety, liberty, and happiness, of the people.

CHAPTER 6

Federalists and Republicans:

1789 to 1801

On March 4, 1789, the new Constitution was little more than a paper project for a government of the United States. Yet in spite of the severe conflict over ratification of the Constitution, the new Washington administration began with impressive public support. The President, whose name was a symbol of national unity, had been the unanimous choice of the electors, and the Congress was filled with able men who had favored the Constitution.

Much of the initial business of government was a kind of supplementary constitution-making. The amendments forming the Bill of Rights were passed decisively by Congress on September 25, 1789, and transmitted to the states. In separate Congressional acts the executive departments—State, War, and Treasury—were instituted. The Judiciary Act of 1789 defined the forms, jurisdictions, and procedures of a federal court system which alone could establish the Constitution, statutes, and treaties of the United States as "the supreme law of the land." The several authorities felt their way toward effective operating procedures, no simple matter in a complex political system employing checks and balances among the separate branches of government. Many of these early decisions created precedents for the future organization and administration of the federal government. Thus presidential rather than Congressional control over the executive departments was introduced; and the Cabinet began to take shape as an advisory body to the President. While a serviceable governing instrument was being formed, President Washington's administration turned to the great questions of public policy which had defied solution under the Articles of Confederation.

The Confederation government had proved too weak to solve its pressing financial problems. A burdensome public debt (the price of independence), an uncertain tax revenue, a shortage of capital, and a depreciated currency left the Union in a perilous position. To place the new government on firm ground, it was necessary to find economic remedies. Not entirely by accident, Washington selected for the Treasury Department the boldest and most skillful of his administrative officers.

Alexander Hamilton, with the steady backing of his chief, seized the initiative in setting the policy of the administration. His aims and methods were, and still remain, the subject of warm controversy. In the Constitutional Convention he had candidly declared his "private opinion" that "the British Government was the best in the world." He proposed a republican equivalent for King and Lords to balance "the amazing violence and turbulence of the democratic spirit." The state governments seemed to him a source of mischief and confusion which could be tolerated only as a concession to popular prejudice. Yet Hamilton provided excellent arguments in defense of the Constitution (Document 62) and contributed greatly to the strength of Washington's administrations. The Constitution, he wrote in 1802, is "a frail and worthless fabric which I have been endeavoring to prop up." That formulation states, if it does not solve, the enigma of Hamilton's purposes.

Hamilton's masterly *Reports* to Congress on the public credit, on the national bank, and on manufactures defined the major policies of the first Washington administration. Underlying the specific measures was a broad conception of the relation between government and the economy. A poor and stagnant economic society could not sustain a strong and secure nation. A flimsy government could not maintain the property rights or promote the welfare of its citizens. In Hamilton's view, a great nation, sound public finance, and a highly developed commercial economy were interdependent objects. To accomplish such objects a firm central government would have to take command.

The *Report on Public Credit* (Document 66) laid the groundwork for the Hamiltonian system. No one doubted that the public credit was dangerously low in 1790 or that decisive measures were required. The general government had accumulated a debt of some fifty millions under the previous regimes. The states owed above twenty-two millions more. Failure to meet interest payments or provide for the retirement of the debt had shaken the faith of public creditors. Government certificates of debt were selling in the market far below face value. The sellers were men who could not or would not wait to see if the government would redeem its promises. The purchasers were men of means who were willing to buy cheap on the chance that the government would make good.

Hamilton did not see the remedy as a simple matter of government house-keeping. His program for *funding* the federal debt and *assuming* the war debts of the states was part of his bold political and economic design. Under his plan, the depreciated certificates of debt issued by the state and federal governments would be exchanged at face value for long-term, interest-paying government bonds. Import duties and internal excise taxes would provide the means for meeting interest charges. A sinking fund would be formed to retire the bonds as they matured. Thus men of substance throughout the union—public creditors and the moneyed classes generally—would find a strong motive for sustaining the national government (and its Federalist administration). Their confidence in the solvency and good faith of the government would raise property values and stimulate business activity. In addition, the funded debt, in the form of negotiable government bonds, would serve the holders as capital to finance new enterprises. In sum, Hamilton proposed to strengthen the federal government and promote national prosperity by setting the public finances in order.

Establishment of the first Bank of the United States (1791), with branches spread over the Union, continued Hamilton's basic program. The national government would gain a source of short-term loans for emergencies and a convenient agency for depositing and disbursing public moneys. For the business community, large capital resources would be provided, and a dependable paper currency would be circulated through the economy. Again, political strength and economic growth would advance together under the guidance of national policy.

The *Report on Manufactures* (1791) had only a delayed impact on public policy. Logically, the proposals formed a part of Hamilton's grand design. By a system of protective tariffs and other encouragements, he hoped to create a diversified national economy in which factory and farm, town and country, would exchange a growing volume of commodities. The wealth of the nation would increase with the development of mechanized industry and the fuller employment of the labor force. Diverse economic and sectional interests would be interwoven in a continental market economy. And national security would be served by providing a domestic source of strategic manufactures. At first, Hamilton's argument for a protective tariff failed to register with farmers and merchants, who saw their primary interest in a relatively free trade among nations. After 1815 the case was revived successfully by Henry Clay and other advocates of the "American System."

The last of Hamilton's major financial measures, the excise tax on distilled liquors (1791), had been promised (or threatened) in the earlier *Report on Public Credit.* The funding of the state and federal debt required increased revenues to meet the heavy interest charges. Import tariffs remained the principal government resource, but Hamilton hoped to draw additional contributions from domestic distillers of rum and whiskey. The farmers of western Pennsylvania and the Southern frontier, who could get their grain to market most readily by converting it into whiskey, denounced the excise tax as an instrument of oppression devised by an overreaching central power at the behest of Eastern commercial interests. The Whiskey Rebellion (1794) in western Pennsylvania, directed against the federal "revenuers" who came to collect the hated excise from the still operators, was the extreme expression of a steadily rising opposition to the Hamiltonian system.

Hamilton's financial program succeeded, most writers agree, in restoring public credit and stimulating economic development. It did unite men of commerce and finance and many others behind the national government and the Federalist party. That a few men in and around the government—*not* including Hamilton—used advance information to make speculative gains was an unfortunate by-product not unknown to later times. Far more serious was Hamilton's failure to convince an ever-increasing body of farmers, Southerners, and men of democratic principle that his financial measures were designed for the common good and were consistent with the requirements of a free federal republic.

PARTY BATTLES AND THE STRIFE OF EUROPE

A loose Republican opposition began to form with the introduction of the public credit measures. Why, critics asked, should speculators receive full face value for securities they had picked up at bargain prices from hard-pressed citizens? Why should the federal government assume responsibility for the mass of state debts? Was Hamilton's grand design really a plot to establish a commercial and financial oligarchy enriched by government favors and thus dependent on the great dispenser of favor, the ambitious Secretary of the Treasury? Were the Northeastern commercial interests to exploit the agricultural West and South with the assistance of the national government? Was the national government to grow all powerful while the states dwindled to nothing? Such doubts almost defeated the debt "assumption" bill. (See Jefferson's comments in Document 68.)

The creation of the national bank added another dimension to the opposition's attack. Nowhere did the Constitution *authorize* the central government to charter corporations, particularly banking corporations with monopolistic privileges. Neither did the Constitution *prohibit* such a measure. With great force, Hamilton argued that Congress must be free to choose the appropriate means for carrying out its enumerated powers, as long as the means bore a reasonable relation to the stated ends and were not forbidden by the letter or spirit of the Constitution (Document 67). To Jefferson and the Republicans this meant the end of a limited Constitution and the beginning of an all-powerful national government. The bank, the funding program, the assumption of state debts, broad construction: all seemed pieces in a sinister pattern (Document 68).

The standards by which Republicans judged the Hamiltonian system were implicit in their criticisms. Perhaps Jefferson's occasional writings offer the best broad definition. (See especially the Jefferson selections in Chapter 8.) The Republican ideal was a predominantly rural society based on the independent freehold farmers. Their needs called for a simple, frugal government designed to secure men's equal rights. Concentrated power was the way to corruption, tyranny, and inequality. Therefore, let the limited powers of government be distributed through the several levels of political society, from nation to locality, confiding the larger share of necessary authority to the state and local agencies where men could closely supervise and control their representatives. A maximum of liberty should remain with individual citizens educated by schools and press and by their experience as independent farmers to appreciate their rights and pursue their interests rightly understood.

By 1792 the outlines of an opposition party were becoming sharper. Jefferson in the State Department and Madison in the House of Representatives were called upon to provide a lead. Disaffected Virginians and New Yorkers concerted political plans. The Federalists in power moved steadily toward coordinated action in behalf of their candidates and program. A party system was in the making. Issues of foreign policy became the center of concern after 1792 and completed the division into antagonistic parties.

The French Revolution of 1789 divided Europe into warring camps for a generation. America felt the consequences in a series of diplomatic crises over relations with the belligerents and in the fierce rivalry of political parties whose sympathies were attached to the French side (Republicans) or the British (Federalists). In retrospect one can see that the young American Republic derived advantage as well as injury from the strife of Europe. The major powers of the West were absorbed in an exhausting conflict during the years when America was first gathering its strength as a nation.

After the outbreak of European war in 1792, the commerce with belligerents opened an immediate and most attractive source of profit to Americans. The French alliance of 1778, under which vital support had been given to the American Revolution, seemed to oblige the United States to side with France. Washington (again preferring Hamilton's advice to Jefferson's) determined that the national interest required, and the French treaty permitted, a Proclamation of Neutrality (1793). (See Document 69 for Washington's approach to foreign policy.) British attacks on neutral trade provoked a diplomatic crisis which was more or less controlled when John Jay negotiated a treaty with England in 1794. To France, and to American Republicans, Jay's treaty was a base capitulation to English demands. The Federalists were denounced as tools of England in a storm of popular protest.

As French raids on American shipping increased to an intolerable point, the focus of conflict shifted. John Adams, Washington's successor, sent three commissioners to France in hopes of finding an accommodation. The French Directory, which was then in power, treated the commissioners with contempt. Confirmed reports that French agents had demanded a bribe as the condition of formal negotiations (the "XYZ Affair" of 1797) turned public outrage against France and the Republican "Jacobins." Only the coolness of John Adams kept the undeclared sea war with France (1798-1800) from growing into a full-scale conflict, with America a partner in the British coalition.

Thus the great Anglo-French encounter in Europe was reflected in American party politics. Party lines were sharply drawn, and party quarrels rose to a furious pitch. The warnings against foreign loyalties and party spirit in Washington's *Farewell Address* were a direct response to the growing turbulence of American politics that seemed to threaten the existence of the Union. Under such conditions, John Adams signed the punitive Alien and Sedition Acts of 1798. To Federalists these were necessary security measures for meeting a clear and present danger to the nation from disloyal Francophile Republicans. To Republicans the Acts showed the cloven hoof of British monarchy, the final stage in the Federalist design for building a splendid despotism on the ruins of the Republic. Thus the Virginia and Kentucky Resolutions of 1798-1799 (Document 70) attacked not only specified invasions of constitutional liberties by the Adams administration but the whole tendency toward consolidated national power demonstrated during a decade of Federalist rule. The principles of state rights developed by Jefferson and Madison would have a long and dangerous career in nineteenth-century politics.

By 1800 a large majority of Americans had abandoned Federalism permanently. Jefferson and his successors of the Virginia line were called upon to restore the American Republic.

Setting the Course of Government

65

INAUGURAL DAY IN NEW YORK

from William Maclay, *Journal*, 1789

To translate a written constitution into a living government was the responsibility of the new Senators and Representatives who slowly gathered in New York through the March days of 1789. They found an empty treasury, a skeleton civil service, no legal machinery, no accepted etiquette, no made-to-order procedures and precedents; in short, they found no government suitable to their purposes. It was for them, and for the President they would install, to create one according to the broad prescriptions of the Constitution.

Among the Senators who claimed their seats in Federal Hall was William Maclay, a lawyer and state officeholder from central Pennsylvania. Maclay was born in 1737;

his experience spanned the colonial, revolutionary, and confederation periods. He recorded in his salty journal the rising suspicions of a homespun democrat watching the new government unfold amidst the splendors of New York. Vice-President John Adams was dubbed "His Rotundity" both for his figure and for his efforts to dignify the proceedings of the Senate by introducing the formalities of Parliamentary ceremony. Others who showed a similar hankering for "high-toned" government got no kinder treatment in the journal. Senator Maclay did not hesitate to remind the testy Adams on the floor—to the vast annoyance of the presiding officer—that simpler ways would better suit an American legislature.

Not even the great Washington was above Maclay's censure, as the following eye-witness account of the first inauguration shows. No one, it seems, knew just how to act under the unfamiliar circumstances. How should the Congress meet the President, or he them? How should the President "advise" with the Senate on treaties and appointments? How should he place before the Congress his proposals for legislative action? How should the executive departments be organized and employed? In a year of trial and error the new government carved its own procedural grooves and gave enduring form to such new institutions as the Cabinet and the federal judiciary. Thus the terms of the Constitution were filled out while new terms of the greatest import were proposed with the transmission of the Bill of Rights to the states for ratification.

30th April [1789], *Thursday.*—This is a great, important day. Goddess of etiquette, assist me while I describe it. The Senate stood adjourned to half after eleven o'clock. About ten dressed in my best clothes; went for Mr. Morris' lodgings, but met his son, who told me that his father would not be in town until Saturday. Turned into the Hall. The crowd already great. The Senate met. The Vice-President rose in the most solemn manner. This son of *Adam* seemed impressed with deeper gravity, yet what shall I think of him? He often, in the midst of his most important airs—I believe when he is at loss for expressions (and this he often is, wrapped up, I suppose, in the contemplation of his own importance)—suffers an unmeaning kind of vacant laugh to escape him. This was the case to-day, and really to me bore the air of ridiculing the farce he was acting. "Gentlemen, I wish for the direction of the Senate. The President will, I suppose, address the Congress. How shall I behave? How shall we receive it? Shall it be standing or sitting?"

Here followed a considerable deal of talk from him which I could make nothing of. Mr. Lee began with the House of Commons (as is usual with him), then the House of Lords, then the King, and then back again. The result of his information was, that the Lords sat and the Commons stood on the delivery of the King's speech. Mr. Izard got up and told how often he had been in the Houses of Parliament. He said a great deal of what he had seen there. [He] made, however, this sagacious discovery, that the Com-

mons stood because they had no seats to sit on, being arrived at the bar of the House of Lords. It was discovered after some time that the King sat, too, and had his robes and crown on. . . .

. . . Here we sat an hour and ten minutes before the President arrived—this delay was owing to Lee, Izard, and Dalton, who had stayed with us while the Speaker came in, instead of going to attend the President. The President advanced between the Senate and Representatives, bowing to each. He was placed in the chair by the Vice-President; the Senate with their president on the right, the Speaker and the Representatives on his left. The Vice-President rose and addressed a short sentence to him. The import of it was that he should now take the oath of office as President. He seemed to have forgot half what he was to say, for he made a dead pause and stood for some time, to appearance, in a vacant mood. He finished with a formal bow, and the President was conducted out of the middle window into the gallery, and the oath was administered by the Chancellor. Notice that the business done was communicated to the crowd by proclamation, etc., who gave three cheers, and repeated it on the President's bowing to them.

As the company returned into the Senate chamber, the President took the chair and the Senators and Representatives their seats. He rose, and all arose also, and addressed them. . . . This great man was agitated and embarrassed more than ever he was by the leveled cannon or pointed musket. He trembled, and several times could scarce make out to read, though it must be supposed he had often read it before. He put part of the fingers of his left hand into the side of what I think the tailors call the fall of the

Text: William Maclay, *Journal,* ed. Edgar S. Maclay (New York: D. Appleton & Co., 1890), pp. 7-10.

breeches [corresponding to the modern sidepocket], changing the paper into his left [right] hand. After some time he then did the same with some of the fingers of his right hand. When he came to the words *all the world,* he made a flourish with his right hand, which left rather an ungainly impression. I sincerely, for my part, wished all set ceremony in the hands of the dancing-masters, and that this first of men had read off his address in the plainest manner, without ever taking his eyes from the paper, for I felt hurt that he was not first in everything. He was dressed in deep brown, with metal buttons, with an eagle on them, white stockings, a bag, and sword.

From the hall there was a grand procession to Saint Paul's Church, where prayers were said by the Bishop. The procession was well conducted and without accident, as far as I have heard. The militia were all under arms, lined the street near the church, made a good figure, and behaved well.

The Senate returned to their chamber after service, formed, and took up the address. Our Vice-President called it *his most gracious speech.* I can not approve of this. A committee was appointed on it—Johnson, Carrol, Patterson. Adjourned. In the evening there were grand fireworks. The Spanish Ambassador's house was adorned with transparent paintings; the French Minister's house was illuminated, and had some transparent pieces; the Hall was grandly illuminated, and after all this the people went to bed.

66

DESIGN FOR UNITY: THE FINANCIAL SYSTEM

from Alexander Hamilton, *First Report on the Public Credit,* 1790

With genuine reluctance George Washington had once more left Mount Vernon to assume America's highest public office, the Presidency—feeling, he said, rather like a culprit marching to his execution. Washington brought to the precarious new government a matchless reputation, extraordinary patriotism, a prudent mind, and a firm hand. He brought, too, a brilliant young Secretary of the Treasury—Alexander Hamilton—whose "enlightened zeal for the energy and efficiency of government," in the prophetic language of *Federalist* No. 1, would be "stigmatized as the offspring of a temper fond of despotic power and hostile to the principles of liberty."

Alexander Hamilton (1757-1804), the guiding genius of the Federalist administration, was a mere thirty-two years old when he assumed his post as Secretary of the Treasury and virtually as Washington's first minister. An amazing career had carried him from obscure beginnings on the British island of Nevis (in the West Indies) to a distinguished position in American public life. By 1789 he had already won high reputation as a spokesman in the Revolutionary debate, as General Washington's trusted military adviser, as a financial expert, as a leading New York lawyer, as an influential promoter of the Constitutional Convention, and as co-author of the *Federalist* papers.

In a series of closely reasoned public papers on public credit, the national bank, and manufacturing, Hamilton proposed systematic policy for the Congress to follow. Hamilton's *Reports* are informed by a bold conception of the role of central government in establishing the public credit and promoting economic development. Agriculture, commerce, industry, and finance would be integrated in an expanding national economy. This was a design for prosperity within a design for national power.

The *First Report on the Public Credit* (January 9, 1790) revealed the direction of the Hamiltonian system. Congress and President approved the Secretary's recommendations to assume responsibility for both state and federal debts at face value and to raise an adequate public revenue. With little question the financial program helped to stabilize and strengthen the new regime at a moment when its fate was doubtful. But Hamilton's measures also aroused an opposition, based in New York, Pennsylvania, and especially in the Southern states, that would gather momentum through the 1790's and lift Jefferson to power.

The nascent opposition had no such clearly formulated aims as did the Secretary of the Treasury. Specific inequities provoked sharp criticism. Hamilton's proposal for "funding" old government obligations at par—i.e., exchanging the various depreciated certificates of debt issued under the previous governments for interest-bearing bonds—provoked a serious protest. A few moneyed men had bought up large parts of the debt on speculation from the original creditors at a fraction of the face value. Still worse from the point of view of critics was the "assumption" of the state war debts by the federal government, a measure which benefited some states (like Massachusetts) more than others (like Virginia).

Some of Hamilton's persuasive arguments in defense of his measures are reprinted here. For the Jeffersonian reaction see Document 68.

Report on Public Credit.

Communicated to the House of Representatives, January 14, 1790.

The Secretary of the Treasury, in obedience to the resolution of the House of Representatives of the twenty-first day of September last, has, during the recess of Congress, applied himself to the consideration of a proper plan for the support of the public credit, with all the attention which was due to the authority of the House, and to the magnitude of the object. . . .

With an ardent desire that his well meant endeavors may be conducive to the real advantage of the nation, and with the utmost deference to the superior judgment of the House, he now respectfully submits the result of his inquiries and reflections to their indulgent construction.

In the opinion of the Secretary, the wisdom of the House, in giving their explicit sanction to the proposition which has been stated, cannot but be applauded by all who will seriously consider and trace, through their obvious consequences, these plain and undeniable truths:

That exigencies are to be expected to occur, in the affairs of nations, in which there will be a necessity for borrowing.

That loans in times of public danger, especially from foreign war, are found an indispensable resource, even to the wealthiest of them.

And that, in a country which, like this, is possessed of little active wealth, or, in other words, little moneyed capital, the necessity for that resource must, in such emergencies, be proportionably urgent.

And as, on the one hand, the necessity for borrowing, in particular emergencies, cannot be doubted, so, on the other, it is equally evident, that, to be able to borrow upon good terms, it is essential that the credit of a nation should be well established.

For, when the credit of a country is in any degree questionable, it never fails to give an extravagant premium, in one shape or another, upon all the loans it has occasion to make. Nor does the evil end here; the same disadvantage must be sustained upon whatever is to be bought on terms of future payment.

Text: Alexander Hamilton, *Works,* ed. John C. Hamilton (New York: Charles S. Francis & Co., 1850), III, 1-15, 20, 41.

From this constant necessity of borrowing and buying dear, it is easy to conceive how immensely the expenses of a nation, in a course of time, will be augmented by an unsound state of the public credit.

To attempt to enumerate the complicated variety of mischiefs in the whole system of the social economy, which proceed from a neglect of the maxims that uphold public credit, and justify the solicitude manifested by the House on this point, would be an improper intrusion on their time and patience.

In so strong a light, nevertheless, do they appear to the Secretary, that, on their due observance, at the present critical juncture, materially depends, in his judgment, the individual and aggregate prosperity of the citizens of the United States; their relief from the embarrassments they now experience; their character as a people; the cause of good government.

If the maintenance of public credit, then, be truly so important, the next inquiry which suggests itself is, By what means is it to be effected? The ready answer to which question is, by good faith; by a punctual performance of contracts. States, like individuals, who observe their engagements, are respected and trusted, while the reverse is the fate of those who pursue an opposite conduct.

Every breach of the public engagements, whether from choice or necessity, is, in different degrees, hurtful to public credit. When such a necessity does truly exist, the evils of it are only to be palliated by a scrupulous attention, on the part of the Government to carry the violation no further than the necessity absolutely requires, and to manifest, if the nature of the case admit of it, a sincere disposition to make reparation whenever circumstances shall permit. But, with every possible mitigation, credit must suffer, and numerous mischiefs ensue. It is, therefore, highly important, when an appearance of necessity seems to press upon the public councils, that they should examine well its reality, and be perfectly assured that there is no method of escaping from it, before they yield to its suggestions. . . .

While the observance of that good faith, which is the basis of public credit, is recommended by the strongest inducements of political expediency, it is enforced by considerations of still greater authority. There are arguments for it which rest on the immutable principles of moral obligation. And in proportion as the mind is disposed to contemplate, in the order of Providence, an intimate connection between public virtue and public happiness, will be its repugnancy to a violation of those principles.

This reflection derives additional strength from the nature of the debt of the United States. It was the price of liberty. The faith of America has been repeatedly pledged for it, and with solemnities that give peculiar force to the obligation. There is, indeed, reason to regret that it has not hitherto been kept; that the necessities of the war, conspiring with inexperience in the subjects of finance, produced direct infractions; and that the subsequent period has been a continued scene of negative violation or non-compliance. But a diminution of this regret arises from the reflection, that the last seven years have exhibited an earnest and uniform effort, on the part of the Government of the Union, to retrieve the national credit, by doing justice to the creditors of the nation; and that the embarrassments of a defective constitution, which defeated this laudable effort, have ceased.

From this evidence of a favorable disposition given by the former Government, the institution of a new one, clothed with powers competent to calling forth the resources of the community, has excited correspondent expectations. A general belief accordingly prevails, that the credit of the United States will quickly be established on the firm foundation of an effectual provision for the existing debt. The influence which this has had at home, is witnessed by the rapid increase that has taken place in the market value of the public securities. From January to November, they rose thirty-three and a third per cent.; and, from that period to this time, they have risen fifty per cent. more; and the intelligence from abroad announces effects proportionably favorable to our national credit and consequence.

It cannot but merit particular attention, that, among ourselves, the most enlightened friends of good government are those whose expectations are the highest.

To justify and preserve their confidence; to promote the increasing respectability of the American name; to answer the calls of justice; to restore landed property to its due value; to furnish new resources, both to agriculture and commerce; to cement more closely the union of the States; to add to their security against foreign attack; to establish public order on the basis of an upright and liberal policy;—these are the great and invaluable ends to be secured by a proper and adequate provision, at the present period, for the support of public credit.

To this provision we are invited, not only by the general considerations which have been noticed, but by others of a more particular nature. It will procure, to every class of the community, some important advantages, and remove some no less important disadvantages.

The advantage to the public creditors, from the increased value of that part of their property which constitutes the public debt, needs no explanation.

But there is a consequence of this, less obvious, though not less true, in which every other citizen is interested. It is a well known fact, that, in countries in which the national debt is properly funded, and an object of established confidence, it answers most of the purposes of money. Transfers of stock or public debt, are there equivalent to payments in specie; or, in other words, stock, in the principal transactions of business, passes current as specie. The same thing would, in all probability, happen here under the like circumstances.

The benefits of this are various and obvious:

First. Trade is extended by it, because there is a larger capital to carry it on, and the merchant can, at the same time, afford to trade for smaller profits; as his stock, which, when unemployed, brings him in an interest from the Government, serves him also as money when he has a call for it in his commercial operations.

Secondly. Agriculture and manufactures are also promoted by it, for the like reason, that more capital can be commanded to be employed in both; and because the merchant, whose enterprise in foreign trade gives to them activity and extension, has greater means for enterprise.

Thirdly. The interest of money will be lowered by it; for this is always in a ratio to the quantity of money, and to the quickness of circulation. This circumstance will enable both the public and individuals to borrow on easier and cheaper terms.

And from the combination of these effects, additional aids will be furnished to labor, to industry, and to arts of every kind. But these good effects of a public debt are only to be looked for, when, by being well funded, it has acquired an adequate and stable value; till then, it has rather a contrary tendency. The fluctuation and insecurity incident to it, in an unfunded state, render it a mere commodity, and a precarious one. As such, being only an object of occasional and particular speculation, all the money applied to it is so much diverted from the more useful channels of circulation, for which the thing itself affords no substitute; so that, in fact, one serious inconvenience of an unfunded debt is, that it contributes to the scarcity of money.

This distinction, which has been little if at all attended to, is of the greatest moment; it involves a question immediately interesting to every part of the community, which is no other than this: Whether the public debt, by a provision for it on true principles, shall be rendered a substitute for money; or whether, by being left as it is, or by being provided for in such a manner as will wound those principles, and destroy confidence, it shall be suffered to continue as it is, a pernicious drain of our cash from the channels of productive industry? . . .

Having now taken a concise view of the inducements to a proper provision for the public debt, the next inquiry which presents itself is, What ought to be the nature of such a provision? This requires some preliminary discussions.

It is agreed, on all hands, that that part of the debt which has been contracted abroad, and is denominated the foreign debt, ought to be provided for according to the precise terms of the contracts relating to it. The discussions which can arise, therefore, will have reference essentially to the domestic part of it, or to that which has been contracted at home. It is to be regretted that there is not the same unanimity of sentiment on this part as on the other.

The Secretary has too much deference for the opinions of every part of the community, not to have observed one, which has more than once made its appearance in the public prints, and which is occasionally to be met with in conversation. It involves this question: Whether a discrimination ought not to be made between original holders of the public securities, and present possessors, by purchase? Those who advocate a discrimination, are for making a full provision for the securities of the former at their nominal value; but contend that the latter ought to receive no more than the cost to them, and the interest. And the idea is sometimes suggested, of making good the difference to the primitive possessor. . . .

The Secretary, after the most mature reflection on the force of this argument, is induced to reject the doctrine it contains, as equally unjust and impolitic; as highly injurious, even to the original holders of public securities; as ruinous to public credit.

It is inconsistent with justice, because, in the first place, it is a breach of contract—a violation of the rights of a fair purchaser. . . .

That he is to be considered as a fair purchaser, results from this: whatever necessity the seller may have been under, was occasioned by the Government, in not making a proper provision for its debts. The buyer had no agency in it, and therefore ought not to suffer. He is not even chargeable with having taken an undue advantage. He paid what the commodity was worth in the market, and took the risks of reimbursement upon himself. He, of course, gave a fair equivalent, and ought to reap the benefit of his hazard—a hazard which was far from inconsiderable, and which, perhaps, turned on little less than a revolution in government. . . .

But, though many of the original holders sold from necessity, it does not follow that this was the case with all of them. It may well be supposed that some of them did it either through want of confidence in an eventual provision, or from the allurements of some profitable speculation. How shall these different classes be discriminated from each other? How shall it be ascertained, in any case, that the money which the original holder obtained for his security, was not more beneficial to him, than if he had held it to the present time, to avail himself of the provision which shall be made? How shall it be known whether, if the purchaser had employed his money in some other way, he would not be in a better situation than by having applied it in the purchase of securities, though he should now receive their full amount? And, if neither of these things can be known, how shall it be determined, whether a discrimination, independent of the breach of contract, would not do a real injury to purchasers; and, if it included a compensation to the primitive proprietors, would not give them an advantage to which they had no equitable pretension? . . .

Questions of this sort, on a close inspection, multiply themselves without end, and demonstrate the injustice of a discrimination, even on the most subtile calculations of equity, abstracted from the obligation of contract. . . .

The impolicy of a discrimination results from two considerations: one, that it proceeds upon a principle destructive of that quality of the public debt, or the stock of the nation, which is essential to its capacity for answering the purposes of money, that is, the security of transfer; the other, that, as well on this account as because it includes a breach of faith, it renders property, in the funds, less valuable, consequently, induces lenders to demand a higher premium for what they lend, and produces every other inconvenience of a bad state of public credit. . . .

But there is still a point of view, in which it will appear perhaps even more exceptionable than in either of the former. It would be repugnant to an express provision of the Constitution of the United States. This provision is, that "all debts contracted, and engagements entered into, before the adoption of that Constitution, shall be as valid against the United States under it, as under the Confederation;" which amounts to a constitutional ratification of the contracts respecting the debt, in the state in which they existed under the Confederation. And, resorting to that standard, there can be no doubt that the rights of assignees and original holders must be considered as equal. . . .

The Secretary, concluding that a discrimination between the different classes of creditors of the United States cannot, with propriety, be made, proceeds to examine whether a difference ought to be permitted to remain between them and another description of public creditors—those of the States, individually. The Secretary, after mature reflection on this point, entertains a full conviction, that an assumption of the debts of the particular States by the Union, and a like provision for them, as for those of the Union, will be a measure of sound policy and substantial justice.

It would, in the opinion of the Secretary, contribute, in an eminent degree, to an orderly, stable, and satisfactory arrangement of the national finances. Admitting, as ought to be the case, that a provision must be made, in some way or other, for the entire debt, it will follow that no greater revenues will be required, whether that provision be made wholly by the United States, or partly by them, and partly by the States separately.

The principal question, then, must be, whether such a provision cannot be more conveniently and effectually made, by one general plan, issuing from one authority, than by different plans, originating in different authorities? In the first case, there can be no competition for resources; in the last, there must be such a competition. The consequences of this, without the greatest caution on both sides, might be interfering regulations, and thence, collision and confusion. Particular branches of industry might also be oppressed by it. The most productive objects of revenue are not numerous. Either these must be wholly engrossed by one side, which might lessen the efficacy of the provisions by the other, or both must have recourse to the same objects, in different modes, which might occasion an ac-cumulation upon them, beyond what they could properly bear. . . .

If all the public creditors receive their dues from one source, distributed with an equal hand, their interest will be the same. And, having the same interests, they will unite in the support of the fiscal arrangements of the Government—as these, too, can be made with more convenience where there is no competition. These circumstances combined, will insure to the revenue laws a more ready and more satisfactory execution.

If, on the contrary, there are distinct provisions, there will be distinct interests, drawing different ways. That union and concert of views, among the creditors, which in every Government is of great importance to their security, and to that of public credit, will not only not exist, but will be likely to give place to mutual jealousy and opposition. And from this cause, the operation of the systems which may be adopted, both by the particular States and by the Union, with relation to their respective debts, will be in danger of being counteracted. . . .

The result of the foregoing discussions is this: That there ought to be no discrimination between the original holders of the debt, and present possessors by purchase; that it is expedient there should be an assumption of the State debts by the Union; and that the arrears of interest should be provided for on an equal footing with the principal. . . .

Persuaded, as the Secretary is, that the proper funding of the present debt will render it a national blessing, yet he is so far from acceding to the position, in the latitude in which it is sometimes laid down, that "public debts are public benefits"—a position inviting to prodigality, and liable to dangerous abuse—that he ardently wishes to see it incorporated, as a fundamental maxim, in the system of public credit of the United States, that the creation of debt should always be accompanied with the means of extinguishment. This he regards as the true secret for rendering public credit immortal. And he presumes that it is difficult to conceive a situation in which there may not be an adherence to the maxim. At least, he feels an unfeigned solicitude that this may be attempted by the United States, and that they may commence their measures for the establishment of credit with the observance of it.

67

ENDS AND MEANS: THE DOCTRINE OF IMPLIED POWERS

from Alexander Hamilton, Opinion on the Constitutionality of the Bank, February 23, 1791

Establishment of the first Bank of the United States was necessary to the completion of the Hamiltonian economic design, the Secretary of the Treasury argued in his *Report* to Congress of December 14, 1790. Such an institution, broadly modeled on the Bank of England, would increase the capital available to the business community, support the value of government bonds, provide a source of public loans, facilitate the collection and disbursement of government funds, and quicken the general circulation of money. The Bank was formed as a quasi-public institution. The federal government would absorb one fifth of the $10,000,000 capital stock; the rest would be subscribed by private investors, paying for their shares in specie (hard coin) and new government securities. Notes issued by the Bank were made receivable for all payments to the United States, and thus became a kind of legal tender currency. The federal charter placed some limitations on banking operations and gave some general supervisory powers to the Secretary of the Treasury.

Again Hamilton's critics were alarmed, especially by the monopolistic features of the charter. The Bank was guaranteed an exclusive position as the sole federally incorporated institution in the field for twenty years, with authority to establish branches in the states. The monopoly question led into a grave constitutional debate. President Washington, uncertain of the Congressional power to charter a banking corporation, requested legal opinions of Hamilton, Secretary of State Jefferson, and Attorney General Randolph before signing the bill. The Virginians questioned the constitutionality of the Bank, and Jefferson went on to argue vehemently for a strict construction of the Constitution. If Congress were free to choose *any convenient means* for "carrying into execution the foregoing [enumerated] powers" (Article I, Sec. 8 of the Constitution), then the whole object of a limited Constitution would be destroyed. There is no measure "which ingenuity may not torture into a *convenience* . . . to *some one* of so long a list of enumerated powers," Jefferson warned.

Hamilton's opinion, a classic defense of broad constitutional construction, persuaded Washington to sign the bank bill. Under the long reign of John Marshall as Chief Justice of the Supreme Court (1801-1835), the Hamiltonian view was read into the Constitution (see Document 86). The public controversy over broad construction in the 1790's did much to enflame party differences between Hamiltonian Federalists and Jeffersonian Republicans. The Alien and Sedition Acts of 1798 broadened and sharpened the conflict. (See Document 70.)

If it would be necessary to bring proof to a proposition so clear, as that which affirms that the powers of the federal government, as to *its objects*, were sovereign, there is a clause of its Constitution which would be decisive. It is that which declares that the Constitution, and the laws of the United States made in pursuance of it, and all treaties made, or which shall be made, under their authority, shall be the *supreme law of the land.* The power which can create the *supreme law of the land* in *any case* is doubtless *sovereign* as to such case.

This general and indisputable principle puts at once an end to the *abstract* question whether the United States have power to erect a *corporation;* that is to say, to give a *legal* or *artificial*

Text: Alexander Hamilton, *Works,* ed. John C. Hamilton (New York: Charles S. Francis & Co., 1850), IV, 104-138 *passim.*

capacity to one or more persons, distinct from the *natural.* For it is unquestionably incident to *sovereign power* to erect corporations, and consequently to *that* of the United States, in *relation* to the *objects* intrusted to the management of the government. The difference is this: where the authority of the government is general, it can create corporations in *all cases;* where it is confined to certain branches of legislation, it can create corporations *only* in those cases. . . .

. . . It is not denied that there are *implied* as well as *express* powers and that the *former* are as effectually delegated as the *latter.* And for the sake of accuracy it shall be mentioned that there is another class of powers which may be properly denominated *resulting powers.* It will not be doubted that, if the United States should make a conquest of any of the territories of its neighbors, they would possess sovereign jurisdiction over the conquered territory. This would be rather a result, from the whole mass of the powers of the government, and from the nature of political society, than a consequence of either of the powers specially enumerated. . . .

. . . It is conceded that *implied powers* are to be considered as delegated equally with *express ones*. Then it follows that, as a power of erecting a corporation may as well be *implied* as any other thing, it may as well be employed as an *instrument* or *mean* of carrying into execution any of the specified powers, as any other *instrument* or *mean* whatever. The only question must be, in this, as in every other case, whether the mean to be employed or, in this instance, the corporation to be erected, has a natural relation to any of the acknowledged objects or lawful ends of the government. Thus a corporation may not be erected by Congress for superintending the police of the city of Philadelphia, because they are not authorized to *regulate* the *police* of that city. But one may be erected in relation to the collection of taxes, or to the trade with foreign countries, or to the trade between the states, or with the Indian tribes; because it is the province of the federal government to *regulate* those objects, and because it is incident to a general *sovereign* or *legislative* power to *regulate* a thing, to employ all the means which relate to its regulation to the best and greatest advantage. . . .

Through this mode of reasoning respecting the right of employing all the means requisite to the execution of the specified powers of the government, it is objected that none but necessary and proper means are to be employed; and the Secretary of State maintains that no means are to be considered as *necessary* but those without which the grant of the power would be *nugatory*. Nay, so far does he go in his restrictive interpretation of the *word*, as even to make the case of the *necessity* which shall warrant the constitutional exercise of the power to depend on *casual* and *temporary* circumstances; an idea which alone refutes the construction. The *expediency* of exercising a particular power, at a particular time, must, indeed, depend on circumstances; but the constitutional right of exercising it must be uniform and invariable, the same today as tomorrow. . . .

It is essential to the being of the national government that so erroneous a conception of the meaning of the word *necessary* should be exploded.

It is certain that neither the grammatical nor popular sense of the term requires that construction. According to both, *necessary* often means no more than *needful, requisite, incidental, use-*ful, or *conducive to.* It is a common mode of expression to say that it is *necessary* for a government or a person to do this or that thing, when nothing more is intended or understood than that the interests of the government or person require, or will be promoted by, the doing of this or that thing. The imagination can be at no loss for exemplifications of the use of the word in this sense. And it is the true one in which it is to be understood as used in the Constitution. . . .

To understand the word as the Secretary of State does would be to depart from its obvious and popular sense and to give it a restrictive operation, an idea never before entertained. It would be to give it the same force as if the word *absolutely* or *indispensably* had been prefixed to it.

Such a construction would beget endless uncertainty and embarrassment. The cases must be palpable and extreme, in which it could be pronounced, with certainty, that a measure was absolutely necessary, or one, without which, the exercise of a given power would be nugatory. There are few measures of any government which would stand so severe a test. To insist upon it would be to make the criterion of the exercise of any implied power a *case of extreme necessity;* which is rather a rule to justify the overleaping of the bounds of constitutional authority than to govern the ordinary exercise of it. . . .

This restrictive interpretation of the word *necessary* is also contrary to this sound maxim of construction, namely, that the powers contained in a constitution of government, especially those which concern the general administration of the affairs of a country, its finances, trade, defense, etc., ought to be construed liberally in advancement of the public good. This rule does not depend on the particular form of a government, or on the particular demarcation of the boundaries of its powers, but on the nature and objects of government itself. The means by which national exigencies are to be provided for, national inconveniences obviated, national prosperity promoted, are of such infinite variety, extent, and complexity, that there must of necessity be great latitude of discretion in the selection and application of those means. Hence, consequently, the necessity and propriety of exercising the authorities intrusted to a government on principles of liberal construction. . . .

. . . The doctrine which is contended for is not chargeable with the consequences imputed to it. It does not affirm that the national government is sovereign in all respects but that it is sovereign to a certain extent; that is, to the extent of the objects of its specified powers.

It leaves, therefore, a criterion of what is constitutional and of what is not so. This criterion is the *end,* to which the measure relates as a *mean.* If the *end* be clearly comprehended within any of the specified powers, and if the measures have an obvious relation to that *end,* and is not forbidden by a particular provision of the Constitution, it may safely be deemed to come within the compass of the national authority. There is also this further criterion, which may materially assist the decision: Does the proposed measure abridge a pre-existing right of any state or of any individual? If it does not, there is a strong presumption in favor of its constitutionality, and slighter relations to any declared object of the Constitution may be permitted to turn the scale. . . .

. . . A bank has a natural relation to the power of collecting taxes—to that of regulating trade—to that of providing for the common defense—and . . . as the bill under consideration contemplates the government in the light of a joint proprietor of the stock of the bank, it brings the case within the provision of the clause of the Constitution which immediately respects the property of the United States.

Under a conviction that such a relation subsists, the Secretary of the Treasury, with all deference, conceives, that it will result as a necessary consequence from the position, that all the specified powers of government are sovereign, as to the proper objects; that the incorporation of a bank is a constitutional measure; and that the objections taken to the bill, in this respect, are ill founded. . . .

68   SHADES OF MONARCHY: THE JEFFERSONIAN ATTACK

from Thomas Jefferson, *The Anas,* 1790

It is difficult to imagine a modern President appointing, let us say, a man of Herbert Hoover's convictions to head the Treasury Department and a full-blooded New Dealer to direct the State Department. In calling both Hamilton and Jefferson into his cabinet, Washington acquired an explosive combination of talents. Their exceptional qualifications for high office were beyond question. Hopefully, their presence might help to unite diverse sections and interests behind the national administration. The new government mainly followed Hamilton's course, and Jefferson soon found himself in a painful position. The gathering opposition to Hamiltonian policies, headed by James Madison in the House of Representatives, began to turn to Jefferson for leadership. Jefferson's first important act on joining the administration, as he ruefully recounts it in the following selection, was to arrange the bargain whereby Virginia got the capital moved south while Hamilton got the votes he needed to pass his bill for the assumption of state debts.

Jefferson's *Anas*—notes recorded while he was Secretary of State (1789-1793) and revised several decades later—presents a scathing indictment of Federalists in general, and specifically of the ambitious "monarchist" in the Treasury Department. This partisan interpretation of Hamilton's political and economic designs cannot be taken as a fair historical verdict. *The Anas* does reveal the terms in which a growing body of Americans in the 1790's came to believe that the republican order must be rescued from Hamilton's "mercenary phalanx" or be lost. By 1800 a majority of voters in the nation had abandoned Hamilton and the Federalists for good, believing with Jefferson that Federalism was the road to reaction: to British monarchy, financial oligarchy, and oppressive nationalism.

Conflicting sentiments were soon supported by rival political groupings. In Congress and in the states, opposing sets of leaders began to organize their forces for electoral and legislative battles during Washington's first term. The views of the administration were defined in John Fenno's *Gazette of the United States* and echoed in sympathetic journals of New England and elsewhere. Republican critics took their lead from Philip Freneau's *National Gazette,* established in Philadelphia (1790) under the sponsorship of Jefferson and Madison. The Virginians formed a working alliance with leading New York politicians, gaining enough strength to make their vice-presidential candidate, New Yorker George Clinton, a close competitor to John Adams in the 1792 election and to make Adams' election as President in 1796 so marginal that he was taunted as the "President by three votes." The Republican party formed around this New York-Virginia axis.

I returned from that mission [to France] in the 1st. year of the new government, having landed in Virginia in Dec. [17]89. & proceeded to N. York in March [17]90. to enter on the office of Secretary of State. Here certainly I found a state of things which, of all I had ever contemplated, I the least expected. I had left France in the first year of its revolution, in the fervor of natural rights, and zeal for reformation. My conscientious devotion to these rights could not be heightened, but it had been aroused and excited by daily exercise. The President received me cordially, and my Colleagues & the circle of principal citizens, apparently, with welcome. The courtesies of dinner parties given me as a stranger newly arrived among them, placed me at once in their familiar society. But I cannot describe the wonder and mortification with which the table conversations filled me. Politics were the chief topic, and a preference of kingly, over republican, government, was evidently the favorite sentiment. An apostate I could not be; nor yet a hypocrite: and I found myself, for the most part, the only advocate on the republican side of the question, unless, among the guests, there chanced to be some member of that party from the legislative Houses. Hamilton's financial system had then past. It had two objects: 1st as a puzzle, to exclude popular understanding & inquiry. 2dly, as a machine for the corruption of the legislature; for he avowed the opinion that man could be governed by one of two motives only, force or interest: force he observed, in this country, was out of the question; and the interests therefore of the members must be laid hold of, to keep the legislature in unison with the Executive. And with grief and shame it must be acknowledged that his machine was not without effect. That even in this, the birth of our government, some members were found sordid enough to bend their duty to their interests, and to look after personal, rather than public good. It is well-known that, during the war, the greatest difficulty we encountered was the want of money or means, to pay our souldiers who fought, or our farmers, manufacturers & merchants who furnished the necessary supplies of food & clothing for them. After the expedient of paper money had exhausted itself, certificates of debt were given to the individual creditors, with assurance of payment, so soon as the U.S. should be able. But the distresses of these people often obliged them to part with these for the half, the fifth, and even a tenth of their value; and Speculators had made a trade of cozening them from the holders, by the most fraudulent practices and persuasions that they would never be paid. In the bill for funding & paying these, Hamilton made no difference between the original holders, & the fraudulent purchasers of this paper. Great & just repugnance arose at putting these two classes of creditors on the same footing, and great exertions were used to pay to the former the full value, and to the latter the price only which he had paid, with interest. But this would have prevented the game which was to be played, & for which the minds of greedy members were already tutored and prepared. When the trial of strength on these several efforts had indicated the form in which the bill would finally pass, this being known within doors sooner than without, and especially than to those who were in distant parts of the Union, the base scramble began. Couriers & relay horses by land, and swift sailing pilot boats by sea, were flying in all directions. Active part[n]ers & agents were associated & employed in every state, town and country neighborhood, and this paper was bought up at 5/ and even as low as 2/ in the pound, before the holder knew that Congress had already provided for it's redemption at par. Immense sums were thus filched from the poor & ignorant, and fortunes accumulated by those who had themselves been poor enough before. Men thus enriched by the dexterity of a leader, would follow of course the chief who was leading them to fortune, and become the zealous instruments of all his enterprises. . . . Another [game] was on the carpet at the moment of my arrival; and to this I was most ignorantly & innocently made to hold the candle. This fiscal maneuvre is well known by the name of the Assumption. Independantly of the debts of Congress, the states had, during the war, contracted separate and heavy debts; and Massachusetts particularly in an absurd attempt, absurdly conducted, on the British post of Penobscot: and the more debt Hamilton could rake up, the more plunder for his mercenaries. This money, whether wisely or foolishly spent, was pretended to have been spent for general purposes, and ought therefore to be paid from the general purse. But it was objected that nobody knew what these debts were, what their amount, or what their proofs. No matter; we will guess them to be 20. millions. But of these 20. millions we do not know how much should be reimbursed to one state, nor how much to another. No matter; we will guess. And so another scramble was set on foot among the several states, and some got much, some little, some nothing. But the main object was obtained, the phalanx of the

Text: Thomas Jefferson, *Writings*, ed. Paul Leicester Ford (New York: G. P. Putnam's Sons, 1894), I, 159-66.

treasury was reinforced by additional recruits. This measure produced the most bitter & angry contests ever known in Congress, before or since the union of the states. I arrived in the midst of it. But a stranger to the ground, a stranger to the actors on it, so long absent as to have lost all familiarity with the subject, and as yet unaware of it's object, I took no concern in it. The great and trying question however was lost in the H. of Representatives. So high were the feuds excited by this subject, that on it's rejection, business was suspended. Congress met and adjourned from day to day without doing any thing, the parties being too much out of temper to do business together. The Eastern members particularly, who, with Smith from South Carolina, were the principal gamblers in these scenes, threatened a secession and dissolution. Hamilton was in despair. As I was going to the President's one day, I met him in the street. He walked me backwards & forwards before the President's door for half an hour. He painted pathetically the temper into which the legislature had been wrought, the disgust of those who were called the Creditor states, the danger of the secession of their members, and the separation of the states. He observed that the members of the administration ought to act in concert, that tho' this question was not of my department, yet a common duty should make it a common concern; that the President was the center on which all administrative questions ultimately rested, and that all of us should rally around him, and support with joint efforts measures approved by him; and that the question having been lost by a small majority only, it was probable that an appeal from me to the judgment and discretion of some of my friends might effect a change in the vote, and the machine of government, now suspended, might be again set into motion. I told him that I was really a stranger to the whole subject; not having yet informed myself of the system of finances adopted, I knew not how far this was a necessary sequence; that undoubtedly if it's rejection endangered a dissolution of our union at this incipient stage, I should deem that the most unfortunate of all consequences, to avert which all partial and temporary evils should be yielded. I proposed to him however to dine with me the next day, and I would invite another friend or two, bring them into conference together, and I thought it impossible that reasonable men, consulting together coolly, could fail, by some mutual sacrifices of opinion, to form a compromise which was to save the union. The discussion took place. I could take no part in it, but an exhortatory one, because I was a stranger to the circumstances

which should govern it. But it was finally agreed that, whatever importance had been attached to the rejection of this proposition, the preservation of the union, & and of concord among the states was more important, and that therefore it would be better that the vote of rejection should be rescinded, to effect which some members should change their votes. But it was observed that this pill would be peculiarly bitter to the Southern States, and that some concomitant measure should be adopted to sweeten it a little to them. There had before been propositions to fix the seat of government either at Philadelphia, or at Georgetown on the Potomac; and it was thought that by giving it to Philadelphia for ten years, and to Georgetown permanently afterwards, this might, as an anodyne, calm in some degree the ferment which might be excited by the other measure alone. So two of the Potomac members ([Alexander] White & [Richard Henry] Lee, but White with a revulsion of stomach almost convulsive) agreed to change their votes, & Hamilton undertook to carry the other point. In doing this the influence he had established over the Eastern members, with the agency of Robert Morris with those of the middle states, effected his side of the engagement, and so the assumption was passed, and 20. millions of stock divided among favored states, and thrown in as pabulum to the stock-jobbing herd. This added to the number of votaries to the treasury and made its Chief the master of every vote in the legislature which might give to the government the direction suited to his political views. I know well, and so must be understood, that nothing like a majority in Congress had yielded to this corruption. Far from it. But a division, not very unequal, had already taken place in the honest part of that body, between the parties styled republican and federal. The latter being monarchists in principle, adhered to Hamilton of course, as their leader in that principle, and this mercenary phalanx added to them ensured him always a majority in both houses: so that the whole action of the legislature was now under the direction of the treasury. Still the machine was not compleat. The effect of the funding system, & of the assumption, would be temporary. It would be lost with the loss of the individual members whom it had enriched, and some engine of influence more permanent must be contrived, while these myrmidons were yet in place to carry it thro' all opposition. This engine was the Bank of the U.S. All that history is known; so I shall say nothing about it. While the government remained at Philadelphia, a selection of members of both houses were constantly kept as Directors, who, on every question interesting to that institution, or to the views of the federal head, voted at the will of that head; and, together with the stockholding members, could always make the federal vote that of the majority. By this combination, legislative expositions were given to the constitution, and all the administrative laws were shaped on the model of England, & so passed. And from this influence we were not relieved until the removal from the precincts of the bank, to Washington. Here then was the real ground of the opposition which was made to the course of administration. It's object was to preserve the legislature pure and independent of the Executive, to restrain the administration to republican forms and principles, and not permit the constitution to be construed into a monarchy, and to be warped in practice into all the principles and pollutions of their favorite English model. Nor was this an opposition to Genl. Washington. He was true to the republican charge confided to him; & has solemnly and repeatedly protested to me, in our private conversations, that he would lose the last drop of his blood in support of it, and he did this the oftener, and with the more earnestness, because he knew my suspicions of Hamilton's designs against it; & wished to quiet them. For he was not aware of the drift, or of the effect of Hamilton's schemes. Unversed in financial projects & calculations, & budgets, his approbation of them was bottomed on his confidence in the man. But Hamilton was not only a monarchist, but for a monarchy bottomed on corruption. In proof of this I will relate an anecdote, for the truth of which I attest the God who made me. Before the President set out on his Southern tour in April 1791. he addressed a letter of the 4th. of that month, from Mt. Vernon to the Secretaries of State, Treasury & War, desiring that, if any serious and important cases should arise during his absence, they would consult & act on them, and he requested that the Vice-president should also be consulted. This was the only occasion on which that officer was ever requested to take part in a Cabinet question. Some occasion for consultation arising, I invited those gentlemen (and the Attorney genl. as well as I remember) to dine with me in order to confer on the subject. After the cloth was removed, and our question agreed & dismissed, conversation began on other matters and, by some circumstance, was led to the British constitution, on which Mr. Adams observed "purge that constitution of it's corruption, and give to it's popular branch equality of representation, and it would be the most perfect constitution ever devised by the wit of man." Hamilton paused and said, "purge it of it's corruption, and give to it's popular branch equality of representation, & it would become an *impracticable* government: as it stands at present, with all it's supposed defects, it is the most perfect government which ever existed." And this was assuredly the exact line which separated the political creeds of these two gentlemen. The one was for two hereditary branches and an honest elective one; the other for a hereditary king with a house of lords & commons, corrupted to his will, and standing between him and the people. Hamilton was indeed a singular character. Of acute understanding, disinterested, honest, and honorable in all private transactions, amiable in society, and duly valuing virtue in private life, yet so bewitched & perverted by the British example, as to be under thoro' conviction that corruption was essential to the government of a nation. . . .

National Unity and World Politics

69

THE LEGACY OF WASHINGTON

from George Washington, *Farewell Address*, September 17, 1796

Perhaps Washington was the indispensable man of his time in a way no other American has ever been. Could he have grasped royal powers for himself? Of course, one cannot answer such "iffy" questions about the past with any confidence. We know that the possibility of a crown was hinted to him more than once and that he denounced all plots against the republic as madness which would "deluge our rising empire in blood." Washington was not an ambitious man. The closing sentiments of his *Farewell Address* carry the convictions of a lifetime: "I anticipate with pleasing expectation that retreat in which I promise myself to realize, without alloy, the sweet enjoyment of partaking, in the midst of my fellow-citizens, the benign influence of good laws under a free government,—the ever favorite object of my heart. . . ."

In September of 1796 Washington determined to exclude himself from consideration for a third term. Only the urgent persuasions of friends, including both Jefferson and Hamilton, had prevented him from retiring in 1792. The *Farewell Address* was given directly to the press; it was never spoken. Hamilton, and to a lesser degree Madison, had a hand in the composition, but the final form is distinctively Washington's own political testament to the nation.

His theme is union. Love of liberty, Washington believed, had taken root in the American character and needed little encouragement. But liberty without obedience to law, without loyalty to the nation and its Constitution, could work its own destruction. In his "disinterested warnings of a parting friend" one can read a history of the troubles of the early republic: the rising bitterness of party warfare, the sharp clash of sectional interest, the passionate sympathies of Americans for one or the other side in the wars of the French Revolution, the resistance western Pennsylvanians had raised against federal tax collectors, the rumors of secessionist conspiracies in the Southwest.

In the face of such disturbing omens, Washington pronounced again the essential virtues of a firm, constitutional union that alone could guarantee independence, safety, tranquillity, prosperity, and liberty itself. The comments on a neutral foreign policy are the best remembered passages of the *Farewell Address*. Isolationists have found their gospel in Washington's advice, while other interpreters have seen a flexible, realistic approach to the concrete circumstances of the 1790's which invites an equally flexible and realistic policy for new conditions of world politics.

Friends, and Fellow-Citizens,

The period for a new election of a Citizen, to administer the Executive Government of the United States, being not far distant, and the time actually arrived, when your thoughts must be employed in designating the person, who is to be clothed with that important trust, it appears to me proper, especially as it may conduce to a more distinct expression of the public voice, that I should now apprise you of the resolution I have formed, to decline being considered among the number of those, out of whom a choice is to be made. . . .

The impressions, with which I first undertook the arduous trust, were explained on the proper occasion.—In the discharge of this trust, I will only say, that I have, with good intentions, contributed towards the organization and administration of the government, the best exertions of which a very fallible judgment was capable.— Not unconscious, in the outset, of the inferiority of my qualifications, experience in my own eyes, perhaps still more in the eyes of others, has strengthened the motives to diffidence of myself; and every day the increasing weight of years admonishes me more and more, that the shade of retirement is as necessary to me as it will be welcome.—Satisfied, that, if any circumstances have given peculiar value to my services, they

Text: George Washington, *Writings*, ed. John C. Fitz-patrick ("George Washington Bicentennial Edition" [Washington, D.C.: Government Printing Office, 1940]), XXXV, 214-38.

were temporary, I have the consolation to believe, that, while choice and prudence invite me to quit the political scene, patriotism does not forbid it. . . .

Here, perhaps, I ought to stop.—But a solicitude for your welfare, which cannot end but with my life, and the apprehension of danger, natural to that solicitude, urge me on an occasion like the present, to offer to your solemn contemplation, and to recommend to your frequent review, some sentiments; which are the result of much reflection, of no inconsiderable observation and which appear to me all important to the permanency of your felicity as a People.—These will be offered to you with the more freedom, as you can only see in them the disinterested warnings of a parting friend, who can possibly have no personal motive to bias his counsels.—Nor can I forget, as an encouragement to it your indulgent reception of my sentiments on a former and not dissimilar occasion.

Interwoven as is the love of liberty, with every ligament of your hearts, no recommendation of mine is necessary to fortify or confirm the attachment.—

The Unity of Government which constitutes you one people, is also now dear to you.—It is justly so;—for it is a main Pillar in the Edifice of your real independence; the support of your tranquillity at home; your peace abroad; of your safety; of your prosperity in every shape; of that very Liberty, which you so highly prize.—But as it is easy to foresee, that, from different causes, and from different quarters, much pains will be taken, many artifices employed, to weaken in your minds the conviction of this truth;—as this is the point in your political fortress against which the batteries of internal and external enemies will be most constantly and actively (though often covertly and insidiously) directed, it is of infinite moment, that you should properly estimate the immense value of your national Union to your collective and individual happiness;—that you should cherish a cordial, habitual, and immovable attachment to it; accustoming yourselves to think and speak of it as of the Palladium of your political safety and prosperity; watching for its preservation with jealous anxiety; discountenancing whatever may suggest even a suspicion that it can in any event be abandoned, and indignantly frowning upon the first dawning of every attempt to alienate any portion of our Country from the rest, or to enfeeble the sacred ties which now link together the various parts.

For this you have every inducement of sympathy and interest.—Citizens by birth or choice of a common country, that country has a right to concentrate your affections.—The name of AMERICAN, which belongs to you, in your national capacity, must always exalt the just pride of Patriotism, more than any appellation derived from local discriminations.—With slight shades of difference, you have the same Religion, Manners, Habits, and political Principles.—You have in a common cause fought and triumphed together. The Independence and Liberty you possess are the work of joint councils, and joint efforts—of common dangers, sufferings and successes.—

But these considerations, however powerfully they address themselves to your sensibility, are greatly outweighed by those, which apply more immediately to your Interest.—Here every portion of our country finds the most commanding motives for carefully guarding and preserving the Union of the whole.

The *North* in an unrestrained intercourse with the *South*, protected by the equal Laws of a common government, finds in the productions of the latter great additional resources of maritime and commercial enterprise—and precious materials of manufacturing industry.—The *South*, in the same intercourse, benefiting by the agency of the *North*, sees its agriculture grow and its commerce expand. Turning partly into its own channels the seamen of the *North*, it finds its particular navigation envigorated;—and, while it contributes, in different ways, to nourish and increase the general mass of the national navigation, it looks forward to the protection of a maritime strength to which itself is unequally adapted. —The *East*, in a like intercourse with the *West*,

already finds, and in the progressive improvement of interior communications, by land and water, will more and more find, a valuable vent for the commodities which it brings from abroad, or manufactures at home.—The *West* derives from the *East* supplies requisite to its growth and comfort,—and what is perhaps of still greater consequence, it must of necessity owe the *secure* enjoyment of indispensable *outlets* for its own productions to the weight, influence, and the future maritime strength of the Atlantic side of the Union, directed by an indissoluble community of interest, as *one Nation*.—Any other tenure by which the *West* can hold this essential advantage, whether derived from its own separate strength, or from an apostate and unnatural connexion with any foreign Power, must be intrinsically precarious.

While then every part of our Country thus feels an immediate and particular interest in Union, all the parts combined in the united mass of means and efforts cannot fail to find greater strength, greater resource, proportionably greater security from external danger, a less frequent interruption of their Peace by foreign Nations; and, what is of inestimable value! they must derive from Union an exemption from those broils and wars between themselves, which so frequently afflict neighboring countries, not tied together by the same government; which their own rivalships alone would be sufficient to produce; but which opposite foreign alliances, attachments, and intrigues would stimulate and embitter.— Hence likewise they will avoid the necessity of those overgrown Military establishments, which under any form of government, are inauspicious to liberty, and which are to be regarded as particularly hostile to Republican Liberty: In this sense it is, that your Union ought to be considered as a main prop of your liberty, and that the love of the one ought to endear to you the preservation of the other.

These considerations speak a persuasive language to every reflecting and virtuous mind,— and exhibit the continuance of the UNION as a primary object of Patriotic desire.—Is there a doubt, whether a common government can embrace so large a sphere?—Let experience solve it.—To listen to mere speculation in such a case were criminal.—We are authorized to hope that a proper organization of the whole, with the auxiliary agency of governments for the respective subdivisions, will afford a happy issue to the experiment. 'Tis well worth a fair and full experiment. With such powerful and obvious motives to Union, affecting all parts of our country, while experience shall not have demonstrated its impracticability, there will always be reason to distrust the patriotism of those, who in any quarter may endeavor to weaken its bands.—

In contemplating the causes which may disturb our Union, it occurs as matter of serious concern, that any ground should have been furnished for characterizing parties by *Geographical* discriminations—*Northern* and *Southern*—*Atlantic* and *Western;* whence designing men may endeavor to excite a belief, that there is a real difference of local interests and views. One of the expedients of Party to acquire influence, within particular districts, is to misrepresent the opinions and aims of other districts.—You cannot shield yourselves too much against the jealousies and heart burnings which spring from these misrepresentations;—They tend to render alien to each other those who ought to be bound together by fraternal affection. . . .

To the efficacy and permanency of your Union, a Government for the whole is indispensable.— No alliances however strict between the parts can be an adequate substitute.—They must inevitably experience the infractions and interruptions which all alliances in all times have experienced.—Sensible of this momentous truth, you have improved upon your first essay, by the adoption of a Constitution of Government, better calculated than your former for an intimate Union, and for the efficacious management of your common concerns.—This government, the offspring of our own choice uninfluenced and unawed, adopted upon full investigation and mature deliberation, completely free in its principles, in the distribution of its powers, uniting security with energy, and containing within itself a provision for its own amendment, has a just claim to your confidence and your support.—Respect for its authority, compliance with its Laws, acquiescence in its measures, are duties enjoined by the fundamental maxims of true Liberty.—The basis of our political systems is the right of the people to make and to alter their Constitutions of Government.—But the Constitution which at any time exists, 'till changed by an explicit and authentic act of the whole People, is sacredly obligatory upon all.—The very idea of the power and the right of the People to establish Government, presupposed the duty of every individual to obey the established Government. . . .

Towards the preservation of your Government and the permanency of your present happy state, it is requisite, not only that you steadily discountenance irregular oppositions to its acknowledged authority, but also that you resist with care the spirit of innovation upon its principles, however specious the pretexts.—One method of as-

sault may be to effect, in the forms of the Constitution, alterations which will impair the energy of the system, and thus to undermine what cannot be directly overthrown.—In all the changes to which you may be invited, remember that time and habit are at least as necessary to fix the true character of Governments, as of other human institutions—that experience is the surest standard, by which to test the real tendency of the existing Constitution of a Country—that facility in changes upon the credit of mere hypothesis and opinion exposes to perpetual change, from the endless variety of hypothesis and opinion:— and remember, especially, that, for the efficient management of your common interests, in a country so extensive as ours, a Government of as much vigor as is consistent with the perfect security of Liberty is indispensable.—Liberty itself will find in such a Government, with powers properly distributed and adjusted, its surest Guardian.—It is, indeed, little else than a name, where the Government is too feeble to withstand the enterprises of faction, to confine each member of the society within the limits prescribed by the laws, and to maintain all in the secure and tranquil enjoyment of the rights of person and property.

I have already intimated to you the danger of Parties in the State, with particular reference to the founding of them on Geographical discriminations.—Let me now take a more comprehensive view, and warn you in the most solemn manner against the baneful effects of the Spirit of Party, generally.

This Spirit, unfortunately, is inseparable from our nature, having its root in the strongest passions of the human mind.—It exists under different shapes in all Governments, more or less stifled, controuled, or repressed; but, in those of the popular form, it is seen in its greatest rankness, and is truly their worst enemy.

The alternate domination of one faction over another, sharpened by the spirit of revenge natural to party dissension, which in different ages and countries has perpetrated the most horrid enormities, is itself a frightful despotism.—But this leads at length to a more formal and permanent despotism.—The disorders and miseries, which result, gradually incline the minds of men to seek security and repose in the absolute power of an Individual: and sooner or later the chief of some prevailing faction, more able or more fortunate than his competitors, turns this disposition to the purposes of his own elevation, on the ruins of Public Liberty.

Without looking forward to an extremity of this kind, (which nevertheless ought not to be entirely out of sight), the common and continual mischiefs of the spirit of Party are sufficient to make it the interest and duty of a wise People to discourage and restrain it.—

It serves always to distract the Public Councils, and enfeeble the Public administration.—It agitates the community with ill founded jealousies and false alarms, kindles the animosity of one part against another, foments occasionally riot and insurrection.—It opens the doors to foreign influence and corruption, which find a facilitated access to the Government itself through the channels of party passions. Thus the policy and the will of one country, are subjected to the policy and will of another.

There is an opinion that parties in free countries are useful checks upon the Administration of the Government, and serve to keep alive the Spirit of Liberty.—This within certain limits is probably true—and in Governments of a Monarchial cast, Patriotism may look with indulgence, if not with favour, upon the spirit of party.— But in those of the popular character, in Governments purely elective, it is a spirit not to be encouraged.—From their natural tendency, it is certain there will always be enough of that spirit for every salutary purpose,—and there being constant danger of excess, the effort ought to be, by force of public opinion, to mitigate and assuage it.—A fire not to be quenched; it demands a uniform vigilance to prevent its bursting into a flame, lest, instead of warming, it should consume.

It is important, likewise, that the habits of thinking in a free country should inspire caution in those entrusted with its administration, to confine themselves within their respective constitutional spheres; avoiding in the exercise of the powers of one department to encroach upon another.—The spirit of encroachment tends to consolidate the powers of all the departments in one, and thus to create, whatever the form of government, a real despotism. . . . If in the opinion of the People, the distribution or modification of the Constitutional powers be in any particular wrong, let it be corrected by an amendment in the way which the Constitution designates.—But let there be no change by usurpation; for though this, in one instance, may be the instrument of good, it is the customary weapon by which free governments are destroyed.—The precedent must always greatly overbalance in permanent evil any partial or transient benefit which the use can at any time yield.—

Of all the dispositions and habits, which lead to political prosperity, Religion and morality are indispensable supports.—In vain would that

man claim the tribute of Patriotism, who should labour to subvert these great Pillars of human happiness, these firmest props of the duties of Men and Citizens.—The mere Politician, equally with the pious man, ought to respect and to cherish them.—A volume could not trace all their connexions with private and public felicity.—Let it simply be asked where is the security for property, for reputation, for life, if the sense of religious obligation *desert* the oaths, which are the instruments of investigation in Courts of Justice? And let us with caution indulge the supposition, that morality can be maintained without religion.—Whatever may be conceded to the influence of refined education on minds of peculiar structure—reason and experience both forbid us to expect, that national morality can prevail in exclusion of religious principle.—

'T is substantially true, that virtue or morality is a necessary spring of popular government.— The rule indeed extends with more or less force to every species of Free Government.—Who that is a sincere friend to it can look with indifference upon attempts to shake the foundation of the fabric?—

Promote, then, as an object of primary importance, institutions for the general diffusion of knowledge. In proportion as the structure of a government gives force to public opinion, it is essential that public opinion should be enlightened.—

As a very important source of strength and security, cherish public credit.—One method of preserving it is, to use it as sparingly as possible: —avoiding occasions of expense by cultivating peace, but remembering also that timely disbursements to prepare for danger frequently prevent much greater disbursements to repel it—avoiding likewise the accumulation of debt, not only by shunning occasions of expense, but by vigorous exertions in time of Peace to discharge the debts which unavoidable wars may have occasioned, not ungenerously throwing upon posterity the burthen which we ourselves ought to bear. . . .

Observe good faith and justice towards all Nations. Cultivate peace and harmony with all. —Religion and Morality enjoin this conduct; and can it be that good policy does not equally enjoin it?—It will be worthy of a free, enlightened, and, at no distant period, a great nation, to give to mankind the magnanimous and too novel example of a People always guided by an exalted justice and benevolence.—Who can doubt that in the course of time and things, the fruits of such a plan would richly repay any temporary advantages, which might be lost by a steady adherence to it? Can it be that Providence has not connected the permanent felicity of a Nation with its virtue? The experiment, at least, is recommended by every sentiment which ennobles human nature.—Alas! is it rendered impossible by its vices?

In the execution of such a plan nothing is more essential than that permanent, inveterate antipathies against particular nations and passionate attachments for others should be excluded; and that in place of them just and amicable feelings towards all should be cultivated.—The Nation, which indulges towards another an habitual hatred or an habitual fondness, is in some degree a slave. It is a slave to its animosity or to its affection, either of which is sufficient to lead it astray from its duty and its interest.—Antipathy in one nation against another disposes each more readily to offer insult and injury, to lay hold of slight causes of umbrage, and to be haughty and intractable, when accidental or trifling occasions of dispute occur. . . .

So likewise a passionate attachment of one Nation for another produces a variety of evils.—Sympathy for the favourite nation, facilitating the illusion of an imaginary common interest in cases where no real common interest exists, and infusing into one the enmities of the other, betrays the former into a participation in the quarrels and wars of the latter, without adequate inducement or justification: It leads also to concessions to the favourite Nation of privileges denied to others, which is apt doubly to injure the Nation making the concessions; by unnecessarily parting with what ought to have been retained, and by exciting jealousy, ill-will, and a disposition to retaliate, in the parties from whom equal privileges are withheld; and it gives to ambitious, corrupted, or deluded citizens, (who devote themselves to the favourite Nation) facility to betray, or sacrifice the interests of their own country, without odium, sometimes even with popularity:—gilding with the appearances of a virtuous sense of obligation, a commendable deference for public opinion, or a laudable zeal for public good, the base of foolish compliances of ambition, corruption or infatuation. . . .

Against the insidious wiles of foreign influence, I conjure you to believe me, fellow-citizens, the jealousy of a free people ought to be *constantly* awake, since history and experience prove that foreign influence is one of the most baneful foes of republican Government.—But that jealousy, to be useful, must be impartial; else it becomes the instrument of the very influence to be avoided, instead of a defence against it.—Excessive partiality for one foreign nation and excessive dislike of another, cause those whom they actuate to see danger only on one side, and serve to veil and even second the arts of influence on the other. —Real Patriots, who may resist the intrigues of the favourite, are liable to become suspected and odious; while its tools and dupes usurp the applause and confidence of the people, to surrender their interests.—

The great rule of conduct for us, in regard to foreign Nations, is, in extending our commercial relations, to have with them as little *Political* connection as possible.—So far as we have already formed engagements, let them be fulfilled with perfect good faith.—Here let us stop.—

Europe has a set of primary interests, which to us have none, or a very remote relation.—Hence she must be engaged in frequent controversies, the causes of which are essentially foreign to our concerns.—Hence therefore it must be unwise in us to implicate ourselves, by artificial ties in the ordinary vicissitudes of her politics, or the ordinary combinations and collisions of her friendships, or enmities.

Our detached and distant situation invites and enables us to pursue a different course.—If we remain one People, under an efficient government, the period is not far off, when we may defy material injury from external annoyance; when we may take such an attitude as will cause the neutrality we may at any time resolve upon to be scrupulously respected. When belligerent nations, under the impossibility of making acquisitions upon us, will not lightly hazard the giving us provocation[;] when we may choose peace or war, as our interest guided by our justice shall counsel.

Why forego the advantages of so peculiar a situation?—Why quit our own to stand upon foreign ground?—Why, by interweaving our destiny with that of any part of Europe, entangle our peace and prosperity in the toils of European ambition, rivalship, interest, humour, or caprice?—

'T is our true policy to steer clear of permanent alliances, with any portion of the foreign world;—so far, I mean, as we are now at liberty to do it—for let me not be understood as capable of patronizing infidelity to existing engagements, (I hold the maxim no less applicable to public than to private affairs, that honesty is always the best policy).—I repeat it therefore let those engagements be observed in their genuine sense. —But in my opinion it is unnecessary and would be unwise to extend them.—

Taking care always to keep ourselves, by suitable establishments, on a respectably defensive posture, we may safely trust to temporary alliances for extraordinary emergencies.—

Harmony, liberal intercourse with all nations, are recommended by policy, humanity, and interest. But even our commercial policy should hold an equal and impartial hand:—neither seeking nor granting exclusive favours or preferences;—consulting the natural course of things; —diffusing and diversifying by gentle means the streams of commerce, but forcing nothing;— establishing with Powers so disposed—in order to give trade a stable course, to define the rights of our Merchants, and to enable the Government to support them—conventional rules of intercourse, the best that present circumstances and mutual opinion will permit; but temporary, and liable to be from time to time abandoned or varied, as experience and circumstances shall dictate; constantly keeping in view that 't is folly in one nation to look for disinterested favors from another,—that it must pay with a portion of its independence for whatever it may accept under that character—that by such acceptance, it may place itself in the condition of having given equivalents for nominal favours and yet of being reproached with ingratitude for not giving more.—There can be no greater error than to expect, or calculate upon real favours from Nation to Nation.—'T is an illusion which experience must cure, which a just pride ought to discard. . . .

Though, in reviewing the incidents of my Administration, I am unconscious of intentional error—I am nevertheless too sensible of my defects not to think it probable that I may have committed many errors.—Whatever they may be, I fervently beseech the Almighty to avert or mitigate the evils to which they may tend.—I shall also carry with me the hope that my country will never cease to view them with indulgence; and that after forty-five years of my life dedicated to its service, with an upright zeal, the faults of incompetent abilities will be consigned to oblivion, as myself must soon be to the mansions of rest.

Relying on its kindness in this as in other things, and actuated by that fervent love towards it, which is so natural to a man, who views in it the native soil of himself and his progenitors for several generations;—I anticipate with pleasing expectation that retreat, in which I promise myself to realize, without alloy, the sweet enjoyment of partaking, in the midst of my fellow-citizens, the benign influence of good Laws under a free Government,—the ever favourite object of my heart, and the happy reward, as I trust, of our mutual cares, labours, and dangers.

Politics in the Adams Administration

70

WHO SHALL JUDGE?: THE KENTUCKY RESOLUTIONS OF 1798

from *The Kentucky Resolutions*, November 16, 1798

The stature of Washington as the great national hero helped to restrain domestic conflicts during the first years of Federalist rule. Washington's successor would inherit his problems, his policies, but not his awesome reputation. Trouble began for John Adams in the campaign of 1796, when Hamilton and other leading Federalists showed a distinct preference for Thomas Pinckney of South Carolina. As the new term opened, Adams faced perplexing policy choices, with a divided administration in which many Federalist Congressmen and even Cabinet officials turned to Hamilton for guidance, and with an unsparing Republican opposition waiting for an opening.

A coalition of powers led by England was then at war with revolutionary France. Under Washington's Neutrality Proclamation (1793), American merchants and shippers reaped the rich rewards of wartime trade. British attempts to cut off American trade with the French brought diplomatic relations to the breaking point. Jay's treaty between England and the United States (1794) calmed that crisis momentarily, only to enrage the French and their Republican sympathizers in America, who saw in the treaty a shameless surrender to British interests. New French attacks on American shipping aroused a martial spirit. A French effort to bribe American peace commissioners (the "XYZ Affair" of 1797) precipitated an undeclared war on the seas in 1798. At home the party battle grew more intense. Federalist "Anglomen" and Republican "Jacobins" (to give each party a label preferred by its opponents) exchanged furious charges of treachery in the press and at public meetings.

In this tense atmosphere the Adams Federalists passed a series of punitive measures: the Naturalization, Alien, Alien Enemies, and Sedition acts of 1798. The first prescribed a fourteen-year residence before an alien could be admitted to citizenship. The Alien Act gave the President power to register and deport aliens considered by him to be dangerous to "peace and safety." The Sedition Act threatened with fine and imprisonment all persons unlawfully combining or conspiring "with intent to oppose any measure or measures of the government of the United States." A more drastic provision of the same act applied severe penalties to any person who should write, speak, or publish "any false, scandalous, and malicious" sentiments with intent to defame the government or the President or excite popular hatred against them. The unmistakable object of the attack was to curb the Republican opposition, which included a number of prominent aliens among its spokesmen and supporters.

Jefferson and Madison used the state legislatures of Kentucky and Virginia to broadcast the Republican reply in a series of challenging resolutions (1798-1799). The Kentucky Resolutions of 1798 were written anonymously by Jefferson. His argument, it will be noted, moves from the unconstitutionality of the specific acts to a general theory of the Constitution as a compact between each state and its co-states, granting limited powers to the general government. Thus ultimate authority in disputes over the meaning and application of the Constitution rests with the original parties to the compact. In declaring the acts "void and of no force" and demanding their repeal, Virginia and Kentucky failed to enlist the support of other states. The resolutions did serve to focus popular resentment against Federalist oppression, however, and aided the Republican victory of 1800. Southern leaders of the South Carolina school later found in the Virginia and Kentucky Resolutions support for their nullification (1832) and secession (1860) doctrines. Whether or not the connection is legitimate is a matter of scholarly dispute; but Jefferson and Madison did not contemplate such extreme remedies in 1798.

I. *Resolved,* that the several States composing the United States of America, are not united on the principle of unlimited submission to their general government; but that by compact under the style and title of a Constitution for the United States and of amendments thereto, they constituted a general government for special purposes, delegated to that government certain definite powers, reserving each State to itself, the residuary mass of right to their own self-government; and that whensoever the general government assumes undelegated powers, its acts are unauthoritative, void, and of no force: That to this compact each State acceded as a State, and is an integral party, its co-States forming, as to itself, the other party: That the government created by this compact was not made the exclusive or final judge of the extent of the powers delegated to itself; since that would have made its discretion, and not the Constitution, the measure of its powers; but that as in all other cases of compact among parties having no common Judge, each party has an equal right to judge for itself, as well of infractions as of the mode and measure of redress.

Text: The Virginia and Kentucky Resolutions with the Alien, Sedition, and Other Acts, 1798-1799, ed. Albert Bushnell Hart and Edward Channing ("American History Leaflets" No. 15 [New York: A. Lovell & Co., 1894]), pp. 10-17.

II. *Resolved,* that the Constitution of the United States having delegated to Congress a power to punish treason, counterfeiting the securities and current coin of the United States, piracies and felonies committed on the high seas, and offenses against the laws of nations, and no other crimes whatever, and it being true as a general principle, and one of the amendments to the Constitution having also declared "that the powers not delegated to the United States by the Constitution, nor prohibited by it to the States, are reserved to the States respectively, or to the people," therefore also the same act of Congress passed on the 14th day of July, 1798, and entitled "An act in addition to the act entitled an act for the punishment of certain crimes against the United States;" as also the act passed by them on the 27th day of June, 1798, entitled "An act to punish frauds committed on the Bank of the United States" (and all their other acts which assume to create, define, or punish crimes other than those enumerated in the Constitution), are altogether void and of no force, and that the power to create, define, and punish such other crimes is reserved, and of right appertains solely and exclusively to the respective States, each within its own Territory.

III. *Resolved,* that it is true as a general principle, and is also expressly declared by one of the amendments to the Constitution that "the powers not delegated to the United States by the Constitution, nor prohibited by it to the States, are reserved to the States respectively or to the people;" and that no power over the freedom of religion, freedom of speech, or freedom of the press being delegated to the United States by the Constitution, nor prohibited by it to the States, all lawful powers respecting the same did of right remain, and were reserved to the States, or to the people.

VI. *Resolved*, that the imprisonment of a person under the protection of the laws of this Commonwealth on his failure to obey the simple order of the President to depart out of the United States, as is undertaken by the said act entitled "An act concerning aliens," is contrary to the Constitution, one amendment to which has provided, that "no person shall be deprived of liberty without due process of law," and that another having provided "that in all criminal prosecutions, the accused shall enjoy the right to a public trial by an impartial jury, to be informed of the nature and cause of the accusation, to be confronted with the witnesses against him, to have compulsory process for obtaining witnesses in his favour, and to have the assistance of counsel for his defense," the same act undertaking to authorize the President to remove a person out of the United States who is under the protection of the law, on his own suspicion, without accusation, without jury, without public trial, without confrontation of the witnesses against him, without having witnesses in his favour, without defense, without counsel, is contrary to these provisions also of the Constitution, is therefore not law, but utterly void and of no force. That transferring the power of judging any person who is under the protection of the laws, from the courts to the President of the United States, as is undertaken by the same act concerning aliens, is against the article of the Constitution which provides, that "the judicial power of the United States shall be vested in courts, the judges of which shall hold their offices during good behavior," and that the said act is void for that reason also; and it is further to be noted, that this transfer of judiciary power is to that magistrate of the general government who already possesses all the executive, and a qualified negative in all the legislative powers.

VII. *Resolved*, that the construction applied by the general government (as is evinced by sundry of their proceedings) to those parts of the Constitution of the United States which delegate to Congress a power to lay and collect taxes, duties, imposts, and excises; to pay the debts, and provide for the common defense, and general welfare of the United States, and to make all laws which shall be necessary and proper for carrying into execution the powers vested by the Constitution in the government of the United States, or any department thereof, goes to the destruction of all the limits prescribed to their power by the Constitution: That words meant by that instrument to be subsidiary only to the execution of the limited powers ought not to be so construed as themselves to give unlimited powers, nor a part so to be taken as to destroy the whole residue of the instrument: That the proceedings of the general government under color of these articles will be a fit and necessary subject for revisal and correction at a time of greater tranquillity, while those specified in the preceding resolutions call for immediate redress.

VIII. *Resolved*, that the preceding Resolutions be transmitted to the Senators and Representatives in Congress from this Commonwealth, who are hereby enjoined to present the same to their respective Houses, and to use their best endeavors to procure, at the next session of Congress, a repeal of the aforesaid unconstitutional and obnoxious acts.

IX. *Resolved*, lastly, that the Governor of this Commonwealth be, and is hereby authorized and requested to communicate the preceding Resolutions to the Legislatures of the several States, to assure them that this Commonwealth considers Union for specified National purposes, and particularly for those specified in their late Federal Compact, to be friendly to the peace, happiness, and prosperity of all the States: that faithful to that compact according to the plain intent and meaning in which it was understood and acceded to by the several parties, it is sincerely anxious for its preservation; that it does also believe, that to take from the States all the powers of self-government, and transfer them to a general and consolidated government, without regard to the special delegations and reservations solemnly agreed to in that compact, is not for the peace, happiness, or prosperity of these States: And that, therefore, this Commonwealth is determined, as it doubts not its co-States are, tamely to submit to undelegated and consequently unlimited powers in no man or body of men on earth: that if the acts before specified should stand, these conclusions would flow from them; that the general government may place any act they think proper on the list of crimes and punish it themselves, whether enumerated or not enumerated by the Constitution as cognizable by them: that they may transfer its cognizance to the President or any other person, who may himself be the accuser, counsel, judge, and jury, whose suspicions may be the evidence, his order the sentence, his officer the executioner, and his breast the sole record of the transaction: that a very numerous and valuable description of the inhabitants of these States being by this precedent reduced as outlaws to the absolute dominion of one man, and the barrier of the Constitution thus swept away from us all, no rampart now remains against the passions and the powers of a majority of Congress, to protect from a like exportation or other more grievous punishment the minority of the same body, the legislatures, judges, governors, and counselors of the States, nor their other peaceable inhabitants who may venture to reclaim the constitutional rights and liberties of the State and people, or who for other causes, good or bad, may be obnoxious to the views or marked by the suspicions of the President, or be thought dangerous to his or their elections or other interests, public or personal: that the friendless alien has indeed been selected as the safest subject of a first experiment, but the citizen will soon follow, or rather has already followed: for, already has a sedition act marked him as its prey: that these and successive acts of the same character, unless arrested on the threshold, may tend to drive these States into revolution and blood, and will furnish new calumnies against Republican governments, and new pretexts for those who wish it to be believed, that man cannot be governed but by a rod of iron: that it would be a dangerous delusion were a confidence in the men of our choice to silence our fears for the safety of our rights: that confidence is everywhere the parent of despotism: free government is founded in jealousy and not in confidence; it is jealousy and not confidence which prescribes limited Constitutions to bind down those whom we are obliged to trust with power: that our Constitution has accordingly fixed the limits to which and no further our confidence may go; and let the honest advocate of confidence read the alien and sedition acts, and say if the Constitution has not been wise in fixing limits to the government it created, and whether we should be wise in destroying those limits; let him say what the government is if it be not a tyranny, which the men of our choice have conferred on the President, and the President of our choice has assented to and accepted over the friendly strangers, to whom the mild spirit of our country and its laws had pledged hospitality and protection: that the men of our choice have more respected the bare suspicions of the President than the solid rights of innocence, the claims of justification, the sacred force of truth, and the forms and substance of law and justice. In questions of power then let no more be heard of confidence in man, but bind him down from mischief by the claims of the Constitution. That this Commonwealth does therefore call on its co-States for an expression of their sentiments on the acts concerning aliens, and for the punishment of certain crimes herein before specified, plainly declaring whether these acts are or are not authorized by the Federal Compact. And it doubts not that their sense will be so announced as to prove their attachment unaltered to limited government, whether general or particular, and that the rights and liberties of their co-States will be exposed to no dangers by remaining embarked on a common bottom with their own: That they will concur with this Commonwealth in considering the said acts so palpably against the Constitution as to amount to an undisguised declaration, that the compact is not meant to be the measure of the powers of the general government, but that it will proceed in the exercise over these States of all powers whatsoever: That they will view this as seizing the rights of the States and consolidating them in the hands of the general government with a power assumed to bind the States (not merely in cases made Federal) but in all cases whatsoever, by laws made, not with their consent, but by others against their consent: That this would be to surrender the form of government we have chosen, and to live under one deriving its powers from its own will, and not from our authority; and that the co-States recurring to their natural right in cases not made Federal, will concur in declaring these acts void and of no force, and will each unite with this Commonwealth in requesting their repeal at the next session of Congress.

71

FEDERALISM CORNERED: TACTICS OF THE "JACOBIN" PARTY

from Fisher Ames, *Laocoon* No. 1, 1799

Fisher Ames (1758-1808) stood high in the Federalist councils of Massachusetts. Writing in the Boston press under the signature of "Brutus" or "Camillus," he had helped to unite conservative opinion behind the new Constitution of the United States in the 1780's. In 1788 Ames defeated Sam Adams of Revolutionary fame for a seat in the first Congress, a place he held through four terms. Following Hamilton's lead, he supported the Federalist program for strengthening the national government and cooperating with the British in their war against France. His fame as a Federalist orator was spread by a fervid speech (1796) warning Congress that if the Jay Treaty were not carried out, "even I, slender and almost broken as my hold upon life is, may outlive the government and constitution of my country."

Federalism was deeply entrenched in Massachusetts. Yet even there, Fisher Ames and his fearful friends of the "Essex Junto" (a powerful clique of Federalist leaders) sensed the growing popular influence of the Republicans, "bawlers or whisperers against government" who invaded the threshing floor, the house-raising party, and even the funeral to organize their followers. Ames spoke for those Federalist diehards, especially prominent in Massachusetts and Connecticut politics, who would never come to terms with a new democracy that raised "the worst" to power. They combined rigid conservatism with a New England sectionalism (once the Republicans gained national control) that led a few of them into secessionist conspiracies in 1803-1804 and again in 1814.

It would be difficult to explain the views of Fisher Ames—views "saturated with the despair of the tomb," as Henry Ames wrote—by reference to the condition of Massachusetts society. His nights were made "restless with visions of horror" by the fixed idea that Republican rule would reproduce in America the "open hell" of Revolutionary France. (Ironically, his brother Nathaniel, a respected Dedham physician, was an outspoken "Jacobin," i.e., Republican.) The *Laocoon* papers, published in the *Boston Gazette* in 1799, recall the venomous spirit of party journalism in the years when Republicans anticipated a monarchist reaction playing into English hands and Federalists prepared for the impending reign of terror under French domination.

Laocoon. No. 1.

First Published in the Boston Gazette, April, 1799

. . . We have to sustain an everlasting conflict with faction; a foe, destined to be the companion of liberty, and, at last, its assassin. However we may flatter ourselves with the idea that our blows will prove fatal to this foe, yet, though smitten to the ground, it will rise again like Anteus, untired, invulnerable, and immortal. Nothing can more strikingly illustrate the folly of the jacobins [i.e., Jefferson's Democratic Republican following], in their pretensions to a superior vigilance for the people, than the natural and indeed experienced tendency of their turbulence to strengthen the powers of government. The danger these men create must be repelled by arming our rulers with force enough, and appointing them to watch in our stead. Thus good citizens find that they must submit to laws of the more rigor, because the desperate licentiousness and wickedness of the bad could not be otherwise restrained. If the laws they complain of [e.g., the Alien and Sedition Acts] really abridge liberty, as they pretend, which however is positively denied, it is their own wickedness that has supplied to government the pretext, and varnished it over with the appearance of necessity. Quiet, satisfied people, need the least law; but as the jacobins are of a very different character, it is clear that all the fruit of their

perverseness must be to abridge the liberty of the people; and this too if they fail of success. But if they should prevail, the people would be crushed, as in France, under tyranny more vindictive, unfeeling, and rapacious, than that of Tiberius, Nero, or Caligula, or any single despot that ever existed. . . .

Behold France, that open hell, still ringing with agonies and blasphemies, still smoking with sufferings and crimes, in which we see their state of torment, and perhaps our future state. There we see the wretchedness and degradation of a people, who once had the offer of liberty, but have trifled it away; and there we have seen crimes so monstrous, that, even after we know they have been perpetrated, they still seem incredible.

If, however, the real people will wake, when their own government is in danger; if, like a body of minute-men, they will rally in its defence, we may long preserve our excellent system unimpaired in the degree of its liberty; we may preserve every thing but our tranquillity.

It is however difficult, if not impossible, to excite and maintain as much zeal and ardor in defence of government, as will animate the jacobins for its subversion; for to them action is ease, to us it is effort; to be at rest costs them more constraint, than us to stir. The machinery

Text: Fisher Ames, *Works,* ed. Seth Ames (Boston: Little, Brown & Co., 1854), II, 110-18.

of our zeal is wrought by a feeble and intermitting momentum, and is impeded by its own friction; their rage beats like the pulse of life, and to stop it would be mortal. Like the whirlwind, it clears away obstacles, and gathers speed in its progress. Any great exertion not only tires, but disgusts the federalists; their spirit, after flaming brightly, soon sleeps in its embers; but the jacobins, like salamanders, can breathe only in fire. Like toads, they suck no aliment from the earth but its poisons. When they rest in their lurking places, as they did after the publication of the [XYZ] despatches, it is, like serpents in winter, the better to concoct their venom; and when they are in action, it is to shed it. Without digressing to make an analysis of the jacobin character, whether it is envy that sickens at the fame of superiors, cupidity that seeks political power for the sake of plunder, or ambition that considers plunder as the instrument to get power; whether their characters are formed by the weak facility of their faith, or their faith determined by the sour, malignant, and suspicious cast of their temperment, yet all agree in this one point, all are moved by some fixed prejudice or strong passion, some powerful spring of action, so blended with self-interest, or self-love, and so exalted into fanaticism, that the ordinary powers of the man, and the extraordinary powers conferred on the enthusiast, are equally devoted to their cause of anarchy. Hatred of the government becomes a mania, . . . and their dread of all power but their own, resembles the hydrophobia, baffling our attempts to describe its nature or its remedies. These are the fanatics whom the federalists must oppose; and what in common times is to excite their zeal and secure the constancy of their opposition? A sense of duty, which a few men of abstraction will deduce from just principles, and the foresight of a few more, who will be terrified by the tendencies of democracy to anarchy? But sober duty and a timorous forecast are feeble antagonists against jacobinism; it is flat tranquillity against passion; dry leaves against the whirlwind; the weight of gunpowder against its kindled force. Such federalists may serve as weathercocks to show how the wind blows, but are no shelter against its violence. The quiet citizens may be compared to the still water in the lake; the jacobins to that part of it which falls over a cataract at its outlet; the former having a thousand times the greatest mass, but no energy, and scarcely motion enough to keep it sweet; the latter dashed into foam, and scooping deeper channels in the rocks of adamant. To weight we must impart motion; correct good sense must acquire the energy of zeal. . . .

A frame of government less free and popular might perhaps have been left to take some care of itself; but the people choose to have it as it is, and therefore they must not complain of the burden, but come forward and support it; it has not strength to stand alone without such help from the wise and honest citizens. The time to do this, is at the elections. There, if anywhere, the sovereignty of the citizens is to be exercised; and there the privilege is open to the most excessive and most fatal abuse.

Here at last the jacobins have taken their post, and here they have intrenched themselves to assail our sober and orderly liberty. Here we see of late, indeed within a single year, an almost total change in the tactics and management of parties. The jacobins have at last made their own discipline perfect; they are trained, officered, regimented, and formed to subordination, in a manner that our militia have never yet equalled. Emissaries are sent to every class of men, and even to every individual man, that can be gained. Every threshing-floor, every husking, every party at work on a house-frame or raising a building, the very funerals are infected with bawlers or whisperers against government. In one of our towns, it is a fact, that the vote would have been unanimous for our worthy chief magistrate; but a turbulent man who kept two great dogs, but could not keep his estate, had influence enough to gain five or six votes for the anti-candidate; the only complaint he had to urge against the governor was, that he had signed the act for the dog-tax.

The extreme industry of this faction shows the extent of their designs; even the town governments are not below their scheme of influence. It is plain, that they intend to get the State government into their hands. They will make the attempt, and if they get only one-fifth jacobin members, they will try again next year, never despairing of their final success; should they succeed, they would use the power of Massachusetts against the laws and government of the United States. No longer hoping much aid from the fleets and armies of France, which they but lately declared they wished to see on our shores and coast, they rely on themselves. In every State they are exerting themselves rather more like an armed force beating up for recruits, than a sect of political disputants; and it is as certain as any future event can be, that they will take arms against the laws as soon as they dare; probably within a year, if they get the countenance of the New England State governments. They are already in arms in Pennsylvania, and Virginia holds forth all possible encouragement to their rising, by

resolutions and remonstrances calculated to excite civil war, and to infuse into the bosoms of
the factions all the fury with which such wars
are carried on.

If they would rise and try the issue in the
field, they would be beaten. Let them then come
out; but while they depend on lies and industry
in spreading them, they will beat us.

They are overmatched by the federalists in
argument. Every public question that has been
keenly investigated and sifted by the political
writers and debaters on both sides, has been
clearly decided against them. In the resources
of money, and that sort of credit which grows
out of confidence in the virtue and morals of
political men, the jacobins are weak indeed. The
federalists, throughout New England at least,
probably pay nineteen shillings in the pound of
the taxes; and as to credit, the chiefs of the party
would consider an inquiry into their title to any
as a cruel irony. For talents as statesmen, the
New England jacobin leaders are despicable;
their ignorance of commerce, of finance, and of
the "diplomatic skill" of France, is not only
obvious, but they are concerned to urge the last
as an excuse, for if they are not ignorant, they
are wicked; it is possible they are both. As to
talents in the field, on which side do they appear?
The reader may be left to look up jacobin generals and heroes.

With all these undoubted titles to contempt,
are the jacobins to be despised? Individually,
it may be so; though great numbers are rather
to be pitied; but, collectively, they are formidable,
and a party is never more to be feared than when
it is despised. Then they are let alone to undermine the pillars of the public order; then it
happens, as at the present moment, that they
bestir themselves to get jacobins elected into the
general court; and the friends of government,
despising their foe, sleep in a dangerous security.

The jacobins know that they are as yet weak
in force, though powerful in lies and low cunning.
They will not appear in arms at present, for
that would make their weakness the antagonist
of our strength. But lies and cunning are always
formidable at elections; thus they oppose their
strength to our weakness; we cannot and will not
resort to lies. But we can overmatch them when
we take the alarm in season, and rouse the federal zeal; that zeal has more than once saved
the country. Now is the time and the occasion
again to display it, for the faction turns its evil
eyes to the elections of the house of representatives of the State; and if they obtain even a large
minority, they will spread the infection with more
ardor than even a majority, as minorities are ever
the most industrious and most firmly united. So
large a mass of poison in the general court,
lying in fermentation for a year, would vitiate
and corrupt our political health; and by another
year a jacobin majority would appear there to
overturn, and overturn, and overturn, till property
shall take wings, and true liberty and good government find their graves. By getting a majority
of jacobins into the New England State legislatures, they would make civil war, disunion, and
perhaps a foreign yoke, the lot of the present
generation. Friends of virtue, if you will not
attend the election, and lend to liberty the help
of your votes, within two years you will have to
defend her cause with your swords.

CHAPTER 7

Jeffersonian Democracy

in Power: 1801 to 1825

Thomas Jefferson's victory in the presidential election of 1800 meant that the party which had grown up in opposition to the Hamiltonian system—the Democratic Republican—would now face the responsibility of translating political criticism into a positive program. For Hamilton's broad construction of the Constitution, the Jeffersonians were pledged to substitute strict construction. Federalism allegedly preferred the minority interests of commerce, industry, and finance; Republicans would restore the great mass of planters and farmers to their rightful eminence. Hamiltonian finance—the funding system, the national bank, the internal excise—was charged with creating an engine of corruption and political oppression. Simplicity and frugality in the conduct of the government would be the Republican standards. If Hamilton envisioned the promotion and guidance of economic development by national authority, Jeffersonians would rely upon the free pursuit of private interest policed by the states, regulated by the central government only in those special cases where the national interest was obviously of first importance.

In retrospect, Jefferson viewed his victory over Federalism as the "Revolution of 1800." Modern writers are inclined rather to emphasize the continuities with the Hamiltonian past and the striking Republican change toward a nationalist outlook during the first quarter of the nineteenth century. Still, there can be little doubt that over the long run the rule of the Jeffersonian Republicans furthered the democratization of American public life; they strengthened the tendency toward decentralization of power and broadened the range of individual liberty, political and economic, in opposition to the claims of governmental authority. Perhaps the irony of Jefferson's career is not so much that events in his and following administrations conspired to block fulfillment of his policy objectives as that the Jeffersonian tradition of liberty and equality was used during the nineteenth century to justify a sectional recalcitrance, a corrupt democracy on the state and local levels, and an unbridled business enterprise that travestied the original purposes of the great Virginian.

REPUBLICAN SOCIETY

American society did not experience a dramatic turn with the Republican rise to power. The United States in 1800 formed a relatively simple agrarian society, concentrated along the Atlantic seaboard but moving steadily westward to the Alleghenies and beyond. Much the same thing could be said of the nation a generation later, if one shifts the line of frontier settlement to the Mississippi. The America of 1825 would not have seemed strange to a citizen of 1800. Growth continued, building upon prior growth. Changes accumulated, swelling the current of prior change. The historian Frederick Jackson Turner found the constant element throughout the nineteenth century to be the presence of a moving frontier where succeeding generations of Americans relived the experience of their fathers and so acquired similar habits and values.

However this may be, the elements of difference in 1825 are not to be dismissed because they did not constitute an arrestingly novel condition of society. If one looks forward to consequences for the next generation, then the new departures of the Republican era become highly significant. The continuous migration of Americans was creating a new West beyond the mountains and along the Gulf coast: a new center of economic activity, a new political force, a new section that would deeply influence the character of the Union. (Eight new states were added to the Union between 1801 and 1825, four of them slave and four free.) In the South the cotton gin (invented by the Yankee Eli Whitney in 1793) began to work a major transformation. King Cotton soon became the staple product over large parts of the section, giving a boost to the system of plantation slavery and stimulating the rapid settlement of the region from Georgia to the Mississippi valley. New England after 1800 experienced a decline in relative importance but found toward the end of the Republican era the new economic formula that would create textile wealth from the combination of enterprise, labor, water power, machines, raw fiber, and the capital gained from foreign commerce. New York in 1825 had just completed a bold enterprise, the Erie Canal, that would tap the riches of the West and help to build the future commercial metropolis of the nation.

The successful steamboat experiments in 1807 of a New Yorker, Robert Fulton, made their largest impress on Western navigation. A faster water carrier that could run upstream as well as down reduced freight rates and quickened the flow of commerce through the Mississippi River system. New Orleans, as the focal point of the river trade, would grow to almost 50,000 by 1830 and double its population in another decade.

In these and other ways the development of American society in the Republican era was distinguished more by what was undertaken than by what was concluded.

FOREIGN POLICY

The conduct of foreign affairs demands a unity, a readiness, a disciplined efficiency of action that would seem far better suited to Hamiltonian Federalism than to Jeffersonian Republicanism. The Federalism of Hamilton centered much of its argument on the need for a central authority strong and firm enough to "provide for the common defense" and promote the national interest of the United States in its relations with external powers. There is a certain irony in the fact that critical foreign policy issues assumed a dominating importance in the Republican administrations of Jefferson and Madison. The party created under the slogans of decentralization and strict construction, the party most apprehensive of public debt and military power, the party, in short, that inherited much of the "Little Americanism" of the Anti-Federalists, was forced to meet external challenges with the concerted strength of the republic. By a further irony, the political heirs of Hamilton—the post-1800 Federalist Party—became the voice of provincialism, strict construction, and almost of disunion in the years of conflict with Great Britain.

The foreign policy of the United States first took shape amidst the turmoil of the War of Independence and developed in an age of European conflict. For most of the period from 1793 to 1815, Revolutionary and Napoleonic France was at war with England and its allies for control of the European continent and the surrounding seas. Washington, in the 1790's, had resisted the clamor of Anglophiles (mainly Federalists) and Francophiles (mainly Republicans) in order to establish a course of neutrality. After walking on the edge of open war with France, John Adams had closed his administration with a peaceful settlement. During the Federalist years and after, bold American shippers reaped the profits of a booming neutral commerce and bore the corresponding losses when the belligerents attacked the forms of trade serving their enemies.

A period of truce in Europe and of comparative self-restraint by France and England in the treatment of American commerce eased diplomatic tensions during the first Jefferson administration.

But the years from 1805 to 1812 told a different and sadder story. Northeastern merchants and shippers continued to take the profits with the risks of neutral commerce. France and England, locked in mortal combat, widened their restrictions on American trade, enforcing maritime rules that met their own strategic requirements.

As affairs moved from crisis to crisis, the Republicans introduced their ill-fated remedy of "peaceful coercion." If American shipping provided the economic lifeline for the hard-pressed belligerents of Europe, Jefferson and Madison reasoned, then the cutting of that line would force the powers to respect the maritime rights of neutrals. A series of enactments—the Embargo Act (1807), the Non-Intercourse Act (1809), and Macon's Bill No. 2 (1810)—put some economic pressure on France and England but still more on the commercial regions of New England and New York.

Madison's administration was caught between a rising Federalist opposition, including a secessionist fringe, in the Northeast and an aggressive war party with visions of territorial expansion along the western frontier and in Canada. These latter War Hawks led by Henry Clay and John C. Calhoun pushed Congress into military preparations while James Madison was deciding that economic coercion would not work, that the honor and interest of the nation were threatened by attacks on her maritime rights, and that England was for the time the main enemy.

The War of 1812 brought the United States no concessions on the major issues concerning maritime rights, no territorial gains, and little glory. American fortunes reached their low point when the British captured and burned Washington in 1814; their high point when Andrew Jackson humbled the enemy at New Orleans on January 8, 1815, two weeks after the peace treaty was signed at Ghent but before the news was out. Perhaps the greatest gain for the United States was the crippling of Indian resistance to further settlement in both the northwest and the southwest. The nation gained still more from the success of England and its allies in vanquishing Napoleon and opening a long, peaceful era of world politics.

The "expansionists of 1812" failed to wrest new territories from British rule. In the postwar years negotiation won some valuable advantages that war could not obtain. Joint commissioners agreed upon a boundary line between the United States and Canada running from the Great Lakes region to the Rockies, and an enduring arrangement was concluded for disarmament along the northern frontier. Thus a long-standing grievance over British meddling in the Old Northwest was removed. In the same period the declining power of Spain invited aggressive diplomatic action that led to the American acquisition of East Florida (1819-1821).

Spanish weakness was further evidenced in the crumbling of Spain's Latin American empire. Great Britain and the United States discovered a strong common interest in preventing intervention by the European powers in Western Hemisphere affairs. Latin-American independence was guaranteed primarily by British naval superiority. Acting separately, the United States in the Monroe Doctrine (1823) asserted its national interest in preventing further colonization or interference in the New World by the European powers. The contrasting circumstances, interests, and principles of America and Europe, it was argued, required that each hemisphere abstain from interference in the internal concerns of the other. Of limited authority in its own time, the Monroe Doctrine slowly gained the status of a basic American policy which would be enforced so far as the nation's power permitted.

REPUBLICAN NATIONALISM

The straight and narrow path of government prescribed by Jeffersonian Democracy began to wind and broaden as the new Republican regime entered rough country. Strict construction and public frugality yielded to national interest when Napoleon put Louisiana up for sale in 1803. Pacific intentions did not prevent Jefferson from using naval force against the Barbary pirates of the Mediterranean in 1805. The libertarian principles so firmly stated in opposing and terminating the Alien and Sedition Acts were a little tarnished by the Jeffersonian campaign to hang Aaron Burr for treason in 1807. Above all, critical relations with France and England and the War of 1812 forced the Republicans into strange positions.

The Embargo Act of 1807, for example, was a far more sweeping regulation of commerce than anything Hamilton had proposed. Under the stress of national emergency, federal agents were charged with the ungrateful task of closing down every American port. When war came, it was a Republican government under Jefferson's appointed heir, James Madison, that had to contract debts and raise taxes for military purposes and had to demand the compliance of the recalcitrant New England states with national troop requisitions.

A new breed of nationalist Republicans, raised to prominence by the war crisis, followed the lead of Clay and Calhoun in seeking to establish the "American System," a system combining Hamiltonian measures with democratic rhetoric. Before the close of Madison's second administration, a protective tariff had been adopted to encourage manufacturing, and a new national bank had been created to bring the national economy out of the chaos of wartime finance. Federal contributions to the construction of internal improvements (principally roads and canals) went little beyond the financing of the National Road from Cumberland, Maryland, across the mountains to Wheeling in western Virginia; but this restraint was due less to policy differences than to the constitutional doubts of Presidents Madison and Monroe. When President John Quincy Adams proposed in 1825 to revive and enlarge the "American System," the tide of public opinion was already turning. The spectacular success of New York's Erie Canal, among other things, turned attention to the state governments as the most effective promoters of economic development.

Party politics in the early years of Jefferson's administration largely echoed the quarrels of the preceding decade, with the positions of majority and minority reversed. Federalism, however, proved ill-suited to the opposition role and soon became the rather carping voice of New England provincialism, striking an occasional note of outright secession. The Federalists recovered strength in the Northeast as critics of Republican foreign trade restrictions and of "Mr. Madison's War," both generally unpopular in that region. The Federalist record of wartime obstruction and the secessionist designs imputed to the Hartford Convention of 1814-1815 gave a taint of disloyalty to that party from which it never recovered. The period of Monroe's presidency (1817-1825) came to be called the "Era of Good Feelings" not because all sectional and group differences had been reconciled, not because politicians had come to love one another as brothers, but rather because the Federalist opposition was dead and sharp new party lines were not yet drawn. The ominous Missouri crisis of 1818-1821 proved how violent party feelings could grow when a divisive issue did emerge: in this case the issue of extending slavery into the Louisiana Purchase country.

Through all the political changes of the Republican era one certainty remained: that Chief Justice John Marshall sat in judgment over the conduct of the Republic and would permit no deviation from the word or spirit of the Founding Fathers as he construed them. Again and again his masterly opinions enforced the teachings that the Constitution and the nation it established were creatures of the people, not the dependencies of sovereign states; that the national government had full power to achieve the great objects assigned to its discretion unless an explicit constitutional prohibition stood in the way; that vested private rights were secured against state interference under the contract clause of the Constitution even if such rights had been created directly by grant of the state; that the Constitution and the legitimate acts of Congress were the supreme law of the land; and that the Supreme Court was the final arbiter, short of the amendment process, in determining the constitutional bounds of national and state legislation. Justice Marshall could not make laws; but he could and did establish by construction the frame within which legislators and lesser courts must act.

The election of 1824 and the subsequent voting in the House of Representatives gave the presidency to John Quincy Adams; but it promised the future to a new man and a new movement. John Adams, Jefferson, Madison, Monroe, and the second Adams all had advanced to the presidency from positions of high responsibility in the national administration. General Andrew Jackson of Tennessee was the popular hero of the Battle of New Orleans. If no man knew exactly where he stood on all the perplexing issues of public policy, a majority of the people seemed to know that this Westerner, with no significant record of accomplishment in statesmanship, would serve their needs and purposes. Politicians who sensed the popular mood had begun by 1824 to make the hard arrangements for the victory of Jacksonian Democracy. Yet this was no mere *coup* of the political bosses. Deep social and political currents had cleared the way for an age of democratic growth and sectional conflict.

Republican Society

72

LAND OF STEADY HABITS: THE CONNECTICUT TOWN, ca. 1800

from Timothy Dwight, *Travels in New England and New York*, 1821

The new American nation at the turn of the century seemed to one French observer "like a youth who from the state of a boy is growing into manhood, and whose features, after the expiration of a year, no longer resemble the original picture that had been drawn of him." If there was a fixed point in that turning world, it might be found in the older New England countryside, above all in Connecticut, "the land of steady habits." Yankees (in the broad sense) were to be remarkable community-builders in upstate New York and the Old Northwest; they would direct bold commercial and industrial enterprises for the Eastern cities; they would lead movements for cultural innovation and social reform. And yet, paradoxically, Massachusetts and Connecticut remained, in the years around 1800, the conservative heartland of America.

Timothy Dwight, Congregational minister and president of Yale (1795-1817), was a pillar of Yankee orthodoxy. Dwight's credentials as a member of the New England élite read according to form: his Massachusetts father was a prosperous merchant; his maternal grandfather was Jonathan Edwards; and he was educated in the sound Calvinism of Yale College. Uncompromising Federalism seemed a natural trait of that close-knit circle of merchants, lawyers, and Congregationalist divines that gave tone and direction to Connecticut political and intellectual life. To men like Timothy Dwight (compare the views of Fisher Ames, Document 71), the Jeffersonian Republicans were infidels and anarchists threatening the faith, the morals, and the order of New England society. "Is it," Dwight asked, "that we may change our holy worship into a dance of Jacobin frenzy . . . ?"

Such dark forebodings did not lead Dwight to withdraw from active concerns. He was a voluminous if not a gifted poet (one youthful epic filled nearly ten thousand lines) and a leader of the "Hartford Wits," a lively regional literary school. As president of Yale he put his mark on higher education in America. His vacation rambles on foot and horseback through the northern countryside, begun as a remedy for broken health, made him one of the most experienced and knowing travelers in America.

Indeed, this high Federalist of Yale had no difficulty making contact with the common New England folk. Democracy as an abstract political doctrine in the mouth of a Jeffersonian made Timothy Dwight explode with anger; but the decorous democracy of a New England town seemed to him a triumph of good sense and good morals. Here men of sound habits and religious training met in moderate numbers at town meetings to arrange their mutual business. Rules were respected; reputable citizens were given public trusts; and policy could not go far astray, since those who ruled would feel the consequences of their actions on their own interests.

One amazing result of this town democracy could be found in the long history of colonial elections in Connecticut. Although the people had chosen their governors and other high officials in annual elections, the same men were returned decade after decade. Moreover, the town meeting and the widely distributed responsibilities of local offices trained Yankees in the practical business of governing and prepared the best of them for higher duties.

Note especially the valuable distinction Dwight draws between the "village manner" of settling, followed by New Englanders since early colonial times, and the more common American mode of scattered occupation of new areas. American society seemed often about to run off into space; perhaps this Yankee notion of community, nurtured by the town experience, helped to introduce a counterforce of social discipline.

. . . In my last letter I gave you a summary view of the Towns, and Counties, in this State; from which you will perceive, that they are both

Text: Timothy Dwight, *Travels in New England and New York* (New Haven, Conn.: Timothy Dwight, 1821), I, 248-52, 335-38.

Republics, subordinate to the State; and each town, in some respects, subordinate to the County, in which it exists. It will be unnecessary for me to make any particular observations concerning the Counties. The towns, you will perceive, have many peculiar interests of great importance; are required to perform many important duties; are invested with many valuable powers, rights, and privileges; and are protected from injustice, and imposition, in the enjoyment of their rights, and the performance of their duties.

The Legislature of each town is, like that of Athens, composed of the inhabitants, personally present; a majority of whom decides every question. The proceedings of this Legislature are all controlled by exact rules; and are under the direction of the proper officers. The confusion, incident to popular meetings, and so often disgraceful to those of Athens and Rome, is effectually prevented.

To this state of things many causes contribute. The towns are all of a moderate size, and population. The numbers, assembled at any town meeting, must, therefore, be always moderate. Of course, the noisy, tumultuous proceedings, and rash measures, so generally found in great assemblies of men, are here unknown. The regulations, also, are marked with the strictest propriety. No person speaks without leave. The person, who rises first, speaks first; and no person interrupts him. The votes, and all the other proceedings, are conducted with a very honourable decorum. The most powerful cause, perhaps, of all this propriety is to be found in the education, and habits, of the people; under the influence of which every person, after the meeting is adjourned, usually retires to his house; and riot, noise, and indecency, so common on similar occasions in other countries, are here unknown.

All the proceedings of these Assemblies are, also, matters of record; and can be re-examined, complained of, and rectified, at any subsequent period.

Their measures affect only their own concerns. They will not injure themselves: they cannot injure others. No clashing can exist between the towns themselves; nor between any town and the public: for their proceedings are valid, only by law; and, whenever they contravene it, are nothing.

By these local Legislatures a multitude of important concerns are managed, too numerous, and unwieldy, to be adjusted by the Legislature of the State; and far better known by those, who actually superintend them, than by any other persons. They have a deep interest in these concerns; and therefore will not neglect them; understand them perfectly, and will therefore regulate them wisely; are always present, and therefore can meet, and act, on every emergency.

In these little schools men commence their apprenticeship to public life; and learn to do public business. . . .

The Select-men, the proper town Executive, are intrusted with powers, which at first sight may seem enormous. They are undoubtedly great: and the trust, (the sphere of action being considered,) is high; of course, it ought always to be, and usually is, committed to respectable citizens. But experience has abundantly proved, that these powers are intrusted with perfect safety, and incalculable advantage to the Public. An instance, in which they have been abused, has hardly been known, since the settlement of the State. Numerous, and troublesome, as their services are; these officers have, in very few towns, ever received any compensation, beside the consciousness of having been useful, and the esteem of their fellow citizens.

I have remarked above, that men learn to do public business by being conversant with the affairs of Towns. You will remember, that every town annually elects a considerable number of Officers. Even the humblest of these offices furnishes opportunities for information, and exercise for sagacity; and, collectively, they are suited to every age, and capacity, of man. Virtues are here tried, and talents occupied, in a manner, safe alike to the employer and the agent. On the one hand the capacity for business is enlarged; and on the other the best proof is given, which can be given, of the proper preparatory qualifications for business of a superiour and more extensive nature. In the closet no man ever becomes acquainted with either the concerns, or the character, of men; or with the manner in which business ought to be conducted. The general principles of political science a scholar may understand, equally with those of other sciences. But of business, which is necessarily done in detail, if done to any purpose, the mere scholar literally knows nothing. He may be able to write a good political book: but he cannot do political business, because he never has done it. A plain man, educated in the business of a town, will easily shew him, that in knowledge of this kind he is an infant; and *that,* whatever may be his genius, or his acquisitions.

At the same time, the business, done here, is so various, so similar in many respects to that of a Legislature, and so connected with the public police; it returns so often, occupies so many hands, and involves so many public offices; that the inhabitants become not a little versed in public affairs. Hence they are peculiarly qualified to judge of their nature. A Republican Government is founded on general opinion. It is, therefore, of the highest importance, that this opinion should be correct. No method, hitherto adopted by mankind, has been equally successful with this, in forming that opinion, and in fitting men to judge well concerning governmental measures. A large proportion of the citizens of this State, have actually sustained one public office; and multitudes, several; and have of course been personally concerned in transacting public business. Hence they have already known by experience, the difficulties incident to public concerns; and are, in a degree superiour to what is usually found elsewhere, prepared to form judicious opinions concerning the measures of the Legislature. I have heard laws discussed by plain men with more good sense, than any mere scholar could have displayed on the same subjects. By these men they were canvassed as to their operation on the actual interests of themselves, and others. By a scholar they would have been examined as to their accordance with preconceived general principles. The former were certain means of determining on the merits of a law; the latter, only probable, and very imperfect.

From these facts it arises in no small measure, that the citizens of Connecticut have ever exhibited a peculiar skill and discretion, in both judging, and acting, concerning public affairs. Every man, who arrives at the higher offices of magistracy, serves, almost of course, an apprenticeship in the concerns of the town. Here his character is tried. If he acquires the general approbation; he is elected to the Legislature. There he undergoes a new trial; and, if sufficiently approved, is, in the end, chosen by the Freemen at large into the Council. In this body, if his conduct is not materially altered, he is regularly placed by the same suffrage, until he declines an election; becomes disqualified by age; or dies. It may, I believe, be truly said, that under no Government are the incumbents of the higher offices equally secure of their places, as under that of Connecticut; notwithstanding they are all annually elected by the voice of the Freemen. In the eighteenth century three Governours only vacated the chair by a deficiency of suffrages in their favour.

In several instances, powerful attacks have been made on men in high office, either by rivals, or enemies. Almost every such attack, however, has been fruitless. So far as my information extends, such attacks have secured to the objects of them all their former friends; and gained them many more: and, instead of diminishing their reputation and influence, have increased both, beyond what they could otherwise have acquired. . . .

. . . It is a remarkable fact, that New-England was colonized in a manner, widely different from that, which prevailed in the other British Colonies. All the ancient, and a great part of the modern, townships were settled in what may be called *the village manner:* the inhabitants having originally planted themselves in small towns. In many other parts of this country the planters have almost universally fixed themselves on their several farms: each placing his house where his own convenience dictated. In this manner, it is evident, the farmer can more advantageously manage his property; can oversee it more readily; and labour on it with fewer interruptions; than when it is dispersed in fields at some distance from each other.

But scattered plantations are subject to many serious disadvantages. Neither schools, nor churches, can without difficulty be either built by the planters, or supported. The children must be too remote from the school and the families from the Church, not to discourage all strenuous efforts to provide these interesting accommodations. Whenever it is proposed to erect either of them, the thought that one's self, and one's family, are too distant from the spot to derive any material benefit, will check the feeble relentings of avarice, the more liberal dispositions of frugality, and even the noble designs of a generous disposition. Should all the first difficulties be overcome, trifling infirmities, foul weather, and the ill state of roads, will prevent a regular attendance. But the family, or the children, who do not go with some good degree of regularity to the Church, or the School, will in the end scarcely go at all. The education of the one, and the religion of both, will therefore, in many cases be prevented.

At the same time, persons, who live on scattered plantations, are in a great measure cut off from that daily intercourse, which softens and polishes man. When we live at a distance from every neighbour, a call demands an effort; and a visit becomes a formal enterprize. A family, thus situated, must in a great measure be confined to its own little circle of domestic objects, and wrought insensibly into an insulated character. At the sight of a stranger the children, having been unaccustomed to such an object, are abashed; and the parents awkward and uneasy. That which generally gives pain, will be regarded with apprehension, and repeated only from necessity. Social intercourse therefore, exercised too little to begin to be pleasant, will be considered as an incumbrance: and the affections, which cherish it, and which it cherishes, and refines, in its turn, will either sleep, or expire. The gentle and pleasing manners, naturally growing out of it, can never be formed here. On the contrary, that rough and forbidding deportment, which springs from intercourse with oxen and horses, or with those who converse only to make bargains about oxen and horses, a rustic sheepishness, or a more awkward and provoking impudence, take possession of the man; and manifest their dominion in his conduct. The state of the manners, and that of the mind, are mutually causes and effects. The mind, like the manners, will be distant, rough, forbidding, gross, solitary, and universally disagreeable. A nation, planted in this manner, can scarcely be more than half civilized; and to refinement of character and life must necessarily be a stranger.

In such settlements schools are accordingly, few and solitary: and a great multitude of the inhabitants, of both sexes, are unable either to write, or read. Churches are still more rare; and the number of persons is usually, not small, who have hardly ever been present either at a prayer, or a sermon. Unaccustomed to objects of this nature, they neither wish for them, nor know what they are. The Preachers, whom they hear, are, at the same time, very frequently uneducated itinerants, started into the desk by the spirit of propagandism; recommended by nothing but enthusiasm and zeal; unable to teach; and often even to learn. . . .

New-England presents a direct contrast to this picture. Almost the whole country is covered with villages: and every village has its church, and its suit of schools. Nearly every child, even those of beggars and blacks, in considerable numbers, can read, write, and keep accounts. Every child is carried to the church from the cradle;

nor leaves the church but for the grave. All the people are neighbours: social beings; converse; feel; sympathize; mingle minds; cherish sentiments; and are subjects of at least some degree of refinement. More than six hundred youths, natives of New-England are always in the Colleges, erected here. In almost every village are found literary men, and social libraries. A great number of men also, not liberally educated, addict themselves to reading, and acquire extensive information. Of all these advantages the mode of settlement has been one, and, it is believed, a powerful cause. Even the scattered plantations in New-England have retained in a great measure the national characteristics of their country. Those, by whom these plantations were formed, had their education in the villages; and, when they emigrated, were too far advanced in life to relinquish their character and habits. Accordingly they built churches, and schools; and in the midst of various difficulties maintained the same social intercourse.

This mode of settling in villages resulted partly from the original habits of the New-England Colonists, and partly from the danger, with which they were threatened by the surrounding savages. Happily for their descendants, these circumstances collected them in such bodies; and thus originated a variety of blessings, without which life, even in the most desirable climate, is to a great extent destitute both of usefulness and enjoyment. . . .

73

THE OTHER VIRGINIA: MOUNTAIN AND VALLEY WAYS

from Duke de la Rochefoucauld–Liancourt, *Travels*, 1799

Timothy Dwight's Connecticut town (Document 72) represents old and stable elements in American life. The western Virginia country observed by the Duke de la Rochefoucauld-Liancourt (1747-1827) illustrates elements of growth and change at the turn of the century. Not that growth was something new in America; in a sense, the most consistent fact about the country from the beginning had been the continuous process of expansion, converting wilderness into communities.

Tidewater Virginia was in serious trouble as the nineteenth century opened. Tobacco culture, the economic basis of plantation society, had exhausted much of the soil in the eastern parts of Virginia, while the turmoil of war and revolution in Europe following 1789 disrupted the normal export markets of the planters. Eastern Virginia neither developed important commercial centers nor attracted a proportionate share of European immigrants to give a new impulse to society. The old Virginia was, however, far from dead in 1800. The state was still the most populous and powerful in the union, and plantation society would supply the nation with its principal leaders and doctrines for a generation to come.

Yet young men in search of opportunity were moving west in growing numbers, across the Blue Ridge Mountains to the Shenandoah Valley and then across the Alleghenies to Kentucky and the new West. Some families stuck along the way to form isolated pockets of settlement such as Rochefoucauld found high in the Blue Ridge Mountains. Meanwhile, Germans and Scots moving down the great valley from

Pennsylvania created prosperous agricultural communities along the Shenandoah. The following account of Winchester, a thriving western market town, illustrates some leading features of the valley region. Wheat was the leading product of the independent farmers and small planters who worked their land with a few slaves or none and sent their surplus grain by wagon to Philadelphia, Baltimore, or Alexandria merchants in exchange for store goods.

The author of these *Travels* was a French nobleman in exile from the French Revolution, who toured large areas of the United States and Upper Canada on horseback from 1795 to 1797. Rochefoucauld had taken a prominent role in the early stages of the French Revolution, serving as a deputy to the States-General and as President of the National Assembly His efforts to assist King Louis XVI brought him under radical suspicion, and in 1792 he fled to England. Much of his life was devoted to philanthropic enterprises: to agricultural experiments, popular education, prison reform, antislavery, and other causes. His *Travels* were published in Paris in 1799 and issued in English translation the same year.

. . . During the whole journey, until you reach the foot of the *Rockfish*, you continually ascend and descend, but the ground rises all along by sensible degrees; the plantations are more numerous, but the buildings consist of small miserable log-houses, although the cultivated fields which surround them are tolerably extensive. The nearer you approach the mountains the more the tobacco-fields grow scarce, and you at last see nothing but wheat and Indian corn. Among all the farmers I have met with, I found but one who was not dissatisfied with the fall in the price of wheat, and who expressed himself on this subject with moderation and judgement; all the rest perceive in the decrease of the value of their commodities their approaching ruin, and lament it with the utmost grief. At length you reach the foot of the Blue-Mountains, which you ascend by a road two miles in length, that has a gentle rise, and is well cut. A small additional expence would have rendered it completely good by turning off several springs, which spoil it in different places. From this mountain you enjoy an extensive prospect over all the heights you have just traversed; but the country is covered with wood to such a degree, that their tops only can be discerned. On the summit of Rockfish-Mountain you find a few miserable houses, the most considerable of which is an abominable inn, full of bugs, fleas, and all kinds of ordure. I stopped there, for I had no choice. All the inhabitants of the place meet here, as they generally do in the small inns in America, to smoke their pipes, to drink whisky, and relate the toils of the day: politics take up but little of their conversation. Newspapers do not reach Rockfish, and the number of families is too small to supply matter for the *"chronique Scandaleuse;"* but

segars and whisky satisfy these good people, who thus spend in a quarter of an hour in the evening the earnings of the whole day. The landlord of the inn has also a distillery of whisky, which he distills from Indian corn and wheat, mixed in equal proportion, and thus increases its strength. This whisky fetches eight shillings per gallon. The addition of Indian corn augments, in my opinion, the unwholesomeness of this liquor; but this is immaterial for the inn-keeper, whose only care is to dispose of it at a profitable rate. A store, established on the top of the mountain, buys the produce of the adjoining country, which is offered there for sale, and retails the merchandize drawn from Richmond by the way of Milford. The store-keeper transmits also to Milford the commodities of the country, if they are not sent by direct conveyance to Richmond. The carriage to Milford costs two thirds of a dollar per hundred weight. All the goods sold at this store are seventy-five per cent dearer than in Philadelphia. . . .

. . . The plantations increase both in number and size, as we approach Winchester, which lies but eight miles from New-Town. It is the capital of Frederick-County, contains upwards of two thousand inhabitants, and is built tolerably well, in the midst of rocks, which circumstance, however, does not prevent many of the inhabitants from building houses of wood . . . Winchester carries on a considerable trade for its inland position, in the midst of a country which is, as yet, so thinly inhabited. It sends to Alexandria the whole produce of the upper country, and draws from Baltimore, but especially from Philadelphia, all sorts of dry goods: the traffic, both in buying and selling, is carried on with ready money.

The preference which is given here to Philadelphia over Alexandria, in regard to the purchase of dry goods, rests on the same grounds as it does in other places of this upper part of Virginia. From the greater wealth possessed by

Text: Duke de la Rochefoucauld–Liancourt, *Travels Through the United States of North America in the Years 1795, 1796, and 1797* (London: R. Phillips, 1799), II, 87-88, 102-06.

the merchants of that city, they are able to give longer credit; they receive the goods from the first hands, and consequently can sell them cheaper; their warehouses being plentifully stocked with merchandize, the buyers can also suit themselves better—circumstances, none of which take place at Alexandria, and which being less combined at Baltimore than at Philadelphia, caused the latter to be resorted to in preference to the former, notwithstanding its greater distance: it is by land that all these productions and commodities are conveyed to Alexandria, and arrive from Philadelphia. The carriage from Philadelphia to Winchester costs from four to five dollars per hundred weight; and from Winchester to Alexandria, two dollars and a half, as it does from New-Town. Heavy merchandize, such as grocery, is at times sent by sea from Philadelphia to Alexandria, whence it is conveyed to Winchester in waggons, which, if not obliged to go back empty from want of a load, are paid at the rate of one dollar and a half per hundred weight. The produce sent from Winchester consists chiefly of flour. The environs of this place, as well as the back country, whence it draws the necessary supplies of provisions, abound in wheat; mills are very numerous in that district; hemp, some linseed, hats and hardware, great quantities of which are manufactured in Frederick-County, are also productions of this country. Upwards of thirty well-stocked stores, or shops, have been opened at Winchester; the value of European goods which it yearly draws from Philadelphia, or Baltimore, is estimated at two hundred thousand pounds, or six hundred sixty-six thousand six hundred and sixty-six dollars; they sell at Winchester thirty per cent dearer than in the former places.

The profession of a lawyer is as lucrative in Winchester as in all the other parts of Virginia.

More than twenty of them find constant practice, and are in thriving circumstances. Mechanics are found in abundance; even a coachmaker, and several watch-makers, have settled there. Five churches have been built at Winchester; a Roman Catholic, an Anglican, a Presbyterian, a German Lutheran church, and a Methodist meeting-house, but without any ministers being peculiarly attached to them. The English minister resides on the other side of the Blue Ridge, and only comes from time to time. The Roman Catholic curate, who lives in Maryland, visits this place also when he chooses; and so do the rest. The methodist meeting-house excepted, divine service is thus performed here by itinerant priests, who are not in the habit of travelling much in Virginia for the purpose of propagating religious truths. But, on the other hand, it is certain that the number of gaming-tables has of late much increased in this town, and they are all of them assiduously frequented. This is a sort of worship, in the observance of which but few Virginians incur the charge of infidelity. . . .

Two or three pitiful schools form all the resources of the inhabitants of Winchester for the education of their children.

The town contains ten or twelve inns, large and small, which are often full. It lies in the way of all travellers who proceed to the back parts of Virginia, to Tenessee, or to the mineral springs in the counties of Augusta and Berkley. Many families which are emigrating into the new countries also pass through Winchester. In the course of last year upwards of four thousand persons passed through the place, who were going to settle in Tenessee or Kentucky. . . .

The population of the county amounts to above twenty-one thousand souls, four thousand five hundred of whom are negro slaves. . . .

A New Regime

THE SUM OF GOOD GOVERNMENT

74

THE REPUBLICAN CREDO: LIMITED GOVERNMENT

from Thomas Jefferson, First Inaugural Address, March 4, 1801

The "Revolution of 1800," as Jefferson later referred to his first election, lacked all of the obvious marks of a radical upheaval in the social and political order. The new President had been Vice-President in the previous Adams administration and before that Secretary of State under Washington. He was elected in a normal constitutional manner and could take the oath of office without reservations. His Inaugural Address of March 4, 1801, was exemplary in its tone of moderation and conciliation. Certainly the accession of Jeffersonian Democracy to power brought a significant shift in men and views. The "Virginia Dynasty" would lead the country for a generation. Hamiltonian Federalism was dead as an organized national political force; in a few decades it would be worth a politician's life in many parts of the country to speak openly in praise of Hamilton or the Federalist party. *If* one agreed with Jefferson that the Hamiltonians conspired to build a monarchical regime resting on an aristocratic society, then 1800 was indeed a revolution.

In the 1800 elections the Republicans gained control of both houses of Congress, while Jefferson and Aaron Burr won seventy-three electoral votes to sixty-five for the Federalist candidate, John Adams. Despite the coolness or hostility of Hamilton and other leading Federalists, Adams carried New England solidly and picked up scattered support elsewhere. Republican strength lay mainly in New York and the South. The Federalists had a second chance to defeat Jefferson in the House of Representatives and almost used it. Under the original Constitution, presidential electors did not specify their votes for President or Vice-President. Thus the tie between Jefferson and Burr threw the election into the House. Hamilton's judgment that Burr was a dangerous man helped to arrest a Federalist scheme for electing Burr as President, but only after six days of high tension in the capital and only on the thirty-sixth ballot. Amendment XII of the Constitution (1804) required distinct votes for President and Vice-President.

Finally, on March 4, Jefferson walked from his boarding house to the Senate chamber of the unfinished Capitol to take the oath of office. The national capital had just been moved to the federal city of Washington in the summer of 1800. Swamps separated the small clusters of boarding houses, shops, homes, and half-completed public buildings which were spread around the town. In the President's mansion the main staircase was not yet started, the roof leaked, and the green timbers in the floors were sagging. Some 3200 souls (one fifth of them slaves) inhabited the raw new capital.

Bad roads, crowded accommodations, and an unhealthy summer climate were only the nuisances confronting the new regime in Washington. The real problem was to construct a fresh administration which could give effect to Jefferson's faith in "a wise and frugal government"—to the Republican credo set forth in the following address.

Friends and Fellow-Citizens:

Called upon to undertake the duties of the first executive office of our country, I avail myself of the presence of that portion of my fellow-citizens which is here assembled to express my grateful thanks for the favor with which they have been pleased to look toward me, to declare a sincere consciousness that the task is above my talents, and that I approach it with those anxious and awful presentiments which the greatness of the charge and the weakness of my powers so justly inspire. A rising nation, spread over a wide and fruitful land, traversing all the seas with the rich productions of their industry, engaged in commerce with nations who feel power and forget right, advancing rapidly to destinies beyond the reach of mortal eye—when I contemplate these transcendent objects, and see the honor, the happiness, and the hopes of this beloved country committed to the issue and the auspices of this day, I shrink from the contemplation, and humble

Text: James D. Richardson (ed.), *A Compilation of the Messages and Papers of the Presidents, 1789-1897* (Washington, D.C.: Government Printing Office, 1897), I, 321-24.

myself before the magnitude of the undertaking. Utterly, indeed, should I despair did not the presence of many whom I here see remind me that in the other high authorities provided by our Constitution I shall find resources of wisdom, of virtue, and of zeal on which to rely under all difficulties. To you, then, gentlemen, who are charged with the sovereign functions of legislation, and to those associated with you, I look with encouragement for that guidance and support which may enable us to steer with safety the vessel in which we are all embarked amidst the conflicting elements of a troubled world.

During the contest of opinion through which we have passed the animation of discussions and of exertions has sometimes worn an aspect which might impose on strangers unused to think freely and to speak and to write what they think; but this being now decided by the voice of the nation, announced according to the rules of the Constitution, all will, of course, arrange themselves under the will of the law, and unite in common efforts for the common good. All, too, will bear in mind this sacred principle, that though the will of the majority is in all cases to prevail, that will to be rightful must be reasonable; that the minority possess their equal rights, which equal law must protect, and to violate would be oppression. Let us, then, fellow-citizens, unite with one heart and one mind. Let us restore to social intercourse that harmony and affection without which liberty and even life itself are but dreary things. And let us reflect that, having banished from our land that religious intolerance under which mankind so long bled and suffered, we have yet gained little if we countenance a political intolerance as despotic, as wicked, and capable of as bitter and bloody persecutions. During the throes and convulsions of the ancient world, during the agonizing spasms of infuriated man, seeking through blood and slaughter his long-lost liberty, it was not wonderful that the agitation of the billows should reach even this distant and peaceful shore; that this should be more felt and feared by some and less by others, and should divide opinions as to measures of safety. But every difference of opinion is not a difference of principle. We have called by different names brethren of the same principle. We are all Republicans, we are all Federalists. If there be any among us who would wish to dissolve this Union or to change its republican form, let them stand undisturbed as monuments of the safety with which error of opinion may be tolerated where reason is left free to combat it. I know, indeed, that some honest men fear that a republican government can not be strong, that this Government is not strong enough; but would the honest patriot, in the full tide of successful experiment, abandon a government which has so far kept us free and firm on the theoretic and visionary fear that this Government, the world's best hope, may by possibility want energy to preserve itself? I trust not. I believe this, on the contrary, the strongest Government on earth. I believe it the only one where every man, at the call of the law, would fly to the standard of the law, and would meet invasions of the public order as his own personal concern. Sometimes it is said that man can not be trusted with the government of himself. Can he, then, be trusted with the government of others? Or have we found angels in the forms of kings to govern him? Let history answer this question.

Let us, then, with courage and confidence pursue our own Federal and Republican principles, our attachment to union and representative government. Kindly separated by nature and a wide ocean from the exterminating havoc of one quarter of the globe; too high-minded to endure the degradations of the others; possessing a chosen country, with room enough for our descendants to the thousandth and thousandth generation; entertaining a due sense of our equal right to

the use of our own faculties, to the acquisitions of our own industry, to honor and confidence from our fellow-citizens, resulting not from birth, but from our actions and their sense of them; enlightened by a benign religion, professed, indeed, and practiced in various forms, yet all of them inculcating honesty, truth, temperance, gratitude, and the love of man; acknowledging and adoring an overruling Providence, which by all its dispensations proves that it delights in the happiness of man here and his greater happiness hereafter—with all these blessings, what more is necessary to make us a happy and a prosperous people? Still one thing more, fellow-citizens—a wise and frugal Government, which shall restrain men from injuring one another, shall leave them otherwise free to regulate their own pursuits of industry and improvement, and shall not take from the mouth of labor the bread it has earned. This is the sum of good government, and this is necessary to close the circle of our felicities.

About to enter, fellow-citizens, on the exercise of duties which comprehend everything dear and valuable to you, it is proper you should understand what I deem the essential principles of our Government, and consequently those which ought to shape its Administration. I will compress them within the narrowest compass they will bear, stating the general principle, but not all its limitations. Equal and exact justice to all men, of whatever state or persuasion, religious or political; peace, commerce, and honest friendship with all nations, entangling alliances with none; the support of the State governments in all their rights, as the most competent administrations for our domestic concerns and the surest bulwarks against antirepublican tendencies; the preservation of the General Government in its whole constitutional vigor, as the sheet anchor of our peace at home and safety abroad; a jealous care of the right of election by the people—a mild and safe corrective of abuses which are lopped by the sword of revolution where peaceable remedies are unprovided; absolute acquiescence in the decisions of the majority, the vital principle of republics, from which is no appeal but to force, the vital principle and immediate parent of despotism; a well-disciplined militia, our best reliance in peace and for the first moments of war, till regulars may relieve them; the supremacy of the civil over the military authority; economy in the public expense, that labor may be lightly burthened; the honest payment of our debts and sacred preservation of the public faith; encouragement of agriculture, and of commerce as its handmain; the diffusion of information and arraignment of all abuses at the bar of the public reason; freedom of religion; freedom of the press, and freedom of person under the protection of the habeas corpus, and trial by juries impartially selected. These principles form the bright constellation which has gone before us and guided our steps through an age of revolution and reformation. The wisdom of our sages and blood of our heroes have been devoted to their attainment. They should be the creed of our political faith, the text of civic instruction, the touchstone by which to try the services of those we trust; and should we wander from them in moments of error or of alarm, let us hasten to retrace our steps and to regain the road which alone leads to peace, liberty, and safety. . . .

75

REPUBLICANISM REVIEWED

from Thomas Jefferson, Second Inaugural Address, March 4, 1805

The first Republican administration under Thomas Jefferson was on most counts a glowing success. The President's second Inaugural Address breathed confidence and contentment after his sweeping victory in the 1804 elections. Jefferson won all but fourteen electoral votes (even New England, excepting intransigent Connecticut, went Republican), while Republicans increased their preponderance in both the House and the Senate.

The strength of the first Jefferson administration was due in part to the quality of the President's chief advisers: Secretary of State James Madison, an old and trusted friend, and Secretary of the Treasury Albert Gallatin, a Swiss immigrant who had first risen to prominence in western Pennsylvania politics. Both were exceptionally accomplished public servants in full sympathy with Jefferson's political aims.

The President was in control of his administration. He gave a tone of democratic simplicity to the new capital by cutting away much of the ceremony and court etiquette which had grown up around the Federalist administrations in New York and Philadelphia. (The fact that Jefferson was a widower with no First Lady in social command made the change easier, it has been suggested.) Jefferson's decision to submit written messages to Congress rather than deliver his annual reports in person (a precedent followed by every President down to Woodrow Wilson) made the executive seem less an awesome personage dictating his will to the legislators. Nevertheless, he did not hesitate to influence governmental action by informal means (such as the use of patronage), and when occasion demanded, he exercised executive authority in a decisive way.

As the Second Inaugural Address makes clear, Jefferson took great pride in the progress of Republican financial policies. In 1802 the internal excise taxes which had earned Hamilton such popular hatred were withdrawn. Under Gallatin's lead the expenses of government were sharply cut, although this meant a reduction of army personnel to 2500 and a comparable weakening of the navy. Rising tariff revenues made it possible to reduce the public debt substantially.

Foreign relations were generally harmonious in the first administration. A breathing spell in the Napoleonic Wars checked depredations on neutral trade and shipping, the source of major diplomatic blowups since 1793. However, the pacific Jefferson did not hesitate to employ the navy (with some success) against the Barbary pirates of Tripoli in North Africa, who had long exacted tribute from users of the Mediterranean seaways.

The most conspicuous failure of the first Republican administration was the attempt to discipline the national judiciary, which had become a stronghold of Federalism. The most glorious achievement was the doubling of the national territory with the purchase of Louisiana. (Documents 76-77)

. . . On taking this station on a former occasion I declared the principles on which I believed it my duty to administer the affairs of our Commonwealth. My conscience tells me I have on every occasion acted up to that declaration according to its obvious import and to the understanding of every candid mind.

In the transaction of your foreign affairs we have endeavored to cultivate the friendship of all nations, and especially of those with which we have the most important relations. We have done them justice on all occasions, favored

Text: James D. Richardson (ed.), A Compilation of the Messages and Papers of the Presidents, 1789-1897 (Washington, D.C.: Government Printing Office, 1897), I, 378-82.

where favor was lawful, and cherished mutual interests and intercourse on fair and equal terms. We are firmly convinced, and we act on that conviction, that with nations as with individuals our interests soundly calculated will ever be found inseparable from our moral duties, and history bears witness to the fact that a just nation is trusted on its word when recourse is had to armaments and wars to bridle others.

At home, fellow-citizens, you best know whether we have done well or ill. The suppression of unnecessary offices, of useless establishments and expenses, enabled us to discontinue our internal taxes. These, covering our land with officers and opening our doors to their intrusions, had already begun that process of domiciliary vexation which once entered is scarcely to be restrained from reaching successively every article of property and produce. If among these taxes some minor ones fell which had not been inconvenient, it was because their amount would not have paid the officers who collected them, and because, if they had any merit, the State authorities might adopt them instead of others less approved.

The remaining revenue on the consumption of foreign articles is paid chiefly by those who can afford to add foreign luxuries to domestic comforts, being collected on our seaboard and frontiers only, and, incorporated with the transactions of our mercantile citizens, it may be the pleasure and the pride of an American to ask, What farmer, what mechanic, what laborer ever sees a taxgatherer of the United States? These contributions enable us to support the current expenses of the Government, to fulfill contracts with foreign nations, to extinguish the native right of soil within our limits, to extend those limits, and to apply such a surplus to our public debts as places at a short day their final redemption, and that redemption once effected the revenue thereby liberated may, by a just repartition of it among the States and a corresponding amendment of the Constitution, be applied *in time of peace* to rivers, canals, roads, arts, manufactures, education, and other great objects within each State. *In time of war,* if injustice by ourselves or others must sometimes produce war, increased as the same revenue will be by increased population and consumption, and aided by other resources reserved for that crisis, it may meet within the year all the expenses of the year without encroaching on the rights of future generations by burthening them with the debts of the past. War will then be but a suspension of useful works, and a return to a state of peace a return to the progress of improvement. . . .

The aboriginal inhabitants of these countries I have regarded with the commiseration their history inspires. Endowed with the faculties and the rights of men, breathing an ardent love of liberty and independence, and occupying a country which left them no desire but to be undisturbed, the stream of overflowing population from other regions directed itself on these shores; without power to divert or habits to contend against it, they have been overwhelmed by the current or driven before it; now reduced within limits too narrow for the hunter's state, humanity enjoins us to teach them agriculture and the domestic arts; to encourage them to that industry which alone can enable them to maintain their place in existence and to prepare them in time for that state of society which to bodily comforts adds the improvement of the mind and morals. We have therefore liberally furnished them with the implements of husbandry and household use; we have placed among them instructors in the arts of first necessity, and they are covered with the aegis of the law against aggressors from among ourselves.

But the endeavors to enlighten them on the fate which awaits their present course of life, to induce them to exercise their reason, follow its dictates, and change their pursuits with the change of circumstances have powerful obstacles to encounter; they are combated by the habits of their bodies, prejudices of their minds, ignorance, pride, and the influence of interested and crafty individuals among them who feel themselves something in the present order of things and fear to become nothing in any other. These persons inculcate a sanctimonious reverence for the customs of their ancestors; that whatsoever they did must be done through all time; that reason is a false guide, and to advance under its counsel in their physical, moral, or political condition is perilous innovation; that their duty is to remain as their Creator made them, ignorance being safety and knowledge full of danger; in short, my friends, among them also is seen the action and counteraction of good sense and of bigotry; they too have their antiphilosophists who find an interest in keeping things in their present state, who dread reformation, and exert all their faculties to maintain the ascendency of habit over the duty of improving our reason and obeying its mandates.

In giving these outlines I do not mean, fellow-citizens, to arrogate to myself the merit of the measures. That is due, in the first place, to the reflecting character of our citizens at large, who, by the weight of public opinion, influence and strengthen the public measures. It is due to the sound discretion with which they select from among themselves those to whom they confide the legislative duties. It is due to the zeal and wisdom of the characters thus selected, who lay the foundations of public happiness in wholesome laws, the execution of which alone remains for others, and it is due to the able and faithful auxiliaries, whose patriotism has associated them with me in the executive functions.

During this course of administration, and in order to disturb it, the artillery of the press has been leveled against us, charged with whatsoever its licentiousness could devise or dare. These abuses of an institution so important to freedom and science are deeply to be regretted, inasmuch as they tend to lessen its usefulness and to sap its safety. They might, indeed, have been corrected by the wholesome punishments reserved to and provided by the laws of the several States against falsehood and defamation, but public duties more urgent press on the time of public servants, and the offenders have therefore been left to find their punishment in the public indignation.

Nor was it uninteresting to the world that an experiment should be fairly and fully made, whether freedom of discussion, unaided by power, is not sufficient for the propagation and protection of truth—whether a government conducting itself in the true spirit of its constitution, with zeal and purity, and doing no act which it would be unwilling the whole world should witness, can be written down by falsehood and defamation. The experiment has been tried; you have witnessed the scene; our fellow-citizens looked on, cool and collected; they saw the latent source from which these outrages proceeded; they gathered around their public functionaries, and when the Constitution called them to the decision by suffrage, they pronounced their verdict, honorable to those who had served them and consolatory to the friend of man who believes that he may be trusted with the control of his own affairs.

No inference is here intended that the laws provided by the States against false and defamatory publications should not be enforced; he who has time renders a service to public morals and public tranquillity in reforming these abuses by the salutary coercions of the law; but the experiment is noted to prove that, since truth and reason have maintained their ground against false opinions in league with false facts, the press, confined to truth, needs no other legal restraint; the public judgment will correct false reasonings and opinions on a full hearing of all parties; and no other definite line can be drawn between the inestimable liberty of the press and its demoralizing licentiousness. If there be still improprieties which this rule would not restrain, its supplement must be sought in the censorship of public opinion.

Contemplating the union of sentiment now manifested so generally as auguring harmony and happiness to our future course, I offer to our country sincere congratulations. With those, too, not yet rallied to the same point the disposition to do so is gaining strength; facts are piercing through the veil drawn over them, and our doubting brethren will at length see that the mass of their fellow-citizens with whom they can not yet resolve to act as to principles and measures, think as they think and desire what they desire; that our wish as well as theirs is that the public efforts may be directed honestly to the public good, that peace be cultivated, civil and religious liberty unassailed, law and order preserved, equality of rights maintained, and that state of property, equal or unequal, which results to every man from his own industry or that of his father's. When satisfied of these views it is not in human nature that they should not approve and support them. In the meantime let us cherish them with patient affection, let us do them justice, and more than justice, in all competitions of interest, and we need not doubt that truth, reason, and their own interests will at length prevail, will gather them into the fold of their country, and will complete that entire union of opinion which gives to a nation the blessing of harmony and the benefit of all its strength.

I shall now enter on the duties to which my fellow-citizens have again called me, and shall proceed in the spirit of those principles which they have approved. I fear not that any motives of interest may lead me astray; I am sensible of no passion which could seduce me knowingly from the path of justice, but the weaknesses of human nature and the limits of my own understanding will produce errors of judgment sometimes injurious to your interests. I shall need, therefore, all the indulgence which I have heretofore experienced from my constituents; the want of it will certainly not lessen with increasing years. I shall need, too, the favor of that Being in whose hands we are, who led our fathers, as Israel of old, from their native land and planted them in a country flowing with all the necessaries and comforts of life; who has covered our infancy with His providence and our riper years with His wisdom and power, and to whose goodness I ask you to join in supplications with me that He will so enlighten the minds of your servants, guide their councils, and prosper their measures that whatsoever they do shall result in your good, and shall secure to you the peace, friendship, and approbation of all nations.

March 4, 1805.

LOUISIANA PURCHASE

76

POLITICAL REALITIES AND CONSTITUTIONAL SCRUPLES

from Thomas Jefferson, Letter to John Breckenridge, August 12, 1803

The severest test for an opposition party is success. The Jeffersonians had tried and condemned the Federalist regime by exacting principles. Those same principles would, after 1800, become the standard for judging their own conduct in power. Republicans assumed the responsibility of governing the nation under a political code that narrowly construed the powers of the national administration: a code of frugality, simplicity, and self-denial.

In important respects the Jefferson administration did act consistently with past Republican professions. (See Document 74.) Yet the most splendid of Jefferson's achievements, the acquisition of the Louisiana Territory, was perhaps the measure that most troubled his political conscience. To attach a vast empire to the United States at a bargain price, the President violated his own conception of his constitutional powers.

Napoleon Bonaparte ruled France after 1800 as First Consul and then as Emperor. Ambitious for world empire, he set out to restore French power in America. By the secret treaty of San Ildefonso (1800), Spain ceded back to France the Louisiana country, including New Orleans and the western Mississippi Valley. When Jefferson heard of the secret transfer, he reversed his pro-French foreign policy. If France were to control New Orleans and the navigation of the Mississippi, he wrote in 1802, "we must marry ourselves to the British fleet and nation." The uncertain loyalty of the Western settlements might be lost for good and the Union confined within the Allegheny wall, if Napoleonic France could dictate conditions for using the Mississippi route.

Jefferson instructed Robert R. Livingston, minister to France, to negotiate with Napoleon for the purchase of New Orleans or some other outlet to the Gulf. Livingston and James Monroe (who was sent to aid in the negotiations) found Napoleon ready to sell not merely New Orleans but the whole Louisiana country. Among other reasons, ruinous French losses in Santo Domingo (where a bloody slave revolt threatened French control) persuaded Napoleon to reduce his overseas commitments. Monroe and Livingston determined on their own initiative to close the bargain on April 30, 1803, at a price of about fifteen million dollars.

On his strict reading of the Constitution, Jefferson could not justify the acquisition of new territory. Amending the Constitution would take too long. His reluctant choice to proceed under the treaty power and leave the final judgment to the nation is explained in the following letter. The treaty was ratified, the purchase money was appropriated, and the United States acquired an imperial domain beyond the Mississippi. By judicial construction the Supreme Court later affirmed the constitutionality of such territorial acquisitions.

Monticello, *August 12, 1803.*

Dear Sir,— . . . Our information as to the [Louisiana] country is very incomplete; we have taken measures to obtain it full as to the settled part, which I hope to receive in time for Congress. The boundaries, which I deem not admitting question, are the high lands on the western side of the Mississippi enclosing all its waters, the Missouri of course, and terminating in the line drawn from the northwestern point of the Lake of the Woods to the nearest source of the Mississippi, as lately settled between Great Britain and the United States. We have some claims, to extend on the seacoast westwardly to the Rio Norte or Bravo, and better, to go east-

wardly to the Rio Perdido, between Mobile and Pensacola, the ancient boundary of Louisiana. These claims will be a subject of negotiation with Spain, and if, as soon as she is at war, we push them strongly with one hand, holding out a price in the other, we shall certainly obtain the Floridas, and all in good time. In the meanwhile, without waiting for permission, we shall enter into the exercise of the natural right we have always insisted on with Spain, to-wit, that of a nation holding the upper part of streams, having a right of innocent passage through them to the ocean. We shall prepare her

Text: State Papers and Correspondence Bearing upon the Purchase of the Territory of Louisiana (Washington, D.C.: Government Printing Office, 1803), pp. 233-35.

to see us practice on this, and she will not oppose it by force.

Objections are raising to the eastward [i.e., in New England] against the vast extent of our boundaries, and propositions are made to exchange Louisiana, or a part of it, for the Floridas. But, as I have said, we shall get the Floridas without, and I would not give one inch of the waters of the Mississippi to any nation, because I see in a light very important to our peace the exclusive right to its navigation, and the admission of no nation into it, but as into the Potomac or Delaware, with our consent and under our police. These federalists see in this acquisition the formation of a new confederacy, embracing all the waters of the Mississippi, on both sides of it, and a separation of its eastern waters from us. These combinations depend on so many circumstances which we can not foresee, that I place little reliance on them. We have seldom seen neighborhood produce affection among nations. The reverse is almost the universal truth. Besides, if it should become the great interest of those nations to separate from this, if their happiness should depend on it so strongly as to induce them to go through that convulsion, why should the Atlantic States dread it? But especially why should we, their present inhabitants, take side in such a question? When I view the Atlantic States, procuring for those on the eastern waters of the Mississippi friendly instead of hostile neighbors on its western waters, I do not view it as an Englishman would the procuring future blessings for the French nation, with whom he has no relations of blood or affection. The future inhabitants of the Atlantic and Mississippi States will be our sons. We leave them in distinct but bordering establishments. We think we see their happiness in their union, and we wish it. Events may prove it otherwise; and if they see their interest in separation, why should we take side with our Atlantic rather than our Mississippi descendants? It is the elder and the younger son differing. God bless them both, and keep them in union, if it be for their good, but separate them, if it be better. The in-habited part of Louisiana, from Point Coupée to the sea, will of course be immediately a territorial government, and soon a State. But above that, the best use we can make of the country for some time, will be to give establishments in it to the Indians on the east side of the Mississippi, in exchange for their present country, and open land offices in the last, and thus make this acquisition the means of filling up the eastern side, instead of drawing off its population. When we shall be full on this side, we may lay off a range of States on the western bank from the head to the mouth, and so, range after range, advancing compactly as we multiply.

This treaty must of course be laid before both Houses, because both have important functions to exercise respecting it. They, I presume, will see their duty to their country in ratifying and paying for it, so as to secure a good which would otherwise probably be never again in their power. But I suppose they must then appeal to *the nation* for an additional article to the Constitution, approving and confirming an act which the nation had not previously authorized. The Constitution has made no provision for our holding foreign territory, still less for incorporating foreign nations into our Union. The executive in seizing the fugitive occurrence which so much advances the good of their country, have done an act beyond the Constitution. The Legislature in casting behind them metaphysical subtleties, and risking themselves like faithful servants, must ratify and pay for it, and throw themselves on their country for doing for them unauthorized, what we know they would have done for themselves had they been in a situation to do it. It is the case of a guardian investing the money of his ward in purchasing an important adjacent territory; and saying to him when of age, I did this for your good; I pretend to no right to bind you: you may disavow me, and I must get out of the scrape as I can: I thought it my duty to risk myself for you. But we shall not be disavowed by the nation, and their act of indemnity will confirm and not weaken the Constitution, by more strongly marking out its lines.

7 7   **THE MENACE OF WESTERN EXPANSION**

from Samuel White, Speech in the U.S. Senate, November 2, 1803

To maintain opposition to the Louisiana Purchase was difficult. For something like three cents an acre the United States could add almost a million acres to the national territory, secure the vital Mississippi route, exclude the French from the southwestern frontier, and clear the way for future expansion across the continent. Faced with such rich opportunities, Jefferson overcame his constitutional scruples (Document 76), and

Hamilton too gave approval, resisting the temptation to play politics with the Louisiana question. In the Senate the treaty of purchase was approved in 1803 by a vote of twenty-four to seven, and the House promptly appropriated the necessary funds.

Nevertheless, some Federalists, including Senator Samuel White of Delaware and, especially a group of embittered New Englanders, found grave errors in the acquisition of the Louisiana Territory. Previously, when the Spanish authorities denied to Americans the right to deposit goods at New Orleans (1802), Federalists had demanded aggressive military action. (Spanish officials continued to govern Louisiana in 1802 although the secret treaty retroceding the territory to France had been signed two years before.) Federalists, among them Senator White, played up to Western sympathies with their appeal for the seizure of New Orleans while Jefferson and Madison were pursuing their plan for the purchase of a Gulf port.

Napoleon's amazing offer to sell the whole Louisiana country, quickly accepted by the American negotiators, presented a wholly new prospect. Seeking an outlet for frontier trade, the United States had gained an imperial domain—the western Mississippi Valley—which would change the shape and course of the Union. As settlers spread over the western territories, creating new states, the political center of gravity would shift inevitably away from the eastern seaboard. To Samuel White and other Federalists, the Louisiana acquisition meant that the American people would be dispersed over the western wilderness, thus weakening the hold of national authority and strengthening the influence of crude frontier agrarians in the national councils. By a curious reversal, Federalists who had worked for an expansive "Great America" since the 1780's now became apprehensive "Little Americans." They criticized the broad construction of the Constitution used to justify the addition of new territories. They denounced the extravagance of purchasing a "desert" with fifteen millions of the nation's funds. In New England the intemperate Essex Junto entertained secessionist schemes, not for the last time. (See Document 82.)

Technically, the soundest of the Federalist objections was that which questioned Napoleon's right to sell the territory to the United States under the terms of his agreement with Spain. Clouded or not, the American title gained recognition, and prompt American occupation ended further dispute. By 1812, Louisiana, the first state formed within the new territory, was ready for admission to the Union.

. . . Mr. [Samuel] WHITE [Delaware] rose and made the following remarks:

. . . Admitting then, Mr. President, that His Catholic Majesty [The King of Spain] is hostile to the cession of this territory to the United States, and no honorable gentleman will deny it, what reasons have we to suppose that the French Prefect, provided the Spaniards should interfere, can give to us peaceable possession of the country? He is acknowledged there in no public character, is clothed with no authority, nor has he a single soldier to enforce his orders. I speak now, sir, from mere probabilities. I wish not to be understood as predicting that the French will not cede to us the actual and quiet possession of the territory. I hope to God they may, for possession of it we must have—I mean of New Orleans, and of such other positions on the Mississippi as may be necessary to secure to us forever the complete and uninterrupted navigation of that river. This I have ever been in favor of; I think it essential to the peace of the United States, and to the prosperity of our Western country. But as to Louisiana, this new, immense, unbounded world, if it should ever be incorporated into this Union, which I have no idea can be

done but by altering the Constitution, I believe it will be the greatest curse that could at present befall us; it may be productive of innumerable evils, and especially of one that I fear even to look upon. Gentlemen on all sides, with very few exceptions, agree that the settlement of this country will be highly injurious and dangerous to the United States; but as to what has been suggested of removing the Creeks and other nations of Indians from the eastern to the western banks of the Mississippi, and of making the fertile regions of Louisiana a howling wilderness, never to be trodden by the foot of civilized man, it is impracticable. The gentleman from Tennessee (Mr. COCKE) has shown his usual candor on this subject, and I believe with him, to use his strong language, that you had as well pretend to inhibit the fish from swimming in the sea as to prevent the population of that country after its sovereignty shall become ours. To every man acquainted with the adventurous, roving, and enterprising temper of our people, and with the

Text: *The Debates and Proceedings in the Congress of the United States, First to Eighteenth Congress, March 3, 1789, to May 27, 1824, Inclusive* (Washington, D.C.: Gales & Seaton, 1852), XIII, 31-35.

manner in which our Western country has been settled, such an idea must be chimerical. The inducements will be so strong that it will be impossible to restrain our citizens from crossing the river. Louisiana must and will become settled, if we hold it, and with the very population that would otherwise occupy part of our present territory. Thus our citizens will be removed to the immense distance of two or three thousand miles from the capital of the Union, where they will scarcely ever feel the rays of the General Government; their affections will become alienated; they will gradually begin to view us as strangers; they will form other commercial connexions, and our interests will become distinct.

These, with other causes that human wisdom may not now foresee, will in time effect a separation, and I fear our bounds will be fixed nearer to our houses than the waters of the Mississippi. We have already territory enough, and when I contemplate the evils that may arise to these States, from this intended incorporation of Louisiana into the Union, I would rather see it given to France, to Spain, or to any other nation of the earth, upon the mere condition that no citizen of the United States should ever settle within its limits, than to see the territory sold for an hundred millions of dollars, and we retain the sovereignty. But however dangerous the possession of Louisiana might prove to us, I do not presume to say that the retention of it would not have been very convenient to France, and we know that at the time of the mission of Mr. Monroe, our Administration had never thought of the

purchase of Louisiana, and that nothing short of the fullest conviction on the part of the First Consul that he was on the very eve of a war with England; that this being the most defenceless point of his possessions, if such they could be called, was the one at which the British would first strike, and that it must inevitably fall into their hands, could ever have induced his pride and ambition to make the sale. He judged wisely, that he had better sell it for as much as he could get than lose it entirely. And I do say that under existing circumstances, even supposing that this extent of territory was a desirable acquisition, fifteen millions of dollars was a most enormous sum to give. Our Commissioners were negotiating in Paris—they must have known the relative situation of France and England—they must have known at the moment that a war was unavoidable between the two countries, and they knew the pecuniary necessities of France and the naval power of Great Britain. These imperious circumstances should have been turned to our advantage, and if we were to purchase, should have lessened the consideration. Viewing, Mr. President, this subject in any point of light—either as it regards the territory purchased, the high consideration to be given, the contract itself, or any of the circumstances attending it, I see no necessity for precipitating the passage of this bill; and if this motion for postponement should fail, and the question on the final passage of the bill be taken now, I shall certainly vote against it.

EDGE OF TREASON

78 THE BURR CONSPIRACY

from Reports of the Trials of Aaron Burr, 1808

The trial of Aaron Burr (1756-1836) brought both acquittal and political ruin to a brilliant and unprincipled adventurer whose ambition had carried him to the threshold of the presidency (see headnote to Document 74) and then to the edge of treason. That Burr played a dangerous game of intrigue with foreign ministers, high government officials, and influential citizens is certain. That he hungered to rule an empire of his own in the Southwest is highly probable. Whether that imagined empire was to be built on the ruins of Spanish Mexico, or carved out of the Western United States, or both, is still a point of scholarly dispute. The evidence is fragmentary and often contradictory. Burr himself said different things to different men, according to his view of their susceptibilities. A key witness against Burr, General James Wilkinson, can hardly be taken seriously since historians have revealed his record as a shameless liar and intriguer who had long been in the pay of Spain. A definitive verdict on the Burr conspiracy will perhaps never be possible.

The Burr conspiracy became a comic opera episode. Sixty men at most formed the expeditionary force that floated down the Ohio River from the island home of Harman Blennerhassett, a romantic Irish exile who had come under Burr's spell. The thousands of discontented Westerners Burr expected to join his enterprise never materialized. Burr with good reason counted on the support of the governor of the Louisiana Territory, General Wilkinson. Instead, Wilkinson betrayed his confederate to President Jefferson—and secretly applied to the Spanish for a sizable reward as the savior of Mexico from American invaders. With the total collapse of Burr's conspiracy, the danger of Western secession that had often alarmed the nation since the 1780's was at an end.

By the time Burr had been captured and brought to trial in the Federal District Court at Richmond (August 1807), the center of interest shifted from a dead conspiracy to a live encounter between President Jefferson and Chief Justice John Marshall, who conducted the trial as part of his circuit duties. Jefferson, convinced that Burr was guilty of treason, used all his influence behind the scenes to secure a vigorous and successful prosecution of the case. His great Federalist adversary, the Chief Justice of the Supreme Court, was equally determined that the passions of the moment should not influence the interpretation of treason as narrowly defined by the Constitution. Republicans saw rank partisanship in Marshall's conduct of the trial and in his unsuccessful efforts to command the President's attendance at court by issuing a subpoena.

John Marshall had his way with the jury. Treason in peacetime, according to the Constitution, consists in an overt act of levying war against the United States, an act established by two witnesses or by confession in open court. Marshall excluded much evidence bearing on the launching of the expedition from Blennerhassett's Island, since Burr was not present and since there were no witnesses to an overt act by which Burr joined directly in a movement levying war against the United States. Again, Marshall insisted, testimony demonstrating Burr's prior associations with the men who launched the expedition or showing that Burr presented treasonable projects to a number of men could not convict the prisoner of an *act* of treason. The jury resentfully complied with Marshall's dictates, stating that Burr was not guilty of treason according to the evidence legally submitted to it.

If John Marshall set an almost impossible standard for proving treason—as against the looser requirements proposed by William Wirt, George Hay, and other Jeffersonian counsellors for the prosecution—he also helped preserve the intention of the Founders that "constructive treason," treason established only by presumption, should not become an instrument of political persecution in the United States.

The following summary of the prosecution view by George Hay, U.S. Attorney for the District of Virginia, must be read, of course, with the understanding that the alleged facts of the conspiracy, as well as the constitutional interpretation of treason, were then and are now subjects of dispute.

After his acquittal Burr went into voluntary European exile, where he continued his dark intrigues. From 1812 until his death in 1836 he practised law in New York City. The man who had slain Alexander Hamilton in a duel in 1803 and who had touched the edge of treason could take no further role in public life.

I should . . . take it for granted, . . . that the overt act of treason was complete, if there were an assemblage of men on Blannerhassett's island, in the county of Wood, whether they were armed or not, and whether they used force or not. It is incumbent on those who prosecute, to shew, 1st, That there was a treasonable design; and 2d, That there was an assemblage of men, for the purpose of effectuating that design. It will be proved to you, gentlemen of the jury, that the design of the prisoner, was not only to wage war against the Spanish provinces, but to take possession of the city of New-Orleans, as preparatory to that design; to detach the people of that country from this, and establish an independent government there, and to dismember the union, separate the western from the eastern states,

making the Allegany mountains the boundary line. You will perceive from the evidence, that he intended to take possession of New-Orleans, to excite the people there to insurrection, and to take advantage of the hostile sentiments, which prevailed to the west of the Allegany against the Spaniards. If either of these be proved; if it be established that his design was to separate the states; or after seizing New-Orleans, to invade the Spanish provinces, he is guilty of treason. If in fact, it be proved, that he intended to take New-Orleans at all, he is completely guilty of treason; whether he designed to take possession of the whole or of a part, he is equally guilty of

Text: David Robertson (ed.), *Reports of the Trials of Aaron Burr* (Philadelphia: Hopkins and Earle, 1808), I, 446-49.

treason. It would be absurd, to suppose, that a man who had revolved in his mind, a scheme so gigantic as this, would communicate it to many persons. But he did disclose it to a few; and fortunately for our country, he was mistaken in his opinion of those persons in whom he confided; and the evidences of his design have been disclosed to our government. I am warranted in saying, gentlemen of the jury, that evidence the most positive and direct, and circumstances numerous and conclusive, will prove to your satisfaction, that the intentions of the accused were precisely such as I have mentioned.

For the purpose of accomplishing these great designs; of establishing an empire in the west, of which New-Orleans was to be the capital, and the accused was to be the chief, he made two long visits to the western country. He went to Ohio, Tennessee and Kentucky, in fact to all the western world, and travelled in various directions, till he went finally to New-Orleans. Wherever he went, he spoke disrespectfully of the government of his country, with a view to facilitate the consummation of his own designs. He represented it as destitute of energy to support or defend our national rights against foreign enemies, and of spirit to maintain our national character. He uniformly said, that we had no character either at home or abroad. To those in whom he confided, he asserted, that all the men of property and influence were dissatisfied with its arrangements, because they were not in the proper situation to which they were entitled: that with five hundred men he could effect a revolution by which he could send the president to Monticello, intimidate congress, and take the government of the United States into his own hands; that the people of the United States had so little knowledge of their rights, and so little disposition to maintain them, that they would meanly and tamely acquiesce in this shameful usurpation. This is the very language of the prisoner, about the government and people; representing the one as totally destitute of all energy and talents, and the other of all patriotism and virtue. But he confined this language to the people of the east; he spoke a different language to the people of the west. He told them, that they were in a state of colonial dependence on those of the Atlantic states, and annually paid millions to the government of the United States, for which they derived no benefit whatever; for which they received no protection, no return. The people on the other side of the Allegany were told, that a separation was necessary and would unquestionably take place; that it was not likely to take effect by the operation of natural,

of moral and political causes, but as determined by a particular chain of events; that the destiny of the republic was fixed, and that this revolution would be accomplished in less than two years. I thank God that this prediction has not been fulfilled, and I hope our posterity to the latest generation will thank God that it has not been fulfilled before their time! Such was the language of the accused; such the sentiments which he avowed, and the doctrines which he endeavoured to propagate. He said every thing to dissatisfy them with their brethren of the east, though all this time he pretended that his objects were of a purely agricultural nature. Nor did he confine himself to conversation with intelligent men only; there were writings published that came from the pen of the person who is indicted, as connected with him, calculated to scatter disaffection among the people and prepare them for his plans.

To accomplish these plans, in the summer and fall of 1806, men were actually inlisted, boats were built on the waters of the Ohio, provisions purchased to an enormous amount, and arms and ammunition provided, as if the object was meant to be carried into effect in a foreign nation; and as if some hostile expedition were on foot. Some of these men, about 40 in number, assembled with arms, on Blannerhassett's island, in order to descend the river. Burr was not there then; he had been there only a short time before, and intended to return, but was warned not to return, but his absence at the time when the people assembled is totally immaterial. A man may *"levy war"* against his country, when not present. A man may *"levy war"* against a country, though three thousand miles distant. This we may probably have an experience of in the course of a very few months. But this principle has been sufficiently established by the decision of the supreme court. "If war be actually levied, all those who perform any part, however minute, *or however remote from the scene of action,* and who are actually leagued in the general conspiracy, are to be considered as traitors."

These troops on the island, seeing the country alarmed, and apprehending that they would be attacked by the militia of Wood county, made a precipitate retreat by night, in company with Blannerhassett, and went down the Ohio to the mouth of Cumberland river, where the accused joined them and took the command. But this time their numbers increased to about one hundred. These men under the command of Burr and Blannerhassett, descended the Mississippi to Bayou Pierre, a point not far from Natchez. It was here, gentlemen of the jury, that he first learned that all his schemes would be frustrated by the exertions of the commander in chief [General Wilkinson]; that his letter in cypher had been communicated to the president; and it was here that in the first moment of surprize, he expressed to another person his astonishment and indignation, at being (as he said) thus betrayed. Finding that the commander in chief, had baffled all his schemes, by communicating his letter to the president, he entered into a kind of capitulation with Cowles Meade, was bound to appear before a tribunal at Natchez, from whence, it is said, he came off without leave of the court, in violation of his recognisance, and in his flight was taken by Perkins.

It will be proved to you, by express and direct evidence, that a settlement of lands on the Washita, was merely a cover to conceal the *real design,* which was to separate the union, take possession of New-Orleans, and attack the Span-ish provinces. But the utmost mystery and circumspection prevailed on this subject. To the world at large, and to those with whom he had not tampered, the object was held up to be, the settlement of lands up the Red river. To some, intimations were dropped, of an approaching rupture with Spain, against whose provinces the expedition was intended, and the conquest of Mexico was alluded to; his language varied according to the character of the man with whom he conversed. To a few only his real design was developed; but to all he said that there was a great scheme in view. All were told, that the design was just and honorable; known and approved by the government; in which the cooperation of the army was to be expected; in which great wealth was to be acquired, and that it would be developed as soon as the proper time for the disclosure arrived. The time, however, never did arrive. . . .

America and the Napoleonic Wars

NEUTRAL TRADE

79 NEUTRAL RIGHTS: CASE FOR THE EMBARGO

from William B. Giles, Speech in the U.S. Senate, November 24, 1808

The European wars following the French Revolution had, in important ways, defined the opportunities and necessities of American action. The richest opportunities were those for expanding neutral trade and shipping while the European powers were preoccupied with a great war. The price of such opportunities, however, was exposure to the attacks of France and Britain on American maritime rights. The belligerents welcomed neutral trade and shipping so far as it served their own war needs, but they could hardly be expected to tolerate forms of neutral commerce which increased the power of the enemy.

By 1805 England had won undisputed mastery of the seas, while Napoleon dominated the European continent. Napoleon's Continental System, established by the Berlin and Milan decrees of 1806-1807, was designed to cut off English trade with Europe. Neutral merchantmen bound to or from British ports were subject to capture. More damaging to American interests was the decision of the English courts (in the *Essex* case of 1805) that neutral ships proceeding from the French West Indies to a port in the United States, and then to France, could be taken as prizes. The "broken voyage," it was claimed, had become a pretext for illicit trading with the French enemy. This decision was followed by the British Orders in Council of 1807, laying a blockade on all French-occupied ports and thus excluding American ships from trade with Europe and the French colonies. The English continued their policy of impressment, under which American ships were boarded at sea and several classes of sailors forcibly removed: British deserters, naturalized Americans (whose right to renounce British citizenship was denied), and—by inevitable error—some native Americans. Impressment was justified as a necessary measure to discourage the enticement of British seamen into the American merchant marine. The provocative attack on the American warship *Chesapeake* by the *Leopard* in June 1807, prepared American public opinion for drastic countermeasures.

President Jefferson and Secretary of State Madison built their foreign policy on the premise that economic coercion could bring the European belligerents to respect America's maritime rights without precipitating war. The Embargo Act of December 1807 prohibited all American trade with foreign ports. The measure proved more painful to Americans than to the intended victims. The shipping and commercial interests of New England and the Middle States felt the major impact of the embargo and raised a storm of protest.

In the speech of November 24, 1808 that follows, Senator William Branch Giles of Virginia defends the Jeffersonian policy as a "painful alternative" to war or submission. The Embargo Act was repealed in response to general complaint a few days before Jefferson left office, only to be replaced by the Non-Intercourse Act of 1809 and later by Macon's Bill No. 2 in 1810. The latter two measures were more flexible attempts to win concessions from France and England by offering economic advantages to the nation that would remove its restrictions on American commerce. No substantial concessions were obtained, and the cry for war grew louder along the frontier and in the South.

Mr. President, I have always understood that there were two objects contemplated by the embargo laws—The first, precautionary, operating upon ourselves—The second, coercive, operating upon the aggressing belligerents. Precautionary, in saving our seamen, our ships and our merchandize from the plunder of our enemies, and avoiding the calamities of war. Coercive, by addressing strong appeals to the interests of both the belligerents. The first object has been answered beyond my most sanguine expectations. To make a fair and just estimate of this measure, reference should be had to our situation at the time of its adoption. At that time, the aggressions of both the belligerents were such, as to leave the United States but a painful alternative in the choice of one of three measures, to wit, the embargo, war, or submission. . . .

It was found that merchandize to the value of one hundred millions of dollars was actually afloat, in vessels amounting in value to twenty millions more—That an amount of merchandize and vessels equal to fifty millions more, was expected to be shortly put afloat, and that it would require fifty thousand seamen to be employed in the navigation of that enormous amount of property. The administration was informed of the hostile edicts of France previously issued, and then in a state of execution, and of an intention on the part of Great Britain to issue her orders, the character and object of which were also known. The object was, to sweep this valuable commerce from the ocean.—The situation of this commerce was as well known to Great Britain, as to ourselves, and her inordinate cupidity could not withstand the temptation of the rich booty, she vainly thought within her

power. This was the state of information at the time this measure was recommended.

The President of the United States ever watchful and anxious for the preservation of the persons and property of all our fellow citizens, but particularly of the merchants, whose property is most exposed to danger, and of the seamen whose persons are also most exposed, recommended the embargo for the protection of both; and it has saved and protected both. . . . It is admitted by all, that the embargo laws have saved this enormous amount of property, and this number of seamen, which, without them, would have forcibly gone into the hands of our enemies, to pamper their arrogance, stimulate their injustice, and increase their means of annoyance.

I should suppose, Mr. President, this saving worth some notice. But, Sir, we are told that instead of protecting our seamen, it has driven them out of the country, and into foreign service. I believe, Sir, that this fact is greatly exaggerated. But, Sir, suppose for a moment that it is so, the government has done all, in this respect, it was bound to do. It placed these seamen in the bosoms of their friends and families, in a state of perfect security; and if they have since thought proper to abandon these blessings, and emigrate from their country, it was an act of choice, not of necessity. . . .

. . . But, Sir, these are not the only good effects of the embargo. It has *preserved our peace—it has saved our honor—it has saved our national independence.* Are these savings not worth notice? Are these blessings not worth preserving? . . .

The gentleman next triumphantly tells us that the embargo laws have not had their expected effects upon the aggressing belligerents. That they have not had their complete effects; that they have not caused a revocation of the British

Text: William B. Giles, *Speech on the Resolution of Mr. Hillhouse, to Repeal the Embargo Laws* (Boston, 1808), pp. 4-15 *passim.*

orders and French decrees, will readily be admitted; but they certainly have not been without beneficial effects upon those nations. . . .

The first effect of the embargo, upon the aggressing belligerents, was to lessen their inducements to war, by keeping out of their way, the rich spoils of our commerce, which had invited their cupidity, and which was saved by those laws. . . .

The second effect, which the embargo laws have had on the aggressing belligerents, is to enhance [the] prices of all American produce, especially articles of the first necessity to them, to a considerable degree, and, if it be a little longer persisted in, will either banish our produce, (which I believe indispensable to them,) from their markets altogether, or increase the prices to an enormous amount—and, of course, we may hope will furnish irresistible inducements for a relaxation of their hostile orders & edicts. . . .

All these considerations must present strong inducements to Great Britain to revoke her hostile orders; but she has hitherto refused to do so. . . .

It is asked, Sir, how do the embargo laws operate on France? It is readily admitted, that the commercial connection between the United States and France, is not of such a nature as to make a suspension of it operate as injuriously to France herself particularly in the interior, as on G. Britain. But our commerce cannot be deemed unimportant to France in the feeble state of her navy. . . .

The French West India islands too, have felt the pressure with great severity. . . .

I think . . . Sir, I am warranted in concluding, that if the embargo laws have failed of complete success, their failure has been owing to extraordinary causes which could neither have been foreseen nor anticipated at the time of the adoption of the measure, and therefore cannot furnish any imputation against its policy or wisdom.

. . . I have said, Sir, that there are no substitutes for the embargo, but *war or submission.* I will now proceed to prove this position—a repeal of the embargo without a substitute, is *submission,* if with a substitute, it is *war.* Gentlemen in the opposition, seem fully sensible of the delicacy and urgency of this part of the question. When pressed for their substitute, they manifest vast reluctance in producing it. . . .

. . . the gentleman from Connecticut . . . intimates merely that he is in favor of an armed commerce. . . .

. . . Would he extend it to acts of reprisal? If so, it is immediate war.—Would he stop short of that. It would still be war; but of a more inefficient kind. If our vessels are to arm, I presume their arms are to be used in self defence; they would be used against both the belligerents. In the present temper of Great-Britain, the first gun fired in a spirit of hostility, even with a blank cartridge; or if it were a popgun, would be instant war. It would be the signal to her navy to seize upon the whole of our commerce, which would be spread over the ocean, the moment of raising the embargo. The gentleman's substitute I, therefore, believe to be war, and war of the most inefficient kind. A repeal of the embargo, without a substitute, is submission.—Submis-[s]ion to what! to colonization, to taxation, to tribute! !

WAR OF 1812

80

OLD REPUBLICANS VS. WAR HAWKS: THE CASE AGAINST WAR

from John Randolph, Speech in the U.S. House of Representatives, December 10, 1811

The main diplomatic grievances of the United States in the first decade of the nineteenth century pertained to the British impressment of sailors and to the denial of neutral trading rights of England and France. Yet the commercial and shipping interests of the Northeast—ostensibly the primary victims of European policy—generally opposed Republican measures for "peaceable coercion" (see Document 82) and after 1812 severely criticized, when they did not impede, the conduct of "Mr. Madison's War." To such men the restraints and depredations of the belligerents still left room for a risky but profitable neutral trade. Embargo or war would simply kill their opportunities. Of great importance to the Federalist opposition centered in New England, and to other Americans as well, was their stake in the defeat of the rampant conqueror Napoleon. The Federalists, it will be recalled, had been the anti-French party since the 1790's.

Jefferson and Madison found their main support in the South and West. Planters and farmers felt a threat to economic prosperity and national honor in the actions of the belligerents, especially England. A hunger for new territory in Spanish Florida and

British Canada made war seem attractive. The Shawnee chief, Tecumseh, and his brother, the Prophet, threatened to consolidate Indian resistance to the further encroachment of Western settlers. In the opinion of frontiersmen, British agents were the principal source of Indian troubles. By 1811 the Republican policy of economic coercion no longer satisfied the aggressive young men led by Henry Clay of Kentucky and John C. Calhoun of the South Carolina back country, who came to Congress to talk the language of nationalism, expansion, and war.

The new leaders were dubbed "War Hawks" by John Randolph (1773-1833), an eccentric Virginia Republican who had broken earlier with Jefferson and Madison and now extended his vitriolic enmity to the advocates of war for conquest. Clay as Speaker of the House and Calhoun as Chairman of the House Committee on Foreign Affairs, together with their militant allies in the Senate, were driving Congress toward war preparations in December of 1811. John Randolph's speech of December 10, responding to the remarks of the Tennessee War Hawk, Felix Grundy, ascribed both crime and folly to a policy which would turn the peaceful American Republic into the ways of militarism and imperialism while undermining English resistance to Napoleon, "the arch enemy of mankind." Some support for the thesis that Western expansionists provoked the War of 1812 can be found in Randolph's charges.

Mr. Randolph rose. . . .

It was a question, as it had been presented to the House, of peace or war. In that light it had been argued; in no other light could he consider it, after the declarations made by members of the Committee of Foreign Relations. . . .

An insinuation had fallen from the gentleman from Tennessee, (Mr. Grundy,) that the late massacre of our brethren on the Wabash had been instigated by the British Government. Has the President given any such information? has the gentleman received any such, even informally, from any officer of this Government? Is it so believed by the Administration? He had cause to think the contrary to be the fact; that such was not their opinion. This insinuation was of the grossest kind—a presumption the most rash, the most unjustifiable. Show but good ground for it, he would give up the question at the threshold— he was ready to march to Canada. It was indeed well calculated to excite the feelings of the Western people particularly, who were not quite so tenderly attached to our red brethren as some modern philosophers; but it was destitute of any foundation, beyond mere surmise and suspicion. . . . He was sorry to say that for this signal calamity and disgrace the House was, in part, at least, answerable. Session after session, their table had been piled up with Indian treaties, for which the appropriations had been voted as a matter of course, without examination. Advantage had been taken of the spirit of the Indians, broken by the war which ended in the Treaty of Greenville. Under the ascendency then acquired over them,

Text: The Debates and Proceedings in the Congress of the United States, First to Eighteenth Congress, March 3, 1789, to May 27, 1824, Inclusive (Washington, D.C.: Gales & Seaton, 1854), XXIII, 441, 445-50, 454-55.

they had been pent up by subsequent treaties into nooks, straightened in their quarters by a blind cupidity, seeking to extinguish their title to immense wildernesses, for which, (possessing, as we do already, more land than we can sell or use) we shall not have occasion, for half a century to come. It was our own thirst for territory, our own want of moderation, that had driven these sons of nature to desperation, of which we felt the effects. . . .

He could but smile at the liberality of the gentleman, in giving Canada to New York, in order to strengthen the Northern balance of power, while at the same time he forwarned her that the Western scale must preponderate. Mr. R. [Randolph] said he could almost fancy that he saw the Capitol in motion towards the falls of Ohio—after a short sojourn taking its flight to the Mississippi, and finally alighting on Darien; which, when the gentleman's dreams are realized, will be a most eligible seat of Government for the new Republic (or Empire) of the two Americas! . . .

This war of conquest, a war for the acquisition of territory and subjects, is to be a new commentary on the doctrine that Republics are destitute of ambition—that they are addicted to peace, wedded to the happiness and safety of the great body of their people. But it seems this is to be a holiday campaign—there is to be no expense of blood, or treasure, on our part—Canada is to conquer herself—she is to be subdued by the principles of fraternity. The people of that country are first to be seduced from their allegiance, and converted into traitors, as preparatory to the making them good citizens. Although he must acknowledge that some of our flaming patriots were thus manufactured, he did not think the process would hold good with a whole community. It was a dangerous experiment. We were to succeed in the French mode by the system of fraternization—all is French! but how dreadfully it might be retorted on the Southern and Western slaveholding States. He detested this subornation of treason. No—if he must have them, let them fall by the valor of our arms, by fair, legitimate conquest; not become the victims of treacherous seduction.

He was not surprised at the war spirit which was manifesting itself in gentlemen from the South. In the year 1805-6, in a struggle for the carrying trade of belligerent colonial produce, this country had been most unwisely brought into collision with the great Powers of Europe. By a series of most impolitic and ruinous measures, utterly incomprehensible to every rational, sober-minded man, the Southern planters, by their own votes, had succeeded in knocking down the price of cotton to seven cents, and of tobacco (a few choice crops excepted) to nothing—and in raising the price of blankets, (of which a few would not be amiss in a Canadian campaign,) coarse woolens, and every article of first necessity, three or four hundred per cent. And now that, by our own acts, we have brought ourselves into this unprecedented condition, we must get out of it in any way, but by an acknowledgement of our own want of wisdom and forecast. But is war the true remedy? Who will profit by it? Speculators—a few lucky merchants, who draw prizes in the lottery—commissaries and contractors. Who must suffer by it? The people. It is their blood, their taxes, that must flow to support it. . . .

He was gratified to find gentlemen acknowledging the demoralizing and destructive consequences of the non-importation law—confessing the truth of all that its opponents foretold when it was enacted. And will you plunge yourselves in war, because you have passed a foolish and ruinous law, and are ashamed to repeal it? "But our good friend the French Emperor stands in the way of its repeal," and as we cannot go too far in making sacrifices to him, who has given such demonstration of his love for the Americans, we must, in point of fact, become parties to his war. "Who can be so cruel as to refuse him this favor?" His imagination shrunk from the miseries of such a connexion. He called upon the House to reflect whether they were not about to abandon all reclamation for the unparalleled outrages, "insults and injuries" of the French Government, to give up our claim for plundered millions; and asked what reparation or atonement they could expect to obtain in hours of future dalliance, after they should have made a tender of their

person to this great deflowerer of the virginity of republics. . . . Go! march to Canada! leave the broad bosom of the Chesapeake and her hundred tributary rivers—the whole line of seacoast from Machias to St. Mary's, unprotected! You have taken Quebec—have you conquered England? Will you seek for the deep foundations of her power in the frozen deserts of Labrador? . . .

Will you call upon her to leave your ports and harbors untouched, only just till you can return from Canada, to defend them? The coast is to be left defenceless, whilst men of the interior are revelling in conquest and spoil. But grant for a moment, for mere argument's sake, that in Canada you touched the sinews of her strength, instead of removing a clog upon her resources—an encumbrance, but one, which, from a spirit of honor, she will vigorously defend. In what situation would you then place some of the best men of the nation? As Chatham and Burke, and the whole band of her patriots, prayed for her defeat in 1776, so must some of the truest friends to their country deprecate the success of our arms against the only Power that holds in check the archenemy of mankind [Napoleon]. . . .

Our people will not submit to be taxed for this war of conquest and dominion. The Government of the United States was not calculated to wage offensive foreign war—it was instituted for the common defence and general welfare; and whosoever should embark it in a war of offence, would put it to a test which it was by no means calculated to endure. Make it out that Great Britain had instigated the Indians on the late occasion, and he was ready for battle; but not for dominion. He was unwilling, however, under present circumstances, to take Canada, at the risk of the Constitution—to embark in a common cause with France and be dragged at the wheels of the car of some Burr or Bonaparte. For a gentleman from Tennessee or Gennessee, or Lake Champlain, there may be some prospect of advantage. Their hemp would bear a great price by the exclusion of foreign supply. In that too the great importers were deeply interested. The upper country on the Hudson and the Lakes would be enriched by the supplies for the troops, which they alone could furnish. They would have the exclusive market: to say nothing of the increased preponderance from the acquisition of Canada and that section of the Union, which the Southern and Western States had already felt so severely in the apportionment bill. . . .

And shall Republicans become the instruments of him who had effaced the title of Attila to the "Scourge of God!" Yet even Attila, in the falling fortunes of civilization, had, no doubt,

his advocates, his tools, his minions, his parasites in the very countries that he overran—sons
of that soil whereon his horse had trod; where
grass could never after grow. . . . He could not
give utterance to that strong detestation which
he felt towards (above all other works of the
creation) such characters as Zingis, Tamerlane,
Kouli-Khan, or Bonaparte. His instincts involuntarily revolted at their bare idea. Malefactors of
the human race, who ground down man to a mere
machine of their impious and bloody ambition.
Yet under all the accumulated wrongs and insults
and robberies of the last of these chieftains, are

we not in point of fact about to become a party
to his views, a partner in his wars? . . .

He called upon those professing to be Republicans to make good the promises held out by
their Republican predecessors when they came
into power—promises, which for years afterwards
they had honestly, faithfully fulfilled. We had
vaunted of paying off the national debt, of re-
trenching useless establishments; and yet had
now become as infatuated with standing armies,
loans, taxes, navies, and war, as ever were the
Essex Junto. What Republicanism is this? . . .

81

THE NATIONALIST'S REPLY

from John C. Calhoun, Speech in the U.S. House of Representatives, December 12, 1811

John C. Calhoun (1782-1850) is best remembered as the powerful advocate of state
rights and sectional interests in the period 1828-1850. This was, in effect, his second
political career. Calhoun first entered South Carolina politics as a militant nationalist,
taking his place with Clay and the young War Hawks after his election to Congress in
1810. For almost two decades in Washington he was mainly identified with measures
designed to strengthen and expand the nation: with the enlargement of the military
establishment, the protective tariff, the national bank, and the like.

In the Congressional debate over military preparations (December 1811), Calhoun
gave the War Hawks' answer to those like Randolph who proposed a cautious and
conciliatory policy toward England. The injustice of French and English violations of
commercial and maritime rights needed no proof. The failure of economic coercion he
considered no less obvious. The question, Calhoun insisted, was simply one of cowardly
submission or war. Not only the honor but the future greatness of the nation were at
stake. Point by point Calhoun met the Randolph charges that America was too weak
for war, that the costs of war would outweigh the gains, that the conquest of Canada
would transgress republican principles, that the West and South were merely greedy
for war profits, and that America must not further the cause of Napoleon by harassing
England.

Calhoun and the other War Hawks converted neither Randolph nor the New England
Federalists. The War Hawks did help to move the cautious Madison administration
toward the decision for war. In February of 1811, Madison, acting under the provisions
of Macon's Bill No. 2, responded to a deceptive French offer to repeal the Continental
System by prohibiting trade with England. The President's confidential message of
June 1, 1812, argued that the impressment of American sailors, the indiscriminate
application of blockades, the plundering of American commerce, and the presumed
encouragement of Indian attacks on Western settlements by the British already constituted a state of war against the United States. Despite the strong opposition of members from New England and the Middle States, Congress voted a declaration of war;
the House took action on June 4, and two weeks later, on June 18, the Senate
followed suit.

The Treaty of Ghent in 1814, following an indecisive war, resolved none of the issues
that had provoked the fighting. However, several commissions created under the treaty
did in time work out agreements on disputed questions of trade, boundaries, border
armaments, and fishing rights. During the war American armies broke the back of
Indian resistance in both the Northwest and the Southwest. Most important, the defeat
of Napoleon by the English introduced a long era of European peace during which the
United States could concentrate on the settlement and development of the American
continent.

Mr. Calhoun.—Mr. Speaker: I understood the opinion of the Committee of Foreign Relations differently from what the gentleman from Virginia (Mr. Randolph) has stated to be his impression. . . . The report could mean nothing but war or empty menace. I hope no member of this House is in favor of the latter. A bullying, menacing system has everything to condemn and nothing to recommend it; in expense, it is almost as considerable as war; it excites contempt abroad, and destroys confidence at home. Menaces are serious things; and, if we expect any good from them, they ought to be resorted to with as much caution and seriousness as war itself, and should, if not successful, be invariably followed by it. It was not the gentleman from Tennessee (Mr. Grundy) that made this a war question. The resolve contemplates an additional regular force; a measure confessedly improper but as a preparation for war, but undoubtedly necessary in that event. . . .

Sir, I might prove the war, should it ensue, justifiable, by the express admission of the gentleman from Virginia; and necessary, by facts undoubted and universally admitted, such as that gentleman did not pretend to controvert. The extent, duration, and character of the injuries received; the failure of those peaceful means heretofore resorted to for the redress of our wrongs, is my proof that it is necessary. Why should I mention the impressment of our seamen; depredation on every branch of our commerce, including the direct export trade, continued for years, and made under laws which professedly undertake to regulate our trade with other nations; negotiation resorted to time after time, till it is become hopeless; the restrictive system persisted in to avoid war, and in the vain expectation of returning justice? The evil still grows, and in each succeeding year swells in extent and pretension beyond the preceding. The question, even in the opinion and admission of our opponents, is reduced to this single point—which shall we do, abandon or defend our own commercial and maritime rights, and the personal liberties of our citizens employed in exercising them? These rights are essentially attacked, and war is the only means of redress. The gentleman from Virginia has suggested none—unless we consider the whole of his speech as recommending patient and resigned submission as the best remedy. Sir, which alternative this House ought to embrace, it is not for me to say. I hope the decision is made already, by a higher authority than the voice of any man. It is not for the human tongue to instill the sense of independence and honor. This is the work of nature—a generous nature, that disdains tame submission to wrongs. . . .

. . . The first argument of the gentleman which I shall notice, is the unprepared state of the country. Whatever weight this argument might have, in a question of immediate war, it surely has little in that of preparation for it. If our country is unprepared, let us remedy the evil as soon as possible. Let the gentleman submit his plan; and, if a reasonable one, I doubt not it will be supported by the House. But, sir, let us admit the fact and the whole force of the argument, I ask whose is the fault? Who has been a member for many years past, and has seen the defenceless state of his country even near home, under his own eyes, without a single endeavor to remedy so serious an evil? Let him not say "I have acted in a minority." It is no less the duty of the minority than a majority to endeavor to serve our country. For that purpose we are sent here and not for that of opposition. We are next told of the expenses of the war, and that the people will not pay taxes. Why not? Is it a want of capacity? What, with one million tons of shipping, a trade of near $100,000,000, manufactures of $150,000,000, and agriculture of thrice that amount, shall we be told the country wants capacity to raise and support ten thousand or fifteen thousand additional regulars? No; it has the ability, that is admitted; but will it not have the disposition? Is not the course a just and necessary one? Shall we, then, utter this libel on the nation? Where will proof be found of a fact so disgraceful? It is said, in the history of the country twelve or fifteen years ago. The case is not parallel. The ability of the country is greatly increased since. The object of that tax was unpopular. But on this, as well as my memory and almost infant observation at that time serve me, the objection was not to the tax, or its amount, but the mode of collection. The eye of the nation was frightened by the number of officers; its love of liberty shocked with the multiplicity of regulations. We, in the vile spirit of imitation, copied from the most oppressive part of European laws on that subject, and imposed on a young and virtuous nation all the severe provisions made necessary by corruption and long growing chicane. If taxes should become necessary, I do not hesitate to say the people will pay cheerfully. It is for their Government and their cause, and would be their interest and duty to pay. But it may be, and I believe was said, that the nation will not pay taxes, because the rights violated are not worth defending, or that the defence will cost

Text: The Debates and Proceedings in the Congress of the United States, First to Eighteenth Congress, March 3, 1789, to May 27, 1824, Inclusive (Washington, D.C.: Gales & Seaton, 1854), XXIII, 476-83.

more than the profit. Sir, I here enter my solemn protest against this low and "calculating avarice" entering this hall of legislation. It is only fit for shops and counting-houses, and ought not to disgrace the seat of sovereignty by its squalid and vile appearance. Whenever it touches sovereign power, the nation is ruined. It is too short-sighted to defend itself. It is an unpromising spirit, always ready to yield a part to save the balance. It is too timid to have in itself the laws of self-preservation. It is never safe but under the shield of honor. Sir, I only know of one principle to make a nation great, to produce in this country not the form but real spirit of union, and that is, to protect every citizen in the lawful pursuit of his business. He will then feel that he is backed by the Government; that its arm is his arms; and will rejoice in its increased strength and prosperity. Protection and patriotism are reciprocal. This is the road that all great nations have trod. Sir, I am not versed in this calculating policy; and will not, therefore, pretend to estimate in dollars and cents the value of national independence, or national affection. I cannot dare to measure, in shillings and pence, the misery, the stripes, and the slavery of our impressed seamen; nor even to value our shipping, commercial, and agricultural losses, under the Orders in Council and the British system of blockade. I hope I have not condemned any prudent estimate of the means of a country, before it enters on a war. This is wisdom, the other folly. Sir, the gentleman from Virginia has not failed to touch on the calamity of war; that fruitful source of declamation, by which pity becomes the advocate of cowardice; but I know not what we have to do with that subject. If the gentleman desires to repress the gallant ardor of our countrymen by such topics, let me inform him, that true courage regards only the cause—that it is just and necessary—and that it despises the pain and danger of war. If he really wishes to promote the cause of humanity, let his eloquence be addressed to Lord Wellesley or Mr. Percival, and not the American Congress. Tell them, if they persist in such daring insult and injury to a neutral nation, that, however inclined to peace, it will be bound in honor and interest to resist; that their patience and benevolence, however great, will be exhausted; that the calamity of war will ensue; and that they, in the opinion of wounded humanity, will be answerable for all its devastation and misery. Let melting pity, a regard to the interest of humanity, stay the hand of injustice. and, my life on it, the gentleman will not find it difficult to call off his country from the bloody scenes of war. . . .

. . . But we have not yet come to the end of the chapter of dangers. The gentleman's imagination, so fruitful on this subject, conceives that our Constitution is not calculated for war, and that it cannot stand its rude shock. This is rather extraordinary—we must depend upon the pity or contempt of other nations, for our existence. The Constitution, it seems, has failed in its essential part, "to provide for the common defence." No, says the gentleman from Virginia, it is competent for a defensive, but not an offensive war. It is not necessary for me to expose the error of this opinion. Why make the distinction in this instance? Will he pretend to say, that this is an offensive war; a war of conquest? Yes, the gentleman has dared to make this assertion; and for reasons no less extraordinary than the assertion itself. He says, our rights are violated on the ocean, and that these violations affect our shipping, and commercial rights, to which the Canadas have no relation. The doctrine of retaliation has been much abused of late by an unnatural extension; we have now to witness a new abuse. The gentleman from Virginia has limited it down to a point. By his system, if you receive a blow on the breast, you dare not return it on the head; you are obliged to measure and return it on the precise point on which it was received. If you do not proceed with mathematical accuracy, it ceases to be just self-defence; it becomes an unprovoked attack. . . .

Sir, said Mr. C. [Calhoun], the gentleman from Virginia attributes preparation for war to everything but its true cause. He endeavored to find it in the probable rise of the price of hemp. He represents the people of the Western States as willing to plunge our country into war for such base and precarious motives. I will not reason on this point. I see the cause of their ardor, not in such base motives, but in their known patriotism and disinterestedness. No less mercenary is the reason which he attributes to the Southern States. He says, that the non-importation act has reduced cotton to nothing, which has produced a feverish impatience. Sir, I acknowledge the cotton of our farms is worth but little; but not for the cause assigned by the gentleman from Virginia. The people of that section do not reason as he does; they do not attribute it to the efforts of their Government to maintain the peace and independence of their country; they see in the low price of the produce, the hand of foreign injustice; they know well, without the market to the Continent, the deep and steady current of supply will glut that of Great Britain; they are not prepared for the colonial state to which again that Power is endeavoring to reduce us. The manly spirit of that section of our country will not submit to be regulated by any foreign Power. The love of France and the hatred of England has also been assigned as the cause of the present measure. France has not done us justice, says the gentleman from Virginia, and how can we without partiality resist the aggressions of England? I know, sir, we have still cause of complaint against France; but it is of a different character from those against England. She professes now to respect our rights, and there cannot be a reasonable doubt but that the most objectionable parts of her decrees, as far as they respect us, are repealed. We have already formally acknowledged this to be a fact. I, however, protest against the whole of the principles on which this doctrine is founded. It is a novel doctrine, and nowhere to be found out of this House, that you cannot select your antagonist without being guilty of partiality. Sir, when two invade your rights you may resist both or either, at your pleasure. It is regulated by prudence and not by right. The stale imputation of partiality to France is better calculated for the columns of a newspaper than for the walls of this House. . . .

. . . The balance of power has also been introduced as an argument for submission. England is said to be a barrier against the military despotism of France. There is, sir, one great error in our legislation. We are ready enough to protect the interest of the States; and it should seem from this argument to watch over those of a foreign nation, while we grossly neglect our own immediate concerns. This argument of the balance of power is well calculated for the British Parliament, but not at all fitted to the American Congress. Tell them that they have to contend with a mighty Power, and that if they persist in insult and injury to the American people, they will compel them to throw the whole weight of their force into the scale of their enemy. Paint the danger to them, and if they desist from injury, we, I answer for it, will not disturb the balance. But it is absurd for us to talk of the balance of power, while they by their conduct smile with contempt at our simple good-natured policy. If, however, in the contest, it should be found that they underrate us, which I hope and believe, and that we can affect the balance of power, it will not be difficult for us to obtain such terms as our rights demand. . . .

82 DISUNION: THE HARTFORD CONVENTION

from John Quincy Adams, "Reply to the Appeal of the Massachusetts Federalists," 1815

John Quincy Adams (1767-1848), son of the second President, was a Yankee who made his peace with Republicanism and refused to countenance the extreme Federalist opposition to the War of 1812. His "Reply to the Appeal of the Massachusetts Federalists" (1815) analyzes the motives and purposes of those ultra-Federalist leaders in New England who had tried several times since 1803 to push their party and section toward secession.

Under the rule of the Virginia Dynasty (1801-1825) the political temper of New England was not unlike that of the Southern states in the following generation. Federalists complained that the original balance of power among the sections was being destroyed by the admission of new Western states and that Northeastern principles and interests were being sacrificed to the demands of the Republican South and West. Secessionist talk was heard in New England during the Embargo crisis (1807-1809). After opposing the declaration of war in 1812, New England leaders using state-rights arguments continued to criticize and obstruct the conduct of war. New England banks refused to buy government bonds, while New England state officials discouraged military enlistments and on occasion refused presidential requisitions for militia. Daniel Webster, the future nationalist spokesman, made his name in Congress as the opposition leader who tried to block Calhoun's measures for strengthening the war effort.

An administration proposal to conscript militiamen into the United States Army brought New England dissidence to a head. At the call of the Massachusetts legislature, official delegates from Massachusetts, Connecticut, and Rhode Island, joined by men from New Hampshire and Vermont, met secretly at Hartford from December 15, 1814, to January 5, 1815, to consider grievances and remedies. Undoubtedly some of the promoters of the Hartford Convention looked forward to secession and a New England Confederacy which would make a separate peace with England. How far the main body of delegates were prepared to go is a matter of dispute. Prudent men like Harrison Gray Otis and George Cabot helped to moderate the public demands that issued from the Convention. The official statement counselled a form of state nullification and urged a series of constitutional amendments that would protect New England rights and interests against a national majority dominated by the South and West. (For example, the Convention called for the abolition of the "three-fifths" rule assigning partial representation to the slave population of the South and proposed a two-thirds majority in Congress on votes to admit new states or to lay restraints on foreign commerce.)

There was no call for secession or a separate peace. As John Quincy Adams points out, however, the Convention statement hints of further drastic actions to be considered if the "moderate" demands should be refused and the peace negotiations with England should fail.

The news of Andrew Jackson's stunning victory over the British at New Orleans on January 8, 1815, followed by the announcement a few days later that a peace treaty had been signed at Ghent on December 24, 1814, cut the ground from under the Hartford men. The Federalist party came to be identified in popular opinion with disloyalty and secession and soon became extinct. Doctrines of state rights, nullification, and secession migrated southward to be used by slave-state leaders who saw their section as an oppressed minority in the decades preceding the Civil War.

The [Hartford] Convention represented the extreme portion of the Federalism of New England, —the party spirit of the school of Alexander Hamilton combined with the sectional Yankee spirit. I use this somewhat vulgar word, because, though somewhat humble in its original, it has gathered many a laurel in the field of glory, and because —like Brother Jonathan and Uncle Sam—it has an energy of significancy for which no other can be substituted. The Yankee spirit is a social spirit, and carries with it the fire of the flint. It was not well or naturally associated with the Federalism of Alexander Hamilton; and he himself once complained of it as clannish. And so it was, and that was its inherent defect. In itself it was good: it was the distillation from the spirit of the Puritan fathers of New England; but it was not American patriotism; on the contrary, it was that virtue which, in its excess, turns to vice. . . . But with this spirit was associated the ultra-Federalism of Hamilton, execrating Mr. Jefferson and all his principles and administration; hating Mr. Madison and my father, whom they had sacrificed to Hamilton and his policy seventeen years before. This was the composition; and this was not patriotism. It was the very reverse.

This coalition of Hamiltonian Federalism with the Yankee spirit had produced as incongruous and absurd a system of politics as ever was exhibited in the vagaries of the human mind. It was compounded of the following prejudices:—

1. An utter detestation of the French Revolution and of France, and a corresponding excess of attachment to Great Britain, as the only barrier against the universal, dreaded empire of France.

2. A strong aversion to republics and republican government, with a profound impression that our experiment of a confederated republic had failed for want of virtue in the people.

3. A deep jealousy of the Southern and Western States, and a strong disgust at the effect of the slave representation in the Constitution of the United States.

4. A belief that Mr. Jefferson and Mr. Madison were servilely devoted to France, and under French influence.

Every one of these sentiments weakened the attachments of those who held them to the Union, and consequently their patriotism. The sentiment itself, in a great measure, changed its object. The feeling against the general administration was so strong that it extended itself to the States and people by which it was supported; and all the impulses of patriotism became concentrated upon New England; and the temper of hostility, instead of patriotism, connected itself with every thought of the general government. . . .

These were the opinions, aggravated by the pressure of the embargo, and afterwards of the war, represented by the Hartford Convention; but they were still not entertained by a large portion of the Federal party,—by very few to the degree of those represented in the Convention. They were utterly and totally disapproved by the whole Republican party. . . .

The closing paragraph of the final report [of the Hartford Convention] is dictated by the same spirit [of disunion]. It is an apology for not proposing an immediate secession from the Union. It says, "Nothing more could be attempted on this occasion than a digest of general principles, and of recommendations suited to the present state of public affairs." It refers to the difficulties of the crisis; to the pending negotiation

Text: Henry Adams (ed.), *Documents Relating to New England Federalism, 1800-1815* (Boston: Little, Brown & Co., 1877), pp. 283-85, 320-22.

for peace, and to the duty of abstaining from measures which might unfavorably affect that issue. It then concludes thus:—

"It is also devoutly to be wished that an occasion may be afforded to all friends of the country, of all parties and in all places, to pause and consider the awful state to which pernicious counsels and blind passions have brought this people. The number of those who perceive, and who are ready to retrace, errors, must, it is believed, be yet sufficient to redeem the nation. It is necessary to rally and unite them by the assurance that no hostility to the Constitution is meditated, and to obtain their aid in placing it under guardians who alone can save it from destruction. Should this fortunate change be effected, the hope of happiness and honor may once more dispel the surrounding gloom. Our nation may yet be great, our Union durable; but, should this prospect be utterly hopeless, the time will not have been lost which shall have ripened a general sentiment of the necessity of more mighty efforts to rescue from ruin at least some portion of our beloved country."

The same predominating ideas which have pervaded the whole report are here concentrated in this summary at its close. The expedient for assuring those who might be disposed to retrace their errors, that no hostility to the Constitution was meditated, was, to be sure, of singular consistency with the seven proposed amendments to it, beginning with the abolition of the slave representation; but it is very apparent that the Hartford Convention were prepared for a continuance of the Union, and of the Constitution too, if they could obtain sufficient aid for placing them under the guardianship of the representative moral, intellectual, and patriotic worth of the New England character [i.e., the Hartford men as they saw themselves]. But if that fortunate change could not be effected, and the prospect of it should prove utterly hopeless, then their time would not have been lost in "ripening" the general sentiment of a "necessity" of more mighty efforts to rescue from ruin at least "some portion of the country;" or, in other words, that the time for a change was at hand.

It will be no longer necessary to search for the objects of the Hartford Convention. They are apparent from the whole tenor of their report and resolutions, compared with the journal of their proceedings. They are admitted in the first and last paragraphs of the report, and they were,—

To wait for the issue of the negotiation at Ghent.

In the event of the continuance of the war, to take one more chance of getting into their own hands the administration of the general government.

On failure of that, a secession from the Union and a New England confederacy.

To these ends, and not to the defence of this part of the country against the foreign enemy, all the measures of the Hartford Convention were adapted; and, of these ends, that of ripening the sentiment of a necessity for the last of these measures was the greatest object of the solicitude of the Convention, and the consummation of all their labors. . . .

Broad Construction and National Progress

THE NEW NATION

83

PARADISE LOST: FROM AGRICULTURE TO MANUFACTURING

from Thomas Jefferson, Letter to William Short, November 28, 1814

Jefferson's brief comments in the following letter to his friend William Short suggest the ex-President's view of the American future as he contemplated the effects of the War of 1812. A society based upon the independent freehold farmer and his way of life, Jefferson formerly had argued, was necessary to sustain a republican polity. Great cities and factories bred poverty, dependence, corruption, and despotism.

Yet Jefferson was prepared to sacrifice the moral advantages of an agrarian republic when external dangers threatened the security of the nation. Without industrial resources America would be at the mercy of hostile powers which could close off foreign markets and sources of supply. Hamilton in his *Report on Manufactures* (1791) had defended industrialization as a positive good for the nation; significantly, Jefferson accepted the development of manufacturing and military strength as a necessary evil signifying the loss of a peaceful agrarian paradise.

One should not conclude from Jefferson's prophetic remarks that the America of 1814 had already been transformed from an agrarian to an industrial society. The second decade of the nineteenth century was a period of small but significant beginnings in a new direction. Particularly in New England, the Republican policies of embargo and war encouraged a shift of capital from foreign commerce to domestic manufacturing that rapidly created a major textile industry in the postwar years. In 1813 (just a year before Jefferson wrote the following comments to Short) Francis Cabot Lowell with a group of great Boston merchants organized the Boston Manufacturing Company in Waltham, Massachusetts; this was a new kind of large-scale enterprise that would integrate the processes of cotton manufacturing from the spinning of the thread to the printing of the cloth. Of more general importance for the nation was a new spirit of enterprise, both private and public, directed primarily toward the improvement of land and water routes linking farms to markets, West to East.

In the domain of public policy, the heirs to the leadership of the Republican party during the postwar "Era of Good Feelings," including some Southerners like Calhoun, departed sharply from the strict principles of Jefferson's First Inaugural to support internal improvements, a protective tariff, and a national bank. Thus policies of a Hamiltonian nationalist cast had a new birth under Republican auspices.

Monticello, November 28, 1814. . . .

I consider the war . . . as entirely justifiable on our part, although I am still sensible it is a deplorable misfortune to us. It has arrested the course of the most remarkable tide of prosperity any nation ever experienced, and has closed such prospects of future improvement as were never before in the view of any people. Farewell all

Text: Thomas Jefferson, *Writings,* ed. H. A. Washington (New York: Riker, Thorne & Co., 1854), VI, 398-400.

hopes of extinguishing public debt! farewell all visions of applying surpluses of revenue to the improvements of peace rather than the ravages of war. Our enemy has indeed the consolation of Satan on removing our first parents from Paradise: from a peaceable and agricultural nation, he makes us a military and manufacturing one. We shall indeed survive the conflict. Breeders enough will remain to carry on population. We shall retain our country, and rapid advances in the art of war will soon enable us to beat our enemy, and probably drive him from the continent. . . .

84 FOREIGN COMMERCE

from David B. Warden, *A Statistical, Political, and Historical Account of the United States of North America,* 1819

The following report by Daniel Bailie Warden, American consul at Paris during Madison's administration, notes the striking success of the nation's overseas merchants and shippers. Since colonial times the leading businessmen of Boston, Philadelphia, New York, and lesser seaport towns had won fortune and reputation by their enterprise as shipbuilders, ocean carriers, and merchants. Following the Revolution bold sea captains took an increasing share of the Atlantic trade, sailed whaling ships over the oceans of the world, and crowded their British rivals in Canton. Before 1800 the United States had built a merchant marine and a foreign commerce second only to England's.

The period of European wars introduced by the French Revolution offered unique opportunities to neutral shippers and traders that Americans were quick to seize. Although the War of 1812 gravely injured the country's maritime and commercial interests, their postwar recovery was strong. Thus by 1824 the sleek sailing packets of Boston and New York had captured the carrying trade with Liverpool. American wheat and cotton sustained a growing export trade. Yankee ships achieved pre-eminence for their speed and efficiency, and enterprising American carriers were to be met in all the great ports of the world. A generation after the Peace of Ghent the maritime interests of the United States were entering their greatest era.

During and after the war, however, businessmen began to shift the main focus of their economic activity from the ocean to the American continent. A nation hungry for expansion and economic development drew an increasing share of capital and enterprise into land speculation, transportation, domestic trade, banking, and manufacturing. With the additional support of foreign investments and immigrant workers, Americans settled a continent, completed a national transportation network, and effected an industrial revolution, all within three generations.

Foreign commerce remained, of course, a vital link between the United States and European markets. Yet the growing importance of domestic industry can be estimated, for example, in the votes of such New England spokesmen as Daniel Webster, who opposed the tariff of 1816 as a burden on shipping and commerce but by 1830 became a leading advocate of protection for the rising manufacturing interests.

In commerce and navigation, the progress of the United States has been rapid beyond example. Besides the natural advantages of excellent harbours, extensive inland bays and navigable rivers, it has been greatly in favour of their commerce, that it has not been fettered by monopolies or exclusive privileges. Goods or merchandise circulate through all the states free of duty, and a full drawback, or restitution of duties of importation, is granted upon articles exported to a foreign port, in the course of the year in which they have been imported. Commerce is considered by all those engaged in it as a most honourable employment. In the sea-port towns, the richest members of society are merchants. Youths of sixteen are sent abroad as factors, or supercargoes, to every commercial country, intrusted with the management of great concerns. Stimulated by the prospect of independence, they study the manufactures and markets of foreign states; the quality, value, and profits of every commercial article, while the youth of other countries, of the same age and rank, have not formed a thought of a provision for future life. Maritime and commercial business is executed with more celerity and less expence than in any other country. Vessels in the ports of the United States are laden and unladen in the course of a few days, whilst in those of other countries, as many months are required for the same purposes, owing to tedious regulations and less enterprise. Merchant vessels are built and prepared for sea in the course of four or five months, and they sail faster than those of any other country. The schooners constructed at Baltimore, and known by the name of "pilot-boat schooners," have often sailed with a cargo from an American to an English or French port in seventeen or eighteen days. The American seamen are extremely active and enterprising. Sloops of sixty tons, and eleven men, have sailed from Albany, (160 miles up the Hudson's river,) to the coast of China. The first of this description which arrived there was believed by the natives of the country to be the long-boat of a large merchant vessel, which they vainly looked for during several days. Nantucket sloops of eighty tons, with ten men, double Cape Horn, and pursue the whale fishery in the South Seas. With similar vessels, numerous voyages have been made from the port of New York to the cold regions of Southern Georgia, for the skins and oil of seals and sea-elephants. The American whalemen, after visiting the south-western coast of New Holland, and California, the Malouin, or Falkland, and other isles, touch for refreshments at the Cape of Good Hope, at the Sandwich Islands, or ports of Chili. A commerce with the Fegee Islands has been carried on by small vessels in trifling articles of hardware, which they exchanged for sandal-wood; and with this article they proceeded to Canton, where it was sold for the purpose of incense in religious ceremonies, at the rate of 400 dollars per ton. The American pilot-boats have lately visited the ports of Santa Fe, Caraccas, and Buenos Ayres, for the commerce in dollars and raw materials. Without any previous knowledge of routes, winds, tides, or harbours, the American whalemen and pilot-boat seamen have visited every coast, and, to the astonishment of Europe, have made shorter voyages than old and experienced navigators. Falkland's Island, which seemed too remote and romantic an object for the grasp of national ambition, is but a stage and resting place in the progress of their victorious industry. "No sea but what is vexed with their fisheries, no climate that is not witness to their toils.["] Since the commencement of the war in 1812, the American public and private armed vessels have visited every sea, from Kamschatka to the Irish Channel, and have captured British merchant ships at the very mouths of British harbours. The great injury done to the commerce of England during that war, notwithstanding her powerful navy, bears strong testimony to the activity and enterprise of American seamen. More than 1700 of her vessels were captured during the course of the war; and it has been stated, that only one out of three

Text: David Bailie Warden, *A Statistical, Political, and Historical Account of the United States of North America* (Edinburgh, 1819), III, 280-86.

American vessels employed in commerce were taken by the English during the same period. The state of European warfare, from the year 1802 to 1812, gave to America almost all the carrying trade, or freight of the commercial world, valued at ten *per cent.* upon the capital. The United States also gained five *per cent.* by exchange, so that the annual profits of commerce and foreign navigation have been estimated at fifteen *per cent.* upon the capital.

SLAVERY

85

THE MISSOURI COMPROMISE

from Hezekiah Niles, *Niles' Weekly Register*, December 23, 1820

The Missouri controversy, wrote Jefferson, "like a fire bell in the night, awakened and filled me with terror." John Quincy Adams saw in the Missouri episode the "title page to a great tragic volume." Indeed to many thoughtful Americans the fierce political quarrels touched off by Missouri's bid for statehood in 1818 carried a warning of sectional conflict and disunion.

Under the Constitution, Congress has the power to govern the national territory and admit new states. Eight states had been added to the original thirteen by the end of 1818, and the admission of Alabama the next year again restored the even balance of slave and free states. When the Missouri petition for statehood reached Congress, a group of Northern leaders determined to arrest the further spread of slavery. Representative Tallmadge of New York introduced an amendment requiring the state to prohibit slavery as a condition of acceptance into the Union. The House, where Representatives from the more populous North predominated, approved; the Senate rejected the amendment.

In the great public debate that followed, men chose sides largely in accordance with their sectional affiliations. The broad political issue underlying the Missouri question was the extension of slavery into the Western territories. (Missouri formed a part of the Louisiana Purchase.) Northern spokesmen insisted on the constitutional powers of Congress to check the growth of a pernicious institution by imposing an anti-slavery condition on new states seeking admission. Although few Southerners at this time defended slavery as a positive good, most argued the justice of permitting slaveholders to carry their property into the new territories and to enjoy the necessary legal protection once states were formed. On constitutional grounds they denied the authority of Congress to lay down admission requirements that would deprive a new state of powers held by older members of the Union: in this case, the power to establish the institution of slavery.

When Congress reopened the Missouri debate in 1820, the House again adopted an anti-slavery amendment. The Senate endorsed a moderate proposal, the Thomas amendment, which would permit slavery in Missouri but exclude the institution from the rest of the Louisiana Territory north of 36° 30'. Congress agreed to a solution admitting Missouri as a slave state with the Thomas amendment while adding Maine to the free state side. The Missouri Constitution of 1820 provoked a fresh controversy over admission. A clause requiring future state legislatures to prevent the entry of free Negroes was denounced by many Congressmen as unconstitutional. Finally in 1821 a second compromise was reached. Missouri would be admitted on condition that the state should not construe the offensive clause to authorize the denial of privileges and immunities guaranteed to the citizens of the several states under the Federal Constitution. In rather defiant language Missouri offered an acceptable pledge, and the process of admission was completed. Apparently statesmen had found a compromise settlement of the explosive issue of slavery extension. The growing antagonisms between North and South, however, were to give the question a new urgency in the decade before the Civil War. The section of the Missouri Compromise prohibiting slavery in the Louisiana Territory north of 36° 30' was repealed by the Kansas-Nebraska Act (1854) and declared unconstitutional in the Dred Scott decision (1857). See Chapter 11 for the later developments.

Hezekiah Niles was the founder and first editor of *Niles' Weekly Register*, a highly influential and informative journal of national affairs published in Baltimore from 1811 to 1849. His argument supporting the Missouri Compromise as the best available way out of a bad situation—not as a good in itself—represents the views of many moderate men in all sections. The evils of slavery and the power of Congress to check the spread of the institution into the national territories were plain to Niles. Yet no less obvious were the formidable presence of slavery, the strong commitment of the South to this valuable interest, and the baffling problems of emancipation. Niles thus defends the Compromise as an expedient measure for soothing sectional feelings and promoting national harmony.

. . . So much has been said, written and published on the "Missouri question" that the people, in general, are displeased with the mere sight of the words in print, and few are willing to read much more on the subject. Articles, too, have appeared on both sides of the question, which ought not to have appeared;—hard words will never obtain a victory in matter like this; railing begets railing, and opposition produces opposition. It is human nature even to resist a just claim, if indecently or improperly urged.

Under these circumstances we should have passed over the *new* crisis which the matter has arrived at, but for the consideration that our motives may be misconstrued, as they were on another highly interesting occasion. While we hold ourselves irresponsible to any men or set of men for our own opinions, "a decent respect" for those of others will always induce us to a liberal exposition of them, if the case requires it. Truth is often times elicited from the conflict of opinion; and the hypothesis of Mr. *Jefferson,* that its "errors may be tolerated when reason is left free to combat it," is as a first principle in the mind of every *genuine* republican, whether his complexion is bleached by the northern blast, or darkened by a southern sun.

When the main matter in dispute was under consideration, it was our misfortune not to please either of the great parties to it; yet both of them united and agreed to the principle which we advocated, as being both right and expedient. It is *established* (so far as large majorities in both houses of congress can establish it), that the *power* to check the progress of a slave population within the *territories* of the United States, exists by the constitution; but admitted, that it was not expedient to exert that power in regard to Missouri and Arkansaw. The latter depended on many considerations of no ordinary importance: the safety and feelings of the white population in several of the states appeared to be involved in it, and the rights and feelings of others were as deeply concerned in the subject at large. In this conflict of interests, among persons who possibly desired the same ultimate issue, though their views of it were diametrically opposed, a spirit of conciliation prevailed and

a compromise was effected. The people of those sections of country in which there are few or no slaves or persons of color, very imperfectly appreciate the wants, necessities or general principle of others differently situated. Collectively, the latter deprecate slavery as severely as the former, and dread its increase—but individual cupidity and rashness acts against the common sentiment, in the hope that an event which every body believes must happen, may not happen in their day. It is thus that too many of us act about death; we are sure it must come, yet we commit wrong to acquire property, just as if we should hold and enjoy it forever! That the slave population will, at some certain period, cause the most horrible catastrophe, cannot be doubted—those who possess them act defensively in behalf of all that is nearest and dearest to them, when they endeavor to acquire all the strength and influence to meet that period which they can; and hence the political and civil opposition of these to the restriction which was proposed to be laid on Missouri, &c. They *have* the offensive population, and no feasible plan has yet been contrived to rid them of it, if they were disposed so to do. Will the people of any of the states, so much alive to humanity, pass acts to encourage emancipation by agreeing to receive the emancipated—what will they do, what *can* they do, to assist the people of others to relieve themselves of their unfortunate condition? It is easy to use severe terms against the practice of slavery—but let us first tell the southern people what they can safely do to abolish it, before we, by wholesale, condemn them. No one can hate slavery more than I do—it is a thing opposed to every principle that operates on my mind, as an individual—and, in my own private circle, I do much to discourage it. I am, also, exceedingly jealous of it, so far as it affects my political rights as a citizen of the United States, entitled to be fairly and fully represented, and no more. But I can make great allowances for those who hold slaves in districts where they abound—where, in many cases, their emancipation might be an act

Text: Hezekiah Niles, Editorial in *Niles' Weekly Register,* XIX (December 23, 1820), 265-66.

of cruelty to them and of most serious injury to the white population. Their difference of color is an insuperable barrier to their incorporation within the society; and the mixture of free blacks with slaves is detrimental to the happiness of both, the cause of uncounted crimes. Yet I think that some have urged their defensive character too far—without a proper respect for the rights and feelings of others, whose business it is also [to] judge on the matter, as applicable to an extension of the evil. But we advocated the compromise, as fixing certain points for the future government of all the parties concerned; believing that the moral and political evil of spreading slavery over Missouri and even in Arkansaw, was not greater than that which might have arisen from restriction, though to restrict was right in itself. The harmony of the union, and the peace and prosperity of the white population, most excited our sympathies. We did not fear the dreadful things which some silly folks talked of, but apprehended *geographical* oppositions which might lead to the worst of calamities. We had no pleasant feeling on the compromise, for bad was the best that could be done. Nevertheless, we hoped that the contest was at an end, and that things would settle down and adopt [adapt] themselves to the agreement which necessity imposed.

Thus situated, it was with no little concern that we saw in the constitution which Missouri was about to offer for the sanction of congress, *new* causes of collision. The objectionable provisions cannot be of any use to the new state, as to the things which they aim at. We are willing to believe that they were unthinkingly introduced; but they have the appearance of braving opposition, and of manifesting a spirit which the meekest man feels disposed to resist—to say nothing of one of them as being contrary to the constitution of the United States—that to prevent the emigration and settlement of free blacks and mulattoes. It appears that some of the former and a number of the latter are entitled to bounty lands, for services rendered in the late war: if their lots should be in Missouri, it is idle to pretend they may not settle upon and enjoy them, if they please. But we are not disposed to examine the subject in detail—the *principle* adopted by the convention of Missouri, to give our opinion of it in a few words, is destructive of the *federative* character of our great compact, and may just as well apply to the exclusion of persons with black hair or blue eyes; and no one can seriously apprehend injury from the emigration of free people of color to a slave-holding state. It would be about as reasonable as to expect that the Mississippi will discharge her waters into the lakes, instead of naturally to disembogue them into the Gulf of Mexico. The result, in the house of representatives, was anticipated; but we did think that both houses, with large majorities, would have so decided, as to striking out the offensive provisions, for the sake of harmony, in the spirit of the compromise: all would then have been well, and a great deal of time, trouble and anxiety saved. We totally reject the idea that any thing which it is the business of congress to do, should be left to the judiciary or any other power. With due deference to the eminent gentleman who proposed it, we regret that he did it; for had his plan been adopted, who can tell where the precedent would have stopped? But we think it more strange that, because Missouri was empowered to *make* a constitution, it should be argued that congress was bound to *accept* it. Why, then, are constitutions offered, referred to committees, and sanctioned by both houses? All this is mere mummery, if they are to be accepted at any rate—as contended for by some of the members. No one wishes harm to the people of Missouri—they are of our own kindred and lineage; they may have urged their claims imprudently, and, in our belief, have mistaken their true interests—but they have a right to judge for themselves; and if that judgment is repugnant to the general opinion or principle on the matter, they will yield it, we trust, to the law, and respect the majority.

We had written thus far when we first saw the resolution offered by Mr. Eustis, in the house of representatives, on Tuesday last . . . It precisely meets our wishes, so far as it goes, and may accomplish all that either party is *really* just now disposed to contend for. The anti-restriction members, as well as others, regretted the existence of certain clauses in the constitution of Missouri, as unnecessary, and calculated only to create doubts and excite opposition. Let them be expunged by the *unanimous* voice of congress, and then we shall hope for an obliteration of the feelings which this unfortunate controversy has given birth to, and that all will be willing to disavow sectional interests within the body of the republic; the peace and p[r]osperity of which can only be maintained by a spirit of forbearance and moderation:—and, if we must differ in opinion, let us differ like rational beings, and grant to others the rights which we assume for ourselves, always recollecting that the fairly expressed will of the majority must govern.

86

CHIEF JUSTICE MARSHALL AND THE COMMERCE POWER

from *Gibbons v. Ogden*, 1824

The political history of the United States from 1801 to 1825 is characterized by the triumph of Jeffersonian Democracy and by the changing course of Republican policy in response to problems of European war and national growth. There is, however, another significant history to be noticed, one that depended not upon election results, legislative deliberations, and presidential leadership but rather upon the interpretations of the Constitution by John Marshall, Chief Justice of the Supreme Court from 1801 to 1835 and probably the most influential shaper of constitutional law in the nation's history.

Marshall (1755-1835) was appointed Chief Justice by John Adams a few months before Jefferson assumed the presidency. He had been a Revolutionary officer, a Richmond lawyer, a member of the Virginia Assembly, a diplomatic agent, and a Congressman. In politics he was a lifelong Federalist of the old school of 1787; and he used his great authority as Chief Justice to make the Supreme Court a defender of national supremacy through an age when state-rights doctrines generally dominated public opinion. During his long tenure Marshall raised the court to a position of equality with the other branches of the Federal government (to a position of supremacy, his critics charged); he established his interpretation of crucial features of the Constitution with a series of powerful judicial opinions that were less technical expositions of the law than broad judgments of the nature of the American political system.

In *Marbury v. Madison* (1803) Marshall laid the basis for judicial review of national legislation. In the Dartmouth College case (1819) he developed the doctrine that certain state grants—such as Dartmouth's corporate charter—were in the nature of contracts and so could not be revoked or altered by the legislature without violating the constitutional rule prohibiting impairment of the obligation of contracts. This ruling sharply limited the authority of states to control vested private interests. Marshall's opinion in *McCulloch v. Maryland* (1819) was a compelling defense of the broad construction of congressional powers (cf. Hamilton's view in Document 67) and a resounding denial of the right of states to impede the exercise of such powers.

A distinguished scholar, Edward S. Corwin, has named Marshall's opinion in *Gibbons v. Ogden* (1824) his "profoundest, most statesmanlike" contribution to constitutional law. In 1808 New York had granted a monopoly over steamboat navigation to Robert R. Livingston and Robert Fulton. This exclusive right had passed to Aaron Ogden. Under an act of Congress, Thomas Gibbons had obtained a license to run steamboats between New Jersey and New York. Ogden successfully sued in the New York courts to prevent Gibbons from entering state waters. Gibbons appealed the case to the Supreme Court of the United States and won Marshall's support. By the reasoning shown in the selection that follows, Marshall established the exclusive control of the national government over interstate and foreign commerce, free of state interference. Thus competing state interests could not frustrate the pursuit of broad national objectives in the field of commercial regulation.

Marshall's construction of the commerce clause had its greatest impact in the twentieth century, when pressing social problems led to the expansion of the economic role of the national government. Those judges who upheld New Deal legislation from the late 1930's on were working largely in the Marshall tradition. To many of his own contemporaries, however—and most conspicuously to Presidents Jefferson and Jackson—John Marshall was the infuriating arch-reactionary whose decisions tended to destroy state authority and subject the people to the domination of private business and financial interests.

The appellant contends that this decree is erroneous, because the laws, which purport to give the exclusive privilege it sustains, are repugnant to the constitution and laws of the United States.

They are said to be repugnant—

1st. To that clause in the constitution which authorizes congress to regulate commerce.

Text: Gibbons v. Ogden, 1824 (9 Wheaton 1), in *The Writings of John Marshall upon the Federal Constitution* (Boston: James Munroe & Co., 1839), pp. 287-98, 304-06, 313-14.

2d. To that which authorizes congress to promote the progress of science and useful arts.

The state of New York maintains the constitutionality of these laws; and their legislature, their council of revision, and their judges, have repeatedly concurred in this opinion. It is supported by great names—by names which have all the titles to consideration that virtue, intelligence, and office can bestow. No tribunal can approach the decision of this question without feeling a just and real respect for that opinion which is sustained by such authority; but it is the province of this court, while it respects, not to bow to it implicitly; and the judges must exercise, in the examination of the subject, that understanding which Providence has bestowed upon them, with that independence which the people of the United States expect from this department of the government. . . .

This instrument [the Constitution] contains an enumeration of powers expressly granted by the people to their government. It has been said that these powers ought to be construed strictly. But why ought they to be so construed? Is there one sentence in the constitution which gives countenance to this rule? In the last of the enumerated powers, that which grants expressly the means for carrying all others into execution, congress is authorized "to make all laws which shall be necessary and proper" for the purpose. But this limitation on the means which may be used is not extended to the powers which are conferred; nor is there one sentence in the constitution, which has been pointed out by the gentlemen of the bar, or which we have been able to discern, that prescribes this rule. We do not, therefore, think ourselves justified in adopting it. What do gentlemen mean by a strict construction? If they contend only against that enlarged construction which would extend words beyond their natural and obvious import, we might question the application of the term, but should not controvert the principle. If they contend for that narrow construction which, in support of some theory not to be found in the constitution, would deny to the government those powers which the words of the grant, as usually understood, import, and which are consistent with the general views and objects of the instrument; for that narrow construction which would cripple the government, and render it unequal to the objects for which it is declared to be instituted, and to which the powers given, as fairly understood, render it competent; then we cannot perceive the propriety of this strict construction, nor adopt it as the rule by which the constitution is to be expounded. As men, whose intentions require no concealment, generally employ the words which most directly and aptly express the ideas they intend to convey, the enlightened patriots who framed our constitution, and the people who adopted it, must be understood to have employed words in their natural sense, and to have intended what they have said. If, from the imperfection of human language, there should be serious doubts respecting the extent of any given power, it is a well settled rule that the objects for which it was given, especially when those objects are expressed in the instrument itself, should have great influence in the construction. . . .

The words are, "Congress shall have power to regulate commerce with foreign nations, and among the several states, and with the Indian tribes."

The subject to be regulated is commerce; and our constitution being, as was aptly said at the bar, one of enumeration, and not of definition, to ascertain the extent of the power it becomes necessary to settle the meaning of the word. The counsel for the appellee would limit it to traffic, to buying and selling, or the interchange of commodities, and do not admit that it comprehends navigation. This would restrict a general term, applicable to many objects, to one of its significations. Commerce, undoubtedly, is traffic, but it is something more; it is intercourse. It describes the commercial intercourse between nations, and parts of nations, in all its branches, and is regulated by prescribing rules for carrying on that intercourse. The mind can scarcely conceive a system for regulating commerce between nations, which shall exclude all laws concerning navigation, which shall be silent on the admission of the vessels of the one nation into the ports of the other, and be confined to prescribing rules for the conduct of individuals in the actual employment of buying and selling, or of barter. . . .

To what commerce does this power extend? The constitution informs us, to commerce "with foreign nations, and among the several states, and with the Indian tribes."

It has, we believe, been universally admitted that these words comprehend every species of commercial intercourse between the United States and foreign nations. No sort of trade can be carried on between this country and any other, to which this power does not extend. It has been truly said that commerce, as the word is used in the constitution, is a unit, every part of which is indicated by the term.

If this be the admitted meaning of the word, in its application to foreign nations, it must carry the same meaning throughout the sentence, and remain a unit, unless there be some plain, intelligible cause which alters it.

The subject to which the power is next applied is to commerce "among the several states." The word "among" means intermingled with. A thing which is among others is intermingled with them. Commerce among the states cannot stop at the external boundary line of each state, but may be introduced into the interior.

It is not intended to say that these words comprehend that commerce which is completely internal, which is carried on between man and man in a state, or between different parts of the same state, and which does not extend to or affect other states. Such a power would be inconvenient; and is certainly unnecessary.

Comprehensive as the word "among" is, it may very properly be restricted to that commerce which concerns more states than one. The phrase is not one which would probably have been selected to indicate the completely interior traffic of a state, because it is not an apt phrase for that purpose; and the enumeration of the particular classes of commerce to which the power was to be extended would not have been made, had the intention been to extend the power to every description. The enumeration presupposes something not enumerated; and that something, if we regard the language or the subject of the sentence, must be the exclusively internal commerce of a state. The genius and character of the whole government seem to be, that its action is to be applied to all the external concerns of the nation, and to those internal concerns which affect the states generally; but not to those which are completely within a particular state, which do not affect other states, and with which it is not necessary to interfere for the purpose of executing some of the general powers of the government. The completely internal commerce of a state, then, may be considered as reserved for the state itself. . . .

We are now arrived at the inquiry, What is this power?

It is the power to regulate; that is, to prescribe the rule by which commerce is to be governed. This power, like all others vested in congress, is complete in itself, may be exercised to its utmost extent, and acknowledges no limitations other than are prescribed in the constitution. These are expressed in plain terms, and do not affect the questions which arise in this case, or which have been discussed at the bar. If, as has always been understood, the sovereignty of congress, though limited to specified objects, is plenary as to those objects, the power

over commerce with foreign nations, and among the several states, is vested in congress as absolutely as it would be in a single government, having in its constitution the same restrictions on the exercise of the power as are found in the constitution of the United States. The wisdom and the discretion of congress, their identity with the people, and the influence which their constituents possess at elections, are, in this, as in many other instances, as that, for example, of declaring war, the sole restraints on which they have relied to secure them from its abuse. They are the restraints on which the people must often rely solely, in all representative governments.

The power of congress, then, comprehends navigation within the limits of every state in the union; so far as that navigation may be, in any manner, connected with "commerce with foreign nations, or among the several states or with the Indian tribes." It may, of consequence, pass the jurisdictional line of New York, and act upon the very waters to which the prohibition now under consideration applies.

But it has been urged with great earnestness, that, although the power of congress to regulate commerce with foreign nations, and among the several states, be coëxtensive with the subject itself, and have no other limits than are prescribed in the constitution, yet the states may severally exercise the same power within their respective jurisdictions. In support of this argument it is said that they possessed it, as an inseparable attribute of sovereignty, before the formation of the constitution, and still retain it, except so far as they have surrendered it by that instrument; that this principle results from the nature of the government, and is secured by the tenth amendment, that an affirmative grant of power is not exclusive, unless in its own nature it be such that the continued exercise of it by the former possessor is inconsistent with the grant, and that this is not of that description.

The appellant, conceding these postulates, except the last, contends that full power to regulate a particular subject implies the whole power, and leaves no residuum; that a grant of the whole is incompatible with the existence of a right in another to any part of it. . . .

In discussing the question, whether this power is still in the states, in the case under consideration, we may dismiss from it the inquiry, whether it is surrendered by the mere grant to congress, or is retained until congress shall exercise the power. We may dismiss that inquiry, because it has been exercised, and the regulations which congress deemed it proper to make are now in full operation. The sole question is, Can a state regulate commerce with foreign nations and among the states, while congress is regulating it? . . .

It has been contended by the counsel for the appellant, that, as the word "to regulate" implies in its nature full power over the thing to be regulated, it excludes, necessarily, the action of all others that would perform the same operation on the same thing. That regulation is designed for the entire result, applying to those parts which remain as they were, as well as to those which are altered. It produces a uniform whole, which is as much disturbed and deranged by changing what the regulating power designs to leave untouched as that on which it has operated.

There is great force in this argument, and the court is not satisfied that it has been refuted.

Since, however, in exercising the power of regulating their own purely internal affairs, whether of trading or police, the states may sometimes enact laws the validity of which depends on their interfering with, and being contrary to, an act of congress passed in pursuance of the constitution, the court will enter upon the inquiry, whether the laws of New York, as expounded by the highest tribunal of that state, have, in their application to this case, come into collision with an act of congress, and deprived a citizen of a right to which that act entitles him. Should this collision exist, it will be immaterial whether those laws were passed in virtue of a concurrent power "to regulate commerce with foreign nations and among the several states," or, in virtue of a power to regulate their domestic trade and police. In one case and the other the acts of New York must yield to the law of congress; and the decision, sustaining the privilege they confer against a right given by a law of the union, must be erroneous.

This opinion has been frequently expressed in this court, and is founded as well on the nature of the government as on the words of the constitution. In argument, however, it has been contended, that, if a law passed by a state, in the exercise of its acknowledged sovereignty, comes into conflict with a law passed by congress in pursuance of the constitution, they affect the subject, and each other, like equal opposing powers.

But the framers of our constitution foresaw this state of things, and provided for it, by declaring the supremacy not only of itself, but of the laws made in pursuance of it. The nullity of any act inconsistent with the constitution is produced by the declaration that the constitution is the supreme law. The appropriate application of that part of the clause, which confers the same supremacy on laws and treaties, is to such acts of the state legislatures as do not transcend their powers, but, though enacted in the execution of acknowledged state powers, interfere with, or are contrary to, the laws of congress made in pursuance of the constitution, or some treaty made under the authority of the United States. In every such case the act of congress, or the treaty, is supreme; and the law of the state, though enacted in the exercise of powers not controverted, must yield to it. . . .

Powerful and ingenious minds, taking, as postulates, that the powers expressly granted to the government of the union are to be contracted, by construction, into the narrowest possible compass, and that the original powers of the states are retained, if any possible construction will retain them, may, by a course of well digested, but refined and metaphysical reasoning, founded on these premises, explain away the constitution of our country, and leave it, a magnificent structure, indeed, to look at, but totally unfit for use. They may so entangle and perplex the understanding as to obscure principles which were before thought quite plain, and induce doubts where, if the mind were to pursue its own course, none would be perceived. In such a case it is peculiarly necessary to recur to safe and fundamental principles, to sustain those principles, and, when sustained, to make them the tests of the arguments to be examined.

FOREIGN POLICY

87   TWO WORLDS: THE MONROE DOCTRINE

from James Monroe, Seventh Annual Message, December 2, 1823

James Monroe (1758-1831), the last in the Virginia line of presidents, ranks well below his distinguished predecessors, Washington, Jefferson, and Madison. Monroe's overwhelming electoral victories in 1816 and 1820 were not a tribute to a remarkable presidential leader so much as a sign of the fall of Federalism, which left the Republican party virtually unopposed in the field. The men who placed their original mark upon the so-called "Era of Good Feelings" (1816-1824) were such figures as Clay and Calhoun, the bold General Jackson, the great Chief Justice Marshall, and the masterful Secretary of State, John Quincy Adams.

The Monroe administration made its most important contributions in the field of foreign policy. East Florida was acquired from Spain (1819-1821) by a combination of military threats and diplomatic pressures. The Florida treaty wrote off American claims to Texas but transferred to the United States the Spanish claim to the Oregon country. The striking event in the diplomatic record, however, is the announcement of the Monroe Doctrine.

After the destruction of the Napoleonic Empire, the great powers of Europe formed a political "Concert"—commonly but inaccurately referred to as the Holy Alliance—to sustain "legitimate" monarchies against the threat of revolution. England drew away from the alliance when it appeared that her own national interests might be threatened by a powerful Continental bloc. The French invasion of Spain in 1823 to put down an anti-Bourbon revolution especially stirred English apprehensions and led Foreign Secretary Canning to approach the United States minister in London with a scheme for Anglo-American collaboration.

The joint concern of the two nations lay in Latin America, where the former Spanish colonies had been in the process of establishing independent republics since 1809. After a period of cautious waiting, the United States decided in 1822 to recognize the new governments. Although Spain alone was too weak to recover its American empire, the European alliance ("Holy Alliance") offered a serious threat of intervention in the New World. Strategic and commercial interests gave both England and the United States strong reasons for opposing such intervention. Moreover, the United States was alarmed by the recent action of the Czar, extending Russian jurisdiction southward from Alaska (Russian America) into the Oregon country of the Pacific Northwest.

Leading Americans, including Jefferson and Madison, advised President Monroe to answer favorably England's invitation to joint action. But Secretary of State John Quincy Adams convinced Monroe of the advantages of an independent course. Adams was persuaded (correctly, as it turned out) that the strength of the British Navy would discourage French intervention in any case, and he recognized that a joint declaration with England would require a pledge by the United States itself to forego future territorial acquisitions in the former Spanish territories.

Monroe decided to place his declaration of policy in the Annual Message of December 2, 1823. The terms are recorded in the following selection. Historians have traced the leading foreign policy principles of the Monroe Doctrine to earlier sources, including Washington and Jefferson. Yet Monroe with the substantial aid of John Quincy Adams drew the elements together in a distinctive formulation that would in the course of the century acquire the force of tradition. In the setting of the times, however, the Monroe Doctrine was but a unilateral declaration of American intentions, without standing in international law, which commanded far less respect among the European powers than did the presence of a British Navy ready to sustain England's interest in Latin-American independence.

Washington, December 2, 1823.

Fellow-Citizens of the Senate and House of Representatives: . . .

At the proposal of the Russian Imperial Government, made through the minister of the Emperor residing here, a full power and instructions have been transmitted to the minister of the United States at St. Petersburg to arrange by amicable negotiation the respective rights and interests of the two nations on the northwest coast of this continent. A similar proposal had been made by His Imperial Majesty to the Government of Great Britain, which likewise been acceded to. The Government of the United States has been desirous by this friendly proceeding of manifesting the great value which they have invariably attached to the friendship of the Emperor and their solicitude to cultivate the best understanding with his Government. In the discussions to which this interest has given rise and in the arrangements by which they may terminate the occasion has been judged proper for asserting, as a principle in which the rights and interests of the United States are involved, that the American continents, by the free and independent condition which they have assumed

Text: James D. Richardson (ed.), *A Compilation of the Messages and Papers of the Presidents, 1789-1897* (Washington, D.C.: Government Printing Office, 1897), II, 207, 209, 217-19.

and maintain, are henceforth not to be considered as subjects for future colonization by any European powers. . . .

It was stated at the commencement of the last session that a great effort was then making in Spain and Portugal to improve the condition of the people of those countries, and that it appeared to be conducted with extraordinary moderation. It need scarcely be remarked that the result has been so far very different from what was then anticipated. Of events in that quarter of the globe, with which we have so much intercourse and from which we derive our origin, we have always been anxious and interested spectators. The citizens of the United States cherish sentiments the most friendly in favor of the liberty and happiness of their fellow-men on that side of the Atlantic. In the wars of the European powers in matters relating to themselves we have never taken any part, nor does it comport with our policy so to do. It is only when our rights are invaded or seriously menaced that we resent injuries or make preparation for our defense. With the movements in this hemisphere we are of necessity more immediately connected, and by causes which must be obvious to all enlightened and impartial observers. The political system of the allied powers is essentially different in this respect from that of America. This difference proceeds from that which exists in their respective Governments; and to the defense of our own, which has been achieved by the loss of so much blood and treasure, and matured by the wisdom of their most enlightened citizens, and under which we have enjoyed unexampled felicity, this whole nation is devoted. We owe it, therefore, to candor and to the amicable relations existing between the United States and those powers to declare that we should consider any attempt on their part to extend their system to any portion of this hemisphere as dangerous to our peace and safety. With the existing colonies or dependencies of any European power we have not interfered and shall not interfere. But with the Governments who have declared their independence and maintained it, and whose independence we have, on great consideration and on just principles, acknowledged, we could not view any interposition for the purpose of oppressing them, or controlling in any other manner their destiny, by any European power in any other light than as the manifestation of an unfriendly disposition toward the United States. In the war between those new Governments and Spain we declared our neutrality at the time of their recognition, and to this we have adhered, and shall continue to adhere, provided no change shall occur which, in the judgment of the competent authorities of this Government, shall make a corresponding change on the part of the United States indispensable to their security.

The late events in Spain and Portugal shew that Europe is still unsettled. Of this important fact no stronger proof can be adduced than that the allied powers should have thought it proper, on any principle satisfactory to themselves, to have interposed by force in the internal concerns of Spain. To what extent such interposition may be carried, on the same principle, is a question in which all independent powers whose governments differ from theirs are interested, even those most remote, and surely none more so than the United States. Our policy in regard to Europe, which was adopted at an early stage of the wars which have so long agitated that quarter of the globe, nevertheless remains the same, which is, not to interfere in the internal concerns of any of its powers; to consider the government *de facto* as the legitimate government for us; to cultivate friendly relations with it, and to preserve those relations by a frank, firm, and manly policy, meeting in all instances the just claims of every power, submitting to injuries from none. But in regard to those continents circumstances are eminently and conspicuously different. It is impossible that the allied powers should extend their political system to any portion of either continent without endangering our peace and happiness; nor can anyone believe that our southern brethren, if left to themselves, would adopt it of their own accord. It is equally impossible, therefore, that we should behold such interposition in any form with indifference. If we look to the comparative strength and resources of Spain and those new Governments, and their distance from each other, it must be obvious that she can never subdue them. It is still the true policy of the United States to leave the parties to themselves, in the hope that other powers will pursue the same course. . . .

NATIONAL REPUBLICANISM

88

THE NEW ADAMS

from John Quincy Adams, Inaugural Address, March 4, 1825

John Adams was defeated for re-election in the "Revolution of 1800" which carried Jeffersonian democracy to power. His son, John Quincy, met a similar fate at the end of his first administration, when Jacksonian Democracy won control of the national government. Both Adamses were men of virtue and talent who made distinguished contributions to the American republic; both conspicuously lacked the gifts for attracting popular support.

As the son of an eminent diplomat and political leader, John Quincy Adams was bred in the public service of the nation. While still in his twenties, he was appointed minister to the Netherlands by George Washington. After practicing law in Boston, he served as United States Senator for Massachusetts (1803-1808), held the chair of rhetoric and oratory at Harvard, and then in 1809 became American minister to St. Petersburg by appointment of James Madison. In 1814 he helped to negotiate the peace treaty with Great Britain and later went to England as American minister. During the Monroe administrations (1817-1825), Adams was the notably vigorous and effective Secretary of State. (See Document 87.)

Echoing the politics of his father, the young John Quincy Adams published strictures on the Federalist side during the party battles of the 1790's. He soon separated himself from the bitter-end Federalism of New England, however, and built his diplomatic career under the Republican administrations. The firm nationalism of his foreign policies was equally evident in his approach to domestic affairs. In the election of 1824, Adams and Clay were the presidential candidates clearly identified with the program of tariffs, internal improvements, and national banking that had enlisted widespread support since 1816. William H. Crawford of Georgia represented the "Old Republican" view, while Andrew Jackson of Tennessee was the popular hero of the Battle of New Orleans who symbolized equalitarian democracy. Jackson led in the electoral vote but failed of a majority. In the House of Representatives a coalition of Clay and Adams men won the presidency for John Quincy Adams, who later gave Clay the State Department. The alliance came to be denounced by Jackson men as the "corrupt bargain," and the charge, though lacking much credible evidence, seriously damaged Adams' popular reputation.

The Inaugural Address of John Quincy Adams (1825) reflects the history of a decade when party lines were blurred and common principles and purposes seemed to overshadow the differences among Americans. Peace in Europe promised a further relaxation of domestic tensions under a regime that would combine the best elements of the Republican and the Federalist heritage. Before the end of his administration Adams would undergo a harsh education in domestic politics. The old hostility to Hamiltonian measures revived with new intensity. Opposing factions gave the Adams administration little peace and soon began to take the shape of the organized and disciplined parties that would compete for power in the following decades under the names of Democrats and Whigs.

It is a source of gratification and of encouragement to me to observe that the great result of this [republican] experiment upon the theory of human rights has at the close of that generation by which it was formed been crowned with success equal to the most sanguine expectations of its founders. Union, justice, tranquillity, the common defense, the general welfare, and the blessings of liberty—all have been promoted by the Government under which we have lived. Standing at this point of time, looking back to that generation which has gone by and forward to that which is advancing, we may at once indulge in grateful exultation and in cheering hope. From the experience of the past we derive instructive lessons for the future. Of the two great political parties which have divided the opinions and feelings of our country, the candid and the just will now admit that both have contributed splendid talents, spotless integrity, ardent pa-

Text: James D. Richardson (ed.), *A Compilation of the Messages and Papers of the Presidents, 1789-1897* (Washington, D.C.: Government Printing Office, 1897), II, 294-97.

triotism, and disinterested sacrifices to the forma- tion and administration of this Government, and that both have required a liberal indulgence for a portion of human infirmity and error. The revolutionary wars of Europe, commencing pre- cisely at the moment when the Government of the United States first went into operation under this Constitution, excited a collision of sentiments and of sympathies which kindled all the passions and imbittered the conflict of parties till the nation was involved in war and the Union was shaken to its center. This time of trial embraced a period of five and twenty years, during which the policy of the Union in its relations with Europe constituted the principal basis of our political divisions and the most arduous part of the action of our Federal Government. With the catastrophe in which the wars of the French Revolution terminated, and our own subsequent peace with Great Britain, this baneful weed of party strife was uprooted. From that time no difference of principle, connected either with the theory of government or with our intercourse with foreign nations, has existed or been called forth in force sufficient to sustain a continued combination of parties or to give more than wholesome animation to public sentiment or legislative debate. Our political creed is, without a dissenting voice that can be heard, that the will of the people is the source and the happiness of the people the end of all legitimate government upon earth; that the best security for the benefi- cence and the best guaranty against the abuse of power consists in the freedom, the purity, and the frequency of popular elections; that the Gen- eral Government of the Union and the separate governments of the States are all sovereignties of limited powers, fellow-servants of the same mas-

ters, uncontrolled within their respective spheres, uncontrollable by encroachments upon each other; that the firmest security of peace is the preparation during peace of the defenses of war; that a rigorous economy and accountability of public expenditures should guard against the aggravation and alleviate when possible the bur- den of taxation; that the military should be kept in strict subordination to the civil power; that the freedom of the press and of religious opinion should be inviolate; that the policy of our country is peace and the ark of our salvation union are articles of faith upon which we are all now agreed. If there have been those who doubted whether a confederated representative democracy were a government competent to the wise and orderly management of the common concerns of a mighty nation, those doubts have been dis- pelled; if there have been projects of partial con- federacies to be erected upon the ruins of the Union, they have been scattered to the winds; if there have been dangerous attachments to one foreign nation and antipathies against another, they have been extinguished. Ten years of peace, at home and abroad, have assuaged the animos- ities of political contention and blended into harmony the most discordant elements of public opinion. There still remains one effort of mag- nanimity, one sacrifice of prejudice and passion, to be made by the individuals throughout the na- tion who have heretofore followed the standards of political party. It is that of discarding every remnant of rancor against each other, of embrac- ing as countrymen and friends, and of yielding to talents and virtue alone that confidence which in times of contention for principle was bestowed only upon those who bore the badge of party communion. . . .

89

THE BENEFITS OF INTERNAL IMPROVEMENTS

from John Quincy Adams, First Annual Message, December 6, 1825

In his first Annual Message (1825), John Quincy Adams sketched a grand design for employing the powers of the national government to achieve "the progressive improve- ment of the condition of the governed." This, he argued, was the "great object of the institution of civil government." Roads and canals linking the sections of the nation would contribute to material improvement; and no less important was the moral, political, and intellectual progress that would follow such measures as the establish- ment of a national university, the encouragement of explorations in the Northwest, and the building of an astronomical observatory. The surplus revenue of the federal government, Adams believed, would support his program for promoting national progress.

Although Congress responded with increased grants for river and harbor improve- ment and for the extension of the National Road beyond Wheeling (in what is now West Virginia), neither legislators nor the broad public sympathized with Adams' ambitious program. Southern leaders were openly hostile. In his efforts to satisfy the grievances of the Creek and Cherokee Indians, Adams ran into resistance from the governor of Georgia and aroused further Southern and Western resentment. Congressional opponents embarrassed his efforts to send delegates to a Pan-American conference. The "tariff of abominations" (1828), loaded with heavy duties on raw materials as well as manufactures, further discredited the Adams administration in the South, although low-tariff men had helped to incorporate offensive terms in the hope of defeating the whole measure. Despite the talents and experience of the President, the administration was an inglorious failure.

Adams' message of 1835 expresses a view of the energetic role of national government that was passing into popular disfavor. (Compare Henry Clay's version of the "American System" in Document 118 below.) More restrained versions of this position would guide the National Republican and Whig party oppositions of the next decade. Of greater significance, the basic view of government responsibility for promoting "progressive improvement" was applied *within* the states. The successful completion of New York's Erie Canal in 1825 introduced an era of bold state spending for public improvements, especially canals.

Washington, December 6, 1825

Fellow-Citizens of the Senate and of the House of Representatives: . . .

Upon this first occasion of addressing the Legislature of the Union, with which I have been honored, in presenting to their view the execution so far as it has been effected of the measures sanctioned by them for promoting the internal improvement of our country, I can not close the communication without recommending to their calm and persevering consideration the general principle in a more enlarged extent. The great object of the institution of civil government is the improvement of the condition of those who are parties to the social compact, and no government, in whatever form constituted, can accomplish the lawful ends of its institution but in proportion as it improves the condition of those over whom it is established. Roads and canals, by multiplying and facilitating the communications and intercourse between distant regions and multitudes of men, are among the most important means of improvement. But moral political, intellectual improvement are duties assigned by the Author of Our Existence to social no less than to individual man. For the fulfillment of those duties governments are invested with power, and to the attainment of the end—the progressive improvement of the condition of the governed—the exercise of delegated powers is a duty as sacred and indispensable as the usurpation of powers not granted is criminal and odious. Among the first, perhaps the very first, instrument for the improvement of the condition of men is knowledge, and to the acquisition of much of the knowledge adapted to the wants, the comforts, and enjoyments of human life public institutions and seminaries of learning

are essential. So convinced of this was the first of my predecessors in this office, now first in the memory, as, living, he was first in the hearts, of our countrymen, that once and again in his addresses to the Congresses with whom he cooperated in the public service he earnestly recommended the establishment of seminaries of learning, to prepare for all the emergencies of peace and war—a national university and a military academy. With respect to the latter, had he lived to the present day, in turning his eyes to the institution at West Point he would have enjoyed the gratification of his most earnest wishes; but in surveying the city which has been honored with his name he would have seen the spot of earth which he had destined and bequeathed to the use and benefit of his country as the site for an university still bare and barren.

In assuming her station among the civilized nations of the earth it would seem that our country had contracted the engagement to contribute her share of mind, of labor, and of expense to the improvement of those parts of knowledge which lie beyond the reach of individual acquisition, and particularly to geographical and astronomical science. Looking back to the history only of the half century since the declaration of our independence, and observing the generous emulation with which the Governments of France, Great Britain, and Russia have devoted the genius, the intelligence, the treasures of their respective nations to the common improvement of the species in these branches of science, is it not incumbent upon us to inquire whether we are not bound by obligations of a high and honorable character to contribute our portion of

Text: James D. Richardson (ed.), *A Compilation of the Messages and Papers of the Presidents, 1789-1897* (Washington, D.C.: Government Printing Office, 1897), II, 299, 311-17.

energy and exertion to the common stock? The voyages of discovery prosecuted in the course of that time at the expense of those nations have not only redounded to their glory, but to the improvement of human knowledge. We have been partakers of that improvement and owe for it a sacred debt, not only of gratitude, but of equal or proportional exertion in the same common cause. Of the cost of these undertakings, if the mere expenditures of outfit, equipment, and completion of the expeditions were to be considered the only charges, it would be unworthy of a great and generous nation to take a second thought. One hundred expeditions of circumnavigation like those of Cook and La Perouse would not burden the exchequer of the nation fitting them out so much as the ways and means of defraying a single campaign in war. But if we take into the account the lives of those benefactors of mankind of which their services in the cause of their species were the purchase, how shall the cost of those heroic enterprises be estimated, and what compensation can be made to them or to their countries for them? Is it not by bearing them in affectionate remembrance? Is it not still more by imitating their example—by enabling countrymen of our own to pursue the same career and to hazard their lives in the same cause?

In inviting the attention of Congress to the subject of internal improvements upon a view thus enlarged it is not my design to recommend the equipment of an expedition for circumnavigating the globe for purposes of scientific research and inquiry. We have objects of useful investigation nearer ·home, and to which our cares may be more beneficially applied. The interior of our own territories has yet been very imperfectly explored. Our coasts along many degrees of latitude upon the shores of the Pacific Ocean, though much frequented by our spirited commercial navigators, have been barely visited by our public ships. The River of the West [the Columbia], first fully discovered and navigated by a countryman of our own, still bears the name of the ship in which he ascended its waters, and claims the protection of our armed national flag at its mouth. With the establishment of a military post there or at some other point of that coast, recommended by my predecessor and already matured in the deliberations of the last Congress, I would suggest the expediency of connecting the equipment of a public ship for the exploration of the whole northwest coast of this continent. . . .

Connected with the establishment of an university, or separate from it, might be undertaken the erection of an astronomical observatory, with provision for the support of an astronomer, to be in constant attendance of observation upon the phenomena of the heavens, and for the periodical publication of his observations. It is with no feeling of pride as an American that the remark may be made that on the comparatively small territorial surface of Europe there are existing upward of 130 of these light-houses of the skies, while throughout the whole American hemisphere there is not one. If we reflect a moment upon the discoveries which in the last four centuries have been made in the physical constitution of the universe by the means of these buildings and of observers stationed in them, shall we doubt of their usefulness to every nation? And while scarcely a year passes over our heads without bringing some new astronomical discovery to light, which we must fain receive at second hand from Europe, are we not cutting ourselves off from the means of returning light for light while we have neither observatory nor observer upon our half of the globe and the earth revolves in perpetual darkness to our unsearching eyes? . . .

The Constitution under which you are assembled is a charter of limited powers. After full and solemn deliberation upon all or any of the objects which, urged by an irresistible sense of my own duty, I have recommended to your attention should you come to the conclusion that, however desirable in themselves, the enactment of laws for effecting them would transcend the powers committed to you by that venerable instrument which we are all bound to support, let no consideration induce you to assume the exercise of powers not granted to you by the people. But if the power to exercise exclusive legislation in all cases whatsoever over the District of Columbia; if the power to lay and collect taxes, duties, imposts, and excises, to pay the debts and provide for the common defense and general welfare of the United States; if the power to regulate commerce with foreign nations and among the several States and with the Indian tribes, to fix the standard of weights and measures, to establish post-offices and post-roads, to declare war, to raise and support armies, to provide and maintain a navy, to dispose of and make all needful rules and regulations respecting the territory or other property belonging to the United States, and to make all laws which shall be necessary and proper for carrying these powers into execution—if these powers and others enumerated in the Constitution may be effectually brought into action by laws promoting the improvement of agriculture, commerce, and manufactures, the cultivation and encouragement of the mechanic and of the elegant arts, the advancement of literature, and the progress of the sciences, ornamental and profound, to refrain from exercising them for the benefit of the people themselves would be to hide in the earth the talent committed to our charge—would be treachery to the most sacred of trusts.

The spirit of improvement is abroad upon the earth. It stimulates the hearts and sharpens the faculties not of our fellow-citizens alone, but of the nations of Europe and of their rulers. While dwelling with pleasing satisfaction upon the superior excellence of our political institutions, let us not be unmindful that liberty is power; that the nation blessed with the largest portion of liberty must in proportion to its numbers be the most powerful nation upon earth, and that the tenure of power by man is, in the moral purposes of his Creator, upon condition that it shall be exercised to ends of beneficence, to improve the condition of himself and his fellowmen. While foreign nations less blessed with that freedom which is power than ourselves are advancing with gigantic strides in the career of public improvement, were we to slumber in indolence or fold up our arms and proclaim to the world that we are palsied by the will of our constituents, would it not be to cast away the bounties of Providence and doom ourselves to perpetual inferiority? In the course of the year now drawing to its close we have beheld, under the auspices and at the expense of one State of this Union, a new university unfolding its portals to the sons of science and holding up the torch of human improvement to eyes that seek the light. We have seen under the persevering and enlightened enterprise of another State the waters of our Western lakes mingle with those of the ocean. If undertakings like these have been accomplished in the compass of a few years by the authority of single members of our Confederation, can we, the representative authorities of the whole Union, fall behind our fellow-servants in the exercise of the trust committed to us for the benefit of our common sovereign by the accomplishment of works important to the whole and to which neither the authority nor the resources of any one State can be adequate?

Finally, fellow-citizens, I shall await with cheering hope and faithful cooperation the result of your deliberations, assured that, without encroaching upon the powers reserved to the authorities of the respective States or to the people, you will, with a due sense of your obligations to your country and of the high responsibilities weighing upon yourselves, give efficacy to the means committed to you for the common good. And may He who searches the hearts of the children of men prosper your exertions to secure the blessings of peace and promote the highest welfare of our country.

CHAPTER 8

Reason, Nature, and Republicanism

The period of American history which inspired a revolution and gave birth to a new nation saw also the formulation of a general pattern of political and moral principles. These principles are not only the foundation of American democratic ideas but also a classic statement of political ideals for all time.

In terms of intellectual movements, the period from 1763 to 1825 was the culmination of the American Enlightenment, which had begun in the early eighteenth century. The general characteristics of the Enlightenment are discussed in the introduction to Part I, Chapter 2. Men like Thomas Jefferson and John Adams were influenced by the same ideas which earlier had been developed by Benjamin Franklin and others. Some new tendencies in thought also appeared in this period, heralding the appearance in America of a new intellectual movement, *Romanticism,* discussed in Part III.

THE REPUBLIC OF REASON

The end of the eighteenth century was a time of violent political controversy, influencing the entire intellectual life of the time. Arguments were sought for and against the Revolution, the Constitution, and the policies of the first two Federalist administrations. By the end of Jefferson's ·administration, however, most of the virulence had faded from these debates. Political battles were waged after 1808 largely over specific means and policies, for out of the revolutionary and constitutional debates had developed a number of philosophical and political principles which became generally accepted by most American thinkers. Though changed somewhat in filtering through a century and a half of new experiences, these principles not only have survived but still constitute the root of our American political faith.

In form these principles were a series of ideas about man, nature, society, and the meaning of America. The philosophy that they constitute is usually called republicanism.[1]

The most eloquent and profound definition of the republican *philosophy* was made by Thomas Jefferson (1743-1826), who, like many of the "Founding Fathers," was a philosopher as well as a practical politician. Jefferson believed that man was basically rational and moral and that God had given him certain inalienable rights. As the Declaration of Independence illustrates, Jefferson felt that the purpose of government was essentially the protection of these rights. Jefferson further insisted that all men had a right to as much self-government as was possible within the boundaries of civil society. In this sense he was an equalitarian. However, Jefferson did not think that all men are equal in talents and virtue nor that all men are equally qualified to rule. In the best kind of society, as he conceived it, all men should have considerable freedom of opportunity and choice, thereby governing themselves in many ways; *but* only the few most talented, educated, and virtuous should be delegated the power to make laws and govern others.

A particular group of ideas about *nature* was also an important part of Jefferson's republicanism. To him, as to most men of the Enlightenment, nature was defined as the non-human physical universe. Nature—like man—was created by God to follow certain moral and physical laws, such as the laws of liberty, and equality of opportunity. For this reason nature had a certain superiority to the artificial societies which men of the past, being ignorant of these natural laws, had created and which denied individual liberty and contained class structures violating equal rights. However, Jefferson did not think, like many Americans of a later period, that man could intuitively discover true and right principles by going directly to nature. On the contrary, nature held for him primarily the material and discipline for the exercise of man's reason and creativity; nature was a benevolent force to be understood and controlled for man's benefit rather than a direct source of inspiration and truth.

The creation of the good republican society required also, in Jefferson's eyes, the victory of man over his own ignorance and passions, as well as the elimination of the false ideas and institutions he had accumulated over the course of history. Therefore the education of the mass of the people to an understanding of their rights and obligations as members of a free society was an essential tenet of his political creed.

Jefferson did believe that with the help of education the majority of men could be brought into the light of reason and morality. For this reason, the new nation of the United States had a crucial place in his philosophy. America was man's first real opportunity in all history to free himself from the tyranny of the past, a new and virgin land where men might recreate society in accordance with the natural laws of the universe.

Although Jefferson's basic philosophical and political principles were accepted in theory by most of his contemporaries, many men were not as sanguine as he about the realization of these principles in actual life. The most profound of these friendly but skeptical critics of republican ideals was John Adams (1735-1826), Jefferson's predecessor as president. Like many others, Adams felt that man's reason and morality are constantly overbalanced by his greed, ambition, and

---

[1] The term "republicanism," as used here, of course, denotes a general philosophy of government and does not refer to the policies of any specific political party.

ignorance. He believed, therefore, that an effective republican government was obliged to compromise and give a strong role to such irrational and "unnatural" but powerful social forces as religion, tradition, and social rank in order to provide a check to the passions and appetites of men. What often happened at the polling places of the early republic, as illustrated in the biting satire of Document 96, suggests that there was much to be said for Adams' reservations.

A NEW MAN IN A NEW WORLD

Besides being a key concept in the republican philosophy, *nature* had many other meanings for Americans of the early republic. It was the wilderness environment of the "New Man" reported by Crèvecoeur. This French emigrant saw a free and independent American character growing out of a close contact with nature. Nature was also the new continent that Lewis and Clark explored and that Jefferson opened for settlement with the Louisiana Purchase. It was the setting for a new society which ardent patriots proudly offered as a model for Old World imitation, and the raw material for a new American language and literature.

The Enlightenment's emphasis on nature was so strong that some thinkers came to equate nature and morality, feeling that civilization itself was an artificial restraint on man's natural goodness and genius. As the advance of the frontier made the wilderness less an immediate experience than a source of romance for most Americans, legends began to grow up around extraordinary frontier characters like Daniel Boone (1734-1820). Along with these legends there developed an ideal of the *natural man,* who was thought to be in many respects the superior of the polished product of civilized society. This idea was an important precursor of *romanticism,* which was to dominate American thought between 1825 and the Civil War.

THE USES OF REASON: ENLIGHTENMENT VS. CHRISTIAN ORTHODOXY

The Enlightenment's confidence in human reason led to a lessening of faith in the authority of the Bible and consequently to some dissatisfaction with orthodox Protestant Christianity. The philosophical religion known as *deism*[2] became the faith of many leading Americans, including Franklin, Washington, Adams, and Jefferson. Despite their unorthodoxy, these men continued to think of themselves as Christians and, believing in every man's right to freedom of conscience, looked on their religious beliefs as a private affair. They did not become involved in controversy with the many orthodox Americans.

In the late eighteenth century, however, more radical deists like Thomas Paine (1737-1809) openly attacked Biblical Christianity as irrational. This criticism, along with the growth of more moderate rational religions like Unitarianism, aroused orthodox Protestants to a great furor of activity. There was a wave of religious revivals strong enough to eliminate deism and revitalize religion as a force in American intellectual life. As in the eighteenth century, the center of religious orthodoxy was in the less settled areas; revivalism flourished along the frontier.

In the frenzy and chaos of the frontier camp meetings, the calm and rational thinkers of the American Enlightenment could see only too clearly a living rejoinder to some of their hopes for America.

[2]See p. 61.

The Republic of Reason

THOMAS JEFFERSON: PHILOSOPHER AND POLITICIAN

Like Benjamin Franklin, Thomas Jefferson (1743-1826) was a man of extraordinary breadth. Practically a walking encyclopedia, he was a scientist, scholar, architect, inventor, educator, and most importantly, a philosopher and a politician. By temperament and training a refined gentleman, he was as jealous a guardian of the rights of the people as any man. Though he loved better than any other spot on earth his peaceful Virginia estate Monticello, with the beautiful house he had himself designed, he was always ready to descend into the political arena to struggle for the realization of his political principles.

Thus, though some philosopher-rulers have tried to wrench human experience to fit some abstract philosophical scheme, Jefferson's republicanism grew out of practical political experience as well as from his philosophical beliefs. In fact he never systematized his ideas in a formal philosophical work but embedded them in official papers and in his brilliant correspondence with all the leading figures of his day. The following selections, mainly from the correspondence of his later years (1813-1820), give a rounded view of his republican philosophy: his ideas on the nature of man, man's rights as the basis of society, political arrangements and the proper rulers, and the necessity of freedom of thought. A general view of Jefferson's philosophy is offered in the introduction to this chapter, while his more specific political activities and some of his official papers can be found in Chapters 5, 6, and 7.

90

REASON'S VOICE: THE MORAL INSTINCT AS THE FOUNDATION OF MAN'S MORALITY

from Thomas Jefferson, Letter to Thomas Law, June 13, 1814

If, as the seventeenth-century Puritan colonists believed, man is by nature irrational and immoral, democracy is a highly impractical government; for how can ignorant and sinful men govern themselves? Jefferson, however, believed that God had planted in men an innate moral sense, which, if properly cultivated, would make him choose the right.

In this letter to Thomas Law, the author of a treatise on moral philosophy, Jefferson develops his idea of a moral instinct in man. He argues for the existence of the moral sense by showing the inadequacies in other ideas of the foundation of morality: truth, love of God, sense of beauty, and self-love. His criticism of those theories which make self-love the basis of morality is especially interesting, because he indicates his belief that the moral instinct planted in man by God is the basis of man as a social animal.

Jefferson's remarks on the "want or imperfection of the moral sense in some men" should be particularly noticed. Here he gives an important argument for the necessity of widespread education to republican society. It is also interesting that he makes *utility* the standard and test of virtue. This belief has important implications for the understanding of his own political career and his willingness to accept social institutions of which he did not entirely approve. As he says, men in different circumstances may have different needs. Thus we cannot expect to create an ideal republican society until men's minds are educated or conditioned for it.

The copy of your Second Thoughts on Instinctive Impulses, with the letter accompanying it, was received just as I was setting out on a journey to this place, two or three days distant from Monticello. I brought it with me and read it with great satisfaction, and with the more as it

Text: Thomas Jefferson, *Writings,* ed. Andrew A. Lipscomb (Washington, D.C.: Thomas Jefferson Memorial Association, 1905), XIV, 138-43.

contained exactly my own creed on the foundation of morality in man. It is really curious that on a question so fundamental, such a variety of opinions should have prevailed among men, and those, too, of the most exemplary virtue and first order of understanding. It shows how necessary was the care of the Creator in making the moral principle so much a part of our constitution as that no errors of reasoning or of speculation might lead us astray from its observance in practice. Of all the theories on this question, the most whimsical seems to have been that of Wollaston, who considers *truth* as the foundation of morality. The thief who steals your guinea does wrong only inasmuch as he acts a lie in using your guinea as if it were his own. Truth is certainly a branch of morality, and a very important one to society. But presented as its foundation, it is as if a tree taken up by the roots, had its stem reversed in the air, and one of its branches planted in the ground. Some have made the *love of God* the foundation of morality. This, too, is but a branch of our moral duties, which are generally divided into duties to God and duties to man. If we did a good act merely from the love of God and a belief that it is pleasing to Him, whence arises the morality of the Atheist? It is idle to say, as some do, that no such being exists. We have the same evidence of the fact as of most of those we act on, to wit: their own affirmations, and their reasonings in support of them. I have observed, indeed, generally, that while in Protestant countries the defections from the Platonic Christianity of the priests is to Deism, in Catholic countries they are to Atheism. Diderot, D'Alembert, D'Holbach, Condorcet, are known to have been among the most virtuous of men. Their virtue, then, must have had some other foundation than the love of God.

The Το κυλαν (sense of beauty) of others is founded in a different faculty, that of taste, which is not even a branch of morality. We have indeed an innate sense of what we call beautiful, but that is exercised chiefly on subjects addressed to the fancy, whether through the eye in visible forms, as landscape, animal figure, dress, drapery, architecture, the composition of colors, etc., or to the imagination directly, as imagery, style, or measure in prose or poetry, or whatever else constitutes the domain of criticism or taste, a faculty entirely distinct from the moral one. Self-interest, or rather self-love, or *egoism*, has been more plausibly substituted as the basis of morality. But I consider our relations with others as constituting the boundaries of morality. With ourselves we stand on the ground of identity, not of relation, which last, requiring two subjects, excludes self-love confined to a single one. To ourselves, in strict language, we can owe no duties, obligation requiring also two parties. Self-love, therefore, is no part of morality. Indeed it is exactly its counterpart. It is the sole antagonist of virtue, leading us constantly by our propensities to self-gratification in violation of our moral duties to others. Accordingly, it is against this enemy that are erected the batteries of

moralists and religionists, as the only obstacle to the practice of morality. Take from man his selfish propensities, and he can have nothing to seduce him from the practice of virtue. Or subdue those propensities by education, instruction or restraint, and virtue remains without a competitor. Egoism, in a broader sense, has been thus presented as the source of moral action. It has been said that we feed the hungry, clothe the naked, bind up the wounds of the man beaten by thieves, pour oil and wine into them, set him on our own beast and bring him to the inn, because we receive ourselves pleasure from these acts. So Helvetius, one of the best men on earth, and the most ingenious advocate of this principle, after defining "interest" to mean not merely that which is pecuniary, but whatever may procure us pleasure or withdraw us from pain, [*de l'esprit* 2, 1,] says, [ib. 2, 2,] "the humane man is he to whom the sight of misfortune is insupportable, and who to rescue himself from this spectacle, is forced to succor the unfortunate object." This indeed is true. But it is one step short of the ultimate question. These good acts give us pleasure, but how happens it that they give us pleasure? Because nature hath implanted in our breasts a love of others, a sense of duty to them, a moral instinct, in short, which prompts us irresistibly to feel and to succor their distresses, and protests against the language of Helvetius, [ib. 2, 5,] "what other motive than self-interest could determine a man to generous actions? It is as impossible for him to love what is good for the sake of good, as to love evil for the sake of evil." The Creator would indeed have been a bungling artist, had he intended man for a social animal, without planting in him social dispositions. It is true they are not planted in every man, because there is no rule without exceptions; but it is false reasoning which converts exceptions into the general rule. Some men are born without the organs of sight, or of hearing, or without hands. Yet it would be wrong to say that man is born without these faculties, and sight, hearing, and hands may with truth enter into the general definition of man.

The want or imperfection of the moral sense in some men, like the want or imperfection of the senses of sight and hearing in others, is no proof that it is a general characteristic of the species. When it is wanting, we endeavor to supply the defect by education, by appeals to reason and calculation, by presenting to the being so unhappily conformed, other motives to do good and to eschew evil, such as the love, or the hatred, or rejection of those among whom he lives, and whose society is necessary to his happiness and even existence; demonstrations by sound calculation that honesty promotes interest in the long run; the rewards and penalties established by the laws; and ultimately the prospects of a future state of retribution for the evil as well as the good done while here. These are the correctives which are supplied by education, and which exercise the functions of the moralist, the preacher, and legislator; and they lead into a course of correct action all those whose disparity is not too profound to be eradicated. Some have argued against the existence of a moral sense, by saying that if nature had given us such a sense, impelling us to virtuous actions, and warning us against those which are vicious, then nature would also have designated, by some particular ear-marks, the two sets of actions which are, in themselves, the one virtuous and the other vicious. Whereas, we find, in fact, that the same actions are deemed virtuous in one country and vicious in another. The answer is, that nature has constituted *utility* to man, the standard and test of virtue. Men living in different countries, under different circumstances, different habits and regimens, may have different utilities; the same act, therefore, may be useful, and consequently virtuous in one country which is injurious and vicious in another differently circumstanced. I sincerely, then, believe with you in the general existence of a moral instinct. I think it the brightest gem with which the human character is studded, and the want of it as more degrading than the most hideous of the bodily deformities. . . .

91

THE ESSENCE OF A REPUBLIC: COMPETENT REPRESENTATIVES CHOSEN BY AN ENLIGHTENED PEOPLE

from Thomas Jefferson, Letter to Pierre S. Du Pont de Nemours, April 24, 1816

Like most men of his time Jefferson was strongly influenced by the political theories of the *social contract philosophers* (discussed in the introduction to Part I, Chapter 2). Like John Locke, the great seventeenth-century English philosopher whose influence was pervasive in republican America, he felt that political society ought to be based on the God-given natural rights of men.

Pierre Samuel Du Pont de Nemours (1739-1817), a Frenchman who migrated to America and became the founder of a long line of scientists and industrialists, had sent Jefferson a letter concerning constitutions that he was preparing for some South American republics. In his reply Jefferson expresses his own ideas about the formation of civil society and the moral principles on which governments ought to be based.

His comments about the role of the mass of the people in government should be especially noted. Jefferson was not one of those who found in the voice of the people the commands of God. On the contrary, he thought the uneducated mass of the people one important factor in the "tyranny and oppression of body and mind" of which history is so full. Jefferson did feel that education would enlighten the people, but even then he limits their role in the formulation of larger governmental policy to the selection of representatives to act for them; they are "unqualified for the management of affairs requiring intelligence above the common level, yet competent judges of human character." Jefferson's idea of a "natural aristocracy," expressed in Document 93, grows directly out of this conviction.

. . . We of the United States, you know, are constitutionally and conscientiously democrats. We consider society as one of the natural wants with which man has been created; that he has been endowed with faculties and qualities to effect its satisfaction by concurrence of others having the same want; that when, by the exercise of these faculties, he has procured a state of society, it is one of his acquisitions which he has a right to regulate and control, jointly indeed with all those who have concurred in the procurement, whom he cannot exclude from its use or direction more than they him. We think experience has proved it safer, for the mass of individuals composing the society, to reserve to themselves personally the exercise of all rightful powers to which they are competent, and to delegate those to which they are not competent to deputies named, and removable for unfaithful conduct, by themselves immediately. Hence, with us, the people (by which is meant the mass of individuals composing the society) being competent to judge of the facts occurring in ordinary

Text: Thomas Jefferson, *Writings*, ed. Andrew A. Lipscomb (Washington, D.C.: Thomas Jefferson Memorial Association, 1905), XIV, 487-88, 490-92.

life, they have retained the functions of judges of facts, under the name of jurors; but being unqualified for the management of affairs requiring intelligence above the common level, yet competent judges of human character, they chose, for their management, representatives, some by themselves immediately, others by electors chosen by themselves. . . .

But when we come to the moral principles on which the government is to be administered, we come to what is proper for all conditions of society. I meet you there in all the benevolence and rectitude of your native character; and I love myself always most where I concur most with you. Liberty, truth, probity, honor, are declared to be the four cardinal principles of your society. I believe with you that morality, compassion, generosity, are innate elements of the human constitution; that there exists a right independent of force; that a right to property is founded in our natural wants, in the means with which we are endowed to satisfy these wants, and the right to what we acquire by those means without violating the similar rights of other sensible beings; that no one has a right to obstruct another, exercising his faculties innocently for the relief of sensibilities made a part of his nature; that justice is the fundamental law of society; that the majority, oppressing an individual, is guilty of a crime, abuses its strength, and by acting on the law of the strongest, breaks up the foundations of society; that action by the citizens in person, in affairs within their reach and competence, and in all others by representatives, chosen immediately, and removable by themselves, constitutes the essence of a republic; that all governments are more or less republican in proportion as this principle enters more or less into their composition; and that a government by representation is capable of extension over a greater surface of country than one of any other form. These, my friend, are the essentials in which you and I agree; however, in our zeal for their maintenance, we may be perplexed and divaricate, as to the structure of society most likely to secure them.

In the Constitution of Spain, as proposed by the late Cortes, there was a principle entirely new to me, and not noticed in yours, that no person, born after that day, should ever acquire the rights of citizenship until he could read and write. It is impossible sufficiently to estimate the wisdom of this provision. Of all those which have been thought of for securing fidelity in the administration of the government, constant ralliance to the principles of the Constitution, and progressive amendments with the progressive advances of the human mind, or changes in human affairs, it is the most effectual. Enlighten the people generally, and tyranny and oppressions of body and mind will vanish like evil spirits at the dawn of day. Although I do not, with some enthusiasts, believe that the human condition will ever advance to such a state of perfection as that there shall no longer be pain or vice in the world, yet I believe it susceptible of much improvement, and most of all, in matters of government and religion; and that the diffusion of knowledge among the people is to be the instrument by which it is to be effected. . . .

92

THE STRUCTURE OF A REPUBLIC: GOVERNMENT AT SEVERAL LEVELS, REVISION AT STATED PERIODS

from Thomas Jefferson, Letter to Samuel Kercheval, July 12, 1816

As a philosopher, Jefferson hoped that ultimately man would progress to the point where a truly free society with maximum self-government might be workable. But as a responsible politician and a leader of a specific country at a specific time, he was aware that man had not yet reached this ideal. The size of the United States and its responsibility for the welfare of several million people made a central government with definite powers absolutely necessary. Therefore, as the best political arrangement for his time Jefferson favored representative government at several levels. He hoped that ultimately a system of wards at the lower levels of government would develop. These wards would be small enough so that all the citizens could meet to deliberate about their affairs, thereby training the people in their civic rights and duties and eventually creating a vigorous democracy. It is interesting to compare Jefferson's views on this matter with Timothy Dwight's description of New England township government in Document 72.

This selection from a letter to an individual who had asked for Jefferson's views on the improvement of the Constitution also provides a good illustration of Jefferson, the politician, seeking ways to realize his principles through political arrangements. In the letter he gives a concise statement of his views on the functions and powers of the different levels of republican government—federal, state, county, and ward—and also expresses his general confidence in the people's ability to live under a republican government. Another aspect of this letter should be especially noticed: Jefferson's suspicion of traditional laws and institutions. Convinced that men would continually progress in the discovery and understanding of the laws of nature, Jefferson was a strong believer in the change of laws and institutions in accordance with such discoveries.

. . . The true foundation of republican government is the equal right of every citizen, in his person and property, and in their management. Try by this, as a tally, every provision of our Constitution, and see if it hangs directly on the will of the people. Reduce your legislature to a convenient number for full, but orderly discussion. Let every man who fights or pays, exercise his just and equal right in their election. Submit them to approbation or rejection at short intervals. Let the executive be chosen in the same way, and for the same term, by those whose agent he is to be; and leave no screen of a council behind which to skulk from responsibility. It has been thought that the people are not competent electors of judges *learned in the law.* But I do not know that this is true, and, if doubtful, we should follow principle. In this, as in many other elections, they would be guided by reputation, which would not err oftener, perhaps, than the present mode of appointment. In one State of the Union, at least, it has long been tried, and with the most satisfactory success. The judges of Connecticut have been chosen by the people every six months, for nearly two centuries, and I believe there has hardly ever been an instance of change; so powerful is the curb of incessant responsibility. If prejudice, however, derived from a monarchical institution, is still to prevail against the vital elective principle of our own, and if the existing example among ourselves of periodical election of judges by the people be still mistrusted, let us at least not adopt the evil, and reject the good, of the English precedent; let us retain a movability on the concurrence of the executive and legislative branches, and nomination by the executive alone. Nomination to office is an executive function. To give it to the legislature, as we do, is a violation of the principle of the separation of powers. It swerves the members from correctness, by temptations to intrigue for office themselves, and to a corrupt barter of votes; and destroys responsibility by dividing it among a multitude. By leaving nomination in its proper place, among executive functions, the principle of the distribution of power is preserved, and responsibility weighs with its heaviest force on a single head.

The organization of our county administrations may be thought more difficult. But follow principle, and the knot unties itself. Divide the counties into wards of such size as that every citizen can attend, when called on, and act in person. Ascribe to them the government of their wards in all things relating to themselves exclusively. A justice, chosen by themselves, in each, a constable, a military company, a patrol, a school, the care of their own poor, their own portion of the public roads, the choice of one or more jurors to serve in some court, and the delivery, within their own wards, of their own votes for all elective officers of higher sphere, will relieve the county administration of nearly all its business, will have it better done, and by making every citizen an acting member of the government, and in the offices nearest and most interesting to him, will attach him by his strongest feelings to the independence of his country, and its republican Constitution. The justices thus chosen by every ward, would constitute the county court, would do its judiciary business, direct roads and bridges, levy county and poor rates, and administer all the matters of common interest to the whole country. These wards, called townships in New England, are the vital principle of their governments, and have proved themselves the wisest invention ever devised by the wit of man for the perfect exercise of self-government, and for its preservation. We should thus marshal our government into, 1, the general federal republic, for all concerns foreign and federal; 2, that of the State, for what relates to our own citizens exclusively; 3, the county republics, for the duties and concerns of the county; and 4, the ward republics, for the small, and yet numerous and interesting concerns of the neighborhood; and in government, as well as in every other business of life, it is by division and subdivision of duties alone, that all matters, great and small, can be managed to perfection. And the whole is cemented by giving to every citizen, personally, a part in the administration of the public affairs. . . .

Text: Thomas Jefferson, *Writings,* ed. Andrew A. Lipscomb (Washington, D.C.: Thomas Jefferson Memorial Association, 1905), XV, 36-38, 40-43.

Some men look at constitutions with sancti-monious reverence, and deem them like the ark of the covenant, too sacred to be touched. They ascribe to the men of the preceding age a wisdom more than human, and suppose what they did to be beyond amendment. I knew that age well; I belonged to it, and labored with it. It deserved well of its country. It was very like the present, but without the experience of the present; and forty years of experience in government is worth a century of book-reading; and this they would say themselves, were they to rise from the dead. I am certainly not an advocate for frequent and untried changes in laws and constitutions. I think moderate imperfections had better be borne with; because, when once known, we accommodate ourselves to them, and find practical means of correcting their ill effects. But I know also, that laws and institu-tions must go hand in hand with the progress of the human mind. As that becomes more developed, more enlightened, as new discoveries are made, new truths disclosed, and manners and opinions change with the change of circumstances, institu-tions must advance also, and keep pace with the times. We might as well require a man to wear still the coat which fitted him when a boy, as civilized society to remain ever under the regimen of their barbarous ancestors. It is this preposter-ous idea which has lately deluged Europe in blood. Their monarchs, instead of wisely yielding to the gradual change of circumstances, of favor-ing progressive accommodation to progressive im-provement, have clung to old abuses, entrenched themselves behind steady habits, and obliged their subjects to seek through blood and violence rash and ruinous innovations, which, had they been referred to the peaceful deliberations and collected wisdom of the nation, would have been put into acceptable and salutary forms. Let us follow no such examples, nor weakly believe that one generation is not as capable as another of taking care of itself, and of ordering its own affairs. Let us, as our sister States have done, avail ourselves of our reason and experience, to correct the crude essays of our first and unexperienced, although wise, virtuous, and well-meaning councils. And lastly, let us pro-vide in our Constitution for its revision at stated periods. . . .

Each generation is as independent of the one preceding, as that was of all which had gone be-fore. It has then, like them, a right to choose for itself the form of government it believes most promotive of its own happiness; conse-quently, to accommodate to the circumstances in which it finds itself, that received from its pred-ecessors; and it is for the peace and good of man-kind, that a solemn opportunity of doing this every nineteen or twenty years, should be pro-vided by the Constitution; so that it may be handed on, with periodical repairs, from genera-tion to generation, to the end of time, if anything human can so long endure. . . .

This corporeal globe, and everything upon it, belong to its present corporeal inhabitants, dur-ing their generation. They alone have a right to direct what is the concern of themselves alone, and to declare the law of that direction; and this declaration can only be made by their majority. That majority, then, has a right to depute rep-resentatives to a convention, and to make the Constitution what they think will be the best for themselves. But how collect their voice? This is the real difficulty. If invited by private authority, or county or district meetings, these divisions are so large that few will attend; and their voice will be imperfectly, or falsely, pronounced. Here, then, would be one of the advantages of the ward divisions I have proposed. The mayor of every ward, on a question like the present, would call his ward together, take the simple yea or nay of its members, convey these to the county court, who would hand on those of all its wards to the proper general authority; and the voice of the whole people would be thus fairly, fully, and peaceably expressed, discussed, and decided by the common reason of the society. If this avenue be shut to the call of sufferance, it will make itself heard through that of force, and we shall go on, as other nations are doing, in the endless circle of oppression, rebellion, reformation; and op-pression, rebellion, reformation, again; and so on forever.

93   THE RULERS IN A REPUBLIC: THE NATURAL ARISTOCRACY

from Thomas Jefferson, Letter to John Adams, October 28, 1813

Though Jefferson believed in the equality of men with respect to rights, he was highly conscious of their inequalities in abilities and virtue. No society could succeed, he felt, unless the most talented and virtuous men were chosen as rulers. For him, a leading argument in favor of popular election was that the people would ultimately select from among themselves a "natural aristocracy," while the existence of an "artificial aristocracy" of heredity and birth would hold down many men of talent.

In this letter to John Adams (1735-1826), he explains his distinction between a natural and an artificial aristocracy and insists upon the importance of a natural aristocracy to republican society. As in his other letters, Jefferson stresses the urgency of education as a means whereby the natural aristocracy may be sought out and prepared for public trusts.

The republican ideal of a natural aristocracy is not necessarily an undemocratic idea, but it has been the least popular of Jefferson's principles. From the beginning, the idea faced criticism from two sides. On the one hand, John Adams (whose reply to Jefferson's letter is printed in Document 95) argued that an aristocracy of wealth and birth being inevitable, it should be legalized and thereby controlled. And to Jeffersonians like H. H. Brackenridge (see Document 96), it seemed that the people often purposely elected the worst possible men. On the other hand, the majority of the American people held to the idea that any man is good enough for political office.

. . . For I agree with you that there is a natural aristocracy among men. The grounds of this are virtue and talents. Formerly, bodily powers gave place among the aristoi. But since the invention of gunpowder has armed the weak as well as the strong with missile death, bodily strength, like beauty, good humor, politeness and other accomplishments, has become but an auxiliary ground of distinction. There is also an artificial aristocracy, founded on wealth and birth, without either virtue or talents; for with these it would belong to the first class. The natural aristocracy I consider as the most precious gift of nature, for the instruction, the trusts, and government of society. And indeed, it would have been inconsistent in creation to have formed man for the social state, and not to have provided virtue and wisdom enough to manage the concerns of the society. May we not even say, that that form of government is the best, which provides the most effectually for a pure selection of these natural aristoi into the offices of government? The artificial aristocracy is a mischievous ingredient in government, and provision should be made to prevent its ascendency. On the question, what is the best provision, you and I differ; but we differ as rational friends, using the free exercise of our own reason, and mutually indulging its errors. You think it best to put the pseudo-aristoi into a separate chamber of legislation, where they may be hindered from doing mischief by their coordinate branches, and where, also, they may be a protection to wealth against the agrarian and plundering enterprises of the majority of the people. I think that to give them power in order to prevent them from doing mischief,

is arming them for it, and increasing instead of remedying the evil. For if the co-ordinate branches can arrest their action, so may they that of the co-ordinates. Mischief may be done negatively as well as positively. Of this, a cabal in the Senate of the United States has furnished many proofs. Nor do I believe them necessary to protect the wealthy; because enough of these will find their way into every branch of the legislation, to protect themselves. From fifteen to twenty legislatures of our own, in action for thirty years past, have proved that no fears of an equalization of property are to be apprehended from them. I think the best remedy is exactly that provided by all our constitutions, to leave to the citizens the free election and separation of the aristoi from the pseudo-aristoi, of the wheat from the chaff. In general they will elect the really good and wise. In some instances, wealth may corrupt, and birth blind them; but not in sufficient degree to endanger the society.

It is probable that our difference of opinion may, in some measure, be produced by a difference of character in those among whom we live. From what I have seen of Massachusetts and Connecticut myself, and still more from what I have heard, and the character given of the former by yourself, (volume 1, page 111,) who know them so much better, there seems to be in those two States a traditionary reverence for certain families, which has rendered the offices of the government nearly hereditary in those families. I presume that from an early period of your history, members of those families happening to possess virtue and talents, have honestly exercised them for the good of the people, and by their services have endeared their names to them. In coupling Connecticut with you, I mean it politically only, not morally. For having made the Bible the

Text: Thomas Jefferson, *Writings*, ed. Andrew A. Lipscomb (Washington, D.C.: Thomas Jefferson Memorial Association, 1905), XIII, 396-402.

common law of their land, they seem to have modeled their morality on the story of Jacob and Laban. But although this hereditary succession to office with you, may, in some degree, be founded in real family merit, yet in a much higher degree, it has proceeded from your strict alliance of Church and State. These families are canonized in the eyes of the people on common principles, "you tickle me, and I will tickle you." In Virginia we have nothing of this. Our clergy, before the revolution, having been secured against rivalship by fixed salaries, did not give themselves the trouble of acquiring influence over the people. Of wealth, there were great accumulations in particular families, handed down from generation to generation, under the English law of entails. But the only object of ambition for the wealthy was a seat in the King's Council. All their court then was paid to the crown and its creatures; and they Philipized in all collisions between the King and the people. Hence they were unpopular; and that unpopularity continues attached to their names. A Randolph, a Carter, or a Burwell must have great personal superiority over a common competitor to be elected by the people even at this day. At the first session of our legislature after the Declaration of Independence, we passed a law abolishing entails. And this was followed by one abolishing the privilege of primogeniture, and dividing the lands of intestates equally among all their children, or other representatives. These laws, drawn by myself, laid the axe to the foot of pseudo-aristocracy. And had another which I prepared been adopted by the legislature, our work would have been complete. It was a bill for the more general diffusion of learning. This proposed to divide every county into wards of five or six miles square, like your townships; to establish in each ward a free school for reading, writing and common arithmetic; to provide for the annual selection of the best subjects from these schools, who might receive, at the public expense, a higher degree of education at a district school; and from these district schools to select a certain number of the most promising subjects, to be completed at an university, where all the useful sciences should be taught. Worth and genius would thus have been sought out from every condition of life, and completely prepared by education for defeating the competition of wealth and birth for public trusts. My proposition had, for a further object, to impart to these wards those portions of self-government for which they are best qualified, by confiding to them the care of their poor, their roads, police, elections, the nomination of jurors, administration of justice in small cases, elemen-

tary exercises of militia; in short, to have made them little republics, with a warden at the head of each, for all those concerns which, being under their eye, they would better manage than the larger republics of the county or State. A general call of ward meetings by their wardens on the same day through the State, would at any time produce the genuine sense of the people on any required point, and would enable the State to act in mass, as your people have so often done, and with so much effect by their town meetings. The law for religious freedom, which made a part of this system, having put down the aristocracy of the clergy, and restored to the citizen the freedom of the mind, and those of entails and descents nurturing an equality of condition among them, this on education would have raised the mass of the people to the high ground of moral respectability necessary to their own safety, and to orderly government; and would have completed the great object of qualifying them to select the veritable aristoi, for the trusts of government, to the exclusion of the pseudalists; and the same Theognis who has furnished the epigraphs of your two letters, assures us that "Ουδεμιαν πω, Κυρν', αγαθοι πολιν ωλεσαν ανδρες." Although this law has not yet been acted on but in a small and inefficient degree, it is still considered as before the legislature, with other bills of the revised code, not yet taken up, and I have great hope that some patriotic spirit will, at a favorable moment, call it up, and make it the keystone of the arch of our government.

With respect to aristocracy, we should further consider, that before the establishment of the American States, nothing was known to history but the man of the old world, crowded within limits either small or overcharged, and steeped in the vices which that situation generates. A government adapted to such men would be one thing; but a very different one, that for the man of these States. Here every one may have land to labor for himself, if he chooses; or, preferring the exercise of any other industry, may exact for it such compensation as not only to afford a comfortable subsistence, but wherewith to provide for a cessation from labor in old age. Every one, by his property, or by his satisfactory situation, is interested in the support of law and order. And such men may safely and advantageously reserve to themselves a wholesome control over their public affairs, and a degree of freedom, which, in the hands of the *canaille* of the cities of Europe, would be instantly perverted to the demolition and destruction of everything public and private. The history of the last twenty-five years of France, and of the last forty years in America, nay of its last two hundred years, proves the truth of both parts of this observation.

But even in Europe a change has sensibly taken place in the mind of man. Science had liberated the ideas of those who read and reflect, and the American example had kindled feelings of right in the people. An insurrection has consequently begun, of science, talents, and courage, against rank and birth, which have fallen into contempt. It has failed in its first effort, because the mobs of the cities, the instrument used for its accomplishment, debased by ignorance, poverty, and vice, could not be restrained to rational action. But the world will recover from the panic of this first catastrophe. Science is progressive, and talents and enterprise on the alert. Resort may be had to the people of the country, a more governable power from their principles and subordination; and rank, and birth, and tinsel-aristocracy will finally shrink into insignificance, even there. This, however, we have no right to meddle with. It suffices for us, if the moral and physical condition of our own citizens qualifies them to select the able and good for the direction of their government, with a recurrence of elections at such short periods as will enable them to displace an unfaithful servant, before the mischief he meditates may be irremediable.

94

A NECESSITY OF REPUBLICANISM: FREEDOM OF INQUIRY AND RELIGION

from Thomas Jefferson, *Notes on Virginia*, 1787

In Jefferson's view, no society that had an established church or any governmental control of thought and inquiry could be a decent environment for men. Not only did he think freedom of the mind one of man's inherent and inalienable rights, but he also believed that men could not progress toward a better life without the free inquiry into nature and society.

In this eloquent passage from his *Notes on Virginia*, Jefferson presents a magnificent series of arguments against what he conceived to be the great error, that the operations of the mind, like those of the body, should be subject to legislation and coercion.

Jefferson never hesitated to fight for the rights of free inquiry in his own political career, and one of the most enduring monuments to his political activities are the first ten amendments to the Constitution, guaranteeing these rights. It is a tragic commentary on our own times that some Americans have felt it necessary to agitate for the limitation of freedom of inquiry.

. . . The error seems not sufficiently eradicated, that the operations of the mind, as well as the acts of the body, are subject to the coercion of the laws. But our rulers can have no authority over such natural rights, only as we have submitted to them. The rights of conscience we never submitted, we could not submit. We are answerable for them to our God. The legitimate powers of government extend to such acts only as are injurious to others. But it does me no injury for my neighbor to say there are twenty gods, or no God. It neither picks my pocket nor breaks my leg. If it be said, his testimony in a court of justice cannot be relied on, reject it then, and be the stigma on him. Constraint may make him worse by making him a hypocrite, but it will never make him a truer man. It may fix him obstinately in his errors, but will not cure them. Reason and free inquiry are the only effectual agents against error. Give a loose to them, they will support the true religion by bringing every false one to their tribunal, to the test of their investigation. They are the natural enemies of error, and of error only. Had not the Roman government permitted free inquiry, Christianity could never have been introduced. Had not free inquiry been indulged at the era of the reformation, the corruptions of Christianity could not have been purged away. If it be restrained now, the present corruptions will be protected, and new ones encouraged. Was the government to prescribe to us our medicine and diet, our bodies would be in such keeping as our souls are now. Thus in France the emetic was once forbidden as a medicine, and the potato as an article of food. Government is just as infallible, too, when it fixes systems in physics. Galileo was sent to the Inquisition for affirming that the earth was a sphere; the government had declared it to be as flat as a trencher, and Galileo was obliged to abjure his error. This error, however, at length prevailed, the earth became a globe, and

Text: Thomas Jefferson, *Writings*, ed. H. A. Washington (New York: Taylor & Maury, 1853), VIII, 400-01.

Descartes declared it was whirled round its axis by a vortex. The government in which he lived was wise enough to see that this was no question of civil jurisdiction, or we should all have been involved by authority in vortices. In fact, the vortices have been exploded, and the Newtonian principle of gravitation is now more firmly established, on the basis of reason, than it would be were the government to step in, and to make it an article of necessary faith. Reason and experiment have been indulged, and error has fled before them. It is error alone which needs the support of government. Truth can stand by itself. Subject opinion to coercion: whom will you make your inquisitors? Fallible men; men governed by bad passions, by private as well as public reasons. And why subject it to coercion? To produce uniformity. But is uniformity of opinion desirable? No more than of face and stature. Introduce the bed of Procrustes then, and as there is danger that the large men may beat the small, make us all of a size, by lopping the former and stretching the latter. Difference of opinion is advantageous in religion. The several sects perform the office of a *censor morum* over such other. Is uniformity attainable? Millions of innocent men, women, and children, since the introduction of Christianity, have been burnt, tortured, fined, imprisoned; yet we have not advanced one inch towards uniformity. What has been the effect of coercion? To make one half the world fools, and the other half hypocrites. To support roguery and error all over the earth. Let us reflect that it is inhabited by a thousand millions of people. That these profess probably a thousand different systems of religion. That ours is but one of that thousand. That if there be but one right, and ours that one, we should wish to see the nine hundred and ninety-nine wandering sects gathered into the fold of truth. But against such a majority we cannot effect this by force. Reason and persuasion are the only practicable instruments. To make way for these, free inquiry must be indulged; and how can we wish others to indulge it while we refuse it ourselves. . . .

CRITICISM OF REPUBLICANISM

95

A HEREDITARY ARISTOCRACY: THE ONLY REMEDY FOR POPULAR STUPIDITY

from John Adams, Letter to Thomas Jefferson, November 15, 1813

John Adams (1735-1826), revolutionary statesman and second President of the United States, was, like Thomas Jefferson, a convinced republican. However, he feared the passions, appetites, and stupidity of the mass of the people. These evils, he felt, inevitably led to the development of an aristocracy based on those things of most influence with the multitude: wealth, birth, and beauty. Since the development of such an aristocracy was inevitable, he felt that it could best be controlled and prevented from wrecking the republican government by legalizing and institutionalizing it. In other words, he was in favor of establishing, for political purposes, what Jefferson called an "artificial aristocracy."

Adams and Jefferson had been co-workers and friends during the Revolution and the administration of Washington. At the time of Jefferson's election to succeed Adams, however, they became estranged, partially through misunderstanding. In early 1811, through the ministrations of mutual friends, the two retired statesmen began to correspond again, surprising even themselves at their basic agreement on most political and philosophical matters. They again became friends, and their correspondence continued until the end of their lives. The letters between the two are fascinating and frequently brilliant, representing as they do the interplay of two of the world's finest minds looking back over a series of events of extraordinary significance.

The letter reproduced here, and Jefferson's letter on natural aristocracy (Document 93), to which Adams' letter is a reply, are part of this old-age correspondence between two of the "Founding Fathers."

We are now explicitly agreed upon one important point, viz., that there is a natural aristocracy among men, the grounds of which are virtue and talents. You very justly indulge a little merriment upon this solemn subject of aristocracy. I often laugh at it too, for there is nothing in this laughable world more ridiculous than the management

Text: Thomas Jefferson, *Writings*, ed. Andrew A. Lipscomb (Washington, D.C.: Thomas Jefferson Memorial Association, 1905), XIV, 1-2, 5-8.

of it by all the nations of the earth; but while we smile, mankind have reason to say to us, as the frogs said to the boys, what is sport to you, are wounds and death to us. When I consider the weakness, the folly, the pride, the vanity, the selfishness, the artifice, the low craft and mean cunning, the want of principle, the avarice, the unbounded ambition, the unfeeling cruelty of a majority of those (in all nations) who are allowed an aristocratical influence, and, on the other hand, the stupidity with which the more numerous multitude not only become their dupes, but even love to be taken in by their tricks, I feel a stronger disposition to weep at their destiny, than to laugh at their folly. But though we have agreed in one point, in words, it is not yet certain that we are perfectly agreed in sense. Fashion has introduced an indeterminate use of the word talents. Education, wealth, strength, beauty, stature, birth, marriage, graceful attitudes and motions, gait, air, complexion, physiognomy, are talents, as well as genius, science, and learning. Any one of these talents that in fact commands or influences two votes in society, gives to the man who possesses it the character of an aristocrat, in my sense of the word. Pick up the first hundred men you meet, and make a republic. Every man will have an equal vote; but when deliberations and discussions are opened, it will be found that twenty-five, by their talents, virtues being equal, will be able to carry fifty votes. Every one of these twenty-five is an aristocrat in my sense of the word; whether he obtains his one vote in addition to his own, by his birth, fortune, figure, eloquence, science, learning, craft, cunning, or even his character for good fellowship, and a *bon vivant.* . . .

. . . Your distinction between natural and artificial aristocracy, does not appear to me founded. Birth and wealth are conferred upon some men as imperiously by nature as genius, strength, or beauty. The heir to honors, and riches, and power, has often no more merit in procuring these advantages, than he has in obtaining a handsome face, or an elegant figure. When aristocracies are established by human laws, and honor, wealth and power are made hereditary by municipal laws and political institutions, then I acknowledge artificial aristocracy to commence; but this never commences till corruption in elections become dominant and uncontrollable. But this artificial aristocracy can never last. The everlasting envies, jealousies, rivalries, and quarrels among them; their cruel rapacity upon the poor ignorant people, their followers, compel them to set up Caesar, a demagogue, to be a monarch, a master; *pour mettre chacun à sa place.* Here you have the origin of all artificial aristocracy, which is the origin of all monarchies. And both artificial aristocracy and monarchy, and civil, military, political, and hierarchical despotism, have all grown out of the natural aristocracy of virtues and talents. . . .

You suppose a difference of opinion between you and me on the subject of aristocracy. I can find none. I dislike and detest hereditary honors, offices, emoluments, established by law. So do you. I am for excluding legal, hereditary distinctions from the United States as long as possible. So are you. I only say that mankind have not yet discovered any remedy against irresistible corruption in elections to offices of great power and profit, but making them hereditary.

96

CAPTAIN FARRAGO ATTENDING AN ELECTION: THE EXCESSES OF FRONTIER DEMOCRACY

from Hugh Henry Brackenridge, *Modern Chivalry*, 1792

Hugh Henry Brackenridge (1748-1816) was only a little less broad in his interests and activities than Jefferson himself. Born in Scotland, he came to America in 1753. After graduating from the College of New Jersey (now Princeton University), he became successively a minister, a teacher, an editor, a poet and dramatist, a lawyer, and finally a judge. He is most remembered today for his long satirical novel *Modern Chivalry*, published in parts between 1792 and 1815. This picaresque novel tells of the adventures of Captain John Farrago, a country squire who resembles a Jeffersonian "natural aristocrat." Farrago is accompanied on his adventures by a Sancho Panza, Teague O'Regan, an incredibly ignorant Irish immigrant. Teague is symbolic of the popular mass, unjustifiably trying to push its way to political, social, and intellectual leadership.

In the episode reprinted here, the Captain and Teague happen upon an election. The results are a commentary on Jefferson's hopes that the people would choose the most intelligent and virtuous among them as their representatives and rulers.

The Captain rising early next morning, and setting out on his way, had now arrived at a place where a number of people were convened, for the purpose of electing persons to represent them in the legislature of the state. There was a weaver who was a candidate for this appointment, and seemed to have a good deal of interest among the people. . . .

. . . the Captain addressed him in the following words:

Mr. Traddle, said he, for that was the name of the manufacturer, I have not the smallest idea of wounding your sensibility; but it would seem to me, it would be more your interest to pursue your occupation, than to launch out into that of which you have no knowledge. When you go to the senate house, the application to you will not be to warp a web; but to make laws for the commonwealth. Now, suppose that the making these laws, requires a knowledge of commerce, or of the interests of agriculture, or those principles upon which the different manufactures depend, what service could you render. It is possible you might think justly enough; but could you speak? You are not in the habit of public speaking. You are not furnished with those common place ideas, with which even very ignorant men can pass for knowing something. There is nothing makes a man so ridiculous as to attempt what is above his sphere. You are no tumbler for instance; yet should you give out that you could vault upon a man's back; or turn head over heels, like the wheels of a cart; the stiffness of your joints would encumber you; and you would fall upon your backside to the ground. Such a squash as that would do you damage. The getting up to ride on the state is an unsafe thing to those who are not accustomed to such horsemanship. It is a disagreeable thing for a man to be laughed at, and there is no way of keeping ones self from it but by avoiding all affectation.

While they were thus discoursing, a bustle had taken place among the croud. Teague hearing so much about elections, and serving the government, took it into his head, that he could be a legislator himself. The thing was not displeasing to the people, who seemed to favour his pretensions; owing, in some degree, to there being several of his countrymen among the croud; but more especially to the fluctuation of the popular mind, and a disposition to what is new and ignoble. For though the weaver was not the most elevated object of choice, yet he was still preferable to this tatter-demalion, who was but a menial servant, and had so much of what is called the brogue on his tongue, as to fall far short of an elegant speaker.

The Captain coming up, and finding what was on the carpet, was greatly chagrined at not having been able to give the multitude a better idea of the importance of a legislative trust; alarmed also, from an apprehension of the loss of his servant. Under these impressions he resumed his address to the multitude. Said he, This is making the matter still worse, gentlemen: this servant of mine is but a bog-trotter; who can scarcely speak the dialect in which your laws ought to be written; but certainly has never read a single treatise on any political subject; for the truth is, he cannot read at all. The young people of the lower class, in Ireland, have seldom the advantage of a good education; especially the descendants of the ancient Irish, who have most of them a great assurance of countenance, but little information, or literature. This young man, whose family name is Oregan, has been my servant for several years. And, except a too great fondness for women, which now and then brings him into scrapes, he has demeaned himself in a manner tolerable enough. But he is totally ignorant of the great principles of legislation; and more especially, the particular interests of the government. A free government is a noble possession to a people: and this freedom consists in an equal right to make laws, and to have the benefit of the laws when made. Though doubtless, in such a government, the lowest citizen may become chief magistrate; yet it is sufficient to possess the right; not absolutely necessary to exercise it. Or even if you should think proper, now and then, to shew your privilege, and exert, in a signal manner, the democratic prerogative, yet is it not descending too low to filch away from me a hireling, which I cannot well spare, to serve your purpose. You are surely carrying the matter too far, in thinking to make a senator of this hostler; to take him away from an employment to which he has been bred, and put him to another, to which he has served no apprenticeship: to set those hands which have been lately employed in currying my horse, to the draughting bills, and preparing business for the house.

The people were tenacious of their choice, and insisted on giving Teague their suffrages; and by the frown upon their brows, seemed to indicate resentment at what has been said; as indirectly charging them with want of judgment; or calling in question their privilege to do what they thought proper. It is a very strange thing, said one of them, who was a speaker for the rest, that after having conquered Burgoyne and Cornwallis, and got a

Text: Hugh Henry Brackenridge, *Modern Chivalry* (Philadelphia: J. Conrad & Co., 1804), I, 10-17.

government of our own, we cannot put in it whom we please. This young man may be your servant, or another man's servant; but if we chuse to make him a delegate, what is that to you. He may not be yet skilled in the matter, but there is a good day a-coming. We will impower him; and it is better to trust a plain man like him, than one of your high flyers, that will make laws to suit their own purposes. . . .

Finding it answered no end to expostulate with the multitude, he requested to speak a word with Teague by himself. . . .

When a man becomes a member of a public body, he is like a racoon, or other beast that climbs up the fork of a tree; the boys pushing at him with pitch-forks, or throwing stones, or shooting at him with an arrow, the dogs barking in the mean time. One will find fault with your not speaking; another with your speaking, if you speak at all. They will have you in the newspapers, and ridicule you as a perfect beast. There is what they call the caricatura; that is, representing you with a dog's head, or a cat's claw. As you have a red head, they will very probably make a fox of you, or a sorrel horse, or a brindled cow. It is the devil in hell to be exposed to the squibs and crackers of the gazette wits and publications.

You know no more about these matters than a goose; and yet you would undertake rashly, without advice, to enter on the office; nay, contrary to advice. For I would not for a thousand guineas, though I have not the half of it to spare, that the breed of the Oregans should come to this; bringing on them a worse stain than stealing sheep; to which they are addicted. You have nothing but your character, Teague, in a new country to depend upon. Let it never be said, that you quitted an honest livelihood, the taking care of my horse, to follow the new fangled whims of the times, and to be a statesman.

Teague was moved chiefly with the last part of the address, and consented to give up the object.

The Captain, glad of this, took him back to the people, and announced his disposition to decline the honour which they had intended him.

Teague acknowledged that he had changed his mind, and was willing to remain in a private station.

The people did not seem well pleased with the Captain; but as nothing more could be said about the matter, they turned their attention to the weaver, and gave him their suffrages.

A New Man in a New World

THE FLOWERING OF NATIONALISM

97

AMERICA, THE REFUGE FROM EUROPEAN POVERTY AND TYRANNY

from J. Hector St. John de Crèvecoeur, "What is an American?" 1782

The hope of men like Jefferson was that the new environment of the virgin American continent and the free institutions of republican society would produce a new man, capable of assuming his place as a citizen of a free society.

This hope was stated as early as 1781 by J. Hector St. John de Crèvecoeur[1] (1735-1813), a French emigrant who came to America in 1754 and settled with an American wife on a farm in Orange County, New York. Ironically, Crèvecoeur himself did not accept the full implications of his observations, for during the Revolution he became a Loyalist and went back to Europe. Returning to America in 1783 as an emissary of the French government, he found his home burned, his wife dead, and his children gone. Disillusioned with his American dreams, he returned to France, where he spent the rest of his life.

In this selection from his *Letters from an American Farmer*, written before his tragic experiences, Crèvecoeur is in the full flush of his enthusiasm for the promise of American life. Like Jefferson and his contemporaries, he sees America as a great asylum for mankind from the corruption and tyranny of the Old World. Out of the new conditions and the mixture of European races, a new man has developed who is industrious and independent, free at last from the poverty, hunger, and war of the Old World.

[1]His more familiar name. Crèvecoeur's true given name was Michel Guillaume Jean de Crèvecoeur.

In this great American asylum, the poor of Europe have by some means met together, and in consequence of various causes; to what purpose should they ask one another what countrymen they are? Alas, two thirds of them had no country. Can a wretch who wanders about, who works and starves, whose life is a continual scene of sore affliction or pinching penury; can that man call England or any other kingdom his country? A country that had no bread for him, whose fields procured him no harvest, who met with nothing but the frowns of the rich, the severity of the laws, with jails and punishments; who owned not a single foot of the extensive surface of this planet? No! urged by a variety of motives, here they came. Every thing has tended to regenerate them; new laws, a new mode of living, a new social system; here they are become men: in Europe they were as so many useless plants, wanting vegitative mould, and refreshing showers; they withered, and were mowed down by want, hunger, and war; but now by the power of transplantation, like all other plants they have taken root and flourished! Formerly they were not numbered in any civil lists of their country, except in those of the poor; here they rank as citizens. By what invisible power has this surprising metamorphosis been performed? By that of the laws and that of their industry. . . .

What then is the American, this new man? He is either an European, or the descendant of an European, hence that strange mixture of blood, which you will find in no other country. I could point out to you a family whose grandfather was an Englishman, whose wife was Dutch, whose son married a French woman, and whose present four sons have now four wives of different nations. *He* is an American, who leaving behind him all his ancient prejudices and manners, receives new ones from the new mode of life he has embraced, the new government he obeys, and the new rank he holds. He becomes an American by being received in the broad lap of our great *Alma Mater.* Here individuals of all nations are melted into a new race of men, whose labours and posterity will one day cause great changes in the world. Americans are the western pilgrims, who are carrying along with them that great mass of arts, sciences, vigour, and industry which began long since in the east; they will finish the great circle. The Americans were once scattered all over Europe; here they are incorporated into one of the finest systems of population which has ever appeared, and which will hereafter become distinct by the power of the different climates they inhabit. The American ought therefore to love this country much better than that wherein either he or his forefathers were born. Here the rewards of his industry follow with equal steps the progress of his labour; his labour is founded on the basis of nature, *self-interest;* can it want a stronger allurement? Wives and children, who before in vain demanded of him a morsel of bread, now, fat and frolicsome, gladly help their father to clear those fields whence exuberant crops are to arise to feed and to clothe them all; without any part being claimed, either by a despotic prince, a rich abbot, or a mighty lord. Here religion demands but little of him; a small voluntary salary to the minister, and gratitude to God; can he refuse these? The American is a new man, who acts upon new principles; he must therefore entertain new ideas, and form new opinions. From involuntary idleness, servile dependence, penury, and useless labour, he has passed to toils of a very different nature, rewarded by ample subsistence.—This is an American.

Text: J. Hector St. John de Crèvecoeur, *Letters from an American Farmer* (London: Thomas Davies & Lockyer Davis, 1782), pp. 49-50, 51-53.

98

ADVICE TO THE PRIVILEGED ORDERS: EUROPE, IMITATE AMERICA!

from Joel Barlow, "Advice to the Privileged Orders," 1792

The rapid success of the republican attempt to create a new social environment for human life filled Americans with patriotic pride. As this selection illustrates, a rampant nationalism quickly followed upon the establishment of the new nation.

One aspect of this nationalism, Jefferson's feeling that America has a vital mission and a sacred duty to mankind, is illustrated in his inaugural addresses, Documents 74 and 75. Joel Barlow (1754-1812), poet, lawyer and diplomat, and a Jefferson supporter, shows in his works two other aspects of American nationalism. As a poet he attempted rather unsuccessfully to create an American literature by writing grandiose national epics. As a political pamphleteer he defended and explained American republicanism to European audiences.

In his "Advice to the Privileged Orders" (1792-1793), Barlow attacks Old World tyranny and suggests that Europeans would do well to imitate the American system.

Within a few years the fifteen states have not only framed each its own state constitution, and two successive federal constitutions; but since the settlement of the present general government in the year 1789, three of the states, Pennsylvania, South Carolina, and Georgia, have totally new modelled their own. And all this is done without the least confusion; the operation being scarcely known beyond the limits of the state where it is performed. Thus they are in the habit of "*choosing their own governors,* of "*cashiering them for misconduct,*" of "*framing a government for themselves,*" and all those abominable things, the mere naming of which, in Mr. Burke's opinion, has polluted the pulpit in the Old Jewry.

But it is said, These things will do very well for America, where the people are less numerous, less indigent, and better instructed; but they will not apply to Europe. This objection deserves a reply, not because it is solid, but because it is fashionable. It may be answered, that some parts of Spain, much of Poland, and almost the whole of Russia, are less peopled than the settled country in the United States; that poverty and ignorance are *effects* of slavery rather than its *causes;* but the best answer to be given, is the example of France. To the event of that revolution I will trust the argument. Let the people have time to become thoroughly and soberly grounded in the doctrine of *equality,* and there is no danger of oppression either from government or from anarchy. Very little instruction is necessary to teach a man his rights; and there is no person of common intellects, in the most ignorant corner of Europe, but receives lessons enough, if they were of the proper kind. For writing and reading are not indispensable to the object; it is *thinking* right which makes them act right. Every child is taught to repeat about fifty Latin prayers, which set up the Pope, the Bishop, and the King, as the trinity of his adoration; he is taught that *the powers that be, are ordained of*

Text: Joel Barlow, *Political Writings* (New York: Mott & Lyon, 1796), pp. 23, 26-28.

God, and therefore the soldier quartered in the parish has a right to cut his throat. Half this instruction, upon opposite principles, would go a great way; in that case nature would be assisted, while here she is counteracted. Engrave it on the heart of a man, *that all men are equal* in rights, and that the *government is their own,* and then persuade him to sell his crucifix and buy a musket,—and you have made him a good citizen. . . .

Another consequence of a settled belief in the equality of rights is, that under this belief *there is no danger from anarchy.* This word has likewise acquired a different meaning in America from what we read of it in books. In Europe it means confusion, attended with mobs and carnage, where the innocent perish with the guilty. But it is very different where a country is *used* to a representative government, though it should have an interval of no government at all. Where the people at large feel and know that they *can do every thing* by themselves personally, they really *do nothing* by themselves personally. In the heat of the American revolution, when the people in some states were for a long time without the least shadow of law or government, they always acted by committees and representation. This they must call anarchy, for they know no other.

These are materials for the formation of governments, which need not be dreaded, though disjointed and laid asunder to make some repairs. They are deep-rooted habits of thinking, which almost change the moral nature of man; they are principles as much unknown to the ancient republics as to the modern monarchies of Europe.

We must not therefore rely upon systems drawn from the experimental reasonings of Aristotle, when we find them contradicted by what we feel to be the eternal truth of nature, and see them brought to the test of our own experience. Aristotle was certainly a great politician; and Claudius Ptolemy was a great geographer; but the latter has said not a word of America, the largest quarter of the globe; nor the former, of representative republics, the resource of afflicted humanity.

99

A NEW LANGUAGE FOR A NEW MAN

from Noah Webster, Preface to *An American Dictionary of the English Language,* 1828

Americans' pride in their new world and new society extended even to matters of language. Noah Webster (1758-1843), a journalist, educator, and lexicographer, was an early exponent of the distinction between American and British English. In his *Grammatical Institute of the English Language* (1783) he called for literary and linguistic as well as political independence from England. In 1800 Webster began work on *An American Dictionary of the English Language,* which he completed in 1828.

The following selection, from the preface to Webster's dictionary, illustrates quite clearly this American pride in all aspects of their republican society, right down to new words like "land-office" that their new experiences and institutions had created.

It is not only important, but in a degree necessary, that the people of this country should have an *American Dictionary of the English Language;* for, although the body of the language is the same as in England, and it is desirable to perpetuate that sameness, yet some differences must exist. Language is the expression of ideas; and if the people of one country can not preserve an identity of ideas, they can not retain an identity of language. Now, an identity of ideas depends materially upon a sameness of things or objects with which the people of the two countries are conversant. But in no two portions of the earth, remote from each other, can such identity be found. Even physical objects must be different. But the principal differences between the people of this country and of all others, arise from different forms of government, different laws, institutions, and customs. Thus the practice of *hawking* and *hunting,* the institution of *heraldry,* and the *feudal system* of England originated terms which formed, and some of which now form, a necessary part of the language of that country; but, in the United States, many of these terms are no part of our present language,—and they can not be, for the things which they express do not exist in this country. They can be known to us only as obsolete or as foreign words. On the other hand, the institutions in this country which are new and peculiar, give rise to new terms or to new applications of old terms, unknown to the people of England; which can not be explained by them, and which will not be inserted in their dictionaries, unless copied from ours. Thus the terms *land-office; land-warrant; location of land; consociation* of churches; *regent* of a university; *intendant* of a city; *plantation, selectmen, senate, congress, court, assembly, escheat,* &c., are either words not belonging to the language of England, or they are applied to things in this country which do not exist in that. No person in this country will be satisfied with the English definitions of the words *congress, senate,* and *assembly, court,* &c.; for although these are words used in England, yet they are applied in this country to express ideas which they do not express in that

country. With our present constitutions of government, *escheat* can never have its feudal sense in the United States.

But this is not all. In many cases, the nature of our governments, and of our civil institutions, requires an appropriate language in the definition of words, even when the words express the same thing as in England. Thus the English dictionaries inform us that a *justice* is one deputed by the *king* to do right by way of judgment—he is a *lord* by his office—justices of the peace are appointed by the *king's commission* —language which is inaccurate in respect to this officer in the United States. So *constitutionally* is defined, by CHALMERS, *legally;* but in this country the distinction between *constitution* and *law* requires a different definition. In the United States, a *plantation* is a very different thing from what it is in England. The word *marshal,* in this country, has one important application unknown in England, or in Europe.

A great number of words in our language require to be defined in a phraseology accommodated to the condition and institutions of the people in these States, and the people of England must look to an *American Dictionary* for a correct understanding of such terms.

The necessity, therefore, of a dictionary suited to the people of the United States is obvious. . . .

The United States commenced their existence under circumstances wholly novel and unexampled in the history of nations. They commenced with civilization, with learning, with science, with constitutions of free government, and with that best gift of God to man, the Christian religion. Their population is now equal to that of England; in arts and sciences, our citizens are very little behind the most enlightened people on earth; in some respects, they have no superiors; and our language, within two centuries, will be spoken by more people in this country than any other language on earth, except the Chinese, in Asia; and even that may not be an exception. . . .

Text: Noah Webster, "Preface" in *An American Dictionary of the English Language* (New York: S. Converse, 1828).

THE NATURAL MAN: THREE VERSIONS

100

SAVAGES AND THE MORAL INSTINCT: A CAROLINA INDIAN

from William Bartram, *Travels*, 1791

Although the men of the Enlightenment found in nature a free and natural moral order which they felt was in many respects superior to the artificial societies of the past, they were usually well aware of its savage and dangerous aspects as well. There was a balance in their thinking between the values of civilized society and the freedom, simplicity, and naturalness that they saw in nature.

Some men, however, particularly those far removed from the real wilderness, had considerably more faith in the virtues of the purely natural than had men like Jefferson. These thinkers developed an ideal of a "natural man," who, untouched by education and civilized artificiality, could fully develop his human potentialities.

Something of the tension between nature and civilization in Enlightenment thought is illustrated by this episode from William Bartram's travel book, *Travels Through North and South Carolina, Georgia, East and West Florida, the Cherokee Country, the Extensive Territories of the Muscogulges or Creek Confederacy, and the Country of the Chactaws*. Bartram (1739-1823), the son of America's first great naturalist, was an associate of the extraordinary group of scientists who clustered around Benjamin Franklin's recently founded American Philosophical Society at Philadelphia. Bartram, too, was a naturalist; and his expeditions in the Carolinas and Florida in search of botanical specimens are described in his *Travels*, published in 1791.

In the encounter with a murderous Indian, described in this selection, Bartram discovers both morality and savagery in this "natural man." His idea of an innate moral principle is the same as Jefferson's concept of a moral instinct (see Document 90).

It may be proper to observe, that I had now passed the utmost frontier of the white settlements on that border. It was drawing on towards the close of day, the skies serene and calm, the air temperately cool, and gentle zephyrs breathing through the fragrant pines; the prospect around enchantingly varied and beautiful; endless green savannas, checquered with coppices of fragrant shrubs, filled the air with the richest perfume. The gaily attired plants which enamelled the green had begun to imbibe the pearly dew of evening; nature seemed silent, and nothing appeared to ruffle the happy moments of evening contemplation: when, on a sudden, an Indian appeared crossing the path, at a considerable distance before me. On perceiving that he was armed with a rifle, the first sight of him startled me, and I endeavoured to elude his sight, by stopping my pace, and keeping large trees between us; but he espied me, and turning short about, set spurs to his horse, and came up on full gallop. I never before this was afraid at the sight of an Indian, but at this time, I must own that

Text: William Bartram, *Travels Through North and South Carolina, Georgia, East and West Florida, the Cherokee Country, the Extensive Territories of the Muscogulges or Creek Confederacy, and the Country of the Chactaws* (Philadelphia: James & Johnson, 1792), pp. 20-23.

my spirits were very much agitated: I saw at once, that being unarmed, I was in his power, and having now but a few moments to prepare, I resigned myself entirely to the will of the Almighty, trusting to his mercies for my preservation; my mind then became tranquil, and I resolved to meet the dreaded foe with resolution and chearful confidence. The intrepid Siminole stopped suddenly, three or four yards before me, and silently viewed me, his countenance angry and fierce, shifting his rifle from shoulder to shoulder, and looking about instantly on all sides. I advanced towards him, and with an air of confidence offered him my hand, hailing him, brother; at this he hastily jerked back his arm, with a look of malice, rage and disdain, seeming every way disconcerted; when again looking at me more attentively, he instantly spurred up to me, and, with dignity in his look and action, gave me his hand. Possibly the silent language of his soul, during the moment of suspense (for I believe his design was to kill me when he first came up) was after this manner: "White man, thou art my enemy, and thou and thy brethren may have killed mine; yet it may not be so, and even were that the case, thou art now alone, and in my power. Live; the Great Spirit forbids me to touch thy life; go to thy brethren, tell them thou sawest an Indian in the forests, who knew how to be humane and compassionate." In fine, we shook hands, and parted in a friendly manner, in the midst of a dreary wilderness; and he informed me of the course and distance to the trading-house, where I found he had been extremely ill treated the day before.

I now set forward again, and after eight or ten miles riding, arrived at the banks of St. Mary's, opposite the stores, and got safe over before dark. The river is here about one hundred yards across, has ten feet water, and, following its course, about sixty miles to the sea, though but about twenty miles by land. The trading company here received and treated me with great civility. On relating my adventures on the road, particularly the last with the Indian, the chief replied, with a countenance that at once bespoke surprise and pleasure, "My friend, consider yourself a fortunate man: that fellow," said he, "is one of the greatest villains on earth, a noted murderer, and outlawed by his countrymen. Last evening he was here, we took his gun from him, broke it in pieces, and gave him a severe drubbing: he,

however, made his escape, carrying off a new rifle gun, with which, he said, going off, he would kill the first white man he met."

On seriously contemplating the behaviour of this Indian towards me, so soon after his ill treatment, the following train of sentiments insensibly crouded in upon my mind.

Can it be denied, but that the moral principle, which directs the savages to virtuous and praiseworthy actions, is natural or innate? It is certain they have not the assistance of letters, or those means of education in the schools of philosophy, where the virtuous sentiments and actions of the most illustrious characters are recorded, and carefully laid before the youth of civilized nations: therefore this moral principle must be innate, or they must be under the immediate influence and guidance of a more divine and powerful preceptor, who, on these occasions, instantly inspires them, and as with a ray of divine light, points out to them at once the dignity, propriety, and beauty of virtue.

101

OLD KENTUCKE: DANIEL BOONE PENETRATING THE WILDERNESS
from John Filson, "Autobiography of Daniel Boone," 1784

Frontier figures like Daniel Boone of Kentucky greatly influenced the development of an ideal of the natural man—a man who, in his uneducated and uncivilized simplicity, was thought to be superior to the polished products of artificial culture. In this selection, taken from a narrative of Boone's adventures supposedly told by the hero himself to historian and explorer John Filson (1747-1788), we can already see some of the tendency to idealize the frontier and the frontier heroes. This tendency reached its high point in the first half of the nineteenth century in such works as the "Leatherstocking Tales" of James Fenimore Cooper (1781-1851).

The stilted style and conventional moral reflections of Boone's narrative suggest that it was heavily doctored by Filson to make Boone appear more of a natural sage than he probably was in reality. Nonetheless, there is much less of a legendary air about this narrative than was usual in later treatments of Boone's life and character. It is interesting to compare this selection with the following statement from Timothy Flint's *Biographical Memoir of Daniel Boone* (1833):

Those who have hearts to admire nobility imported by nature's great seal . . . will not fail to be interested in a sketch of the life of the pioneer and hunter of Kentucky, Daniel Boone. Contemplated in any light, we shall find him in his way and walk, a man as truly great as Penn, Marion, and Franklin in theirs. True, he was not learned in the lore of books, or trained in the etiquette of cities. But he possessed a knowledge far more important in the sphere which Providence called him to fill. He felt, too, the conscious dignity of self-respect, and would have been seen as erect, firm, and unembarrassed amid the pomp and splendor of the proudest court in Christendom.

It is also interesting to note in Filson's narrative the strong sense that the wilderness was a virgin paradise where men might live in true happiness. This belief was an important element in American attitudes toward the West and helped to stimulate westward expansion in the nineteenth century. See Part III, Documents 163-165, for further discussion of the meaning of the West in American life.

Daniel Boone was born in Berks County, Pa., in 1734 and earned fame as a hunter at an early age. While still a young boy he was taken by his father to settle on the Yadkin River in North Carolina, and from his new home he hunted and explored along the boundary line between what are now Tennessee and Kentucky. In 1755 he took part in General Edward Braddock's famous campaign against the French and Indians. In 1767, accompanied by William Hill, he explored westward, pushing for his first time into Kentucky, where he spent the winter. In 1769 he ventured forth with five other trained woodsmen, engaged to explore the country thoroughly, purchase land from the Cherokees, and blaze the Wilderness Road for the movement of settlers into Kentucky. On this expedition he was held captive temporarily by Indians and placed his foot for the first time in the Blue Grass region. Boonesborough was founded in 1775. Boone died in Missouri in 1820.

It was on the first of May, in the year 1769, that I resigned my domestic happiness for a time, and left my family and peaceable habitation on the Yadkin River, in North Carolina, to wander through the wilderness of America, in quest of the country of Kentucke, in company with John Finley, John Stewart, Joseph Holden, James Monay, and William Cool. We proceeded successfully, and after a long and fatiguing journey through a mountainous wilderness, in a westward direction, on the seventh day of June following, we found ourselves on Red River, where John Finley had formerly been trading with the Indians, and, from the top of an eminence, saw with pleasure the beautiful level of Kentucke. Here let me observe, that for some time we had experienced the most uncomfortable weather as a prelibation of our future sufferings. At this place we encamped, and made a shelter to defend us from the inclement season, and began to hunt and reconnoitre the country. We found everywhere abundance of wild beasts of all sorts, through this vast forest. The buffaloes were more frequent than I have seen cattle in settlements, browzing on the leaves of the cane, or croping the herbage on those extensive plains, fearless, because ignorant, of the violence of man. Sometimes we saw hundreds in a drove, and the numbers about the salt springs were amazing. In this forest, the habitation of beasts of every kind natural to America, we practised hunting with great success until the twenty-second day of December following.

This day John Stewart and I had a pleasing ramble, but fortune changed the scene in the close of it. We had passed through a great forest, on which stood myriads of trees, some gay with blossoms, others rich with fruits. Nature was here a series of wonders, and a fund of delight. Here she displayed her ingenuity and industry in a variety of flowers and fruits, beautifully

coloured, elegantly shaped, and charmingly flavoured; and we were diverted with innumerable animals presenting themselves perpetually to our view.—In the decline of the day, near Kentucke river, as we ascended the brow of a small hill, a number of Indians rushed out of a thick cane brake upon us, and made us prisoners. The time of our sorrow was now arrived, and the scene fully opened. The Indians plundered us of what we had, and kept us in confinement seven days, treating us with common savage usage. During this time we discovered no uneasiness or desire to escape, which made them less suspicious of us; but in the dead of night, as we lay in a thick cane brake by a large fire, when sleep had locked up their senses, my situation not disposing me for rest, I touched my companion and gently awoke him. We improved this favourable opportunity, and departed, leaving them to take their rest, and speedily directed our course towards our old camp, but found it plundered, and the company dispersed and gone home. . . .

. . . We were then in a dangerous, helpless situation, exposed daily to perils and death amongst savages and wild beasts, not a white man in the country but ourselves.

Thus situated, many hundred miles from our families in the howling wilderness, I believe few would have equally enjoyed the happiness we experienced. I often observed to my brother, You see now how little nature requires to be satisfied. Felicity, the companion of content, is rather found in our own breasts than in the enjoyment of external things: And I firmly believe it requires but a little philosophy to make a man happy in whatsoever state he is. This consists in a full resignation to the will of Providence; and a resigned soul finds pleasure in a path strewed with briars and thorns. . . .

One day I undertook a tour through the country, and the diversity and beauties of nature I met with in this charming season, expelled every gloomy and vexatious thought. Just at the close of day the gentle gales retired, and left the place to

Text: John Filson, *The Discovery, Settlement, and Present State of Kentucke* (Philadelphia, 1784), pp. 49-57.

the disposal of a profound calm. Not a breeze shook the most tremulous leaf. I had gained the summit of a commanding ridge, and, looking round with astonishing delight, beheld the ample plains, the beauteious tracts below. On the other hand, I surveyed the famous river Ohio that rolled in silent dignity, marking the western boundary of Kentucke with inconceivable grandeur. At a vast distance I beheld the mountains lift their venerable brows, and penetrate the clouds. All things were still. I kindled a fire near a fountain of sweet water, and feasted on the loin of a buck, which a few hours before I had killed. The sullen shades of night soon overspread the whole hemisphere, and the earth seemed to gasp after the hovering moisture. My roving excursion this day had fatigued my body, and diverted my imagination. I laid me down to sleep, and I awoke not until the sun had chased away the night. I continued this tour, and in a few days explored a considerable part of the country, each day equally pleased as the first. I returned again to my old camp, which was not disturbed in my absence. I did not confine my lodging to it, but often reposed in thick cane brakes, to avoid the savages,

who, I believe, often visited my camp, but fortunately for me, in my absence. In this situation I was constantly exposed to danger, and death. How unhappy such a situation for a man tormented with fear, which is vain if no danger comes, and if it does, only augments the pain. It was my happiness to be destitute of this afflicting passion, with which I had the greatest reason to be affected. The prowling wolves diverted my nocturnal hours with perpetual howlings; and the various species of animals in this vast forest, in the daytime, were continually in my view.

Thus I was surrounded with plenty in the midst of want. I was happy in the midst of dangers and inconveniences. In such a diversity it was impossible I should be disposed to melancholy. No populous city, with all the varieties of commerce and stately structures, could afford so much pleasure to my mind, as the beauties of nature I found here. . . .

Soon after, I returned home to my family with a determination to bring them as soon as possible to live in Kentucke, which I esteemed a second paradise, at the risk of my life and fortune.

102

THE AMERICAN SUCCESS STORY: THE COUNTRY MAN IN THE ARTFUL CITY

from Charles Brockden Brown, *Arthur Mervyn*, 1799-1800

Charles Brockden Brown (1771-1810), America's first novelist of any significance, was a firm convert to the ideal of the natural man. His *Arthur Mervyn* (1799-1800) is one of the first treatments of one of the most durable themes of American fiction: the story of the young man from the country who comes to the city to make his fortune. Brown's version of this plot is an incredibly complicated tale involving all kinds of murders, robberies, swindles, and seductions against the background of the Philadelphia Yellow Fever epidemic of 1793. His hero, Arthur Mervyn, the young man from the country, eventually outwits one of the most accomplished and complicated villains in fiction and marries a beautiful, brilliant, and wealthy young widow, solely through the power of his natural innocence, intelligence, and benevolence.

Brown's work is an excellent illustration of the way in which Enlightenment ideas gradually changed and developed—under the influence of European Romantic literature and philosophy—into an American Romanticism which we shall discuss in Part III. This particular selection from *Arthur Mervyn* shows young Arthur on his first trip to the city and demonstrates the particular ambivalence about urban life that Americans felt as early as the end of the eighteenth century. Jefferson and most of his followers felt that the independent farmer was the best foundation of a republican society. To them the city was a symbol of the corruption of masses of people jammed together without the sobering responsibilities of property of their own, a condition that they associated with the hated Old World tyrannies. As Americans became a city-building as well as an agricultural people, this attitude led to very mixed feelings about cities on the part of many Americans. This ambivalence can be seen in the mixed reactions— fear and fascination, resentment and delight—of the young country boy, Arthur Mervyn, to his first urban experiences.

I rose at the dawn, and, without asking or bestowing a blessing, sallied forth into the highroad to the city, which passed near the house. I left nothing behind, the loss of which I regretted. I had purchased most of my own books with the product of my own separate industry, and, their number being, of course, small, I had, by incessant application, gotten the whole of them by rote. They had ceased, therefore, to be of any further use. I left them, without reluctance, to the fate for which I knew them to be reserved, that of affording food and habitation to mice.

I trod this unwonted path with all the fearlessness of youth. In spite of the motives to despondency and apprehension incident to my state, my heels were light and my heart joyous. "Now," said I, "I am mounted into man. I must build a name and a fortune for myself. Strange if this intellect and these hands will not supply me with an honest livelihood. I will try the city in the first place; but, if that should fail, resources are still left to me. I will resume my post in the cornfield and threshing-floor, to which I shall always have access, and where I shall always be happy."

I had proceeded some miles on my journey, when I began to feel the inroads of hunger. I might have stopped at any farm-house, and have breakfasted for nothing. It was prudent to husband, with the utmost care, my slender stock; but I felt reluctance to beg as long as I had the means of buying, and I imagined that coarse bread and a little milk would cost little even at a tavern, when any farmer was willing to bestow them for nothing. My resolution was further influenced by the appearance of a signpost. What excuse could I make for begging a breakfast with an inn at hand and silver in my pocket?

I stopped, accordingly, and breakfasted. The landlord was remarkably attentive and obliging, but his bread was stale, his milk sour, and his cheese the greenest imaginable. I disdained to animadvert on these defects, naturally supposing that his house could furnish no better.

Having finished my meal, I put, without speaking, one of my pieces into his hand. This deportment I conceived to be highly becoming, and to indicate a liberal and manly spirit. I always regarded with contempt a scrupulous maker of bargains. He received the money with a complaisant obeisance. "Right," said he. "*Just* the money, sir. You are on foot, sir. A pleasant way of travelling, sir. I wish you a good day, sir." So saying, he walked away.

Text: Charles Brockden Brown, Arthur Mervyn; or, Memoirs of the Year 1793 (Philadelphia: David McKay, 1889), I, 25-28; II, 3.

This proceeding was wholly unexpected. I conceived myself entitled to at least three-fourths of it in change. The first impulse was to call him back, and contest the equity of his demand; but a moment's reflection showed me the absurdity of such conduct. I resumed my journey with spirits somewhat depressed. I have heard of voyagers and wanderers in deserts, who were willing to give a casket of gems for a cup of cold water. I had not supposed my own condition to be, in any respect, similar; yet I had just given one-third of my estate for a breakfast.

I stopped at noon at another inn. I counted on purchasing a dinner for the same price, since I meant to content myself with the same fare. A large company was just sitting down to a smoking banquet. The landlord invited me to join them. I took my place at the table, but was furnished with bread and milk. Being prepared to depart, I took him aside. "What is to pay?" said I.—"Did you drink any thing, sir?"—"Certainly. I drank the milk which was furnished."—"But any liquors, sir?"—"No."

He deliberated a moment, and then, assuming an air of disinterestedness, " 'Tis our custom to charge dinner and club; but, as you drank nothing, we'll let the club go. A mere dinner is half a dollar, sir."

He had no leisure to attend to my fluctuations. After debating with myself on what was to be done, I concluded that compliance was best, and, leaving the money at the bar, resumed my way.

I had not performed more than half my journey, yet my purse was entirely exhausted. This was a specimen of the cost incurred by living at an inn. If I entered the city, a tavern must, at least for some time, be my abode; but I had not a farthing remaining to defray my charges. My father had formerly entertained a boarder for a dollar per week, and, in case of need, I was willing to subsist upon coarser fare and lie on a harder bed than those with which our guest had been supplied. These facts had been the foundation of my negligence on this occasion.

What was now to be done? To return to my paternal mansion was impossible. To relinquish my design of entering the city and to seek a temporary asylum, if not permanent employment, at some one of the plantations within view, was the most obvious expedient. . . .

I adhered to the crossways, till I reached Market Street. Night had fallen, and a triple row of lamps presented a spectacle enchanting and new. My personal cares were, for a time, lost in the tumultuous sensations with which I was now engrossed. I had never visited the city at this hour. When my last visit was paid, I was a mere child. The novelty which environed every object, was, therefore, nearly absolute. I proceeded with more cautious steps, but was still absorbed in attention to passing objects. I reached the market-house, and, entering it, indulged myself in new delight and new wonder.

I need not remark that our ideas of magnificence and splendour are merely comparative; yet you may be prompted to smile when I tell you that, in walking through this avenue, I, for a moment, conceived myself transported to the hall "pendent with many a row of starry lamps and blazing crescents fed by naphtha and asphaltos." That this transition from my homely and quiet retreat had been effected in so few hours wore the aspect of miracle or magic. . . .

Surely the youth had displayed inimitable and heroic qualities. His courage was the growth of benevolence and reason, and not the child of

insensibility and the nursling of habit. He had been qualified for the encounter of gigantic dangers by no laborious education. He stepped forth upon the stage, unfurnished, by anticipation or experience, with the means of security against fraud; and yet, by the aid of pure intentions, had frustrated the wiles of an accomplished and veteran deceiver.

I blessed the chance which placed the youth under my protection. When I reflected on that tissue of nice contingencies which led him to my door, and enabled me to save from death a being of such rare endowments, my heart overflowed with joy, not unmingled with regrets and trepidation. How many have been cut off by this disease, in their career of virtue and their blossom-time of genius! How many deeds of heroism and self-devotion are ravished from existence, and consigned to hopeless oblivion!

The Uses of Reason: Enlightenment vs. Christian Orthodoxy

A RATIONAL FAITH

103 DEISM

from Thomas Paine, *The Age of Reason*, 1793

Like Thomas Jefferson, Thomas Paine (1737-1809) was a great believer in the efficacy of human reason. However, in personality and career an enormous contrast divides the two. Paine was a fire-breathing revolutionary agitator. In the Revolution, his *Common Sense* and *Crisis* papers gave impassioned and eloquent support for the cause of independence. Not content with a peaceful life after the success of the American struggle for independence, Paine went to France where he was an active leader of the French Revolution. He became disgusted with the excesses of the French Revolutionary government, however, and was thrown into prison by the Jacobins. He was released only after the exercise of American influence.

During his stay in Europe, Paine wrote *The Rights of Man*, a defense of the French Revolution, and *The Age of Reason*, a rationalistic attack on Christianity. When he finally returned to the United States, he found that his radical religious views, expressed in the latter book, had made him a pariah. He spent most of the rest of his life in poverty and obscurity.

In religion, Paine like many leading Americans was a follower of deism, a rationalistic and philosophical religion that had originated with the philosophers of the European Enlightenment. Most of the American deists were content to hold their religious views as private matters, but Paine, an agitator as always, insisted on pointing out what he considered to be the ridiculous errors of traditional Christianity. Statements like those made in the selection following aroused the anger of orthodox Christians. Paine summarized his own religious creed as follows:

I believe in one God and no more; and I hope for happiness beyond this life.

I believe in the equality of man, and I believe that religious duties consist in doing justice, loving mercy, and endeavouring to make our fellow-creatures happy. . . .

I do not believe in the creed professed by the Jewish church, by the Roman church, by the Greek church, by the Turkish church, by the Protestant church, nor by any church that I know of. My own mind is my own church.

If we consider the nature of our condition here, we must see there is no occasion for such a thing as *revealed religion*. What is it we want to know? Does not the creation, the universe we behold, preach to us the existence of an Almighty power, that governs and regulates the whole? And is not the evidence that this creation holds out to our senses infinitely stronger than any thing we can read in a book, that any imposter might make and call the word of God? As for morality, the knowledge of it exists in every man's conscience.

Here we are. The existence of an Almighty power is sufficiently demonstrated to us, though we cannot conceive, as it is impossible we should, the nature and manner of its existence. We cannot conceive how we came here ourselves, and yet we know for a fact that we are here. We must know also, that the power that called us into being, can if he please, and when he pleases, call us to account for the manner in which we have lived here; and therefore, without seeking any other motive for the belief, it is rational to believe that he will, for we know beforehand that he can. The probability or even possibility of the thing is all that we ought to know; for if we knew it as a fact, we should be the mere slaves of terror; our belief would have no merit, and our best actions no virtue.

Deism then teaches us, without the possibility of being deceived, all that is necessary or proper to be known. The creation is the Bible of the deist. He there reads, in the hand-writing of the Creator himself, the certainty of his existence, and the immutability of his power; and all other Bibles and Testaments are to him forgeries. The probability that we may be called to account hereafter, will, to reflecting minds, have the influence of belief; for it is not our belief or disbelief that can make or unmake the fact. As this is the state we are in, and which it is proper we should be in, as free agents, it is the fool only, and not the philosopher, nor even the prudent man, that will live as if there were no God.

But the belief of a God is so weakened by being mixed with the strange fable of the Christian creed, and with the wild adventures related in the Bible, and the obscurity and obscene nonsense of the Testament, that the mind of man is bewildered as in a fog. Viewing all these things in a confused mass, he confounds fact with fable; and as he cannot believe all, he feels a disposition to reject all. But the belief of a God is a belief distinct from all other things, and ought not to be confounded with any. The notion of a Trinity of Gods has enfeebled the belief of *one* God. A multiplication of beliefs acts as a division of belief; and in proportion as anything is divided, it is weakened.

Religion, by such means, becomes a thing of form instead of fact; of notion instead of principle: morality is banished to make room for an imaginary thing called faith, and this faith has its origin in a supposed debauchery; a man is preached instead of a God; an execution is an object for gratitude; the preachers daub themselves with the blood, like a troop of assassins, and pretend to admire the brilliancy it gives them; they preach a humdrum sermon on the merits of the execution; then praise Jesus Christ for being executed, and condemn the Jews for doing it.

A man, by hearing all this nonsense lumped and preached together, confounds the God of the Creation with the imagined God of the Christians, and lives as if there were none.

Of all the systems of religion that ever were invented, there is none more derogatory to the Almighty, more unedifying to man, more repugnant to reason, and more contradictory in itself, than this thing called Christianity. Too absurd for belief, too impossible to convince, and too inconsistent for practice, it renders the heart torpid, or produces only atheists and fanatics. As an engine of power, it serves the purpose of despotism; and as a means of wealth, the avarice of priests; but so far as respects the good of man in general, it leads to nothing here or hereafter.

The only religion that has not been invented, and that has in it every evidence of divine originality, is pure and simple deism. It must have been the first and will probably be the last that man believes. But pure and simple deism does not answer the purpose of despotic governments. They cannot lay hold of religion as an engine but by mixing it with human inventions, and making their own authority a part; neither does it answer the avarice of priests, but by incorporating themselves and their functions with it, and becoming, like the government, a party in the system. It is this that forms the otherwise mysterious connection of church and state; the church human, and the state tyrannic.

Were a man impressed as fully and strongly as he ought to be with the belief of a God, his moral life would be regulated by the force of belief; he would stand in awe of God, and of himself, and would not do the thing that could not be concealed from either. To give this belief the full opportunity of force, it is necessary that it acts alone. This is deism.

Text: Thomas Paine, *Writings,* ed. Moncure D. Conway (New York: G. P. Putnam's Sons, 1896), IV, 188-90.

104 UNITARIAN CHRISTIANITY

from William Ellery Channing, "Unitarian Christianity," 1819

Unitarianism, as a wag had it, was centered about the fatherhood of God, the brotherhood of man, and the neighborhood of Boston. In form it was a mildly rationalistic religion, accepting some of the traditional Christian revelation but only so far as that revelation was in accordance with man's reason. Therefore, the Unitarians denied such traditional articles of faith as the divinity of Christ, whom they saw as an inspired ethical teacher but not in any sense a god.

Growing out of the thoughts of Enlightenment Protestants like Charles Chauncy, whose attack on revivalistic Calvinism we saw in Document 36, Unitarianism was practiced in one form or another at the beginning of the nineteenth century by several Boston congregations. Among them was that of the Federal Street Church,' whose minister was William Ellery Channing. When sharp differences arose among New England congregations around 1815, Channing at first took a neutral position, wishing to avoid the formation of a new sect, but finally became leader of the Unitarian ranks. The new faith received a definite formulation in 1819, when, at the ordination of Jared Sparks, William Ellery Channing delivered a sermon on "Unitarian Christianity." With this sermon the lines were firmly drawn between the orthodox Christians and the new Unitarians, and considerable controversy resulted.

Unitarianism has always been a cool, rational, and decorous religion that has had a particular appeal to upper-class groups and intellectuals, never becoming widely popular because of its lack of fire and emotionalism. At first it was mainly confined to relatively aristocratic congregations in the vicinity of Boston, but beginning in the mid-nineteenth century, Unitarianism spread all over the country; today most cities of any size have at least one Unitarian congregation.

William Ellery Channing, the first philosopher of the Unitarian movement, was well equipped in terms of both intellect and personality to be the Unitarian leader. Born in 1780 in Newport, R. I., Channing was educated at Harvard, from which he received his degree in 1798. In 1803 he was ordained and installed as minister of the Federal Street Church of Boston, a post he held until his death. In 1820 he organized the Berry Street Conference of Ministers, out of which the American Unitarian Association grew in 1825. Channing was a brilliant and highly educated man of great integrity, with a cool and rational personality which made him a moderate in all things. His only enthusiasm was humanitarianism; he fervently opposed slavery, war, and social injustice. He died in Bennington, Vt., in 1842.

In this selection from his sermon at the ordination of Jared Sparks, his emphasis on reason in the analysis of religious matters shows his close relationship to the American Enlightenment.

The peculiar circumstances of this occasion not only justify but seem to demand a departure from the course generally followed by preachers at the introduction of a brother into the sacred office. It is usual to speak of the nature, design, duties, and advantages of the Christian ministry; and on these topics I should now be happy to insist, did I not remember that a minister is to be given this day to a religious society whose peculiarities of opinion have drawn upon them much remark, and, may I not add, much reproach. Many good minds, many sincere Christians, I am aware, are apprehensive that the solemnities of this day are to give a degree of influence to principles which they deem false and injurious. The fears and anxieties of such men I respect; and, believing that they are grounded in part on mis-

take, I have thought it my duty to lay before you, as clearly as I can, some of the distinguishing opinions of that class of Christians in our country who are known to sympathize with this religious society. I must ask your patience, for such a subject is not to be despatched in a narrow compass. I must also ask you to remember that it is impossible to exhibit, in a single discourse, our views of every doctrine of revelation, much less the differences of opinion which are known to subsist among ourselves. I shall confine myself to topics on which our sentiments have been misrepresented, or which distinguish us most widely from others. May I not hope to be heard

Text: William Ellery Channing, *Works* (Boston: James Munroe & Co., 1841), III, 59-62, 65-66, 84-86, 93-94.

with candor? God deliver us all from prejudice and unkindness, and fill us with the love of truth and virtue! . . .

I. We regard the Scriptures as the records of God's successive relations to mankind, and particularly of the last and most perfect revelation of his will by Jesus Christ. Whatever doctrines seem to us to be clearly taught in the Scriptures, we receive without reserve or exception. We do not, however, attach equal importance to all the books in this collection. Our religion, we believe, lies chiefly in the New Testament. The dispensation of Moses, compared with that of Jesus, we consider as adapted to the childhood of the human race, a preparation for a nobler system, and chiefly useful now as serving to confirm and illustrate the Christian Scriptures. Jesus Christ is the only master of Christians, and whatever he taught, either during his personal ministry or by his inspired Apostles, we regard as of divine authority, and profess to make the rule of our lives.

Our leading principle in interpreting Scriptures is this, that the Bible is a book written for men, in the language of men, and that its meaning is to be sought in the same manner as that of other books. We believe that God, when He speaks to the human race, conforms, if we may so say, to the established rules of speaking and writing. How else would the Scriptures avail us more than if communicated in an unknown tongue?

Now all books and all conversation require in the reader or hearer the constant exercise of reason; for their true import is only to be obtained by continual comparison and inference. Human language, you well know, admits various interpretations; and every word and every sentence must be modified and explained according to the subject which is discussed, according to the purposes, feelings, circumstances, and principles of the writer, and according to the genius and idioms of the language which he uses. These are acknowledged principles in the interpretation of human writings; and a man whose words we should explain without reference to these principles would reproach us justly with a criminal want of candor, and an intention of obscuring or distorting his meaning. . . .

We object strongly to the contemptuous manner in which human reason is often spoken of by our adversaries, because it leads, we believe, to universal scepticism. If reason be so dreadfully darkened by the fall that its most decisive judgments on religion are unworthy of trust, then Christianity, and even natural theology, must be abandoned; for the existence and veracity of God, and the divine original of Christianity, are conclusions of reason, and must stand or fall with

it. If revelation be at war with this faculty, it subverts itself, for the great question of its truth is left by God to be decided at the bar of reason. It is worthy of remark, how nearly the bigot and the sceptic approach. Both would annihilate our confidence in our faculties, and both throw doubt and confusion over truth. We honor revelation too highly to make it the antagonist of reason, or to believe that it calls us to renounce our highest powers. . . .

To give our views of God in one word, we believe in his parental character. We ascribe to him not only the name, but the dispositions and principles of a father. We believe that he has a father's concern for his creatures, a father's desire for their improvement, a father's equity in proportioning his commands to their powers, a father's joy in their progress, a father's readiness to receive the penitent, and a father's justice for the incorrigible. We look upon this world as a place of education, in which he is training men by prosperity and adversity, by aids and obstructions, by conflicts of reason and passion, by motives to duty and temptations to sin, by a various discipline suited to free and moral beings, for union with himself, and for a sublime and ever-growing virtue in heaven.

Now, we object to the systems of religion which prevail among us, that they are adverse, in a greater or less degree, to these purifying, comforting, and honorable views of God; that they take from us our Father in heaven, and substitute for him a being whom we cannot love if we would, and whom we ought not to love if we could. We object, particularly on this ground, to that system which arrogates to itself the name of Orthodoxy, and which is now industriously propagated through our country. This system indeed takes various shapes, but in all it casts dishonor on the Creator. According to its old and genuine form, it teaches that God brings us into life wholly depraved, so that under the innocent features of our childhood is hidden a nature averse to all good and propense to all evil, a nature which exposes us to God's displeasure and wrath, even before we have acquired power to understand our duties or to reflect upon our actions. According to a more modern exposition, it teaches that we came from the hands of our Maker with such a constitution, and are placed under such influences and circumstances, as to render certain and infallible the total depravity of every human being from the first moment of his moral agency; and it also teaches that the offence of the child, who brings into life this ceaseless tendency to unmingled crime, exposes him to the sentence of everlasting damnation. Now, according to the plainest principles of morality, we maintain that a natural constitution of the mind, unfailingly disposing it to evil, and to evil alone, would absolve it from guilt; that to give existence under this condition would argue unspeakable cruelty; and that to punish the sin of this unhappily constituted child with endless ruin would be a wrong unparalleled by the most merciless despotism. . . .

. . . I shall now, in the last place, give our views of the nature of Christian virtue, or true holiness. We believe that all virtue has its foundation in the moral nature of man, that is, in conscience, or his sense of duty, and in the power of forming his temper and life according to conscience. We believe that these moral faculties are the grounds of responsibility, and the highest distinctions of human nature, and that no act is praiseworthy any farther than it springs from their exertion. We believe that no dispositions infused into us without our own moral activity are of the nature of virtue, and therefore we reject the doctrine of

irresistible divine influence on the human mind, moulding it into goodness as marble is hewn into a statue. Such goodness, if this word may be used, would not be the object of moral approbation, any more than the instinctive affections of inferior animals, or the constitutional amiableness of human beings.

By these remarks, we do not mean to deny the importance of God's aid or Spirit; but by his Spirit we mean a moral, illuminating, and persuasive influence, not physical, not compulsory, not involving a necessity of virtue. We object, strongly, to the idea of many Christians respecting man's impotence and God's irresistible agency on the heart, believing that they subvert our responsibility and the laws of our moral nature, that they make men machines, that they cast on God the blame of all evil deeds, that they discourage good minds, and inflate the fanatical with wild conceits of immediate and sensible inspiration.

105

REFORM OF THE MIND: PSYCHOLOGY AND CONTROL OF THE MORAL INSTINCT

from Benjamin Rush, "The Influence of Physical Causes on the Moral Faculty," 1815

Benjamin Rush, physician and signer of the Declaration of Independence, was one of a group of extraordinarily capable Enlightenment scientists who worked together through Benjamin Franklin's American Philosophical Society, centered at Philadelphia. The members of this group shared ideas and interests similar to those of Thomas Jefferson, being, like him, republican and rationalistic.

In this selection from Rush's fascinating paper on "The Influence of Physical Causes on the Moral Faculty," we see an extreme statement of the Enlightenment's hope that human reason, unaided by divine revelation, could bring man "to the likeness of God Himself" through the discovery of the natural laws of morality. Rush felt that man's "moral instinct" or "faculty" (which Jefferson discusses in his letter to Thomas Law, Document 90) is partially controlled by physical agents like climate, diet, pain, disease, and habits. He suggests that an understanding of these elements could lead to the elimination of those elements which have a bad influence on man, thereby progressively improving the moral character of the human race.

Though Rush, like Jefferson, considered himself a Christian and was by no means an opponent of religion, it is not surprising that his ideas about the moral faculty aroused great opposition among the orthodox. In traditional Christian thought, man's morality was determined solely by his relationship to God, physical causes having nothing to do with the matter.

Rush's paper is also interesting as a rationale for the new science of psychology, which first appeared during the Enlightenment. Throughout the nineteenth and early twentieth centuries, American psychological and sociological research was strongly influenced by the hope of finding some way to improve the moral character of man, a hope for which Benjamin Rush was one of the earliest exponents.

Born near Philadelphia in 1745, Benjamin Rush was graduated from Princeton at the age of fourteen and from the University of Edinburgh at twenty-two. After becoming professor of chemistry at the College of Philadelphia, he engaged actively in Revolutionary movements and later in the debates over the Constitution. In 1789 he assumed a professorship of the theory and practice of medicine, followed by a professorship in the medical college of the University of Pennsylvania. He became a strong advocate of slavery abolition, was associated with various religious and scientific societies, and from 1799 until his death from typhus in Philadelphia in 1813 was treasurer of the United States Mint. His best-known works are *Medical Inquiries and Observations* (5 volumes, 1789-1798) and *Diseases of the Mind* (1812).

The Influence of Physical Causes Upon the Moral Faculty

By the moral faculty I mean a capacity in the human mind of distinguishing and choosing good and evil, or, in other words, virtue and vice. It is a native principle, and though it be capable of improvement by experience and reflection, it is not derived from either of them. . . . The moral faculty is what the schoolmen call the "regula regulans;" the conscience is their "regula regulata;" or, to speak in more modern terms, the moral faculty performs the office of a lawgiver, while the business of conscience is to perform the duty of a judge. The moral faculty is to the conscience, what taste is to the judgment, and sensation to perception. It is quick in its operations, and like the sensitive plant, acts without reflection, while conscience follows with deliberate steps, and measures all her actions by the unerring square of right and wrong. The moral faculty exercises itself upon the actions of others. It approves, even in books, of the virtues of a Trajan, and disapproves of the vices of a Marius, while conscience confines its operations only to its own actions. These two capacities of the mind are generally in an exact ratio to each other, but they sometimes exist in different degrees in the same person. Hence we often find conscience in its full vigour, with a diminished tone, or total absence of the moral faculty. . . .

Our books of medicine contain many records of the effects of physical causes upon the memory, the imagination, and the judgment. In some instances we behold their operation only on one, in others on two, and in many cases, upon the whole of these faculties. Their derangement has received different names, according to the number or nature of the faculties that are affected. The loss of memory has been called "amnesia;" false judgment upon one subject has been called "melancholia;" false judgment upon all subjects has been called "mania;" and a defect of all the three intellectual faculties that have been mentioned has received the name of "amentia." Persons who labour under the derangement, or want, of these faculties of the mind, are considered, very properly, as subjects of medicine; and there are many cases upon record, that prove that their diseases have yielded to the healing art.

Text: Benjamin Rush, *Medical Inquiries and Observations* (Philadelphia: Johnson & Warner, 1815), I, 95-97, 106, 120-22.

I am aware, that in venturing upon this subject I step upon untrodden ground. I feel as Aeneas did, when he was about to enter the gates of Avernus, but without a sybil to instruct me in the mysteries that are before me. I foresee, that men who have been educated in the mechanical habits of adopting popular or established opinions will revolt at the doctrine I am about to deliver, while men of sense and genius will hear my propositions with candour, and if they do not adopt them, will commend that boldness of inquiry, that prompted me to broach them. . . .

The extent of the moral powers and habits in man is unknown. It is not improbable, but the human mind contains principles of virtue, which have never yet been excited into action. We behold with surprise the versatility of the human body in the exploits of tumblers and rope-dancers. Even the agility of a wild beast has been demonstrated in a girl of France, and an amphibious nature has been discovered in the human species, in a young man in Spain. We listen with astonishment to the accounts of the *memories* of Mithridates, Cyrus, and Servin. We feel a veneration bordering upon divine homage, in contemplating the stupendous *understandings* of Lord Verulam and Sir Isaac Newton; and our eyes grow dim, in attempting to pursue Shakspeare and Milton in their immeasurable flights of *imagination*. And if the history of mankind does not furnish similar instances of the versatility and perfection of our species in virtue, it is because the moral faculty has been the subject of less culture and fewer experiments than the body, and the intellectual powers of the mind. From what has been said, the reason of this is obvious. Hitherto the cultivation of the moral faculty has been the business of parents, schoolmasters and divines. But if the principles, we have laid down, be just, the improvement and extension of this principle should be equally the business of the legislator—the natural philosopher—and the physician; and a physical regimen should as necessarily accompany a moral precept, as directions with respect to the air—exercise—and diet, generally accompany prescriptions for the consumption and the gout. To encourage us to undertake experiments for the improvement of morals, let us recollect the success of philosophy in lessening the number, and mitigating the violence of incurable diseases. The intermitting fever, which proved fatal to two of the monarchs of Britain, is now under absolute subjection to medicine. Continual fevers are much less fatal than formerly. The small-pox is disarmed of its mortality by inoculation, and even the tetanus and the cancer have lately received a check in their ravages upon mankind. But medicine has done more. It has penetrated the deep and gloomy abyss of death, and acquired fresh honours in his cold embraces.—Witness the many hundred people who have lately been brought back to life, by the successful efforts of the humane societies, which are now established in many parts of Europe, and in some parts of America. Should the same industry and ingenuity, which have produced these triumphs of medicine over diseases and death, be applied to the moral science, it is highly probable, that most of those baneful vices, which deform the human breast, and convulse the nations of the earth, might be banished from the world. I am not so sanguine as to suppose, that it is possible for man to acquire so much perfection from science, religion, liberty and good government, as to cease to be mortal; but I am fully persuaded, that from the combined action of causes, which operate at once upon the reason, the moral faculty, the passions, the senses, the brain, the nerves, the blood and the heart, it is possible to produce such a change in his moral character, as shall raise him to a resemblance of angels—nay more, to the likeness of GOD himself. . . .

ORTHODOXY REPLIES

106

REVELATION IS THE HIGHEST REASON: AN ORTHODOX ATTACK ON RATIONALISM

from Archibald Alexander, *Evidences*, 1836

Although many social and intellectual leaders of the early republic were strongly imbued with the rationalism of the Enlightenment, the majority of Americans, though convinced republicans, remained orthodox Protestant Christians. So long as the deists and Unitarians kept their beliefs a matter of their own private consciences there was little concern among the orthodox. Reaction against Enlightenment ideas in religious matters were largely confined to sporadic but intense outbursts of religious revivalism like the mid-eighteenth-century Great Awakening. However, when deists like Thomas Paine began to attack Christianity, and Enlightenment scientists like Benjamin Rush began to suggest that moral matters could be investigated scientifically, the orthodox reaction became more vociferous. It took two main forms: a continuation of emotional revivalism (illustrated by Document 107) and, on a more intellectual level, a search for arguments in support of the divine inspiration of the Bible and the necessity of orthodox Christianity for a republican society.

Since most citizens were supporters of orthodox Protestantism, the forces of orthodoxy had control of almost all the schools and colleges. One of the courses which was required in almost every academic institution in America was that in "Evidences of Christianity," in which students were shown all the arguments in favor of the validity and authority of the Bible and Christian beliefs. One of the popular texts for this course was the "Evidences" of Archibald Alexander, professor of theology at Princeton University from 1813 to 1851.

In this selection from Alexander's book, he criticizes the Rational Christians, a variety of Unitarians, for their use of reason in the analysis of God's revelation.

Before I leave the consideration of the various classes of persons who, while they profess to be guided by reason, make an improper use of this faculty, I ought to mention a set of men, distinguished for their learning and ingenuity, who profess to receive the Christian revelation and glory in the appellation of Rational Christians. They proceed on the plausible and (if rightly understood) correct principle of receiving nothing as true but what their reason approves; but these very men, with all their fair appearances of rationality, are chargeable with as gross a dereliction of reason as can well be conceived; and, in regard to consistency, are more vulnerable than any of those already mentioned. While they admit that God has made a revelation, they insist upon the right of bringing the truths revealed to the test of human judgment and opinion, and reject

Text: Archibald Alexander, *Evidences of the Authenticity, Inspiration, and Canonical Authority of the Holy Scriptures* (Philadelphia: Presbyterian Board of Publication, 1836), pp. 14-15.

them as unreasonable if they do not accord with this standard. But the declaration of God is the highest reason which we can have for believing any thing. To set up our opinion against the plain expression of his will, is surely presumption of the highest kind. Perhaps, however, I do not represent the case with perfect accuracy. Perhaps no man is chargeable with such an inconsistency, as to admit a thing to be contained in an undoubted revelation, and yet reject it. The exact state of the matter is this. The Scriptures, it is admitted, contain a revelation from God; but there are many things in the Bible, which if taken in the most obvious sense, are inconsistent with reason; and as nothing inconsistent with reason can be from God, it is concluded that this cannot be the true sense of Scripture. Accordingly, their wits are set to work, and their learning laid under contribution, to invent and defend some other sense. Upon these principles, a man may believe just as much, or as little as he pleases of what the Bible contains; for it has been found, that no text is so stubborn as not to yield to some of the modes of treatment which have been adopted. This whole procedure is contrary to right reason. The plain course which reason directs us to pursue, is, after examining the evidences of revelation until we are satisfied, to come to the interpretation of the Scriptures with an unbiased mind; and in the exercise of a sound judgment, and with the aid of those helps and rules which reason and experience suggest, to obtain the sense of the several parts of the document; and although this sense may contradict our preconceived opinions, or clash with our inclinations, we ought implicitly to receive it; and not by a refined ingenuity, and laboured critical process, to extort a meaning that will suit our own notions. This is not to form our opinions by the word of God, but to cut down the sublime and mysterious doctrines of revelation to the measure of our narrow conceptions. In the creed of many, called Rational Christians, the divine system of heavenly truth is shorn of its glory, and comes forth little more than an improved theory of Natural Religion. There is no reason in this.

FRONTIER REVIVALISM

107

A FRESH, GREEN, LIVE YANKEE: A METHODIST CIRCUIT RIDER LAUGHING AT A RATIONAL MISSIONARY

from Peter Cartwright, *Autobiography*, 1857

Revivalist techniques developed by eighteenth-century Calvinists like Jonathan Edwards were continued by other religious groups on the early nineteenth-century frontier as part of the strong orthodox reaction to the Enlightenment's rationalism.

One unique American institution developed by these groups around 1800 was the frontier camp meeting. Large groups would assemble in tents or out in the open air to hear the preaching of the rousing and spirited itinerant preachers, the circuit riders. The preacher would go through the assembly, singing, exhorting, praying, and admonishing poor sinners, and the crowd would become tumultuous, shouting, "jerking," falling down, tumbling, and evincing other signs of emotional release. These camp meetings were an important part of frontier life, one of the few opportunities for isolated farmers to get together and let off steam and at the same time catch up on the news of the day.

The Methodists were among the most successful of religious groups on the frontier, because their use of uneducated but gifted circuit riders allowed them to cover the area more adequately than their Congregationalist and Presbyterian rivals, who generally tried to set up congregations and erect church buildings. Also, the circuit riders were frequently frontier men themselves and had a better understanding of the psychology of the pioneer settler than did the highly educated New Englanders whom the Presbyterians and Congregationalists sent out as missionaries.

Peter Cartwright was a typical Methodist circuit rider. Somewhat more literate than many of his colleagues, he left us an autobiography which is one of the most fascinating documents of the period. Born in Virginia in 1785, Cartwright moved to the Kentucky wilderness with his parents when he was five and became a Methodist circuit rider at the age of eighteen, traveling in Kentucky, Tennessee, Indiana, Ohio, and Illinois for nearly fifty years. His death came in 1872 at the age of eighty-seven. Among many interesting incidents in his long and colorful career was his campaign for Congress in 1846, when he was defeated by another American of some note, Abraham Lincoln.

This selection from Cartwright's autobiography tells what happened when a calm, rational, and highly educated New England missionary appeared in Cartwright's territory in the midst of a revival meeting. It illustrates nicely the feelings of a strenuously orthodox Christian toward a moderate and rational Christian of the American Enlightenment.

There happened to be at our quarterly meeting a fresh, green, live Yankee from down east. He had regularly graduated, and had his diploma, and was regularly called, by the Home Missionary Society, to visit the far-off west—a perfect moral waste, in his view of the subject; and having been taught to believe that we were almost cannibals, and that Methodist preachers were nothing but a poor, illiterate set of ignoramuses, he longed for an opportunity to display his superior tact and talent, and throw us poor upstarts of preachers in the west, especially Methodist preachers, into the shades of everlasting darkness. He, of course, was very forward and officious. He would, if I had permitted it, have taken the lead of our meeting. At length I thought I would give him a chance to ease himself of his mighty burden, so I put him up one night to read his sermon. The frame building we were worshiping in was not plastered, and the wind blew hard; our candles flared and gave a bad light, and our ministerial hero made a very awkward out in reading his sermon. The congregation paid a heavy penance and became restive; he balked, and hemmed, and coughed at a disgusting rate. At the end of about thirty minutes the great blessing came: he closed, to the great satisfaction of all the congregation.

I rose and gave an exhortation, and had a bench prepared, to which I invited the mourners. They came in crowds; and there was a solemn power rested on the congregation. My little hothouse reader seemed to recover from his paroxysm of a total failure, as though he had done all right, and, uninvited, he turned in to talk to the mourners. He would ask them if they did not love Christ; then he would try to show them that Christ was lovely; then he would tell them it was a very easy thing to become a Christian; that they had only to resolve to be a Christian, and instantly he or she was a Christian. I listened a moment, and saw this heterodoxy would not do; that it produced jargon and confusion. I stepped up to him and said:

"Brother, you don't know how to talk to mourners. I want you to go out into the congregation, and exhort sinners."

He did not appear the least disconcerted, but at my bidding he left the altar, and out he went into the crowd, and turned in to talking to sinners.

There was a very large man, who stood a few steps from the mourners, who weighed about two hundred and thirty pounds; he had been a professor, but was backslidden. The power of God arrested him, and he cried out aloud for mercy, standing on his feet. My little preacher turned round, and pressed back through the crowd; and coming up to this large man, reached up, and tapped him on the shoulder, saying,

"Be composed; be composed."

Seeing, and indistinctly hearing this, I made my way to him, and cried out at the top of my voice,

"Pray on, brother; pray on, brother; there's no composure in hell or damnation."

And just as I crowded my way to this convicted man, who was still crying aloud for mercy, the little preacher tapped him again on the shoulder, saying,

"Be composed; be composed, brother."

I again responded:

"Pray on, brother; pray on, brother; there is no composure in hell."

I said to the throng that crowded the aisle that led to the altar,

"Do, friends, stand back, till I get this man to the mourners' bench."

But they were so completely jammed together that it seemed almost impossible for me to get through with my mourner. I let go his arm, and stepped forward to open the way to the altar, and just as I had opened the aisle, and turned to go back, and lead him to the mourners' bench, the Lord spoke peace to his soul, standing on his feet; and he cried, "Glory to God," and in the ecstasy of his joy, he reached forward to take me in his arms; but, fortunately for me, two men were crowded into the aisle between him and myself, and he could not reach me. Missing his aim in catching me, he wheeled round and caught my little preacher in his arms, and lifted him up from the floor; and being a large, strong man, having great physical power, he jumped from bench to bench, knocking the people against one another on the right and left, front and rear, holding up in his arms the little preacher. The little fellow stretched out both arms and both

Text: Peter Cartwright, *Autobiography,* ed. W. P. Strickland (New York: Carlton & Porter, 1857), pp. 370-72.

feet, expecting every moment to be his last, when he would have his neck broken. O! how I desired to be near this preacher at that moment, and tap him on the shoulder, and say, "Be composed; be composed, brother!" But as solemn as the times were, I, with many others, could not command my risibilities, and for the moment, it had like to have checked the rapid flow of good feeling with those that beheld the scene; but you may depend on it, as soon as the little hot-bed parson could make his escape, he was missing.

CHAPTER 9

Interpretations of the Revolution

and the New Republic

It is almost a fixed rule that great historical controversies lead to controversial history. Thus it is with the American Revolution, the formation of the Constitution, Jacksonian Democracy, the Civil War, the New Deal, and other critical events or movements in American history. And though time lends perspective to historical understanding, the great encounters of American history involve enduring issues that are usually no less real, no less divisive to latter-day interpreters who come to assess the motives and achievements of the past than they were to the original participants.

That the Revolution and the founding of the new republic should inspire conflicting historical interpretations does not seem strange. At stake were fundamental choices that would set the course of national development—choices concerning the centralization of political power, the scope of individual liberty, the role of the popular majority in government, and the direction of social and economic development. A powerful, original historian, Charles A. Beard (1874-1948), did much to set the terms of a scholarly debate that has continued for a generation. The modern "Beardian" synthesis combines elements from several major contributors— J. Franklin Jameson, *The American Revolution Considered as a Social Movement* (1926); Carl Becker, *History of Political Parties in the Province of New York, 1760-1776* (1909); and Merrill Jensen, *The New Nation* (1950)—as well as from Beard's own works, especially *An Economic Interpretation of the Constitution* (1913) and *The Rise of American Civilization* (1927).

In simplified form, the "Beardian" view emphasizes the *political* conflict of democrats and aristocratic forces, based upon the *social* conflict of agrarian and commercial economic interests. Thus it is argued that the Revolution was a dual movement: a fight for home rule, as Carl Becker put it, and equally a fight about who should rule at home. The agrarian-democrats won substantial victories in the states and secured their influence under the Articles of Confederation, which left effective sovereignty with the states. In the Constitutional Convention of 1787 and in the state ratifying conventions—the "Beardian" argument continues—a commercial-aristocratic minority employed wealth, talent, prestige, personal influence, and clever strategy to effect a "counterrevolution." In consequence, a political élite, entrenched in the central government and protected by checks and balances, could restrain the passions of the many, block agrarian debtor legislation, and promote the interests of investors and business enterprisers. The struggle between agrarian democracy and commercial aristocracy continued under the new Constitution, with Jefferson and Hamilton as the two great leaders (and symbols) of this basic antagonism in American society and politics. (A careful, scholarly application of the "Beardian" view to the American Revolution is presented in Professor Merrill Jensen's essay, Document 108.)

Professor Daniel Boorstin offers one significant challenge to the "Beardian" thesis (Document 109). Boorstin not only questions the importance of internal social and political divisions in the Revolution but also—more emphatically—attacks the whole conventional notion of the Revolution as a struggle for philosophic ideals. According to his reading, the Declaration of Independence is less concerned with self-evident universal truths about the natural rights of man than it is with the felt grievances of a set of law-minded Britons.

Professor Edmund Morgan in his approach to the birth of the Republic disputes the crucial proposition of the "Beardian" school: the contention that the Constitution represents a conservative class reaction against the democratic principles of the Declaration (Document 110). But he does so while rejecting equally Boorstin's conception that the Revolution and the Constitution were relatively free of dogma. To Morgan, the Revolution was indeed inspired and guided by the dogma—he would say doctrine or principles—of John Locke and the Declaration. *Ideas* of man's equal natural rights and of government as the product of popular consent gave meaning to *experience*, and not the other way around. In this respect Morgan returns to the traditional view of the Revolution, given classical definition by George Bancroft in the nineteenth century.

The passage from Revolution to Constitution was not, Morgan contends, a case of democratic backsliding, nor was it essentially a consequence of class strategem. Rather the Constitution was a practical adaptation of liberal principles to hard realities, in terms consistent with the Declaration. Class interests sometimes coincided with and reinforced the common interest, but they did not dictate the form and content of the Constitution. Morgan's view expresses, in part, the conclusions of recent research indicating that, contrary to Beard's suggestions, (1) political participation was open to a large majority of white, male Americans when the Constitution was adopted, and remained so, and (2) supporters and opponents of the Constitution did not divide neatly according to their economic interests into agrarian debtors and commercial creditors.

Henry Adams' classic study of the Republican regime under Jefferson and Madison is not concerned with the "Beardian" battle. In his *History of the United States* Adams instead provides a masterly examination of Thomas Jefferson's dilemma: how Jefferson, as President, should employ the concentrated powers of the national government for the public good, while holding the political conviction that all power tends to corrupt and that concentrated power corrupts absolutely.

108

DEMOCRACY AND THE AMERICAN REVOLUTION

from Merrill Jensen, "Democracy and the American Revolution," 1957

Professor Merrill Jensen of the University of Wisconsin has done much to shape the prevailing historical view of the Confederation period. His major contributions are *The Articles of Confederation* (1940) and *The New Nation* (1950), works which have persuaded most historians to place quotation marks around the phrase "Critical Period" as a designation for the 1780's. (See Document 58.)

The following selection is from a brief reformation of his position he delivered at the Conference of Early American History at the Henry E. Huntington Library, February 9, 1957. Here the author attempts to meet recent criticisms of his work, with special reference to the "internal revolution" thesis (see the Introduction to this chapter); he does so by clarifying the definition of democracy and reviewing significant examples of democratic protest and conservative alarm.

A contrasting view of the American Revolution appears in Document 109, and an implicit contrast is suggested in Professor Morgan's discussion of the Constitutional Convention in Document 110.

The historian who ventures to talk about democracy in early America is in danger because there are almost as many opinions as there are writers on the subject. The Puritans have been pictured as the founders of American democracy, and it is vigorously denied that they had anything to do with it. Some have seen in Roger Williams the father of American democracy, and others have denied that he was a democrat, whatever his putative progeny may be. The conflict is equally obvious when it comes to the American Revolution, and the problems of solution are far more complex than they are for the seventeenth century. The difficulty is compounded, for all too often men's emotions seem to become involved.

It is sometimes suggested that we avoid the use of the word "democracy" when discussing the seventeenth and eighteenth centuries. It seems to me that this is a flat evasion of the problem, for the Americans of those centuries used the word and they meant something by it. Our task, then, is not to avoid the issue but to try to understand what they meant, and understand what they meant in the context of the times in which they lived. What we must not do is to measure the seventeenth and eighteenth centuries in terms of our own assumptions about what democracy is or should be. This is all the more important since many of us do not seem to be too clear about our assumptions, even for the century in which we live.

A number of years ago I took the position that "in spite of the paradoxes involved one may still maintain that the Revolution was essentially, though relatively, a democratic movement within the thirteen American colonies, and that its significance for the political and constitutional history of the United States lay in its tendency to

elevate the political and economic status of the majority of the people." And then, with a somewhat rhetorical flourish which I have sometimes regretted but have not as yet withdrawn, I went on to say that "the Articles of Confederation were the constitutional expression of this movement and the embodiment in governmental form of the philosophy of the Declaration of Independence." One thing can be said for this statement at least: reviewers read it and quoted it, some with raised eyebrows, and some with approval, whether or not they said anything at all about the rest of the book. . . .

It is clear that a considerable diversity of opinion prevails. It is also clear that the time has come to set forth certain propositions or generalizations which seem to me to have a measure of validity.

First of all, a definition of democracy is called for. And just to face the issue squarely, I will offer one stated at Newport, Rhode Island, in 1641 when a meeting declared that "the government which this body politic doth attend unto . . . is a democracy or popular government; . . . that is to say: It is in the power of the body of freemen, orderly assembled, or the major part of them, to make or constitute just laws, by which they will be regulated, and to depute from among themselves such ministers as shall see them faithfully executed between man and man." That such an idea was not confined to Newport was shown six years later when the little towns in Rhode Island formed a confederation, the preamble of which states: "It is agreed, by this present assembly

Text: Merrill Jensen, "Democracy and the American Revolution," The Huntington Library Quarterly, XX (August 1957), 321-32, 338-41 *passim.*

thus incorporate, and by this present act declared, that the form of government established in Providence Plantations is democratical; that is to say, a government held by the free and voluntary consent of all, or the greater part of the free inhabitants." . . .

The second proposition is that colonial governments on the eve of the Revolution did not function democratically, nor did the men who controlled them believe in democracy. Even if we agree that there was virtually manhood suffrage in Massachusetts, it is difficult, for me at least, to see it as a democracy. In 1760 the government was controlled by a superb political machine headed by Thomas Hutchinson, who with his relatives and political allies occupied nearly every important political office in the colony except the governorship. The Hutchinson oligarchy controlled the superior court, the council, the county courts, and the justices of the peace; with this structure of appointive office spread throughout the colony, it was able to control the house of representatives elected by the towns. For six years after 1760 the popular party in Boston, led by Oxenbridge Thacher and James Otis, suffered one defeat after another at the hands of the Hutchinson machine. The popular leaders in the town of Boston tried everything from slander to mob violence to get control of the government of the colony but it was not until after the Stamp Act crisis that they were able to win a majority of the house of representatives to their side. Even then, men like James Otis did not at first realize that the Stamp Act could be turned to advantage in the fight against the Hutchinson oligarchy. In terms of political support between 1760 and 1765, if Massachusetts had a democratic leader, that man was Thomas Hutchinson, a charge to which he would have been the first to issue a horrified denial.

The third proposition is that before 1774 or 1775 the revolutionary movement was not a democratic movement, except by inadvertence. The pamphleteers who wrote on political and constitutional questions, and the town and county meetings and legislatures that resolved endlessly between 1763 and 1774, were concerned with the formulation of constitutional arguments to defend the colonies and their legislatures from interference by parliament.

The colonial theorists wrote much about the British constitution, the rights of Englishmen, and even of the laws of nature, but they accepted the British assumption that colonial governments derived from British charters and commissions. Their essential concern was with the relationship that existed, or ought to exist, between the British government and the colonial governments, and not with the relationship between man as man, and government itself. Such writers showed no interest in domestic problems, and when it was suggested that the arguments against taxation by parliament were equally applicable to the taxation of under-represented areas in the colonies, or to dissenting religious groups, such suggestions were looked upon as being quite out of order.

The same indifference was displayed in the realm of political realities. The ardent leaders of the fight against British policies showed no interest in, or sympathy for, the discontent of back-country farmers or religious groups such as the Baptists. Instead, they temporarily joined with their political enemies to suppress or ignore it. Such sympathy as the discontented got, they got from the British government, or from colonial leaders charged with being tools of the British power.

The fact is that the popular leaders of the revolutionary movement had no program of domestic reform. Instead, their program was a combination of a continuous assault on the local officeholding aristocracies and an ardent attack on British policies; and in the course of time they identified one with the other. It is sometimes difficult to tell with which side of the program the popular leaders were more concerned. In Massachusetts, for instance, before 1765 they were so violent in their attack on Hutchinson that they prevented Massachusetts from joining the other colonies in making formal protests against British legislation.

The fourth proposition is related to the third. It is that although the popular leaders in the colonies showed no interest in internal political and social change, they were still able to build up a political following, particularly in the seacoast towns. They were superb organizers, propagandists with a touch of genius, and possessed of an almost demonic energy in their dual fight against the local political aristocracies and British policies. After a few false starts such as that of James Otis, who at first called the Virginia Stamp Act Resolves treason, the popular leaders took an extreme stand on the subject of colonial rights. The political aristocracies might object to British policies, as most of them did, but considering what they owed to British backing, they displayed an understandable caution, a caution that made it impossible for them to pose as patriotic leaders.

The popular leaders were also willing to take extreme measures in practical opposition to British policies, ranging all the way from mob violence to non-importation agreements forced upon unwilling merchants. And with ever more force and violence they accused Americans who did not agree with them or their methods of knuckling under to British tyranny and of readiness to sell the liberties of their country for a little pelf. In the course of this campaign they appealed to the people at large. Men who normally could not or did not take part in political life, particularly in the cities, were invited to mass meetings where the rules of suffrage were ignored and where they could shout approval of resolutions carefully prepared in advance by their leaders. In addition, the mob was a constant factor in political life, particularly in Boston where it was efficiently organized. Mobs were used to nullify the Stamp Act, to harass British soldiers, to hamper the operations of the customs service, and to intimidate office holders.

All these activities on the part of the disfranchised, or the hitherto politically inactive, accustomed men to taking part in public affairs as never before; and it gave them an appetite for more. From the beginning of the crisis in 1774 onward, more and more "new men," which was the politest name their opponents called them, played an ever more active role, both on the level of practical politics and on the level of political theory. They began writing about and talking about what they called "democracy." And this was a frightening experience, not only to the conservative-minded leaders of the colonies, but to many of the popular leaders as well.

For instance, when a New York mass meeting gathered in May 1774 to answer the letter of the Boston Town Meeting asking for a complete stoppage of trade with Britain as an answer to the Boston Port Act, the people talked about far more than letter writing. One alarmed observer wrote: "I beheld my fellow-citizens very accurately counting all their chickens, not only before any of them were hatched, but before above one half of the eggs were laid. In short, they fairly contended about the future forms of our government, whether it should be founded upon aristocratic or democratic principles." The leaders had "gulled" the mob for years, and now, said Gouverneur Morris, the mob was waking up and could no longer be fooled. The only salvation for the aristocracy of New York was peace with Britain at almost any price.

By early 1776 the debate over future governments to be adopted was in full swing. Disliking intensely the ideas of government set forth in *Common Sense*, John Adams drafted his *Thoughts on Government*. His plan was modeled on the old government of Massachusetts, with an elective rather than a royal governor, of course, but it certainly contemplated no radical change in the political structure. John Adams was no innovator. He deplored what he called "the rage for innovation" which had appeared in Massachusetts by June of 1776. The projects, said he, are not for repairing the building but for tearing it down. "The projects of county assemblies, town registers, and town probates of wills are founded in narrow notions, sordid stinginess, and profound ignorance, and tend directly to barbarism." . . .

But change was in the air, and writer after writer sought to formulate new ideas about government and to offer concrete suggestions for the theoretical foundations and political structures of the new states to be. In 1775, on hearing that congress had given advice to New Hampshire on the establishment of a government, General John Sullivan offered his thoughts to the revolutionary congress of his colony. All government, he wrote, ought to be instituted for the good of the people. There should be no conflicting branches in imitation of the British constitution "so much celebrated by those who understand nothing of it. . . ." The two houses of the legislature and a governor should all be elected by the people. No danger can arise to a state "from giving the people a free and full voice in their own government." The so-called checks upon the licentiousness of the people "are only the children of designing or ambitious men, no such thing being necessary. . . ."

It seems clear, to me at least, that by 1776 there were people in America demanding the establishment of democratic state governments, by which they meant legislatures controlled by a majority of the voters, and with none of the checks upon their actions such as had existed in the colonies. At the same time there were many Americans who were determined that there should be no changes except those made inevitable by separation from Great Britain.

The history of the writing of the first state constitutions is to a large extent the history of the conflict between these two ideals of government. The conflict can be exaggerated, of course, for there was considerable agreement on structural details. Most of the state constitutions worked out in written form the structure of government that had existed in the colonies, all the way from governors, two-house legislatures, and judicial systems, to the forms of local government. In terms of structure, little that is revolutionary is to be found. Even the much maligned unicameral legislature of Pennsylvania was only a continuation of what Pennsylvania had had since the beginning of the century.

The significant thing is not the continuity of governmental structure, but the alteration of the balance of power within the structure, and in the political situation resulting from the break away from the supervising power of a central government—that of Great Britain.

The first and most revolutionary change was in the field of basic theory. In May 1776, to help bring about the overthrow of the Pennsylvania assembly, the chief stumbling block in the way of independence, Congress resolved that all governments exercising authority under the crown of Great Britain should be suppressed, and that "all the powers of government [be] exerted under the authority of the people of the colonies. . . ." John Adams described it as "the most important resolution that ever was taken in America." The Declaration of Independence spelled it out in terms of the equality of men, the sovereignty of the people, and the right of a people to change their governments as they pleased.

Second: the Revolution ended the power of a sovereign central government over the colonies. Britain had had the power to appoint and remove governors; members of upper houses of legislatures, judges, and other officials. It had the power to veto colonial legislation, to review cases appealed from colonial supreme courts, and to use armed force. All of this superintending power was wiped out by independence.

Third: the new central government created in America by the Articles of Confederation was, in a negative sense at least, a democratic government. The Congress of the United States had no power over either the states or their citizens. Hence, each state could govern itself as it pleased, and as a result of some of the new state constitutions, this often meant by a majority of the voters within a state.

Fourth: in writing the state constitutions, change was inevitable. The hierarchy of appointed legislative, executive, and judicial officials which had served as a check upon the elective legislatures was gone. The elective legislature became the supreme power in every state, and the lower houses, representing people however inadequately, became the dominant branch. The appointive houses of colonial times were replaced by elective senates, which in theory were supposed to represent property. They were expected to, and sometimes did, act as a check upon the lower houses, but their power was far less than that of pre-war councils.

Fifth: the office of governor underwent a real revolution. The governors of the royal colonies had, in theory at least, vast powers, including an absolute veto. In the new constitutions, most Americans united in shearing the office of governor of virtually all power.

Sixth: state supreme courts underwent a similar revolution. Under the state constitutions they were elected by the legislatures or appointed by governors who were elected officials. And woe betide a supreme court that tried to interfere with the actions of a legislature.

What such changes meant in terms of political realities was that a majority of voters within a state, if agreed upon a program and persistent enough, could do what it wanted, unchecked by governors or courts or appeals to a higher power outside the state.

There were other areas in which changes took place, although they were only beginnings. A start was made in the direction of ending the property qualification for voting and office-holding. A few states established what amounted to manhood suffrage, and a few years later even women voted in New Jersey although that was stopped when it appeared that woman suffrage meant only a means of stuffing ballot boxes. A few states took steps in the direction of representation according to population, a process as yet unsolved in the United States. A large step was taken in the direction of disestablishing state churches, but on the whole one still had to be a Protestant, and a Trinitarian at that, to hold office.

In connection with office-holding, there is one eighteenth-century American idea that is worthy of a whole study by itself, and that is the concept of rotation in office. Many Americans were convinced that office-holding bred a lust for power in the holder. Therefore there must be frequent, if not annual, elections; and there must be a limitation on the time one might spend in certain offices. There is probably no more remarkable self-denying ordinance in the history of politics than the provision in the Articles of Confederation that no man could be a member of Congress more than three years out of any six. . . .

109

CONSERVATISM OF THE AMERICAN REVOLUTION

from Daniel Boorstin, "Revolution Without Dogma," 1953

The "Beardian" view of the Revolution and Constitution is associated with the liberal, progressive outlook prevalent in the early years of the twentieth century and again in the New Deal era. Similarly, the point of view expressed in Professor Daniel J. Boorstin's writings is one shared by many scholars and intellectuals of the post-World War II era: men who have grown skeptical of the liberal philosophy, indeed toward all "abstract" philosophy, and have derived from Edmund Burke a new respect for tradition and experience as the sovereign guides to political conduct. Boorstin's discussion of the "Revolution without Dogma" might be taken as a special modern version of Burke's famous Conciliation speech of 1775, in which that eloquent critic of imperial policy argued that American principles of liberty arose out of English tradition and even that the American mind was in part the product of an extreme preoccupation with English legal writings.

Professor Boorstin of the University of Chicago has developed his view of the admirably pragmatic, non-doctrinaire quality of American thought and practice in a series of challenging studies: *The Lost World of Thomas Jefferson* (1948), *The Genius of American Politics* (1953), and *The Americans* (1958). The following selection is taken from the second of these works, originally presented in a series of public lectures at the University of Chicago.

The most obvious peculiarity of our American Revolution is that, in the modern European sense of the word, it was hardly a revolution at all. The Daughters of the American Revolution, who have been understandably sensitive on this subject, have always insisted in their literature that the American Revolution was no revolution but merely a colonial rebellion. The more I have looked into the subject, the more convinced I have become of the wisdom of their naïveté. "The social condition and the Constitution of the Americans are democratic," De Tocqueville observed about a hundred years ago. "But they have not had a democratic revolution." This fact is surely one of the most important of our history.

A number of historians (J. Franklin Jameson and Merrill Jensen, for example) have pointed out the ways in which a social revolution, including a redistribution of property, accompanied the American Revolution. These are facts which no student of the period should neglect. Yet it seems to me that these historians have by no means succeeded in showing that such changes were so basic and so far-reaching as actually in themselves to have established our national republican institutions. When we speak of the Revolution therefore, we are still fully justified in referring to something other than what Jameson's disciples mean by "the American Revolution as a social movement." If we consider the American Revolution in that sense, it would not be a great deal more notable than a number of other social

movements in our history, such as Jacksonianism, populism, progressivism, and the New Deal.

The Revolution, as the birthday of our nation, must mean something very different from all this. It is the series of events by which we separated ourselves from the British Empire and acquired a national identity. Looking at our Revolution from this point of view, what are some features which distinguish it from the French Revolution of 1789 or the other revolutions to which western European nations trace their national identity? And, especially, what are those peculiarities which have affected the place of theory in our political life?

1. First, and most important, the United States was born in a *colonial* rebellion. Our national birth certificate is a Declaration of Independence and not a Declaration of the Rights of Man. The vast significance of this simple fact is too often forgotten. Compared even with other colonial rebellions, the American Revolution is notably lacking in cultural self-consciousness and in any passion for national unity. The more familiar type of colonial rebellion—like that which recently occurred in India—is one in which a subject people vindicates its local culture against foreign rulers. But the American Revolution had very little of this character. On the contrary, ours was one of the few conservative colonial rebellions of modern times.

Text: Daniel J. Boorstin, *The Genius of American Politics* (Chicago: University of Chicago Press, 1953), pp. 68-74, 98.

We should recall several of the peculiar circumstances (most of them obvious) which had made this kind of revolution possible. At the time of the Revolution, the major part of the population of the American colonies was of British stock. Therefore, no plausible racial or national argument could be found for the superiority either of the inhabitants of the mother-country or of the continental American colonies. Even when Jefferson, in his *Notes on Virginia,* went to some trouble to refute Buffon and the Abbé Raynal and others who had argued that all races, including man, deteriorated on the American continent, he did not go so far as to say that the American races were distinctly superior.

Since the climate and topography of substantial parts of the American colonies were similar to those of the mother-country (and for a number of other reasons), there had been a pretty wholesale transplantation of British legal and political institutions to North America. Unlike the Spanish colonies in South America, which were to rebel, at least in part, because they had had so little home rule, the British colonies in North America were to rebel because, among other reasons, they had had so much. Finally, the North American continent was (except for sparse Indian settlements) empty of indigenous populations, hence barren of such local institutions and traditions as could have competed with what the colonists had brought with them.

All these facts were to make it easy, then, for the American Revolution to seem in the minds of most of its leaders an affirmation of the tradition of British institutions. The argument of the best theorists of the Revolution—perhaps we should call them lawyers rather than theorists —was not, on the whole, that America had institutions or a culture superior to that of the British. Rather their position, often misrepresented and sometimes simply forgotten, was that the British by their treatment of the American colonies were being untrue to the ancient spirit of their own institutions. The slogan "Taxation without Representation Is Tyranny" was clearly founded on a British assumption. As James Otis put it in his pamphlet, *The Rights of the British Colonies* (1764), he believed "that this [British] constitution is the most free one, and by far the best, now existing on earth: that by this constitution, every man in the dominions is a free man: that no parts of His Majesty's dominions can be taxed without their consent: that every part has a right to be represented in the supreme or some subordinate legislature: that the refusal of this would seem to be a contradiction in practice to the theory of the constitution."

According to their own account, then, the Americans were to have forced on them the need to defend the ancient British tradition; to be truer to the spirit of that tradition than George III and Lord North and Townshend knew how to be. They were fighting not so much to establish new rights as to preserve old ones: "for the preservation of our liberties . . . in defence of the freedom that is our birthright, and which we ever enjoyed till the late violation of it" (Declaration of Causes of Taking up Arms, July 6, 1775). From the colonists' point of view, until 1776 it was Parliament that had been revolutionary, by exercising a power for which there was no warrant in English constitutional precedent. The ablest defender of the Revolution—in fact, the greatest political theorist of the American Revolution—was also the great theorist of British conservatism, Edmund Burke.

2. Second, the American Revolution was *not* the product of a nationalistic spirit. We had no Bismarck or Cavour or any nationalist philosophy. We were singularly free from most of the philosophical baggage of modern nationalism.

Perhaps never was a new nation created with less enthusiasm. To read the history of our Revolution is to discover that the United States was a kind of *pis aller.* This fact explains many of the difficulties encountered in conducting the Revolution and in framing a federal constitution. The original creation of a United States was the work of doubly reluctant men: men reluctant, both because of their local loyalties—to Virginia, Massachusetts, Rhode Island, and New York— and because of their imperial loyalty. The story of the "critical period" of American history, of the Articles of Confederation and the Constitution, tells of the gradual overcoming of this reluctance. It was overcome not by any widespread conversion to a nationalist theory—even the *Federalist* papers are conspicuously lacking in such a theory—but by gradual realization of the need for effective union.

In the period of the American Revolution we do discover a number of enthusiasms: for the safety and prosperity of Virginia or New York, for the cause of justice, for the rights of Englishmen. What is missing is anything that might be called widespread enthusiasm for the birth of a new nation: the United States of America. Until well into the nineteenth century, Jefferson—and he was not alone in this—was using the phrase "my country" to refer to his native state of Virginia. . . .

The Revolution itself, as we have seen, had been a kind of affirmation of faith in ancient British institutions. In the greater part of the institutional life of the community the Revolution thus required no basic change. If any of this helps to illustrate or explain our characteristic lack of interest in political philosophy, it also helps to account for the value which we still attach to our inheritance from the British constitution: trial by jury, due process of law, representation before taxation, habeas corpus, freedom from attainder, independence of the judiciary, and the rights of free speech, free petition, and free assembly, as well as our narrow definition of treason and our antipathy to standing armies in peacetime. It also explains our continuing—sometimes bizarre, but usually fortunate—readiness to think of these traditional rights of Englishmen as if they were indigenous to our continent. In the proceedings of the San Francisco Vigilance Committee of 1851, we hear crude adventurers on the western frontier describing the technicalities of habeas corpus as if they were fruits of the American environment, as natural as human equality.

110 THE CONSTITUTIONAL CONVENTION

from Edmund S. Morgan, *The Birth of the Republic*, 1956

To Professor Edmund S. Morgan of Yale University the writings of Beard and his followers have seriously distorted our understanding of the Constitution. The work of the "demigods" of 1787, Morgan suggests, established a fundamentally democratic political system adapted to the needs of the American Union. If precautions were taken against popular misrule, these were not the devices of aristocracy but the means of securing individual rights (including property rights) suggested by the principles of the Declaration. If there were clauses in the Constitution favorable to public creditors and great merchants, these were not examples of raw class legislation but—at bottom—provisions for national strength and prosperity. In these respects, Morgan returns to the "patriotic" view of national origins set forth in the works of older writers like George Bancroft (1800-1891). Perhaps Bancroft is an especially valuable guide for Morgan, since the eminent Jacksonian historian wrote that the Constitution was the fulfillment (not the denial) of the democratic equal-rights tradition.

Morgan's works include a study of the *Puritan Family* (1944), a fresh account of *The Stamp Act Crisis* (1953), and the elegant historical essay from which the following selection is taken, *The Birth of the Republic* (1956), a volume in the *Chicago History of Civilization*.

. . . [Twenty-nine] of the most distinguished men in the United States made their appearance in the Philadelphia State House on May 25, 1787. In the course of the meetings twenty-six more took their seats. Rhode Island alone failed to participate. Washington, who was chosen president of the convention on its first day, lent it a dignity everyone was bound to respect, a dignity further enhanced by the venerable presence of Benjamin Franklin. The other members were mostly younger men in their thirties and forties, old enough to have lived and fought and thought through the crowded years of the Revolution, old enough to have digested the significance of those years, not old enough to think them all vanity and vexation of spirit.

There were a few conspicuous absences. Sam Adams of Massachusetts and Patrick Henry of Virginia were not there, the latter because he "smelled a rat" in the whole proceeding. Both had become politically myopic in their old age and were well left at home. Thomas Jefferson and John Adams, who might have contributed much, were in Europe, but Jefferson's views were ably represented by James Madison, and Adams' by Gouverneur Morris of Pennsylvania, a dazzling speaker and thinker of conservative tastes.

Much has been written about these men and their work, and since we are still intimately affected by what they did, we cannot view them with complete detachment. Indeed, as long as patriotism remained the principal ingredient of American historical writing, the constitutional convention was regarded as an assemblage of the gods. But in 1913 Charles Beard published *An Economic Interpretation of the Constitution of the United States*, and, ever since, historians have striven to look at the convention as a meeting of ordinary human beings. Beard's achievement was extraordinary: he examined the career of every member of the convention and discovered

Text: Reprinted from *The Birth of the Republic* by Edmund S. Morgan, pp. 130-37, 155-57 *passim*, by permission of The University of Chicago Press. Copyright 1956 by The University of Chicago.

that most of them had invested in public securities of the United States and therefore stood to gain by strengthening public credit. He also examined their political ideas as expressed in the convention and found that most of them wished to restrain the people from legislation that would adversely affect the value of public securities. The conclusion was obvious that the makers of the Constitution, consciously or unconsciously, were seeking to protect their own economic interests, a characteristic that historians of the present age have frequently discovered in the actions of men both past and present.

We have discovered signs of economic interest in the events of the decades preceding the convention. The colonists did not wish to see their trade ruined or their property endangered by Parliamentary taxation and fought to protect themselves; land speculators wished to profit by settling the West and helped to secure a national domain. In each case self-interest led to the enunciation of principles which went far beyond the point at issue. In each case the people of the United States were committed to doctrines which helped to mold their future in ways they could not have anticipated. At the constitutional convention much the same thing occurred. The members had a selfish interest in bringing about a public good. But in this case, contrary to the impression given by Beard, it is all but impossible to differentiate private selfishness from public spirit.

Patriotism led responsible Americans to invest in public securities in wartime, and patriotism guided their efforts to revive the languishing nation which their money and blood had purchased. That personal economic interests were also involved is undeniable, but we learn very little about the convention by knowing that its members held public securities and believed in the sacredness of property. The principles they carried with them to Philadelphia would not all have fitted in their pocketbooks. . . .

. . . There was scarcely a member of the convention whose views can be explained by any simple formula, economic or otherwise. Even Alexander Hamilton, who deserted the convention for a time when it would not establish an executive and a senate with life terms, argued for a larger house of representatives than the convention would agree to: "He was seriously of opinion that the House of Representatives was on so narrow a scale as to be really dangerous, and to warrant a jealousy in the people for their liberties." Pierce Butler of South Carolina, who held public securities himself and argued vociferously that representation in the legislature should be apportioned among the different states

according to wealth . . . was against placing any property qualification on the suffrage, saying, "There is no right of which the people are more jealous than that of suffrage." Holland, he observed, where the right had been abridged, had turned into a "rank aristocracy." As for those who speculated in public securities, he was against requiring the new government to pay the public debt in full "lest it should compel payment as well to the Blood-suckers who had speculated on the distresses of others, as to those who had fought and bled for their country."

The members of the convention were certainly human, which is to say they were complex, unpredictable, paradoxical, compounded of rationality and irrationality, moved by selfishness and by altruism, by love and by hate and by anger—and by principle. If the convention succeeded, it was not simply because the members possessed a common economic or class interest but because they held common principles, principles learned in twenty years of British tyranny and American seeking, in colonial assemblies, in state legislatures, and in Congress. Their work has often been described as a bundle of compromises, and so it was, but the compromises were almost all on matters of detail. They could afford to give and take where they disagreed, because there were so many important things about which they did agree.

They agreed, to begin with, on the urgency of their task. Most of them were convinced that unless they came up with an acceptable, and at the same time workable, scheme of national government, the union would dissolve. Charles Pinckney of South Carolina, who had just been serving in Congress, believed that body would have collapsed already if the appointment of the convention had not given hope that the union might continue. But he did not need to tell the other members. Whenever arguments became heated, they would remind each other of the dreadful consequences if they failed. "The condition of the United States requires that something should be immediately done," cried Gunning Bedford of Delaware, himself a strong advocate of states' rights. "The fate of the Union will be decided by the Convention," said Elbridge Gerry of Massachusetts. "It is agreed on all hands," said his colleague Caleb Strong, "that Congress are nearly at an end. If no Accommodation takes place, the Union itself must soon be dissolved." . . .

Dickinson and the other members agreed not only on the desperateness of the situation but, in broad outlines at least, on what must be done about it. They almost all believed that the central government should be strengthened by enabling it to act without the mediation of state governments, to levy and collect its own taxes, and to make laws and enforce them through its own administrative agencies. There were a few members, notably from the smaller states, who felt that the task of the convention could be fulfilled simply by granting more authority to the existing government, in other words to Congress. But this solution was generally regarded as dangerous. Congress was not, strictly speaking, a representative body: its members were not elected directly by the people. To give it powers of taxation and legislation would therefore be to violate a cardinal principle of the Revolution. Moreover, even if popularly elected, Congress might by means of these powers get out of control. While it operated through the state governments, they served as a restraint on it, far too great a one. Before it could be safely freed from that restraint and given the strength everyone agreed it should have, it must be made truly representative and must be furnished with some new safeguard against abuse of its authority.

The new safeguard that most of the delegates at Philadelphia had in mind was a division of the central government into several different departments, each independent of the others, each with carefully specified powers. The appeal of this method was obvious: it had undergone testing for ten years in the state governments; therefore Americans could with some confidence judge its success and measure its failure.

The state constitutions, as we have seen, were constructed with this very intention of keeping the different departments separate and independent, but it was now felt that this intention had not been carried out with complete success. The state legislatures, except in Pennsylvania, were bicameral, but the upper houses were not much wiser or more virtuous or more conservative than the lower houses and did not constitute a sufficient check. And while the legislatures had been protected from the governors, the governors had not been protected from the legislatures. John Adams' warning that the executive must be given strength had gone unheeded. The legislatures had run away with the governments, and the lower houses had run away with the legislatures.

These failures to keep the different departments adequately separated did not reduce the general confidence in the principle of separation itself. They were failures of application, from which the convention could learn what to avoid in forming the national government. Under the Articles of Confederation there had been the even more serious failure of not applying the principle at all. All the functions and powers of government had been concentrated in a single body of men, a mistake that might have resulted in tyranny if Congress had not been kept so weak by the jealousy of the states. As Edmund Randolph of Virginia put it, "If the union of these powers heretofore in Congress has been safe, it has been owing to the general impotency of that body." The problem then was to construct a representative government of divided powers on the model of the state governments but without the flaws which ten years' wear and tear had brought to light.

There was no serious consideration of any radically different design: a few members, notably Alexander Hamilton and John Dickinson, thought highly of constitutional monarchy as a form of government, but they knew that Americans could not be sold that idea. And the other members, the great majority, wanted nothing but a republic: they were committed irrevocably to the principle of equality as expressed in the Declaration of Independence, and that principle, they believed demanded republican government. Some of them had doubts about the durability of a large republic but were willing to leave the proof to time. Even Elbridge Gerry, who said that "the evils we experience flow from the excess of democracy," and that democracy was "the worst . . . of all political evils," nevertheless believed that the United States should remain a republic. . . .

In spite of the bitter fights that preceded ratification, the differences between Federalists and anti-Federalists were primarily differences of opinion about means, not fundamental differences of principle. Both sides wanted an effective national government. Both sides wanted to guard that government against tyranny. Their disagreement was over the question whether the proposed separation of powers would be an adequate guard. The anti-Federalists thought not, and the amendments they recommended were digested by James Madison (who was also the principal author of the Constitution itself) to become the first ten amendments, usually called the Bill of Rights. These amendments in no way threatened the workability of the new government. Had Madison and his friends had the foresight to include them in the original document, ratification would have been much easier. Instead, it was obtained by the narrowest of margins and by methods that cannot be defended.

The result achieved was so happy that for a century or more these methods were forgotten, and the founding fathers escaped serious criticism. The present century has looked upon the vilification, the pressure, and the politicking, and has sometimes condemned not only the methods but, by implication at least, the result. The Constitution, it has been suggested, represented a reaction from the democratic principles of the Revolution, a reaction engineered by the rich and well-born, which was only overcome by the Jeffersonian and Jacksonian movements that followed.

Everyone who studies the Revolution and the Constitution must decide for himself whether this was true. It is worth pointing out, however, that if the Revolution was a struggle to make property secure, the Constitution was the final fulfilment of that struggle. If the Revolution called for the coupling of taxation with representation, the Constitution made the central government representative before giving it powers to tax. If the Revolution was built upon the principle that all men are created equal, the Constitution gave men a more equal share in the national government than the Confederation did. If the Revolution opened for Americans the discovery of their own nationality, the Constitution gave them the instrument for expressing it. If the Revolution taught them the danger of tyranny, the aim of the Constitution was to prevent tyranny.

Most of us will think it was successful. But the men who make it knew it was not the end of the search. They had come a long way in twenty-five years, perhaps as far as men have ever come in so short a time, but the farther they traveled, the fairer the prospect that lay ahead. The Constitution was a bulwark to protect what they had gained, but it was also a base from which to continue the exploration. The bulwark still stands, and in spite of halts and pauses along the way the exploration still goes on. As long as any man remains less free than another, it cannot honorably cease.

111 THE JEFFERSONIAN REPUBLIC

from Henry Adams, *History of the United States*, 1889

Henry Adams' *History of the United States* (1889-91) is the last in a distinguished line of nineteenth-century historical classics, a series including the works of George Bancroft, Francis Parkman, and W. H. Prescott. (See Document 38.) The breadth of mind, the elegance of style, the architectonic sense of the American classics are still evident in Adams' *History*. Yet Henry Adams stands unmistakably at the end of the older line and suggests some of the directions American historiography would take in the new century.

The grandeur of Parkman's themes, tracing the march of centuries and the clash of cultures, cannot be recaptured in a precise study of the Jefferson and Madison administrations which focuses upon presidential politics and foreign affairs. When Henry Adams did approach majestic themes, he wrote not history in any conventional sense but philosophic reflections on past and present: thus his interpretation of the medieval mind and spirit in *Mont-Saint-Michel and Chartres* (1904), his searching personal essay on the making of the modern temper, *The Education of Henry Adams* (1907), or his bold speculations on the application of physical law to the philosophy of history.

What a Henry Adams (1838-1918) born a generation earlier might have written—or might have been—is an interesting subject for the imagination. What he did write in his *History* is a unique contribution to our understanding of the early republic. No other historian of the Republican era brings to the task comparable gifts of mind and style; none shares the distinctive heritage, experience, and point of view of Henry Adams. He was the great-grandson of one President (John Adams), the grandson of another (John Quincy Adams), and the son of Charles Francis Adams, the notable minister to England during the Civil War years. Being an Adams of Massachusetts defined a character, an education, a commitment, a special destiny.

In Washington during the secession Winter of 1860-1861, the young secretary to an eminent father met and observed the greats of American politics (some of them old family friends) as they confronted the tragedy of a breaking Union. The continuing education of Henry Adams in England during the 1860's consisted not only of a priceless training in the ways of great-power diplomacy (Henry remained his father's secretary) but of exciting intellectual adventures in the company of such distinguished men as the poet Browning and the geologist Lyell at a time when English thought was coming to grips with the new evolutionary theories of Darwin and others.

Adams returned to his country to witness and report the degradation of democracy under Grant's administration. A position in history at Harvard seemed a welcome retreat for a while, but Adams found Boston tame and returned to his observation post at Washington, where the brilliant *salon* formed by him and his New England friends (including the future Secretary of State, John Hay) became the intellectual center of the capital. He wrote political novels, biographies of Albert Gallatin and John Randolph, and then his nine-volume *History of the United States*. His later years were spent in traveling the world, in reading and conversation, and in bringing out small private editions of his book on Chartres and of the work best known to later generations, *The Education of Henry Adams*.

The following selection from the *History* captures the mood and tone of the "Revolution of 1800," as Jefferson and his Republican disciples took over from John Adams the responsibility of governing the nation.

Jefferson was the first President inaugurated at Washington, and the ceremony, necessarily simple, was made still simpler for political reasons. The retiring President was not present at the installation of his successor. In Jefferson's eyes a revolution had taken place as vast as that of 1776; and if this was his belief, perhaps the late President was wise to retire from a stage where everything was arranged to point a censure upon his principles, and where he would have seemed, in his successor's opinion, as little in place as George III. would have appeared at the installation of President Washington. The collapse of government which marked the last weeks of February, 1801, had been such as to leave of the old Cabinet only Samuel Dexter of Massachusetts, the Secretary of the Treasury, and Benjamin Stoddert of Maryland, the Secretary of the Navy, still in office. John Marshall, the late Secretary of State, had been appointed, six weeks before, Chief-Justice of the Supreme Court.

In this first appearance of John Marshall as Chief-Justice, to administer the oath of office, lay the dramatic climax of the inauguration. The retiring President, acting for what he supposed to be the best interests of the country, by one of his last acts of power, deliberately intended to perpetuate the principles of his administration, placed at the head of the judiciary, for life, a man as obnoxious to Jefferson as the bitterest New England Calvinist could have been; for he belonged to that class of conservative Virginians whose devotion to President Washington, and whose education in the common law, caused them to hold Jefferson and his theories in antipathy. The new President and his two Secretaries were political philanthropists, bent on restricting the powers of the national government in the interests of human liberty. The Chief-Justice, a man who in grasp of mind and steadiness of purpose had no superior, perhaps no equal, was bent on enlarging the powers of government in the interests of justice and nationality. As they stood face to face on this threshold of their power, each could foresee that the contest between them would end only with life. . . .

Not . . . in the Inaugural Address, with its amiable professions of harmony, could President Jefferson's full view of his own reforms be discovered. Judged by his inaugural addresses and annual messages, Jefferson's Administration seemed a colorless continuation of Washington's; but when seen in the light of private correspondence, the difference was complete. So strong was the new President's persuasion of the monarchical bent of his predecessors, that his joy at obtaining the government was mingled with a shade of surprise that his enemies should have handed to him, without question, the power they had so long held. He shared his fears of monarchy with politicians like William B. Giles, young John Randolph, and many Southern voters; and although neither Madison nor Gallatin seemed to think monarchists formidable, they gladly encouraged the President to pursue a conservative and conciliatory path. Jefferson and his Southern friends took power as republicans opposed to monarchists, not as democrats opposed to oligarchy. Jefferson himself was not in a social sense a democrat, and was called so only as a term of opprobrium. His Northern followers were in the main democrats; but he and most of his Southern partisans claimed to be republicans, opposed by secret monarchists.

The conflict of ideas between Southern republicanism, Northern democracy, and Federal monarchism marked much of Jefferson's writing; but especially when he began his career as President his mind was filled with the conviction that he had wrung power from monarchy, and that in this sense he was the founder of a new republic. Henceforward, as he hoped, republicanism was forever safe; he had but to conciliate the misguided, and give an example to the world, for centralization was only a monarchical principle. Nearly twenty years passed before he woke to a doubt on this subject; but even then he did not admit a mistake. In the tendency to centralization he still saw no democratic instinct, but only

Text: Henry Adams, *History of the United States of America* (New York: Charles Scribner's Sons, 1889), I, 191-92, 208-17 *passim*.

the influence of monarchical Federalists "under the pseudo-republican mask."

The republic which Jefferson believed himself to be founding or securing in 1801 was an enlarged Virginia,—a society to be kept pure and free by the absence of complicated interests, by the encouragement of agriculture and of commerce as its handmaid, but not of industry in a larger sense. "The agricultural capacities of our country," he wrote long afterward, "constitute its distinguishing feature; and the adapting our policy and pursuits to that is more likely to make us a numerous and happy people than the mimicry of an Amsterdam, a Hamburg, or a city of London." He did not love mechanics or manufactures, or the capital without which they could not exist. "Banking establishments are more dangerous than standing armies," he said; and added, "that the principle of spending money to be paid by posterity, under the name of funding, is but swindling futurity on a large scale." Such theories were republican in the Virginia sense, but not democratic; they had nothing in common with the democracy of Pennsylvania and New England, except their love of freedom; and Virginia freedom was not the same conception as the democratic freedom of the North.

In 1801 this Virginia type was still the popular form of republicanism. Although the Northern democrat had already developed a tendency toward cities, manufactures, and "the mimicry of an Amsterdam, a Hamburg, or a city of London," while the republican of the South was distinguished by his dislike of every condition except that of agriculture, the two wings of the party had so much in common that they could afford to disregard for a time these divergencies of interest; and if the Virginians cared nothing for cities, banks, and manufactures, or if the Northern democrats troubled themselves little about the dangers of centralization, they could unite with one heart in overthrowing monarchy, and in effecting a social revolution.

Henceforward, as Jefferson conceived, government might act directly for the encouragement of agriculture and of commerce as its handmaid, for the diffusion of information and the arraignment of abuses; but there its positive functions stopped. Beyond that point only negative action remained,—respect for States' rights, preservation of constitutional powers, economy, and the maintenance of a pure and simple society such as already existed. With a political system which would not take from the mouth of labor the bread it had earned, and which should leave men free to follow whatever paths of industry or improve-

ment they might find most profitable, "the circle of felicities" was closed.

The possibility of foreign war alone disturbed this dream. President Washington himself might have been glad to accept these ideas of domestic politics, had not France, England, and Spain shown an unequivocal wish to take advantage of American weakness in arms in order to withhold rights vital to national welfare. How did Jefferson propose to convert a government of judiciary and police into the strongest government on earth? His answer to this question, omitted from the Inaugural Address, was to be found in his private correspondence and in the speeches of Gallatin and Madison as leaders of the opposition. He meant to prevent war. He was convinced that governments, like human beings, were on the whole controlled by their interests, and that the interests of Europe required peace and free commerce with America. Believing a union of European Powers to be impossible, he was willing to trust their jealousies of each other to secure their good treatment of the United States. Knowing that Congress could by a single act divert a stream of wealth from one European country to another, foreign Governments would hardly challenge the use of such a weapon, or long resist their own overpowering interests. The new President found in the Constitutional power "to regulate commerce with foreign nations" the machinery for doing away with navies, armies, and wars. . . .

That these views were new as a system in government could not be denied. In later life Jefferson frequently asserted, and took pains to impress upon his friends, the difference between his opinions and those of his Federalist opponents. The radical distinction lay in their opposite conceptions of the national government. The Federalists wished to extend its functions; Jefferson wished to exclude its influence from domestic affairs:—

"The people," he declared in 1821, "to whom all authority belongs, have divided the powers of government into two distinct departments, the leading characters of which are foreign and domestic; and they have appointed for each a distinct set of functionaries. These they have made co-ordinate, checking and balancing each other, like the three cardinal departments in the individual States,—each equally supreme as to the powers delegated to itself, and neither authorized ultimately to decide what belongs to itself or to its coparcener in government. As independent, in fact, as different nations, a spirit of forbearance and compromise, therefore, and not of encroachment and usurpation, is the healing balm of such a Constitution."

In the year 1824 Jefferson still maintained the same doctrine, and expressed it more concisely than ever:—

"The federal is in truth our foreign government, which department alone is taken from the sovereignty of the separate States." "I recollect no case where a question simply between citizens of the same State has been transferred to the foreign department, except that of inhibiting tenders but of metallic money, and *ex post facto* legislation."

These expressions, taken together, partly explain why Jefferson thought his assumption of power to be "as real a revolution in the principles of our government as that of 1776 was in its form." His view of governmental functions was simple and clearly expressed. The national government, as he conceived it, was a foreign department as independent from the domestic department, which belonged to the States, as though they were governments of different nations. He intended that the general government should "be reduced to foreign concerns only;" and his theory of foreign concerns was equally simple and clear. He meant to enforce against foreign nations such principles as national objects required, not by war, but by "peaceable coercion" through commercial restrictions. "Our commerce is so valuable to them that they will be glad to purchase it, when the only price we ask is to do us justice."

PART THREE

Democratic Growth and the

Sectional Conflict

1825–1865

Alexis de Tocqueville shocked many of his English and European readers when he insisted, in the 1830's, that democracy—conspicuously, American democracy—was far more likely to err on the side of excessive conformity and stability than on the side of excessive liberty and disorder. In the traditional view, the combination of freedom and popular rule was expected to lead by way of anarchy to dictatorship. Jacksonian Americans could accept De Tocqueville's case more readily: first, because their democratic theory maintained that a government representing the many and serving their common interest could claim a deeper loyalty than a government of the few that imposed its will on society; second, because their own society did exhibit a remarkable degree of uniformity and consensus on fundamentals.

Americans of the 1820's felt a sense of great achievement in the establishment of a thriving nation conceived in liberty and dedicated to the proposition that all men are created equal. North-South sectionalism had reared its head more than once in the early history of the Republic, but few men saw in this conflict an insoluble dilemma for the Union. The great party issues of the Jacksonian age sometimes touched sectional concerns, as in the case of the tariff and the South Carolina nullification crisis, but these seemed only marginal to the main business of politics. Jackson's war against the Second Bank of the United States, which did so much to fix political alignments, divided men not by their geographic locations but by their attitudes toward corporate power, government intervention, paper money, and the future shape of republican society. In the general culture of Jacksonian times, the leading themes were the affirmation of national democratic values and the amelioration of the human condition by social reforms.

In the mid-1840's politics and culture took a sharp turn. The gradual expansion of slavery during the nineteenth century had given that "peculiar institution" a dominant position in the Southern economy—dominant not in *extent* but in the strategic *role* it played. In social terms, slavery was the South's seemingly indispensable system for regulating a large mass of "inferiors." In cultural terms, slavery came to be understood in the South as the necessary basis for a superior civilization. In politics, slavery gave a sharp sectional cast to major national decisions, for slavery was a sectional institution.

The total absence of slavery in the Northern states is evidence enough of almost universal antislavery sentiments there. Antislavery, not abolitionist. As late as the 1830's, an abolitionist speaker in many Northern towns and cities risked mob violence. Political conflict over slavery came with westward expansion. The Mexican War (1846-48) and the acquisition of new territories posed the question of the *expansion* of slavery and the *balance* of free and slave states.

Here North and South took their stand, with Stephen A. Douglas somewhere in the middle, trying to avoid a sectional collision by leaving the choice of slavery or freedom to the people of the territories. Douglas' remedy failed in Kansas. Political parties which had been founded on a national basis were divided into their sectional components. Crisis bred crisis until in 1860 the victory of Lincoln and the new Republican party convinced the Southern leaders that they could find neither safety nor justice in the Union.

The terrible four-year struggle of Blue and Gray established Lincoln's principle that the nation was indivisible. The South, desolate and powerless, had to face the consequences of forced emancipation and Northern dominance. The nation had to face the task of reconstruction and resolve the dilemma of force and freedom. In the meantime, a surging industrial revolution in the North was transforming the character of American society and politics. The year 1865 marks a new age in American history.

Chronological Chart: 1825 to 1865

THE AMERICAN SCENE . . . .

POLITICAL

1825–1829 John Quincy Adams, president.
1828 "Tariff of Abominations" enacted, *May 19.*
Calhoun's *South Carolina Exposition and Protest* issued.
1829–1837 Andrew Jackson, president.
1829 "Spoils system" introduced on large scale.
1830 Webster-Hayne debate in Senate, *Jan. 19-27.*
Jackson vetoed Maysville Road bill, *May 27.*
1831–1842 Indians removed to west of Mississippi River.

1832 Jackson vetoed charter for 2nd Bank of the U.S.
South Carolina adopted tariff nullification ordinance.
1833 Compromise tariff and Force Bill enacted.
Jackson removed public deposits from Bank of the U.S.
1836 Republic of Texas won independence from Mexico.
"Specie Circular" issued.
1st "gag rule" on slavery petitions adopted by Congress.
1837–1841 Martin Van Buren, president.
1840 Independent Treasury Act passed.
1841 William Henry Harrison, president *(Mar. 4-Apr. 4).*
1841–1845 John Tyler, president.
1842 Webster-Ashburton Treaty signed.
1845 Texas annexed by joint resolution of Congress.
1845–1849 James K. Polk, president.
1846–1848 War with Mexico.
1846 Oregon boundary treaty signed with Britain.
Wilmot Proviso 1st introduced.
1848 Treaty of Guadalupe Hidalgo ceded Texas, California, and New Mexico territory to U.S.
1849–1850 Zachary Taylor, president.
1850–1853 Millard Fillmore, president.
1850 Compromise of 1850 enacted, *Sept. 9-20.*
1853–1857 Franklin Pierce, president.
1854 Perry opened Japanese trade relations.
Kansas-Nebraska Act passed.
Republican party founded.
1855–1856 Civil War in Kansas.
1857–1861 James Buchanan, president.
1857 Dred Scott decision, *Mar. 6.*
1858 Lincoln-Douglas debates, *Aug. 21-Oct. 15.*
1859 John Brown raided Harper's Ferry, Va., *Oct. 16-18.*
1860 Lincoln elected president, *Sept.-Oct.*
South Carolina seceded, *Dec. 20.*
1861 Confederacy formed at Montgomery, *Feb. 4.*
Morrill tariff act passed, *Mar. 2.*
Abraham Lincoln inaugurated, *Mar. 4.*
Fort Sumter fired on, *Apr. 12.*
Lincoln called for volunteer troops. *Apr. 15.*
1862 Congress abolished slavery in District of Columbia and the territories.
1863 Emancipation Proclamation issued, *Jan. 1.*
National Banking System established.
Battle of Gettysburg, *July 1-3.*
1865 Lee surrendered at Appomattox, *Apr. 9.*
Lincoln assassinated, *Apr. 14.*

ECONOMIC AND SOCIAL

1825–1860 Cotton remained No. 1 U.S. export.
1825 Erie Canal opened in New York state.

1830 U.S. census: 12,866,020 (8.8% urban).
Pre-emption Act provided cheap land for squatters.
1830–1845 Power weaving and Waltham system became widespread in New England textile industry.
1831 1st American railroads began operations.
Reaper developed by Cyrus H. McCormick.
Nat Turner slave insurrection crushed in Virginia.
1832 1st American clipper ship launched at Baltimore.
1833 Chicago organized as a town.
American Antislavery Society founded by W. L. Garrison.

1837 Steel plow introduced to U.S.
1837–1843 Panic of 1837 caused wholesale failures of state banks, followed by general business depression.
1839 Vulcanized rubber developed by Charles Goodyear.
1841–1846 Brook Farm established by George Ripley.
1842–1843 Great migration to Oregon country began.
1844 Samuel Morse developed 1st practical telegraph.
1845–1882 Great Irish and German immigration.
1846 Sewing machine invented by Elias Howe.
1847 Brigham Young's Mormons founded Salt Lake City.
American Medical Association founded.
1848 Gold discovered at Sutter's Mill in California.
The Associated Press founded in New York.

1850 Land grants to railroads adopted by Congress.
1851 Maine became 1st state to adopt prohibition.
1853 Chicago and New York linked by railway.

1855 Soo Canal opened, linking Lakes Superior and Huron.
1857–1858 Panic of 1857, due to overspeculation in land and railroads, caused sharp business depression.
1858 Silver discovered in Nevada.
1859 1st successful oil well drilled at Titusville, Pa.
1860 U.S. census: 31,443,321 (19.8% urban).
1860–1861 Pony Express ran from St. Joseph to Sacramento.
1861–1865 War business boom caused by government spending and inflationary price rise.
1861 Federal income tax imposed for 1st time.
1st transcontinental telegraph opened.
1862 "Greenbacks" issued by Federal government.
1st Homestead Act passed, *May 20.*

1864 George M. Pullman built 1st sleeping car.
1865 Union Stockyards opened in Chicago.

. . . . THE WORLD SCENE

INTELLECTUAL

1826 Lyceum movement begun in Millbury, Mass.
American Temperance Society founded.
James Fenimore Cooper's *Last of the Mohicans* published.
1830 Mormon church founded by Joseph Smith.
Oberlin College founded as 1st college to admit women.
1830–1860 Hudson River School of landscape painters was most prominent group of pre-Civil War artists.
1831 Garrison's abolitionist *Liberator* founded.

1832 J. P. Kennedy's *Swallow Barn* published.
1834 Firm of Currier & Ives founded.
George Bancroft's 1st volume of his nationalistic *History of the United States* published.
1836 1st of "McGuffey's Readers" published.
"Transcendental Club" began as casual discussion group.

1840–1860 Gothic revival began in architecture.
1841 Emerson's *Essays* (1st series) published.

1843 William Prescott's *Conquest of Mexico* published.
1845 Edgar Allan Poe's "The Raven" published.
1846 Smithsonian Institution founded by Congress.

1849 Amelia Bloomer published 1st issues of *Lily*, a journal devoted to temperance and women's rights.
1850 *Harper's Magazine* founded in New York.
Nathaniel Hawthorne's *The Scarlet Letter* published.
1852 Harriet Beecher Stowe's *Uncle Tom's Cabin* published.
1854 Michigan State Agricultural College opened as 1st agricultural school in U.S.
Henry Thoreau's *Walden* published.
1855 Walt Whitman's *Leaves of Grass* 1st published.
1857 *Atlantic Monthly* founded.
Hinton Rowan Helper's *The Impending Crisis* published.
1858 Religious revival, begun in New York and Philadelphia, swept the country.
1859 Massachusetts Institute of Technology founded.

1862 Morrill Act for land-grant colleges passed by Congress.

1865 Yale University opened 1st fine arts department in a U.S. college.

1825 Russian "Decembrist rising" quelled by Nicholas I.
1st railway line opened in England.
1828 Friedrich Wöhler founded organic chemistry.
1829 Catholic Emancipation Act granted suffrage to English Catholics.
1830 Belgium won independence from the Netherlands.
The "July Revolution" in France enthroned the "bourgeois monarch," Louis Philippe (1830-1848).
1832 English Reform Bill redistributed parliamentary representation and extended the franchise.
Slavery abolished throughout the British Empire.
Zollverein, a German customs union, established.
1833 British Factory Act restricted child labor.
1835–1837 Dutch Boers made "great trek" from British-held Cape Colony to the Transvaal.
1836 Republic of Texas proclaimed.
1837–1901 Victoria, Queen of England.
1839 English "Chartists" agitated for political reform.
1840 1st English colonists arrived in New Zealand.
Upper and Lower Canada united.
1842 China ceded Hong Kong to Britain.

1845 Famine in Ireland.
1846 Repeal of Corn Laws provided almost complete free trade for Britain.
1847 Republic of Liberia established in Africa.
1848 "Revolutions of 1848" in France, Germany, Austria, Italy, and elsewhere finally crushed by aristocrats.
Communist Manifesto issued by Marx and Engels.
1850 Australia given partial self-government.
1850–1864 Taiping Rebellion in China.
1852–1870 Napoleon III, emperor of France.
1853–1856 The Crimean War.
1853–1856 David Livingstone crossed African continent.

1855 Newfoundland given virtual self-government.
1856 Bessemer steel-making process developed.
1857–1858 Sepoy Mutiny in India.

1859 Darwin's *Origin of Species* published.
1860 Garibaldi's "Red Shirts" conquered Sicily and Naples, which were annexed to Sardinia-Piedmont.
c1860–1870 Russian "Nihilists" agitated for reforms.
1861 Kingdom of Italy proclaimed.
Russian serfs emancipated by Alexander II.
1862–1890 Otto von Bismarck, chancellor of Prussia.
1863–1867 Maximilian, emperor of Mexico.
1863 Impressionists exhibited in Salon des Refusés.
1864 International Red Cross founded.
1865 Lister announced new antiseptic methods for wounds.
1865–1866 1st transatlantic cables laid.

CHAPTER 10

The Age of Jacksonian Democracy:

1825 to 1850

What makes the age of Jacksonian Democracy a distinctive chapter of American history? The answer is not so simple as it seems. Andrew Jackson somehow represented a unique force in American political life, but what he stood for and what he accomplished will long remain disputed questions. (See Document 166.) Democracy? Certainly democracy by any definition greatly enlarged its sphere during the second quarter of the nineteenth century; but democracy had been growing in America since Jamestown. The traditional tale of the Tennessee frontiersman with his horde of Western farmers and Eastern workers sweeping aristocracy from power will not stand close scrutiny. If one will settle for a less dramatic story, however, then "the Age of Jacksonian Democracy" remains an apt designation for the period from 1825 to 1850.

VOX POPULI

Jacksonian Democracy did not create a democratic polity in the United States. It was there in essence from the beginning. Democracy, in Lincoln's lucid definition, is "government of the people, by the people, for the people." Of the people: "deriving their just powers from the consent of the governed." By the people: in practice, by agents selected and controlled—more or less directly—by the votes of a majority of the people. For the people: "to secure these rights" of all men to life, liberty, and the pursuit of happiness.

Now government of and for the people, as defined above, was declared to be the fundamental principle of the American Revolution and of the new republics formed in the 1770's. If, as some argued, the Federal Constitution was a creature of the states, still it was the *people* of the states acting through special conventions who ratified the instrument; and the preamble acknowledged the ultimate source of political authority in the phrase, "We, the people of the United States." The federal and state constitutions carefully specified the objects and limits of government for the people.

What then of government *by* the people in the early republic? Here one encounters difficulties of fact and interpretation. We can only suggest a tentative conclusion: government by the people—popular government—was accepted in principle by the founders of the new state and federal regimes. But over the whole range of responsible opinion from Jefferson to Hamilton there was no inclination to make government *unconditionally* the tool of the numerical majority. Thus the republican principle of representation, the separation of powers, checks and balances, the federal structure, and indeed the very concept of a fundamental law (the Constitution) prescribing the ends, forms, and limits of government. All of these restrictions were generally accepted by "radicals" as well as "conservatives."

Agreement in broad principle did not preclude sharp and significant practical differences. Government by the people might be more or less direct, and the people (political society) might be defined to include or exclude various segments of the population. Recent scholarship suggests that a large majority of free, white, adult males could vote, if they would, in the early republic and that a persistent popular majority could sooner or later impose its will on government.

If democracy by all the terms of Lincoln's definition was formed in outline and in many details before the Jacksonians arrived upon the political scene, what was left for Jacksonian Democracy to accomplish? A great deal. During the age of Jackson, every man with the least claim to substantial membership in the political community gained a vote. Public offices from justice of the peace to high executive and judicial posts were filled by popular election. State legislatures and constituency meetings claimed the right to "instruct" members of Congress on how to vote. In the seaboard states, the western districts won fuller representation; in the nation as a whole, the balance of power shifted toward the newly-settled Western states where society was fluid and politics relatively open to popular influence. At the same time there was a tendency to hobble the actions of the people's representatives. State constitutions became long catalogues of detailed prescriptions governing the use of legislative power, especially in the areas of corporations, banking, and public finance. These restrictive measures were a kind of democracy too: the kind that distrusts men in power, even democratic representatives, and wishes above all for government to leave society alone.

In the Jacksonian period the most profound changes in political life were not explicitly recorded in laws and constitutions. Such changes can best be seen in the evolving party system. The political party was not the invention of Jacksonian Democracy. As early as the 1790's, we have seen, parties had become much more than temporary alliances of political leaders to effect specific projects, though the rapid decline and fall of Federalism after 1800 arrested the development·of a national two-party system. At the state and local level, however, notable changes were in progress. Master politicians like Martin Van Buren of New York were building stable party organizations that reached from the neighborhood to the statehouse. A network of little journals in the towns and villages spoke in unison on candidates and measures, taking their cues from an authoritative "party organ." Party discipline was enforced in the legislatures by a system of rewards and punishments—i.e., by the selective distribution of appointments, nominations, and other valuable considerations.

By 1828 organized parties of the modern type had matured in New York and Pennsylvania and were rapidly taking shape elsewhere. As one illustration of the process, New York's Tammany society was already a.symbol of machine politics. Did the party development advance or retard the cause of government by the people? The party came to mediate between the people and their government. Its very nature as an organization whose success depends upon winning popular favor makes the party highly responsive to public opinion. Moreover, the party serves to give its supporters a unified and therefore a powerful voice on candidates and programs. But the party also has a tendency to serve its own organizational needs—*i.e.*, to manipulate the electorate and manage the government for the power and profit of professional politicians. Many of the ugly features of boss and machine rule were already matters of concern in the Jacksonian era, especially in the larger cities. The argument over the role of parties in achieving government by the people will no doubt continue as long as democracy endures. There is no argument, however, over the tremendous influence of parties in the age of Jackson.

The presidential campaign of 1828 foreshadowed a new political epoch: the age of Jacksonian Democracy. The successful candidate was not a leading statesman of a previous administration who had won the approval of the Congressional inner circle. Andrew Jackson (1767-1845) was a political outsider, a victorious general from Tennessee whose name had become a symbol of muscular patriotism and republican simplicity. Martin Van Buren, James Buchanan, William B. Lewis, and other state party managers knew what to do with such a candidate. On the surface they fought a campaign of personal vituperation and demogogic tricks; beneath the surface they appealed to the people to take control of the national government in the person of Old Hickory.

In power the Jacksonians steadily closed party ranks and perfected party discipline. An unofficial "kitchen cabinet" not only advised the President on policy questions but carefully managed organizational details: the members maintained close communications with party leaders over the country, looked to the circulation of administrative views, and calculated the most effective use of patronage. The greatest argument for party loyalty, however, was the unexampled popularity of Andrew Jackson. The words and deeds of a commanding President became the touchstone of American politics. A *national* party formed around the Jackson administration; and in the 1830's a national opposition—the National Republicans, later the Whigs—was consolidated.

Thus (in broad outline) government by the people found new expressions in the Jacksonian era. Through the medium of parties, the tastes, moods, and desires of the almost all-inclusive voting public impressed themselves on every phase of the political process. The political genius of Andrew Jackson, it has been suggested, lay in his instinctive understanding of public sentiments and his total confidence that his actions would be confirmed by the people.

DEMOCRATS AND WHIGS

Jeffersonian Democracy came to power in 1801 with a relatively firm set of policy objectives which had been defined in the decade-long opposition to Hamiltonian Federalism. Jacksonian Democracy in 1829 was not identified with a clearcut program. Andrew Jackson's reputation suggested only that he would approach the problems of his administration as an uncompromising defender of the Union and its interests, as a veteran Republican who found what little doctrine he needed in the old Jeffersonian school, and as a sworn enemy of class privilege in politics or economics.

Jacksonian Democracy in office did not disappoint popular expectations. The use of patronage to strengthen the administration party was nothing new in state or national politics; Jackson, however, made a democratic principle of "rotation in office." Although the President used the power of removal and appointment with restraint, his argument against a permanent federal civil service as an aristocratic institution encouraged the growth of the "spoils system." Jackson, moreover, gave the presidential office new meaning and authority. He viewed the chief executive as the unique representative of the whole people and thus did not hesitate to oppose the Supreme Court or Congress when they obstructed the common interest—as he saw it. He imposed an unprecedented number of vetoes.

The two burning issues of Jacksonian politics concerned the national bank and nullification. The latter was not a party but a sectional question. Jackson's allies in the South Carolina crisis included political opponents like Senator Daniel Webster of New Hampshire; his chief adversary was the Vice-President, South Carolinian John C. Calhoun. To Calhoun and his followers, all the benefits of protective tariffs went to Northern manufacturers while Southern planters (who exported three-fourths or more of their cotton crop) bore the burden of higher prices. Acting on the Calhoun doctrine of state sovereignty, a South Carolina convention declared the tariff of 1832 oppressive, unconstitutional, and therefore null and void within the limits of the state. Andrew Jackson was no advocate of high protective tariffs and generally supported a strict (Jeffersonian) construction of federal powers; but he condemned the extreme South Carolina doctrine of state sovereignty and nullification as an invitation to treason. Jackson's Nullification Proclamation (1832) sternly announced his intention to execute the laws of the United States in South Carolina, by force if necessary. The compromise tariff of 1833, introduced by Senator Henry Clay, permitted South Carolina a dignified retreat from a perilous and isolated position.

The nullification crisis held the seeds of future catastrophe. It was Andrew Jackson's war against the Second Bank of the United States, however, that most thoroughly aroused the political passions of the Jacksonian generation. The Bank was an economic giant, a thirty-five million dollar private corporation chartered by Congress in 1816 to receive federal deposits, issue paper money, and do a general commercial banking business. Under the direction of a master financier, Nicholas Biddle, the Philadelphia bank with its twenty-nine branches played a decisive role in the national economy. Supporters of the Bank, and most modern scholars, agree that Biddle used the great power of the institution effectively to serve the financial needs of a growing country.

Andrew Jackson did not agree. Whatever merits a national bank might have were overbalanced in his eyes by the dangers of perpetuating an unconstitutional monopoly which tended to make the rich richer with government aid and thus tended to undermine the republican principle of equal rights. In July of 1832 Jackson declared open war on the Bank, issuing a stirring veto of a bill to renew the Bank's charter. Following his victory in the presidential election of 1832 over Henry Clay, a leading Bank supporter, Jackson found a new Secretary of the Treasury, Roger B. Taney, who would order the removal of the public deposits from the Bank of the United States (1833). Nicholas Biddle and his friends fought back with every means at their disposal, but they could not budge Old Hickory from his grim determination to kill the "Monster."

Jackson intended not only to strike down a dangerous monopoly but to check "the paper system": the uncontrolled creation of money and credit by privileged banking corporations which, he argued, shook society with extreme business fluctuations and engendered "a spirit of speculation injurious to the habits and character of the people." Yet Jackson's transfer of government deposits to a group of "pet" state banks fed a runaway speculative boom in the mid-1830's; and his condemnation of the national bank encouraged a reckless proliferation of state banks and "soft" paper currency. The Panic of 1837 and the ensuing depression wrote a harsh conclusion (but not a permanent one) to the inflationary episode.

Jacksonian Democracy under Martin Van Buren met its first national defeat in the midst of depression. The rival Whig party successfully employed such political devices as slogans, songs, parades, and a non-committal candidate in their "Log Cabin and Hard Cider" campaign of 1840. Any real hope of restoring the national bank ended with the death of William Henry Harrison shortly after his inauguration and the succession of Vice-President John Tyler, a Virginian who opposed the broad construction and economic nationalism of Northern and Western Whigs. The election of Democrat James K. Polk ("Young Hickory") in 1844 guaranteed a return to strict Jacksonian economic policies. Problems of banking, paper money, and corporate monopoly remained a vital concern in the states; and the Democratic party did its best to keep alive the memory of Jackson's war against the monster Bank and its Whig allies. But new issues of territorial expansion and slavery now dominated national politics.

THE WEST AND MANIFEST DESTINY

During the quarter-century from 1825 to 1850 Americans and Northern European immigrants settled the Great Lakes region, advanced the agricultural frontier to the edge of the Great Plains, occupied Texas, and sent vanguards to the Pacific coast. By 1850 nearly half the population of the United States lived west of the Alleghenies. Westward expansion was paralleled by a growing concentration of population in the commercial and industrial centers of the Northeast. The great metropolis of New York had half a million inhabitants by 1850—a sign of the city's success in trapping the commerce of the West through the Erie Canal, in financing the cotton trade of the Lower South, and in drawing the major share of foreign commerce to its docks.

Westward migration in search of fresh lands and new opportunities was a continuous theme of American history. Expansionism became a *political* issue when American ambitions in the Far West encountered resistance. Should the United States annex the Lone Star Republic of Texas, which had won its independence in 1836, despite the threatening objections of Mexico? Should the nation enforce its claims to the Oregon country, jointly occupied by British and American soldiers? How far should the government go in forcing Mexico to release its precarious hold on California? Politicians and publicists in the 1840's began to talk of America's "Manifest Destiny" to occupy the continent, extend the blessings of republican dominion to the lands of the Far West, and prepare for a leading role in the commerce of the Pacific.

. The election of 1844 was a popular verdict in favor of the outspoken expansionist James K. Polk. Negotiations with Great Britain confirmed the American claim to Oregon up to the 49th parallel (1846). The outgoing President, John Tyler, signed a joint Congressional resolution for the annexation of Texas (1845), and Polk completed the process. Determined to acquire California and to extend the Texas boundary to the Rio Grande, Polk first attempted diplomatic negotiations with Mexico and then invited hostile action by sending troops into a disputed border area. The Mexican War (1846-48) gave the United States possession of California and the Southwest for the modest price of $15,000,000 plus a few additional millions for settling the claims of United States citizens against Mexico.

Once again the expansion of national territory raised the issue of slavery and sectional balance. Many Whigs and "Free Soil" Democrats denounced the war as an imperialist adventure and insisted that slavery be excluded from the conquered territory. The anti-slavery Wilmot Proviso, first introduced in 1846, stirred a fierce national debate that would not cease until the house had been divided into warring sections.

Vox Populi

112

THE PEOPLE'S DAY: INAUGURATION, 1829

from Margaret Bayard Smith, *The First Forty Years of Washington Society*, 1906

Andrew Jackson (1767-1845) was the first President of the United States to rise from humble origins, the first to be identified with the Western frontier, and the first to claim the office as a military hero without significant accomplishments in statesmanship. (Washington was, of course, far more than a triumphant general to his devoted public.) Jackson's Scotch-Irish immigrant parents made their way from Charleston to the primitive Waxhaw settlement at the far western border of the two Carolinas. An ambitious young frontiersman, Jackson picked up a hasty legal education in the neighborhood, followed the early migration to the West, and soon won a place among the leading citizens of Nashville when Tennessee was still a part of North Carolina. Strong natural gifts of mind and character gained for Jackson a succession of high offices in the new community: at the age of thirty he was appointed United States Senator (his legislative career was brief and unimpressive); at thirty-five he served as major general of the Tennessee militia.

The War of 1812 gave Jackson his opportunity for national fame. A tough, resourceful frontier general, he destroyed the power of the Creeks in the southwestern campaigns of 1813. His militia forces at New Orleans (January 8, 1815) crushed an imposing British army of invasion to give the United States its only decisive land victory of the war. The Hero of New Orleans enhanced his popular reputation when he later invaded Spanish Florida to punish the troublesome Seminoles and incidentally to arrange a military hanging for two Britishers accused of stirring up the Indians. Cautious statesmen might denounce the hot-headed general; but there is little evidence that the electors were alarmed by charges of military despotism against the man who had successfully defied two favorite enemies, the British and the Indians. In the presidential campaign of 1824 Jackson led in the electoral vote but lost in the House of Representatives. In 1828 he swept to victory over John Quincy Adams by a vote of 178 to 83, carrying New York and Pennsylvania with the West and South.

After the ferociously fought campaign of 1828 the people who had recognized a champion in Andrew Jackson (including many with their hands out for the spoils of victory) swarmed to Washington for the inauguration. Although policy issues had not been sharply drawn, there was a general sense that a new age of equalitarian democracy was dawning. Margaret Bayard Smith, wife of a prominent Washington editor, banker, and public official during the Republican era, recorded her impressions of the Inaugural ceremonies and of the riotous reception at the President's house. A selection from her correspondence, published later as *The First Forty Years of Washington Society*, offers an unrivalled inside view of men and manners in the early years of the national capital.

. . . I left the rest of this sheet for an account of the inauguration. It was not a thing of detail

Text: Margaret Bayard Smith, *The First Forty Years of Washington Society*, ed. Gaillard Hunt (New York: Charles Scribner's Sons, 1906), pp. 290-92, 295-96.

of a succession of small incidents. No, it was one grand whole, an imposing and majestic spectacle and to a reflective mind one of moral sublimity. Thousands and thousands of people, without distinction of rank, collected in an immense mass round the Capitol, silent, orderly and tranquil, with their eyes fixed on the front of that edifice, waiting the appearance of the President in the portico. The door from the Rotunda opens, preceded by the marshals, surrounded by the Judges of the Supreme Court, the old man with his grey locks, that crown of glory, advances, bows to the people, who greet him with a shout that rends the air, the Cannons, from the heights around, from Alexandria and Fort Warburton proclaim the oath he has taken and all the hills reverberate the sound. It was grand,—it was sublime! An almost breathless silence, succeeded and the multitude was still,—listening to catch the sound of his voice, tho' it was so low, as to be heard only by those nearest to him. After reading his speech, the oath was administered to him by the Chief Justice. The Marshal presented the Bible. The President took it from his hands, pressed his lips to it, laid it reverently down, then bowed again to the people—Yes, to the people in all their majesty. And had the spectacle closed here, even Europeans must have acknowledged that a free people, collected in their might, silent and tranquil, restrained solely by a moral power, without a shadow around of military force, was majesty, rising to sublimity, and far surpassing the majesty of Kings and Princes, surrounded with armies and glittering in gold. But I will not anticipate, but will give you an account of the inauguration in mere detail. The whole of the preceding day, immense crowds were coming into the city from all parts, lodgings could not be obtained, and the newcomers had to go to George Town, which soon overflowed and others had to go to Alexandria. I was told the Avenue and adjoining streets were so crowded on Tuesday afternoon that it was difficult to pass.

A national salute was fired early in the morning, and ushered in the 4th of March. By ten oclock the Avenue was crowded with carriages of every description, from the splendid Barronet and coach, down to waggons and carts, filled with women and children, some in finery and some in rags, for it was the people's President, and all would see him. . . . Some one came and in-

formed us the crowd before the President's house, was so far lessen'd, that they thought we might enter. This time we effected our purpose. But what a scene did we witness! *The Majesty of the People* had disappeared, and a rabble, a mob, of boys, negros, women, children, scrambling fighting, romping. What a pity what a pity! No arrangements had been made no police officers placed on duty and the whole house had been inundated by the rabble mob. We came too late. The President, after having been *literally* nearly pressed to death and almost suffocated and torn to pieces by the people in their eagerness to shake hands with Old Hickory, had retreated through the back way or south front and had escaped to his lodgings at Gadsby's. Cut glass and china to the amount of several thousand dollars had been broken in the struggle to get the refreshments, punch and other articles had been carried out in tubs and buckets, but had it been in hogsheads it would have been insufficient, ice-creams, and cake and lemonade, for 20,000 people, for it is said that number were there, tho' I think the estimate exaggerated. Ladies fainted, men were seen with bloody noses and such a scene of confusion took place as is impossible to describe,—those who got in could not get out by the door again, but had to scramble out of windows. At one time, the President who had retreated and retreated until he was pressed against the wall, could only be secured by a number of gentlemen forming round him and making a kind of barrier of their own bodies, and the pressure was so great that Col Bomford who was one said that at one time he was afraid they should have been pushed down, or on the President. It was then the windows were thrown open, and the torrent found an outlet, which otherwise might have proved fatal.

This concourse had not been anticipated and therefore not provided against. Ladies and gentlemen, only had been expected at this Levee, not the people en masse. But it was the People's day, and the People's President and the People would rule. God grant that one day or other, the People, do not put down all rule and rulers. . . .

113   THE REGIME OF DEMOCRACY

from Alexis de Tocqueville, *Democracy in America*, 1835

A new writer on the nature of American democracy still receives his highest praise when a critic labels him a worthy successor to Alexis de Tocqueville. For that curious and reflective Frenchman in his twenties drew from a nine-months' tour of the United States (1831-1832) the materials for a unique masterpiece: *Democracy in America*, published in France between 1835 and 1840, and soon translated into English and many other languages. Alexis Charles Henri Clerel de Tocqueville (1805-1859) was born into the lesser nobility of Normandy. His grandfather was guillotined in the French Revolution; his father was a court official under the restored Bourbon monarchy. De Tocqueville was himself a young magistrate at Versailles when the July Revolution of 1830 unsettled his position and led him to undertake a trip to Jacksonian America in company with his friend Gustave de Beaumont. Their official object was an investigation of the renowned American penal system; their underlying purpose, however, was to gain an understanding of the new social and political order of democracy that had reached full development in America and seemed to prefigure the destiny of Europe.

De Tocqueville traveled some seven thousand miles through the United States, recording his impressions of democratic character, customs, and institutions. The volumes he prepared for publication after his return to France scarcely resembled the usual "Travels in America" that were becoming a drug on the market, for the brilliant Frenchman transformed his observations into the stuff of philosophical inquiry. The reader seeking colorful vignettes of American life must look elsewhere. As De Tocqueville wrote of his own purposes: "I sought there the image of democracy itself, with its inclinations, its character, its prejudices, and its passions, in order to learn what we have to fear or to hope from its progress." Perhaps it is a tribute to the method as well as to the distinguished author that Americans over a century later continue to discover themselves and the essential problems of their community in De Tocqueville's pages.

The selection reprinted below is taken from the first part of De Tocqueville's analysis, concerning the character of political society in democratic America. Here he advances his thesis that the American polity derives from a dominant principle, popular sovereignty, which has unfolded over the course of the nation's history and now (in Jackson's time) presents its consequences, good and ill, for reflection. Other themes from *Democracy in America* may be examined in Documents 116 and 149.

[The People Reign]

. . . In America the principle of the sovereignty of the people is neither barren nor concealed, as it is with some other nations; it is recognized by the customs and proclaimed by the laws; it spreads freely, and arrives without impediment at its most remote consequences. If there is a country in the world where the doctrine of the sovereignty of the people can be fairly appreciated, where it can be studied in its application to the affairs of society, and where its dangers and its advantages may be judged, that country is assuredly America.

I have already observed that, from their origin, the sovereignty of the people was the fundamental principle of most of the British colonies in America. It was far, however, from then exercising as much influence on the government of society as it now does. Two obstacles, the one external, the other internal, checked its invasive progress.

It could not ostensibly disclose itself in the laws of colonies which were still forced to obey the mother country; it was therefore obliged to rule secretly in the provincial assemblies, and especially in the townships.

American society at that time was not yet prepared to adopt it with all its consequences.

Text: Alexis de Tocqueville, *Democracy in America*, ed. and trans. Henry Reeve (Cambridge, Mass.: Sever & Francis, 1862), I, 69-72, 318-23.

Intelligence in New England and wealth in the country to the south of the Hudson (as I have shown in the preceding chapter) long exercised a sort of aristocratic influence, which tended to keep the exercise of social power in the hands of a few. Not all the public functionaries were chosen by popular vote, nor were all the citizens voters. The electoral franchise was everywhere somewhat restricted and made dependent on a certain qualification, which was very low in the North and more considerable in the South.

The American Revolution broke out, and the doctrine of the sovereignty of the people came out of the townships and took possession of the state. Every class was enlisted in its cause; battles were fought and victories obtained for it; it became the law of laws.

A change almost as rapid was effected in the interior of society, where the law of inheritance completed the abolition of local influences.

As soon as this effect of the laws and of the Revolution became apparent to every eye, victory was irrevocably pronounced in favor of the democratic cause. All power was, in fact, in its hands, and resistance was no longer possible. The higher orders submitted without a murmur and without a struggle to an evil that was thenceforth inevitable. The ordinary fate of falling powers awaited them: each of their members followed his own interest; and as it was impossible to wring the power from the hands of a people whom they did not detest sufficiently to brave, their only aim was to secure its goodwill at any price. The most democratic laws were conse-'uently voted by the very men whose interests they impaired: and thus, although the higher classes did not excite the passions of the people against their order, they themselves accelerated the triumph of the new state of things; so that, by a singular change, the democratic impulse was found to be most irresistible in the very states where the aristocracy had the firmest hold. The state of Maryland, which had been founded by men of rank, was the first to proclaim universal suffrage and to introduce the most democratic forms into the whole of its government.

When a nation begins to modify the elective qualification, it may easily be foreseen that, sooner or later, that qualification will be entirely abolished. There is no more invariable rule in the history of society: the further electoral rights are extended, the greater is the need of extending them; for after each concession the strength of the democracy increases, and its demands increase with its strength. The ambition of those who are below the appointed rate is irritated in exact proportion to the great number of those who are above it. The exception at last becomes the rule, concession follows concession, and no stop can be made short of universal suffrage.

At the present day the principle of the sovereignty of the people has acquired in the United States all the practical development that the imagination can conceive. It is unencumbered by those fictions that are thrown over it in other countries, and it appears in every possible form, according to the exigency of the occasion. Sometimes the laws are made by the people in a body, as at Athens; and sometimes its representatives, chosen by universal suffrage, transact business in its name and under its immediate supervision.

In some countries a power exists which, though it is in a degree foreign to the social body, directs it, and forces it to pursue a certain track. In others the ruling force is divided, being partly within and partly without the ranks of the people. But nothing of the kind is to be seen in the United States; there society governs itself for itself. All power centers in its bosom, and scarcely an individual is to be met with who would venture to conceive or, still less, to express the idea of seeking it elsewhere. The nation participates in the making of its laws by the choice of its legislators, and in the execution of them by the choice of the agents of the executive government; it may almost be said to govern itself, so feeble and so restricted is the share left to the administration, so little do the authorities forget their popular origin and the power from which they emanate. The people reign in the American political world as the Deity does in the universe. They are the cause and the aim of all things; everything comes from them, and everything is absorbed in them. . . .

[*The Habits of Freedom*]

. . . It is not impossible to conceive the surprising liberty that the Americans enjoy; some idea may likewise be formed of their extreme equality; but the political activity that pervades the United States must be seen in order to be understood. No sooner do you set foot upon American ground than you are stunned by a kind of tumult; a confused clamor is heard on every side, and a thousand simultaneous voices demand the satisfaction of their social wants. Everything is in motion around you; here the people of one quarter of a town are met to decide upon the building of a church; there the election of a representative is going on; a little farther, the delegates of a district are hastening to the town in order to consult upon some local improvements; in another place, the laborers of a village quit their plows to deliberate upon the project of a road or a public school. Meetings are called for the sole purpose of declaring their disapprobation of the conduct of the government; while in other assemblies citizens salute the authorities of the day as the fathers of their country. Societies are formed which regard drunkenness as the principal cause of the evils of the state and solemnly bind themselves to give an example of temperance.

The great political agitation of American legislative bodies, which is the only one that attracts the attention of foreigners, is a mere episode, or a sort of continuation, of that universal movement which originates in the lowest classes of the people and extends successively to all the ranks of society. It is impossible to spend more effort in the pursuit of happiness.

It is difficult to say what place is taken up in the life of an inhabitant of the United States by his concern for politics. To take a hand in the regulation of society and to discuss it is his biggest concern and, so to speak, the only pleasure an American knows. This feeling pervades the most trifling habits of life; even the women frequently attend public meetings and listen to political harangues as a recreation from their household labors. Debating clubs are, to a certain extent, a substitute for theatrical entertainments: an American cannot converse, but he can discuss, and his talk falls into a dissertation. He speaks to you as if he was addressing a meeting; and if he should chance to become warm in the discussion, he will say "Gentlemen" to the person with whom he is conversing.

In some countries the inhabitants seem unwilling to avail themselves of the political privileges which the law gives them; it would seem that they set too high a value upon their time to spend it on the interests of the community; and that they shut themselves up in a narrow selfishness, marked out by four sunk fences and a quickset hedge. But if an American were condemned to confine his activity to his own affairs, he would be robbed of one half of his existence; he would feel an immense void in the life which he is accustomed to lead, and his wretchedness would be unbearable. I am persuaded that if ever a despotism should be established in America, it will be more difficult to overcome the habits that freedom has formed than to conquer the love of freedom itself.

This ceaseless agitation which democratic government has introduced into the political world influences all social intercourse. I am not sure that, on the whole, this is not the greatest advantage of democracy; and I am less inclined to applaud it for what it does than for what it causes to be done.

It is incontestable that the people frequently conduct public business very badly; but it is impossible that the lower orders should take a part in public business without extending the circle of their ideas and quitting the ordinary routine of their thoughts. The humblest individual who co-operates in the government of society acquires a certain degree of self-respect; and as he possesses authority, he can command the services of minds more enlightened than his own. He is canvassed by a multitude of applicants, and in seeking to deceive him in a thousand ways, they really enlighten him. He takes a part in political undertakings which he did not originate, but which give him a taste for undertakings of the kind. New improvements are daily pointed out to him in the common property, and this gives him the desire of improving that property which is his own. He is perhaps neither happier nor better than those who came before him, but he is better informed and more active. I have no doubt that the democratic institutions of the United States, joined to the physical constitution of the country, are the cause (not the direct, as is so often asserted, but the indirect cause) of the prodigious commercial activity of the inhabitants. It is not created by the laws, but the people learn how to promote it by the experience derived from legislation.

When the opponents of democracy assert that a single man performs what he undertakes better than the government of all, it appears to me that they are right. The government of an individual, supposing an equality of knowledge on either side, is more consistent, more persevering, more uniform, and more accurate in details than that of a multitude, and it selects with more discrimination the men whom it employs. If any deny this, they have never seen a democratic government, or have judged upon partial evidence. It is true that, even when local circumstances and the dispositions of the people allow democratic institutions to exist, they do not display a regular and methodical system of government. Democratic liberty is far from accomplishing all its projects with the skill of an adroit despotism. It frequently abandons them before they have borne their fruits, or risks them when the consequences may be dangerous; but in the end it produces more than any absolute government; if it does fewer things well, it does a greater number of things. Under its sway the grandeur is not in what the public administration does, but in what is done without it or outside of it. Democracy does not give the people the most skillful government, but it produces what the ablest governments are frequently unable to create: namely, an all-pervading and restless activity, a super abundant force, and an energy which is inseparable from it and which may, however unfavorable circumstances may be, produce wonders. These are the true advantages of democracy.

In the present age, when the destinies of Christendom seem to be in suspense, some hasten to assail democracy as a hostile power while it is yet growing; and others already adore this new deity which is springing forth from chaos. But both parties are imperfectly acquainted with the object of their hatred or their worship; they strike in the dark and distribute their blows at random.

We must first understand what is wanted of society and its government. Do you wish to give a certain elevation to the human mind and teach it to regard the things of this world with generous feelings, to inspire men with a scorn of mere temporal advantages, to form and nourish strong convictions and keep alive the spirit of honorable devotedness? Is it your object to refine the habits, embellish the manners, and cultivate the arts, to promote the love of poetry, beauty, and glory? Would you constitute a people fitted to act powerfully upon all other nations, and prepared for those high enterprises which, whatever be their results, will leave a name forever famous in history? If you believe such to be the principal object of society, avoid the government of the democracy, for it would not lead you with certainty to the goal.

But if you hold it expedient to divert the moral and intellectual activity of man to the production of comfort and the promotion of general well-being; if a clear understanding be more profitable to man than genius; if your object is not to stimulate the virtues of heroism, but the habits of peace; if you had rather witness vices than crimes, and are content to meet with fewer noble deeds, provided offenses be diminished in the same proportion; if, instead of living in the midst of a brilliant society, you are contented to have prosperity around you; if, in short, you are of the opinion that the principal object of a government is not to confer the greatest possible power and glory upon the body of the nation, but to ensure the greatest enjoyment and to avoid the most misery to each of the individuals who compose it—if such be your desire, then equalize the conditions of men and establish democratic institutions.

114 THE ART AND CRAFT OF PARTY POLITICS

from Thomas Ford, A History of Illinois, 1854

A Jacksonian lawyer, judge, and governor of Illinois (from 1842 to 1846), Thomas Ford observed the evolution of party politics in his frontier community with a penetrating and critical eye. Ford's *History of Illinois* contains one of the most rewarding contemporary records of the process by which parties assumed a major role in American political life.

Parties of some sort are perhaps an inevitable feature of popular government. James Madison in *Federalist* No. 10 (Document 61) argued that "factions" would spring up wherever men were free both to pursue their private interests and to combine with others of similar interest in order to grasp advantages from government. Washington in his *Farewell Address* (Document 69), considering the violent party battles between Federalists and Republicans in the 1790's, sought to moderate that extreme party spirit which would divide and destroy the Union. We have also seen in Fisher Ames' diatribes against the "Jacobins" (Document 71) some evidence of the growing power of local party organization, a Republican evil which the bitter Massachusetts Federalist proposed to remedy by imitation.

The admission of new Western states with highly democratic constitutions, as well as the gradual revision of the older state constitutions in the early decades of the nineteenth century, reduced voting and officeholding qualifications and increased the number of elective offices. Ingenious politicians, especially in New York and Pennsylvania, improved the arts of managing a mass electorate and enforcing party discipline by such modern devices as the partisan press, patronage, and the like. In national politics the Congressional caucus lost its control of presidential nominations in 1824, and the whole caucus system gradually gave way to party nominating conventions at all political levels. In these and other ways the political party in the Jacksonian era—Whig as well as Democratic—assumed a set of essential functions: nominating candidates, conducting electoral campaigns, framing issues and alternatives, organizing legislative action, dispensing public appointments, and—not least—perpetuating the party organization itself.

How such developments came about in early Illinois and how they affected the qualities of political life are the subject of the following selection. Thomas Ford's findings offer interesting comparisons with De Tocqueville's general analysis of democratic politics (Document 113) and with the story of young Abe Lincoln in Illinois (Document 115).

. . . Personal politics, intrigue, and a disregard of the public welfare, were carried from the primary elections into the legislature. Almost everything there was done from personal motives. Special legislation for the benefit of friends occupied members, and diverted their attention from such measures as were for the general benefit. The man of the most tact and address, who could make the most friends and the most skil-

Text: Thomas Ford, *A History of Illinois* (Chicago: S. C. Griggs, 1854), pp. 88-90, 198-208 *passim.*

ful combinations of individual interests, was always the most successful in accomplishing his purposes. A smooth, sleek, supple, friendly manner, which by gaining favor imposed upon credulity, made a politician formidable. Truly, the man who could approach another with a graceful and friendly impudence, and readily conciliate good-will, was potent indeed. The genius and humor of the times invented or imported a slang language, very expressive of the achievements of these political heroes. Such an operator in politics was said to carry "a gourd of *possum fat*," with which to "grease" the members. It is not known why the fat of the opossum was selected for the emblem of this kind of tact, unless because it was the most fluid and slippery of oils then known in the country. The easy, facile credulous fool who was the victim of artful fascination, was said to be "*greased and swallowed*." A man was "greased" when he was won over to the purposes of another by a feigned show of friendship and condescension; and he was "swallowed" when he was made to act to suit the purposes of "the intrigue," whatever it might be. Sometimes the act of lubrication, by which a man was fitted to be "swallowed," was supposed to be performed with "*soft soap*." It was no uncommon thing to hear that such a one "had a great deal of soft soap about him," and was a "great hand to swallow people." Gov. Edwards was said to be the greatest hand to swallow people in all the country; and when he was last a candidate for governor, it was charged on him that he had not only swallowed a great many of his former enemies, but that he had actually performed the grand operation of swallowing himself. The simpleton who suffered himself to be made a mere instrument in the hands of another to do something discreditable or unpopular, whereby he was unable to be elected again, was said to be "used up," meaning that he had been used like the aforesaid soft soap, or other household article, until there was no more of him left.

During this period of twelve years [1818-1830], neither the people nor their public servants ever dreamed that government might be made the instrument to accomplish a higher destiny for the people. There seemed to be no aim to advance the civilization and real happiness of the human family. . . . In fact, the great mass of the people, politicians and all, had a mere selfish destiny in view. The people were, most of them, pioneers and adventurers, who came to a new country hoping to get a living with more ease than they had been accustomed to, or to better their condition as to property. Such persons cared but little for matters of government, except when stirred up by their demagogues; and then they had no definite object to accomplish except to punish their representatives for a single act or vote, which was, nine times out of ten, a good one. The politicians took advantage of this lethargic state of indifference of the people to advance their own projects, to get offices and special favors from the legislature, which were all they busied their heads about. . . .

And here is a proper place for some further account of political parties. In their origin, such parties seem to be founded partly in the nature of man, and much upon artifice. There is undoubtedly a difference in the mental and physical constitution of men, inclining them one way or the other in political affairs. Some distrust the people, others confide in their capacity for self-government. Some prefer a quiet government, others a stormy turbulence. The condition of men, also, has much to do with party; some are poor and lowly as to property, but proud in their hearts; others rich and well-born, with a power to make their pride felt by others. Some are ignorant and feeble-minded, others shrewd and intelligent; some are rough and ill-bred, others polished and graceful. In a word, some have superior advantages, which create them into a caste of their own. That portion enjoying these superior advantages, are apt to look down upon their less-gifted fellow-citizens with contempt or indifference; and to feel that as they are superior in some respects, they ought to be in all. They can have but little patience with the idea that the rabble is to govern the country. The people in humble condition look up to them with resentment and detestation. These remarks are not invariably true of either side, but it will be accorded to me that almost every neighborhood has some one richer than the rest, who puts on airs of importance, and manifests such a want of sympathy with his fellows, as to disgust his humbler neighbors; amongst whom there are those who, full of ill-nature, look upon such pretensions with envious resentment. These little big men, on both sides, of the neighborhood sort, are apt to feel the most thorough hatred for each other; their malice often supplying the place of principle and patriotism. They think they are devoted to a cause, when they only hate an opponent; and the more thoroughly they hate, the more thoroughly are they partisans. Here originates the hostility between democracy and aristocracy, as it is said to exist in this country; and here originates the feeling of proscription, which is more violent amongst mere neighborhood politicians, men who never expect an office, than among politicians who have risen to distinction. The eminent politicians on each side frequently feel a liberality, personally to an adversary, which cannot be manifested without losing the confidence of their humbler friends.

And this state of things are kept up by the party newspapers on each side, the editors of which well know that their most profitable harvest is during an excited contest. Newspapers are then more sought for and read; and then it is that an editor's funds best support him with money and patronage. It may be said with truth that a partisan editor is a continual candidate for the favor of his party; for which reason, it is his interest to make political contests interminable. The great mass of the people, who take newspapers at all, generally content themselves with one political paper of their own party. This and no other, except in the towns, they read from week to week, and from year to year, until they become thoroughly enlisted in all the quarrels of the editor, and imbued with all his malice and prejudice; and thus they become bound up in the most ill-natured, narrow-minded, pedantic conceits; fully convinced that their way, and no other, is right, and that all persons of the opposite party know it to be so. They feel assured that their political opponents, and particularly those of them who are elected to office, are a set of insufferable rogues, bent upon the enslavement of the people, or the ruin of the country. The rascality of the whigs, in the opinion of the democrats, is to end in enslaving the people, or to transfer the government to some foreign power; and the rascality of the democrats, in the opinion of the whigs, is to ruin the country. It is probably true that in something like this, is the natural difference, founded upon which parties will continue to be built, and that all efforts to get up third parties, not founded upon this difference, and all efforts to make new and merely temporary issues the permanent foundation of party, must be abortive. . . .

Our old way of conducting elections required each aspirant for office to announce himself as a candidate. The more prudent, however, always first consulted a little caucus of select, influential friends. The candidates then travelled around the county or State, in proper person, making speeches, conversing with the people, soliciting votes, whispering slanders against their opponents, and defending themselves against the attacks of their adversaries. . . .

. . . As party spirit increased more and more, the necessity of some mode of concentrating the party strength became more and more apparent.

The large emigration from the old States, bringing with it the zeal and party organization in which it had been trained from infancy, gave a new impulse to the consolidation of the strength of party. An attempt at this was early made by the New England and New York people living in the north part of the State, by introducing the convention system of nominating candidates. . . .

At a great meeting of the lobby, during the special session of 1835-'6, at Vandalia, Mr. Peck made the first speech ever made in the lower part of the State in favor of the convention system. . . . From this time the system won its way slowly, and now [ca. 1847] all the candidates for governor, lieutenant governor, and members of Congress, are brought before the people by conventions, and it pervades two-thirds of the State in nominating candidates for the legislature.

The system has some advantages and disadvantages in this country. Those in favor of it say that it furnishes the only mode of concentrating the action of a party, and giving effect to the will of the majority. They justly urge, that since the organization of parties, the old system of electing from personal preference is carried into each party in the mere selection of candidates, which distracts the harmony of a party by introducing competition amongst distinguished men for the mere privilege of becoming candidates, without any means of deciding between them, except at the polls. . . . Without a nomination, a party may be greatly in the majority, but by being divided on men, the minority may succeed in the elections, and actually govern the majority. To remedy this evil, it was proposed by conventions of delegates, previously elected by the people, to provide but a single set of candidates for the same party. It was also urged by some, that these bodies would be composed of the best-informed and principal men of a party, and would be more competent than the people at large, to select good men for candidates. . . .

On the other side, it was urged, that the whole convention system was a fraud on the people; that it was a mere fungus growth engrafted upon the constitution; that conventions themselves were got up and packed by cunning, active, intriguing politicians, to suit the wishes of a few. The mode of getting them up, was for some active man to procure a few friends in each precinct of a county, to hold primary meetings, where delegates were elected to county conventions, who met at the county seats, and nominated candidates for the legislature and for county offices; and appointed other delegates to district and State conventions, to nominate candidates for Congress and for governor. The great difficulty was in the primary meetings in the precincts. In the Eastern States, where conventions originated, they had township governments, little democracies, where the whole people met in person at least once a year, to lay taxes for roads and for the support of schools and the poor. This called the whole people of a township together, enlightened their minds and accustomed them to take a lively interest in their government; and whilst assembled they could and did elect their delegates to conventions. In this mode a convention reflected the will of a party, as much as the legislature reflected the will of the whole people. But how is it in Illinois? We had no township governments, no occasions for a general meeting of the people, except at the elections themselves; the people did not attend the primary meetings; a few only assembled, who were nearest the places of meeting, and these were too often mere professional politicians, the loafers about the towns, who having but little business of their own, were ever ready to attend to the affairs of the public. This threw the political power out of the hands of the people, merely because they would not exercise it, into the hands of idlers—of a few active men, who controlled them. If any one desired an office, he never thought of applying to the people for it; but passed them by, and applied himself to conciliate the managers and idlers about the towns, many of whom could only

be conciliated at an immense sacrifice of the public interest. It is true that a party had the reserved right of rebellion against all this machinery; no one could be punished for treason in so doing, otherwise than by losing the favor of his party, and being denounced as a traitor; which was almost as efficacious in restraining the refractory as the pains and penalties of treason, the hanging and embowelling of former times. . . .

By means of the convention system, and many exciting contests, the two parties of whigs and democrats were thoroughly organized and disciplined by the year 1840. No regular army could have excelled them in discipline. They were organized upon the principles of national politics only, and not in any degree upon those of the State. . . . The President was the leader of his party in the nation, and there was no principle of party in the State but this. Men were elected to office upon the popularity of the President, and upon the principles which the President put forth; and they were thus compelled, in self-defence, to support and defend him, through good and evil, right or wrong, as much as if they owed their offices to his gift. Besides this, their parties absolutely required them to do so. It may be remarked here as a curious fact, that the politicians all over the nation, pretending to be most in favor of State rights and State sovereignty, have contributed most to overthrow them, by forever insisting upon the organization of parties, purely upon national questions. . . .

115 WESTERN POLITICKING: ABE LINCOLN IN ILLINOIS

from William H. Herndon and Jesse W. Weik, *Herndon's Lincoln*, 1889

Historians have had a gay time demolishing the "Lincoln myth," yet the myth is not so mythical after all. Abraham Lincoln (1809-1865) did spring from pioneer folk who followed the frontier line from Kentucky to Illinois. He did split rails; he did educate himself; he did emerge from the rough and tumble politics of the frontier to become a great President and an authentic national hero. If Lincoln's career did not prove that any boy could rise from log cabin to White House, it did testify that one with Lincoln's qualities could achieve the highest honors in American public life without benefit of family prestige, wealth, or formal education.

An autobiography which Lincoln wrote in 1859 tells his early life in his own characteristically earthy style:

"I was born February 12, 1809, in Hardin County, Kentucky. My parents were both born in Virginia, of undistinguished families. . . . My mother, who died in my tenth year, was of a family of the name of Hanks. . . . My father, at the death of his father, was but six years of age, and he grew up literally without education. He removed from Kentucky to what is now Spencer County, Indiana, in my eighth year. . . . It was a wild region, with many bears and other wild animals still in the woods. There I grew up. There were some schools, so called, but no qualification was ever required of a teacher beyond 'readin', writin', and cipherin',' to the rule of three. . . . There was absolutely nothing to excite ambition for education. Of course, when I came of age, I did not know much. Still, somehow, I could read, write, and cipher to the rule of three, but that was all. I have not been to school since. The little advance I now have upon this store of education, I have picked up from time to time under the pressure of necessity.

"I was raised to farm work, which I continued till I was twenty-two. At twenty-one I came to Illinois, Macon County. Then I got to New Salem . . . where I remained a year as a sort of clerk in a store. Then came The Black Hawk War; and I was elected a captain of volunteers, a success which gave me more pleasure than any I have had since. I went the campaign, was elected, ran for the legislature the same year (1832), and was beaten—the only time I ever have been beaten by the people. The next and three succeeding biennial elections I was elected to the legislature. I was not a candidate afterward. During this legislative period I had studied law, and removed to Springfield to practice it. In 1846 I was once elected to the lower House of Congress. Was not a candidate for reelection. From 1849 to 1854, both inclusive, practised law more assiduously than ever before. . . . I was losing interest in politics when the repeal of the Missouri Compromise aroused me again. What I have done since then is pretty well known.

"If any personal description of me is thought desirable, it may be said I am, in height, six feet four inches, nearly; lean in flesh, weighing on an average one hundred and eighty pounds; dark complexion, with coarse black hair and gray eyes. No other marks or brands recollected."

William H. Herndon, the co-author of the following selection, was Lincoln's long-time law partner and friend. His biography of Lincoln preserves some doubtful stories—for instance, the Ann Rutledge romance—and some doubtful judgments—as of Mary Todd Lincoln's character. Still it remains a priceless document among the innumerable writings about Abe Lincoln in Illinois, for Herndon knew his subject and his scene intimately and was not lacking in shrewdness or candor. Especially valuable is the account of the years after Lincoln had come to New Salem, Illinois, from Indiana.

The closing scene in the selection below shows Lincoln in 1834 borrowing $200 to dress and maintain himself in a style befitting a newly elected Illinois legislator. Little more than two decades later one will meet the masterly spokesman for the Republican cause, ready to challenge Stephen A. Douglas for the leadership of Illinois and thereby to earn his place in the first rank of presidential candidates (Document 134).

The return of the Black Hawk warriors to New Salem occurred in the month of August, but a short time before the general election. A new Legislature was to be chosen, and as Lincoln had declared to his comrades in the army he would, and in obedience to the effusive declaration of principles which he had issued over his signature in March, before he went to the war, he presented himself to the people of his newly adopted county as a candidate for the Legislature. . . . Though he may not have distinctly avowed himself a Whig, yet, as one of his friends asserted, "he stood openly on Whig principles." He favored a national bank, a liberal system of internal improvements, and a high protective tariff. The handbill or circular alluded to announcing his candidacy was a sort of literary fulmination, but on account of its length I deem it unnecessary to insert the whole of it here. I have been told that it was prepared by Lincoln, but purged of its most glaring grammatical errors by James Mc-Namar, who afterwards became Lincoln's rival in an important love affair.

The circular is dated March 9, 1832, and addressed to the "People of Sangamon County." In it he takes up all the leading questions of the day: railroads, river navigation, internal improvements, and usury. He dwells particularly on the matter of public education, alluding to it as the most important subject before the people. Realizing his own defects arising from a lack of school instruction he contends that every man and his children, however poor, should be permitted to obtain at least a moderate education, and thereby be enabled "to read the Scriptures and other works both of a moral and religious nature for themselves." The closing paragraph was so constructed as to appeal to the chivalrous sentiments of Clary's Grove. "I was born and have ever remained," he declares, "in the most humble walks of life. I have no wealthy or popular relatives or friends to recommend me. My case is thrown exclusively upon the independent

Text: William H. Herndon and Jesse W. Weik, *Herndon's Lincoln* (Chicago: Belford, Clarke & Co., 1889), I, 101-06, 109-10, 112, 118-20, 125-27.

voters of the county; and if elected they will have conferred a favor upon me for which I shall be unremitting in my labors to compensate. But if," he dryly concludes, "the good people in their wisdom shall see fit to keep me in the background, I have been too familiar with disappointments to be very much chagrined."

The election being near at hand only a few days remained for his canvass. One who was with him at the time describing his appearance, says: "He wore a mixed jeans coat, clawhammer style, short in the sleeves and bobtail—in fact it was so short in the tail he could not sit on it; flax and towlinen pantaloons, and a straw hat. I think he wore a vest, but do not remember how it looked. He wore pot-metal boots." His maiden effort on the stump was a speech on the occasion of a public sale at Pappsville, a village eleven miles west of Springfield. After the sale was over and speechmaking had begun, a fight—a "general fight," as one of the bystanders relates—ensued, and Lincoln, noticing one of his friends about to succumb to the energetic attack of an infuriated ruffian, interposed to prevent it. He did so most effectually. Hastily descending from the rude platform he edged his way through the crowd, and seizing the bully by the neck and seat of his trowsers, threw him by means of his strength and long arms, as one witness stoutly insists, "twelve feet away." Returning to the stand and throwing aside his hat he inaugurated his campaign with the following brief but juicy declaration:

"Fellow Citizens, I presume you all know who I am. I am humble Abraham Lincoln. I have been solicited by many friends to become a candidate for the Legislature. My politics are short and sweet, like the old woman's dance. I am in favor of a national bank. I am in favor of the internal improvement system and a high protective tariff. These are my sentiments and political principles. If elected I shall be thankful; if not it will be all the same."

I obtained this speech from A. Y. Ellis, who in 1865 wrote it out. Ellis was his friend and supporter, and took no little interest in his canvass. "I accompanied him," he relates, "on one of his electioneering trips to Island Grove, and he made a speech which pleased his party friends very well indeed, though some of the Jackson men tried to make sport of it. He told several anecdotes, and applied them, as I thought, very well. He also told the boys several stories which drew them after him. I remember them, but modesty and my veneration for his memory forbid me to relate them." His story-telling propensity, and the striking fitness of his yarns—

many of them being of the bar-room order—in illustrating public questions . . . was really one of the secrets of his popularity and strength.

The election, as he had predicted, resulted in his defeat—the only defeat, as he himself afterward stated, that he ever suffered at the hands of the people. But there was little defeat in it after all. Out of the eight unsuccessful candidates he stood third from the head of the list, receiving 657 votes. Five others received less. The most gratifying feature of it all was the hearty support of his neighbors at New Salem. . . .

The unsuccessful result of the election did not dampen his hopes nor sour his ambition. The extensive acquaintance, the practice in public speaking, the confidence gained with the people, together with what was augmented in himself, made a surplus of capital on which he was free to draw and of which he afterwards frequently availed himself. The election being over, however, he found himself without money, though with a goodly supply of experience, drifting again. His political experience had forever weaned him from the dull routine of common labor. Labor afforded him no time for study and no incentive to profitable reflection. What he seemed to want was some lighter work, employment in a store or tavern where he could meet the village celebrities, exchange views with strangers, discuss politics, horse-races, cock-fights, and narrate to listening loafers his striking and significant stories. In the communities where he had lived, the village storekeeper held undisturbed sway. He took the only newspaper, owned the only collection of books and half the property in the village; and in general was the social, and oftentimes the political head of the community. Naturally, therefore the prominence the store gave the merchant attracted Lincoln. . . .

Conscious of his many shortcomings as a merchant, . . . Lincoln returned to his books. Rowan Herndon, with whom he had been living, having removed to the country, he became for the first time a sojourner at the tavern, as it was then called—a public-house kept by Rutledge, Onstatt, and Alley in succession. "It was a small log house," he explained to me in later years, "covered with clapboards, and contained four rooms." It was second only in importance to the store, for there he had the opportunity of meeting passing strangers—lawyers and others from the county seat, whom he frequently impressed with his knowledge as well as wit. He had, doubtless, long before determined to prepare himself for the law; in fact, had begun to read Blackstone while in the store, and now went at it with renewed zeal. He borrowed law-books of his former comrade in the Black Hawk war, John T. Stuart, who was practicing law in Springfield, frequently walking there to return one and borrow another. His determination to master any subject he undertook and his application to study were of the most intense order. On the road to and from Springfield he would read and recite from the book he carried open in his hand, and claimed to have mastered forty pages of Blackstone during the first day after his return from Stuart's office. At New Salem he frequently sat barefooted under the shade of a tree near the store, poring over a volume of Chitty or Blackstone, sometimes lying on his back, putting his feet up the tree, which provokes one of his biographers to denote the latter posture as one which might have been "unfavorable to mental application, in the case of a man with shorter extremities." . . .

It was not long until he was able to draw up deeds, contracts, mortgages, and other legal papers for his neighbors. He figured conspicuously as a pettifogger before the justice of the peace, but regarding it merely as a kind of preliminary practice, seldom made any charge for his services. Meanwhile he was reading not only law books but natural philosophy and other scientific subjects. He was a careful and patient reader of newspapers, the *Sangamon Journal*—published at Springfield—*Louisville Journal, St. Louis Republican,* and *Cincinnati Gazette* being usually within his reach. He paid a less degree of attention to historical works, although he read Rollin and Gibbon while in business with Berry. He had a more pronounced fondness for fictitious literature, and read with evident relish Mrs. Lee Hentz's novels, which were very popular books in that day, and which were kindly loaned by his friend A. Y. Ellis. . . .

While wooing that jealous-eyed mistress, the law, Lincoln was earning no money. As another has said, "he had a running board bill to pay, and nothing to pay it with." By dint of sundry jobs here and there, helping Ellis in his store today, splitting rails for James Short tomorrow, he managed to keep his head above the waves. His friends were firm—no young man ever had truer or better ones—but he was of too independent a turn to appeal to them or complain of his condition. He never at any time abandoned the idea of becoming a lawyer. That was always a spirit which beckoned him on in the darkest hour of his adversity. Someone, probably a Democrat who voted for him in the preceding fall, recommended him to John Calhoun, then surveyor of the county, as suitable material for an assistant. This office, in view of the prevailing speculation in lands and town lots, was the most

important and possibly the most profitable in the county. Calhoun, the incumbent, was a Yankee and a typical gentleman. . . .

. . . The recommendation of Lincoln's friends was sufficient to induce Calhoun to appoint him one of his deputies. At the time he received notice of his selection by Calhoun, Lincoln was out in the woods near New Salem splitting rails. A friend named Pollard Simmons, who still survives and has related the incident to me, walked out to the point where he was working with the cheering news. Lincoln, being a Whig and knowing Calhoun's pronounced Democratic tendencies, inquired if he had to sacrifice any principle in accepting the position. "If I can be perfectly free in my political action I will take the office," he remarked; "but if my sentiments or even expression of them is to be abridged in any way I would not have it or any other office." A young man hampered by poverty as Lincoln was at this time, who had the courage to deal with public office as he did, was certainly made of unalloyed material. . . .

No little of Lincoln's influence with the men of New Salem can be attributed to his extraordinary feats of strength. By an arrangement of ropes and straps, harnessed about his hips, he was enabled one day at the mill to astonish a crowd of village celebrities by lifting a box of stones weighing near a thousand pounds. There is no fiction either, as suggested by some of his biographers, in the story that he lifted a barrel of whisky from the ground and drank from the bung; but in performing this latter almost incredible feat he did not stand erect and elevate the barrel, but squatted down and lifted it to his knees, rolling it over until his mouth came opposite the bung. His strength, kindness of manner, love of fairness and justice, his original and unique sayings, his power of mimicry, his perseverance—all made a combination rarely met with on the frontier. Nature had burnt him in her holy fire, and stamped him with the seal of her greatness.

In the summer of 1834 Lincoln determined to make another race for the legislature; but this time he ran distinctly as a Whig. He made, it is presumed, the usual number of speeches, but as the art of newspaper reporting had not reached the perfection it has since attained, we are not favored with even the substance of his efforts on the stump. I have Lincoln's word for it that it was more of a hand-shaking campaign than anything else. Rowan Herndon relates that he came to his house during harvest, when there were a large number of men at work in the field. He was introduced to them, but they did not hesitate to apprize him of their esteem for a man who could labor; and their admiration for a candidate for office was gauged somewhat by the amount of work he could do. Learning these facts, Lincoln took hold of a cradle, and handling it with ease and remarkable speed, soon distanced those who undertook to follow him. The men were satisfied, and it is presumed he lost no votes in that crowd. One Dr. Barrett, seeing Lincoln, inquired of the latter's friends: "Can't the party raise any better material thán that?" but after hearing his speech the doctor's opinion was considerably altered, for he declared that Lincoln filled him with amazement: "that he knew more than all of the other candidates put together." The election took place in August. Lincoln's

friend, John T. Stuart, was also a candidate on the legislative ticket. He encouraged Lincoln's canvass in every way, even at the risk of sacrificing his own chances. But both were elected. The four successful candidates were Dawson, who received 1390 votes, Lincoln 1376, Carpenter 1170, and Stuart 1164.

At last Lincoln had been elected to the legislature, and by a very flattering majority. In order, as he himself said, "to make a decent appearance in the legislature," he had to borrow money to buy suitable clothing and to maintain his new dignity. Coleman Smoot, one of his friends, advanced him "two hundred dollars, which he returned, relates the generous Smoot, according to promise." . . .

The Open Society

116 THE DEMOCRATIC CAREER

from Alexis de Tocqueville, *Democracy in America*, 1840

The passages reprinted below are from the second part of *Democracy in America* (see headnote to Document 113), published some eight years after the author's return from the United States (1840). Here De Tocqueville considered the ideas, feelings, and manners of the Americans before closing the circle at the original point of departure: the political order of democracy. Underlying the sequence of short essays is the author's leading proposition, announced in the introduction to the first volume: "equality of condition is the fundamental fact from which all others seem to be derived and the central point at which all my observations constantly terminated."

That American life in the Jacksonian era showed an unprecedented mobility of men, breathtaking fluidity of affairs and institutions, was a commonplace among observers, especially Europeans accustomed to a world where rank and status, custom and tradition still maintained a certain hold over society. It was De Tocqueville's task in the following selection to account for the mutability of American life as a consequence of "equality of condition." The issues De Tocqueville defines have a most familiar ring.

. . . A native of the United States clings to this world's goods as if he were certain never to die; and he is so hasty in grasping at all within his reach that one would suppose he was constantly afraid of not living long enough to enjoy them. He clutches everything, he holds nothing fast, but soon loosens his grasp to pursue fresh gratifications.

In the United States a man builds a house in which to spend his old age, and he sells it before the roof is on; he plants a garden and lets it just as the trees are coming into bearing;

Text: Alexis de Tocqueville, *Democracy in America,* ed. and trans. Henry Reeve (Cambridge, Mass.: Sever & Francis, 1862), II, 163-67, 308-14 *passim.*

he brings a field into tillage and leaves other men to gather the crops; he embraces a profession and gives it up; he settles in a place, which he soon afterwards leaves to carry his changeable longings elsewhere. If his private affairs leave him any leisure, he instantly plunges into the vortex of politics; and if at the end of a year of unremitting labor he finds he has a few days' vacation, his eager curiosity whirls him over the vast extent of the United States, and he will travel fifteen hundred miles in a few days to shake off his happiness. Death at length overtakes him, but it is before he is weary of his bootless chase of that complete felicity which forever escapes him.

At first sight there is something surprising in this strange unrest of so many happy men, restless in the midst of abundance. The spectacle itself, however, is as old as the world; the novelty is to see a whole people furnish an exemplification of it.

Their taste for physical gratifications must be regarded as the original source of that secret disquietude which the actions of the Americans betray and of that inconstancy of which they daily afford fresh examples. He who has set his heart exclusively upon the pursuit of worldly welfare is always in a hurry, for he has but a limited time at his disposal to reach, to grasp, and to enjoy it. The recollection of the shortness of life is a constant spur to him. Besides the good things that he possesses, he every instant fancies a thousand others that death will prevent him from trying if he does not try them soon. This thought fills him with anxiety, fear, and regret and keeps his mind in ceaseless trepidation, which leads him perpetually to change his plans and his abode.

If in addition to the taste for physical well-being a social condition be added in which neither laws nor customs retain any person in his place, there is a great additional stimulant to this restlessness of temper. Men will then be seen continually to change their track for fear of missing the shortest cut to happiness.

It may readily be conceived that if men passionately bent upon physical gratifications desire eagerly, they are also easily discouraged; as their ultimate object is to enjoy, the means to reach that object must be prompt and easy or the trouble of acquiring the gratification would be greater than the gratification itself. Their prevailing frame of mind, then, is at once ardent and relaxed, violent and enervated. Death is often less dreaded by them than perseverance in continuous efforts to one end.

The equality of conditions leads by a still straighter road to several of the effects that I have here described. When all the privileges of birth and fortune are abolished, when all professions are accessible to all, and a man's own energies may place him at the top of any one of them, an easy and unbounded career seems open to his ambition and he will readily persuade himself that he is born to no common destinies. But this is an erroneous notion, which is corrected by daily experience. The same equality that allows every citizen to conceive these lofty hopes renders all the citizens less able to realize them; it circumscribes their powers on every side, while it gives freer scope to their desires. Not only are they themselves powerless, but they

are met at every step by immense obstacles, which they did not at first perceive. They have swept away the privileges of some of their fellow creatures which stood in their way, but they have opened the door to universal competition; the barrier has changed its shape rather than its position. When men are nearly alike and all follow the same track, it is very difficult for any one individual to walk quickly and cleave a way through the dense throng that surrounds and presses on him. This constant strife between the inclination springing from the equality of condition and the means it supplies to satisfy them harasses and wearies the mind.

It is possible to conceive of men arrived at a degree of freedom that should completely content them; they would then enjoy their independence without anxiety and without impatience. But men will never establish any equality with which they can be contented. Whatever efforts a people may make, they will never succeed in reducing all the conditions of society to a perfect level; and even if they unhappily attained that absolute and complete equality of position, the inequality of minds would still remain, which, coming directly from the hand of God, will forever escape the laws of man. However democratic, then, the social state and the political constitution of a people may be, it is certain that every member of the community will always find out several points about him which overlook his own position; and we may foresee that his looks will be doggedly fixed in that direction. When inequality of conditions is the common law of society, the most marked inequalities do not strike the eye; when everything is nearly on the same level, the slightest are marked enough to hurt it. Hence the desire of equality always becomes more insatiable in proportion as equality is more complete.

Amongst democratic nations, men easily attain a certain equality of condition, but they can never attain as much as they desire. It perpetually retires from before them, yet without hiding itself from their sight, and in retiring draws them on. At every moment they think they are about to grasp it; it escapes at every moment from their hold. They are near enough to see its charms, but too far off to enjoy them; and before they have fully tasted its delights, they die. . . .

In democratic times enjoyments are more intense than in the ages of aristocracy, and the number of those who partake in them is vastly larger: but, on the other hand, it must be admitted that man's hopes and desires are oftener blasted, the soul is more stricken and perturbed, and care itself more keen. . . .

. . . Amongst a people whose ranks are nearly equal, no ostensible bond connects men together or keeps them settled in their station. None of them have either a permanent right or power to command, none are forced by their condition to obey; but every man, finding himself possessed of some education and some resources, may choose his own path and proceed apart from all his fellow men. The same causes that make the members of the community independent of each other continually impel them to new and restless desires and constantly spur them onwards. It therefore seems natural that in a democratic community men, things, and opinions should be forever changing their form and place, and that democratic ages should be times of rapid and incessant transformation.

But is this really the case? Does the equality of social conditions habitually and permanently lead men to revolution? Does that state of society contain some perturbing principle which prevents the community from ever subsiding into calm and disposes the citizens to alter incessantly their laws, their principles, and their manners? I do not believe it; and as the subject is important, I beg for the reader's close attention.

Almost all the revolutions that have changed the aspect of nations have been made to consolidate or to destroy social inequality. Remove the secondary causes that have produced the great convulsions of the world and you will almost always find the principle of inequality at the bottom. Either the poor have attempted to plunder the rich, or the rich to enslave the poor. If, then, a state of society can ever be founded in which every man shall have something to keep and little to take from others, much will have been done for the peace of the world. . . .

Not only are the men of democracies not naturally desirous of revolutions, but they are afraid of them. All revolutions more or less threaten the tenure of property; but most of those who live in democratic countries are possessed of property; not only do they possess property, but they live in the condition where men set the greatest store upon their property.

If we attentively consider each of the classes of which society is composed, it is easy to see that the passions created by property are keenest and most tenacious among the middle classes. The poor often care but little for what they possess, because they suffer much more from the want of what they have not than they enjoy the little they have. The rich have many other passions besides that of riches to satisfy; and, besides, the long and arduous enjoyment of a great fortune sometimes makes them in the end insensible to its charms. But the men who have a competency, alike removed from opulence and from penury, attach an enormous value to their possessions. As they are still almost within the reach of poverty, they see its privations near at hand and dread them; between poverty and themselves there is nothing but a scanty fortune, upon which they immediately fix their apprehensions and their hopes. Every day increases the interest they take in it, by the constant cares which it occasions; and they are the more attached to it by their continual exertions to increase the amount. The notion of surrendering the smallest part of it is insupportable to them, and they consider its total loss as the worst of misfortunes.

Now, these eager and apprehensive men of small property constitute the class that is constantly increased by the equality of conditions. Hence in democratic communities the majority of the people do not clearly see what they have to gain by a revolution, but they continually and in a thousand ways feel that they might lose by one. . . .

It is a mistake to believe that, when once equality of condition has become the old and uncontested state of society and has imparted its characteristics to the manners of a nation, men will easily allow themselves to be thrust into perilous risks by an imprudent leader or a bold innovator. Not indeed that they will resist him openly, by well-contrived schemes, or even by a premeditated plan of resistance. They will not struggle energetically against him, sometimes they will even applaud him; but they do not follow him. To his vehemence they secretly oppose their inertia, to his revolutionary tendencies their conservative interests, their homely tastes to his adventurous passions, their good sense to the flights of his genius, to his poetry their prose. With immense exertion he raises them for an instant, but they speedily escape from him and fall back, as it were, by their own weight. He strains himself to rouse the indifferent and distracted multitude and finds at last that he is reduced to impotence, not because he is conquered, but because he is alone.

I do not assert that men living in democratic communities are naturally stationary; I think, on the contrary, that a perpetual stir prevails in the bosom of those societies, and that rest is unknown there; but I think that men bestir themselves within certain limits, beyond which they hardly ever go. They are forever varying, altering, and restoring secondary matters; but they carefully abstain from touching what is fundamental. They love change, but they dread revolutions. . . .

The Commonwealth and Party Doctrine

117 JACKSON REVIEWING HIS POLICIES

from Andrew Jackson, *Farewell Address*, March 4, 1837

To evaluate past Presidents is no more simple than to evaluate current ones. Time settles reputations only in the sense that the evidence is controlled by fewer judges, who may for a period adopt a common appraisal. The analysis of changing historical estimates of Andrew Jackson by Charles Grier Sellers, Jr., (Document 166) could be matched by comparable histories of history in the case of each significant administration from that of Washington and Hamilton to that of Franklin Delano Roosevelt.

To his political enemies Andrew Jackson was a crude, hot-blooded border chieftain who appealed to ignorance and prejudice to gain his popularity and who used his executive power blindly to upset the peace of society, the dignity of republican government, and the progress of the national economy. (See the contemporary criticisms in Documents 118 and 119.) To friends he was the people's champion who drove the moneyed aristocracy from their entrenched position in the government and restored the Jeffersonian Republic to its original principles.

At the end of his eight years in office Jackson reviewed the purposes and policies of his administration with solid satisfaction. He had destroyed the "Monster Bank" (the Second Bank of the United States) after a titanic struggle. He had scotched nullification in South Carolina. (See pages 323-324.) He had won a major diplomatic settlement with France over "spoilation claims" (financial claims for which the United States had long sued as a result of Napoleon's pirating of American shipping). He had reduced the national debt almost to nothing and had resisted efforts to revive Clay's American System. Jackson had, as he saw it, restored control of the nation to "the planter, the farmer, the mechanic, and the laborer," to "the bone and sinew of the country." His satisfaction was the greater because he knew that the republic would be safe in the hands of his trusted adviser and lieutenant Martin Van Buren for the next four years (1837-1841). The crowd that cheered the Old Hero's departure from the Capitol on March 4, 1837, was more solemn than the shouting mob of 1829 (see Document 112). Their farewell cry, wrote Senator Benton, was a testimony of "affection, gratitude and admiration." Perhaps no other political leader of the nineteenth century stirred such profound popular feelings of veneration and—on the other side—of hatred.

. . . We have now lived almost fifty years under the Constitution framed by the sages and patriots of the Revolution. The conflicts in which the nations of Europe were engaged during a great part of this period, the spirit in which they waged war against each other, and our intimate commercial connections with every part of the civilized world rendered it a time of much difficulty for the Government of the United States. We have had our seasons of peace and of war, with all the evils which precede or follow a state of hostility with powerful nations. We encountered these trials with our Constitution yet in its infancy, and under the disadvantages which a new and untried government must always feel when it is called upon to put forth its whole strength without the lights of experience to guide it or the weight of precedents to justify its measures. But we have passed triumphantly through all these difficulties. Our Constitution is no longer a doubtful experiment, and at the end of nearly half a century we find that it has preserved unimpaired the liberties of the people, secured the rights of property, and that our country has improved and is flourishing beyond any former example in the history of nations. . . .

. . . Forty years have passed since this imperishable document was given to [Washington's] countrymen. The Federal Constitution was then regarded by him as an experiment—and he so speaks of it in his Address—but an experiment upon the success of which the best hopes of his country depended; and we all know that he was prepared to lay down his life, if necessary, to se-

Text: James D. Richardson (ed.), *A Compilation of the Messages and Papers of the Presidents, 1789-1897* (Washington, D.C.: Government Printing Office, 1897), III, 293-306 *passim*.

cure to it a full and a fair trial. The trial has been made. It has succeeded beyond the proudest hopes of those who framed it. Every quarter of this widely extended nation has felt its blessings and shared in the general prosperity produced by its adoption. But amid this general prosperity and splendid success the dangers of which he warned us are becoming every day more evident, and the signs of evil are sufficiently apparent to awaken the deepest anxiety in the bosom of the patriot. We behold systematic efforts publicly made to sow the seeds of discord between different parts of the United States and to place party divisions directly upon geographical distinctions; to excite the *South* against the *North* and the *North* against the *South*, and to force into the controversy the most delicate and exciting topics—topics upon which it is impossible that a large portion of the Union can ever speak without strong emotion. Appeals, too, are constantly made to sectional interests in order to influence the election of the Chief Magistrate, as if it were desired that he should favor a particular quarter of the country instead of fulfilling the duties of his station with impartial justice to all; and the possible dissolution of the Union has at length become an ordinary and familiar subject of discussion. . . .

What have you to gain by division and dissension? Delude not yourselves with the belief that a breach once made may be afterwards repaired. If the Union is once severed, the line of separation will grow wider and wider, and the controversies which are now debated and settled in the halls of legislation will then be tried in fields of battle and determined by the sword. Neither should you deceive yourselves with the hope that the first line of separation would be the permanent one, and that nothing but harmony and concord would be found in the new associations formed upon the dissolution of this Union. Local interests would still be found there and unchastened ambition. And if the recollection of common dangers, in which the people of these United States stood side by side against the common foe, the memory of victories won by their united valor, the prosperity and happiness they have enjoyed under the present Constitution, the proud name they bear as citizens of this great Republic—if all these recollections and proofs of common interest are not strong enough to bind us together as one people, what tie will hold united the new divisions of empire when these bonds have been broken and this Union dissevered? The first line of separation would not last for a single generation; new fragments would be torn off, new leaders would spring up, and

this great and glorious Republic would soon be broken into a multitude of petty States, without commerce, without credit, jealous of one another, armed for mutual aggression, loaded with taxes to pay armies and leaders, seeking aid against each other from foreign powers, insulted and trampled upon by the nations of Europe, until, harassed with conflicts and humbled and debased in spirit, they would be ready to submit to the absolute dominion of any military adventurer and to surrender their liberty for the sake of repose. It is impossible to look on the consequences that would inevitably follow the destruction of this Government and not feel indignant when we hear cold calculations about the value of the Union and have so constantly before us a line of conduct so well calculated to weaken its ties. . . .

But in order to maintain the Union unimpaired it is absolutely necessary that the laws passed by the constituted authorities should be faithfully executed in every part of the country, and that every good citizen should at all times stand ready to put down, with the combined force of the nation, every attempt at unlawful resistance, under whatever pretext it may be made or whatever shape it may assume. Unconstitutional or oppressive laws may no doubt be passed by Congress, either from erroneous views or the want of due consideration; if they are within the reach of judicial authority, the remedy is easy and peaceful; and if, from the character of the law, it is an abuse of power not within the control of the judiciary, then free discussion and calm appeals to reason and to the justice of the people will not fail to redress the wrong. But until the law shall be declared void by the courts or repealed by Congress no individual or combination of individuals can be justified in forcibly resisting its execution. It is impossible that any government can continue to exist upon any other principles. It would cease to be a government and be unworthy of the name if it had not the power to enforce the execution of its own laws within its own sphere of action. . . .

It is well known that there have always been those amongst us who wish to enlarge the powers of the General Government, and experience would seem to indicate that there is a tendency on the part of this Government to overstep the boundaries marked out for it by the Constitution. . . . From the extent of our country, its diversified interests, different pursuits, and different habits, it is too obvious for argument that a single consolidated government would be wholly inadequate to watch over and protect its interests; and every friend of our free institutions should be always prepared to maintain unimpaired and in full vigor the rights and sovereignty of the States and to confine the action of the General Government strictly to the sphere of its appropriate duties.

There is, perhaps, no one of the powers conferred on the Federal Government so liable to abuse as the taxing power. The most productive and convenient sources of revenue were necessarily given to it, that it might be able to perform the important duties imposed upon it; and the taxes which it lays upon commerce being concealed from the real payer in the price of the article, they do not so readily attract the attention of the people as smaller sums demanded from them directly by the taxgatherer. But the tax imposed on goods enhances by so much the price of the commodity to the consumer, and as many of these duties are imposed on articles of necessity which are daily used by the great body of the people, the money raised by these imposts is drawn from their pockets. Congress has no right under the Constitution to take money from the people unless it is required to execute some one of the specific powers intrusted to the Government; and if they raise more than is necessary for such purposes, it is an abuse of the power of taxation, and unjust and oppressive. It may indeed happen that the revenue will sometimes exceed the amount anticipated when the taxes were laid. When, however, this is ascertained, it is easy to reduce them, and in such a case it is unquestionably the duty of the Government to reduce them, for no circumstances can justify it in assuming a power not given to it by the Constitution nor in taking away the money of the people when it is not needed for the legitimate wants of the Government.

Plain as these principles appear to be, you will yet find there is a constant effort to induce the General Government to go beyond the limits of its taxing power and to impose unnecessary burdens upon the people. Many powerful interests are continually at work to procure heavy duties on commerce and to swell the revenue beyond the real necessities of the public service, and the country has already felt the injurious effects of their combined influence. They succeeded in obtaining a tariff of duties bearing most oppressively on the agricultural and laboring classes of society and producing a revenue that could not be usefully employed within the range of the powers conferred upon Congress, and in order to fasten upon the people this unjust and unequal system of taxation extravagant schemes of internal improvement were got up in various quarters to squander the money and to purchase support. Thus one unconstitutional

measure was intended to be upheld by another, and the abuse of the power of taxation was to be maintained by usurping the power of expending the money in internal improvements. You can not have forgotten the severe and doubtful struggle through which we passed when the executive department of the Government by its veto endeavored to arrest this prodigal scheme of injustice and to bring back the legislation of Congress to the boundaries prescribed by the Constitution. The good sense and practical judgment of the people when the subject was brought before them sustained the course of the Executive, and this plan of unconstitutional expenditures for the purposes of corrupt influence is, I trust, finally overthrown. . . .

In reviewing the conflicts which have taken place between different interests in the United States and the policy pursued since the adoption of our present form of Government, we find nothing that has produced such deep-seated evil as the course of legislation in relation to the currency. The Constitution of the United States unquestionably intended to secure to the people a circulating medium of gold and silver. But the establishment of a national bank by Congress, with the privilege of issuing paper money receivable in the payment of the public dues, and the unfortunate course of legislation in the several States upon the same subject, drove from general circulation the constitutional currency and substituted one of paper in its place. . . .

The paper system being founded on public confidence and having of itself no intrinsic value, it is liable to great and sudden fluctuations, thereby rendering property insecure and the wage of labor unsteady and uncertain. The corporations which create the paper money can not be relied upon to keep the circulating medium uniform in amount. In times of prosperity, when confidence is high, they are tempted by the prospect of gain or by the influence of those who hope to profit by it to extend their issues of paper beyond the bounds of discretion and the reasonable demands of business; and when these issues have been pushed on from day to day, until public confidence is at length shaken, then a reaction takes place, and they immediately withdraw the credits they have given, suddenly curtail their issues, and produce an unexpected and ruinous contraction of the circulating medium, which is felt by the whole community. The banks by this means save themselves, and the mischievous consequences of their imprudence or cupidity are visited upon the public. Nor does the evil stop here. These ebbs and flows in the currency and these indiscreet extensions of credit naturally engender a spirit of speculation injurious to the habits and character of the people. We have already seen its effects in the wild spirit of speculation in the public lands and various kinds of stock which within the last year or two seized upon such a multitude of our citizens and threatened to pervade all classes of society and to withdraw their attention from the sober pursuits of honest industry. It is not by encouraging this spirit that we shall best preserve public virtue and promote the true interests of our country; but if your currency continues as exclusively paper as it now is, it will foster this eager desire to amass wealth without labor; it will multiply the number of dependents on bank accommodations and bank favors; the temptation to obtain money at any sacrifice will become stronger and stronger, and inevitably lead to corruption, which will find its way into your public councils and destroy at no distant day the purity of your Government. Some of the evils which arise from this system of paper press with peculiar hardship upon the class of society least able to bear it. A portion of this currency frequently becomes depreciated or worthless, and all of it is easily counterfeited in such a manner as to require peculiar skill and much experience to distinguish the counterfeit from the genuine note. These frauds are most generally perpetrated in the smaller notes, which are used in the daily transactions of ordinary business, and the losses occasioned by them are commonly thrown upon the laboring classes of society, whose situation and pursuits put it out of their power to guard themselves from these impositions, and whose daily wages are necessary for their subsistence. It is the duty of every government so to regulate its currency as to protect this numerous class, as far as practicable, from the impositions of avarice and fraud. It is more especially the duty of the United States, where the Government is emphatically the Government of the people, and where this respectable portion of our citizens are so proudly distinguished from the laboring classes of all other nations by their independent spirit, their love of liberty, their intelligence, and their high tone of moral character. Their industry in peace is the source of our wealth and their bravery in war has covered us with glory; and the Government of the United States will but ill discharge its duties if it leaves them a prey to such dishonest impositions. Yet it is evident that their interests can not be effectually protected unless silver and gold are restored to circulation.

These views alone of the paper currency are sufficient to call for immediate reform; but there is another consideration which should still more strongly press it upon your attention. . . .

. . . When the charter for the Bank of the United States was obtained from Congress it perfected the schemes of the paper system and gave to its advocates the position they have struggled to obtain from the commencement of the Federal Government to the present hour. The immense capital and peculiar privileges bestowed upon it enabled it to exercise despotic sway over the other banks in every part of the country. From its superior strength it could seriously injure, if not destroy, the business of any one of them which might incur its resentment; and it openly claimed for itself the power of regulating the currency throughout the United States. In other words, it asserted (and it undoubtedly possessed) the power to make money plenty or scarce at its pleasure, at any time and in any quarter of the Union, by controlling the issues of other banks and permitting an expansion or compelling a general contraction of the circulating medium, according to its own will. The other banking institutions were sensible of its strength, and they soon generally became its obedient instruments, ready at all times to execute its mandates; and with the banks necessarily went also that numerous class of persons in our commercial cities who depend altogether on bank credits for their solvency and means of business, and who are therefore obliged, for their own safety, to propitiate the favor of the money power by distinguished zeal and devotion in its service. The result of the ill-advised legislation which established this great monopoly was to concentrate the whole moneyed power of the Union, with its boundless means of corruption and its numerous dependents, under the direction and command of one acknowledged head, thus organizing this particular interest as one body and securing to it unity and concert of action throughout the United States, and enabling it to bring forward upon any occasion its entire and undivided strength to support or defeat any measure of the Government. In the hands of this formidable power, thus perfectly organized, was also placed unlimited dominion over the amount of the circulating medium, giving it the power to regulate the value of property and the fruits of labor in every quarter of the Union, and to bestow prosperity or bring ruin upon any city or section of the country as might best comport with its own interest or policy.

We are not left to conjecture how the moneyed power, thus organized and with such a weapon in its hands, would be likely to use it. The distress and alarm which pervaded and agitated the whole country when the Bank of the United States waged war upon the people in order to compel them to submit to its demands can not yet be forgotten. The ruthless and unsparing temper with which whole cities and communities were oppressed, individuals impoverished and ruined, and a scene of cheerful prosperity suddenly changed into one of gloom and despondency ought to be indelibly impressed on the memory of the people of the United States. If such was its power in a time of peace, what would it not have been in a season of war, with an enemy at your doors? No nation but the freemen of the United States could have come out victorious from such a contest; yet, if you had not conquered, the Government would have passed from the hands of the many to the hands of the few, and this organized money power from its secret conclave would have dictated the choice of your highest officers and compelled you to make peace or war, as best suited their own wishes. The forms of your Government might for a time have remained, but its living spirit would have departed from it. . . .

It is one of the serious evils of our present system of banking that it enables one class of society—and that by no means a numerous one —by its control over the currency, to act injuriously upon the interests of all the others and to exercise more than its just proportion of influence in political affairs. The agricultural, the mechanical, and the laboring classes have little or no share in the direction of the great moneyed corporations, and from their habits and the nature of their pursuits they are incapable of forming extensive combinations to act together with united force. Such concert of action may sometimes be produced in a single city or in a small district of country by means of personal communications with each other, but they have no regular or active correspondence with those who are en-

gaged in similar pursuits in distant places; they have but little patronage to give to the press, and exercise but a small share of influence over it; they have no crowd of dependents about them who hope to grow rich without labor by their countenance and favor, and who are therefore always ready to execute their wishes. The planter, the farmer, the mechanic, and the laborer all know that their success depends upon their own industry and economy, and that they must not expect to become suddenly rich by the fruits of their toil. Yet these classes of society form the great body of the people of the United States; they are the bone and sinew of the country—men who love liberty and desire nothing but equal rights and equal laws, and who, moreover, hold the great mass of our national wealth, although it is distributed in moderate amounts among the millions of freemen who possess it. But with overwhelming numbers and wealth on their side they are in constant danger of losing their fair influence in the Government, and with difficulty maintain their just rights against the incessant efforts daily made to encroach upon them. The mischief springs from the power which the moneyed interest derives from a paper currency which they are able to control, from the multitude of corporations with exclusive privileges which they have succeeded in obtaining in the different States, and which are employed altogether for their benefit; and unless you become more watchful in your States and check this spirit of monopoly and thirst for exclusive privileges you will in the end find that the most important powers of Government have been given or bartered away, and the control over your dearest interests has passed into the hands of these corporations. . . .

WHIGGERY

118

THE AMERICAN SYSTEM

from Henry Clay, Speech in the U.S. Senate, February 2, 3, and 6, 1832

Andrew Jackson had against him most of the political greats of the Republican era: John Quincy Adams, Henry Clay, Daniel Webster, and finally his own Vice-President, John C. Calhoun. (The Jackson supporters, it should be added, included men of respectable talents: among others, Martin Van Buren, Thomas Hart Benton, Edward Livingston, Roger B. Taney, and Silas Wright.) Clashing personalities and rival ambitions had some part in shaping the anti-Jackson opposition; conflicts over policy played an even greater role.

The leading figure in the opposition coalition, and in the National Republican (later, the Whig) party that was forming to challenge Jackson's rule, was Henry Clay of Kentucky (1777-1852). "Harry of the West" first won his national reputation as a War Hawk before the War of 1812 and sustained it as the leading spokesman for the American System in Congress (1811-1825). It was to Clay that the National Republican party turned in 1832 as a presidential candidate to drive Jackson and the Democrats from power and thus effectively to override the Bank veto of 1832 by the force of public opinion. Clay was badly beaten, 219 to 49, in the electoral vote.

Clay's Senate speech of February 1832 presents the standard arguments for a protective tariff to foster the growth of industry. Since 1816 a series of protective measures had been adopted, reaching a high point in the 1828 "Tariff of Abominations." Jackson in 1831 sought a modest reduction in duties that would tame the rising fury of the South, but the resulting tariff of 1832 only heightened resentment. Calhoun, who had once been a protectionist and nationalist, now taught South Carolinians that the tariffs of 1828 and 1832 were deadly weapons of sectional exploitation and that the state must exercise its right to nullify such intolerable measures.

In November 1832 a South Carolina convention adopted a nullification ordinance, answered promptly by Jackson's stern Nullification Proclamation (December 10, 1832) and by the passage early in the next year of the Force Bill, threatening military coercion if South Carolina should defy federal authorities. At this point Henry Clay showed himself a statesman more devoted to the Union than to a particular tariff policy. He helped prepare a compromise tariff bill providing for a gradual reduction of duties to 20 per cent. South Carolina was appeased (although it reasserted the right to nullify federal laws), and the crisis passed. Both Jackson and Clay gained stature in the nullification controversy, each in his characteristic way. Jackson confronted the threat of disunion with a commanding show of executive authority, Henry Clay with his skillful direction of the legislative process to achieve compromise.

Henry Clay's attempts to further the American System had met defeat on several fronts during the Jackson administration. The President's Maysville veto (1830) blocked the way to enlarged federal appropriations for internal improvements. The Bank veto (1832) dealt a mortal blow to the national banking system. The compromise tariff (1833) was a partial abandonment of protection. In 1836 Clay sponsored a measure for distributing the national treasury surplus among the states, to be used in support of internal improvements. Before the funds could be employed, a major economic crisis struck (1837) and turned the surplus into a deficit. Yet Clay's failure was only superficial. By 1860 a transportation revolution had been effected by state and private enterprise. An interdependent national economy had been created; industrialization had made giant strides; and a new party—the Republican—was ready to erect protective tariffs, form a national banking system, and underwrite vast railroad enterprises with national resources.

I pass . . . to two general propositions which cover the entire ground of debate. The first is, that under the operation of the American system, the objects which it protects and fosters are brought to the consumer at cheaper prices than they commanded prior to its introduction, or, than they would command if it did not exist. If that be true, ought not the country to be contented and satisfied with the system, unless the second proposition, which I mean presently also to consider, is unfounded? And that is, that the tendency of the system is to sustain, and that it has upheld, the prices of all our agricultural and other produce, including cotton.

And is the fact not indisputable, that all essential objects of consumption affected by the tariff, are cheaper and better since the act of 1824, than they were for several years prior to that law? I appeal for its truth to common observation, and to all practical men. I appeal to the farmer of the country, whether he does not

Text: Henry Clay, *Works*, ed. Calvin Colton (New York: A. S. Barnes and Burr, 1857), V, 464-67, 472-78 *passim.*

purchase on better terms his iron, salt, brown sugar, cotton goods, and woolens, for his laboring people? And I ask the cotton planter if he has not been better and more cheaply supplied with his cotton-bagging? . . .

. . . Will gentlemen believe the fact, which I am authorized now to state, that the United States, at this time, manufacture one half the quantity of cotton which Great Britain did in 1816! We possess three great advantages: first, the raw material; second, water-power instead of that of steam, generally used in England; and, third, the cheaper labor of females. In England, males spin with the mule and weave; in this country, women and girls spin with the throstle, and superintend the power-loom. And can there be any employment more appropriate? Who has not been delighted with contemplating the clock-work regularity of a large cotton manufactory? I have often visited them at Cincinnati and other places, and always with increased admiration. The women, separated from the other sex, work in apartments, large, airy, well warmed, and spacious. Neatly dressed, with ruddy complexions, and happy countenances, they watch the work before them, mend the broken threads, and replace the exhausted balls or broaches. At stated hours they are called to their meals, and go and return with light and cheerful step. At night they separate, and repair to their respective houses, under the care of a mother, guardian, or friend. "Six days shalt thou labor and do all that thou hast to do, but the seventh day is the sabbath of the Lord thy God." Accordingly, we behold them on that sacred day, assembled together in His temples, and in devotional attitudes and with pious countenances offering their prayers to heaven for all its blessings; of which it is not the least, that a system of policy has been adopted by their country, which admits of their obtaining a comfortable subsistence. Manufactures have brought into profitable employment a vast amount of female labor, which, without them, would be lost to the country. . . .

Gentlemen have allowed to the manufacturing portions of the community no peace; they have been constantly threatened with the overthrow of the American system. From the year 1820, if not from 1816, down to this time, they have been held in a condition of constant alarm and insecurity. Nothing is more prejudicial to the great interests of a nation than unsettled and varying policy. Although every appeal to the national legislature has been responded to in conformity with the wishes and sentiments of the great majority of the people, measures of protection have only been carried by such small majorities as to excite hopes on the one hand, and fears on the other. Let the country breathe, let its vast resources be developed, let its energies be fully put forth, let it have tranquillity, and my word for it, the degree of perfection in the arts which it will exhibit, will be greater than that which has been presented, astonishing as our progress has been. Although some branches of our manufactures might, and in foreign markets now do, fearlessly contend with similar foreign fabrics, there are many others yet in their infancy, struggling with the difficulties which encompass them. We should look at the whole system, and recollect that time, when we contemplate the great movements of a nation, is very different from the short period which is allotted for the duration of individual life. . . .

Second, . . . under the operation of the American system, the products of our agriculture command a higher price than they would do without it, by the creation of a home market; and by the augmentation of wealth produced by manufacturing industry, which enlarges our powers of consumption both of domestic and foreign articles.

The importance of the home market is among the established maxims which are universally recognized by all writers and all men. However some may differ as to the relative advantages of the foreign and the home market, none deny to the latter great value and high consideration. It is nearer to us; beyond the control of foreign legislation; and undisturbed by those vicissitudes to which all international intercourse is more or less exposed. The most stupid are sensible of the benefit of a residence in the vicinity of a large manufactory, or of a market town, of a good road, or of a navigable stream, which connects their farms with some great capital. If the pursuits of all men were perfectly the same, although they would be in possession of the greatest abundance of the particular produce of their industry, they might, at the same time, be in extreme want of other necessary articles of human subsistence. The uniformity of the general occupation would preclude all exchanges, all commerce. It is only in the diversity of the vocations of the members of a community that the means can be found for those salutary exchanges which conduce to the general prosperity. And the greater that diversity, the more extensive and the more animating is the circle of exchange. Even if foreign markets were freely and widely open to the reception of our agricultural produce, from its bulky nature, and the distance of the interior, and the dangers of the ocean, large portions of it could never profitably reach the foreign market. . . .

What would be the condition of the farming country of the United States—of all that portion which lies north, east, and west of James river, including a large part of North Carolina—if a home market did not exist for this immense amount of agricultural produce? Without the market, where could it be sold? In foreign markets? If their restrictive laws did not exist, their capacity would not enable them to purchase and consume this vast addition to their present supplies, which must be thrown in, or thrown away, but for the home market. But their laws exclude us from their markets. I shall content myself by calling the attention of the Senate to Great Britain only. The duties in the ports of the United Kingdom on breadstuffs are prohibitory, except in times of dearth . . . and yet Great Britain is the power in whose behalf we are called upon to legislate, so that we may enable her to purchase our cotton!—Great Britain, that thinks only of herself in her own legislation! When have we experienced justice, much less favor, at her hands? When did she shape her legislation in reference to the interests of any foreign power? She is a great, opulent, and powerful nation; but haughty, arrogant, and supercilious; not more separated from the rest of the world by the sea that girts her island, than she is separated in feeling, sympathy, or friendly consideration of their welfare. Gentlemen, in supposing it impracticable that we should successfully compete with her in manufactures, do injustice to the skill and enterprise of their own country. Gallant as Great Britain undoubtedly is, we have gloriously contended with her, man to man, gun to gun, ship to ship, fleet to fleet, and army to army. And I have no doubt we are destined to achieve equal success in the more useful, if not nobler contest for superiority in the arts of civil life.

I could extend and dwell on the long list of articles—the hemp, iron, lead, coal, and other items—for which a demand is created in the home market by the operation of the American system; but I should exhaust the patience of the Senate. Where, where should we find a market for all these articles, if it did not exist at home? What would be the condition of the largest portion of our people, and of the territory, if this home market were annihilated? How could they be supplied with objects of prime necessity? What would not be the certain and inevitable decline in the price of all these articles, but for the home market? And allow me, Mr. President, to say, that of all the agricultural parts of the United States which are benefited by the operation of this system, none are equally so with those which border the Chesapeake bay, the lower parts of North Carolina, Virginia, and the two shores of Maryland. Their facilities of transportation, and proximity to the north, give them decided advantages. . . .

I have hitherto considered the question in reference only to a state of peace; but a season of war ought not to be entirely overlooked. We have enjoyed nearly twenty years of peace; but who can tell when the storm of war shall again break forth? Have we forgotton so soon, the privations to which not merely our brave soldiers and our gallant tars were subjected, but the whole community, during the last war, for the want of absolute necessaries? To what an enormous price they rose! And how inadequate the supply was at any price! The statesman who justly elevates his views will look behind as well as

forward, and at the existing state of things; and he will graduate the policy, which he recommends, to the probable exigencies which may arise in the Republic. Taking this comprehensive range, it would be easy to show that the higher prices of peace, if prices were higher in peace, were more than compensated by the lower prices of war, during which, supplies of all essential articles are indispensable to its vigorous, effectual, and glorious prosecution. I conclude this part of the argument with the hope that my humble exertions have not been altogether unsuccessful in showing,

First, that the policy which we have been considering ought to continue to be regarded as the genuine American system.

Secondly, that the free trade system, which is proposed as its substitute, ought really to be considered as the British colonial system.

Thirdly, that the American system is beneficial to all parts of the Union, and absolutely necessary to much the larger portion.

Fourthly, that the price of the great staple of cotton, and of all our chief productions of agriculture, has been sustained and upheld, and a decline averted, by the protective system.

Fifthly, that if the foreign demand for cotton has been at all diminished by the operation of that system, the diminution has been more than compensated in the additional demand created at home.

Sixthly, that the constant tendency of the system, by creating competition among ourselves, and between American and European industry, reciprocally acting upon each other, is to reduce prices of manufactured objects.

Seventhly, that in point of fact, objects within the scope of the policy of protection have greatly fallen in price.

Eighthly, that if, in a season of peace, these benefits are experienced, in a season of war, when the foreign supply might be cut off, they would be much more extensively felt.

Ninthly, and finally, that the substitution of the British colonial system for the American system, without benefiting any section of the Union, by subjecting us to a foreign legislation, regulated by foreign interests, would lead to the prostration of our manufactories, general impoverishment, and ultimate ruin. . . .

119

DISASTROUS EXPERIMENT: AN ATTACK ON JACKSONIAN FINANCE

from Daniel Webster, Speech at the Merchants' Meeting, New York, September 28, 1840

By 1832 Senators John C. Calhoun and Daniel Webster had completed their curious exchange of positions. The former nationalist and South Carolina War Hawk became the open advocate of nullification and state rights. The early Yankee sectionalist and critic of the American System won a new reputation as a protectionist and a formidable defender of Nicholas Biddle's Bank of the United States.

The Second Bank (1816-1836) was built broadly along the lines of its Hamiltonian predecessor. It combined the attributes of a great financial corporation with those of a public fiscal agent. Thus on the public side the bank held an exclusive federal charter, included federal directors on its ruling board, and received and paid out government funds. Yet it was a profit-making institution (a highly successful one) which extended loans, facilitated national and international exchanges, and—in common with other banking institutions of the time—issued paper notes that circulated as money. Under the direction of Nicholas Biddle, a brilliant and ambitious Philadelphia financier, the Second Bank used its great resources somewhat in the manner of a modern central bank—i.e., it regulated the flow of money and credit through the national economy in an effort to offset inflationary or deflationary trends.

The ambiguous nature of the institution—part public, part private—was one source of its vulnerability to political attack. The government, Jackson feared, had created a "Monster" that threatened to dominate its lawful master, the people and government of the United States. The very success of Nicholas ·Biddle in restraining the wildcat tendencies of local banks not only made him bitter enemies but reinforced the image of his vast power over the economic life of the nation. Biddle's use of bank funds to sweeten politicians and editors, to maintain lobbyists, and to conduct pro-bank publicity campaigns was at the least imprudent, persuading Jackson and his followers that the Second Bank would corrupt the political order in order to have its way.

Henry Clay and Webster (the latter a well-paid legal counselor as well as a convinced advocate of the bank) helped to push a charter-renewal bill through Congress in 1832. "The Bank, Mr. Van Buren, is trying to kill me, but I will kill it." In the spirit of this remark, Jackson thundered back his veto and made it stick by winning re-election. The following autumn he found a Secretary of the Treasury, Roger B. Taney, who would order the gradual removal of government deposits from the bank and their relocation in a number of "pet" state banks.

The current verdict of historians holds that Jackson's victory in the Bank War was the prelude to economic disaster. With the restraining power of the Second Bank crippled, the nation entered a wildly speculative boom (1834-1836) and paid the price in the Panic of 1837 and a bitter depression lasting into the 1840's. Martin Van Buren, Jackson's heir to the presidency, reaped the whirlwind. A revived Whig party in 1840 passed over its greats to give the nomination to an old Indian fighter of nondescript political views—William Henry Harrison—and swept to victory with a "Log Cabin and Hard Cider" campaign.

Daniel Webster's 1840 speech in Wall Street reviews the financial heresies of Jackson and Van Buren and restates the Whig case for a national bank. More typical of Whig campaign oratory in that year were passionate denunciations of the executive despotism established by Jackson and Van Buren, crude jibes at Van Buren's taste for gold spoons and other sybaritic trappings, and tearful tributes to the moral beauty of the log cabin. Whig success turned sour when Harrison died a month after his inauguration, leaving the presidency in the hands of a Virginian, John Tyler, who had no taste for national banks, protective tariffs, or internal improvements.

I am duly sensible, fellow-citizens, both of the honor and of the responsibility of the present occasion. An honor it certainly is to be requested to address a body of merchants such as I behold before me, as intelligent, as enterprising, and as respectable as any in the world. A responsible undertaking it is to address such an assembly, and on a subject which many of you understand scientifically and in its elements at least as well

Text: Daniel Webster, *Writings and Speeches,* National ed. (Boston: Little, Brown & Co., 1903), III, 55-57, 63-66 *passim.*

as I do, and with which most of you have more or less of practical acquaintance. The currency of a country is a subject always important, and in some measure complex; but it has become the great leading question of our time. I have not shrunk from the expression of my opinions, since I have been in public life, nor shall I now, especially since on this question another great political question seems likely to turn; namely, the question whether one administration is about to go out of power, and another administration to come into power. . . .

I will, in the first place, state a few general propositions, which I believe to be founded on true principles of good, practical political economy, as understood in their application to the condition of a country like ours.

And first, I hold the opinion that a mixed currency, composed partly of gold and silver and partly of good paper, redeemable and steadily redeemed in specie on demand, is the most useful and convenient for such a country as we inhabit, and is sure to continue to be used, to a greater or less extent, in these United States; the idea of an exclusive metallic currency being either the mere fancy of theorists, or, what is probably nearer the truth, being employed as a means of popular delusion. . . .

In the next place, I hold that the regulation of the currency, whether metallic or paper,—that a just and safe supervision over that which virtually performs the office of money, and constitutes the medium of exchange, whatever it may be,—necessarily pertains to government; that it is one of the necessary and indispensable prerogatives of government.

Every bank, as banks are now constituted in this country, performs two distinct offices or functions. First, it discounts bills or notes. This is merely the lending of money, and may be performed by corporations, by individuals, or by banks without circulation, acting as banks of discount merely. In this country our banks are all banks of circulation, issuing paper with an express view to circulation. When such a bank discounts notes, it pays the amount of discount in its own bills, and thereby adds so much to the actual amount of circulation, every such operation being, by so much, an increase of the circulating medium of the country. Hence it is true, that, in the absence of all government control and supervision, the wisdom and discretion regulating the amount of money afloat at any time in the community are but the aggregate of the wisdom and discretion of all the banks collectively considered; each individual bank acting from the promptings of its own interest,

without concert with others, and not from any sense of public duty. In my judgment, such a regulator, or such a mode of regulating the currency, and of deciding what shall be the amount of money at any time existing in the community, is unsafe and untrustworthy, and is one to which we never can look to guard us against those excessive expansions and contractions which have produced such injurious consequences. Hence arises my view of the duty of government to take the care and control of the issues of these local institutions, and thereby to guard the community against the evils of an excessive circulation. . . . You all know, and from experience, perfectly well, that a general institution for the circulation of a currency, which shall be as good in one part of the country as in another, if it shall possess a competent capital and shall be empowered to act as the fiscal agent of the government, is capable of controlling excessive issues, and keeping the bank paper in circulation in a community within reasonable limits. Such an institution acts also beneficially by supplying a currency which is of general credit, and uniform in value throughout the country. . . .

When the national bank was destroyed, or rather when its charter expired, and was not renewed, in consequence of the executive veto, what followed? I say that the government then put the entire business of this country, its commercial, its manufacturing, its shipping interest, its fisheries,—in a word, all that the people possessed,—on the tenterhooks of experiment; it put to the stretch every interest of the nation; it held them up, and tried curious devices upon them, just as if the institutions of our country were things not to be cherished and fostered with the most solicitous anxiety and care, but matters for political philosophers to try experiments upon. I need not remind you that General Jackson said he could give the country a better currency; that he took the national treasure from where it had been deposited by Congress, to place it in the State banks; and that Congress, by subsequent legislation, legalized the transfer, under the assurance that it would work well for the country. Yet I may be permitted to remind you that there were some of us who from the first declared that these State banks never could perform the duties of a national institution; that the functions of such an institution were beyond their scope, without the range of their powers; that they were, after all, but small arms, and not artillery, and could not reach an object so distant. The State bank system exploded; but the administration did not expect it to explode. At that day, they no more looked to the subtreasury scheme than they looked for an eclipse, and they did not expect an eclipse half as much as they do just now. When the United States Bank was overthrown, they turned, as the next expedient, to the State institutions; and they had full confidence in them, for confidence is a quality in which experimenters are seldom found wanting; but the expedient failed,—the banks exploded. And what then? . . .

. . . They instantly turned about, and, with the utmost bitterness of remark, reviled the banks which their experiment had crushed. They were vile, corrupt, faithless, treacherous institutions, leagued from the very beginning with the opposition, and not much better than British Whigs! And when we, who had opposed the placing of the national treasure in these banks, declared that they had failed only because they were applied to a purpose for which they never were calculated, and had perished in consequence of a rash and unwise experiment, we were instantly told, "You are bank aristocrats; you are leagued with a thousand corrupt banks, and are seeking, by the power of British gold, to destroy the purest administration that ever breathed the air of heaven!" Thus, when we said that State banks, though good for some purposes, were not good as a substitute for a national bank, we were denounced as the enemies of banks; but when we wished to shield these same banks from misapplied censure, and protect them from being totally destroyed by acts of bankruptcy, then we were reviled as "bank aristocrats."

I ask you, Gentlemen, as merchants, what confidence can you place in such an administration? Do you see any thing that they are disposed to do to restore the times you once enjoyed? (Loud cries of "No!" "No!") I perceive that your opinion corresponds with my own, and that you cannot lend your support to men who turn their backs on the experience, the interests, and the institutions of their country, and who openly declare that they will not exercise the powers which have been conferred on them for the public good. . . .

Expansion and Manifest Destiny

COMMERCE AND CORPORATIONS

120 GROWTH OF THE RAILROADS: LAND GRANTS

from *The Western Journal and Civilian*, 1851

Between the War of 1812 and the Civil War, Americans effected a transportation revolution. The continuous migration into the vast spaces of the continent could be sustained only by linking the scattered settlements to market centers. With the development of the steamboat the Mississippi River system served some of the needs of the growing Western population. But Americans of the nineteenth century were far too eager for expansion and economic growth to be satisfied with natural lines of communication. Henry Clay's repeated calls for federal aid to internal improvements were but one expression of a general conviction that human enterprise, public or private, must be employed to join farm to market, town to town, section to section.

A rage for turnpikes constructed by private companies with local government aid was succeeded in the 1820's and 1830's by ambitious state canal-building programs that created over 3000 miles of artificial waterways by 1850. Over their heads in debt, many states faced bankruptcy in the crash of 1837 and turned a cold eye on deficit spending for public enterprise. Yet the insatiable demand for better transportation survived the shock and found a new answer in the railroad corporation.

A series of English and American experiments with steam-powered locomotion on rails led to the first successful railroad operations in the United States by the Baltimore and Ohio in 1830. By 1840 small railroad companies in the Atlantic states had opened over 3000 miles of track, roughly equal in extent to the existing canal system. These early local lines, impeded by novel technological problems, limited capital, and the political opposition of canal interests, could not compete for the heavy freight traffic of the water carriers; but the inherent superiority of the railroad as a fast and flexible carrier soon attracted the enterprise and money necessary to create the dominant transportation system of the nation, covering some 30,000 miles by 1860. Groups of New York and Boston capitalists in the 1840's and 1850's consolidated local roads to form trunk lines—for example, the New York Central—extending from the Atlantic to Lake Erie and the Ohio River and connecting with Western roads that reached the Mississippi.

The selection of a railroad route became a life or death matter for the rising towns and cities of the West. Local governments pledged their resources and their credit to gain a rail connection. The Congressman from the Chicago district had a bolder scheme: Stephen A. Douglas with the support of Southern representatives persuaded Congress (1850) to grant some 3.7 million acres of the national domain to Illinois and other states along the line of a projected railroad from Chicago to the Gulf. The states would convey the land to private railroad corporations, which in turn could use the property as collateral when raising capital in the New York money market. Under this arrangement the Illinois Central completed by 1858 a north-south route through the state, with Chicago as the major terminal. The city on Lake Michigan rapidly became the great rail crossroad of the nation.

The Illinois Central grant opened the floodgates of federal aid to railroads. As the following selection indicates, St. Louis and other contenders for the commerce of the Mississippi Valley demanded their share of government support for railroad projects. By 1860 Congress had granted eighteen million acres of public land to railroad corporations in ten states, and the end was not yet in sight. The contemporary argument favoring such gifts of public resources to encourage settlement and growth is represented in the passages below.

The right of Congress to apply any portion of the public lands, in aid of leading canals or railroads, is questioned by some, and the principle involved in any such right has neither been definitely admitted nor denied, but to this moment remains so far undetermined as to make every new grant an act of special favor of Congress, obtained through a concurrence of accidental and favorable circumstances, and under a kind of protest from a certain fraction of the national legislature.

Now it is admitted by all, that it is the interest of the Government to have the lands occupied as speedily as possible; and yet it is denied in the same breath, that the steps necessary to be taken to secure the occupation of these lands within a reasonable time, are competent to be taken by the government. It is admitted and contended on all hands, that the land should, if possible, be disposed of only to actual occupiers, men who would settle upon it, and improve it; and yet it is denied by some, that the only steps which would render that occupation (in the case of all lands away from the rivers,) desirable to that class of men, viz., ease of access to a market, should be facilitated and endorsed by Congress.

What are those steps but the opening up of the interior lands by means of great leading lines of communication, enabling those resident on them, to send their produce with profit to the local markets. As the lands are situated now,

they fall by the very inaction of Congress into the hands of the speculators. The farmer or the miner, who seeks a field for constitutional activity of disposition, or for the application of a healthy industry, has no inducement to settle on these back lands, however rich they may be. He cannot find a market on the spot, and there are no mechanical facilities of transportation within his reach to neutralise the distance of his position from the market cities of his section of country. This is the case with all the lands of the Western states away from the rivers, except on the few belts where canals or railroads are being established. If by accident, such a man settles in such a position, he lives along in the hope of something being done for his section of country, until his early activity of disposition is unsettled by the absence of compensation for his labors. He fills up his leisure time by hunting, loses his regular habits, and discouraged and disappointed, ends by doing the little that he had to do to sustain his family, in a slovenly and imperfect manner. The result is, that these back lands are entered very slowly; that the speculator with some capital to back him, acquires and holds large parts of them, in the faith that the gradual progress of population, which time will assure, or some lucky chance, will ultimately enable him to dispose of them to advantage. A large extent of public land is held in this way, which but for the absence of competition consequent on its inaccessible position, would never have fallen into such hands. The men who would have made those lands valuable are not there; the railroads

Text: The Western Journal and Civilian, III (1851), 174-178 *passim.*

which would have made them accessible are not building for want of that encouragement which in every sense it would be the interest of the government to give; and the men with idle capital called speculators, with a foresight for which they should receive credit, are enabled, by the timidity, the indifference or the inaction of Congress, to obtain for a trifle, large portions of the very rich lands, which while we are framing laws, ostensibly and on paper to secure them to the hard working man, we are taking especial pains to render by their position not worth his purchase. . . .

The principle acted upon in the railroad land bills for Alabama, Mississippi and Illinois has been to donate every alternate section for six miles in width on either side, and to double the price of the land on the remaining alternate sections. The cost of the land donated is thus provided for and recovered, for the remaining land will easily command the increased price. The condition admits of the government conferring a vast benefit upon a state without pecuniary loss, and with certain benefit in other respects to itself.

And does the Government gain any thing by this timely benefit so easily conferred?

Take the case of the Illinois Central railroad, the Mobile and Ohio railroad, the Missouri railroads, the proposed Arkansas railroad, or the proposed railroad through Iowa. In the case of all these railroads, public lands, which are at present entirely inaccessible for any practical purpose, are made available and profitable, without charge or risk to the Government. A large extent of territory will, as these railroads are made, be industriously settled. Its produce will swell the commerce of the country East, West and South, and its trade and wants add to the revenues of the Government. An active population will settle along these railroads, as a matter of course, for they are not less prolific than rivers of ample water power, in the creation and support of industrial pursuits.—The wealth and power of the country are increased, and what was formerly an idle range for the hunter, becomes noisy with the activities of civilized life. Surely, the difference is worth some sacrifice and might excuse some effort, and yet such advantages, following the progress of railroad communications through such territories, as surely as the plant grows from the seed, are begrudged or delayed in subservience to party or sectional jealousies, as if the consequences involved were of the most secondary importance.

121   GENERAL VS. SPECIAL INCORPORATION: A JACKSONIAN VIEW

from William Leggett, *Political Writings*, 1839

In the early republic the corporation was regarded as a quasi-public institution created by law to accomplish objectives of general value to the community. Colleges and academies might receive a corporate charter from the state legislature; so too might certain "public-utility" business enterprises, especially bridge and turnpike companies which served important transportation needs. Increasingly during the Jacksonian era, the corporate form was made available to banks, insurance firms, factories, and railroads.

Down to the 1830's, the granting of a corporate charter typically required a special legislative act defining the privileges and responsibilities of the corporation. As distinguished from an ordinary business partnership, the corporate body had a legal existence of its own, continuing indefinitely or for a stated term. Thus individual members (stockholders) of a corporation might pass their shares of ownership to others, but the corporate "person" lived on and retained its functions. Moreover, the early American corporate charter often carried with it some public promise of an exclusive privilege (monopoly) to perform a given task in a given place. By the 1830's the law recognized a principle of incalculable advantage to the corporation: the rule of *limited liability*, under which a stockholder was responsible for corporate debts only to the extent of his investment in the company.

The eager solicitation of corporate charters for banks and other enterprises—leading sometimes to "logrolling" and outright corruption in the state legislatures—is well explained by the special legal privileges attached to the grant and by the related *economic* advantages. The corporation could concentrate the funds of many investors in a single large-scale enterprise. This was a peculiarly valuable function in mid-nineteenth-century America, where large private accumulations of capital were too scarce to support the undertakings required by a rapidly expanding economy. Many Whigs also made a case for the corporation as an instrument of what now might be called "people's capitalism." That is, the corporation both freed the new enterpriser seeking capital from dependence on a few rich men and invited the small investor to share in the profits of the most successful businesses.

Hostility to business corporations in recent times has been associated with a "left-wing" position. Jacksonian Democrats, like their Jeffersonian predecessors, could trace their criticism of the corporation to the father of laissez-faire (or free-enterprise) doctrine, Adam Smith. The natural economic order for Adam Smith—and for Jefferson and Jackson—consisted of individuals freely competing for material gain under conditions of equal opportunity and equal risk. Every grant of corporate privilege required critical scrutiny, for it awarded advantages to a few and denied them to the rest of society. In opposing the incorporated national bank, both Jefferson and Jackson denounced the *monopolistic* features of the institution and its tendency to create a *privileged class.*

William Leggett (1801-1839) was a New York City author and editor who helped to formulate the position of the Locofoco (or Equal Rights) wing of Jacksonian Democracy in the mid-1830's. (The popular name of the group was derived from a type of matches used by their supporters at a New York Democratic meeting after the opposing faction had turned off the gas lights.) Leggett and the Locofocos insisted on a strict application of the Jacksonian equal-rights doctrine to state banks and other corporations. At first the Locofoco demands for "free banking" and "general incorporation" laws were considered dangerously radical; but gradually, from the 1830's on, Whigs joined Democrats to make corporate charters available to all comers who could meet certain general legal requirements. The proliferation of corporations under the new system of general laws (as against special charter grants) disturbed many Jacksonians who had helped to effect the change; and in the state legislatures and constitutional conventions of the 1840's and 1850's they fought for tighter rules governing such matters as stockholder liability and corporate taxation. They were especially concerned to check the evils of paper-money banking corporations.

The following selections are taken from editorials contributed by Leggett to the *New York Evening Post,* where he served as assistant to William Cullen Bryant from 1829 to 1836, and the *Plaindealer,* which he established in 1836. William Leggett's political writings presented an uncompromising laissez-faire position. He supported free enterprise against both corporate privilege and government regulation. His defense of the legal rights of trade unions added to his reputation for radicalism, while his appeals for the civil liberties of abolitionists (whose meetings were often broken up by Northern city mobs in the 1830's) angered large segments of his own New York Democratic party.

One of the newspapers which has done us the honour to notice this journal, animadverts, with considerable asperity, upon our declaration of interminable hostility to the principle of special incorporation, and points our attention to certain incorporated institutions, which, according to the universal sense of mankind, are established with the purest motives, and effect the most excellent objects. The ready and obvious answer to the strictures we have provoked is, that it is the means, not the end, which furnishes the subject of our condemnation. An act of special incorporation may frequently afford the persons associated under it facilities of accomplishing much public good; but if those facilities can only be given at the expense of rights of paramount importance, they ought to be denied by all whose political morality rejects the odious maxim that the end justifies the means. It would be a very

strained and unwarrantable inference from any remarks we have made, to say that we are an enemy to churches, public libraries, or charitable associations, because we express hostility to special legislation. It would be an unwarranted inference to say that we are even opposed to the principle of incorporation; since it is only to the principle of *special incorporation* that we have expressed hostility. We are opposed, not to the object, but to the mode by which the object is effected. We are opposed, not to corporation partnerships, but to the right of forming such partnerships being specially granted to the few, and wholly denied to the many. We are opposed, in short, to unequal legislation, whatever form it may assume, or whatever object it may ostensibly seek to accomplish.

It has been beautifully and truly said, by the illustrious man who presides over the affairs of our Confederacy, that "there are no necessary evils in government. Its evils exist only in its abuses. If it would confine itself to *equal pro-*

Text: William Leggett, *A Collection of the Political Writings,* ed. Theodore Sedgwick, Jr. (New York: Taylor & Dodd, 1839), II, 135-39; I, 142-43.

tection, and, as heaven does its rains, shower its favours alike on the high and the low, the rich and the poor, it would be an unqualified blessing." But it departs from its legitimate office, it widely departs from the cardinal principle of government in this country, the equal political rights of all, when it confers privileges on one set of men, no matter for what purpose, which are withheld from the rest. It is in this light we look upon all special acts of incorporation. They convey privileges not previously enjoyed, and limit the use of them to those on whom they are bestowed. That special charters are, in many instances, given for objects of intrinsic excellence and importance, is freely admitted; nor do we desire to withhold our unqualified acknowledgment that they have been the means of effecting many improvements of great value to the community at large. Let it be clearly understood, then, that we do not war against the good achieved; but seek only to illustrate the inherent evil of the means. A special charter is a powerful weapon; but it is one which should have no place in the armory of the democracy. It is an instrument which may hew down forests, and open fountains of wealth in barren places; but these advantages are purchased at too dear a rate, if we give for them one jot or tittle of our equal freedom. As a general rule, too, corporations act for themselves, not for the community. If they cultivate the wilderness, it is to monopolize its fruits. If they delve the mine, it is to enrich themselves with its treasures. If they dig new channels for the streams of industry, it is that they may gather the golden sands for themselves, as those of Pactolus were gathered to swell the hoards of Croesus. . . .

Every special act of incorporation is, in a certain sense, a grant of a monopoly. Every special act of incorporation is a charter of privileges to a few, not enjoyed by the community at large. There is no single object can be named, for which, consistently with a sincere respect for the equal rights of men, a special charter of incorporation can be bestowed. It should not be given to establish a bank, nor to erect a manufactory; to open a road, nor to build a bridge. Neither trust companies nor insurance companies should be invested with exclusive rights. Nay, acting in strict accordance with the true principles both of democracy and political economy, no legislature would, by special act, incorporate even a college or a church. Let it not be supposed, however, that we would withhold from such institutions the intrinsic advantages of a charter. We would only substitute general, for partial legislation, and extend to all, the privileges proper to be bestowed upon any. . . .

It is not against the objects effected by incorporated companies that we contend; but simply against the false principle, politically and politico-economically, of special grants and privileges. Instead of renewing the charters of Insurance Companies, or any other companies, about to expire, or granting charters to new applicants, we would recommend the passing of one general law of joint stock partnerships, allowing any number of persons to associate for any object, (with one single temporary exception, which we shall state in the proper place) permitting them to sue and be sued under their partnership name, to be secure from liability beyond the amount of capital invested, to conduct their business according to their own good pleasure, and, in short, to possess all the powers defined by the revised statutes as belonging to corporations. There is nothing not perfectly equitable in the principle which exempts men from liability to any greater amount than the capital actually invested in any business, provided proper notoriety be given of the extent and circumstances of that investment. If such a law were passed, the stockholders in an insurance company, or the stockholders in any other chartered company, when their corporate privileges were about to expire, would have merely to give the proper public notification of their intention to continue their business in the mode specified in the general joint-stock partnership law, and they might go on precisely the same as if their special privileges had been renewed. The only difference would be that those privileges would no longer be special, but would belong to the whole community, any number of which might associate together, form a new company for the same objects, give due notification to the public, and enter into free competition with pre-existing companies or partnerships; precisely as one man, or set of associated men, may now enter into mercantile business by the side of other merchants, import the same kinds of goods, dispose of them on the same terms, and compete with them in all the branches of their business.

There has been a great deal said about our ultraism and Utopianism; and this is the extent of it. By a general law of joint-stock partnerships all the good effects of private incorporations would be secured, and all the evil ones avoided. The humblest citizens might associate together, and wield, through the agency of skilful and intelligent directors, chosen by themselves, a vast aggregate capital, composed of the little separate sums which they could afford to invest in such an enterprise, in competition with the capitals of the purse-proud men who now almost monopolize certain branches of business.

122 FLUSH TIMES IN THE SOUTHWEST

from Joseph G. Baldwin, *The Flush Times of Alabama and Mississippi*, 1853

The cotton boom in the new Gulf states of Alabama and Mississippi drew hordes of fortune seekers from depressed areas of the older South, among them Joseph Baldwin (1815-64), a young lawyer from western Virginia who made the trek in 1836. The cotton boom was real; the wild inflation of the time, fantastic. In the spirit of Illinois and New York, then of the whole nation, the Southwest had plunged into the current of unbounded speculation. The fever ran especially high in pioneer communities where imagination and desire met few institutional restraints.

Government land sales, for example, more than quadrupled between 1834 and 1836, most of the purchases representing an exchange of borrowed paper money (hot off the printing press) for land titles which the buyer hoped to resell to another paper-money borrower at a steep rise. Jackson's Specie Circular of July 1836 required the payment of hard money for government lands; as Baldwin observes below, it exploded the great land bubble. The Panic of 1837 and the subsequent depression completed the cruel work of deflating fictitious values. State governments, as well as individuals who had committed themselves to glorious enterprises far beyond their means, now faced bankruptcy.

Joseph Baldwin's sketch of flush times in Alabama and Mississippi reveals at once a general experience of Jacksonian America and the particular atmosphere of frontier society in the new Gulf States. The rest of his volume presents anecdotes, humorous sketches, and biographical portraits drawn from the life of the region. Baldwin writes in the style of Davy Crockett, August B. Longstreet, and other contemporary authors of folk humor. *The Flush Times* first appeared in 1853 and won a wide audience. The following year the writer-lawyer settled in San Francisco, then perhaps a wilder place than Mississippi had been two decades earlier. His growing legal reputation won him a seat on the California Supreme Court.

In the fulness of time the new era had set in—the era of the second great experiment of independence: the experiment, namely, of credit without capital, and enterprise without honesty. The Age of Brass had succeeded the Arcadian period when men got rich by saving a part of their earnings, and lived at their own cost and in ignorance of the new plan of making fortunes on the profits of what they owed. A new theory, not found in the works on political economy, was broached. It was found out that the prejudice in favor of the metals (brass excluded) was an absurd superstition; and that, in reality, any thing else, which the parties interested in giving it currency chose, might serve as a representative of value and medium for exchange of property; and as gold and silver had served for a number of years as representatives, the republican doctrine of rotation in office required they should give way. Accordingly it was decided that Rags [*i.e.*, paper money], a very familiar character, and very popular and easy of access, should take their place. Rags belonged to the

school of progress. He was representative of the then Young America. His administration was not tame. It was *very* spirited. It was based on the Bonapartist idea of keeping the imagination of the people excited. The leading fiscal idea of his system was to *democratize* capital, and to make, for all purposes of trade, credit and enjoyment of wealth, the man that had *no* money a little richer, if anything, than the man that had a million. The principle of success and basis of operation, though inexplicable in the hurry of the time, is plain enough now: it was faith. Let the public believe that a smutted rag is money, it is money: in other words, it was a sort of financial biology, which made, at night, the thing conjured for, the thing that was seen, so far as the patient was concerned, while the fit was on him—except that now a man does not do his trading when under the mesmeric influence: in the flush times he did.

This country was just settling up. Marvellous accounts had gone forth of the fertility of its virgin lands; and the productions of the soil were commanding a price remunerating to slave labor as it had never been remunerated before. Emigrants came flocking in from all quarters

Text: Joseph G. Baldwin, *The Flush Times of Alabama and Mississippi* (New York: A. Appleton & Co., 1853), pp. 81-91.

of the Union, especially from the slave-holding States. The new country seemed to be a reservoir, and every road leading to it a vagrant stream of enterprise and adventure. Money, or what passed for money, was the only cheap thing to be had. Every crossroad and avocation presented an opening,—through which a fortune was seen by the adventurer in near perspective. Credit was a thing of course. To refuse it—if the thing was ever done—were an insult for which a bowie-knife were not a too summary or exemplary a means of redress. The State banks were issuing their bills by the sheet, like a patent steam printing-press *its* issues; and no other showing was asked of the applicant for the loan than an authentication of his great distress for money. Finance, even in its most exclusive quarter, had thus already got, in this wonderful revolution, to work upon the principles of the charity hospital. If an overseer grew tired of supervising a plantation and felt a call to the mercantile life, even if he omitted the compendious method of buying out a merchant wholesale, stock, house and good will, and laying down, at once, his bullwhip for the yard-stick—all he had to do was to go on to New-York, and present himself in Pearl-street with a letter avouching his citizenship, and a clean shirt, and he was regularly given a through ticket to speedy bankruptcy.

Under this stimulating process prices rose like smoke. Lots in obscure villages were held at city prices; lands, bought at the minimum cost of government, were sold at from thirty to forty dollars per acre, and considered dirt cheap at that. In short, the country had got to be a full ante-type of California, in all except the gold. Society was wholly unorganized: there was no restraining public opinion: the law was well-nigh powerless—and religion scarcely was heard of except as furnishing the oaths and *technics* of profanity. The world saw a fair experiment of what it would have been, if the fiat had never been pronounced which decreed subsistence as the price of labor.

Money, got without work, by those unaccustomed to it, turned the heads of its possessors, and they spent it with a recklessness like that with which they gained it. The pursuits of industry neglected, riot and coarse debauchery filled up the vacant hours. . . .

The old rules of business and the calculations of prudence were alike disregarded, and profligacy, in all the departments of the *crimen falsi*, held riotous carnival. Larceny grew not only respectable, but genteel, and ruffled it in all the pomp of purple and fine linen. Swindling was raised to the dignity of the fine arts. Felony

came forth from its covert, put on more seemly habiliments, and took its seat with unabashed front in the upper places of the synagogue. . . .

"Commerce was king"—and Rags, Tag and Bobtail his cabinet council. Rags was treasurer. Banks, chartered on a specie basis, did a very flourishing business on the promissory notes of the individual stockholders ingeniously substituted in lieu of cash. They issued ten for one, the *one* being fictitious. They generously loaned all the directors could not use themselves, and were not choice whether Bardolph was the endorser for Falstaff, or Falstaff borrowed on his own proper credit, or the funds advanced him by Shallow. The stampede towards the golden temple became general: the delusion prevailed far and wide that this thing was not a burlesque on commerce and finance. Even the directors of the banks began to have their doubts whether the intended swindle was not a failure. Like Lord Clive, when reproached for extortion to the extent of some millions in Bengal, they exclaimed, after the bubble burst, "When they thought of what they had got, and what they might have got, they were astounded at their own moderation."

The old capitalists for a while stood out. With the Tory conservatism of cash in hand, worked for, they couldn't reconcile their old notions to the new regime. They looked for the thing's ending, and *then* their time. But the stampede still kept on. Paper fortunes still multiplied—houses and lands changed hands—real estate see-sawed up as morals went down on the other end of the plank—men of straw, corpulent with bank bills, strutted past them on 'Change. They began, too, to think there might be something in this new thing. Peeping cautiously, like hedge-hogs out of their holes, they saw the stream of wealth and adventurers passing by—then, looking carefully around, they inched themselves half way out—then, sallying forth and snatching up a morsel, ran back, until, at last, grown more bold, *they* ran out too with their hoarded store, in full chase with the other unclean beasts of adventure. They never got back again. Jonah's gourd withered one night, and the next morning the vermin that had nestled under its broad shade were left unprotected, a prey to the swift retribution that came upon them. They were left naked, or only clothed themselves with cursing (the Specie Circular on the United States Bank) as with a garment. . . .

The condition of society may be imagined:—vulgarity—ignorance—fussy and arrogant pretension—unmitigated rowdyism—bullying insolence, if they did not rule the hour, *seemed* to wield unchecked dominion. The workings of these choice spirits were patent upon the face of society; and the modest, unobtrusive, retiring men of worth and character (for there were many, perhaps a large majority of such) were almost lost sight of in the hurly-burly of those strange and shifting scenes.

Even in the professions were the same characteristics visible. Men dropped down into their places as from the clouds. Nobody knew who or what they were, except as they claimed, or as a surface view of their characters indicated. Instead of taking to the highway and magnanimously calling upon the wayfarer to stand and deliver, or to the fashionable larceny of credit without prospect or design of paying, some unscrupulous horse-doctor would set up his sign as "Physician and Surgeon," and draw his lancet on you, or fire at random a box of his pills into your bowels, with a vague chance of hitting some disease unknown to him, but with a better prospect of killing the patient, whom or whose administrator he charged some ten dollars a trial for his marksmanship. . . .

But this state of things could not last for ever: society cannot always stand on its head with its heels in the air.

The Jupiter Tonans of the White House saw the monster of a free credit prowling about like a beast of apocalyptic vision, and marked him for his prey. Gathering all his bolts in his sinewy grasp, and standing back on his heels, and waving his wiry arm, he let them all fly, hard and swift upon all the hydra's heads. Then came a crash, as "if the ribs of nature broke," and a scattering, like the bursting of a thousand magazines, and a smell of brimstone, as if Pandemonium had opened a window next to earth for ventilation, —and all was silent. The beast never stirred in his tracks. To get down from the clouds to level ground, the Specie Circular was issued without warning, and the splendid lie of a false credit burst into fragments. It came in the midst of the dance and the frolic—as Tam O'Shanter came to disturb the infernal glee of the warlocks, and to disperse the rioters. Its effect was like that of a general creditor's bill in the chancery court, and a marshalling of all the assets of the tradespeople. Gen. Jackson was no fairy: but he did some very pretty fairy work, in converting the bank bills back again into rags and oak-leaves. Men worth a million were insolvent for two millions: promising young cities marched back again into the wilderness. The ambitious town plat was re-annexed to the plantation, like a country girl taken home from the city. The frolic was ended, and what headaches, and feverish limbs the next morning! The retreat from Moscow was performed over again, and "Devil take the hindmost" was the tune to which the soldiers of fortune marched. The only question was as to the means of escape, and the nearest and best route to Texas. The sheriff was as busy as a militia adjutant on review day; and the lawyers were mere wreckers, earning salvage. Where are ye now my ruffling gallants? Where now the braw cloths and watch chains and rings and fine horses? Alas! for ye—they are glimmering among the things that were—the wonder of an hour! They live only in memory, as unsubstantial as the promissory notes ye gave for them. When it came to be tested, the whole matter was found to be hollow and fallacious. Like a sum ciphered out through a long column, the first figure an error, the whole, and all the parts were wrong, throughout the entire calculation.

Such is a charcoal sketch of the interesting region—now inferior to none in resources, and the character of its population—during the FLUSH TIMES; a period constituting an episode in the commercial history of the world—the reign of humbug, and wholesale insanity, just overthrown in time to save the whole country from ruin. . . .

123 MANIFEST DESTINY

from John L. O'Sullivan, "Annexation," 1845

"Manifest Destiny" was a rhetorical flourish probably concocted in 1845 by a Democratic editor, John L. O'Sullivan, and promptly taken up by a host of Western orators to justify American expansion across the continent (and perhaps a little beyond). Whatever the language used, the spirit and practice of expansion had been a leading force in American national life from the beginning. The promise of good, cheap land continuously drew American pioneers westward. The purchase of Louisiana under Jefferson not only solved a problem of national security but opened the vision of a freehold empire. The expansionists of 1812 hungered for new lands in Canada and Florida; the latter soon was added to the national domain by aggressive diplomacy. The Monroe

Doctrine was in form a defensive policy, but it carried the implicit meaning that the United States had a primary interest in Western Hemisphere affairs and might find it necessary to acquire new territories.

American expansion into the Mexican lands of the Southwest encountered resistance and led the nation into war. American claims to Texas as part of the Louisiana Purchase had slight foundation and were abandoned by Monroe in the Spanish treaty of 1819. In the 1820's, however, the independent Mexican government encouraged settlers from the United States to take up Texas lands. Under the early leadership of Stephen Austin the English-speaking population grew steadily, numbering by 1834 some eighteen thousand whites with two thousand slaves. Conflicts with Mexican authorities led to the bloody debacle at the Alamo in 1836 and the subsequent Texan victory at San Jacinto under General Sam Houston which established the independent Lone Star Republic. President Jackson recognized the new government on March 3, 1837.

The 1844 election went to Democrat James K. Polk, in part because he had committed himself to annexation of Texas and an aggressive Oregon policy while his Whig opponent, Henry Clay, voiced doubts on Texas. Just before Polk took office in March of 1845, Congress passed a joint resolution admitting Texas to the Union. The public debate over the annexation of the former Mexican territory had grown very sharp indeed. It was the Missouri question over again. Proslavery forces demanded annexation to preserve the position of the South in the sectional tug of war; anti-slavery men replied in kind, with the further argument that the United States should not receive the stolen property of Mexico.

Finally, the national interest in excluding British or French influence from Texas and the national spirit of expansionism summed up in the Manifest Destiny slogan overrode other considerations. The dominant attitude was expressed by John Louis O'Sullivan (1813-95), founder and long-time editor of *The United States Magazine and Democratic Review*. This Democratic lawyer and journalist from New York appealed in spread-eagle style to destiny, to aggressive national pride, and to practical interest in his effort to silence criticism of the Texas annexation. In the 1850's O'Sullivan held diplomatic posts at Lisbon. He was several times indicted under United States neutrality laws for promoting filibustering expeditions to Cuba. (See Documents 124 and 125 for the military sequel to the Texas affair.)

It is time now for opposition to the Annexation of Texas to cease, all further agitation of the waters of bitterness and strife, at least in connexion with this question,—even though it may perhaps be required of us as a necessary condition of the freedom of our institutions, that we must live on for ever in a state of unpausing struggle and excitement upon some subject of party division or other. But, in regard to Texas, enough has now been given to Party. It is time for the common duty of Patriotism to the Country to succeed;—or if this claim will not be recognized, it is at least time for common sense to acquiesce with decent grace in the inevitable and the irrevocable.

Texas is now ours. Already, before these words are written, her Convention has undoubtedly ratified the acceptance, by her Congress, of our proffered invitation into the Union; and made the requisite changes in her already republican form of constitution to adopt it to its future federal relations. Her star and her stripe may already be said to have taken their place in the glorious blazon of our common nationality; and the sweep of our eagle's wing already includes within its circuit the wide extent of her fair and fertile land. She is no longer to us a mere geographical space—a certain combination of coast, plain, mountain, valley, forest and stream. She is no longer to us a mere country on the map. She comes within the dear and sacred designation of Our Country; no longer a *"pays,"* she is a part of *"la patrie;"* and that which is at once a sentiment and a virtue, Patriotism, already begins to thrill for her too within the national heart. . . .

Why, were other reasoning wanting, in favor of now elevating this question of the reception of Texas into the Union, out of the lower region of our past party dissensions, up to its proper level of a high and broad nationality, it surely is to be found, found abundantly, in the manner in which other nations have undertaken to intrude themselves into it, between us and the proper parties to the case, in a spirit of hostile interference against us, for the avowed object of thwarting our policy and hampering our power, limiting our greatness and checking the fulfilment of our

Text: John L. O'Sullivan, "Annexation," *The United States Magazine and Democratic Review*, XVII (July and August, 1845), 5-10 *passim*.

manifest destiny to overspread the continent allotted by Providence for the free development of our yearly multiplying millions. . . .

It is wholly untrue, and unjust to ourselves, the pretence that the Annexation has been a measure of spoliation, unrightful and unrighteous—of military conquest under forms of peace and law—of territorial aggrandizement at the expense of justice, and justice due by a double sanctity to the weak. This view of the question is wholly unfounded, and has been before so amply refuted in these pages, as well as in a thousand other modes, that we shall not again dwell upon it. The independence of Texas was complete and absolute. It was an independence, not only in fact but of right. No obligation of duty towards Mexico tended in the least degree to restrain our right to effect the desired recovery of the fair province once our own—whatever motives of policy might have prompted a more deferential consideration of her feelings and her pride, as involved in the question. If Texas became peopled with an American population, it was by no contrivance of our government, but on the express invitation of that of Mexico herself; accompanied with such guaranties of State independence, and the maintenance of a federal system analogous to our own, as constituted a compact fully justifying the strongest measures of redress on the part of those afterwards deceived in this guaranty, and sought to be enslaved under the yoke imposed by its violation. She was released, rightfully and absolutely released, from all Mexican allegiance, or duty of cohesion to the Mexican political body, by the acts and fault of Mexico herself, and Mexico alone. There never was a clearer case. It was not revolution; it was resistance to revolution; and resistance under such circumstances as left independence the necessary resulting state, caused by the abandonment of those with whom her former federal association had existed. What then can be more preposterous than all this clamor by Mexico and the Mexican interest, against Annexation, as a violation of any rights of hers, any duties of ours? . . .

Nor is there any just foundation of the charge that Annexation is a great pro-slavery measure —calculated to increase and perpetuate that institution. Slavery had nothing to do with it. . . . The country which was the subject of Annexation in this case, from its geographical position and relations, happens to be—or rather the portion of it now actually settled, happens to be —a slave country. But a similar process might have taken place in proximity to a different section of our Union; and indeed there is a great deal of Annexation yet to take place, within the life of the present generation, along the whole line of our northern border. Texas has been absorbed into the Union in the inevitable fulfilment of the general law which is rolling our population westward; the connexion of which with that ratio of growth in population which is destined within a hundred years to swell our numbers to the enormous population of *two hundred and fifty millions* (if not more), is too evident to leave us in doubt of the manifest design of Providence in regard to the occupation of this continent. It was disintegrated from Mexico in the natural course of events, by a process perfectly legitimate on its own part, blameless on ours; and in which all the censures due to wrong, perfidy and folly, rest on Mexico alone. And possessed as it was by a population which was in truth but a colonial detachment from our own, and which was still bound by myriad ties of the very heartstrings to its old relations, domestic and political, their incorporation into the Union was not only inevitable, but the most natural, right and proper thing in the world— and it is only astonishing that there should be any among ourselves to say it nay. . . .

California will, probably, next fall away from the loose adhesion which, in such a country as Mexico, holds a remote province in a slight equivocal kind of dependence on the metropolis. Imbecile and distracted, Mexico never can exert any real governmental authority over such a country. The impotence of the one and the distance of the other, must make the relation one of virtual independence; unless, by stunting the province of all natural growth, and forbidding that immigration which can alone develope its capabilities and fulfil the purposes of its creation, tyranny may retain a military dominion which is no government in the legitimate sense of the term. In the case of California this is now impossible. The Anglo-Saxon foot is already on its borders. Already the advance guard of the irresistible army of Anglo-Saxon emigration has begun to pour down upon it, armed with the plough and the rifle, and marking its trail with schools and colleges, courts and representative halls, mills and meeting-houses. A population will soon be in actual occupation of California, over which it will be idle for Mexico to dream of dominion. They will necessarily become independent. All this without agency of our government, without responsibility of our people—in the natural flow of events, the spontaneous working of principles, and the adaptation of the tendencies and wants of the human race to the elemental circumstances in the midst of which they find themselves placed. And they will have a right to independence—to self-government—to the possession of the homes conquered from the wilderness by their own labors and dangers, sufferings and sacrifices—a better and a truer right than the artificial title of sovereignty in Mexico a thousand miles distant, inheriting from Spain a title good only against those who have none better. Their right to independence will be the natural right of self-government belonging to any community strong enough to maintain it—distinct in position, origin and character, and free from any mutual obligations of membership of a common political body, binding it to others by the duty of loyalty and compact of public faith. This will be their title to independence; and by this title, there can be no doubt that the population now fast streaming down upon California will both assert and maintain that independence. Whether they will then attach themselves to our Union or not, is not to be predicted with any certainty. Unless the projected rail-road across the continent to the Pacific be carried into effect, perhaps they may not; though even in that case, the day is not distant when the Empires of the Atlantic and Pacific would again flow together into one, as soon as their inland border should approach each other. But that great work, colossal as appears the plan on its first suggestion, cannot remain long unbuilt. Its necessity for this very purpose of binding and holding together in its iron clasp our fast settling Pacific region with that of the Mississippi valley—the natural facility of the route—the ease with which any amount of labor for the construction can be drawn in from the overcrowded populations of Europe, to be paid in the lands made valuable by the progress of the work itself—and its immense utility to the commerce of the world with the whole eastern coast of Asia, alone almost sufficient for the support of such a road—these considerations give assurance that the day cannot be distant which shall witness the conveyance of the representatives from Oregon and California to Washington within less time than a few years ago was devoted to a similar journey by those from Ohio; while the magnetic telegraph will enable the editors of the "San Francisco Union," the "Astoria Evening Post," or the "Nootka Morning News" to set up in type the first half of the President's Inaugural, before the echoes of the latter half shall have died away beneath the lofty porch of the Capitol, as spoken from his lips.

Away, then, with all idle French talk of *balances of power* on the American Continent. There is no growth in Spanish America! Whatever progress of population there may be in the British Canadas, is only for their own early severance of their present colonial relation to the little island three thousand miles across the Atlantic; soon to be followed by Annexation, and destined to swell the still accumulating momentum of our progress. And whatsoever may hold the balance, though they should cast into the opposite scale all the bayonets and cannon, not only of France and England, but of Europe entire, how would it kick the beam against the simple solid weight of the two hundred and fifty or three hundred millions—and American millions—destined to gather beneath the flutter of the stripes and stars, in the fast hastening year of the Lord 1945?

THE MEXICAN WAR

124 THE PRESIDENT'S CALL FOR WAR

from James K. Polk, Message to Congress, May 11, 1846

The annexation of Texas (Document 123) pointed directly toward war with Mexico. The outraged Mexicans broke off diplomatic relations and threatened to redress their grievances against the United States by force. Whether this was more than brave talk it is difficult to say. Certainly Mexico had done nothing to reëstablish its authority over Texas while the independent Republic stood alone (1836-1845); and the entry of Texas into the Union would have made coercion a much more perilous experiment. At any rate, the first provocative actions were taken by an expansionist President of the United States.

James K. Polk (1795-1849), a Jacksonian Democrat from Tennessee, had proved a stalwart party man in his determined rise to the Speaker's chair in the United States House of Representatives. To orthodox Jacksonian political and economic views he added an intense commitment to national expansion that made him the successful dark-horse candidate in the 1844 Democratic Convention and boosted him to victory over Henry Clay. Master of his administration, President Polk led the nation toward a set of bold objectives. He would have the Oregon Country for American settlers. He would collect long-standing American claims against the Mexican government. He would protect the new state of Texas and establish its boundary along the course of the Rio Grande. And he would have California, by one means or another, to advance the American interest in the potential commerce of the Pacific. If Polk could win his objectives peacefully (as he did in the case of Oregon), then he would be a man of peace.

The Slidell mission to Mexico (1845-1846) did not go quite as Polk describes it in the following passages. Mexico had agreed to receive a commissioner for discussion of American claims; Polk sent a full minister with instructions to purchase up to half of Mexico's territory, including New Mexico and California. When the Mexican government refused to receive Slidell, Polk made his provocative move. He ordered General Zachary Taylor to occupy the country between the Nueces and the Rio Grande, in the southeastern corner of Texas, although the American claim to this area was doubtful at best. A predictable border incident, involving a Mexican attack on a detachment of Taylor's army, gave Polk the occasion to advocate publicly the choice of war that he had already presented to his Cabinet.

On May 12, 1846, the day after receiving the President's statement of the case for action, Congress voted a declaration of war by large majorities in both houses. Few historians have accepted Polk's version of the events leading to war, as given in the following selection, although some writers do credit Polk with a legitimate concern for Mexican aggression in Texas and for British designs on California. The point at issue has been primarily one of underlying motive: was the Mexican War of 1846-1848 a part of the design of an "aggressive slavocracy"? Or was it rather the product of that imperious expansionism, shared by North and South, which demanded a whole continent for the fulfillment of America's destiny and would brook no interference by a backward and chaotic Mexico?

The existing state of the relations between the United States and Mexico renders it proper that I should bring the subject to the consideration of Congress. In my message at the commencement of your present session the state of these relations, the causes which led to the suspension of diplomatic intercourse between the two countries in March, 1845, and the long-continued and unredressed wrongs and injuries committed by the Mexican Government on citizens of the United States in their persons and property were briefly set forth. . . .

Mr. Slidell arrived at Vera Cruz on the 30th of November [1845], and was courteously received by the authorities of that city. But the Government of General Herrera was then tottering to its fall. The revolutionary party had seized upon the Texas question to effect or hasten its overthrow. Its determination to restore friendly relations with the United States, and to receive our minister to negotiate for the settlement of this question, was violently assailed, and was made the great theme of denunciation against it. The Government of General Herrera, there is good reason to believe, was sincerely desirous to receive our minister; but it yielded to the storm raised by its enemies, and on the 21st of December

Text: James D. Richardson (ed.), *A Compilation of the Messages and Papers of the Presidents, 1789-1897* (Washington, D.C.: Government Printing Office, 1897), IV, 437-42 *passim*.

ber refused to accredit Mr. Slidell upon the most frivolous pretexts. These are so fully and ably exposed in the note of Mr. Slidell of the 24th of December last to the Mexican minister of foreign relations, herewith transmitted, that I deem it unnecessary to enter into further detail on this portion of the subject.

Five days after the date of Mr. Slidell's note General Herrera yielded the Government to General Paredes without a struggle, and on the 30th of December resigned the Presidency. This revolution was accomplished solely by the army, the people having taken little part in the contest; and thus the supreme power in Mexico passed into the hands of a military leader. . . .

Under these circumstances, Mr. Slidell, in obedience to my direction, addressed a note to the Mexican minister of foreign relations, under date of the 1st of March last, asking to be received by that Government in the diplomatic character to which he had been appointed. This minister in his reply, under date of the 12th of March, reiterated the arguments of his predecessor, and in terms that may be considered as giving just grounds of offense to the Government and people of the United States denied the application of Mr. Slidell. Nothing therefore remained for our envoy but to demand his passports and return to his own country.

Thus the Government of Mexico, though solemnly pledged by official acts in October last to receive and accredit an American envoy, violated their plighted faith and refused the offer of a peaceful adjustment of our difficulties. Not only was the offer rejected, but the indignity of its rejection was enhanced by the manifest breach of faith in refusing to admit the envoy who came because they had bound themselves to receive him. Nor can it be said that the offer was fruitless from the want of opportunity of discussing it; our envoy was present on their own soil. Nor can it be ascribed to a want of sufficient powers; our envoy had full powers to adjust every question of difference. Nor was there room for complaint that our propositions for settlement were unreasonable; permission was not even given our envoy to make any proposition whatever. Nor can it be objected that we, on our part, would not listen to any reasonable terms of their suggestion; the Mexican Government refused all negotiation, and have made no proposition of any kind.

In my message at the commencement of the present session I informed you that upon the earnest appeal both of the Congress and convention of Texas I had ordered an efficient military force to take a position "between the Nueces and the Del Norte." This had become necessary to meet a threatened invasion of Texas by the Mexican forces, for which extensive military preparations had been made. The invasion was threatened solely because Texas had determined, in accordance with a solemn resolution of the Congress of the United States, to annex herself to our Union, and under these circumstances it was plainly our duty to extend our protection over her citizens and soil.

This force was concentrated at Corpus Christi, and remained there until after I had received such information from Mexico as rendered it probable, if not certain, that the Mexican Government would refuse to receive our envoy.

Meantime Texas, by the final action of our Congress, had become an integral part of our Union. The Congress of Texas, by its act of December 19, 1836, had declared the Rio del Norte to be the boundary of that Republic. Its jurisdiction had been extended and exercised beyond the Nueces. The country between that river and the Del Norte had been represented in the Congress and in the convention of Texas, had thus taken part in the act of annexation itself, and is now included within one of our Congressional districts. Our own Congress had, moreover, with great unanimity, by the act approved December 31, 1845, recognized the country beyond the Nueces as a part of our territory by including it within our own revenue system, and a revenue

officer to reside within that district has been appointed by and with the advice and consent of the Senate. It became, therefore, of urgent necessity to provide for the defense of that portion of our country. Accordingly, on the 13th of January last instructions were issued to the general in command of these troops to occupy the left bank of the Del Norte. This river, which is the southwestern boundary of the State of Texas, is an exposed frontier. . . .

The movement of the troops to the Del Norte was made by the commanding general under positive instructions to abstain from all agressive acts toward Mexico or Mexican citizens and to regard the relations between that Republic and the United States as peaceful unless she should declare war or commit acts of hostility indicative of a state of war. He was specially directed to protect private property and respect personal rights.

The Army moved from Corpus Christi on the 11th of March, and on the 28th of that month arrived on the left bank of the Del Norte opposite to Matamoras, where it encamped on a commanding position, which has since been strengthened by the erection of fieldworks. A depot has also been established at Point Isabel, near the Brazos Santiago, 30 miles in rear of the encampment. The selection of his position was necessarily confided to the judgment of the general in command.

The Mexican forces at Matamoras assumed a belligerent attitude, and on the 12th of April General Ampudia, then in command, notified General Taylor to break up his camp within twenty-four hours and to retire beyond the Nueces River, and in the event of his failure to comply with these demands announced that arms, and arms alone, must decide the question. But no open act of hostility was committed until the 24th of April. On that day General Arista, who had succeeded to the command of the Mexican forces, communicated to General Taylor that "he considered hostilities commenced and should prosecute them." A party of dragoons of 63 men and officers were on the same day dispatched from the American camp up the Rio del Norte, on its left bank, to ascertain whether the Mexican troops had crossed or were preparing to cross the river, "became engaged with a large body of these troops, and after a short affair, in which some 16 were killed and wounded, appear to have been surrounded and compelled to surrender."

The grievous wrongs perpetrated by Mexico upon our citizens throughout a long period of years remain unredressed, and solemn treaties pledging her public faith for this redress have been disregarded. A government either unable or unwilling to enforce the execution of such treaties fails to perform one of its plainest duties.

Our commerce with Mexico has been almost annihilated. It was formerly highly beneficial to both nations, but our merchants have been deterred from prosecuting it by the system of outrage and extortion which the Mexican authorities have pursued against them, whilst their appeals through their own Government for indemnity have been made in vain. Our forbearance has gone to such an extreme as to be mistaken in its character. Had we acted with vigor in repelling the insults and redressing the injuries inflicted by Mexico at the commencement, we should doubtless have escaped all the difficulties in which we are now involved.

Instead of this, however, we have been exerting our best efforts to propitiate her good will. Upon the pretext that Texas, a nation as independent as herself, thought proper to unite its destinies

with our own, she has affected to believe that we have severed her rightful territory, and in official proclamations and manifestoes has repeatedly threatened to make war upon us for the purpose of reconquering Texas. In the meantime we have tried every effort at reconciliation. The cup of forbearance had been exhausted even before the recent information from the frontier of the Del Norte. But now, after reiterated menaces, Mexico has passed the boundary of the United States, has invaded our territory and shed American blood upon the American soil. She has proclaimed that hostilities have commenced, and that the two nations are now at war.

As war exists, and, notwithstanding all our efforts to avoid it, exists by the act of Mexico herself, we are called upon by every consideration of duty and patriotism to vindicate with decision the honor, the rights, and the interests of our country.

125 WHIG OPPOSITION TO WAR

from Thomas Corwin, Speech in the U. S. Senate, February 11, 1847

President James K. Polk could carry Congress and the country into war with Mexico because his policy expressed the dominant public mood of the time and specifically because the Mexican attack on American soldiers was understood as an act of aggression violating the national honor. The martial spirit was most enthusiastic in the Mississippi Valley, growing weaker toward the Atlantic seaboard. As Polk's war aims grew clearer, the Whig opposition took a bolder line. Defending the Texas border was one thing; marching to Mexico City with the obvious purpose of extorting territorial concessions in New Mexico and California was quite another.

Thomas Corwin of Ohio, an antislavery Whig Senator since 1844, created a sensation with this biting speech of February 11, 1847, denouncing "the shame, the crime, of an aggressive, unprovoked war." It seemed to many little short of treason to oppose war appropriations as Corwin did, with the pronouncement that if he were a Mexican, he would greet the American invaders with bloody hands. Most leading Whigs prudently voted for war credits and supplies, while attacking the Polk administration in terms not much gentler than Tom Corwin's. Daniel Webster, Horace Greeley, and the new young Congressman from Illinois, Abraham Lincoln, were among the stinging critics of the war. New England intellectuals might not follow Henry David Thoreau to jail as a protest against an unjust war (Document 153); but many of them took up the charge of a Southern conspiracy "to lug new slave-states in," in the language of James Russell Lowell's *Biglow Papers:* "They may talk o' Freedom's airy/ Tell they're pupple in the face;/ It's a grand gret cemetary/ Fer the barthrights of our race. . . ."

Despite severe Congressional opposition and a sharp decline in popular support, the war was pressed to a victorious conclusion. While small American forces were taking over California and New Mexico with comparative ease (1846), General Zachary Taylor and General Winfield Scott pressed the invasion of Mexico proper. Taylor decisively defeated the Mexicans under Santa Anna at Buena Vista (February 1847). Scott, with such promising subalterns as Captain Robert E. Lee and Lieutenant Ulysses S. Grant under his command, marched inland from Vera Cruz to Mexico City against determined resistance. On December 14, 1847, the capital fell.

By the Treaty of Guadalope Hidalgo (1848) Mexico ceded Texas with the Rio Grande boundary, New Mexico, and Upper California, receiving $15 million in compensation (some called it conscience money) from the victors. In addition, the United States assumed responsibility for the claims of American citizens against the Mexican government. The treaty had been negotiated by a diplomatic agent, Nicholas Trist, after Polk had canceled his authority. The President nevertheless submitted the unauthorized treaty to the Senate for ratification, in part to silence a growing demand for the absorption of all Mexico.

Thoughtful men understood that the acquisition of some half a million square miles of Mexican territory would cost the United States far more than the treaty price. The ominous note of opposition sounded by the Corwins and Thoreaus announced that the issue of slavery extension would divide the conquerors of Mexico. During the war (August 1846) a Pennsylvania Democrat, David Wilmot, introduced his "proviso" banning slavery from the Mexican cessions. The Wilmot Proviso never passed both Houses of Congress, but it touched off a passionate sectional controversy that would dominate the politics of the 1850's.

Mr. President, I . . . beg the indulgence of the Senate to some reflections on the particular bill now under consideration. I voted for a bill somewhat like the present at the last session—our army was then in the neighborhood of our line. I then hoped that the President did sincerely desire a peace. Our army had not then penetrated far into Mexico, and I did hope, that with the two millions then proposed, we might get peace, and avoid the slaughter, the shame, the crime, of an aggressive, unprovoked war. But now you have overrun half of Mexico—you have exasperated and irritated her people—you claim indemnity for all expenses incurred in doing this mischief, and boldly ask her to give up New Mexico and California; and, as a bribe to her patriotism, seizing on her property, you offer three millions to pay the soldiers she has called out to repel your invasion, on condition that she will give up to you at least one-third of her whole territory. . . .

But, sir, let us see what, as the chairman of the Committee on Foreign Relations explains it, we are to get by the combined processes of conquest and treaty.

What is the territory, Mr. President, which you propose to wrest from Mexico? It is consecrated to the heart of the Mexican by many a well-fought battle with his old Castilian master. His Bunker Hills, and Saratogas, and Yorktowns, are there! The Mexican can say, "There I bled for liberty! and shall I surrender that consecrated home of my affections to the Anglo-Saxon invaders? What do they want with it? They have Texas already. They have possessed themselves of the territory between the Nueces and the Rio Grande. What else do they want? To what shall I point my children as memorials of that independence which I bequeath to them when those battlefields shall have passed from my possession?"

Sir, had one come and demanded Bunker Hill of the people of Massachusetts, had England's Lion ever showed himself there, is there a man over thirteen and under ninety who would not have been ready to meet him? Is there a river

on this continent that would not have run red with blood? Is there a field but would have been piled high with the unburied bones of slaughtered Americans before these consecrated battlefields of liberty should have been wrested from us? But this same American goes into a sister republic and says to poor, weak Mexico, "Give up your territory, you are unworthy to possess it; I have got one-half already, and all I ask of you is to give up the other!" England might as well, in the circumstances I have described, have come and demanded of us, "Give up the Atlantic slope —give up this trifling territory from the Alleghany Mountains to the sea; it is only from Maine to St. Mary's—only about one-third of your republic, and the least interesting portion of it." What would be the response? They would say, we must give this up to John Bull. Why? "He wants room." The Senator from Michigan says he must have this. Why, my worthy Christian brother, on what principle of justice? "I want room!"

Sir, look at this pretence of want of room. With twenty millions of people, you have about one thousand millions of acres of land, inviting settlement by every conceivable argument, bringing them down to a quarter of a dollar an acre, and allowing every man to squat where he pleases. But the Senator from Michigan says we will be two hundred millions in a few years, and we want room. If I were a Mexican I would tell you, "Have you not room in your own country to bury your dead men? If you come into mine, we will greet you with bloody hands, and welcome you to hospitable graves."

Why, says the chairman of this Committee on Foreign Relations, it is the most reasonable thing in the world! We ought to have the Bay of San Francisco. Why? Because it is the best harbor on the Pacific! It has been my fortune, Mr. President, to have practised a good deal in criminal courts in the course of my life, but I

Text: Appendix to the Congressional Globe, 29th Congress, 2nd session (Washington, D.C.: Blair and Rives, 1847), pp. 216-17 passim.

never yet heard a thief, arraigned for stealing a horse, plead that it was the best horse that he could find in the country! We want California. What for? Why, says the Senator from Michigan, we will have it; and the Senator from South Carolina, with a very mistaken view, I think, of policy, says you can't keep our people from going there. I don't desire to prevent them. Let them go and seek their happiness in whatever country or clime it pleases them.

All I ask of them is, not to require this Government to protect them with that banner consecrated to war waged for principles—eternal, enduring truth. Sir, it is not meet that our old flag should throw its protecting folds over expeditions for lucre or for land. But you still say you want room for your people. This has been the plea of every robber chief from Nimrod to the present hour. . . .

CHAPTER 11

House Divided—The Nation and the Sections: 1850 to 1860

The American Union has survived the test of war and depression, of social and sectional antagonisms, of absorbing new lands and strange peoples. Once only did the Union break, and that tragic Civil War has possessed the minds of Americans as has no other historical encounter. Perhaps beneath the endless fascination with the War Between the States—with the heroics and the sufferings, the strategies and maneuvers—lies a national absorption with the question: How did it happen to us? Americans have always hoped, when they could not quite believe, that they were immune from the tragic fate of other peoples. A rich and isolated continent, a moral and comfortable society, a resourceful and energetic character, an enlightened political order, and a fresh start in a new world: advantages such as these made Jefferson, for example, speak of his country as "the world's best hope" and enabled Lincoln to discover "the last best hope of earth" even in his war-torn Union.

Historians have offered many useful answers but never *the* answer to the problem of why war came in 1861. It would only be misleading to propose a quick solution here. Without much question, however, one can assert that slavery was somehow at the source of the conflict. Some have argued (with Lincoln) that slavery posed a moral dilemma demanding political choice. (See Document 168.) Others that slavery was used by irresponsible politicians to *create* a fighting issue. (See Document 167.) Still others that slavery characterized a rigid agrarian economic order in conflict with the dynamic commercial and industrial economy of the North. Briefly, in all the diverse accounts of the coming of the Civil War, one overwhelming fact commands attention: the struggle was fought out between two geographical sections, one of which embraced the "peculiar institution," while the other rejected it.

THE PECULIAR INSTITUTION

Had North and South found some escape from the crisis of the 1850's—a bargain as successful, let us say, as the Missouri Compromise of 1820—one might not speak so confidently of two contrasting social worlds in fundamental conflict. Many of the political, social, and economic features of the age of Jacksonian Democracy were common national traits. The democratization of political institutions, for instance, or the rage for speculation, or the expansionist drive could be observed on either side of the slavery line. Both sections were predominantly peopled by free farmers. The qualities of frontier society spread over the Ohio River boundary. Significantly, the issues of Jacksonian politics were not radically different in North and South. Democrats and Whigs were national parties which divided the allegiance of both sections. There were, moreover, strong bonds of memory, faith, and interest uniting both North and South.

The mystery of separation grows deeper when one adds that slavery was no novel feature of the Southern scene but an institution that had evolved over two centuries. Slavery had been present when the sections fought together in the Revolution, when they formed a common nation, and when they sustained the Union through the first half of the nineteenth century. As late as the 1830's, *Northern* mobs could still be gathered to harass abolitionists. Elijah Lovejoy was murdered by a mob in Lincoln's Illinois and William Lloyd Garrison was dragged through the streets of Boston.

Nevertheless there *was* a Civil War between North and South—no accidental border encounter but a mighty four-year struggle that cost the nation well over half a million lives. That enormous fact compels one to emphasize the forces of separation over the forces of unity in reviewing the antebellum decade. And again it is the "peculiar institution" of the South, chattel slavery, that looms as the great divider of the sections.

Slavery, it must be recognized, was not only a labor system applied to the plantation economy but a general social system for regulating race relations in the South. The *economic* function explains the original introduction of slavery in the seventeenth-century South and the steady growth of the institution and its renewed vigor in the expanding Cotton Kingdom of the nineteenth century. Thus the South came to hold some four million Negro slaves (and another quarter of a million free Negroes) by 1860, when the white population had reached about eight million. The presence of that large servile population, set off by color, culture, and experience, was a great *social* fact which helps to explain why the South became a self-conscious political body with a common purpose.

Probably only one Southern white family out of four owned slaves on the eve of the Civil War. Among this slaveholding minority only a small fraction would qualify as major planters; fully one half of the total number of slave owners held four slaves or less. Thus the overwhelming majority of white Southerners had no direct economic stake, or a small one, in the institution of slavery. (Of course, the whole section had a very substantial *indirect* interest in the plantation economy, based on slavery, which produced the great money-making staple crops: cotton, sugar, rice, and tobacco.) Yet the majority of non-slaveholding yeoman farmers followed the minority of planters into political battles, and eventually into a civil war, in which the slavery issue was decisive. They did so, historians have suggested, because they aspired to join the planter elite, because they shared the planter's resentment against economic exploitation of the agrarian South by

Northern commercial and industrial interests, because they shared a Southern heritage of manners, customs, and values distinct from those of the North. Above all, it is argued, the white South stood together because it saw no method but slavery to maintain control over the large Negro population and because it saw the North as threatening the existence of slavery and thus of social order—even civilization—in the South.

THE POLITICS OF SLAVERY

"A house divided against itself cannot stand," said Lincoln in 1858, quoting the Scriptures. But the house has stood divided for many decades, replied his adversary, Stephen Douglas, and will stand indefinitely if only the Republicans stop pushing it. It has stood, Lincoln rejoined, because the Founders of the Union and their successors committed themselves to the containment and ultimate extinction of slavery. In the expectation that the house would cease to be divided, men could wait patiently for the result: a united free republic. But the advocates of slavery seek to unite the house by moving it from its foundations on the principles of the Declaration of Independence. On the contrary, Southerner John Calhoun would object, the Union was founded on a bargain between two radically different interest groups—North and South—whose power once was in balance. The house must remain divided and obey the concurrent voice of both the major and the minor parties in matters of vital concern. In one sense, the radical abolitionists like Garrison agreed with Calhoun, for they too rejected the Constitution and laws of the Union as final authority where higher interests were concerned.

From broad terms such as these the sectional argument proceeded, finding its principal concrete issues in the area of slavery extension. Americans generally shared the hunger for expansion in the Far West, but each new acquisition posed the divisive question: slave or free? It was at once a question of giving slavery new fields for growth and of changing the balance between slave and free states. A crisis came and passed in 1850 when the compromise sponsored by Henry Clay, Stephen Douglas, and Daniel Webster gained majority support. California was added to the free-state side; New Mexico and Utah Territories were in effect left to determine the status of slavery for themselves; the North was offered the abolition of the slave trade in the nation's capital; and the South received a more effective law for the return of fugitive slaves. (See the arguments pro and con in Documents 130 and 131.)

The political settlement of 1850 brought a moment of calm, but the forces of dissension lay just beneath the surface. Douglas believed that he had found a permanent cure for sectional conflict in the principle of "popular sovereignty" (called "squatter sovereignty" by opponents) and experimented with it in the Kansas-Nebraska Act of 1854. Under this arrangement the territorial settlers would at some undetermined point make their own decision for or against slavery. To secure Southern backing, Douglas included an explicit repeal of the Missouri Compromise of 1820, knowing that this would raise a "hell of a storm" in the North, as he remarked. In that storm the national Whig party was blown apart, and the Republican party emerged to take its place in the North. Douglas had not anticipated the still more violent storm that struck Kansas when the "Border Ruffians" up from Missouri and the free-state settlers financed and armed by New England abolitionists fought tooth-and-claw to capture political control of the territory. Intended by Douglas to heal the sectional quarrel over slavery in the territories, popular sovereignty became instead a call to battle and created "Bleeding Kansas."

For reasons that remain unclear, the Supreme Court at this critical stage undertook to settle the territorial question by judicial authority. In the *Dred Scott* decision (1857) Chief Justice Taney announced that the thirty-seven-year-old Missouri Compromise was unconstitutional, since Congress lacked authority to exclude slavery from the territories. (See Document 132.) The South was grateful, the North enraged, and Douglas Democrats were placed in a dilemma. Did the *Dred Scott* ruling put an end to popular sovereignty as a legal remedy? This became one of the great issues of the Lincoln-Douglas debates; this and the more fundamental question of the rightness and practicability of local as against national determination of slavery extension. (See Documents 133 and 134.)

But time for debate was running out. The chaos in Kansas stirred the passions of North and South. Incendiary episodes multiplied. In the Senate Chamber, a South Carolinian caned Senator Charles Sumner of Massachusetts within an inch of his life in retaliation for his fierce denunciation of slavery and its supporters (1856). In Massachusetts, Wisconsin, and other Northern states, the spectacle of slaves being forced back into bondage under the national fugitive slave law aroused popular resistance and led local courts and legislatures to interfere with the operation of the law.

When John Brown and a handful of disciples made their raid on Harper's Ferry (1859) as part of a visionary scheme to liberate the slaves by direct action, the whole South felt a chill of horror. When Virginia sent Brown to the gallows, the antislavery radicals of the North gained a martyr.

The fundamental differences between slave and free society, the clash of sectional principles and policies, and the provocative incidents of the 1850's all served to build up tensions to the breaking point. The political schedule called for an election in 1860; but the charged emotional atmosphere indicated an explosion.

The Peculiar Institution

126

THE PLANTATION AS BIG BUSINESS

from Frederick Law Olmsted, *The Cotton Kingdom*, 1861

In the closing decades of the eighteenth century, when Americans of North and South were full of brave hopes for the new republican world, there seemed a chance to resolve the contradiction of slavery in a free society. "The spirit of the master is abating," Jefferson wrote, "that of the slave rising from the dust, his condition mollifying, the way I hope preparing under the auspices of heaven, for a total emancipation, and that this is disposed, in the order of events, to be with the consent of the masters, rather than by their extirpation." Within a generation that hope was nearly dead. The invention of the cotton gin and the vast expansion of the textile industry in England and the Northern states gave a new thrust to the institution of plantation slavery. Cotton culture spread from the eastern tidewater to the Piedmont and then advanced into the fertile regions along the Gulf of Mexico and the lower Mississippi Valley. By mid-century, King Cotton dominated the Southern economy. Despite the effective legal ban on slave importing, the slave population multiplied from about 700,000 in 1790 to nearly two and a half million by 1840 and four million in 1860. Only the rare Southerner could imagine or wish his section without its "peculiar institution," for slavery had become not only a powerful and dynamic economic system but an orthodox creed of Southern society.

The American South was the last great stronghold of slavery in the Western world. It required a perceptive eye and a judicious mind to comprehend the variety within the unity of that unique Cotton Kingdom. Slavery was not all of one type from Maryland to Texas; even within a state or region of the South there were many degrees and kinds of slave-holding; and—the most arresting fact of internal variety—an estimated three out of four white Southerners in 1860 held no slaves. Frederick Law Olmsted (1822-1903), a Northern landscape architect, world traveler, author, and gentleman farmer, is one of the most discerning contemporary guides to slavery in the antebellum South. Commissioned by the New York *Daily Times* to provide a series of articles, Olmsted set out in 1852 to discover for himself the realities of society and economy throughout the slave states. His fourteen-month journey in the seaboard states, through Texas, and in the "back country" was recorded in a series of distinguished travel reports. The essence of Olmsted's articles and books on the South can be found in his own summary work, *The Cotton Kingdom* (1861), or in a recently published paperback, *The Slave States*, edited by Harvey Wish (1959).

The following selection offers a view of slavery on one of the great cotton plantations of the lower Mississippi Valley. Large-scale enterprises of this sort represented only a small sector of Southern agriculture—holders of a hundred or more slaves numbered less than eighteen hundred in 1850—but a sector of great and growing economic importance. Moreover, the small class of major planters constituted the social and political aristocracy of the South. Clearly disapproving of slavery on moral and economic grounds, Olmsted remained a keen reporter of the actualities of the institution.

. . . I am now about to describe what I judged to be the most profitable estate that I visited. . . . It was situated upon a tributary of the Mississippi, and accessible only by occasional steamboats; even this mode of communication being frequently interrupted at low stages of the rivers. The slaves upon it formed about one twentieth of the whole population of the county, in which the blacks considerably outnumber the whites. At the time of my visit, the owner was sojourning upon it, with his family and several invited guests, but his usual residence was upon a small plantation, of little productive value, situated in a neighbourhood somewhat noted for the luxury and hospitality of its citizens, and having a daily mail, and direct railroad and telegraphic communication with New York. This was, if I am not mistaken, his second visit in five years.

The property consisted of four adjoining plantations, each with its own negro-cabins, stables, and overseer, and each worked to a great extent independently of the others, but all contributing their crop to one gin-house and warehouse, and all under the general superintendence of a bailiff or manager, who constantly resided upon the estate, and in the absence of the owner, had viceregal power over the overseers, controlling, so far as he thought fit, the economy of all the plantations. . . .

In the main, the negroes appeared to be well taken care of and abundantly supplied with the necessaries of vigorous physical existence. A large part of them lived in commodious and well-built cottages, with broad galleries in front, so that each family of five had two rooms on the lower floor, and a loft. The remainder lived in log huts, small and mean in appearance, but those of their overseers were little better, and preparations were being made to replace all of these by neat boarded cottages. Each family had a fowl-house and hog-sty (constructed by the negroes themselves), and kept fowls and swine, feeding the latter during the summer on weeds and fattening them in the autumn on corn, stolen (this was mentioned to me by the overseers as if it were a matter of course) from their master's cornfields. I several times saw gangs of them eating the dinner which they had brought, each man for himself, to the field, and observed that they generally had plenty, often more than they could eat, of bacon, corn-bread, and molasses. The allowance of food is weighed and measured under the eye of the manager by the drivers, and distributed to the head of each family weekly: consisting of—for each person, 3 pounds of pork, 1 peck of meal; and from January to July, 1 quart of molasses. Monthly, in addition, 1 pound tobacco, and 4 pints salt. No drink is ever served but water, except after unusual exposure, or to ditchers working in water, who get a glass of whisky at night. All hands cook for themselves after work at night, or whenever they please between nightfall and daybreak, each family in its own cabin. Each family has a garden, the products of which, together with eggs, fowls, and bacon, they frequently sell, or use in addition to their regular allowance of food. Most of the

Text: Frederick Law Olmsted, *The Cotton Kingdom* (New York: Mason Brothers, 1861), II, 193-207, 232-34 *passim.*

families buy a barrel of flour every year. The manager endeavours to encourage this practice; and that they may spend their money for flour instead of liquor, he furnishes it to them at rather less than what it costs him at wholesale. There are many poor whites within a few miles who will always sell liquor to the negroes, and encourage them to steal, to obtain the means to buy it of them. These poor whites are always spoken of with anger by the overseers, and they each have a standing offer of much more than the intrinsic value of their land, from the manager, to induce them to move away. . . .

On reaching the nearest "quarters," we stopped at a house, a little larger than the ordinary cabins, which was called the loom-house, in which a dozen negroes were at work making shoes, and manufacturing coarse cotton stuff for negro clothing. One of the hands so employed was insane, and most of the others were cripples, invalids with chronic complaints, or unfitted by age, or some infirmity, for fieldwork. . . .

Near the first quarters we visited there was a large blacksmith's and wheelwright's shop, in which a number of mechanics were at work. Most of them, as we rode up, were eating their breakfast, which they warmed at their fires. Within and around the shop there were some fifty ploughs which they were putting in order. The manager inspected the work, found some of it faulty, sharply reprimanded the workmen for not getting on faster, and threatened one of them with a whipping for not paying closer attention to the directions which had been given him. . . .

Each overseer regulated the hours of work on his own plantation. I saw the negroes at work before sunrise and after sunset. At about eight o'clock they were allowed to stop for breakfast, and again about noon, to dine. The length of these rests was at the discretion of the overseer or drivers, usually, I should say, from half an hour to an hour. There was no rule.

The number of hands directed by each overseer was considerably over one hundred. The manager thought it would be better economy to have a white man over every fifty hands, but the difficulty of obtaining trustworthy overseers prevented it. Three of those he then had were the best he had ever known. He described the great majority as being passionate, careless, inefficient men, generally intemperate, and totally unfitted for the duties of the position. The best overseers, ordinarily, are young men, the sons of small planters, who take up the business temporarily, as a means of acquiring a little capital with which to purchase negroes for themselves.

The ploughs at work, both with single and double mule teams, were generally held by women, and very well held, too. I watched with some interest for any indication that their sex unfitted them for the occupation. Twenty of them were ploughing together, with double teams and heavy ploughs. They were superintended by a negro man who carried a whip, which he frequently cracked at them, permitting no dawdling or delay at the turning; and they twitched their ploughs around on the head-land, jerking their reins, and yelling to their mules, with apparent ease, energy, and rapidity. Throughout the Southwest the negroes, as a rule, appear to be worked much harder than in the Eastern and Northern Slave States. I do not think they accomplish as much in the same time as agricultural labourers at the North usually do, but they certainly labour much harder, and more unremittingly. They are constantly and steadily driven up to their work, and the stupid, plodding, machine-like manner in which they labour, is painful to witness. This was especially the case with the hoe-gangs. One of them numbered nearly two hundred hands (for the force of two plantations was working together), moving across the field in parallel lines, with a considerable degree of precision. I repeatedly rode through the lines at a canter, with other horsemen, often coming upon them suddenly, without producing the smallest change or interruption in the dogged action of the labourers, or causing one of them, so far as I could see, to lift an eye from the ground. I had noticed the same thing with smaller numbers before, but here, considering that I was a stranger, and that strangers could but very rarely visit the plantation, it amazed me very much. I think it told a more painful story than any I had ever heard, of the cruelty of slavery. It was emphasized by a tall and powerful negro who walked to and fro in the rear of the line, frequently cracking his whip, and calling out in the surliest manner, to one and another, "Shove your hoe, there! shove your hoe!" But I never saw him strike any one with the whip.

The whip was evidently in constant use, however. There were no rules on the subject, that I learned; the overseers and drivers punished the negroes whenever they deemed it necessary, and in such manner, and with such severity, as they thought fit. . . .

I happened to see the severest corporeal punishment of a negro that I witnessed at the South while visiting this estate. . . . The manner of the overseer who inflicted the punishment, and his subsequent conversation with me about it, indicated that it was by no means unusual in severity. I had accidentally encountered him, and he was showing me his plantation. In going from one side of it to the other, we had twice crossed a deep gully, at the bottom of which was a thick covert of brushwood. We were crossing it a third time, and had nearly passed through the brush, when the overseer suddenly stopped his horse exclaiming, "What's that? Hallo! who are you, there?"

It was a girl lying at full length on the ground at the bottom of the gully, evidently intending to hide herself from us in the bushes.

"Who are you, there?"

"Sam's Sall, sir."

"What are you skulking there for?"

The girl half rose, but gave no answer.

"Have you been here all day?"

"No, sir."

"How did you get here?"

The girl made no reply.

"Where have you been all day?"

The answer was unintelligible.

After some further questioning, she said her father accidentally locked her in, when he went out in the morning.

"How did you manage to get out?"

"Pushed a plank off, sir, and crawled out."

The overseer was silent for a moment, looking at the girl, and then said, "That won't do; come out here." The girl arose at once, and walked towards him. She was about eighteen years of age. A bunch of keys hung at her waist, which the overseer espied, and he said, "Your father locked you in; but you have got the keys." After a little hesitation, she replied that these were the keys of some other locks; her father had the door-key.

Whether her story were true or false, could have been ascertained in two minutes by riding on to the gang with which her father was at work, but the overseer had made up his mind.

"That won't do;" said he, "get down." The girl knelt on the ground; he got off his horse, and holding him with his left hand, struck her thirty or forty blows across the shoulders with his tough, flexible, "raw-hide" whip (a terrible instrument for the purpose). They were well laid on, at arm's length, but with no appearance of angry excitement on the part of the overseer. At every stroke the girl winced and exclaimed, "Yes, sir!" or "Ah, sir!" or "Please, sir!" not groaning or screaming. At length he stopped and said, "Now tell me the truth." The girl repeated the same story. "You have not got enough yet," said he; "pull up your clothes—lie down." The girl without any hesitation, without a word or look of remonstrance or entreaty, drew closely all her garments under her shoulders, and lay down upon the ground with her face toward the overseer, who continued to flog her with the raw hide, across her naked loins and thighs, with as much strength as before. She now shrunk away from him, not rising, but writhing, grovelling, and screaming, "Oh, don't sir! oh, please stop, master! please, sir! please, sir! oh, that's enough, master! oh, Lord! oh, master, master! oh, God master, do stop! oh God, master! oh, God, master!" . . .

"Was it necessary to punish her so severely?"

"Oh yes, sir," (laughing again.) "If I hadn't, she would have done the same thing again to-morrow, and half the people on the plantation would have followed her example. Oh, you've no idea how lazy these niggers are; you Northern people don't know anything about it. They'd never do any work at all if they were not afraid of being whipped." . . .

What proportion of the larger cotton plantations are resided upon by their owners, I am unable to estimate with confidence. Of those having cabin accommodations for fifty slaves each, which came under my observation from the road, while I was travelling through the rich cotton district bordering the Mississippi river, I think more than half were unprovided with a habitation which I could suppose to be the ordinary residence of a man of moderate wealth. I should judge that a large majority of all the slaves in this district, were left by their owners to the nearly unlimited government of hireling overseers the greater part of the time. Some of these plantations are owned by capitalists, who reside permanently and constantly in the North or in Europe. Many are owned by wealthy Virginians and Carolinians, who reside on the "show plantations" of those States—country seats, the exhausted soil of which will scarcely produce sufficient to feed and clothe the resident slaves, whose increase is constantly removed to colonize these richer fields of the West. . . .

The number of plantations of this class, and the proportion of those employed upon them to the whole body of negroes in the country, is, as I have said, rapidly increasing. At the present prices of cotton the large grower has such advantages over the small, that the owner of a plantation of fifty slaves, favourably situated, unless he lives very recklessly, will increase in wealth so rapidly and possess such a credit that he may very soon establish or purchase other plantations, so that at his death his children may be provided for without reducing the effective force of negroes on any division of his landed estate. The excessive credit given to such planters by negro dealers and tradesmen renders this the more practicable. The higher the price of cotton the higher is that of negroes, and the higher the price of negroes the less is it in the power of men of small capital to buy them. Large plantations of course pay a much larger per centage on the capital invested in them than smaller ones; indeed the only plausible economical defence of slavery is simply an explanation of the advantages of associated labour, advantages which are possessed equally by large manufacturing establishments in which free labourers are brought together and employed in the most effective manner, and which I can see no sufficient reason for supposing could not be made available for agriculture did not the good results flowing from small holdings, on the whole,

counterbalance them. If the present high price of cotton and the present scarcity of labour at the South continues, the cultivation of cotton on small plantations will by-and-by become unusual, for the same reason that hand-loom weaving has become unusual in the farm houses of Massachusetts.

But whatever advantages large plantations have, they accrue only to their owners and to the buyers of cotton; the mass of the white inhabitants are dispersed over a greater surface, discouraged and driven toward barbarism by them, and the blacks upon them while rapidly degenerating from all that is redeeming in savage-life, are, it is to be feared, gaining little that is valuable of civilization. . . .

127 MASTERS AND POOR WHITES: DISSENT FROM WITHIN

from Hinton Rowan Helper, *The Impending Crisis of the South,* 1857

The non-slaveholding majority in the South—the yeoman farmers, highlanders, and "poor whites"—generally identified themselves with the slavery interest and accepted the political leadership of the planter class. No Northern abolitionist tract could be so subversive of the established order as an attack on slavery from within Southern society, addressed to the grievances of the small farmer. Such an incendiary book was Hinton Rowan Helper's *The Impending Crisis* (1857). So violently was the work condemned by leaders of Southern opinion that it was dangerous to own a copy. The North Carolina author prudently removed himself to New York. In the North a fund was started to print 100,000 copies for use in the Republican campaign of 1860.

Helper (1829-1909) was a crude and intemperate writer, but he made a powerful point. By statistical comparisons of economic progress in the North and South, Helper emphasized the costs of slavery to the white farmers and mechanics of the South. In biting terms he sought to arouse "the white victims of slavery" to liberate themselves from their abject submission to the planter aristocracy and to follow their own economic interests. He openly demanded abolition, but he had no sympathy for Negroes, slave or free. In this respect Helper anticipated later Southern leaders like "Pitchfork Ben" Tillman of South Carolina, who in the name of the small farmer attacked both the rights of Negroes and the privileges of white "aristocrats." During the Reconstruction era Helper published violent anti-Negro tracts in opposition to the Radical Republican policies.

. . . And now to the point. In our opinion, an opinion which has been formed from data obtained by assiduous researches, and comparisons, from laborious investigation, logical reasoning, and earnest reflection, the causes which have impeded the progress and prosperity of the South, which have dwindled our commerce, and other similar pursuits, into the most contemptible insignificance; sunk a large majority of our people in galling poverty and ignorance, rendered a small minority conceited and tyrannical, and driven the rest away from their homes; entailed upon

Text: Hinton Rowan Helper, *The Impending Crisis of the South* (New York: A. B. Burdick, 1857), pp. 25, 42-45 *passim.*

us a humiliating dependence on the Free States; disgraced us in the recesses of our own souls, and brought us under reproach in the eyes of all civilized and enlightened nations—may all be traced to one common source, and there find solution in the most hateful and horrible word, that was ever incorporated into the vocabulary of human economy—*Slavery!*

Reared amidst the institution of slavery, believing it to be wrong both in principle and in practice, and having seen and felt its evil influences upon individuals, communities and states, we deem it a duty, no less than a privilege, to enter our protest against it, and to use our most strenuous efforts to overturn and abolish it! Then we are an abolitionist? Yes! not merely a freesoiler, but an abolitionist, in the fullest sense of the term. . . .

. . . Our soul involuntarily, but justly, we believe, cries out for retribution against the treacherous, slavedriving legislators, who have so basely and unpatriotically neglected the interests of their poor white constituents and bargained away the rights of posterity. Notwithstanding the fact that the white non-slaveholders of the South, are in the majority, as five to one, they have never yet had any part or lot in framing the laws under which they live. There is no legislation except for the benefit of slavery, and slaveholders. As a general rule, poor white persons are regarded with less esteem and attention than negroes, and though the condition of the latter is wretched beyond description, vast numbers of the former are infinitely worse off. A cunningly devised mockery of freedom is guarantied to them, and that is all. To all intents and purposes they are disfranchised, and outlawed, and the only privilege extended to them, is a shallow and circumscribed participation in the political movements that usher slaveholders into office.

We have not breathed away seven and twenty years in the South, without becoming acquainted with the demagogical manoeuverings of the oligarchy. Their intrigues and tricks of legerdemain are as familiar to us as household words; in vain might the world be ransacked for a more precious junto of flatterers and cajolers. It is amusing to ignorance, amazing to credulity, and insulting to intelligence, to hear them in their blattering efforts to mystify and pervert the sacred principles of liberty, and turn the curse of slavery into a blessing. To the illiterate poor whites—made poor and ignorant by the system of slavery—they hold out the idea that slavery is the very bulwark of our liberties, and the foundation of American independence! For hours at a time, day after day, will they expatiate upon the inexpressible beauties and excellencies of this great, *free* and *independent* nation; and finally,

with the most extravagant gesticulations and rhetorical flourishes, conclude their nonsensical ravings, by attributing all the glory and prosperity of the country, from Maine to Texas, and from Georgia to California, to the "invaluable institutions of the South!" With what patience we could command, we have frequently listened to the incoherent and truth-murdering declamations of these champions of slavery, and, in the absence of a more politic method of giving vent to our disgust and indignation, have involuntarily bit our lips into blisters.

The lords of the lash are not only absolute masters of the blacks, who are bought and sold, and driven about like so many cattle, but they are also the oracles and arbiters of all non-slaveholding whites, whose freedom is merely nominal, and whose unparalleled illiteracy and degradation is purposely and fiendishly perpetuated. How little the "poor white trash," the great majority of the Southern people, know of the real condition of the country is, indeed, sadly astonishing. The truth is, they know nothing of public measures, and little of private affairs, except what their imperious masters, the slave-drivers, condescend to tell, and that is but precious little, and even that little, always garbled and one-sided, is never told except in public harangues; for the haughty cavaliers of shackles and handcuffs will not degrade themselves by holding private converse with those who have neither dimes nor hereditary rights in human flesh. . . .

It is expected that the stupid and sequacious masses, the white victims of slavery, will believe, and, as a general thing, they do believe, whatever the slaveholders tell them; and thus it is that they are cajoled into the notion that they are the freest, happiest and most intelligent people in the world, and are taught to look with prejudice and disapprobation upon every new principle or progressive movement. Thus it is that the South, woefully inert and inventionless, has lagged behind the North, and is now weltering in the cesspool of ignorance and degradation. . . .

128 THE ETHIC OF THE MASTER RACE

from George Fitzhugh, *Cannibals All! or, Slaves Without Masters*, 1857

The rise of abolitionism in the North from the 1830's on was paralleled by a shift among Southern spokesmen from apologies for slavery on the grounds of law, history, interest, and necessity to the justification of slave society as the best order for man. Historians like Avery Craven (see Document 167) have emphasized the importance of this development in converting a manageable sectional argument over practical interests into an "irrepressible conflict" of ideals.

John C. Calhoun observed with satisfaction in 1835 that Southerners had come to recognize slavery as a positive good. The South Carolina statesman helped to strengthen that conviction with his argument that liberty is a reward to be earned by superior men and not "a boon to be bestowed on a people too ignorant, degraded, and vicious to be capable either of appreciating or of enjoying it." The most comprehensive and aggressive pro-slavery arguments came in the 1850's from a variety of lawyers, journalists, politicians, professors, and ministers. Not the most influential of Southern writers, George Fitzhugh (1806-1881) of Virginia was in many respects the boldest and most challenging advocate of slavery as a principle and as a way of life. His words were taken seriously in the North as a revelation of the South's ultimate designs.

Fitzhugh grew up in the aristocratic society of Alexandria, Virginia, and later practiced law in Port Royal. He contributed pro-slavery articles to *DeBow's Review* and other journals and published his major statements in two books: *Sociology for the South; or the Failure of Free Society* (1854) and *Cannibals All! or, Slaves Without Masters* (1857). Granting the contradiction between slavery and Jefferson's Declaration of Independence, Fitzhugh decisively rejected the fundamental doctrines of free society as (in a borrowed phrase) "exuberantly false, and arborescently fallacious." He challenged Americans to explain why the principle of *equal rights* applied to *unequal men* would not lead to the exploitation of the weak by the strong. Slavery, as Fitzhugh conceived it, was a system of social cooperation in which superior men assumed responsibility for governing their inferiors. The chattel slavery of the South was required by the childlike qualities of the Negro. But some lesser degree of "slavery"— of the rule of inferiors by superiors—must be found for all civilized societies.

The following selection from *Cannibals All!* represents Fitzhugh's provocative attack on Northern society as a system using liberty as a sham excuse for reducing the white workers to "slaves without masters."

We are, all, North and South, engaged in the White Slave Trade, and he who succeeds best, is esteemed most respectable. It is far more cruel than the Black Slave Trade, because it exacts more of its slaves, and neither protects nor governs them. We boast, that it exacts more, when we say, "that the *profits* made from employing free labor are greater than those from slave labor." The profits, made from free labor, are the amount of the products of such labor, which the employer, by means of the command which capital or skill gives him, takes away, exacts or "exploitates" from the free laborer. The profits of slave labor are that portion of the products of such labor which the power of the master enables him to appropriate. These profits are less, because the master allows the slave to retain a larger share of the results of his own labor, than do the employers of free labor. But we not only boast that the White Slave Trade is more exacting and fraudulent (in fact, though not in intention,) than Black Slavery; but we also boast, that it is more cruel, in leaving the laborer to take care of himself and family out of the pittance which skill or capital have allowed him to retain. When the day's labor is ended, he is free, but is overburdened with the cares of family and household, which make his freedom

Text: George Fitzhugh, *Cannibals All! or, Slaves Without Masters* (Richmond, Va.: A. Morris, 1857), pp. 25-32 *passim.*

an empty and delusive mockery. But his employer is really free, and may enjoy the profits made by others' labor, without a care, or a trouble, as to their well-being. The negro slave is free, too, when the labors of the day are over, and free in mind as well as body; for the master provides food, raiment, house, fuel, and everything else necessary to the physical well-being of himself and family. The master's labors commence just when the slave's end. No wonder men should prefer white slavery to capital, to negro slavery, since it is more profitable, and is free from all the cares and labors of black slave-holding.

Now, reader, if you wish to know yourself —to "descant on your own deformity"—read on. But if you would cherish self-conceit, self-esteem, or self-appreciation, throw down our book; for we will dispel illusions which have promoted your happiness, and shew you that what you have considered and practiced as virtue, is little better than moral Cannibalism. But you will find yourself in numerous and respectable company; for all good and respectable people are "Cannibals all," who do not labor, or who are successfully trying to live without labor, on the unrequited labor of other people:—Whilst low, bad, and disreputable people, are those who labor to support themselves, and to support said respectable people besides. Throwing the negro slaves out of the account, and society is divided in Christendom into four classes: The rich, or independent respectable people, who live well and labor not at all; the professional and skillful respectable people, who do a little light work, for enormous wages; the poor hard-working people, who support every body, and starve themselves; and the poor thieves, swindlers and sturdy beggars, who live like gentlemen, without labor, on the labor of other people. The gentlemen exploitate, which being done on a large scale, and requiring a great many victims, is highly respectable—whilst the rogues and beggars take so little from others, that they fare little better than those who labor.

But, reader, we do not wish to fire into the flock. "Thou art the man!" You are a Cannibal! and if a successful one, pride yourself on the number of your victims, quite as much as any Feejee chieftain, who breakfasts, dines and sups on human flesh.—And your conscience smites you, if you have failed to succeed, quite as much as his, when he returns from an unsuccessful foray.

Probably, you are a lawyer, or a merchant, or a doctor, who have made by your business fifty thousand dollars, and retired to live on your capital. But, mark! not to spend your capital. That would be vulgar, disreputable, criminal. That would be, to live by your own labor; for your capital is your amassed labor. That would be, to do as common working men do; for they take the pittance which their employers leave them, to live on. They live by labor; for they exchange the results of their own labor for the products of other people's labor. It is, no doubt, an honest, vulgar way of living; but not at all a respectable way. The respectable way of living is, to make other people work for you, and to pay them nothing for so doing—and to have no concern about them after their work is done. Hence, white slave-holding is much more respectable than negro slavery—for the master works nearly as hard for the negro, as he for the master. But you, my virtuous, respectable reader, exact three thousand dollars per annum from white labor, (for your income is the product of white labor,) and make not one cent of return in any form. You retain your capital, and never labor, and yet live in luxury on the labor of others. Capital commands labor, as the master does the slave. Neither pays for labor; but the master permits the slave to retain a larger allowance from the proceeds of his own labor, and hence "free labor is cheaper than slave labor." You, with the command over labor which your capital gives you, are a slave owner—a master, without the obligations of a master. They who work for you, who create your income, are slaves, without the rights of slaves. Slaves without a master! Whilst you were engaged in amassing your cap-

ital, in seeking to become independent, you were in the White Slave Trade. To become independent, is to be able to make other people support you, without being obliged to labor for *them*. Now, what man in society is not seeking to attain this situation? He who attains it, is a slave owner, in the worst sense. He who is in pursuit of it, is engaged in the slave trade. You, reader, belong to the one or other class. The men without property, in free society, are theoretically in a worse condition than slaves. Practically, their condition corresponds with this theory, as history and statistics every where demonstrate. The capitalists, in free society, live in ten times the luxury and show that Southern masters do, because the slaves to capital work harder and cost less, than negro slaves.

The negro slaves of the South are the happiest, and, in some sense, the freest people in the world. The children and the aged and infirm work not at all, and yet have all the comforts and necessaries of life provided for them. They enjoy liberty, because they are oppressed neither by care nor labor. The women do little hard work, and are protected from the despotism of their husbands by their masters. The negro men and stout boys work, on the average, in good weather, not more than nine hours a day. The balance of their time is spent in perfect abandon. Besides, they have their Sabbaths and holidays. White men, with so much of license and liberty, would die of ennui; but negroes luxuriate in corporeal and mental repose. With their faces upturned to the sun, they can sleep at any hour; and quiet sleep is the greatest of human enjoyments. "Blessed be the man who invented sleep." 'Tis happiness in itself—and results from contentment with the present, and confident assurance of the future. We do not know whether free laborers ever sleep. They are fools to do so; for, whilst they sleep, the wily and watchful capitalist is devising means to ensnare and exploitate them. The free laborer must work or starve. He is more of a slave than the negro, because he works longer and harder for less allowance than the slave, and has no holiday, because the cares of life with him begin when its labors end. He has no liberty, and not a single right. . . .

Free laborers have not a thousandth part of the rights and liberties of negro slaves. Indeed, they have not a single right or a single liberty, unless it be the right or liberty to die. But the reader may think that he and other capitalists and employers are freer than negro slaves. Your capital would soon vanish, if you dared indulge in the liberty and abandon of negroes. You hold your wealth and position by the tenure of constant watchfulness, care and circumspection. You never labor; but you are never free.

Where a few own the soil, they have unlimited power over the balance of society, until domestic slavery comes in, to compel them to permit this balance of society to draw a sufficient and comfortable living from "terra mater." Free society, asserts the right of a few to the earth—slavery, maintains that it belongs, in different degrees, to all.

But, reader, well may you follow the slave trade. It is the only trade worth following, and slaves the only property worth owning. All other is worthless, a mere *caput mortuum,* except in so far as it vests the owner with the power to command the labors of others—to enslave them. Give you a palace, ten thousand acres of land, sumptuous clothes, equipage and every other luxury; and with your artificial wants, you are poorer than Robinson Crusoe, or the lowest working man, if you have no slaves to capital, or domestic slaves. Your capital will not bring you an income of a cent, nor supply one of your wants, without labor. Labor is indispensable to give value to property, and if you owned every thing else, and did not own labor, you would be poor. But fifty thousand dollars means, and is, fifty thousand dollars worth of slaves. You can command, without touching on that capital, three thousand dollars' worth of labor per annum. You could do no more were you to buy slaves with it, and then you would be cumbered with the cares of governing and providing for them. You are a slaveholder now, to the amount of fifty thousand dollars, with all the advantages, and none of the cares and responsibilities of a master.

"Property in man" is what all are struggling to obtain. Why should they not be obliged to take care of man, their property, as they do of their horses and their hounds, their cattle and their sheep. Now, under the delusive name of liberty, you work him, "from morn to dewy eve"—from infancy to old age—then turn him out to starve. You treat your horses and hounds better. Capital is a cruel master. The free slave trade, the commonest, yet the cruellest of trades.

129

NARRATIVE OF ELLEN BETTS, AN EX-SLAVE

from B. A. Botkin, *Lay My Burden Down,* 1945

The truth about the condition of the bondsman is most difficult to come by. At one extreme is Fitzhugh's picture of the contented slave enjoying all the advantages that his simple nature can require—a situation far more comfortable and secure than that of the free "white slave" of the North. (See Document 128.) At the opposite limit are the pathetic images in *Uncle Tom's Cabin.* (See Document 162.) The difficulty in reaching an accurate understanding is *partially* one of fact. The contrasting situations of, say, the one- or two-slave farming operation in the back country of the Upper South and the massive enterprise of a Louisiana sugar plantation make simple generalizations doubtful. Moreover, the diverse attitudes and temperaments among slaveholders in a relationship that was controlled essentially by the master's will meant that the treatment of the slave would vary from case to case. Finally, one indispensable witness has remained largely silent: the slave himself.

Beyond such problems of evidence concerning the lot of the bondsman lie still more challenging issues of principle and interpretation. *If* the African slave was destined by racial inheritance to be no more than an irresponsible hewer of wood and drawer of water, then a social system that gave him an assured place and a useful task, kept his belly full and his bones warm, offered him some simple pleasures, and broadly regulated his life under the authority of his natural superiors might be approved as necessary and even praiseworthy. An older school of Southern historians has judged the evidence largely from this point of view, reserving criticism of the master-slave relationship for the undoubted excesses of the system: instances of brutality, of slave-breeding for the market, of callous family separations, and the like.

If, on the contrary, the slave was but a man with a dark skin, potentially capable of sharing in a free life, then the whole system was radically unjust. So long as the slave remained a piece of movable property subject to the will of his master, no amount of care and kindness could balance the crime of reducing the Negro to a permanent state of helpless dependence. Historians of this conviction not only give greater emphasis to the cruelties of slavery but insist that such excesses were made inevitable by the very nature of the system. These writers further distinguish between humane treatment with respect to bodily needs and pleasures and the general determination of the planters (in the pre-Civil War decades) to withhold the means by which a slave might elevate himself, the prevalent refusal to educate the Negro or to offer him a chance to accumulate property with which he might purchase his freedom.

The reader can imagine how the contending schools might quarrel over the following narrative of Ellen Betts, a former slave on a large Louisiana sugar plantation. How does one judge a human relationship that was warm and kindly yet one that empowered the master to determine all the important conditions of a slave's life? How representative were the considerate and protective "Marse William" and the affectionately grateful Ellen? (Compare the observations of slavery by Frederick Law Olmsted in Document 126.) Further recollections of bondage may be found in the record of oral interviews with former slaves, *Lay My Burden Down; A Folk History of Slavery*, edited by the distinguished folklorist B. A. Botkin. A rather different impression of the bondsman's lot is given in the few reminiscences published by fugitive slaves, the exceptional men and women who risked their lives to gain the dignity of freedom. A notable example of such writing is Frederick Douglass' *Life and Times* (1881). Even the mildest forms of bondage were unbearably oppressive to this promising young slave, who had discovered pride, ambition, and a little learning.

I got borned on the Bayou Teche, clost to Opelousas. That in St. Mary's Parish, in Louisiana, and I belonged to Tolas Parsons, what had 'bout five hundred slaves, counting the big ones and the little ones, and he had God know what else. When my eyes just barely fresh open, Marse Tolas die and will the whole lot of us to he brother, William Tolas Parsons. And I tells you that Marse William am the greatest man what ever walk this earth. That's the truth. I can't lie on him when the poor man's in he grave.

When a whupping got to be done, Old Marse do it heself. He don't 'low no overseer to throw he gals down and pull up their dress and whup on their bottoms like I hear tell some of 'em do. Was he still living I 'spect one part of he hands be with him today. I knows I would.

When us niggers go down the road, folks say, "Them's Parsons' niggers. Don't hit one them niggers for God's sake, or Parsons sure eat your jacket up."

Aunt Rachel what cook in the big house for Miss Cornelia had four younguns and them children fat and slick as I ever seen. All the niggers have to stoop to Aunt Rachel just like they curtsy to Missy. I mind the time her husband, Uncle Jim, git mad and hit her over the head with the poker. A big knot raise up on Aunt Rachel's head, and when Marse 'quire 'bout it, she say she done bump the head. She dasn't tell on Uncle Jim or Marse sure beat him. Marse sure proud them black, slick children of Rachel's. You couldn't find a yaller child on he place. He sure got no use for mixing black and white.

Marse William have the prettiest place up and down that bayou, with the fine house and fine trees and such. From where we live it's five

mile to Centerville one way and five mile to Patterson t'other. They hauls the lumber from one place or t'other to make wood houses for the slaves. Sometime Marse buy the furniture, and sometime the carpenter make it.

Miss Sidney was Marse's first wife, and he had six boys by her. Then he marry the widow Cornelia, and she give him four boys. With ten children springing up quick like that and all the colored children coming 'long fast as pig litters, I don't do nothing all my days, but nurse, nurse, nurse. I nurse so many children it done went and stunted my growth, and that's why I ain't nothing but bones to this day.

When the colored women has to cut cane all day till midnight come and after, I has to nurse the babies for them and tend the white children, too. Some them babies so fat and big I had to tote the feet while 'nother gal tote the head. I was such a little one, 'bout seven or eight year old. The big folks leave some toddy for colic and crying and such, and I done drink the toddy and let the children have the milk. I don't know no better. Lawsy me, it a wonder I ain't the biggest drunker in this here country, counting all the toddy I done put in my young belly!

When late of night come, iffen them babies wake up and bawl, I set up a screech and outscreech them till they shut their mouth. The louder they bawl, the louder I bawl. Sometime when Marse hear the babies cry, he come down and say, "Why the children cry like that, Ellen?" I say, "Marse, I git so hongry and tired I done drink the milk up." When I talk sassy like that, Marse just shake he finger at me, 'cause he

Text: B. A. Botkin, *Lay My Burden Down; A Folk History of Slavery* (Chicago: University of Chicago Press, 1945), pp. 125-29 *passim*.

knowed I's a good one and don't let no little mite starve. . . .

I wanted to git the papers for midwifing but, Law, I don't never have no time for larning in slave time. If Marse cotch a paper in you hand he sure whup you. He don't 'low no bright niggers round, he sell 'em quick. He always say, "Book larning don't raise no good sugar cane." The only larning he 'low was when they larn the colored children the Methodist catechism. The only writing a nigger ever git am when he git born or marry or die, then Marse put the name in the big book.

Law, I 'lect the time Marse marry Miss Cornelia. He went on the mail boat and brung her from New Orleans. She the prettiest woman in the world almost, 'cepting she have the biggest mouth I nearly ever seed. He brung her up to the house, and all the niggers and boys and girls and cats and dogs and such come and salute her. There she stand on the gallery, with a pretty white dress on with red stripes running up and down. Marse say to her, "Honey, see all the black folks, they 'longs to you now." She wave to us and smile on us, and next day she give her wedding dress to my ma. That the finest dress I ever seen. It was purple and green silk and all the nigger gals wear that dress when they git marry. My sister Sidney wore it and Sary and Mary.

Miss Cornelia was the finest woman in the world. Come Sunday morning she done put a bucket of dimes on the front gallery and stand there and throw dimes to the nigger children just like feeding chickens. I sure right here to testify, 'cause I's right there helping grab. Sometime she done put the washtub of buttermilk on the back gallery, and us children bring us gourds and dip up that good old buttermilk till it all git drunk up. Sometime she fotch bread and butter to the back gallery and pass it out when it don't even come mealtime. . . .

Lawsy me, I seen thousands and thousands sugar barrels and kettles of syrup in my day. Lord knows how much cane Old Marse have. To them cutting the cane it don't seem so much, but to them what work hour in, hour out, them sugar cane fields sure stretch from one end the earth to the other. Marse ship hogs and hogs of sugar down the bayou. I seen the river boats go down with big signs what say, "Buy this here 'lasses" on the side. And he raise a world of rice and 'taters and corn and peanuts, too.

When the work slight, us black folks sure have the balls and dinners and such. We git all day to barbecue meat down on the bayou, and the white folks come done and eat 'longside the colored.

When a black gal marry, Marse marry her hisself in the big house. He marry 'em Saturday, so they git Sunday off, too. One time the river boat come bearing the license for niggers to git marry with. Marse chase 'em off and say, "Don't you come trucking no no-'count papers round my niggers. When I marry 'em, they marry as good as if the Lord God hisself marry 'em and it don't take no paper to bind the tie." Marse don't stand no messing round, neither. A gal have to be of age and ask her pa and ma and Marse and Missy, and if they 'gree, they go ahead and git marry. Marse have the marry book to put the name down. . . .

. . . When me and my husband, John, come to Texas the folks say that Louisiana masters the meanest in the world, and I say right back at 'em that they is good and mean in every spot of the earth. . . .

North, South, West: The Bounds of Compromise

130 UNION IN BALANCE: SECTIONAL LOGIC

from John C. Calhoun, Speech in the U. S. Senate, March 4, 1850

As early as 1820, in the Missouri crisis, sectional passions were aroused by the question of extending slavery into the national territories and of altering the balance of free and slave states. (See Document 85.) The annexation of Texas (1845), the war with Mexico (1846-1848), and the acquisition of the New Mexico and California country (1848) reopened the dangerous controversy.

But the new conflict was far more ominous than the old. In thirty years the sections had grown apart to a point where men could see two antagonistic societies, opposed in their interests, their principles, and their ways of life. Increasingly, Northerners viewed the South as a barbarous, backward country obsessed with the idea of spreading its "peculiar institution" over the West and perhaps in time into the free states. Increasingly, Southerners viewed themselves as an oppressed minority defending their superior civilization against the teeming, polyglot, avaricious North.

When Representative David Wilmot introduced his "Proviso" banning slavery from all territory taken from Mexico (August 1846), the sectional debate flared up menacingly. The hedging tactics of the major parties (Whigs and Democrats) in the 1848 election campaign led to the formation of the new Free Soil party, whose candidate—the Jacksonian, Martin Van Buren—drew about 10 per cent of the popular vote from among the political abolitionists and the antislavery elements in the old parties ("Barnburner" Democrats and "Conscience" Whigs). Following the election of the Whig general, Zachary Taylor, California and New Mexico applied for admission to the Union under antislavery constitutions. The threatening language of secession could now be heard in the angry Congressional debate.

Henry Clay, the "Great Pacificator" of Kentucky, and Stephen A. Douglas, the "Little Giant" of Illinois, sponsored a package deal containing the elements of the eventual "Compromise of 1850." California (which had suddenly gained 100,000 inhabitants with the gold rush of the Forty-Niners) would be admitted as a free state. The territories of Utah and New Mexico would be organized without any federal restriction on slavery. Texas would be compensated for abandoning its claim to the lands between the present western boundary of the state and the line of the Rio Grande. The slave trade, but not slavery, would be abolished in the District of Columbia. And more rigorous federal rules would govern the return of fugitive slaves.

Behind the compromise stood the two Whig ancients, Clay and Webster, and a substantial contingent of moderate Democrats, following the lead of Douglas. In grim opposition were the Southern "fire-eaters"—Calhoun, Jefferson Davis, and their supporters—and unyielding Northern antislavery Whigs like William H. Seward of New York and Charles Sumner of Massachusetts. On March 4, 1850, the gravely ill Calhoun (then within a month of his death) listened from his Senate seat while an associate read his powerful denunciation of the Compromise. Although Calhoun has the reputation (with some reason) for being a doctrinaire, a legalist and logic-chopper, his appeal for union on Southern terms as the sole alternative to secession contains a trenchant analysis of social and political realities: of the Southern decline to a permanent minority status in the Union and of the gradual unraveling of the many spiritual, political, and social "cords that bind the States together." For the political theory underlying Calhoun's speech, consult his important essay "A Disquisition on Government," reprinted in most editions of his writings.

Mr. Calhoun. I have, Senators, believed from the first that the agitation of the subject of slavery would, if not prevented by some timely and effective measure, end in disunion. Entertaining this opinion, I have, on all proper occasions, endeavored to call the attention of each of the two great parties which divide the country to adopt some measure to prevent so great a disaster, but without success. The agitation has been permitted to proceed, with almost no attempt to resist it, until it has reached a period when it can no longer be disguised or denied that the Union is in danger. You have thus had forced upon you the greatest and the gravest question that can ever come under your consideration: How can the Union be preserved?

To give a satisfactory answer to this mighty question, it is indispensable to have an accurate and thorough knowledge of the nature and the character of the cause by which the Union is endangered. Without such knowledge it is impossible to pronounce, with any certainty, by what measure it can be saved; just as it would be impossible for a physician to pronounce, in the case of some dangerous disease, with any certainty by what remedy the patient could be saved, without familiar knowledge of the nature and character of the cause of the disease. The first question, then, presented for consideration, in the investigation I propose to make, in order to obtain such knowledge, is: What is it that has endangered the Union?

To this question there can be but one answer: that the immediate cause is the almost universal discontent which pervades all the States composing the southern section of the Union. This widely-extended discontent is not of recent origin. It

Text: The Congressional Globe, 31st Congress, 1st Session, XXI (Part 1), 451-55 passim.

commenced with the agitation of the slavery question, and has been increasing ever since. The next question, going one step further back, is: What has caused this widely-diffused and almost universal discontent?

It is a great mistake to suppose, as is by some, that it originated with demagogues, who excited the discontent with the intention of aiding their personal advancement, or with the disappointed ambition of certain politicians, who resorted to it as the means of retrieving their fortunes. On the contrary, all the great political influences of the section were arrayed against excitement, and exerted to the utmost to keep the people quiet. The great mass of the people of the South were divided, as in the other section, into Whigs and Democrats. The leaders and the presses of both parties in the South were very solicitous to prevent excitement and to preserve quiet; because it was seen that the effects of the former would necessarily tend to weaken, if not destroy, the political ties which united them with their respective parties in the other section. Those who know the strength of party ties will readily appreciate the immense force which this cause exerted against agitation and in favor of preserving quiet. But, as great as it was, it was not sufficiently so to prevent the wide-spread discontent which now pervades the section. No; some cause, far deeper and more powerful than the one supposed, must exist, to account for discontent so wide and deep. The question, then, recurs: What is the cause of this discontent? It will be found in the belief of the people of the southern States, as prevalent as the discontent itself, that they cannot remain, as things now are, consistently with honor and safety, in the Union. The next question to be considered is: What has caused this belief?

One of the causes is, undoubtedly, to be traced to the long-continued agitation of the slave question on the part of the North, and the many aggressions which they have made on the rights of the South during the time. I will not enumerate them at present, as it will be done hereafter, in its proper place.

There is another, lying back of it, with which this is intimately connected, that may be regarded as the great and primary cause. That is to be found in the fact that the equilibrium between the two sections in the Government, as it stood when the constitution was ratified and the Government put in action, has been destroyed. At that time there was nearly a perfect equilibrium between the two, which afforded ample means to each to protect itself against the aggression of the other; but, as it now stands, one section

has the exclusive power of controlling the Government, which leaves the other without any adequate means of protecting itself against its encroachment and oppression. . . .

But we are just at the close of the sixth decade, and the commencement of the seventh. The census is to be taken this year, which must add greatly to the decided preponderance of the North in the House of Representatives and in the electoral college. The prospect is, also, that a great increase will be added to its present preponderance in the Senate during the period of the decade, by the addition of new States. Two Territories, Oregon and Minnesota, are already in progress, and strenuous efforts are making to bring in three additional States from the territory recently conquered from Mexico; which, if successful, will add three other States in a short time to the northern section, making five States; and increasing the present number of its States from fifteen to twenty, and of its Senators from thirty to forty. On the contrary, there is not a single territory in progress in the southern section, and no certainty that any additional State will be added to it during the decade. The prospect then, is, that the two sections in the Senate, should the efforts now made to exclude the South from the newly-acquired territories succeed, will stand, before the end of the decade, twenty northern States to twelve southern, (considering Delaware as neutral,) and forty northern Senators to twenty-four southern. This great increase of Senators, added to the great increase of members of the House of Representatives and the electoral college on the part of the North, which must take place under the next decade, will effectually and irretrievably destroy the equilibrium which existed when the Government commenced.

Had this destruction been the operation of time, without the interference of Government, the South would have had no reason to complain; but such was not the fact. It was caused by the legislation of this Government, which was appointed as the common agent of all, and charged with the protection of the interests and security of all. The legislation by which it has been effected may be classed under three heads. The first is, that series of acts by which the South has been excluded from the common territory belonging to all of the States, as the members of the Federal Union, and which have had the effect of extending vastly the portion allotted to the Northern section, and restricting within narrow limits the portion left the South; the next consists in adopting a system of revenue and disbursements, by which an undue proportion of the burden of taxation has been imposed upon the South, and an undue proportion of its proceeds appropriated to the North; and the last is a system of political measures by which the original character of the Government has been radically changed. . . .

That the [Federal] Government claims, and practically maintains, the right to decide in the last resort as to the extent of its powers, will scarcely be denied by any one conversant with the political history of the country. That it also claims the right to resort to force to maintain whatever power she claims, against all opposition, is equally certain. Indeed it is apparent, from what we daily hear, that this has become the prevailing and fixed opinion of a great majority of the community. Now, I ask, what limitation can possibly be placed upon the powers of a Government claiming and exercising such rights? And, if none can be, how can the separate governments of the States maintain and protect the powers reserved to them by the Constitution, or the people of the several States maintain those which are reserved to them, and among others, the sovereign powers by which they ordained and established, not only their separate State constitutions and governments, but also the Constitution and Government of the United States? But, if they have no constitutional means of maintaining them against the right claimed by this Government, it necessarily follows that they hold them at its pleasure and discretion, and that all the powers of the system are in reality concentrated in it. It also follows that the character of the Government has been changed, in consequence, from a Federal Republic, as it originally came from the hands of its framers, and that it has been changed into a great national consolidated democracy. It has indeed, at present, all the characteristics of the latter, and not one of the former, although it still retains its outward form.

The result of the whole of these causes combined is, that the North has acquired a decided ascendancy over every department of this Government, and through it a control over all the powers of the system. A single section, governed by the will of the numerical majority, has now, in fact, the control of the Government and the entire powers of the system. What was once a constitutional Federal Republic is now converted, in reality, into one as absolute as that of the Autocrat of Russia, and as despotic in its tendency as any absolute Government that ever existed.

As, then, the North has the absolute control over the Government, it is manifest that on all questions between it and the South, where there is a diversity of interests, the interests of the latter will be sacrificed to the former, however oppressive the effects may be, as the South possesses no means by which it can resist through the action of the Government. But if there was no question of vital importance to the South, in reference to which there was a diversity of views between the two sections, this state of things might be endured without the hazard of destruction to the South. But such is not the fact. There is a question of vital importance to the southern section, in reference to which the views and feelings of the two sections are as opposite and hostile as they can possibly be.

I refer to the relation between the two races in the southern section, which constitutes a vital portion of her social organization. Every portion of the North entertains views and feelings more or less hostile to it. Those most opposed and hostile regard it as a sin, and consider themselves under the most sacred obligation to use every effort to destroy it. Indeed to the extent that they conceive they have power, they regard themselves as implicated in the sin, and responsible for suppressing it by the use of all and every means. Those less opposed and hostile, regard it as a crime—an offence against humanity, as they call it; and although not so fanatical, feel themselves bound to use all efforts to effect the same object; while those who are least opposed and hostile, regard it as a blot and a stain on the character of what they call the nation, and feel themselves accordingly bound to give it no countenance or support. On the contrary, the southern section, regards the relation as one which cannot be destroyed without subjecting the two races to the greatest calamity, and the section to poverty, desolation, and wretchedness; and accordingly they feel bound by every consideration of interest and safety, to defend it.

This hostile feeling on the part of the North towards the social organization of the South long lay dormant, but it only required some cause to act on those who felt most intensely that they were responsible for its continuance, to call it into action. The increasing power of this Government, and of the control of the northern section over all its departments, furnished the cause. It was this which made an impression on the minds of many that there was little or no restraint to prevent the Government from doing whatever it might choose to do. This was sufficient of itself to put the most fanatical portion of the North in action for the purpose of destroying the existing relation between the two races in the South. . . .

What has since followed are but the natural consequences. With the success of their first movement, this small fanatical party began to acquire strength; and with that to become an object of courtship to both the great parties. The necessary consequence was a further increase of power, and a gradual tainting of the opinions of both of the other parties with their doctrines until the infection has extended over both; and the great mass of the population of the North who, whatever may be their opinion of the original abolition party, which still preserves its distinctive organization, hardly ever fail, when it comes to acting, to cooperate in carrying out their measures. With the increase of their influence, they extended the sphere of their action. . . .

Such is a brief history of the agitation, as far as it has yet advanced. Now, I ask Senators, what is there to prevent its further progress, until it fulfills the ultimate end proposed, unless some decisive measure should be adopted to prevent it? Has any one of the causes, which has added to its increase from its original small and contemptible beginning until it has attained its present magnitude, diminished in force? Is the original cause of the movement, that slavery is a sin, and ought to be suppressed, weaker now than at the commencement? Or is the Abolition party less numerous or influential, or have they less influence over, or control over the two great parties of the North in elections? Or has the South greater means of influencing or controlling the movements of this Government now than it had when the agitation commenced? To all these questions but one answer can be given: no, no, no! The very reverse is true. Instead of being weaker, all the elements in favor of agitation are stronger now than they were in 1835, when it first commenced, while all the elements of influence on the part of the South are weaker. Unless something decisive is done, I again ask what is to stop this agitation, before the great and final object at which it aims—the abolition of slavery in the States—is consummated? Is it, then, not certain that if something decisive is not now done to arrest it, the South will be forced to choose between abolition and secession? Indeed, as events are now moving, it will not require the South to secede to dissolve the Union. Agitation will of itself effect it, of which its past history furnishes abundant proof, as I shall next proceed to show.

It is a great mistake to suppose that disunion can be effected by a single blow. The cords which bind these States together in one common Union are far too numerous and powerful for that. Disunion must be the work of time. It is only through a long process, and successively,

that the cords can be snapped, until the whole fabric falls asunder. Already the agitation of the slavery question has snapped some of the most important, and has greatly weakened all the others, as I shall proceed to show.

The cords that bind the States together are not only many, but various in character. Some are spiritual or ecclesiastical; some political; others social. Some appertain to the benefit conferred by the Union, and others to the feeling of duty and obligation.

The strongest of those of a spiritual and ecclesiastical nature consisted in the unity of the great religious denominations, all of which originally embraced the whole Union. All these denominations, with the exception, perhaps, of the Catholics, were organized very much upon the principle of our political institutions; beginning with smaller meetings corresponding with the political divisions of the country, their organization terminated in one great central assemblage, corresponding very much with the character of Congress. At these meetings the principal clergymen and lay members of the respective denominations from all parts of the Union met to transact business relating to their common concerns. It was not confined to what appertained to the doctrines and discipline of the respective denominations, but extended to plans for disseminating the Bible, establishing missionaries, distributing tracts, and of establishing presses for the publication of tracts, newspapers, and periodicals, with a view of diffusing religious information, and for the support of the doctrines and creeds of the denomination. All this combined, contributed greatly to strengthen the bonds of the Union. The strong ties which held each denomination together formed a strong cord to hold the whole Union together; but, as powerful as they were, they have not been able to resist the explosive effect of slavery agitation. . . .

The strongest cord of a political character consists of the many and strong ties that have held together the two great parties, which have, with some modifications, existed from the beginning of the Government. They both extended to every portion of the Union, and strongly contributed to hold all its parts together. But this powerful cord has fared no better than the spiritual. It resisted for a long time the explosive tendency of the agitation, but has finally snapped under its force—if not entirely, in a great measure. Nor is there one of the remaining cords which have not been greatly weakened. To this extent the Union has already been destroyed by agitation, in the only way it can be, by snapping asunder and weakening the cords which bind it together.

If the agitation goes on, the same force, acting with increased intensity, as has been shown, will finally snap every cord, when nothing will be left to hold the States together except force. But surely that can, with no propriety of language, be called a union, when the only means by which the weaker is held connected with the stronger portion is force. It may, indeed, keep them connected; but the connection will partake much more of the character of subjugation, on the part of the weaker to the stronger, than the union of free, independent, and sovereign States, in one confederation, as they stood in the early stages of the Government, and which only is worthy of the sacred name of union.

Having now, Senators, explained what it is that endangers the Union, and traced it to its cause, and explained its nature and character, the question again recurs, How can the Union be saved? To this I answer, there is but one way by which it can be, and that is, by adopting such measures as will satisfy the States belonging to the southern section that they can remain in the Union consistently with their honor and their safety. There is, again, only one way by which that can be effected, and that is, by removing the causes by which this belief has been produced. Do that, and discontent will cease, harmony and kind feelings between the sections be restored, and every apprehension of danger to the Union removed. The question is, By what can this be done? . . .

The plan of the Administration cannot save the Union, because it can have no effect whatever towards satisfying the States composing the southern section of the Union that they can, consistently with safety and honor, remain in the Union. It is, in fact, but a modification of the Wilmot proviso. It proposes to effect the same object, to exclude the South from all territory acquired by the Mexican treaty. . . .

Having now shown what cannot save the Union, I return to the question with which I commenced, How can the Union be saved? There is but one way by which it can with any certainty; and that is, by a full and final settlement, on the principle of justice, of all the questions at issue between the two sections. The South asks for justice, simple justice, and less she ought not to take. She has no compromise to offer but the Constitution, and no concession or surrender to make. She has already surrendered so much that she has little left to surrender. Such a settlement would go to the root of the evil, and remove all cause of discontent, by satisfying the South she could remain honorably and safely in the Union, and thereby restore the harmony and fraternal feelings between the sections which existed anterior to the Missouri agitation. Nothing else can, with any certainty, finally and forever settle the questions at issue, terminate agitation, and save the Union.

But can this be done? Yes, easily; not by the weaker party, for it can of itself do nothing—not even protect itself—but by the stronger. The North has only to will it to accomplish it—to do justice by conceding to the South an equal right in the acquired territory, and to do her duty by causing the stipulations relative to fugitive slaves to be faithfully fulfilled—to cease the agitation of the slave question, and to provide for the insertion of a provision in the Constitution, by an amendment, which will restore to the South in substance the power she possessed of protecting herself, before the equilibrium between the sections was destroyed by the action of this Government. There will be no difficulty in devising such a provision—one that will protect the South, and which at the same time will improve and strengthen the Government, instead of impairing and weakening it.

But will the North agree to do this? It is for her to answer this question. But, I will say, she cannot refuse, if she has half the love of the Union which she professes to have, or without justly exposing herself to the charge that her love of power and aggrandizement is far greater than her love of the Union. At all events, the responsibility of saving the Union rests on the North, and not the South. The South cannot save it by any act of hers, and the North may save it without any sacrifice whatever, unless to do justice, and to perform her duties under the Constitution should be regarded by her as a sacrifice.

It is time, Senators, that there should be an open and manly avowal on all sides, as to what is intended to be done. If the question is not now settled, it is uncertain whether it ever can hereafter be; and we, as the representatives of the States of this Union, regarded as governments, should come to a distinct understanding as to our respective views, in order to ascertain whether the great questions at issue can be settled or not. If you, who represent the stronger portion, cannot agree to settle them on the broad principle of justice and duty, say so, and let the States we both represent agree to separate and part in peace. If you are unwilling we should part in peace, tell us so, and we shall know what to do, when you reduce the question to submission or resistance. If you remain silent, you will compel us to infer by your acts what you intend. In that case, California will become the test question. If you admit her, under all the difficulties that oppose her admission, you compel us to infer that you intend to exclude us from the whole of the acquired territories, with the intention of destroying irretrievably the equilibrium between the two sections. We would be blind not to perceive, in that case, that your real objects are power and aggrandizement, and infatuated not to act accordingly.

I have now, Senators, done my duty in expressing my opinions fully, freely, and candidly, on this solemn occasion. In doing so, I have been governed by the motives which have governed me in all the stages of the agitation of the slavery question since its commencement. I have exerted myself, during the whole period, to arrest it, with the intention of saving the Union, if it could be done; and, if it could not, to save the section where it has pleased Providence to cast my lot, and which I sincerely believe has justice and the Constitution on its side. Having faithfully done my duty to the best of my ability, both to the Union and my section, throughout this agitation, I shall have the consolation, let what will come, that I am free from all responsibility.

131 UNION BY CONCESSION: NATIONALIST LOGIC

from Daniel Webster, Speech in the U.S. Senate, March 7, 1850

The Free Soil revolt of 1848 was one of many signs of the weakening of national parties under the pressure of the slavery issue. The nominal unity of the Democratic party barely concealed a mounting struggle among Northern free-soilers (some of whom deserted to the Republicans in the mid-1850's), Douglas moderates (who relied on "popular sovereignty," or the determination of the slavery-expansion question by the people of the several territories), and Southern extremists (who would bolt in the 1860 campaign and then would choose secession after political defeat). Whig unity was still more severely strained by sectional antagonisms and broke down completely in 1856 when the antislavery wing of the party went over to the newly formed Republican party while the Southern membership dissolved.

Daniel Webster's Seventh of March speech in defense of the 1850 Compromise was—according to one's point of view—either a noble Whig effort to preserve the Union by offering reasonable concessions to the South or a terrible betrayal of conscience and principle by a man from whom "the soul has fled" (in the language of the Quaker poet Whittier). Webster's speech helped to gain a limited and temporary support for the Compromise of 1850 in the North. The death in 1852 of the two great Compromise Whigs, Clay and Webster, made way for a new breed of Northern antislavery leaders: men like William H. Seward, Whig Senator from New York, who denounced the Compromise of 1850 in the name of a *higher law* than our Constitution" pronouncing slavery immoral and who later spoke of "an irrepressible conflict between opposing and enduring forces," the forces of slavery and freedom.

Compare Webster's view with Calhoun's (Document 130) on the nature and value of the Union and on the sources of sectional conflict. Note especially Webster's argument, shared with Clay and others, that natural forces—climate, soil, topography—would limit the spread of slavery without the intervention of national policy. Many historians have accepted this position as objectively sound, although to Lincoln and those who defend his policies this was a "lullabye" argument attempting to evade the overwhelming moral and political question of slavery extension.

Mr. President, I wish to speak to-day, not as a Massachusetts man, nor as a northern man, but as an American, and a member of the Senate of the United States. It is fortunate that there is a Senate of the United States; a body not yet moved from its propriety, not lost to a just sense of its own dignity, and its own high responsibilities, and a body to which the country looks with confidence, for wise, moderate, patriotic, and healing counsels. It is not to be denied that we live in the midst of strong agitations, and surrounded by very considerable dangers to our institutions of government. The imprisoned winds are let loose. The East, the West, the North and the stormy South, all combine to throw the whole ocean into commotion, to toss its billows to the skies, and to disclose its pro-

Text: The Congressional Globe, 31st Congress, 1st Session, XXI (Part 1), 476-83 *passim.*

foundest depths. I do not expect, Mr. President, to hold, or to be fit to hold, the helm in this combat of the political elements; but I have a duty to perform, and I mean to perform it with fidelity—not without a sense of the surrounding dangers, but not without hope. I have a part to act, not for my own security or safety, for I am looking out for no fragment upon which to float away from the wreck, if wreck there must be, but for the good of the whole, and the preservation of the whole; and there is that which will keep me to my duty during this struggle, whether the sun and the stars shall appear, or shall not appear, for many days. I speak to-day for the preservation of the Union. "Hear me for my cause." I speak to-day, out of a solicitous and anxious heart, for the restoration to the country of that quiet and that harmony which make the blessings of this Union so rich and so dear to us all. These are the topics that I propose to myself to discuss; these are the motives, and the sole motives, that influence me in the wish to communicate my opinions to the Senate and the country; and if I can do anything, however little, for the promotion of these ends, I shall have accomplished all that I desire. . . .

And now let us consider, sir, for a moment, what was the state of sentiment, North and South, in regard to slavery at the time this Constitution was adopted. A remarkable change has taken place since, but what did the wise and great men of all parts of the country think of slavery? In what estimation did they hold it in 1787, when this Constitution was adopted? Now, it will be found, sir, if we will carry ourselves by historical research back to that day, and ascertain men's opinions by authentic records still existing among us, that there was no great diversity of opinion between the North and the South upon the subject of slavery; and it will be found that both parts of the country held it equally an evil— a moral and political evil. It will not be found, that either at the North or at the South, there was much, though there was some, invective against slavery as inhuman and cruel. The great ground of objection to it was political; that it weakened the social fabric; that, taking the place of free labor, society was less strong, and labor was less productive; and, therefore, we find, from all the eminent men of the time, the clearest expression of their opinion that slavery was an evil. And they ascribed it, not without truth, and not without some acerbity of temper and force of language, to the injurious policy of the mother country, who, to favor the navigator, had entailed these evils upon the colonies. I need hardly refer, sir, to the publications of the day. They

are matters of history on the record. The eminent men, the most eminent men, and nearly all the conspicuous of the South, held the same sentiments, that slavery was an evil, a blight, a blast, a mildew, a scourge, and a curse. There are no terms of reprobation of slavery so vehement in the North of that day as in the South. The North was not so much excited against it as the South, and the reason is, I suppose, because there was much less at the North; and the people did not see, or think they saw, the evils so prominently as they were seen, or thought to be seen, at the South. . . .

This was the state of things, sir, and this the state of opinion under which those two very important matters were arranged, and those two important things done; that is, the establishment of the Constitution, with a recognition of slavery as it existed in the States, and the establishment of the ordinance prohibiting, to the full extent of all territory owned by the United States, the introduction of slavery into those territories. And here, sir, we may pause. We may reflect for a moment upon the entire coincidence and concurrence of sentiment between the North and the South upon this question, at the period of the adoption of the Constitution. But opinions, sir, have changed—greatly changed—changed North and changed South. . . .

The North growing much more warm and strong against slavery, and the South growing much more warm and strong in its support. Sir, there is no generation of mankind whose opinions are not subject to be influenced by what appears to them to be their present, and emergent, and exigent interest. I impute to the South no particularly interested view, in the change which has come over her. I impute to her certainly no dishonest view. All that has happened has been natural. It has followed those causes which always influence the human mind and operate upon it. What, then, have been the causes which have created so new a feeling in favor of slavery in the South—which have changed the whole nomenclature of the South on the subject—and from being thought of and described in the terms I have mentioned, but will not repeat, it has now become an institution, a cherished institution there; no evil, no scourge, but a great religious, social, and moral blessing, as I think I have heard it lately described? I suppose this, sir, is owing to the sudden uprising and rapid growth of the cotton plantations of the South. So far as any motive of honor, justice, and general judgment could act, it was the cotton interest that gave a new desire to promote slavery, to spread it and to use its labor. I again say that this is produced by the causes, which we must always expect to produce like effects—their whole interests became connected with it. If we look back to the history of the commerce of this country, at the early commencement of this Government, what were our exports? Cotton was hardly, or but to a very limited extent, known. The tables will show that the exports of cotton for the years 1790 and '91, were hardly more than forty or fifty thousand dollars a year. It has gone on increasing rapidly until it may now be, perhaps, in a season of great product and high prices, a hundred millions of dollars. . . .

Well, sir, we know what follows. The age of cotton became a golden age for our southern brethren. It gratified their desire for improvement and accumulation, at the same time that it excited it. The desire grew by what it fed upon, and there soon came to be an eagerness for other territory—a new area or new areas for the cultivation of the cotton crop; and measures were brought about, somewhat rapidly, one after another, under the lead of southern men at the head of the Government—they having a majority in both branches of the Government—to accomplish their ends. The honorable member from Carolina observed, that there has been a majority all along in favor of the North. If that be true, sir, the North acted either very liberally and kindly, or very weakly; for they never exercised that majority five times in the history of the Government. Never. Whether they were outgeneralled, or whether it was owing to other causes, I shall not stop to consider, but no man acquainted with the history of the country can deny, that the general lead in the politics of the country, for three-fourths of the period that has elapsed since the adoption of the Constitution, has been a southern lead. . . .

Now, as to California and New Mexico, I hold slavery to be excluded from those territories by a law even superior to that which admits and sanctions it in Texas—I mean the law of nature—of physical geography—the law of the formation of the earth. That law settles forever, with a strength beyond all terms of human enactment, that slavery cannot exist in California or New Mexico. Understand me, sir—I mean slavery as we regard it; slaves in the gross, of the colored race, transferable by sale and delivery, like other property. . . . California and New Mexico are Asiatic in their formation and scenery. They are composed of vast ridges of mountains, of enormous height, with sometimes broken ridges and deep valleys. The sides of these mountains are barren—entirely barren—their tops capped by perennial snow. There may be in California,

now made free by its constitution—and no doubt there are—some tracts of valuable land. But it is not so in New Mexico. Pray, what is the evidence which any gentleman has obtained on this subject, from information sought by himself or communicated by others? I have inquired, and read all I could, to obtain information on this subject. What is there in New Mexico that could by any possibility induce any body to go there with slaves? There are some narrow strips of tillable land on the borders of the rivers; but the rivers themselves dry up before midsummer is gone. All that the people can do is to raise some little articles—some little wheat for their tortillas—and all that by irrigation. And who expects to see a hundred black men cultivating tobacco, corn, cotton, rice, or anything else, on lands in New Mexico, made fertile only by irrigation? I look upon it, therefore, as a fixed fact, to use an expression current to the day, that both California and New Mexico are destined to be free, so far as they are settled at all, which I believe, especially in regard to New Mexico, will be very little for a great length of time—free by the arrangement of things by the Power above us. I have therefore to say, in this respect also, that this country is fixed for freedom, to as many persons as shall ever live there, by as irrepealable and a more irrepealable law, than the law that attaches to the right of holding slaves in Texas; and I will say further, that if a resolution, or a law, were now before us, to provide a territorial government for New Mexico, I would not vote to put any prohibition into it whatever. The use of such a prohibition would be idle, as it respects any effect it would have upon the territory; and I would not take pains to reaffirm an ordinance of nature, nor to reenact the will of God. And I would put in no Wilmot proviso, for the purpose of a taunt or a reproach. I would put into it no evidence of the votes of superior power, to wound the pride, even whether a just pride, a rational pride, or an irrational pride—to wound the pride of the gentlemen who belong to the southern States. I have no such object—no such purpose. They would think it a taunt—an indignity. They would think it to be an act taking away from them what they regard a proper equality or privilege; and whether they expect to realize any benefit from it or not, they would think it a theoretic wrong—that something more or less derogatory to their character and their rights had taken place. I propose to inflict no such wound upon any body, unless something essentially important to the country, and efficient to the preservation of liberty and freedom, is to be effected. Therefore, I repeat, sir—and I repeat it because I wish it to be understood—that I do not propose to address the Senate often on this subject. I desire to pour out all my heart in as plain a manner as possible; and I say again, that if a proposition were now here for a government for New Mexico, and it was moved to insert a provision for a prohibition of slavery, I would not vote for it. . . .

Sir, wherever there is a particular good to be done—wherever there is a foot of land to be staid back from becoming slave territory—I am ready to assert the principle of the exclusion of slavery. I am pledged to it from the year 1837; I have been pledged to it again and again; and I will perform those pledges; but I will not do a thing unnecessary, that wounds the feelings of others, or that does disgrace to my own understanding.

Mr. President, in the excited times in which we live, there is found to exist a state of crimination and recrimination between the North and the South. There are lists of grievances produced by each; and those grievances, real or supposed, alienate the minds of one portion of the country from the other, exasperate the feelings, subdue the sense of fraternal connection, and patriotic love, and mutual regard. I shall bestow a little attention, sir, upon these various grievances, produced on the one side and on the other. I begin with the complaints of the South: I will now answer, farther than I have, the general statements of the honorable Senator from South Carolina [John C. Calhoun], that the North has grown upon the South in consequence of the manner of administering this Government, in the collecting of its revenues, and so forth. These are disputed topics, and I have no inclination to enter into them. But I will state these complaints, especially one complaint of the South, which has in my opinion just foundation; and that is, that there has been found at the North, among individuals and among the Legislatures of the North, a disinclination to perform, fully, their constitutional duties, in regard to the return of persons bound to service, who have escaped into the free States. In that respect, it is my judgment that the South is right, and the North is wrong. Every member of every northern Legislature is bound, by oath, like every other officer in the country, to support the Constitution of the United States; and this article of the Constitution, which says to these States, they shall deliver up fugitives from service, is as binding in honor and conscience as any other article. . . .

Therefore, I repeat, sir, that here is a ground of complaint against the North, well founded, which ought to be removed—which it is now in the power of the different departments of this Government to remove—which calls for the enactment of proper laws, authorizing the judicature of this Government, in the several States, to do all that is necessary for the recapture of fugitive slaves, and for the restoration of them to those who claim them. Wherever I go, and whenever I speak on the subject—and when I speak here, I desire to speak to the whole North—I say that the South has been injured in this respect, and has a right to complain; and the North has been too careless of what I think the Constitution peremptorily and emphatically enjoins upon it as a duty. . . .

There can be no such thing as a peaceable secession. Peaceable secession is an utter impossibility. Is the great Constitution under which we live here—covering this whole country—is it to be thawed and melted away by secession, as the snows on the mountain melt under the influence of a vernal sun—disappear almost unobserved, and die off? No, sir! no, sir! I will not state what might produce the disruption of the States; but, sir, I see it as plainly as I see the sun in heaven—I see that disruption must produce such a war as I will not describe, in its twofold characters.

Peaceable secession! peaceable secession! The concurrent agreement of all the members of this great Republic to separate! A voluntary separation, with alimony on one side and on the other. Why, what would be the result? Where is the line to be drawn? What States are to secede? What is to remain American? What am I to be?—an American no longer? Where is the flag of the Republic to remain? Where is the eagle still to tower? or is he to cower, and shrink, and fall to the ground? Why, sir, our ancestors—our fathers, and our grandfathers, those of them that are yet living among us with prolonged lives—would rebuke and reproach us; and our children, and our grandchildren, would cry out, Shame upon us! if we, of this generation, should dishonor these ensigns of the power of the Government, and the harmony of the Union, which is every day felt among us with so much joy and gratitude. What is to become of the army? What is to become of the navy? What is to become of the public lands? How is each of the thirty States to defend itself? I know, although the idea has not been stated distinctly, there is to be a southern Confederacy. I do not mean, when I allude to this statement, that any one seriously contemplates such a state of things. I do not mean to say that it is true, but I have heard it suggested elsewhere, that that idea has originated in a design to separate. I am sorry, sir, that it has ever been thought of, talked of, or dreamed of, in the wildest flights of human imagination. But the idea must be of a separation, including the slave States upon one side, and the free States on the other. Sir, there is not—I may express myself too strongly perhaps—but some things, some moral things, are almost as impossible, as other natural or physical things; and I hold the idea of a separation of these States—those that are free to form one government, and those that are slaveholding to form another—as a moral impossibility. We could not separate the States by any such line, if we were to draw it. We could not sit down here to-day, and draw a line of separation, that would satisfy any five men in the country. There are natural causes that would keep and tie us together, and there are social and domestic relations which we could not break, if we would, and which we should not, if we could. Sir, nobody can look over the face of this country at the present moment—nobody can see where its population is the most dense and growing—without being ready to admit, and compelled to admit, that, ere long, America will be in the valley of the Mississippi.

Well, now sir, I beg to inquire what the wildest enthusiast has to say, on the possibility of cutting off that river, and leaving free States at its source and its branches, and slave States down near its mouth? Pray, sir—pray, sir, let me say to the people of this country, that these things are worthy of their pondering and of their consideration. Here, sir, are five millions of freemen in the free States north of the river Ohio: can anybody suppose that this population can be severed by a line that divides them from the territory of a foreign and an alien government, down somewhere, the Lord knows where, upon the lower banks of the Mississippi? What will become of Missouri? Will she join the arrondisse-

ment of the slave States? Shall the man from the Yellow Stone and the Platte be connected in the new Republic with the man who lives on the southern extremity of the Cape of Florida? Sir, I am ashamed to pursue this line of remark. I dislike it—I have an utter disgust for it. I would rather hear of natural blasts and mildews, war, pestilence, and famine, than to hear gentlemen talk of secession. To break up! to break up this great Government! to dismember this great country! to astonish Europe with an act of folly, such as Europe for two centuries has never beheld in any government! No, sir! no, sir! There will be no secession. Gentlemen are not serious when they talk of secession. . . .

And now, Mr. President, instead of speaking of the possibility or utility of secession, instead of dwelling in these caverns of darkness, instead of groping with those ideas so full of all that is horrid and horrible, let us come out into the light of day; let us enjoy the fresh air of liberty and union; let us cherish those hopes which belong to us; let us devote ourselves to those great objects that are fit for our consideration and our action; let us raise our conceptions to the magnitude and the importance of the duties that devolve upon us; let our comprehension be as broad as the country for which we act, our aspirations as high as its certain destiny; let us not be pigmies in a case that calls for men. Never did there devolve, on any generation of men, higher trusts than now devolve upon us for the preservation of this Constitution, and the harmony and peace of all who are destined to live under it. Let us make our generation one of the strongest, and the brightest link, in that golden chain which is destined, I fully believe, to grapple the people of all the States to this Constitution, for ages to come.

132 THE CONSTITUTION AND THE SLAVE

from Dred Scott v. Sandford, 1857

The French commentator Alexis de Tocqueville (see Documents 113, 116, and 149) observed that Americans characteristically translate political questions into legal terms and thus permit the relatively cool and conservative bench and bar to shape important public decisions. He was especially impressed by the unique position of the United States Supreme Court as final arbiter in the federal political system. This feature of American politics was conspicuous, for example, in the great Hamilton-Jefferson debates of the 1790's, which presented major policy differences in the language of constitutional interpretation. Again, during the long judicial reign of John Marshall, fundamental questions of politics were restated and resolved within the judicial process.

It is not surprising then that Southern spokesmen should have formulated many of their political demands in constitutional terms, including the demand that the national territory remain open to slaveholders. Since 1820 slavery had been excluded by Congressional authority from the Louisiana Purchase country north of the Missouri border. More than three decades later the increasingly restive South won a political reversal when the Kansas-Nebraska Act (1854) included an explicit repeal of the venerable Missouri Compromise. But the constitutional question of Congressional authority over slavery in the territories remained; and the bloody chaos that prevailed in Kansas, as proslavery and antislavery forces fought for control of the territory, prompted men on both sides of the issue to seek an authoritative ruling by the Supreme Court.

With affairs in this troubled state, the appeal of the Missouri slave Dred Scott reached the Supreme Court in 1856. By then the Dred Scott case was of little importance either to the slave or to his nominal master, for Scott was in the hands of anti-slavery owners who intended to free him however the court should decide. Rather, the case became an occasion for testing a great constitutional (ultimately, a political) question.

The background must be stated very briefly. In 1834 Dred Scott, a household slave, had been taken by Dr. John Emerson, an army surgeon, from St. Louis, Missouri, to the free state of Illinois and later to Fort Snelling in Wisconsin Territory (now part of Minnesota), where slavery was prohibited by the Missouri Compromise. In 1838, after some four years of residence on free soil, Scott was carried back to the slave state of Missouri. Supported by abolitionist friends, Scott in 1846 commenced his legal pursuit of freedom in the Missouri courts. A lower court, following Missouri precedents, upheld his claim that Dr. Emerson (in effect, if unknowingly) had emancipated Scott by taking him into the zone of freedom. This judgment, however, was overruled in 1852 by a divided state supreme court.

In order to appeal the question to the federal courts, Scott's new antislavery owners arranged a fictitious sale to John F. A. Sanford (whose name is misspelled in the court records) of New York. The suit of a Missouri citizen against a New York citizen would come under federal jurisdiction. Finally, in 1856, the Dred Scott case was argued at length before the United States Supreme Court. As noted earlier, the case aroused great political expectations. Indeed, the newly elected President, James Buchanan, took the questionable step of sounding out two of the justices before including in his Inaugural Address (March 4, 1857) a reference to a forthcoming Court decision that would close the bitter controversy over slavery in the territories. Two days later, Chief Justice Roger Taney (1777-1864), speaking for the Court, ruled against Dred Scott on the broadest possible grounds: (1) as a slave, or a descendant of slaves, or simply as a Negro, he could not claim citizenship under the Constitution and so he could not enter the Court's jurisdiction; (2) Scott's residence in Wisconsin Territory could not support a claim to freedom, since the Missouri Compromise excluding slavery from that area violated the Constitution, particularly the Fifth Amendment; (3) Scott's residence in free territory could not support his claim to freedom since the laws and judicial decisions of Missouri determined his status once he had returned. Taney's chief arguments are included in the following selection.

The South, in brief, got everything it hoped for, short of an endorsement of the extreme state-sovereignty doctrine. But the Court's decision wholly failed to quiet the political dispute; if anything, debate grew angrier. Most Northerners refused to recognize Taney's "majority" opinion as an authoritative reading of the Constitution on the matters of Negro citizenship and Congressional control of the territories. Each of the nine justices, the critics pointed out, had submitted a separate opinion. Although a majority of seven justices agreed that Scott remained a slave, they combined in different ways on the several leading points set forth in Taney's opinion (see above); moreover, the majority justices followed several distinct lines of legal reasoning to reach their common conclusions. Critics did not hesitate to mention that five of the majority were Southerners and all of them Democrats, while two of the dissenters, Curtis and McLean, were of opposing party persuasions. Finally, it was charged, the Court's rulings on Negro citizenship and territorial slavery were *obiter dicta* (pronouncements not required for determination of the case) resting on doctrines without judicial precedent.

On these and other grounds Republicans like Lincoln insisted on their right to seek a new ruling, consonant with the dissenting views of Justices Curtis and McLean; some critics openly announced their intention to change the political and sectional composition of the Supreme Court. In the meantime, the Republicans continued to demand a Congressional ban on the spread of slavery into the territories. Perhaps the worst effect of the Dred Scott decision was to damage the prestige of the Court and thus to sap its authority at the threshold of an era when political passions would run high and an independent judiciary would be sorely needed as a moderating influence.

Mr. Chief Justice Taney delivered the opinion of the Court. . . .

It is true, every person, and every class and description of persons, who were at the time of the adoption of the Constitution recognized as citizens in the several states, became also citizens of this new political body; but none other; it was formed by them, and for them and their posterity, but for no one else. And the personal rights and privileges guaranteed to citizens of this new sovereignty were intended to embrace those only who were then members of the several state communities or who should afterward by birthright or otherwise become members, according to the provisions of the Constitution and the principles on which it was founded. . . .

In the opinion of the Court the legislation and histories of the times, and the language used in the Declaration of Independence, show that neither the class of persons who had been imported as slaves nor their descendants, whether they had become free or not, were then acknowledged as a part of the people nor intended to be included in the general words used in that memorable instrument.

It is difficult at this day to realize the state of public opinion in relation to that unfortunate race which prevailed in the civilized and enlightened portions of the world at the time of the Declaration of Independence and when the Constitution of the United States was framed and adopted. But the public history of every European nation displays it in a manner too plain to be mistaken.

They had for more than a century before been regarded as beings of an inferior order and altogether unfit to associate with the white race, either in social or political relations; and so far inferior that they had no rights which the white man was bound to respect; and that the Negro might justly and lawfully be reduced to slavery for his benefit. He was bought and sold and treated as an ordinary article of merchandise and traffic whenever a profit could be made by it. This opinion was at that time fixed and universal in the civilized portion of the white race. It was regarded as an axiom in morals as well as in politics, which no one thought of disputing, or supposed to be open to dispute; and men in every grade and position in society daily and habitually acted upon it in their private pursuits, as well as in matters of public concern, without doubting for a moment the correctness of this opinion. . . .

Text: Dred Scott v. *Sandford* 19 Howard 393 (1857), pp. 399, 406-12, 426-27, 430, 432, 447-52 *passim.*

The opinion thus entertained and acted upon . . . was naturally impressed upon the colonies they founded on this side of the Atlantic. And, accordingly, a Negro of the African race was regarded by them as an article of property and, held and bought and sold as such in every one of the thirteen colonies which united in the Declaration of Independence and afterward formed the Constitution of the United States. The slaves were more or less numerous in the different colonies, as slave labor was found more or less profitable. But no one seems to have doubted the correctness of the prevailing opinion of the time.

The legislation of the different colonies furnishes positive and indisputable proof of this fact. . . .

The language of the Declaration of Independence is equally conclusive:

It begins by declaring that "when, in the course of human events, it becomes necessary for one people to dissolve the political bands which have connected them with another, and to assume, among the powers of the earth the separate and equal station to which the laws of nature and nature's God entitle them, a decent respect for the opinions of mankind requires that they should declare the causes which impel them to the separation."

It then proceeds to say: "We hold these truths to be self-evident: that all men are created equal; that they are endowed by their Creator with certain inalienable rights; that among these are life, liberty, and the pursuit of happiness; that to secure these rights, governments are instituted, deriving their just powers from the consent of the governed."

The general words above quoted would seem to embrace the whole human family, and if they were used in a similar instrument at this day would be so understood. But it is too clear for dispute that the enslaved African race were not intended to be included and formed no part of the people who framed and adopted this declaration; for if the language, as understood in that day, would embrace them, the conduct of the distinguished men who framed the Declaration of Independence would have been utterly and flagrantly inconsistent with the principles they asserted; and instead of the sympathy of mankind, to which they so confidently appealed, they would have deserved and received universal rebuke and reprobation.

Yet the men who framed this declaration were great men—high in literary acquirements—high in their sense of honor, and incapable of asserting principles inconsistent with those on which they were acting. They perfectly understood the meaning of the language they used and how it would be understood by others; and they knew that it would not in any part of the civilized world be supposed to embrace the Negro race, which, by common consent, had been excluded from civilized governments and the family of nations and doomed to slavery. They spoke and acted according to the then established doctrines and principles and in the ordinary language of the day, and no one misunderstood them. The unhappy black race were separated from the white by indelible marks, and laws long before established, and were never thought of or spoken of except as property and when the claims of the owner or the profit of the trader were supposed to need protection.

This state of public opinion had undergone no change when the Constitution was adopted, as is equally evident from its provisions and language. . . .

No one, we presume, supposes that any change in public opinion or feeling, in relation to this unfortunate race, in the civilized nations of Europe or in this country should induce the Court to give to the words of the Constitution a more liberal construction in their favor than they were intended to bear when the instrument was framed and adopted. Such an argument would be altogether inadmissible in any tribunal called on to interpret it. If any of its provisions are deemed unjust, there is a mode prescribed in the instrument itself by which it may be amended; but, while it remains unaltered, it must be construed now as it was understood at the time of its adoption. It is not only the same in words but the same in meaning and delegates the same powers to the government and reserves and secures the same rights and privileges to the citizen; and, as long as it continues to exist in its present form, it speaks not only in the same words but with the same meaning and intent with which it spoke when it came from the hands of its framers and was voted on and adopted by the people of the United States. Any other rule of construction would abrogate the judicial character of this Court and make it the mere reflex of the popular opinion or passion of the day. This Court was not created by the Constitution for such purposes. Higher and graver trusts have been confided to it, and it must not falter in the path of duty.

What the construction was at that time, we think, can hardly admit of doubt. We have the language of the Declaration of Independence and of the Articles of Confederation, in addition to the plain words of the Constitution itself; we have the legislation of the different states before, about the time, and since the Constitution was adopted; we have the legislation of Congress, from the time of its adoption to a recent period; and we have the constant and uniform action of the Executive department, all concurring together and leading to the same result. And, if anything in relation to the construction of the Constitution can be regarded as settled, it is that which we now give to the word "citizen" and the word "people."

And upon a full and careful consideration of the subject, the Court is of opinion that, upon the facts stated in the plea in abatement, Dred Scott was not a citizen of Missouri within the meaning of the Constitution of the United States and not entitled as such to sue in its courts; and, consequently, that the circuit court had no jurisdiction of the case and that the judgment on the plea in abatement is erroneous. . . .

We proceed . . . to inquire whether the facts relied on by the plaintiff entitled him to his freedom. . . .

The act of Congress, upon which the plaintiff relies, declares that slavery and involuntary servitude, except as a punishment for crime, shall be forever prohibited in all that part of the territory ceded by France, under the name of Louisiana, which lies north of thirty-six degrees thirty minutes north latitude and not included within the limits of Missouri. And the difficulty which meets us at the threshold of this part of the inquiry is whether Congress was authorized to pass this law under any of the powers granted to it by the Constitution; for, if the authority is not given by that instrument, it is the duty of this Court to declare it void and inoperative and incapable of conferring freedom upon anyone who is held as a slave under the laws of any one of the states. . . .

We do not mean . . . to question the power of Congress in this respect. The power to expand the territory of the United States by the admission of new states is plainly given; and in the construction of this power by all the departments of the government, it has been held to authorize the acquisition of territory, not fit for admission at the time, but to be admitted as soon as its population and situation would entitle it to admission. . . . All we mean to say on this point is that, as there is no express regulation in the Constitution defining the power which the general government may exercise over the person or property of a citizen in a territory thus acquired, the Court must necessarily look to the provisions and principles of the Constitution, and its distribution of powers, for the rules and principles by which its decision must be governed.

Taking this rule to guide us, it may be safely assumed that citizens of the United States who migrate to a territory belonging to the people of the United States cannot be ruled as mere colonists, dependent upon the will of the general government, and to be governed by any laws it may think proper to impose. The principle upon which our governments rest, and upon which alone they continue to exist, is the union of states, sovereign and independent within their own limits in their internal and domestic concerns, and bound together as one people by a general government, possessing certain enumerated and restricted powers, delegated to it by the people of the several states, and exercising supreme authority within the scope of the powers granted to it, throughout the dominion of the United States. A power, therefore, in the general government to obtain and hold colonies and dependent territories, over which they might legislate without restriction, would be inconsistent with its own existence in its present form. Whatever it acquires, it acquires for the benefit of the people of the several states who created it. It is their trustee acting for them and charged with the duty of promoting the interests of the whole people of the Union in the exercise of the powers specifically granted. . . .

A reference to a few of the provisions of the Constitution will illustrate this proposition.

For example, no one, we presume, will contend that Congress can make any law in a territory respecting the establishment of religion, or the free exercise thereof, or abridging the freedom of speech or of the press, or the right of the people of the territory peaceably to assemble, and to petition the government for the redress of grievances.

Nor can Congress deny to the people the right to keep and bear arms, nor the right to trial by jury, nor compel anyone to be a witness against himself in a criminal proceeding.

These powers, and others, in relation to rights of person, which it is not necessary here to enumerate, are, in express and positive terms, denied to the general government; and the rights of private property have been guarded with equal care. Thus the rights of property are united with the rights of person and placed on the same ground by the Fifth Amendment to the Constitution, which provides that no person shall be deprived of life, liberty, and property without due process of law. And an act of Congress which deprives a citizen of the United States of his liberty or property, without due process of law, merely because he came himself or brought his property into a particular territory of the United States, and who had committed no offense against

the laws, could hardly be dignified with the name of due process of law. . . .

The powers over person and property of which we speak are not only not granted to Congress but are in express terms denied, and they are forbidden to exercise them. And this prohibition is not confined to the states, but the words are general and extend to the whole territory over which the Constitution gives it power to legislate, including those portions of it remaining under territorial government as well as that covered by states. It is a total absence of power everywhere within the dominion of the United States and places the citizens of a territory, so far as these rights are concerned, on the same footing with citizens of the states and guards them as firmly and plainly against any inroads which the general government might attempt under the plea of implied or incidental powers. And if Congress itself cannot do this—if it is beyond the powers conferred on the federal government—it will be admitted, we presume, that it could not authorize a territorial government to exercise them. It could confer no power on any local government, established by its authority, to violate the provisions of the Constitution.

It seems, however, to be supposed that there is a difference between property in a slave and other property and that different rules may be applied to it in expounding the Constitution of the United States. And the laws and usages of nations, and the writings of eminent jurists upon the relation of master and slave and their mutual rights and duties, and the powers which governments may exercise over it, have been dwelt upon in the argument. . . .

Now, as we have already said in an earlier part of this opinion, upon a different point, the right of property in a slave is distinctly and expressly affirmed in the Constitution. The right to traffic in it, like an ordinary article of merchandise and property, was guaranteed to the citizens of the United States, in every state that might desire it, for twenty years. And the government in express terms is pledged to protect it in all future time if the slave escapes from his owner. This is done in plain words—too plain to be misunderstood. And no word can be found in the Constitution which gives Congress a greater power over slave property or which entitles property of that kind to less protection than property of any other description. The only power conferred is the power coupled with the duty of guarding and protecting the owner in his rights.

Upon these considerations it is the opinion of the Court that the act of Congress which prohibited a citizen from holding and owning property of this kind in the territory of the United States north of the line therein mentioned is not warranted by the Constitution and is therefore void; and that neither Dred Scott himself, nor any of his family, were made free by being carried into this territory; even if they had been carried there by the owner with the intention of becoming a permanent resident. . . .

Squatter Sovereignty: A Lincoln-Douglas Debate

133 TO EACH HIS OWN

from Stephen A. Douglas, Opening Speech at Alton, Illinois, October 15, 1858

The seven joint debates between Stephen A. Douglas and Abraham Lincoln, contestants for the senatorial choice in Illinois, commanded the attention of the nation, and the records of their encounter still serve as an indispensable textbook on the coming of the Civil War. Douglas, the leading Northern Democrat, had recently broken with the Buchanan administration over its attempt to bring Kansas into the Union with the proslavery Lecompton constitution plainly opposed by a majority of Kansans (1857-1858). At the same time, Chief Justice Taney's opinion in the *Dred Scott* case (1857) cast grave doubts on the constitutionality of Douglas's chief political remedy for the sectional crisis—"popular sovereignty" (see pages 368-369)—since Taney's denial of Congressional power to restrict slavery would seem to apply equally as a check upon the power of the territorial governments created by Congress. Douglas then was fighting for the only policy, as he believed, which would save a nation torn between the "Black Republicans" of the North and the proslavery extremists of the South, who dominated Buchanan's administration. And he was fighting for his own political life against a worthy challenger.

For Lincoln, too, the personal and political stakes were incalculably high. Entering Illinois politics in the 1830's as a devoted Henry Clay Whig (see Document 115), Lincoln had attained some local reputation and won a Congressional seat in 1846, only to retire to law practice after a single term. By his own account: "I was losing interest in politics when the repeal of the Missouri Compromise [the Kansas-Nebraska Act of 1854] aroused me again." To Lincoln and those who went with him into the new Republican party, the Missouri repeal violated a sacred bargain that had preserved the sectional peace for thirty-four years. Stephen A. Douglas had been the chief author of this alleged political crime. And Douglas was Lincoln's natural adversary for another reason: by fighting Buchanan and the Southern Democrats over Kansas in the name of "popular sovereignty," Douglas was making a serious bid for leadership of the "free-soil" forces of the North. But Lincoln insisted that "popular sovereignty" was a dangerous delusion, a policy that could not (as he argued at Springfield, June 16, 1858) "arrest the further spread of [slavery], and place it where the public mind shall rest in the belief that it is in course of ultimate extinction." Thus Lincoln entered the debates with Douglas in the summer and fall of 1858 determined to sustain the Union as it was conceived by the Founders and to improve an ideal opportunity to win a leading role in national politics.

Douglas was the incumbent Senator with the imposing name. Lincoln trailed his famous rival from town to town in the first stages of the 1858 campaign until Douglas accepted a challenge to a series of seven joint debates, one in each congressional district where they had not yet spoken. With brass bands and provincial pomp the prairie towns of Illinois turned out to receive the political champions: the stubby, energetic "Little Giant" with the look of a dignitary, past master of the frenetic style of Western oratory; and the lanky, shambling, long-necked Lincoln in battered stovepipe hat—a grotesque backwoods figure in the eyes of sophisticated observers—who could rise from crude "stump" banter to miracles of simple eloquence.

Douglas would attack Lincoln as an abolitionist "Black Republican" whose doctrines would divide the Union into warring camps and force racial equality on a nation "established on the white basis." Lincoln would attack Douglas as a moral cripple who "don't care" about the great principles of the Declaration and whose policy "squatter sovereignty" had become an invitation to chaos. At Freeport, under Lincoln's shrewd questioning, Douglas argued that a territory still could exclude slavery, despite the Dred Scott decision, by refusing to enact the local "police regulations" necessary to sustain the institution. Lincoln pressed his opening and thus helped to alienate Douglas's Southern supporters, who insisted that *Dred Scott* unequivocally opened the territories to slavery. In the final debate at Alton, from which the following selections are taken, each man reviewed the basic points at issue as he conceived them and formulated the essential case for his own position.

Here Douglas makes a forceful appeal for "popular sovereignty" as the true democratic doctrine and as the sole alternative to civil war.

It is now nearly four months since the canvass between Mr. Lincoln and myself commenced. On the sixteenth of June the Republican Convention assembled at Springfield and nominated Mr. Lincoln as their candidate for the United States Senate, and he, on that occasion, delivered a speech in which he laid down what he understood to be the Republican creed and the platform on which he proposed to stand during the contest.

The principal points in that speech of Mr. Lincoln's were: First, that this government could not endure permanently divided into free and slave states, as our fathers made it; that they must all become free or all become slave; all become one thing or all become the other, otherwise this Union could not continue to exist. I give you his opinions almost in the identical language he used. His second proposition was a crusade against the Supreme Court of the United States because of the Dred Scott decision; urging as an especial reason for his opposition to that decision that it deprived the Negroes of the rights and benefits of that clause in the Constitution of the United States which guarantees to the citizens of each state all the rights, privileges, and immunities of the citizens of the several states. . . .

On the . . . eleventh of July, Mr. Lincoln replied to me at Chicago, explaining at some length, and reaffirming the positions which he had taken in his Springfield speech. In that Chicago speech he even went further than he had before and uttered sentiments in regard to the Negro being on an equality with the white man. He adopted in support of this position the argument which Lovejoy and Codding, and other abolition lecturers had made familiar in the northern and central portions of the state, to wit: that the Declaration of Independence

Text: Political Debates Between Hon. Abraham Lincoln and Hon. Stephen A. Douglas, in the Celebrated Campaign of 1858 (Columbus, Ohio: Follett, Foster & Co., 1860), pp. 215-23 passim.

having declared all men free and equal, by divine law, also that Negro equality was an inalienable right, of which they could not be deprived. He insisted, in that speech, that the Declaration of Independence included the Negro in the clause, asserting that all men were created equal, and went so far as to say that if one man was allowed to take the position that it did not include the Negro, others might take the position that it did not include other men. He said that all these distinctions between this man and that man, this race and the other race, must be discarded, and we must all stand by the Declaration of Independence, declaring that all men were created equal.

The issue thus being made up between Mr. Lincoln and myself on three points, we went before the people of the state. . . . I took up Mr. Lincoln's three propositions in my several speeches, analyzed them, and pointed out what I believed to be the radical errors contained in them, First, in regard to his doctrine that this government was in violation of the law of God, which says that a house divided against itself cannot stand, I repudiated it as a slander upon the immortal framers of our Constitution. I then said, I have often repeated, and now again assert, that in my opinion our government can endure forever, divided into free and slave states as our fathers made it—each state having the right to prohibit, abolish, or sustain slavery, just as it pleases. This government was made upon the great basis of the sovereignty of the states, the right of each state to regulate its own domestic institutions to suit itself, and that right was conferred with the understanding and expectation that, inasmuch as each locality had separate interests, each locality must have different and distinct local and domestic institutions, corresponding to its wants and interests. Our fathers knew when they made the government that the laws and institutions which were well adapted to the Green Mountains of Vermont were unsuited to the rice plantations of

South Carolina. They knew then, as well as we know now, that the laws and institutions which would be well adapted to the beautiful prairies of Illinois would not be suited to the mining regions of California. They knew that in a republic as broad as this, having such a variety of soil, climate, and interest, there must necessarily be a corresponding variety of local laws—the policy and institutions of each state adapted to its condition and wants. For this reason this Union was established on the right of each state to do as it pleased on the question of slavery and every other question; and the various states were not allowed to complain of, much less interfere with, the policy of their neighbors. . . .

My friends, there never was a time when it was as important for the Democratic party, for all national men, to rally and stand together as it is today. We find all sectional men giving up past differences and continuing the one question of slavery, and, when we find sectional men thus uniting, we should unite to resist them and their treasonable designs. . . . It was so in 1850, when abolitionism had even so far divided this country, North and South, as to endanger the peace of the Union; Whigs and Democrats united in establishing the compromise measures of that year and restoring tranquillity and good feeling. These measures passed on the joint action of the two parties. They rested on the great principle that the people of each state and each territory should be left perfectly free to form and regulate their domestic institutions to suit themselves. You Whigs and we Democrats justified them in that principle. In 1854, when it became necessary to organize the territories of Kansas and Nebraska, I brought forward the bill on the same principle. In the Kansas-Nebraska Bill you find it declared to be the true intent and meaning of the act not to legislate slavery into any state or territory, nor to exclude it therefrom, but to leave the people thereof perfectly free to form and regulate their domestic institutions in their own way. I stand on that same platform in 1858 that I did in 1850, 1854, and 1856. . . .

I answer specifically if you want a further answer and say that, while under the decision of the Supreme Court, as recorded in the opinion of Chief Justice Taney, slaves are property like all other property, and can be carried into any territory of the United States the same as any other description of property, yet when you get them there they are subject to the local law of the territory just like all other property. . . .

The whole South are rallying to the support of the doctrine that, if the people of a territory want slavery, they have a right to have it, and

if they do not want it, that no power on earth can force it upon them. I hold that there is no principle on earth more sacred to all the friends of freedom than that which says that no institution, no law, no constitution, should be forced on an unwilling people contrary to their wishes; and I assert that the Kansas and Nebraska Bill contains that principle. . . . I will never violate or abandon that doctrine if I have to stand alone. I have resisted the blandishments and threats of power on the one side, and seduction on the other, and have stood immovably for that principle, fighting for it when assailed by northern mobs or threatened by southern hostility. I have defended it against the North and the South, and I will defend it against whoever assails it, and I will follow it wherever its logical conclusions lead me. I say to you that there is but one hope, one safety, for this country, and that is to stand immovably by that principle which declares the right of each state and each territory to decide these questions for themselves. This government was founded on that principle and must be administered in the same sense in which it was founded.

But the Abolition party really think that under the Declaration of Independence the Negro is equal to the white man and that Negro equality is an inalienable right conferred by the Almighty, and hence that all human laws in violation of it are null and void. With such men it is no use for me to argue. I hold that the signers of the Declaration of Independence had no reference to Negroes at all when they declared all men to be created equal. They did not mean Negro, nor the savage Indians, nor the Fiji Islanders, nor any other barbarous race. They were speaking of white men. They alluded to men of European birth and European descent—to white men and to none others—when they declared that doctrine. I hold that this government was established on the white basis. It was established by white men for the benefit of white men and their posterity forever and should be administered by white men and none others. But it does not follow, by any means, that merely because the Negro is not a citizen, and merely because he is not our equal, that, therefore, he should be a slave. On the contrary, it does follow that we ought to extend to the Negro race, and to all other dependent races all the rights, all the privileges, and all the immunities which they can exercise consistently with the safety of society. Humanity requires that we should give them all these privileges; Christianity commands that we should extend those privileges to them. The question then arises: What are those privileges and what is the nature and extent of them. My answer is that that is a question which each state must answer for itself. We in Illinois have decided it for ourselves. We tried slavery, kept it up for twelve years, and, finding that it was not profitable, we abolished it for that reason, and became a free state. We adopted in its stead the policy that a Negro in this state shall not be a slave and shall not be a citizen. We have a right to adopt that policy. For my part I think it is a wise and sound policy for us. You in Missouri must judge for yourselves whether it is a wise policy for you. If you choose to follow our example, very good; if you reject it, still well, it is your business, not ours. So with Kentucky. Let Kentucky adopt a policy to suit herself. If we do not like it, we will keep away from it, and if she does not like ours let her stay at home, mind her own business and let us alone. If the people of all the states will act on that great principle, and each state mind its own business, attend its own affairs, take care of its own Negroes, and not meddle with its neighbors, then there will be peace between the North and the South,

the East and the West, throughout the whole Union. Why can we not thus have peace? Why should we thus allow a sectional party to agitate this country, to array the North against the South, and convert us into enemies instead of friends, merely that a few ambitious men may ride into power on a sectional hobby? How long is it since these ambitious northern men wished for a sectional organization? Did any one of them dream of a sectional party as long as the North was the weaker section and the South the stronger? Then all were opposed to sectional parties; but the moment the North obtained the majority in the House and Senate by the admission of California, and could elect a President without the aid of southern votes, that moment ambitious northern men formed a scheme to excite the North against the South, and make the people be governed in their votes by geographical lines, thinking that the North, being the stronger section, would outvote the South, and consequently they, the leaders, would ride into office on a sectional hobby. I am told that my hour is out. It is very short.

134

RIGHT OR WRONG?: A NATIONAL QUESTION

from Abraham Lincoln, Reply at Alton, Illinois, October 15, 1858

Since 1854 Abraham Lincoln had set his face against the "Nebraska" remedy of Douglas and had defined a policy toward slavery that would become the position of the Republican party. Lincoln, like the founders of the nation, held the traditional conception of statecraft as "the art of the possible." Some recent writers have suggested that this was equivalent to the rule "anything goes" and that Lincoln was at bottom a shrewd politico making his way to the presidency. But the evidence provides a more persuasive account.

Lincoln was not prepared to offer an ultimate solution of the race question in America. Should Negroes be granted political and social equality? "My own feelings will not admit of this," he announced at Peoria (1854), "and if mine would, we well know that those of the great mass of white people will not. Whether this feeling accords with justice and sound judgment, is not the sole question, if indeed, it is any part of it."

Slavery was quite another matter. At Springfield (1857) Lincoln entered his protest "against that counterfeit logic which concludes that, because I do not want a black woman for a *slave* I must necessarily want her for a *wife*. . . . I can just leave her alone. In some respects she certainly is not my equal; but in her natural right to eat the bread she earns with her own hands without asking leave of anyone else, she is my equal, and the equal of all others." This was not simply a private credo but the teaching of the Declaration upon which the American Republic was founded. As Lincoln wrote: "*Most governments* have been based, practically, on the denial of equal rights of men. . . . We proposed to give *all* a chance; and we expected the weak to grow stronger, the ignorant, wiser; and all better, and happier together."

Was Lincoln then bound logically to demand immediate emancipation, if not full equality, for Negroes? Once again Lincoln turned to his understanding of the Founders for an answer: "They meant simply to declare the *right*, so that the *enforcement* of it might follow as fast as circumstances should permit. They meant to set up a standard maxim for free society" (Springfield 1857). Slavery was an established *fact* of American life in 1776, in 1787, and—most formidably—in the 1850's; it could not be wished away; nor did the Constitution permit interference with slavery in the states where it already existed. The task of Lincoln's generation, as he saw it, was to arrest the further spread of slavery, to chain the institution within its present bounds, to re-assert the national commitment to the original principle of equal rights, and thus to condemn slavery to "ultimate extinction." But read the argument as Lincoln makes it in his Alton speech below and in the documents of Chapter 12.

The immediate outcome of the 1858 campaign was the election of Douglas to the Senate by the Illinois legislature, although Lincoln had a small edge in the popular vote. Lincoln had done considerable political damage to Douglas among Northern voters by exposing his "indifference" to slavery extension and in the South by eliciting from Douglas the "Freeport doctrine," which would permit the territories to exclude slavery even under the Dred Scott ruling. For himself, Lincoln won the national reputation as an inspiring antislavery moderate that would bring him the Republican nomination in 1860.

. . . I have stated upon former occasions, and I may as well state again, what I understand to be the real issue in this controversy between Judge Douglas and myself. On the point of my wanting to make war between the free and the slave states, there has been no issue between us. So, too, when he assumes that I am in favor of introducing a perfect social and political equality between the white and black races. These are false issues, upon which Judge Douglas has tried to force the controversy. There is no foundation in truth for the charge that I maintain either of these propositions. The real issue in this controversy—the one pressing upon every mind —is the sentiment on the part of one class that looks upon the institution of slavery *as a wrong* and of another class that *does not* look upon it as a wrong. The sentiment that contemplates the institution of slavery in this country as a wrong is the sentiment of the Republican party. It is the sentiment around which all their actions —all their arguments circle—from which all their propositions radiate. They look upon it as being a moral, social, and political wrong; and, while they contemplate it as such, they nevertheless have due regard for its actual existence among us, and the difficulties of getting rid of it in any satisfactory way and to all the constitutional obligations thrown about it. Yet having a due regard for these, they desire a policy in regard to it that looks to its not creating any more danger. They insist that it should, as far as may be, *be treated* as a wrong, and one of the methods of treating it as a wrong is to *make provision that it shall grow no larger.* They also desire a policy that looks to a peaceful end of slavery at sometime as being wrong. These are the views they entertain in regard to it as I understand them; and all their sentiments—all their arguments and propositions—are brought within this range. I have said, and I repeat it here, that if there be a man amongst us who does not think that the institution of slavery is wrong in

any one of the aspects of which I have spoken, he is misplaced and ought not to be with us. And if there be a man amongst us who is so impatient of it as a wrong as to disregard its actual presence among us and the difficulty of getting rid of it suddenly in a satisfactory way, and to disregard the constitutional obligations thrown about it, that man is misplaced if he is on our platform. We disclaim sympathy with him in practical action. He is not placed properly with us.

On this subject of treating it as a wrong, and limiting its spread, let me say a word. Has anything ever threatened the existence of this Union save and except this very institution of slavery? What is it that we hold most dear amongst us? Our own liberty and prosperity. What has ever threatened our liberty and prosperity save and except this institution of slavery? If this is true, how do you propose to improve the condition of things by enlarging slavery—by spreading it out and making it bigger? You may have a wen or cancer upon your person and not be able to cut it out lest you bleed to death; but surely it is no way to cure it, to engraft it and spread it over your whole body. That is no proper way of treating what you regard a wrong. You see this peaceful way of dealing with it as a wrong— restricting the spread of it, and not allowing it to go into new countries where it has not already existed. That is the peaceful way, the old-fashioned way, the way in which the fathers themselves set us the example.

On the other hand, I have said there is a sentiment which treats it as *not* being wrong. That is the Democratic sentiment of this day. I do not mean to say that every man who stands within that range positively asserts that it is right. That class will include all who positively assert that

Text: Political Debates Between Hon. Abraham Lincoln and Hon. Stephen A. Douglas, in the Celebrated Campaign of 1858 (Columbus, Ohio: Follett, Foster & Co., 1860), pp. 232-35 *passim.*

it is right, and all who like Judge Douglas treat it as indifferent and do not say it is either right or wrong. These two classes of men fall within the general class of those who do not look upon it as a wrong. . . .

The Democratic policy in regard to that institution will not tolerate the merest breath, the slightest hint, of the least degree of wrong about it. Try it by some of Judge Douglas' arguments. He says he "don't care whether it is voted up or voted down" in the territories. I do not care myself in dealing with that expression, whether it is intended to be expressive of his individual sentiments on the subject or only of the national policy he desires to have established. It is alike valuable for my purpose. Any man can say that who does not see anything wrong in slavery, but no man can logically say it who does see a wrong in it; because no man can logically say he does not care whether a wrong is voted up or voted down. He may say he does not care whether an indifferent thing is voted up or down, but he must logically have a choice between a right thing and a wrong thing. He contends that whatever community wants slaves has a right to have them. So they have if it is not a wrong. But if it is a wrong, he cannot say people have a right to do wrong. He says that, upon the score of equality, slaves should be allowed to go in a new territory, like other property. This is strictly logical if there is no difference between it and other property. If it and other property are equal, his argument is entirely logical. But if you insist that one is wrong and the other right, there is no use to institute a comparison between right and wrong. You may turn over everything in the Democratic policy from beginning to end, whether in the shape it takes on the statute book, in the shape it takes in the Dred Scott decision, in the shape it takes in conversation, or the shape it takes in short maxim-like arguments—it everywhere carefully excludes the idea that there is anything wrong in it.

That is the real issue. That is the issue that will continue in this country when these poor tongues of Judge Douglas and myself shall be silent. It is the eternal struggle between these two principles—right and wrong—throughout the world. They are the two principles that have stood face to face from the beginning of time and will ever continue to struggle. The one is the common right of humanity and the other the divine right of kings. It is the same principle in whatever shape it develops itself. It is the same spirit that says, "You work and toil and earn bread, and I'll eat it." No matter in what shape it comes, whether from the mouth of a king who seeks to bestride the people of his own nation and live by the fruit of their labor, or from one race of men as an apology for enslaving another race, it is the same tyrannical principle. . . .

I understood I have ten minutes yet. I will employ it in saying something about this argument Judge Douglas uses, while he sustains the Dred Scott decision, that the people of the territories can still somehow exclude slavery. The first thing I ask attention to is the fact that Judge Douglas constantly said, before the decision, that whether they could or not, *was a question for the Supreme Court.* But after the Court has made the decision, he virtually says it is *not* a question for the Supreme Court but for the people. And how is it he tells us they can exclude it? He says it needs "police regulations," and that admits of "unfriendly legislation." Although it is a right established by the Constitution of the United States to take a slave into a territory of the United States and hold him as property, yet unless the territorial legislature will give friendly legislation, and, more especially, if they adopt unfriendly legislation, they can practically exclude him. Now, without meeting this proposition as a matter of fact, I pass to consider the real constitutional obligation. Let me take the gentleman who looks me in the face before me, and let us suppose that he is a member of the territorial legislature. The first thing he will do will be to swear that he will support the Constitution of the United States. His neighbor by his side in the territory has slaves and needs territorial legislation to enable him to enjoy that constitutional right. Can he withhold the legislation which his neighbor needs for the enjoyment of a right which is fixed in his favor in the Constitution of the United States which he has sworn to support? Can he withhold it without violating his oath? And, more especially, can he pass unfriendly legislation to violate his oath? Why, this is a *monstrous* sort of talk about the Constitution of the United States! *There has never been as outlandish or lawless a doctrine from the mouth of any respectable man on earth.* I do not believe it is a constitutional right to hold slaves in a territory of the United States. I believe the decision was improperly made, and I go for reversing it. Judge Douglas is furious against those who go for reversing a decision. But he is for legislating it out of all force while the law itself stands. I repeat that there has never been so monstrous a doctrine uttered from the mouth of a respectable man. . . .

Grapes of Wrath

135 HARPER'S FERRY

from U.S. Senate, *Report on the Invasion at Harper's Ferry*, 1859

In 1858 Lincoln Republicans and Douglas Democrats still had some grounds for discussion within the constitutional framework. But Douglas was rapidly losing his influence in the South to impatient sectionalists who would not swallow a Republican victory. And Lincoln in the North could not control the actions of such abolitionists as John Brown. If the zealots on both sides did not command majority support, they could provoke crisis which would force opinion in their direction.

The nightmare vision of slave insurrection had troubled the South at least since the Nat Turner Rebellion of 1831. No abolitionist dared show his face in a Southern community during the ante-bellum decades, and few pieces of abolitionist literature escaped the censorious eye of Southern postmasters. Every state enacted severe codes to meet the menace of slave uprisings. Slave conspiracies, whether real or (more commonly) rumored, could spread alarm through the countryside. For all their proud assertions of the beneficence of slavery, Southerners could not quiet their own dark forebodings of blood and terror.

Thus old John Brown's abortive raid on the federal arsenal at Harper's Ferry (1859), probing the already raw nerves of the South, seemed to confirm the worst fears of a coming slave insurrection provoked and directed by Northern conspirators. If Brown commanded a mere handful of dedicated followers and failed utterly to enlist the voluntary support of slaves, still he brought guns and pikes enough to arm thousands and almost got the full equipment of the arsenal in his hands. If responsible Northern opinion in both parties condemned Brown as a fanatic, still he had found influential friends to encourage and finance his mission. Southerners were not in a mood to distinguish between a Lincoln who compared John Brown to the brooding assassins of history attempting to end injustice with one wild blow and a Thoreau who said: "Some eighteen hundred years ago Christ was crucified; this morning, perchance, Captain Brown was hung."

To Southern minds, in short, John Brown's raid was the bitter fruit of years of abolitionist and "Black Republican" agitation. What had been tried once would be tried again. The North had a dagger pointed at the heart of the South and would strike when it could. Secessionists made the most of their opportunity.

The following selection relates the main circumstances of the raid as seen by Jefferson Davis and his majority colleagues on a senatorial investigating committee. The language of the official report is far more restrained than that commonly employed in the press and forums of the South concerning John Brown, his confederates, and his Northern patrons.

. . . As to the attack itself at Harper's Ferry, the committee find that Brown first appeared in that neighborhood early in July, 1859. He came there under the assumed name of Isaac Smith, attended by two of his sons and a son-in-law. He gave out in the neighborhood that he was a farmer from New York, who desired to rent or purchase land in that vicinity, with a view to agricultural pursuits, and soon afterwards rented a small farm on the Maryland side of the river, and some four or five miles from Harper's Ferry, having on it convenient houses, and began farming operations in a very small way. He had little or no intercourse with the people of the country; and when questioned through the curiosity of his neighbors, stated further that

he was accustomed to mining operations, and expected to find deposits of metal in the adjacent mountains. He lived in an obscure manner, and attracted but little attention, and certainly no suspicion whatever as to his ulterior objects. Whilst there, he kept some two or three of his party, under assumed names, at Chambersburg, Pennsylvania, who there received, and from time to time forwarded to him, the arms of different kinds of which he was subsequently found in possession. Cook, one of his men spoken of above, it appears, had resided at Harper's Ferry

Text: James M. Mason, Jefferson Davis, and Graham N. Fitch, *Report on the Invasion at Harper's Ferry*, U.S. Senate Reports, 36th Congress, 1st Session, No. 278, pp. 3-8, 13 *passim*.

and its neighborhood for some twelve months before Brown appeared, pursuing various occupations. He left the Ferry a few days before the attack was made, and joined Brown at his country place. The whole number assembled with Brown at the time of the invasion were twenty-one men, making with himself in all twenty-two.

On Sunday night, the 16th of October, 1859, between 11 and 12 o'clock at night, Brown, attended by probably eighteen of his company, crossed the bridge connecting the village of Harper's Ferry with the Maryland shore, and, on reaching the Virginia side, proceeded immediately to take possession of the buildings of the armory and arsenal of the United States. These men were armed, each, with a Sharp's rifled carbine, and with revolving pistols. The inhabitants of the village asleep, the presence of this party was not known until they appeared and demanded admittance at the gate leading to the public works, which was locked. The watchman in charge states that on his refusal to admit them, the gate was opened by violence and the party entered, made him prisoner, and established themselves immediately in a strong brick building used as an engine-house, with a room for the watchmen adjoining it. They brought with them a wagon, with one horse, containing arms and some prepared torches.

The invasion thus silently commenced, was as silently conducted, none of the inhabitants having been aroused. Armed parties were then stationed at corners of the streets. Their next movement was to take possession, by detached parties of three or four, of the arsenal of the United States, where the public arms were chiefly deposited, a building not far from the engine-house; and by another party, of the workshops and other buildings of the armory, about half a mile off, on the Shenandoah river, called "Hall's rifle works." These dispositions made, an armed party was sent into the adjoining country, with a view to the seizure of two or three of the principal inhabitants, with such of their slaves as might be found, and to bring them to Harper's Ferry (in the language of Brown) as "hostages"; Cook, who had become well acquainted with the country around Harper's Ferry, acting as their guide. . . .

When daylight came, as the inhabitants left their houses, consisting chiefly of workmen and others employed in the public works, on their way to their usual occupations, and unconscious of what had occurred during the night, they were seized in the streets by Brown's men and carried as prisoners to the engine-house, until, with those previously there, they amounted to some

thirty or forty in number. Pikes were put in the hands of such of the slaves as they had taken, and they were kept under the eyes of their captors, as sentinels, near the buildings they occupied. But their movements being conducted at night, it was not until the morning was well advanced that the presence and character of the party was generally known in the village.

The nearest towns to Harper's Ferry were Charlestown, distant some ten miles, and Martinsburg, about 20. As soon as information could reach those points, the citizens assembled, hurriedly enrolled themselves into military bands, and with such arms as they could find, proceeded to the Ferry. Before their arrival, however, it would seem that some four or five of the marauders, who were stationed at "Hall's rifle works," were driven out by the citizens of the village, and either killed or captured. In the course of the day, an attack was made on the engine and watch-house by those of the armed citizens of the adjoining country who had thus hurriedly arrived, and the prisoners in the watch-house, adjoining the engine-house, were liberated. The attacking parties were fired on by the marauders in the engine-house, and some were severely wounded. It should have been stated that during the night Brown selected ten of those whom he considered the principal men of his prisoners, and carried them into the engine-house, where they were detained. The rest thus left in the watch-house were those who were liberated during the attack spoken of. The engine-house is a strong building, and was occupied by Brown, with seven or eight of his men. . . .

To conclude this narrative, it appears that as soon as intelligence could be conveyed to Washington of the state of things at Harper's Ferry, the marines on duty at the navy-yard were ordered to the scene of action, under the command of Colonel Robert E. Lee, of the army. . . .

Colonel Lee, it will be seen, found it necessary to carry the house by storm, the party within refusing to surrender except on terms properly held inadmissible. In this affair one marine was killed, and another slightly wounded.

Such, it is believed, are succinctly the facts attending this great outrage; and the committee find in response to so much of the resolutions of the Senate, that the armory and other public works of the United States were in the possession and under the control of his hostile party more than thirty hours; that besides the resistance offered by them to the military force of Virginia, they resisted by force the lawful authority of the United States sent there to dispossess them, killing one, and wounding another of the troops of the United States, and as shown that, before they were thus overpowered, they killed in the streets three of the citizens of Virginia who were alone and not even in military array, beside the negro who was killed by them on their first arrival. . . .

In answer to the inquiry contained in the third resolution of the series, "Whether such invasion and seizure was made under color of any organization, intended to subvert the government of any of the States of the Union, what was the character and extent of such organization, and whether any citizens of the United States, not present, were implicated therein, or accessory thereto, by contributions of money, arms, munitions, or otherwise," the committee report: . . .

. . . It clearly appeared that the scheme of Brown was [to] take with him comparatively but few men, but those had been carefully trained by military instruction previously, and were to act as officers. For his military force he relied, very clearly, on inciting insurrection amongst the slaves, who he supposed would flock to him as soon as it became known that he had entered the State and had been able to retain his position—an expectation to no extent realized, though it was owing alone to the loyalty and well-affected disposition of the slaves that he did not succeed in inciting a servile war, with its necessary attendants of rapine and murder of all sexes, ages, and conditions. It is very certain from the proofs before the committee, that not one of the captured slaves, although arms were placed in their hands, attempted to use them; but on the contrary, as soon as their safety would admit, in the absence of their captors, their arms were thrown away and they hastened back to their homes.

It is shown that Brown brought with him for this expedition arms sufficient to have placed an effective weapon in the hands of not less than 1,500 men; besides which, had he succeeded in obtaining the aid he looked to from the slaves, he had entirely under his control all the arms of the United States deposited in the arsenal at Harper's Ferry. After his capture, beside the arms he brought in the wagon to the Ferry, there were found on the Maryland side, where he had left them, 200 Sharp's rifled carbines, and 200 revolver pistols, packed in the boxes of the manufacturers, with 900 or 1,000 pikes, carefully and strongly made, the blade of steel being securely riveted to a handle about five feet in length; many thousand percussion caps in boxes, and ample stores of fixed ammunition, besides a large supply of powder in kegs, and a chest that contained hospital and other military stores, beside a quantity of extra clothing for troops.

For an answer to the inquiry, how far "any citizens of the United States, not present, were implicated therein or accessory thereto by contributions of money, arms, munitions, or otherwise," the committee deem it best to refer to the evidence which accompanies this report. It does not appear that such contributions were made with actual knowledge of the use for which they were designed by Brown, although it does appear that money was freely contributed by those styling themselves friends of this man Brown, and friends alike of what they styled "the cause of freedom," (of which they claimed him to be an especial apostle,) without inquiry as to the way in which the money would be used by him to advance such pretended cause. . . .

. . . With such elements at work, unchecked by law and not rebuked but encouraged by public opinion, with money freely contributed and placed in irresponsible hands, it may easily be seen how this expedition to excite servile war in one of the States of the Union was got up, and it may equally be seen how like expeditions may certainly be anticipated in future whenever desperadoes offer themselves to carry them into execution. . . . It may not become the committee to suggest a duty in those States to provide by proper legislation against machinations by their citizens or within their borders destructive of the peace of their confederate republics; but it does become them fully to expose the consequences resulting from the present license there existing, because the peace and integrity of the Union is necessarily involved in its continuance. . . .

136 JOHN BROWN'S BODY

from John Brown, Last Speech in Court, November 2, 1859

John Brown's invasion of Virginia with an "army" of twenty-one disciples (eighteen followers, it is reported, joined in the actual raid on Harper's Ferry) was a wildly improbable adventure. Apparently, Brown (1800-1859) hoped to establish himself in an Appalachian mountain stronghold and add to his numbers by forcibly liberating slaves or recruiting fugitives. The arms he brought plus those he hoped to seize from the federal arsenal would be used for further raids and for the defense of an independent freedmen's state in the Virginia mountains. Eventually so many slaves would desert their masters that the South would be forced to accept general emancipation. In his own eyes, Brown aimed at "liberation" rather than "rebellion." The practical distinction seemed insignificant to the Virginia court that tried, convicted, and hanged John Brown (with six followers) for "treason, and conspiring and advising with slaves and other rebels, and murder in the first degree."

John Brown's conduct at the trial (October 1859) was in keeping with his character and career. To plead insanity as his lawyer counseled would have robbed his mission of its significance, and Brown refused. His case was simple: he had transgressed the laws of Virginia, founded on human injustice, to serve "the law of God." His legal wrong was a moral right. So in Kansas the grim patriarch and his sons had made free use of "Beecher's Bibles"—the efficient Sharps rifles sent out from New England—in the border warfare of the mid-1850's. On May 25, 1856, men under Brown's command perpetrated the "Pottawatomie Massacre," the shooting of five proslavery settlers to avenge the previous murders of free-state men. Believing himself a soldier of the Lord, John Brown did not hesitate to sacrifice his life or his sons (two died at Harper's Ferry); nor did he hesitate to take the lives of men who stood in the way of his cause. If his violent adventures helped to destroy the grounds of sectional compromise, then, as he felt, all the better for the abolitionist cause. God's truth was not a proper subject for political bargaining.

Of such stuff are martyrs made. Emerson hailed John Brown as "that new saint," and thousands of antislavery men (but not the responsible party leaders of the North) took fresh inspiration from his death. In the South the specter of John Brown, inciter of slave rebellion, made many ponder desperate measures. In the end the old man had his way. "John Brown's Body" became a song of Union soldiers marching south.

I have, may it please the Court, a few words to say.

In the first place, I deny everything but what I have all along admitted,—the design on my part to free the slaves. I intended certainly to have made a clean thing of that matter, as I did last winter, when I went into Missouri and there took slaves without the snapping of a gun on either side, moved them through the country, and finally left them in Canada. I designed to have done the same thing again, on a larger scale. That was all I intended. I never did intend murder, or treason, or the destruction of property, or to excite or incite slaves to rebellion, or to make insurrection.

I have another objection: and that is, it is unjust that I should suffer such a penalty. Had I interfered in the manner which I admit, and which I admit has been fairly proved (for I admire the truthfulness and candor of the greater portion of the witnesses who have testified in this case),—had I so interfered in behalf of the rich, the powerful, the intelligent, the so-called

great, or in behalf of any of their friends,—either father, mother, brother, sister, wife, or children, or any of that class,—and suffered and sacrificed what I have in this interference, it would have been all right; and every man in this court would have deemed it an act worthy of reward rather than punishment.

This court acknowledges, as I suppose, the validity of the law of God. I see a book kissed here which I suppose to be the Bible, or at least the New Testament. That teaches me that all things whatsoever I would that men should do to me, I should do even so to them. It teaches me, further, to 'remember them that are in bonds, as bound with them.' I endeavored to act up to that instruction. I say, I am yet too young to understand that God is any respecter of persons. I believe that to have interfered as I have done—as I have always freely admitted I have done—in behalf of His despised poor, was not wrong, but right. Now, if it is deemed necessary that I should forfeit my life for the furtherance of the ends of justice, and mingle my blood further with the blood of my children and with the blood of millions in this slave country whose rights are disregarded by wicked, cruel, and unjust enactments,—I submit; so let it be done! . . .

Text: Franklin B. Sandborn, *The Life and Letters of John Brown* (Boston: Roberts Brothers, 1885), pp. 584-85.

CHAPTER 12

An American Tragedy—Civil War: 1860 to 1865

By 1860 the strains of sectional struggle had gravely weakened the framework and the very foundations of the American political order. One more thrust from either side and the whole structure would go. If the sections could not reach a tolerable equilibrium within the constitutional system, then it was most improbable that they could remain at peace once they met as two separate and hostile powers sharing one land. The election of Lincoln in November 1860 signaled the breakup of the Union. The firing on Fort Sumter in April 1861 brought the war. The Union and constitutional democracy failed and were restored only after four years of the most dreadful warfare the world had known.

THE BREAKING POINT

Of course the system failed because the people and their leaders responsible for its operation failed. Yet this is an evasive answer. Why this time and never before or after? Why indeed any time? It was the hope and the intention of the Founders to employ the "new science of politics" in constructing a polity that would control the classic disorders of popular government—above all, the disease of "faction." (See Madison's discussion in *Federalist* No. 10, Document 61.) The Constitution was built to contain, and restrain, diverse interests, each with a passionate determination to impose its will on the body politic. The Founders rested their case not on the angelic character of men or on the saving intervention of "enlightened statesmen" but rather on the political and social structure of the Federal Republic under the Constitution. The system was designed explicitly to account for human error.

In an important sense, then, the Civil War represented a failure of the political order. In 1860 the Constitution was still in force; elections were free; public discussion was still possible, though somewhat limited by local law and prejudice; and the courts remained open. Tolerable compromises had been found in 1820 and (briefly) in 1850. Why not again in 1860, when everyone with the least political awareness knew that the nation stood on the verge of disaster? As Calhoun had pointed out, the success of majority rule depends upon the willingness of the minority to accept defeat as preferable to rebellion. Such acceptance presupposes a *common interest* greater and more compelling than the special interest in dispute. But, he continued, once a community is split by fundamental differences of interest into a permanent majority and minority, then the majority can no longer speak legitimately for the whole, and the minority can no longer tolerate defeat. Such was the case of North and South in the Union, as Calhoun saw it.

Calhoun's vague remedy of a two-headed nation convinced no one. Here Lincoln's logic supervened: "A house divided against itself cannot stand." "I believe this government cannot endure permanently half-slave and half-free. . . . It will become all one thing or all the other." Lincoln was speaking of the long-run tendency. The leaders of the South believed him and decided not to wait. The Constitution, with its checks and balances and its recognition of slavery as a domestic institution subject to state control, could be reinterpreted and rewritten by a large, persistent Northern majority. Defeat at this point threatened disaster to the slave society of the South. Defeat seemed intolerable; and in 1860-1861 the South broke through the legal framework of democracy, claiming a right as sovereign states to refuse further obedience to national majority decisions.

In some such terms, suggested by contemporary political thought, one might view the dramatic events of 1860 and 1861 as the Union reached and passed the breaking point. Even before Lincoln could assume office on March 4, 1861, and declare his official policy intentions, seven states of the Deep South and Southwest had seceded and established the Confederate States of America.[1] For all the inexorable logic of majority tyranny, state sovereignty, and constitutional secession, the decision was hard and often close. Few downright Unionists spoke up at the Southern state secession conventions, but a substantial minority of conservatives—Alexander H. Stephens of Georgia was a distinguished example— held out as long as they could for prudence and delay. However, most of these moderates, when forced to choose between state and nation, gave their support to secession and the new Confederacy. Thus Robert E. Lee, recently the Superintendent of West Point and a man who had freed his own slaves and opposed secession, refused the high command of the Union army to serve Virginia and the Confederacy.

With secession an actuality, the outgoing President, James Buchanan, was paralyzed. He would neither accept the fact nor do anything about it. The North poured mixed counsels into Lincoln's ear, but the new President would not be the creature of imperious editors or party chiefs. He would rule as well as reign. In his Inaugural Address, Lincoln squarely faced the arguments and the fact of

---

[1] The seven seceding states of the Lower South were South Carolina (December 20, 1860), Mississippi (January 9, 1861), Florida (January 10), Alabama (January 11), Georgia (January 19), Louisiana (January 26), and Texas (February 1). The firing on Fort Sumter (April 12-13, 1861) prompted further secession: Virginia (April 17), Arkansas (May 6), Tennessee (May 7), and North Carolina (May 20). The border slave states of Delaware, Maryland, Kentucky, and Missouri remained in the Union, but not without protracted struggles in the last three. The mountainous western parts of Virginia refused secession, and a convention at Wheeling (June 11, 1861) established a Union government; eventually fifty western counties were admitted to the Union as the State of West Virginia on June 20, 1863.

secession. He pleaded for reunion; he promised consideration for the South's legitimate fears; but he would not yield either his basic policy of containment of slavery or his commitment to maintain the supremacy of the Constitution and the national laws. In the following months, against the judgment of powerful advisers, Lincoln determined to maintain the federal garrison at Fort Sumter in Charleston harbor.

THE ARGUMENT OF GUNS

When the South Carolina shore batteries opened fire on Fort Sumter, indecision ended. Almost with relief the two sides exchanged the tortuous complexities of politics for the shining simplicities (as they seemed) of war. The Upper South, but not the border, fell into line with the Confederacy. Volunteers sprang up for what appeared to be a short and glorious fight for the Union or for Southern independence. And then the shock of battle.

No bare summary can suggest the qualities of that massive four-year struggle, which cost over half a million lives, consumed billions in property, changed the face of the nation, and transformed the character of warfare itself. The South assumed the posture of defense. Its aim was independence, and Jefferson Davis adopted the strategy of beating back invasions of Confederate soil wherever they came until the Union should learn the hopelessness of restoring the nation by force. A superb set of commanders (largely drawn from the U.S. Army), the fighting qualities of the Southern people, and the compelling diplomatic powers of King Cotton were confidently expected to sustain the Confederacy against the more populous, richer, and far more self-sufficient North.

Lincoln, who fully exercised his constitutional powers as Commander in Chief, was bound to fight a war of offense. To restore the Union he must destroy the sword of the rebellion: the Confederate armies. At the same time, he would attempt to blockade the long Southern coastline, split the Confederacy at the Mississippi, and drive a wedge through Tennessee into the Gulf states. Not until 1864 did Lincoln find a general to match Lee in Virginia. In the West, Grant, Sherman, Thomas, and their subordinates gave him crucial victories, while Lee and his lieutenants were dominating the Eastern theater.

The turning point of the war came in 1863. Lee's alarming invasion of Pennsylvania was repelled decisively at Gettysburg. Grant seized control of the Mississippi at Vicksburg and pressed forward into Tennessee. Sherman was poised for the drive to Atlanta, effected in 1864, and the ensuing march through Georgia and the Carolinas. Numbers, supplies, fighting generals at last, and the coordinated strategy gave the Union a rapidly mounting superiority. Lee exacted a heavy price for every mile of Virginia soil he abandoned to the enemy, but finally in April 1865 his back was to the wall. At Appomattox Court House in Virginia, Grant accepted Lee's surrender in the best tradition of generosity for an honorable adversary. Within the month the guns of Blue and Gray were silent.

THE AIMS OF LINCOLN

The first question one asks about the Civil War is: why did the South secede? Some aspects of that question have been considered in Chapter 11 and in the preceding pages. Less meaningful to us now but urgently important to contemporaries was the corresponding question: why did the North fight? At any time from December 1860 to April 1865 the Union could have had peace by recognizing Southern independence. The slavery question could have been resolved, in a sense, by the simplest of remedies: separation. Did the North, if it stood alone, lack land, people, or resources for a prosperous career? Why could not two nations share a spacious continent? Just before Sumter not a few thoughtful and influential men were tempted by the slogan: "Let the erring sister go in peace."

Lincoln never gave serious consideration to the possibility of peaceful separation. The nation was in origin, form, and destiny a single body politic. There was no lawful way for a part of the Union to withdraw its allegiance. If a minority should exercise its right of revolution, then the government must execute its sworn pledge under the Constitution to maintain the national authority. This was more than a formal, legal theory for Lincoln. Secession put a test question "to the whole family of man": "Is there, in all republics, this inherent, and fatal weakness? Must a government, of necessity, be too *strong* for the liberties of its own people, or too *weak* to maintain its own existence?" Secession in short put democracy on trial before the world, and Lincoln was determined to vindicate the great experiment of the Founders. And something more:

> Physically speaking, we cannot separate. . . . A husband and wife may be divorced, and go out of the presence and beyond the reach of each other; but the different parts of our country cannot do this. They cannot but remain face to face, and intercourse, either amicable or hostile, must continue between them. . . . Can aliens make treaties easier than friends can make laws?

At first, then, Lincoln's object was to restore the Union as it had been. Until late in 1862 he resisted Radical Republican demands that he enlarge the war aims of the North to include emancipation. He detested slavery, but he would not risk dividing the supporters of the Union and imperiling the primary object of the struggle. Finally, on January 1, 1863, he proclaimed emancipation as a military necessity. What justice had always recommended, prudence now approved. The decision Lincoln understood to be irreversible. With his full support the Thirteenth Amendment abolishing slavery was moved through Congress and awaited ratification at the time of his death in April 1865.

Emancipation for Lincoln was not an act of vengeance against the South or in itself a final solution to the profound race problem. Lincoln never used his powerful voice or his supreme authority to excite hatred or exact punishment. He had hoped for a gradual transition from slavery to freedom, with the North bearing its part of the cost. He offered the South a relatively easy and honorable road to reunion. Emancipation was one minimum condition of reconstruction, but he counseled patience in advancing the freedmen by degrees to citizenship.

The work of finishing the war and rebuilding the nation should proceed "with malice toward none; with charity for all." But it should be carried forward "with firmness in the right, as God gives us to see the right." Lincoln offered generosity and understanding to the South; yet he demanded as he had always done that the principles of the Declaration of Independence should remain

> a standard maxim for free society, which should be familiar to all, and revered by all, constantly looked to, constantly labored for, and even though never perfectly attained, constantly approximated, and thereby constantly spreading and deepening its influence, and augmenting the happiness and value of life to all people of all colors everywhere.

The mad act of an assassin put the decisions of peace and reconstruction in other, cruder hands. One cannot doubt that the South, the freedmen, and the nation paid a cruel price for one man's deadly theatrical performance on the night of April 14, 1865. The South would endure an ill-planned revolution from above and undo as much of the work as it dared when the nation lost its zeal for vengeance and for reform. The North would experience its own industrial revolution, energized by the war economy of 1861-1865, and in a mood of irresponsible indifference permit the degradation of the democratic dogma.

The Breaking Point

137

FOR GEORGIA AND THE UNION: A PLEA FOR PRUDENCE

from Alexander H. Stephens, Speech in the Georgia House of Representatives, November 14, 1860

After a decade of furious sectional conflict, something had to give. The partisans of North and South would not recede from their demands; on the contrary they grew more adamant, more hostile, with each new crisis. It was the Union that gave way.

The first clear sign that the nation had reached the breaking point appeared at Baltimore in April of 1860, when the delegates from eight Southern states bolted the Democratic party convention rather than accept Douglas and popular sovereignty. Finally, in June, the Southern Democrats picked their own presidential candidate, John C. Breckinridge of Kentucky, and wrote a platform demanding federal protection for slavery in the territories. With the splitting of the only remaining national party, the election of 1860 became a test of sectional strength, and Lincoln's victory was assured. The Republican candidate won 40 per cent of the popular vote and 180 electoral votes out of the total of 303, carrying every free state from Maine to California. Douglas followed with 29 per cent of the popular vote but captured only a dozen electoral votes. His Democratic rival, Breckinridge, swept the South from the Carolinas to Texas, piling up 72 electoral votes with only 18 per cent of the popular ballot. The border area of Virginia, Kentucky, and Tennessee followed John Bell and his makeshift compromise party of Constitutional Unionists. The two salient features of the election were the sharply sectional character of the voting and the heavy preponderance of pro-Union sentiment (Lincoln and Douglas polled over 69 per cent of the popular vote).

However badly the South might have misjudged Lincoln's purposes and its own immediate peril, it did not mistake the obvious lesson of the vote. Calhoun had been warning the slave states since the 1830's that they were fated to remain a permanent minority in the Union. When the Georgia legislature learned of Lincoln's victory, it promptly turned to the proposal for a special state convention that would decide the question of secession. The Assembly called a series of evening meetings to be addressed by Georgia's leading spokesmen. On the first two nights the legislators heard the belligerent appeals of "fire-eaters" Thomas R. R. Cobb and Robert Toombs. On the third night Alexander H. Stephens (1812-1883), an old-time Whig and Unionist who had represented Georgia in the Congress since 1843, tried to turn the tide.

Stephens' moving speech reveals the double loyalties of many Southerners who valued the Union, respected the Constitution, feared for the rights and interests of the slave states, and hoped somehow to put off the terrible choice between home and nation. Stephens continued his battle for delay and compromise in the Georgia Convention of January 1861. But like nearly all distinguished Southern moderates he accepted the decision of his state for secession, and he served the Confederacy as Vice-President through the Civil War.

. . . FELLOW-CITIZENS: I appear before you tonight at the request of members of the Legislature and others to speak of matters of the deepest interest that can possibly concern us all of an earthly character. There is nothing—no question or subject connected with this life—that concerns a free people so intimately as that of the Government under which they live. We are now,

Text: *The Rebellion Record: A Diary of American Events, with Documents, Narratives, Illustrative Incidents, Poetry, etc.*, ed. Frank Moore (New York: D. Van Nostrand, 1867), I, 219-21, 224-27 *passim*.

indeed, surrounded by evils. Never since I entered upon the public stage has the country been so environed with difficulties and dangers that threatened the public peace and the very existence of society as now. . . .

My object is not to stir up strife, but to allay it; not to appeal to your passions, but to your reason. Good governments can never be built up or sustained by the impulse of passion. I wish to address myself to your good sense, to your good judgment, and if after hearing you disagree, let us agree to disagree, and part as we met, friends. We all have the same object, the same interest. That people should disagree in republican governments, upon questions of public policy, is natural. That men should disagree upon all matters connected with human investigation, whether relating to science or human conduct, is natural. Hence, in free governments parties will arise. But a free people should express their different opinions with liberality and charity, with no acrimony toward those of their fellows, when honestly and sincerely given. These are my feelings to-night. . . .

The first question that presents itself is shall the people of the South secede from the Union in consequence of the election of Mr. Lincoln to the presidency of the United States? My countrymen, *I tell you frankly, candidly, and earnestly, that I do not think that they ought*. In my judgment, the election of no man, constitutionally chosen to that high office, is sufficient cause for any State to separate from the Union. It ought to stand by and aid still in maintaining the constitution of the country. To make a point of resistance to the Government, to withdraw from it because a man has been constitutionally elected, puts us in the wrong. We are pledged to maintain the Constitution. Many of us have sworn to support it. Can we, therefore, for the mere election of a man to the Presidency, and that too in accordance with the prescribed forms of the Constitution, make a point of resistance to the Government without becoming the breakers of that sacred instrument ourselves, withdraw ourselves from it? Would we not be in the wrong? Whatever fate is to befall this country, let it never be laid to the charge of the people of the South, and especially to the people of Georgia, that we were untrue to our national engagements. Let the fault and the wrong rest upon others. If all our hopes are to be blasted, if the Republic is to go down, let us be found to the last moment standing on the deck, with the Constitution of the United States waving over our heads. (Applause.) Let the fanatics of the North break the Constitution, if such is their fell purpose.

Let the responsibility be upon them. I shall speak presently more of their acts; but let not the South, let us not be the ones to commit the aggression. We went into the election with this people. The result was different from what we wished; but the election has been constitutionally held. Were we to make a point of resistance to the Government and go out of the Union on that account, the record would be made up hereafter against us.

But it is said Mr. Lincoln's policy and principles are against the Constitution, and that if he carries them out it will be destructive of our rights. Let us not anticipate a threatened evil. If he violates the Constitution then will come our time to act. Do not let us break it because, forsooth, he may. If he does, that is the time for us to strike. (Applause.) I think it would be injudicious and unwise to do this sooner. I do not anticipate that Mr. Lincoln will do any thing to jeopard our safety or security, whatever may be his spirit to do it; for he is bound by the constitutional checks which are thrown around him, which at this time renders him powerless to do any great mischief. This shows the wisdom of our system. The President of the United States is no emperor, no dictator—he is clothed with no absolute power. He can do nothing unless he is backed by power in Congress. The House of Representatives is largely in the majority against him.

In the Senate he will also be powerless. There will be a majority of four against him. . . . Mr. Lincoln cannot appoint an officer without the consent of the Senate—he cannot form a Cabinet without the same consent. He will be in the condition of George III., (the embodiment of Toryism,) who had to ask the Whigs to appoint his ministers, and was compelled to receive a cabinet utterly opposed to his views; and so Mr. Lincoln will be compelled to ask of the Senate to choose for him a cabinet, if the Democracy of that body choose to put him on such terms. He will be compelled to do this or let the Government stop, if the National Democratic men—for that is their name at the North—the conservative men in the Senate, should so determine. Then, how can Mr. Lincoln obtain a cabinet which would aid him, or allow him to violate the Constitution?

Why then, I say, should we disrupt the ties of this Union when his hands are tied, when he can do nothing against us? . . .

My honorable friend who addressed you last night, (Mr. Toombs,) and to whom I listened with the profoundest attention, asks if we would submit to Black Republican rule? I say to you and to him, as a Georgian, I never would submit to any Black Republican *aggression* upon our constitutional rights. I will never consent myself, as much as I admire this Union for the glories of the past, or the blessings of the present, as much as it has done for the people of all these States, as much as it has done for civilization, as much as the hopes of the world hang upon it, I would never submit to aggression upon my rights to maintain it longer; and if they cannot be maintained in the Union, standing on the Georgia platform, where I have stood from the time of its adoption, I would be in favor of disrupting every tie which binds the States together.

I will have equality for Georgia and for the citizens of Georgia in this Union, or I will look for new safeguards elsewhere. This is my position. The only question now is, can they be secured in the Union? That is what I am counselling with you to-night about. Can it be secured? In my judgment it may be, but it may not be; but let us do all we can, so that in the future, if the worst come, it may never be said we were negligent in doing our duty to the last.

My countrymen, I am not of those who believe this Union has been a curse up to this time. True men, men of integrity, entertain different views from me on this subject. I do not question their right to do so; I would not impugn their motives in so doing. Nor will I undertake to say that this Government of our fathers is perfect. There is nothing perfect in this world of a human origin. Nothing connected with human nature, from man himself to any of his works. You may select the wisest and best men for your judges, and yet how many defects are there in the administration of justice? You may select the wisest and best men for your legislators, and yet how many defects are apparent in your laws? And it is so in our Government.

But that this Government of our fathers, with all its defects, comes nearer the objects of all good Governments than any other on the face of the earth is my settled conviction. . . .

When I look around and see our prosperity in every thing, agriculture, commerce, art, science, and every department of education, physical and mental, as well as moral advancement, and our colleges, I think, in the face of such an exhibition, if we can without the loss of power, or any essential right or interest, remain in the Union, it is our duty to ourselves and to posterity to— let us not too readily yield to this temptation— do so. Our first parents, the great progenitors of the human race, were not without a like temptation when in the garden of Eden. They were led to believe that their condition would be bettered—that their eyes would be opened—and that they would become as gods. They in an evil

hour yielded—instead of becoming gods they only saw their own nakedness.

I look upon this country with our institutions as the Eden of the world, the paradise of the universe. It may be that out of it we may become greater and more prosperous, but I am candid and sincere in telling you that I fear if we rashly evince passion and without sufficient cause shall take that step, that instead of becoming greater or more peaceful, prosperous, and happy—instead of becoming gods, we will become demons, and at no distant day commence cutting one another's throats. This is my apprehension. Let us, therefore, whatever we do, meet these difficulties, great as they are, like wise and sensible men, and consider them in the light of all the consequences which may attend our action. Let us see first clearly where the path of duty leads, and then we may not fear to tread therein. . . .

My honorable friend said last night, "I ask you to give me the sword, for if you do not give it to me, as God lives, I will take it myself."

Mr. Toombs—I will. (Applause on the other side.)

Mr. Stephens—I have no doubt that my honorable friend feels as he says. It is only his excessive ardor that makes him use such an expression; but this will pass off with the excitement of the hour. When the people in their majesty shall speak, I have no doubt that he will bow to their will, whatever it may be, upon the "sober second thought." (Applause.)

Should Georgia determine to go out of the Union, I speak for one, though my views might not agree with them, whatever the result may be, I shall bow to the will of her people. Their cause is my cause, and their destiny is my destiny; and I trust this will be the ultimate course of all. The greatest curse that can befall a free people is civil war. . . .

I am for exhausting all that patriotism can demand before taking the last step. I would invite, therefore, South Carolina to a conference. I would ask the same of all the other Southern States, so that if the evil has got beyond our control, which God, in his mercy, grant may not be the case, let us not be divided among ourselves—(cheers,)—but, if possible, secure the united coöperation of all the Southern States; and then, in the face of the civilized world, we may justify our action; and, with the wrong all on the other side, we can appeal to the God of battles to aid us in our cause. (Loud applause.) But let us not do any thing in which any portion of our people may charge us with rash or hasty action. It is certainly a matter of great importance to tear this Government asunder. You were not sent here for that purpose. I would wish the whole South to be united if this is to

be done; and I believe if we pursue the policy which I have indicated, this can be effected. . . .

138   DECLARATION OF INDEPENDENCE: SOUTH CAROLINA

from *South Carolina Declaration of the Causes of Secession*, December 21, 1860

The Southern people, Alexander Stephens wrote on the eve of secession, "are wild with passion and frenzy, doing they know not what." Lincoln's election was taken as a deadly challenge to the essential interests of the South, as the last irremediable act of what South Carolina called "this sectional combination for the subversion of the Constitution." In state after state, the secessionist radicals forced the issue to a decision, over the substantial opposition of moderates like Stephens, and won majorities in the state conventions. South Carolina, long the spearhead of extremist forces, led the way out of the Union on December 20, 1860. Mississippi, Florida, Alabama, Georgia, Louisiana, and Texas all had followed by February 1861, a month before the inauguration of Lincoln. On February 4 the seceding states assembled in convention at Montgomery, Alabama, to frame a constitution and establish a provisional government for the Confederate States of America. Within a week they completed their task and elected Jefferson Davis provisional President and Alexander H. Stephens Vice-President of the new regime.

The reasons for secession must be found not only in official explanations (such as that of South Carolina given in the following selection) but in the full history of the preceding decades. The sharpening contrast of slave and free society, the clash of ideas, the policy disputes over the territories and the fugitives, the argument of blood that came with Kansas and John Brown: all helped prepare the South for its tragic choice. By 1860 the Union began to appear as an enemy, and an independent Southern nation gradually became the focus for common hopes and plans.

The legal argument for secession was the one Calhoun had taught the South. If the Union was but a confederacy of fully sovereign states, then each state became the final judge of its constitutional rights. A state that found itself oppressed and without other remedy might withdraw its allegiance from the Union, not as a revolutionary act but as a normal exercise of constitutional right. South Carolina and the other seceding states made plain their view of the nature of the oppression which they had suffered under the Union. Each grievance came down to a Northern threat against slavery. Northern states had interfered with the return of fugitive slaves by passing so-called "personal liberty" laws (a case, it should be noted, of the South demanding the use of federal authority and the North appealing to "state rights"). Northern leaders, notably Lincoln and the "Black Republicans," were sworn to exclude slavery from the territories, to refuse admission to new slave states, and generally to work toward the ultimate extinction of the institution.

Why not then stand up to tyranny before it was too late? Would the North dare to confront a united Southern Confederacy? If it dared, how long could it sustain a way of coercion when the South stood on its own soil, defending its sacred rights and vital interests? Would not the power of King Cotton beggar the North and buy the recognition and support of foreign nations?

The floundering lame-duck President, James Buchanan, could only wait and hope for some deliverance; but Lincoln would reply on March 4 with a message of stunning force and eloquence. (See Document 139.)

. . . And now the State of South Carolina having resumed her separate and equal place among nations, deems it due to herself, to the remaining United States of America, and to the nations of

Text: The Rebellion Record: A Diary of American Events, with Documents, Narratives, Illustrative Incidents, Poetry, etc., ed. Frank Moore (New York: D. Van Nostrand, 1867), I, 3-4.

the world, that she should declare the immediate causes which have led to this act.

In the year 1765, that portion of the British Empire embracing Great Britain undertook to make laws for the Government of that portion composed of the thirteen American Colonies. A struggle for the right of self-government ensued, which resulted, on the 4th of July, 1776, in a

Declaration, by the Colonies, "that they are, and of right ought to be, FREE AND INDEPENDENT STATES; and that, as free and independent States, they have full power to levy war, conclude peace, contract alliances, establish commerce, and to do all other acts and things which independent States may of right do."

They further solemnly declared that whenever any "form of government becomes destructive of the ends for which it was established, it is the right of the people to alter or abolish it, and to institute a new government." Deeming the Government of Great Britain to have become destructive of these ends, they declared that the Colonies "are absolved from all allegiance to the British Crown, and that all political connection between them and the State of Great Britain is, and ought to be, totally dissolved." . . .

Thus were established the two great principles asserted by the Colonies, namely, the right of a State to govern itself; and the right of a people to abolish a Government when it becomes destructive of the ends for which it was instituted. And concurrent with the establishment of these principles, was the fact, that each Colony became and was recognized by the mother country as a FREE, SOVEREIGN AND INDEPENDENT STATE.

In 1787, Deputies were appointed by the States to revise the articles of Confederation; and on 17th September, 1787, these Deputies recommended, for the adoption of the States, the Articles of Union, known as the Constitution of the United States.

The parties to whom this constitution was submitted were the several sovereign States; they were to agree or disagree, and when nine of them agreed, the compact was to take effect among those concurring; and the General Government, as the common agent, was then to be invested with their authority. . . .

Thus was established, by compact between the States, a Government with defined objects and powers, limited to the express words of the grant. This limitation left the whole remaining mass of power subject to the clause reserving it to the States or the people, and rendered unnecessary any specification of reserved rights. We hold that the Government thus established is subject to the two great principles asserted in the Declaration of Independence; and we hold further, that the mode of its formation subjects it to a third fundamental principle, namely, the law of compact. We maintain that in every compact between two or more parties, the obligation is mutual; that the failure of one of the contracting parties to perform a material part of the agreement, entirely releases the obligation of the

other; and that, where no arbiter is provided, each party is remitted to his own judgment to determine the fact of failure, with all its consequences.

In the present case, the fact is established with certainty. We assert that fourteen of the States have deliberately refused for years past to fulfil their constitutional obligations, and we refer to their own statutes for the proof.

The Constitution of the United States, in its fourth Article, provides as follows: "No person held to service or labor in one State under the laws thereof, escaping into another, shall, in consequence of any law or regulation therein, be discharged from such service or labor, but shall be delivered up, on claim of the party to whom such service or labor may be due."

This stipulation was so material to the compact that without it that compact would not have been made. The greater number of the contracting parties held slaves, and they had previously evinced their estimate of the value of such a stipulation by making it a condition in the Ordinance for the government of the territory ceded by Virginia, which obligations, and the laws of the General Government, have ceased to effect the objects of the Constitution. The States of Maine, New Hampshire, Vermont, Massachusetts, Connecticut, Rhode Island, New York, Pennsylvania, Illinois, Indiana, Michigan, Wisconsin, and Iowa, have enacted laws which either nullify the acts of Congress, or render useless any attempt to execute them. In many of these States the fugitive is discharged from the service of labor claimed, and in none of them has the State Government complied with the stipulation made in the Constitution. . . . Thus the constitutional compact has been deliberately broken and disregarded by the non-slaveholding States; and the consequence follows that South Carolina is released from her obligation.

The ends for which this Constitution was framed are declared by itself to be "to form a more perfect union, establish justice, insure domestic tranquillity, provide for the common defence, promote the general welfare, and secure the blessings of liberty to ourselves and our posterity."

These ends it endeavored to accomplish by a Federal Government, in which each State was recognized as an equal, and had separate control over its own institutions. The right of property in slaves was recognized by giving to free persons distinct political rights; by giving them the right to represent, and burdening them with direct taxes for, three-fifths of their slaves; by authorizing the importation of slaves for twenty years; and by stipulating for the rendition of fugitives from labor.

We affirm that these ends for which this Government was instituted have been defeated, and the Government itself has been destructive of them by the action of the non-slaveholding States. Those States have assumed the right of deciding upon the propriety of our domestic institutions; and have denied the rights of property established in fifteen of the States and recognized by the Constitution; they have denounced as sinful the institution of Slavery; they have permitted the open establishment among them of societies, whose avowed object is to disturb the peace of and eloin the property of the citizens of other States. They have encouraged and assisted thousands of our slaves to leave their homes; and those who remain, have been incited by emissaries, books, and pictures, to servile insurrection.

For twenty-five years this agitation has been steadily increasing, until it has now secured to its aid the power of the common Government. Observing the *forms* of the Constitution, a sectional party has found within that article establishing the Executive Department, the means of subverting the Constitution itself. A geographical line has been drawn across the Union, and all the States north of that line have united in the election of a man to the high office of President of the United States whose opinions and purposes are hostile to Slavery. He is to be intrusted with the administration of the common Government, because he has declared that that "Government cannot endure permanently half slave, half free," and that the public mind must rest in the belief that Slavery is in the course of ultimate extinction.

This sectional combination for the subversion of the Constitution has been aided, in some of the States, by elevating to citizenship persons who, by the supreme law of the land, are incapable of becoming citizens; and their votes have been used to inaugurate a new policy, hostile to the South, and destructive of its peace and safety.

On the 4th of March next this party will take possession of the Government. It has announced that the South shall be excluded from the common territory, that the Judicial tribunal shall be made sectional, and that a war must be waged against Slavery until it shall cease throughout the United States.

The guarantees of the Constitution will then no longer exist; the equal rights of the States will be lost. The Slaveholding States will no longer have the power of self-government, or self-protection, and the Federal Government will have become their enemy.

Sectional interest and animosity will deepen the irritation; and all hope of remedy is rendered vain, by the fact that the public opinion at the North has invested a great political error with the sanctions of a more erroneous religious belief.

We, therefore, the people of South Carolina, by our delegates in Convention assembled, appealing to the Supreme Judge of the world for the rectitude of our intentions, have solemnly declared that the Union heretofore existing between this State and the other States of North America is dissolved, and that the State of South Carolina has resumed her position among the nations of the world, as separate and independent state, with full power to levy war, conclude peace, contract alliances, establish commerce, and to do all other acts and things which independent States may of right do.

139

NOT ENEMIES BUT FRIENDS: LINCOLN'S FIRST INAUGURAL

from Abraham Lincoln, First Inaugural Address, March 4, 1861

The choice of Lincoln by the Republican party convention of 1860 was favored by his western background, his appealing career (the "Railsplitter"), his rugged simplicity ("Honest Abe"), his eloquence, even by his comparative obscurity and lack of a troublesome public record. Yet Lincoln's greatest asset was his firm but temperate position on slavery, defined in a series of notable speeches since 1854 and brought to national attention in the great debates with Douglas (see Documents 133 and 134). There could be little doubt among his supporters that Abraham Lincoln as President would respect the constitutional limits on his powers to interfere with slavery in the Southern states, would accept his constitutional obligation to enforce a reasonable fugitive slave law, and would in general approach his task with an understanding that slavery was a deep-rooted and perplexing problem of American life which would not yield to crude and hasty remedies.

Still clearer was Lincoln's determination both to arrest the growth of slavery and to maintain the integrity of the nation. As inaugural day, March 4, approached, the available alternatives were few and sharp. Desultory efforts at compromise during the secession winter of 1860-1861 had failed hopelessly to satisfy either Northern Republicans or Southern Democrats. Horace Greeley of the New York *Tribune* and other antislavery spokesmen had turned to counsels of despair in the face of an impending civil war: "Wayward sisters, depart in peace!"

Lincoln boarded his special train from Springfield to Washington on February 11, 1861, "with a task before me greater than that which rested upon Washington." Along the way he made dozens of short speeches, mostly vague and reassuring, and a few major statements of broad purpose: for example, his affirmation at Independence Hall in Philadelphia (February 22) that the great purpose of the nation was embodied in the promise of the Declaration "that in due time the weights should be lifted from the shoulders of all men, and that *all* should have an equal chance." "If," Lincoln concluded, "this country cannot be saved without giving up that principle—I was about to say I would rather be assassinated on this spot than surrender to it."

Assassination was not an idle notion. Ugly rumors of a plot in Baltimore led Lincoln's managers to get him secretly aboard his special train, which traveled through the night to Washington. Soldiers were placed at strategic points along Pennsylvania Avenue as the inaugural parade moved slowly to the Capitol. There Lincoln—in the strange company of James Buchanan, the Northern "doughface" who had bent readily to Southern demands, and Chief Justice Taney, the author of the Dred Scott decision—pronounced his judgments on the error of "constitutional secession," on the safety of the South's domestic institutions against federal invasion, on the obligation to return fugitive slaves, on the binding force of majority decisions, on the perpetuity and supreme value of the Union. Without specifying in precise terms the methods he would follow to meet Southern resistance, Lincoln revealed his determination to maintain the authority of the nation under the Constitution.

There was a plain threat to rebels in his words, but above that threat there was a whole-hearted appeal to common memories and purposes and interests. Threat and appeal were equally useless, however, for Lincoln yielded nothing to the South's demands on slavery extension. Perhaps by March 4, 1861, no concession short of full capitulation would have been sufficient.

Fellow Citizens of the United States: In compliance with a custom as old as the government itself, I appear before you to address you briefly, and to take in your presence the oath prescribed by the Constitution of the United States to be taken by the President "before he enters on the execution of his office."

I do not consider it necessary at present for me to discuss those matters of administration about which there is no special anxiety or excitement.

Apprehension seems to exist among the people of the Southern states that by the accession of a Republican administration their property and their peace and personal security are to be endangered. There has never been any reasonable cause for such apprehension. Indeed, the most ample evidence to the contrary has all the while existed and been open to their inspection. It is found in nearly all the published speeches of him who now addresses you. I do but quote from one of those speeches when I declare that "I have no purpose, directly or indirectly, to interfere with the institution of slavery in the states where it exists. I believe I have no lawful right to do so, and I have no inclination to do so." Those who nominated and elected me did so with full knowledge that I had made this

and many similar declarations, and had never recanted them. And, more than this, they placed in the platform for my acceptance, and as a law to themselves and to me, the clear and emphatic resolution which I now read:

"*Resolved*, That the maintenance inviolate of the rights of the states, and especially the right of each state to order and control its own domestic institutions according to its own judgment exclusively, is essential to that balance of power on which the perfection and endurance of our political fabric depend, and we denounce the lawless invasion by armed force of the soil of any state or territory, no matter under what pretext, as among the gravest of crimes."

I now reiterate these sentiments; and, in doing so, I only press upon the public attention the most conclusive evidence of which the case is susceptible, that the property, peace, and security of no section are to be in any wise endangered by the now incoming administration. I add, too, that all the protection which, consistently with the Constitution and the laws, can be given, will be cheerfully given to all the states when lawfully

Text: Abraham Lincoln, *Complete Works*, ed. John G. Nicolay and John Hay (New York: The Century Co., 1902), II, 1-7.

demanded, for whatever cause—as cheerfully to one section as to another.

There is much controversy about the delivering up of fugitives from service or labor. The clause I now read is as plainly written in the Constitution as any other of its provisions:

"No person held to service or labor in one state, under the laws thereof, escaping into another, shall in consequence of any law or regulation therein be discharged from such service or labor, but shall be delivered up on claim of the party to whom such service or labor may be due."

It is scarcely questioned that this provision was intended by those who made it for the reclaiming of what we call fugitive slaves; and the intention of the lawgiver is the law. All members of Congress swear their support to the whole Constitution—to this provision as much as to any other. To the proposition, then, that slaves whose cases come within the terms of this clause "shall be delivered up," their oaths are unanimous. Now, if they would make the effort in good temper, could they not with nearly equal unanimity frame and pass a law by means of which to keep good that unanimous oath?

There is some difference of opinion whether this clause should be enforced by national or by state authority; but surely that difference is not a very material one. If the slave is to be surrendered, it can be of but little consequence to him or to others by which authority it is done. And should anyone in any case be content that his oath shall go unkept on a merely unsubstantial controversy as to how it shall be kept?

Again, in any law upon this subject, ought not all the safeguards of liberty known in civilized and humane jurisprudence to be introduced, so that a free man be not, in any case, surrendered as a slave? And might it not be well at the same time to provide by law for the enforcement of that clause in the Constitution which guarantees that "the citizen of each state shall be entitled to all privileges and immunities of citizens in the several states"?

I take the official oath today with no mental reservations, and with no purpose to construe the Constitution or laws by any hypercritical rules. And while I do not choose now to specify particular acts of Congress as proper to be enforced, I do suggest that it will be much safer for all, both in official and private stations, to conform to and abide by all those acts which stand unrepealed, than to violate any of them, trusting to find impunity in having them held to be unconstitutional.

It is seventy-two years since the first inauguration of a president under our national Constitution. During that period fifteen different and greatly distinguished citizens have, in succession, administered the executive branch of the government. They have conducted it through many perils, and generally with great success. Yet, with all this scope of precedent, I now enter upon the same task for the brief constitutional term of four years under great and peculiar difficulty. A disruption of the federal Union, heretofore only menaced, is now formidably attempted.

I hold that, in contemplation of universal law and of the Constitution, the union of these states is perpetual. Perpetuity is implied, if not expressed, in the fundamental law of all national governments. It is safe to assert that no government proper ever had a provision in its organic law for its own termination. Continue to execute all the express provisions of our national Constitution, and the Union will endure forever—it being impossible to destroy it except by some action not provided for in the instrument itself.

Again, if the United States be not a government proper, but an association of states in the nature of contract merely, can it, as a contract, be peaceably unmade by less than all the parties who made it? One party to a contract may violate it—break it, so to speak; but does it not require all to lawfully rescind it?

Descending from these general principles, we find the proposition that, in legal contemplation the Union is perpetual confirmed by the history of the Union itself. The Union is much older than the Constitution. It was formed, in fact, by the Articles of Association in 1774. It was matured and continued by the Declaration of Independence in 1776. It was further matured, and the faith of all the then thirteen states expressly plighted and engaged that it should be perpetual, by the Articles of Confederation in 1778. And, finally, in 1787 one of the declared objects for ordaining and establishing the Constitution was "to form a more perfect Union."

But if the destruction of the Union by one or by a part only of the states be lawfully possible, the Union is less perfect than before the Constitution, having lost the vital element of perpetuity.

It follows from these views that no state upon its own mere motion can lawfully get out of the Union; that resolves and ordinances to that effect are legally void; and that acts of violence, within any state or states, against the authority of the United States, are insurrectionary or revolutionary, according to circumstances.

I therefore consider that, in view of the Constitution and the laws, the Union is unbroken and to the extent of my ability I shall take care, as the Constitution itself expressly enjoins upon me, that the laws of the Union be faithfully executed in all the states. Doing this I deem to be only a simple duty on my part; and I shall perform it so far as practicable, unless my rightful masters, the American people, shall withhold the requisite means, or in some authoritative manner direct the contrary. I trust this will not be regarded as a menace, but only as the declared purpose of the Union that it will constitutionally defend and maintain itself.

In doing this there needs to be no bloodshed or violence; and there shall be none, unless it be forced upon the national authority. The power confided to me will be used to hold, occupy, and possess the property and places belonging to the government, and to collect the duties and imposts; but beyond what may be necessary for these objects, there will be no invasion, no using of force against or among the people anywhere. Where hostility to the United States, in any interior locality, shall be so great and universal as to prevent competent resident citizens from holding the federal offices, there will be no attempt to force obnoxious strangers among the people for that object. While the strict legal right may exist in the government to enforce the exercise of these offices, the attempt to do so would be so irritating, and so nearly impracticable withal, that I deem it better to forego for the time the uses of such offices.

The mails, unless repelled, will continue to be furnished in all parts of the Union. So far as possible, the people everywhere shall have that sense of perfect security which is most favorable to calm thought and reflection. The course here indicated will be followed unless current events and experience shall show a modification or change to be proper, and in every case and exigency my best discretion will be exercised according to circumstances actually existing, and with a view and a hope of a peaceful solution of the national troubles and the restoration of fraternal sympathies and affections.

That there are persons in one section or another who seek to destroy the Union at all events, and are glad of any pretext to do it, I will neither affirm nor deny; but if there be such, I need address no word to them. To those, however, who really love the Union may I not speak?

Before entering upon so grave a matter as the destruction of our national fabric, with all its benefits, its memories, and its hopes, would it not be wise to ascertain precisely why we do it? Will you hazard so desperate a step while there is any possibility that any portion of the ills you fly from have no real existence? Will you, while the certain ills you fly to are greater than all the real ones you fly from—will you risk the commission of so fearful a mistake?

All profess to be content in the Union if all constitutional rights can be maintained. Is it true, then, that any right, plainly written in the Constitution, has been denied? I think not. Happily the human mind is so constituted that no party can reach to the audacity of doing this. Think, if you can, of a single instance in which a plainly written provision of the Constitution has ever been denied. If by the mere force of numbers a majority should deprive a minority of any clearly written constitutional right, it might, in a moral point of view, justify revolution—certainly would if such a right were a vital one. But such is not our case. All the vital rights of minorities and of individuals are so plainly assured to them by affirmations and negations, guarantees and prohibitions, in the Constitution, that controversies never arise concerning them. But no organic law can ever be framed with a provision specifically applicable to every question which may occur in practical administration. No foresight can anticipate, nor any document of reasonable length contain, express provisions for all possible questions. Shall fugitives from labor be surrendered by national or by state authority? The Constitution does not expressly say. *May* Congress prohibit slavery in the territories? The Constitution does not expressly say. *Must* Congress protect slavery in the territories? The Constitution does not expressly say.

From questions of this class spring all our constitutional controversies, and we divide upon them into majorities and minorities. If the minority will not acquiesce, the majority must, or the government must cease. There is no other alternative; for continuing the government is acquiescence on one side or the other.

If a minority in such case will secede rather than acquiesce, they make a precedent which in turn will divide and ruin them; for a minority of their own will secede from them whenever a majority refuses to be controlled by such minority. For instance, why may not any portion of a new confederacy a year or two hence arbitrarily secede again, precisely as portions of the present Union now claim to secede from it? All who cherish disunion sentiments are now being educated to the exact temper of doing this.

Is there such perfect identity of interests among the states to compose a new Union, as to produce harmony only, and prevent renewed secession?

Plainly, the central idea of secession is the essence of anarchy. A majority held in restraint by constitutional checks and limitations, and always changing easily with deliberate changes of popular opinions and sentiments, is the only true sovereign of a free people. Whoever rejects it does, of necessity, fly to anarchy or to despotism. Unanimity is impossible; the rule of a minority, as a permanent arrangement, is wholly inadmissible, so that, rejecting the majority principle, anarchy or despotism in some form is all that is left.

I do not forget the position, assumed by some, that constitutional questions are to be decided by the Supreme Court; nor do I deny that such decisions must be binding, in any case, upon the parties to a suit, as to the object of that suit, while they are also entitled to very high respect and consideration in all parallel cases by all other departments of the government. And while it is obviously possible that such decisions may be erroneous in any given case, still the evil effect following it, being limited to that particular case, with the chance that it may be overruled and never become a precedent for other cases, can better be borne than could the evils of a different practice. At the same time, the candid citizen must confess that if the policy of the government, upon vital questions affecting the whole people, is to be irrevocably fixed by decisions of the Supreme Court, the instant they are made, in ordinary litigation between parties in personal actions, the people will have ceased to be their own rulers, having to that extent practically resigned their government into the hands of that eminent tribunal. Nor is there in this view any assault upon the court or the judges. It is a duty from which they may not shrink to decide cases properly brought before them, and it is no fault of theirs if others seek to turn their decisions to political purposes.

One section of our country believes slavery is right, and ought to be extended, while the other believes it is wrong, and ought not be extended. This is the only substantial dispute. The fugitive-slave clause of the Constitution, and the law for the suppression of the foreign slave-trade, are each as well enforced, perhaps, as any law can ever be in a community where the moral sense of the people imperfectly supports the law itself. The great body of the people abide by the dry legal obligation in both cases, and a few break over in each. This, I think, cannot be perfectly cured; and it would be worse in both cases after the separation of the sections than before. The foreign slave-trade, now imperfectly suppressed, would be ultimately revived, without restriction, in one section, while fugitive slaves, now only partially surrendered, would not be surrendered at all by the other.

Physically speaking, we cannot separate. We cannot remove our respective sections from each other, nor build an impassable wall between them. A husband and wife may be divorced, and go out of the presence and beyond the reach of each other; but the different parts of our country cannot do this. They cannot but remain face to face, and intercourse, either amicable or hostile, must continue between them. Is it possible, then, to make that intercourse more advantageous or more satisfactory after separation than before? Can aliens make treaties easier than friends can make laws? Can treaties be more faithfully enforced between aliens than laws can among friends? Suppose you go to war, you cannot fight always; and when, after much loss on both sides, and no gain on either, you cease fighting, the identical old questions as to terms of intercourse are again upon you.

This country, with its institutions, belongs to the people who inhabit it. Whenever they shall grow weary of the existing government, they can exercise their constitutional right of amending it, or their revolutionary right to dismember or overthrow it. I cannot be ignorant of the fact that many worthy and patriotic citizens are desirous of having the national Constitution amended. While I make no recommendation of amendments, I fully recognize the rightful authority of the people over the whole subject, to be exercised in either of the modes prescribed in the instrument itself; and I should, under existing circumstances, favor rather than oppose a fair opportunity being afforded the people to act upon it. I will venture to add that to me the convention mode seems preferable, in that it allows amendments to originate with the people themselves, instead of only permitting them to take or reject propositions originated by others not especially chosen for the purpose, and which might not be precisely such as they would wish to either accept or refuse. I understand a proposed amendment to the Constitution—which amendment, however, I have not seen—has passed Congress, to the effect that the federal government shall never interfere with the domestic institutions of the states, including that of persons held to service. To avoid misconstruction of what I have said, I depart from my purpose not to speak of particular amendments so far as to say that, holding such a provision to now be implied constitutional law, I have no objections to its being made express and irrevocable.

The chief magistrate derives all his authority from the people, and they have conferred none upon him to fix terms for the separation of the states. The people themselves can do this also if they choose; but the executive, as such, has nothing to do with it. His duty is to administer the present government, as it came to his hands, and to transmit it, unimpaired by him, to his successor.

Why should there not be a patient confidence in the ultimate justice of the people? Is there any better or equal hope in the world? In our present differences is either party without faith of being in the right? If the Almighty Ruler of Nations, with His eternal truth and justice, be on your side of the North, or on yours of the South, that truth and that justice will surely prevail by the judgment of this great tribunal of the American people.

By the frame of the government under which we live, this same people have wisely given their public servants but little power for mischief; and have, with equal wisdom, provided for the return of that little to their own hands at very short intervals. While the people retain their virtue and vigilance, no administration, by any extreme of wickedness or folly, can very seriously injure the government in the short space of four years.

My countrymen, one and all, think calmly and well upon this whole subject. Nothing valuable can be lost by taking time. If there be an object to hurry any of you in hot haste to a step which you would never take deliberately, that object will be frustrated by taking time; but no good object can be frustrated by it. Such of you as are now dissatisfied, still have the old Constitution unimpaired, and, on the sensitive point, the laws of your own framing under it; while the new administration will have no immediate power, if it would, to change either. If it were admitted that you who are dissatisfied hold the right side in the dispute, there still is no single good reason for precipitate action. Intelligence, patriotism, Christianity, and a firm reliance on Him who has never yet forsaken this favored land, are still competent to adjust in the best way all our present difficulty.

In your hands, my dissatisfied fellow-countrymen, and not in mine, is the momentous issue of civil war. The government will not assail you. You can have no conflict without being yourselves the aggressors. You have no oath registered in heaven to destroy the government, while I shall have the most solemn one to "preserve, protect, and defend it."

I am loath to close. We are not enemies, but friends. We must not be enemies. Though passion may have strained, it must not break our bonds of affection. The mystic chords of memory, stretching from every battlefield and patriot grave to every living heart and hearthstone all over this broad land, will yet swell the chorus of the Union when again touched, as surely they will be, by the better angels of our nature.

The Argument of Guns

FORT SUMTER

140

SUMTER IS LOST: THE NORTH IS UNITED

from an Editorial, New York *Tribune*, April ?, 1861

The Deep South had given its final word by forming the Confederate States of America at Montgomery, Alabama, on February 8, 1861. Lincoln had made his final response at Washington on March 4. Two hostile nations were poised for action. The border states from North Carolina to Arkansas and north to the Mason-Dixon and Ohio Line swayed in the balance. One false move on either side would start the shooting. Yet no one wanted the terrible responsibility. All eyes were fixed on Fort Sumter.

On December 26, 1860—just after South Carolina had seceded—Major Robert Anderson, commander of the United States troops in Charleston harbor, withdrew to a strong defensive position at Fort Sumter on an island in the harbor. President Buchanan screwed up enough courage to send an unarmed ship with reinforcements but lost his nerve again when shore batteries drove the ship away on January 9. From this point on, the overt facts are clear, but their meaning lies hidden beneath a cloud of charges and countercharges.

Did Lincoln deliberately provoke the South into striking the first blow by declaring his intention in April to provision the fort? Did the Confederate leaders order the attack on Sumter to take their followers beyond the point of no return and to force Virginia and the border states to commit themselves? ("I tell you, gentlemen," said Roger Pryor of Virginia just before the decision was taken, "what will put Virginia in the Southern Confederacy in less than an hour by Shrewsbury clock—strike a blow.") Each of the loaded questions touches an element of truth but puts the truth in a hostile light. Thus Lincoln would have avoided war if he could have gained peaceful recognition of the federal authority, but if war had to come, he wanted the first act of aggression to be the Confederacy's. Confederate leaders saw the plan to provision Sumter as a direct challenge to their existence; acceptance would signify surrender to Lincoln. They chose an act of war timed to hold the seceding states together and enlist the support of their logical allies in the Upper South.

At any rate, each side got results from Sumter that seemed to confirm the charges of its opponents. General Pierre G. T. Beauregard, commanding the Confederate forces at Charleston, demanded the surrender of the fort. Major Robert Anderson refused. After two days of Confederate bombardment (April 12-13, 1861), the Union garrison was helpless and Anderson surrendered. In the North the days of indecision and prudence were over. Men were ready for the argument of guns. Horace Greeley's *Tribune* spoke the dominant opinion of the Union: "Fort Sumter is lost, but freedom is saved." On April 15, Lincoln declared that an "insurrection" was in progress and called for 75,000 three-month volunteers.

Fort Sumter is lost, but freedom is saved. There is no more thought of bribing or coaxing the traitors who have dared to aim their cannon balls at the flag of the Union, and those who gave their lives to defend it. It seems but yesterday that at least two-thirds of the journals of this city were the virtual allies of the Secessionists, their apologists, their champions. The roar of the great circle of batteries pouring their iron hail upon devoted Sumter, has struck them all dumb. It is as if one had made a brilliant and effective speech, setting forth the innocence of murder, and having just bidden adieu to the cheers and the gas-light, were to be confronted by the gory form and staring eyes of a victim of assassination, the first fruit of his oratorical success. For months before the late Presidential election, a majority of our journals predicted forcible resistance to the government as the natural and necessary consequence of a Republican triumph; for months since they have been cherishing and encouraging the Slaveholder's Rebellion, as if it were a very natural and proper proceeding. Their object was purely partisan—they wished to bully the Republican Administration into shameful recreancy to Republican principle, and then call upon the people to expel from power a party so profligate and cowardly. They did not

Text: The Rebellion Record: A Diary of American Events, with Documents, Narratives, Illustrative Incidents, Poetry, etc., ed. Frank Moore (New York: D. Van Nostrand, 1867), I, 57-58.

succeed in this; they *have* succeeded in enticing their Southern *protegés* and some time allies into flagrant treason.

There cannot be a rational doubt that every man who aided or abetted the attack on Fort Sumter is involved in the guilt of treason. That all the besiegers of Forts Sumter and Pickens have incurred the penalty of treason—which is death—is indisputable.

Most of our journals lately parading the pranks of the Secessionists with scarcely disguised exultation, have been suddenly sobered by the culmination of the slaveholding conspiracy. They would evidently like to justify and encourage the traitors further, but they dare not; so the Amen sticks in their throat. The aspect of the people appals them. Democrat as well as Republican, Conservative and Radical, instinctively feel that the guns fired at Sumter were aimed at the heart of the American Republic. Not even in the lowest groggery of our city would it be safe to propose cheers for Beauregard and Gov. Pickens. The Tories of the Revolution were relatively ten times as numerous here as are the open sympathizers with the Palmetto Rebels. It is hard to lose Sumter; it is a consolation to know that in losing it we have gained a united people. Henceforth, the loyal States are a unit in uncompromising hostility to treason, wherever plotted, however justified. Fort Sumter is temporarily lost, but the country is saved. Live the Republic! . . .

141

SOUTHERN RESISTANCE BECOMES A PATRIOTIC VIRTUE

from an Editorial, Louisville *Democrat*, April ?, 1861

Less than a week after the bombardment of Fort Sumter, Virginia joined the Confederacy (April 17, 1861). Arkansas, North Carolina, and Tennessee followed in May and June. Maryland and Delaware were caught, so to speak, behind the Union lines and remained more or less loyal. Kentucky and Missouri anguished, argued, fought within themselves, and finally stayed in officially, sending some brothers North and others South. Sumter had done its work for the Confederacy too. Lincoln had threatened war, and now, as the editor of the border-state Louisville (Ky.) *Democrat* insisted, "Resistance becomes exalted into a patriotic virtue."

By the fall of 1861 there had been significant encounters of Blue and Gray in Missouri (a Union state with many Rebel sympathizers) and in western Virginia (a Unionist enclave in a Confederate state). In the area just south of Washington the rival commanders were working desperately to shape up their raw recruits when Lincoln in mid-July ordered an attack on General Beauregard's army at Manassas, Virginia. The two armies, each roughly thirty thousand strong, clashed in the vicinity of a small stream called Bull Run. The end of a hard day's fighting found the Union army in wild retreat toward Washington. An English journalist in Washington (William H. Russell) witnessed an incredible scene on the gray morning of July 22, as a steady stream of men covered with mud, soaked through with rain, came pouring in confusion up Pennsylvania Avenue toward the Capitol. The writer asked a pale young officer where the men were coming from. "Well, sir, I guess we're all coming out of Virginny as fast as we can, and pretty well whipped too." "What! the whole army sir?" "That's more than I know. They may stay that like. I know I'm going home. I've had enough of fighting to last my lifetime."

Official Washington seemed paralyzed in the face of disaster; but the journalist could see that "this prick in the great Northern balloon will let out a quality of poisonous gas, and rouse the people to a sense of the nature of the conflict on which they have entered." Indeed both sides were learning by the end of 1861 that this was not to be a three-months escapade but a long, grim, bloody war to the finish. Sumter and even Bull Run (or Manassas) gave but a slight hint of what the argument of guns would cost.

The authorities at Washington are now for raising seventy-five thousand troops, and fancy they will do exploits. They ought to reflect that the few they can spare to the South go far from home, into an intensely hostile country, and to them most unpropitious climate. They will have, after the excitement is over, little heart in the business. There will be no laurels to win. The rest of mankind will give them no credit. Even England and France deplore the strife, and offer prayers that it may cease. Every patriot will feel ashamed of the fratricidal war. They will meet an enemy skilled in war, as proud and vain as ever trod a battle-field—an enemy fighting for his home and his firesides, and who can bring into the field any number of fighting men that he may need. We say *any* number, and it is true— one hundred thousand if needed. If they doubt it, they can try the experiment, and it will be another Fort Sumter experiment.

We don't doubt the bravery of the North; but in this contest they will lack the stimulus of their foes, and meet their equals at great dis-

advantage. Then there is a sentiment in this country that all just governments are founded on the consent of the governed. If a whole tier of States seek other arrangements in government; if their old government is odious to them, and they seek a release from it, and resist with determination the old government, what shall be done about it? There is our Declaration of Independence, and the strong expressions of States when they entered the Union, which, if they do not recognize the right of secession, squint so much that way that they are easily applied to that purpose. It is an odious task to force a government on an unwilling people. Resistance becomes exalted into a patriotic virtue. No matter how little cause really provokes the resistance. How easy it is to inflame the South against this conduct of coercion! What, they will say, is the motive? Is it any love for us that all this blood

Text: The Rebellion Record: A Diary of American Events, with Documents, Narratives, Illustrative Incidents, Poetry, etc., ed. Frank Moore (New York: D. Van Nostrand, 1867), I, 66.

is shed to retain us in the same Union? No, they will say; they hate us! They abhor slavery and slaveholders! They tried to keep us out of the Union, and they swear it as a part of their religion that they will have no more Slave States! Why do they wish to retain us, but to play the tyrant over us? Why are they not ready to let us go in peace? They preach against us, pray against us; and what do they want with us but to subjugate us—to indulge their preaching and prayer at our expense?

The terms now used in all these irrepressible prints are, rebels, traitors, and the empty threats to punish them. The bluster and gasconade about having a government, only reminds men of George III., who used empty words after they had lost their meaning. We say nothing about the similarity of the cases upon their merits. George & Co. thought the Colonies had no more reason than the Southern States now have; and the latter

think they have more reason to rebel than their fathers had, and they know that these threats against them are more imbecile than the threat of His Majesty against the Colonies.

Depend upon it, Messrs. Lincoln & Co., you are wasting treasure and blood to no purpose. All your professions of peace will count nothing. You talk like enemies and act like them. Even these border Slave States, who have stood by their government, who feel a patriotic attachment to the Union their fathers made, are unheeded. Their advice disregarded, and their wise counsels spurned. They ask for peace most earnestly, as essential to a restoration of confidence and salvation of the Union; and Lincoln & Co. call for troops, and are mustering armies, when all the effect will be to gratify their own resentment and make the breach incurable. They mistake altogether our government and people. No power can restore a State to this Union but its people.

1864-1865

142

WAR IS HELL: SHERMAN IN GEORGIA

from William T. Sherman, *Memoirs*, 1875

The military victory of the Union over the Confederacy seemed inevitable—after the fact. From the first Battle of Bull Run (or Manassas) in July of 1861 until the Battle of Gettysburg in July of 1863, few dispassionate judges would have given odds favoring the "inevitable" Northern victory. Again and again in the early years, Robert E. Lee and his remarkable lieutenants of the Army of Northern Virginia—"Stonewall" Jackson, James Longstreet, J. E. B. Stuart, and the rest—struck telling blows against the numerically superior but poorly commanded Army of the Potomac. The initial advantages of the North in man power and material were real enough, but they did not become decisive until the middle of the war, when Confederate strategy could no longer compensate for dwindling reserves and resources.

In 1861 the North outnumbered the South by more than two to one, although the strength of the rival armies was fairly even in most of the early battles. Northern preponderance in supplies, transportation facilities, and productive capacity was overwhelming from the start and steadily increased through the war years. Yet Lincoln had by far the more demanding objective. To restore the Union it was necessary to invade the South, destroy its fighting power, and possess the major centers of resistance. For Jefferson Davis the great end was to maintain Southern independence by holding on to the home ground. Thus Lincoln—after rejecting as inadequate General Winfield Scott's proposed "anaconda" plan for sealing off and slowly starving out the South—turned to a broad strategy of striking relentlessly at the major Confederate army defending Richmond, while dividing the South first along the Mississippi line, then along the Tennessee River, and finally by a march through Georgia and the Carolinas. Scott's blockade scheme was combined with this strategy. Jefferson Davis, in contrast, adopted a strategy of "dispersed defense" designed to meet Northern invasions wherever they came and hold the entire Confederate territory intact. Up to Gettysburg he counted on foreign support to redress the balance of numbers and supplies.

In the Eastern theater of operations Lee more than held his own through 1863, although his major northward thrust was beaten back at Gettysburg. Indeed until the final months of the war he stood off the bloody hammer blows of Grant, who had assumed general command of the Union forces in March of 1864 after directing the all-important Western triumphs at Vicksburg (Mississippi) and Chattanooga (Tennessee).

While seeking a showdown fight in northern Virginia, Grant planned in 1864 to press the Union advantage in the Western theater. He sent William Tecumseh Sherman, a seasoned fighting general built to his own taste, to smash the Confederate army under "Joe" Johnston and knock Atlanta, Georgia, out of the war. In the spring of 1864 Sherman with a force approaching a hundred thousand struck southeastward from Chattanooga into the heart of the Confederacy, driving the wily but outnumbered Johnston before him. The aggressive General John B. Hood, who replaced Johnston in July, could not stop Sherman's war machine and retired into Atlanta. Cut off from his supplies, Hood was finally forced to evacuate the city (September 1864) and stake everything on the chance that he could draw Sherman off by threatening the Union positions in Tennessee.

Sherman's heavy numbers permitted him to send thirty thousand of his troops to reinforce Tennessee while driving his main army through three hundred miles of undefended Georgia country from Atlanta to the sea (November 14 to December 22, 1864). With Savannah firmly secured, Sherman swept northward through the Carolinas (January 16 to March 21, 1865) to complete his mastery of the Lower South and tighten the vise around the Confederate capital at Richmond, Virginia, and its stubborn defending army under Robert E. Lee.

Sherman's startling achievements in 1864-1865 show why the Civil War has been called the first of the modern wars. On the march to Atlanta, Sherman's engineers accomplished miracles in constructing and maintaining bridge, rail, and telegraph communications with the Union base in Tennessee. Both armies developed the new art of entrenchment as a mode of strengthening field positions and reducing losses in the clash of massive armies. When his extended supply lines became too vulnerable to hit-and-run attacks, Sherman reversed his tactics. From Atlanta to the sea he cut a path three hundred miles long and thirty miles wide, taking what he needed from the country and destroying much of what remained. His engineers became masters in the art of demolition. They not only ripped out Southern rails but heated them and draped them around trees. The scars, physical and mental, left by Sherman's army took many long decades to heal.

The advanced technology and daring logistics employed by Sherman were not the only modern features of his command. The march through Georgia and the Carolinas was above all a master stroke of psychological warfare, bringing ruin and terror to the farms and cities of the enemy heartland and thus weakening the Southern will to resist. Sherman was not *personally* a cruel or vindictive man, but he had a cold, unsentimental view of the nature of war. The following communications concerning the evacuation of the civilian population of Atlanta and the system of confiscation and destruction suggest some of the moral dilemmas that haunt the modern age of total war.

[*General Sherman to General Halleck, Sept. 20, 1864*]

GENERAL: I have the honor herewith to submit copies of a correspondence between General Hood, of the Confederate Army, the Mayor of Atlanta, and myself, touching the removal of the inhabitants of Atlanta. . . .

It is sufficient for my Government to know that the removal of the inhabitants has been made with liberality and fairness, that it has been attended with no force, and that no women or children have suffered, unless for want of provisions by their natural protectors and friends.

My real reasons for this step were:

We want all the houses of Atlanta for military storage and occupation.

We want to contract the lines of defense, so as to diminish the garrison to the limit necessary to defend its narrow and vital parts, instead of embracing, as the lines now do, the vast suburbs. This contraction of the lines, with

the necessary citadels and redoubts, will make it necessary to destroy the very houses used by families as residences.

Atlanta is a fortified town, was stubbornly defended, and fairly captured. As captors, we have a right to it.

The residence here of a poor population would compel us, sooner or later, to feed them or to see them starve under our eyes.

The residence here of the families of our enemies would be a temptation and a means to keep up a correspondence dangerous and hurtful to our cause; a civil population calls for provost-guards, and absorbs the attention of officers in listening to everlasting complaints and special grievances that are not military.

These are my reasons; and, if satisfactory to the Government of the United States, it makes

Text: William T. Sherman, *Memoirs* (New York: D. Appleton & Co., 1875), II, 117-18, 121-27, 175-79 *passim.*

no difference whether it pleases General Hood and *his* people or not. . . .

[General Hood to General Sherman, Sept. 12, 1864]

GENERAL: I have the honor to acknowledge the receipt of your letter of the 9th inst., with its inclosure in reference to the women, children, and others, whom you have thought proper to expel from their homes in the city of Atlanta. Had you seen proper to let the matter rest there, I would gladly have allowed your letter to close this correspondence, and, without your expressing it in words, would have been willing to believe that, while "the interests of the United States," in your opinion, compelled you to an act of barbarous cruelty, you regretted the necessity, and we would have dropped the subject; but you have chosen to indulge in statements which I feel compelled to notice, at least so far as to signify my dissent, and not allow silence in regard to them to be construed as acquiescence. . . .

You order into exile the whole population of a city; drive men, women, and children from their homes at the point of the bayonet, under the plea that it is to the interest of your Government, and on the claim that it is an act of "kindness to these families of Atlanta." Butler only banished from New Orleans the registered enemies of his Government, and acknowledged that he did it as a punishment. You issue a sweeping edict, covering all the inhabitants of a city, and add insult to the injury heaped upon the defenseless by assuming that you have done them a kindness. This you follow by the assertion that you will "make as much sacrifice for the peace and honor of the South as the best-born Southerner." And, because I characterize what you call a kindness as being real cruelty, you presume to sit in judgment between me and my God; and you decide that my earnest prayer to the Almighty Father to save our women and children from what you call kindness, is a "sacrilegious, hypocritical appeal."

You came into our country with your army, avowedly for the purpose of subjugating free white men, women, and children, and not only intend to rule over them, but you make negroes your allies, and desire to place over us an inferior race, which we have raised from barbarism to its present position, which is the highest ever attained by that race, in any country, in all time. I must, therefore, decline to accept your statements in reference to your kindness toward the people of Atlanta, and your willingness to sacrifice every thing for the peace and honor of the South, and refuse to be governed by your decision in regard to matters between myself, my country, and my God.

You say, "Let us fight it out like men." To this my reply is—for myself, and I believe for all the true men, ay, and women and children, in my country—we will fight you to the death! Better die a thousand deaths than submit to live under you or your Government and your negro allies! . . .

[Mayor Calhoun to General Sherman, Sept. 11, 1864]

SIR: We the undersigned, Mayor and two of the Council for the city of Atlanta, for the time being the only legal organ of the people of the said city, to express their wants and wishes, ask leave most earnestly but respectfully to petition you to reconsider the order requiring them to leave Atlanta.

At first view, it struck us that the measure would involve extraordinary hardship and loss, but since we have seen the practical execution of it so far as it has progressed, and the individual condition of the people, and heard their statements as to the inconveniences, loss, and suffering attending it, we are satisfied that the amount of it will involve in the aggregate consequences appalling and heart-rending.

Many poor women are in advanced state of pregnancy, others now having young children, and whose husbands for the greater part are either in the army, prisoners, or dead. Some say: "I have such a one sick at my house; who will wait on them when I am gone?" Others say: "What are we to do? We have no house to go to, and no means to buy, build, or rent any; no parents, relatives, or friends, to go to." Another says: "I will try and take this or that article of property, but such and such things I must leave behind, though I need them much." We reply to them: "General Sherman will carry your property to Rough and Ready, and General Hood will take it thence on." And they will reply to that: "But I want to leave the railroad at such a place, and cannot get conveyance from there on."

We only refer to a few facts, to try to illustrate in part how this measure will operate in practice. As you advanced, the people north of this fell back; and before your arrival here, a large portion of the people had retired south, so that the country south of this is already crowded, and without houses enough to accommodate the people, and we are informed that many are now staying in churches and other outbuildings.

This being so, how is it possible for the people still here (mostly women and children) to find any shelter? And how can they live through the winter in the woods—no shelter or subsistence, in the midst of strangers who know them not, and without the power to assist them much, if they were willing to do so?

This is but a feeble picture of the consequences of this measure. You know the woe, the horrors, and the suffering, cannot be described by words; imagination can only conceive of it, and we ask you to take these things into consideration.

We know your mind and time are constantly occupied with the duties of your command, which almost deters us from asking your attention to this matter, but thought it might be that you had not considered this subject in all of its awful consequences, and that on more reflection you, we hope, would not make this people an exception to all mankind, for we know of no such instance ever having occurred—surely never in the United States—and what has this *helpless* people done, that they should be driven from their homes, to wander strangers and outcasts, and exiles, and to subsist on charity?

We do not know as yet the number of people still here; of those who are here, we are satisfied a respectable number, if allowed to remain at home, could subsist for several months without assistance, and a respectable number for a much longer time, and who might not need assistance at any time.

In conclusion, we most earnestly and solemnly petition you to reconsider this order, or modify it, and suffer this unfortunate people to remain at home, and enjoy what little means they have. . . .

[*General Sherman to Mayor Calhoun, Sept. 12, 1864*]

GENTLEMEN: I have your letter of the 11th, in the nature of a petition to revoke my orders removing all the inhabitants from Atlanta. I have read it carefully, and give full credit to your statements of the distress that will be occasioned, and yet shall not revoke my orders, because they were not designed to meet the humanities of the case, but to prepare for the future struggles in which millions of good people outside of Atlanta have a deep interest. We must have peace, not only at Atlanta, but in all America. To secure this, we must stop the war that now desolates our once happy and favored country. To stop war, we must defeat the rebel armies which are arrayed against the laws and Constitution that all must respect and obey. To defeat those armies, we must prepare the way to reach them in their recesses, provided with the arms and instruments which enable us to accomplish our purpose. Now, I know the vindictive nature of our enemy, that we may have

many years of military operations from this quarter; and, therefore, deem it wise and prudent to prepare in time. The use of Atlanta for warlike purposes is inconsistent with its character as a home for families. There will be no manufactures, commerce, or agriculture here, for the maintenance of families, and sooner or later want will compel the inhabitants to go. Why not go now, when all the arrangements are completed for the transfer, instead of waiting till the plunging shot of contending armies will renew the scenes of the past month? Of course, I do not apprehend any such thing at this moment, but you do not suppose this army will be here until the war is over. I cannot discuss this subject with you fairly, because I cannot impart to you what we propose to do, but I assert that our military plans make it necessary for the inhabitants to go away, and I can only renew my offer of services to make their exodus in any direction as easy and comfortable as possible.

You cannot qualify war in harsher terms than I will. War is cruelty, and you cannot refine it; and those who brought war into our country deserve all the curses and maledictions a people can pour out. I know I had no hand in making this war, and I know I will make more sacrifices to-day than any of you to secure peace. But you cannot have peace and a division of our country. . . .

You might as well appeal against the thunderstorm as against these terrible hardships of war. They are inevitable, and the only way the people of Atlanta can hope once more to live in peace and quiet at home, is to stop the war, which can only be done by admitting that it began in error and is perpetuated in pride.

We don't want your negroes, or your horses, or your houses, or your lands, or any thing you have, but we do want and will have a just obedience to the laws of the United States. That we will have, and if it involves the destruction of your improvements, we cannot help it. . . .

Now you must go, and take with you the old and feeble, feed and nurse them, and build for them, in more quiet places, proper habitations to shield them against the weather until the mad passions of men cool down, and allow the Union and peace once more to settle over your old homes at Atlanta. . . .

[*General Sherman's Special Field Orders, No. 120, Nov. 9, 1864*]

. . . 3. There will be no general train of supplies, but each corps will have its ammunition-train and provision-train, distributed habitually as follows: Behind each regiment should follow one wagon and one ambulance; behind each brigade should follow a due proportion of ammunition-wagons, provision-wagons, and ambulances. In case of danger, each corps commander should change this order of march, by having his advance and rear brigades unencumbered by wheels. The separate columns will start habitually at 7 A. M., and make about fifteen miles per day, unless otherwise fixed in orders.

4. The army will forage liberally on the country during the march. To this end, each brigade commander will organize a good and sufficient foraging party, under the command of one or more discreet officers, who will gather, near the route traveled, corn or forage of any kind, meat of any kind, vegetables, corn-meal, or whatever is needed by the command, aiming at all times to keep in the wagons at least ten days' provisions for his command, and three days' forage. Soldiers must not enter the dwellings of the inhabitants, or commit any trespass; but, during a halt or camp, they may be permitted to gather turnips, potatoes, and other vegetables, and to drive in stock in sight of their camp. To regular foraging-parties must be intrusted the gathering of provisions and forage, at any distance from the road traveled.

5. To corps commanders alone is intrusted the power to destroy mills, houses, cotton-gins, etc.; and for them this general principle is laid down: In districts and neighborhoods where the army is unmolested, no destruction of such property should be permitted; but should guerrillas or bushwhackers molest our march, or should the inhabitants burn bridges, obstruct roads, or otherwise manifest local hostility, then army commanders should order and enforce a devastation more or less relentless, according to the measure of such hostility.

6. As for horses, mules, wagons, etc., belonging to the inhabitants, the cavalry and artillery may appropriate freely and without limit; discriminating, however, between the rich, who are usually hostile, and the poor and industrious, usually neutral or friendly. Foraging-parties may also take mules or horses, to replace the jaded animals of their trains, or to serve as pack-mules for the regiments or brigades. In all foraging, of whatever kind, the parties engaged will refrain from abusive or threatening language, and may,

where the officer in command thinks proper, give written certificates of facts, but no receipts; and they will endeavor to leave with each family a reasonable portion for their maintenance.

7. Negroes who are able-bodied and can be of service to the several columns may be taken along; but each army commander will bear in mind that the question of supplies is a very important one, and that his first duty is to see to those who bear arms.

8. The organization, at once, of a good pioneer battalion for each army corps, composed if possible of negroes, should be attended to. This battalion should follow the advance-guard, repair roads and double them if possible, so that the columns will not be delayed after reaching bad places. Also, the army commanders should practise the habit of giving the artillery and wagons the road, marching their troops on one side, and instruct their troops to assist wagons at steep hills or bad crossings of streams. . . .

About 7 A.M. of November 16th we rode out of Atlanta by the Decatur road, filled by the marching troops and wagons of the Fourteenth Corps; and reaching the hill, just outside of the old rebel works, we naturally paused to look back upon the scenes of our past battles. We stood upon the very ground whereon was fought the bloody battle of July 22d, and could see the copse of wood where McPherson fell. Behind us lay Atlanta, smouldering and in ruins, the black smoke rising high in air, and hanging like a pall over the ruined city. Away off in the distance, on the McDonough road, was the rear of Howard's column, the gun-barrels glistening in the sun, the white-topped wagons stretching away to the south; and right before us the Fourteenth Corps, marching steadily and rapidly, with a cheery look and swinging pace, that made light of the thousand miles that lay between us and Richmond. Some band, by accident, struck up the anthem of "John Brown's soul goes marching on;" the men caught up the strain, and never before or since have I heard the chorus of "Glory, glory, hallelujah!" done with more spirit, or in better harmony of time and place. . . .

143

STILLNESS AT APPOMATTOX

from Ulysses S. Grant, *Personal Memoirs*, 1886

By the end of 1864 Northern victory was inevitable. The only question was how long and how painful the death struggle would be. Confederate forces were outnumbered five to one. The Northern industrial machine had expanded under the stimulus of war, while the South was approaching economic exhaustion. All hope of foreign aid for the Confederacy was gone, and as the Union blockade pressed tighter, the South was nearly walled off from the outside world. After seizing control of the Mississippi River in 1863 (and thus effectively splitting off the Confederate Southwest), the Union armies had driven a wedge through Tennessee and Georgia and faced an open path into the Carolinas. (See Document 142.) Only Lee's isolated and exhausted Army of Northern Virginia stood in the way of final victory.

Mile by mile, Grant slugged his way into Virginia through the spring and summer of 1864. With decisive numerical superiority, he deliberately accepted shocking losses—some 55,000 casualties from the Battle of the Wilderness (May 5-6) to Cold Harbor (June 1-3)—to force a decision. For almost a year the two entrenched armies fought a punishing battle for Petersburg (due south of Richmond) until Grant finally broke through to seize the railroad supply lines to Richmond. The Confederate capital was abandoned; and Lee, left with only a worn remnant of his gallant army, could do nothing more.

On April 9, 1865, Lee met Grant at Appomattox to surrender the Army of Northern Virginia. That moving scene is well described in the following selection from Grant's *Memoirs.* The two great generals were in many ways the symbols of the Blue and Gray: Ulysses Simpson Grant (1822-1885), the rough-cut Midwestern farm boy who was master of the massive strategy, the relentless attack; and Robert E. Lee (1807-1870), the tall, graceful, dignified Virginia aristocrat who maneuvered his dwindling forces brilliantly in defense of the Confederate capital and, above all, in defense of his native state.

Through April and May of 1865 the remaining Confederate armies were surrendered, and the South could only wait amidst the ruins for the victor to decree the terms of reconstruction.

I [Grant] was conducted at once to where Sheridan was located with his troops drawn up in line of battle facing the Confederate army near by. They were very much excited, and expressed their view that this was all a ruse employed to enable the Confederates to get away. They said they believed that Johnston was marching up from North Carolina now, and Lee was moving to join him; and they would whip the rebels where they now were in five minutes if I would only let them go in. But I had no doubt about the good faith of Lee, and pretty soon was conducted to where he was. I found him at the house of a Mr. McLean, at Appomattox Court House, with Colonel Marshall, one of his staff officers, awaiting my arrival. . . .

I had known General Lee in the old army, and had served with him in the Mexican War; but did not suppose, owing to the difference in our age and rank, that he would remember me; while I would more naturally remember him distinctly, because he was the chief of staff of General Scott in the Mexican War.

When I had left camp that morning I had not expected so soon the result that was then taking place, and consequently was in rough garb. I was without a sword, as I usually was when on horseback on the field, and wore a soldier's blouse for a coat, with the shoulder straps of my rank to indicate to the army who I was. When I went into the house I found General Lee. We greeted each other, and after shaking hands took our seats. I had my staff with me, a good portion of whom were in the room during the whole of the interview.

What General Lee's feelings were I do not know. As he was a man of much dignity, with an impassible face, it was impossible to say whether he felt inwardly glad that the end had finally come, or felt sad over the result, and was too manly to show it. Whatever his feelings, they were entirely concealed from my observation; but my own feelings, which had been quite

Text: Ulysses S. Grant, *Personal Memoirs* (New York: Charles L. Webster, 1886), II, 486-95 *passim.*

jubilant on the receipt of his letter, were sad and depressed. I felt like anything rather than rejoicing at the downfall of a foe who had fought so long and valiantly, and had suffered so much for a cause, though that cause was, I believe, one of the worst for which a people ever fought, and one for which there was the least excuse. I do not question, however, the sincerity of the great mass of those who were opposed to us.

General Lee was dressed in a full uniform which was entirely new, and was wearing a sword of considerable value, very likely the sword which had been presented by the State of Virginia; at all events, it was an entirely different sword from the one that would ordinarily be worn in the field. In my rough traveling suit, the uniform of a private with the straps of a lieutenant-general, I must have contrasted very strangely with a man so handsomely dressed, six feet high and of faultless form. But this was not a matter that I thought of until afterwards.

We soon fell into a conversation about old army times. He remarked that he remembered me very well in the old army; and I told him that as a matter of course I remembered him perfectly, but from the difference in our rank and years (there being about sixteen years' difference in our ages), I had thought it very likely that I had not attracted his attention sufficiently to be remembered by him after such a long interval. Our conversation grew so pleasant that I almost forgot the object of our meeting. After the conversation had run on in this style for some time, General Lee called my attention to the object of our meeting, and said that he had asked for this interview for the purpose of getting from me the terms I proposed to give his army. I said that I meant merely that his army should lay down their arms, not to take them up again during the continuance of the war unless duly and properly exchanged. He said that he had so understood my letter.

Then we gradually fell off again into conversation about matters foreign to the subject which had brought us together. This continued for some little time, when General Lee again interrupted the course of the conversation by suggesting that the terms I proposed to give his army ought to be written out. I called to General Parker, secretary on my staff, for writing materials, and commenced writing out the following terms:

Appomattox C. H., Va.,
Ap l 9th, 1865.

Gen. R. E. Lee,
Comd'g C. S. A.

GEN: In accordance with the substance of my letter to you of the 8th inst., I propose to receive the surrender of the Army of N. Va. on the following terms, to wit: Rolls of all the officers and men to be made in duplicate. One copy to be given to an officer designated by me, the other to be retained by such officer or officers as you may designate. The officers to give their individual paroles not to take up arms against the Government of the United States until properly exchanged, and each company or regimental commander sign a like parole for the men of their commands. The arms, artillery and public property to be parked and stacked, and turned over to the officer appointed by me to receive them. This will not embrace the side-arms of the officers, nor their private horses or baggage. This done, each officer and man will be allowed to return to their homes, not to be disturbed by United States authority so long as they observe their paroles and the laws in force where they may reside.

Very respectfully,
U. S. GRANT,
Lt. Gen.

When I put my pen to the paper I did not know the first word that I should make use of in writing the terms. I only knew what was in my mind, and I wished to express it clearly, so that there could be no mistaking it. As I wrote on, the thought occurred to me that the officers had their own private horses and effects, which were important to them, but of no value to us; also that it would be an unnecessary humiliation to call upon them to deliver their side arms.

No conversation, not one word, passed between General Lee and myself, either about private property, side arms, or kindred subjects. He appeared to have no objections to the terms first proposed; or if he had a point to make against them he wished to wait until they were in writing to make it. When he read over that part of the terms about side arms, horses and private property of the officers, he remarked, with some feeling, I thought, that this would have a happy effect upon his army.

Then, after a little further conversation, General Lee remarked to me again that their army was organized a little differently from the army of the United States (still maintaining by implication that we were two countries); that in their army the cavalrymen and artillerists owned their own horses; and he asked if he was to understand that the men who so owned their horses were to be permitted to retain them. I told him that as the terms were written they would not; that only the officers were permitted to take their private property. He then after reading over the terms a second time, remarked that that was clear.

I then said to him that I thought this would be about the last battle of the war—I sincerely hoped so; and I said further I took it that most of the men in the ranks were small farmers. The whole country had been so raided by the two armies that it was doubtful whether they would be able to put in a crop to carry themselves and their families through the next winter without the aid of the horses they were then riding. The United States did not want them and I would, therefore, instruct the officers I left behind to receive the paroles of his troops to let every man of the Confederate army who claimed to own a horse or mule take the animal to his home. Lee remarked again that this would have a happy effect. . . .

General Lee, after all was completed and before taking his leave, remarked that his army was in a very bad condition for want of food, and that they were without forage; that his men had been living for some days on parched corn exclusively, and that he would have to ask me for rations and forage. I told him "certainly," and asked for how many men he wanted rations. His answer was "about twenty-five thousand:" and I authorized him to send his own commissary and quartermaster to Appomattox Station, two or three miles away, where he could have, out of the trains we had stopped, all the provisions wanted. As for forage, we had ourselves depended almost entirely upon the country for that.

Generals Gibbon, Griffin and Merritt were designated by me to carry into effect the paroling of Lee's troops before they should start for their homes—General Lee leaving Generals Longstreet, Gordon and Pendleton for them to confer with in order to facilitate this work. Lee and I then separated as cordially as we had met, he returning to his own lines, and all went into bivouac for the night at Appomattox. . . .

The Aims of Lincoln

PRIORITIES: RESTORATION AND EMANCIPATION

144

I WOULD SAVE THE UNION

from Abraham Lincoln, Letter to Horace Greeley, August 22, 1862

Lincoln has sometimes been portrayed as a political juggler tossing a set of balls labeled "preservation of the Union," "military victory," "emancipation," and "party control." Some balls were always coming down as others were rising, until by a combination of genius, luck, and magic Lincoln got them all in the air at once. As the selections from Lincoln's views in the 1850's suggest (see Documents 115 and 134), this image overrates the President's manipulative powers, impressive as they were, and underrates his intellectual powers. Lincoln did have a multiplicity of goals; but he placed them in an ordered sequence. His particular genius as a national leader was to know when the times were ripe for the next move and how to combine his moves in order to realize his whole purpose.

Before Sumter, Lincoln accepted a double responsibility: to uphold the Constitution (including the provisions that secured existing slavery) and—within the Constitution— to arrest the spread of slavery and thus prepare the way for the ultimate extinction of that divisive institution. He meant to preserve the Union. But the Union for Lincoln was not a mere collection of territories, peoples, and powers; it was a body politic with a high mission in the world defined by the Declaration of Independence. It was necessary to move patiently and prudently, to respect the law and custom of the land, and even to concede something to deep-rooted prejudice. It was no less necessary to move forward in the direction set by the Founders: toward a free society united under the Constitution.

After Sumter, Lincoln confronted a new situation. If the war were lost, there would be no Union to preserve—only two mutilated powers in perpetual conflict—and consequently no progress toward the ideals of the Declaration. Victory came first. During the years of peace Lincoln had subordinated his *personal* preference for abolition to his duty under the Constitution and to his political judgment that the nation was not ready for a radical leap forward. During the early years of the war, Lincoln believed he had the emergency *power* to deal decisively with slavery as the chief executive and high commander of the Union; but still his political *judgment* restrained him. The Union was fighting for its life. His paramount object "in this struggle," as he wrote to Horace Greeley, was to save the Union. Under the circumstances of war—and a war that was going badly for the North—Lincoln would subordinate his feelings and ultimate intentions toward slavery to the urgent task of the day.

Horace Greeley, the influential editor of the Republican New York *Tribune*, voiced the sentiments of the antislavery Radicals who dominated Congress and sought to control the military and civil policies of the executive branch through their "Joint Committee on the Conduct of the War." Greeley's aggressive editorial of August 19, 1862—"The Prayer of 20,000,000 People"—rudely questioned Lincoln's motives in postponing abolition. In sure but temperate terms Lincoln reminded his critic of the priorities set by the military situation of the Union. To contemporaries Lincoln's answer meant that he was concerned about the loyalty of the border states, where slavery still existed, and the support of Northern "war Democrats." Insiders knew, however, that Lincoln had decided for a policy of emancipation by July of 1862 and was waiting for a favorable turn in military fortunes so that his proclamation would not be construed at home or abroad as an act of desperation.

Executive Mansion, Washington,
August 22, 1862

Hon. Horace Greeley.

Dear Sir: I have just read yours of the 19th, addressed to myself through the New York *Tribune*. If there be in it any statements or assumptions of fact which I may know to be erroneous, I do not, now and here, controvert them. If there be in it any inferences which I may believe to be falsely drawn, I do not, now and here, argue against them. If there be perceptible in it an impatient and dictatorial tone, I waive it in deference to an old friend whose heart I have always supposed to be right.

As to the policy I "seem to be pursuing," as you say, I have not meant to leave any one in doubt.

I would save the Union. I would save it the shortest way under the Constitution. The sooner the national authority can be restored, the nearer the Union will be "the Union as it was." If there be those who would not save the Union unless they could at the same time save slavery, I do not agree with them. If there be those who would not save the Union unless they could at the same time destroy slavery, I do not agree with them. My paramount object in this struggle is to save the Union, and is not either to save or to destroy slavery. If I could save the Union without freeing any slave, I would do it; and if I could save it by freeing all the slaves, I would do it; and if I could save it by freeing some and leaving others alone, I would also do that. What I do about slavery and the coloured race, I do because I believe it helps to save the Union; and what I forbear, I forbear because I do not believe it would help to save the Union. I shall do less whenever I shall believe what I am doing hurts the cause, and I shall do more whenever I shall believe doing more will help the cause. I shall try to correct errors when shown to be errors, and I shall adopt new views so fast as they shall appear to be true views.

I have here stated my purpose according to my view of official duty; and I intend no modification of my oft-expressed personal wish that all men everywhere could be free.

Yours,
A. LINCOLN

Text: Abraham Lincoln, *Complete Works*, ed. John G. Nicolay and John Hay (New York: The Century Co., 1902), II, 227-28.

145

UPON MILITARY NECESSITY: EMANCIPATION PROCLAMATION

from Abraham Lincoln, *Final Emancipation Proclamation*, January 1, 1863

Lincoln's preliminary Emancipation Proclamation of September 22, 1862, and his final Proclamation of January 1, 1863, gave immediate freedom to few slaves; indeed the Executive Proclamation added nothing significantly new to existing national policy and practice. The only slaves affected by the Emancipation Proclamation were those beyond the reach of federal power, in areas controlled by the Confederacy. As early as May of 1861, General Benjamin F. Butler, in command of Union forces at Fortress Monroe, Virginia, had declared captured slaves "contraband of war" and so not subject to the claims of their masters. Congress in 1861 and again in July of 1862 had passed Confiscation Acts declaring free the slaves of all who supported the rebellion. Further laws antedating the Emancipation Proclamation had abolished slavery in the District of Columbia (with compensation to the owners) and in the national territories.

What then was the importance of Lincoln's Act, so carefully postponed until the partial Union success at Antietam (September 17, 1862) provided an appropriate occasion? Primarily the document served as a symbolic pronouncement that the war aims of the Union now included the emancipation of slaves. If the terms of the proclamation were limited, still there could be no doubt that the Union would never restore the institution of slavery as it existed before the war. Lincoln formally justified his act "as a fit and necessary war measure" adopted by the Commander in Chief "upon military necessity." But he also justified the Proclamation as "an act of justice" for which he would stand in judgment before God and man. Henceforth the Civil War would be fought not only to preserve the Union but to secure "a new birth of freedom."

Even as he moved forward to the emancipation policy under the pressure of military necessity, Lincoln did not forget the profound economic and social disturbances that such a revolution would create. Lincoln's greatest failure, from his own point of view, was his inability to persuade Congress to plan a gradual transition from slavery to freedom. In his message of December 1, 1862, he pleaded with Congress to introduce a comprehensive policy of gradual compensated emancipation: "In giving freedom to the slave, we assure freedom to the free. . . . We shall nobly save, or meanly lose, the last best hope of earth." But the border states were not interested in any scheme of abolition and the Radicals were not inclined to buy piecemeal a result that might be seized at once for nothing—nothing, Lincoln added, but more lives and further bitterness.

By issuing the Emancipation Proclamation, Lincoln stole the thunder of the Radicals and established his political leadership on a firmer basis. He met the antislavery sentiments of European nations, thus strengthening his diplomatic position. And in the long run he gained an additional force of some 186,000 former slaves, who fought and worked with the Union forces to put an end to human bondage. The process of emancipation was completed only with the defeat of the Confederacy and the ratification in 1865 of the Thirteenth Amendment to the Constitution.

Whereas on the 22d day of September, A.D. 1862, a proclamation was issued by the President of the United States, containing, among other things, the following, to wit:

That on the 1st day of January, A.D. 1863, all persons held as slaves within any State or designated part of a State the people whereof shall then be in rebellion against the United States shall be then, thenceforward, and forever free; and the executive government of the United States, including the military and naval authority thereof, will recognize and maintain the freedom of such persons and will do no act or acts to repress such persons, or any of them, in any efforts they may make for their actual freedom.

That the Executive will on the 1st day of January aforesaid, by proclamation designate the States and parts of States, if any, in which the people thereof, respectively, shall then be in rebellion against the United States; and the fact that any State or the people thereof shall on that day be in good faith represented in the Congress of the United States by members chosen thereto at elections wherein a majority of the qualified voters of such States shall have participated shall, in the absence of strong countervailing testimony, be deemed conclusive evidence that such State and the people thereof are not then in rebellion against the United States.

Now, therefore, I, Abraham Lincoln, President of the United States, by virtue of the power in me vested as Commander in Chief of the Army and Navy of the United States in time of actual armed rebellion against the authority and Government of the United States, and as a fit and necessary war measure for suppressing said rebellion, do, on this 1st day of January, A.D. 1863, and in accordance with my purpose so to do, publicly proclaimed for the full period of one hundred days from the day first above mentioned, order and designate as the States and parts of States

Text: Abraham Lincoln, Complete Works, ed. John G. Nicolay and John Hay (New York: The Century Co., 1902), II, 287-88.

wherein the people thereof, respectively, are this day in rebellion against the United States the following, to wit:

Arkansas, Texas, Louisiana (except the parishes of St. Bernard, Plaquemines, Jefferson, St. John, St. Charles, St. James, Ascension, Assumption, Terrebonne, Lafourche, St. Mary, St. Martin, and Orleans, including the city of New Orleans), Mississippi, Alabama, Florida, Georgia, South Carolina, North Carolina, and Virginia (except the forty-eight counties designated as West Virginia, and also the counties of Berkeley, Accomac, Northampton, Elizabeth City, York, Princess Anne, and Norfolk, including the cities of Norfolk and Portsmouth), and which excepted parts are for the present left precisely as if this proclamation were not issued.

And by virtue of the power and for the purpose aforesaid, I do order and declare that all persons held as slaves within said designated States and parts of States are and henceforward shall be free, and that the executive government of the United States, including the military and naval authorities thereof, will recognize and maintain the freedom of said persons.

And I hereby enjoin upon the people so declared to be free to abstain from all violence, unless in necessary self-defense; and I recommend to them that in all cases when allowed they labor faithfully for reasonable wages.

And I further declare and make known that such persons of suitable condition will be received into the armed service of the United States to garrison forts, positions, stations, and other places and to man vessels of all sorts in said service.

And upon this act, sincerely believed to be an act of justice, warranted by the Constitution upon military necessity, I invoke the considerate judgment of mankind and the gracious favor of Almighty God. . . .

146

EXILE OR INDEPENDENCE: CONFEDERATE RETORT

from Jefferson Davis, Message to the Confederate Congress, January 12, 1863

By the almost universal judgment of history, Abraham Lincoln was *the* great leader of the Union. The quality of greatness, on the Confederate side, has commonly been found not in the President, Jefferson Davis (1808-1889), but in the Commander of the Army of Northern Virginia, Robert E. Lee. In part, of course, those judgments reflect the run of events beyond the control of leaders. Lincoln, who was bitterly criticized by his Northern contemporaries, presided over a victorious cause, died a martyr, and gained in retrospect the glory of the Union triumph. Lee won brilliant victories and went to gallant defeat in "the lost cause." Davis bore the concentrated guilt for a failure that was compounded of many men's faults and some natural deficiencies of man power and resources that no one could remove.

The strong suspicion remains, however, that apart from circumstances and the misleading wisdom of hindsight, Jefferson Davis was not a great leader, although he was an honorable, intelligent, and dedicated servant of the Southern cause. He managed to alienate many of the men of character and brains on his own side. He failed to win the powerful state-righters in the Confederate government and in the states to a policy of centralized control over the war effort—an enormous task but an essential one for the leader of a massive struggle for independence. He imposed his own strategic concept of "dispersed defense" upon the conduct of the war, indeed held the supreme command of Confederate military operations firmly in his own hands, and thus incurred the responsibility for defeat insofar as defeat was a consequence of human error.

In his message of January 12, 1863, Davis voiced the outrage of the South at Lincoln's Emancipation Proclamation. Now, he contended, the cloven hoof of the Republicans was plainly exposed. From the beginning, despite their smooth assurance of noninterference with slavery, Lincoln and his followers had designed to revolutionize the South. This measure of "impotent rage" must convince Southerners of the wisdom of secession and the final impossibility of any settlement short of independence. Neutral nations and Northern citizens alike, he claimed (or hoped), would see Lincoln's Proclamation as a confession of military failure.

By his argument and his tone of utter indignation, Davis confirmed what his Vice-President, Alexander Stephens, had asserted in 1861 and the North had charged before and after: that slavery was the "cornerstone" of Southern unity, the essential and untouchable principle of the Confederacy. If emancipation were attempted, Davis said, it could only mean the extermination of the slaves or "the exile of the whole white population from the Confederacy." (In the last desperate months of the Confederacy, Davis would himself propose the arming of the slaves to postpone disaster.)

The note of high confidence in the Davis message can be taken both as a sign of strength, reflecting the military triumphs of the Army of Northern Virginia, and as a sign of weakness, reflecting the President's unpromising domestic struggle to subordinate state rights and interests to the common cause of the Southern nation. His dream of foreign aid and economic self-sufficiency proved empty. Holding out for Southern independence to the bitter end, Jefferson Davis was captured in Georgia on May 10, 1865, imprisoned for two years, threatened with a trial for treason, but finally released.

His last years were spent at his home in Beauvoir, Mississippi. The fall of the Confederacy ended the active career of a man who had been a model of the "new aristocracy" of the ante-bellum South. Born in Kentucky of yeoman stock—not many miles from Lincoln's birthplace—he had entered the Mississippi planter elite with the economic success of his family, had served respectably in the U.S. Army as a West Point graduate, won a considerable reputation as a Representative, Senator, and Secretary of War in the federal government, and found his greatest triumph and his ultimate failure as the controversial leader of the Confederacy through four years of war. Jefferson Davis and the self-made aristocracy of the Lower South—who largely dominated the Confederacy—had risked everything on an audacious bid for independence and lost.

. . . The public journals of the North have been received, containing a proclamation, dated on the 1st day of the present month, signed by the President of the United States, in which he orders and declares all slaves within ten of the States of the Confederacy to be free, except such as are found within certain districts now occupied in part by the armed forces of the enemy. We may well leave it to the instincts of that common humanity which a beneficent Creator has implanted in the breasts of our fellowmen of all countries to pass judgment on a measure by which several millions of human beings of an inferior race, peaceful and contented laborers in their sphere, are doomed to extermination, while at the same time they are encouraged to a general assassination of their masters by the insidious recommendation "to abstain from violence unless in necessary self-defense." Our own detestation of those who have attempted the most execrable measure recorded in the history of guilty man is tempered by profound contempt for the impotent rage which it discloses. So far as regards the action of this Government on such criminals as may attempt its execution, I confine myself to informing you that I shall, unless in your wisdom you deem some other course more expedient, deliver to the several State authorities all commissioned officers of the United States that may hereafter be captured by our forces in any of the States embraced in the proclamation, that they may be dealt with in accordance with the laws of those States providing for the punishment of criminals engaged in exciting servile insurrection. The enlisted soldiers I shall continue to treat as unwilling instruments in the commission of these crimes, and shall direct their dis-

charge and return to their homes on the proper and usual parole.

In its political aspect this measure possesses great significance, and to it in this light I invite your attention. It affords to our whole people the complete and crowning proof of the true nature of the designs of the party which elevated to power the present occupant of the Presidential chair at Washington and which sought to conceal its purpose by every variety of artful device and by the perfidious use of the most solemn and repeated pledges on every possible occasion. . . .

The people of this Confederacy, then, cannot fail to receive this proclamation as the fullest vindication of their own sagacity in foreseeing the uses to which the dominant party in the United States intended from the beginning to apply their power, nor can they cease to remember with devout thankfulness that it is to their own vigilance in resisting the first stealthy progress of approaching despotism that they owe their escape from consequences now apparent to the most skeptical. This proclamation will have another salutary effect in calming the fears of those who have constantly evinced the apprehension that this war might end by some reconstruction of the old Union or some renewal of close political relations with the United States. These fears have never been shared by me, nor have I ever been able to perceive on what basis they could rest. But the proclamation affords the fullest guarantee of the impossibility of such a result; it has established a state of things which can lead to but one of three possible consequences—the ex-

Text: Jefferson Davis, *Letters, Papers and Speeches,* ed. Dunbar Rowland (Jackson, Miss.: Mississippi Department of Archives and History, 1923), V, 409-11, 414-15.

termination of the slaves, the exile of the whole white population from the Confederacy, or absolute and total separation of these States from the United States.

This proclamation is also an authentic statement by the Government of the United States of its inability to subjugate the South by force of arms, and as such must be accepted by neutral nations, which can no longer find any justification in withholding our just claims to formal recognition. It is also in effect an intimation to the people of the North that they must prepare to submit to a separation, now become inevitable, for that people are too acute not to understand a restoration of the Union has been rendered forever impossible by the adoption of a measure which from its very nature neither admits of retraction nor can coexist with union. . . .

. . . Our Government, born of the spirit of freedom and of the equality and independence of the States, could not have survived a selfish or jealous disposition, making each only careful of its own interest or safety. The fate of the Confederacy, under the blessing of Divine Providence, depends upon the harmony, energy, and unity of the States. It especially devolves on you, their representatives, as far as practicable, to reform abuses, to correct errors, to cultivate fraternity, and to sustain in the people a just confidence in the Government of their choice. To that confidence and to the unity and self-sacrificing patriotism hitherto displayed is due the success which has marked the unequal contest, and has brought our country into a condition at the present time such as the most sanguine would not have ventured to predict at the commencement of our struggle. Our armies are larger, better disciplined, and more thoroughly armed and equipped than at any previous period of the war. The energies of a whole nation devoted to the single object of success in this war have accomplished marvels, and many of our trials have, by a beneficent Providence, been converted into blessings. The magnitude of the perils which we encountered has developed the true qualities and illustrated the heroic character of our people, thus gaining for the Confederacy from its birth a just appreciation from the other nations of the earth. The injuries resulting from the interruption of foreign commerce have received compensation by the development of our internal resources. Cannon crown our fortresses that were cast from the products of mines opened and furnaces built during the war. Our mountain caves yield much of the niter for the manufacture of powder, and promise increase of product. From our own foundries and laboratories, from our own armories and workshops, we derive in a great measure the warlike material, the ordnance and ordnance stores which are expended so profusely in the numerous and desperate engagements that rapidly succeed each other. Cotton and woolen fabrics, shoes and harness, wagons and gun carriages are produced in daily increasing quantities by the factories springing into existence. Our fields, no longer whitened by cotton that cannot be exported, are devoted to the production of cereals and the growth of stock formerly purchased with the proceeds of cotton. In the homes of our noble and devoted women, without whose sublime sacrifices our success would have been impossible, the noise of the loom and of the spinning wheel may be heard throughout the land. With hearts swelling with gratitude let us, then, join in returning thanks to God, and in beseeching the continuance of his protecting care over our cause and the restoration of peace with its manifold blessings to our beloved country.

ABRAHAM LINCOLN

147 A NEW BIRTH OF FREEDOM

from Abraham Lincoln, *Gettysburg Address*, November 19, 1863

Not many years ago American school children learned to round their letters by endlessly copying the Gettysburg Address. They might not know the exact length of "four score and seven years" or understand just how the Battle of Gettysburg preserved "government of the people, by the people, for the people"; but the words of Lincoln were stamped in memory as the sort of thing one said on solemn political occasions. Thus (not for the first time) a noble credo was emptied of meaning by what the publicists now call overexposure. The Gettysburg Address deserves a better fate, for it is a little masterpiece: a quintessential statement of the Union aims and of the ends of the Republic.

In the spring of 1863 with Grant closing in on Vicksburg (the key to control of the Mississippi), Lee persuaded President Davis to authorize an invasion of Pennsylvania.

By carrying the war into Northern territory, Lee might relieve the dangerous pressure on the West and strike a death blow at the morale and diplomatic prestige of the Union. Lee's forces moved up the Shenandoah Valley into Pennsylvania and turned to face the concentrated Union army under General George G. Meade, entrenched in a strong defensive position at the town of Gettysburg. In three days of bloody fighting (July 1-3) the outnumbered Lee made a splendid but futile effort to crack the center of the Union line on Cemetery Ridge by frontal assault. Badly mauled, Lee's army backed off into Virginia, never again to resume the offensive. Only the caution and sluggishness of Meade saved the Confederacy from total disaster.

On November 19, 1863, the National Cemetery at Gettysburg was opened with appropriate ceremony. The principal orator of the day was Edward Everett of Massachusetts. His two-hour speech has long been forgotten. The overburdened President, accepting an invitation to dedicate the grounds "by a few appropriate remarks," spoke his mind in two minutes. His words endure. The beautiful economy of Lincoln's statement is one source of its power. More important by far is Lincoln's gift for touching the heart of the matter, directly and simply. He understood the tragedy of war and would not mock death with threats or boasting. What could justify the sacrifice at Gettysburg and all the other battlefields? Only, Lincoln said, the high purpose that a nation conceived in liberty and dedicated to human equality should endure and have a new birth of freedom.

Four score and seven years ago our fathers brought forth on this continent, a new nation, conceived in Liberty, and dedicated to the proposition that all men are created equal.

Now we are engaged in a great civil war, testing whether that nation, or any nation so conceived and so dedicated, can long endure. We are met on a great battle-field of that war. We have come to dedicate a portion of that field, as a final resting place for those who here gave their lives that that nation might live. It is altogether fitting and proper that we should do this.

But, in a larger sense, we can not dedicate—we can not consecrate—we can not hallow—this ground. The brave men, living and dead, who struggled here, have consecrated it, far above our poor power to add or detract. The world will little note, nor long remember what we say here, but it can never forget what they did here. It is for us the living, rather, to be dedicated here to the unfinished work which they who fought here have thus far so nobly advanced. It is rather for us to be here dedicated to the great task remaining before us—that from these honored dead we take increased devotion to that cause for which they gave the last full measure of devotion—that we here highly resolve that these dead shall not have died in vain—that this nation, under God, shall have a new birth of freedom—and that government of the people, by the people, for the people, shall not perish from the earth.

Text: Abraham Lincoln, *Complete Works*, ed. John G. Nicolay and John Hay (New York: The Century Co., 1902), II, 439.

148   WITH MALICE TOWARD NONE

from Abraham Lincoln, *Second Inaugural Address*, March 4, 1865

One cannot help speculating on the "iffy" questions that arise at each critical juncture of American history. None is more fascinating or more baffling than the query: what sort of peace might have come if Lincoln had survived the assassin's bullet and served out his second term? Here one can only suggest a fragmentary answer, relating to Lincoln's ends and proposed means.

From the beginning to the end of the Civil War, Lincoln's constant, overriding object was victory and the restoration of the Union. But gradually a wider purpose unfolded. As Lincoln explained in a letter to a Kentucky critic (April 4, 1864): "I claim not to have controlled events, but confess plainly that events have controlled me. Now, at the end of three years struggle the nation's condition is not what either party, or any man devised, or expected. . . . If God now wills the removal of a great wrong [slavery] . . . impartial history will find therein new cause to attest and revere the justice and goodness of God." A year later he would enlarge and deepen the theme in his Second Inaugural Address.

On the eve of the presidential election of 1864 Lincoln and his friends took a gloomy view of their chances. Caught between the sharpshooting Radicals on his left and the war-weary Democrats on his right, Lincoln doubted that his moderate policy of vigorous military effort and cautious progress toward emancipation would survive a popular test. However, his own skillful political management and General Sherman's timely conquest of Atlanta gave Lincoln a decisive electoral victory and an opportunity to shape the terms of peace and reconstruction. By March 4, 1865, the final triumph was in sight. General Hood's Confederate army had been smashed in Tennessee. Sherman had offered Savannah to the President as his Christmas gift and was cutting his way through South Carolina. Grant was putting intolerable pressure on Lee south of Richmond.

Lincoln's thoughts on entering his second term turned backward and forward. He could not conceive the tragic four-year struggle in the simple terms of winners and losers. On the political level the war came because one party sought to destroy the Union and the other chose to fight rather than submit to peaceful dissolution. On the moral level war came because one party was so committed to the "peculiar and powerful" interest of slavery that it would break the Union rather than accept restrictions on the spread of the institution.

But the very magnitude of the tragedy demanded a still higher point of view. The guilt of slavery rested upon all and the terrible punishment fell upon all. The case, said Lincoln, went beyond ordinary human judgment. It was for the Lord to judge, and it was for man to act "with malice toward none, with charity for all, with firmness in the right as God gives us to see the right." Thus he returned to the theme stated in his First Inaugural: "We are not enemies, but friends. We must not be enemies."

For Lincoln in 1865 a "just and lasting peace" meant generous terms of surrender, the restoration of the national authority, the abolition of slavery, and the prompt return of the seceded states into "their proper practical relation with the Union." Resisting the demands of the Congressional Radicals for a harsh settlement, Lincoln in December of 1863 had proclaimed his readiness to grant liberal pardons to Southerners and to recognize new state governments established by ten per cent of the qualified voters, provided that they abolish slavery. Before the President's death four Confederate states—Tennessee, Louisiana, Arkansas, and Virginia—had followed the executive plan of reconstruction and were seeking recognition by the Congress.

But the Radicals controlling Congress, Ben Wade and Charles Sumner and Thad Stevens, would not budge. Lincoln had arrested their drastic scheme of Reconstruction by a "pocket veto" of the Wade-Davis bill in July of 1864. When Lincoln died from bullet wounds inflicted by John Wilkes Booth (April 15, 1865), the Radicals renewed their campaign against a far more vulnerable opponent, the new President Andrew Johnson. Finally, they had their way. Reconstruction was to be an experiment in social and political change imposed by an army of occupation.

Would Lincoln have done otherwise? Certainly he would have offered more generous conditions to the conquered South. Possibly he could have carried the country with him. Certainly he would have counseled a more gradual advance toward full citizenship for the freedmen. Possibly Lincoln, too, would have turned to force when faced with Black Codes and a general refusal of the Southern leadership to move in the direction of Negro equality. Here speculation must end.

FELLOW-COUNTRYMEN: At this second appearing to take the oath of the Presidential office there is less occasion for an extended address than there was at the first. Then a statement somewhat in detail of a course to be pursued seemed fitting and proper. Now, at the expiration of four years, during which public declarations have been constantly called forth on every point and phase of the great contest which still absorbs the attention and engrosses the energies of the

Text: Abraham Lincoln, *Complete Works,* ed. John G. Nicolay and John Hay (New York: The Century Co., 1902), II, 656-57.

nation, little that is new could be presented. The progress of our arms, upon which all else chiefly depends, is as well known to the public as to myself, and it is, I trust, reasonably satisfactory and encouraging to all. With high hope for the future, no prediction in regard to it is ventured.

On the occasion corresponding to this four years ago all thoughts were anxiously directed to an impending civil war. All dreaded it; all sought to avert it. While the inaugural address was being delivered from this place, devoted altogether to *saving* the Union without war, insurgent agents were in the city seeking to *destroy* it without war—seeking to dissolve the Union and divide effects by negotiation. Both parties deprecated war, but one of them would *make* war rather than let the nation survive, and the other would *accept* war rather than let it perish, and the war came.

One-eighth of the whole population were colored slaves, not distributed generally over the Union, but localized in the southern part of it. These slaves constituted a peculiar and powerful interest. All knew that this interest was somehow the cause of the war. To strengthen, perpetuate, and extend this interest was the object for which the insurgents would rend the Union even by war, while the Government claimed no right to do more than to restrict the territorial enlargement of it. Neither party expected for the war the magnitude or the duration which it has already attained. Neither anticipated that the *cause* of the conflict might cease with or even before the conflict itself should cease. Each looked for an easier triumph, and a result less fundamental and astounding. Both read the same Bible and pray to the same God, and each invokes His aid against the other. It may seem strange that any men should dare to ask a just God's assistance in wringing their bread from the sweat of other men's faces, but let us judge not, that we be not judged. The prayers of both could not be answered. That of neither has been answered fully. The Almighty has His own purposes. "Woe unto the world because of offenses; for it must needs be that offenses come, but woe to that man by whom the offense cometh." If we shall suppose that American slavery is one of those offenses which, in the providence of God, must needs come, but which, having continued through His appointed time, He now wills to remove, and that He gives to both North and South this terrible war as the woe due to those by whom the offense came, shall we discern therein any departure from those divine attributes which the believers in a living God always ascribe to Him? Fondly do we hope, fervently do we pray, that this mighty scourge of war may speedily pass away. Yet, if God wills that it continue until all the wealth piled by the bondsman's two hundred and fifty years of unrequited toil shall be sunk, and until every drop of blood drawn with the lash shall be paid by another drawn with the sword, as was said three thousand years ago, so still it must be said "the judgments of the Lord are true and righteous altogether."

With malice toward none, with charity for all, with firmness in the right as God gives us to see the right, let us strive on to finish the work we are in, to bind up the nation's wounds, to care for him who shall have borne the battle and for his widow and his orphan, to do all which may achieve and cherish a just and lasting peace among ourselves and with all nations.

CHAPTER 13

Romanticism, Democracy, and Sectional Culture

At the end of the eighteenth century and the beginning of the nineteenth, just as the American republic was taking form, a new philosophical, literary, and social movement began spreading over the continent of Europe. For over a century and a half, the intellectual movement known as the Enlightenment had maintained aristocratic standards of expression and inquiry which—in accordance with the emphasis on reason and the intellect—aimed at clarity, rationality, decorum, and moderation. Its literature and art was founded to a large extent on rules and models from classical antiquity, and its science was concerned with observable laws. Romanticism revolted against these rational principles and emphasized the imagination and the emotions and the freer expression of the individual. In Germany, Immanuel Kant ushered in philosophical idealism, and Beethoven unleashed emotions never before expressed in music. France gave birth to the "natural" philosophy of Rousseau, to the "liberty, equality, fraternity" of the Revolution, and to the nationalism of the Napoleonic era, firing the imagination of men the world over. And England offered a new and exciting literature, filled with passionate emotion and lyrical idealism.

As it gained power, Romanticism took on diverse characteristics in different lands and among various persons. But in general the Romanticists shared several preoccupations: they reacted against the view that the universe and man were fairly simple machines created by God to run with the regularity of clocks. They rejected the materialism, coldness, and lack of spirituality implicit in such a view. Instead they tended to assert that the force of the universe was spiritual, that human intuition and poetic sensibility were more likely than reason to lead man to truth, and that, properly viewed, the world was not a machine but a constantly changing and developing kaleidoscope, full of the unexpected, the irrational, and the unknowable.

Their view of the universe led the Romanticists to a revived interest in the common man and to an enthusiasm for nature, as opposed to "society"—particularly man and nature in their "natural," untamed state. Both politics and poetry enjoyed the expression of emotions. Both scholars and poets turned to the legends and lore of the Middle Ages. In biology there later arose the first major statement of the historical ideal of evolution. In political theory the European Romantic movement achieved a significant new conception of society, not as a fixed system but rather as an evolving organism susceptible to refashioning and improvement. The Romantic nineteenth century saw a succession of revolutions and reform movements in Europe aiming at larger political freedoms and rights for the individual.

In America, European Romantic influences were strengthened by native forces: the republican political freedom realized in the Revolution and the Constitution; the individualism and unbounded optimism aroused by the frontier experience; the love of nature growing out of the predominant agrarian life and the proximity of the primeval forest; and the humanitarianism inherited from Quakerism and from the Calvinism of Jonathan Edwards and others in whom a latent optimism prevailed. Because most Americans believed that the Founding Fathers had firmly established the necessary political foundations for rapid progress toward perfection, American Romantics tended to concern themselves relatively more with aspects of society other than its political institutions; they turned to social and humanitarian reforms and to the cultivation of the arts.

THE ROMANTIC PHILOSOPHER

Ralph Waldo Emerson (1803-1882) was one of the leaders of the American Romantic movement. Of an old New England family, Emerson was educated for the ministry at Harvard but left even the liberal Unitarian church because he did not approve of its forms and rituals. As a writer and lecturer, he became around 1830 the leading figure in an informal group of New England ministers and other intellectuals who called themselves "Transcendentalists."

Like Thomas Jefferson, Emerson was essentially a man of hope who looked on America as man's chance to develop a good society. However, his conception of the ideal society was significantly different from Jefferson's. For Jefferson, man was first and foremost a social creature who found his fulfillment in interaction with other men. For Emerson, on the other hand, man could fulfill himself only through maximum individual development. These different social views reflected different conceptions of the nature of the universe. Emerson believed that the many different aspects of the universe were really diverse manifestations of one all-encompassing central Spirit, which he called the Over-Soul. The individual man, Emerson believed, could become a channel for the higher truths of the Over-Soul if he would only develop his intuitive powers to the fullest. Thus, he felt that the "natural laws" which the men of the Enlightenment tried to discover through the exercise of reason represented a lower level of truth than the "higher laws" intuited by the individual soul in communion with the Over-Soul.

Because he believed in each individual's ability to intuit higher laws, Emerson had great faith in the benevolence of nature and man's continual progress toward perfection. Therefore, like Jefferson, he believed in limited government, but for a different reason: Jefferson had opposed strong central governments in order that men might meet in smaller, more manageable groups to govern themselves; Emerson, however, opposed strong government because he felt it inevitably limited the fullest development of each individual.

VERSIONS OF ROMANTICISM

Thought and action in the Romantic Age centered about the liberation of man and the full development of individual potentialities. A large group of intellectuals worked toward social and humanitarian reforms of all kinds, but their idea of reform was typically Romantic. Instead of agitating for government regulations and controls, as reformers of the later nineteenth century would do, they sought to eliminate social institutions that they felt were repressing the full development of individual men. Even a relatively advanced social thinker like Orestes Brownson suggested the elimination of the institution of property inheritance as the panacea for the class struggle which he saw coming. This tendency is further illustrated by the two most powerful reform movements of the period: the abolition movement, which sought to end the institution of slavery, and the temperance movement, which tried to eliminate drinking. It was also at this time that the movement for women's rights first began. Margaret Fuller, a friend of Emerson, was one of the earliest workers for this cause.

Emerson, himself, was sympathetic to, but skeptical of, the work of the active social and humanitarian reformers. He felt that the only true reform could come from the creation of "great individuals." His follower, Henry Thoreau, attempted to put Emersonian ideas on politics and reform into action by refusing to pay his taxes during the Mexican War. He justified his conduct by arguing that the individual is morally obligated to disobey the government when its orders conflict with the higher laws he intuitively believes.

The American Romantic ideal of individualism—emphasizing as it did the value of each individual man apart from his role as an atom in the complex institutional structure of society—reflected the influence of the ideal of the natural man which developed in the later Enlightenment (see Documents 100-102). These two ideas were in turn related to the Jacksonian movement's emphasis on popular democracy and the virtues of the common man. Jackson himself was frequently presented to the public as a natural man from the West who was going to free America from the corrupt and artificial manipulations of Eastern bankers.

Popular culture was also strongly influenced by the ideals of Romanticism, though in a version which was watered down and mixed with a sizeable dose of orthodox Protestant Christianity. Sentimental novelists, who flourished in this period, warmly espoused such Romantic reforms as temperance and found the makings of full-blown Romantic heroes in such unpromising figures as urban newsboys.

Interestingly enough, Herman Melville and Nathaniel Hawthorne, the two greatest American novelists of the pre-Civil War period, rejected most of the Romantic ideas about man and society, though they were both strongly influenced by Romantic concepts of art. Hawthorne's biting satire on progress in "The Celestial Railroad" is typical of their criticism of Romantic optimism.

THE SECTIONS IN AMERICAN LIFE AND THOUGHT

Although America today is an extremely homogeneous nation culturally speaking, the North, South, and West before the Civil War not only had their own distinctive economic interests and social systems but were in many ways different in manners, customs, and thought. Even within the sections there were strikingly different ways of life in different places and among different classes. In the North the traditional village culture of New England with its distinct social classes, quiet orderliness, and staunch resistance to change was still prominent. However, the social and economic developments discussed in Chapter 10 were gradually bringing about many important changes in manners and ideas, the full significance of which was not generally realized until after the Civil War. The growing city with its disturbing new ways of life was a particular object of concern to many Northerners. Accustomed to the stability, placidity, and general homogeneity of the villages, many Americans were shocked as they gradually became aware of new social phenomenon like slums, crime, and the presence of large groups of immigrants in the rapidly developing Northern cities.

Despite the efforts of a few brilliant literary figures like Edgar Allan Poe, the dominant Romantic influence in the South was the fiction of Sir Walter Scott, whose exciting narratives of adventure and gracious living in feudal England gave Southern plantation folk a model for imitation. Southerners of the upper classes tended to idealize the cotton plantation as a happy feudal manor where faithful slaves were cared for and protected by dashing, gallant gentlemen and pure, highborn ladies. These idealizations found their way into much of both the serious and the popular fiction created by Southerners before and after the war. A very different kind of Southern life, that of the small farmers of the less developed interior, was reflected in the writings of a few individuals who were less bemused by the romanticized version of plantation life and the elevated literary ideals of men like Emerson. A remarkable group of humorists, delighted, inspired, and disgusted by the rough-and-tumble antics they saw about them in the rapidly developing area of the Old Southwest (Tennessee, Alabama, Georgia, Mississippi and Louisiana), developed in their sketches a new and more realistic literary tradition which was later to bear fruit in the great works of Mark Twain.

The West was particularly important in American thought in the early nineteenth century, when its untapped economic and social opportunities stimulated many Americans to seek new homes in the continental interior. As it was portrayed in novel and story, however, the West had many different meanings. To some writers the West was a beautiful virgin land populated only by noble Indians and fugitives from civilization who bore a notable resemblance to the natural man of Enlightenment and Romantic thought. In the popular tall tales which proliferated around both historical and mythical figures, the West was a land of legendary frontiersmen who could whip their weight in wildcats and even, in one of the first great American engineering feats, grease up the axles of the earth to get it moving on a cold day. The real Western frontier, of course, bore little resemblance to literary legend or to the popular tall tale. Rather the frontier posed terrible problems of adjustment for the more cultured and educated of its settlers, who soon discovered that Romantic idealizations of a wilderness utopia in frontier Michigan and Illinois were poor preparation for the realistics of mud, isolation, and brutality.

Romantic Democracy

149

THE DEMOCRATIC MIND: FAITH IN PUBLIC OPINION, FAITH IN HUMAN PERFECTIBILITY

from Alexis de Tocqueville, *Democracy in America*, 1835

French traveler Alexis de Tocqueville's famous book, *Democracy in America*, is filled with incisive comments on American ways of thinking. De Tocqueville was particularly struck by the Americans' tendency toward the practical, their avoidance of traditions, and their optimistic hope that in the new American social system men would be able to progress rapidly toward perfection. He attributed these traits primarily to the all-pervasive influence of relative political and social equality.

In this selection De Tocqueville begins by characterizing American thought in the Romantic Age. Then he analyzes the concept of the perfectibility of man, which he felt was one of the key beliefs generated by American democracy. He points out that in an aristocratic society, where class lines are firmly drawn, men look for some betterment but not for drastic change. In a democratic society, however, where all men have a chance to better themselves, there arises the idea that society as a whole might improve infinitely. Such an idea not only filled the thought of men like Emerson but also influenced the many reform movements of the day; it even stimulated some individuals to found ideal utopian communities like Brook Farm.

For other selections from De Tocqueville's observations, see Documents 113 and 116.

I think that in no country in the civilized world is less attention paid to philosophy than in the United States. The Americans have no philosophical school of their own, and they care but little for all the schools into which Europe is divided, the very names of which are scarcely known to them.

Yet it is easy to perceive that almost all the inhabitants of the United States use their minds in the same manner, and direct them according to the same rules; that is to say, without ever having taken the trouble to define the rules, they have a philosophical method common to the whole people.

To evade the bondage of system and habit, of family maxims, class opinions, and, in some degree, of national prejudices; to accept tradition only as a means of information, and existing facts only as a lesson to be used in doing otherwise and doing better; to seek the reason of things for oneself, and in oneself alone; to tend to results without being bound to means, and to strike through the form to the substance—such are the principal characteristics of what I shall call the philosophical method of the Americans.

But if I go further and seek among these characteristics the principal one, which includes almost all the rest, I discover that in most of the operations of the mind each American appeals only to the individual effort of his own understanding. . . .

In the midst of the continual movement that agitates a democratic community, the tie that unites one generation to another is relaxed or broken; every man there readily loses all trace of the ideas of his forefathers or takes no care about them.

Men living in this state of society cannot derive their belief from the opinions of the class to which they belong; for, so to speak, there are no longer any classes, or those which still exist are composed of such mobile elements that the body can never exercise any real control over its members.

As to the influence which the intellect of one man may have on that of another, it must necessarily be very limited in a country where the citizens, placed on an equal footing, are all closely seen by one another; and where, as no signs of incontestable greatness or superiority are perceived in any one of them, they are constantly brought back to their own reason as the most obvious and proximate source of truth. It is not only confidence in this or that man which is destroyed, but the disposition to trust the authority

Text: Alexis de Tocqueville, *Democracy in America*, ed. and trans. Henry Reeve (Cambridge, Mass.: Sever & Francis, 1862), II, 1-3, 6-7, 10-11, 37-39.

of any man whatsoever. Everyone shuts himself up tightly within himself and insists upon judging the world from there.

The practice of Americans leads their minds to other habits, to fixing the standard of their judgment in themselves alone. As they perceive that they succeed in resolving without assistance all the little difficulties which their practical life presents, they readily conclude that everything in the world may be explained, and that nothing in it transcends the limits of the understanding. Thus they fall to denying what they cannot comprehend; which leaves them but little faith for whatever is extraordinary and an almost insurmountable distaste for whatever is supernatural. As it is on their own testimony that they are accustomed to rely, they like to discern the object which engages their attention with extreme clearness; they therefore strip off as much as possible all that covers it; they rid themselves of whatever separates them from it, they remove whatever conceals it from sight, in order to view it more closely and in the broad light of day. This disposition of mind soon leads them to condemn forms, which they regard as useless and inconvenient veils placed between them and the truth.

The Americans, then, have found no need of drawing philosophical method out of books; they have found it in themselves. . . .

There are no revolutions that do not shake existing belief, enervate authority, and throw doubts over commonly received ideas. Every revolution has more or less the effect of releasing men to their own conduct and of opening before the mind of each one of them an almost limitless perspective. When equality of conditions succeeds a protracted conflict between the different classes of which the elder society was composed, envy, hatred, and uncharitableness, pride and exaggerated self-confidence seize upon the human heart, and plant their sway in it for a time. This, independently of equality itself, tends powerfully to divide men, to lead them to mistrust the judgment of one another, and to seek the light of truth nowhere but in themselves. Everyone then attempts to be his own sufficient guide and makes it his boast to form his own opinions on all subjects. Men are no longer bound together by ideas, but by interests; and it would seem as if human opinions were reduced to a sort of intellectual dust, scattered on every side, unable to collect, unable to cohere.

Thus that independence of mind which equality supposes to exist is never so great, never appears so excessive, as at the time when equality is beginning to establish itself and in the course of that painful labor by which it is established.

That sort of intellectual freedom which equality may give ought, therefore, to be very carefully distinguished from the anarchy which revolution brings. Each of these two things must be separately considered in order not to conceive exaggerated hopes or fears of the future.

I believe that the men who will live under the new forms of society will make frequent use of their private judgment, but I am far from thinking that they will often abuse it. This is attributable to a cause which is more generally applicable to democratic countries, and which, in the long run, must restrain, within fixed and sometimes narrow limits, individual freedom of thought. . . .

I have shown . . . how equality of conditions leads men to entertain a sort of instinctive incredulity of the supernatural and a very lofty and often exaggerated opinion of human understanding. The men who live at a period of social equality are not therefore easily led to place that intellectual authority to which they bow either beyond or above humanity. They commonly seek for the sources of truth in themselves or in those who are like themselves. This would be enough to prove that at such periods no new religion could be established, and that all schemes for such a purpose would be not only impious, but absurd and irrational. It may be foreseen that a democratic people will not easily give credence to divine missions; that to discover the chief arbiter of their belief within, and not beyond, the limits of their kind.

When the ranks of society are unequal, and men unlike one another in condition, there are some individuals wielding the power of superior intelligence, learning, and enlightenment, while the multitude are sunk in ignorance and prejudice. Men living at these aristocratic periods are therefore naturally induced to shape their opinions by the standard of a superior person, or a superior class of persons, while they are averse to recognizing the infallibility of the mass of the people.

The contrary takes place in ages of equality. The nearer the people are drawn to the common level of an equal and similar condition, the less prone does each man become to place implicit faith in a certain man or a certain class of men. But his readiness to believe the multitude increases, and opinion is more than ever mistress of the world. Not only is common opinion the only guide which private judgment retains among a democratic people, but among such a people it possesses a power infinitely beyond what it has elsewhere. At periods of equality men have no faith in one another, by reason of their common resemblance; but this very resemblance gives them almost unbounded confidence in the judgment of the public; for it would seem probable that, as they are all endowed with equal means of judging, the greater truth should go with the greater number.

When the inhabitant of a democratic country compares himself individually with all those about him, he feels with pride that he is the equal of any one of them; but when he comes to survey the totality of his fellows and to place himself in contrast with so huge a body, he is instantly overwhelmed by the sense of his own insignificance and weakness. The same equality that renders him independent of each of his fellow citizens, taken severally, exposes him alone and unprotected to the influence of the greater number. The public, therefore, among a democratic people, has a singular power, which aristocratic nations cannot conceive; for it does not persuade others to its beliefs, but it imposes them and makes them permeate the thinking of everyone by a sort of enormous pressure of the mind of all upon the individual intelligence.

In the United States the majority undertakes to supply a multitude of ready-made opinions for the use of individuals, who are thus relieved from the necessity of forming opinions of their own. Everybody there adopts great numbers of theories, on philosophy, morals, and politics, without inquiry, upon public trust; and if we examine it very closely, it will be perceived that religion itself holds sway there much less as a doctrine of revelation than as a commonly received opinion. . . .

Equality suggests to the human mind several ideas that would not have originated from any other source, and it modifies almost all those previously entertained. I take as an example the idea of human perfectibility, because it is one of the principal notions that the intellect can conceive and because it constitutes of itself a great philosophical theory, which is everywhere to be traced by its consequences in the conduct of human affairs.

Although man has many points of resemblance with the brutes, one trait is peculiar to himself: he improves; they are incapable of improvement. Mankind could not fail to discover this difference from the beginning. The idea of perfectibility is therefore as old as the world; equality did not give birth to it, but has imparted to it a new character.

When the citizens of a community are classed according to rank, profession, or birth and when all men are forced to follow the career which chance has opened before them, everyone thinks that the utmost limits of human power are to be discerned in proximity to himself, and no one seeks any longer to resist the inevitable law of his destiny. Not, indeed, that an aristocratic people absolutely deny man's faculty of self-improvement, but they do not hold it to be indefinite; they can conceive amelioration, but not change: they imagine that the future condition of society may be better, but not essentially different; and, while they admit that humanity has made progress and may still have some to make, they assign to it beforehand certain impassable limits.

Thus they do not presume that they have arrived at the supreme good or at absolute truth (what people or what man was ever wild enough to imagine it?), but they cherish an opinion that they have pretty nearly reached that degree of greatness and knowledge which our imperfect nature admits of; and as nothing moves about them, they are willing to fancy that everything is in its fit place. Then it is that the legislator affects to lay down eternal laws; that kings and nations will raise none but imperishable monuments; and that the present generation undertakes to spare generations to come the care of regulating their destinies.

In proportion as castes disappear and the classes of society draw together, as manners, customs, and laws vary, because of the tumultuous intercourse of men, as new facts arise, as new truths are brought to light, as ancient opinions are dissipated and others take their place, the image of an ideal but always fugitive perfection presents itself to the human mind. Continual changes are then every instant occurring under the observation of every man; the position of some is rendered worse, and he learns but too well that no people and no individual, however enlightened they may be, can lay claim to infallibility; the condition of others is improved, whence he infers that man is endowed with an indefinite faculty for improvement. His reverses teach him that none have discovered absolute good; his success stimulates him to the never ending pursuit of it. Thus, forever seeking, forever falling to rise again, often disappointed, but not discouraged, he tends unceasingly towards that unmeasured greatness so indistinctly visible at the end of the long track which humanity has yet to tread.

It can hardly be believed how many facts naturally flow from the philosophical theory of the indefinite perfectibility of man or how strong an influence it exercises even on those who, living entirely for the purposes of action and not of thought, seem to conform their actions to it without knowing anything about it.

I accost an American sailor and inquire why the ships of his country are built so as to last for only a short time; he answers without hesitation that the art of navigation is every day making such rapid progress that the finest vessel would become almost useless if it lasted beyond a few years. In these words, which fell accidentally, and on a particular subject, from an uninstructed man, I recognize the general and systematic idea upon which a great people direct all their concerns.

Aristocratic nations are naturally too liable to narrow the scope of human perfectibility; democratic nations, to expand it beyond reason.

RALPH WALDO EMERSON: PHILOSOPHER OF ROMANTIC DEMOCRACY

Ralph Waldo Emerson, the unofficial leader of the Romantic movement in America, was born in Boston on May 25, 1803, a descendant of nine successive generations of ministers. His father, minister of the First Church, Unitarian, in Boston, died when Emerson was eight years of age, leaving his widow and four sons in financial difficulties. However, all four sons were able to go through Harvard, from which Emerson graduated in 1821. Emerson became pastor of the Second Church, Unitarian, of Boston in 1829 but resigned in 1832 because of his distaste for ritual, as demonstrated in his unwillingness to administer the Lord's Supper. For the remainder of his life he was a writer and lecturer, publishing essays and poems and delivering addresses on all kinds of philosophical, artistic, and political subjects. He died in Concord in 1882, one of the most widely respected men in America.

Emerson left Unitarianism and formal religion at the age of twenty-nine because he felt that each individual should rely upon his own intuitive perceptions, even to the extent of setting aside the authority of the Bible. "Make your own Bible," he said. "Select and collect all the words and sentences that in all your reading have been to you like the blast of a trumpet, out of Shakespeare, Seneca, Moses, John, and Paul." All impositions of authority—traditions and laws—upon the individual should be resisted. "I hope in these days we have heard the last of conformity and consistency," he announced in his essay "Self-Reliance." Emerson was not an anarchical romanticist, however; he was not opposed to society. In his mind a good society was the sum of self-reliant individuals, each free to develop perfection and virtue in his own life. This conception of man's role in the universe, together with the ideas expressed in the following selections, made Emerson the representative philosopher of Romantic democracy.

150 THE OVER-SOUL: MAN'S ONENESS WITH THE UNIVERSE

from Ralph Waldo Emerson, "The Over-Soul," 1841

Emerson's philosophy—often called "transcendentalism" from the Romantic belief that the intuitive and spiritual transcend, or go beyond, the rational and physical—was far more complex than can be indicated by a few brief selections. It was based on the idea that all beings and objects both animate and inanimate are diverse manifestations of one universal spirit. This spirit, which Emerson called the "Over-Soul," generates out of itself all the diverse forms which make up the world as we know it, including our own souls.

Emerson did not draw from this belief the conclusion that an Indian mystic might have. Far from considering the physical world of the senses an unreal delusion and urging men to renounce it for mystic communion with God, or the Over-Soul, Emerson had enough Yankee practicality in his make-up to seek instead a way of realizing *in this life* some of the higher truth, beauty, and goodness of the Over-Soul. In this approach we probably see the influence of American democratic ideals to which Emerson was deeply committed.

Emerson believed that every man is potentially capable of insight into the meaning of existence, because the all-knowing, all-pervading Over-Soul is in a sense contained within each individual soul. If a man can develop certain intuitive powers within himself, he can gain some knowledge of the "laws" of the Over-Soul and thereby become truly wise and happy.

(The Supreme Critic on the errors of the past and the present, and the only prophet of that which must be, is that great nature in which we rest, as the earth lies in the soft arms of the atmosphere; that Unity, that Over-soul, within which every man's particular being is contained and made one with all other; that common heart, of which all sincere conversation is the worship, to which all right action is submission; that overpowering reality which confutes our tricks and talents, and constrains every one to pass for what he is, and to speak from his character, and not from his tongue, and which evermore tends to pass into our thought and hand, and become wisdom, and virtue, and power, and beauty.) We live in succession, in division, in parts, in particles. (Meantime within man is the soul of the whole; the wise silence; the universal beauty, to which every part and particle is equally related; the eternal ONE.) And this deep power in which we exist, and whose beatitude is all accessible to us, is not only self-sufficing and perfect in every hour, but the act of seeing and the thing seen, the seer and the spectacle, the sub-ject and the object, are one. We see the world piece by piece, as the sun, the moon, the animal, the tree; but the whole, of which these are the shining parts, is the soul. Only by the vision of that Wisdom can the horoscope of the ages be read, and by falling back on our better thoughts, by yielding to the spirit of prophecy which is innate in every man, we can know what it saith. Every man's words, who speaks from that life, must sound vain to those who do not dwell in the same thought on their own part. I dare not speak for it. My words do not carry its august sense; they fall short and cold. Only itself can inspire whom it will, and behold! their speech shall be lyrical, and sweet, and universal as the rising of the wind. Yet I desire, even by profane words, if I may not use sacred, to indicate the heaven of this deity, and to report what hints I have collected of the transcendent simplicity and energy of the Highest Law.

Text: Ralph Waldo Emerson, *Complete Works,* ed. Edward Waldo Emerson (Boston: Houghton Mifflin & Co., 1903), II, 268-70.

151

MAN, THE REFORMER: THE DREAM OF HUMAN PERFECTIBILITY

from Ralph Waldo Emerson, "Man, the Reformer," 1841

With a few significant exceptions, American intellectuals have always been reformers and social critics. In Emersonian fashion, they have considered society to be a flexible and fluid thing constantly needing improvement and readjustment in accordance with new insights. At times the American people as a whole have also been reform-conscious and have followed the lead of clergymen, philosophers, and other thinkers in attempts to renovate American society. One of these times was the Romantic Age, when individuals from all classes participated in reform organizations aimed at all kinds of changes and improvements in American institutions. Naturally, many particular reforms were strongly opposed by those groups whose specific interests were threatened by the changes proposed. Such conflict was aroused by the movement to abolish slavery, a reform which became increasingly popular in the North while it met with almost complete antagonism in the South. Nonetheless, to improve society was a general urge, which manifested itself in scores of diverse movements, political, economic, and humanitarian.

In the following selection, Emerson analyzes this general spirit of reform and points out some of its essential components. Reform in the Romantic Age was based particularly on faith in the potentialities of individual men, and most reformers were marching against customs and institutions which they felt were hindrances to individual development. The most popular reform of the time aside from abolition, and strangely enough one of the most powerful forces in American popular thought throughout the nineteenth century, was the temperance movement. Prohibition of alcohol was popular both because of Biblical injunctions and because of the popular feeling that liquor obstructed the economic and moral development of individuals who fell under its baneful influence. Many sincerely believed that drink was *the* major cause of vice and crime, and thus the prime source of human unhappiness.

Other reforms growing out of the romantic desire to liberate and develop the potentialities of individual human beings included the movement for women's rights and the first important work with the handicapped, the blind, the deaf, the dumb, and the insane.

But the idea which now begins to agitate society has a wider scope than our daily employments, our households, and the institutions of property. We are to revise the whole of our social structure, the state, the school, religion, marriage, trade, science, and explore their foundations in our own nature; we are to see that the world not only fitted the former men, but fits us, and to clear ourselves of every usage which has not its roots in our own mind. What is a man born for but to be a Reformer, a Re-maker of what man has made; a renouncer of lies; a restorer of truth and good, imitating that great Nature which embosoms us all, and which sleeps no moment on an old past, but every hour repairs herself, yielding us every morning a new day, and with every pulsation a new life? Let him renounce everything which is not true to him, and put all his practices back on their first thoughts, and do nothing for which he has not the whole world for his reason. If there are inconveniences, and what is called ruin in the way, because we have so enervated and maimed ourselves, yet it would be like dying of perfumes to sink in the effort to reattach the deeds of every day to the holy and mysterious recesses of life.

The power, which is at once spring and regulator in all efforts of reform, is faith in Man, the conviction that there is an infinite worthiness in him which will appear at the call of worth, and that all particular reforms are the removing of some impediment. Is it not the highest duty that man should be honored in us? I ought not to allow any man, because he has broad lands, to feel that he is rich in my presence. I ought to make him feel that I can do without his riches, that I cannot be bought,—neither by comfort, neither by pride,—and though I be utterly penniless, and receiving bread from him, that he is the poor man beside me. And if,

Text: Ralph Waldo Emerson, *Complete Works*, ed. Edward Waldo Emerson (Boston: Houghton Mifflin & Co., 1903), I, 247-51.

at the same time, a woman or a child discovers a sentiment of piety, or a juster way of thinking than mine, I ought to confess it by my respect and obedience, though it go to alter my whole way of life.

The Americans have many virtues, but they have not Faith and Hope. I know no two words whose meaning is more lost sight of. We use these words as if they were as obsolete as Selah and Amen. And yet they have the broadest meaning and the most cogent application to Boston in 1841. The Americans have no faith. They rely on the power of a dollar; they are deaf to a sentiment. They think you may talk the north wind down as easily as raise society; and no class more faithless than the scholars or intellectual men. Now if I talk with a sincere wise man and my friend, with a poet, with a conscientious youth who is still under the dominion of his own wild thoughts, and not yet harnessed in the team of society to drag with us all in the ruts of custom, I see at once how paltry is all this generation of unbelievers, and what a house of cards their institutions are, and I see what one brave man, what one great thought executed might effect. I see that the reason of the distrust of the practical man in all theory, is his inability to perceive the means whereby we work. Look, he says, at the tools with which this world of yours is to be built. As we cannot make a planet, with atmosphere, rivers, and forests, by means of the best carpenters' or engineers' tools, with chemist's laboratory and smith's forge to boot,—so neither can we ever construct that heavenly society you prate of, out of foolish, sick, selfish men and women, such as we know them to be. But the believer not only beholds his heaven to be possible, but already to begin to exist,—but not by the men or materials the statesman uses, but by men transfigured and raised above themselves by the power of principles. To principles something else is possible that transcends all the power of expedients.

152

POLITICS AND PERSONAL LIBERTY: THE ROMANTIC INSISTENCE ON LIMITED GOVERNMENT

from Ralph Waldo Emerson, "Politics," 1844

One important base of Romantic reform—as well as of American reform movements throughout the nineteenth century—was the idea that society is fluid and capable of being refashioned by men. Therefore society can and ought to be molded to accord with the current needs of its citizens. Emerson expresses this idea in his essay "Politics," along with several other ideas reflecting the political theory of American Romantic democracy. According to the theory, the state tends to lag behind the thought of the most intelligent and perceptive individuals of a particular time and is therefore invariably a repressing influence on the fullest development of individual men. This belief leads Emerson to two main conclusions: "the less government we have, the better," and "good men must not obey the laws too well."

On the surface this would appear to be a recommendation for lawlessness, but Emerson actually makes no such appeal for irresponsibility. On the contrary, his criticism of contemporary political processes and relations is based on the idea, expressed in the latter part of the selection, that traditional political institutions are simply less effective than certain basic, more just and loving types of human relations. The good society is one composed of good individuals—individuals who have perfected their sense of justice and wisdom in dealing with their fellows. Government is an expedient, a "proxy," a temporary regulatory force, awaiting the moral and spiritual development of the individuals who make up society. Thus, in criticizing traditional political processes and institutions, Emerson is not advocating their instant elimination but reminding men that they are capable of progress toward a better kind of human relations than those based on the force of organized government.

Although Henry Thoreau (see Document 153) attempted personally to belie Emerson's criticism that "I do not call to mind a single human being who has steadily denied the authority of the laws, on the simple ground of his own moral nature," Emerson's statement of his political theory is far more radical than most Americans of his time would have accepted. His basic ideas, however, were an important part of the political convictions of many Americans.

In dealing with the State, we ought to remember that its institutions are not aboriginal, though they existed before we were born: that they are not superior to the citizen: that every one of them was once the act of a single man: every law and usage was a man's expedient to meet a particular case: that they all are imitable, all alterable; we may make as good; we may make better. Society is an illusion to the young citizen. It lies before him in rigid repose, with certain names, men, and institutions, rooted like oak-trees to the centre, round which all arrange themselves the best they can. But the old statesman knows that society is fluid, there are no such roots and centres; but any particle may suddenly become the centre of the movement, and compel the system to gyrate round it, as every man of strong will, like Pisistratus, or Cromwell, does for a time, and every man of truth, like Plato, or Paul, does forever. But politics rest on necessary foundations, and cannot be treated with levity. Republics abound in young civilians, who believe that the laws make the city, that grave modifications of the policy and modes of living, and employments of the population, that commerce, education, and religion, may be voted in or out; and that any measure, though it were absurd, may be imposed on a people, if only you can get sufficient voices to make it a law. But the wise know that foolish legislation is a rope of sand, which perishes in the twisting; that the State must follow, and not lead the character and progress of the citizen; the strongest usurper is quickly got rid of; and they only who build on Ideas, build for eternity; and that the form of government which prevails, is the expression of what cultivation exists in the population which permits it. The law is only a memorandum. We are superstitious, and esteem the statute somewhat: so much life as it has in the character of living men, is its force. The statute stands there to say, yesterday we agreed so and so, but how feel ye this article to-day? Our statute is a currency, which we stamp with our own portrait: it soon becomes unrecognizable, and in process of time will return to the mint. Nature is not democratic, nor limited-monarchical, but despotic, and will not be fooled or abated of any jot of her authority, by the pertest of her sons: and as fast as the public mind is opened to more intelligence, the code is seen to be brute and stammering. It speaks not articulately and must be made to. Meantime the education of the general mind never stops. The reveries of the true and simple are prophetic. What the tender poetic youth dreams, and prays, and paints to-day, but shuns the ridicule of saying aloud, shall presently be the resolutions of public bodies, then shall be carried as grievance and bill of rights through conflict and war, and then shall be triumphant law and establishment for a hundred years, until it gives place, in turn, to new prayers and pictures. The history of the State sketches in coarse outline the progress of thought, and follows at a distance the delicacy of culture and of aspiration. . . .

The same necessity which secures the rights of person and property against the malignity of folly of the magistrate, determines the form and

Text: Ralph Waldo Emerson, *Complete Works*, ed. Edward Waldo Emerson (Boston: Houghton Mifflin & Co., 1903), III, 199-201, 207-08, 212-16, 220-21.

methods of governing, which are proper to each nation, and to its habit of thought, and nowise transferable to other states of society. In this country, we are very vain of our political institutions, which are singular in this, that they sprung, within the memory of living men, from the character and condition of the people, which they still express with sufficient fidelity,—and we ostentatiously prefer them to any other in history. They are not better, but only fitter for us. We may be wise in asserting the advantage in modern times of the democratic form, but to other states of society, in which religion consecrated the monarchical, that and not this was expedient. Democracy is better for us, because the religious sentiment of the present time accords better with it. Born democrats, we are nowise qualified to judge of monarchy, which, to our fathers living in the monarchical idea, was also relatively right. But our institutions, though in coincidence with the spirit of the age, have not any exemption from the practical defects which have discredited other forms. Every actual State is corrupt. Good men must not obey the laws too well. What satire on government can equal the severity of censure conveyed in the word *politic,* which now for ages has signified *cunning,* intimating that the State is a trick. . . .

We must trust infinitely to the beneficent necessity which shines through all laws. Human nature expresses itself in them as characteristically as in statues, or songs, or railroads, and an abstract of the codes of nations would be a transcript of the common conscience. Governments have their origin in the moral identity of men. Reason for one is seen to be reason for another, and for every other. There is a middle measure which satisfies all parties, be they never so many, or so resolute for their own. Every man finds a sanction for his simplest claims and deeds in decisions of his own mind, which he calls Truth and Holiness. In these decisions all the citizens find a perfect agreement, and only in these; not in what is good to eat, good to wear, good use of time, or what amount of land, or of public aid, each is entitled to claim. This truth and justice men presently endeavor to make application of, to the measuring of land, the apportionment of service, the protection of life and property. Their first endeavors, no doubt, are very awkward. Yet absolute right is the first governor; or, every government is an impure theocracy. The idea after which each community is aiming to make and mend its law, is, the will of the wise man. The wise man, it cannot find in nature, and it makes awkward but earnest efforts to secure his government by contrivance; as, by

causing the entire people to give their voices on every measure; or, by a double choice to get the representation of the whole; or, by a selection of the best citizens; or, to secure the advantages of efficiency and internal peace, by confiding the government to one, who may himself select his agents. All forms of government symbolize an immortal government, common to all dynasties and independent of numbers, perfect where two men exist, perfect where there is only one man. . . .

Hence, the less government we have, the better,—the fewer laws, and the less confided power. The antidote to this abuse of formal Government, is, the influence of private character, the growth of the Individual; the appearance of the principal to supersede the proxy; the appearance of the wise man, of whom the existing government is, it must be owned, but a shabby imitation. That which all things tend to educe, which freedom, cultivation, intercourse, revolutions, go to form and deliver, is character; that is the end of nature, to reach unto this coronation of her king. To educate the wise man, the State exists; and with the appearance of the wise man, the State expires. . . .

We live in a very low state of the world, and pay unwilling tribute to governments founded on force. There is not, among the most religious and instructed men of the most religious and civil nations, a reliance on the moral sentiment, and a sufficient belief in the unity of things to persuade them that society can be maintained without artificial restraints, as well as the solar system; or that the private citizen might be reasonable, and a good neighbor, without the hint of a jail or a confiscation. What is strange too, there never was in any man sufficient faith in the power of rectitude, to inspire him with the broad design of renovating the State on the principle of right and love. All those who have pretended this design, have been partial reformers, and have admitted in some manner the supremacy of the bad State. I do not call to mind a single human being who has steadily denied the authority of the laws, on the simple ground of his own moral nature. Such designs, full of genius and full of fate as they are, are not entertained except avowedly as air-pictures. If the individual who exhibits them, dare to think them practicable, he disgusts scholars and churchmen; and men of talent, and women of superior sentiments, cannot hide their contempt. Not the less does nature continue to fill the heart of youth with suggestions of this enthusiasm, and there are now men,—if indeed I can speak in the plural number,—more exactly, I will say, I have just been conversing with one man, to whom no weight of adverse experience will make it for a moment appear impossible, that thousands of human beings might exercise towards each other the grandest and simplest sentiments, as well as a knot of friends, or a pair of lovers.

VERSIONS OF ROMANTIC DEMOCRACY

153

CIVIL DISOBEDIENCE: A ROMANTIC INDIVIDUALIST SECEDES FROM THE UNION

from Henry David Thoreau, "Civil Disobedience," 1849

Henry David Thoreau, perhaps the greatest of all American nature writers and surely the most noted of Romantic individualists, was born in Concord, Massachusetts, July 12, 1817. He was graduated without distinction from Harvard in 1837, helped his brother for a while teaching in a private school, assisted his father in the manufacture of lead pencils in the 1840's, did odd jobs in Emerson's household in 1841 and again in 1847-48, contributed essays and poems to the transcendentalist magazine, *The Dial*, and delivered several not very popular or remunerative lectures in various northeastern cities. He refused to undertake a regular occupation. Throughout his life he felt he had no special obligations to society; he wished to live free and uncommitted, untrammeled by institutions. He never married, never attended church, never voted, and even went to jail for refusing to pay taxes. He died of tuberculosis in Concord, May 6, 1862. When on his deathbed his Aunt Louisa asked if he had "made his peace with God," he replied, "I have never quarreled with Him."

Thoreau is particularly known for two events in his life. The first is his famous "experiment" at Walden Pond. On July 4, 1845, he "went into the woods," he explains in *Walden*, the immortal account of his sojourn, "because I wished to live deliberately, to front only the essential facts of life," in essence, to study nature and read and write "with the fewest obstacles." He built himself a small hut beside the pond above Concord and lived alone there until September 6, 1847. He was not a hermit, however, for he often visited the village, received visitors at the Pond, and performed various odd jobs for a living: house painting, fence building, carpentering, gardening, surveying.

The second major event of his life occurred in 1846, during his residence at Walden. Sometime around 1843 Thoreau had decided to refuse to pay his poll tax to the government on the ground that his principles forbade him to give financial support to any government tolerating slavery. In 1846, he was arrested for this rebellion and, persisting in his refusal, was sent to jail, where he spent the night. There is a charming story, unfortunately apocryphal, that it was his friend and master Emerson who bailed him out the next day.

More important than his brief stay in the village jail is the eloquent essay Thoreau composed on the basis of his experience, from which the following selection is taken. In his act Thoreau carried out the political theories expressed by men like Emerson; in his essay "Civil Disobedience" he demanded that men should refuse to support a government that goes against their conscience. Thoreau did not advocate forcible revolution but a peaceful resistance, at the climax of which the individual willingly enters prison rather than support the government in what he considers an immoral policy.

Thoreau's theories had little practical effect on history until, at the beginning of the twentieth century, an obscure young Indian lawyer named Mohandas Gandhi developed them into the political technique of "passive resistance," which had such dramatic results in India's struggle for independence from Great Britain. In recent years, Thoreau's ideas, returning to America, have influenced the techniques adopted by Negro groups in combatting discrimination in the South.

I heartily accept the motto,—"That government is best which governs least"; and I should like to see it acted up to more rapidly and systematically. Carried out, it finally amounts to this, which also I believe,—"That government is best which governs not at all"; and when men are prepared for it, that will be the kind of govern-

Text: Henry D. Thoreau, *Writings* (Boston: Houghton Mifflin & Co., 1906), IV, 356-57, 360-61, 370-76, 382-87.

ment which they will have. Government is at best but an expedient; but most governments are usually, and all governments are sometimes, inexpedient. The objections which have been brought against a standing army, and they are many and weighty, and deserve to prevail, may also at last be brought against a standing government. The standing army is only an arm of the standing government. The government itself, which is only the mode which the people have chosen to execute their will, is equally liable to be abused and perverted before the people can act through it. Witness the present Mexican war, the work of comparatively a few individuals using the standing government as their tool; for, in the outset, the people would not have consented to this measure.

This American government,—what is it but a tradition, though a recent one, endeavoring to transmit itself unimpaired to posterity, but each instant losing some of its integrity? It has not the vitality and force of a single living man; for a single man can bend it to his will. It is a sort of wooden gun to the people themselves. But it is not the less necessary for this; for the people must have some complicated machinery or other, and hear its din, to satisfy that idea of government which they have. Governments show thus how successfully men can be imposed on, even impose on themselves, for their own advantage. . . .

But, to speak practically and as a citizen, unlike those who call themselves no-government men, I ask for, not at once no government, but *at once* a better government. Let every man make known what kind of government would command his respect, and that will be one step toward obtaining it.

After all, the practical reason why, when the power is once in the hands of the people, a majority are permitted, and for a long period continue, to rule, is not because they are most likely to be in the right, nor because this seems fairest to the minority, but because they are physically the strongest. But a government in which the majority rule in all cases cannot be based on justice, even as far as men understand it. Can there not be a government in which majorities do not virtually decide right and wrong, but conscience?—in which majorities decide only those questions to which the rule of expediency is applicable? Must the citizen ever for a moment, or in the least degree, resign his conscience to the legislator? Why has every man a conscience, then? I think that we should be men first, and subjects afterward. It is not desirable to cultivate a respect for the law, so much as for the right. The only obligation which I have a right to assume, is to do at any time what I think right. It is truly enough said, that a corporation has no conscience; but a corporation of conscientious men is a corporation *with* a conscience. Law never made men a whit more just; and, by means of their respect for it, even the well-disposed are daily made the agents of injustice. A common and natural result of an undue respect for law is, that you may see a file of soldiers, colonel, captain, corporal, privates, powder-monkeys, and all, marching in admirable order over hill and dale to the wars, against their wills, ay, against their common sense and consciences, which makes it very steep marching indeed, and produces a palpitation of the heart. They have no doubt that it is a damnable business in which they are concerned; they are all peaceably inclined. Now, what are they? Men at all? or small movable forts and magazines, at the service of some unscrupulous man in power? . . .

The mass of men serve the state thus, not as men mainly, but as machines, with their bodies. . . .

How does it become a man to behave toward this American government to-day? I answer, that he cannot without disgrace be associated with it. I cannot for an instant recognize that political organization as *my* government which is the *slave's* government also.

All men recognize the right of revolution; that is, the right to refuse allegiance to, and to resist, the government, when its tyranny or its inefficiency are great and unendurable. But almost all say that such is not the case now. But such was the case, they think, in the Revolution of '75. If one were to tell me that this was a bad government because it taxed certain foreign commodities brought to its ports, it is most probable that I should not make an ado about it, for I can do without them. All machines have their friction, and possibly this does enough good to counterbalance the evil. At any rate, it is a great evil to make a stir about it. But when the friction comes to have its machine, and oppression and robbery are organized, I say, let us not have such a machine any longer. In other words, when a sixth of the population of a nation which has undertaken to be the refuge of liberty are slaves, and a whole country is unjustly overrun and conquered by a foreign army, and subjected to military law, I think that it is not too soon for honest men to rebel and revolutionize. What makes this duty the more urgent is the fact, that the country so overrun is not our own, but ours is the invading army. . . .

It is not a man's duty, as a matter of course, to devote himself to the eradication of any, even the most enormous wrong; he may still properly have other concerns to engage him; but it is his duty, at least, to wash his hands of it, and, if he gives it no thought longer, not to give it practically his support. If I devote myself to other pursuits and contemplations, I must first see, at least, that I do not pursue them sitting upon another man's shoulders. I must get off him first, that he may pursue his contemplations too. . . .

. . . Action from principle, the perception and the performance of right, changes things and relations; it is essentially revolutionary, and does not consist wholly with anything which was. It not only divides states and churches, it divides families; ay, it divides the *individual*, separating the diabolical in him from the divine.

Unjust laws exist: shall we be content to obey them, or shall we endeavor to amend them, and obey them until we have succeeded, or shall we transgress them at once? Men generally, under such a government as this, think that they ought to wait until they have persuaded the majority to alter them. They think that, if they should resist, the remedy would be worse than the evil. But it is the fault of the government itself that the remedy *is* worse than the evil. *It* makes it worse. Why is it not more apt to anticipate and provide for reform? Why does it not cherish its wise minority? Why does it cry and resist before it is hurt? Why does it not encourage its citizens to be on the alert to point out its faults, and *do* better than it would have them? Why does it always crucify Christ, and excommunicate Copernicus and Luther, and pronounce Washington and Franklin rebels? . . .

Under a government which imprisons any unjustly, the true place for a just man is also a prison. The proper place to-day, the only place which Massachusetts has provided for her freer and less desponding spirits, is in her prisons, to be put out and locked out of the State by her own act, as they have already put themselves out by their principles. It is there that the fugitive slave, and the Mexican prisoner on parole, and the Indian come to plead the wrongs of his race, should find them; on that separate, but more free and honorable ground, where the State places those who are not *with* her, but *against* her,— the only house in a slave State in which a free man can abide with honor. If any think that their influence would be lost there, and their voices no longer afflict the ear of the State, that they would not be as an enemy within its walls, they do not know by how much truth is stronger than error, nor how much more eloquently and effectively he can combat injustice who has experienced a lit-

tle in his own person. Cast your whole vote, not a strip of paper merely, but your whole influence. A minority is powerless while it conforms to the majority; it is not even a minority then; but it is irresistible when it clogs by its whole weight. If the alternative is to keep all just men in prison, or give up war and slavery, the State will not hesitate which to choose. . . .

I have paid no poll-tax for six years. I was put into a jail once on this account, for one night; and, as I stood considering the walls of solid stone, two or three feet thick, the door of wood and iron, a foot thick, and the iron grating which strained the light, I could not help being struck with the foolishness of that institution which treated me as if I were mere flesh and blood and bones, to be locked up. I wondered that it should have concluded at length that this was the best use it could put me to, and had never thought to avail itself of my services in some way. I saw that, if there was a wall of stone between me and my townsmen, there was a still more difficult one to climb or break through, before they could get to be as free as I was. I did not for a moment feel confined, and the walls seemed a great waste of stone and mortar. I felt as if I alone of all my townsmen had paid my tax. They plainly did not know how to treat me, but behaved like persons who are underbred. In every threat and in every compliment there was a blunder; for they thought that my chief desire was to stand the other side of that stone wall. I could not but smile to see how industriously they locked the door on my meditations, which followed them out again without let or hindrance, and *they* were really all that was dangerous. As they could not reach me, they had resolved to punish my body; just as boys, if they cannot come at some person against whom they have a spite, will abuse his dog. I saw that the State was half-witted, that it was timid as a lone woman with her silver spoons, and that it did not know its friends from its foes, and I lost all my remaining respect for it, and pitied it. . . .

However, the government does not concern me much, and I shall bestow the fewest possible thoughts on it. It is not many moments that I live under a government, even in this world. If a man is thought-free, fancy-free, imagination-free, that which *is not* never for a long time appearing *to be* to him, unwise rulers or reformers cannot fatally interrupt him. . . .

The authority of government, even such as I am willing to submit to,—for I will cheerfully obey those who know and can do better than I, and in many things even those who neither know nor can do so well,—is still an impure one: to be strictly just, it must have the sanction and consent of the governed. It can have no pure right over my person and property but what I concede to it. The progress from an absolute to a limited monarchy, from a limited monarchy to a democracy, is a progress toward a true respect for the individual. Even the Chinese philosopher was wise enough to regard the individual as the basis of the empire. Is a democracy, such as we know it, the last improvement possible in government? Is it not possible to take a step further towards recognizing and organizing the rights of man? There will never be a really free and enlightened State, until the State comes to recognize the individual as a higher and independent power, from which all its own power and authority are derived, and treats him accordingly. I please myself with imagining a State at last which can afford to be just to all men, and to treat the individual with respect as a neighbor; which even would not think it inconsistent with its own repose, if a few were to live aloof from it, not meddling with it, nor embraced by it, who fulfilled all the duties of neighbors and fellow-men. A State which bore this kind of fruit, and suffered it to drop off as fast as it ripened, would prepare the way for a still more perfect and glorious State, which also I have imagined, but not yet anywhere seen.

154

EMANCIPATION OF THE LABORING CLASSES: A ROMANTIC APPEAL FOR ECONOMIC REFORM

from Orestes Brownson, "The Laboring Classes," 1840

Romantic ideas greatly influenced social thinking of all kinds in the pre-Civil War period. An example is this selection from an article by Orestes Brownson (1803-1876) on the necessity of economic reform. Much of Brownson's thinking is reminiscent of what we associate today with Marxism: his image of history as the struggle between political and economic classes; his emphasis on the crucial role of the proletariat, or laboring classes, in contemporary society; and his belief that religious and philosophical ideas tend to be a reflection of the social and economic interests of those who hold them. Such ideas are not uniquely Marxian, however, and they were held by many men in the Romantic Age. Of crucial importance is the fact that Brownson does not draw the Marxian conclusions from his ideas. Where Marx advocated the violent overthrow of the governing classes by the proletariat, Brownson propounds a typically romantic idea of reform: the elimination of the institution of property inheritance, a reform which he believes will give every individual a chance to develop himself, without some men having from the start an unfair advantage over others.

Brownson's own career illustrates the intellectual ferment of the Romantic Age and the search on the part of many individuals for a personally satisfying faith. Reared a Presbyterian, Brownson went through a whole series of religious and political systems before his final conversion to Catholicism in 1844.

No one can observe the signs of the times with much care, without perceiving that a crisis as to the relation of wealth and labor is approaching. It is useless to shut our eyes to the fact, and like the ostrich fancy ourselves secure because we have so concealed our heads that we see not the danger. We or our children will have to meet this crisis. The old war between the King and the Barons is well nigh ended, and so is that between the Barons and the Merchants and Manufacturers,—landed capital and commercial capital. The business man has become the peer of my Lord. And now commences the new struggle between the operative and his employer, between wealth and labor. Every day does this struggle extend further and wax stronger and fiercer; what or when the end will be God only knows. . . .

We pass through our manufacturing villages; most of them appear neat and flourishing. The operatives are well dressed, and we are told, well paid. They are said to be healthy, contented, and happy. This is the fair side of the picture; the side exhibited to distinguished visitors. There is a dark side, moral as well as physical. Of the common operatives, few, if any, by their wages, acquire a competence. A few of what Carlyle terms not inaptly the *body-servants* are well paid, and now and then an agent or an overseer rides in his coach. But the great mass

Text: Orestes A. Brownson, *The Laboring Classes* (Boston: Benjamin H. Greene, 1840), pp. 9, 11-14, 23-24.

wear out their health, spirits, and morals, without becoming one whit better off than when they commenced labor. The bills of mortality in these factory villages are not striking, we admit, for the poor girls when they can toil no longer go home to die. The average life, working life we mean, of the girls that come to Lowell, for instance, from Maine, New Hampshire, and Vermont, we have been assured, is only about three years. What becomes of them then? Few of them ever marry; fewer still ever return to their native places with reputations unimpaired. "She has worked in a Factory," is almost enough to damn to infamy the most worthy and virtuous girl. We know no sadder sight on earth than one of our factory villages presents, when the bell at break of day, or at the hour of breakfast, or dinner, calls out its hundreds or thousands of operatives. . . .

Now the great work for this age and the coming, is to raise up the laborer, and to realize in our own social arrangements and in the actual condition of all men, that equality between man and man, which God has established between the rights of one and those of another. In other words, our business is to emancipate the proletaries, as the past has emancipated the slaves. This is our work. There must be no class of our fellow men doomed to toil through life as mere workmen at wages. If wages are tolerated it must be, in the case of the individual operative, only under such conditions that by the time he is of a proper age to settle in life, he shall have accumulated enough to be an independent laborer on his own capital,—on his own farm, or in his own shop. Here is our work. How is it to be done?

Reformers in general answer this question, or what they deem its equivalent, in a manner which we cannot but regard as very unsatisfactory. They would have all men wise, good, and happy; but in order to make them so, they tell us that we want not external changes, but internal; and therefore instead of declaiming against society and seeking to disturb existing social arrangements, we should confine ourselves to the individual reason and conscience; seek merely to lead the individual to repentance, and to reformation of life; make the individual a practical, a truly religious man, and all evils will either disappear, or be sanctified to the spiritual growth of the soul.

This is doubtless a capital theory, and has the advantage that kings, hierarchies, nobilities, —in a word, all who fatten on the toil and blood of their fellows, will feel no difficulty in supporting it. . . .

This theory, however, is exposed to one slight objection, that of being condemned by something like six thousand years' experience. For six thousand years its beauty has been extolled, its praises sung and its blessings sought, under every advantage which learning, fashion, wealth, and power can secure; and yet under its practical operations, we are assured, that mankind, though totally depraved at first, have been growing worse and worse ever since.

For our part, we yield to none in our reverence for science and religion; but we confess that we look not for the regeneration of the race from priests and pedagogues. They have had a fair trial. They cannot construct the temple of God. They cannot conceive its plan, and they know not how to build. They daub with untempered mortar, and the walls they erect tumble down if so much as a fox attempt to go up thereon. In a word they always league with the people's masters, and seek to reform without disturbing the social arrangements which render reform necessary. They would change the consequents without changing the antecedents, secure to men the rewards of holiness, while they continue their allegiance to the devil. We have no faith in priests and pedagogues. They merely cry peace, peace, and that too when there is no peace, and can be none.

We admit the importance of what Dr. Channing in his lectures on the subject we are treating recommends as "self-culture." Self-culture is a good thing, but it cannot abolish inequality, nor restore men to their rights. As a means of quickening moral and intellectual energy, exalting the sentiments, and preparing the laborer to contend manfully for his rights, we admit its importance, and insist as strenuously as any one on making it as universal as possible; but as constituting in itself a remedy for the vices of the social state, we have no faith in it. As a means it is well, as the end it is nothing. . . .

Now the evils of which we have complained are of a social nature. That is, they have their root in the constitution of society as it is, and they have attained to their present growth by means of social influences, the action of government, of laws, and of systems and institutions upheld by society, and of which individuals are the slaves. This being the case, it is evident that they are to be removed only by the action of society, that is, by government for the action of society is government.

But what shall government do? Its first doing must be an *undoing*. There has been thus far quite too much government, as well as government of the wrong kind. The first act of government we want, is a still further limitation of itself. It must begin by circumscribing within narrower limits its powers. And then it must proceed to repeal all laws which bear against the laboring classes, and then to enact such laws as are necessary to enable them to maintain their equality. We have no faith in those systems of elevating the working classes which propose to elevate them without calling in the aid of government. We must have government, and legislation expressly directed to this end.

But again what legislation do we want so far as this country is concerned? We want first the legislation which shall free the government, whether State or Federal, from the control of the Banks. The Banks represent the interest of the employer, and therefore of necessity interests adverse to those of the employed; that is they represent the interests of the business community in opposition to the laboring community. So long as the government remains under the control of the Banks, so long it must be in the hands of the natural enemies of the laboring classes, and may be made, nay, will be made, an instrument of depressing them yet lower. It is obvious then that, if our object be the elevation of the laboring classes, we must destroy the power of the Banks over the government, and place the government in the hands of the laboring classes themselves, or in the hands of those, if such there be, who have an identity of interest with them. But this cannot be done so long as the Banks exist. . . .

Following the destruction of the Banks, must come that of all monopolies, of all PRIVILEGE. There are many of these. We cannot specify them all; we therefore select only one, the greatest of them all, the privilege which some have of being born rich while others are born poor. It will be seen at once that we allude to the hereditary descent of property, an anomaly in our American system, which must be removed, or the system itself will be destroyed. We cannot now go into a discussion of this subject, but we promise to resume it at our earliest opportunity. We only say now, that as we have abolished hereditary monarchy and hereditary nobility, we must complete the work by abolishing hereditary property. A man shall have all he honestly acquires, so long as he himself belongs to the world in which he acquires it. But his power over his property must cease with his life, and his property must then become the property of the state, to be disposed of by some equitable law for the use of the generation which takes his place. Here is the principle without any of its details, and this is the grand legislative measure to which we look forward. We see no means of elevating the laboring classes which can be effectual without this. And is this a measure to be easily carried? Not at all. It will cost infinitely more than it cost to abolish either hereditary monarchy or hereditary nobility. It is a great measure, and a startling. The rich, the business community, will never voluntarily consent to it, and we think we know too much of human nature to believe that it will ever be effected peaceably. It will be effected only by the strong arm of physical force. It will come, if it ever come at all, only at the conclusion of war, the like of which the world as yet has never witnessed, and from which, however inevitable it may seem to the eye of philosophy, the heart of Humanity recoils with horror.

155

EMANCIPATION OF WOMEN: WOMEN'S RIGHTS AS ROMANTIC REFORM

from Margaret Fuller, *Woman in the Nineteenth Century*, 1845

The Romantic Age saw widespread agitation for the extension of social and political rights to various classes, and one of these classes was women. The exponents of women's rights sought not only the rights of suffrage and equal justice but also the acceptance of women in many social roles hitherto filled only by men. The movement was at first strenuously denounced or ridiculed by the majority of American males, but in the latter part of the nineteenth century, as women organized and their economic importance and political potential became more apparent, many men, including some shrewd politicians, were won to their cause. In the Romantic Age, however, most of the male support for women's rights came from reforming intellectuals, like Emerson and his associates, who insisted on the equal right of women to develop intellectual needs and capacities.

Sarah Margaret Fuller (1810-1850), a friend and associate of Ralph Waldo Emerson, was one of the earliest agitators for women's rights, not only in her writings but in her career, wherein she rejected many of the traditional taboos which then controlled women's behavior. She was brilliant and scholarly and amazingly well-read; Emerson claimed that her reading was on the level of the historian Gibbon's. A light in any intellectual conversation, she was accepted as a cultural equal by many of the leading thinkers and writers of her time. Her book, *Woman in the Nineteenth Century,* from which the following selection is taken, is thus more than a courageous plea for greater equality between the sexes; it is also an appeal for recognition of woman's intellectual capabilities.

. . . Knowing that there exists in the minds of men a tone of feeling toward women as toward slaves, such as is expressed in the common phrase, "Tell that to women and children;" that the infinite soul can only work through them in already ascertained limits; that the gift of reason, Man's highest prerogative, is allotted to them in much lower degree; that they must be kept from mischief and melancholy by being constantly engaged in active labor, which is to be furnished and directed by those better able to think, &c, &c,—we need not multiply instances, for who can review the experience of last week without recalling words which imply, whether in jest or earnest, these views, or views like these,—knowing this, can we wonder that many reformers think that measures are not likely to be taken in behalf of women, unless their wishes could be publicly represented by women?

"That can never be necessary," cry the other side. "All men are privately influenced by women; each has his wife, sister, or female friends, and is too much biased by these relations to fail of representing their interests; and, if this is not enough, let them propose and enforce their wishes with the pen. The beauty of home would be destroyed, the delicacy of the sex be violated, the dignity of halls of legislation degraded, by an attempt to introduce them there. Such duties are inconsistent with those of a mother:" and then we have ludicrous pictures of ladies in hysterics at the polls, and senate-chambers filled with cradles. . . .

As to the use of the pen, there was quite as much opposition to Woman's possessing herself of that help to free agency as there is now to her seizing on the rostrum or the desk; and she is likely to draw, from a permission to plead her cause that way, opposite inferences to what might be wished by those who now grant it.

As to the possibility of her filling with grace and dignity any such position, we should think those who had seen the great actresses, and heard the Quaker preachers of modern times, would not doubt that Woman can express publicly the fulness of thought and creation, without losing any of the peculiar beauty of her sex. What can pollute and tarnish is to act thus from any motive except that something needs to be said or done. Woman could take part in the processions, the songs, the dances of old religion; no one fancied her delicacy was impaired by appearing in public for such a cause. . . .

As to men's representing women fairly at present, while we hear from men who owe to their wives not only all that is comfortable or graceful, but all that is wise, in the arrangement of their lives, the frequent remark, "You cannot reason with a woman,"—when from those of delicacy, nobleness, and poetic culture, falls the contemptuous phrase "women and children," and that in no light sally of the hour, but in works intended to give a permanent statement of the best experiences,—when not one man, in the million, shall I say? no, not in the hundred million, can rise above the belief that Woman was made *for Man,*—when such traits as these are daily forced upon the attention, can we feel that Man will always do justice to the interests of Woman? Can we think that he takes a sufficiently discerning and religious view of her office and destiny *ever* to do her justice, except when prompted by sentiment,—accidentally or transiently, that is, for the sentiment will vary according to the relations in which he is placed? The lover, the poet, the artist, are likely to view her nobly. The father and the philosopher have some chance of liberality; the man of the world, the legislator for expediency, none.

Under these circumstances, without attaching importance, in themselves, to the changes demanded by the champions of Woman, we hail them as signs of the times. We would have every arbitrary barrier thrown down. We would have every path laid open to Woman as freely as to Man. Were this done, and a slight temporary fermentation allowed to subside, we should see crystallizations more pure and of more various beauty. We believe the divine energy would pervade nature to a degree unknown in the history of former ages, and that no discordant collision, but a ravishing harmony of the spheres, would ensue.

Yet, then and only then will mankind be ripe for this, when inward and outward freedom for

Text: Margaret Fuller, *Woman in the Nineteenth Century* (New York: Greeley & McElrath, 1845), pp. 25-26, 50-51.

Woman as much as for Man shall be acknowledged as a *right*, not yielded as a concession. As the friend of the negro assumes that one man cannot by right hold another in bondage, so should the friend of Woman assume that Man cannot by right lay even well-meant restrictions on Woman. If the negro be a soul, if the woman be a soul, apparelled in flesh, to one Master only are they accountable. There is but one law for souls, and, if there is to be an interpreter of it, he must come not as man, or son of man, but as son of God. . . .

It is not the transient breath of poetic incense that women want; each can receive that from a lover. It is not life-long sway; it needs but to become a coquette, a shrew, or a good cook, to be sure of that. It is not money, nor notoriety, nor the badges of authority which men have appropriated to themselves. If demands, made in their behalf, lay stress on any of these particulars, those who make them have not searched deeply into the need. The want is for that which at once includes these and precludes them; which would not be forbidden power, lest there be temptation to steal and misuse it; which would not have the mind perverted by flattery from a worthiness of esteem: it is for that which is the birthright of every being capable of receiving it—the freedom, the religious, the intelligent freedom of the universe to use its means, to learn its secret, as far as Nature has enabled them, with God alone for their guide and their judge.

Ye cannot believe it, men; but the only reason why women ever assume what is more appropriate to you, is because you prevent them from finding out what is fit for themselves. Were they free, were they wise fully to develop the strength and beauty of Woman; they would never wish to be men, or man-like. . . .

156

SENTIMENTAL FICTION: THE ROMANTIC HERO IN THE LAND OF OPPORTUNITY

from A. L. Stimson, *Easy Nat*, 1854
from Elizabeth Oakes Smith, *The Newsboy*, 1854

Sentimental fiction, which provided one of the favorite avenues of escape from the unpleasantness of real life for multitudes of nineteenth-century Americans, was one of the many popular offshoots of the general climate of Romantic ideas which we have seen in other contexts. The sentimental novel generally told of the trials and tribulations of an inanely pure hero or heroine, whose character frequently resembled a Christianized version of the natural man of romantic thought. This hero or heroine was usually faced with the machinations of some bold villain, whose evil nature revealed few human qualities. The success or failure of the central character usually depended on whether he or she was able to resist the temptations offered by the villain; these temptations tended to be liquor in the case of the young men and seduction in the case of the women. Religion was a prominent feature in almost all these novels. An intense but cloying faith in a sentimentalized version of orthodox Protestantism was the major bulwark of the hero or heroine against the temptations of their satanic adversaries.

The two brief selections that follow give some idea of the characteristic themes and devices of sentimental fiction. The first selection presents one of an almost infinite number of climactic moments from an incredibly rambling novel dealing mainly with the rise of the noble young Edwin Fairbanks from rags to riches. In the course of his rise he is temporarily distracted from his true love, the pure seamstress Susan Midge, by the wiles of the aristocratic Helen Bogardus. However, discovering from the faint aroma of "the 1770," an old wine, on her breath that she indulges in liquor, he is saved from the male equivalent of a fate worse than death. The author sarcastically recommends that young women who indulge in drink take a sugared cubeb, the nineteenth-century equivalent to chlorophyll gum for freshening the breath. As the episode suggests, this novel, among other things, strenuously propagandizes for the cause of temperance, a typical Romantic reform.

The second selection is from the beginning of a novel recounting the trials and tribulations of newsboy life in New York. As this beginning suggests, however, the story hardly offers the sort of urban realism one might expect from such a subject. The author sees the newsboy's plight not as a manifestation of a social injustice but as a sight to stimulate rhapsodies about the nobility of man. It was this sort of romanticizing of poverty and deprivation that prevented many Americans from sensing until later in the nineteenth century the need for the creation of new social institutions to deal with some of the problems that the American economic and social system was producing as a result of the growth of industrial capitalism. The figure of the noble newsboy will reappear in Volume II as one of the leading characters in the juvenile romances of Horatio Alger.

Easy Nat

Then she performed the overture to the last opera with brilliant execution. It was superbly, gloriously done, and Edwin Fairbanks could not adequately express his admiration. His enthusiasm delighted her, for she inferred from it the existence of a reciprocal passion—the thought being, unconsciously, the offspring of the desire.

Next, she sang a love song from the same opera, in Italian—'burning, yet tender'—and rendering it *con expressione,* with all the power of a voice so rich and flexible, that the most eminent prima donna in the world might well envy her its possession; it lapped the sensuous soul in elysium, and thrilled the heart of the hearer with the most intense ecstasy.

As bending over her symmetrical form, he turned the leaves of her music, her glowing cheek nearly touched his own; and when she looked into his countenance (as she did almost continually while singing), and saw it beaming upon her as if he thought her the very embodiment of delicious sound, and her warm breath saluted his lips as the zephyr does the rosebud which it woos to open; Edwin (shall we confess it? It was too bad, gentle reader, but it is our duty to be candid with you,) thought that he detected the flavor, or aroma, rather, of her father's rare old wine!

The truth was, that some old familiar friends of her own sex had made a call about noon, and she had treated them to a sandwich and a glass of 'the 1770.'

The spell was broken, and Edwin was enabled to tear himself away from the siren, who had held him for some minutes, lost to all self-consciousness by the power of her fascination!

O! ye young ladies, seeking temperate husbands, and yet loving a little wine occasionally yourselves, be warned by the unhappy Helen's example—and always eat a sugared cubeb, or two, after drinking!

The Newsboy

. . . I was thinking of such possibilities, and so I looked out in the morning, (I am sure it was in the morning, for that is the time for pleasant thoughts,) when under my window I saw a little Newsboy calling in a lusty voice the names of several of the morning papers. He was a skin of a boy, little, and old before his time.

I should as soon have thought of taking Tom Thumb, or the Aztecs for a hero as this newsboy. Wasn't he poor, and ragged, and ignorant, and wouldn't everybody laugh at the idea! Little by little, Bob (I afterward learned his name was Bob) grew into my mind, not as a poor, forsaken, ignorant, neglected child, who ought to be taken up and sent to the Orphan Asylum, or asylum for vagrants, but as a great-soul'd boy, whose nobleness I dared not fathom, but which I could appreciate, the latchet of whose old, dilapidated shoes I was not worthy to unloose. He had walked through fiery furnaces unscathed, and sat amid lions, and their savageness had been rebuked before him.

I learned to await the coming of the Newsboy with solemn expectancy, and the shuffling of his weary feet grew to have a majesty about them; his ragged habiliments were right royal robes over his great heart, and the brimless hat became him like a regal crown, for Bob had that innate dignity of soul which neither crown nor sceptre could augment.

Little by little I learned his story—little by little, for I was not great enough to take in all the greatness of the Newsboy. I with my conventional life, and years of training, and ancestors of forecast—how could I comprehend a being who had stood up naked from the hands of nature, and said "come behold a man!" Who had owed nothing to the schools, the preacher, the tailor, and little to the cook; who was a philosopher in his way, seeing things through his own eyes, and drawing his own conclusions unaided of any man.

The image of the Newsboy haunted me, and at length I felt I must write his history. I saw that the race would soon be so modified by the genialities of some benevolent souls, that the newsboy of our time would pass away and be only a tradition, and even the nobleness of Bob come to be regarded as a fable. I looked into the newsboy lodging rooms, and saw how these benevolent souls (God comfort them in every hour of need, and do them good even as they have done good) were making this wilderness life of the newsboy to blossom as the rose, and soon the newsboy of

Texts: A. L. Stimson, *Easy Nat; or The Three Apprentices; A Tale of Life in New York and Boston* (New York: J. O. Derby, 1854), pp. 448-49. Elizabeth Oakes Smith, *The Newsboy* (New York: J. C. Derby, 1854), pp. 8-10.

Bob's time, sleeping by the wayside, in areas, under steps, about the Parks, in old crates and hogsheads, in the markets, and everywhere that a shelter could be found, would be forgotten; and then it was that the Ishmael-like wander-ings of Bob, fatherless and motherless, friendless and forsaken, going up and down the great city, grew to have a genuine pathos about them, and I put myself to the study of his character, and learned he was a hero.

CRITICISM OF ROMANTIC DEMOCRACY

157

THE CELESTIAL RAILROAD: A SATIRE OF ROMANTIC AND RELIGIOUS LIBERALISM

from Nathaniel Hawthorne, "The Celestial Railroad," 1843

Although Romanticism was the leading cultural movement of the pre-Civil War period, it was not without its opponents. Emersonian optimism and the more liberal political and religious ideas of the Transcendentalists were certainly suspect to many groups of Americans, some of whom held to orthodox Protestantism, others of whom opposed the reforms or the political theories of the Romantic democrats, and a few of whom had vision of the character of human existence more tragic than optimistic. One of these last was Nathaniel Hawthorne, whose keen sense of the depravity and evil in man's nature made it difficult for him to accept many of the assumptions of Emersonian Romanticism, though he was strongly influenced by Romantic ideas about art.

Hawthorne, one of America's greatest novelists, was born in Salem, Massachusetts, in 1804. In a brilliant group of stories, sketches and novels, including *The Scarlet Letter* (1850), *The House of the Seven Gables* (1851), *The Blithedale Romance* (1852) and *The Marble Faun* (1860), he probed deeply into the problems of evil and human sin. He was generally popular throughout the nineteenth century (unlike his great contemporary Melville, who was almost forgotten); and today his works, with their symbolism and psychological analyses, are being read with new interest as precursors of later nineteenth- and twentieth-century novels.

"The Celestial Railroad" illustrates another side of Hawthorne: his keen satirical sense of the moral and philosophical shortcomings of his contemporaries. Modeled on John Bunyan's *Pilgrim's Progress*, the great seventeenth-century allegory of the Christian's journey toward salvation, Hawthorne's sketch is an "up-to-date" version of this pilgrimage. Social and technological progress has replaced the hard trek of Bunyan's pilgrim with a fast train ride with all the modern conveniences over a bridge built by the "advances" of philosophy. Satirized, thus, is the Romantic liberal who considers the Christian life as pleasant and not too difficult to attain.

In this selection, from the beginning of the work, Mr. Smooth-it-away, a director of the Celestial Railroad, explains to the author some of these improvements. It is not difficult to infer what Hawthorne thought about these "modern advances" over the traditional Christian idea of the soul's pilgrimage through doubt and temptation; and it is no surprise when at the end the destination of the Celestial Railroad turns out to be a somewhat darker and more hellish place than that expected by its liberalistic passengers.

Not a great while ago, passing through the gate of dreams, I visited that region of the earth in which lies the famous City of Destruction. It interested me much to learn that by the public spirit of some of the inhabitants a railroad has recently been established between this populous and flourishing town and the Celestial City. Having a little time upon my hands, I resolved to gratify a liberal curiosity by making a trip thither.

Text: Nathaniel Hawthorne, *Works* (Boston: Houghton Mifflin & Co., 1882), V, 212-15.

Accordingly, one fine morning after paying my bill at the hotel, and directing the porter to stow my luggage behind a coach, I took my seat in the vehicle and set out for the station-house. It was my good fortune to enjoy the company of a gentleman—one Mr. Smooth-it-away—who, though he had never actually visited the Celestial City, yet seemed as well acquainted with its laws, customs, policy, and statistics, as with those of the City of Destruction, of which he was a native townsman. Being, moreover, a director of the railroad corporation and one of its largest stockholders, he had it in his power to give me all desirable information respecting that praiseworthy enterprise.

Our coach rattled out of the city, and at a short distance from its outskirts passed over a bridge of elegant construction, but somewhat too slight, as I imagined, to sustain any considerable weight. On both sides lay an extensive quagmire, which could not have been more disagreeable either to sight or smell, had all the kennels of the earth emptied their pollution there.

"This," remarked Mr. Smooth-it-away, "is the famous Slough of Despond—a disgrace to all the neighborhood; and the greater that it might so easily be converted into firm ground."

"I have understood," said I, "that efforts have been made for that purpose from time immemorial. Bunyan mentions that above twenty thousand cartloads of wholesome instructions had been thrown in here without effect."

"Very probably! And what effect could be anticipated from such unsubstantial stuff?" cried Mr. Smooth-it-away. "You observe this convenient bridge. We obtained a sufficient foundation for it by throwing into the slough some editions of books of morality; volumes of French philosophy and German rationalism; tracts, sermons, and essays of modern clergymen; extracts from Plato, Confucius, and various Hindoo sages, together with a few ingenious commentaries upon texts of Scripture,—all of which by some scientific process, have been converted into a mass like granite. The whole bog might be filled up with similar matter."

It really seemed to me, however, that the bridge vibrated and heaved up and down in a very formidable manner; and, in spite of Mr. Smooth-it-away's testimony to the solidity of its foundation, I should be loath to cross it in a crowded omnibus, especially if each passenger were encumbered with as heavy luggage as that gentleman and myself. Nevertheless we got over without accident, and soon found ourselves at the station-house. This very neat and spacious edifice is erected on the site of the little wicket gate, which formerly, as all old pilgrims will recollect, stood directly across the highway, and, by its inconvenient narrowness, was a great obstruction to the traveller of liberal mind and expansive stomach. The reader of John Bunyan will be glad to know that Christian's old friend Evangelist, who was accustomed to supply each pilgrim with a mystic roll, now presides at the ticket office. Some malicious persons it is true deny the identity of this reputable character with the Evangelist of old times, and even pretend to bring competent evidence of an imposture. Without involving myself in a dispute I shall merely observe that, so far as my experience goes, the square pieces of pasteboard now delivered to passengers are much more convenient and useful along the road than the antique roll of parchment. Whether they will be as readily received at the gate of the Celestial city I decline giving an opinion.

A large number of passengers were already at the station-house awaiting the departure of the cars. By the aspect and demeanor of these persons it was easy to judge that the feelings of the community had undergone a very favorable change in reference to the celestial pilgrimage. It would have done Bunyan's heart good to see it. Instead of a lonely and ragged man with a huge burden on his back, plodding along sorrowfully on foot while the whole city hooted after him, here were parties of the first gentry and most respectable people in the neighborhood setting forth towards the Celestial City as cheerfully as if the pilgrimage were merely a summer tour. Among the gentlemen were characters of deserved eminence—magistrates, politicians, and men of wealth, by whose example religion could not but be greatly recommended to their meaner brethren. In the ladies' apartment, too, I rejoiced to distinguish some of those flowers of fashionable society who are so well fitted to adorn the most elevated circles of the Celestial City. There was much pleasant conversation about the news of the day, topics of business and politics, or the lighter matters of amusement; while religion, though indubitably the main thing at heart, was thrown tastefully into the background. Even an infidel would have heard little or nothing to shock his sensibility.

One great convenience of the new method of going on pilgrimage I must not forget to mention. Our enormous burdens, instead of being carried on our shoulders as had been the custom of old, were all snugly deposited in the baggage car, and, as I was assured, would be delivered to their respective owners at the journey's end. Another thing, likewise, the benevolent reader will be delighted to understand. It may be remembered that there was an ancient feud between Prince Beelzebub and the keeper of the wicket gate, and that the adherents of the former distinguished personage were accustomed to shoot deadly arrows at honest pilgrims while knocking at the door. This dispute, much to the credit as well of the illustrious potentate above mentioned as of the worthy and enlightened directors of the railroad, has been pacifically arranged on the principle of mutual compromise. The prince's subjects are now pretty numerously employed about the station-house, some in taking care of the baggage, others in collecting fuel, feeding the engines, and such congenial occupations; and I can conscientiously affirm that persons more attentive to their business, more willing to accommodate, or more generally agreeable to the passengers, are not to be found on any railroad. Every good heart must surely exult at so satisfactory an arrangement of an immemorial difficulty.

Sectionalism

THE NORTHERN STATES: THE OLD AND THE NEW

158 A BOSTON BRAHMIN DESCRIBING AN OLD NEW ENGLAND TOWN

from Oliver Wendell Holmes, *Elsie Venner*, 1861

Ironically, one of the major centers of opposition to Romantic democracy was the very city that produced its leading exponent, Ralph Waldo Emerson. Boston, as the cultural center of New England, was the home of a social and intellectual aristocracy which, though quite liberal in its religious and philosophical views, tended to be socially and politically conservative. Its most articulate spokesman was the doctor, scholar, and wit, Oliver Wendell Holmes (1809-1894), who also gave this group its most familiar name: the "Brahmin caste of New England." Though a strong opponent of traditional Calvinistic Protestantism, he was a firm upholder of the aristocratic principle in social life and was very skeptical of the Romantic belief in the intelligence and insight of the common man.

For all his belief in aristocracy, Holmes himself was in no sense a wealthy idler. Indeed, he was nearly great in several fields. A pioneer in medical research and an early exponent of scientific determinism in the area of human behavior, he was also a fine essayist, a capable poet, and a conversationalist of superior powers. His *Autocrat of the Breakfast Table* and its sequels were collections of charming essays on a variety of topics given in the form of conversations carried on by a group of individuals in a genteel New England boarding house. These works were considered by many readers in the later nineteenth century to represent the apex of American culture, and many writers strove to imitate Holmes' blend of gentle, aristocratic wit and whimsy.

Holmes was also the author of an unusual group of novels, books he jokingly referred to as his "medicated novels." Though lacking in real force as fictional narratives, these works are interesting early attempts to analyze mentally disturbed characters from a scientific point of view. From one of these novels, *Elsie Venner*, the following selection is taken. In his description of the houses of a New England village, Holmes shows himself a keen social observer; he makes the point that even in relatively fluid and democratic New England, social class distinctions play an important role in the life of the people.

A New England "mansion-house" is naturally square, with dormer windows projecting from the roof, which has a balustrade with turned posts round it. It shows a good breadth of front-yard before its door, as its owner shows a respectable expanse of clean shirt-front. It has a lateral margin beyond its stables and offices, as its master wears his white wrist-bands showing beyond his coat-cuffs. It may not have what can properly be called grounds, but it must have elbow-room, at any rate. Without it, it is like a man who is always tight-buttoned for want of any linen to show. The mansion-house which has had to button itself up tight in fences, for want of green or gravel margin, will be advertising for boarders presently. . . .

Next to the mansion-houses, came the two-story trim, white-painted, "genteel" houses, which, being more gossipy and less nicely bred, crowded close up to the street, instead of standing back from it with arms akimbo, like the mansion-houses. Their little front-yards were very commonly full of lilac and syringa and other bushes,

Text: Oliver Wendell Holmes, *Works* (Boston: Houghton Mifflin & Co., 1891), V, 57-60.

which were allowed to smother the lower story almost to the exclusion of light and air, so that, what with small windows and small window-panes, and the darkness made by these choking growths of shrubbery, the front parlors of some of these houses were the most tomb-like, melancholy places that could be found anywhere among the abodes of the living. Their garnishing was apt to assist this impression. Large-patterned carpets, which always look discontented in little rooms, hair-cloth furniture, black and shiny as beetles' wing cases, and centre-tables, with a sullen oil-lamp of the kind called astral by our imaginative ancestors, in the centre,—these things were inevitable. In set piles round the lamp was ranged the current literature of the day, in the form of Temperance Documents, unbound numbers of one of the Unknown Public's Magazines with worn-out steel engravings and high-colored fashion-plates, the Poems of a distinguished British author whom it is unnecessary to mention, a volume of sermons, or a novel or two, or both, according to the tastes of the family, and the Good Book, which is always Itself in the cheapest and commonest company. The father of the family with his hand in the breast of his coat, the mother of the same in a wide-bordered cap, sometimes a print of the Last Supper, by no means Morghen's, or the Father of his Country, or the old General, or the Defender of the Constitution, or an unknown clergyman with an open book before him,—these were the usual ornaments of the walls, the first two a matter of rigor, the others according to politics and other tendencies.

This intermediate class of houses, wherever one finds them in New England towns, are very apt to be cheerless and unsatisfactory. They have neither the luxury of the mansion-house nor the comfort of the farm-house. They are rarely kept at an agreeable temperature. The mansion-house has large fireplaces and generous chimneys, and is open to the sunshine. The farm-house makes no pretensions, but it has a good warm kitchen, at any rate, and one can be comfortable there with the rest of the family, without fear and without reproach. These lesser country-houses of genteel aspirations are much given to patent subterfuges of one kind and another to get heat without combustion. The chilly parlor and the slippery hair-cloth seat take the life out of the warmest welcome. If one would make these places wholesome, happy, and cheerful, the first precept would be,—The dearest fuel, plenty of it, and let half the heat go up the chimney. If you can't afford this, don't try to live in a "genteel" fashion, but stick to the ways of the honest farm-house.

There were a good many comfortable farm-houses scattered about Rockland. The best of them were something of the following pattern, which is too often superseded of late by a more pretentious, but infinitely less pleasing kind of rustic architecture. A little back from the road, seated directly on the green sod, rose a plain wooden building, two stories in front, with a long roof sloping backwards to within a few feet of the ground. This, like the "mansion-house," is copied from an old English pattern. Cottages of this model may be seen in Lancashire, for instance, always with the same honest, homely look, as if their roofs acknowledged their relationship to the soil out of which they sprung. The walls were unpainted, but turned by the slow action of sun and air and rain to a quiet dove or slate color. An old broken millstone at the door,—a well-sweep pointing like a finger to the heavens, which the shining round of water beneath looked up at like a dark unsleeping eye,—a single large elm a little at one side,—a barn twice as big as the house,—a cattle-yard, with

"The white horns tossing above the wall,"—

some fields, in pasture or in crops, with low stone walls round them,—a row of beehives,—a garden-patch, with roots, and currant-bushes, and many-hued hollyhocks, and swollen-stemmed, globe-headed, seedling onions, and marigolds and flower-de-luces, and lady's-delights, and peonies, crowding in together, with southernwood in the borders, and woodbine and hops and morning-glories climbing as they got a chance,—these were the features by which the Rockland-born children remembered the farm-house, when they had grown to be men. Such are the recollections that come over poor sailor-boys crawling out on reeling yards to reef topsails as their vessels stagger round the stormy Cape; and such are the flitting images that make the eyes of old country-born merchants look dim and dreamy, as they sit in their city palaces, warm with the after-dinner flush of the red wave out of which Memory arises, as Aphrodite arose from the green waves of the ocean.

Two meeting-houses stood on two eminences, facing each other, and looking like a couple of fighting-cocks with their necks straight up in the air,—as if they would flap their roofs, the next thing, and crow out of their upstretched steeples, and peck at each other's glass eyes with their sharp-pointed weathercocks.

The first was a good pattern of the real old-fashioned New England meeting-house. It was a large barn with windows, fronted by a square tower crowned with a kind of wooden bell inverted and raised on legs, out of which rose a slender spire with the sharp-billed weathercock at its summit. Inside, tall, square pews with flapping seats, and a gallery running round three sides of the building. On the fourth side the pulpit, with a huge, dusty sounding-board hanging over it. Here preached the Reverend Pierrepont Honeywood, D.D., successor, after a number of generations, to the office and the parsonage of the Reverend Didymus Bean, before mentioned, but not suspected of any of his alleged heresies. He held to the old faith of the Puritans, and occasionally delivered a discourse which was considered by the hard-headed theologians of his parish to have settled the whole matter fully and finally, so that now there was a good logical basis laid down for the Millennium, which might begin at once upon the platform of his demonstrations. Yet the Reverend Dr. Honeywood was fonder of preaching plain, practical sermons about the duties of life, and showing his Christianity in abundant good works among his people. It was noticed by some few of his flock, not without comment, that the great majority of his texts came from the Gospels, and this more and more as he became interested in various benevolent enterprises which brought him into relations with ministers and kind-hearted laymen of other denominations. He was in fact a man of a very warm, open, and exceedingly *human* disposition, and, although bred by a clerical father, whose motto was "*Sit anima mea cum Puritanis,*" he exercised his human faculties in the harness of his ancient faith with such freedom that the straps of it got so loose they did not interfere greatly with the circulation of the warm blood through his system. Once in a while he seemed to think it necessary to come out with a grand doctrinal sermon, and then he would lapse away for a while into preaching on men's duties to each other and to society, and hit hard, perhaps, at some of the actual vices of the time and place, and insist with such tenderness and eloquence on the great depth and breadth of true Christian love and charity, that his oldest deacon shook his head, and wished he had shown as much interest when he was preaching, three Sabbaths back, on Predestination, or in his discourse against the Sabellians. But he was sound in the faith; no doubt of that. Did he not preside at the council held in the town of Tamarack, on the other side of the mountain, which expelled its clergyman for maintaining heretical doctrines? As presiding officer, he did not vote, of course, but there was no doubt that he was all right; he had some of the Edwards blood in him, and that couldn't very well let him go wrong.

The meeting-house on the other and opposite summit was of a more modern style, considered by many a great improvement on the old New England model, so that it is not uncommon for a country parish to pull down its old meeting-house, which has been preached in for a hundred years or so, and put up one of these more elegant edifices. The new building was in what may be called the florid shingle-Gothic manner. Its pinnacles and crockets and other ornaments were, like the body of the building, all of pine wood, —an admirable material, as it is very soft and easily worked, and can be painted of any color desired. Inside, the walls were stuccoed in imitation of stone,—first a dark brown square, then two light brown squares, then another dark brown square, and so on, to represent the accidental differences of shade always noticeable in the real stones of which walls are built. To be sure, the architect could not help getting his party-colored squares in almost as regular rhythmical order as those of a chess-board; but nobody can avoid doing things in a systematic and serial way. . . . The pews of this meeting-house were the usual oblong ones, where people sit close together, with a ledge before them to support their hymn-books, liable only to occasional contact with the back of the next pew's heads or bonnets, and a place running under the seat of that pew where hats could be deposited,—always at the risk of the owner, in case of injury by boots or crickets.

In this meeting-house preached the Reverend Chauncy Fairweather, a divine of the "Liberal" school, as it is commonly called, bred at that famous college which used to be thought, twenty or thirty years ago, to have the monopoly of training young men in the milder forms of heresy. His ministrations were attended with decency, but not followed with enthusiasm. "The beauty of virtue" got to be an old story at last. "The moral dignity of human nature" ceased to excite a thrill of satisfaction, after some hundred repetitions. It grew to be a dull business, this preaching against stealing and intemperance, while he knew very well that the thieves were prowling round orchards and empty houses, instead of being there to hear the sermon, and that the drunkards, being rarely church-goers, got little good by the statistics and eloquent appeals of the preacher. Every now and then, however, the Reverend Mr. Fairweather let off a polemic discourse against his neighbor opposite, which waked his people up a little; but it was a languid congregation, at best,—very apt to stay away from meeting in the afternoon, and not at all given to extra evening services. The minister, unlike his rival of the other side of the way, was a downhearted and timid kind of man. He went on preaching as he had been taught to preach, but he had misgivings at times. There was a little Roman Catholic church at the foot of the hill where his own was placed, which he always had to pass on Sundays. He could never look on the thronging multitudes that crowded its pews and aisles or knelt bare-headed on its steps, without a longing to get in among them and go down on his knees and enjoy that luxury of devotional contact which makes a worshipping throng as different from the same numbers praying apart as a bed of coals is from a trail of scattered cinders. . . .

A mile or two from the centre of Rockland was a pretty little Episcopal church, with a roof like a wedge of cheese, a square tower, a stained window, and a trained rector, who read the service with such ventral depth of utterance and rrre-duplication of the rrresonant letter, that his own mother would not have known him for her son, if the good woman had not ironed his surplice and put it on with her own hands.

There were two public-houses in the place: one dignified with the name of the Mountain House, somewhat frequented by city people in the summer months, large-fronted, three-storied, balconied, boasting a distinct ladies'-drawing-room, and spreading a *table d'hôte* of some pretensions; the other "Pollard's Tahvern," in the common speech,—a two-story building, with a bar-room, once famous, where there was a great smell of hay and boots and pipes and all other bucolic-flavored elements,—where games of checkers were played on the back of the bellows with red and white kernels of corn, or with beans and coffee,—where a man slept in a box-settle at night, to wake up early passengers,—where teamsters came in, with wooden-handled whips and coarse frocks, reinforcing the bucolic flavor of the atmosphere, and middle-aged male gossips, sometimes including the squire of the neighboring law-office, gathered to exchange a question or two about the news, and then fall into that solemn state of suspended animation which the temperance bar-rooms of modern days produce in human beings, as the Grotta del Cane does in dogs in the well-known experiments related by travellers. This bar-room used to be famous for drinking and story-telling, and sometimes fighting, in old times. . . .

But the bar of Pollard's Tahvern no longer presented its old attractions, and the loggerheads had long disappeared from the fire. In place of the decanters, were boxes containing "lozengers," as they were commonly called, sticks of candy in jars, cigars in tumblers, a few lemons, grown hard-skinned and marvellously shrunken by long exposure, but still feebly suggestive of possible lemonade,—the whole ornamented by festoons of yellow and blue cut flypaper. On the front shelf of the bar stood a large German-silver pitcher of water, and scattered about were ill-conditioned lamps, with wicks that always wanted picking, which burned red and smoked a good deal, and were apt to go out without any obvious cause, leaving strong reminiscences of the whale-fishery in the circumambient air. . . .

159

THE NIGHTMARE OF THE CITY: THE IMPACT OF A NEW URBAN WAY OF LIFE

from Herman Melville, *Pierre*, 1852

The New England village described by Oliver Wendell Holmes (see Document 158), with its quiet stability and respect for tradition, represents an older pattern of American life. The commercial cities rapidly growing up in the North in the pre-Civil War period had long been an object of concern to many Americans, who associated crowded cities with the decadent and corrupt social structure of Europe. When they discovered that their own cities, filling with immigrants, had developed the slums, vice, and crime that they had hoped the new American society would somehow avoid, they were shocked and deeply disturbed. This selection from the novel *Pierre* by Herman Melville describes the impact of such a discovery on a young man from the country.

Pierre Glendenning, who has decided to seek his fortune as a writer in the city of New York, has arrived in the city with his half-sister Isabel and her maid Delly. Because the trio reach New York in the evening, Pierre leaves Isabel and Delly at a watch-house, or police station, while he seeks aid and counsel from his cousin, Glendenning Stanly. Stanly refuses to help him. When the selection begins, Pierre has just left his cousin's house and is looking for a cab to take him back to the watch-house where Isabel and Delly are waiting. The nightmarish scene which greets him when he arrives at the station effectively suggests the shock that many Americans experienced when they began to discover the underworld of their growing cities.

The greatness of Herman Melville (1819-1891), the author of this selection, is now generally recognized, though in the middle of the nineteenth century his books—notably *Moby Dick* (1851)—were so poorly received that Melville actually gave up his career as a novelist after a little more than ten years of writing. From 1857 to about 1889 he wrote little but poetry. In his last years he wrote the superb novelette *Billy Budd*, which was not published until 1924, long after his death. Forgotten for many years, Melville's work was dramatically revived after the First World War, when world events had made men better able to appreciate his deep and tragic pessimism. Even today, when most literate Americans know his *Moby Dick*, Melville's other fine works, *Typee* (1846), *Omoo* (1847), *Mardi* (1849), *White Jacket* (1850), *Pierre* (1852), and *The Confidence-Man* (1857), are surprisingly little known.

'Hack, sir? Hack, sir? Hack, sir?'

'Cab, Sir? Cab, sir? Cab, sir?'

'This way, sir! This way, sir! This way, sir!'

'He's a rogue! Not him! he's a rogue!'

Pierre was surrounded by a crowd of contending hackmen; all holding long whips in their hands; while others eagerly beckoned to him from their boxes, where they sat elevated between their two coach-lamps like shabby, discarded saints. The whip-stalks thickened around him, and several reports of the cracking lashes sharply sounded in his ears. Just bursting from a scene so goading as his interview with the scornful Glen in the dazzling drawing-room, to Pierre, this sudden tumultuous surrounding of him by whip-stalks and lashes, seemed like the onset of the chastising fiends upon Orestes. But, breaking away from them, he seized the first plated door-handle near him, and, leaping into the hack, shouted for whoever was the keeper of it, to mount his box forthwith and drive off in a given direction.

The vehicle had proceeded some way down the great avenue when it paused, and the driver demanded whither now; what place?

'The Watch-house of the —— Ward,' cried Pierre.

'Hi! hi! Goin' to deliver himself up, hey?' grinned the fellow to himself. 'Well, that's a sort of honest, anyway:—g'lang, you dogs!—whist! whee! wha!—g'lang!'

The sights and sounds which met the eye of Pierre on re-entering the watch-house, filled him with inexpressible horror and fury. The before decent, drowsy place, now fairly reeked with all things unseemly. Hardly possible was it to tell what conceivable cause or occasion had, in the comparatively short absence of Pierre, collected such a base congregation. In indescribable disorder, frantic, diseased-looking men and women of all colours, and in all imaginable flaunting, immodest, grotesque, and shattered dresses, were

leaping, yelling, and cursing around him. The torn Madras handkerchiefs of negresses, and the red gowns of yellow girls, hanging in tatters from their naked bosoms, mixed with the rent dresses of deep-rouged white women, and the split coats, checkered vests, and protruding shirts of pale, or whiskered, or haggard, or moustached fellows of all nations, some of whom seemed scared from their beds, and others seemingly arrested in the midst of some crazy and wanton dance. On all sides, were heard drunken male and female voices, in English, French, Spanish, and Portuguese, interlarded now and then, with the foulest of all human lingoes, that dialect of sin and death, known as the Cant language, or the Flash.

Running among this combined babel of persons and voices, several of the police were vainly striving to still the tumult; while others were busy handcuffing the more desperate; and here and there the distracted wretches, both men and women, gave downright battle to the officers; and still others already handcuffed struck out at them with their joined ironed arms. Meanwhile words and phrases unrepeatable in God's sunlight, and whose very existence was utterly unknown, and undreamed of by tens of thousands of the decent people of the city; syllables obscene and accursed were shouted forth in tones plainly evincing that they were the common household breath of their utterers. The thieves'-quarters, and all the brothels, Lock-and-Sin hospitals for incurables, and infirmaries and infernoes of hell seemed to have made one combined sortie, and poured out upon earth through the vile vomitory of some unmentionable cellar.

Though the hitherto imperfect and casual city experiences of Pierre, illy fitted him entirely to comprehend the specific purport of this terrific spectacle; still he knew enough by hearsay of the more infamous life of the town, to imagine from whence, and who, were the objects before him. But all his consciousness at the time was absorbed by the one horrified thought of Isabel and Delly, forced to witness a sight hardly en-

Text: Herman Melville, *Pierre; or, The Ambiguities* (New York: Harper & Bros., 1852), pp. 326-32.

durable for Pierre himself; or, possibly, sucked into the tumult, and in close personal contact with its loathsomeness. Rushing into the crowd, regardless of the random blows and curses he encountered, he wildly sought for Isabel, and soon descried her struggling from the delirious reaching arms of a half-clad, reeling whiskerando. With an immense blow of his mailed fist, he sent the wretch humming, and seizing Isabel, cried out to two officers near, to clear a path for him to the door. They did so. And in a few minutes the panting Isabel was safe in the open air. He would have stayed by her, but she conjured him to return for Delly, exposed to worse insults than herself. An additional posse of officers now approaching, Pierre committing her to the care of one of them, and summoning two others to join himself, now re-entered the room. In another quarter of it, he saw Delly seized on each hand by two bleared and half-bloody women, who with fiendish grimaces were ironically twitting her upon her close-necked dress, and had already stripped her handkerchief from her. She uttered a cry of mixed anguish and joy at the sight of him; and Pierre soon succeeded in returning with her to Isabel.

During the absence of Pierre in quest of the hack, and while Isabel and Delly were quietly awaiting his return, the door had suddenly burst open, and a detachment of the police drove in, and caged, the entire miscellaneous night-occupants of a notorious stew, which they had stormed and carried during the height of some outrageous orgy. The first sight of the interior of the watch-house, and their being so quickly huddled together within its four blank walls, had suddenly lashed the mob into frenzy; so that for the time, oblivious of all other considerations, the entire force of the police was directed to the quelling of the indoor riot; and consequently, abandoned to their own protection, Isabel and Delly had been temporarily left to its mercy.

It was no time for Pierre to manifest his indignation at the officer—even if he could now find him—who had thus falsified his individual pledge concerning the precious charge committed to him. Nor was it any time to distress himself about his luggage, still somewhere within. Quitting all, he thrust the bewildered and half-lifeless girls into the waiting hack, which, by his orders, drove back in the direction of the stand, where Pierre had first taken it up.

When the coach had rolled them well away from the tumult, Pierre stopped it, and said to the man, that he desired to be taken to the nearest respectable hotel or boarding-house of any kind, that he knew of. The fellow—maliciously diverted

by what had happened thus far—made some ambiguous and rudely merry rejoinder. But warned by his previous rash quarrel with the stage-driver, Pierre passed this unnoticed, and in a controlled, calm, decided manner repeated his directions.

The issue was, that after a rather roundabout drive they drew up in a very respectable side-street, before a large respectable-looking house, illuminated by two tall white lights flanking its portico. Pierre was glad to notice some little remaining stir within, spite of the comparative lateness of the hour. A bare-headed, tidily dressed, and very intelligent-looking man, with a broom clothes-brush in his hand, appearing, scrutinised him rather sharply at first; but as Pierre advanced further into the light, and his countenance became visible, the man, assuming a respectful but still slightly perplexed air, invited the whole party into a closely adjoining parlour, whose disordered chairs and general dustiness, evinced that after a day's activity it now awaited the morning offices of the housemaids.

'Baggage, sir?'

'I have left my baggage at another place,' said Pierre, 'I shall send for it to-morrow.'

'Ah!' exclaimed the very intelligent-looking man, rather dubiously, 'shall I discharge the hack, then?'

'Stay,' said Pierre, bethinking him, that it would be well not to let the man know from whence they had last come, 'I will discharge it myself, thank you.'

So returning to the sidewalk, without debate, he paid the hackman an exorbitant fare, who, anxious to secure such illegal gains beyond all hope of recovery, quickly mounted his box and drove off at a gallop.

'Will you step into the office, sir, now?' said the man, slightly flourishing with his brush—'this way, sir, if you please.'

Pierre followed him, into an almost deserted, dimly lit room with a stand in it. Going behind the stand, the man turned round to him a large ledger-like book, thickly inscribed with names like any directory, and offered him a pen ready dipped in ink.

Understanding the general hint, though secretly irritated at something in the manner of the man, Pierre drew the book to him, and wrote in a firm hand, at the bottom of the last-named column:

'Mr. and Mrs. Pierre Glendinning, and Miss Ulver.'

The man glanced at the writing inquiringly, and then said, 'The other column, sir—where from.'

'True,' said Pierre, and wrote 'Saddle Meadows.'

The very intelligent-looking man re-examined the page, and then slowly stroking his shaven chin, with a fork, made of his thumb for one tine, and his united four fingers for the other, said softly and whisperingly, 'Anywheres in this country, sir?'

'Yes, in the country,' said Pierre, evasively, and bridling his ire. 'But now show me to two chambers, will you; the one for myself and wife, I desire to have opening into another, a third one, never mind how small; but I must have a dressing-room.'

'Dressing-room,' repeated the man, in an ironically deliberative voice—'Dressing-room;—Hem! —You will have your luggage taken into the dressing-room, then, I suppose.—Oh, I forgot—your luggage ain't come yet—ah, yes, yes, yes—luggage is coming to-morrow—Oh, yes, yes,—certainly —to-morrow—of course. By the way, sir; I dislike to seem at all uncivil, and I am sure you will not deem me so; but——'

'Well,' said Pierre, mustering all his self-command for the coming impertinence.

'When stranger gentlemen come to this house without luggage, we think ourselves bound to ask them to pay their bills in advance, sir; that is all, sir.'

'I shall stay here to-night and the whole of to-morrow, at any rate,' rejoined Pierre, thankful that this was all; 'how much will it be?' and he drew out his purse.

The man's eyes fastened with eagerness on the purse; he looked from it to the face of him who held it; then seemed half hesitating an instant; then brightening up, said, with sudden suavity, 'Never mind, sir, never mind, sir; though rogues sometimes be gentlemanly; gentlemen that are gentlemen never go abroad without their diplomas. Their diplomas are their friends; and their only friends are their dollars; you have a purseful of friends.—We have chambers, sir, that will exactly suit you, I think. Bring your ladies and I will show you up to them immediately.' So saying, dropping his brush, the very intelligent-looking man lighted one lamp, and taking two unlighted ones in his other hand, led the way down the dusky lead-sheeted hall, Pierre following him with Isabel and Delly.

THE ANTEBELLUM SOUTH

160

SUMMER MORNINGS IN THE OLD DOMINION: FEUDAL PLANTATION LIFE

from John Pendleton Kennedy, *Swallow Barn*, 1832

Plantation life in the Old South was in many respects coarse and brutal, but it had its gracious and dignified features as well. Due partly to the social system and partly to the influence of English novels of Romantic chivalry, which were the most popular reading among the plantation aristocracy, there developed a Southern ideal of a quasi-feudal system in which a noble group of gentry graciously ruled a host of lesser creatures. This ideal not only motivated the pro-slavery feelings of the South before the Civil War but also influenced the postwar fiction writers portraying the antebellum South. Margaret Mitchell's *Gone With the Wind*, a novel of enormous popularity just before World War II, was squarely in the tradition of John Pendleton Kennedy's *Swallow Barn*, from which this selection was taken. First published in 1832, this novel was one of the first and best of the romantic and idyllic pictures of life in the "feudal" area of the Old South.

In the country every thing wears a Sunday look. The skies have a deeper blue, the clouds rest upon them like painting. The soft flutter of the groves hushes one into silence. The chirp of the grasshopper, as he leaps in his short semi-circles along your path, has the feebleness of a whisper; and the great vagabond butterfly, which gads amongst the thistles, moves noiseless as a straggling leaf borne upon a zephyr. Then, there is a lowing of cows upon a distant meadow, and a scream of jay-birds, heard at intervals; the sullen hammer of a lonely woodpecker resounds from some withered trunk; and, high above, a soaring troop of crows, hoarse with cawing, send forth a far-off note. Sometimes a huge and miry mother of the sty, with her litter of querulous pigs, steps leisurely across the foreground; and a choir of locusts in the neighboring woods spin out a long stave of music, like the pupils of a singing-school

Text: John Pendleton Kennedy, *Swallow Barn; A Sojourn in the Old Dominion* (Philadelphia: J. B. Lippincott & Co., 1861), pp. 307-11.

practising the elements of psalmody. Still, this varied concert falls faintly upon the ear, and only seems to measure silence.

Our morning pursuits at Swallow Barn partake somewhat of the quiet character of the scenery. Frank Meriwether is an early riser at this season, and generally breakfasts before the rest of the family. This gives him time to make a circuit on horseback, to inspect the progress of his farm concerns. He returns before the heat of the day, and, about noon, may be found stretched upon a broad settee in the hall, with a pile of books on the floor beneath him, and a dozen newspapers thrown around in great confusion: not unfrequently, too, he is overtaken with a deep sleep, with a volume straddling his nose; and he will continue in this position, gradually snoring from a lower to a higher key, until he awakens himself by a sudden and alarming burst that resembles the bark of a mastiff. He says the old clock puts him asleep, and, in truth, it has a very narcotic vibration; but Frank is manifestly growing corpulent. And, what is a little amusing, he protests in the face of the whole family that he does not snore.

The girls get at the piano immediately after breakfast; and Ned and myself usually commence the morning with a stroll. If there happen to be visitors at Swallow Barn, this after-breakfast hour is famous for debates. We then all assemble in the porch, and fall into grave discussions upon agriculture, hunting, or horsemanship, in neither of which do I profess any great proficiency, though I take care not to let that appear. Some of the party amuse themselves with throwing pebbles picked from the gravel walk, or draw figures upon the earth with a cane, as if to assist their cogitations; and when our topics grow scarce, we saunter towards the bridge, and string ourselves out upon the rail, to watch the bubbles that float down the stream; and are sometimes a good deal perplexed to know what we shall do until dinner time.

There is a numerous herd of little negroes about the estate; and these sometimes afford us a new diversion. A few mornings since, we encountered a horde of them, who were darting about the bushes like untamed monkeys. They are afraid of me, because I am a stranger, and take to their heels as soon as they see me. If I ever chance to get near enough to speak to one of them, he stares at me with a suspicious gaze; and, after a moment, makes off at full speed, very much frightened, towards the cabins at some distance from the house. They are almost all clad in a long coarse shirt which reaches below the knee, without any other garment: but one of the group we met on the morning I speak of, was oddly decked in a pair of ragged trowsers, conspicuous for their ample dimensions in the seat. These had evidently belonged to some grown-up person, but were cut short in the legs to make them fit the wearer. A piece of twine across the shoulder of this grotesque imp, served for suspenders, and kept his habiliments from falling about his feet. Ned ordered this crew to prepare for a foot-race, and proposed a reward of a piece of money to the winner. They were to run from a given point, about a hundred paces distant, to the margin of the brook. Our whole suite of dogs were in attendance, and seemed to understand our pastime. At the word, away went the bevy, accompanied by every dog of the pack, the negroes shouting and the dogs yelling in unison. The *shirts* ran with prodigious vehemence, their speed exposing their bare, black, and meager shanks, to the scandal of all beholders; and the strange baboon in trowsers struggled close in their rear, with ludicrous earnestness, holding up his redundant and troublesome apparel with his hand. In a moment they reached the brook with unchecked speed; and, as the banks were muddy, and the dogs had become tangled with the racers in their path, two or three were precipitated into the water. This only increased the merriment, and they continued the contest in this new element, by floundering, kicking, and splashing about, like a brood of ducks in their first descent upon a pool. These young negroes have wonderfully flat noses, and the most oddly disproportioned mouths, which were now opened to their full dimensions, so as to display their white teeth in striking contrast with their complexions. They are a strange pack of antic and careless animals, and furnish the liveliest picture that is to be found in nature, of that race of swart fairies which, in the old time, were supposed to play their pranks in the forest at moonlight. Ned stood by, enjoying this scene like an amateur; encouraging the negroes in their gambols, and hallooing to the dogs, that by a kindred instinct entered tumultuously into the sport and kept up the confusion. It was difficult to decide the contest. So the money was thrown into the air, and as it fell to the ground, there was another rush, in which the hero of the trowsers succeeded in getting the small coin from the ground in his teeth, somewhat to the prejudice of his finery.

Rip asserts a special pre-eminence over these young serfs, and has drilled them into a kind of local militia. He sometimes has them all marshalled in the yard, and entertains us with a review. They have an old watering-pot for a drum, and a dingy pocket-handkerchief for a standard, under which they are arrayed in military order. As they have no hats amongst them, Rip makes each stick a cock's feather in his wool; and in this guise they parade over the grounds with a riotous clamor, in which Rip's shrill voice, and the clink of the old watering-pot, may be heard at a great distance.

Besides these occupations, Hazard and myself frequently ride out during the morning; and we are apt to let our horses take their own way. This brings us into all the by-places of the neighborhood, and makes me many acquaintances. Lucy and Victorine often accompany us, and I have occasion to admire their expert horsemanship. They have each a brisk, little pony and these are wonderful favorites with them; and, to hear them talk, you would suppose them versed in all the affairs of the stable.

With such amusements, we contrive to pass our mornings, not listlessly, but idly. This course of life has a winning quality that already begins to exercise its influence upon my habits. There is a fascination in the quiet, irresponsible, and reckless nature of these country pursuits, that is apt to seize upon the imagination of a man who has felt the perplexities of business. Ever since I have been at Swallow Barn, I have entertained a very philosophical longing for the calm and dignified retirement of the woods. I begin to grow moderate in my desires; that is, I only want a thousand acres of good land, an old manor-house, on a pleasant site, a hundred negroes, a large library, a host of friends, and a reserve of a few thousands a year in the stocks,—in case of bad crops,—and, finally, a house full of pretty, intelligent, and docile children, with some few et ceteras not worth mentioning.

I doubt not, after this, I shall be considered a man of few wants, and great resources within myself.

161

THE KNOB DANCE: A TENNESSEE POOR-WHITE FROLIC

from George Washington Harris, "The Knob Dance," 1845

Though much of Southern life centered around the plantation and its gentry, the larger part of the Southern population consisted of poor independent farmers whose relationship with the plantation aristocracy varied from mutual toleration to outright hostility. The working life of the small farmer was dreary, and perhaps in reaction to this, his religious and social life tended to be volatile and violent. The two main leisure activities of the farmer in the less developed areas were attending revival meetings and taking part in such frolics as the one described in this selection. In the comically exaggerated antics of George Washington Harris' "The Knob Dance," there is enough realistic description of characters and manners for the reader to sense the spirit of life among these people.

The colorful character of life in the western part of the Old South found literary representation in the works of an exceptionally able group of humorous writers, of whom the author of the present selection was perhaps the greatest. The pungent and realistic quality of this humor of the Old Southwest was an important influence on other literary realists, whose work we will discuss in Part I, Volume II.

Knoxville, July 16, 1845

You may talk of your bar hunts, Mister Porter, and your deer hunts, and knottin tigers' tails through the bung-holes of barrels, an cock fitin, and all that but if a regular bilt frolick in the Nobs of "Old Knox," don't beat 'em all blind for fun, then I'm no judge of fun, that's all! I said *fun*, and I say it agin, from a *kiss* that cracks like a wagin-whip up to a *fite* that rouses up all out-doors—and as to laffin, why they *invented* laffin, and the *last* laff will be hearn at a

Text: William T. Porter (ed.), *A Quarter Race in Kentucky and Other Tales* (Philadelphia: T. B. Peterson Bros., 1854), pp. 82-90.

Nob dance about three in the morning! I'm jest gettin so I can ride arter the motions I made at one at Jo Spraggins's a few days ago.

I'll try and tell you who Jo Spraggins is. He's a squire, a school comishner, overlooker of a mile of Nob road *that leads towards Rody's still-house*—a fiddler, a judge of a hoss, and a hoss himself! He can belt six shillins worth of corn-juice at still-house rates and travel—can out shute and out lie any feller from the Smoky Mounting to Noxville, and, if they'll bar one feller in Nox, I'll say to the old Kaintuck Line! (I'm sorter feared of him for they say that he lied a jassack to death in two hours!)—can make more spinin-wheels, kiss more spinners, thrash more wheat an more men than any one-eyed man I know on. He hates a circuit rider, a nigger, and a shot gun—loves a woman, old sledge, and sin in eny shape. He lives in a log hous about ten yards squar; it has two rooms one at the bottom an one at the top of the ladder —has all out ove doors fur a yard, and all the South fur its ocupants at times. He gives a frolic onst in three weeks in plowin time and one every Saturday-nite the ballance of the year, and only axes a "fip" for a reel, and two "bits" fur what corn-juice you suck; he throws the galls in, and a bed too in the hay, if you git too hot to locomote. The supper is made up by the fellers; every one fetches sumthin; sum a lick of meal, sum a middlin of bacon, sum a hen, sum a possum, sum a punkin, sum a grab of taters, or a pocket full of peas, or dried apples, an sum only fetches a good appetite and a skin chock full of perticular deviltry, and if thars been a shutin match for beef the day before, why a *leg* finds its way to Jo's, sure, without eny help from the ballance of the critter. He gives Jim Smith, (the store-keeper over Bay's Mounting,) *warnin* to fetch a skane of silk fur fiddle-strings, and sum "Or-leans" for sweetnin, or not to fetch himself; the silk and sugar has never failed to be thar yet. Jo then mounts Punkinslinger bar backed, about three hours afore sun down and gives all the galls *item*. He does this a leetle of the slickest —jist rides past in a peart rack, singing,

"Oh, I met a frog, with a fiddle on his back,
A axin his way to the fro-l-i-c-k!
Wha-a he! wha he! wha he! wha he!
he-ke-he!"

That's enuf! The galls nows *that* aint a jack-ass, so by sun-down they come pourin out of the woods like pissants out of an old log when tother end's afire, jest "as fine as silk" and full of fun, fixed out in all sorts of fancy doins, from the broad-striped homespun to the sunflower callico, with the thunder-and-lightnin ground. As for silk, if one had a silk gown she's be too smart to wear it to Jo Spraggins's, fur if she did she'd go home in her petticote-tale *sartin*, for the home-spun wud tare it off of hir quicker nor winkin, and if the sunflowers dident help the homespuns, they wouldn't do the silk eny good, so you see that silk is never ratlin about your ears at a Nob dance.

The sun had about sot afore I got the things fed an had Barkmill saddled (you'll larn directly why I call my poney Barkmill), but an owl couldent have cotch a rat afore I was in site of Jo's with my gall, Jule Sawyers, up behind me.

She hugged me mity tite she was *"so feerd of fallin off that drated poney."* She said she didn't mind a fall but it mought break hir leg an then good bye frolicks—she'd be fit fur nuthin but to nuss brats ollers arterwards. I now hearn the fiddle ting-tong-ding-domb. The yard was full of fellers and two tall fine lookin galls was standin in the door, face to face holdin up the door posts with their backs, laffin, an castin sly looks into the house, an now an then kickin each other with their knees, an then the one kicked wud bow so perlite, and quick at that, and then they'd laff agin an turn red. Jo was a standin in the hous helpin the galls to hold the facins up, an when they'd kick each other he'd wink at the fellers in the yard an grin. Jule, she bounced off just like a bag of wool-rolls, and I hitched my bark-machine up to a saplin that warnt skinned, so he'd get a craw-full of good fresh bark afore mornin. I giv Jule a kiss to sorter molify my natur an put hir in heart like, and in we walked. "Hey! hurray!" said the boys, "my gracious!" said the galls, "if here aint Dick an Jule!" jist like we hadent been *rite thar* only last Saturday nite. "Well, I know we'll have reel now!" "Hurraw! Go it while you're young!" "Hurraw for the brimstone kiln—every man praise his country!" "Clar the ring!" "Misses Spraggins drive out these dratted tow-headed brats of your'n—give room!" "Who-oo-whoop! whar's that crock of baldface, and that gourd of honey? Jim Smith, hand over that spoon, an quit a lickin it like "sank in a bean-pot." "You, Jake Snyder, don't holler so!" says the old oman—"why you are worse nor a painter." "Holler! why I was jist *whispering* to that gall on the bed—*who-a-whoopee!* now I'm beginning to *holler!* Did you hear *that*, Misses Spraggins, and be darned to your bar legs? You'd make a nice hemp-brake, you would." "Come here, Suse Thompson, and let me pin your dress behind? Your back looks adzactly like a blaze on a white oak!" "My *back* aint nuffin to you, Mister Smarty!" "Bill Jones, quit a smashin that ar cat's tail!" "Well, let hir keep hir tail clar of my ant killers!" "Het Goins, stop tumblin that bed an tie your *sock!*" "Thankee marm, its a longer stockin than you've got—look at it!" "Jim Clark has gone to the woods for fat pine, and Peggy Willet is along to take a lite for him—they've been gone a coon's age. Oh, here comes the lost 'babes in the wood,' and no *lite!*" "Whar's that lite! whar's that torch! I say, Peggy, whar *is* that bundle of lite wood?" "Why, I fell over a log and lost it, and we hunted clar to the foot of the holler for it, and never found it. It's no account, no how—nuthin but a little pine— who cares?" "Hello, thar, gin us 'Forked Deer,' old fiddle-teazer, or I'll give you forked litnin! *Ar* you a goin to tum-tum all nite on that pot-gutted old pine box of a fiddle, *say?*" "Give him a sock at the crock and a lick at the patent bee-hive—it'll *ile* his elbows." "Misses Spraggins you're a hoss! cook on, don't mind me—I dident aim to slap *you;* it was Suze Winters I *wanted* to hit; but you stooped so fair—" "Yes, and it's well for your good looks that you didn't hit to hurt me, old feller!" "Turn over them rashers of bacon, they're a burnin!" "Mind your own business, Bob Proffit, I've cooked for frolicks afore you shed your petticotes—so jist hush an talk to Marth Giffin! See! she is beckonin to you!" "That's a lie, marm! If he comes a near me I'll unjint his dratted neck! No sech fool that when a gall puts hir arm round his neck will break and run, shall look at *me*, that's flat! Go an try Bet Holden!" "Thankee, marm, I don't take your leavins," says Bet, hir face lookin like a full cross between a gridiron and a steel-trap.

Whoop! hurraw! Gether your galls for a break down! Give us "Forked Deer!" "No, give us 'Natchez-under-the-hill!' " "Oh, Shucks! give us 'Rocky Mounting,' or 'Misses McCloud!' " " 'Misses McCloud' be darned, and 'Rocky Mounting' too! jist give us

"She woudent, and she coudent, and she dident come at all!"

"Thar! that's it! Now make a brake! *Tang!* Thar is a brake—a string's gone!" "Thar'll be a head broke afore long!" "Giv him goss—no giv him a horn and every time he stops repeat the dose, and nar another string'll brake to nite. Tink-tong! Ting-tong! all rite! Now go it!" and if I know what *goin it* is, we *did* go it.

About midnite, Misses Spraggins sung out "stop that ar dancin and come and get your supper!" It was sot in the yard on a table made of forks stuck in the ground and plank of the stable loft, with sheets for table cloths. We had danced, kissed and drank ourselves into a perfect thrasin-machine apetite, and the vittals *hid* themselves in a way quite alarmin to tavern-keepers. Jo sung out "nives is scase, so give what thar is to the galls and let the ballance use thar paws—they was invented afore nives, eney how. Now, Gents, jist walk into the fat of this land. I'm sorter feerd the honey wont last till day break, but the liquor will, I *think*, so you men when you drink your'n, run an kiss the galls fur sweetnin —let them have the honey—it belongs to them, naturaly!"—"Hurraw, my Jo! You know how to do things rite." "Well, I rayther think I do; I never was rong but onst in my life and then I mistook a camp meetin for a political speechifyin, so I rid up an axed the speaker 'how much Tarrif

there was on rot-gut?' and he said 'about here there *appeared* to be none!' That rayther sot me, as I was right smartly smoked, myself, jist at that time. I had enough liquor plumb in me to swim a skunk, so I come agin at him. I axed him 'who was the bigest fool the Bible told of?' an he said 'Noah for he'd get tite!' I *thought*, mind, I only thought he might be a pokin his dead cat at somebody what lives in this holler; I felt my bristles a raisin my jacket-back up like a tent cloth, so I axed him if he'd *'ever seed the Ele-phant?'* He said no, but he had seen *a grocery walk*, and he expected to see one *rot down* from its *totterin* looks, purty soon!' Thinks I, Jo you're beat at your own game; I sorter felt mean, so I spurr'd and sot old Punkinslinger to cavortin like he was skeered, and I wheeled and twisted out of *that* crowd, an when I *did* git out of site the way I did sail was a caution to turkles and all the other slow varmints."

Well, we danced, and hurrawed without eny thing of *very* particular interest to happen, till about three o'clock, when the darndest muss was kicked up you ever did see. Jim Smith sot down on the bed alongside of Bet Holden (the steel-trap gall), and jist fell to huggin of hir bar fashion. She tuck it very kind till she seed Sam Henry a looking on from behind about a dozen galls, *then* she fell to kickin *an* a hollerin, *an* a screechin like all rath. Sam he come up an told Jim to let Bet go! Jim told him to go to a far off countrie whar they give away brimestone and throw in the fire to burn it. Sam hit him strate atween the eyes an after a few licks the fitin *started*. Oh hush! It makes my mouth water now to think what a beautiful row we had. One feller from Cady's Grove, nocked a hole in the bottom of a fryin-pan over Dan Turner's head, and left it a hangin round his neck, the handle flyin about like a long que, and thar it hung till Jabe Thurman cut it off with a cold chissel next day! That was *his share*, fur that nite, sure. Another feller got nocked into a meal-barrel; he was as mealy as an Irish tater, and as *hot* as hoss-radish; when he bursted the hoops and cum out he rared a few. Two fellers fit out of the door, down the hill, and into the creek, and thar ended it, in a quiet way, all alone. A perfect mule from Stock Creek hit *me* a wipe with a pair of windin blades; he made kindlin-wood of them, an I lit on him. We had it head-and-tails fur a very long time, all over the house, but the truth must come and shame my kin, he warped me·nice, so, jist to save his time I *hollered!* The lickin he give me made me sorter oneasy and hostile like; it weak-ened my wolf wide awake, so I begin to look about for a man I *could* lick and *no mistake!*

The little fiddler cum a scrougin past, holdin his fiddle up over his head to keep it *in tune,* for the fitin was gettin tolerable brisk. You're the one, thinks I, and jist I grabbed the dough-tray and split it plumb open over his head. *He* rotted down, right thar, and I paddled his 'tother end with one of the pieces!—while I was a molifyin my feelins in that way his gall slip'd up behind me and fetcht'd me a rake with the pot-hooks. Jule Sawyer was *thar,* and jist *anexed to her rite* off, and a mity nice fite it was. Jule carried enuf har from hir hed to make a sifter, and striped and checked her face nice, like a partridge-net hung on a white fence. She hollered fur hir fiddler, but oh, shaw! he coudent do hir a bit of good; he was too buisy a rubbin first his broken head and then his blistered extremities, so when I thought Jule had given her a plenty I pulled hir off and put hir in a good humor by given hir about as many kisses as would cover a barn door.

Well, I thought at last, if I had a drink I'd be *about done,* so I started for the creek; *and* the first thing I saw was more stars with my eyes shut than I ever did with them open. I looked round, and it was the little fiddler's *big brother! I know'd what it meant,* so we locked horns without a word, thar all alone, and I do think we fit an hour. At last some fellers hearn the jolts at the house, and they cum and *dug us out,* for we had fit into a hole whar a big pine stump had burnt out, and thar we was, up to our girths a peggin away, face to face, an *no dodgin!*

Well, it is now sixteen days since that fite, and last night Jule picked gravels out of my knees as big as squirell shot. Luck rayther run agin me that nite, fur I dident lick eny body but the fiddler, and had three fites—but Jule licked her gall, that's some comfort, and I suppose a feller cant *always* win! Arter my fite in the ground we made friends all round (except the fiddler—he's hot yet,) and danced and liquored at the tail of every Reel till sun up, when them that was sober enuff went home, and them that was *wounded* staid whar they fell. *I* was in the list of wounded, but could have got away if my bark-mill hadn't *ground* off the saplin and gone home without a parting word; so Dick and Jule had to ride "Shanks' mar," and a rite pert *four-legged* nag she is. She was *weak* in *two* of hir legs, but 'tother two—oh, my stars and possum dogs! they make a man swaller tobacker jist to look at 'em, and feel sorter like a June bug was crawlin up his trowsers and the waistband too tite for it to git out. I'm agoin to marry Jule, I swar I am, and *sich* a cross! Think of a locomotive and a cotton gin! Who! whoopee!

That's Dick Harlan's story, Mr. Editor, and if the man "In the Swamp" could see Dick at a *Knob Dance* he would think that something besides politicks and religion occupied the mind of *some* of the inhabitants of the "peaceful valley."

Is Mr. Free dead? I have a yarn to spin on him, also, one about "Sleep Walking," and I will do it some day if I can over come my laziness. You see I am a *hot* hand at the *location* of capital letters and puntuation, (the spelling is Dick's). If you think I have made one "capital" letter I shall be agreeably disappointed.

Your Friend,
SUGARTAIL.

162 THE SLAVE MARKET: A NORTHERN VIEW

from Harriet Beecher Stowe, *Uncle Tom's Cabin,* 1852

Harriet Beecher Stowe's anti-slavery novel *Uncle Tom's Cabin* (1852) incited millions of readers to pity and anger not only before the Civil War, when a half million copies sold within the first year and translations appeared almost everywhere in Europe, but also throughout the later nineteenth century, when, transformed into a play, it drew packed theater houses all over the country. The book is one of the striking phenomena of American culture. It furnishes a perfect illustration of the sentimental Christianity permeating Romantic fiction, and its popularity undoubtedly reflects the vigor of orthodox religiosity among the American people. It is also overflowing with sympathy for the underdog, a characteristic so persistently a part of popular causes in America.

Daughter, sister, and wife of clergymen and educators, Mrs. Harriet Beecher Stowe (1811-1896), like so many other reformers of the period, was born in New England. Her family's removal to southern Ohio in 1832, where her father became head of Lane Theological Seminary, brought her into contact with slavery and converted her to moderate abolitionism. *Uncle Tom's Cabin* was published serially in 1851 and 1852 and in book form in 1852. Its picture of the hardships of slave life and the tragic repercussions of the "peculiar institution" on the life of other people was perhaps the most powerful argument against slavery. Full of memorable characters—like the title figure, whose death had obvious overtones of Christian martyrdom; little Eva, whose pure and religious death set millions to sobbing; and that classic villain, the slave overseer Simon Legree—the novel rapidly entered the national mythology. Its impact on the South is suggested by the fact that over fourteen pro-slavery novels appeared within a few years, directly answering the charges made by Mrs. Stowe.

This selection from *Uncle Tom's Cabin* describes a slave market in the South. Particularly worthy of note is the humanitarian feeling which permeates the narrative and which was so typical of Northern Romantic reform.

A slave warehouse! Perhaps some of my readers conjure up horrible visions of such a place. They fancy some foul, obscure den, some horrible *Tartarus* "*informis, ingens, cui lumen ademptum.*" But no, innocent friend; in these days men have learned the art of sinning expertly and genteelly, so as not to shock the eyes and senses of respectable society. Human property is high in the market; and is, therefore, well fed, well cleaned, tended, and looked after, that it may come to sale sleek, and strong, and shining. A slave warehouse in New Orleans is a house externally not much unlike many others, kept with neatness; and where every day you may see arranged, under a sort of shed along the outside, rows of men and women, who stand there as a sign of the property sold within.

Then you shall be courteously entreated to call and examine, and shall find an abundance of husbands, wives, brothers, sisters, fathers, mothers, and young children, to be "sold separately, or in lots, to suit the convenience of the purchaser;" and that soul immortal, once bought with blood and anguish by the Son of God, when the earth shook, and the rocks were rent, and the graves were opened, can be sold, leased, mortgaged, exchanged for groceries or dry goods, to suit the phases of trade, or the fancy of the purchaser.

It was a day or two after the conversation between Marie and Miss Ophelia, that Tom, Adolph, and about half a dozen others of the St. Clare estate, were turned over to the loving kindness of Mr. Skeggs, the keeper of a depot on —— street, to await the auction next day.

Tom had with him quite a sizable trunk full of clothing, as had most others of them. They were ushered, for the night, into a long room, where many other men, of all ages, sizes and shades of complexion, were assembled, and from which roars of laughter and unthinking merriment were proceeding.

"Ah, ha! that's right. Go it, boys,—go it!" said Mr. Skeggs, the keeper. "My people are always

so merry! Sambo, I see!" he said, speaking approvingly to a burly negro who was performing tricks of low buffoonery, which occasioned the shouts which Tom had heard.

As might be imagined, Tom was in no humor to join these proceedings; and, therefore, setting his trunk as far as possible from the noisy group, he sat down on it, and leaned his face against the wall.

The dealers in the human article make scrupulous and systematic efforts to promote noisy mirth among them, as a means of drowning reflection, and rendering them insensible to their condition. The whole object of the training to which the negro is put, from the time he is sold in the northern market till he arrives south, is systematically directed towards making him callous, unthinking, and brutal. The slave-dealer collects his gang in Virginia or Kentucky, and drives them to some convenient, healthy place,— often a watering-place,—to be fattened. Here they are fed full daily; and, because some incline to pine, a fiddle is kept commonly going among them, and they are made to dance daily; and he who refuses to be merry—in whose soul thoughts of wife, or child, or home, are too strong for him to be gay—is marked as sullen and dangerous, and subjected to all the evils which the ill-will of an utterly irresponsible and hardened man can inflict upon him. Briskness, alertness, and cheerfulness of appearance, especially before observers, are constantly enforced upon them, both by the hope of thereby getting a good master, and the fear of all that the driver may bring upon them, if they prove unsalable.

"What dat ar nigger doin' here?" said Sambo, coming up to Tom, after Mr. Skeggs had left the room. Sambo was a full black, of great size, very lively, voluble, and full of trick and grimace.

"What you doin' here?" said Sambo, coming up to Tom, and poking him facetiously in the side. "Meditatin', eh?"

"I am to be sold at the auction, to-morrow!" said Tom, quietly.

"Sold at auction,—haw! haw! boys, an't this yer fun? I wish't I was gwine that ar way!—tell ye, wouldn't I make 'em laugh? But how is it,—dis

Text: Harriet Beecher Stowe, *Uncle Tom's Cabin; or, Life Among the Lowly* (Boston: Houghton Mifflin & Co., 1890), pp. 365-70.

yer whole lot gwine to-morrow?" said Sambo, laying his hand freely on Adolph's shoulder.

"Please to let me alone!" said Adolph, fiercely, straightening himself up, with extreme disgust.

"Law, now, boys! dis yer's one o' yer white niggers,—kind o' cream-color, ye know, scented!" said he, coming up to Adolph and snuffing. "O Lor! he'd do for a tobaccer-shop; they could keep him to scent snuff! Lor, he'd keep a whole shop agwine,—he would!"

"I say, keep off, can't you?" said Adolph, enraged.

"Lor, now, how touchy we is,—we white niggers! Look at us, now!" and Sambo gave a ludicrous imitation of Adolph's manner; "here's de airs and graces. We's been in a good family, I specs."

"Yes," said Adolph; "I had a master that could have bought you all for old truck!"

"Laws, now, only think," said Sambo, "the gentlemens that we is!"

"I belonged to the St. Clare family," said Adolph, proudly.

"Lor, you did! Be hanged if they ar'n't lucky to get shet of ye. Spects they's gwine to trade ye off with a lot o' cracked teapots and sich like!" said Sambo, with a provoking grin.

Adolph, enraged at this taunt, flew furiously at his adversary, swearing and striking on every side of him. The rest laughed and shouted, and the uproar brought the keeper to the door.

"What now, boys? Order,—order!" he said, coming in and flourishing a large whip.

All fled in different directions, except Sambo, who, presuming on the favor which the keeper had to him as a licensed wag, stood his ground, ducking his head with a facetious grin, whenever the master made a dive at him.

"Lor, Mas'r, 't an't us,—we's reg'lar stiddy,— it's these yer new hands; they's real aggravatin',— kinder pickin' at us, all time!"

The keeper, at this, turned upon Tom and Adolph, and distributing a few kicks and cuffs without much inquiry, and leaving general orders for all to be good boys and go to sleep, left the apartment.

While this scene was going on in the men's sleeping-room, the reader may be curious to take a peep at the corresponding apartment allotted to the women. Stretched out in various attitudes over the floor, he may see numberless sleeping forms of every shade of complexion, from the purest ebony to white, and of all years, from childhood to old age, lying now asleep. Here is a fine bright girl, of ten years, whose mother was sold out yesterday, and who to-night cried herself to sleep when nobody was looking at her. Here,

a worn old negress, whose thin arms and callous fingers tell of hard toil, waiting to be sold tomorrow, as a cast-off article, for what can be got for her; and some forty or fifty others, with heads variously enveloped in blankets or articles of clothing, lie stretched around them. But, in a corner, sitting apart from the rest, are two females of a more interesting appearance than common. One of these is a respectably dressed mulatto woman between forty and fifty, with soft eyes and a gentle and pleasing physiognomy. She has on her head a high-raised turban, made of a gay red Madras handkerchief, of the first quality, and her dress is neatly fitted, and of good material, showing that she has been provided for with a careful hand. By her side, and nestling closely to her, is a young girl of fifteen,—her daughter. She is a quadroon, as may be seen from her fairer complexion, though her likeness to her mother is quite discernible. She has the same soft, dark eye, with longer lashes, and her curling hair is of a luxuriant brown. She also is dressed with great neatness, and her white, delicate hands betray very little acquaintance with servile toil. These two are to be sold to-morrow, in the same lot with the St. Clare servants; and the gentleman to whom they belong, and to whom the money for their sale is to be transmitted, is a member of a Christian church in New York, who will receive the money, and go thereafter to the sacrament of his Lord and theirs, and think no more of it.

These two, whom we shall call Susan and Emmeline, had been the personal attendants of an amiable and pious lady of New Orleans, by whom they had been carefully and piously instructed and trained. They had been taught to read and write, diligently instructed in the truths of religion, and their lot had been as happy an one as in their condition it was possible to be. But the only son of their protectress had the management of her property; and, by carelessness and extravagance, involved it to a large amount, and at last failed. One of the largest creditors was the respectable firm of B. & Co., in New York. B. & Co. wrote to their lawyer in New Orleans, who attached the real estate (these two articles and a lot of plantation hands formed the most valuable part of it), and wrote word to that effect to New York. Brother B., being, as we have said, a Christian man, and a resident in a free state, felt some uneasiness on the subject. He didn't like trading slaves and souls of men,—of course, he didn't; but, then, there were thirty thousand dollars in the case, and that was rather too much money to be lost for a principle; and so, after much considering, and asking advice from those that he knew would advise to suit him, Brother B. wrote to his lawyer to dispose of the business in the way that seemed to him the most suitable, and remit the proceeds.

The day after the letter arrived in New Orleans, Susan and Emmeline were attached, and sent to the depot to await a general auction on the following morning; and as they glimmer faintly upon us in the moonlight which steals through the grated window, we may listen to their conversation. Both are weeping, but each quietly, that the other may not hear.

"Mother, just lay your head on my lap, and see if you can't sleep a little," says the girl, trying to appear calm.

"I haven't any heart to sleep, Em; I can't; it's the last night we may be together!"

"Oh, mother, don't say so! perhaps we shall get sold together,—who knows?"

"If't was anybody's else case, I should say so, too, Em," said the woman; "but I'm so 'feared of losin' you that I don't see anything but the danger."

"Why, mother, the man said we were both likely, and would sell well."

Susan remembered the man's looks and words. With a deadly sickness at her heart, she remembered how he had looked at Emmeline's hands, and lifted up her curly hair, and pronounced her a first-rate article. Susan had been trained as a Christian, brought up in the daily reading of the Bible, and had the same horror of her child's being sold to a life of shame that any other Christian mother might have; but she had no hope,—no protection.

"Mother, I think we might do first-rate, if you could get a place as cook, and I as chambermaid or seamstress, in some family. I dare say we shall. Let's both look as bright and lively as we can, and tell all we can do, and perhaps we shall," said Emmeline.

"I want you to brush your hair all back straight, to-morrow," said Susan.

"What for, mother? I don't look near so well, that way."

"Yes, but you'll sell better so."

"I don't see why!" said the child.

"Respectable families would be more apt to buy you, if they saw you looked plain and decent, as if you wasn't trying to look handsome. I know their ways better'n you do," said Susan.

"Well, mother, then I will."

"And, Emmeline, if we shouldn't ever see each other again, after to-morrow,—if I'm sold way up on a plantation somewhere, and you somewhere else,—always remember how you've been brought up, and all Missis has told you; take your Bible with you, and your hymn-book; and if you're faithful to the Lord, he'll be faithful to you."

So speaks the poor soul, in sore discouragement; for she knows that to-morrow any man, however vile and brutal, however godless and merciless, if he only has money to pay for her, may become owner of her daughter, body and soul; and then, how is the child to be faithful? She thinks of all this, as she holds her daughter in her arms, and wishes that she were not handsome and attractive. It seems almost an aggravation to her to remember how purely and piously, how much above the ordinary lot, she has been brought up. But she has no resort but to *pray*; and many such prayers to God have gone up from those same trim, neatly arranged, respectable slave-prisons,—prayers which God has not forgotten, as a coming day shall show; for it is written, "Whoso causeth one of these little ones to offend, it were better for him that a mill-stone were hanged about his neck, and that he were drowned in the depths of the sea."

THE WESTERN FRONTIER AND AMERICAN IMAGINATION

163

THE ROMANTIC FRONTIER: LEATHERSTOCKING AND THE VIRGIN WILDERNESS

from James Fenimore Cooper, *The Pioneers*, 1823

Students of American culture have long been aware of the great impact of the West both on American life and institutions and on American thought. In the Romantic Age the presence of an untouched and uncivilized wilderness in the interior of the American continent constantly reminded Americans of the promise of their new world and of the chance to create in this wilderness a society whose ways would be closer to the intentions of God.

With such dreams widely prevalent, the actual settlement of the West was a great disappointment, especially to thinkers influenced by the Romantic ideal of the natural man. For in many respects the conditions of Western settlement brought out the worst in men: life was harsh and there was little time for the amenities of civilized life; land speculation, political chicanery, and immorality were rife in the relatively lawless and poorly organized Western towns. The tension between the dream of a good society in the virgin wilderness and the actuality of frontier life is frequently reflected in American thought and literature of the Romantic Age.

James Fenimore Cooper's "Leatherstocking Tales," one of the most popular of American literary series, illustrates both the idealization of the virgin wilderness and the sense of loss and betrayal that many Americans felt when they became aware of the crude fashion in which the wilderness was being settled. Comprising a series of five novels—*The Deerslayer* (1841), *The Last of the Mohicans* (1826), *The Pathfinder* (1840), *The Pioneers* (1823) and *The Prairie* (1827)—the "Leatherstocking Tales" present the character Natty Bumppo, a frontiersman from whose characteristic dress the series of novels take their title. Natty Bumppo, also called Hawkeye and Deerslayer, is a man who from his earliest youth in upper New York state has chosen to live in the wilderness. Noted for his prowess as a hunter and fighter, he is also in his primitive way a man of deep religious and moral feeling, resembling in this respect the Romantic ideal of the natural man. In most of the novels he is accompanied on his travels and hunts by a single Indian companion, the Mohican, Chingachgook, who is, like him, one of nature's noblemen. Although, as has often been pointed out, Cooper's Indians have scant resemblance to the real American aborigine, Cooper convincingly expresses the pathos of the situation in which the American Indian is pushed out of his ancestral lands by the advancing white man.

In most of the Leatherstocking novels, Natty is pictured as fleeing the encroachments of civilization by moving farther and farther west in search of untouched nature. In this selection from *The Pioneers*, Natty voices the beauty and meaning he finds in the virgin wilderness and the sense of loss he feels at its destruction.

. . . For a short time a profound silence prevailed, during which each man was very busy with his hook and line; but Edwards, probably feeling that it remained with him to renew the discourse, soon observed, with the air of one who knew not what he said,—

"How beautifully tranquil and glassy the lake is! Saw you it ever more calm and even than at this moment, Natty?"

"I have known the Otsego water for five-and-forty years," said Leather-Stocking; "and I will say that for it, which is, that a cleaner spring or better fishing is not to be found in the land. Yes, yes; I had the place to myself, once, and a cheerful time I had of it. The game was plenty as heart could wish; and there was none to meddle with the ground, unless there might have been a hunting party of the Delawares crossing the hills, or, maybe, a rifling scout of them thieves, the Iroquois. There was one or two Frenchmen that squatted in the flats, farther west, and married squaws; and some of the Scotch-Irishers from the Cherry Valley, would come on to the lake, and borrow my canoe to take a mess of parch, or drop a line for salmon-trout; but, in the main, it was a cheerful place, and I had but little to disturb me in it. John would come, and John knows."

Mohegan turned his dark face at this appeal; and, moving his hand forward with a graceful motion of assent, he spoke, using the Delaware language:—

"The land was owned by my people; we gave it to my brother, in council—to the Fire-eater; and what the Delawares give lasts as long as the waters run. Hawkeye smoked at that council, for we loved him."

"No, no, John," said Natty; "I was no chief, seeing that I knowed nothing of scholarship, and had a white skin. But it was a comfortable hunting-ground then, lad, and would have been so to this day, but for the money of Marmaduke Temple, and the twisty ways of the law."

"It must have been a sight of melancholy pleasure, indeed," said Edwards, while his eye roved along the shores and over the hills, where the clearings, groaning with the golden corn, were cheering the forests with the signs of life, "to have roamed over these mountains, and along this sheet of beautiful water, without a living soul to speak to, or to thwart your humor."

"Haven't I said it was cheerful?" said Leather-Stocking. "Yes, yes; when the trees began to be covered with leaves, and the ice was out of the lake, it was a second paradise. I have travelled the woods for fifty-three years, and have made them my home for more than forty; and I can

Text: James Fenimore Cooper, "The Pioneers; or, The Sources of the Susquehanna," in *Works* (New York: G. P. Putnam's Sons, 1896), pp. 298-302.

say that I have met but one place that was more to my liking; and that was only to eye-sight, and not for hunting or fishing."

"And where was that?" asked Edwards.

"Where! why up on the Cattskills. I used often to go up into the mountains after wolves' skins and bears; once they paid me to get them a stuffed painter, and so I often went. There's a place in them hills that I used to climb to when I wanted to see the carryings on of the world, that would well pay any man for a barked shin or a torn moccasin. You know the Cattskills, lad; for you must have seen them on your left, as you followed the river up from York, looking as blue as a piece of clear sky, and holding the clouds on their tops, as the smoke curls over the head of an Indian chief at the council fire. Well, there's the High-peak and the Round-top which lay back like a father and mother among their children, seeing they are far above all the other hills. But the place I mean is next to the river, where one of the ridges juts out a little from the rest, and where the rocks fall, for the best part of a thousand feet, so much up and down, that a man standing on their edges is fool enough to think he can jump from top to bottom."

"What see you when you get there?" asked Edwards.

"Creation," said Natty, dropping the end of his rod into the water, and sweeping one hand around him in a circle: "all creation, lad. I was on that hill when Vaughan burned 'Sopus in the last war; and I saw the vessels come out of the Highlands as plain as I can see that lime-scow rowing into the Susquehanna, though one was twenty times farther from me than the other. The river was in sight for seventy miles, looking like a curled shaving under my feet, though it was eight long miles to its banks. I saw the hills in the Hampshire grants, the Highlands of the river, and all that God had done, or man could do, far as eye could reach—you know that the Indians named me for my sight, lad; and from the flat on the top of that mountain, I have often found the place where Albany stands. And as for 'Sopus' the day the royal troops burnt the town, the smoke seemed so nigh, that I thought I could hear the screeches of the women."

"It must have been worth the toil to meet with such a glorious view."

"If being the best part of a mile in the air, and having men's farms and houses at your feet, with rivers looking like ribbons, and mountains bigger than the 'Vision,' seeming to be hay-stacks of green grass under you, gives any satisfaction to a man, I can recommend the spot.

When I first came into the woods to live, I used to have weak spells when I felt lonesome; and then I would go into the Cattskills, and spend a few days on that hill to look at the ways of man; but it's now many a year since I felt any such longings, and I am getting too old for rugged rocks. But there's a place, a short two miles back of that very hill, that in late times I relished better than the mountain; for it was more covered with the trees, and natural."

"And where was that?" inquired Edwards, whose curiosity was strongly excited by the simple description of the hunter.

"Why, there's a fall in the hills where the water of two little ponds, that lie near each other, breaks out of their bounds and runs over the rocks into the valley. The stream is, maybe, such a one as would turn a mill, if so useless a thing was wanted in the wilderness. But the hand that made that 'Leap' never made a mill. There the water comes crooking and winding among the rocks; first so slow that a trout could swim in it, and then starting and running like a creatur' that wanted to make a far spring, till it gets to where the mountain divides, like the cleft hoof of a deer, leaving a deep hollow for the brook to tumble into. The first pitch is nigh two hundred feet, and the water looks like flakes of driven snow afore it touches the bottom; and there the stream gathers itself together again for a new start, and maybe flutters over fifty feet of flat rock before it falls for another hundred, when it jumps about from shelf to shelf, first turning thisaway and then turning thataway, striving to get out of the hollow, till it finally comes to the plain."

"I have never heard of this spot before; it is not mentioned in the books."

"I never read a book in my life," said Leather-Stocking; "and how should a man who has lived in towns and schools know anything about the wonders of the woods? No, no, lad; there has that little stream of water been playing among the hills since He made the world, and not a dozen white men have ever laid eyes on it. The rock sweeps like mason-work, in a half-round, on both sides of the fall, and shelves over the bottom for fifty feet; so that when I've been sitting at the foot of the first pitch, and my hounds have run into the caverns behind the sheet of water, they've looked no bigger than so many rabbits. To my judgment, lad, it's the best piece of work that I've met with in the woods; and none know how often the hand of God is seen in the wilderness, but them that rove it for a man's life."

164

THE LEGENDARY FRONTIER: DAVY CROCKETT AND THE TALL TALE

from Anonymous, 1840?

The appeal of legendary frontier is suggested by the popularity of that doughty frontiersman Davy Crockett (1786-1836), whose fame underwent a brief renaissance a few years ago in an immensely popular song, a couple of movies, and a television program. Crockett, despite the welter of myths that have clustered about him, was a real man. He first came to national attention as a minor figure in the Jacksonian movement, but coming to Washington as a Congressman, he quarreled with Jackson and went over to the Whigs, who were then in need of an authentic Westerner in their campaigns against Jackson and his policies. Crockett's own gift for telling tall tales about himself inspired Whig politicians to make up still other legends about him, and even during his own lifetime he was rapidly becoming the center of fantastic stories about frontier exploits. His death at the Alamo under heroic circumstances added the lustre of martyrdom to his fame, and throughout the mid-nineteenth century his legend was kept alive through biographies and short stories in almanacs and magazines. An *Autobiography* largely written by others was very popular and remains a classic of American tall tales.

As the following selection—a brief anecdote from a Crockett almanac—illustrates, Crockett most particularly embodied the optimistic spirit of adventure and enterprise that had so much to do with the settlement of the West. His own motto, "Go ahead," expressed the pride of Americans in their ability to solve any problems that might face them by the use of a little inspired common sense; here with exaggerated practicality he averts a cosmic catastrophe by the judicious application of a little bear grease.

One January morning it was so all screwen cold that the forest trees were stiff and they couldn't shake, and the very daybreak froze fast as it was trying to dawn. The tinder box in my cabin would no more ketch fire than a sunk raft at the bottom of the sea. Well, seein' daylight war so far behind time I thought creation war in a fair way for freezen fast: so, thinks I, I must strike a little fire from my fingers, light my pipe, an' travel out a few leagues, and see about it. Then I brought my knuckles together like two thunderclouds, but the sparks froze up afore I could begin to collect 'em, so out I walked, whistlin' "Fire in the mountains!" as I went along in three double quick time. Well, arter I had walked about twenty miles up the Peak O'Day and Daybreak Hill I soon discovered what war the matter. The airth had actually friz fast on her axes, and couldn't turn round; the sun had got jammed between two cakes o' ice under the wheels, an' thar he had been shinin' an' workin' to get loose till he friz fast in his cold sweat. C-r-e-a-t-i-o-n! thought I, this ar the toughest sort of suspension, an' it mustn't be endured.

Somethin' must be done, or human creation is done for. It war then so anteluvian an' premature cold that my upper and lower teeth an' tongue war all collapsed together as tight as a friz oyster; but I took a fresh twenty-pound bear off my back that I'd picked up on my road, and beat the animal agin the ice till the hot ile began to walk out on him at all sides. I then took an' held him over the airth's axes an' squeezed him till I'd thawed 'em loose, poured about a ton on't over the sun's face, give the airth's cog-wheel one kick backward till I got the sun loose—whistled "Push along, keep movin'!" an' in about fifteen seconds the airth gave a grunt, an' began movin'. The sun walked up beautiful, salutin' me with sich a wind o' gratitude that it made me sneeze. I lit my pipe by the blaze o' his top-knot, shouldered my bear, an' walked home, introducin' people to the fresh daylight with a piece of sunrise in my pocket.

Text: Constance Rourke, *American Humor; A Study of the National Character*, pp. 58-59. From *American Humor* by Constance Rourke, copyright, 1931, by Harcourt, Brace and Company, Inc.; renewed by Alice D. Fore. Used by permission of the publishers.

165

THE REAL FRONTIER: AN EARLY SETTLER SPEAKING
HER MIND ON FRONTIER CUSTOMS

from Caroline Kirkland, *A New Home—Who'll Follow?*, 1839

The real West was a rather different place from the West of the romantic legends of Cooper or the tall tales of Davy Crockett. Frontier settlers faced the task of felling timber, grubbing stumps, and tilling the fields in a land of scorching summers, punctuated by fierce thunderstorms, and long winters of freezing winds and heavy snow. Preoccupied as they were with the problems of food and shelter, the early settlers had little spare time to establish the amenities of civilized life. Thus, many of the more educated and genteel of those who joined the westward migrations endured particular hardship in adjusting themselves to frontier customs and manners, so different from those of the civilized towns and cities they had left behind.

In this selection from Mrs. Caroline Kirkland's description of frontier life in Michigan, *A New Home—Who'll Follow?*, first published in 1839, the author describes some of the problems she faced in her relations with her neighbors. Though she recommends frontier life as a salutary change for the jaded palates of urban epicures, she does not romanticize what she thinks are its shortcomings.

One must come quite away from the conveniences and refined indulgences of civilized life to know any thing about them. To be always inundated with comforts, is but too apt to make us proud, selfish, and ungrateful. The mind's health, as well as the body's, is promoted by occasional privation or abstinence. Many a sour-faced grumbler I wot of, would be marvellously transformed by a year's residence in the woods, or even in a Michigan village of as high pretensions as Montacute. If it were not for casting a sort of dishonor on a country life, turning into a magnificent "beterinhaus" these

> "Haunts of deer,
> And lanes in which the primrose ere her time
> Peeps through the moss,"

I should be disposed to recommend a course of Michigan to the Sybarites, the puny exquisites, the world-worn and sated Epicureans of our cities. If I mistake not, they would make surprising advances in philosophy in the course of a few months' training. I should not be severe either. I should not require them to come in their strictly natural condition as featherless bipeds. I would allow them to bring many a comfort—nay, even some real luxuries; books, for instance, and a reasonable supply of New York Safety-Fund notes, the most tempting form which "world's gear" can possibly assume for our western, wild-cat wearied eyes. I would grant to each Neophyte a ready-made loggery, a garden fenced with tamarack poles, and every facility and convenience which

Text: Caroline Kirkland (Mary Clavers, pseudonym), *A New Home—Who'll Follow? or, Glimpses of Western Life* (New York: C. S. Francis, 1839), pp. 325-32.

is now enjoyed by the better class of our settlers, yet I think I might after all hope to send home a reasonable proportion of my subjects completely cured, sane for life.

I have in the course of these detached and desultory chapters, hinted at various deficiencies and peculiarities, which strike, with rather unpleasant force, the new resident in the backwoods; but it would require volumes to enumerate all the cases in which the fastidiousness, the taste, the pride, the self-esteem of the refined child of civilization, must be wounded by a familiar intercourse with the persons among whom he will find himself thrown, in the ordinary course of rural life. He is continually reminded in how great a variety of particulars his necessities, his materials for comfort, and his sources of pain, are precisely those of the humblest of his neighbors. The humblest, did I say? He will find that he has no humble neighbors. He will very soon discover, that in his new sphere, no act of kindness, no offer of aid, will be considered as any thing, short of insult, if the least suspicion of *condescension* peep out. Equality, perfect and practical, is the *sine qua non;* and any appearance of a desire to avoid this rather trying fraternization, is invariably met by a fierce and indignant resistance. The spirit in which was conceived the motto of the French revolution, "La fraternité ou la mort," exists in full force among us, though modified as to results. In cities we bestow charity—in the country we can only exchange kind offices, nominally at least. If you are perfectly well aware that your nearest neighbor has not tasted meat in a month, nor found in his pocket the semblance of a shilling to purchase it, you must not be surprised, when you have sent him a piece, to receive for reply, "Oh! your pa wants to *change*, does he? Well, you may put it down." And this without the remotest idea that the time for repayment ever will arrive, but merely to avoid saying, "I thank you," a phrase especially eschewed, so far as I have had opportunity to observe.

This same republican spirit is evinced rather amusingly, in the reluctance to admire, or even to approve, any thing like luxury or convenience which is not in common use among the settlers. Your carpets are spoken of as "*one* way to hide dirt;" your mahogany tables, as "dreadful plaguy to scour;" your kitchen conveniences, as "lumberin' up the house for nothin';" and so on to the end of the chapter. One lady informed me, that if she had such a pantry full of "dishes," under which general term is included every variety of china, glass and earthenware, she should set up store, and "sell them off pretty quick," for she would not "be plagued with them." Another, giving a slighting glance at a French mirror of rather unusual dimensions, larger by two thirds, I verily believe, than she had ever seen, remarked, "that would be quite a nice glass, if the frame was done over."

Others take up the matter reprovingly. They "don't think it right to spend money so;" they think too, that "pride never did nobody no good;" and some will go so far as to suggest modes of disposing of your superfluities. "Any body that's got so many dresses, might afford to give away half on 'em;" or, "I should think you'd got so much land, you might give a poor man a lot, and never miss it." A store of any thing, however simple or necessary, is, as I have elsewhere observed, a subject of reproach, if you decline supplying whomsoever may be deficient.

This simplification of life, this bringing down the transactions of daily intercourse to the original principles of society, is neither very eagerly adopted, nor very keenly relished, by those who have been accustomed to the politer atmospheres. They rebel most determinedly, at first. They perceive that the operation of the golden rule, in circumstances where it is all *give* on one side, and all *take* on the other, must necessarily be rather severe; and they declare manfully against all impertinent intrusiveness. But, sooth to say, there are in the country so many ways of being made uncomfortable by one's most insignificant enemy, that it is soon discovered that warfare is even more costly than submission.

And all this forms part of the schooling which I propose for my spoiled child of refined civilization. And although many of these remarks and requisitions of our unpolished neighbors are unreasonable and absurd enough, yet some of them commend themselves to our better feelings in such a sort, that we find ourselves ashamed to refuse what it seemed at first impertinent to ask; and after the barriers of pride and prejudice are once broken, we discover a certain satisfaction in this homely fellowship with our kind, which goes far towards repaying whatever sacrifices or concessions we may have been induced to make. This has its limits of course; and one cannot help observing that "levelling upwards" is much more congenial to "human natur'," than levelling downwards. The man who thinks you ought to spare him a piece of ground for a garden, because you have more than he thinks you need, would be far from sharing with his poorer neighbor the superior advantages of his lot. He would tell him to work for them as *he* had done.

But then there are, in the one case, some absolute and evident superfluities, according to the primitive estimate of these regions; in the other, none. The doll of Fortune, who may cast a languid eye on this homely page, from the luxurious depths of a velvet-cushioned library-chair, can scarce be expected to conceive how natural it may be, for those who possess nothing beyond the absolute requisites of existence, to look with a certain degree of envy on the extra comforts which seem to cluster around the path of another; and to feel as if a little might well be spared, where so much would still be left. To the tenant of a log-cabin whose family, whatever be its numbers, must burrow in a single room, while a bed or two, a chest, a table, and a wretched handful of cooking utensils, form the chief materials of comfort, an ordinary house, small and plain it may be, yet amply supplied, looks like the very home of luxury. The woman who owns but a suit a-piece for herself and her children, considers the possession of an abundant though simple and inexpensive wardrobe, as needless extravagance; and we must scarcely blame her too severely, if she should be disposed to condemn as penurious, any reluctance to supply her pressing need, though she may have no shadow of claim on us beyond that which arises from her being a daughter of Eve. We look at the matter from opposite points of view. *Her* light shows her very plainly, as she thinks, what is *our* Christian duty; we must take care that ours does not exhibit too exclusively her envy and her impertinence.

The inequalities in the distribution of the gifts of fortune are not greater in the country than in town, but the contrary; yet circumstances render them more offensive to the less favored class. The denizens of the crowded alleys and swarming lofts of our great cities see, it is true, the lofty mansions, the splendid equipages of the wealthy—but they are seldom or never brought into contact or collision with the owners of these glittering advantages. And the extreme width of the great gulf between, is almost a barrier, even to all-reaching envy. But in the ruder stages of society, where no one has yet begun to expend any thing for show, the difference lies chiefly in the ordinary requisites of comfort; and this comes home at once "to men's business and bosoms." The keenness of their appreciation, and the strength of their envy, bear a direct proportion to the *real* value of the objects of their desire; and when they are in habits of entire equality and daily familiarity with those who own ten or twenty times as much of the *matériel* of earthly enjoyment as themselves, it is surely natural, however provoking, that they should not be studious to veil their longings after a share of the good, which has been so bounteously showered upon their neighbors.

I am only making a sort of apology for the foibles of my rustic friends. I cannot say that I feel much respect for any thing which looks like a willingness to live at others' cost, save as a matter of the last necessity.

I was adverting to a certain unreservedness of communication on these points, as often bringing wholesome and much needed instruction home to those whom prosperity and indulgence may have rendered unsympathizing, or neglectful of the kindly feelings which are among the best ornaments of our nature.

But I am aware that I have already been adventurous, far beyond the bounds of prudence. To hint that it may be better not to cultivate *too* far that haughty spirit of exclusiveness which is the glory of the fashionable world, is, I know, hazardous in the extreme. I have not so far forgotten the rules of the sublime *clique* as not to realize, that in acknowledging even a leaning toward the "vulgar" side, I place myself forever beyond its pale. But I am now a denizen of the wild woods—in my view, "no mean city" to own as one's home; and I feel no ambition to aid in the formation of a Montacute aristocracy, for which an ample field is now open, and all the proper materials are at hand. What lack we? Several of us have as many as three cows; some few, carpets and shanty-kitchens; and one or two, piano-fortes and silver tea-sets. I myself, as *dame de la seigneurie,* have had secret thoughts of an astral lamp! but even if I should go so far, I am resolved not to be either vain-glorious or over-bearing, although this kind of superiority forms the usual ground for exclusiveness. I shall visit my neighbors just as usual, and take care not to say a single word about dipped candles, if I can possibly help it.

CHAPTER 14

Interpretations of Democratic

Growth and the Sectional Conflict

No historical synthesis of classical dimensions has yet been written for the age of democratic growth and sectional conflict, 1825-1865. There is, of course, no strict accounting for the wayward path of genius in historiography or any other human enterprise. Possibly the logical author of such a mid-nineteenth-century synthesis would have been Frederick Jackson Turner, a first-rank historian whose themes were democracy, the frontier, and the sections. Yet Turner's nearest approach to the task (in *The United States: 1830-1850*) remained unfinished at his death, gave only passing notice to major political issues, and showed in any case but a hint of the writer's undoubted historical mastery. Only his biographer might say why.

A major historical synthesis seems best to fit a dramatic order of events: one in which protagonist and antagonist come to grips with a profound dilemma and reach a necessary (if not a happy or proper) resolution. There was drama enough in Jacksonian Democracy, and greater drama in the sectional struggle. Unfortunately for literature, the break between Act One and Act Two has proved too difficult to bridge convincingly. The concerns of Jacksonian Democracy are swallowed up in a new dominant plot. The expansion of popular power gives way to the expansion of national territory as a theme of politics. The argument turns from, say, free banking to free soil. Parties built to fight one sort of battle confront the issues of slavery and expansion, change their primary character, and finally are pulled apart into Northern and Southern components.

One important interpretation of the period from 1825 to 1865 does focus upon the continuities between Jacksonian Democracy and the sectional conflict. Professor Avery Craven (see Document 167) associates the party battles of the

Jacksonian era with the clash of interests between the agrarian South and the industrial, capitalistic North. Thus the Civil War can be viewed as the climax of a long struggle between social forces with a sectional base. Craven suggests a further link of still greater significance. If the Civil War is conceived essentially as a breakdown of the normal democratic process, then one would look for democratic flaws that developed during the Jacksonian decades. The "ferment of reform" in Northern society during the second quarter of the nineteenth century, Professor Craven argues, produced a heady brew of ideology—of abstract and rigid dogmas of right and wrong. The sober, limited politics of *quid pro quo*, which permitted a diverse nation to reconcile its differences peaceably, became the all-or-none politics of reckless Northern and Southern ideologues. The democratic system was not built to take such violent shocks.

The Craven thesis has been questioned from both sides. The controversial historiography of Jacksonian Democracy (see Document 166) lends only limited support to the view that sectional traits, interests, and values dominated the battle of Whigs and Jacksonian Democrats. On the other side, Professor Allan Nevins (see Document 168) and many other interpreters of the Civil War insist that slavery did in fact pose a moral issue which had to be met head-on. War came not because propagandists *created* an irreconcilable conflict of ideologies but rather because statesmen lacked the courage and imagination to conceive fundamental solutions and lacked the prudence to plan a gradual transition to the ultimate and inevitable goal of freedom.

If ever someone is to offer an historical synthesis for the age of democratic growth and sectional conflict, perhaps he will borrow from Craven and Nevins and others the notion of democracy, its expansion, its natural tendencies, and its inner conflicts, as the unifying principle. Historians might in the end return to the prophetic hint of De Tocqueville (see Documents 113, 116, and 149) that the great source of revolutions in the modern era has been the glaring contradiction of inequality in the midst of growing equality, and that Jacksonian America, the most uniformly egalitarian of all societies, could not in the long run tolerate slavery, the most shocking form of human inequality.

166

CHANGING VIEWS OF ANDREW JACKSON

from Charles Grier Sellers, Jr., "Andrew Jackson Versus the Historians," 1958

Historians "make" history. Just as a journalist puts together elements from the public and private record to give a standard identity to "Dwight Eisenhower" or the "New Deal," so the historian selects his sources and organizes his findings to give a standard identity to "Abraham Lincoln" or "Jacksonian Democracy." Neither journalist nor historian can sell fancy as plain truth so long as informed critics are free to correct inventions or distortions. History has some advantage over journalism in this respect, since the scholar can claim years, not hours, for patient inquiry; he can second-guess his subjects; and he can enjoy a certain professional detachment and independence.

If the competition of historical appraisals helps to set the record straight, it does not remove important conflicts of interpretation. As Charles Grier Sellers, Jr., demonstrates in the following review of Jacksonian historiography, the shifting course of interpretation often has more to do with changing political and intellectual perspectives than with the accumulation of new evidence as such. Thus Sellers' history of history provides an opportunity to inspect the long-term process by which scholarly opinion— indirectly public opinion—of an historical age is formed. It should be noted carefully that Sellers does not conclude from his review of diversity and conflict in historical judgments that one view is as good as another and that it is all a matter of private taste. On the contrary, he finds in the record a challenge to further research on disputed questions and to the more rigorous exercise of critical judgment.

Professor Sellers is a member of the University of California (Berkeley) faculty. His articles on Southern politics in the Jacksonian era are important contributions to party history, and his biography-in-progress of James K. Polk promises a new understanding of that controversial figure, who bridges the gap between the age of Jackson and the Civil War era.

Andrew Jackson's masterful personality was enough by itself to make him one of the most controversial figures ever to stride across the American stage. "It can hardly be expected that the present generation will do justice to the character of Jackson," complained the compiler of his funeral eulogies in 1846, for "his opponents have ever been most bitter enemies, and his friends almost his worshippers." And when James Parton sat down fifteen years later to attempt the first impartial biography of Old Hickory, he despairingly concluded from the mountain of conflicting sources before him that his subject "was a patriot and a traitor. He was one of the greatest of generals, and wholly ignorant of the art of war. A writer brilliant, elegant, eloquent, without being able to compose a correct sentence, or spell words of four syllables. The first of statesmen, he never devised, he never framed a measure. He was the most candid of men, and was capable of the profoundest dissimulation. A most law-defying, law-obeying citizen. A stickler for discipline, he never hesitated to disobey his superior. A democratic autocrat. An urbane savage. An atrocious saint."

Such radical opposites could not be reconciled simply by splitting the difference; Parton and all who followed him on this difficult terrain have been forced pretty substantially either into the Jackson camp or into the camp of Jackson's enemies. Indeed, Parton's lament could almost stand today as the conclusion to a review of Jacksonian historiography.

The reasons for such continuing disagreement run far deeper than the individual characteristics of any historical personality. Andrew Jackson was intimately identified with the full flowering of American democracy; and as long as democracy remains pre-eminently the distinguishing feature of our society, the period and symbol of its triumph will remain controversial.

While American democracy emerged victorious on the plane of political ideology around 1776 or 1800, and on the plane of political practice around 1828, it did not achieve respectability in American historiography (for all George Bancroft's efforts) until about 1900. From the Jacksonian era to the end of the nineteenth century the writing of American history was dominated, as Charles H. Peck observed in 1899, by men "who were educated under the sway of the Whiggish culture of the country." This "Whig" school of Jacksonian historiography included the first two important Jackson biographers, James Parton and William Graham Sumner; the authors of the first two detailed American histories extending to the Civil War, Hermann E. von Holst and James Schouler; and Moisei Ostrogorski, author of the enormously influential study of *Democracy and the Organization of Political Parties.* . . .

Yet it was not fundamentally Jackson's personality that turned the Whig historians against him, nor was it the general policies he pursued as president. These writers were all liberals of the nineteenth-century stripe and actually approved the laissez-faire tendencies of most of the Jacksonian measures. Sumner was outraged that Jackson had "unjustly, passionately, ignorantly, and without regard to truth assailed a great and valuable financial institution," for the Yale economist was a stout champion of sound money and vested interests. But Sumner was an even more strenuous champion of Herbert Spencer's doctrine of unfettered individual enterprise, and his philosophy compelled him to admit that "it came in Jackson's way to do some good, to check some bad tendencies and to strengthen some good ones." . . . And all the Whig historians were ardent nationalists and applauded Jackson's bold stand against the South Carolina nullifiers.

How, then, could Parton say that "notwithstanding the good done by General Jackson during his presidency, his election to power was a mistake"? How could von Holst speak of "the frightful influence . . . which he exercised during the eight years of his presidency"? A clue may be found in the abhorrence with which the Whig historians uniformly treated Jackson's policy of removing his political enemies from federal office and replacing them with his friends. Indeed, for these scholarly mugwumps, the institution of the spoils system on a large scale

Text: Charles Grier Sellers, Jr., "Andrew Jackson Versus the Historians," *The Mississippi Valley Historical Review,* XLIV (March 1958), 615-33 *passim.*

became almost the distinguishing feature of Jackson's administration. "If all his other public acts had been perfectly wise and right," said Parton, "this single feature of his administration would suffice to render it deplorable."

Yet the spoils system was only a symptom of the real disease—the new system of democratic politics that both Jackson and the spoils system symbolized. "Popular sovereignty," said von Holst, would be "a dreadful condition of things"; and Schouler lamented the fact that, all too often, "the great body of our American democracy . . . slips back unconsciously into the mire whence the poverty-stricken millions emerge and falls too easy a prey to vice and ignorance." Ostrogorski got to the heart of the Whig historians' case against Jacksonian Democracy when he complained that it "excluded men of sterling worth and high principles from public life." Von Holst similarly argued that since Jackson "the people have begun to exchange the leadership of a small number of statesmen and politicians of a higher order for the rule of an ever increasing crowd of politicians of high and low degree, down even to the pothouse politician and the common thief, in the protecting mantle of demagogism." And as a result, said Parton, "the public affairs of the United States have been conducted with a stupidity which has excited the wonder of mankind." . . .

By the 1890's patrician liberalism was giving way to the broader movement which under the name Progressivism was soon to effect a profound shift in the mood and direction of American life. A corresponding shift in the mood of American historiography was signaled in 1893, when the young Wisconsin historian, Frederick Jackson Turner, read his famous paper emphasizing "The Significance of the Frontier in American History." Yet Turner's real significance lies less in his controversial frontier thesis than in his influence as leader of the massive shift of American historiography to a pro-democratic orientation. A whole new generation of young historians—men like Woodrow Wilson, William E. Dodd, John Spencer Bassett, Charles A. Beard, and Vernon L. Parrington—stood ready to echo Turner's vibrantly sympathetic description of democracy emerging "stark and strong and full of life, from the American forest." . . .

Andrew Jackson and his Democracy were naturally among the leading beneficiaries of the new pro-democratic orientation of American historiography. Out of the "frontier democratic society" of the West, said Turner, "where the freedom and abundance of land in the great Valley opened a refuge to the oppressed in all regions, came the Jacksonian democracy which governed the nation after the downfall of the party of John Quincy Adams." This Jacksonian Democracy was "strong in the faith of the intrinsic excellence of the common man, and in his capacity to share in government." . . .

The earliest major product of the democratic school of Jacksonian historiography was John Spencer Bassett's *Life of Andrew Jackson,* published in 1911. Bassett was the first scholar since Parton to work thoroughly through the extant Jacksonian sources, which now seemed to reveal "a man who was great, spite of many limitations." Bassett was generally sympathetic to Jackson's purposes and policies, but he was not uncritical, and his final chapter remains the most successful attempt to appraise Jackson's baffling character. Jackson had plenty of shortcomings—"lack of education, his crude judgments in many affairs, his occasional outbreaks of passion, his habitual hatred of those enemies with whom he had not made friends for party purposes, and his crude ideas of some political policies"—yet, for Bassett, "all lose some of their infelicity in the face of his brave, frank, masterly leadership of the democratic movement which then established itself in our life. . . . Few American Presidents have better lived up to the demands of the movement which brought them into power." . . .

The pro-democratic orientation that transformed Jacksonian historiography at the turn of the century has continued to be the dominant influence on writings about the Jackson period ever since. It permeated Marquis James's impressive Jackson biography of the 1930's, as well as the extensive studies of the Jackson period by Claude G. Bowers in the 1920's and Arthur M. Schlesinger, Jr., in the 1940's. More significantly, it has controlled the interpretations of Jacksonian Democracy to be found in nearly all the general works on American history written in the twentieth century, from the widely influential accounts of Vernon L. Parrington and Charles and Mary Beard to the most obscure textbooks. Political scientists have joined in the chorus of approval, with such writers as John W. Burgess, Wilfred E. Binkley, and Leonard D. White praising Jackson and his followers for strengthening the presidency and developing the new-style political party as an indispensable democratic institution.

Despite this widespread acceptance, the twentieth-century democratic school of Jacksonian historiography has attained neither the unchallenged hegemony nor the unity of outlook that the Whig school enjoyed in the nineteenth century. For one thing, the Whig interpretation would not play dead. Most embarrassing to the democratic view of Andrew Jackson has been the interpretation of Old Hickory's role in early Tennessee politics advanced by Thomas P. Abernethy. Abernethy presents Jackson as a frontier nabob who took sides against the democratic movement in his own state. Actually, this leader of the democratic movement in national politics was a demagogic aristocrat, says Abernethy, an "opportunist" for whom "Democracy was good talk with which to win the favor of the people and thereby accomplish ulterior objectives." . . .

Yet the democratic historians have suffered less from these dissenting views than from their own inability to make clear just what they mean by "democracy." The men of Turner's generation who originated democratic historiography conceived of the democratic process in a characteristically middle-class, Progressive way. Hating monopoly and plutocracy, they rejoiced in the egalitarian, anti-monopolistic tradition that stemmed from Jacksonian Democracy. But hating the class consciousness of Populism and Socialism as much or more, they shrank from any interpretation of the American past that smacked of social conflict. Their enthusiasm for democracy rested on an essentially romantic faith in the whole people, whom they saw as an undifferentiated mass, virtually free of inequalities and conflicts. Democracy, in the view which informed both Progressive politics and Turnerean historiography, was the process by which the whole people's fundamentally virtuous impulses were translated into public policy. . . .

The democratic historians' aversion to social conflict was a major factor in causing them to supplement the frontier thesis with a heavy emphasis on sectionalism. Conflict was simply too obvious in the Jackson era to be ignored, but Turner and his followers muted the discordant note of class struggle by transposing it into conflict between distinct geographical sections. Thus, alongside the Jacksonian rise of the whole people, we find in their writings a three-way contest among the democratic West (epitomized by Jackson), the capitalist Northeast, and the planting and increasingly aristocratic South. Beard and Parrington, to be sure, made social conflict central to their interpretations. But even their dramas of struggle against privileged minorities were grounded on the same Rousseauistic concept of the whole people as the conventional democratic interpretation; and more often than not they, too, fell back upon oversimplified sectional categories.

This vague conception of democracy remained prevalent in Jacksonian historiography until 1945, when Arthur M. Schlesinger, Jr., published *The Age of Jackson*. Schlesinger's thesis was that "more can be understood about Jacksonian democracy if it is regarded as a problem not of sections but of classes." Defining the central theme of American political history to be the efforts "on the part of the other sections of society to restrain the power of the business community," he interpreted Jacksonian Democracy as a movement "to control the power of the capitalistic groups, mainly Eastern, for the benefit of noncapitalist groups, farmers and laboring men, East, West, and South." Schlesinger traced the movement to the economic hardships of the 1820's, and he saw the East and the workingmen as playing the crucial roles in the Jacksonian coalition.

Schlesinger not only provided a sharper definition of the democratic movement and a clearer explanation of its origins, but he also stirred up a warm debate which prompted other historians to offer alternative definitions. The attack on *The Age of Jackson* was launched by a scholarly official of the Federal Reserve Board, Bray Hammond, who was irritated in the first instance by Schlesinger's failure to appreciate the central banking functions that the national bank had exercised so beneficially before it was attacked by Jackson. Emphasizing the role of the state banks in fomenting the Jacksonian assault on the national bank, Hammond insisted that the real animus of Jacksonian Democracy was not against business but against the exclusion of new entrepreneurs from business opportunities. Schlesinger "represents the age of Jackson as one of triumphant liberalism," he complained, "when it was as much or more an age of triumphant exploitation."

Hammond was quickly joined in his criticism of Schlesinger by a group of historians at Columbia University. Joseph Dorfman argued that the "labor" spokesmen whom Schlesinger had emphasized did not represent a genuine labor movement, and that their views were far from anti-business. Richard B. Morris contended that Jackson was anti-labor rather than pro-labor, while several of Morris' students attempted, with questionable success, to demonstrate that workingmen did not vote for Jackson.

These historians showed a considerable affinity for the Whig view of Jackson personally, especially in the version advanced by Thomas P. Abernethy. Their own interpretation of the Jackson movement was expressed best, perhaps, by Richard Hofstadter, who described it as "a phase in the expansion of liberated capitalism," and as "closely linked to the ambitions of the small capitalist."

Thus the recent historiography of Jacksonian Democracy has been dominated by the debate over Schlesinger's "class-conflict" or "labor" thesis on the one hand and the "entrepreneurial" thesis put forward by Schlesinger's critics on the other. Schlesinger and his supporters picture the democratic impulse largely as a movement of protest against the unfair privileges claimed by an exploitative business elite, while the Columbia historians defend the diametrically opposed view that the democratic movement was itself strongly capitalist in spirit and objected only to any limitation on free entry into the game of capitalist exploitation. . . .

But what of Old Hickory himself and Jacksonian Democracy? What are we to conclude when, after a century of scholarship, historians still squarely contradict each other about the essential nature of both the man and the movement? Has the frame of reference cut us off from the past as it actually was? Do historical writings tell us more about their authors than they do about their purported subjects?

Before accepting these disheartening conclusions, it may be well to remind ourselves that an interpretation is not necessarily wrong merely because a writer seems to have been impelled toward that interpretation by a particular frame of reference. The conclusions of honest men, working within limits set by an abundance of reliable and relatively unmalleable evidence, must have some basis in the reality of the past they seek to interpret. This may suggest that each school of Jacksonian historiography has been correct up to a point, and that the real problem of interpreting Jacksonian Democracy is to define the proper relationship among the various elements emphasized by the different schools.

Several recent writers, in attempting to do just this, have concluded that the Jacksonian movement was essentially paradoxical. Louis Hartz describes the American democrat of the Jackson era as a hybrid personality—both a class-conscious democrat and an incipient entrepreneur —at once the "man of the land, the factory, and the forge . . . who has all the proletarian virtues that Marx was forever contrasting with the pettiness of the petit-bourgeois," and "an aggressive entrepreneur, buying 'on speculation,'

combining 'some trade with agriculture,' making 'agriculture itself a trade'." He had "a certain smallness of entrepreneurial preoccupation which has never been glamorous in Western thought," Hartz concludes, but at the same time he was involved in "two heroic dramas, the covered wagon drama of the American frontier and the strike-ridden drama of a rising labor movement, so that when we come to men like Jackson and Leggett we are never quite sure whether we are dealing with a petty hope or a glorious dream."

Another scholar has defined the paradox of Jacksonian Democracy somewhat differently. Judging from Jackson's own public papers, says Marvin Meyers, the Jacksonians appealed "not to some workingman's yearning for a brave new world; not to the possibilities of a fresh creation at the western limits of civilization; not to the ambitions of a rising laissez-faire capitalism— not to any of these so much as to a *restoration* of old virtues and a (perhaps imaginary) old republican way of life." Meyers states the paradox thus: "The movement which in many ways cleared the path for the triumph of laissez-faire capitalism and its culture in America, and the public which in its daily life acted out that victory, held nevertheless in their conscience an image of a chaste republican order, resisting the seductions of risk and novelty, greed and extravagance, rapid motion and complex dealings." Still another scholar, John W. Ward, has found confirmation for this mood of Old Republican restorationism in the symbolic uses to which Jackson was put by his generation.

If these scholars are right about the paradoxical character of the Jacksonian democratic impulse, then it is easy to see why historians, in emphasizing different elements of the paradox, have reached such different interpretations. Viewed in this light, the frame of reference has served a valuable purpose after all, by leading historians to the different elements of the complex Jacksonian past out of which an over-all synthesis must eventually be constructed.

167 EMOTIONAL ORIGINS OF THE CIVIL WAR

from Avery Craven, *The Repressible Conflict*, 1939

The controversy over Andrew Jackson has been but a gentle stirring as compared with the storm over the Civil War. The early histories were almost literally continuations of the war by other means. Thus the writings of Alexander H. Stephens and Jefferson Davis on the Confederate side, or the Unionist work of Henry Wilson. In a subtler and more discriminating way, even modern works of scholarship choose sides among competing leaders and programs. One thinks, for instance, of Professor James

G. Randall, leader of the "revisionist" school of interpretation, whose writings show an unmistakable leaning toward the politics of Stephen A. Douglas; or of Professor Allan Nevins, who tends to take the view of a qualified Lincolnian. Indeed, an impressive recent analysis of the Lincoln-Douglas debates by Professor Harry Jaffa insists that this is as it must be, for historical judgment rests on a prior political judgment of the merits of the case.

Professor Avery Craven of the University of Chicago has done much to advance the "revisionist" view of the coming of the Civil War. "Revisionism" describes a tendency in recent decades to disprove the inevitability of the Civil War. Neither the clash of sectional principles nor the conflict of sectional interests, it is argued, provides a sufficient explanation of the break-up of the Union. Craven, in particular, has contended that emotional factors were decisive in carrying the sectional quarrel beyond the limits of compromise. The thrust and counterthrust of propaganda, beginning with the Abolitionist attacks in the 1830's, hardened sectional loyalties, brought extremist leaders forward on both sides, and translated ordinary differences of interest and opinion into a final conflict of sacred values.

Professor Craven's view was introduced in *The Repressible Conflict* (1939) and developed with some modifications (and much learning) in *The Coming of the Civil War* (1942; revised edition, 1957) and *The Growth of Southern Nationalism, 1848-1861* (1953).

The move for an independent South which came to a climax in 1861 did not arise from permanent physical and social conditions. It sprang rather from temporary emotional factors cultivated both without and within the section. Men fought because they had come to fear and hate—because they had at last accepted a distorted picture of both themselves and the people in other sections.

We have found little in the natural setup of the South to make a unity out of the varied states and regions stretching from Virginia to Texas. That had to be achieved through conflict. Nor have we found inherent differences great enough to make war "inevitable" or "irrepressible" between this section and other sections within the nation. That was to be an artificial creation of inflamed minds. Around the institution of slavery was engendered most of the bitterness which made war necessary. Yet slavery in itself, as we have seen, was not an all-inclusive institution. If it had not become a symbol first of sectional differences and then of southern depravity, or superiority, according to the point of view—it might have been faced as a national question and dealt with as successfully as the South American countries dealt with the same problem. Lincoln said he was fighting to save the Union, and most certainly men of the South had been struggling for decades to save the Constitution on which that Union rested and was made possible. What we are slowly coming to realize is that war was the product, not so much of sectional differences as of emotions developed about differences, which by 1861 made it impossible longer to reason, to trust, or to compromise. Both sides believed the other to be composed of persons who could only be handled by force—fiends in human form whose lives need not be spared, whose homes could be pillaged and burned, and whose institutions must be destroyed. The North could say that it was fighting to save a Union which God had established as a great experiment in democracy and which Southerners would destroy and replace with chaos, aristocracy, and human bondage. That is the whole substance of Lincoln's Gettysburg Address. The South, on the other hand, could say that it was fighting to save the original Constitution and to defend rights granted under that Constitution; that Yankees would not respect either constitutions or rights—they would even, in John Brown fashion, stir racial wars. . . .

To trace the steps by which the South was pounded into self-consciousness and moved to ultimate secession is not simple. We will ignore the early recognition of differences in colonial days as the manifestation of a provincialism common to all the colonies. The old notion of Puritan in New England and Cavalier in Virginia does not hold water. The real distinction between the sections was one of commerce as against agriculture—a difference which manifested itself almost as soon as the colonists came together under a government of their own. In the Constitutional Convention, Charles Pinckney observed "a real distinction between the northern and southern interests arising from the character of their means of livelihood." Madison declared that "the great division of interest did not lie between the large and small states; it lay between the northern and southern." . . .

But real division did not appear until Hamilton began his program of centralization under funding, banking, and tariff schemes, and did not bring wide sectional response until that movement

Text: Avery Craven, *The Repressible Conflict, 1830-1861* (Baton Rouge, La.: Louisiana State University Press, 1939), pp. 63-72, 74-76, 79-80, 85-87, 89-91, 93-96 *passim.*

found its greater champion in John Marshall. When the struggle was fully developed, it revealed itself as a contest between those who farmed and those whose economic efforts were confined to the urban centers. Southern men assumed the leadership of the rural group only because their intellectual and social qualifications gave them the right to do so. . . . They accepted as a matter of course the superiority of farming over all other forms of endeavor and assumed that, if economic affairs were left alone by government, the great mass of the people would be tillers of the soil and the great proportion of the nation's wealth would come from farming and remain in the hands of farmers. They believed that democratic government could succeed only when the people were largely engaged in agricultural pursuits and when their virtues were those developed and sustained by rural living. . . .

When John Marshall gave constitutional approbation to the centralizing trends which Hamilton had inaugurated and added his own contributions by decisions which subjected even the state courts to federal review, the agrarian spokesmen saw it all as a continuation of the scheme to exploit farmers in the interests of "legal factions." The passage of protective tariffs in the same period showed the aggressive interest of those in control of central government in the industrial parasites, and the efforts of the same group to lay restrictions on the state of Missouri as the price of admission to the Union had a like purpose when rightly understood. Agriculture was being crowded aside and plundered through the centralization of government in the interests of its own creatures—paper and industrial monopolies. . . .

The checking of this evil was not wholly a southern problem. It was the farmer's problem wherever he might be. But since the South was the home of those who had most completely accepted the old physiocratic doctrines; since her planters had achieved the highest station reached by American agriculturists through the plantation system and staple crops; since her leaders had long served as spokesmen for the rural groups, it was her destiny to be thought of as the champion of these interests and to have thrown against her all the hatred and force which the opposing element could muster. The defense, based on states' rights, which the farmers offered was destined to be considered her especial property even though it had wide and common use throughout the nation up to 1860! In the fight to defend agriculture through local democracy, the South came to be thought of as a section of peculiar unity and unusual self-consciousness. . . .

It is not necessary to follow in detail this constitutional struggle. The significant point is that the states' rights doctrine had been brought forward in peculiar form to defend an agricultural group or "interest" against a commercial-urban-industrial group or "interest." The important fact to be emphasized is that this was not in reality a sectional struggle. The support for it was found among farmers and .lesser elements throughout the *nation.* New England farmers and the agricultural and labor groups in the Middle States combined with southern men in what was a class struggle—an economic conflict. Their votes helped Jefferson to the presidency; Andrew Jackson found them behind him in the fight against the Bank. They resented the new-rich factory owner with a zeal quite comparable to that of the South Carolinian and not until slavery entered the picture did they desert. . . .

A survey of any southern state in the period of the 1820's and early 1830's will reveal internal conflict of the most intense kind. In legislatures and in conventions, every question which was later to divide North and South was being fought out: the rights of minorities and majorities; the rights of property; the correct interpretation of constitutions; the merits of wide central government activity as against local action, including aid to economic endeavors; even the merits and the evils of slavery. In this contest appeared a group of leaders, perhaps representing a majority of the people of the South, who upheld the very positions which the North was to uphold on the eve of civil war. Every weapon of defense later used to combat the North was used to protect southern men from their fellow southern citizens! It is absurd to talk of a unique southern consciousness and common southern attitudes in this period!

If this analysis be correct, then the growth of southern consciousness and the final stroke for independent nationalism was the product of events and developments belonging in the main to the period after 1830. They had largely to do with the institution of slavery. Other issues, of course, entered into the picture, but in most cases slavery, sooner or later, managed to cast its distorting shadow over them and, ultimately, to make itself the symbol of sectional differences. The old idea of superiority and inferiority in social-economic life grew to new proportions as conflict became more bitter and the weapon of states' rights under the Constitution took on sharper edges as antagonisms developed. But the moral implications of the slavery controversy alone made hatred and distrust in degree great enough to require war.

Slavery as a reality and slavery as a symbol of southern life in its conflict with the North were, as we have seen, two quite different things. The one was important only as a very ancient labor system, probably at this time rather near the end of its existence; the other was a creation of inflamed imaginations which endowed southern men and institutions with every quality desired and extended its scope to cover all that was peculiar to the life of a section. The first was an economic fact, the other a psychological one. The first we can almost ignore in our study of sectional conflict; the second leaves few pages of history from 1830 to 1860 untouched. . . .

The rise of the professional spokesmen—called "abolitionists" on the one side and "fire-eaters" on the other—needs notice only because of the emotional flavor which they added to the contest. William Lloyd Garrison had the gift for making everyone mad—including himself. He had an unusual capacity for hating. If Southerners like Dew and Harper and Ruffin were more dignified and logical, they were no less positive and one-sided. When the clergymen entered the field, and thousands of them did, they added righteous indignation to the conflict. The clan is notoriously efficient in uncomprising assertion of "right" and "wrong." When one speaks for God, argument is useless; only combat is possible.

The significant thing about the antislavery men and movements and those who developed the abstract defense of the South is the picture of slavery and of society which they created. They were too extreme for any great following. Conservative men of the day dismissed them as fanatics and hastened to assure their friends in other sections that such voices did not represent the true opinions and feelings of their people. But these fanatics, unrestrained by fact, were creating clear-cut pictures of slavery, slaves, slaveholders, and southern and northern life positive enough to suit the needs of those engaged in conflict. When politicians became enraged in debate, when the sections became entangled in strife, then these pictures were to serve wider purposes. The time would come when opponents needed just such distorted weapons—when false propaganda could take the place of truth. Then the conceptions of men and societies woven by these intense emotional voices of heaven would pass as sober truth. Enemies would become devils; friends, the incarnation of right and justice. Blood would have to be spilled. . . .

The final logical conclusion of all this discussion was stated by Theodore Parker in 1851 when he declared that:

The South, in the main, had a very different origin from the North. I think few if any persons settled there for religion's sake; or for the sake of the freedom of the State. It was not a moral idea which sent men to Virginia, Georgia, or Carolina. "Men do not gather grapes of thorns." The difference in the seed will appear in the difference of the crop. In the character of the people of the North, and South, it appears at this day. . . . Here, now, is the great cause of the difference in the material results, represented in towns and villages, by farms and factories, ships and shops. Here is the cause of differences in the schools and colleges, churches, and in the literature; the cause of difference in men. The South with its despotic idea, dishonors labor, but wishes to compromise between its idleness and its appetite, and so kidnaps men to do its work.

"Two opposing civilizations are in conflict here, and have been from the infancy of our Union," said Professor Austin Phelps of Andover Theological Seminary. . . .

For a generation southern men and women lived under such an attack. It began, as we have said, as a simple questioning of the justice of human slavery by a few earnest, if fanatical, humanitarians. It ended on the level of a high moral crusade, the justice of which few northern men questioned, and tended to include in its sweep of purpose the overthrow of the whole southern way of life. Garrison and Phillips and Parker became as well known in the South as in the North. In fact, one writer has recently evaluated Garrison in the antislavery impulse as more important for the hatred he stirred below Mason and Dixon's line than for the influence he wielded above it. Gradually the South became conscious and bitter. It turned in self-defense. . . .

A . . . positive reply was offered in the ingenious "proslavery argument" which was evolved in the South from 1820 to 1860. From a half-apologetic defense of slavery as a necessary evil, it grew to an aggressive glorification of a way of life. The Bible, the Past, Nature, and Civilization were all appealed to, and when the task was completed the Southerner stood before the world a superior man in a superior society. An early group attempted to point out the benefits of slavery to the Negro himself. . . .

From such beginnings, the defense went on to ingenious refinements, as men discovered that slaves were better off than factory workers; that all labor, regardless of the system, was exploited; that republican government could exist only where all white men were free from drudgery; and that without slavery in agriculture all farmers were destined to a degrading peasantry. It reached its fullness in the staunch belief that under slavery, the South had achieved a vastly superior civilization, toward which the rest of the world must move. Here was a society without a labor conflict, without race conflict, and without social agitation. There was no unemployment and no old-age worries for its toilers. Culture and refinement prevailed, and the ruin which urban life produced in "depravity of morals . . . increase of want, and of crime," as Edward Fisher charged, was lacking. Slavery had marked the beginning of man's upward climb, as Professor Dew had early declared, and it now marked its highest peak. When war broke, the Reverend J. H. Thornwell could say:

The parties in this conflict are not merely abolitionists and slaveholders; they are atheists, socialists, communists, red republicans, jacobins on the one side, and the friends of order and regulated freedom on the other. In one word, the world is the battle ground, Christianity and atheism the combatants, and the progress of humanity the stake.

What stands out in all this is the belief in the peculiar quality and character of the South; the growing emotion involved in attack and defense; the assumption of differences inherent and persistent. There was a North, and there was a South. They represented entirely different values and qualities. They were by nature enemies. And, what is most significant, *moral* values were involved—things affecting humanity, civilization, God's purposes in this world. Those are things for which men give their lives; for which holy wars are fought. National consciousness is woven from fear and resentment as well as from conviction and faith. Material realities shrink into insignificance when brought into comparison. . . .

After 1840 few issues were allowed to stand on their own merits. Individuals and groups, consciously and unconsciously, used slavery to aid their interests. John C. Calhoun and John Quincy Adams, seeking political advantage, tangled slavery hopelessly with the western demand for the annexation of Texas. David Wilmot introduced his trouble-making Proviso as part of a political game which he and his friends were playing. The repeal clause in the Kansas-Nebraska Act was the afterthought of a mere handful of politicians and not a move in response to southern demands. The Appeal to Independent Democrats, which Chase and his group used to stir the Northwest, was false in its assertions and unfair in its purposes, but it was politically effective. The damaging section in the Dred Scott decision was an *obiter dictum,* forced, according to the late Professor Hodder, by the political ambitions of dissenting judges. John Brown, who reduced rabid talk to action, is frankly considered insane by his most able biographer.

Yet these uncalled-for moves and this irresponsible leadership were the very things which lifted the crusade of a band of "crack-pot reformers" in the North and an extravagant group of "fire-eaters" in the South to the proportions of a national conflict adjustable only by civil war. Texas and slavery combined begot the Wilmot Proviso, which, in turn, forced the crisis of 1850. The repeal of the Missouri Compromise begot the Republican party and ultimately the combination of a political party and a moral crusade. The Dred Scott *obiter dictum* justified the continuation of that party as a perpetual guard against the aggressions of the South. John Brown brought the race question to the fore and added the final emotional appeal needed to pound the divergent classes of the South into a working unity.

The politician thus gave an air of reality to the abstractions of those who had evolved the slavery question into a struggle of civilizations. In his hands the conflict between freedom and slavery became a sectional contest for lands, internal improvements, tariffs, and new areas for expansion. The continuation of material well-being and the existence of fundamental rights were linked with the spread or the restriction of the "peculiar institution." An emotional fervor and moral force, which only slavery could create, was thus thrown about a whole set of very practical and concrete problems. Two ways of life and two opposing sets of constitutional principles were thus forced into an irrepressible contest for supremacy. Yet, as a matter of fact, few actual gains or losses were involved. Texas would have come along about as it did if slavery had never been mentioned. There were only three slaves in Kansas in 1860, and there never was the slightest chance of slavery's entering Kansas or Nebraska. All well-informed men knew that by 1857, and many were saying so at the very time Lincoln was making political capital out of proslavery danger. A dozen *obiter dicta* would not have spread slavery over the North, and a hundred John Browns could not have produced a general revolution among the slaves.

The combined efforts of reformer and politician gradually created the notion of the "Slave Power" and of "Black Republicanism." Each of these creations was supposed to consist of a well-organized force and program. The one was determined to spread slavery throughout the land. The other was determined to wipe out the institution of slavery even at the cost of a race war. Both were fictions. Yet partisans were able to bring all the fears and apprehensions, all the noble purposes and sentiments aroused by the antislavery and the proslavery crusades to their side and to pour all the bitter distortions of that conflict upon their op-

ponents. They made a conscious North and a conscious South. Each could fight for God against
the Devil and his human allies. One would struggle for Union and democracy; the other for self-

rule and the Constitution untarnished. Sane men
on both sides, and they constituted a majority even
in 1861, were helpless before fanatics armed with
such holy weapons. . . .

168 SLAVERY AND THE CIVIL WAR

from Allan Nevins, *The Emergence of Lincoln*, 1952

Professor Allan Nevins' majestic narrative of the Civil War era recalls the grand
manner of the nineteenth-century American historical classics. Character and episode
and setting unfold in ample detail as Nevins makes his stately progress through the
decades of *The Ordeal of the Union*. Four stout volumes carry the story from the
Mexican War to the election of Lincoln; at least several more will be devoted to the
war itself. This is not "thesis" history—writing dominated by *analytic* concerns—as
the work of men like Beard or Turner or Craven tends to be. Nevins' chief business is
the narration of a great story in all its fullness.

Such narrative writing does not, of course, avoid the problems of interpretation.
If Nevins does not try to demonstrate a thesis, he does introduce a broad point of
view toward statesmanship in general and the slavery crisis in particular to give
shape and meaning to his story. Like most historians, he praises moderation and
compromise as essentials of statecraft; unlike some, he insists that compromise be
grounded in firm principle and that the great statesman in times of crisis is one who
confronts the real issue, however explosive it may be.

For Nevins the real issue underlying the Civil War was the vast and infinitely
complicated problem of race relations. Slavery was the particular form for regulating
race relations sanctioned by experience and belief in the South. This form violated
both the principles of the American republican system and the moral judgment of
the Western world. Slavery was an intolerable anachronism that sooner or later had
to go. Southern leadership failed by blindly refusing to confront this ultimate necessity.
Northern leadership failed by ignoring the problem of race relations which slavery
was designed to answer in one way and by offering no reasonable alternative solution.
Out of this joint failure came the tragedy of civil war.

Allan Nevins recently retired from the Columbia University faculty to accept a
research appointment at the Huntington Library. He was president of the American
Historical Association in 1959. His large shelf of historical writings covers every period
and phase of American development from the Revolution to the Second World War.
Notable items include biographies of Frémont, Cleveland, Rockefeller, and Henry Ford,
useful diplomatic studies of the nineteenth and twentieth centuries, and the modern
classic from which the following selection is taken: *The Ordeal of the Union*, which
reaches its fifth volume, and the opening of the Civil War, in 1959. Volumes II and III
are published under the title *The Emergence of Lincoln*. Nevins has twice been
awarded the Pulitzer prize—in 1933 for the biography *Grover Cleveland* and in 1937
for the biography *Hamilton Fish*.

Great and complex events have great and complex causes. Burke, in his *Reflections on the Revolution in France,* wrote that "a state without
the means of some change is without the means
of its conservation," and that a constant reconciliation of "the two principles of conservation
and correction" is indispensable to healthy national growth. It is safe to say that every such
revolutionary era as that on which the United
States entered in 1860 finds its genesis in an
inadequate adjustment of these two forces. It
is also safe to say that when a tragic national
failure occurs, it is largely a failure of leader-

ship. . . . To explain the failure of American
leadership in 1846-1861, and the revolution that
ensued, is a bafflingly complicated problem.

Looking backward from the verge of war in
March, 1861, Americans could survey a series of
ill-fated decisions by their chosen agents. One
unfortunate decision was embodied in Douglas's

Text: Allan Nevins, *The Emergence of Lincoln* (New
York: Charles Scribner's Sons, 1950), II, 462-71 *passim.*
Reprinted with the permission of Charles Scribner's Sons
from *The Emergence of Lincoln* by Allan Nevins; copyright 1950 by Charles Scribner's Sons.

Kansas-Nebraska Act of 1854. Had an overwhelming majority of Americans been ready to accept the squatter sovereignty principle, this law might have proved a statesmanlike stroke; but it was so certain that powerful elements North and South would resist it to the last that it accentuated the strife and confusion. Another disastrous decision was made by Taney and his associates in the Dred Scott pronouncement of 1857. Still another was made by Buchanan when he weakly accepted the Lecompton Constitution and tried to force that fraudulent document through Congress. The Northern legislatures which passed Personal Liberty Acts made an unhappy decision. Most irresponsible, wanton, and disastrous of all was the decision of those Southern leaders who in 1858-60 turned to the provocative demand for Congressional protection of slavery in all the Territories of the republic. Still other errors might be named. Obviously, however, it is the forces behind these decisions which demand our study; the waters pouring down the gorge, not the rocks which threw their spray into the air.

At this point we meet a confused clamor of voices as various students attempt an explanation of the tragic denouement of 1861. Some writers are as content with a simple explanation as Lord Clarendon was when he attributed the English Civil War to the desire of Parliament for an egregious domination of the government. The bloody conflict, declared James Ford Rhodes, had "a single cause, slavery." He was but echoing what Henry Wilson and other early historians had written, that the aggressions of the Slave Power offered the central explanation. That opinion had been challenged as early as 1861 by the London *Saturday Review,* which remarked that "slavery is but a surface question in American politics," and by such Southern propagandists as Yancey, who tried to popularize a commercial theory of the war, emphasizing a supposed Southern revolt against the tariff and other Yankee exactions. A later school of writers was to find the key to the tragedy in an inexorable conflict between the business-minded North and the agrarian-minded South, a thrusting industrialism colliding with a rather static agricultural society. Still another group of writers has accepted the theory that the war resulted from psychological causes. They declare that agitators, propagandists, and alarmists on both sides, exaggerating the real differences of interest, created a state of mind, a hysterical excitement, which made armed conflict inevitable.

At the very outset of the war Senator Mason of Virginia, writing to his daughter, asserted that two systems of society were in conflict; systems, he implied, as different as those of Carthage and Rome, Protestant Holland and Catholic Spain. That view, too, was later to be elaborated by a considerable school of writers. Two separate nations, they declared, had arisen within the United States in 1861, much as two separate nations had emerged within the first British Empire by 1776. Contrasting ways of life, rival group consciousness, divergent hopes and fears made a movement for separation logical; and the minority people, believing its peculiar civilization in danger of suppression, began a war for independence. We are told, indeed, that two types of nationalism came into conflict: a Northern nationalism which wished to preserve the unity of the whole republic, and a Southern nationalism intent on creating an entirely new republic. . . .

One fact needs emphatic statement: of all the monistic explanations for the drift to war, that posited upon supposed economic causes is the flimsiest. This theory was sharply rejected at the time by so astute an observer as Alexander H. Stephens. South Carolina, he wrote his brother on New Year's Day, 1861, was seceding from a tariff "which is just what her own Senators and members in Congress made it." As for the charges of consolidation and despotism made by some Carolinians, he thought they arose from peevishness rather than a calm analysis of facts. "The truth is, the South, almost in mass, has voted, I think, for every measure of general legislation that has passed both houses and become law for the last ten years." The South, far from groaning under tyranny, had controlled the government almost from its beginning, and Stephens believed that its only real grievance lay in the Northern refusal to return fugitive slaves and to stop the antislavery agitation. "All other complaints are founded on threatened dangers which may never come, and which I feel very sure would be averted if the South would pursue a judicious and wise course." Stephens was right. It was true that the whole tendency of Federal legislation 1842-1860 was toward free trade; true that the tariff in force when secession began was largely Southern-made; true that it was the lowest tariff the country had known since 1816; true that it cost a nation of thirty million people but sixty million dollars in indirect revenue; true that without secession no new tariff law, obnoxious to the Democratic Party, could have passed before 1863—if then. . . .

. . . In short, the divisive economic issues are easily exaggerated. At the same time, the unifying economic factors were both numerous and powerful. North and South had economies which were largely complementary. It was no misfortune to the South that Massachusetts cotton mills wanted its staple, and that New York ironmasters like Hewitt were eager to sell rails dirt-cheap to Southern railway builders; and sober business-men on both sides, merchants, bankers, and man-ufacturers, were the men most anxious to keep the peace and hold the Union together.

We must seek further for an explanation; and in so doing, we must give special weight to the observations of penetrating leaders of the time, who knew at firsthand the spirit of the people. Henry J. Raymond, moderate editor of the New York *Times*, a sagacious man who disliked North-ern abolitionists and Southern radicals, wrote in January, 1860, an analysis of the impending con-flict which attributed it to a competition for power:

In every country there must be a just and equal balance of powers in the government, an equal distribution of the national forces. Each section and each interest must exercise its due share of influence and control. It is always more or less difficult to preserve their just equipoise, and the larger the country, and the more varied its great interests, the more difficult does the task become, and the greater the shock and disturbance caused by an attempt to adjust it when once disturbed. I believe I state only what is generally conceded to be a fact, when I say that the growth of the Northern States in population, in wealth, in all the elements of political influence and control, has been out of proportion to their political influ-ence in the Federal Councils. While the Southern States have less than a third of the aggregate population of the Union, their interests have influ-enced the policy of the government far more than the interests of the Northern States. . . . Now the North has made rapid advances within the last five years, and it naturally claims a proportionate share of influence and power in the affairs of the Confederacy.

It is inevitable that this claim should be put forward, and it is also inevitable that it should be conceded. No party can long resist it; it overrides all parties, and makes them the mere instruments of its will. It is quite as strong today in the heart of the Democratic party of the North as in the Republican ranks; and any party which ignores it will lose its hold on the public mind.

Why does the South resist this claim? Not because it is unjust in itself, but because it has become involved with the question of slavery, and has drawn so much of its vigor and vitality from that quarter, that it is almost merged in that issue. The North bases its demand for increased power, in a very great degree, on the action of the government in regard to slavery—and the just and rightful ascendency of the North in the Federal councils comes thus to be regarded as an element of danger to the institutions of the Southern States.

In brief, Raymond, who held that slavery was a moral wrong, that its economic and social tendencies were vicious, and that the time had come to halt its growth with a view to its final eradication, believed that the contest was pri-marily one for power, and for the application of that power to the slave system. With this opinion Alexander H. Stephens agreed. The Georgian said he believed slavery both morally and politically right. In his letter to Lincoln on December 30, 1860, he declared that the South did not fear that the new Republican Administration would interfere directly and immediately with slavery in the States. What Southerners did fear was the ultimate result of the shift of power which had just occurred—in its application to slavery:

Now this subject, which is confessedly on all sides outside of the constitutional action of the Government, so far as the States are concerned, is made the 'central idea' in the platform of prin-ciples announced by the triumphant party. The leading object seems to be simply, and wantonly, if you please, to put the institutions of nearly half the States under the ban of public opinion and national condemnation. This, upon general princi-ples, is quite enough of itself to arouse a spirit not only of general indignation, but of revolt on the part of the proscribed. Let me illustrate. It is gen-erally conceded by the Republicans even, that Congress cannot interfere with slavery in the States. It is equally conceded that Congress can-not establish any form of religious worship. Now suppose that any one of the present Christian churches or sects prevailed in all the Southern States, but had no existence in any one of the Northern States,—under such circumstances sup-pose the people of the Northern States should organize a political party, not upon a foreign or domestic policy, but, with one leading idea of condemnation of the doctrines and tenets of that particular church, and with an avowed object of preventing its extension into the common Terri-tories, even after the highest judicial tribunal of the land had decided they had no such constitu-tional power. And suppose that a party so organ-ized should carry a Presidential election. Is it not apparent that a general feeling of resistance to the success, aims, and objects of such a party would necessarily and rightfully ensue?

Raymond and Stephens agreed that the two sections were competing for power; that a momentous transfer of power had just occurred; and that it held fateful consequences because it was involved with the issue of slavery, taking authority from a section which believed slavery moral and healthy, and giving it to a section which held slavery immoral and pernicious. To Stephens this transfer was ground for resuming the ultimate sovereignty of the States. Here we find a somewhat more complex statement of James Ford Rhodes's thesis that the central cause of the Civil War lay in slavery. Here, too, we revert to the assertions of Yancey and Lincoln that the vital conflict was between those who thought slavery right and those who thought it wrong. But this definition we can accept only if we probe a little deeper for a concept which both modifies and enlarges the basic source of perplexity and quarrel.

The main root of the conflict (and there were minor roots) was the problem of slavery *with its complementary problem of race-adjustment;* the main source of the tragedy was the refusal of either section to face these conjoined problems squarely and pay the heavy costs of a peaceful settlement. Had it not been for the difference in race, the slavery issue would have presented no great difficulties. But as the racial gulf existed, the South inarticulately but clearly perceived that elimination of this issue would still leave it the terrible problem of the Negro. Those historians who write that if slavery had simply been left alone it would soon have withered overlook this heavy impediment. The South as a whole in 1846-61 was not moving toward emancipation, but away from it. It was not relaxing the laws which guarded the system, but reinforcing them. It was not ameliorating slavery, but making it harsher and more implacable. The South was further from a just solution of the slavery problem in 1830 than it had been in 1789. It was further from a tenable solution in 1860 than it had been in 1830. Why was it going from bad to worse? Because Southern leaders refused to nerve their people to pay the heavy price of race-adjustment. These leaders never made up their mind to deal with the problem as the progressive temper of civilization demanded. They would not adopt the new outlook which the upward march of mankind required because they saw that the gradual abolition of slavery would bring a measure of political privilege; that political privilege would usher in a measure of economic equality; that on the heels of economic equality would come a rising social status for the Negro. Southern leadership dared not ask the people to pay this price.

A heavy responsibility for the failure of America in this period rests with this Southern leadership, which lacked imagination, ability, and courage. But the North was by no means without its full share, for the North equally refused to give a constructive examination to the central question of slavery as linked with race adjustment. This was because of two principal reasons. Most abolitionists and many other sentimental-minded Northerners simply denied that the problem existed. Regarding all Negroes as white men with dark skins, whom a few years of schooling would bring abreast of the dominant race, they thought that no difficult adjustment was required. A much more numerous body of Northerners would have granted that a great and terrible task of race adjustment existed—but they were reluctant to help shoulder any part of it. Take a million or two million Negroes into the Northern States? Indiana, Illinois, and even Kansas were unwilling to take a single additional person of color. Pay tens of millions to help educate and elevate the colored population? Take even a first step by offering to pay the Southern slaveholders some recompense for a gradual liberation of their human property? No Northern politician dared ask his constituents to make so unpopular a sacrifice. The North, like the South, found it easier to drift blindly toward disaster.

The hope of solving the slavery problem without a civil war rested upon several interrelated factors, of which one merits special emphasis. We have said that the South as a whole was laboring to bolster and stiffen slavery—which was much to its discredit. But it is nevertheless true that slavery was dying all around the edges of its domain; it was steadily decaying in Delaware, Maryland, western Virginia, parts of Kentucky and Missouri. Much of the harshness of Southern legislation in the period sprang from a sense that slavery was in danger from *internal* weaknesses. In no great time Delaware, Maryland, and Missouri were likely to enter the column of free States; and if they did, reducing the roster to twelve, the doom of the institution would be clearly written. Allied with this factor was the rapid comparative increase of Northern strength, and the steady knitting of economic, social, and moral ties between the North and West, leaving the South in a position of manifest inferiority. A Southern Confederacy had a fair fighting chance in 1861; by 1880 it would have had very little. If secession could have been postponed by two decades, natural forces might well have placed a solution full in sight. Then, too, the growing pressure of world sentiment must in time have produced its effect. But to point out these considerations is not to suggest that in 1861 a policy of procrastination and appeasement would have done anything but harm. All hope of bringing Southern majority sentiment to a better attitude would have been lost if Lincoln and his party had flinched on the basic issue of the restriction of slavery; for by the seventh decade of nineteenth century history, the time had come when that demand had to be maintained. . . .

Still another element in the tragic chronicle of the time must be mentioned. Much that happens in human affairs is accidental. When a country is guided by true statesmen the role of accident is minimized; when it is not, unforseen occurrences are numerous and dangerous. In the summer and fall of 1858, as we have seen, the revival of a conservative opposition party in the upper South, devoted to the Union, furnished a real gleam of hope. If this opposition had been given unity and determined leadership, if moderate Southerners had stood firm against the plot of Yancey and others to disrupt the Democratic Party, if Floyd had been vigilant enough to read the warning letter about John Brown and act on it, the situation might even then have been saved. Instead, John Brown's mad raid fell on public opinion like a thunderstroke, exasperating men everywhere and dividing North and South more tragically than ever. The last chance of persuading the South to submit to an essential step, the containment of slavery, was gone.

The war, when it came, was not primarily a conflict over State Rights, although that issue had become involved in it. It was not primarily a war born of economic grievances, although many Southerners had been led to think that they were suffering, or would soon suffer, economic wrongs. It was not a war created by politicians and publicists who fomented hysteric excitement; for while hysteria was important, we have always to ask what basic reasons made possible the propaganda which aroused it. It was not primarily a war about slavery alone, although that institution seemed to many the grand cause. It was a war over slavery *and* the future position of the Negro race in North America. Was the Negro to be allowed, as a result of the shift of power signalized by Lincoln's election, to take the first step toward an ultimate position of general economic, political, and social equality with the white man? Or was he to be held immobile in a degraded, servile position, unchanging for the next hundred years as it had remained essentially unchanged for the hundred years past? These questions were implicit in Lincoln's demand that slavery be placed in a position where the public mind could rest assured of its ultimate extinction.

Evasion by the South, evasion by the North, were no longer possible. The alternatives faced were an unpopular but curative adjustment of the situation by the opposed parties, or a war that would force an adjustment upon the loser. For Americans in 1861, as for many other peoples throughout history, war was easier than wisdom and courage.